CONCISE DICTIONARY ENGLISH-ENGLISH

A Perfect Reference tool for Aspirants of Competitive Examinations, Educationists, Students & General Readers

Published by:

F-2/16, Ansari road, Daryaganj, New Delhi-110002
☎ 23240026, 23240027 • *Fax:* 011-23240028
info@vspublishers.com • www.vspublishers.com

Online Brandstore: amazon.in/vspublishers

Regional Office : Hyderabad
5-1-707/1, Brij Bhawan (Beside Central Bank of India Lane)
Bank Street, Koti, Hyderabad - 500 095
☎ 040-24737290
vspublishershyd@gmail.com

Follow us on:  

BUY OUR BOOKS FROM: AMAZON FLIPKART

ISBN 978-93-505713-8-5
New Edition

Printed at : Param Offsetters, Okhla, New Delhi–110020

Publisher's Note

A fairly good response received from readers to our previously published concise dictionaries on science, commerce and language subjects has encouraged us to undertake yet another publication commanding everlasting demand - An **English-English Dictionary**. Like earlier ones this is a pocket-type concise version. This edition is expected to fulfil the academic and writing requirements of students, researchers, scholars, translators, educationists, and writers. This dictionary is quite different from others in that the 'Terms' have been drawn from areas of universal usage - literature, science, geography, commerce & business etc. Terms used in common parlance, compound words, syntax and other grammatical details along with a sentence (in English) to improve writing have been given.

Terms have been serialized in Alphabetical order, i.e., A-Z for ease in making searches easy. Terms carry meaning in simple English. To the extent possible, Terms used in common parlance have been included, avoiding less frequent ones.

It is hoped that this dictionary will be found useful by student community besides others such as, educationists, writers, and translators.

Every effort has been made to keep this dictionary error-free. However, should you come across any mistake, misprint, unsatisfactory annotation or explanation, please intimate us. We would incorporate your valuable suggestion while acknowledging your contribution.

How to use this Dictionary

Umpire - (*noun*) 1. In certain sports an official who watches a game or match closely to enforce the rules and arbitrate on matters arising from the play. *Umpires play a significant part in a cricket match.* 2. A person chosen to arbitrate between contending parties. *Both parties agreed to have him act as umpire to arbitrate in their dispute. (verb) act as an umpire; act as umpire in a game or match. He is umpiring the match between class X and XII.*

1. The Lead word (here **Umpire** is the lead word) is shown in dark bold lettering.
2. A hyphen follows the lead word.
3. Part of Speech (noun, pronoun, verb, adverb etc) of the lead word is shown in italic and duly enclosed within a bracket like this ( ).
4. Core sense of the lead word comes next.
5. To clarify the meaning of the lead word, a sentence is written. The sentence is shown in *italic*.
6. After this, sub-sense of the lead word is shown (if the lead word has more than one meaning); followed by another sentence in *italic*.
7. Similarly other meanings (sub-senses) and corresponding sentences follow.
8. If the lead word comes under another Parts of Speech, then the new Part of Speech (noun, pronoun, verb etc as the case may be) is given. As before, it is in *italic* and within bracket ( ).
9. As before, meaning and sentence formation is given along with sub-senses.
10. If there are other parts of speech also of the lead word, identical method - parts of speech, meaning, sentence, then sub-sense and sentences follows.

Symbols used

noun – noun
pronoun – pronoun
verb – verb
adverb- adverb
adjective - adjective
proposition - proposition
prefix – prefix

Grammar in Short

abbr.	abbreviation
adv.	adverb
adj.	adjective
conj.	conjunction
det.	*determiner*
excl.	exclamatory
noun	noun
prep.	preposition
pl.	plural
verb	verb
[American English]	American English
[British English]	British English

Aa

A–the first letter of the English alphabet. (1) First note in music.(2) First known quantity in Algebra.

Aback – *(adv.)* **1** [archaic] towards or situated to the rear. **2** sailing with the sail pressed back against the mast by a headwind. *The ship came into the harbour with all sails aback.*

Abaction *(adj.)* – **1** *A large herd* of cattle was stolen. *Police have registered a case of abaction.*

Abandon – *(verb)* **1** give up (an action or practice) completely. **2** desert or leave permanently. *We abandoned the old car in an empty parking lot.* **3** (abandon oneself to) indulge in (a desire or impulse) without restraint. *She danced with abandon.* [as adjective abandoned] unrestrained; uninhibited: a wild, abandoned dance. Noun lack of inhibition or restraint.

Abase – *(verb)* belittle or degrade. *He was angry with his friend and abased him in public.*

Abash – *(verb)* cause to feel embarrassed, disconcerted, or ashamed. *His father abashed him by criticizing him before his friends.*

Abashment – *(noun)* felt feeling embarrassed due to modesty. *I felt abashment as it was my first time to perform on stage.*

Abba – *(noun)* **1** [in the New Testament] God as father. *Abba will certainly listen to our prayers.* **2** [in the Syrian Orthodox and Coptic Churches] a title given to bishops and patriarchs. *He was given the honored title of Abba.*

Abbess – *(noun)* a woman who is the head of an abbey of nouns. *He wanted the abbess to hear his confession.*

Abbey – *(noun)* an establishment occupied by a community of monks or nuns. *Once, there was an abbey here, now the building is dilapidated and deserted.*

Abbot – *(noun)* a man who is the head of an abbey of monks. *The abbot here very popular, he listen to the grievances of all people.*

Abbreviate – *(verb)* shorten (a word, phrase, or text). *Etc. is an abbreviated form of etcetera.*

Abdomen – *(noun)* the part of the body containing the digestive and reproductive organs; the belly. [Zoology] the hinder part of the body of an arthropod. *His abdomen is flat because he does a lot of exercise.*

Abdominal – *(adj.)* of or relating to or near the abdomen. *We took our brother to doctor as he complained of severe abdominal pain.*

Abduce – *(verb)* to draw or take away. *The problem was big but he soon abduced the conclusion.*

Abduct – *(verb)* **1** take (someone) away illegally by force or deception. *Ashok's son has been abducted. The police are investing the case.* **2** [Physiology] (of a muscle) move (a limb or part) away from the midline of the body or from another part. The opposite of Adduct.

Abduction – *(noun)* the action of forcibly taking someone away against their will. *Abduction of children has increased and the police have become active.*

Abecedarian – *(noun)* a novice learning the rudiments of some subject. *He is an abecedarian learning the basics of computer.*

Abed – *(adv.)* [archaic] in bed. *He was so tired that he went abed at once and slept.*

Abberrance – *(noun)* a state or condition markedly different from norm. *Aberrance from the right path usually occurs in young age.*

Abet – *(verb)* [abetted, abetting] encourage or assist (someone) to do something wrong, in particular to commit a crime. *He doesn't want to abet a crime.*

Abhor – *(verb)* (abhorred, abhorring) detest; hate. *I abhor scenes of crime and violence.*

Abide – *(verb)* **1** [abide by] accept act in accordance with (a rule or decision). *We must abide by the rules of traffic.* **2** [of a feeling or memory] endure. *I shall abide by the memories of my childhood.* **4** [archaic] live; dwell.

Ability – *(noun)* **1** the capacity to do something. *He has the ability of speaking five languages.* **2** skill or talent. *His ability in driving is remarkable.*

Abiogenesis – *(noun)* technical term for spontaneous generation.

Abject – *(adj.)* **1** extremely unpleasant and degrading living in poverty. *He lives in abject poverty on footpath.* **2** without pride or dignity; *an abject apology. Being charged with a crime he died in abject disgrace.*

Ablactate – *(verb)* deprive of mother's milk. *The mother got sick and the infant was ablactated.*

Ablactation – *(noun)* the act of substituting other food for the mothers mild in diet of a child or young mammal. *Ablacation is usually advised by doctors when babies can't get mother's milk.*

Ablation – *(noun)* **1** The loss of solid material (especially ice) by melting or evaporation. The erosion of rock by wind action. *If exposed to strong winds over long periods even rocks undergo ablation.* **2** The surgical removal of body tissue.

Ablative – *(adj.)* **1** [Grammar] denoting a case indicating an agent, instrument, or source, expressed by 'by', 'with', or 'from' in English. **2** Involving ablation. *(noun)* [Grammar] a word in the ablative case.

Ablaze – *(adj.)* burning fiercely. *The bus was set ablaze by miscreants.*

Able – *(adj.)* **1** Having the power, skill, or means to do something. *He is able to lift such a heavy weight.* **2** Having considerable proficiency or intelligence.

Abloom – *(adj.)* bursting into flower. *The whole garden is abloom with flowers.*

Ablush – *(adj.)* having a red face from embarrassment, agitation or emotional upset *She felt ablush when he expressed his love for her.*

Ablution – *(noun)* the ritual of washing of a priest's hands or of sacred vessels. *Ablution is usually done by priests early in the morning.*

Ably – *(adverb)* with competence. *He played ably and scored a centuary.*

Abnegate – *(verb)* [formal] renounce or reject (something desired or valuable). *Babar abnegated wine when Humayu was seriously sick.*

Aboard – *(adv.&prep.)* **1** On or into (a ship, train, or other vehicle). *If aboard the ship in time.* **2** [Baseball] on base.

Abode – *(noun)* [formal or poetic – literary] a house or home. Residence: *Their right of adobe in Britain Himalya is the abode of gods.*

Abode – *(verb)* [archaic] past of abide.

Abolish – *(verb)* formally put an end to (a practice or institution). *Sati pratha was abolished during the British rule.*

Abolition – *(noun)* the act of abolishing a system practice or invitation. *The credit to abolition of Sati pratha must go to Raja Ram Mohan Rai.*

Abominate – *(verb)* [formal] detest. *I abominate such rude behaviour.*

Aboral – *(adj.)* [zoology] furthest from or leading away from the mouth.

Aboriginial – *(adj.)* inhabiting or existing in a land from the earliest times or from before the arrival of colonists. *Santhals are an aboriginal race of India.* indigenous. *Aboriginal rituals are fascinating.* (Aboriginal) of or relating to the Australian Aboriginals or their languages. *(noun)* **1** An aboriginal inhabitant (Aboriginal), a person belonging to one of the indigenous peoples of Australia. *Dances of Australian aborigins are interesting to watch.* **2** (Aboriginal) any of the Australian Aboriginal languages.

Aborigines – *(noun)* an aboriginal person, animal, or plant. (Aborigine) an Australian aboriginal. *Aborigines of Australia are known all over the world.*

Abort – *(verb)* **1** Carry out or undergo the abortion of (a fetus). *She wanted to abort her child.* **2** bring to a premature end because of a problem or fault. *Attempts of terrorists were aborted because of timely action taken by police.* *(noun)* [informal or technical] an act of aborting a flight or other enterprise. *Aborted my business enterprise.*

Abound – *(verb)* exist in large numbers or amounts. (abound in – with) have in large numbers or amounts. *This pond abounds in fish.*

About – *(adv. & prep.)* **1** on the subject of; concerning. *I know nothing about him.* **2** Used to indicate movement within a particular area or location in a particular place. **3** approximately. *The train was about to leave when I reached the station.*

Above – *(adv.&prep.)* **1** At a higher level than. *High above the mountains a plane was flying.* **2** In preference to. *I would prefer coffee above tea.* **3** (in printed text) mentioned earlier.

Abracadabra – *(exclamation)* a word said by conjurors when performing a magic trick. *The magician said Abracadabra and the lady disappeared.*

Abrade – *(verb)* scrape or wear away by friction or erosion. *Strong winds abrade away the fertile earth.*

Abreast – *(adv.)* **1** Side by side and facing the same way. *While climbing over we found a huge rock abreast us.* **2** Alongside. *Abreast of the long wall of the fort there were huge statues.* **3** (abreast of) up to date with. *I keep abreast with latest news.*

Abridge – *(verb)* **1** Shorten (a text or film) without losing the sense. *This is the abridge edition of Mahabharata, you won't have to read the lengthy book now.* **2** [Law] curtail (a right or privilege). *The court has abridged the encroachment of historical monuments.*

Abrogate – *(verb)* [formal] repeal or do away with (a law or agreement).

Abrupt – *(adj.)* **1** Sudden and unexpected. *Her abrupt speech shocked me,* **2** Brief to the point of rudeness; curt. *He broke into speech abroptly.*

Abruption – *(noun)* technical the sudden breaking away of a portion from a mass. Medicine premature separation of the placenta from the wall of the womb during pregnancy. *The sudden abruption of the rock from the mountain was shocking.*

Abruptly – *(adverb)* quickly and actual warning. *He left the room abruptly.*

Abscess – *(noun)* a swollen area within body tissue, containing an accumulation of pus. *After the accident an abscess formed on his left leg.*

Abscond – *(verb)* **1** Leave hurriedly and secretly to escape from custody or avoid arrest. *He absconded from the prison through a tunnel.* **2** (of bees) entirely abandon a hive.

Absence – *(noun)* **1** The state of being away from a place or person. *Her parents were worried because of the absence of their daughter from home.* **2** (absence of) the non-existence or lack of. *The absence of salt in vegetable spoiled it.*

Absent – *(adj.)* **1** Not present. *Many students were absent from the class.* **2** Showing a lack of attention. *Although the lecture was going on he seemed absent and lost in his thought.* *(verb)* (absent oneself) stay or go away. *He absented himself from the meeting.* *(prep.)* N. Amer. without.

Absinth – *(noun)* **1** The shrub wormwood. *He became an addict to absinth.* **2** (usu. absinthe) a green aniseed-flavoured liqueure formerly made with wormwood.

Absolute – *(adj.)* **1** Not qualified or diminished in any way; total. not subject to any limitation of power. *A dictator is an absolute ruler.* **2** not relative or comparative. *This is an absolute truth.* **3** grammar (of a construction) syntactically independent of the rest of the sentence, as in dinner being over; we left the table. (of a transitive verb) used without an expressed object (e.g. guns kill). (of an adjective) used without an expressed *(noun)* (e.g. the brave). **4** law (of a decree) final. *(noun)* [Philosophy] a value or principle regarded as universally valid or able to be viewed without relation to other things. *God is an absolute truth.*

Absorb – *(verb)* **1** soak up (liquid or another substance). *The sponge soaked up the liquid.* **2** take in (information). *I have absorbed all the information.* **3** assimilate (a less powerful entity). *Sea absorbs all the river waters.* **4** use up (time or resources). *The research absorbed all my time.* **5** reduce the effect or intensity of (sound or an impact). *Noise of plane absorbed all other sounds.* **6** engross the attention of. *The speech absorbed the attention of all the people.*

Abstain – *(verb)* **1** restrain oneself from doing something. *You are sick with an infection lungs, so abstain from smoking.* **2** formally decline to vote.

Abstemious – *(adj.)* not self-indulgent, especially as regards eating and drinking. *He is an abstemious man and never touches alcohol.*

Abstention – *(noun)* **1** an instance of abstaining from a vote. *Due to high abstention he lost the election.* **2** Abstinence. *He was on abstinence from alccohol.*

Abstinent – *(noun)* a person who refrains from drinking intoxicating beverages. *My friends is an abstinent and he would never drink a beverage which has even the least alcohol.*

Abstract – *(adj.)* **1** theoretical rather than physical or concrete. **2** relating to or denoting art that does not attempt to represent external, recognizable reality. *(verb)* **1** consider theoretically or separately from something else. **2** extract or remove. (abstract oneself) withdraw. **3** [as adjective abstracted] not concentrating **4** make a written summary of. *(noun)* **1** a summary of a book or article. *I am writing an abstract of this book.* **2** an abstract work of art.

Absurd – *(adj.)* wildly unreasonable, illogical or inappropriate. *It is an highly absurd theory, nobody can make head or tail of it.*

Abundance – *(noun)* **1** a very large quantity of something. plentifulness; prosperity. *This garden is famous for its abundance of flowers.* **2** the amount of something present in a particular area or sample. **3** (in solo whist) a bid by which a player undertakes to make nine or more tricks.

Abuse – *(verb)* **1** use to bad effect or for a bad purpose. *During a fight the men abused one another a lot.* **2** treat with cruelty or violence, assault sexually. *The abused his wife sexually.* **3** address in an insulting ana offensive way. *(noun)* **1** the improper use of something. *The abuse of alcohol makes you alcoholic.* **2** cruel and violent treatment. sexual assault. **3** insulting and offensive language. *We shouldn't use abusive language.*

Abut – *(verb)* [abutted, abutting] **1** (of land or a building) be next to or have a common boundary with. *Me and my friend's house are abutting.* **2** touch or lean on.

Acacia – *(noun)* a tree or shrub of warm climates which has yellow or white flowers and is trypically thorny. [Genus Acacia: numerous species.]. *The villages of India abound in Keeker (acacia) trees.*

Academy – *(noun)* **1** a place of study or training in a special field. [chiefly in names] US & Scottish a secondary school. *The academy is famous all over the world.* **2** a society or institution of distinguished scholars, artists, or scientists. *I am happy and proud to say that the distinguished Academy of England has invited me to give a lecture.*

Acarpous – *(adj.)* producing me fruit. *This plant is acarpous* as it produces no flower or fruit.

Accelerate – *(verb)* begin to move more quickly. Increase in rate, amount, or extent. [physics] undergo a change in velocity. *If you accelerate highly the car will rush madly.*

Accentuation – *(noun)* the use or application of an accent. *Proper accentuation helps a lot in correct pronunciation.*

Accept – *(verb)* **1** consent to receive (something offered). *I'll accept this job offer.* **2** regard favourably or with approval. *We accept your proposals.* **3** Believe to be valid or correct. **4** Take on (a responsibility or liability). Tolerate or submit to.

Acceptation – *(noun)* the accepted meaning of a word or phrase. *There is acceptation of many Hindi words into English language.*

Access – *(noun)* **1** the means or opportunity to approach or enter a place. the right or opportunity to use something or see someone. *I have direct access to the minister office.* **2** retrieval of inforemation stored in a computer's memory. *I can't gain access to this computer system.* **3** an attack or outburst of an emotion. *In an access of rage the man killed his friend.* *(verb)* **1** gain access to, make accessible. computing obtain, examine, or retrieve (data). **2** approach or enter (a place).

Accession – *(noun)* **1** The attainment of position of rank. *He has gained accession to the rank of*

Admiral. **2** The formal acceptance of a treaty or joining of an association. *You have my accession to this treaty.* **3** A new item added to a collection of books or arte-facts. *(verb)* record the addition of (a new item) to a library or museum.

Accidence – *(noun)* the part of grammar concerned with the inflections of words.

Accidented – *(noun)* **1** An unfortunate incident that happens unexpectedly and unintentionally. *He met an accident on his way.* **2** Something that happens by chance or without apparent cause. *I came across my lost old friend by accident.* Chance. **3** [Philosophy] a property of a thing which is not essential to its nature.

Acclaim – *(verb)* praise enthusiastically and publicly. *His efforts were acclaimed.* *(noun)* enthusiastic public praise. *A great acclaim waited him at the airport.*

Acclamation – *(noun)* Enthusiastic approval. *He received great acclamation for his speech.*

Acclivity – *(noun)* an upward slope.

Accommodate – *(verb)* **1** provide lodging or sufficient space for: *I can accommodate you at least for one night.* **2** fit in with the wishes or needs of. fitting in helpfully with another's wishes or demands. *He is so good natured that he can accommodate with anyone.*

Accompanier – *(noun)* one who accompanier. *My friend is my accompanier in this journey.*

Accompany – *(verb)* **1** go somewhere with. *My father accompanied me to my school.* **2** be present or occur at the same time as. provide something as a complement to. *Wherever I went my bad luck accompanied me.* **3** play a musical accompaniment for. *My guitar accompanies me where I go.*

Accomplice – *(noun)* a person who helps another commit a crime. *He was my accomplice in the crime.*

Accomplish – *(verb)* achieve or complete successfully. *I have yet to accomplish this difficult task.*

Accord – *(verb)* **1** give or grant someone (power or recognition). *His services have been accorded.* **2** (accord with) be harmonious or consistent with. *(noun)* **1** an official agreement or treaty. **2** agreement or harmony. *The accord between the two countries has been signed.*

According – *(adv.)* **1** (according to) as stated by or in. in a manner corresponding or in proportion to. *According to an announcement by the government petrol will be cheaper by two rupees.* **2** (according as) depending on whether.

Accost – *(verb)* approach and address boldly or aggressively.

Accouncheur – *(noun)* a male midwife.

Accouchement – *(noun)* [archaic] the action of giving birth.

Account – *(noun)* **1** a description of an event or experience. *Your application has been taken into account.* **2** a record of financial expenditure and receipts. a bill taking the form of such a record. *The whole account of the accident is here.* **3** a service through a bank or similar organization by which funds are held on behalf of a client or goods or services are supplied on credit. *If you have a problem with accounts go the accounts section.* **4** a facility allowing access to a computer or computational facility. *I have taken accounts as one of my subjects.* **5** importance. *Money was of no account to him.* *(verb)* **1** consider or regard in a specified way. **2** supply or make up (a specified amount). **3** give a satisfactory record or explanation of. *He accounts the accident to the Police.* **4** succeed in killing or defeating.

Accredit – *(verb)* **1** Give credit to (someone) for something. *He has been accredited with a lot of praise.* Attribute something to. **2** Give official authorization or sanction to. **3** Send (a diplomat or journalist) to a particular place or post.

Accure – *(verb)* **1** (of a benefit or sum or money) be received in regular or increasing amounts. **2** make provision for (a charge) at the end of a financial period.

Accumulate – *(verb)* gather together a number or quantity of. build up. *He accumulated a lot of wealth.*

Accurate – *(adj.)* **1** correct in all details. *Accurate shooting got him a gold in games* **2** capable of or successful in reaching the intended target.

Accusal – *(noun)* another term for accusation.

Accusatory – *(adj.)* expressing accusation. *Out of anger she gave me black accusatory looks.*

Accuse – *(verb)* charge with an offence or crime. claim that someone has done something wrong. *He was accused of murder. The court trial went on for 7 years.*

Accustom – *(verb)* **1** make used to. (be accustomed to) be used to. *I am not accustomed to waiting for such long hours.* **2** customary. *It is accustom to take your shoes off before entering the temple.*

Acentric – *(adj.)* **1** without a centre; not centralized. *He was turned out of the meeting because of acentric behaviour.* **2** Genetics (of a chromosome) having no centromere.

Acephalous – *(adj.)* **1** Without a head. *Worms who don't have a clear defined head are called acephalous* **2** [Prosody] lacking syllables in the first foot.

Acerbate – *(verb)* cause to be bitter or resentful. *The injustice acerbated him now more.*

Acerbic – *(adj.)* **1** Sharp and forthright. *He was acerbic in his speech which angered many people.* **2** [archaic or technical] tasting sour or better.

Acerbity – *(noun)* a rough and bitter manner. *Acerbity developed between two brothers on a land dispute.*

Acervate – *(adj.)* pertaining to a growth of fungi that forms a leaped-up mass. *This is an acervate fungus sporo phores.*

Acetic – *(adj.)* relating to or containing acetic acid. *Thin object contains acetic acid, let us give it a medical test.*

Acetify – *(verb)* make sour or more sour. *This solution has been acetified let's take it to the laboratory.*

Acetous – *(adj.)* producing or resembling vinegar. *This substances is acetous resembling vinegar.*

Acharnement – *(noun)* [archaic] bloodthirsty fury or ferocity. *The acharnement of his fury made everyone fear for their lives.*

Achieve – *(verb)* bring about or accomplish by effort, skill, or courage. *He has achieved a lot in such a short time*

Acholia – *(noun)* **1** A member of a farming and pastoral people of northern Uganda and southern Sudan. **2** The Nilotic language of this people.

Achromatic – *(adj.)* **1** relation to or denoting lenses that transmit light without separating it into constituent colours. *These glass are achromatic.* **2** without colour. *Water is achromatic, i.e. it has no colour.*

Acid – *(noun)* **1** A substance (typically, a corrosive or sourtasting liquid) with particular chemical properties including turning litmus red, neutralizing alkalis, and dissolving some metals. *I made the maud clear the floor with acid.* [Chemistry] any molecule able to donate a proton or accept electrons in reactions. *Some rowdy boys threw hydrochloric acid over a girl; her skin was burnt away.* **2** [informal] the drug LSD. *(adj.)* **1** containing or having the properties of an acid; having a pH of less than 7. [Geology & Metallurgy] rich in silica. **2** sharp-tasting or sour. *her acid remark cut me.* **3** (of remarks) bitter or cutting. chemical. *The acidity of this dish is amplified by the sugar added to it.*

Acidification – *(noun)* the process of becoming acid or being converted into an acid.*Acidification of this liquid has taken place.*

Acidulate – *(verb)* make slightly acidic.

Aclinic – *(noun)* another term for magnetic equator.

Acme – *(noun)* the highest point of achievement or excellence. *He has become very rich and touched acme at last.*

Acne – *(noun)* a skin condition marked by numerous red pimples resulting from inflamed sebaceous glands. *In young age acne often appears on the face.*

Aconite – *(noun)* **1** A poisonous plant bearing spiels of hooded pink or purple flowers. *Aconite is a plant used in homeopathic medicines.* [Genus Aconitum: many species, including monkshood.] **2** (also winter aconite) a small plant bearing yellow flowers in early spring.

Acorn – *(noun)* the fruit of the oak, a smooth oval nut in a cuplike base. *Acorn is used in Ayurvedic therapy.*

Acoustic – *(adj.)* **1** relating to sound or hearing. (of building materials) used for soundproofing or modifying sound. (of an explosive mine) set off by sound waves. *The acoustic system* *of the auditorium failed and there was no performance for a long time.* **2** (of popular musical instruments) not having electrical amplification. *Many guitars are acoustic and have no electric amplification.* *(noun)* **1** the properties of a room or building that determine how sound is transmitted in it. **2** the branch of physics concerned with the properties of sound.

Acquaint – *(verb)* **1** (acquaint someone with) make someone aware of or familiar with. *Why should you talk to me? I am not acquainted with you.* **2** (be acquainted with) know personality. (of two or more people) know each other personally.

Acquiesce – *(verb)* accept or consent to something without protest. *I acquiesce to your suggestion.*

Acquire – *(verb)* come to possess. Learn or develop (a skill, quality etc.). *She has acquired great skill in designing clothes.*

Acquisition – *(noun)* **1** a recently acquired asset or object. *A painting by Picasso is his latest acquisition.* **2** the act of acquiring. *This land has been in the process of acquisition by government.*

Acquit – *(verb)* **1** formally declare not guilty of a criminal charge. *He has been acquitted from the charge of murder.* **2** conduct oneself or perform in a specified way. discharge (a duty or responsibility). *She acquitted herself gracefully on the stage.*

Acrid – *(adj.)* unpleasantly bitter or pungent. *The food in this place smells acrid.*

Acrobat – *(noun)* an entertainer who performs acrobatics. *Acrobats in the circus gave stunning performance.*

Acropolis – *(noun)* a citadel or fortified part of an ancient greek city, built on high ground. *I visited an acropolis when I was in Greece.*

Across – *(prep. & adv.)* from one side to the other of (something). expressing movement over a place or region. on or towards the other side of. *He went across the room and opened the door.*

Act – *(verb)* **1** take action; do something. (act up) [informal] behave badly. *According to police the bomb explosion was an act of sabotage.* **2** represent on a contractual or legal basis. Temporarily doing the duties of another. **3** Take effect or have a particular effect. *We all act differently in one way or the other. Act of hamlet is superb.* **4** Perform a fictional role in a play or film. Be have so as to appear to be. *He acted excellently in the role of an old man.* (act something out) perform a narrative as if it were a play. *(noun)* **1** A thing done. *The act of murder landed him in jail.* **2** A simulation or pretence. A particular type of behaviour or routine. **3** Law a written ordinance of Parliament, congress, etc. *If you don't believe me go read act 329 of the parliament.* **4** a record to the decisions or proceedings of a committee or an academic body. **5** A main division of a play, ballet, or opera. **6** A set performance.

Acting – *(noun)* **1** the performance of a part or role in a drama. *His acting in the film was so powerful that it become an all time hit.* **2** temporarity. *The acting director will soon be retired.* *(adj.)* serving especially as substitute.

Actinic – *(adj.)* [technical] (of light or lighting) able to cause photochemical reactions, as in photography, having a significant short-wavelength or ultraviolet component.

Action – *(noun)* **1** the process of doing something to achieve an aim. *If you don't take action in time things may go out of control.* **2** a thing done. *The chemical action between Hydrogen and Oxygen results in the formation of water.* **3** the effect or influence of something such as a chemical. **4** a legal process; a lawsuit. *I'll take legal action against him.* **5** armed conflict. *The two groups took action and soon indulged into armed fight.* **6** the way in which something works or moves. *(verb)* take action on.

Actively – *(adverb)* **1** in or active manner. *He actively helps the needy.*

Active – *(adj.)* **1** moving or tending to move about vigorously or frequently. (of a person's mind or imagination) alert and lively. *On account of his sharp mind and active imagination he has become a popular writer.* **2** participating in a particular sphere or activity. *Children are usually very active.* **3** Working. *This is an active volcano it has erupted many times.* **4** (of an electric circuit) capable of modifying its state or characteristics automatically in response to input or feedback.

The disease of AIDS is very active in some parts of Africa. 5. (of a volcano) erupting or having erupted in the historical times. **6** (of a disease) not in remission or latent. **7** having a chemical or biological effect on something. **8** denoting a voice of verbs in which the subject is typically the person or thing performing the action and which can take a direct object the opposite or passive [Grammar]. noun [Grammar] an active form of a verb.

Actor – *(noun)* **1** a person whose profession is acting. *He is a very fine actor* he has always given powerful performances. **2** a participant in an action or process.

Actual – *(adj.)***1** existing in fact. *In actual sense he is a very intelligent man.* **2** current. *It is actually raining.*

Actuary – *(noun)* a person who compiles and analyses statistics in order to calculated insurance risks and premiums.

Acuity – *(noun)* sharpness or keenness of thought, vision, or hearing. *He has great acuity, that is why he is considered an authority over history.*

Aculeated – *(adj.)* **1** entomology denoting hymenopterans insects with stings, e.g. bees and wasps. **2** [botany] sharply pointed; prickly.

Acumen – *(noun)* the ability to make good judgments and take quick decisions. *He has great business acumen, that is why he is so successful.*

Acuminate – *(adj.)* **1** [biology] (of a plant or animal structure) tapering to a point. *This acuminate plant has a sharp tapering point.*

Adage – *(noun)* a proverb or short statement expressing a general truth. *Adages are popular even today.*

Adam – *(old testament)* in Judaism-Christian mythology, the first man and the husband of Eve and the progenitor of the human race. *Adam ate the apple and sin entered his mind.*

Adamant – *(adj.)* refusing to be persuaded or to change one's mind. *He is very adamant by nature and won't change his opinion about you.*

Adapt – *(verb)* **1** make suitable for a new use or purpose. *Creatures who could not adapt to changing environment gradually died away.* **2** become adjusted to new conditions.

Add – *(verb)* **1** join to or put with something else. Increase in amount, number, or degree. *If we add two and two it makes four.* **2** put together (two or more number, or amounts) to calculate their total value. amount to. **3** [Informal] make sense. *Whatever you have said adds up and I'll help you.* **4** Say as a further remark. *This all adds up to fact that you can't escape a court sentence.*

Addict – *(noun)* a person who is addicted to something. *He is a drug addict.*

Addle – *(verb)* **1** confuse. *His addled behaviour surprised all people.* **2** (of an egg) become rotten, producing no chick. *(adj.)* **1** Unsound; muddled. **2** [archaic] (of an egg) rotten.

Address – *(noun)* **1** the particular of the place where someone lives or an organization is situated. *This letter has come back from the post office because the address was wrong.* **2** a formal speech [archaic] a person's manner of speaking. *The president of the association presented his formal address.* [archaic] courteous or amorous approaches. *You must address me as sir.* **3** dated skill, dexterity, or readiness. *"At what address do you live" the policeman asked. (verb)* **1** write someone's name and address on (an envelope or parcel). speak formally to. direct one's remarks to. **3** think about and begin to deal with. **4** golf prepare to hit (the ball).

Adduce – *(verb)* cote as evidence.

Adept – *(adj.)* very skilled or proficient. *(noun)* a person who is adept at something. *He is adept at oil painting.*

Adequate – *(adj.)* satisfactory or acceptable. *Children should be given adequate supply of milk.*

Adhere – *(verb)* **1** stick fast to. *I'll adhere to my words no matter what comes.* **2** believe in and follow the practices of. *I strictly adhere to tenets of Lord Buddha.* **3** represent truthfully and in detail.

Adhesion – *(noun)* the action or process of adhering. *Adhesion to good habits always pays.* [physics] the sticking together of particles of different substances. [medicine] an abnormal union of surfaces due to inflammation or injury.

Adhibit - *(verb)* [formal] apply or affix to something else.

Adieu - *(exclamatory)* chiefly poetic - literary goodbye. *When we had reached the airport I said adieu to my friend.*

Adit - *noun* an access or drainage passage leading horizontally into a mine. *We reached the mine through an adit.*

Adjacent - *(adj.)* **1** next to or adjoining something else. *My house is adjacent to my school.* **2** [geometry] (of a pair of angles) formed on the same side of a straight line when intersected by another line. *Can you draw a pair of adjacent angles?*

Adjective - *(noun)* [grammar] a word naming an attribute of a noun, such as sweet, red, or technical. *In the words dark prince dark is an adjective noun is prince.*

Adjoin - *(verb)* be next to and joined with. *These two pieces of wood are adjoined together with a strong adhesive.*

Adjourn - *(verb)* **1** break off (a meeting) with the intention of resuming it later. *The court is adjourned for today.* **2** postpone (a resolution or sentence).

Adjudge - *(verb)* **1** consider or declare to be true or the case. *The witness was adjudged to be true* **2** (in legal use) award (compensation). **3** (in legal use) condemn to pay a penalty.

Adjunct - *(noun)* **1** an additional and supplementary part. *This tool is an adjunct to the big machine over running there.* **2** an assistant. *This person is my adjunct and will remain with me wherever I go.* **3** [grammar] a word or phrase in a sentence other than the verb or predicate. *(adj.)* connected or added in an auxiliary way.

Adjuration - *(noun)* [mathematic] the joining of two sets to form a large set. **2** [logic] the asserting in a single formula of two previously asserted formulae.

Adjure - *(verb)* [formal] solemnly urge to do something. *He adjured to do sometime destructive.*

Adjust - *(verb)* **1** alter slightly in order to achieve a correct or desired result. adapt or become used to a new situation. *I have adjusted to my new home.* **2** assess (loss or damages) when settling an insurance claim. *Though it is not much money but other I'll adjust.*

Adjutant - *(noun)* **1** a military officer acting as an administrative assistant to a senior officer. *He is an adjutant to the general.* **2** a large black and white stork with a massive bill and a bare head and neck, found in India and SE Asia. *Adjutant is a kind of stork found in India.*

Adjuvant - *(adj.)* (of therapy) applied after initial treatment for cancer to suppress secondary tumour formation. *Adjuvant therapy has started and doctors are looking for complete recovery.* *(noun)* a substance which enhances the body's immune response to an antigen. *Adjuvant is a substance which enhance immune response of the body.*

Admeasure - *(verb)* [archaic], apportion.

Administer - *(verb)* **1** attend to the organization or implementation of. *The chemist administered the drug to me.* **2** dispense (a drug or remedy). deal out (punishment). **3** (of a priest) perform the rites or (a sacrament). *He was busy enough to be administered a light sentence by court.* [archaic] or law direct the taking of (an oath). *The priest administered the rites of marriage*

Administrator - *(noun)* **1** someone who administers a business. *My father is a good administrator and ably handles a flourishing business.* **2** the party appointed by a probate court to distribute the estate of someone who does without a will. *The court has appointed an administrator because my uncle died without making a will.*

Admirable - *(adj.)* deserving respect and approval. *You have done admirable work.*

Admissible - *(adj.)* **1** acceptable or valid. **2** having the right to be admitted to a place. *I am a lifelong member of this club and hence admissible to it any time.*

Admission - *(noun)* **1** a confession. *Due to his quick admission of crime the judge passed a light sentence.* **2** the process or fact of being admitted to a place. *These days it is very difficult to find admission a good school.*

Admissive - *(adj.)* cheracterised by or allowing admission. *All children up to 14 are admissive to free education in government schools.*

Admix - *(verb)* [chiefly technical] mix with something else.

Admonish - *(verb)* reprimand firmly. earnestly urge or warn. *I admonished him for his rude behaviour.*

Ado - *(noun)* trouble; fuss. *It was much ado about nothing.*

Adobe - *(noun)* a kind of clay used to make sun-dried bricks. *Hermites build their adobe in jungle.*

Adolescence - *(noun)* the time period between the beginning of puberty and adulthood. *The time period between adolescence (14-15 years) and adulthood is very critical from many angles.*

Adolescent - *(adj.)* in the process of developing from a child into an adult. *(noun)* an adolescent boy or girl. *Adolescents often remain confused if not properly guided.*

Adopt - *(verb)* **1** legally take (another's child) and bring it up as one's own. *Since they had no children they adopted one from the orphanage.* **2** choose to take up or follow (an option or course of action). *He adopted an attitude of innocence.* **3** choose as a candidate for office. formally approve or accept. **4** (of a local authority) accept responsibility for the maintenance of (a road). **5** assume (an attitude or position). *I'll have to adopt some other course of action to achieve my goal.*

Adorable - *(adj.)* inspiring great affection. *My mother is very adorable.*

Adore - *(verb)* **1** love and respect deeply. **2** worship or venerate (a deity.) *I simply adore my English teacher.*

Adown - *(prep.)* [archaic] down. **1** *The liquid was poured adown his throat.*

Adrift - *(adj. & adv.)* **1** (of a boat) drifting without control. *This boat was found adrift in the sea.* **2** [informal] no longer fixed in position. *She was adrift in her own misery.*

Adscititious - *(adj.)* rare additional. *It is an adscititious habit rather than an inherent taste.*

Adult - *(noun)* a person who is fully grown and developed. [law] a person who has reached the age of majority. *(adj.)* fully grown and development. of, for, or characteristic of adults. *He is an adult and can take his own decision*

Adulterant - *(adj.)* making impure by adding extraneous materials.

Adust - *(adj.)* [archaic] **1** burnt. **2** gloomy.

Adultery - *(noun)* voluntary sexual intercourse between a married person and a person who is not their spouse. *Adultery is crime and severely punished in Muslim countries.*

Advanced - *(verb)* **1** move forwards. cause to occur at an earlier date than planned. *The work has completed before the advanced date.* **2** make or cause to make progress. *As the bull advanced towards me I got afraid.* **3** put forward (a theory or suggestion). **4** hand over (payment) to (someone) as a loan or before. it is due. *(noun)* **1** a forwarded movement. **2** a development or improvement. **3** an amount of money advanced. *He was in need of money so I gave him some advance.* **4** an approach made with the aim of initiating a sexual or amorous relationship. *(adjective)* done, sent, or supplied beforehand.

Advantage - *(noun)* **1** a condition or circumstance that puts one in a favourable position. benefit; profit. *His being elected as a party candidate is of advantage to me.* **2** [tennis] a score marking a point interim between deuce and winning the game. *(verb)* be of benefit to. prosperous.

Adventure - *(noun)* **1** an unusual, exciting, and daring experience. excitement arising from this. *We have planned great adventure in the jungles of east Africa.* **2** [archaic] a commercial speculation. *(verb)* dated engage in an adventure. *The adventurous journey thrilled me.*

Adverb - *(noun)* [grammar] a word or phrase that modifies the meaning of an adjective, verb, or other adverb, or of a sentence. *She walked slowly. In this sentence slowly is an adverb.*

Adversary - *(noun)* an opponent. *(adj.)* another term for *adversarila. He is my adversary in estate business.*

Adversative – *(adj.)* [grammar] (of a word or phrase) expressing opposition or antithesis. *His adversative attitude upset me.*

Adverse – *(adj.)* harmful; unfavourable. *This medicine may have adverse effects.*

Advert – *(noun)* [informal] an advertisement. *There was an advert in the newspaper regarding sale of summer clothes. (verb)* formal refer to.

Advertise – *(verb)* **1** promote or publicize. *If you want tenant one way is to advertise in the newspaper.* **2** [archaic] notify.

Advice – *(noun)* **1** guidance or recommendations offered with regard to future action. *The advice the doctor gives is to quit smoking as soon as possible.* **2** a formal notive of a sale, delivery, or other transaction. **3** [archaic] news.

Advisability – *(noun)* the quality of being advisable. *The chairman questioned the advisability of our plan.*

Advisable – *(adj.)* to be recommended; sensible. *It is an advisable step you took.*

Advise – *(verb)* **1** recommend (a course of action). offer advice to. **2** inform about a fact or situation. *I advise you to leave this place at once.*

Advocacy – *(noun)* active support of an idea or cause. *This advocacy is the court was brilliant.*

Advocate – *(noun)* **1** a person who publicly supports or recommends a particular cause or policy. *My father was a famous advocate.* **2** a person who pleads a case on someone else's behalf. Scottish term for BARRISTER. *(verb)* publicly recommend or support.

Adynamia – *(noun)* lack of strength or vigour. *Adynamia in him is the result of long disease from which he is recovering.*

Aegis – *(noun)* **1** the protection, backing, or support of someone. *The negotiations were conducted under the aegis of the UN.* **2** (in classical art and mythology) an attribute of certain gods represented as a goatskin shield. *Aegis is an attribute of Zeus and Athene.*

Aeon – *(noun)* **1** an indefinite and very long period. *Such astrological wonders among planets happen in aeons.* **2** [Astronomy & Geology] a period of a thougsand million years. **3** [geology] a major division of geological time, subdivided into erase. **4** [philosophy] (in Neoplatonism, Platonism, and Genosticism) a power existing outside time, deriving from the supreme deity.

Aeration – *(noun)* the process of exposing to air *Aeration of clothes makes them dry.*

Aerial – *(noun)* **1** a structure that transmits or receivers radio or television signals. *If the aerial is in right direction TV transmits good pictures.* **2** a type of freestyle skiing in which the skier jumps from a ramp and carries out manoeuvres in the air. *Aerial shows are often held during winters. (adj.)* **1** existing or taking place in the air or atmosphere. (of a bird) spending much of its time in flight. *Do you see these diving planes? Air force is holding one of its aerial shows.* **2** involving the use of aircraft. **3** (of a part of a plant) growing above ground.

Aeriferous – *(adj.)* conveying air. *Bronchial tubes are auriferous.*

Aeriform – *(adj.)* resembling air or having the form of air. *Water is not as aeriform as wind.*

Aerify – *(verb)* turn into gas. *This water has been aerified, i.e. turned into gas.*

Aero – *(combining)* **1** form relating to air: aerobic. *The Aerobic dance was beautifully executed by the dancers.* **2** of or relating to aircraft: aerodrome.

Aesthetics – *(pl. noun)* a set of principles concerned with the nature and appreciation of beauty, especially in art. the branch of philosophy which deals with questions of beauty and artistic taste. *We should never lose sense of aesthetics.*

Aestival – *(adj.)* [technical] belonging to or appearing in summer.

Aether – *(noun)* variant spelling of ether (in senses 3 and 4). *Our earth is surrounded by aether.*

Afar – *(noun)* **1** a member of a people living in Djibouti and NE Ethiopia. **2** the Cushitic language of this people.

Affable – *(adj.)* good-natured and sociable. *He is very affable by nature; always laughing mixing and socializing.*

Affect – *(verb)* have an effect on; make a difference to. touch the feeling of. *His words have affected me so much. I am going to apologize to him.*

Affectation – *(noun)*. behaviour, speech, or writing that is artificial and designed to impress. a studied display of feeling. *His speech shows a lot of affectation; these can't be his genuine feelings.*

Affected – *(adj.)* **1** artificial, pretentious, and designed to impress. *His behaviour is clearly affected. He can't be that gentle.* **2** [archaic] disposed or inclined in a specified way.

Affection – *(noun)* **1** a feeling of fondness or liking. *I have great affection for my granddaughter.* **2** [archaic] the action or process of affecting or being affected. a disease. a mental state; an emotion.

Affective – *(adj.)* [chiefly psychology] relating to moods, feelings, and attitudes. *His affective cheerfulness touched all people.*

Afferent – *(adj.)* relating to or denoting the conduction of nerve impulses or blood inwards or towards something. the opposite of efferent. *(noun)* an afferent nerve fibre or vessel.

Affiance – *(verb)* poetic – literary be engaged to marry. *She is affiance with her boyfriend.*

Affidavit – *(noun)* [law] a written statement confirmed by oath or affirmation, for use as evidence in court. *I had to produce an affidavit in police station to the effect that I had lost my ID.*

Affiliate – *(verb)* officially attach or connect to an organization. (of an organization) admit as a member. *noun* an affiliated person or organization. *This collage is affiliated with Delhi University.*

Affined – *(adj.)* [mathematics] allowing for or preserving parallel relationships. *noun* [anthropology] a relative by marriage.

Affinity – *(noun)* **1** a spontaneous or natural liking or sympathy. a close relationship based on a common origin or structure. relationship by marriage. *I enjoyed great affinity with her and consequently I married her* **2** [chiefly biochemistry] the degree to which a substance tends to combine with another.

Affirm – *(verb)* state emphatically or publicly. [law] ratify (a judgment or agreement). [law] make a formal declaration rather than taking an oath. *I publicly affirmed that I had never seen that man before.*

Affirmative – *(adj.)* **1** agreeing with or consenting to a statement or request. [Grammar] &logic stating that a fact is so. Contrasted with negative and interrogative. **2** relating to or denoting proposed legislation which must receive an affirmative parliamentary vote before it can come into force. *(noun)* an affirmative statement or word. *My affirmative reply encouraged him a lot.* [logic] a statement asserting that something is true of the subject of a proposition. exclamatory [chiefly N. Amer.] yes.

Affix – *(verb)* attach or fasten to something else. *Affix this stamp on the envelope and drop it into a letterbox.* *(noun)* [Grammar] an addition to the base form or stem of a word in order to modify its meaning or create a new word.

Afflict – *(verb)* cause pain or suffering to. *He is afflicted with a terrible wound.*

Affluence – *(noun)* abundant wealth. *His affluence carried a lot of weigh and he became the President of the club.*

Affluent – *(adj.)* **1** wealthy. *He is an affluent person and owns a chain of malls.* **2** [archaic] (of water) flowing freely or copiously. *(noun)* [archaic] a tributary stream.

Afflux – *(noun* [archaic] a flow of water or air.

Afford – *(verb)* **1** have sufficient money, time, or means for. be able to do something without risk of adverse consequences. *I can't afford such a costly TV.* **2** provide (an opportunity or facility).

Afforest – *(verb)* **1** convert (land) into forest for commercial exploitation. *The land mafia has afforested large chutiks land for commercial gain.***2** [historical] bring (woodland) under the jurisdiction of forest law for the purpose of hunting.

Affray – *(noun)* [law] a breach of the peace by fighting in a public place. *Affray near the cinema hall caused the police to intervene.*

Affright – *(verb)* frighten. *The lonely jungle in the night a frightened.* *(noun)* fright. *There was a fright in the air as he entered an old and dark tunnel.*

Affront - *(noun)* an action or remark that causes outrage or offence. *(verb)* offend the modesty or values of. *It was an affront on his part to insult his senior.* **2** He affronted the modesty of a women and was arrested.

Affuse - *(verb)* pour out. *I affused a lot of affection on her.*

Afield - *(adv.)* **1** to or at a distance. Afield I chanced to see a lion. **2** in the field (in reference to hunting). *He was afield for hunting.*

Afire - *(adv.&adj.)* in flames. *The mob set afire the police jeep.*

Aflame - *(adv. & adj.)* in flames. *The aeroplane went down aflame as it hit a mountain.*

Afloat - *(adv. & adj.)* **1** floating in water. on board a ship or boat. *There is nobody in the ship. It must have been afloat for a long time.* **2** out of debt or difficulty.

Afore - *(prep.)* [archaic or dialect] before. *Please send the aforementioned documents.*

Afraid - *(adj.)* (often afraid of - to do) fearful or anxious. anxious about the well-being of. *I am afraid that my father might not have another heart attack.*

Afresh - *(adverb)* in a new or different way. *He started afresh even after total bankruptcy.*

After - *(prep.)* **1** in the time following (an event or another period of time). N. Amer. past (used in specifying a time). *I entered the house after my father had gone.* **2** behind. in the direction of someone who is moving away. *I am coming right after you.* **3** in pursuit or quest of. *The police is after the dacoit.* **4** next to and following in order or importance. *The digit 5 comes after 4.* **5** in allusion or reference to. *He was named after his grandfather.* In the style or following the example of. [conjunction & adverb] in the time following (an event). *(adj.)* [archaic] later. **2** nearer the stern of a ship.

Again - *(adv.)* **1** once more. *Again he won the trophy.* **2** returning to a previous position or condition. *After the court decided in his favour he again got his job* **3** in addition to what has already been mentioned. on the other hand. *He is a brilliant chess player and again a good mathematician.*

Against - *(prep.)* **1** in opposition to. to the disadvantage of. in resistance to. *I am totally against this project.* **2** in anticipation of and preparation for (a difficulty). (in betting) in anticipation of the failure of. *How dare you speak against me?* **3** in relation to (money owed, due, or lent) so as to reduce, canncel, or secure it. in or into contact with. in contrast to. *Doctors and hospitals are preparing against the breakout of an epidemic.* **4** Next week India will play against Pakistan. *The odds are against England in this match.*

Agape - *(adj.)* (of a person's mouth) wide open. *The surprise news left him agape.*

Agate - *(noun)* an ornamental stone consisting of a hard variety of chalcedony, typically banded in appearance.

Agenda - *(noun)* a list of items to be discussed at a meeting. a list of matters to be addressed. *The chairman was given the agenda as soon as the meeting started.*

Agent - *(noun)* **1** a person that provides a particular service, typically one organizing transactions between two other parties. a person who manages financial or contractual matters for an actor, performer, or writer. *Travel and property agents are useful people.* **2** a person who works in secret to obtain information for a government. *Actors and writers have their own agents.* **3** a person or thing that takes an active role or produces a specified effect. Grammar the doer of an action. *A Russian agent was caught in America.* **4** Computing an independently operating Internet program, typically one set up to locate information on a specified subject and deliver it on a regular basis.

Agglutinate - *(verb)* **1** firmly stick or be stuck together to form a mass. *The jelly agglutinate.* **2** [linguistics] (of a language) combine (word elements) to express compound ideas. *He agglutinated jargons to sound high and mighty.*

Aggravate - *(verb)* **1** make worse. **2** [informal] annoy. *His drunken behaviour has aggravated an already bad situation.*

Aggregate - *(noun)* **1** a whole formed by combining several disparate elements. *The* *aggregate of points gained by her in the match is very impressive.* **2** the total score of a player or team in a fixture comprising more than one game or round. *My aggregate is 400 out of 500.* **3** a material or structure formed from a loosely compacted mass of fragments or particles. pieces of broken or crushed stone or gravel used to make concrete. *(adj.)* **1** formed or calculated by the combination of many separate units or items. **2** [Botany] (of a group of species) comprising several very similar species formerly regarded as a single species. **3** [Economics] denoting the total supply or demand for goods and services in an economy at a particular time. *(verb)* combine into a whole.

Aggrieve - *(adj.)* characterized by or resulting from aggression. unduly forceful. *As he was attacked upon he is the aggrieved party.*

Aghast - *(adj.)* filled with horror or shock. *I felt aghast at his cheap behaviour.*

Agile - *(adj.)* able to move quickly and easily. *Snake is an agile creature.*

Agist - *(verb)* take in and feed (livestock) for payment. *My profession was to agist the cattle.*

Agitate - *(verb)* **1** make troubled or nervous. *The news of accident agitated him* **2** campaign to arouse public concern about an issue. *The agitation of people against the cuts in electric supply went on for long time.* **3** stir or disturb (a liquid) briskly.

Agitation - *(noun)* a mental state of extreme emotional disturbance. *In a state of agitation he attacked his opponent.* **2** a state of turbulent change or development. *People agitated against the poor water supply.* **3** the feeling of being agitated. *I was in an agitated state of mind when my friend called me liar.*

Aglet - *(noun)* a metal or plastic tube fixed tightly round each end of a shoelace. *The aglets of my shoes have become loose.*

Aglow - *(adj.)* softly bright or radiant. *The palace was aglow with lights.*

Agnate - *(adj.)* related on the faiher's side.

Agnus - *(noun)* **1** a figure of a lamb bearing a cross or flag, as an emblem of Christ. **2** Christian church an invocation beginning with the words 'Lamb of God' forming a set part of the Mass.

Agog - *(adj.)* very eager to hear or see something. *He was agog with excitement as he entered the movie hall.*

Agonic - *(noun)* an imaginary line round the earth passing through both the north pole and the north magnetic pole, at any point on which a compass needle points to true north. *The needle is pointing to the North so it must be a point on the agonic.*

Agonist - *(noun)* [biochemistry] a substance which initiates a physiological response when combined with a part of the body directly. **2** a protagonist. *He is an agonist in the field of boxing.*

Agonize - *(verb)* **1** undergo great mental anguish through worrying over something. *I was agonized to hear about his accident.* **2** (agonizing) cause agony to.

Agony - *(noun)* extreme suffering. *I am far away from my family and thus living in great agony.*

Agoraphobia - *(noun)* extreme or irrational fear of open or public places. *He is afraid of vast open space. Doctors say it is a disease named agoraphobia.*

Agrarian - *(adj.)* of or relating to cultivated land or agriculture. relating to landed property. *Agrarian revolution in France showed good result.* *(noun)* a person who advocates a redistribution of landed property.

Agree - *(verb)* **1** have the same opinion about something. (of two or more parties) be in agreement. *I agree with you in this matter.* **2** consent to do something. reach agreement about. *We shall soon agree over this point.* **3** be consistent with. be good for. *Such kind of food doesn't agree with my stomach.* [Grammar] have the same number, gender, case, or person as.

Agrestic - *(adj.)* characteristic of the fields or country. *Rural people have agrestic simplicity.*

Agriculture - *(noun)* the science or practice of farming, including the rearing of crops and animals. *Agriculture forms an important part of a country's economy.*

Aground - *(adj.&adv.)* (with reference to a ship) on or on to the bottom in shallow water. *The ship ran aground and was damaged.*

Ague – *(noun)* [archaic] malaria or some other illness involving fever and shivering. a fever or shivering fit.

Ahead – *(adv.)* further forward in space or time. in advance. in the lead. *America is far ahead than any other country in space science.*

Ahem – *(exclamatory)* used to attract attention or express disapproval or embarrassment. *He didn't like the talks going on and to show his disagreement loudly said ahem.*

Aid – *(noun)* **1** help or support. *He provides aid me in times of crisis.* **2** material help given to a country in need. *India gives aid many neighboring countries in times of disaster like floods and earthquakes.* **3** [historical] a grant of subsidy or tax to a king. *(verb)* help.

Aigrette – *(noun)* a headdress consisting of white egret's feather or other decoration such as a spray of gems. *She ware an aigrette for Halloween.*

Ail – *(verb)* [archaic] trouble or afflict in mind or body. *He is ailing from TB.*

Aim – *(verb)* point (a weapon or camera) at a target. direct at someone or something. *I aimed my rifle at the wolf and shot him.* **2** try to achieve something. *My aim in life is to become a doctor.* *(noun)* **1** a purpose or intention. **2** the aiming of a weapon or missile. *His anger was aimed at me.*

Air – *(noun)* **1** the invisible gaseous substance surrounding the earth, a mixture mainly or oxygen and nitrogen. *Air surrounded earth; if there were no air we won't be able to breath and would die.* **2** the indicating the use of aircraft. the earth's atmosphere as a medium for transmitting radio waves. Radio waves pass through the air. *Election news will be aired at TV at 12'O' clock noon.* **3** one of the four elements in ancient and medieval philosophy and in astrology. **4** a breeze or light wind. *Put these damp clothes in the air so that they become ary.* **5** an impression given. an annoyingly affected and condescending manner. **6** music a tune or short melodious composition. *(verb)* **1** express (an opinion or grievance) publicly. broadcast (a program me) on radio or television. *He aired his grievences publicly.* **2** expose (a room) to the open air. brit. put (washed laundry) in the open air or a warm place to remove dampness.

Aisle – *(noun)* **1** a passage between rows of seat, pews, or supermarket shelves. *I walked through the aisle in the church and reached the pulpit.* **2** [architecture] a lateral division of a church parallel to, and divided by pillars from, a nave, choir, or transept. *I walked briskly through the aisle and found my seal.* **3** Supermarkets put their goods in aisles also.

Ajar – *(adv. & adj.)* (of a door or window) slightly open. *I left the door ajar to watch his activities.*

Akin – *(adj.)* **1** of similar character. **2** related by blood. *He being my brother is akin to me.*

Alack – *(exclamatory)* [archaic] an expression of regret or dismay.

Alacrity – *(noun)* brisk and cheerful readiness. *The alacrity in his nature makes him good companion.*

Alamode – *(adj.)* in the current fashion or style *Jeans are alamode these days.*

Alarm – *(noun)* **1** anxious or frightened awareness of danger. a warning of danger. *The news has set alarm bells ringing in my mind.* **2** a warning sound or device. *I have set the alarm at 5 'o' clock.* *(verb)* **1** frighten or disturb. *His sudden appearance has alarmed me.* **2** be filled or protected with an alarm. **3** *There is an alarm bells at the door.*

Albeit – *(conj.)*– though. *He is poor albeit honest.*

Albert – *(noun)* a watch chain with a bar at one end for attaching to a buttonhole.

Albescent – *(adj.)* growing or shading into white.

Albino – *(noun)* a person or animal having a congenital absence of pigment in the skin and hair (which are white) and the eyes (which are usually pink). *A strange child was born to her having no colouring in eyes skin or hair, it was an albino.*

Album – *(noun)* **1** a blank book for the insertion of photographs, stamps, with feathery leaves and plume-like flowers. *This album consists all my pictures of childhood.*

Albumen – *(noun)* egg white, or the protein contained in it. *Albumen in the egg has lots of protienes.*

Albuminoid – *(noun)* a simple protein found horny and cartilaginous tissues and in the lens of the eye. *There is albuminoid.*

Alchemy – *(noun)* **1** the medieval forerunner of chemistry, concerned particularly with attempts to convert base metals into gold or to find a universal elixir. **2** a process by which paradoxical results are achieved or incompatible elements combined.

Alcove – *(noun)* a recess, typically in the wall of a room. *I fitted my almirah in the alcove.*

Alee – *(adj.&adv.)* [nautical] on the leeward side of a ship. *Move round to leeward.*

Alert – *(adj.)* quick to notice and respond to potential danger or problems. intellectually active. *This watchmen is very alert, you can't enter the compound without his permission.* *(noun)* **1** the state of being alert. **2** a warning of danger. *We are all on the alert and nobody can pass through this place.* **3** a reminder or prompt. *verb* warm of a danger or problem. **4** Not understand

Algebra – *(noun)* the part of mathematics in which letters and other general symbols are used to represent numbers and quantities in formulae and equations. a system of this based on given axioms. *So far mathematics is concerned he is very weak in algebra.*

Algid – *(adj.)* chilly. *In winter this room becomes very algid.*

Alias – *(adv.)* also known as. *Raj alias Raju was a notorious thug.* *(noun)* **1** a false or assumed identity. **2** computing an alternative name or label that refers to a file, command, or address, and can be used to locate or access it. **3** [physics & telecommunications] each of a set of signal frequencies which, when sampled at a given uniform rate, would give the same set of sampled values and thus be indistinguishable. *(verb)* [physics & telecommunication] misidentify (a signal frequency), introducing distortion or error.

Alien – *(adj.)* **1** belonging to a foreign country. *He hails from USA. He is an alien.* **2** unfamiliar and distasteful. *This is something alien to my tongue and I don't like it.* **3** introduced from another country and later naturalized. **4** relating to or denoting beings from other worlds. *(noun)* **1** a foreigner, especially one who is not a natrualized citizen of the country where they are living. **2** an alien plant or animal species. **3** a being from another world. *Someday aliens from other planets may attack earth.*

Alienate – *(verb)* **1** cause to feel isolated. lose of destroy the support or sympathy of. *On account of his bad behaviour he has been alienated from his family.* **2** [law] transfer ownership of (property rights) to another. *The father has legally alienated the rights of his property to his son.*

Alienist – *(noun)* former term for phychiatrist. [chiefly US] a psychiatrist who assesses the competence of a defendant in a law court.

Aliform – *(adj.)* wing-shaped. *An aliform kite flew in the sky.*

Alight – *(verb)* **1** [formal] descend form public transport. *He alighted from the moving bus.* **2** chance to notice.

Alike – *(adj)* similar. *(adverb)* in a similar way. Both the brother are alike. *They also behave alike.*

Aliment – *(noun)* **1** [archaic] food; nourishment. Scots law maintenance; alimony. *The judge fixed the aliment for the divorced women.*

Alimony – *(noun)* maintenance for a spouse after separation or divorce. *After the divorce he was ordered to pay a huge amount as alimony to his divorced wife.*

Aliquot – *(noun)* **1** a portion of a larger whole, especially a sample taken for chemical analysis or other treatment. *When an aliquot of the river water was taken it was found to be contaminated.* **2** [mathematics] a quantity which can be divided into another. an integral number of times. *(verb)* divided (a whole) into aliquots; take aliquots from (a whole).

Alive – *(adj.)* **1** living, not dead. continuing in existence or use. *The river was alive with fish.* **2** alert and active. don't be I am very alive or this project. having interest and meaning. aware of and interested in. swarming or teeming with. *I am very much alive to the music.*

Alkali – *(noun)* a compound, e.g. lime or caustic soda, with particular chemical properties including turning litmus blue and neutralizing or effervescing with acids. *This mixture seems to be alkaline.*

Alkaloid – *(noun)* [chemistry] any of a class of nitrogenous organic compounds of plant origin which have pronounced physiological actions on humans. *Alkaloid compounds of a plant act physiologically on humans.*

Alkanet – *(noun)* a plant of the borage family with a hairy stem and blue flowers. *This blue flowered plant is called alkanet.*

All – *(predeterminer, determiner & pronoun)* the whole quantity or extent of. any whatever. the greatest possible. everything. *In all only ten students are present.* *(adverb)* **1** completely. *All people present here should raise their lands.* **2** used after a number to indicate an equal score.

Allay – *(verb)* diminish (fare are concern), alleviate (pain or hunger). *His talk allayed my fears.*

Allegation – *(noun)* **1** [law] a formal accusation against somebody. *The allegation against him is that of murder.* **2** a statement affirming or denying certain matters of fact that you are performed to prove. *I am ready to prove that all allegation against him are false.*

Allege – *(verb)* claim that someone has done something wrong, typically without proof. *It is alleged that he got drunk and hit his wife.*

Allegiant – *(adj.)* steadfast in devotion. *It is not possible to be allegiant to two masters.*

Allegoric – *(adj.)* used in or characteristic of or containing allegory. *In ancient times allegoric tales occupied an important place.*

Allegro – *(adv. & adj.)* at a brisk speed. *(noun)* an allegro movement, passage, or composition. *The allegro movement on women's rights succeeded in the end.*

Alleviate – *(verb)* make (pain or difficulty) less severe. *The doctor's treatment alleviated my pain.*

Alley – *(noun)* **1** a narrow passageway between or behind buildings. a path in a park or garden. *I saw two cats fighting in the alley.* **2** a long, narrow area in which skittles and bowling are played. *Some boys are playing in the alley.* **3** [N. Amer.] [Tennis] either of the two side strips between the service court and the sidelines. baseball the area between the outfielders in left-centre or right centerfield.

Alliance – *(noun)* **1** a union or association formed for natural benefit. a relationship based on an affinity. the state of being joined or associated. [Ecology] a group of closely related plant associations. *There is alliance between the two states to preserve wild life.*

Alligator – *(noun)* **1** a large semiaquatic reptile similar to a crocodile but with a broader and shorter head, native to the Americas and China. *Alligator looks like crocodile but there is some difference.* **2** the skin of the alligator.

Alliterate – *(verb)* [poetry] use alliteration as a form of poetry.

Allocate – *(verb)* assign or distribute (resources or duties) to. *All person were allocated their duties by the election officer.*

Allocution – *(noun)* a formal speech giving advice or a warning. *He was given an allocution before delivering the speech.*

Allograph – *(noun)* **1** [linguistics] each of two or more alternative forms of a letter of an alphabet or other unit of a writing system. **2** [phonetics] each of two or more letters or letter combinations representing a single phoneme in different words (e.g. the (f) of 'fake' and the (ph) of 'phase').

Allot – *(verb)* apportion or assign (something) to someone. *I have been allotted a flat by DDA.*

Allotment – *(noun)* **1** a plot of land rented by an individual from a local authority, for growing vegetables or flowers. *People said there were lots of irregularities in the allotment of flats by DDA.* **2** the action of allotting. an amount of something allotted. *Rupees one lakh was allotted by the centre to the flood hill areas.*

Allow – *(verb)* **1** admit as legal or acceptable. permit to do something. *The pan was allowed to go on leave.* **2** (often allow for) take into consideration when making plans or calculations. provide or set aside for a particular purpose. *I'll* *allow only half the amount to be spent.* **3** admit the truth of. *Allow the truth to shine out.*

Allowance – *(noun)* the amount of something allowed. a sum of money paid regularly to a person, typically to meet specified expenses. an amount of money that can be earned or received free of tax. *My tax allowance does not allow me to lead a luxurious life.* [horse racing] a deduction in the weight that a horse is required to carry in a race. *(verb)* [archaic] give a sum of money regularly as an allowance. *You'll get an allowance of Rs. 2000 per month to run the house.*

Alloy – *(noun)* a metal made by combining two or more metallic elements, especially to give greater strength or resistance to corrosion. an inferior metal mixed with a precious one. *This is an alloy of nickel, bronze and zinc.* *(verb)* mix to make an alloy. *I am alloying tin with copper to make bronze.*

Allspice – *(noun)* **1** the dried aromatic fruit of a Caribbean tree, used as a culinary spice. *While visiting Caribbean island I ate the fruit allspice. It was very nice.* **2** a tree of the myrtle family from which this spice is obtained. **3** an aromatic north American tree or shrub.

Allude – *(verb)* hint at. mention in passing. *While in restaurant I alluded at having an ice cream.*

Allcure – *(noun)* powerful attraction or fascination. *He had allcure for discovering lost cities of ancient times.* *(verb)* [often as *(adj.)* alluring] powerfully attract. **2** *The sight of her allcured me.* **3** *The fascinating jungle all around me allcured me.*

Allusion – *(noun)* the practice or device of making indirect or implicit references. a reference of this type. *I alluded to a similar case in the court where the sentence of hanging was withdrawn.*

Alluvial – *(adj.)* of or relating to alluvium. *The alluvial soil is greatly fertile.*

Alluvion – *(noun)* [law] the formation of new land by deposition of sediment by the sea or a river. compare with avulsion. *Formation of alluvion land by deposition the sea or river of sedimentation has made this piece of land very fertile.*

Ally – *(noun)* a person or organization that cooperates with another. *In 2nd world war America was an ally of France and UK.* a state formally cooperating with another for a military or other purpose. *The two countries were allied formally by treaty.* the countries that fought with Britain in the first and second world wars. verb combine a resource or commodity with for mutual benefit. side with.

Almanac – *(noun)* an annual calendar containing important dates and statistical information, such as astronomical data. an annual handbook containing information of general or specialist interest. *Let me consult the almanac to find an auspicious date for marriage.*

Almanographer - *(noun)* one who makes almanac. *Every year almanographers get busy in making the almanac.*

Almighty – *(adj.)* **1** omnipotent. *God is almighty.* **2** [informal] enormous. *(noun)* a name or title for God.

Almond – *(noun)* **1** the oval edible nut-like kernel of the almond tree, growing in a woody shell. *It is said that five almonds in the morning everyday are greatly beneficial for health.* **2** The tree that produces this, related to the peach and plum.

Almoner – *(noun)* [historical] an official distributor of alms. *He is on the important part of almoner because he distributes alms.*

Almost – *(adverb)* nearly. *He almost died of malaria.*

Alms – *(pl. noun)* (in historical contexts) charitable donations of money of food to the poor. *Alms have been distributed among the poor.*

Aloe – *(noun)* **1** a succulent tropical plant with a rosette of thick tapering leaves and bell-shaped or tubular flowers on long stems. a strong laxative obtained from the bitter juice of various kinds of aloe. another term for centurey palnt. *This bitter juice is that of aloe drink. It is a good laxative, you'll get rid of your constipation also.* **2** the fragrant heartwood of a tropical asian tree. the resin obtained from this wood, used in perfume, incense, and medicine.

Alone – *(adj.&adv.)* **1** on one's own; by oneself. *I went into the jungle all alone.* isolated and lonely. *Of all I alone supported him.* **2** only; exclusively. *At this age I prefer to live alone.*

Along -*(prep.&adv.)* **1** moving in a constant direction on (a more or less horizontal surface). *I went along the railing and soon reached the hall.* **2** in or into company with others. *I went to picnic along with my friends.*

Alopecia - *(noun)* [medicine] the absence of hair from areas of the body where it normally grows. *He suffers from alopecia and has lost a lot of hair.*

Aloud - *(adv.)* audibly. [archaic] loudly. *Please speak aloud I can't hear you.*

Alow - *(adv.)* [archaic or dialect] below; downwards. *Alow there is a lake.*

Alps - *(noun)* a high mountain. the high range of mountains in Switzerland and adjourning countries. (in Switzerland) an area of green pasture on a mountain side. *When in Europe I tried to climb alps.*

Alpaca - *(noun)* a long-haired domesticated south American mammal related to the llama. the wool of the alpaca, or fabric made from it. *When I went to South America I saw alpaca related to ilama.*

Alpha - *(noun)* **1** the first letter of the Greek alphabet transliterated as 'a'. denoting the first of a series of items or categories. a first-class mark given for a piece of work. a code word representing the letter. A, used in radio communication.

Alphabet - *(noun)* a set of letters or symbols a fixed order used to represent the basic set of speech sounds of a language. *Without alphabets there can be no language.*

Alpine - *(adj.)* **1** of or relating to high mountains. (in the names of plants and animals) growing or found on high mountains. of or relating to the Alps. *This is a giant tree almost alpine in height.* **2** (also alpine) relating to or denoting skiing downhill. *(noun)* **1** an alpine plant. *This plant grows on alps hence we can call it alpine plant.* **2** a north American butterfly which has brownish-black wings with orange-red markings.

Alpinist - *(noun)* a climber of high mountains, especially in the alps. *He is a famous alpinist, he has climbed alps many times.*

Already - *(adv.)* **1** before the time in question. as surprisingly soon or early as this. *I have already finished the book* **2** [North American, informal] an expression of impatience: enough already with these crazy kids! *I am already late. Come to the point quickly.*

Also - *(adv.)* in addition. *He is handsome and also intelligent.*

Altar - *(noun)* the table in a Christian church at which the bread and wine are consecrated in communion services. *Wine and bread were put on the altar in the church.* a table or flat-topped block used as the focus for a religious ritual. *In ancient times people were sacrificed on altar for rituals.*

Alter - *(verb)* change in character, appearance, direction, etc. [North American & Austral], castrate or spay (a domestic animal). *He completely altered his appearance.*

Altercate - *(verb)* have a disagreement over something my brother altercates with me over this point. *An altercation took place between me and my brother over this point.*

Altered - *(adj.)* **1** change in form or cheracter without becoming something else. *The altered outfit of this shop will certainly attract customers.* **2** changes in order to improve or made more fit for particular purpose. *He has altered his personality to succeed in the interview.*

Alternate - *(verb)* occur or do in turn repeatedly. (of a thing) change repeatedly between two contrasting conditions. *Bouts of depression alternate with periods of elation.* *(adj.)* **1** every other. other in a regular pattern. *She was asked to attend every alternate day.* [Botany] (of leaves or shoots) placed alternately on the two sides of the stem. *Another term for alternate. This is a novel set alternative universe.*

Although - *(conj.)* **1** in spite of the fact that. *Although he is a high class officer he has no manners.* **2** but. *He is good looking although a fool.*

Alimeter - *(noun)* an instrument for determining altitude attained, especially a barometric or radar device fitted in an aircraft. *The alimeter fitted in the plane showed the altitude it was flying at.*

Altitude – *(noun)* the height of an object or point in relation to sea level or ground level. *He dived into the sea from the altitude of 50 meters.* [Astronomy] the apparent height of a celestial object above the horizon, measured in angular distance. *Everest is at the altitude of 29 thousand & 7 ft from the sea level.* [geometry] the length of the perpendicular line from a vertex to the opposite side of a figure. *I drew an altitude from one point of the triangle to its base at the opposite side. If measured in angular distance that star is at the altitude of four hundred thousand kms from the earth.*

Alto – *(noun)* **1** [especially in church music] the highest adult male singing voice. the lowest female singing voice; contralto. denoting the member of a family of instruments pitched second or third highest. *Do you hear the alto, it is the high singing male voice and the low tone of the women singing together.*

Altogether – *(adv.)* completely. in total. on the whole. *Altogether the plan seems reasonable. Altogether the scene was lovely.*

Alum – *(noun)* [chemistry] **1** (also potash alum) a colourless astringent compound which is a hydrated double sulphate of aluminum and potassium, used in solution in dyeing and tanning. *The tanner uses alum in solution for dyeing and tanning.* **2** any of a series of analogous compounds of other metals.

Aluminum – *(noun)* a strong, light, corrosion-resistant silvery-grey metal, the chemical element of atomic number **1** *Aluminum is used in the manufacture of planes and window frames with other materials.*

Alumina – *(noun)* aluminum oxide, a white solid that is a major constituent of many clays and is found crystallized as corundum and sapphire. [Al_2O_3].

Alumnus – *(noun)* a former pupil or student of a particular school, college, or university. *I have been an alumnus of K.M. college.*

Alveolate – *(adj.)* pitted with cell-like cavaties. *This alveolate like object is full of cell like cavities, may be it is an old honeycomb.*

Alvine - *(adj.)* of or rilating to the intestines. *He is suffering from alvine wounds and is on high antibiotics.*

Always – *(adv.)* **1** on all occasions. throughout a long period of the past. forever; repeatedly. *You always get what you deserve.* **2** failing all else. *If the marriage fails, we can always divorce.*

Amain – *(adverb)* with great harte, at full speed. *The boys quickly ran away amain.* **2** with all strength. *They pulled the door amain.*

Amalgam – *(noun)* **1** a mixture or blend. *Don't amalgamate the various chemicals rashly, it may explode.* **2** [chemistry] an alloy of mercury with another metal, especially one used for dental fillings.

Amaranth – *(noun)* a plant of a chiefly tropical family that includes love-lies-bleeding. *Amaranth plant is used as a medicine.*

Amass – *(verb)* accumulate over time. [archaic] (of people) gather together. *The fungus amassed overnight almost in no time.*

Amative – *(adj.)* inclined forward or displaying love. *During talks with her he suddenly became amative she didn't appreciate it.*

Amatory – *(adj.)* relating to or induced by sexual love or desire. *He has an amatory character and has relation with many women.*

Amaurosis – *(noun)* [medicine] partial or total blindness without visible change in the eye, typically due to disease of the optic nerve, spinal cord, or brain. *His optical nerve was damaged and thus amaurosis occurred.*

Amaze – *(verb)* surprise greatly. *I was amazed at his sudden appearance after a long time.*

Amazon – *(noun)* **1** a member of a legendary race of female warriors believed by the ancient Greeks to exist in Scythia or elsewhere. a very tall, strong woman. *She is so broad and toll almost like an Amazon.* **2** a green parrot with a broad rounded tail, found in central and south America. *I bought an Amazon parrot.*

Amabagious – *(adj.)* [of language] having more than one meaning. unclear because not distinguishing between alternatives. *You were amabagious in your speech mainly because you presented so many alternatives and your words had more than one meaning.*

Ambassador – *(noun)* a diplomat sent by a state as its permanent representative in a foreign country. *This ambassador from Bolivia is very smart and evasive.* a representative or promoter of a specified activity. *Many actors are brand ambassador of many companies.*

Ambassadress – *(verb)* a women ambassader. *That lady over there in the thick of the party is an ambassadress. She is very glamorous and smart.*

Amber *(noun)* **1** hard translucent fossilized resin originating from extinct coniferous trees, typically yellowish in colour and used in jewellery. *Jewelers use amber to give yellow tinge to their jewelry.* **2** a honey-yellow colour. a yellow light used as a cautionary signal between green for 'go' and red for 'stop'.

Ambient – *(adj.)* **1** of or relating to the immediate environs of something. **2** denoting a style of instrumental music with electronic textures and no persistent beat, used to create atmosphere.

Ambidextrous – *(adj.)* equally skillful with call hand. *He is on ambidextrous surgeon.*

Ambiguity – *(noun)* an expression of who meaning cannot be determined from its contact. *His dialogues are full of ambiguity.* **2** unclearness by ristue of having more than one meaning.

Ambit – *(noun)* the scope, extent, or bounds of something. *The sky has no ambit.*

Ambition – *(noun)* a strong desire to do or achieve something, desire for success, wealth, of fame. *His ambition is to become a doctor.*

Ambo – *(noun)* [in an early Christian church]an oblong pulpit with steps at each end. *The priest has started speaking from the ambo.*

Ambrosia – *(noun)* **1** [Greek & Roman Mythology] the food of the gods. something very pleasing to taste or smell. *He is a very good cook. The food prepared by him tastes and smells of ambrosia.* **2** a fungal product used as food by ambrosia beetles or their larvae. *Ambrosia is used as food by insects like beetles.*

Ambry – *(noun)* variant spelling of AUMBRY. *Same as aumbry.*

Ambulance – *(noun)* a vehicle equipped for taking sick or injured people to and from hospital. *I'm eagerly awaiting the ambulance as my father is very sick.*

Ambulant – *(adj.)* medicine able to walk about; not confined to bed. *He is ambulant; quite mobile on his two feels.*

Ambulate – *(verb)* formal or technical walk; move about. *He ambulated from kitchen to the garden.*

Ambuscade – *(noun)* an ambush. *(verb)* [archaic] lie in wait; ambush. *He ambuscaded to attack his enemy by surprise.*

Ambush – *(noun)* a surprise attack by people lying in wait in a concealed position. *(verb)* attack in such a way. *Babar's army lay in ambush for a surprise attack.*

Ameliorate – *(verb)* make better; *His condition in the hospital has ameliorated and he can walk hour.* reduce the undesirable effect of. *The medicine ameliorated the grip of disease.*

Amen – *(exclamatory)* said at the end of a prayer or hymn, meaning 'so be it'. *At the end of the prayer the priest said amen.*

Amenable – *(adj.)* responsive to suggestion. (amenable to) capable of being acted on. *Go talk to him; he is an amenable fellow and will respond to you.*

Amend – *(verb)* **1** make minor improvements to (a document, proposal, etc.). *I shall have to amend this speech.*

Amenity – *(noun)* a useful or desirable feature of a place. the pleasantness or attractiveness of a place. *The amentity of this place is appreciable.*

Amenorrhoea – *(noun)* an abnormal absence of menstruation. *This amenorrhoea is not to be taken lightly; let's take her at once to the hospital and consult a gyno.*

Amerce – *(verb)* punish with an orbitary penalty; punish by a fine imposed arbitrarily by the direction of the court. *The court has amerced him.*

Amercement – *(noun)* English law, [historical] a fine. *Amercement imposed by the court is very huge.*

Amethyst – *(noun)* a transparent purple variety of quartz; used as a gemstone. *My watch shines in the night because it has fine particles of amethyst.*

Amiable – *(adj.)* friendly and pleasant in manner. *He is an amiable fellow.*

Amid – *(prep.)* surrounded by; in the middle of. *He was lost somewhere amid the huge crowd.*

Amidships – *(adv.& adj.)* in the middle of a ship, either longitudinally or laterally. *As he stood amidships he was hit by a cannon.*

Amity – *(noun)* friendly relations. *There is perfect amity between us friends.*

Ammeter– *(noun)* an instrument for measuring electric current in amperes. *Please bring the ammeter I have to measure the current.*

Ammonia – *(noun)* a colourless, intensely pungent gas which dissolves in water to give a strongly alkaline solution. [NH_3] a solution of this, used as a cleaning fluid. *I am making a cleaning fluid with ammonia and water.*

Ammunition – *(noun)* a supply or quantity of bullets and shells. *The government does not allow civilians to live near ammunition depot because it is very dangerous.*

Amnesia – *(noun)* a partial or total loss of memory. *He has been suffering from amnesia for a long time.*

Amoeba – *(noun)* a single-called animal which catches food and moves about by extending finger-like projections of protoplasm. *For reproduction proceses amoeba divides itself into two.*

Amoral – *(adj.)* lacking a moral sense; unconcerned whether something is right. or wrong. *He is an amoral person, not knowing what should be done and what shouldn't be.*

Amorist – *(noun)* a person who is in love or who writes about love. *He is a big amorist. He has written about a dozen books on love.*

Amoroso – *(adv.&adj.)* [music] in a loving or tender manner. *The music in the café was very amoroso.*

Amorous – *(adj.)* showing or feeling sexual desire. *He is very amorous by nature having many girl friends.*

Amortize – *(verb)* **1** gradually write off the initial cost of (an asset) over a period. reduce or cancel (a debt) by money regularly put aside. *My loan has been amortized by the society.* **2** [historical] transfer (land) to a corporation in mortmain. *The cost of your land has been amortized.*

Amount – *(noun)* the total of something in number; size, value, or extent. a quantity: *I have a large amount of money at my disposal and can buy anything I want.* *(verb)* (amount to) **1** come to be (a total) when added together. *His whole expression amounted to nothing but hate.*

Amour – *(noun)* a love affair or lover; *The amour was wounded in a sword fight.* especially a secret one. *Her amour leaked out although she had guarded it well.*

Ampere – *(noun)* the SI base unit of electric current, equal to a flow of one coulomb per second. *How many ampere of electricity have been used?*

Amphibian – *(noun)* **1** [zoology] a cold-blooded vertebrate animal of a class (Amphibia) that comprises the forges, toads, newts, salamanders and caecilians, distinguished by an aquatic gill-breathing adult stage. *Frog etc. are amphibian animals which can live on both land and water.* **2** a seaplane, tank, or other vehicle that can operate on land and on water. *This rich man has a amphibian seaplane which can operate both on land and water.*

Amphibious – *(adj.)* **1** living in or suited for both land and water. *Many snakes are amphibious* **2** (of a military operation) involving forces landed from the sea. *Amphibious allied forces landed from the sea.*

Amphigory – *(noun)* nonsensical writing. *All his work amounts to amphigory.*

Amphitheatre – *(noun)* **1** round building consisting of tiers of seats surrounding a central space for dramatic or sporting events. a semicircular seating gallery in a theatre. *When I went to Rome I saw the famous amphitheatre there.*

Amphora – *(noun)* a tall ancient Greek or Roman jar or jug with two handles and a narrow neck. *I saw an amphora at a museum. I would have loved to drink from it.*

Amplification – *(noun)* **1** addition of extra material, illustration or classifying detail. *He added a few remarks in amplification and* *defence.* **2** the amount of increase in signal power, voltage or current expressed as the ratio of output to input. *In physics, the process of increasing the magnitude of a variable quantity is known as amplification.*

Amplitude – **1** [physic] the maximum extent or magnitude of a vibration or other oscillating phenomenon, measured from the equilibrium position or average value. **2** breadth, range, or magnitude. **3** [astronomy] the angular distance of a celestial object from the true east or west point of the horizon at rising or setting.

Amply – *(adv.)* **1** in or ample manner. *The opinions of people were amply represented.* **2** sufficiently; more than adequately. *I amply fed myself at the feast.*

Amputate – *(verb)* cut of (a limb) by surgical operation. *The doctors had to amputate to save the patient's life.*

Amuck – *(adv.)* variant spelling of AMOK. *The elephant ran amuck.*

Amulet – *(noun)* an ornament or small piece of jewellery thought to give protection against evil or danger. *I always wear an amulet given by a Sadhu.*

Amuse – *(verb)* **1** cause to laugh or smile. *I was amused by the pranks played by him.* **2** entertain.

An – determine the form of the indefinite article used before words beginning with a vowel sound. *I saw a hen laying an egg.*

Anabaptism – *(noun)* the doctrine that baptism should only be administered to believing adults, held by a protestant sect of the 16th century. *I am a non-believer and as such I would never Anabaptism allow to be administered to me.*

Anachronism – *(noun)* **1** a thing appropriate to a period other than that in which it exists. **2** the attrubution of something to a period to which it does not belong.

Anaclisis – *(noun)* [psychoanalysis] relationship marked by strong dependence on others. *He is suffering from anaclisis for which he is seeing psychologist.*

Anaemia – *(noun)* a condition in which there is a deficiency of red cells or hemoglobin in the blood, resulting in pallor and weariness. *He is suffering from anaemia. He should have checked hemoglobin.*

Anaesthesia – *(noun)* insensitivity to pain, especially as artificially induced by the administration of gases or drugs before a surgical operation. *His body has been made insensitive to pain by anaesthesia because he is to undergo an operation.*

Anal – *(adj.)* **1** of, relating to, or situated near the anus. *He had to undergo anal surgery to get rid of piles.* **2** [psychoanalysis] denoting a stage of infantile psychosexual development in which defecation is the major source of sensuous pleasure. anal-retentive.

Analeptic – *(adj.)* restorative, especially through stimulating the central nervous system. *(noun)* an analeptic drug. *It is an analeptic drug, it will stimulate your mind.*

Analgesia – *(noun)* [medicine] relief of pain through administration of drugs or other methods. *Take an analgesia tablet to get relief from your pain.*

Analogical – *(adj.)* expressing composed of, or based on an analogy. *The two poems are analogical in content.*

Analogy – *(noun)* a comparison between one thing and another made for the purpose of explanation or clarification. the process of making such a comparison. a thing regarded as analogous to another; an analogue. *There is a great analogy between the two brothers.*

Analysable – *(adj.)* capable of being partitioned. *This sentence is Analysable.*

Analyse – *(verb)* **1** examine methodically and in detail the constitution or structure of. identify and measure the chemical constituents of. *If you analyse this chemical properly you will know its constituent.* **2** psychoanalyse.

Analysis – *(noun)* **1** a detailed examination of the elements or structure of something. *Analysis of his DNA sample must be done as soon as possible.* **2** the process of separating something into its constituent elements. often contrasted with synthesis. the process of analysing the chemical constituents of a substance. *Analysis of a sentence is the opposite of its synthesis.*

3 short for psychoanalysis. *The analysis of his mind brought no result although it took a long time.* **4** [mathematics] the part of mathematics concerned with the theory of functions and the use of limits, continuity, and the operations of calculus.

Analytical - *(adj.)* relating to or using analysis or logical reasoning. *Analytical discussion of a thing leads to its logical conclusion.*

Anamnesis - **1** recollection, especially of a supposed previous existence. *Anamnesis occurred to him at the age of eight and she remembered many facts of his past birth.* **2** [Christian church] the part of the educharist in which the passion, resurrection, and ascension of Christ are recalled.

Anamorphous - *(noun)* the evolution of one type of organism from another by a long series of gradual changes. *Fish has evolved from another organism which is known as anamorphous.*

Anarchic - *(adj.)* with no controlling rules or principles to give order. *The state was declared anarchic.*

Anarchy - *(noun)* **1** a state of disorder due to lack of government or control. *Anarchists had spread anarchy all over the city.* **2** a society or political system founded on the principles of anarchism.

Anathema - *(noun)* **1** something that one vehemently dislikes. *Casteism was anathema to her.* **2** a formal curse of the church, excommunicating a person or denouncing a doctrine.

Anatomy - *(noun)* **1** the branch of biology and medicine concerned with bodily structure, especially as reveled by dissection. the bodly structure of a person, animal, or plant. *Anatomy interests me greatly.* **2** a detailed examination: the anatomy of change. a complex structure.

Ancestor - *(noun)* a person, typically one more remote than a grandparent, from whom one is descended. something from which a later species or version has evolved. *Our ancestor belonged to India.*

Anchor - *(noun)* **1** a heavy object used to moor a ship to the sea bottom, typically having a metal shank with a pair of curved, barbed flukes. the brakes of a car. *The ship has dropped anchor and is secured firmly in a position.* **2** an anchorman or achorwoman. *(verb)* **1** moor with an anchor. secure firmly in position. *The ship was anchored firmly.* **2** present and coordinate (a television or radio programme). *She is an anchor is a top news channel.*

Anchorite - *(noun)* [historical] a religious recluse. *He is an anchorite, remaining alone and talking to nobody.*

Ancient - *(adj.)* belonging to or originating in the very distant past. *In ancient times there were very funny and dangerous animals.* [chiefly humorous] very old. *(noun)* **1** [archaic or humorous] an old man. *Don't you bother your head about him he is an ancient old man.* **2** the people of ancient times, especially the classical Greeks and Romans. *Greeks and Roman were people of ancient times.*

Ancillary - *(adj.)* providing support to the primary activities of an organization; additional; subsidiary. *This branch is an ancillary of the food department.* *(noun)* an ancillary person or thing. *He is ancillary to the director.*

Ancon - *(noun)* **1** a console, typically consisting or two volutes, that supports or appears to support a cornice. **2** each of a pair of projection on either side of a block of stone or other material, used for lifting it.

And - *(conj.)* **1** used to connect words of the same part of speech, clauses, or sentences. connecting two identical comparatives, to emphasize a progressive change. connecting two identical words, implying great duration or great extent. *Love and kindness two great virtues.* **2** used to connect two numbers to indicate that they are being added together. [archaic] connecting two numbers, implying succession. *You and me are going to see a movie.* **3** used to introduce an additional comment or interjection. *I wanted to study a lot and become a doctor.* **4** [informal] used after some verbs and before another verb to indicate intention, instead of 'to'. *(noun)* a logical operation which gives the value one if and only if all the operands are one, and otherwise gives a value of zero. *I went to the bus stand and boarded a bus.*

Andiron – *(noun)* a metal support, typically one of a pair, for wood burning in a fireplace. *It was very cold. He put an andiron into the hearth for supporting fire logs.*

Anecdote – *(noun)* a short entertaining story about a real incident or person. an account regarded as unreliable or as being hearsay. *I'll feel you an anecdote about my brother. Whatever you are saying is not reliable. It seems an anecdote.*

Anemograph – *(noun)* an anemometer which records the speed, duration, and sometimes also the direction of the wind. *The anemograph shows that a strong wind is developing.*

Anemometer – *(noun)* an instrument for measuring the speed of the wind or other flowing gas. *According to the anemometer the speed of the wind is 200 kms an hour.*

Aneroid – *(adj.)* relating to or denoting a barometer that measures air pressure by the action of the air in deforming the elastic lid of an evacuated box. *This is an instrument called barometer or aneroid which tells us about the air pressure.*

Anew – *(adv.)* [chiefly poetic – literary] in a new or different way. once more; again. *Now that you have served your term you must start anew.*

Anfroctuous – *(adj.)* sinuous or circuitous. *Catacombs are always anfroctuous in construction.*

Angel – *(noun)* **1** a spiritual being believed to act as an attendant or messenger of God, conventionally represented as being of human form with wings. *You have proved yourself an angel by helping me in this hour of need.* **2** a person of great beauty, kindness, or virtue. *She is beautiful and virtuous like an angle.* **3** [informal] (especially in the theatre) a financial backer: **4** [aviation] slang used with a numeral to indicate an aircraft's altitude in thousands of feel. *We rendezvous at angels nine.* **5** a former English coin bearing the figure of the archangel Michael killing a dragon. **6** [informal] an unexplained radar signal.

Anger – *(noun)* a strong feeling of annoyance, displeasure, or hostility. *By his behaviour he angesed me. (verb)* provoke anger in. *Anger was his doing he couldn't console himself in time.*

Angina – *(noun)* [medicine] **1** a condition marked by severe pain in the chest, arising from an inadequate blood supply to the heart. *Your father is suffering from angina pain. You should call a doctor at once.* **2** used in names of disorders involving pain in the throat: *Ludwig's angina.*

Angle – *(noun)* **1** the space (usually measured in degrees) between two intersecting lines or surfaces at or close to the point where they meet. a corner, especially an external projection or internal recess. a measure of the indlination of one line or surface with respect to another. *A triangle has three angles.* **2** a position from which something is viewed or along which it travels or acts. a particular way of approaching an issue or problem. *Please look at this problem from my angle then you'll understand my difficulty.* **3** [astrology] each of the four cardinal points of a chart. **4** angle iron or a similar constructional material. *This wash basin needs the support an angle iron. (verb)* **1** direct, move, or incline at an angle. **2** present (information) to reflect a particular view or have a particular focus. *I discussed the problem from every conceivable angle.*

Angler – *(noun)* a scheming person; someone who schemes to gain an advantage. *He is an angler and has thousand tricks up his sleeve, so beware of him.* **2** a fisherman who uses a hook and line. *An angler who is trying to catch a fish with a hook and line must have great patience and skill.* **3** fishes having large mouths with a worm like filament attached for luring prey. *This is angler fish having a large mouth.*

Anglican – *(adj.)* relating to or denoting the church of England or any church in communion with it. *I visited an Anglican church during my visit to England. (noun)* a member of any of these churches. *He is an Anglican because he belong to the church of England.*

Angling – *(verb)* **1** fishing with a hook. *The fisherman is Angling for hours by the river side with a hook and line.* **2** move or proceed at an age. *He has turned and now is angling towards my house.*

Anglo - *(noun)* **1** a white english-speaking person, especially one of British or non-hispanic origin. *He is an Anglo descending from British race.* **2** [brit. informal] a person selected for a scottish, lrish, or welsh national sports team who plays for an English club. *Although Irish he is called Anglo because he is playing for an English club.*

Anglo saxon - *(noun)* **1** a Germanic inhabitant of England between the 5th century and the Norman conquest. a person of English descent. [chiefly North American] any white, English-speaker person. *The Anglo Saxon were fierce.* **2** the old English language. informal plain English, in particular vulgar slang. *This book is written in Anglo Saxon.*

Angrily - *(adv.)* with anger. *She angrily shouted at him.*

Angriness - *(noun)* the state of being angry. *In his angriness he couldn't think properly.*

Angry - *(adj.)* **1** feeling or showing anger. *I'm very angry with you over your stupid remars.* **2** (of a wound or sore) red and inflamed. *This dog looks angry and dangerous.*

Anguine - *(adj.)* [zoology] of or related to or resembling a snake. *This creature looks like anguine.*

Anguish - *(noun)* extreme distress of body or mind. *He caused my emotional anguish by his scandalous remarks.*

Angular - *(adj.)* having angles of an angular shape. *This house is built is an angular shape and has lots of angles in it.*

Angulate - *(verb)* [technical] hold or bend (a part of the body) so as to form an angle or angles. skiing incline sideways and outwards during a turn. *We angulate our body a lot of time while doing yoga.*

Anil - *(noun)* **1** a blue dye obtained from plants or made synthetically. *I got my clothes died in Anil blue.* **2** shrub of West Indies and South America that is source of Indigo dye. *Indigo dye is obtained from a Shorub called Anil.*

Anile - *(adj.)* like a feeble old woman. *He walked like an anile weak and trumbling.*

Aniline - *(noun)* [chemistry] a colourless oily liquid present in coal tar, used in the manufacture of dyes, drugs, and plastics.

Animadvert - *(verb)* [formal] criticize or censure. *He animadverted me before my friends and I felt insulted.*

Animal- *(noun)* **1** a living organism which is typically distinguished from a plant by feeding on organic matter; having specialized sense organs and nervous system, and being able to move about and to respond rapidly to stimuli. a mammal, as opposed to a bird, reptile, fish, or insect. *In contrast to tree animals can move.* **2** a very cruel, violent, or uncivilized person. *He is a very cruel person just like an animal.* **3** of the flesh rather than the spirit or intellect. *He suffers from animal lust.* **4** a particular type of person or thing. *(adj.)* [biology] denoting the pole or extremity of an embryo containing the more active cytoplasm. the opposite of vegetal. *My brother is a political animal and I am a party animal.*

Animalcule - *(noun)* [archaic] a microscopic animal. *Bacteria is an animalcule.*

Animalism - *(noun)* **1** behaviour characteristic of animals; animality. *This animalism knows no bounds. He almost worship all animals.* **2** religious worship of or concerning animals. *This animalism knows no bounds. He almost worship all animals.*

Animality - *(noun)* behaviour or nature characteristic of animal, especially in being physical and instinctive. *The animality in him is too pronounced, don't go to near him.*

Animation - *(noun)* **1** the state of being full of life or vigour. [archaic] the state of being alive. **2** the technique of filing successive drawings, or positions of models, to create a film giving an illusion of movement. (also computer animation) the manipulation of electronic images by means of a computer to create moving images. *The various comics today especially computer graphics and animation and give the images an illusion of movement of life.*

Animism – *(noun)* **1** the attribution of a living soul to plants, inanimate objects, and natural phenomena. *I believe in animism, i.e. all plants and inanimate objects have a soul and the whole universe was organized by a supernatural power.* **2** belief in a supernatural power that organized and animals the material universe.

Animosity – *(noun)* strong hostility. *I bear great animosity from this murderer, get him away from here.*

Animus - *(noun)* **1** hostility or ill feeling. *He has great animus towards his partners.* **2** motivation to do something. *The reformist animus came from within the party.*

Anise – *(noun)* **1** a mediterranean plant of the parsley family, cultivated for its aromatic seeds (aniseed). *I have great liking for the aroma of anise.* **2** used in names of asian or american trees or shrubs bearing fruit with an aniseed-like odour, e.g. *Star anise.*

Aniseed – *(noun)* the seed of the anise, used as a flavouring and in herbal medicine. *When once I was hurt in a village the local physician cured me with aniseeds.*

Ankle – *(noun)* the joint connecting the foot with the leg. the narrow part of the leg between this and the calf. *(verb)* [informal, chiefly US] walk. leave. *The American tourist wore anklets and the socks just up to her ankles.*

Anklet – *(noun)* **1** an ornament worn round ankle. *She was wearing the anklets which suited her very well.* **2** chiefly North american a sock that reaches just above the ankle.

Anna – *(noun)* a former monetary unit of India and Pakistan, equal to one sixteenth of a rupee. *Annas become obsolete currency.*

Annals – *(noun)* a record of the events of one year. a record of one item in a chronicle. *Let me consult the annals in the library. I may find something worthy.*

Annalist – *(noun)* a historian who writes annals. *The retired professor of history was employed as an annalist by the college.*

Annex – *(verb)* add as an extra or subordinate part. add to one's own territory by appropriation. *Some years back Iraq wanted to annex some territory of Kuwait claiming it as its own.* *(noun)* **1** a building joined to or associated with a main building. *This is the annex where the staff lives. If you want to understand the full document please read the annex.* **2** an addition to a document.

Annihilate – *(verb)* **1** destroy utterly. [informal] defeat utterly. [physics] convert into radiant energy, especially by collision of a particle with an antiparticle. *During wars large chunks of soldiers are completely annihilated by bombarding.*

Anniversary – *(noun)* the date on which an event took place in a previous year or in the past. *He celebrated his birth anniversary with great pomp and show.*

Anno Domini – *(adv.)* full form of AD. *I was born on 1938 Anno Domini i.e. after the birth of Christ.*

Annotate – *(verb)* add notes to (a text or diagram) giving explanation or comment. *If you don't follow the text consult the annotates given below.*

Announce – *(verb)* make a formal public declaration about a fact, occurrence, or intention. make known the arrival of (a guest) at a formal social occasion. *Ladies and gentlemen I proudly announce the engagement of my daughter Tina to Anand.*

Annoy – *(verb)* **1** make a little angry. *Don't amnog me auth such silly mistakes in future.* **2** [archaic] harm or attack repeatedly.

Annual – *(adj.)* **1** occurring once every year. *The school is celebrating its annual sports day.* **2** calculated over or covering a year. *It is an annual plant it'll wither as soon as the year is over.* **3** (of a plant) living only for a year or less, perpetuating itself by seed. compare with biennial, perennial. *noun* **1** a book or magazine of a series published once a year. *This is the annual issue of this magazine.* **2** an annual plant.

Annuitant – *(noun)* [formal] a person who receives an annuity. *This former servant of my father is an annuitant, he gets fixed sum every year.*

Annuity – *(noun)* a fixed sum of money paid to someone each year, typically for the rest of their life. a form of insurance or investment entitling the investor to a series of annual sums. *Each year for the whole life I'll be paying annuity to the insurance company.*

Annular – *(adj.)* [technical] ring-shaped. *It is an annular object may be it is a ring of somebody.*

Annlet – *(noun)* 1 [architecture] a small band encircling a column. 2 [Heraldry] a charge in the form of a small ring.

Anodyne – *(adj.)* unlikely to cause offence or disagreement but somewhat dull. *(noun)* a painkilling drug or medicine. *Please apply some anodyne on your ankle, it wild ease your pain.*

Anoint – *(verb)* smear or rub with oil, especially as part of a religious ceremony. ceremonially confer office on (a priest or monarch) by anointing. nominate as successor. *Before being made monarch he was anointed by a priest.*

Anomaly – *(noun)* 1 something that deviates from what is standard, normal, or expected. *The anomaly in his character didn't let him stick anywhere.* 2 [Astronomy] the angular distance of a planet or satellite from its last perihelion or perigee.

Anon – *(adv.)* [archaic or informal] soon; shortly. *He made a sign and anon a big crowd followed him.*

Anonym – *(noun)* 1 an anonymous person or publication. *This book is written by an anonym.* 2 a pseudonym.

Anonymity – *(noun)* the state of being anonymous. *For years she has been able to retain her anonymity.*

Anonymous – *(adj.)* 1 not identified by name; of unknown identity. *He is a man of anonymous character. No one knows anything about him.* 2 having no individual or unusual features.

Anosmia – *(noun)* [medicine] the loss of the sense of smell, caused by head injury, infection, or blockage of the nose. *He has lost his sense of smell, may be because of the blockage of the nose caused by anosmia.*

Another – *(determine & pronoun)* 1 one more; a further. 2 used to refer to a different person or thing from one already referred to. *Another person is needed for help.*

Anserine – *(adj.)* of or like a goose. *This egg is anserine.*

Answer – *(noun)* 1 something said, written, or done as a reaction to a question, statement, or situation. *I have got the answer to my problems.* 2 the solution to a problem or dilemma. *(verb)* 1 respond with an answer. respond impudently. be responsible or report to. be called. *He answered all the questions in the paper.* 2 defend oneself against (a charge or accusation). *I'll answer myself in my defense.* be responsible or to blame for. 3 be suitable for fulfilling; satisfy. *He answered me rather innocently.*

Ant – *(noun)* a small insect, usually wingless and with a sting, living in a complex social colony with one or more breeding queens. *Ants are very social and hard working insects.*

Antacid – *(adj.)* preventing or correcting acidity in the stomach. *(noun)* an antacid medicine. *You seem to suffer from acidity, take an antacid.*

Antagonism – *(noun)* active hostility or opposition. *The English found a lot of antagonism in Indians.*

Antarctic – *(adj.)* of or relating to the south polar region or Antarctica. *White bears are found in the Antarctic region.*

Ante – *(noun)* a stake put up by a player in poker or brag before receiving cards. *(verb)* put up (an amount) as an ante in poker or brag. [North American informal] pay an amount of money in advance.

Antecede – *(verb)* be earleir in time, go back further. *Stone tools antecede brown fools.*

Antecedence – *(noun)* proceding in time. *I enjoy the privilege of antecedence. All my brothers are younger.*

Antecedent – *(noun)* 1 a thing that existed before or logically precedes another. 2 a person's ancestors and social background. *For marriage purposes we have checked the antecedents of the boy.* [Grammar] an earlier word, phrase, or clause to which a following pronoun refers back. 4 [logic] the statement contained in the 'if' claused of a conditional proposition. *(adj.)* preceding in time or order.

Antechamber – *(noun)* a small room leading to a main one. *Almost all the pyramids used to have a secret antechamber which led to main room or hall.*

Antedate – *(verb)* come before in date. indicate that (a document or event) should be assigned to an earlier date. *There notes in this chapters should be antedate.*

Antelope – *(noun)* a swift-running deer-like ruminant animal with upward-pointing horns, of a group including the gazelles, impala, gnu, and eland.

Antemeridian – *(adj.)* before noon *I'll see you tomorrow at 9 A.M. antemeridian.*

Anterior – *(adj.)* **1** [chiefly anatomy & biology] nearer the front, especially in the front of the body or nearer to the head. The opposite of posterior. [botany] situated further away from the main stem. **2** [formal] prior to. **3** [phonetics] pronounced with an obstruction located in front of the palate-alveolar region of the mouth. e.g. b,p,d,t.

Anteroom – *(noun)* an antechamber, especially one serving as a waiting room. a large room in an officers mess adjacent to the dining room. *I waited in the anteroom to be called in the officer's mess.*

Anthelion – *(noun)* a luminous halo round a shadow projected by the sun on to a cloud or fog bank. a parhelion seen opposite the sun in the sky. *Do you see that beautiful sight of an anthelion projecting a halo on the cloud.*

Anthem – *(noun)* a rousing or uplifting song indentified with a particular group or causes, a solemn patriotic song adopted as an expression of national identity, a musical setting of a religious text to be sung by a choir during a church service. *The foreigner is listening to our alternatively National Anthem.*

Anther – *(noun)* [botany] the part of a stamen that contains the pollen. *You will see many insects sucking pollen at the anther.*

Anthlogy – *(noun)* **1** a collection of literary or musical works, such as poems or short stories. **2** a collection of various things.

Anthropoad – *(adj.)* resembling a human being in form. [zoology] relating to the group of higher primates including monkeys, apes, and humans. belonging to the family of great apes. [zoology] a higher primate. especially an ape or apeman. *All apes and monkeys are anthropoads.*

Anti – *(prep.)* opposed to, against. [informal] an opponent of something. *I am anti-dictatorship.*

Antic – *(adj.)* [archaic] grotesque or bizarre. antico 'antique'. also 'grotesque'. *He bought an interesting antic from the bazaar of Morocco.*

Antichrist – *(noun) a* postulated opponent of christ expected by the early church to appear before the end of the world. *Antichrist will appear at the end of world.*

Anticyclone – *(noun)* a weather system with high barometric pressure at its centre, around which air slowly circulates. *The storm is coming, we should put an anticyclone at the centre.*

Antidote – *(noun)* **1** a medicine taken to counteract a particular poison. *If a snake bites you the doctors will inject an antidote and save you.* **2** something that counteracts an unpleasant feeling or situation. *Laughter is a good antidote to stress.*

Antilogy – *(noun)* [archaic] a contradiction in terms or ideas. *There is great antilogy between us.*

Antimony – *(noun)* the chemical element of atomic number 51, a brittle silvery-white semimetal. *In old times people used a piece of antimony to cure showing cuts.*

Antinomy – *(noun)* a paradox. *It is an antinomy that my long last friend was living in my neighbourhood and I didn't know.*

Antipathetic – *(adj.)* strangly opposed. *He is antipathetic to new ideas.* **2** characterised by antagonism or antipathy. *The antipathetic groups in the party made it weak.*

Antipathy – *(noun)* a deep-seated feeling of aversion. *I have developed deep antipathy towards my cousin. I don't know why?*

Antiphlogistic – *(adj.)* contracting inflammation. *this is an antiphlogistic medicine. It will reduce your inflammation.*

Antiphonal – *(adj.)* (of church music) sung, recited, or played alternately by two groups. *(noun)* another term for antiphonary. *Hymns are being sung in church in an antiphonal way.*

Antiphony – *(noun)* antiphonal singing, playing, or chanting. *I daily practice antiphony in the morning.*

Antipodes – *(pl. noun)* **1** Australia and New Zealand (used by inhabitants of the northern hemisphere). **2** the direct opposite of something.

Antipyretic – *(adj.)* used to prevent or reduce fever. *(noun)* an antipyretic drug. *This is an antipyretic drug; take it and your fever will come down.*

Antiquarian – *(adj.)* relating to or studying antiques. rare books, or antiquities. *(noun)* a person who studies or collects antiques or antiquities.

Antiquate – *(adj.)* old-fashioned or outdated.

Antique – *(noun)* a decorative object or place of furniture that is valuable because of its age. *(adj.)* **1** valuable because of its age. *Today I went to see the race of antique cars. It was fantastic.* **2** belonging to the distant past. old-fashioned or outdated. *(verb)* cause to resemble an antique by artificial means.

Antiseptic – *(adj.)* **1** relating to or denoting substances that prevent the growth of disease-causing micro-organisms. *Before operation doctors use strong antiseptics so as to kill various micro-organisms.* **2** so clean or pure as to be bland or characterless. *Their sequealy clean home epitomizes this antiseptic respectability.* *(noun)* an antiseptic compound or preparation. *The use of appropriate antiseptic is an important part of operation.*

Antisocial – *(adj.)* **1** contrary to the customs of society and causing annoyance to others. [psychiatry] sociopathic. *Most of the persons elements have been arrested by police during a special drive.* **2** not sociable.

Antithesis – *(noun)* **1** a person or thing that is the direct opposite of another. a contrast or opposition between two things. *There is perfect antithesis between the two brothers.* **2** a rhetorical or literary device in which an opposition or contrast of ideas is expressed. *This poem is full of antithesis.* **3** the negation of the thesis as the second stage in the process of dialectical reasoning. compare with synthesis.

Antitoxin – *(noun)* [physiology] an antibody that counteracts a toxin. *We must eat food rich in antitoxins so that they can counteract the toxins.*

Antler – *(noun)* a branched horn on the head of an adult deer. one of the branches on an antler. *I saw an antler in the sanctuary of South Africa. It was so thrilling.*

Antonym – *(noun)* a word opposite in meaning to another. *Cruelty is the antonym of kindness.*

Antrum – *(noun)* **1** a natural chamber or cavity in a bone. *As the zoologist looked into the antrum he found something stuck into him.* **2** the pyloric end of the stomach.

Anus – *(noun)* the opening at the end of the alimentary canal through which solid waste matter leaves the body. *The development of anus was important stage in evolution.*

Anvil – *(noun)* **1** a heavy iron block on which metal can be hammered and shaped. *Blacksmiths shape iron by hammering it on the anvil.* **2** the horizontally extended upper part of a cumulonimbus cloud. **3** [anatomy] another term for INCUS.

Anxiety – *(noun)* a feeling of being anxious. [psychiatry] a nervous disorder marked by excessive uneasiness. *He suffers from anxiety disorders and is consulting a psychiatrist.*

Anxious – *(adj.)* **1** experiencing worry or unease. **2** very eager and concerned to do something. *I am very much anxious about my son's fate. He never succeeds anywhere.*

Any – *(determine & pronoun)* **1** used to refer to one or some of a thing or number of things, no matter how much or how many. *Any of you interested is taking part in debate.* **2** whichever of a specified class might be chosen. *(adverb)* at all; in some degree. *Nobody seems to have any books in the class.*

Aorta – *(noun)* the main artery of the body, supplying oxygenated blood from the heart to the circulatory system. *If due to any reason aorta is cut off the patient will die at once.*

Apace - *(adv.)* [poetic - literary] swiftly; quickly.

Apart - *(adv.)* **1** separated by a specified distance. no longer living together or close emotionally. *The two friends after some distance went apart.* **2** to or on one side. **3** into pieces. *Apart from being friends they are colleagues also.*

Apartment - *(noun)* **1** [chiefly north American] a suite of rooms forming one residence; a flat. a block of apartments. *These city people prefer to live in apartments.* **2** a private suite of rooms in a very large house.

Apathetic - *(adj.)* not interested or enthusiastic. *He was apathetic to her miseries.*

Apathy - *(noun)* lack of interest or enthusiasm. *He developed total apathy to his friend who didn't give up his bad habits.*

Aperient - *(adj.)* used to relieve constipation. *(noun)* an aperients drug. *Take this aperient. It will relieve you in the morning.*

Aperture - *(noun)* [chiefly technical] an opening, hole, or gap. the variable opening by which light enters a camera. *The sun light creeping through an aperture filled the room with light.*

Apetalous - *(adj.)* [botany] having no petals.

Apex - *(noun)* **1** the top or highest part of something, especially one forming a point. [botany] the growing point of a shoot. **2** the highest level of a hierarchy. *The apex court gave a landmark judgment. (verb)* reach a high point or climax. *In royalty monarch is the apex.*

Aphasia - *(noun)* [medicine] inability to understand or produce speech as a result of brain damage. *He can't hear or talk because he is suffering from aphasia.*

Aphelion - *(noun)* [linguistics] omission of the initial sound of a word, as when he is is pronounced he's. *Aphelion is getting very popular these days.*

Aphonia - *(noun)* [medicine] a disorder of the vocal organs that results in the loss of voice. *He is suffering from aphonia.*

Aphorism - *(noun)* a pithy observation which contains a general truth. *A bird in hand is better than two in the bush is a popular aphorism.*

Aphrodisiac - *(noun)* a food, drink, or drug that stimulates sexual desire. *It is believed that a rhino's horn is a great aphrodisiac.*

Apiary - *(noun)* a place where bees are kept.

Apical - *(adj.)* **1** [technical] relating to or denoting an apex. **2** [phonetics] formed with the tip of the tongue at or near the front teeth or the alveolar ridge, for example th or trilled r. *R is an apical letter.*

Apiculture - *(noun)* [technical] term for beekeeping. *He is an expert in apiculture.*

Apiece - *(adv.)* to, for or by each one. *The trench was dug apiece.*

Apocryphal - *(adj.)* **1** authenticity, although widely circulated as being true. **2** of or belonging to the apocrypha. *This document is apocryphal, its authenticity can't be doubled.*

Apollo - *(noun)* a large creamy-white butterfly with black and red spots, found chiefly in the mountains of eurpoe. *I chanced to see an Apollo during my stay while in Europe.*

Apologetic - *(adj.)* **1** expressing an apology. *I apologies to you for my rude behaviour.* **2** constituting a formal justification of a theory or doctrine.

Apologist - *(noun)* a person who offers an argument in defence of something controversial.

Apologize - *(verb)* express regret for something that one has done wrong. *I apologize for having hurt you.*

Apologue - *(noun)* a moral fable, especially one with animals as characters. *Children let me tell you an apologue of a Fox and Monkey.*

Apology - *(noun)* **1** a regretful acknowledgement of an offence or failur. *See an apology having criticized you unfavorably.* a formal expression of regret at being unable to attend a meeting or social function. *My apologies for not being able to come to the function.* **2** a very poor example of. **3** a justification or defence.

Apophthegm - *(noun)* a concise saying or maxim.

Apoplexy - *(noun)* **1** unconsciousness or incapacity resulting from a cerebral hemorrhage or stroke. *He had a stroke of apoplexy and hence* *can't speak.* **2** [informal] inability to act or speak caused by extreme anger. *He had apoplexy and couldn't act or speak.*

Apostate – *(noun)* a person who renounces a belief or principle. *(adj.)* abandoning a belief or principle. *He is an apostate. He has renounced his faith.*

Apostle – *(noun)* **1** each of the twelve chief disciples of Jesus Christ. an important early Christian teacher or missionary. *Judas was an apostle of Christ who betrayed him.* **2** a vigorous and pioneering supporter of an idea or cause. *He is an apostle of democracy.*

Apostolic – *(adj)* **1** of or relating to the apostics. *He will not change his apostolic decision.* **2** of or relating to the pope, especially when he is regarded as the successor to St Peter. *It is an apostolic decision. It won't be changed.*

Apothecary – *(noun)* [archaic] a person who prepared and sold medicines. *You can buy medicines from my apothecary friend.*

Apotheosis – *(noun)* **1** the highest point in the development of something. **2** elevation to diving status.

Appal – *(verb)* **1** greatly dismay or horrify. *I was appaled at his rude behaviour.* **2** [informal] very bad or displeasing.

Apparel – *(noun)* [formal] clothing. embroidered ornamentation on ecclesiastical vestments. *The apparels of royalty used to be very costly.* *(verb)* US appareled, appareling [archaic] clothe.

Apparent – *(adj.)* **1** readily perceived or understood; obvious. *It is very apparent that he is telling a lie.* **2** seeming real or true. *Apparently there is no truth in these statements.*

Apparition – *(noun)* a remarkable thing making a sudden appearance. a ghost. *Suddenly in the dead of night an apparition appeared before me.*

Appear – *(verb)* **1** come into sight. come into existence or use. be published. [informal] arrive. *It was an a long voyage but ultimately the land appeared.* **2** present oneself publicly or formally, especially on stage or as the accused or counsel in a law court. *As the actor appeared on the stage there was loud clapping.* **3** seem; give a specified impression.

Appease – *(verb)* placate by acceding to their demands. *All the small animals appeased lion's demand.*

Appellant – *(noun)* [law] a person who appeals against a court ruling. *The appellant demands that the case be reopened.*

Appellation – *(noun)* [formal] a name or title. *The royal child was conferred the appellation of Prince.*

Append – *(verb)* add to end of a document or piece of writing. *This piece of writing should be appended properly.*

Appendix – *(noun)* **1** [anatomy] a tube-shaped sac attached to the lower end of the large intestine. *He usually has pain in his appendix.* **2** a section of subsidiary matter at the end of a book. *Some books end with an appendix.*

Appendicitis – *(noun)* inflammation of the vermiform appendix. *He has been suffuring form appendicitis.*

Apperception – *(noun)* psychology assimilation into the mind of a new concept. *The psychologist put up a new apperception into his mind.*

Appetency – *(noun)* [archaic] a longing or desire. *Since long he had cherished appetency.*

Appetite – *(noun)* a natural desire to satisfy a bodily need, especially for food. *I have great applauded for non-veg food.*

Appetizer – *(noun)* a small dish of food or a drink taken before a meal to stimulate the appetite. *Hot tomato soup is a good appetizer.*

Applaud – *(verb)* show approval by clapping. praise or approve of. *The show was greatly applanded by people.*

Applause – *(noun)* approval expressed by clapping. *He got huge applause for his acting as Shaheed Bhagat Singh.*

Apple – *(noun)* **1** the rounded fruit of a tree of the rose family, with green or red skin and crisp flesh. *I like apples a lot.* **2** the tree bearing such fruit. *This is an apple tree.* **3** used in names of similar unrelated fruits, e.g. custard apple. *I like custard apple pie.*

Appliance – *(noun)* **1** a device designed to perform a specific task. *Electrical appliances of Bajaj are famous all over India.* **2** a fire engine. *Without appliance of some force you can't move this car.*

Applicable – *(adj.)* relevant; appropriate. *This law is not applicable in this land.*

Applicant – *(noun)* a person who applies for something. *All applicants must appear for interview at 10 A.M.*

Application – *(noun)* **1** a formal request to an authority. *I have submitted an application for leave.* **2** the action of putting something into operation. practical use or relevance. *The process has been put into application.* **3** the action of applying something to a surface. **4** sustained effort. *Only application of a lot of force can move this object.* **5** computing a program or place of software designed to fulfill a particular purpose. *Use this software application it will solve the problem.*

Apply – *(verb)* **1** make a formal request. put oneself forward as a candidate for a job. *I have applied for several jobs.* **2** bring into operation of use. be relevant. **3** put on a surface. **4** work hard. *Apply some pressure so that you can succeed into your mission.*

Appoint – *(verb)* **1** assign a job or role to. *You are appointed as a teacher in directorate of Delhi Education Deptt. Here is your appointment letter.* **2** determine or decide on [archaic] decree. *I have been appointed as head to carry out this mission.* **3** [law] determine the disposal of under powers granted by the owner.

Apportion – *(verb)* share out; assign. *Let me assign you a tough task.*

Apposite – *(adj.)*very appropriate; apt. *It is an apposite decision taken at the right time.*

Appraise – *(verb)* assess the value, quality, or performance of. set a price on. *I have appraised the value of this piece of furniture.*

Appreciable – *(adj.)* large or important enough to be noticed. *Your effort are appreciable.*

Appreciate – *(verb)* **1** recognize the value or significance of. be grateful for. *I appreciate your efforts.* **2** in value or price.

Apprehend – *(verb)* **1** intercept in the course of harmful or illicit action; seize or arrest. *The thief was apprehended at the spot.* **2** understand; perceive. **3** [archaic] anticipate with uneasiness or fear. *I apprehend a bad day.*

Apprehension – *(noun)* **1** anxious or fearful anticipation. *I have apprehension that something will go wrong.* **2** understanding. *Apprehension dawned on me as the scheme was explained in detail.* **3** the action of arresting someone. *The apprehension of the thief took place at a bus stand.*

Apprentice – *(noun)* a person learning a trade from a skilled employer. *(verb)* employ as an apprentice. *The young boy is an apprentice.*

Apprise – *(verb)* inform; tell. *I apprised him of all the facts.*

Apprize – *(verb)* [archaic] put a price on.

Approach – *(verb)* **1** come near or nearer to in distance, time, or standard. [archaic] bring nearer. *I approached him boldly.* **2** make an initial proposal to or request of. **3** start to deal with in a certain way. *(noun)* **1** a way of dealing with something. *I know the kind of approach needed to put him to work.* **2** an initial proposal or request. **3** the action of approaching. a way leading to a place; the northern approaches to london.

Approbate – *(verb)* accept as valid; approval or sanction officially. *His documents have been approbated.*

Approbation – *(noun)* approval; praise. *His work has received a lot of approbation.*

Appropriate – *(adj.)* **1** suitable; proper. *Appropriate action has been taken against the culprit.* **2** [archaic] assigned to a particular person. *(verb)* **1** take for one's own use without permission. **2** devote to a special purpose.

Approval – *(noun)* the action of approving of something. a favourable opinion. *Your scheme has my approval.*

Approximate – *(adj.)* fairly accurate but not totally precise. *The approximate value of this diamond should be 5 lakhs.* *(verb)* come close in quality or quantity. estimate Fairley accurately. *I have approximated 20% grauth.*

Appurtenance – *(noun)* an accessory associated with a particular activity. *A space wheel is an appurtance in a vehicle.*

Apricot – *(noun)* **1** an orange-yellow soft fruit. resembling a small peach. *Apricot is a useful* *dry fruit increasing the activity of brain.* **2** the tree bearing this fruit. **3** an orange-yellow colour.

Apriori - *(adj.&adv.)* based on theoretical deduction rather than empirical observation.

Apropos - *(prep.)* with reference to.

Apse - *(noun)* **1** a large semicircular or polygonal recess with a domed roof, typically at a church's eastern end. **2** another term for APSIS.

Apt - *(adj.)* **1** appropriate; suitable. *I gave him an apt answer; he was happy and surprised.* **2** having a specified tendency. **3** quick to learn. *He is an apt learners of French language.*

Aqua - *(noun)* the colour aquamarine. *Mix this medicine in aqua.*

Aquarium - *(noun)* a transparent tank of water in which live fish and other water creatures and plants are kept.

Aquarius - *(noun)* **1** [astronomy] a large constellation (the water carrier or water bearer). said to represent a man pouring water from a jar. *Do you see that large in the sky? Aquarius.* **2** [Astrology] the eleventh sign of the zodiac, which the sun enters about 21 January.

Aqueduct - *(noun)* **1** an artificial channel for conveying water, especially a bridge or viaduct carrying a waterway. *Water in this canal is being carried through aqueduct.* **2** [anatomy] a small duct containing fluid in the body.

Aqueous - *(adj.)* of, resembling, or containing water. *I have bought an aqueous jar.*

Aquline - *(adj.)* **1** like an eagle. **2** (of a nose) curved like an eagle's beak. *The Bird has an aquline nose. May be it is an eagle.*

Arab - *(noun)* **1** a member of a Semitic people inhabiting much of the middle east and north Africa. *People of Arab are very religious.* **2** a horse of a breed originating in Arabia. *It must be an Arab horse.*

Arabian - *(noun)* [historical] a native or inhabitant of Arabia. *He is an Arabian. It is clear from his features and complexion.* **2** an Arab horse. *This tall and strong horse must be Arabian.* *(adj.)* of or relating to Arabia or its people. *Have you heard the stories of Arabian Nights.*

Arabic - *(noun)* the Semitic language of the Arabs, spoken in many dialects in much of north Africa and the middle east and written from right to left in a cursive script also used for other languages such as Persian, Urdu, and Malay. *I am learning Arabic. It is an interesting language written from right to left.*

Arable - *(adj.)* suitable for growing corps. (of corps) able to be grown on such land. *(noun)* arable land or crops. *The land that I have bought is quite costly but then it is arable.*

Arbiter - *(noun)* **1** a person who setties a dispute. *An arbiter has been appointed to solve the case between two brothers.* **2** a person who has influence over something: an arbiter of taste.

Arbitrary - *(adj.)* **1** based on random choice or personal whim. *It is an arbitrary decision. It isn't fair and I'll not abide by it.* **2** (of power or a ruling body) autocratic. **3** mathematics (of a constant or other quantity) of unspecified value.

Arbitrate - *(verb)* act between parties with a view to reconciling differences. *I am going to arbitrate between the two parties to settle their old dispute.*

Arboreal - *(adj.)* of, relating to, or living in trees. *Birds are arboreal creatures.*

Arc - *(noun)* **1** a curve forming part of the circumference of a circle or other figure. *The new moon is arc like in shape.* a curving trajectory. [mathematics] indicating the inverse of a trigonometrically function: are cosine. **2** a luminous electrical discharge between two points. *(verb)* **1** move with a curving trajectory. **2** the forming of an electric are.

Arcade - *(noun)* **1** a covered passage with arches along one or both sides. chiefly a covered walk with shops along one or both sides. [architecture] a series of arches supporting a wall. *I found him in the amusement arcade.* **2** short for amusement arcade.

Arcadian - *(noun)* **1** a native of Arcadia, a mountainous region of southern Greece. *He is an Arcadian.* **2** [poetic - literary] an idealized country dweller. *(adj.)* of or relating to Arcadia, especially as regarded as an ideal rustic paradise.

Arch - *(adj.)* self-consciously playful or teasing. *The arch villain of the show is Ravana.*

Archaeology - the branch of anthropolgy that studies prehistoric people and thur ....through their material remains.

Archangel - *(noun)* **1** an angel of high rank. *He is an archangel and beloved of God.* **2** a yellow-flowered deadnettle found in woodland.

Archbishop - *(noun)* the chief bishop responsible for a large district. *St. Thomas was the archbishop of Canterbury.*

Arch-enemy - *(noun)* a chief enemy. *Devil is the archenemy of human race.*

Archer - *(noun)* a person who shoots with a bow and arrows. *There were many fine archers in King Richard's army.*

Archetype - *(noun)* **1** a very typical example. *Every man carries in his unconscious mind an archetype of their early ancestors.* **2** an original model. *All the archetypes of space ships are carefully preserved.* **3** [psychoanalysis] a primitive mental image inherited from the earliest human ancestors and supposed to be present in the collective unconscious. **4** a recurrent motif in literature or art.

Architect - *(noun)* **1** a person who designs buildings and supervises their construction. *He is a renowned architect who is designing a hospital.* **2** a person responsible for the invention or realization of something. *(verb)* computing design and make (a program or system).

Archway - *(noun)* a curved structure forming a passage or entrance. *I saw an old archway in building.*

Arctic - *(adj.)* **1** of or relating to the regions around the north pole. living or growing in such regions. *This is an arctic plant.* **2** [informal] very cold. *The cold is almost arctic.* *(noun)* **1** the regions around the north pole. **2** north American a thick water-proof overshoe. **3** a drab-coloured hairy butterfly of the arctic and subarctic regions of the new world.

Arcuate - *(adj.)* [technical] curved.

Ardent - *(adj.)* **1** very enthusiastic or passionate. *He is an ardent lover of mine.* **2** [archaic or poetic - literary] burning; glowing.

Ardour - *(noun)* great enthusiasm or passion. *He has great ardour to become an IAS officer.*

Arduous - *(adj.)* difficult and tiring. *The mountain climbing proved very arduous for me.*

Area - *noun* **1** a region of an expanse or surface. a space allocated for a specific use. *It is an area reserved for airport.* **2** a subject or range of activity. *The area measures 1000*1000 Sq. yards.* **3** the extent or measurement of a surface. **4** a sunken enclosure giving access to a basement.

Areca - *(noun)* any of several tall tropical palms native to southern Asia having egg shaped nuts. *Would you dare to climb the areca and pluck a nut.*

Arena - *noun* **1** a level area surrounded by seating, in which public events and entertainments are held. *In circus public sit circularly and in the middle is round shaped arena where events take place.* **2** a sphere of activity.

Arenaceous - *(adj.)* [geology] consisting of sand or sand-like particles. *This area is arenaceous; it is full of sands and plants.* [biology] living or growing in sand.

Argent - *(adj.&noun)* [poetic - literary & heraldry] silver. *This piece of writing is argent.*

Argil - *(noun)* a artist clay. *The clay models are made of argil.*

Argue - *(verb)* **1** exchange diverging or opposite views heatedly. *To argue is to completely miss the point of discussion.* **2** give reasons or cite evidence in support of something. *I have argued on these basic facts.*

Arguing - *(noun)* a contentious speech act; a dispute where there is strong disagreement. *The members of committee went on arguing for hours but there was no result because all had different news.*

Argument - *(noun)* **1** a heated exchange of diverging or opposite views. *Heated argument were exchanged among the club members but to no avail.* **2** a set of reasons given in support of something. *I submit these reason's is support of my arguments.* **3** [mathematics & logic] an independent variable associated with a function or proposition and determining its value, e.g.

x in y = F(x). **4** [linguistics] any of the noun phrases in a clause that are related directly to the verb. **5** [archaic] a summary of the subject matter of a book.

Argute – *(adj.)* rare shrewd. *He is an argute person.*

Arid – *(adj.)* **1** very dry; having little or no rain. *It is an arid and vast desert.* **2** uninteresting: arid verse.

Aries – *(noun)* **1** [astronomy] a small constellation said to represent the ram whose golden fleece was sought by Jason and the Argonauts. **2** [astrology] the first sign of the zodiac, which the sun enters about 20 march.

Aright – *(adj.)* [dialect] correctly; properly. *He entered the hotel turned aright.*

Arise – *(verb)* **1** originate or become apparent. occur as a result of. **2** [formal of poetic – literary] get or stand up. *With the arise of women emancipation movement in England many countries joined it.*

Arista – *(noun)* bristle like process near the tip of the antenna of certain files.*This is a strange fly called arista. It has bristle like growth near its antenna.*

Aristocracy – *(noun)* the highest class in some societies, comprising people of noble birth with hereditary titles. *Aristocracy was never popular among common man.* a form of government in which power is held by the nobility. *Government controlled aristocracy are out of vogue.*

Aristocrat – *(noun)* a member of the aristocracy. *He is an aristocrat having lots of money and power.*

Arithmetic – *(noun)* the branch of mathematics concerned with the properties and manipulation of numbers. the use of numbers in counting and calculation. *(adj.)* of or relating to arithmetic. *He is very good in Arithmetic.*

Ark – *abbreviation* Arkansas. *Arkansas.*

Arm – *(noun)* **1** each of the two upper limbs of the human body from the shoulder to the hand. a limb of an octopus, starfish, or other animal. *Arms are very important parte of human body.* **2** a side part of a chair supporting a sitter's arm. *The arms of the chair are broken.* **3** a narrow strip of water or land projecting from a larger body. **4** a branch or division of an organization. one of the types of troops of which an army is composed. *Orphanage is an arm of the NGO's.* [mathematics] each of the lines enclosing an angle. *Navy is branch of army.*

Armament – *(noun)* **1** military weapons and equipment. *The armament comprising; big guns anti air guns truck jeeps etc. crawled along the Mountaineous area.* **2** the process of equipping military forces for war.

Armature – *(noun)* the rotating coil or coils of a dynamo or electric motor. any moving part of an electrical machine in which a voltage is induced by a magnetic field. a piece of iron acting as keeper for a magnet. *The armature of this motor is burnt out.* **2** a framework on which a clay sculpture is moulded. **3** [biology] the projective covering of an animal or plant. [archaic] armour.

Armistice – *(noun)* a truce. *Orders for armistice were given by the general.*

Armless – *(adj.)* without arms. *I saw an armless beggar.*

Armlet – *(noun)* a bend warm around the arm for decoration. *Her armlet is very beautiful.*

Armorial – *(adj.)* of or relating to heraldry or heraldic arms. *The coach had armorial bearing.*

Armour – *(noun)* **1** the metal coverings formerly worn by soldiers to protect the body in battle. *The metal armour worn by soldiers in old times used to be very heavy.* **2** the tough metal layer covering a military vehicle or ship. military vehicles collectively. *Military vehicles are covered with armour.* **3** the protective layer or shell of some animals and plants. *The armour of crocodile is very tough.*

Army – *(noun)* **1** an organized military force equipped for fighting on land. *Indian army is very strong and brave.* **2** a large number of similar people or things.

Arose – past of ARISE. *He arose late in the morning.*

Around – *(adj.)* **1** located or situated on every side. *That old building must be somewhere around here.* **2** so as to face in the opposite direction. *Please turn around and face me.* **3** in or to many places throughout a locality. *There is a hotel around the corner, it must be open yet.* **4** here and there. *All around there is greenery here.* 5. available or present. *Oh! Come around and agree to the point.* 6. approximately. *(prep.)* **1** an every side of. **2** in or to many places throughout. **3** so as to encircle or embrace. following an approximately circular route.

Arouse – *(verb)* **1** evoke (a feeling or response). *I was aroused at the news of going to cenema.* provoke to anger or strong emotions. *His behaviour aroused my anger.* excite sexually. awaken from sleep. *He aroused from deep sleep.*

Arraign – *(verb)* call before a court to answer a criminal charge. *The police arraigned for charge of murder.*

Arrange – *(verb)* **1** put in a neat, attractive, or required order. *I have arranged everything in the room.* **2** organize or plan. *All the details of the trip abroad have been arranged.* reach agreement about an action or event in advance. *They arranged to meet at eleven o'clock.* **3** [music] adapt for performance with instruments or voices other than those originally specified. **4** [archaic] settle (a dispute or claim). *I arranged to meet him at the old temple.*

Arrangement – *(noun)* **1** the action, process, or result of arranging. *The arrangement in the hotel was superb.* **2** a plan for a future event. *Arrangements have been made for the travel. The arranged composition of music was mind blowing.* **3** music an arranged composition. **4** [archaic] a settlement of a dispute or claim.

Arrant – *(adj.)* utter; complete: *What arrant stupidity!*

Array – *(noun)* **1** an impressive display or range of a particular thing. *The array of flowers was impressive.* **2** an ordered arrangement of troops. *The general received the salute from the array of the army.* **3** [mathematics] an arrangement of quantities or symbols in rows and columns; a matrix. **4** computing an ordered set of related elements. **5** [law] a list of jurors impanelled. **6** [poetic - literary] elaborate or beautiful clothing. *(verb)* **1** display or arrange in a neat or impressive way. **2** be elaborately clothed in. **3** [law] impanel (a jury).

Arrears – *(plural noun)* payments or debts that are outstanding and due. *My arrears along with investment are worth Rs. 1 lakh.*

Arrest – *verb* **1** seize by legal authority and take them into custody. *He was arrested by police and detained in the lock up.* **2** stop or check. *He suddenly arrested the speed of car.* **3** attract the attention of. *Her beautiful eyes arrested me.* *(noun)* **1** the action of arresting. **2** a sudden cessation of motion.

Arrival – *()* **1** someone and something that arrives *The arrival of train created a commotion on the platform.* **2** accomplishment of an objective. **3** the act of arriving at a certain place. *I awaited your arrival.*

Arrive – *(verb)* **1** reach a destination. *The train has arrived.* **2** be brought or delivered. *I have arrived at my destination* **3** (of a particular moment) come about. *Your parcel has arrived kindly take delivery.* **4** reach (a conclusion or decision). *I have arrived at a conclusion.* **5** [informal] become successful and well known.

Arrogance – *(noun)* overbearing pride evidenced by a superior manner toward inferiors. *All kings used to have arrogance.*

Arrogate – *(verb)* take or claim for oneself without justification. *He arrogated that he had promoted her brother.*

Arrow – *(noun)* a stick with a sharp pointed head, designed to be shot from a bow. *He shot the arrow with a baw.* a symbol resembling this, used to show direction or position. *(verb)* more swiftly and directly.

Arse – *(noun)* a person's buttocks or anus.*I am going to hit his fat arse.* *(verb)* **1** behave in a stupid way. not be bothered to do something. *He arsed all the way in the train.*

Arsenal – *(noun)* a store of weapons and ammunition. *A suspicious was arrested from near the military arsenal.* a military establishment where weapons and ammunition are made and stored. *Don't go near the military arsenal.*

Arsenic - *(noun)* the chemical element of atomic number 33, a brittle steel-grey semimetal with many highly poisonous compounds. *Arsenic is a highly poisonous chemical. It can kill you in second.*

Art - *(noun)* **1** the expression or application of creative skill and imagination especially through a visual medium such as painting or sculpture. works produced in this way. *M.F. Hussain was a great master of art from India.* **2** the various branches of creative activity, such as painting, music, literature, and dance. *You can choose any of the arts-painting, music, literature, dance, they are all creative activities.* **3** subjects of study primarily concerned with human culture (as contrasted with scientific or technical subjects). *I am inserted in arts and humanities.* **4** a skill at doing a specified thing. *She is arty and creative.*

Arterial - *(adj.)* of, involving or contained in the arteries. *The arterial system must be thoroughly understood and any defect should be soon done away with.*

Artery - *(noun)* **1** any of the muscular-walled tubes forming part of the circulation system by which blood is conveyed from the heart to all parts of the body. *Blood must keep flowing through the arteries.* **2** an important route in a traffic or transport system.

Artful - *(adj.)* cunningly clever or skilful. *He is very arful at telling lies.*

Arthritis - *(noun)* a disease causing painful inflammation and stiffness of the joints. *I suffer from arthritis. I cannot bend my knees.*

Artichoke - *(noun)* **1** a plant with large, theistic-like flower heads. *Jerusalem Artichoke is a plant famous for its peculiar flower head.* **2** the unopened flower head of this plant, of which the heart and the fleshy bases of the bracts are edible. **3** see jerusalem arthichoke.

Article - *(noun)* **1** a particular object. **2** a place of writing included with others in a newspaper or magazine. *I want to read this particular article.* **3** a separate clause or paragraph of a legal document. **4** a period of training with a firm as a solicitor; [architect], surveyor, or accountant. the terms on which crew members take service on a ship. **5** [grammar] the definite or indefinite article. *(verb)* bind by articles in order to become qualified. *In grammar there are three articles a, as, The.*

Articular - *(adj.)* anatomy of or relating to a joint. *This piece of wood is articular to that one at 90 degree angle.*

Articulate - *(adj.)* **1** fluent and clear in speech. *He is very articulate in his speech.* **2** [technical] having joints or jointed segments. [zoology] denoting a brachiopod which has projections and sockets that form a hinge joining the two halves of the shell. *(verb)* **1** pronounce distinctly. clearly express (an idea or feeling). *The motion of the speaker is well articulated skillfully articulated.* **2** form a joint. be connected by joints.

Articulation - *(noun)* **1** the action of articulating. music clarity in the production of successive notes. *In this music show articulation is superb.* [phonetics] the formation of a speech sound by constriction of the air flow in the vocal organs. **2** the state of being jointed. a specified joint.

Artificial - *(adj.)* **1** made as a copy of something natural. *She is wearing artificial jewellery.* **2** contrived or affected. **3** bridge conventional as opposed to natural. *It is an artificial bridge and not a natural one.*

Artillery - *(noun)* large-caliber guns used in warfare on land. a branch of the armed forces trained to use artillery. *The artillery moved slowly with large caliber guns.*

Artisan - *(noun)* a skilled worker who makes things by hand. *A potter is an artisan.*

Artist - *(noun)* a person who paints or draws as a profession or hobby. a person who parctise or performs any of the creative arts. *There are many fine artists in our country who either draw or paint.* **2** [informal] a habitual practitioner of a specified activity. *He is a piano artist.*

Artistic - *(adj.)* **1** relating to or characteristic of art or artists. *This artistic background helped him to gain admission in the music academy.* **2** satisfying aesthetic standards and sensibilities. **3** aesthetically pleasing. **4** having or revealing creative skill.

Artless – *(adj.)* **1** without guile or pretension. *He is a artless rather clumsy guy; don't you suspect him on any account.* **2** clumsy.

Arts – *()* studies intended to provide general knowledge and intellectual skills. *He studies in the college of arts and sciences.*

As – *(adj.)* used in comparisons to refer to the extent or degree of something. used to emphasize an amount. *conjunction* **1** used to indicate simultaneous occurrence. *He is as tall as his brother.* **2** used to indicate simultaneous occurrence. *The drove as he read the sign boards.* **2** used to indicate by comparison the way that something happens. **3** because. *As the temperature rises up so does the heat.* **4** even though. *(prep.)* **1** used to refer to the function or character of someone or something. *He couldn't take exam as he was sick.* **2** during the time of being. *He wrote the article as the train raced.*

Asafoetida – *(noun)* **1** a fetid resinous gum obtained from the roots of a herbaceous plant, used in herbal medicine and Indian cooking; a plant of the parsley family, from which this gum is obtained. *Asafoetida is used in Indian looking.*

Asbestos – *(noun)* a highly heat-resistant fibrous silicate mineral able to be woven into fabrics, used in brake linings and in fire-resistant and insulating materials. *I am wearing asbestos woven fabric which will save me from fire.*

Ascend – *(verb)* **1** go up; climb or rise. *He has ascended to the post of principal.* **2** rise in status. *I'll keep on ascending in life and one day become a great man.* **3** (of a voice or sound) rise in pitch. *This voice kept on ascending and after same time he was screaming.*

Ascension – *(noun)* **1** the action of ascending in status. *His ascension to the post of PM filled him with glory.* **2** the ascent of Christ into heaven on the fortieth day after the resurrection. *Ascension is the ascent of Christ.*

Ascent – *(noun)* an instance of ascending. a climb to the summit of a mountain. an upward slope. *The ascent to this mountain is very difficult.*

Ascertain – *(verb)* find out for certain. *I want to ascertain if I have succeeded or not.*

Ascetic – *(adj.)* characterized by the practice of severe self-discipline. *(noun)* an ascetic person. *Saints are Ascetic persons.*

Ascribable – *(adj.)* capable of being assigned or created to. *Ill health is ascribable to poor diet.*

Ascribe – *(verb)* attribute something to (a particular cause, person or period): regard a quality as belonging to. *He ascribed his success to his friend.*

Aseptic – *(adj.)* free of or using methods to keep free of pathological microorganisms *Aseptic surgical instruments are employed during operations.*

Ash – *(noun)* **1** a tree with compound leaves, winged fruits, and hard pale wood. used in names of other trees, e.g. mountain ash. *Mountain ash is very beautiful and wonderful tree.* **2** the residue that remains when something is burned. **3** an old English runic letter. the symbol ae or AE, used in the roman alphabet in place of the runic letter and as a phonetic symbol, see also.

Ashamed – *(adj.)* feeling embarrassed or guilty. *I felt ashamed at having been so rude to her.*

Ashen – *(adj.)* **1** (of a person's face) very pale with shock, fear, or illness. *His face grew ashen as he looked at something in the dark.* **2** [poetic – literary] made of wood from the ash tree.

Ashore – *(adj.)* to or on the shore or land from the direction of the sea. on land as opposed to at sea. *I reached ashore after a long voyage.*

Ashy – *(adj.)* of a light grey. *This piece of cloth looks ashy.*

Asiatic – *(adj.)* relating to or deriving from Asia. *Features of Asiatic people are different from those of Europeans.*

Aside – *(adverb)* **1** on or to one side. *The boy threw the book aside.* **2** out of the way (especially away from one's thoughts). *The man brushes the objections aside.* **3** not taken into account or excluded from consideration. **4** in a different direction. **5** placed or kept separate and distinct as for a purpose. *A day set aside for relaxing.* **6** in reserve; not for immediate use. *(noun)* **1** a line spoken by an actor to the audience but not intended for others on the stage. **2** a message that departs from the main subject.

Asinine - *(adj.)* extremely stupid or foolish. *He is an asinine* person.

Ask - *(verb)* **1** say something in order to obtain an answer or some information. enquire about the well-being of. *I asked him about his father's health.* **2** request to do or give something. request permission. request to speak to. request (a specified amount) as a price for selling something. *The stranger was asking the way to post office.* **3** expect or demand (something) of someone. *He asked me to give him 100 rupees.* **4** invite to a social occasion. invite someone out on a date. *(noun)* [chiefly north American]. *The asking price of a financial security.*

Askew - *(adj.&adv.)* not in a straight or level position. H*e looked at me askew.*

Aslant - *(adj.)* at a slant. *(preposition)* across at a slant. *The child slipped and went aslant on the slope.*

Asleep - *(adj.&adv.)* **1** in or into a state of sleep. not attentive or alert. *My father was fast asleep when I reached home.* **2** numb.

Aslope - *(adj.&adv.)* [poetic - literary] in a sloping position.

Aspect - *(noun)* **1** a particular part or feature. a particular appearance or quality. *I didn't pay attention to this aspect of situation.* **2** the positioning or a building in a particular direction. the side of a building facing a particular direction. *This aspect of building faces east.* **3** [Astrology] any of a number of particular angular relationships between one celestial body or point on the ecliptic and another. **4** [grammar] a category or form of a *verb* which expresses a feature of the action related to time, such as completion or duration. *(verb)* [astrology] (of a planet) form an aspect with (another celestial body).

Asperity - *(noun)* **1** harshness of tone or manner. harsh qualities or conditions. *His asperity hurts me.* **2** a rough edge on a surface.

Asperse - *(verb)* rare cast aspersions on. *People aspersed her but she remained undaunted.*

Aspersion - *(noun)* an attack on someone's character or reputation. *They cast aspersions on him but he answered all their questions fearlessly.*

Asphodel - *(noun)* **1** a plant of the lily family with long, slender leaves and flowers borne on a spike. *Thank you for this rare plant of asphodel.* **2** [poetic - literary] an everlasting flower said to grow in the Elysian fields.

Asphyxia - *(noun)* a condition arising when the body is deprived of oxygen, causing unconsciousness or death. *This man's death has been due to asphyxia.*

Aspirant - *(adj.)* aspiring towards a particular achievement or status. *(noun)* a person who has such aspirations. *He is an aspirant for the job of director.*

Aspirate - *(verb)* **1** [phonetics] pronounce (a sound) with an exhalation of breath. pronounce the sound of h at the beginning of a word. *Please aspirate the sound h in this word as in horse!* **2** [chiefly medicine] draw by suction form a bodily vessel or cavity. *At once aspirate the water from the lungs.* **3** inhale. **4** (of an internal-combustion engine) provided with air. *(noun)* **1** [phonetics] an aspirated consonant. a sound of h. **2** [medicine] matter that has been drawn form the body by aspiration. *(adj.)* [phonetics] aspirated.

Aspiration - *(noun)* **1** a hope or ambition. *My aspiration is to become an army officer.* **2** the action of aspirating.

Aspirator - *(noun)* [medicine] an instrument or apparatus for aspirating. *Bring an aspirator to draw out the air from lungs.*

Aspire - *(verb)* **1** direct one's hopes or ambitions towards achieving something. *I aspire to be a business tycoon.* **2** [poetic - literary] rise high; tower.

Aspirin - *(noun)* a synthetic compound used to relieve pain and reduce fever and inflammation. *Take an aspirin and your fever will come down.*

Asquint - *(adv. & adj.)* with a glance to one side or from the corner of the eyes. *He looked at me asquint.*

Ass - *(noun)* **1** an animal of the horse family which is smaller than a horse and had longer ears and a braying call. (in general use) a donkey. *This animal is known as a jackass.* **2** [informal] a foolish or stupid person. *He is an ass by means.*

Assail - *(verb)* **1** make a concerned or violent attack on. **2** (of an unpleasant feeling) come upon (someone) strongly. *A bad feeling assailed me in the morning.*

Assassin - *(noun)* **1** a person who assassinates. *This is the assassin who shot the president.* **2** a member of the fanatical Nizarl branch of Ismaili Muslims dominant at the time of the crusades.

Assault - *(noun)* **1** a violent attack. [law] an act that threatens physical harm to a person, whether or not actual harm is done. *He assaulted me at a public place.* **2** a concerted attempt to do something demanding. *(verb)* make an assault on. *Assault him!*

Assemble - *(verb)* **1** come or bring together. *I assembled the different parts of the machinery together.* **2** fit together the component parts of. **3** [computing] translate (a program) from a symbolic language into machine code.

Assembly - *(noun)* **1** a group of people gathered together. a group having legislative or decision-making powers. a regular gathering of teachers and pupils in a school. *All the MLA's were asked to assemble at the assembly at 10 AM. sharp for voting.* **2** the action of assembling component parts. a unit consisting of assembled components. **3** computing the conversion of instructions in symbolic code to machine code by an assmebler.

Assent - *(noun)* the expression of approval or agreement. *(verb)* express assent. *I expressed my assent to the proposal.*

Assentient - *(adj.)* expressing agreement or consent. *He was in an assentient mood.*

Assert - *(verb)* **1** state a fact or belief confidently and forcefully. *I asserted my belief in God.* **2** cause others to recognize (one's authority or a right) by confident and forceful behaviour. behave or speak confidently and forcefully.

Assertive - *(adj.)* having or showing a confident and forceful personality. *He is an assertive and energetic man.*

Assertion - *(noun)* **1** declaration that is made emphatically. **2** the act of affirming, asserting or stating something.

Assertor - *(noun)* someone who claims to speak the truth. *He is an assertor and he will not budge from his statement.*

Assess - *(verb)* evaluate or estimate the nature, value, or quality of. set the value of a tax, fine, etc. for (a person or property) at a specified level. *The bank will assess the value of your property before giving you loan.*

Assiduity - *(noun)* constant or close attention to what one is doing. *His assiduity for work is well known* [archaic or poetic - literary] constant attentions to someone.

Assiduous - *(adj.)* showing great care and perseverance. *His assiduous care soon cured him.*

Assign - *(verb)* **1** allocate a task or duty to someone. appoint to a particular task. *I assigned him the task of bringing money from the bank.* **2** designate or set aside for a person. *I'll assign the financial aspect of the plan to him.* **3** transfer (legal rights or liabilities). *(noun)* law another term for assignee.

Asunder - *(adj.)* [archaic or poetic - literary] apart. *They were asunder for years.*

Asylum - *(noun)* **1** the protection granted by a state to someone who has left their native country as a political refugee. shelter or protection form danger. *The diplomat was granted asylum by the state.* **2** institution for the care of the mentally ill. *There are many asylums in the city for mentally ill.*

At - *(prep.)* **1** expressing location or arrival in a particular place or position. *I'll meet you at the railway station.* **2** expressing the time when an event takes place. *I daily rise at 8 AM.* **3** expressing attendance of an educational institution or a workplace. *At school you must behave properly.* **4** denoting a particular point or segment on a scale. referring to someone's age. **5** expressing a particular state or condition. *He threw a stone at me.* **6** expressing the object or target of a look, shot, action, or plan. expressing an incomplete or attempted action. *I am very expert at swimming.* **7** expressing the means by which something is done.

Ate – *(suffix)* forming nouns: **1** denoting status or office: doctorate. denoting a state or function: mandate. **2** denoting a group. **3** [chemistry] denoting a salt or ester, especially of an acid with a corresponding name ending in-ic: chlorate. **4** denoting a product of a chemical process: condensate.

Atelier – *(noun)* a workshop or studio. *We were called for lecture in the atelier.*

Atheism – *(noun)* the theory or belief that god does not exist. *He believes in atheism, for him there is no God.*

Athirst – *(adj.)* extremity desirous. *He is athirst for money.*

Athlete – *(noun)* a person who is proficient in sports, especially one who competes in track and field events. *There is no dearth of good Atheletes in our country.*

Athwart – *(prep.)* **1** from side to side of; across. *The swan athwart the river.* **2** counter to. *(adverb)* **1** across from side to side; transversely. **2** so as to be perverse or contra- dictory.

Atlantic – *(adj.)* **1** of or adjoining the Atlantic ocean. *Cold wind blew over the Atlantic.* **2** [geology] relating to or denoting the third climatic stage of the postglacial period in northern Europe with a moist oceanic climate.

Atlas – *(noun)* **1** a book of maps or charts. *When you open this atlas and you will find maps of all the countries in it.* **2** [anatomy] the topmost vertebra of the backbone, articulating with the occipital bone of the skill. *The doctors are looking at the X-ray of the atlas.* **3** [architecture] a stone carving of a male figure, used as a column to support the entablature of a Greek or Greek-style building.

Atoll – *(noun)* a ring-shaped reef or chain of islands formed of coral.

Atom – *(noun)* the smallest particle of a chemical element, consisting of a positively charged nucleus (containing protons and typically also neutrons) surrounded by negatively charged electrons. *Scientist named the smallest particle as atom.* **2** an extremely small amount.

Atomizer – *(verb)* **1** convert (a substance) into very fine particles or droplets. *We use atomizer to convert any substance into fragments.* **2** fragment.

Atomy – *(noun)* [archaic] a skeleton or emaciated body. *I took pity at his atomy like body.*

Atone – *(verb)* make amends or reparation for. *I went to church to atone for my sins.*

Atop – *(prep.)* on the top of. *(adverb)* on the top. *The bird sat atop the tree.*

Atrophy – *(verb)* **1** (of body tissue or an organ) waste away, especially as a result of the degeneration of cells, or become vestigial during evolution. **2** gradually decline in effectiveness or vigour. *(noun)* the condition or process of atrophying. *Atrophy of muscles is very common in an old age.*

Attach – *(verb)* **1** fasten; join. include (a condition) as part of an agreement. *Please find attached my biodata with the application.* **2** assign or attribute. full of affection or fondness. *I am very much attached to my children.* **3** appoint for special or temporary duties. *He has been attached to the director for special duty.* **4** [law, archaic, seize] (a person or property) by legal authority. *His property has been attached by the government.*

Attack – *(verb)* **1** take aggressive action against. act harmfully on. *He attacked me in open daylight.* **2** criticize or oppose fiercely and publicly. *People criticized their leader openly.* **3** begin to deal with (a problem or task) in a determined way. *Our hockey players made a determined attack upon the opposite team.* **4** make a forceful attempt to score goals or points. *(noun)* **1** an instance of attacking. destructive action by a disease or chemical. **2** a sudden short bout of an illness or disorder. **3** the players in a team whose role is to attack. *I suffered from an attack of malaria.*

Attain – *(verb)* **1** succeed in accomplishing. *I succeeded in attaining my goal.* **2** reach (a specified age, size, or amount). *He has attained the age of sixty.*

Attainder – *(noun)* [historical] the forfeiture of land and civil rights suffered as a consequence of a sentence of death for treason or felony. *He was an attainder so his property was attached and he was executed.*

Attaint - *(verb)* **1** [historical] subject to attainder. **2** [archaic] (of a disease) affect or infect.

Attar - *(noun)* a fragrant essential oil, typically made from rose petals. *I have used special attar in smells.*

Attemper - *(verb)* modify the temperature of.

Attempt - *(verb)* make an effort to achieve or complete. try to climb to the top of (a mountain). *He attempted to climb the mountain and succeeded.* *(noun)* an act of attempting. a bid to kill someone. *They attempted to kill him.*

Attend - *(verb)* **1** be present at. go regularly to (a school, church, or clinic). *I'll certainly attend the class.* **2** deal with. pay attention to. *I attended upon the sick lady.* **3** occur at the same time as or as a result of. *He attended the function dutifully.* **4** escort and wait on (a member of royalty or other important person.) *I'll attend to you presently.*

Attendant - *(noun)* a person employed to provide a service to the public. an assistant to an important person. *I am attendant to the secretary.* **2** a person who attends a particular occasion. *(adj.)* occurring at the same time or as a result of.

Attender - *(noun)* **1** someone who listens attentively. *He is an attender and regularly attends the lectures.* **2** someone who attends to the need of another. *I have hired an attender for my mother.* **3** a person will is present and participates in a meeting. *He was a regular attender at the meeting.*

Attention - *(noun)* **1** the mental faculty of considering. *Don't pay any attention to him he is a fool.* a person's behaviour to another as an indication of affection or sexual interest. *Please pay attention to what I am saying.* **2** [military] position assumed by a soldier, standing very straight with the feet together and the arms straight down the sides of the body. *The officer cried attention and the Jawan stood still.*

Attentive - *(adj.)* **1** paying close attention. *I am attentive to you.* **2** assiduously attending to the comport or wishes of others. *He is always attentive to other people's needs.*

Attest - *(verb)* **1** provide or serve as clear evidence of. *I have my document attested from a gazette officer.* **2** declare that something exists or is the case. *I attested to the existence of my grandfather.*

Attire - *(noun)* clothes, especially fine or formal ones. *He appeared in the fancy show in the attire of a king.* *(verb)* be dressed in clothes of a specified king.

Attitude - *(noun)* **1** a settled way of thinking or feeling. a position of the body indicating a particular. *Doesn't he behave funny? He must have attitude problem.*

Attorney - *(noun)* a person, typically a lawyer, appointed to act for another in legal matters. qualified lawyer. *I have hired an attorney to fight my case*

Attract - *(verb)* **1** draw or bring in by offering something of interest or advantage. *Full moon attracts the sea waters.* **2** evoke (a specified reaction). cause to have a liking for or interest in. *He was attracted to her like anything.* **3** exert a pull on. *Opposite poles attract each other.*

Attribute - *(verb)* regard something as belonging to or being caused by. *I attribute my whole success to my mother.* *(noun)* **1** a quality or feature regarded as characteristic or inherent. *Serving the needy is one of his attributes.* **2** a material object recognized as representative of a person, status, or office.

Attrit - *(verb)* [informal] wear down by sustained action. *His body attrited due to a long disese.*

Attrition - *(noun)* **1** the action or process of gradually wearing down through sustained attack or pressure. *He travelled long through the jungle and his body was in a condition of attrition.* **2** wearing away by friction. **3** (in scholastic theology) sorrow for sin falling short of contrition.

Auburn - *(noun)* a reddish-brown colour. *I got my hair coloured auburn.*

Auction - *(noun)* **1** a public sale in which goods or property are sold to the highest bidder. *He was deeply in debt so his house was auctioned.* **2** [bridge] the part of the game in which players bid to decide the contract in which the hand shall be played. *(verb)* sell or offer for sale at an auction.

Audacious – *(adj.)* recklessly daring. *He is an audacious fellow and will never see sense.* **2** impudent.

Audible – *(adj.)* able to be heard. *He has an audible and clear voice.* *(noun)* [American football] a change of playing tactics called by the quarterback at the line of scrimmage.

Audibly – *(adv.)* in an audible manner. *She spoke audibly to listeners and they understood her.*

Audience – *(noun)* **1** a gathering of spectators or listeners at a performance. *The audience was disturbed.* **2** the part of general public interested in a source of information or entertainment. *Every speaker needs an audience.* **3** a conference. *The speaker requested an audience with the official.*

Audiometer – *(noun)* an instrument used to measure the sensitivity of nearing. *Here is an audiometer whereby you can measure the sensitivity of hearing.*

Audit – *(noun)* an official inspection of an organization's accounts, typically by an independent body. *Audit is going on so I can't attend to you; please come tomorrow.* *(verb)* **1** conduct an audit of. **2** north America attend informally, without working for credit.

Audition – *(noun)* **1** an interview for a musician, actor, etc. consisting of a practical demonstration of the candidate's suitability and skill. *Next is my turn for audition and I'm feeling a bit nervous.* **2** [archaic] the power of hearing. *(verb)* assess or be assessed by an audition.

Auditive – *(adj.)* of or relating to the process of hearing. *This problem is auditive.*

Auditor – *(noun)* **1** a person who conducts an audit. *He is the auditor who is going to audit the company accounts.* **2** a listener. **3** [north American] a person who attends a class informally without working for credit.

Auditorium – *(noun)* **1** the part of a theatre or hall in which the audience sit. *The auditorium was full of people who had come to see the famous drama.* **2** [chiefly north American] a large hall used for public gatherings.

Auditory – *(adj.)* of or relating to the sense of hearing. *This is something that relates to auditory defect.*

Augean – *(adj.)* extremely filthy from long reflect. *The old place smelled Augean.*

Auger – *(noun)* a tool resembling a large corkscrew, for boring holes.

August – *(noun)* the eight month of the year. *August is the 8th month of the year.*

Aunt – *(noun)* **1** the sister of one's father or mother or the wife of one's uncle. *One of my aunts is a director of this company.* **2** [informal] an unrelated audit female friend of a child. *Aunt, will you mind giving me that bag.*

Aural – *(adj.)* of or relating to the ear or the sense of hearing. *He had to consult a specialist because of an aural infection.*

Aureole – *(noun)* **1** a radiant circle surrounding a person's head or body as a way of representing holiness. *You'll find an aureole around the head of saints.* **2** a corona around the sun or moon. **3** [geology] the zone of metamorphosed rock surrounding an igneous intrusion.

Auric – *(adj.)* of or relating to an aura. *The halo around the sun is auric.*

Auriferous – *(adj.)* (of rocks or minerals) containing gold. *These rocks are auriferous.*

Auriform – *(adj.)* harming a shape resembling an car. *I saw a tree leaf which was almost auriform like an ear.*

Aurora – *(noun)* **1** the northern lights or southern lights; a natural phenomenon characterized by the appearance of streamers of coloured light in the sky near the earth's magnetic poles and caused by the interaction of charged particles form the sun with atoms in the supper atmosphere. *At aurora I was half awake and saw a strange dream.* **2** [poetic – literary] the dawn.

Auspice – *(noun)* [archaic] an omen. *Seeing an owl is not a good auspice.*

Auspicious – *(adj.)* indicating a good chance of success; favourable. *Today is my brother's marriage. It is an auspicious day.*

Austere – *(adj.)* **1** servere or strict in appearance or manner. *My father is very austere. I'm afraid of even speaking to him.* **2** lacking comforts, luxureis, or adornment.

Austerity – *(noun)* the trait of great self-denial. *Many saints preach austerity.*

Austral – *(adj.)* [technical] **1** of the southern hemisphere. **2** of Australia or Australasia. *This man seems austral in appearance must be from Australia.*

Authentic– *(adj.)* **1** of undisputed origin or veracity; genuine. *These papers are authentic. I have shown them to a lawyer.* **2** [music] containing notes between the principal note or final and the note an octave higher. compare with plagal.

Authenticity – *(noun)* the property of being genuine or valid. *The authenticity of this document is beyond doubt.*

Author – *(noun)* **1** a writer of a book, article, or report. *He is an author of many novels.* **2** an originator of a plan or idea. *(verb)* be the author or the originator of. *He authored many books.*

Authority – *(noun)* **1** the power or right to give orders and enforce obedience. *He is the authority.* **2** a persons or organizartion exerting control in a particular political or administrative sphere. *The authority in power.* **3** the power to influence others based on recognized knowledge or expertise. an authoritative person, book, or other source. *He is an authoritative person.*

Authorize – *(verb)* give official permission for or approval to. *I authorized him to attend the meeting on my behalf.*

Autobiography – *(noun)* an account of a person's life written by that person. *Almost all great men write their autobiography.*

Autocracy – *(noun)* **1** a system of government by one person with absolute power. *Autocracy is not popular these day's.* **2** a country, state, or society governed in this way.

Autocrat – *(noun)* **1** a ruler who has absolute power. *Autocrats usually meet tragic ends.* **2** a domineering person.

Autograph – *(noun)* **1** a celebrity's signature written for an admirer. *I have with me autograph of Amitabh Bachchan.* **2** a manuscript or musical score in an author's or composer's own handwriting. **3** a person's handwriting. *(verb)* write one's signature on. *(adj.)* written in the author's own handwriting.

Automatic – *(adj.)* **1** working by itself with little or no direct human control. self-loading and able to fire continuously. *These day automatic devices and machines are in vogue with little human intervention.* **2** done or occurring without conscious though. necessary and inevitable, as result of a fixed rule or particular set of circumstances. *(noun)* an automatic machine or device.

Automobile – *(noun)* [chiefly north American] a motor car. *I would like to sit in a racing automobile.*

Autonomous – *(adj.)* not controlled by outside forces; existing as an independent entity. *Judiciary is an autonomous body.*

Autonomy – *(noun)* **1** the possession or right of self-government. *People enjoy autonomy in democracy.* **2** freedom of action.

Autumn – *(noun)* **1** [chiefly brit.] the season after summer and before winter. *Trees shed their leaves in autumn.* **2** [astronomy] the period form the autumn equinox to the winter solstice.

Auxiliary – *(adj.)* providing supplementary or additional help and support. *(noun)* an auxiliary person or thing. *The flood victims were provided auxiliary help.*

Avail – *(verb)* use or take advantage of. *When opportunity comes avail yourself of it.* **2** help or benefit. noun use or benefit.

Avarice – *(noun)* extreme greed for wealth or material gain. *He suffers from avarice.*

Avenge – *(verb)* inflict harm in return for (an injury or wrong). inflict retribution on behalf of (a wronged person). *I avenged myself upon him as he had dishonored me.*

Avenue – *(noun)* **1** a broad road or path, especially one lined with trees. *We had to walk along a long avenue before reaching the house.* **2** a means of approach.

Average – *(noun)* **1** the result obtained by adding several amounts together and then dividing the total by the number of amounts. *We calculate average in arithmetic.* **2** a usual or ordinary amount, level, or rate. *The mangoes are getting silled at average rate.* **3** [law] the apportionment of financial liability resulting from loss of or damage to a ship or its cargo. *(adj.)* of the usual or ordinary amount, level or rate. mediocre: a very average movie. *It is an average movie. (verb)* **1** amount to or achieve as an average. calculate or estimate the average of. *he made an average of the number.* **2** result in an even distribution.

Avert - *(verb)* **1** turn away (one's eyes or thoughts). *He averted his eyes from me.* **2** prevent. or ward off.

Aviary - *(noun)* a large enclosure for keeping birds in. *I have built an aviary for birds.*

Aviate - *(verb)* operate an aeroplane. *He aviated the plane skillfully.*

Aviation - *(noun)* the activity or business of operating and flying aircraft. *He is an expert at aviation.*

Avid - *(adj.)* keenly interested or enthuslastic. *He has an avid interest in music.*

Avocation - *(noun)* auxiliary activity. *Besides his hardware business his avocation is breeding dogs.*

Avoid - *(verb)* **1** keep away or refrain from. prevent form doing or happening. *I always avoid him because he is a non-stop talker.* [law] repudiate, nullity, or render void.

Avulsion - *(noun)* **1** [chiefly medicine] the action of pulling or tearing away. *The avulsion of the tissue from its wound is not a good sign.* **2** [law] the sudden separation of land from one property and its attachment to another, especially by flooding. compare with alluvion.

Await - *(verb)* wait for. *I'll await you here.*

Awake - *(verb)* **1** stop sleeping. *He has long been awake.* **2** make or become active again. *I was awakened. (adj.)* **1** not asleep. **2** aware of. *I was awakened to the truth by my friends.*

Awaken - *(verb)* **1** stop or cause to stop sleeping. *I awakened him from sleep.* **2** rouse.

Award - *(verb)* give or grant officially as a prize or reward. *(noun)* something awarded. *He was given an award for his performance in athletic events.*

Aware - *(adj.)* having knowledge or perception of a situation or fact. *I am aware that he is going to meet my sister..*

Away - *(adj.)* **1** to or at a distance. at a specified future distance in time. *He left his home and went far away.* **2** towards a lower level. **3** into an appropriate place for storage or safe keeping. *Do you see that star far away in the sky.* **4** towards or into non-existence. *Away and away into the space the space craft hurtled and disappeared for ever.* **5** constantly, persistently, or continuously. *10 years away we shall reach mars.* **6** at the opponent's ground. *There is a town here only five miles away where we can stay. (adj.)* played at the opponent's ground. *(noun)* an away game. *For Indian it was an away game but they won it.*

Awe - *(noun)* a feeling of reverential respect mixed with fear or wonder. *(verb)* inspire with awe. *I looked at the big man with awe.*

Awful - *(adj.)* **1** very bad or unpleasant. *It was awful to be in such a dirty place.* **2** used for emphasis. *an awful lot of letters.* [archaic] inspiring awe.

Awhile - *(adj.)* for a short time. *For awhile she was with her mother but awhile* she came back.

Awkward - *(adj.)* **1** hard to do or deal with. *He is such an awkward fellow, he never fits in any place.* **2** uneasily embarrassed. **3** not smooth or graceful.

Awl - *(noun)* a small pointed toll used for placing holes. *A shoe maker sews shoes with an awl.*

Awoke - past of awake. *I awoke late yesterday.*

Axe - *(noun)* **1** a heavy-bladed tool used for chopping wood. *Woodcutter cut wood with an axe.* **2** cost-cutting action, especially redundancy. *Thirty staff are facing the axe.* **3** [informal] a guitar or a saxophone. *(verb)* **1** end, cancel, or dismiss suddenly and ruthlessly. *Thirty workers have been axed.* **2** cut or strike with an axe.

Axial - *(adj.)* forming, relating to, or around and axis. *The earth moves a round the imaginary line namely axial.*

Axilla - *(noun)* **1** [anatomy] an armpit, or the corresponding part in a bird or other animal. *Axilla itching is very common during summer.* **2** [botany] an axil.

Axillary – *(adj.)* [anotomy] of or relating to the armpit. *If there is an axillary growth a doctor should be consulted at once.*

Axiom – *(noun)* **1** an accepted statement or proposition regarded as being self-evidently true. **2** [chiefly mathematics] a statement or proposition on which an abstractly defined structure is based. *In mathematics we can't do without axioms.*

Axis – *(noun)* **1** an imaginary line about which a body rotates or with respect to which it possesses rotational symmetry. *Our earth rotates round an imaginary line called axis* **2** an imaginary line which divides something in half, especially in the direction of its greatest length. **3** [mathematics] a fixed reference line for the measurement of coordinates. **4** a straight central part in a structure to which other parts are connected. **5** [anatomy] the second cervical vertebra, below the atlas at the top of the backbone. **6** the alliance between Germany and Italy in the second world war.

Axle – *(noun)* a rod or spindle passing through the centre of a wheel or group of wheels. *Both the cart wheels are rotating on spindle like axle.*

Aye – *exclamatory* [archaic] a response accepting an order. i assent. *(noun)* an affirmative answer, especially in voting. *Aye! We are moving ahead, increase speed of your boat.*

Azure – *(adj.)* bright blue in colour like a cloudless sky. heraldry blue. *She wore an azure coloured suit which looked amazing.* *(noun)* a bright blue colour.

Bb

B – the second letter of the English alphabet. (1) The seventh note in music. (2) The second known quantity in Algebra.

Baa – *(verb)* (of a sheep or lamb) bleat. *(noun)* the cry of a sheep or lamb. *The lamb cried baa and the shepherd became alert.*

Babble – *(verb)* **1** talk rapidly and continuously in a foolish, excited, or incomprehensible way. reveal something secret. *He babbled away the secret.* **2** (of a stream) make a continuous murmur as the water flows over stones. *We could hear the babbling of the river.* *(noun)* the sound of babbling. foolish, excited, or confused talk. *He kept on babbling about him.*

Babe – *(noun)* **1** [poetic/literary] a baby. *The babe was beautiful and healthy.* **2** [informal] a sexually attractive young woman. *Hey babe you look special today.*

Babel – *(noun)* a confused noise made by a number of voices. *I couldn't hear him clearly in that babel.*

Baboon – *(noun)* a large ground-dwelling social monkey with a long dog-like snout and large teeth. *In Africa I saw herds of baboons dwelling on ground.*

Baby – *(noun)* **1** a child or animal that is newly or recently born. *A baby was born to my sister-in-law.* **2** a timid or childish person. *Although adult he behaves like a baby.* **3** [informal] a person with whom one is having a romantic relationship (often as a form of address). *Baby! You look amazing today.* *(adj.)* comparatively small or immature of its kind. *He is such a baby.* *(verb)* pamper or be over-protective towards. *I pamper my 4 year old baby to no end.*

Baccate – *(adj.)* **1** Resembling a berry. *The fruit looks like berry although it is not; it is baccate.*

Bacchanal – *(noun)* **1** an occasion of wild and drunken revelry. *Today's rave parties remind us of bacchanal parties given in honour of Bacchus the god wine in old times.* **2** a priest, worshipper, or follower of Bacchus, the Greek or roman god of wine. *He is a bacchanal.*

Bachelor – *(noun)* **1** a man who is not and has never been married. *People cast strange glances at bachelors.* **2** [zoology] a male bird or mammal prevented from breeding by a dominant male. *The ostrich stopped the bachelor from mating with female.* **3** a person who holds a first degree from a university or other academic institution (only in titles or set expressions). *After having passed his B.A. he attended Bachelor's convocation in university.*

Bacillary – *(adj.)* [biology] **1** relating to or produced by or containing bacilli. *Bacillary dysentry is a type of dysentry.*

Bacilliform – *(adj.)* [chiefly biology] rod-shaped. *These bacilliformed objects are germs of disease.*

Backbite *(verb)* say near things. *People backbite all the time.*

Backbone – *(noun)* **1** the spine. *I have pain in my backbone.* **2** the chief support of a system or organization. strength of character. *He is the sole earner in the family and hence the backbone of the family.*

Background – *(noun)* **1** part of a scene, picture, or description that forms a setting for the main fighters, events, etc. *The background was full of dust fighters deputing the fight bring.* **2** a persistent low level of radioactivity. radiation, noise, etc. present in a particular environment. *In the film they created a vast dark frightening background to show the battle of Mahabharata.* **3** explanatory or contributory information or circumstances. a person's education, experience, and social circumstances. *I have made enquiries about him; his background is not good.*

Backhand – *(noun)* (in tennis and other racket sports) a stroke played with the back of the hand facing in the direction of the stroke, with the arm across the body. *Boris Becker was famous for his back hand shots. (verb)* strike with a backhanded blow or stroke. *He backhand the stroke.*

Backing – *(noun)* **1** support. a layer of material that forms, protects, or strengthens the back of something. *You have my backing, go on and fight.* **2** (especially in popular music) musical or vocal accompaniment to the main singer or soloist. *The soloist singing has backing of forty singers.* **3** [phonetics] the movement of the place of formation of a sound towards the back of the mouth. *His backing has some problem which shows up during his pronunciations of few words.*

Backside – *(noun)* **1** [informal] a person's buttocks or anus. *I am not fond of seeing the backsides of people.* **2** [chiefly North American] the reverse of rearward side.

Backslide – *(verb)* relapse into bad ways. *After remaining away a long time from alcohol he backslided and took to drinking again.*

Backward – *(adj.)* **1** directed behind or to the rear. *As he advanced the other man began to inch backward.* **2** having made less progress than is normal or expected, having learning difficulties. *He is rather backward in his studies.* **3** lacking the confidence to do. *Though backward he displayed his talents ably.* **4** [cricket] (of a fielding position) behind an imaginary line passing through the stumps at the batsman's end at with angles to the wicket. *(adverb)* variant of backwards. *People living in remote areas are rather backward.*

Backwards – *(adj.)* **1** in the direction of one's back. *I moved backwards as the animal came forward.* **2** back towards the starting point. *The car moved backwards in the reverse gear.* **3** in reverse of the usual direction or order. towards the past. towards a worse state. *Despite such fantastic progress he has again gone backwards. He is back where he used to be at the starting point of poverty.*

Bacon – *(noun)* cured meat from the back or sides of a pig. *He is fond of eating bacon meat.*

Bacteria – *plural* form of bacterium. *Bacteria are everywhere.*

Bad – *(adj.)* **1** of poor quality or a low standard. *To leave food midway are bad manners.* **2** unwelcome; unpleasant. severe; serious. harmful to. *This is a bad wound.* **3** offending moral standards or accepted conventions. *He behaved bad in the party and thus offended all the people.* **4** injured, ill, or diseased. *He has a bad wound it is getting worse.* **5** (of food) decayed. guilty; ashamed. *This piece of bread is decayed and bad.* **6**. inappropriate. *It was bad of you to point out his misfortune.*

Badge – *(noun)* **1** a small piece of metal, plastic, or cloth bearing a design or words, typically worn to indentify a person or to indicate support for a cause. *All scouts wear a badge.* **2** a sign or feature revealing a quality or condition. *He converts the macho stereotype into a badge of honour. (verb)* mark with a badge. *In many hospitals doctors have to wear a badge.*

Badger– *(noun)* a heavily built omnivorous nocturnal mammal of the weasel family, typically having a grey and black coat and a white-striped head. *We could see badger hunting for food. (verb)* repeatedly and annoyingly ask someone to do something. *He badgered me with questions.*

Badly– *(adverb)* **1** in a bad manner. *He behaved badly and angered all.* **2** severely; seriously. *He was badly beaten.* **3** very much. *The boy needs food badly.*

Baffle – *(verb)* **1** totally bewilder. *This question baffled me.* **2** restrain or regulate (a fluid, a sound, etc.) *I baffled the already loud sound by turning the knob. (noun)* a derive used to restrain the flow of a fluid, gas, or loose material or to prevent the spreading of sound or light in a particular direction. *You can cut out glare from a strip light by concealing it behind a baffle.*

Bafta – *(noun)* coarse fabric, typically of cotton. *I have bought a piece of bafta cloth, although coarse it is durable.*

Bag – *(noun)* **1** a flexible container with an opening at the top. a piece of luggage. *Let us put all these things into one bag.* **2** loose folds of skiing under a person's eyes. **3** [British] he loose-fitting trousers. *In England many people wear baggies.* **4** [informal, chiefly British] plenty of. *From overuse his pants look like bulging loose bags.* **5** the amount of game shot by a hunter. *In his hunting expedition he has bagged two foxes.* **6.** [informal] an unpleasant or unattractive women. *She is so thin that she is called a bag of bones.* *(verb)* **1** put in a bag. *You should bag all your shoes.* **2** succeed in killing or catching (an animal). succeed in securing. *The lion bagged down the deer.* **3** (of clothes) form loose bulges due to wear.

Bagasse – *(noun)* the dry pulpy residue left after the extraction of juice from sugar cane. *I wonder in what way they use bagasse.*

Baggage – *(noun)* **1** personal belonging packed in suitcases for travelling. *He appeared at the airport with bag and baggage.* **2** past experiences or long-held opinions perceived as encumbrances; emotional baggage. **3** a cheeky or disagreeable girl or woman.

Bagman – *(noun)* **1** [British informal] a travelling salesman. *He is a very successful bagman.* **2** [Canadain] a political fundraiser. *He is assigned the work of collecting funds. He is the party bagman.* **4** [informal] an agent who collects or distributes the proceeds of illicit activities. *The bagman distributed suspicious package.*

Bagpipe – *(noun)* a musical instrument with reed pipes that are sounded by the pressure of wind emitted from a bag squeezed by the player's arm. *He is expert at playing bagpipe.*

Bail – *(noun)* **1** the temporary release of an accused person awaiting trial, sometimes on condition that a sum of money is lodged on guarantee their appearance in court. *The judge granted him bail against the security of 50,000 rupees.* **2** money paid by or for such a person as security. *He was released on bail. (verb)* releases or secure the release of on payment of bail. *He was released on bail.*

Bailee– *(noun)* [law] a person or party to whom goods are delivered for a purpose, without transfer of ownership. *The property was transferred to bailee but he would not use it for legal purposes.*

Bailiff – *(noun)* an officer of the court who is employed to execute writs and processes and make arrests, etc. *Yesterday a bailiff came to my friend's house to arrest him.*

Bait – *(noun)* **1** food used to entice fish or other animals as prey. *Fisherman use a bait to catch fish. (verb)* **1** deliberately annoy or launt. *He baited me openly and I got angry.* **2** put bait on (a hook) or in (a trap, net, or fishing area). *He baited the worm on the hook.*

Baize – *(noun)* a coarse felt-like woolen material that is typically green used chiefly for covering billiard and card tables. *Cover the billiard and card tables with baize so they do not get damp or dirty.*

Bake – *(verb)* **1** cook by dry heat without direct exposure to a flame, typically in an oven. *Biscuits are baked in the oven.* **2** (of the sun or other agency) subject to dry heat. [informal] be or become extremely hot in prolonged hot weather. *I was baked in hot sun. (noun)* **1** a dish consisting of a number of ingredients at which baked food of a specified kind is eaten. *Baked brinjals were served at dinner.*

Balance-wheel – *(noun)* another term for balance. *Things are weighed in a balance.*

Balance – *(noun)* **1** a state of equilibrium. **2** equality between the totals of the credit and debit sides of an account. **3** harmonious arrangement or relation of parts or elements within a whole (as in a design). **4** equality of distribution. **5** something left after other parts have been taken away. *The man took what he wanted and I got* the balance. **6** the difference between the totals of the credit and debit sides of an account. **7** [mathematics] an attribute of a shape or relation; exact reflection of form on opposite sides of a dividing line ort plane. **8** a weight that balances another weight. **9** a wheel that regulates the rate of movement in a machine; especially a wheel oscillating the hairspring of a timepiece to regulate its beat. **10** a scale for weighing; depends on pull of gravity. *(verb)* **1** bring into balance or equilibrium. **2** compute credits and debits of an account. **3** hold or carry in equilibrium. **4** be in equilibrium. *The young girl was balancing on one foot.*

Balcony- *(noun)* **1** a platform enclosed by a wall or balustrade on the outside of a building. *I usually stand in my balcony and look at the sea.* **2** the highest tier of seats in a theater or cinema. *Only rich can afford balcony in cinema.* [north American] the dress circle in a theatre.

Bald - *(adj.)* **1** having a scalp wholly or partly lacking hair. feathers. *He is a bald man.* **2** having the tread worn away. **3** plain; blunt. *It may hurt you but this is the bald truth.*

Balderdash- *(noun)* senseless talk or writing. *All his talk and writings are balderdash.*

Baldric - *(noun)* [historical] a belt for a sword or other piece of equipment, worn over one shoulder and reaching down to the opposite hip. *In old times soldiers wore their swords on a baldric.*

Bale - *(noun)* **1** a large wrapped or bound bundle of paper. hay, or cotton. *Bales of cotton paper were loaded off from the truck.* **2** the quantity in a bale as a measure, specifically (in the US) 500 lb of cotton. *(verb)* make up into bales.

Baleen - *(noun)* whalebone. *This large bone must be baleen.*

Bale fire - *(noun)* [US] a large open-air fire. *A strange soul of bale fire spread in some cities of a country.*

Balk - *(verb)* & *(noun)* [chiefly US] valiant spelling of baulk. *As we travelled we saw a big balk lying in our way.*

Ballade - *(noun)* **1** a poem consisting of one or more triples of stanzas with a repeated refrain and an envoy. *The old blind man was singing a ballad.* **2** a short, lyrical place of music, especially one for Plano.

Ballet - *(noun)* **1** an artistic dance form performed to music. using precise and formalized set of steps and gestures. *In India we rarely get an opportunity to see live ballet.* **2** a creative work of this form or the music written for it.

Balista - *(noun)* a catapult used in ancient warfare for hurling large boulders. *In old times the soldiers used balista to throw big stones.*

Balloon - *(noun)* **1** a small rubber sac which is inflated and used as a child's toy or a decoration. a rounded outline strip of cartoon. *Children like balloons very much.* **2** a large bag filled with hot air or gas to make it rise in the air, typically having a basket for passengers. *Some adventurous people travel long distance in hot air balloons.* **3** a large rounded drinking glass, used especially for brandy. *Brandy is drunk in balloon shaped glasses.* **4** [Scottish informal] a stupid person. *(verb)* **1** sell out in a spherical shape. increase rapidly. **2** [British] lob or be lobbed high in the air.

Ballot - *(noun)* **1** a procedure by which people vote secretly on an issue. the total number of votes cast in such a process. *These days people cast their vote by ballot.* **2** a lottery held to decide the allocation of tickets or other things among a number of applicant. *The applicants were given tickete in ballot.* *(verb)* **1** elicit a secret vote form cast one's vote. **2** allocate by drawing lots.

Balm - *(noun)* **1** a fragrant ointment used to heal or soothe the skin. something that has a soothing or restorative effect. *If you have headache you can use this balm; it will be very helpful.* **2** a tree which yields a fragrant resinous substance, especially one used in medicine. used in names of other fragrant plants, chiefly of the mint family, e.g. lemon balm.

Balmoral - *(noun)* **1** a round bramless hat with a cockade or ribbons attached, worn by certain scottish regiments. *Scottish regiments was balmoral.* **2** a heavy laced leather walking boot. *Her feet looked pretty in balmoral.*

Balsam - *(noun)* an aromatic resinous substance exuded by various trees and shrubs, used as a base for certain fragrances and medical preparations. a tree or shrub which yields balsam. *Balsam extracted from trees or shrubs is also of medicinal use.* **2** a herbaceous plant cultivated for its helmeted pink or purple flowers. *Balsam was grousing in their yard.*

Balustrade - *(noun)* a railing at the side of a stairccase or saleory to pervent people from falling. *Every staircase should have a secure balustrade.*

Bam - *(noun)* a sudden very loud noise. *We heard a loud bam outside the house.*

Bamboo – *(noun)* a giant woody grass with hollow jointed stems, grown chiefly in the tropics for use in furniture and implements. *Bamboo is largely used in furniture.*

Bamboozle – *(verb)* [informal] cheat or mystify. *I have been bamboozled by a fellow and thus lost a heavy amount of money.*

Ban – *(verb)* officially or legally prohibit. *It is banned for heavy vehicles to enter this street by order magistrate.* *(noun)* an official or legal prohibition. *There is a cigarette ban in particular parts of duty.*

Banana – *(noun)* **1** a long curved fruit which grows in clusters and has soft pulpy flesh and yellow skin when ripe. *I daily eat two bananas in my breakfast.* **2** the tropical and subtropical palm-like plant which bears this fruit.

Band – *(noun)* **1** a flat, thin strip or loop of material used as a easterner, for reinforcement, or as decoration. a belt or strap transmitting motion between two wheels or pulleys. [North American ornithology] a ring of metal placed round a bird's leg to identify it. *I came across a band of robbers and they robbed me.* **2** a stripe, line, or elongated area of a different colour or composition from its surroundings: a band of cloud. *She wore a beautiful red elastic band round her head.* **3** a range of values or a specified category within a series. a range of frequencies or wavelengths in a spectrum: channels in the UHF band. any of several groups into which school pupils of the same age are divided on the basis of similar ability. *In villages we usually see a thick heavy cloth band setting two wheels in motion.* **4** a collar with two hanging strips, worn by certain lawyers clerics, and academics as part of their formal dress. **5** [archaic] a bond. *(verb)* **1** surround or fit with a band. *Do you see that band of cloud in sky? It is going to rain.* **2** mark with a stripe or stripes of a different colour. allocate to a range or category.

Bandit – *(noun)* **1** a violent robber or outlaw belonging to a gang. *This photo is of a notorious bandit.* **2** military slang for an enemy aircraft.

Bandog – *(noun)* a fighting dog bred for its strength and ferocity. *The bandog it is very ferocious.*

Bandoleer – *(noun)* a brood cartridge belt over the shoulder by soldiers worn women.

Bandy – *(adj.)* (of a person's legs) curved outwards so that the knees are wide apart.

Bang – *(noun)* **1** a sudden loud, sharp noise. a sudden painful blow. *There was a loud bang and the gun went off.* **2** [chiefly North American] a hair cut straight across the forehead. **3** computing, [chiefly North American] the character '!' *(verb)* **1** strike or put down forcefully and noisily. *He banged the box on the ground.* make or cause to make a sudden loud noise. *I banged him across the face.* **2** vulgar slang have sexual intercourse with. *(adverb)* [informal, chiefly British] exactly. *The train arrived bang on time.*

Bangle – *(noun)* a rigid ornamental band worn around the arm. *It is customary for Indian women to wear glass bangles.*

Banish – *(verb)* **1** send away, especially from a country, as an official punishment. *He was banished from his country and asked to leave it forever as an official punishment.* **2** dismiss from one's mind. *I banished her from my mind.*

Banjo – *(noun)* a stringed instrument of the guitar family, with an open-backed sound box of vellum stretched over a round hoop. *He plays banjo beautifully.*

Banker – *(noun)* **1** a person who manages or owns a bank or group of banks. *My uncle is a banker; he owns a chain of banks besides being the manager of one.* the person running the table, controlling play, or acting as dealer in some gambling or board games. **2** [British] a supposedly certain bet. a result forecast identically in several football pool entries on the coupon.

Banking – *(noun)* the business conducted or services offered by a bank. *Some private banks offer excellent banking.*

Bankrupt – *(adj.)* **1** declared in law unable to pay one's debts. *My uncle was unable to pay his debts so he was declared bankrupt.* **2** completely lacking in a particular good quality judged by a court to be bankrupt. *(verb)* reduce to a bankrupt state.

Banner - *(noun)* a long strip of cloth bearing a slogan or design. *The procession went on. A lot of them bearing placards and banners.* a flag on a pole used as the standard of a king, knight, or army. *(adj.)* [North American] excellent; outstanding.

Banquet - *(noun)* an elaborate and formal meal for many people. *I went to the banquet hall in a marriage. (verb)* entertain with a banquet.

Bantam - *(noun)* a chicken of a small breed. *My brother rears bantams.*

Banter - *(noun)* the playful and friendly exchange of teasing remarks. *(verb)* engage in banter. *Although I bantered my friend a lot, he didn't mind it and rather bantered me in return.*

Bar — *(noun)* **1** a long rigid piece of wood, metal, or similar material, typically used as an obstruction, fastening, or weapon. *Let us put a heavy bar across the door so that it does not open easily.* a sandbank or shoal at the mouth of a harbour or an estuary. [British] a metal strip below the clasp of a medal, awarded as an additional distinction. [heraldry] a charge in the form of a narrow horizontal stripe across the shield. **2** a counter in a public house or cafe across which alcoholic drinks or refreshments are served. a room in a public house, restaurant, or hotel in which alcohol is served. an establishment where alcohol and other refreshments are served. a small shop or stall snack bar. *I entered the bar and the barman placed a jug of beer on the counter.* **3** a barrier or restriction to action or advance. a plea arresting an action or claim in a law case. *Person was barred from leaving the country.* **4** [music] any of the short sections or measures into which a piece of music is divided, shown on a score by vertical lines across the stave. *Convicts are supposed to stand in bar while trial.* **5** a partition in a court room, now usually notional, beyond which most people may not pass and at which an accused person stands. [British] a rail marking the end of each chamber in the house of parliament. **6** the profession of barrister. [British.] barristers collectively. [North American] lawyers collectively. *(verb)* **1** fasten with a bar or bars. prohibit from doing something or going somewhere. *He was barred from taking further action.* exclude from consideration. law prevent or delay by objection. *The officer's uniform was decorated with bars and medals.* 3 mark with bars or strips. *There were thick colour bass on that wall.*

Barb - *(noun)* **1** sharp projection near the end of an arrow, fish hook, or similar object, which is angled away from the main point so as to make extraction difficult. a barbel at the mouth of some fish. one of the fine hair-like filaments growing from the shaft of a feather, forming the vane. *Barbed wire was placed all around the school.* **2** a deliberately hurtful remark. **3** a fresh water fish with barbels around the mouth, popular in aquaria. *This fish has got a barbel in her mouth.*

Barbarian - *(noun)* **1** (in ancient times) a member of a people not belonging to one of the great civilizations. *In ancient times many kings. They gave horrible punishment to law breakers.* **2** an uncultured or brutish person. *(adj.)* **1** of or relating to ancient barbarians. **2** uncultured; brutish.

Barbaric - *(adj.)* savagely cruel. *People helplessly looked at the barbaric punishment given to a thief.* **2** primitive; unsophisticated.

Barbate - *(adj.)* having hair on the chew and chiw.

Barber - *(noun)* a person who cuts men's hair and shaves or trims beards as an occupation. *I am going to the barber for a haircut. (verb)* cut or trim (a man's hair).

Barbican - *(noun)* the outer defence of a city or castle, especially a double tower above a gate or drawbridge. *In old times castles used to have barbican for defense.*

Bard - *(noun)* [archaic or poetic/literary] a poet, traditionally one reciting epics. (the bard) Shakespeare. *Shakespeare was a bard who recited epics and wrote plays.*

Bare - *(adj.)* **1** (of a person or part of the body) not clothed or covered. without the appropriate or usual covering or contents. (bare of) without.

In the ritual he had to appeare bare bodied with no clothes. **2** without elaboration; basic. *He won by bare majority.* only just sufficient: a bare majority. *(verb)* uncover (a part of the body) and expose it to view. *It is the bare truth.*

Bargain - *(noun)* **1** an agreement between two or more people as to what each will do for the other. *I struck a bargain with the trader and bought the blankets at almost three-fourth the price.* **2** a thing bought or offered for sale for a lower price than normal. *I bought this carpet at a bargain. (verb)* negotiate the terms and conditions of a transaction. *Let us bargain. I'll paint your house and you give a new look to my garden.*

Barge - *(noun)* **1** a long flat-bottomed boat for carrying freight on canals and rivers. *The barges ply in rivers or canals and carry loads.* a long ornamental boat used for pleasure or on ceremonial occasions. *Barges are also used for partying fun and frolic.* **2** a boat used by the chief officers of a warship. *Barges in sea shore gave clear indication of a was. (verb)* move forcefully or roughly. intrude or interrupt rudely or awkwardly.*He barged into my room and frightened me.*

Barium - *(noun)* the chemical element of atomic number 56, a soft white reactive metal of the alkaline earth group, medicine a mixture of barium sulphate and water, opaque to X-rays, which is swallowed to permit radiological examination of the stomach of intestines. *For a medical test I had to drink barium before X-ray.*

Barker - *(noun)* [informal] a tout at an auction or sideshow who calls out to passers-by to attract custom. *He is a barker by profession.*

Barm - *(noun)* **1** the froth on fermenting malt liquor. *Barm (yeast) is good for health.*

Barman - *(noun)* [chiefly British] a man serving behind the bar of a public house. *The barman served me the drink I ordered.*

Barn - *(noun)* **1** a large farm building used for storage or for housing livestock. *The cattle live in barn. It is used for storage also.* **2** [North American] a large shed for storing road or railway vehicles. *Road and railway vehicles are parked in barns.*

Barometer - *(noun)* **1** an instrument measuring atmospheric pressure, used especially in forecasting the weather and determining altitude. *I have a barometer at my house.It gives me information about atmospheric pressure, weather, altitude, etc.* **2** an indicator of change. *Furniture is a barometer of changing tastes.*

Baronet - *(noun)* a member of the lowest hereditary titled british order. *The baronet was expelled for his rude behaviour.*

Baroque - *(adj.)* relating to or denoting a style of European architecture, music, and art of the 17th and 18th centuries characterized by ornate detail. highly ornate and extravagant in style. *(noun)* the baroque style or period. *Baroque style in 17th - 18th century was highly ornate and extravagant.*

Barouche - *(noun)* [historical] a four-wheeled horse-drawn carriage with a collapsible hood over the rear half. *Barouche was a popular mode of transport in old times.*

Barrack - *(verb)* provide with accommodation. *There are some military barracks where jawans live.*

Barracoon - *(noun)* [historical] an enclosure in which black slaves were temporarily confined. *In old time black slaves were confined in barracoons.*

Barrage - *(noun)* **1** a concentrated artillery bombardment over a wide area. *The artillery razed the entire town with heavy barrage.* an overwhelming number of questions or complaints delivered in rapid succession. **2** [British] an artificial barrier across a river, to prevent flooding or to aid irrigation or navigation. *The barrage was constructed to obstruct the flow of river into the village. (verb)* bombard with question or complaints. *The media barraged him with questions.*

Barrator - *(noun)* someone guilty of barratry. *The narrator was condemned by the court.*

Barrel - *(noun)* **1** a cylindrical container bulging out in the middle, traditionally made of wooden staves enclosed by metal hoops. a measure of capacity for oil and beer, equal to 36 imperial gallons for beer and 35 imperial gallons or

42 US gallons for oil. *The captain of the ship ordered various barrels of rum and beer.* **2** a cylindrical tube forming part of an object such as a gun or a pen. *For effi firing barrel of the gun should be clear.*

Barren – *(adj.)* too poor to produce much or any vegetation. (of a tree or plant) not producing fruit or seed. *The desert is a barren place.* **2** (of a animal) unable to bear young. *The couple were barren so they adopted a child.* **3** bleak and lifeless. *The tree is barren. (noun)* [chiefly North American] barren tracts of land. *On the countryside, there are huge tracts of barren land.*

Barricade – *(noun)* an improvised barrier erected to obstruct the movement of opposing forces. *The town people raised a barricade to obstruct the advance of enemy forces. (verb)* block or defend with a barricade.

Barrier – *(noun)* a fence or other obstacle that prevents movement or access. *Now that a barrier has been raised between her and my house I can no longer approach her.* an obstacle to communication, understanding, or progress: a language barrier. *She was from Russia. The language barrier prevented me from talking to her.*

Barring – *(prep.)* except for; if not for. *Barring a few distant relatives all were invited to the birthday party.*

Barter – *(verb)* exchange for other goods or services. *In ancient times when there was no currency people bartered one thing for another. (noun)* the action or system of bartering. *In the barter, we received a cow.*

Basalt – *(noun)* a dark fine-grained volcanic rock composed largely of plagioclase with pyroxene and olivine. *Today, we studied the characteristics of basalt.*

Base – *(noun)* **1** the lowest part or edge of something, especially the part on which it rests or is supported. *The base of this statute is made of teak wood polished black.* [architecture] the part of a column between the shaft and pedestal or pavement. [botany & zoology] the end at which a part or organ is attached to the trunk or main part. **2** a conceptual structure or entity on which something draws or depends. *The town's economic base collapsed.* a foundation or starting point. **3** the main place where a person works or stays. *His base is a remote island he operates from there.* **4** a main or important element or ingredient to which other things are added. a substance into which a pigment is mixed to form paint. *The pigment was mixed with pink colour as base.* **5** [chemistry] a substance capable of reacting with an acid to form a salt and water, or of accepting or neutralizing hydrogen ions. *NH_2SO_4 is a weale base.* **6** [electronics] the middle part of a bipolar transistor, separating the emitter from the collector. *The base characteristics were taught in physics class.* **7** [lingustics] the root or stem of a word or a derivative. the uninflected form of a verb. **8** [mathematics] a number used as the basis of a numberation scale. a number in terms of which other numbers are expressed as logarithms. **9**. [baseball] one of the four stations that must be reached in turn to score a run. *(verb)* **1** use something as the foundation for. *The film is based on a novel.* **2** situate at a place as the centre of operations.

Bash – *(verb)* **1** strike hard and violently. criticize severely. *He bashed me on the head.* **2** produce something rapidly and carelessly. *(noun)* **1** a heavy blow. *She will have a bash at anything.* **2** a party or social event. *He drank heavily at a bash.* [British] an attempt: she'll have a bash at anything.

Bashful – *(adj.)* shy and easily embarrassed. *He is rather bashful and can be easily embarrassed.*

Basil – *(noun)* leaves of the common basil; used fresh or dried. *Use fresh basil leaves to get aroma.*

Basin – *(noun)* **1** a large bowl or open container for washing in, preparing food, or holding liquid. *You can wash your hands in the wash-basin.* **2** a broadly circular valley or natural depression on the earth's surface. an area drained by a river and its tributaries. an enclosed area of water where boats can be moored. [geology] a circumscribed rock formation where the strata dip towards the centre. *In India, Ganga–Brahmaputra basin is very fertile.*

Basis – *(noun)* **1** the underlying support for an idea, argument, or process. *This gentleman is the basis of my argument.* **2** the principles according to which an activity is carried on. *All our activities have some fundamental basis.*

Bask – *(verb)* **1** lie exposed to warmth and sunlight for pleasure. *She was basking in the sun.* **2** revel in (something pleasing). *She basked in the glory of her success.*

Basket – *(noun)* **1** a container used to hold or carry things, made from interwoven strips of cane or wire. *Please take this basket and bring vegetables from the market.* **2** [basketball] a net fixed on a hoop used as the goal. a goal scored. *The player put the ball in the basket.*

Bass – *(noun)* **1** the lowest adult male singing voice. *As the singing went on in the church I could hear the bass in music.* **2** denoting the member of a family of instruments that is the lowest in pitch. [informal] a bass guitar or audio system, corresponding to the bass in music. *I love bass music.*

Bassinet – *(noun)* a child's wicker cradle. *The child was lying is a bassinet.*

Bastard – *(noun)* illegitimate. *He is born out of wedlock, hence people call him illegitimate or bastard.*

Bastille – *(noun)* a jail or prison. *He has been sent to bastille for four years.*

Bastion – *(noun)* **1** a projecting part of a fortification allowing an increased angle of fire. *Heavy firing was coming from bastion.* **2** an institution or person strongly maintaining particular principles, attitudes, or activities. *My grandfather is the bastion of our family.*

Bat – *(noun)* a mainly nocturnal mammal capable of sustained flight, with membranous wings that extend between the fingers and limbs. *Thousands of bats were hanging upside down in the dark cave.*

Batch – *(noun)* a quantity or consignment of goods produced at one time. *A batch of one thousand shirts was made ready overnight.* computing a group of records processed as a single unit. *(verb)* arrange in sets or groups. *All the goods have been arranged in batches.*

Bate – *(noun)* [British informal], an angry mood. *He got into a stinking bate.*

Bath – *(noun)* an ancient Hebrew liquid measure equivalent to about 40 litres or 9 gallons. *Pour 40 baths of water into the tank.*

Batiste – *(noun)* a fine, light linen or cotton fabric resembling cambric. *I would like to have a shirt made of batiste.*

Batman – *(noun)* [in the british armed forces] an officer's personal valet or attendant. *I have handed over my car to my batman.*

Baton – *(noun)* **1** a thin stick used by a conductor to direct an orchestra or choir. *The conductor moved his baton to direct the music.* **2** a short stick passed from runner to runner in a relay race. *The baton is being passed from player to player.* **3** a stick carried and twirled by a drum major. *Look at that drum major how he is carrying and twirling his baton.* **4** a police officer's truncheon. *This police officer is coming towards us waving his baton.*

Batsman – *(noun)* a player who bats in cricket. *Virat Kohli is a fine batsman.*

Batt – *(noun)* a piece of felted material or fiberglass used for insulation. *Batt is being placed in quilt to make it warm.*

Batten – *(verb)* thrive or prosper at the expense of. *He is battening upon the expense of his uncle.*

Battery – *(noun)* **1** a container consisting of one or more cells, in which chemical energy is converted into electricity and used as a source of power. *Charge your cell phone, the battery must be running low.* **2** an extensive series, sequence, or range of things. *I have just put two battery cells in my flash light.* **3** [chiefly British] a series of small cages for the intensive rearing and housing of poultry. *You will find here a battery of small cages in which we rear poultry.* **4** [Law] the infliction of unlawful personal violence on another person, even where the contact does no physical harm. *He was accused of assault and battery.* **5** a fortified emplacement for heavy guns. an artillery subunit of guns, men, and vehicles. *An army unit with battery was seen on the other side of the mountain.*

Battle – *(noun)* **1** a sustained flight between organized armed forces. *A fierce battle between the two countries went on for a long time.* **2** a lengthy and difficult conflict or struggle. *(verb)* flight or struggle tenaciously with an enemy or to achieve something. *I have to battle with my brother for TV remote.*

Bauble – *(noun)* **1** a small, showy trinket or decoration. a decorative hollow ball hung on a Christmas tree. *A few baubles hung on the Christmas tree looked beautiful.* **2** a baton formerly used as an emblem by jesters.

Bawd – *(noun)* [archaic] a women in charge of a brothel. *Arrest her! She is the bawd.*

Bawdy – *(adj.)* humorously indecent. *(noun)* humorously indecent talk or writing. *He is fond of cracking bawdy jokes.*

Bawl – *(verb)* shout out noisily. reprimand someone angrily. *I heard a bawl and became nervous.* **2** weep noisily. *The child bawled whole night.* *(noun)* a loud shout. *When he didn't listen to me I bawled at him.*

Bawn – *(noun)* **1** [Irish & Chadian] an area of grassy land near a house; a meadow. *I have a bawn near my house where a lot of sheep graze.* **2** [Chadian] a flat expanse of rocks on a beach, on which fish are spread to dry. *You can see a lot of fish being dried on bawn.*

Bay – *(noun)* a broad curved inlet of the sea. *When I was in Calcutta I went to see the bay of Bengal.*

Bayonet – *(noun)* **1** a long blade fixed to the muzzle of a rifle for use in hand-to-hand fighting. *The soldier stabbed the enemy with the bayonet.* **2** denoting a type of fitting for a light bulb or other appliance which is pushed into a socket and then twisted into place. *The bulb was not fused but the bayonet was faulty.* *(verb)* stab with a bayonet.

Bay-window – *(noun)* a window built to project outwards from a wall. *Look out of the bay window and you'll see a man.*

Beach – *(noun)* a pebbly or sandy shore at the edge of the sea or a lake. *The beach was crowded today.* *(verb)* bring on to a beach form the water. become or cause to become stranded on a beach. *In Goa there are many beautiful beaches where people bathe in the sea.*

Beacon – *(noun)* **1** a fire lit on the top of a hill as a signal. *The ship saw the beacon interpreted the signal and turned left.* **2** a light serving as a signal for ships or aircraft. a radio transmitter signaling the position of a ship or aircraft. *Do you see that beacon, it is telling us the position of the sinking ship.*

Beadle – *(noun)* [British] **1** a ceremonial officer of a church, college, or similar institution. *He is a beadle, talk to him respectfully.* **2** [historical] a minor parish officer dealing with petty offenders.

Beady – *(adj.)* small, round, and observing things clearly. *Look at this animal; how beady and sharp are its eyes.*

Beak – *(noun)* **1** a bird's horny projecting jaws; a bill. a projecting jaw in some other animals. *The beak of an eagle is very different from that of crow.* **2** a projection at the prow of an ancient warship, used to pierce the hulls of enemy ships. *Beak of the war ships was used to damage the enemy ships.*

Beaker – *(noun)* [british] a tall plastic cup. a lipped cylindrical glass container for laboratory use. *We use beaker in chemistry labs.* [archaic or poetic/literary] a large drinking container with a wide mouth. *In old times people drank from large sized beakers.*

Beam – *(noun)* **1** a long sturdy piece of squared timber or metal used horizontally in building to support a load above. a narrow horizontal length of squared timber used for balancing exercises in gymnastics. **2** a horizontal beam supporting the deck and joining the sides of a ship. the direction of an object visible from the side of a ship when it is perpendicular to the centre line of the vessel. *There was land in sight on the port beam. a ship's breadth at its widest point.* **3** a ray or shaft of light. a directional flow of particles or radiation. a series of radio or radar signals emitted as a navigational guide. *I just saw a beam of light in the darkness.*

4 a radiant smile. *As I praised her she beamed happily.* **5** the crossbar of a balance. *It is very difficult to balance one on the long thin beam.* **6.** an oscillating shaft in a beam engine. **7.** the shank of an anchor. *(verb)* **1** transmit in a specified direction. **2** shine brightly. **3** smile radiantly.

Bean – *(noun)* **1** an edible kidney-shaped seed growing in long pods on certain leguminous plants. the hard seed of coffee, cocoa, and certain other plants. *I like beans a lot, they are so tasty to eat.* **2** a leguminous plant bearing beans. *Some of the best coffee beans come from Brazil.* **3** [informal] a very small amount or nothing at all. **4** [informal], dated a person's head.

Beanfeast – *(noun)* [british informal] a celebratory party with plentiful food and drink. *Come let us go to the beanfeast, there will be a lot to eat.*

Bear – *(verb)* **1** carry have as an attribute or visible mark. conduct oneself in a specified manner. *He bears himself in a dignified way.* **2** manage to tolerate: I can't bear it. *He was so vain I couldn't bear with him.* **3** give birth to (a child). *My wife bore me a child.* (of a tree or plant) produce (full or flowers). *Last year this tree bore a lot of fruit.* **4** turn and proceed in a specified direction: bear left.

Bear – *(noun)* a large, heavy mammal which walks on the soles of its feet, having thick fur and a very short tail. *Bear is a dangerous animal.* **2** stock exchange a person who sells shares hoping to buy them back later at a lower price. often contrasted having BULL. *Stock exchange is a game of bears and bulls.* [said to be from a proverb warring against 'selling the bear's skin before one has caught the bear.

Bearable – *(adj.)* capable of being borne though can be pleasant. *He is merely a bearable person.*

Beard – *(noun)* a growth of hair on the chin and lower cheeks of a man's face. an animal's growth or marking that is likened to a beard, such as the gills of an oyster. a tuft of hairs or bristles on certain plants. *I am thinking of keeping a French cut beard this time.*

Bearing – *(noun)* a person's way of standing, moving, or behaving. *His bearing a awkward.* **2** relation; relevance. *The case has no bearing on this issue.* **3** a device in a machine that allows two parts to rotate or move in contact with each other with reduced friction. *Ball bearings are used in machines to reduce friction.* **4** the direction or position of something relative to a fixed point, normally measured in degrees and with magnetic north as zero. awareness of one's position relative to one's surrounding.

Bearish – *(adj.)* resembling or likened to a bear. **2** stock exchange characterized by falling share prices. inclined to sell because of an anticipated selling.

Bearskin – *(noun)* a tall cap of black fur worn ceremonially by certain troops. *Cap of bearskin with black fur is worn by people in extreme cold.*

Beast – *(noun)* **1** an animal, especially a large or dangerous mammal. a bovine farm animal. *Lion is a big and dangerous beast.* **2** an inhumanly cruel or depraved person. *He is a beast. He killed his wife.*

Beat – *(verb)* **1** strike repeatedly and violently so as to hurt or punish them. strike repeatedly so as make a noise. *The teacher beat the student as he had not done his homework.* flatten or shape by striking it repeatedly with a hammer. *The blacksmith is beating the metal sheet with a hammer.* **2** defeat in a game or other competitive situation. surpass (a record or score). overcome (a problem). [informal] baffle. *It beats me how you manage it.* **3** pulsate. *India beat England by 40 runs.* **4** move the wings up and down. *The bird beat her wings and flew away.* *(noun)* **1** a main accent or rhythmic unit in music or poetry. a rhythm or rhythmic sound or movement. a pulsation of the heart. a periodic variation of sound or amplitude due to the combination of two sounds or other vibrations with similar but not identical frequencies. *I beat the cream vigorously so as to take out ghee.* **2** the movement of bird's wings. **3** an area allocated to a police officer and patrolled on foot a spell of duty allocated to a police officer. a stretch of water fished by an angler. **4** a brief pause or moment of hesitation. *(adj.)* informal completely exhausted. **8** *Don't beat about the* *bush come straight to the point.* **9** *I beat across the field many times so as to raise the game birds for shooting.10 The beat of the music compelled me to dance.* **11** *This policeman is the beat officer of this area.* **12** *I am completely beaten and can walk no further.*

Beatify – *(verb)* [in the roman catholic church] announce the beatification of. *The church has beatified the dead man. He is in a state of bliss.*

Beating – *(noun)* the act of overcoming or outdoing.

Beatitude – *(noun)* **1** supreme blessedness. the blessings listed by Jesus in the sermon on the mount. *He was in a state of supreme beatitude.* **2** a title given to patriarchs in the orthodox church.

Beau-ideal – *(noun)* a person or thing representing the highest possible standard of excellence in a particular respect. *Gandhi ji was a beau-ideal.*

Beautiful – *(adj.)* **1** pleasing the senses or mind aesthetically. *My girlfriend is very beautiful.* **2** of a very high standard; excellent.

Beautifully – *(adv.)* in a beautiful manner. *The cake was beautifully done.*

Beaver – *(noun)* **1** a large semi aquatic board-tailed rodent, noted for its habit of gnawing through trees to fell them in order to make lodges and dams. the soft light brown fur of the beaver. [chiefly historical] a hat made of felted beaver fur. a heavy woolen cloth resembling felted beaver fur. *I am wearing hat made of beaver fur.* **2** a very hard-working person. *The beaver has gnawed through the tree to make it fall.* **3** a boy aged about 6 or 7 who is an affiliated member of the scout association. *(verb)* informal work hard.

Becalm – *(verb)* leave (a sailing ship) of the typical rhythm of this music. *The ship was becalmed because of lack of wind.*

Became – past participle of become. *The sea became calm after sometime.*

Because – conjunction for the reason that; since. *You can't take the exam because you haven't come in time.*

Beck – *(noun)* [archaic] a stream. *Beck blowed through the forest.*

Becoming – *(adj.)* **1** (of clothing) looking well on someone. *This shirt is becoming on you.* **2** decorous.

Bed – *(noun)* **1** a piece of furniture incorporating a mattress or other surface for sleeping or resting on. *It is time for sleep. I am going to bed.* a place for a patient in a hospital. *My mother is sick. Please make arrangement for a bed in the hospital.* [informal] used with reference to a bed as a place for sexual activity. **2** an are of ground where flowers and plants are grown; a flower bed. *This bed of flowers is very beautiful.* **3** a flat base or foundation on which something rests or is supported. [chiefly North American] the open part of a truck or cart, where goods are carried. *Put the fruit on the bed of the truck.* **4** a stratum or layer of rock. **5** the bottom of the ses or a lake or river. a place on the seabed where shellfish breed or are bred. *Shellfish are bred in the seabed.* *(verb)* **1** provide with sleeping accommodation. settle down for the night in an improvised place. **2** [informal] have sexual intercourse with. **3** transfer from a pot or seed tray to the ground. **4** fix firmly; embed. lay or arrange in a layer.

Bedaub – *(verb)* [poetic/literary] smear or daub with a sticky substance. *The doctor bedaubed the wound with a disinfectant.*

Bedazzle – *(verb)* greatly impress with brilliance or skill. *The actress bedazzled the audience with her great beauty.*

Bedchamber – *(noun)* [archaic] a bedroom. *This way leads to the bedchamber.*

Bedding – *(noun)* **1** bedclothes. straw or similar material for animals to sleep on. *The bedding must be washed today.* **2** a base or bottom layer. *Animals are sleeping on the bedding.* **3** [geology] the stratification or layering of rocks.

Bed-fellow – *(noun)* a person or thing that is closely connected with another. *We are great friends. He is my bedfellow.*

Beduin – *(noun)* variant spelling of bedouin. *When I want to an Arab country, I saw many Bedouins.*

Bedstead – *(noun)* the framework of a bed. *I don't like the bed stead change it.*

Bed-time – *(noun)* the usual time when someone goes to bed. *It is bed-time now, all must go to sleep.*

Bee – *(noun)* **1** a stinging social insect which collects nectar and pollen form flowers and produces wax and honey. *Honeybees are dangerous insects; If try to get their honey they will attack you.* **2** an insect of a large group to which the honeybee belongs, including many solitary as well as social kinds. **3** a meeting for communal work or amusement: a sewing bee.

Beech – *(noun)* a large tree with smooth grey bark, glossy leaves, and hard, pale, fine-grained wood. *Mussourie forests are full of beech trees.*

Beef – *(noun)* **1** the flesh of a cow, bull, or ox, used as food. farming a cow, bull, or ox fattened for its meat. *Hindus do not eat beef.*

Beefy – *(adj.)* muscular and heavily built. *He is a beefy fellow with all muscles and power.*

Beehive – *(noun)* **1** a structure in which bees are kept, typically in the form of a dome or box. **2** a woman's domed and lacquered hairstyle popular in the 1960s.

Been – past participle of be. *He has been watching TV for two hours.*

Beesting – *(plural noun)* the first milk produced by a cow or goat after giving birth. *Would you like to taste Beestings?*

Beet – *(noun)* a herbaceous plant cultivated as a source of food for humans and livestock, and for processing into sugar. *Eating beet root is good for health.*

Beeves – plural form of beef (in sense 1 of the noun.) *A lot of Europeans eat beeves.*

Befall – *(verb)* [poetic/literary (especially of something bad)] happen to. *A great misfortune befell him.*

Before – *(prep., conj. & adv.)* **1** during the period of time preceding. *Our ancestors were there before us. I would like to go for a world tour before I die.* **2** in front of. in front of and required to answer to (a court of law, tribunal, or other authority). *I rarely talk before my father.* **3** in preference to; with a higher priority than. *You are before the judge. You must answer the questions asked.*

Befoul – *(verb)* make dirty; pollute. *He has befouled the whole atmosphere by his abusive language.*

Befriend – *(verb)* act as or become a friend to. *Although you have talked ill of me I'll still befriend you.*

Began – past of BEGIN. *He began to earn from the age of eight.*

Beget – *(verb)* [archaic or poetic/literary] produce (a child). *She beget me a son.*

Begging – *(noun)* a solicitation of money or food (in the street by on apparently penniless person). *Begging is something in human.*

Beginner – *(noun)* someone new to a field activity. *He is a beginner in cricket.*

Begone – *(exclamatory)* [archaic] go away at once! *No more talking, begone!*

Begot – past of beget. *I begot a son from her.*

Behalf – *(noun)* (in phrase on behalf of or on someone's behalf) **1** in the interests of a persons, group, or principle. *I am here on behalf of the director.* **2** as a representative of. *I agree to this proposal on behalf of my colleagues.*

Behave – *(verb)* **1** act or conduct oneself in a specified way. *Will you behave yourself?* **2** conduct oneself in accordance with accepted norms.

Behead – *(verb)* cut off the head of (someone), especially as a form of execution. *In old times execution was often done by beheading.*

Behest – *(noun)* [poetic/literary] a person's orders or command. *The troops advanced on behest of their commander.*

Behold – *(verb)* [archaic or poetic/literary] see or observe. *Behold! Here is my son.*

Beholden – *(adj.)* indebted. *I am beholden to you for this favour.*

Beholder – *(noun)* a person who becomes aware through the senses.

Behoof – *(noun)* [archaic] benefit or advantage. *He purchased the food his own behoof.*

Behove – *(verb)* [formal] it is a duty, responsibility, or appropriate response for someone to do something. *It would behove you to be respectful to your elders.*

Being – *(noun)* **1** existence. living; being alive. *It is my being here that matters most.* **2** the nature or essence of a person. *There is something a being in the forest.* **3** a real or imaginary living creature: alien beings. *Alien beings can contact us.*

Belated - *(adj.)* offer the expected or usual time delayed. *I have received your belated birthday greetings.*

Belay - *(verb)* **1** fix round a rock, pin, or other object to secure it. **2** secure a rock climber using a belay. *To belay by spike or rope is necessary for a mountain climber.* **3** [nautical slang] stop! *(noun)* **1** an act of belaying. **2** a spike of rock or other object used for belaying. *Rock climbers use belay for secure footing.*

Belch - *(verb)* **1** emit wind noisily form the stomach through the mouth. *He belched noisily and everyone looked at him.* **2** expel smoke or flames forcefully out or up. *(noun)* a act of belching.

Beleagure - *(verb)* **1** lay siege to. *The army beleagured the town.* **2** make difficulties for; harass. *He beleagured her.*

Belfry - *(noun)* the place in a bell tower or steeple in which bells are housed. *Huge bells are hung in towers in belfry.*

Belie - *(verb)* **1** fail to give a true notion of. *He belied his claim to land in the court.* **2** fail to justify (a claim or expectation).

Belief - *(noun)* **1** an acceptance that something exists or is true, especially one without proof. a firmly held opinion or conviction. a religious conviction. *I have firm belief in god.* **2** trust or confidence in.

Believable - *(adj.)* capable of being believed. *I find your statement believable.*

Belike - *(adv.)* with considerable certainty without much doubt.

Belittle - *(verb)* dismiss as unimportant. *I belittled his importance by ignoring him.*

Belladonna - *(noun)* deadly nightshade. a drug made from this plant, containing atropine. *Belladonna is a famous homeopathy drug.*

Belle - *(noun)* a beautiful girl or woman. *That belle is my fiancée.*

Bellicose - *(adj.)* aggressive; ready to fight. *He is a very bellicose person, ever ready to fight.*

Belligerent - *(adj.)* hostile and aggressive. engaged in a war or conflict. *(noun)* a nation or person engaged in war or conflict. *This one is belligerent country, it sure will pick up a fight with some other country.*

Bell-metal - *(noun)* an alloy of copper and tin for making bells, with a higher tin content than in bronze. *Bells are made of two metals-copper and tin.*

Bellow - *(verb)* emit a loud, deep roar, typically in pain or anger. shout or sing very loudly. *He bellowed in anger.*

Bellows - *(plural noun)* **1** a device with an air bag that emits a stream of air when squeezed together with two handles, used for blowing air into a fire. a similar device used in a harmonium or small organ. *In old times bellows were used to blow air into the furnance.* **2** an object or device with concertinaed sides to allow it to expand and contract, such as a tube joining a lens to a camera body.

Belly - *(noun)* **1** the front part of the human truck below the ribs, containing the stomach and bowels. the stomach, especially as representing the body's need for food. *My belly is only half full give me more food.* a cut of pork form the underside between the legs. **2** the rounded underside of a ship or aircraft. *Luggage is kept in the belly of the plane.* **3** the top surface of an instrument of the violin family, over which the strings are placed. *(verb)* swell or cause to swell or bulge.

Belong *(verb)* **1** be rightly placed in or assigned to a specified position. *I belong to khan family and I am in my right belonging.* **2** fit or be acceptable in a specified place or environment. be a member of. *My family belongs to Kashipur.* **3** be the property of. be the rightful possession of; be due to.

Beloved - *(adj.)* dearly loved. *(noun)* a much loved person. *She is my beloved.*

Belt - *(noun)* **1** a strip of leather or other material worn round the waist to support or hold in clothes or to carry weapons. *He was beaten with a belt.* a belt worn as a sign of rank or achievement, ishment of being struck with a belt. *The conveyor belt was broken.* **2** a continuous band of material used in machinery for transferring motion from one wheel to another. **3** a strip or encircling area of a specified kind. **4** [informal] a heavy blow. *(verb)* **1** fasten or secure with a belt. **2** beat or hit very hard. [informal] sing or play something loudly and without finesse. **3** [informal] rush or dash in a specifies direction. **4** [informal] be quiet.

Belvedere – *(noun)* a summer house or other building positioned to command a fine view. *I stood in the belvedere and looked down on the scene pleasant.*

Bemire – *(verb)* [archaic] cover or stain with mud. *It was raining and my clothes got bemired.*

Bemoan – *(verb)* lament or express sorrow for. *I bemoaned the loss of my friend.*

Bemuse – *(verb)* confuse or bewilder. *I found him in a drunk and bemused condition.*

Bend – *(verb)* **1** shape or force (something straight) into a curve or angle. (of a road, river, or path) deviate from a straight line. *The sudden bend in the road took me by surprise.* **2** (of a person) incline the body downwards; stoop. *I bend the branch and plucked the fruit.* **3** interpret or modify to suit oneself. *I bent his words to suit my purpose. Bending his body he touched his toes.* **4** direct (one's attention or energies) to a task. **5** nautical attach (a sail or cable) by means of a knot. *(noun)* **1** a curved or angled part of something. a curve in a road, path, or river. **2** a king of knot used to join two ropes together, or one rope to another object. **3** decompression sickness.

Beneath – *(prep. & adverb)* **1** extending or directly underneath. *I found the thief beneath the bed.* **2** of lower status or worth than. *You are beneath me in rank.*

Benedick – *(noun)* a newly married man.

Benefaction – *(noun)* [informal] a donation or gift. *The rich man gave the orphanage a big benefaction.*

Benefice – *(noun)* a church office. typically that of a rector or vicar, for which property and income are provided in respect of pastoral duties. *The man sitting in the benefic is our vicar.*

Beneficence – *(noun)* doing good, feeling beneficent.

Beneficiary – *(noun)* a person who gains benefit from something, especially a trust or will. *His father left him a lot of money in his will that makes him a beneficiary.*

Benefit – *(noun)* **1** an advantage or profit gained from something. *He got benefit from an insurance scheme when he was unemployed.* **2** a payment made by the state or an insurance scheme to someone entitled to receive it, e.g. an unemployed person. *His business was a success he earned huge benefits.* **3** a public performance designed to raise money for a charity. *(verb)* receive an advantage; profit. *I have benefitted a lot from your friendship.*

Benevolence – *(noun)* disposition to do good; an inclination to do kind of charitable acts. *His benevolence earned him a lot of fame.*

Benevolent – *(adj.)* **1** well meaning and kingly. *A benevolent person works more for charity than for profit.* **2** (of an organization) serving a charitable rather than a profit making purpose.

Benight – *(verb)* overtake by darkness or night.

Benighted – *(adj.)* **1** in a state of intellectual or moral ignorance. *He is a benighted person not knowing what is moral or intellectual* **2** [archaic] overtaken by darkness. *As the power tripped the place was benighted.*

Benign – *(adj.)* **1** genial kingly. *He is benign and generous like a king.* **2** favourable; not harmful. medicine (of tumour) not malignant. *This tumour is not malign but benign.*

Benison – *(noun)* [poetic/literary] a blessing. *He has received benison from the priest.*

Benjamin – *(noun)* gum resin used in.

Bent – past and past participle of bend. *(adj.)* **1** sharply curved or having an angle. *I saw a bent iron rod in the junkyard.* **2** [informal, chiefly British] dishonest; corrupt. *Don't trust him, he is a bent fellow.* **3** [British informal, derogatory] homosexual. **4** determined to do or have. *(noun)* a natural talent or inclination. *He has natural bent of mind for mathematics.*

Benzene – *(noun)* [chemistry] a volatile liquid hydrocarbon present in coal tar and petroleum, having a hexagonal ring-shaped molecule which is the basis of most aromatic organic compounds. [C_6H_6]. *The molecule present in benzene is the basis of most organic compounds.*

Benzion – *(noun)* a fragrant gum resin obtained from certain East Asian storax trees. **2** [chemistry] a crystalline aromatic ketone present in this resin. *I like the fragrant smell of benzion.*

Bequeath – *(verb)* leave to a person or other beneficiary by a will. hand down or pass on. *He bequeathed all his money to a charity institution.*

Bequest – *(noun)* the action of bequeathing. something that is bequeathed. *The bequest of money took place when he was about to die.*

Bergamot – *(noun)* **1** an oily substance extracted from a variety of Seville orange, used in cosmetics and as flavouring in Earl Grey tea. *Seville orange from bergamot is used in cosmetics and in flavoring tea.* **2** the tree bearing this fruit. *Bergamot is an aromatic herb of mint family.* **3** an aromatic North American herb of the mint family. *The tree bergamot bears the fruit Seville orange.*

Beri-Beri – *(noun)* a disease causing inflammation of the nerves and heart failure, ascribed to a deficiency of vitamin B. *Due to deficiency of vitamin B_1 my uncle was affected with Beriberi.*

Berry – *(noun)* **1** a small roundish juicy fruit without a stone. [botany] any fruit that has its seeds enclosed in a fleshy pulp, for example a banana or tomato. *I am fond of eating berries.* **2** a fish egg or roe of a lobster or similar creature.

Beryl – *(noun)* a transparent pale green, blue, or yellow mineral consisting of a silicate of beryllium and aluminum, sometimes used as a gemstone. *Jwellers sometimes use beryl as a gemstone.*

Beside – *(prep.)* **1** at the side of; next to. compared with. *He sat beside me in the bus.* **2** in addition to; apart from.

Besides – *(prep.)* in addition to; apart from. *Besides being a painter he is a writer as well.* *(adverb)* in addition; as well. used to introduce an additional idea or explanation.

Besiege – *(verb)* **1** surround with armed forces in order to capture it or force its surrender. crowd round oppressively. The *town has been besieged by army.* **2** be inundated by large numbers of requests or complaints.

Besmear – *(verb)* [poetic/literary] smear or cover with. *He had a bullet wound and was besmeared with blood.*

Besmirch – *(verb)* **1** damage (someone's reputation). *I besmirched his reputation.* **2** [poetic/literary] make dirty; soil.

Bespatter – *(verb)* spatter with liquid. *He bespattered me with mud.*

Bespeak – *(verb)* **1** be evidence of. **2** order or reserve in advance. **3** [archaic] speak to. *I bespeak you to reserve a seat for me in Rajdhani Express.*

Besprinkle – *(verb)* [poetic/literary] sprinkle with liquid, powder, etc. *All the wedding guest s were besprinkle with fragrant scent.*

Bestir – *(verb)* exert or rouse oneself. *I woke up and bestirred myself.*

Bestow – *(verb)* **1** confer (an honour, right, or gift). **2** [archaic] put in a specified place. *He was bestowed the little of Sir.*

Bestrew *(verb)* [poetic/literary] scatter or lie scattered over (a surface). *Dry leaves were bestrewed all over the ground.*

Bet – *(verb)* **1** risk a sum of money or other valued item against someone else's on the basis of the outcome of an unpredictable event such as a race or game. *This party team looks a good bet for victory.* **2** [informal] used to express certainty. *He'll be surprised to see me. I'll bet.* *(noun)* an act of betting. a sum of money staked. [informal] a candidate or option offering a specified likelihood of success. *Allen looked a good bet for victory.* [informal] one's opinion.

Beta – *(noun)* **1** the second letter of the Greek alphabet transliterated as 'b'. denoting the second of a series of items or categories. [British] a second-class mark given for a piece of work. *As in Greek alphabet 'B' is the second letter so it is in English language.* **2** relating to beta decay or beta particles. **3** a measure of the movement in price of a security relative to the stock market, used to indicate possible risk.

Betake – *(verb)* [poetic/literary] go to.

Betel – *(noun)* **1** the leaf of an Asian evergreen climbing plant, which in the east is chewed and used as a mild stimulant. *Betel leave is used in religious ceremonies.* **2** the plant, related to pepper, from which these leaves are taken.

Bethink – *(verb)* [informal] come to think. *Bethink he has not come today.*

Betide – *(verb)* [poetic/literary] in good time; early. *We betide that rascal.*

Betimes – *(adverb)* [poetic/literary] in good time; early. *We must be up betimes tomorrow.*

Betoken – *(verb)* [poetic/literary] be a warning or sign of. *Those black clouds betoken rain.*

Betroth – *(verb)* formally engaged to be married. *(noun)* the person to whom one is engaged. *She is betrothed to that gentleman.*

Better – *(adj.)* **1** more desirable, satisfactory, or effective. more appropriate, advantageous, or well advised. *You won't find a better coffee shop than this one.* **2** partly or fully recovered from illness or injury. *I am feeling better than before.* *(adverb)* more excellently or effectively. *(noun)* **1** that which is better; the better one. *This shirt is better one.* **2** one's superiors in social class or ability. *In social circle he holds a better position than me.* *(verb)* improve on or surpass. achieve a higher social position or status. overcome or defeat (someone). *Next year I'll better my record.*

Betwixt – *(prep.)* & adverb [archaic] term for between. *Let this secret be hidden betwixt we two people.*

Beverage – *(noun)* a drink other than water. *In beverages I like coca cola the most.*

Bewail – *(verb)* greatly regret or lament. *She is bewailing the loss of her husband.*

Beware – *(verb)* be cautious and alert to risks or dangers. *Beware of this dog. It is a bad tempered one.*

Bewilder – *(verb)* perplex or confuse. *I was bewildered not to find my friend at home.*

Beyond – *(prep. & adv.)* **1** at or to the further side of. more extensive or extreme than. *The city we have to reach in beyond that jungle.* **2** happening or continuing after. **3** having reached or progressed further than (a specified level or amount). *Supersonic planes fly beyond the sound barrier.* **4** to or in a degree where a specified action is impossible. too advanced for. *There is no speed beyond the speed of light.* **5** apart from; except. *(noun)* the unknown, especially in references to life after death. *Beyond death there seems nothing or is there a life beyond death also?*

Bezique – *(noun)* a trick-taking card game for two, played with a double pack of 64 cards, including the seven to ace only in each suit. the holding of the queen of spades and the jack of diamonds in this game. *He is an expert in the card game of bezique.*

Bi – (symbolic) the chemical element bismuth.

Bias – *(noun)* **1** inclination or prejudice for or against one thing or person. *My boss is biassed against me.* a systematic distortion of a statistical result due to a factor not allowed for in its derivation. *He has a bias against the plan.* **2** a diagonal across the grain of a fabric. **3** the irregular shape given to one side of a bowl. the oblique course taken by such a bowl. **4** [electronics] a steady voltage, magnetic field, or other factor applied to a system to cause it to operate over a pre-determined range. *(verb)* **1** influence unfairly; prejudice. *Speeches bias public opinion.* **2** electronics give a bias to.

Biaxial – *(adj.)* having or relating to two axes. *All four wheelers are biaxial.*

Bib – *(noun)* **1** a piece of cloth or plastic fastened round a child's neck to keep its clothes clean while eating. *Cooks wear a bib like apron covering their front portion.* a loose-fitting sleeveless garment worn for identification, e.g. by competitors and officials at sporting events. the part above the waist of the front of an apron or pair of dungarees. *This child is wearing a beautiful bib round its neck.* **2** a common Europe inshore fish of the cod family.

Bibber – *(noun)* **1** top part of an apron covering the chest. **2** a napkin tied under the chin of a child while cutting.

Bible – *(noun)* **1** the Christian scriptures, consisting of the old and new testaments. the

Jewish scriptures, consisting of the torah or law, the prophets, and the hagiographa or writings. *Bible is the largest selling book in the world.* **2** [informal] a book regarded as authoritative.

Bibliographer – *(noun)* someone trained in compiling bibliographies.

Bibliography – *(noun)* **1** a list of sources referred to in a particular work. a list of the books of a specific author or on a specific subject. *Most books have bibliography at the end.* **2** the study of books in terms of their classification, printing, and publication.

Bibulous – *(adj.)* [formal] excessively fond of drinking alcohol. *He is a bibulous man. Very fond of drinking alcohol.*

Bicameral – *(adj.)* (of a legislative body) having two chambers. *This lawyer's office is bicameral.*

Bicentenary – *(noun)* the two hundredth anniversary of a significant event. *Bicentenary is celebrated of many big events.*

Bicephalous – *(adj.)* having two heads. *These children's heads are bicephalous and only a surgeon can separate them.*

Bicker – *(verb)* **1** argue about petty and trivial matters. *He has a bad habit of bickering nothing of importance appeals to him.* **2** [poetic/literary] flow with a gentle repetitive noise. *The stream flowed with a gentle bickering.*

Bicuspid – *(adj.)* having two cusps or points. *Two of his teeth are bicuspid. (noun)* a tooth with two cusps, especially a human premolar tooth.

Bid – *(verb)* **1** offer for something, especially at an auction. (of a contractor) tender for work. *At auction I'll bid for this painting.* **2** make an effort to obtain or achieve. *I made a bid for the job and got it.* **3** make a statement during the auction undertaking to make (a certain number of tricks). *(noun)* **1** an offer to buy something. an offer to do work or supply goods at a stated price. **2** an effort to obtain or achieve. **3** bridge an undertaking by a player in the auction to make a stated number of tricks with a stated suit as trumps.

Biddable – *(adj.)* **1** meekly ready to accept and follow instructions. *He is a biddable person and will do as you say.* **2** bridge strong enough to justify a bid.

Bidder – *(noun)* someone who makes an offer. *He is a smart bidder.*

Bide – *(verb)* [archaic or dialect] remain or stay in a certain place. *I'll bide by my decision come what may.*

Biennial – *(adj.)* **1** taking place every other year. compare with biannual. *The biennial festival will now take place after two years.* **2** taking two years to grow from seed to fruition and die. compare with annual, perennial. *(noun)* **1** a biennial plant. *It is a biennial plant and will die in two years.* **2** an event celebrated or taking place every two years.

Bier – *(noun)* a movable platform on which a coffin or corpse is placed before burial. *The dead body was carried on a bier to the crematorium.*

Bifacial – *(adj.)* having two faces, or two different faces. *A bifacial child was born to her.*

Bifurcate – *(verb)* divide into two branches or forks. *(adj.)* forked; branched. *This lengthy volume has been bifurcated.*

Bigamist – *(noun)* someone who marries one person while legally married to another. *He is a bigamist having two wives.*

Bigamy – *(noun)* the offence of marrying someone while already married to another person. *Practicing bigamy is against the law.*

Bight – *(noun)* **1** a curve or recess in a coastline or other geographical feature. *The bight was beautiful and many person bathed there.* **2** a loop of rope. *He put his leg in the bight and was pulled up.*

Bigot – *(noun)* a person who is prejudiced in their views and intolerant of the opinions of others. *It is impossible to convince him of anything other than his own belief. He is a bigot.*

Bike – *(noun)* a bicycle or motorcycle. *I have purchased a new bike. (verb)* ride a bicycle or motorcycle.

Bilateral – *(adj.)* **1** having or relating to two sides. involving two parties. *It is a bilateral agreement.*

Bile – *(noun)* **1** a bitter greenish-brown alkaline fluid secreted by the liver and stored in the gall bladder, which aids digestion. *Bile helps digest food.* **2** anger; irritability. *He has too much bile in him.*

Biliary – *(adj.)* medicine of or relating to bile or the bile duct. *His liver is not right; so he is taking some biliary.*

Bilingual – *(adj.)* speaking two languages fluently. expressed in or using two languages. *He is bilingual and can speak Tamil and Hindi fluently.*

Bilious – *(adj.)* affected by or associated with nausea or vomiting. *He is feeling bilious; may be he will vomit.* **2** spiteful; bad-tempered. *He is a very bilious person.* **3** physiology of or relating to bile.

Bilk – *(verb)* [informal] **1** cheat or defraud. obtain fraudulently. *He has bilked me. One million. I am going to lodge an FIR.* **2** [archaic] evade; elude.

Billet – *(noun)* a civilian where soldiers are lodged temporarily. *Right now the troops are lodged in a billet. (verb)* lodge in a civilian house.

Billion – cardinal number **1** the number equivalent to the product of a thousand and a million; 1,000,000,000 or 10^9. [chiefly British] a million million. *He has got a billion rupees, i.e. thousand millions.* **2** [informal] a very large number or amount.

Billow – *(noun)* **1** a large undulating mass of cloud, smoke, or steam. *In the distance we could see a thick line of billows* **2** [archaic] a large sea wave. *(verb)* fill with air and swell outwards. move or flow outward with an undulating motion.

Billy-goat – *(noun)* a male goat. *He has three Billy-goats and two she- goats.*

Bimetallic – *(adj.)* **1** made or consisting of two metals. [historical] of or relating to bimetallism. *This vase is bimetallic which in made of two metals copper and tin.*

Bimonthly – *(adj.)* & adverb appearing or taking place twice a month or every two months. *This magazine is bimonthly. In a month you'll receive two issues.*

Binary – *(adj.)* **1** composed of, or involving two things. **2** using or denoting a system of numerical notation with two as its base, employing the digits 0 and 1 *(noun)* **1** the binary system of notation. **2** [astronomy] a system of two stars revolving round their common centre.

Bind – *(verb)* **1** tie of fasten (something) tightly together. *Bind the two ends of the rope together.* restrain by tying their hands and feet. wrap or encircle tightly. *He is a thief. Bind his hands and feet.* **2** hold in a united or cohesive group or mass, hold or combine with by chemical bonding. *Now we shall bind the elements together by chemical bonding.* **3** impose a legal or contractual obligation on. *You are bound by legal obligation to appear in the court.* indenture as an apprentice. secure typically with a sum of money. (of a court of law) require someone to fulfill an obligation, typically by paying a sum of money as surety. **4** fix together and enclose in a cover. **5** trim with a fabric strip. North American cast of in knitting. **6** [logic] be applied to so that the variable falls within its scope. **7** make (someone) constipated. *(noun)* **1** [informal] an annoyance. a problematical situation. **2** a statutory constraint. **3** [music] another term for tie. **4** another term for bine.

Binocular – *(adj.)* adapted for or using both eyes.

Biogenesis – *(noun)* **1** the synthesis of substances by living organisms. *According to biogenesis a living matter given rise to another living matter.* **2** [historical] the hypothesis that living matter arises only form other living matter.

Biography – *(noun)* an account of someone's life written by someone else. *I have read the biography of Tolstoy. It is fascinating.*

Biological – *(adj.)* **1** of or relating to biology or living organisms. containing enzymes to assist the process of cleaning. **2** related by blood; natural. *They are his biological parents.* **3** relating to, involving, or denoting the use of micro-organisms of toxins of biological origin as weapons of war. *Next war may be biological using toxins of biological origin as weapons.*

Biology – *(noun)* the scientific study of living organisms. the plants and animals of a particular area. the features of a particular organism or class of organisms. *I have taken biology as a main subjuct.*

Biscope – *(noun)* [chiefly south American] a cinema or film. *I want to see a film in bioscope.*

Biparous – *(adj.)* producing two offspring at a time.

Bipedal - *(adj.)* having two feet.

Biplane - *(noun)* an early type of aircraft with two pairs of wings, one above the other. *Early planes used to be called biplanes as they had one wing over the other.*

Bipolar - *(adj.)* **1** having or relating to two poles or extremities. of or occurring in both polar regions. *He is an authority over bipolar animal life.* **2** characterized by both manic and depressive episodes, or manic ones only. *He is suffering from bipolar disorder, he should see a psychiatric.* **3** having two axons, one either side of the cell body. **4** [electronics](of a transistor or other device) using both positive and negative charge carriers.

Birch - *(noun)* **1** a slender hardy tree which has thin, peeling, typically silver-grey or white bark and yields a hard, pale, fine-grained wood. *There are a lot of birch trees in Mussourie.* **2** [chiefly historical] a formal punishment in which a person is flogged with a bundle of birch twigs. *As punishment he was flogged with birch twigs.* *(verb)* [chiefly historical] punish with the birch.

Birdlime - *(noun)* a substance spread on to twigs to trap small birds. *People trap small birds by spreading birdlime over twigs once.*

Bird's eye - *(adj.)* as from an attitude or distance. *I have taken a bird's eye view of the problem. We shall go in detail later.*

Birth - *(noun)* **1** the emergence of a baby or other young from the body of its mother; the start of life as a physically separate being. *My sister gave birth to a daughter.* **2** the beginning of something. origin, descent, or ancestry. *He is of noble birth.* *(verb)* chiefly North American give birth to.

Biscuit - *(noun)* **1** a small, flat, crisp unleavened cake. [North American] a small, soft round cake like a scone. *Biscuits are very popular in European countries.* **2** porcelain or other pottery which has been fired but not glazed. **3** a light brown colour. *This shirt is of biscuit colour.* **4** [carpentry] a small flat piece of wood used to join two larger pieces of wood together, fitting into slots in each.

Bisect - *(verb)* divide into two parts. *Now I'll bisect thin circle.*

Bisexual - *(adj.)* **1** sexually attracted to both men and women. *He is bisexual by nature.* **2** [biology] having characteristics of both sexes. *(noun)* a person who is sexually attracted to both men and women.

Bison - *(noun)* humpbacked shaggyharied wild ox. [Bison bison (the North American buffalo) and b. bonasus (Europe, now only Poland).]

Bisque - *(noun)* a rich soup made from lobster of other shellfish. *I very much like to drink bisque.*

Bistoury - *(noun)* a surgical knife with a straight or curved narrow blade. *Surgeon work with a bistoury.*

Bit - *(noun)* **1** a small piece, quantity, or extent of something. *Let me have a bit of bread.* **2** [informal] a set of actions or ideas associated with a specific group or activity bit. *He did his theatrical bit.* **3** [informal] a girl or young woman.

Bitch - *(noun)* **1** a female dog, wolf, fox or otter. *I have named my bitch Sophie.* **2** [informal] a woman whom one dislikes or considers to be malicious or unpleasant. a black English woman. *This bad tempered woman is sure a bitch.* **3** informal a difficult or unpleasant thing or situation. *(verb)* [informal] make malicious or spitefully critical comments.

Bite - *(verb)* **1** use the teeth to cut into something. wound with a sting, pincers, or fangs. *I bit a loaf of bread.* **2** refrain with difficulty from saying something. *I will bit my tongue before letting out the secret.* **3** grip or take hold on a surface. press into a part of the body, causing pain. *She bit my hand.* **4** corrode a surface. **5** take the bait or lure on the end of a fishing line into the mouth. **6** take effect, with unpleasant consequences. *The cuts in art education were starting to bite.* [informal] annoy or worry. *You are in such a bad mood, what is biting you today?* *(noun)* **1** an act or instance of biting. a piece cut off by biting. dentistry the bringing together of the teeth in occlusion. **2** [informal] a quick snack. **3** a sensation of sharpness or pungency. *The cold wind was biting.*

Bitter - *(adj.)* **1** having a sharp, pungent taste or smell; not sweet. *Bitter gourd is a bitter* *vegetable.* **2** causing pain or unhappiness. feeling or showing angry hurt or resentment. harsh and British beer that is strongly flavoured with hops and has a bitter taste. **2** liquor that is flavoured with bitter plant extracts and used as an additive in cocktails. *As he wept and told his tale bitter feelings rose in my heart.*

Bitterish – *(adj.)* somewhat bitter.

Bitumen – *(noun)* a black viscous mixture of hydrocarbons obtained naturally or as a residue from petroleum distillation, used for road surfacing and roofing. *We need more bitumen for road and roof surfacing.*

Bivalve – *(noun)* an aquatic molluse which has a compressed body enclosed withing two hinged shelles, such as an oyster, mussel, or scallop. *(adj.)* **1** (of a molluse or other aquatic invertebrate) having a hinged double shell. [botany] having two valves.

Bivouac – *(noun)* a temporary camp without tents or cover. *(verb)* stay in such a camp. *We stayed in a bivouac camp, it was so exciting and funny.*

Bizzare – *(adj.)* strange; unusual. *Yes tonight I saw a bizarre dream.*

Blab – *(verb)* reveal secrets or confidential information.

Black – *(adj.)* **1** of the very darkest colour due to the absence of or complete absorption of light. deeply stained with dirt. served without milk. *Black is the opposite of white.* **2** of or relating to a human group having dark-coloured skin, especially of African or Australian aboriginal ancestry. *I want a black coffee.* **3** characterized by tragedy, disaster, or despair. presenting tragic or harrowing situations in comic terms. full of anger or haired. *Africans have a black skin.* **4** [British] not to be handled or undertaken by trade union members, as an expression of solidarity with an industrial dispute elsewhere. *It is a black day our president has passed away.* **5** of the highest level of difficulty. *Spades and clubs are black colour in cards.*6. of or denoting the suits spades and clubs in a pack of cards. *(noun)* **1** black colour or pigment. black clothes or material, worn as a sign of mouring. *These people are wearing black bands because they are mourning.* **2** a member of a dark-skinned people, especially one of African or Australian Aboriginal ancestry. **3** the player of the black pieces in chess or draughts. **4** [British informal] blackcurrant cordial. *(verb)* **1** make black, especially by the application of black polish, make-up, etc. **2** make a room or building dark by extinguishing light, covering windows, etc. obscure something completely. (of a television screen) go blank. **3** undergo a sudden and temporary loss of consciousness. **4** British dated refuse to deal with or undertake as a form of industrial action. **5** decide not to broadcast a controversial programme.

Blacken – *(verb)* make or become black.

Black-guard – *(noun)* a man who behaves in a dishonorable or contemptible way. *He has betrayed us. He is a blackguard.* *(verb)* disparage or denounce.

Blackish – *(adj.)* of something that is somewhat black. *These shoes are rather of blackish colour.*

Blackmail – *(noun)* the action of demanding money from someone in return for not revealing discreditable information. the use of threats or unfair manipulating in an attempt to influence someone's actions. *(verb)* subject to blackmail. *His grandson was kidnapped and he was subjected to blackmail.*

Bladder – *(noun)* **1** a muscular membranous sac in the abdomen which receives urine from the kidneys and stores it for excretion. *My bladder is almost bursting please show me the toilet.* **2** an inflated or hollow flexible bag or chamber.

Blame – *(verb)* assign responsibility for a fault or wrong to. *(noun)* responsibility for a fault or wrong. *There was an accident and the blame fell on the truck driver.*

Blameless – *(adj.)* free of guilt not subject to blame. *I find him blameless so he is free to go.*

Blanch – *(verb)* **1** make or become white or pale. **2** prepare for freezing or further cooking by immersing briefly in boiling water. peel by scalding them.

Bland – *(adj.)* lacking strong features or characteristics and therefore uninteresting. lacking flavour or seasoning insipid. *He* *is a bland fellow without any interesting characteristics. I have no interest in him.*

Blandish – *(verb)* [archaic] coax with kind words or flattery. *I blandished her a lot and she became happy.*

Blanket – *(noun)* **1** a large place of woolen material used as a covering for warmth, as on a bed. *I bought a good quality blanket from the market.* **2** a thick mass or layer of a specified material. *A thick blanket of dark clouds covered the sky.* **3** printing a rubber surface used for transferring the image in ink from the plate to the paper in offset printing. *(adj.)* covering all cases or instances; total. *There should be a blanket ban as tobacco.* *(verb)* **1** cover completely with a thick layer. *A thin blanket of ice covered the ground.* **2** sailing take wind from the sails of by passing to windward.

Blare – *(verb)* sound loudly and harshly. *(noun)* a loud, harsh sound. *A blare of trumpets welcomed the king.*

Blaspheme – *(verb)* speak irreverently about God or sacred things. *He talked ill of God and thus blasphemed.*

Blast – *(noun)* **1** a destructive wave of highly compressed air spreading outwards from an explosion. *Suddenly there was a bomb blast in the market.* **2** a strong gust of wind or air. a strong current of air used in smelting. *Blasts are caused by explosives.* **3** a single loud note of a horn or whistle. *The blast of whistle alerted me.* **4** [informal] a severe reprimand. *The space rocket blasted towards sky from the launching pad.* **5** [North American, informal] an enjoyable experience or lively party. *(verb)* **1** blow up or break apart with explosives. **2** take off from a launching site. **3** produce loud continuous music or noise. **4** [informal] criticize fiercely. **5** kick or strike hard. **6** [poetic/literary] wither or shrivel. *He blasted me with criticism.* **7** strike with diving anger: [British informal] expressing annoyance.

Blatter – *(verb)* [informal] move or strike with a clatter. *The warriors attacked each other with a clatter of swords.*

Blaze – *(noun)* **1** a white stripe down the face of a horse or other animal. *Our horse has a blaze on its face.* **2** a cut made on a tree to mark a route. *In the forest you will find a birch tree with a blaze on its trunk, turn right from there.* *(verb)* **1** mark out a path or route. *I have blazed a path through jungle.*

Blazon – *(verb)* **1** display or report prominently or vividly. *He reported the incident in a blazon way.* **2** [heraldry] describe or depict in a correct heraldic manner. *(noun)* [heraldry] a correct description of armorial bearings. [archaic] a coat of arms.

Bleach – *(verb)* **1** cause to become white or much lighter to a chemical process or by exposure to sunlight. *This shirt has been bleached that is why it is looking so light and white.* **2** clean or sterilize with bleach. *(noun)* a chemical used to bleach things and also to sterilize drains, strike, etc. *The chemical bleach also sterilizes things.*

Blear – *(noun)* a small silvery river fish of the carp family. *I am fond of the silvery blear.*

Bleb – *(noun)* **1** a small blister on the skin. *Doctors have discovered a bleb on the surface of one of my cells.* [biology] a rounded outgrowth on the surface of a cell. **2** a small bubble in glass or in a fluid.

Bleed – *(noun)* **1** lose blood from the body as a result of injury or illness. *He was bleeding profusely after the accident.* **2** draw blood from as a former method of medical treatment. *People in old times drew blood from the body as a method of treatment.* **3** (in phr. bleed someone dry) [informal] drain of money or resources. **4** seep into an adjacent colour or area. printing be printed so that it runs off the page after trimming. **5** allow to escape from a closed system through a valve. *(noun)* the action or an instance of bleeding.

Blemish – *(noun)* **1** a small mark or flaw which spoils the appearance of something. *There is a blemish on this diamond which has spoiled its appearance.* **2** a moral defect or fault. *(verb)* spoil the appearance of.

Blend – *(verb)* **1** mix and combine with something else. **2** from a harmonious combination or part of a whole. *A body guard has to blend in with the surroundings. (noun)* **1** a mixture of different things or people. **2** a word made up to the parts and combining the meanings of two others, for example motel from motor and hotel.

Blent – [poetic/literary] past and past participle of blaen.

Blessed – *(adj.)* highly favoured or fortunate. *Blessed are the meek for they shall also enter heaven'.*

Blessing – *(adj.)* **1** make holly; consecrated. a title preceding the name of a dead person considered to have led a holy life, especially a person formally beatified by the Roman Catholic church. *I am praying for God's favour and blessings.* **2** endowed with divine favour and protection. **3** [informal] used in mild expressions of annoyance of exasperation.

Blest – *(adj.)* [archaic or poetic/literary] term for blessed.

Blight – *(noun)* **1** a plant disease, especially one caused by fungi such as mildews, rusts, and smuts. *The growth of this plant has been infected by blight.* **2** a thing that spoils or damages something. *Hailstones are a blight for the crop.* ugly or neglected urban landscape. *(verb)* **1** infect with blight. *What a deserted blight landscape.* **2** spoil, harm, or destroy. subject to neglect.

Blimp – *(noun)* [informal] **1** [British] a pompous, reactionary person. *He is a blimp fellow.* **2** a small airship or barrage balloon. *He owned a blimp and was fond of flying it.* **3** [North American] an obese person. **4** a soundproof cover for a movie camera.

Blind – *(adj.)* **1** unable to see because of injury, disease, or a congenital condition. *He is blind person.* **2** dóne without being able to see or without certain information. using instruments only. *He fell into a deep pit and became blind to his surroundings.* **3** lacking perception, judgment, or reason. **4** concealed, closed, or blocked off. impossible to see round. *He tried to trick a rich person but it didn't do him a blind of good.* **5** without buds, eyes, or terminal flowers. *He was blinded because of a chemical explosion.* 6. [informal] the slightest. *He is blind to judgment or reason. (verb)* **1** cause to be unable to see. **2** deprive of understanding or judgment. confuse or overawe someone with (something they do not understand). **3** [british informal] move very fast and dangerously. *(noun)* **1** a screen for a window, especially one on a roller or made of slats. *Please cover the windows with a blind.* [British] an awning over a shop window. **3** [North American] a hide, as used by hunters. **4** [British informal] a heavy drinking bout. adverb without being able to see clearly. *He indulged into blind drinking.*

Blindfold – *(noun)* a cloth used to cover the eyes. *He covered his eyes with a blindfold.*

Blindly – *(adv.)* without seeing or looking. *He obeyed me blindly.*

Blindness – *(noun)* the state of being blind or lacking sight. *Blindness occurred to him become of weak eye nerve.*

Blink – *(verb)* **1** shut and open the eyes quickly. *As he suddenly confronted bright lights he blinked his eyes.* **2** react with surprise or disapproval. *He blinked his eyes with disapproval.* **3** shine unsteadily or intermittently. *Suddenly a light blinked in the sky. (noun)* **1** an act of blinking. **2** a momentary gleam of light.

Bliss – *(noun)* perfect happiness. a state of spiritual blessedness. *He has been meditating long and now he is in a state of bliss. (verb)* [informal] be in a state of perfect happiness, oblivious to everything else.

Blister – *(noun)* **1** a small bubble on the skin filled with serum and typically caused by friction or burning. *The sole of his feet got blisters as he walked barefooted in the desert.* **2** a similar swelling, filled with air or fluid, on a surface. **3** [medicine, chiefly historical] a preparation applied to the skin to form a blister. **4** [British informal] an annoying person. *(verb)* be or cause to be affected with blisters.

Blithe – *(adj.)* cheerfully or thoughtlessly indifferent. *She is a blithe child, always happy and playful.* **2** [poetic/literary] happy or joyous.

Blizzard – *(noun)* a severe snowstorm with high winds. *We were trapped in a blizzard.*

Bloat – *(verb)* cure by salting and smoking it lightly.

Blockade – *(noun)* **1** an act of sealing off a place to prevent goods or people from entering or leaving. *There is a police blockade on the road.* **2** an obstruction of a biochemical or other physiological function. *(verb)* set up a blockaded port.

Blockhead – *(noun)* a stupid person, used to express law opinion of someone.

Blockish – *(adj.)* **1** bulky or crude in form. *He is a blockish fellow.* **2** unintelligent; stupid.

Blond – *(noun)* a person with pair skin and hair. *She is a blond a women with fair hair.*

Bloody – *(adj.)* **1** covered with or composed of blood. *The dead body was too bloody.* **2** involving much violence or cruelty. *Skinning dead animals is a bloody business.* *(verb)* cover or stain with blood.

Bloom – *(noun)* a mass of iron or steel hammered or rolled into a thick bar for further working. [historical] an unworked mass of puddle iron. *(verb)* make into such a mass.

Blossom – *(noun)* a flower or a mass of flowers on a tree or bush. the state or period of flowering. *(verb)* **1** produce blossom. *The flowers blossomed on the tree.* **2** mature or develop in a promising or healthy way. *He blossomed into manhood.*

Blot – *(noun)* **1** a dark mark or stain, especially one made by ink. *Here is a blot on this otherwise it is clean page.* **2** a thing that mars something that is otherwise good. *He is a blot on our good family.* **3** [biochemistry] a procedure in which proteins or nucleic acids separated on a gel are transferred directly to an immobilizing medium for identification. *(verb)* **1** dry with an absorbent material. *Please dry this spilled ink with a blotting paper.* **2** mark, stain, or mar. **3** obscure a view. obliterate or disregard a painful memory or thought. *I want to blot out that painful incident from my memory.*

Blotch – *(noun)* a large irregular patch or unsightly mark. *(verb)* cover or mark with blotches. *There was rain last night and the road is covered with blotches.*

Blouse – *(noun)* **1** a woman's upper garment resembling a shirt. *She is wearing a low cut red blouse which goes well with her saree.* **2** a loose smock or tunic of a type worn by peasants and manual workers. a type of jacket worn as part of military uniform. *(verb)* make hang in loose folds.

Blow – *(noun)* **1** a powerful stroke with a hand or weapon. *I gave him a blow on the chin.* **2** a sudden shock or disappointment. *His defeat in boxing was a blow to the trainer.*

Blowy – *(adj.)* windy or windswept. *This valley is very blowy.*

Bluogeon – *(noun)* a thick stick with a heavy end, used as a weapon. *He beat him with a bluogen.* *(verb)* **1** beat with a bludgeon. **2** bully into doing something.

Blue – *(adj.)* **1** of a colour intermediate between green and violet, as of the sky or sea on a sunny day. having fur of a smoky grey colour. *Sky seem to be of blue colour.* **2** [informal] melancholy, sad, or depressed. *Blue suits me very well.* **3** [informal] with sexual or pornographic content. *Blue films are pornographic in content.* **4** [british, informal] politically conservative. **5** of the second-lowest level of difficulty. *(noun)* blue colour, pigment, or material. [poetic/literary] the sky or sea, or the unknown. another term for bluing.

Blue blood – *(noun)* noble birth. *He is a man of blue blood.*

Blue-stone – *(noun)* **1** a bluish or grey building stone. *I would like to use some blue stones on this wall.* **2** any of the smaller dolerite stones forming the inner part of Stonehenge.

Bluff – *(noun)* an attempt to deceive someone into believing that one can or will do something. *(verb)* try to deceive someone as to one's abilities or intentions. *He bluffed me into believing that he could very easily get me the loan.*

Bluish – *(adj.)* having a blue tinge. *Your blazer has a bluish tinge. It works fantastic.*

Blunder – *(noun)* a stupid or careless mistake. *I committed a blunder by delaying the loan* *payment.* *(verb)* **1** make a blunder. *I blundered in the presentation.*

Blunt – *(adj.)* **1** lacking a sharp edge or point. *This knife is blunt. Give me a sharp one.* having a flat or rounded end. *He was hit on head with a blunt object.* **2** uncompromisingly forthright in manner. *He gave me a blunt reply.* *(verb)* **1** make or become less sharp. **2** weaken or reduce the force of. *(noun)* black slang a hollowed out eager filled with cannabis.

Blur– *(verb)* make or become unclear or less distinct. *My eyesight was blurred as something hit me on the head.* *(noun)* something that cannot be seen, heard, or recalled clearly. *I am old and my memory is blurred.*

Blurt – *(verb)* say suddenly and without careful consideration. *Ah! Yes I have committed the crime he blurted out.*

Bluster – *(verb)* **1** talk in a loud, aggressive, or indignant way with little effect. **2** blow or beat fiercely and noisily. *(noun)* blustering talk. *He gave me a blustering talk which had little effect on me.*

Boa – *(noun)* **1** a large snake which kills its prey by constriction. *I saw a boa in jungle; it was crushing its prey to death.* **2** a long, thin stole of feathers or fur worn around a woman's neck, usually as part of evening dress. *Her pink boa was beautiful.*

Boar – *(noun)* **1** a tusked wild pig from which domestic pigs are descended. *If you confront boar in the jungle it can be very dangerous.* **2** an uncastrated domestic male pig. *The boar is still in the form.*

Board – *(noun)* **1** a long, thin, flat piece of wood used for floors or other building purposes. [informal] the stage of a theatre. *I'll need at least a dozen boards for the floor.* **2** a thin, flat, rectangular piece of stiff material, e.g. a chopping board or noticeboard. the piece of equipment on which one stands in surfing, skate boarding, etc. *I'll need board for putting up notices.* **3** the decision-making body of an organization. *Board of directors is considering.* *(verb)* **1** get on or into (a ship, aircraft, or other vehicle.) be ready for passengers to get on. *As soon as I boarded the train it started to move.* **2** live in school in return for payment. *I live in the boarding house of the school.* **3** cover or seal a window or building with pieces of wood. *I have boarded the window shut.* **4** made of wooden boards. **5** ride on a snowboard. *Boarding and lodging is provided here.*

Boast – *(verb)* **1** talk with excessive pride and self-satisfaction about oneself. *He boasted a lot about his inherited wealth.* **2** possess. *(noun)* an act of boasting.

Boat – *(noun)* a small vessel propelled by oars, sails, or an engine. a vessel of any size. *I crossed the river by boat.*

Boating – *(noun)* water travel for pleasure. *Let us go for boating.*

Boatman – *(noun)* a person who provides transport by boat. *The boatman propelled the oars and the boat moved.*

Bodice – *(noun)* the part of a women's dress above the waist. a woman's sleeveless undergarment, often laced at the front. *She wore a perfectly fitting bodice.*

Boding – *(noun)* a feeling of evil to come. *I had a boding for this house.*

Bog – *(noun)* **1** an area of very soft wet muddy ground. *Frogs often live in bog.* [ecology] wetland with acid, party soil. **2** [British informal] a toilet. *(verb)* **1** cause to become stuck; hinder the progress of. *The whole progress was bogged down.* [informal] start a task enthusiastically. **3** [British informal] go away. *He was bogged away.*

Boggle – *(verb)* [informal] be startled or baffled. *My mind boggled at the speed the train ran.* hesitate or be anxious at.

Boggy – *(adj.)* soft and watery soil. *The soil was boggy.*

Bogie – *(noun)* **1** an undercarriage with four or six wheels pivoted beneath the end of a railway vehicle. *There are eight bogies in this train.* **2** [chiefly north English] a low truck on four small wheels. *The stuff was carried over in a bogle.*

Bogle – *(noun)* a phantom or goblin. *It is rumored that a bogle roams here in this forest.*

Bogus - *(adj.)* not genuine or true. *This driving license is bogus, said the policeman.*

Bodkin - *(noun)* **1** a thick, blunt needle with a large eye, used for drawing tape through a hem. *Women fasten their hair with a bodkin.* [historical] a long pin used to fasten women's hair. printing a pointed tool used for removing pieces of metal type for correction.

Boil- *(verb)* **1** reach or cause to reach the temperature at which it bubbles and turns to vapour. *Water boils at 100⁰* c. **2** cook or be cooked by immersing in boiling water. *I would like to boil milk.* **3** be turbulent and stormy. be stirred up or inflamed. become so excited or tense as to lose control. *I am boiling inside. I may lose control of myself and attack him.* **4** amount to. *(noun)* **1** the act or process of boiling; boiling point. **2** fishing a sudden rise of a fish at a fly.

Boisterous - *(noun)* **1** noisy, energetic, and cheerful. *He gave a boisterous laugh at my joke.* **2** (of weather or water) wild or stormy. *The wind was strong and boisterous. Boisterous waters raged into the city.*

Bold - *(adj.)* **1** confident and daring or courageous. audacious; impudent. *He is bold and will certainly succeed.* **2** strong or vivid. having thick strokes. *(noun)* a typeface with thick strokes. *It is a vivid and bold painting with thick strokes.*

Bole - *(noun)* a tree trunk. *Some years ago I engraved some letters on this bole and they are still here.*

Bolster - *(noun)* **1** a long, thick pillow. *Please bring me a bolster, I want to relax thoroughly.* **2** a part on a vehicle or tool providing structural support or reducing friction. building a short timber cap over a post increasing the bearing of type beams it supports. *(verb)* support or strengthen.

Bolter - *(noun)* a person or animal that bolts or runs away. *Deer are the best bolters the moment you make a noise they will run and disappear.* [Austral, historical] an escaped convict or absconder. *The bolter has not been caught go for.*

Bomb - *(noun)* **1** a container of explosive or incendiary material, designed to explode on impact or when detonated by a timing or remote-control device. nuclear weapons collectively. *The bomb blast killed many people.* **2** [British informal] a large sum of money. *If USA have the bomb Russia also have it.* **3** [informal] a thing that fails badly. *That project was a bombs.* **4** a lump of lava thrown out by a volcano. *Volcano eruption expelled bomb out of it.* *(verb)* **1** attack with a bomb or bombs. *The city was bombed by terrorists.* **2** [British, informal] move very quickly. *He bombed post me.*

Bombard - *(verb)* **1** attack continuously with bombs or other missiles. *The bombardment of UK by Germany continued for a long time.* **2** subject to a continuous flow of questions or information. *The journalists bombarded the politician with questions.* **3** [physics] direct a stream of high-speed particles at. *The stream of atoms bombarded at the screen.* *(noun)* an early form of cannon. *The bombard is displayed at museum.*

Bomber - *(noun)* **1** an aircraft that drops bombs. *Planes were largely used as bombers in second world war.* **2** a person who plants bombs, especially as a terrorist. *The bomber had the bomb in a dustbin by the road to be later detonated by remote device.*

Bon - *(noun)* a Japanese Buddhist festival held annually in august to honour the dead. *Many people go to Japan to attend bon.*

Bonafide - *(adj.)* genuine; real. *You should get bonafide birth certificate.* *(adverb)* [chiefly law] without intention to deceive. *It is a bonafide document and you can submit it in the court without hesitation.*

Bondage- *(noun)* **1** the state of being a slave or serf. *He was held in bondage for a long time.* **2** sexual practice that involves the tying up or restraining of one partner. *The bondage act can severely hurt a person.*

Bondman - *(noun)* **1** a person who stands surety for a bond. *In the court you will find lots of bondmen willing to stand surely.* **2** [archaic] a slave or feudal serf.

Bondsman - *(noun)* **1** a male slave. *Earlier bings had bondsman.* **2** someone who signs a bond as surety for someone else. *I was his bondsman in his company.*

Bone – *(noun)* **1** any of the pieces of hard, whitish tissue making up the skeleton in vertebrates. *The bone are made up of calcium.* **2** the calcified material of which bones consist. *The bones in our body are made of calcified material.* a thing made of a substance resembling bone, e.g. a strip of stiffening for an undergarment. *(verb)* remove the bones from before cooking. *Use the boneless chicken for recipe.*

Bonfire – *(noun)* a large openair fire. *Let us camp here and light a bonfire.*

Bonny – *(adj.)* **1** physically attractive; healthy-looking. *He is a bonny child; I would also like to have one like that.* **2** sizeable; considerable. *It's worth a bonny sum.*

Bonus – *(noun)* **1** a sum of money added seasonally to a person's wagés for good performance. *In this firm employees get bonus on every Diwali.* [british] an extra dividend or issue paid to shareholders. **2** an extra and unexpected welcome event.

Boo – *(exclamatory)* **1** said suddenly to surprise someone. *She said 'Boo' in my ear and I was started.* **2** said to show disapproval or contempt. *(verb)* say 'boo' to show disapproval or contempt. *The crowd booed away the performer.*

Booby – *(noun)* **1** [informal] a stupid person. *No use talking to that booby.* **2** a large tropical seabird of the gannet family, with brown, black, or white plumage and brightly coloured feet. *I saw the beautiful bird booby in a zoo.*

Boodle – *(noun)* [informal] money, especially that gained or spent dishonestly. *All money spent or won in gambling is boodle.*

Boohoo – *(exclamatory)* representing the sound of someone crying noisily. *'Boohoo' she cried loudly as she wept over the loss of her jewellery.*

Book-binder – *(noun)* a person who binds books. *My brother is a book-binder.*

Book-case – *(noun)* an open cabinet containing shelves on which to keep books. *I have bought a book-case just to keep books in order.*

Booking - *(noun)* the act of reseving or engaging the services of a person or group.

Book-keeper – *(noun)* someone who records the transactions of a business. *He is a book-keeper in the office.*

Book-keeping – *(noun)* the activity of keeping records of financial affairs. *The job of book-keeping is not an easy one as it involves financial dealings.*

Booklet – *(noun)* a small, thin book with paper covers. *I prefer booklets to books.*

Book-maker – *(noun)* a person whose job is to take bets, calculate odds, and pay out winnings. *A book-maker has an important place in a gambling house.*

Book-seller – *(noun)* **1** the proprie of a bookstore. *The bookseller is a nice person.* **2** a dealer of books; a merchant who sells books. *The bookseller tells all kinds of fiction books.*

Book-worm – *(noun)* **1** [informal] a person who enjoys reading. *He is a bookworm.* **2** the larva of a wood-boring beetle which feeds on the paper and glue in books. *This book has become useless. The larva of the book-worm has eaten into it.*

Boom – *(noun)* a loud, deep, resonant sound. *The firing cannons made of boom- boom sound.* *(verb)* make this sound.

Boon – *(noun)* **1** a thing that is helpful or beneficial. *His having become my partner in business was no less a boon.* **2** [archaic] a favour or request. *He was thankful for his boon.*

Boor – *(noun)* a rough and bad-mannered person. *He is a boor.*

Boost – *(verb)* help or encourage to increase or improve. *My father having come to my help in bad times boosted my morals.* *(noun)* a source of help or encouragement. *A good bank balance is great boost.*

Boot – *(noun)* **1** a sturdy item of footwear covering the foot and ankle, and something the lower leg. *I purchased a pair of boots.* **2** [informal] a hard kick. **3** [British] a space at the back of a car for carrying luggage. *Please open the boot of the car and take out the luggage.* **4** [historical] an instrument of torture crushing the foot. *The army used boot to crush the feet of prisoner.* *(verb)* kick hard. *I booted* *him on the bum.* **2** [informal] force someone to leave unceremoniously. *He was booted out of the ceremony.* **3** start (a computer) and put it into a state of readiness for operation. *Boot the computer.*

Booth – *(noun)* **1** a small temporary structure used for selling goods or staging shows at a market or fair. *There were a lot of booths in the fair.* **2** an enclosed compartment allowing privacy when telephoning voting, etc. *Booths are used for telephonic and voting purposes.*

Boot-lace – *(noun)* a cord or leather strip for lacing boots. *Will someone find my boot-laces I have to tie up shoe.*

Bootless – *(adj.)* [archaic] ineffectual; useless. *Ignore it. It is something bootless.*

Booty – *(noun)* valuable stolen goods. *Let us divide the booty among ourselves before the police come.*

Booze – *(noun)* [informal] alcoholic drink. *(verb)* drink large quantities of alcohol. *He had a lot of booze and was out. He went boozing around from bar to bar.*

Borax – *(noun)* a white mineral consisting of hydrated sodium borate, found in some alkaline salt deposits and used in making glass and as a metallurgical flux. *Borax is used in this glass.*

Border – *(noun)* **1** a line separeating two countries or other areas. *The border line between India and Pakistan is very long.* **2** a decorative band around the edge of something. *The strip of border on the your saree is very beautiful.* a strip of ground along the edge of a lawn for planting flowers or shrubs. *You can see the decorated border around the garden.* *(verb)* **1** form a border around or along. *Border this house.* **2** be adjacent to. *His house is at the border of my house.* **3** come close to an extreme condition. *he was at the border of death.*

Bore – *(noun)* a steep-fronted wave caused by the meeting of two tides or by a tide rushing up a narrow estuary.

Borer – *(noun)* **1** a worm, molluse, or insect which bores into plant material or rock. *The worm called borer has eaten into our plants as well as the rocks around.* **2** a tool for boring. *I have to make a hole in the wall please give me the borer.*

Boric – *(adj.)* [chemistry] of boron. *Boric acid is a chemical.*

Boring – *(adj.)* so lacking in interest as to cause mental weariness. *He is a very boring person. You will soon get tired of him.*

Born – *(adj.)* **1** existing as a result of birth. *I was born in the year 1938.* **2** having a natural ability to do a particular job or task: a born engineer. *Don't worry he'll do well. He is a born engineer.* **3** having a specific nationality. *He is a French born philosopher.*

Borne – past participle of bear. *The weight was borne by him for a long distance.*

Borrow – *(verb)* **1** take and use with the intention of returning it. take and use from a person or bank under agreement to pay it back later. *He borrowed money from the bank when he was in difficult times. I went to my friend to borrow some books.* **2** [Golf] allow when playing a shot to compensate for a slope or other irregularity. *(noun)* [Golf] a slope or other irregularity on a golf course.

Bort – *(noun)* inferior diamonds used in cutting tools. *Please get me a bort, I have to cut glass.*

Bosh – *(noun)* [informal] nonsense. *Oh! He is talking bosh.*

Bosky – *(adj.)* [poetic/literary] covered by trees or bushes. *The garden was bosky.*

Bosom – *(noun)* **1** a woman's breast or chest. *A buxom bosom adds to the beauty of a women.* **2** the breast as the seat of emotions: quivering dread was settling in her went home each night to the bosom of his family. *I am feeling uneasy is my bosom.* *(adj.)* very close. *Come! Come to my bosom son and you will lose all your fear, said the mother.*

Botanic – *(adj.)* of or relating to plants or botony. *This problem is botanic i.e. related with plant life so go and ask a botanist about it.*

Botanist – *(noun)* a biologist specialising in the study of plants. *My brother is a botanist.*

Botany – *(noun)* **1** all the plant life in a particular region or period. *The botany of that garden is beautiful.* **2** the branch of biology that studies plants. *We had a period of botany.*

Botch – *(verb)* carry out badly or carelessly. *He has botched up the plan.* *(noun)* a badly carried out task. *The task was a botch.*

Botchy – *(adj.)* poorly done. *No use acting upon this botchy scheme.*

Both – *(Predetermined, determined, pronoun)* two people or things, regarded and identified together. Both of you are promoted. *(adverb)* applying equally to each of two alternatives. *Both the brothers took up the challenge. Both the alternatives can be used.*

Bother – *(verb)* **1** take the trouble to do something. *He was bothered by his boss.* **2** worry, disturb, or upset. feel concern about or interest in. *The problem is still bothering me.* *(noun)* trouble; fuss. a cause of trouble or fuss. *Don't you bother about it, it is not worth that.* *(exclamatory)* [chiefly British] used to express mild irritation. *Leave this problem to me to bother about I can handle it.*

Bottler – *(noun)* a manufacturer that makes and battles beverages. *In this city, bottler makes fantastic bottles.*

Bottom – *(noun)* **1** the lowest point or part of something. the furthest part or point of something. the lower half of a two-piece garment. *The bottom of the trousers is loose. I'll give it to the tailor to tight it.* **2** [chiefly British] a person's buttocks. *His bottom is hurt.* **3** [archaic] stamina or stregth of character, especially of a horse. *He is not improving he is sinking and going down to bottom.* **4** [physics] one of six flavours of quark. *(adj.)* in the lowest position. in the furthest position away in a downhill direction. *(verb)* **1** touch the bottom of the sea. *The divers often swim upon the bottom of the sea.* **2** reach the lowest point before stabilizing or improving. *He stumbled hill the bottom.*

Boudoir *(noun)* a lady's bedroom or private room. *Her boudoir is beautifully done..*

Bought – past and past participle of buy. *I bought a shirt yesterday. My father had bought the shop before he consulted me.*

Boulder – *(noun)* a large rock. *A boulder fell down and raced past me.*

Bouncer – *(noun)* **1** a person employed by a nightclub or pub to prevent troublemakers entering or to eject them from the premises. *The bouncer stopped him from entering the club because he was too drunk. The bouncers threw the man out because he was proving a nuisance to girls.* **2** [cricket] a ball bowled fast and short so as to rise high after pitching. *The bowler threw a bouncer and the batsman was out.*

Bouncing – *(noun)* rebounding from an impact. *The ball hit the wall and come back bouncing.*

Bound – *(verb)* walk or run with leaping strides. *The leopard leapt and bounded gracefully.* *(noun)* a leaping movement towards or over something. *The tiger bounded upon its prey.*

Boundary – *(noun)* **1** a line marking the limits of an area. *There is a boundary around the play ground.* **2** [cricket] a hit crossing the limits of the field, scoring four or six runs. *Sachin hit again and again across the boundary.*

Boundless – *(adj.)* unlimited. *Sportsmen have boundless energy.*

Bounds *(noun)* line or plane indicating the limit or extent of something. *He was out of his bounds.*

Bounteous – *(adj.)* [archaic] bountiful. *He is very bounteous, his bounty knows no limits.*

Bountiful – *(adj.)* **1** abundant. *There is bountiful food in here.* **2** giving generously. *He is bountiful person and donates generously.*

Bounty– *(noun)* **1** a reward paid for killing or capturing someone. *He was given a bounty by authorities for catching an escaped convict.* **2** [historical] a sum paid by the state to encourage trade. *Government granted a huge bounty to ministry of commerce to promote international trade.* [chiefly historical] a sum paid by the state to enlisting army or navy recruits. *Government gives a bounty to those who enlist in navy army.* **3** [poetic/literary] something given or occurring in generous amounts.

Bouquet – *(noun)* a bunch of flowers. *She received a bouquet from her best friend.*

Bourse – *(noun)* a stock market in a non-English speaking country, especially France. *When I went to France I visited bourse also.*

Bout - *(noun)* **1** a short period of intense activity. an attack of illness or strong emotion. *I had a bout of malaria.* **2** a wresting or boxing match. *In the very first bout of boxing he earned sufficient points.* **3** a curve in the side of a violin or other musical instrument. *The bout of violin was rigged.*

Bovine - *(adj.)* of, relating to, or resembling cattle. *(noun)* an animal of the cattle family. *A cow belongs to bovine family.*

Bovril - *(noun)* an extract of beef.

Bow - *(verb)* **1** bend the head or upper body as a sign of respect, greeting, or shame. *I bowed before my master.* **2** cause to bend with age or under a heavy weight. *He has bowed with age.* **3** submit to pressure of demands. *Ultimately I bowed to the demands of my son.* **4** withdraw or retire from something. *He bowed out of the play.* *(noun)* an act of bowing. *his bow said everything.*

Bowel - *(noun)* the intestine. *There is something wrong, my bowels are troubling me.* **2** the deepest inner parts of something. *Deep inside the bowels of earth is still hot.*

Bower - *(noun)* an anchor carried at a ship's bow. *Bower is placed in the front part of the ship.*

Bowl - *(noun)* **1** a round, deep dish or basin. a rounded, concave part of an object. *There were so many bowls placed at the dining table.* [geography] a natural basin. *The Faqir drank from his bowl.* [chiefly North American] a stadium for sporting or musical events. an American football game played after the season between leading teams. *We went to see a same of boul.*

Bowler - *(noun)* **1** [cricket] a member of the fielding side who bowls. *A good bowler is an asset for a winning team.*2 a player at bowls, tenpin bowling, or skittles. *The bowler was faulty.*

Bow-wow - exclamatory an imitation of a dog's bark. *(noun)* informal a dog. *He irritated the dog and said 'bow-wow!'*

Boxing - *(noun)* fighting with the fists. *I am fond of seeing boxing matches.*

Boy - *(noun)* **1** a male child or youth. *He is a well mannered boy.* **2** [informal] men who mix socially or belong to a particular group. **3** offensive a black male servant or worker. *(exclamatory)* [informal] used to express strong feelings. *Oh boy that is a wonderful scene!*

Boyhood - *(noun)* the childhood of a boy. *My boyhood was pleasent.*

Boyish - *(adj.)* befitting or characteristic of young boy. *Although mature he behaves boyish.*

Brabble - *(verb)* argue over petty thing.

Brace - *(noun)* **1** [British] a pair of straps passing .over the shoulders and fastening to the top of trousers at the front and back to hold them up. *He has a big round belly so he uses braces to hold the trousers.* **2** a wire device fitted in the mouth to straighten the teeth. *She wears braces because her teeth are irregular.* a strengthening piece of iron or timber in building or carpentry. **3** a drilling tool with a crank handle and a socket to hold a bit. *Will you get me a brace? I have to drill a hole.* **4** a rope attached to the yard of a ship for trimming the sail. *He braced the stair case with an iron rod.* **5** a pair of things, especially birds or mammals killed in hunting. **6** either of two connecting marks {and}, used in printing. music a similar mark connecting staves to be performed at the same time. *(verb)* **1** make stronger or firmer with wood, iron, etc. *The structure was braced with wood.* **2** press firmly against something in order to stay balanced. **3** prepare for something difficult or unpleasant.

Bracelet - *(noun)* **1** an ornamental band or chain worn on the wrist or arm. *She bought a diamond bracelet to wear on her wrist* **2** [informal] handcuffs.

Bracer - *(noun)* [informal] an alcoholic drink taken to prepare one for something difficult or unpleasant. *He needed a bracer to prepare that dangerous stunt.*

Bracing - *(adj.)* fresh and invigorating. *This is a bracing drink.*

Braekish - *(adj.)* slightly salty, as in river estuaries. living in or requiring such water. *Some fishes need brakeish water to live in.*

Bradawl – *(noun)* a tool for boring holes, resembling a screwdriver. *I need a bradawl to drill a hole.*

Brag – *(verb)* boast. *(noun)* **1** a simplified form of poker; *He is a bragger.* **2** an act of bragging. *He brags all the time of his wealth, of his power, of his business ventures, etc.*

Braid – *(noun)* **1** threads of silk, cotton etc. woven into a decorative band. *The braid she wore was made of silk and cotton woven finely into a band.* **2** a length of hair made up of three or more interlaced strands. *(verb)* **1** form a braid with three or more stands of hair. *She is wearing her braid gracefully.* **2** edge or trim with braid. *She braidely the end of scarf.* **3** of a river or stream flow into shallow interconnected channels divided by deposited earth.

Braille – *(noun)* a written language for the blind in which characters are represented by patterns of raised dots. *This book has been typed in Braille so that the blind can read it.*

Brain – *(noun)* **1** an organ of soft nervous tissue contained in the skull, functioning as the coordinating centre of sensation and intellectual and nervous activity. *This intellectual and nervous activities show that he has lots of brains.* the substance of an animal's brain used as food. *A plate of mutton for me brings brains.* **2** intellectual capacity. **3** informal the main organizer or planner within a group. *(verb)* informal hit hard on the head with an object.

Brake – *(noun)* [historical] an open horse-drawn carriage with four wheels. *He travelled a long way in brake.*

Bramble – *(noun)* a prickly scrambling shrub of the rose family, especially a blackberry. *The gardener is gathering blackberries from bramble.* [chiefly British] the fruit of the blackberry.

Bran – *(noun)* pieces of grain husk separated from flour after milling. *Bran is good for health.*

Branch – *(noun)* **1** a woody extending part of a tree which grows out from the trunk or a bough. *This branch of tree is full of fruits.* **2** a subdivision extending from the trunk or a bough. a subdivision extending from a river, road, or railway. a division of a large organization. *This bank has branches in almost every city.* a conceptual subdivision of a group of languages, subject, etc. *(verb)* **1** divide into one or more subdivisions. bear or send out branches. *This river divides itself in two branches.* **2** extend one's activity or interests in a new direction. *This branch of Railway goes to the bridge. One branch of this road goes into the forest. This car manufacturing plants has branches all over the country.*

Brand – *(noun)* **1** a type of product manufactured by a company under a particular name. *Woodland brand of shoes are famous all over.* a particular name. a particular type of something: the finish brand of socialism. **2** an identifying mark or characteristic common to the products of a particular company. *Another such brand is Allen Solly.* **3** an identifying mark burned on livestock with a branding iron. *All brown barn cattles are mine.* *(verb)* **1** mark with a branding iron. mark out as having a particular shameful quality. *She was branded a liar.* **2** assign a brand name to. *She wears branded attire.*

Brandish – *(noun)* wave or flourish as a threat or in anger or excitement. *Her brandish attitude scared us.*

Brandy – *(noun)* a strong alcoholic spirit distilled from wine or fermented fruit juice. *If you have cought cold you may take a little brandy, that will help.*

Bravado – *(noun)* boldness intended to impress or intimidate. *He has lot of bravado and creates impression by his boldness.*

Brave – *(adj.)* showing courage. *He proved to be a brave soldier.* *(noun)* an American Indian warrior: *(verb)* endure or face with courage.

Bravo – *(exclamatory)* used to express approval for a performer. *Bravo! You did a great job.* *(noun)* a code word representing the letter B, used in radio communication.

Brawl – *(noun)* a rough or noisy fight or quarrel. *Police found him indulged in a street brawl and arrested him, others ran away.* *(verb)* take part in a brawl.

Bray - *(noun)* the loud, harsh cry of a donkey. *In the morning I heard a donkey's braying and woke up irritated. (verb)* make such a sound. *The man brayed like a donkey.*

Braze - *(verb)* form, fix, or join by soldering with an alloy of copper and zinc. *This is a brazed joint. (noun)* a brazed joint.

Brazen - *(adj.)* **1** bold and shameless.. *Her brazen attitude irritated all in the party.* **2** [chiefly poetic/literary] made of brass. *Bring out the brazen trophy. (verb)* endure a difficult situation with apparent confidence and lack of shame. *he braxened the blow.*

Breach - *(noun)* **1** an act of breaking a law, agreement, or code of conduct. a break in relations. *To enter someone's house without permission is a breach of law.* **2** a gap in a wall or barrier, especially one made by an attacking army. *(verb)* **1** make a breach in. *The army breached the wall.* **2** break (a law, agreement, or code of conduct). *My friend breached the agreement and I took him to the court.*

Bread - *(noun)* **1** food made of flour, water, and yeast mixed together and baked. *Bread is not native Indian food.* **2** [nformal] money. *This is the only source of income which provides me with my bread and butter.*

Breakable - *(adj.)* capable of being braken or damaged. *This stick is thin and surely breakable.*

Breakage - *(noun)* the act of breaking something. *The young men who created a scene in restaurant had to pay for the breakage.*

Breakdown - *(noun)* **1** a failure or collapse. *The breakdown of the car occurred in an isolated place.* **2** chemical or physical decomposition. *She had another nervous breakdown.* **3** an explanatory analysis, especially of statistics. *Following are the breakdown figures of the statistics.*

Breaker - *(noun)* **1** a heavy sea wave that breaks on the shore. *The breaker came and almost the whole ship shook.* **2** a person or thing that breaks. *This person sure is a breaker. He has broken so many plates.* **3** a person who interrupts a conversation on a citizens' band radio channel. indicating that they wish to transmit a message. any CB radio user. *The clutch wire of my scooter usually breaks.* **4** a break dancer. *He is a famous break dancer.*

Breakfast - *(noun)* a meal eaten in the morning, the first of the day. *You must not miss your breakfast as it is the first meal of the day.*

Breakneck - *(adj.)* dangerously or extremely fast. *He drove the car at breakneck speed.*

Breakwater - *(noun)* a barrier built out into the sea to protect a coast or harbour from the force of waves. *This barrier in the sea is named breakwater as it protects the coast from the force of waves.*

Breast - *(noun)* **1** either of the two soft, protruding organs on the upper front of a woman's body which secrete milk after pregnancy. *Mother should breast feed her child after birth.* **2** a person's or animal's chest region. a joint of meat or poultry cut from such a part. *Cook the breast of chicken properly. (verb)* face and move forwards against or through. reach the top of a hill.

Breast-bone - *(noun)* a thin flat bone running down the centre of the chest and connecting the ribs; the sternum. *He was hit hard on his breast-bone.*

Breath - *(noun)* **1** air taken into or expelled form the lungs. an inhalation or exhalation of air form the lungs. *His breath came slow.* **2** a slight movement of air.

Breathe - *(verb)* **1** take air into the lungs and then expel it as a regular physiological process. respire or exchange gases. *Breathing is necessary to maintain life.* **2** be exposed to fresh air. *In yoga we have so many breathing techniques.* **3** admit or emit air or moisture. *Oh mountains we breathe fresh air.* **4** allow to rest after exertion. *Take a breathe from this work.*

Breathing - *(noun)* the bodily process of inhalation and exhalation. *He was breathing steadily.*

Breathless - *(adj.)* **1** gasping for breath, typically due to exertion. *He grew breathless as he ran faster and faster.* feeling or causing great excitement, fear, etc. *I found him breathless with excitement.* **2** stiflingly still.*The patient lay almost breathless.*

Breed – *(verb)* **1** mate and then produce offspring. cause to produce offspring. *Insects breed like anything*. **2** bring up to behave in a particular way. *He has been bred like a prince.* **3** produce or lead to. *Success has bred a certain pride in him.* **4** [physics] create by nuclear reaction. *Uranium was breeded in nuclear reaction.* *(noun)* **1** a distinctive stock of animals or plants within a species, typically one deliberately developed. *You have developed a rare breed of dogs*. **2** a sort or kind.

Breeder – *(noun)* **1** a person or animal that breeds. *We humans and animals are breeders, if we were not so the races would have died.* **2** a heterosexual person. *He is a breeder.* **3** a nuclear reactor which creates another fissile material as a by-product of energy production by fission of uranium 238. *The breeder is coolant was hard water.*

Breeding – *(noun)* good manner regarded as characteristic of the aristocracy and conferred by heredity. *Seeing his aristocratic manners his breeding must have been high class.*

Breviary – *(noun)* a book containing the service for each day, to be recited by those in orders in the roman catholic church. *Roman Catholics daily recite from breviary.*

Brew – *(verb)* **1** make by soaking, boiling, and fermentation. *I would like to have a jug of brew.* **2** make by mixing it with hot water. kind of beer. [informal] a drink of tea. *He brewed the tea.*

Bribe – *(verb)* dishonestly persuade to act in one's favour by a payment or other inducement. *He bribed the office.* *(noun)* an inducement offered in an attempt to bribe. *He gave me a bribe of ten thousand rupees to get his license before due date.*

Bribery – *(noun)* the giving or offering of a bribe. *Bribery is very common in our country.*

Brick – *(noun)* **1** a small rectangular block of fired or sun dried clay, used in building. bricks collectively as a building material. *Without bricks we cannot make a house.* **2** [British, informal] a generous, helpful, and reliable person. *he is a brick.* *(verb)* block or enclose with a wall of bricks. *The door was bricked out last summer.*

Bridal – *(adj.)* of or concerning a bride or a newly married couple. *She is wearing bridal make up.*

Bridegroom – *(noun)* a man on his wedding day or juts before and after the event. *The bridegroom sat on a horse.*

Bridge – *(noun)* a card game related to whist, played by two partnerships of two players who at the beginning of each hand bid for the right to name the trump suit, the highest bid also representing a contract to make a specified number of tricks. *He is an expert bridge player.* **2** a structure that allows people or vehicles to cross on obstacle such as a river or and or railway etc. *Engineers have build a bridge over the river.*

Brief – *(noun)* a structure that allows people or vehicles to cross on obstacle such as a river or and or railway etc. *What I want say in brief is that you must leave tomorrow.* *(verb)* give essential information to someone. *I don't have time right now I'll brief you about the program tomorrow.*

Brigade – *(noun)* **1** a subdivision of an army, typically consisting of a small number of battalions and forming part of a division. *Brigadier commands a brigade which is a sub- division of army.* **2** an organization with a quasi-military structure. *The brigade has strict working environment.* **3** [informal] a group of people with a characteristic in common. *I am going to form an anti-smoking brigade.*

Brigadier – *(noun)* a rank of officer in the British army, above colonel and below major general. *A brigadier is high ranking office above the rank of colonel.*

Bright – *(adj.)* **1** giving out much light, or filled with light. *The room was bright with light.* **2** vivid and bold. *He is very bright you won't be able to defeat him in argumentation* **3** intelligent and quick, witted. *Car headlights were switched to full beam. He is a bright student.* **4** clear and typically high-pitched. *Her voice is really bright.*

Brighten– *(verb)* make lighter or brighter. *Her presence brightened up the room.*

Brilliant – *(adj.)* **1** very bright or vivid. *He is a brilliant student.* **2** exceptionally clever or talented. *Brilliant people usually succeed.* **3** [British, informal] excellent; marvellous. *(noun)* a diamond of brilliant cut.

Brills – *(noun)* Europian food fish. *I love brills.*

Brim – *(noun)* **1** the projecting edge around the bottom of a hat. *The brim of her hat is decorated with a band of flowers.* **2** the lip of a cup, bowl, etc. *The tea was filled to the brim.* *(verb)* fill or be full to the point of overflowing. *The up was brimming with coffee.*

Brimstone – *(noun)* [archaic] sulphur. *A brimstone is of medical use.* **2** a large butterfly, the male of which is bright yellow and the female greenish-white. *I chanced to see a brimstone butterfly.*

Brindle – *(adj.)* (especially of a domestic animal) brownish or tawny with streaks of other colour. *It is a brindle coloured dog.*

Brine – *(noun)* water saturated or strongly impregnated with salt; seawater. technical a strong solution of a salt or salts. *I am not fond of drinking brine water.* *(verb)* soak in or saturate with brine.

Brinjal – *(noun)* [Indian & South African] an aborigine. *I love eating brinjals.*

Brink – *(noun)* **1** the extreme edge of land before a steep slope or a body of water. *I stood on the brink of the slope and shivered as I looked down.* **2** the verge of a state or situation, typically a bad one. *He was on the brink of bankruptcy.*

Briny – *(adj.)* of salty water or the sea; salty. *(noun)* [British, informal] the sea. *This is a briny drink and I don't like it.*

Brisk – *(adj.)* active and energetic. *He has a brisk walk.* *(verb)* quicken something. *Mary brisked up her pace.*

Brisket – *(noun)* meat from the breast of a cow. *Bring me a plate of brisket.*

Bristle – *(noun)* a short, stiff hair or an animal's skin or a man's face. *He has grown a bristle on his chin.* a bristle, or a man-made substitute, used to make a brush. *(verb)* stand upright away from the skin, typically as a sign of anger or fear. react angrily or defensively. *He bristled with anger.*

British – *(adj.)* **1** of or relating to great Britain or the united kingdom. *He is a British citizen.* **2** of the British commonwealth or the British empire. *The British pronounce English differently from Indians.*

Briton – *(noun)* **1** a native or inhabitant of great Britain, or a person of British descent. *My brother is a Briton.* **2** one of the people of southern Britain before and during roman times. *My grandfather was a briton.*

Brittle – *(adj.)* hard but liable to break or shatter easily. *An ice slab is brittle.* *(noun)* a brittle sweet made from nuts and set melted suger. *She loves cooking peanut brittle.*

Broach – *(verb)* **1** raise for discussion. *I broached the issue in the meeting.* **2** pierce or open to draw liquor. *I broached the bottle open.*

Broad – *(adj.)* **1** having a distance larger than usual from side to side; wide. of a specified distance wide. *In monsoon the river becomes very broad.* **2** large in area or scope. *I have a very clear and broad view of the problem.* **3** without detail. **4** clear and unambiguous. *This is a broad outline of the plan no detail have yet come in.* **5** very noticeable and strong. *Her stature is very broad.*

Broadcast – *(noun)* message that is transmitted by radio or television. *The broadcast will come on television tonight.* *(verb)* **1** broadcast over the airwaves, as in radio or television. *We cannot broadcast this vulgar song.* **2** cause to become widely known. *He ordered to broadcast the news.*

Broadcasting – *(noun)* a medium that disseminates via telecommunication. *Broadcasting the issue from radio is one way to solve the problem.*

Brocade – *(noun)* a rich fabric woven with a raised pattern. usually with gold or silver thread. *I would like to have a brocade saree woven with gold and silver threads.* *(verb)* weave with this design. *The end of saree was brocaded.*

Broccoli – *(noun)* a cultivated variety of cabbage with heads of small green or purplish flower buds, eaten as vegetable. *So far as vitamin A is concerned broccoli is far better than cabbage.*

Brochure – *(noun)* a small book or magazine containing pictures and information about a product or service. *I visited the office of a building company and asked for their brochure so that I could read all detail at my home.*

Broil – *(noun)* [archaic] a quarrel or a commotion. *There was a broil out somewhere.*

Broke – *(adj.)* [informal] having completely run out of money. *Give me some money I am completely broke.*

Broken – *(adj.)* spoken falteringly and with many mistakes, as by a foreigner. *The foreigner spoke in broken Hindi.*

Broker – *(noun)* a person who buys and sells goods or assets for others. *He is a very intelligent broker. I feel my money is safe in his hands.* compare with broker-dealer. *(verb)* arrange or negotiate (a deal or plan). *The deal was brokered through.*

Bromide – *(noun)* [Chemistry] a compound of bromine with another element or group: methyl bromide. *People used to drink bromide for sleeplessness.*

Bromine – *(noun)* the chemical element of atomic number 35, a dark red toxic liquid halogen with a choking irritating smell. *The teacher told us the characteristics of Bromine.*

Bronchus – *(noun)* any of the major air passages of the lungs which diverge from the windpipe. *I suffer from bronchitis as my windpipe is inflamed.*

Bronze – *(noun)* **1** a yellowish-brown alloy of copper with up to one-third tin. *India has won many bronze medal in international sport events.* **2** a yellowish-brown colour. *She has worn bronze jeweller.* **3** a work of sculpture or other object made of bronze. *The bronze statue is beautiful.*

Brood – *(noun)* a family of young animals, especially birds, produced at one hatching or birth. *The hen went looking for food with her brood behind her.* *(verb)* think deeply about something that makes one unhappy. *He was sitting in the corner and brooding.*

Brook – *(noun)* a small stream. *There are many brooks in this jungle.*

Broom – *(noun)* **1** a long-handled brush of bristles or twigs, used for sweeping. *A broom is used for and cleaning the room.* **2** a shrub typically having many yellow flowers, long, thin green stems, and small or few leaves. *The broom was growing all over there garden.*

Brothel – *(noun)* building where prostitutes are available. *The politician visited the brothel.*

Brother – *(noun)* **1** a man or boy in relation to other sons and daughters of his parents. *My brother is a famous sportsman.* **2** a male associate or fellow member of an organization. *Brother was present in the Church.* **3** [Christian church] a fellow Christian. a member of a religious order of men. [exclamatory] used to express annoyance or surprise.

Brow – *(noun)* a ship's gangway or landing platform. *Ship sailed till it reached the brow.*

Brown – *(adj.)* **1** of a colour produced by mixing red, yellow, and blue, as of dark wood or rich soil. *Brown colour is my favourite.* **2** dark-skinned or suntanned. *Her brown skin was a result of tan.* *(noun)* **1** brown colour, pigment, or material. **2** used in names of various butterflies with mainly brown wings, e.g. meadow brown. *(verb)* **1** make or become brown by cooking. **2** [informal] be irritated or depressed.

Brownie – *(noun)* a small square of rich chocolate cake, with nuts. austral a piece of sweet currant bread. *Please bring me two brownies it is so rich in chocolate.*

Brownish – *(adj.)* of a colour similar to that of wood or earth. *I would rather buy a brownish pair of shoes.*

Browse – *(verb)* survey goods or text in a leisurely and casual way. computing read or survey via a network. *His favourite pastime is to browse a computer network.*

Bruise – *(noun)* an injury appearing as an area of discolored skin on the body, caused by a blow or impact rupturing underlying blood vessels. *While fighting the robbers he received many bruises.* a similar area of damage on a fruit, vegetable, or plant. *(verb)* **1** inflict a bruise on. be susceptible to bruising. **2** crush or pound.

Bruit – *(verb)* spread widely. *It has been bruited widely that he has won the election. (noun)* **1** [archaic] a report or rumour. *It is a bruit that he has been murdered.* **2** [medicine] a sound, especially an abnormal one, heard through a stethoscope. *The doctor could hear the bruit through his stethoscope.*

Brumal – *(adj.)* characteristics of or relating to winter.

Brumous – *(adj.)* filled or abounding with fog or mist. *The atmespher was brumous.*

Brunt – *(noun)* the chief impact of something bad. *I'll bear the brunt of going bankrupt.*

Brushwood – *(noun)* undergrowth, twigs, and small branches. *There was a lot of brushwood in the jungle.*

Brusque – *(adj.)* abrupt or offhand. *He left me in an brusque manner.*

Brutal – *(adj.)* **1** savagely violent. *Last night there was a brutal attack on him.* **2** without any attempt to disguise unpleasantness. *Brutal honesty.*

Brute – *(noun)* **1** a violent or savage person or animal. informal a cruel or insensitive person. *So far as manners are concerned he is a brute.* **2** an animal as opposed to a human being. *He was a brute better. (adj.)* **1** unreasoning and animal-like. **2** merely physical. *Brute force enabled him to lift the heavy weight.* **3** harsh or inescapable: brute necessity.

Brutish – *(adj.)* resembling a beast showing lack of human sensibility. *The murder was brutish.*

Bubble – *(noun)* **1** a thin sphere of liquid enclosing air or another gas. an air or gas-filled spherical cavity in a liquid or a solidified liquid such as glass. *The water was full of bubbles.* **2** a transparent domed cover or enclosure. *The bubble wrap saved the show piece. (verb)* **1** be agitated by rising bubbles of air or gas. **2** be filled with an irrepressible positive feeling. *He was bubbling with enthusiasm.*

Buccal – *(adj.)* technical of or relating to the cheek or mouth. *This is a buccal disease.*

Buccaneer – *(noun)* [historical] a pirate, originally one preying on ships in the Caribbean. *Captain Hook was a notorious buccaneer of Caribbean pirates.*

Buck – *(noun)* an object placed as a reminder in front of a poker player whose turn it is to deal. *He is to deal the cards so put the buck in front of him.*

Bucket – *(noun)* **1** a cylindrical open container with a handle, used to carry liquids. a compartment on the outer edge of a waterwheel. the scoop of a dredger or grain elevator, or one attached to the front of a digger or tractor. *Please fetch the water in bucket from the well.* **2** [informal] large quantities of liquid. *(verb)* [informal British] rain heavily. *It rained buckets.*

Buckle – *(noun)* a flat rectangular or oval frame with a hinged pin, used for joining the ends of a belt or strap. *I must have the buckle of my belt changed. (verb)* **1** fasten or decorate with a buckle. **2** bend and give way under pressure. *I buckled under the pressure of children and took them to picnic.*

Buckler – *(noun)* [historical] a small round shield held by a handle or worn on the forearm. *In old times fighters used to wear buckler on their forearm.*

Buckshot – *(noun)* coarse lead shot used in shotgun shells. *he still has his buckshot.*

Buckwheat – *(noun)* an asian plant of the dock family, producing starchy seeds used for fodder or milled into flour. *Seeds of buckwheat are milled into flour and eaten during festival when ladies break their fast.*

Bud – *(noun)* **1** a compact knob-like growth on a plant which develops into a leaf, flower, or shoot. *A bud in plant grows into a flower fruit or seed.* **2** [biology] an out-growth from an organism that separates to form a new individual asexually. *Sometimes a bud is grafted an another plant.* **3** [zoology] a rudimentary leg or other appendage of an animal which has not yet grown, or never will grow, to full size. *The human finger if cut remain as a bud. (verb)* [biology] form a bud. graft a bud of on to another plant.

Budge – *(verb)* **1** make or cause to make the slightest movement. *There is no place on the bench and I will not budge.* [informal] make room for another person by moving. **2** change or cause to change an opinion. *I won't budge an inch from my stand.*

Budget - *(noun)* **1** an estimate of income and expenditure for a set period of time. a regular estimate of national revenue and expenditure put forward by a finance minister. *This year's budget does not suit the common man.* **2** the amount of money needed or available for a purpose. *Our family budget for the month has failed due to rising prices.*

Budless - *(noun)* a partially opened flower. *The budless tree well bloom in few days.*

Buff - *(noun)* [informal] a person who is interested in a particular subject. *He is a buff on Mughal history. Ask him and he will answer any question.*

Buffalo - *(noun)* a heavily built wild ox with backswept horns. and genus bubalus. *Buffalo's milk is thicker than that of a cow.*

Buffet - *(verb)* strike repeatedly and violently. *He was buffeted heavily and consequently sent to hospital.* *(noun)* [dated] a blow.

Buffoon - *(noun)* a ridiculous but amusing person. *He amuses all by his buffoonery.*

Bug - *(noun)* **1** [entomology] an insect of a large order having piercing and sucking mouthparts, including aphids, leafhoppers, cicadas, and many other insects. [informal] any small insect. *As I slept in open I found the bugs all over me.* **2** [informal] a harmful micro-organism. an illness caused by a micro-organism. *Some bugs can cause serious harm in body.* **3** [informal] an enthusiasm for something. *These days he is bitten by the bug of mountaineering.* **4** a concealed miniature microphone as used for secret recording. *A small secret bug was fixed on the inside of his table so as to know what was he talking and where?* **5** an error in a computer program or system. *I think there is a bug in this compute.* *(verb)* informal annoy; bother. *He bugged me to no end.*

Buggy - *(noun)* **1** a small motor vehicle with an open top. *In old times people used to travel in buggy.* **2** a baby buggy. *I am going to buy a baby buggy for my child.* **3** [historical] a light horse-drawn vehicle for one or two people. *People in earlier things used to travel in buggy.*

Bugle - *(noun)* an ornamental tube-shaped bead on clothing. *She has a bugle over her Kurta.*

Build - *(verb)* **1** construct by putting parts or materials together. incorporate something as a permanent part of. *I am going to build my house on this plot.* **2** increase in size or intensity over time. use as a basis for further development. *His disease built up because he ignored it for a long.* *(noun)* the proportion of a person's or animal's body. *This animal has a large build.* the style or form of construction of something.

Built - past and past participle of build. *(adj.)* of a specified physical build. *This lady is slightly built.*

Bulge - *(noun)* **1** a rounded swelling distorting a flat surface. *We are going to play on that bulge.* **2** [military] a piece of land projecting outwards form an otherwise regular line. *There was a bulge in the land.* **3** [informal] a temporary increase. *His salary has been bulged.* *(verb)* swell or protrude to an unnatural extent. be full of and distended with.

Bulginess - *(noun)* the property possessed by a rounded convexity. *His bulkiness statue is embarrassing.*

Bulk - *(noun)* **1** the mass or magnitude of something large. a large mass or shape. large in quantity. *He supplied in bulk.* **2** the greater part. *I have received raw material in bulk.* **3** roughage in food. *The dinosaurs had bulk food.*

Bull - *(noun)* uncastrated adult male of domestic cattle. *The bull was on streets.*

Bullet - *(noun)* **1** a projectile fired from a small firearm, typically metal, cylindrical and pointed. *He fired a bullet from his pistol and the bullet went past grazing me.* **2** printing a small solid circle printed before each in a list of items. *Use bullet for points.*

Bulletin - *(noun)* a short official statement or summary of news. a regular newsletter or report. *I just read the sports news in the bulletin.*

Bullion - *(noun)* gold or silver in bulk before coining, or valued by weight. *Bullion must be a sight to see.*

Bullock - *(noun)* a castrated male bovine animal raised for beef. *(verb)* [austral, informal] work very hard. *He works hard like a bullock.*

Bull's eye - *(noun)* **1** the centre of the target in sports such as archery and darts. *Vijay Kumar hit the bull's eyes with pistol in rapid firing.* **2** a large, hard peppermint-flavoured sweet. *I like bulk's eye sweet.*

Bully - *(noun)* a person who deliberately intimidates or persecutes those who are weaker. *He is a school bully and intimidates weaker and smaller children. (verb)* intimidate.

Bulwark - *(noun)* **1** a defensive wall. *We have created the bulwark against the enemy.* **2** an extension of a ship's sides above deck level. *The bulwark of ship was broken.*

Bumper - *(noun)* **1** a horizontal bar across the front or back of a motor vehicle to reduce damage in a collision. *I'll get a bumper fixed to my car at both front and back.* **2** [Austral, informal] a cigarette butt. *(adj.)* exceptionally large or successful. *This year there was a bumper crop of wheat.*

Bumpkin - *(noun)* an unsophisticated country person. *He is a bumpkin.*

Bumpy- *(adj.)* covered with or full of bumps. *The road is bumpy.*

Bunch - *(noun)* a number of things growing or fastened in which the hair is drawn into a tight cull at the back of the head. *Her hair tightened into a bunch at the back looked beautiful.*

Bundle - *(noun)* **1** a collection of things or quantity of material tired or wrapped up together. *He carried a bundle of sticks from the jungle.* a set of nerve, muscle, or other fibers running in parallel close together. *Right now he is very upset and almost a bundle of nerves.* **2** [informal] a large amount of money. *I have got bundles of money with me. (verb)* **1** tie or roll up in or as if in a bundle. *Her clothe were all bundled.* **2** dress in many warm clothes. *I bundled up in sweater.* **3** [informal] push or carry forcibly. move in a disorganized way. *Some goons came and bundled her in the car.* **4** sleep fully clothed with another person, as a former local custom during courtship.

Bung - *(noun)* a stopper for a hole in a container. *I have closed the hole with a bung. (verb)* close with a bung. block something up.

Bunion - *(noun)* a painful swelling on the first joint of the big toe. *My bunion was painful.*

Bunk - *(noun)* a narrow shelf-like bed. *(verb)* [chiefly North American] sleep in a bunk or improvised bed in shared quarters. *Last night due to lack of space I slept on a bunk. (verb)* play truant from work or school. *She bunked the school for a movie.*

Bunker - *(noun)* **1** a large container or compartment for storing fuel. *The bunker contained petrol.* **2** a reinforced underground shelter for use in wartime. *During war soldiers live in bunkers and fight from there.*

Bunt - *(noun)* the baggy centre of a fishing net or a sail.

Bunting - *(noun)* any of a large group of seed-eating song-birds related to the finches, typically with brown streaked plumage and a boldly marked head. and other genera, family emberizidae. *Those singing and seed eating birds belong to bunting family.*

Buoy - *(noun)* an anchored float serving as a navigation mark, to show hazards, or for mooring. *I can see a buoy lets move there we can no longer keep afloat.*

Buoyancy - *(noun)* **1** a sleeveless jacket lined with buoyant material, worn for water sports. *People wear buoyant jackets for water sports.*

Burble - *(verb)* **1** make a continuous murmuring noise. *He has a bad habit of burbling.* **2** speak unintelligibly and at unnecessary length. *He was burbling around.*

Bureau - *(noun)* **1** [British] a writing desk with drawers and an angled top opening downwards to form a writing surface. *I have purchased a bureau because I have to do a lot of writing work.* **2** [North American] a chest of drawers. *Arrange your clothes in a bureau.* **3** a government department. *Central bureau of investigation is an important government department.*

Bureaucracy - *(noun)* a system of government in which most decisions are taken by state officials rather than by elected representatives. a state or organization governed according to such a system. *Bureaucracy has been the misfortune of our nation.*

Bureaucrat – *(noun)* a government official perceived as being overly concerned with procedural correctness. *Bureaucrats are not a popular breed.*

Burette – *(noun)* a graduated glass tube with a tap at one end, for delivering known volumes of a liquid. *We work with burettes in our chemistry labs.*

Burgeon – *(verb)* grow or increase rapidly. *Some plants burgeon at very fast rate.*

Burgess – *(noun)* [British archaic] an inhabitant of a town or borough with full rights of citizenship. **2** [British historical] a member of parliament of a borough, corporate town, or university. **3** a magistrate or member of the governing body of a town. *He is a burgess and an important person in parliament.*

Burglar – *(noun)* a person who commits burglary. *This burglar has been sent many times to jail.*

Burial – *(noun)* **1** the burying of a dead body. a funeral. *A lot of people were present at his burial. The burial procession of the dead leader was very long.* **2** [archaeology] a grave or the remains found in it. *Archaeological department has found many graves deep inside a historical building.*

Burliness – *(adj.)* muscular and heavily built.

Burly – *(adj.)* large and strong. *He is a very burly person.*

Burn – *(noun)* [Scottish & north English] a small stream. *There are many burns in this forest.*

Burner – *(noun)* **1** a part of a cooker, lamp, etc., that emits a flame. *The burner of this gas stove has become choked.* **2** an apparatus for burning something.

Burnish – *(verb)* polish by rubbing. *The furniture in burnished vigorously.* *(noun)* the shine on a polished surface.

Burnt – past and past participle of BURN. *This house has been burnt to ashes.*

Burrow – *(noun)* a hole or tunnel dug by a small animal as a dwelling. *Rats have made a burrow here.* *(verb)* **1** make a burrow. dig into or through something solid. **2** hide underneath or delve into something.

Burst – *(verb)* **1** break or cause to break suddenly and violently apart. *He burst out in anger.* **2** be very full: feel emotion or impulse. *The almirah is bursting with clothes.* **3** move or be opened suddenly and forcibly. issue suddenly and uncontrollably. *The door burst open and police entered.* **4** separate into single sheets. *(noun)* **1** an instance or the result of bursting. **2** a sudden brief outbreak of something violent or noisy. **3** a period of continuous effort.

Bury – *(verb)* **1** put or hide underground. place in the earth or a tomb. **2** cause to disappear or become unnoticeable. **3** involve oneself deeply in something.

Bush – *(noun)* [British] **1** a metal lining for a round hole, especially one in which an axle revolves. *The bushes of this mixer have to be changed.* **2** a sleeve that protects an electric cable where it passes through a panel.

Business – *(noun)* **1** a person's regular occupation or trade. work to be done or matters to be attended to. *I run the business of export and import of clothes.* **2** a person's concern. *You have no business here, please go away.* **3** [informal] a mater. *It is my business to find my mother.*

Businesslike – *(adj.)* efficient and practical. *His attire was all business like.*

Buskin – *(noun)* **1** [historical] a calf-high or knee-high boot. a thick-soled laced boot worn by an ancient Athenian tragic actor to gain height. *Many Americans still wear buskin.*

Bustle – *(noun)* [historical] a pad or frame worn under a skirt to puff it out behind. *Women in old times used to wear bustle under their skirts.*

Busy – *(adj.)* **1** having a great deal to do. [chiefly north American] engaged. *Right now I am very busy, please meet me tomorrow*

Butcher – *(noun)* **1** a person whose trade is cutting up and selling meat in a shop. a person who slaughters and cuts up animals for food. *The butcher living in our street is very conscious of hygiene and is very efficient.* **2** [north American, informal] a person selling refreshments, newspapers, etc. on a train or in a theatre. *(verb)* **1** slaughter or cut up for food. kill brutally. **2** ruin deliberately or through incompetence. *He has butchered his performance on the stage.*

Butter – *(noun)* a pale yellow edible fatty substance made by churning cream and used as a spread or in cooking. *Bread and butter is my favourite.* *(verb)* **1** spread with butter. **2** [informal] flatter someone. *I am buttering him so that he speaks in my favour.*

Butterfly – *(noun)* **1** any of a large group of nectar feeding lepidopterist insects with two pairs of large, typically colourful wings, distinguished from moths by having clubbed or dilated antennae, holding their wings erect when at rest, and being active by day. *It is a sight to see colourul butterflies flying or sitting on a flower. I am against catching them.* **2** having a two-lobed shape resembling the spread wings of a butterfly. *Butterfly clips are popular among girls.* **3** a showy or frivolous person. *She is showy and frivolous. People call her social butterfly.* **4** [informal] a fluttering and nauseous sensation felt in the stomach when one is nervous. *He was feeling butterflies in his stomach before the interview.* **5** a stroke in swimming in which both arms are raised out of the water and lifted forwards together. *Now there will be competition of butterfly swimming.* *(verb)* split almost in two and spread it out flat.

Buttery – *(noun)* [British] a room in a college where food is kept and sold to students. *Will you go to buttery and get some food.*

Buttock – *(noun)* either of the two round fleshy parts of the human body that form the bottom. *I feel like kicking you on buttock.*

Buttony – *(adj.)* small and shing like a shiny bead or button. *The buttony feel off from the shirt.*

Buttress – *(noun)* **1** a projecting support of stone or brick built against a wall. **2** a projecting portion of a hill or mountain. *(verb)* support with buttresses. support or strengthen. *This wall is buttressed by a stone wall. The dictator was buttressed with military force.*

Buxom – *(adj.)* having a large bosom and pleasing curves of a woman's body.

Buzz – *(noun)* **1** a low, continous humming or murmuring sound, made by or simialr to that made by an insect. *Flies were buzzing all around me.* the sound of a buzzer or telephone. [informal] a telephone call. *Suddenly the buzzer sounded and I was called in for interview.* **2** an atmosphere of excitement and activity. informal a thrill. *The room was buzzing with people.* *(verb)* **1** make a humming sound. signal with a buzzer. *When I reached the office the place was buzzing with excitement.* **2** more quickly. [informal] go away. [informal] very close to at high speed. *The car buzzed past me.* **3** have an air or excitement or purposeful activity.*The office is buzzing with the rumour that the boss has been transferred.*

By – *(prep.)* **1** through the agency or means of. indicating how something happens. *I went to Simala by bus.* **2** indicating a quantity or amount, or the size of a margin. indentifying a parameter. expressing multiplication, especially in dimensions. *He sat by me.* **3** indicating the end of a time period. *He was bitten by a dog.* **4** near to; beside. past and beyond. *Oranges are sold by dozen.* **5** during. *He passed by a narrow margin.* **6**. according to. *By the grace of God I have cleared my exam.* **7**. used in mild oaths. adverb so as to go past. *(noun)* variant spelling of bye. *8 multiplied by 8 is 6 4 8 By the time I reached his house he was gone.* **9** *By the end of century Delhi will change a lot.* **10** *Only one way traffic is permitted here by the order of the Magistrate.* **11** *I swear it by God.* **12** *He passed by me at a high speed.*

Byblow – *(noun)* [British] a man's illegitimate child. *This child is a byblow because his father was living with another woman.*

Bye – *(exclamatory)* [informal] goodbye. *Bye-Bye son! Come back soon.*

Byelection – *(noun)* the election of an MP in a single constituency of fill a vacancy arising during a government's term of office. *In the byelection held the candidate of democratic party won.*

Bygone – *(adj.)* belonging to an earlier time. *In the bygone era humans lived in caves.*

Bylaw - *(noun)* **1** [British] a regulation made by a local authority or corporation. *Houses should be built according to the bylaws of corporation.* **2** a rule made by a company or society to control the actions of its members. *There are the bylaws to which every member should adhere.*

Byname - *(noun)* a sobriquet or nickname. *His byname is Tinku.*

Bypath - *(noun)* a side road little travelled.

Byre - *(noun)* [British] a cowshed. *Cows are tied in the byre.*

Byroad - *(noun)* a minor road. *A byroad goes inside the forest.*

Bystander - *(noun)* **1** [historical] a fine textile fiber and fabric of flax. *This cloth is made bystander.* **2** [zoology] a tuft of tough silky filaments by which mussels and some other bivalves adhere to rocks and other object. *These shellfish are attached to the rock by means of tuft or bystander.*

Byword - *(noun)* **1** a person or thing cited as a notable example or embodiment of something. *This man is a byword of honesty.* **2** a word or expression summarizing a thing's characteristic or a person's principles. *The byword written by him explained his principles.*

Cc

C- the third letter of the English alphabet. (1) The first note in the natural major scale in music. (2) An academic mark indicating the third highest standard.

C- *(abbreviation)* **1** (cricket) caught by. *The ball was caught by the fielder.* **2** cent(s). **3** centi-: cst (centistokes). **4** (c.) century or centuries. *Sachin hit a century.* **5** circa.

Cabal - *(noun)* **1** a secret political clique or faction. *Cabal was a much feared organization in Russia during cold war.*

Cabaret - *(noun)* entertainment held in a nightclub or restaurant while the audience eat or drink at tables, a nightclub or restaurant where such entertainment is performed. *I went to a famous cabaret, I dined there as well as enjoyed the dance performance on the stage.*

Cabbage - *(noun)* **1** a cultivated plant eaten as a vegetable, having thick green or purple leaves surrounding a spherical heart or head of young leaves. *Of all the vegetables cabbage is my favourite.* **2** [informal, derogatory] a person whose physical or mental activity is impaired or destroyed as a result of injury or illness. *Due to the least attack last year he is reduced to a cabbage state.*

Cabin - *(noun)* **1** a private room or compartment on a ship. *I am going to my cabin to sleep, please done disturb me.* **2** the passenger compartment in an aircraft. *The lives in a small cabin is jungle. There are cabin for private use in an airport.* **3** a small wooden shelter or house. *(verb)* dated confine in a small place.

Cabinet - *(noun)* **1** a cupboard with drawers or shelves for storing or displaying articles, a wooden box, container, or place of furniture housing a radio, television set, or speaker. *A wooden almirah which has various centimes for radio, TV, etc.* **2** the committee of senior ministers responsible for controlling government policy; a body of advisers to the president, composed of the heads of the exeoutive departments of the government. *Cabinet in the most powerful body in central government made of cabinet ministers. It controls the entire affairs of the country.*

Cable - *(noun)* **1** a thick rope of wire or hemp, typically used for construction, mooring ships, and towing vehicles; the chain of a ship's anchor; architecture a moalding resembling twisted rope. "*An underground cable.*" **2** an insulated wire or wires having a protective casing and used for transmitting electricity or telecommunication signals. *I have just sent a cablegram or wire to my father.* *(verb)* **1** a cablegram. *This is a cable for television, please don't distroy it.* **2** nautical a length of 200 yards or 240 yards. *(verb)* **1** send a cablegram to. **2** provide with power lines or other equipment necessary for cable television.

Caboose - *(noun)* **1** [North American] railway wagon with accommodation for the train crew, typically attached to the end of the train. *A caboose has been attached to the end of of trains in which the train crew is travelling.* **2** [archaic] a kitchen on a ship's deck. *Caboose is at the end of train.*

Cacao - *(noun)* **1** bean-like seeds from which cocoa, cocoa butter, and chocolate are made. **2** the small tropical American evergreen tree, also called chocolate tree.

Cache - *(noun)* **1** a hidden store of things. *You will find this item in cache which is a hidden store of things.* **2** computing an auxiliary memory form which high-speed retrieval is possible. *(verb)* store in a cache.

Cachectic - *(noun)* general ill health with emaciation, usually accruing in association with cancer or a chronic infections disease.

Cachet – *(noun)* **1** prestige. **2** a distinguishing mark or seal. *The MP's car carried a cachet.* **3** a flat capsule enclosing a dose of unpleasant tasting medicine.

Cachexy – *(noun)* Any general reduction in vitality and strength of body and mind resulting from a debilitating chronic disease. *This cachexy has weakened his body.*

Cachinnate – *(verb)* [poetic/literary] laugh loudly. *He is so funny, we cachinnated until our sides hurt.*

Cachou – *(noun)* a pleasant-smelling lozenge sucked to mask bad breath. *He is chewing lozenge. Cachou, so that he can hide the bad smell coming from his mouth.*

Cackle – *(verb)* **1** give a raucous clucking cry; make a similar sound when laughing. **2** talk inconsequentially and at length. *(noun)* a cackling sound.

Cactus – *(noun)* a succulent plant of a large family native to arid regions of the new world, with a thick fleshy stem which typically bears spines, lacks leaves, and has brilliantly coloured flowers. *I have a grand collection of cactus at home.*

Cad – *(noun)* a man who behaves dishonorably, especially towards a woman. *He is a cad.*

Caddish – *(noun)* a small moth-like insect of an order having aquatic larvae that build protective cases of sticks, stones, etc. *I have seen caddish. It is an insect having a watery larvae which sticks to a stone.*

Cadence – *(noun)* **1** a modulation or inflection of the voice. **2** [music] a sequence of notes or chords comprising the close of a musical phrase.

Cadet – *(noun)* a young trainee in the armed services or police; a secondary school pupil; a junior branch of a family.

Cadge – *(verb)* [informal] ask for or obtain. *(noun)* a padded wooden frame on which hooded hawks are carried to the field. *My uncle was carrying a cadge to fields. In the cadge were sitting hooded hawks that was going to hunt.*

Cadmium – *(noun)* the chemical element of atomic number 48, a silvery-white metal resembling zinc. *Have you seen cadmium? It is a silvery white metal resembling zinc.*

Cadre – *(noun)* **1** a small group of people trained for a particular purpose or profession. **2** a group of activists in a communist or other revolutionary organization.

Cafe – *(noun)* **1** a small restaurant selling light meals and drinks. *A cafe suits me very well; there is light and the drinks are excellent.* **2** [north American] a bar or nightclub.

Cage – *(noun)* **1** a structure of bars in which birds or other animals are confined. *The man puts there birds in a cage. What a pity? Can a man be so cruel?* **2** an open framework forming the compartment in a lift. **3** a structure of crossing bares or wires designed to hold or support something; [baseball] a portable mesh backstop used for batting practice. *(verb)* confine in or as in a cage.

Cain – *(noun)* [informal] create trouble or a commotion. *These four men are responsible for caining in the public.*

Cairn – *(noun)* **1** a mound of rough stoned built as a memorial or landmark; a prehistoric burial mound made of stones. *I have just bought a cairn.* **2** a small terrier of a breed with short legs, a longish body, and shaggy coat. *See that cairn! It is a prehistoric burial.*

Caisson – *(noun)* **1** a large water light chamber in which underwater construction work may be carried out. *Water construction can also be carried in caisson caisson.* **2** a vessel or watertight structure used as a gate across the entrance of a dry dock or basin.

Caitiff – *(noun)* [archaic] a contemptible or cowardly person. *He is a caitiff and I am not ready to talk to such people.*

Cajole – *(verb)* persuade to do something by sustained coaxing or flattery. *I cajoled him into going to see a movie with me.*

Cake – *(noun)* **1** an item of soft sweet food made from baking a mixture or flour, fat, eggs, sugar, etc. **2** an item of savoury food formed into a flat round shape, and baked or fried. **3** the amount of money or assets regarded as available for sharing: a fair slice of the education cake. *(verb)* cover and become encrusted on.

Calabash - *(noun)* **1** an ever-green tropical American tree which bears fruit in the form of large woody gourds. **2** a water container, tobacco pipe. or other object made from the dried shell of a gourd.

Calamitous - *(adjective)* [of events] having extremely unfortunate or dire consequences; bringing ruin. *The sudden expanding of the volcano was calamitous.*

Calamity - *(noun)* an event causing great and often sudden damage or distress. *There was an earthquake and sudden calamity followed.*

Calash - *(noun)* another term for caleche.

Calcareous - *(adjective)* containing calcium carbonate; chalky. *This substance is chalky and contains calcium carbonate.*

Calcify - *(verb)* harden by deposition of or conversion into calcium carbonate or some other insoluble calcium compounds. *This compound has calcified.*

Calcine - *(verb)* reduce, oxidize, or desiccate by roasting or strong heat. *My chemistry teacher told me to calcine the compound.*

Calcium - *(noun)* the chemical element of atomic number 20, a soft grey reactive metal of the alkaline earth metal group. *Calcium is essential for bone health.*

Calculate - *(verb)* determine mathematically. *I can calculate this sum easily.* **2** include as an essential element in one's plans. **3** intend to have a particular effect. *Calculated move.*

Calculation - *(noun)* **1** a mathematical determination of quantity or extent. *Calculation of this sum is not possible.* **2** an assessment of the risks or effects of a course of action.

Calculator - *(noun)* something used for making mathematical calculations, in particular a small electronic device with a keyboard and a visual display. *For quick calculation, there is an electronic device called calculator.*

Calendar - *(noun)* **1** a chart or series of pages showing the days, weeks, and months of a particular year. *I have bought a beautiful colourful calendar with important dates and events.* **2** a system by which the beginning, length, and sub-divisions of the year are fixed. **3** a list or schedule of special days, events, etc. *(verb)* enter in a calendar. *It was at their discretion whether to index or calendar the records.*

Calendula - *(noun)* a plant of a genus that includes the common or pot marigold. *Calendula is a famous medicinal plant.*

Calf - *(noun)* **1** a young bovine animal, especially a domestic cow or bull in its first year. *The young one of bovine family is called calf.* **2** the young of some other large mammals, such as elephants. **3** a floating piece of ice detached from an iceberg.

Calibre - *(noun)* **1** quality of character or level of ability; the standard reached by something. *He is a man of high calibre.* **2** the internal diameter of a gun barrel; the diameter of a bullet, shell, or rocket. *This is a 9mm calibre gun.*

Calico - *(noun)* [British] a type of plain white or unbleached cotton cloth. [North American] printed cotton fabric. *(adjective)* [North American] (of an animal, typically a cat) multicoloured or piebald. *I like to wear dresses made of calico cloth, especially the printed ones.*

Calif - *(abbreviation)* California. *California is my favourite city.*

Calix - *(noun)* variant spelling of calyx. *I love to see calix, the thing of leave that covers a flower bed.*

Calk - *(noun & verb)* US spelling of Caulk. *If a mason is not available You can yourself take same calk a water dry substance and can fill the cracks and joints.*

Call - *(verb)* **1** cry out of in order to summon them or attract their attention, telephone. *I called out to my friend to stop.* **2** pay a brief visit, stop to collect. stop at (a specified station) on a particular route. *I will call upon you tomorrow.* **3** give a specified name; address by a specified name, title, etc. consider or describe as being. *I will stop right over here and give you a call.* **4** fix a date or time for (a meeting, strike, or election). predict the result of (an election or a vote). *Out of all Ramesh is the only person I would like to call upon.* **5** [Computing] cause the execution of (a subroutine).

Mr. Pant's name was called out to give evidence. **6** bring into court to give evidence. *I will call a meeting tomorrow to finalize the election agenda.* **7** inspire or urge to do something. *I will now call out the name o the miner candidate.* **8** bridge make during the auction: her partner called. **9** Cricket (of an umpire) no-ball for throwing. *The umpire called out 'No ball'.* *(noun)* **1** a cry made as a summons or to attract attention. a telephone communication. *Soldiers I call upon you to attack the enemy.* **2** an appeal or demand for. a demand or need for: there is little call for antique furniture. *There is little call for antique furniture.* **3** a vocation: his call to a disciple. *His call is to be a doctor.* **4** a brief visit. *I called upon him for a marvel.* **5** a shout by an official in a game indicating that the ball had gone out of play or that a rule has been breached. *The referee called as the ball went out of bonding line.*

Call-boy – *(noun)* a person in a theatre who summons actors when they are due on stage. *The call-boy called out to acters when they had to be present is the stage.*

Calligraphy – *(noun)* decorative handwriting or handwritten lettering, the art of producing this. *If you wish to see the art of calligraphy visit the scribes near Jama Masjid.*

Callisthenic – *(Plural noun)* gymnastic exercises to achieve bodily fitness and grace of movement. *I took up callisthenic to develop grace and fitness of the body.*

Callosity – *(noun)* [technical] callus, cruel. *Many dictators had shoun callocity.*

Callous – *(adjective)* insensitive and cruel. *(noun)* variant spelling of CALLUS. *This boy is simply callous.*

Callow – *(adjective)* inexperienced and immature. *He is callow.*

Callus – *(noun)* a thickened and hardened part of the skin or soft tissue, especially one caused by friction. [medicine] the bony healing tissue which forms around the ends of broken bone. *Do you see the bony healing part which has grown round the broken bone. It is called callus.*

Calm – *(adjective)* **1** not showing or feeling nervousness, anger, or other emotions. *His attitude was calm and cool.* **2** peaceful and undisturbed. *(noun)* **1** the state or fact of being peaceful or tranquil. *He calmed down listening to my soothing works.* **2** an area of the sea without wind. *I have rarely seen such calm sea.* *(verb)* make or become tranquil and quiet.

Calmative – *(adjective)* having a sedative effect. *(noun)* a calmative drug. *Many drugs are calmative by nature.*

Calmly – *(adverb)* in a calm manner. *He calmly responds to my harsh call.*

Calomel – *(noun)* miraculous chloride, a white powder formerly used as a purgative. *Where can I get calomel from?*

Caloric – *(adjective)* [chiefly north Americanor technical] of or relating to heat; calorific. *(noun)* [physics] a hypothetical fluid substance formerly thought to be responsible for the phenomenon of heat. *Caloric was previously thought to be rated to heat.*

Calorie – *(noun)* the energy needed to raise the temperature of 1 gram of water through 1°C, equal to one thousand small calories and often used to measure the energy value of foods. *Don'it eat fried food, it has lots of caloric value.*

Calorimeter – *(noun)* an apparatus for measuring the amount of heat involved in a chemical reaction or other process. *He used a calorimeter to measure the heat generated in the reaction.*

Calumniate – *(verb)* [formal] make false and defamatory statements about someone. *He calumniated me but I kept my calm.*

Calumny – *(noun)* the making of false and defamatory statements about someone. *The calumny he made against me made me furriness and I slapped him.* *(verb)* [formal] calumniate.

Calve – *(verb)* **1** give birth to a calf. *The cow calved.* **2** easily (of a mass of ice) split off from an iceberg or glacier. *A huge mass of ice calved from the iceberg.*

Calx – *(noun)* [chemistry, archaic] a powdery metallic oxide formed when an ore or mineral has been heated. *Calx is a residual substance.*

Calyx - *(noun)* **1** [botany] the sepals of a flower, typically forming a whorl that encloses the petals and forms a protective layer around a flower an bud. **2** [zoology] a cup-like cavity or structure, in particular part of the pelvis of a mammalian kidney.

Cam - *(noun)* **1** a projection on a rotating part in machinery, designed to make sliding contact with another part while rotating and impart reciprocal or variable motion to it.

Cambric - *(noun)* a lightweight, closely woven white linen or cotton fabric. *I always like to wear lightweight cambric shirts.*

Came - *(noun)* each of a number of strips forming a framework for enclosing a pane of glass, especially in a leaded window.

Camel - *(noun)* **1** a large, long-necked, mainly domesticated ungulate mammal of arid country, with long slender legs, broad cushioned feet, and either one or tow humps on the back. *While in desert I rode a camel and enjoyed the ride.* **2** a fabric made from camel hair. *I am sitting on a seat made of camel hair.* **3** an apparatus for raising a sunken ship, consisting of one or more watertight chests to provide buoyancy.

Camelopard - *(noun)* [archaic] a camelopard. *Giraffe is a tall and very long necked animal.*

Cameo - *(noun)* **1** a peace of jewellery consisting of a portrait in profile carved in relief on a background of a different colour. *I would like to buy that cameo with the portrait in the profile.* **2** a short piece of writing which neatly encapsulates something. **3** a small distinctive part in a play or film, played by a distinguished actor. *That cameo in the film played by the great actor was wonderful.*

Camera - *(noun)* a device for recording visual images in the form of photographs, cinema film, or video signals. *I have bought the latest digital camera with multiple devices.*

Camisole - *(noun)* a women's loose-fitting undergarment for the upper body. *The camisole she is wearing is very colourful.*

Camouflage - *(noun)* **1** the disguising of military personnel and equipment by painting or covering them to make them blend in with their surroundings. The clothing or materials used for such a purpose. **2** the natural closuring or form of an animal which enables it to blend in with its surroundings. *The rat camouflaged in the bush.* *(verb)* hide or disguise by means of camouflage.

Camp - *(noun)* a place with temporary accommodation of huts, tents, or other structures. *"I am staying in a camp."* *(verb)* live for some time in a tent, especially while on holiday. *"This is a holiday Park which you can camp."*

Campaign - *(noun)* **1** a series of military operations intended to achieve an objective in a particular area. **2** an organized course of action to achieve a goal. *They behave in a very stylish and effeminate way.* *(verb)* work in an organized and active way towards a goal. *Over 100p.c. literacy campaign will certainly prove a success.*

Camphor - *(noun)* a white volatile crystalline substance with an aromatic smell and bitter taste, occurring in certain essential oils. *Camphor has an aromatic smell.*

Can - *(abbreviation)* Canada or Canadian.

Canal - *(noun)* **1** an artificial waterway allowing the passage of boats inland or conveying water for irrigation. *Our village has a very long canal and we are fond of bathing in it. It was made by government.* **2** a tubular duct in a plant or animal conveying food, liquid, or air.

Canard - *(noun)* **1** an unfounded rumour or story. *It is a canard that he met with an accident. I am just coming after meeting him, he is alright.* **2** a small wing-like projection on an aircraft forward of the main wing, for extra stability or control. *The canard was destroyed.*

Canary - *(noun)* **1** a bright yellow finch with a melodious song, popular as a cage bird. *I have just bought a canary. It cost me a fortune. Come today and we shall hear her singing.* **2** a bright yellow colour. *I love canary colour.* **3** [historical] a sweet wine from the canary islands, similar to Madeira. *The canary wine from canary Islands tastes amazing.*

Cancel - *(verb)* **1** decision that will not take place; annul or revoke. *The meeting has been cancelled.* **2** mark or tear to show that it has been used or invalidate. **3** neutralize or negate the effect of (another). **4** [mathematics] delete from both sides of an equation or from the numerator and denominator of fraction. *(noun)* **1** a mark made on a postage stamp to show that it has been used. *This postage stamp bears a mark which shrews that it has been used.* **2** printing a new page or section inserted in a book to replace the original text. *The orginal page of the book was cancelled and a new one was printed and inserted.*

Cancellation – *(noun)* the act of cancelling calling off some arrangement. *The project was threatened with cancellation.*

Cancer – *(noun)* **1** [Astronomy] a constellation said to represent a crab crushed under the foot of Hercules. **2** [Astrology] the fourth sign of the zodiac, which the sun enters at the northern summer solstice. *Her sun sign is cancer.*

Candle – *(noun)* **1** a cylinder of wax or tallow with a central wick which is lit to produce light as it burns. **2** [physics] a unit of luminous intensity, superseded by the candela. *(verb)* test for freshness or fertility by holding it to the light.

Candlemas – *(noun)* a Christian festival held on 2nd February to commemorate the purification of the virgin marry and the presentation of Christ in the temple. *I joined and candlemas last year loved it.*

Candour – *(noun)* the quality of being open and honest. *I like his candour character.*

Candy – *(noun)* **1** [north American] sweets; confectionery. *Children love candies a lot.* **2** [chiefly British] sugar crystallized by repeated boiling and slow evaporation. *(verb)* preserve by coating and impregnating it with a sugar syrup. *This candied fruit tastes good!*

Cane – *(noun)* **1** the hollow jointed stem of tall reeds, grasses, etc., especially bamboo or the slender; pliant stem of plants such as rattan. a woody stem of a raspberry or related plant. *He was beaten with a cane as punishment.* **2** a length of cane or a slender stick used as a support for plants, a walking stick, or an instrument of punishment. *Sometimes a slender stick of cane is used to support a plant.* *(verb)* **1** beat with a cane as a punishment. **2** [British informal] use recklessly or without restraint. *He caned her remorselessly.*

Canister – *(noun)* **1** a round or cylindrical container used for storing food, chemicals, rolls of film, etc. *We keep chemicall, film rolls, food etc. in canisters.* **2** [historical] small bullets packed in cases that fit the bore of a gun.

Canker – *(noun)* **1** destructive fungal disease of trees that results in damage to the bark. an open lesion in plant tissue caused by infection or injury. fungal rot in parsnips, tomatoes, or other vegetables. **2** an ulcerous condition of an animal, especially an inflammation of the ear caused by a mite infestation. [chiefly North American] a small ulcer of the mouth or lips. *Animals also get infected with canker, having ulcers in mouth or car.* *(verb)* **1** become infected with canker. **2** infect with a pervasive and corrupting bitterness.

Cannon – *(noun)* **1** a large, heavy piece of artillery formerly used in warfare; an automatic heavy gun that fires shells from an aircraft or tank. *Once for a way I saw artillery, an automatic heavy gun fire that fires shells from an aircraft or tank.* **2** [billiards & snooker, chiefly British] a stroke in which the cue ball strikes two balls successively. *That was a cannon shot.* **3** [Engineering] a heavy cylinder or hollow drum rotating independently on a shaft. *(verb)* [chiefly British] collide with something forcefully or at an angle. [billiards & snooker]. *The couple behind almost cannoned into us.*

Cannonade – *(noun)* a period of continuous heavy gunfire. *There was cannonade and a heavy gun fire was discharged continuously at the border.* *(verb)* discharge heavy guns continuously.

Cannula – *(noun)* [surgery] a thin tube inserted into the body to administer medication, drain off fluid, or introduce a surgical instrument. *When my father was being operated upon cannula was inserted in to his body.*

Cannular – *(adjective)* constituting a tube, having hallow tubes. *This is a cannular tree; it is hollow.*

Canny – *(adjective)* **1** shrewd, especially in financial or business matters. *He is a canny fellow smart and shred in business and financial matters.* **2** [North English & Scottish] pleasant; nice. *She is a canny lass.*

Canoe – *(noun)* a narrow keelless boat with pointed ends propelled with a paddle. *(verb)* travel in or paddle a canoe. *Once in a river in Africa I travelled in a canoe. It was great fun. I felt like palling into water any time.*

Canon – *(noun)* **1** a general law, rule principle, or criterion by which something is judged. *The appointment violated the canons of fair play and equal opportunity.* **2** a collection or list of sacred books accepted as genuine. *The Biblical canon.*

Canonical – *(adjective)* **1** according to or ordered by canon law. *The canonical rites of the Roman Church.* **2** inclveled in the list of sacred books officially accepted as genuine. *The canonical Gospels of the New Testament.* *(noun)* the prescribed official dress of the clergy. *Cardinal Bea in full canonicals.*

Canopy – *(noun)* **1** a clothe covering over a throne, bed, etc. *This is a four poster bed complete with drapes and a canopy.* **2** the uppermost branches of the trees in a forest, forming a more or less continuous layer of foliage. *Monkeys spend hours everyday sitting high in the canopy.* *(verb)* cover or provide with a canopy. *I so want a canopied bed.*

Canorous – *(adjective)* rare melodious or resonant. *He has got a canorous voice.*

Cant – *(noun)* **1** hypocritical and sanctimonious talk. **2** derogatory language peculiar to a specified group denoting a phrase or catchword temporarily current. *Thiever's cant.* *(verb)* talk hypocritically and sanctimoniously. *If they'd stop canting about 'honest work' they might get somewhere.*

Cantab – *(abbreviation)* of Cambridge university.

Cantaloupe – *(noun)* a small round melon of a variety with orange flesh and ribbed skin. *In taste I found cantaloupe better them ordinary melon.*

Cantankerous – *(adjective)* bad-tempered, argumentative, and uncooperative. *He is a cantankerous fellow.*

Canteen – *(noun)* **1** a restaurant in a workplace or educational establishment. *I take lunch in my school canteen.* **2** [British] a specially designed case or box containing a set of cutlery. **3** a small water bottle, as used by soldiers or campers. *We are all carrying our canteens because we are going into an arid area.*

Canter – *(noun)* pace of a horse between a trot and a gallop, with not less than one foot on the ground at any time; a ride on a horse at such a speed. *I rode a cantering horse.* *(verb)* move at this pace.

Canticle – *(noun)* a hymn or chant forming a regular part of a church service. *A canticle was being sung in the church.*

Cantilever – *(noun)* a long projecting beam or girder fixed at only one end, used chiefly in bridge construction; a bracket or beam projecting from a wall to support a balcony, cornice, etc. *(verb)* support by a cantilever or cantilevers. *The cantilever projecting from the wall is supporting this balcony.*

Canton – *(noun)* **1** a political or administrative subdivision of a country; a state of the Swiss confederation. *Canton is a state of the Swiss confederation.* **2** [heraldry] a square charge smaller than a quarter and positioned in the upper corner of a shield.

Cantonment – *(noun)* a military camp, especially a permanent military station in British India. *My uncle, a military officer, stays in cantonment area which is a permanent military station.*

Canvas – *(noun)* **1** a strong, coarse unbleached cloth used to make sails, tents, etc., and as a surface for oil painting; a piece of canvas prepared for use as the surface for an oil painting; the floor of a boxing or wrestling ring, having a canvas covering. *I use canvas for oil painting.* **2** either of a racing boat's tapering ends, originally covered with canvas. *(verb)* cover with canvas. *The door had been canvassed over.*

Canvass – *(verb)* **1** solicit votes from (electors); question in order to ascertain their opinion on something. *He is canvassing for election at full speed.* **2** [British] propose for discussion. *(noun)* an act of canvassing. *Canvassing is an art which not many people know of.*

Canyon – *(noun)* a deep gorge, especially one with a river flowing through it. *Grand canyon of America is worth a visit.*

Cap – *(abbreviation)* **1** capacity. *I don't have capacity for such hard work.* **2** capital (city) *Delhi is the capital of India.* **3** capital letter. *Many words are written with capital letters.*

Capability – *(noun)* power or ability to do something; an undeveloped or unused faculty. *I have capability of speaking five languages.*

Capable – *(adjective)* **1** having the ability or quality necessary to do something; open to or admitting of something. *I am capable of crossing this river.* **2** competent. *She looked enthusiastic and capable.*

Capacious – *(adjective)* having a lot of space inside; roomy. *This building is quite capacious.*

Capacitate – *(verb)* **1** [formal or archaic] make capable or legally competent. *He has been capacitated to become a first class lawyer.* **2** [physiology] undergo changes inside the female reproductive tract enabling them to penetrate and fertilize an ovum.

Capacity – *(noun)* **1** the maximum amount that something can contain or produce; fully occupying the available space; the total cylinder volume that is swept by the pistons in an internal-combustion engine. *This glass is full of water. It has no more capacity to contain more.* **2** the ability or power to do something; a person's legal competence. *I caint walk now. I have no more capacity to walk.* **3** a specified role or position. *I have the capacity to lift this weight.*

Cape – *(noun)* a headland or promontory; the former cape province of South Africa. *Cap is a piece of land jutting into the sea; e.g., cape of good hope.*

Caper – *(verb)* skip or dance about in a lively or playful way. *(noun)* **1** a playful skipping movement. *She capered softly and lightly on the stage.* **2** [informal] an illicit or ridiculous activity or escapade. *He often indulges is capers.*

Capful – *(noun)* the amount that a cap can hold. *I gave him a capful of cough syrup.*

Capillarity – *(noun)* the tendency of a liquid in a narrow tube or pore to rise or fall as a result of surface tension. *The first recorded observation of capillarity action was by Leonardo da Vinci*

Capillary – *(noun)* **1** [anatomy] any of the fine branching blood vessels that form a network between the arterioles and venues. *Very small fines capillaries that join the arteries and veins.* **2** a tube with an internal diameter of hair-like thinness. *(adjective)* of or relating to capillaries or capillarity.

Capital – *(noun)* [architecture] the distinct, typically broader section at the head of a pillar or column. *There are three lions on the capital of Ashoka.*

Capitulate – *(verb)* cease to resist an opponent or an unwelcome demand; surrender. *The army capitulated before the enemy forces.*

Capon – *(noun)* a castrated domestic cock fattened for eating. *This is our fattened capon we intend to cut it today.*

Caprice – *(noun)* **1** a sudden and unaccountable change of mood or behaviour. *Her caprices made his life impossible.* **2** [music] another term for CAPRICCIO. *As he is a man of caprice, it is difficult to deal with him.*

Capricious – *(adjective)* relating to or resembling a goat or goats. *He is capricious and covet to be trusted.*

Capricorn – *(noun)* [astrology] the tenth sign of the zodiac which the sun enters at the northern winter solstice. *I was born under the sign of Capricorn.*

Caprine – *(adjective)* relating to or resembling a goat or goats. *"Caprine arthritis."*

Capsicum – *(noun)* **1** the fruit of a tropical American plant, of which sweet peppers and chilli peppers are varieties. *I am very fond of eating capsicum.* **2** the plant of the nightshade family from which such fruits come.

Capsize – *(verb)* be overturned in the water. *The boat capsized and sank into water.*

Captain – *(noun)* **1** the person in command of a ship. the pilot in command of a civil aircraft. a rank of naval officer above commander and below commodore. *It is my ambition to become a captain either of a ship or of an aeroplane.* **2** a rank of officer in the army and in the US and Canadian air forces, above lieutenant and below major. **3** a police officer in charge of a precinct. *In some countries police chiefs are also called captain.* **4** the leader of a team, especially in sports. *Dhoni is a very good cricket captain.* *(verb)* serve as the captain of.

Caption – *(noun)* **1** a title or brief explanation appended to an illustration or cartoon; a piece of text appearing on screen as part of a film or broadcast. *I enjoyed that Russian film simply because it had captions. The cartoon film was provided with captious.* **2** [law] the heading of a legal document. *(verb)* provide with a caption.

Captious – *(adjective)* [formal] tending to find fault or raise petty objections. *She was a captious teacher.*

Captivate – *(verb)* attract and hold the interest and attention of; charm. *The film captivates the audience.*

Captive – *(noun)* a person who has been taken prisoner or confined. *(adjective)* **1** imprisoned or confined. *He has been captive.* **2** having no freedom to choose and alternative. *She held the audience captive by her songs.* **3** controlled by and reserved for a particular orgainzation. *This is a captive power plant.*

Captor – *(noun)* a person who imprisons or confines another. *She is so beautiful as to be my captor.*

Capture – *(verb)* **1** take into one's possession or control by force. make a move that secures the removal of an opposing piece. *We captured the territories of enemy forces.* **2** [physics] absorb. **3** record or express accurately in words or pictures. *I have captured every detail of the scenic beauty of this place in words as well as pictures.* **4** cause to be stored in a computer. *All this matter has been captured in computer.* *(noun)* **1** the action of capturing or of being captured. *Some kidnappers captured a rich man's on for ransom.* **2** a person or thing that has been captured. *The escaped convict has been captured.*

Caracole – *(noun)* a half turn to the right or left by a horse. *(verb)* perform a caracole. *The horse was performing a caracole.*

Carat – *(noun)* **1** a unit of weight for precious stones and pearls, equivalent to 200 milligrams. *Maharaja jewellers is her favourite. She always buys carat gold orna-ments from them.* **2** a measure of the purity of gold, pure gold being 24 carats. *This gold is 24 carats.*

Caravan – *(noun)* **1** [British] a vehicle equipped for living in, usually designed to be towed. *While in Rajsthan I came across a long colourful caravan.* **2** [north American] a covered truck. **3** [historical] a group of people travelling together across a desert in Asia or North Africa. *I went along with the caravan.*

Carbide – *(noun)* [chemistry] a compound of carbon with a metal or other element: silicon carbide. *Carbide is a compound of carbon with a metal.*

Carbon – *(noun)* **1** the chemical element with atomic number 6, non-metal which has two main forms, occurs in impure form in charcoal, soot, and coal, and is present in all organic compounds. *Lots of writing problems have been solved by invention of carbon paper.* **2** a rod of carbon in an are lamp. *All lamps have a carbon rod.* **3** a piece of carbon paper; a carbon copy. *He is a carbon copy of his father.*

Carbonic – *(adjective)* of or relating to carbon or carbon dioxide. *This drink is carbonic.*

Carbuncle – *(noun)* **1** a severe abscess or multiple boil in the skin. *It is a bad boil on year arm. You should at once consult a skin surgeon.* **2** a bright red gem. *He was wearing a round ring of carbuncle.*

Card – *(verb)* comb and clean with a sharp-toothed instrument to disentangle the fibers before spinning. *(noun)* a toothed implement or machine for this purpose. *A sharp toothed comb to clean fibers before spinning.* **2** *A pack of playing cards has 52 cards.* **3** *I am not using my credit card these days.* **4** *I have received your greeting card, thanks.*

Cardamon – *(noun)* the aromatic seeds of a plant of the ginger family, used as a spice. *I like a bit of cardamom in my tea along with ginger.*

Cardiac – *(adjective)* of or relating to the heart. *He died of cardiac arrest.*

Cardinal - *(noun)* **1** a leading dignitary of the roman catholic church, nominated by and having the power to elect the pope. **2** a deep scarlet colour like that of a cardinal's cassock. *The colour of her skirt is deep scarlet like that of cardinal's cassock.* **3** an American songbird of which the male is partly or mostly red and which typically has a crest. cardinals and other species, [subfamily] cardinalinae. *American songbird cardinal has a crest and is of red colour.*

Cardiograph - *(noun)* an instrument for recording heart muscle activity. *Doctors use cardiograph to measure heart activity.*

Care - *(noun)* **1** the provision of what is necessary for the health, welfare, maintenance, and protection of someone or something. *The adopled son was well taken care of.* [British] protective custody or guardianship provided for children by a local authority. *In Britain local authorities take care of children.* **2** serious attention or consideration applied to an action or plan. a feeling of or occasion for anxiety. *I'll take care of you my dear, don't you wary. (verb)* **1** feel concern or interest. *These are uncertain times we should plan out with great care.* feel affection or liking. like to have or be willing to do something.*I care for you therefore I'll never hurt you.* **2** look after and provide for the needs of. *Since I care for you I'll do whatever you say*

Career - *(noun)* **1** an occupation undertaken for a significant period of a person's life, usually with opportunities for progress. *I was very worried as to what career I was going to launch myself upon.* the progress through history of an institution or organization. *Without career there is no life.* working with commitment in a particular profession. *a career diplomat.* pursuing a profession. *Right from class X a student should become career conscious so that he can choose a suitable stream for himself. (verb)* move swiftly and in an uncontrolled way. *The car careered out of control.*

Careful - *(adjective)* **1** taking care to avoid mishap or harm; cautious; protective of; prudent in the use of. *Be careful while driving lest you meet with an accident.* **2** done with or showing thought and attention. *He is a very careful person. He carefully went through.*

Careless - *(adjective)* **1** not giving sufficient attention or thought to avoiding harm or mistakes; not concerned or worried about; showing no interest or effort. *He is careless and stupid with most of the things.* casual. *He takes everything in a careless way. Don't assign any important work to him he is a careless fellow.*

Caress - *(verb)* touch or stroke gently or lovingly. *(noun)* a gentle or loving touch. *I caressed her with love and affection.*

Caret - *(noun)* a mark placed below a line of text to indicate a proposed insertion. *Wherever you wish to in sort insert put a mark or caret under it.*

Cargo - *(noun)* goods carried commercially on a ship, aircraft, or truck. *A cargo ship is different from passenger ship.*

Carking - *(adjective)* [archaic] causing distress or worry. *He is a carking fellow.*

Carl - *(noun)* [archaic] a man of low birth. *He is a Carl and I don't want to have relations with him.*

Carline - *(noun)* a this tile-like European plant with flower heads that bear shing persistent straw-coloured bracts. *Caroline is a plant with medicinal properties.*

Carminative - *(adjective)* relieving flatulence. (noun) a carminative drug. *Carminative is a wind relieving drug from the stomach.*

Carmine - *(noun)* a vivid crimson pigment made from cochineal. *'A carmine rose.'*

Carnage - *(noun)* the killing of a large number of people. *Carnage took place when Nadir Shah entered Delhi.*

Carnal - *(adjective)* relating to physical, especially sexual, needs and activities. *Sexual needs are regarded as carnal. Don't focus more on having carnal pleasure.*

Carnation - *(noun)* a double-lowered cultivated variety of clove pink, with grey-green leaves and showy pink, white, or red flowers. *Carnation is a variety of clove.*

Carnival - *(noun)* **1** an annual period of public revelry involving processions, music, dancing, etc. *in south America, Rio de Jenerio the annual carnival is celebrated with much for fare. It is a tourist attrition as well.* **2** [north American] a travelling funfair or circus.

Carnivora – *(plural noun)* [zoology] an order of mammals comprising the cats, dogs, bears, hyenas, weasels, civets, raccoons, and mongooses, having powerful jaws and teeth adapted for tearing and eating flesh. *Lion belongs to carnivora order of mammals.*

Carnivorous – *(adjective)* feeding on flesh. *Carnivorous animals live upon grass eating animals.*

Carol – *(noun)* a religious song or popular hymn associated with Christmas. *We sang carols happily in the streets. (verb)* sing carols in the streets.

Carouse – *(verb)* drink alcohol and enjoy oneself with others in a noisy, lively way. (noun) a noisy, lively drinking party. *We arranged a party shortly with some other friends and we were carousing.*

Carp – *(verb)* complain or find fault continually. *Don't carp in the morning and make my day horrible.*

Carpal – *(adjective)* of or relating to the carpus. *(noun)* a bone of the carpus. *As she fell down, she felt her carpus strained.*

Carpenter – *(noun)* a person who makes wooden objects and structures. *He is a carpenter by profession. (verb)* make by shaping wood. *The carpenter in carpentering a chair.*

Carpet – *(noun)* **1** a floor covering made from thick woven fabric. a large rug. *I bought a wall to wall carpet.* **2** a thick or soft expanse or layer of something. *The floor was covered with a thick costly carpet.* **3** used in names of geometrid moths with variegated wings. *(verb)* **1** cover with a carpet carpet the floors of the house. *The stairs were corpeted a lovely shade of red.* **2** [British informal] reprimand severely. *The chancellor of the Exchequer carpeted the Bank bosses.*

Carpus – *(noun)* the group of small bones between the main part of the forelimb and the metacarpus, forming the writs in humans. *She strained her carpus.*

Carriage – *(noun)* **1** a four-wheeled passenger vehicle pulled by two or more horses; a wheeled support for moving a heavy object such as a gun. *In old times horse driven carriages were very popular.* **2** [British] the conveying of items or merchandise form one place to another. **3** a moving part of a machine that carries other parts into the required position. **5** a person's bearing or deportment.

Carrier – *(noun)* **1** a person or thing that carries, holds, or coveys something. *He carried the news to me.* **2** a person or company that undertakes the professional conveyance of goods or people. *There are many carriers/ caurriers around the city.* **3** a person or animal that transmits a disease-causing organism to others, especially without suffering from it themselves; an individual possessing a particular gene, especially as a single copy whose effect is masked by a dominant allele, so that the associated characteristic is not displayed but may be passed to offspring. *Rats are the carrier of plague.*

Carriole – *(noun)* [historical] a small open horse-drawn carriage for one person; a light covered cart. *In old time there used to be carriole for one person.* **2** a kind of sledge pulled by a horse or dogs, with space for one or more passengers. *People enjoy sledge rides in Alask or any place where there is thick and solid ice on ground.*

Carry – *(verb)* **1** move or transport form one place to another. *I carried and delivered the parcel to him.* have on one's person wherever one goes. conduct; transmit; be infected with and liable to transmit it to others. **2** support the weight of; be pregnant with stand and move in a specified way; assume or accept. *Dogs carry germs of rabies in their saliva and teeth.* **3** have as a feature or consequence. *He carries himself like a noble man.* **4** take or develop to a specified point; propel to a specified distance. *He carried the argument to a point where nobody could challenge him.* [golf & cricket] hit the ball over and beyond a particular point. **5** approve by a majority of votes; persuade to support one's policy; [north American] gain in an election. *The plane carried itself a few hundred* *meters on ground and then it took off.* **6** publish or broadcast. keep a regular stock of. *After being hit the ball carried itself across the boundary.* **7** be audible at a distance. *The voice carried itself to the far end of ground.* **8** *He swiftly carried the ball to the goal and his team won.* **9** *I always carry a gun with me.* **10** *The bullet from this gun covers the distance of 700 meters.* **11** *The horse carried the weight of more that 80 kgs.* **12** *She is pregnant and her walk is peculiar. She carries himself like a duck.* *(noun)* **1** an act of carrying. American football an act of running or rushing with the ball. chiefly north American the action of keeping a gun on one's person. [north American historical] a portage for boats or supplies. **2** finance the maintenance of an investment position in a securities market, especially with regard to the costs or profits accruing. **3** [golf] the distance a ball travels before reaching the ground. **4** the range of a gun or similar.

Cartilage – *(noun)* a firm, whitish, flexible connective tissue which is the main component of the articulating surfaces of joints and of structures; such as the larynx and respiratory tract and the external ear. *He is suffering from arthritis as the cartilage of both his knees has dried.*

Cartographer – *(noun)* a person who maps makes.

Cartography – *(noun)* the science or practice of drawing maps. *My brother does cartography..*

Carton – *(noun)* a light cardboard container. *The new fridge I bought was enclosed in a big carton.*

Cartouche – *(noun)* **1** a carved tablet or drawing representing a scroll with rolled-up ends, used or name tally or bearing an inscription, a decorative architectural feature resembling a scroll, an ornate frame around a design or inscription. *If you look at Egyptian hieroglyphs bearing the name and title of a monarch, you will usually find them enclosed in an oval or oblong cartouche.* **2** [Archaeology] an oval or oblong enclosing a group of Egyptian hieroglyphs, typically representing the name and title of a monarch. *Ancient carvings, pictures, scrolls etc. used to be called cartouche..*

Cartridge – *(noun)* **1** a container holding a spool of photographic film, a quantity of ink, or other item or substance, designed for insertion into a mechanism. *I have some space cartridges. You can keep your film spools into them.* **2** a casing containing a charge and a bullet or shot for small arms or an explosive charge for blasting. *The cartridge had an explosive charge and when fired, it blasted the small house.*

Caruncle – *(noun)* **1** [zoology] a fleshy outgrowth, such as a bird's wattles or the red prominence at the inner corner of the eye. **2** [botany] a coloured waxy or oily outgrowth from a seed near the micropyle.

Cascade – *(noun)* **1** a small waterfall, especially one in a series. *There is a cascade, we can take a bath here.* **2** a mass of something that falls, hangs, or occurs in copious quantities. *Her thick hair fell down on her face like a cascade.* **3** a process by which information or knowledge is passed on successively. **4** a succession of devices or stages in a process, each of which triggers or initiates the next. *(verb)* **1** pour downwards rapidly and in large quantities. *Water from the water tank cascades through the large pipe.* **2** pass on to a succession of others. **3** arrange in a series or sequence.

Case – *(noun)* **1** a container designed to hold or protect something, the outer protective covering of a natural or manufactured object. *Here is a case for you spectacles. It is strong enough to protect your glasses.* **2** [British] a suitcase. *Where is my case?* **3** a box containing twelve bottles of wine or other drink, sold as a unit. *Here is a case of bear for you to carry away.* **4** Printing a partitioned container for loose metal type. each of the two forms, capital or minuscule, in which a letter of the alphabet may be written or printed. *The hunting knife is enclosed in a case.* *(verb)* **1** enclose within a case. **2** [informal] reconnoiter before carrying out a robbery.

Casement – *(noun)* a window set on a vertical hinge so that it opens like a door. *Please open the window and you will have a nice view of the sea.*

Caseous - *(adjective)* medicine characterized by caseation. *It is caseous like medicine.*

Cash - *(noun)* [historical] a coin of low value from China, southern India, or SE Asia. *This coin seems to be cash either from China or cast India.* **2** *I have ready money in the form of cast-currency notes, coins, silver gold, etc.*

Cashier - *(noun)* person handling payments and receipts in shop, bank, or business. *My father is a cashier in the bank.*

Cashmere - *(noun)* fine soft wool, originally that from the Kashmir goat. *I am wearing a cashmere sweater. It is very worm.*

Casing - *(noun)* **1** a cover or shell that protects or encloses something. *The glass pone of the window is enclosed in a metallic casing.* **2** the frame around a door or window. *This is a casing for a knife.*

Casino - *(noun)* an establishment where gambling games are played. *I visited a casino abroad. There I saw a lot of gambling games being played.*

Cask - *(noun)* a large barrel-like container for the storage of liquid, especially alcoholic drinks. *My uncle has a cask full of rum.*

Casket - *(noun)* a small ornamental box or chest for holding valuable objects. *He keeps his father's ashes in asket.* [British] a small wooden box for cremated ashes. *My aunt keeps her armaments in a casket.* [chiefly north American] a coffin. *A casket was bought for the dead man's body.*

Casque - *(noun)* **1** [historical] a helmet. *Soldiers used to wear a casqued while going to war.* **2** [zoology] a helmet like structure, such as that on the bill of a hornbill.

Cassia - *(noun)* **1** a leguminous tree or plant of warm climates, producing senna and other valuable products. *A lot of cassia trees (cinnamon) grow in our country.* **2** the aromatic bark of an east Asian tree, yielding an inferior kind of cinnamon.

Cassock - *(noun)* a long garment worn by some Christian clergy and members of church choirs. *I have seen many Christian clergy men wearing cassocks.*

Cast - *(noun)* the actors taking part in a play or film. *The cast of the film is impressive.* *(verb)* assign a part to (an actor). allocate parts in a play or film. *He has been cast in to the role of a villain.*

Caste - *(noun)* **1** each of the hereditary classes of Hindu society, distinguished by relative degrees of ritual purity or pollution and of social status. *In India, treatment to different people varies depending upon caste.* **2** [Entomology] a physically distinct kind of individual with a particular function.

Castigate - *(verb)* reprimand severely. *I was castigated by my father for bunking the school.*

Casting - *(noun)* a large and stately mansion. *Casting of the film was done very wisely.*

Cast-iron - *(noun)* **1** a hard, relatively brittle alloy of iron and carbon which can be readily cast in a mould. *My father deals in cast-iron business.* **2** firm and unchangeable. *There are no cast-iron guarantees. You cannot pin me down for murder because I have a cast-iron alibi.*

Castle - *(noun)* the chaice of actors to play poarticular roles in a play or movie. *In old times kings used to live in castles.*

Castor-oil - *(noun)* a pale yellow purgative oil obtained from the seeds of an African shrub. *I took a close of castor-oil as I was suffering from constipation.*

Casual - *(adjective)* **1** relaxed and unconcerned. made, done, or acting without much care or thought. *He takes everything casually.* **2** not regular or firmly established. employed on a temporary or irregular basis. *He is a casual employee.* 3 happening by chance; accidental. *It was a casual happening.* **4** without formality of style, manner, or procedure. *He was dressed casual and talked in a casual manner.* *(noun)* **1** a casual worker. **2** clothes or shoes suitable for everyday wear rather than formal occasion. *The threw me a casual glance. He likes casual clothes and shoes not formal ones.* **3** [British] a youth belonging to a subculture characterized by the wearing of expensive casual clothing.

Casuist - *(noun)* a person who uses clever but false reasoning. *He is a casuist and as such I don't like him.*

Cat - *(noun)* a small domesticated carnivorous mammal which is widely kept as a pet. *I have a pet cat..*

Cataclysm - *(noun)* a violent upheaval or disaster. *The earthquake caused cataclysm.*

Catacomb - *(noun)* an underground cemetery consisting of a gallery with recesses for tombs. *He was lost in the dark and frightening catacomb.*

Catalepsy - *(noun)* a medical condition characterized by a trance or seizure with a loss of sensation and consciousness accompanied by rigidity of the body. *She suffered from catalepsy and at that time she seemed to be dead.*

Catalogue - *(noun)* a complete list of items arranged in alphabetical or other systematic order. *Please give your catalogue, I would like to know what you have got into your shop.* a publication containing details of items for sale. *To find out the book of your choice, please consult the catalogue!* a series of unfortunate or bad things. *His life has been a catalogue of failures.* a series of unfortunate or bad things *(verb)* list in a catalogue. *These items have not been catalogued as yet.*

Catamaran - *(noun)* a yacht or other boat with twin hulls in parallel. *I was offered a ride in catamaran and I enjoyed it.*

Cataplasm - *(noun)* [archaic] a plaster or poultice. *You should apply a cataplasm on your injury.*

Cataract - *(noun)* **1** a large waterfall. *In south America there are a number of cataracts with abundance of water.* **2** a medical condition in which the lens of the eye becomes progressively opaque, resulting in blurred vision. *You have cataract in both of your eyes. I think you should consult on eye surgeons.*

Catarrh - *(noun)* excessive discharge of mucus in the nose or throat. *You are suffering from catarrh. Take some medicine.*

Catastrophe - *(noun)* **1** an event causing great damage or suffering. *Floods brought great catastrophe to the village.* **2** the denouement of a drams, especially a classical tragedy. *The play ends in catastrophe.*

Catch - *(verb)* **1** intercept and hold (something which has been thrown, propelled, or dropped), seize or take hold of. [Cricket] dismiss by catching the ball before it touches the ground. *Dravid caught a brilliant catch.* **2** capture (a person or animal that tries or would try to escape). *We have caught the stray dogs which were trying to escape.* **3** accidentally become entangled or trapped in something. *We have accidently caught a wild boar.* **4** reach in time and board (a train, bus, or aircraft), reach or be in a place in time to see (a person, performance, etc.). *I had to catch a train so I hurried up.* **5** unexpectedly find oneself in an unwelcome situation. surprise in an award or incriminating situation. *I was caught unawares into a bad situation.* **6** engage perceive fleetingly, hear or understand (something said), especially with effort. succeed in evoking or representing. *The surprised given to me caught me unawares.* **7** strike on a part of the body, accidentally strike (a part of one's body) against something. *The bull suddenly caught me and hit me against the all.* **8** contract (an illness) through infection or contagion. *I hurried and caught my friend to say 'good bys' before he could enter the airport.* **9** become ignited and start burning. *I could exactly catch his words.* *(noun)* **1** an act or instance of catching. an amount of fish caught. [informal] a person considered desirable as a partner or spouse. **2** a device for securing something such as a door, window, or box. **3** a hidden problem or disadvantage. **4** an unevenness in a person's voice caused by emotion. **5** Music a round, typically one with words arranged to produce a humorous effect.

Catchy - *(adj.)* likely to attract attention. *It is a catchy song.*

Catechism - *(noun)* a summary of the principles of Christian religion in the form of question and answers, used for teaching. *Principles of christen region are taught in catechism.*

Catechize – *(verb)* instruct by means of question and answer; especially by using a catechize. *Students are instructed by using catechize.*

Catechu – *(noun)* a vegetable extract containing tannin, chiefly obtained form an Indian acacia tree and used for tanning and dyeing. *Catechu is an extract used for dyeing.*

Categorical – *(adjective)* unambiguously explicit and direct. *His statements are usually categorical.*

Category – *(noun)* **1** a class or division of people or things having particular shared characteristics. *So for as social status is concerned we belong to the same category.* **2** [Philosophy] each of a possibly exhaustive set of classes among which all things might be distributed. an a priori conception applied by the mind to sense impressions. *All labour class belongs to one category.*

Cater – *(verb)* [chiefly British] **1** provide food and drink at a social event. *Don't worry a lot of people are here to cater to your needs.* **2** provide with what is needed or required. take into account or make allowances for, satisfy (a need or demand). *The school caters for children with learning difficulties.*

Caterpillar – *(noun)* the larva of butterfly or moth. *Caterpillars are beautiful to look at.*

Cathectic – *(adjective)* psychoanalysis of or relating to cathexis.

Cathedra – *(noun)* a throne that is the official chair of a bishop.

Cathedral – *(noun)* the principal church of a diocese.

Catheter – *(noun)* [medicine] a flexible tube inserted through a narrow opening into a body cavity, particularly the bladder, for removing fluid. *My friend could not pass urine so they inserted catheter in his body through a thin opening and took out the fluid.*

Catholic – *(adjective)* of the roman catholic faith. of or including and practice of the western church. *Many of my friends are Roman Catholic people are scared of earthquakes causing distractions.* *(noun)* a member of the roman catholic church.

Catoptric – *(adjective)* [physics] of or relating to a mirror or reflection. *In are student days we had done lots of catoptric experiments.*

Cat's eye – *(noun)* **1** a semi-precious stone, especially chalcedony, with a chatoyant lustre. *My friend wears cat's eye. It suits him well.* **2** [British] a light-reflecting stud set in a series into a road to mark traffic lanes or the edge of the carriageway. *In England, traffic Police use cat's eye to control traffic.*

Cattle – *(plural noun)* large ruminant animals with horns and cloven hoofs, chiefly domesticated for meat or milk cows and oxen. *This person has the greatest herd of cattle, two hundred heads. He sells a lot of milk.*

Caudal – *(adjective)* of or like a tail, at or near the tail or the posterior part of the body. *Caudal growth in human disappeared a long time back.*

Caught – past and past participle of CATCH. *He was caught off mid wicket.*

Caul – *(noun)* **1** the amniotic membrane enclosing a fetus, part of this membrane occasionally found on a child's head at birth, thought to bring good luck. *The baby was born fully enclosed in the caul.* **2** [historical] a woman's close-fitting indoor headdress or hairnet. *She is fond of wearing caul.*

Cauldron – *(noun)* **1** a large metal pot, used for cooking over an open fire. *The food for the wedding guests are being cooked in a caldron.* **2** a situation characterized by instability and strong emotions. *He is a cauldron of boiling emotions.*

Cauliflower – *(noun)* a cabbage of a variety which bears a large immature flower head of small creamy-white flower buds, eaten as a vegetable. *prefer cauliflower to cabbage.*

Causal – *(adjective)* of, relating to, or acting as a cause. *The causal effect of rain was heavy floods.*

Causality – *(noun)* **1** the relationship between cause and effect. *Without cause there can be no effect.* **2** the principle that everything has a cause.

Causation – *(noun)* **1** the action of causing something. **2** the relationship between cause and effect.

Causative – *(adjective)* **1** acting as a cause. **2** [grammar] expressing causation. *The cause of his illness was being bitten by dangerous mosquitoes.*

Cause – *(noun)* **1** a person or thing that gives rise to an action, phenomenon, or condition. reasonable grounds for a belief or action. *Heavy clouds are the cause and rain is its effects.* **2** a principle or movement which one is prepared to defend or advocate. something deserving of support. *I'll take up and defend your cause.* **3** a matter to be resolved in a court of law. an individual's case offered at law. *(verb)* be the caused of; make happen.

Causeless – *(adj.)* hanging me justifying cause or reason. *This attack seems to be causeless.*

Causeway – *(noun)* a raised road or track across low or wet ground. *There is a causeway here, you can softly drive your car.*

Caustic – *(adjective)* **1** able to burn or corrode organic tissue by chemical action. **2** scathingly sarcastic. *Her caustic remarks upset him.* **3** [physics] formed by the intersection of reflected or refracted parallel rays from a curved surface. *(noun)* **1** a caustic substance. **2** [physics] a caustic surface or curve.

Caution – *(noun)* **1** care taken to avoid danger or mistakes. *Take caution going through while mud road.* **2** [British] an official or legal warning given to someone who has committed a minor offence but has not been charged. *Take every caution while you are travelling.* **3** [informal], dated an amusing or surprising person. *(verb)* **1** say something as a warning. warn or advise against. **2** [British] issue an official or legal warning to. advise of their legal rights when arresting them.

Cautionary – *(adjective)* serving as a warning. *There is a cautionary warning on the board.*

Cavalier – *(noun)* **1** [historical] a supporter of King Charles I in the English civil war. *Cavaliers were soldiers fisting under a king.* **2** [archaic] a gallant. [archaic] a cavalryman. (adjective) showing a lack of proper concern.

Cavalry – *(noun)* historical soldiers who fought on horseback. modern soldiers who fight in armoured vehicles. *Cavalry are the soldiers who fought on a horseback.*

Cave – *(noun)* large natural underground chamber. *As students we looked for caves and often went in.* *(verb)* **1** explore caves as a sport, subside or collapse.

Cavern – *(noun)* **1** a large cave, or chamber in cave. *We were thrilled to explore a cavern.* **2** a vast, dark space.

Cavil – *(verb)* make petty or unnecessary objections. *(noun)* an objection of this kind. *Women are usually cavil.*

Cavity – *(noun)* an empty space within a solid object, a decayed part of a tooth. *Cavities decay a tooth.*

Caw – *(noun)* the harsh cry of a rook, crow, or similar bird. *(verb)* utter a caw. *The crow was cawing harshly.*

Cayenne – *(noun)* a pungent, hot-tasting red powder prepared from dried chillies. *Some people have a fondness for cayenne.*

Cease – *(verb)* come or bring to an end; stop. *When the rain ceased I stepped out of the house.*

Ceaseless – *(adjective)* constant and unending. *Ceaseless rain fell and nobody could go anywhere.*

Cecity – *(noun)* blindness. *She suffers from cecity.*

Cedar – *(noun)* a tall, elegant coniferous tree yielding typically fragment, durable wood. Cedrus libani and other species in the genera cedrus and Thuja. *I would like to have a cedar in my compound.*

Cede – *(verb)* give up (power or territory). *He ceded his lands to enemy forces.*

Ceil – *(verb)* [archaic] line or plaster the roof of (a building). *The nave has been ceiled in wood.*

Ceiling – *(noun)* **1** the upper interior surface of a room. *The ceiling of my room is white coloured.* **2** an upper limit set on prices, wages. etc. *A ceiling has been put on the price of this cammodity.* **3** the maximum altitude that an aircraft can reach. the altitude of the base of a cloud layer. *The plane has a ceiling of flying up to the height of 30 thousand ft.* **4** the inside planking of a ship's bottom and sides. *The ceiling of this strip is very strong.*

Celebrate – *(verb)* **1** mark (a significant time or event) with an enjoyable activity. engage in festivities. *We all took port in holi celebration.* **2** perform in particular officiate at the Eucharist. **3** Hounour or praise publicly.

Celebrity – *(noun)* **1** a famous person. *Most film stars are celebrities.* **2** the state of being famous. *His prestige and celebrity grew.*

Celerity – *(noun)* [archaic] swiftness of movement.

Celeste – *(noun)* a musical instrument consisting graduated steel plates that are struck by hammers activated by keyboard.

Celestial – *(adjective)* **1** positioned in or relating to the sky or outer space. *One day we may begin to live on a celestial planet.* **2** belonging or relating to heaven.

Celibacy – *(noun)* an unmarried status, abstaining from sexual relations.*Saints and faqirs often observe celibacy.*

Celibate – *(adjective)* **1** abstaining from marriage and sexual relations for religious reasons. *He is a celibate priest.* *(noun)* having or involving no sexual relations; a person who is celibate. *He is attracted to women, yet the lives as a celibate.*

Cell – *(noun)* **1** a small room in which a prisoner is locked up or in which a monk or nun sleeps. *Prisoners are locked in cells. Manks and priests live in cells.* a small compartment in a larger structure such as a honeycomb. [historical] a small monastery dependent on a larger one. **2** [biology] the smallest structural and functional unit of an organism, typically microscopic, consisting of cytoplasm and a nucleus enclosed in a membrane. **3** a small group forming a nucleus of political activity. **4** a device containing electrodes immersed in an electrolyte, used for current generation or electrolysis; a unit in a device for converting chemical energy or light into electricity.

Cellar – *(noun)* a storage space or room below ground level in a house; a stock of wine. *(verb)* store in a cellar. *A stock of wine is usually kept in the cellar.*

Cellular – *(adjective)* **1** of, relating to, or consisting of living cells. *Cellular phones have becomes so popular these days.* **2** denoting or relating to a mobile telephone system that uses a number of short-range radio stations. *This house has so many rooms that it is almost cellular.* **3** knitted so as to form holes or hollows that trap air and provide extra insulation. **4** consitsting of small compartments or rooms.

Celluloid – *(noun)* a transparent flammable plastic made in sheets from camphor and nitrocellulose, formerly used for cinematographic film; the cinema as a genre. *Today we use celluloid for making toys as make up material.*

Cellulose – *(noun)* **1** an insoluble substance which is a polysaccharide derived from glucose and is the main constituent of plant cell walls and of vegetable fibers such as cotton. *Cellulose forms the solid frame-work of plants.* **2** paint or lacquer consisting principally of cellulose acetate or nitrate in solution.

Cemetery – *(noun)* a large burial ground. *His body was buried in the cemetery.*

Cense – *(verb)* ritually perfume with burning incense. *Our grandmother's burnt is cense in the temple and it gave out aromatic smell.*

Censer – *(noun)* a container in which incense is burnt. *We keep a censer in which cense is burnt.*

Censor – *(noun)* **1** an official who examines material that is to be published and suppresses parts considered offensive or a threat to security; [psychoanalysis] an aspect of the superego which prevents certain ideas and memories from emerging into consciousness. *Censor is responsible for reaming any part of fiction or film which is objection able to society.* **2** a magistrate who held censuses and supervised public morals. *(verb)* examine officially and suppress unacceptable parts of it. *Superego works on censor and prevents harmful memories from coming in to conscious minds.*

Censorious – *(adjective)* severely critical. *He is very strict, almost censorious.*

Censorship – *(noun)* deleting parts of publications, correspondence or theatrical performances. *Censorship is a must even if it is a democratic country.*

Censure – *(verb)* express severe disapproval of; formally reprove. *My father censured me over my rude behavior.* *(noun)* formal disapproval.

Census – *(noun)* an official count or survey of a population. *During censor count is taken of the people living in a country.*

Cent – *(noun)* **1** a monetary unit equal to one hundredth of a dollar or other decimal currency unit. *I have so many cents but no dollars.* **2** [music] one hundredth of a semitone.

Centenarian – *(noun)* a person a hundred or more years old. *(adjective)* a hundred or more years old. *My grandfather is a centenarian.*

Centenary – *(noun)* [British] the hundredth anniversary of a significant event. *After 100 years we celebrate the centenary of many events or people.*

Centennial – *(adjective)* of or relating to a hundredth anniversary. *(noun)* a hundredth anniversary.

Centesimal – *(adjective)* of or relating to division into hundredths.

Centigrade – *(adjective)* of or denoting a scale of a hundred degrees, in particular the Celsius scale of temperature. *Water boils at 100°C.*

Centipede – *(noun)* an arthropod with a flattened, elongated body composed of many segments, most of which bear a pair of legs. *I am extremely afraid of centipedes.*

Central – *(adjective)* **1** in or near the centre of something. *In the crowd the heroin was of central attraction.* **2** most important; principal.

Centralise – *(verb)* concentrate under a single authority. *In a dictator ship power is centralised in the hands of the dictator.*

Centre – *(noun)* **1** a point in the middle of something that is equally distant form all of its sides, ends, or surfaces, the middle player in some team games. *A centre forward player is the most important one.* a kick, hit, or throw of the ball from the side to the middle of field. *The ball was kiced and thrown from the side to the centre of the field.* **2** a place or group of buildings where a specified activity is concentrated. a point to or from which an activity or process is directed. *(verb)* **1** place in the centre. kick, hit, or throw from the side to the middle of field. [north American] play as the middle player in some team games. **2** (centre on/around) have as a major concern or theme. occur mainly in or around.

Centrifugal – *(adjective)* [physics] moving away from a centre. *Centrifugal force.*

Centripetal – *(adjective)* [physics] moving towards a centre. *Centripetal force.*

Centuple – *(verb)* multiply by a hundred.

Century – *(noun)* **1** a period of one hundred years, in particular each of a number of such periods from the date of the birth of christ. *A lot of centuries have passed since the birth of Christ.* **2** a batsman's score of a hundred runs in cricket. *Sachin has made so many centuries.* **3** a company of a hundred men in the ancient roman army; an electoral division of ancient Rome.

Cephalic – *(adjective)* of, in, or relating to the head. *It is something cephalic and has nothing to with other body parts.*

Ceramics – *(adjective)* **1** made of clay that is permanently hardened by heat. *I bought a ceramics plate.* **2** of or relating to ceramics. *Yesterday I read one article on the art of ceramics.* *(noun)* **1** ceramic articles; the art of making ceramics **2** clay used in this way; any nonmetallic solid which remains hard when heated.

Cereal – *(noun)* **1** a grain used for food, for example wheat, maize, or rye. a grass producing such grain, grown as an agricultural crop. *Cereals make carbohydrates in our body.* **2** a breakfast food made from a cereal grain or grains.

Cerebral – *(adjective)* of the cerebrum of the brain. intellectual rather than emotional or physical. *Cerebral port of his brain is very active.*

Cerebrum – *(noun)* [anatomy] the principal part of the brain, located in the front area of the skull and consisting of left and right hemispheres. *Cerebrum is the largest part of the brain.*

Ceremonial – *(adjective)* **1** relating to or used for ceremonies. *Marriage is a ceremonial affair.* **2** involving only nominal authority or power.

Cerography – *(noun)* the art or process of writing or engraving on wax. *She specializes in cerography.*

Certain – *(adjective)* **1** able to be firmly relied on to happen or be the case. *I am certain that he will come.* **2** completely convinced of something. *These are certain problems upsetting me.* **3** specific but not explicitly named or stated. *Certain problems.* not known to the reader or hearer. *(pronoun)* some but not all. *A certain Mr. Mukherjee called upon you.*

Certainly – *(adverb)* definitely; undoubtedly. yes; by all means. *I'll certainly go to Simla this summer.*

Certificate – *(noun)* **1** an official document attesting or recording a particular fact or event, a level of achievement, the fulfillment of a legal requirement, etc. *I have all my certificates enclosed in a file.* **2** an official classification awarded to a film by a board of censors, indicating its suitability for a particular age group. *(verb)* provide with or attest in an official document. *This film has an 'A' certificate.*

Certify – *(verb)* **1** formally attest or confirm. *It is certified that he has passed his 12th grade.* **2** officially recognize as possessing certain qualifications or meeting certain standards. *It is certified that he is insane.*

Certitude – *(noun)* a feeling of absolute certainty; something considered with certainty to be true. *I have the certitude that he will pass the exam first class first.*

Cerumen – *(noun)* technical term for earwax. *The car specialist took out a lot of cerumen from the car.*

Cervical – *(adjective)* anatomy **1** of or relating to the cervix. *His cervical pain has increased.* **2** of or relating to the neck.

Cervine – *(adj.)* relating to or resembling deer. *She is cervine and deer-like.*

Cess – *(noun)* (in Scotland, Ireland, and India) a tax or levy. *Heavy cess has been imposed on traders.*

Cessation – *(noun)* the fact or process of ceasing. *Cessation of the war brought peace.*

Cession – *(noun)* the formal giving up of rights, property, or territory by a state. *Cession by the defeated state ended the battle.*

Chaff – *(noun)* **1** the husks of grain or other seed separated by winnowing or threshing. chopped hay and straw used as fodder. *Chaff is mainly used on fodder.* **2** strips of metal foil released in the air to obstruct radar detection.

Chaffer – *(verb)* haggle. *(noun)* [archaic] haggling. *It is the habit of ladies to chaffer.*

Chaffing – *(verb)* be silly or tease on another. *They were chaffing and it annoyed me.*

Chagrin – *(noun)* annoyance or shame at having failed. *(verb)* feel annoyed or ashamed. *He chagrined at having failed.*

Chain – *(noun)* a connected flexible series of metal links used for fastening, pulling, etc., of in jewellery, a restricting force or factor. *The chain of my cycle is broken.* **2** a sequence of items of the same type forming a line. a series of connected elements. a group of hotels or shops owned by the same company. a part of a molecule consisting of a number of atoms bounded together in a linear sequence. *I had no control over the chain of events.* **3** a jointed measuring line consisting of linked metal rods. the length of this a structure projecting horizontally from a sailing ship's sides abreast of the masts, used to widen the basis for the shrouds. *(verb)* fasten, secure, or confine with a chain.

Chair – *(noun)* **1** a separate seat for one person, typically with a back and four legs. *I have bought an easy chair today.* **2** the person in charge of a meeting or an organization. an official position of authority, especially on a board of directors. *He is the chairperson of the meeting.* **3** a professorship. **4** [chiefly British] a metal socket holding a rail in place on a railway sleeper. *(verb)* **1** act as chairperson of. **2** British carry aloft in a chair or in a sitting position to celebrate a victory.

Chairman – *(noun)* a person in charge of meeting, committee, company, or other organization. *He is the chairmen of our company.*

Chaise – *(noun)* **1** [chiefly historical] a horse-drawn carriage for one or two people, especially one with an open top and two wheels. *Chaise were very popular 0 century back.* another term for psot-chaise.

Chalice – *(noun)* **1** historical a goblet. *He drank from the chalice.* **2** the wine cup used in the Christian Eucharist.

Chalk – *(noun)* a white soft earthy limestone formed from the skeletal remains of sea creatures. a similar substance and used for drawing or writing. *Teachers write with chalk on the blackboard.* *(verb)* **1** draw or write with chalk. rub the tip of with chalk. **2** [British] charge to a person's account. **3** achieve something noteworthy.

Challenge – *(noun)* **1** a call to someone to participate in a contest or fight to decide who is superior. *He threw me a challenge for a boxing match.* a demanding task or situation; an attempt to win a sporting contest. *I challenge you to a 100 m race.* **2** a call to prove or justify something. *To take IAS exam was a challenge to me.* **3** medicine exposure of the immune system to pathogenic organisms or antigens. *(verb)* **1** dispute the truth or validity of. law object to (a jury member). **2** invite to engage in a contest. compete with. test the abilities. of. **3** [medicine] expose to pathogenic organisms or antigens.

Chamber – *(noun)* **1** a large room used for formal or public events. *The meeting was held in a chamber.* **2** one of the houses of a parliament. *I found my lawyer sitting in the chamber.* **3** law, British rooms used by a barrister or barristers, especially in the inns of court. law a judge's room used for official proceedings not required to be held in open court. *The judge heard the case in private in his own chamber.* **4** [poetic]a private room, especially a gun bore that contains the charge. **5** music or of for a small group of instruments: a chamber orchestra. *I had a chance to hear the chamber orchestra.*

Chamberlain – *(noun)* **1** an officer who managed the household of a monarch or noble. *He looks after the affairs of the noble man.* **2** British an officer who received revenue on behalf of a corporation or public body.

Chameleon – *(noun)* a small slow-moving lizard with a prehensile tail, long extensible tongue, protruding eyes, and the ability to change colour. *Chameleon can change their colour according to the environments.*

Chamois – *(noun)* **1** an agile goat antelope with short hooked horns, found in mountainous areas of southern Europe. *I have seen many chamois.* **2** soft pliable leather made form the skin of sheep, goats, or deer. *I don't use things made from the skin of animals.*

Champ – *(verb)* **1** munch enthusiastically or noisily. make a noisy biting or chewing action. *He champed a lot while eating.* **2** fret impatiently. *He becamed angry and champed.*

Champion – *(noun)* [law] an illegal agreement in which a person with no previous interest in lawsuit finances it with a view to haring the disputed property if the suit succeeds. *He is a champion into entering illegal lawsuits.*

Chance – *(noun)* **1** a possibility of something happening. *You may succeed by chance who knows.* **2** the probability of something happening. *Go and try your luck, chance is waiting for you.* **3** an opportunity. *I'll take a chance and show my cards.* **4** the occurrence of events in the absence of any obvious design or cause.*I met my brother by chance. I chanced to see him at a cinema house.* *(verb)* **1** do something by accident. find or se by accident. **2** informal risk.

Chancel – *(noun)* the part of a church near the altar, reserved for the clergy and choir, and typically separated from the nave by steps or a screen. *The clergy is speaking from the chancel.*

Chancellor – *(noun)* **1** a senior state or legal official of various kinds. *He is the judge o a chancery court.* the head of the government in some European countries, e.g. Germany. [British] the non-resident honorary head of a university. *This gentleman is the chancellor of the university.* US the presiding judge of a chancery court. an officer of an order of knighthood who seals commissions.

Chancery – *(noun)* **1** [law] the lord chancellor's court, a division of the high court of justice. *Right now the case is in chancery.* **2** [US] a court

a void. **3** [archaic] chicanery. *(verb)* [archaic] employ chicanery.

Chicken – *(noun)* **1** a domestic fowl kept for its eggs or meat, especially a young one. *My neighbour has so many chickens.* **2** a coward. *He is a chicken hearted fellow.* **3** informal a game in which the first person to lose their nerve and withdraw from a dangerous situation is the loser. *(adjective)* [informal] cowardly. *(verb)* informal be too scared to do something. *He is a chicken to do anything worthwhile.*

Chide – *(verb)* scold or rebuke. *The teacher chided me on coming late.*

Cheif – *(noun)* **1** a leader or ruler of a people, the head of an organization. *He is the chief of our organization.* **2** [heraldry] an ordinary consisting of a broad horizontal band across the top of the shield; the upper third of the field. *He is the chief of military/police.* *(adjective)* **1** having the highest rank or authority. **2** most important: *the chief reason.*

Cheiftain – *(noun)* the leader of a people or clan. *He is the chieftain of a clan.*

Chiffon – *(noun)* a light, transparent fabric typically made of silk or nylon. *My sister is fond of wearing chiffon sarces.*

Chilblain – *(noun)* a painful, itching swelling on a hand or foot caused by poor blood circulation in the skin when exposed to cold. *He is suffering from chilblain.*

Child – *(noun)* **1** a young human being below the age of full physical development; a son or daughter of any age. *The child is very cute.* **2** [derogatory] an immature or irresponsible person. *Although grown up he still behaves like a child.* **3** [archaic] the descendants of a family or people.

Children – *(plural)* form of child. *Children are making a lot of noise.*

Chill – *(noun)* **1** an unpleasant feeling of coldness. **2** a feverish cold. *He is feverishly cold.* **3** a metal mould designed to aid cooling of metal during casting. *(verb)* **1** make cold; cool in a refrigerator. *The meat has been chilled in frige.* **2** horrify or frighten. **3** informal calm down and relax. *Please chill down.* *(adjective)* chilly.

Chilli – *(noun)* **1** a small hot-tasting pod of a variety of capsicum, used in sauces, relishes, and spice powders. *This vegetable is very chilli, my mouth is burning, please bring some water.* **2** short for chilli powder or chilli concarne.

Chilly – *(adjective)* **1** unpleasantly cold. *It is ice all around. I am feeling chilly.* **2** unfriendly.

Chimera – *(noun)* **1** [creek mythology] a fire-breathing female monster with a lion's head, a goat's body, and serpent's tail. **2** something hoped for but illusory or impossible to achieve. **3** [biology] an organism containing a mixture of genetically different tissues, formed by processes, such as fusion of early embryos, grafting, or mutation. **4** a long tailed cartilaginous marine fish with an erect spine before the first dorsal fin.

Chimpanzee – *(noun)* an anthropoid ape with large ears, mainly black coloration, and lighter skin on the face, native to west and central Africa. *It is fun to see the Chimpanzee see in the zoo.*

Chin – *(noun)* **1** a member of people of SW Burma and neighbouring parts of India and Bangladesh. **2** the Tibeto-Burman language of this people.

China – *(noun)* **1** a fine white or translucent vitrified ceramic material; household tableware or other objects made from china. *I have just bought some china crockery.* **2** [British informal] a friend.

Chinese – *(noun)* **1** the language of China. *He speaks Chinese well.* **2** a native or national of China, or a person of Chinese descent. *(adjective)* of or relating to China, its people or their language. belonging to the dominant ethnic group of China.

Chink – *(noun)* informal, offensive a Chinese person. *He is a chink and I look down upon such people.*

Chintz – *(noun)* printed multicoloured cotton fabric with a glazed finish, used especially for curtains and upholstery. *She has used chintz for curtains.*

Chippy – *(noun)* **1** [British] a fish and chip shop. *I went to a chippy to buy fish.* **2** [British] a carpenter. *I have called a chippy to repair my* *wardrobe.* **3** [north American] a prostitute. *(adjective)* touchy and irritable. *He is a chippy person.*

Chips – *(noun)* strips of potato fried in deep fat many people are fond of chips.

Chirography – *(noun)* handwriting, especially as distinct from typography. *His chirogsophy is very good.*

Chirology – *(noun)* telling fortunes by lines on the palm of the hand.

Chiromancer – *(noun)* for tuneteller who pride its your future by the this a your palm.

Chiromancy – *(noun)* telling fortunes by this on the palm of the hand.

Chirpy – *(adjective)* [informal] cheerful and lively. *She is chirpy; always talking and laughing.*

Chirr – *(verb)* make a prolonged low trilling sound. *(noun)* a low trilling sound. *The bird made a loud chair sound.*

Chisel – *(noun)* a long-bladed hand tool with a beveled cutting edge, struck with a hammer or mallet to cut or shape wood, stone, or metal. *Carpenters use chisel for cutting wood. (verb)* **1** cut or shape with a chisel. **2** strongly and clearly defied. **3** [informal] chiefly north American, cheat or swindle out of something.

Chit – *(noun)* [derogatory] an impudent of arrogant young woman. *Do you think I am going to talk to that chit of a girl.*

Chitchat – *(noun)* inconsequential conversation. *We indulged in chitchat for a long time. (verb)* talk about trivial matters.

Chitty – *(noun)* [British informal] term of chit. *She is sure a chitty girl.*

Chivalric – *(adj.)* characteristic of the time of chivalry and knighthood in the middle Ages. *He is chivalric as well as handsome.*

Chivalry – *(noun)* **1** the medieval knightly system with its religious, moral, and social code. *Chivalry is a custom of the part now.* **2** [archaic] knights, noblemen, and horsemen collectively. **3** the combination of qualities expected of an ideal knight, especially courage, honour, courtesy, justice, and a readiness to help the weak. courteous behaviour, especially that of man towards women.

Chloride – *(noun)* [chemistry] a compound of chlorine with another element or group: sodium chloride. *We daily take sodium chloride, i.e., salt.*

Chlorine – *(noun)* the chemical element of atomic number 17, a toxic, irritant, pale green gas of the halogen group.

Chloroform – *(noun)* a volatile sweet-smelling liquid used as a solvent and formerly as a general anaesthetic. [$CHCl_3$] *(verb)* make unconscious with this substance. *Before operations chloroform is given to patients so that they because unconscious thus in-sensitive to the pain of operation.*

Chock – *(noun)* **1** a wedge or block against a wheel or rounded object to prevent it from moving or to support it. *Chock is placed against a wheel to prevent it from moving.* **2** a ring with a gap at the top, through which a rope or line is run. *(verb)* support or make fast with a chock.

Chocolate – *(noun)* **1** a food made from rested and ground cacao seeds, typically sweetened and eaten as confectionery. a sweet covered with chocolate. *Chocolates or chocolate drink is much liked by children as well as adults.* **2** a drink made by mixing milk or water with chocolate. **3** a deep brown colour.

Choice – *(noun)* **1** an act of choosing, the right or ability to choose. *I made the right choice between house work and job.* **2** a range from which to choose, something chosen. *His choice of good quality of food is famous. (adjective)* **1** especially of food of very good quality. **2** rude and abusive.

Choir – *(noun)* an organized group of singers, especially one that takes part in church services. *Choir song was going on when we reached the church.* **2** a group of instruments of one family playing together. *Choir and clergy use a separate part from the rest of the church.* **3** the part of a cathedral or large church between the altar and the nave, used by the choir and clergy.

Choke – *(verb)* have sever difficulty in breathing be cause of a constricted or obstructed throat or a lack of air. *Willie choked on a mouthful of tea.*

Choler – *(noun)* **1** one of the four bodily humours, identified with bile, believed to be associated with a peevish or irascible temperament. *He is choler by nature.* **2** [archaic] anger or irascibility.

Cholera – *(noun)* **1** an infectious and often fatal bacterial disease of the small intestine, typically contracted from infected water supplies and causing severe vomiting and diarrhoea. *He died of cholera.* **2** an infections form of pasteurellosis affecting fowls.

Choleric – *(adjective)* **1** bad-tempered or irritable. *He has a choleric temperament.* **2**. influenced by or predominating in cholera.

Choose – *(verb)* **1** pick out as being the best of two or more alternatives. *He chose a wrong career for himself.* **2** decide on a course of action. *He has chosen to go back to his country.*

Chopper – *(noun)* **1** [British] a short axe with a large blade used as a machine for chopping*: He bought a chopper to kill his enemy.* **2** a device for regularly interrupting a current or beam. *The chopper landed in the middle of the garden.* **3** [informal] teeth. **4** [informal] a helicopter. **5** [informal] a type of motorcycle with high handlebars. **6** vulgar slang a man's penis.

Choral – *(adjective)* of, for, or sung by a choir or chorus. *Choral songs were being sung in the church.*

Chord – *(noun)* a group of notes sounded together in harmony. *The chord was strong and music rose up in harmony.* *(verb)* play, sing, or arrange notes in chords.

Chorion – *(noun)* [embryology] the outermost membrane surrounding the embryo of a reptile, bird, or mammal.

Chorister – *(noun)* **1** a member of a choir, especially a choir boy or choirgirl. *There were many chorister singing is the choir.* **2** US a person who leads the singing of a church choir or congregation. *A beautiful chorister was leading the congregation.*

Choroid – *(adjective)* resembling the chorion, particularly in containing many blood vessels. *(noun)* the pigmented vascular layer of the eyeball between the retina and the sclera.

Chortle – *(verb)* laugh in a gleeful way. *(noun)* a gleeful laugh. *He chortled when he heard the joke.*

Chorus – *(noun)* **1** a large group of singers, especially one performing with an orchestra. *He sings in chorus.* **2** a piece of choral music, especially one forming part of an opera or oratorio. *In an opera I heard a chorus. it was beautiful.* **3** a part of a song which is repeated after each verse. **4** a group of performers who comment on the main action, typically speaking and moving together. **5** a simultaneous utterance by many people. *The singers typically sing and move together.* **5** a character who speaks the prologue and other linking parts of the play, especially in Elizabethan drama. *In Elizabeth an drama, the character speaks the prologue.* **7** a device used with an amplified musical instrument to give the impression that more than one instrument is being played. *(verb)* say the same thing at the same time.

Chrism – *(noun)* a consecrated oil used for anointing in the catholic, orthodox, and Anglican churches. *In church I was anointed with chrism.*

Christ – *(noun)* the title, also treated as a name, given to Jesus; [exclamatory] an oath used to express irritation, dismay, or surprise.

Christian – *(adjective)* **1** of, relating to, or professing Christianity or its teachings. *I have many Christian friends and I love all of them.* **2** [informal] having qualities associated with Christians, e.g. kindness or fairness. (noun) a person who has received Christian baptism or is a believer in Christianity.

Christmas – *(noun)* **1** the annual Christian festival celebrating Christ's birth, held on 25 December.

Chromatic – *(adjective)* **1** [music] relating to or using notes not belonging to the diatonic scale of the key of a passage. ascending or descending by semitones. **2** of relating to, or produced by colour.

Chrome – *(noun)* **1** chromium plate as a decorative or protective finish. **2** denoting compounds or alloys of chromium: chrome steel.

Chromium – *(noun)* the chemical element of atomic number 24, a hard white metal used in stainless steel and other alloys.

Chronic – *(adjective)* **1** persisting for a long time. *He is a chronic patient of asthma.* **2** having a persistent illness or bad habit. *His TB became chronic.* **3** [British informal] very bad.

Chronicle – *(noun)* a written account of important or historical events in the order of their occurrence. *(verb)* record in a factual and detailed way. *I went to the library to read some British Chronicle.*

Chronograph – *(noun)* an instrument for recording time with great accuracy. *Chronicles are recorded with the help of chronograph to help keep time accuracy.*

Chronological – *(adj.)* relating to or arranged according to temporal order. *A chronological record follows the order in which things occurred.*

Chronology – *(noun)* **1** the study of records to establish the dates of past events. *Professors consult chronology to find out in which order events followed.* **2** the arrangement of events or dates in the order of their occurrence.

Chronometer – *(noun)* an instrument for measuring time accurately in spite of motion or variations in temperature, humidity, and air pressure. *Chronometer is very useful for weather specialists.*

Chronometry – *(noun)* the science of accurate time measurement. *Some people study chronometry.*

Chrysanthemum – *(noun)* a plant of the daisy family with brightly coloured ornamental flowers. *I am very much fond of chrysanthemum.*

Chrysolite – *(noun)* a yellowish-green or brownish variety of olivine, used as a gemstone. *The gemstone that I am wearing is made of chrysolite.*

Chubby – *(adjective)* plump and rounded. *What a beautiful and chubby child!*

Chuckle – *(verb)* laugh quietly or inwardly. *He chuckles at my joke.* *(noun)* a quiet or suppressed laugh.

Chucklehead – *(noun)* [informal] a stupid person. *He is a chucklehead.*

Chuffy – *(verb)* move with a regular sharp puffing sound. *He walked chuffily.*

Chum – *(noun)* a close friend. *You are my best chum.* *(verb)* **1** [chum up] form a friendship with someone. **2** [Scottish] accompany somewhere.

Chump – *(noun)* **1** [informal] a foolish person. *He is a chum a foolish fellow.* **2** [British] the thick end of something, especially a loin of lamb or mutton. *I would like to have chump for lunch.*

Church – *(noun)* **1** a building used for public Christian worship. *I go to church every sunday.* **2** a particular Christian organization with its own distinctive doctrines. **3** institutionalized religion as a political or social force. *(verb)* [archaic] take to church for a service of thanksgiving.

Churl – *(noun)* an impolite and mean-spirited person. [archaic] a miser. *People don't respect a churl.* **2** [archaic] a peasant.

Churn – *(noun)* **1** a machine for making butter by agitating milk or cream. **2** [British] a large metal milk can. *(verb)* **1** agitate in a churn to produce butter. *Churn the milk well and you'll get butter.* **2** move about vigorously. **3** produce something mechanically in large quantities. **4** upset or nervous.

Chute – *(noun)* a sloping channel or slide for conveying things to a lower level; a water slide into a swimming pool. *Water went down the chute.*

Cicatrize – *(verb)* heal by scar formation. *He has a cicatrize across his face.*

Cider – *(noun)* [British] an alcoholic drink made from fermented apple juice. [north American] a cloudy unfermented drink made from crushed apples.

Cigar – *(noun)* a cylinder of tobacco rolled in tobacco leaves for smoking. *Cigar is going out of fashion these days.*

Cigarette – *(noun)* a thin cylinder of finely cut tobacco rolled in paper for smoking. *Cigarette smoking is very harmful.*

Cilia – *plural* form of cilium.

Cilice – *(noun)* haircloth. *In winter people use cilice.*

Cinchona – *(noun)* a medicinal drug containing quinine and related compounds, made from the dried bark of various south American trees. *I had to take cinchona for malaria.*

Cincture – *(noun)* **1** [poetic] a girdle or belt. **2** [architecture] a ring at either end of a column shaft.

Cinder – *(noun)* a piece of burnt coal or wood that has stopped giving off flames but still has combustible matter in it. *We pulled out a cinder which seemed a piece of dead coal*

Cingalese – *(noun & adjective)* [archaic] spelling of sinhalese.

Cinnabar – *(noun)* **1** a bright red mineral consisting of mercury sup hide. **2** a day flying moth with black and red wings.

Cinnamon – *(noun)* **1** an aromatic spice made from the fried and rolled bark of a SE Asian tree. *I am fond of the taste of cinnamon.* **2** the tree which yields this spice. **3** a yellowish-brown colour resembling cinnamon.

Cipher – *(noun)* a continuous sounding of an organ pipe, caused by a defect. *(verb)* sound continuously.

Circa – *(preposition)* approximately.

Circlet – *(noun)* **1** an ornamental circular band worn on the head. **2** a small circular arrangement or object. *I bought a beautiful circlet for wearing on my wrist.*

Circuit – *(noun)* **1** a roughly circular line, route, or movement. **2** [British] a track used for motor racing, house racing, or athletics. *Sport tracks are usually circulars.* **3** a system of electrical conductors and components forming a complete path around which an electric current can flow. **4** an established series of sporting events or entertainments. **5** a series of athletic exercises performed in one training session. **6** a regular journey by a judge around a district to hear court cases. **7** a group of Methodist churches forming an administrative unit. **8** a chin of theatres or cinemas under a single management. *(verb)* move all the way around.

Circuitous – *(adjective)* longer than the most direct way. *It is a circuitous way leading out of the jungle.*

Circular – *(adjective)* **1** having the form of a circle. *The circus animals moved in a circular path.* **2** [logic] already containing an assumption of what is to be proved. *The circular of director was sent to all departments.* **3** for distribution to a large number of people. *(noun)* a circular letter or advertisement.

Circulation – *(noun)* **1** movement to and fro or around something; the continuous motion by while blood travels through the body. *Our blood runs in a circular way.* **2** the public availability or knowledge of something. **3** the number of copies sold of a newspaper or magazine. *The circulation of the newspaper 'Apana Desh' has gone up.*

Circum – *prefix* about; around within the word as an ad(verb) as in circumambulate, or as a preposition as in circumpolar.

Circumference – *(noun)* **1** the enclosing boundary of a circle. *Circumference of this dish is 5".* **2** the distance around something. *Without circumference there can be no circl.*

Circumscribe – *(verb)* **1** restrict; limit. *He has been circumscribed for crossing the limit.* **2** [geometry] draw two circles touching it at points but not cutting it; compare with inscribe. *When two circles drawn touch each other but do not cut this is called to circumscribe.*

Circumsolar – *(adjective)* moving or situated around the sun. *There are many circumsolar stars in the galaxy.*

Circumspect – *(adjective)* cautious or prudent. *He is a very circumspect person.*

Circumstance – *(noun)* **1** a fact or condition connected with or relevant to an event or action. *The circumstance did not allow him to pay back the loan.* **2** one's state of financial or material welfare. *I could not live in his circumstance.*

Circumvent – *(verb)* **1** find a way around. **2** [archaic] outwit. *He circumvented his opponent.*

Circumvolution – *(noun)* a winding movement of one thing round another. *Many machines work on the basis of circumvolution.*

Circus – *(noun)* **1** a travelling company of acrobats, trained animals, and clowns, giving performances typically in a large tent. *The whole of our family went to see a circus show and we enjoyed it a lot.* **2** a rounded sporting arena lined with tiers of seats. **3** [informal] a scene of lively activity. **4** a rounded open space in a town where several steels converge.

Cirrus – *(noun)* **1** cloud forming wispy filamentous tufted streaks at high altitude. *I saw a cirrus it; was around a mountain peak and had streaks of lightening.* **2** [zoology] a slender tendril or hair-like filament, e.g. the appendage of a barnacle or the barbell of a fish. [botany] a tendril.

Cist – *(noun)* a box for sacred utensils. *I keep all my sacred utensils in a cist.*

Cistern – *(noun)* **1** a water storage tank, especially as part of a flushing toilet. *I'll have to call a plumber because there is some problem with the cistern in the toilet.* **2** an underground reservoir for rainwater.

Citadel – *(noun)* **1** a fortress protecting or dominating a city. *Old forts used to have a citadel for protection from enemy.* **2** a meeting hall of the salvation army.

Citation – *(noun)* **1** a quotation from or reference to a book or author. *I give citation of a para of Mahatma Gandhi's autobiography.* **2** a mention of a praiseworthy act in an official report; a note accompanying an award, giving reasons for it. *There will be citation in your name for the act of bravery along with an award.* **3** [law] a reference to a former case, used as guidance or in support of an argument. *Please allow me to cite here a former law case.* **4** [law, chiefly north American] a summons.

Cite – *(verb)* **1** quote as evidence for an argument. *I will now cite a case to further strengthen my argument.* **2** praise for a courageous act in an official dispatch. *In this letter my praise has been cited.* **3** [law] summon to appear in law court.

Citizen – *(noun)* **1** a legally recognized subject or national of a state or commonwealth. *I am a citizen of India.* **2** an inhabitant of a town or city.

Citric – *(adjective)* derived from or related to citrus fruit. *Lemon juice is citric in nature.*

Citrine – *(noun)* a glassy yellow variety of quartz. *I am wearing a citrine ring.*

Citron – *(noun)* a shrubby Asian tree bearing large lemon-like fruits with thick fragrant peel. **2** the fruit of this tree.

City – *(noun)* **1** a large town. *I live in the city of Delhi.* [north American] a municipal centre incorporated by the state or province. **2** the part of London governed by the lord mayor and the corporation. the financial and commercial institutions in this part of London.

Civic – *(adjective)* of or relating to a city or town. *(noun)* [informal] an elected, community-based body concerned with local government in a black township.

Civil – *(adjective)* **1** of or relating to ordinary citizens, as distinct from military or ecclesiastical matters. *Civilians are non military people z.e, different from military personnel.* **2** [law noncriminal] a civil court. **3** courteous and polite. *He is a very civil and polite person.* **4** fixed by custom or law, not natural or astronomical.

Civilization – *(noun)* **1** an advanced stage or system of human social development. the process of achieving this. *As compared to old times, now live a highly civilized society.* **2** a civilized nation or region. *Civilization always marches forward.*

Civilize – *(verb)* **1** bring to an advanced stage of social development. *Civilize the people.* **2** polite and good-mannered.

Clack – *(verb)* **1** make or cause to make a sharp sound as of a hard object striking another. **2** [archaic] chatter loudly. *(noun)* **1** a clacking sound. *There was a clacking sound as the hammer hit the iron.* **2** [archaic], loud chatter.

Claim – *(verb)* **1** assert that something is the case. *I laid claim in the curt to many assets which were mine.* **2** demand as one's property or earnings. *I claim this property to be mine.* request under the terms of an insurance policy. *I claimed my money from the insurance company.* **3** call for (someone's attention). *After some struggle I succeeded in claiming her attention.* **4** caused the loss of someone's like. *I have claimed these there coal mines.* *(noun)* **1** an assertion of the truth of something. a statement of the novel features in a patent. **2** a demand for something considered one's due. a request for compensation under the terms of an insurance policy. **3** a place of land allotted to or taken by someone in order to be mined.

Clamant – *(adjective)* forcing itself urgently on the attention. *'Please, sir, I am clamant to your attention for a second'.*

Clamber – *(verb)* climb or move in an awkward and laborious way. *He clambered over the mountain. (noun)* an act of clambering.

Clamour – *(noun)* a loud and confused noise, especially of vehement shouting. a vehement protest or demand. *(verb)* make a clamour. *After the leader had spoken, there was a clamour in the crowd.*

Clamp – *(noun)* **1** a heap of potatoes or other root vegetables stored under straw or earth. *You will find a lot of potatos and other vegetables under this clamp.* **2** a three-sided structure used to store silage.

Clan – *(noun)* **1** a group of close-knit and interrelated families, especially in the Scottish highlands. **2** a group with a strong common interest. *Clans have religion and rituals of their own and they don't like spongers or any interference.*

Clandestine – *(adjective)* surreptitious. *I don't like his clandestine ways which are of secret nature.*

Clang – *(noun)* a loud, resonant metallic sound. *(verb)* make or cause to make a clang. *Iron clanged against iron and there was a metallic noise.*

Clank – *(noun)* a loud, sharp sound as of pieces of metal being struck together. *(verb)* make or cause to make a clank. *There was a clank as various machines started working.*

Clannish – *(adjective)* tending to exclude others outside the group. *I wanted to join their group but they acted clannish and kept me out.*

Clanship – *(noun)* the system of clan membership or laity. *In school days we had formed a clan and only a few could be granted membership.*

Clansman – *(noun)* a male member of a clan. *We had less clansman and no women.*

Clap – *(noun)* [informal] a venereal disease, especially gonorrhoea.

Clapper – *(noun)* the tongue or striker of a bell.

Claptrap – *(noun)* nonsense. *Whatever you have talked so for is nothing but claptrap.*

Clarence – *(noun)* [historical] a closed four-wheeled horse-drawn carriage, seating four inside and two outside. *In old days Clarence was a popular mode of transport.*

Clarification – *(noun)* an interpretation that remove obstacles to understanding. *You owe me a clarification how did all this happen?*

Clarify – *(verb)* **1** make more comprehensible. *Will you please clarify your stand?* **2** melt to separate out the impurities. *Metals are being melted to clarify them.*

Clarity – *(noun)* **1** the state or quality of being clear, distinct, and easily perceived or understood. *The clarity of his speech is appreciable.* **2** the quality of transparency or purity: the crystal clarity of water. *The water of this place is very clear.*

Clash – *(verb)* **1** come abruptly into violent conflict. have a forceful disagreement. *The two cars clashed head on.* **2** be incompatible. *We can be no longer friends because our ideas have begun to clash.* **3** appear discordant when placed together. *Clash occurred between the two leaders on the stage.* **4** occur inconveniently at the same time. **5** strike together, producing a loud discordant sound. *(noun)* an instance of clashing.

Clasp – *(verb)* **1** grasp tightly with one's hand; place around something so as to hold it tightly; hold tightly; press together with the fingers interlaced. *He clasped my hand warmly.* **2** fasten with a clasp. *I fastened the bag with a clasp and held it tightly. (noun)* **1** a small device with interlocking parts used for fastening things together. **2** an inscribed silver bar on a medal ribbon. **3** an act of clasping.

Classic – *(adjective)* **1** judged over a period of time to be of the highest quality; of a simple, elegant, style not greatly subject to changes in fashion. *Some films and novels are classic. They do not fade with the passage of time.* **2** remarkably typical: the classic symptoms of flu. *Body ache and fever are classic symptoms of flu. (noun)* **1** a work of art of recognized and established value. *The works of Latin and Greek writings are classics.* **2** the study of ancient Greek and

Latin literature, philosophy, and history. the works of ancient Greek and Latin writers and philosophers. **3** a major sports tournament or competition, especially in golf or tennis.

Classify – *(verb)* **1** arrange in classes or categories according to shared qualities or characteristics. assign to a particular class or category. *Some official documents are classified as secret or top secret.* **2** designate as officially secret or to which only authorized people may have access. *Categorization or classification is a must in private as well as government offices.*

Clatter – *(noun)* a loud rattling sound as of hard objects falling or striking each other. *(verb)* make or cause to make a clatter; fall or move with a clatter. *The swords of the two warriors clattered together.*

Clause – *(noun)* **1** a unit of grammatical organization next below the sentence in rank, and in traditional grammar said to consist of a subject and predicate. *Sometimes it becomes difficult to find participle and subordinate clauses in a sentence.* **2** a particular and separate article, stipulation, or proviso in a treaty. bill, or contract. *There is a clause in contract that none of us can resign till this particular job is completed.*

Clavicle – *(noun)* [anatomy] technical term for collarbone. *As he fell down, he broke his clavicle.*

Claviform – *(adjective)* another term of clavate.

Claw – *(noun)* **1** a curved, pointed horny nail on each digit of the foot in birds, lizards, and some mammals. either of a pair of small hooked appendages on an insect's foot. *The claws of carnivorous birds are different from those of other birds.* **2** the pincer of a crab, scorpion, or other arthropod. *I scratched his face with my claws.* **3** a mechanical device resembling a claw, used for gripping or lifting. *I saw a huge mechanical claw lifting heavy objects.* **4** *She keeps her hails sharp, clean and painted.* (verb) **1** scratch or tear at with the claws or fingernails. **2** oneself forward with one's hands. **3** regain or recover money, power, etc. laboriously or harshly. **4** beat to windward.

Clay – *(noun)* **1** a stiff, sticky fine-grained impermeable earth that can be moulded when wet and baked to make bricks and pottery. *Bricks and pottery are mode out of clay.* **2** [poetic] the substance of the human body. *Our body is nothing but lifeless clay.*

Claymore – *(noun)* **1** [historical] a type of two-edged or single edged broadsword used in Scotland. **2** a type of antipersonnel mine.

Clean – *(adjective)* **1** free from dirt, pollutants, or harmful substances. attentive to personal hygiene. *It is a clean place.* **2** morally pure; not obscene; showing or having no record of offences or crimes. played or done according to the rules. *The comedy show was clean without any obscenity or personal remarks.* **3** free from irregularities. smooth; well defined; free from knots. *The job of theft was so cleanly done that it took years for police to solve it.* **4** smoothly and skillfully done. *I am sorry, I clean forgot your birthday.* **5** distinctive and fresh. *Please take away the men and make the room tidy and clean.* *(verb)* **1** make clean; make free of mess. **2** [informal] use up or take all someone's money or resources. strip a place of and steal all its contents. *The thieves cleaned the safe.* **3** [informal] make a substantial gain or profit. *(noun)* chiefly British an act of cleaning.

Cleanse – *(verb)* **1** make thoroughly clean. *She has been cleansed of her sins by a priest.* **2** [archaic] cure a leper. *(noun)* an act of cleansing.

Clearance – *(noun)* **1** the action or process of clearing or of being dispersed. *Clearance sale! 30% rebate on every item?* **2** a kick or hit that sends the ball out of a defensive zone. *He hit the ball across the boundary.* **3** [snooker] the potting of all the balls remaining on the table in a singly break. **4** official authorization for something to proceed or take place. *I have received clearance from the office to start the operation.* **5** clear space allowed for a thing to move past or under another. *The plane got the clearance to land.*

Cleat – *(noun)* **1** a T-shaped or similar projection to which a rope may be attached. *The cow was tied to this cleat.* **2** a projecting wedge on spar, took, etc. to prevent slippage. one of a number of projections on the sole of a boot, to increase its grip.

Cleft - *(noun)* **1** a fissure or split in rock or the ground. *You can put your foot into that cleft and climb upwards.* **2** an indentation or deep hollow in person's forehead or chin, or between two parts of the body. *The cleft on his chin is an added attraction to his handsome features.*

Clemency - *(noun)* leniency and compassion shown to ward off enders by a person or agency charged with administering justice. *Please sir, I plead for clemency.*

Clergy - *(noun)* the body of people ordained for religious duties in the Christian church. *He is the finest speaking clergy in the church.*

Clerical - *(adjective)* concerned with or relating to the routine work of an office clerk. *He was offered a clerical job which he refused.* **2** of or relating to the clergy. *There are a lot of clerical monks in the church.*

Clerk - *(noun)* **1** a person employed in an office or bank to keep records or accounts and to undertake other routine administrative duties. *He is a clerk in an office.* **2** an official in charge of the records of a local council or court. a senior official in parliament. *My father was a clerk in parliament.* a lay officer of a cathedral, church, or chapel. *There are many clerks working in cathedrals and churches.* **3** [north American] receptionist in a hotel. an assistant in a shop; a sales clerk. **4** formal a member of the clergy. *(verb)* north American work as a clerk.

Clew - *(noun)* **1** the lower or after corner of a sail. **2** [nautical] the cords by which a hammock is suspended. *If you go into a labyrinth, don't forget to carry a clew so that you can find your way back.* **3** [archaic] a ball of thread. **4** [archaic] variant of CLUE. *(verb)* draw a sail up or let it down by the clews when preparing for furling or when unfurling.

Click - *(noun)* a short, sharp sound as of two metallic or plastic objects coming smartly into contact. *The two metallic rods clicked together.* a speech sound produced by sudden withdrawal of the tongue form the soft palate, front teeth, or back teeth and hard plate, occurring in some southern African and other languages. *She clicked her tongue as she saw the food on the table.* computing an act of pressing one of the buttons or become secured with such a sound; [computing] press one of the buttons on a mouse. **2** informal become suddenly clear and understandable. become friendly and compatible. *An idea suddenly clicked into my mind and everything became clear.*

Client - *(noun)* **1** a person using the services of a professional person or organisation. *He is the best client to deal with him very carefully.* **2** [computing] a computer or workstation that obtains information and applications from a server; a program that obtains a service provided by another program. **3** a plebian under the protection of a patrician. [archaic] a dependant; a hanger-on.

Cliff - *(noun)* a steep rock face, especially at the edge of the sea. *Climbing cliffs is his favourites hobby.*

Climate - *(noun)* **1** the general weather conditions prevailing in an area over a long period. a prevailing trend or public attitude. *Climate of Africa is hot.*

Climax - *(noun)* **1** the most intense, exciting, or important point of something. *As the climax scene of the film approached, I felt very tense and my heart beat increased.* **2** an orgasm. *He reached climax rather too soon* . **3** [rhetoric] a sequence of propositions or ideas in order of increasing importance, force, or effectiveness of expression. **4** [ecology] the final stage in a succession in a given environment, at which a plant community reaches a state of equilibrium. *(verb)* reach or bring to a climax.

Climb - *(verb)* **1** go or come up to a higher position; go up mountains as a sport; slope or lead up; grow up by clinging to or twining round it. *He is a professional mountain climber.* **2** move with effort into or out of a confined space. *I climbed up out of the hole with great difficulty.* **3** increase in scale, value, or power. *The sale of his songs has climbed.* **4** withdraw from a position taken up in argument or negotiation. *(noun)* **1** an instance of climbing; an ascent. **2** a recognised route up a mountain or cliff.

Clime - *(noun)* [chiefly poetic/literary] a region considered with reference to its climate: jetting oft to sunnier climes. *Summer climes in India are beautiful.*

Cling - *(verb)* **1** hold on tightly to; adhere or stick to. **2** remain persistently faithful to: she clung to her convictions. **3** be emotionally dependent on. *(noun)* a clingstone peach.

Clinic - *(noun)* **1** a place where specialised medical treatment or advice is given. *I went to doctor's clinic for a medical checkup.* **2** a gathering at a hospital bedside for the teaching of medicine or surgery. *We stood close by patient's bed and listened to doctor's lecture about surgery.* **3** chiefly north American a conference or short course on a particular subject: a drum clinic.

Clink - *(noun)* a sharp ringing sound, such as that made when metal or glass are struck. *(verb)* make or cause to make a clink. *They clinked the glasses together and drank.*

Cloak - *(noun)* **1** an over garment that hangs loosely form the shoulders over the arms to the knees or ankles. **2** something that hides or covers. *I don't trust that man, he is covered in a cloak secrecy.* **3** [British] a cloakroom. *If you want to go to toilet, go where it is written cloakroom.* *(verb)* dress or hide in a cloak.

Clock - *(noun)* an ornamental pattern woven or embroidered on the side of a stocking or sock near the ankle.

Clod - *(noun)* **1** a lump of earth or clay. *I took a handful of clod and tried to make a toy out of it.* **2** informal a stupid person. *He is a clod.* **3** [British] a coarse cut of meat from the lower neck of an ox.

Clog - *(noun)* **1** a shoe with a thick wooden sole. **2** an encumbrance. *There look at that shop there is a pair of clogs for sale if you want to buy one.* *(verb)* block or become blocked with something thick or sticky. *The engine of the car is clogged.*

Cloister - *(noun)* **1** a covered, and typically colonnaded, passage round an open court in a convent, monastery, college, or cathedral. *In college we often walk in the cloister.* **2** a convent or monastery; monastic life. *(verb)* seclude or shut up in a convent or monastery.

Close - *(adjective)* **1** only a short distance away or apart in space or time. dense: close very near to being or doing something. *God it was a close shave for me in the morning. As I was crossing the street a vehicle closely passed by me.* **2** denoting someone who is part of a person's immediate family, typically a parent or sibling. strong. *We are the closest of friends.* **3** very affectionate or intimate. *My mother is closer to me than my father is.* **4** done in a careful and through way. **5** carefully guarded. of a person not willing to give away money or information. **6** uncomfortably humid or airless. *This is a close secret and I'll keep it close.* **7** [phonetics] another term for HIGH. *(adverb)* so as to be very near; with very little space between. *The men has closed his mouth, we can't get anything more out of him.* *(noun)* **1** [British] a residential street without through access. **2** [British] the precinct surrounding a cathedral. **3** Scottish an entry form the street to a common stairway or to a court at the back of a building.

Closet - *(noun)* **1** [chiefly north American] a tail cupboard or wardrobe. *I have a closet made up of teak wood.* **2** a small room. *He is alone and lives in a closet.* **3** [archaic] a toilet. *He is in a closet and you can't meet him now.* **4** especially with reference to homosexuality a state of secrecy or concealment. **5** secret; covert: a closet socialist. *(verb)* shut away in private conference or study. keeping something, especially the fact of being homosexual, secret.

Closure - *(noun)* **1** an act or process of closing something. *The closure of the shop will be at 8 p.m.* **2** a device that closes or seals something. *You can seal this shop with this closure.* **3** a procedure for ending a debate and taking a vote. *Now there will be a closure to the debate and voting will take place.* *(verb)* apply the closure to in a legislative assembly.

Clot - *(noun)* **1** a thick mass of coagulated liquid, especially blood, or of material stuck together. *A clot of blood blocked his artery and he died.* **2** [British informal] a foolish or clumsy person. *It is not me talking to him, he is a clot.* *(verb)* form or cause to form into clots. cover with sticky matter.

Clothe – *(verb)* put clothes on; dress. provide someone with clothes. *I put clothe and went to the wedding.*

Cloud – *(noun)* **1** a visible mass of condensed watery vapour floating in the atmosphere, typically high above the general level of the ground. *As the sky became full of dark clouds, it began to rain.* an indistinct or billowing mass of smoke, dust, or something consisting of numerous particles; an opaque patch within a transparent substance. *Clouds make the sky beautiful at dawn or sunset.* **2** an oppressive burden of gloom or anxiety. *As I was under debt a heavy cloud of gloom sat on me.* *(verb)* **1** become full of clouds. **2** make or become less clear or transparent. **3** become expressive of sadness, anxiety, or anger. **4** make unclear or uncertain.

Clough – *(noun)* [north English] a steep valley or ravine. *The jungle was full of cloughs.*

Clove – *(noun)* any of the small bulbs making up a compound bulb of garlic, shallot, etc. *The oil of clove has many medical uses. Many people clew clove for bad breath.*

Clown – *(noun)* **1** a comic entertainer, especially one in a circus, wearing a traditional costume and exaggerated make-up. *All children liked the performance of clowns in the circus.* **2** a playful, extrovert person. **3** [archaic] an unsophisticated country person. *(verb)* act comically or playfully. *He is a clownish person and nobody gets bored in his company.* **3** *'Ah! Don't you worry, he is just a clown.'*

Club – *(noun)* **1** a heavy stick with a thick end, used as a weapon. *Club was a favourite weapon of the cave men.* **2** a club used to hit the ball in golf, with a heavy wooden or metal head on a slender shaft. *He was beaten with a club-like weapon.* **3** one of the four suits in a conventional pack of playing cards, denoted by a black trefoil. a card of such a suit. *(verb)* beat with a club or similar implement.

Clue – *(noun)* a fact or place of evidence serving to reveal a hidden truth or solve a problem. *(verb)* [informal] inform someone about a particular matter. *Police found a clue and caught the gang of thieves.*

Clump – *(noun)* **1** a small group of trees or plants growing closely together. a compacted mass or lump of something. *The wounded animal hid itself in a clump.* [physiology] an agglutinated mass of blood cells or bacteria, especially as an indicator of the presence of an antibody to them. **2** a thick extra sole on a boot or shoe. **3** another term for clomp. *(verb)* **1** form into a clump or mass. **2** another term for clomp.

Cluster – *(noun)* a group of similar things positioned or occurring closely together. *There was a cluster of ants around the piece of sweet.* **2** a natural subgroup of a population, used for statistical sampling or analysis. **3** [chemistry] a group of atoms of the same element, typically a metal, bounded closely together in a molecule. *(verb)* **1** form a cluster. **2** [statistics] have similar numerical values.

Clutch – *(verb)* grasp tightly. *Clutch the rope tightly, I am gong to pull you up.* *(noun)* **1** a tight grasp. **2** power; control. *She was lucky enough not to fall into his clutches.* **3** a mechanism for connecting and disconnecting the engine and the transmission system in a vehicle, or the working parts of any machine. *While learning to drive, I rather use the clutch too much.*

Clutter – *(noun)* things lying about untidily. an untidy state. *(verb)* cover or fill with clutter. *The entire floor of the room was cluttered with a lot of broken and useless things.*

Clyster – *(noun)* [archaic] term for enema. *Doctors used clysters to clean his intestines of all the excreta.*

Coach – *(noun)* **1** an instructor or trainer in sport. *We still remember our hockey coach of college days.* **2** a tutor who gives private or specialized teaching. **3** [austral] a docile cow or bullock used as a decoy to attract wild cattle. *(verb)* train or teach as a coach.

Coadjutor – *(noun)* a bishop appointed to assist and often to succeed a diocesan bishop.

Coal – *(noun)* a combustible rock consisting mainly of carbonized plant matter and used as fuel. [British] a piece of coal. *(verb)* provide with or extract coal.

Coalition - *(noun)* a temporary alliance, especially of political parties forming a government. *Our today's governments is a coalition government.*

Coarse - *(adjective)* **1** rough or harsh in texture; unrefined. consisting of large grains or particles. *He seemed to be a country man. He was wearing coarse clothes.* **2** not elegantly formed or proportioned. *He is coarse by nature, no refinement in him. Even his speech and jokes are coarse.* **3** [British] relating to the sport of angling for coarse fish.

Coast - *(noun)* **1** the part of the land adjoining or near the sea. *There are some coasts very popular in European countries. (verb)* **1** succeed with little effort. *In the hockey match they coasted to victory and won by two goals without much tremble.* **2** sail along the coast. *All of us sailed along the coast. It was great fun.*

Coat - *(noun)* **1** a full-length outer garment with sleeves, a man's jacket. *He wore a blue coloured coat.* **2** an animal's covering of fur or hair. *Our dog has a thick coat of hair.* **3** an enclosing or covering layer or structure. **4** a single application of paint or similar material. *The room has first coat of paint so far. (verb)* provide with or form a layer or covering.

Coating - *(noun)* a thin layer or covering of something. *You have to give three coatings of paint to this room.*

Coax - *(verb)* persuade gradually or by flattery to do something; use such persuasion to obtain; manipulate carefully into a particular situation or position. *I coaxed my friend into going to a movie.*

Cob - *(noun)* **1** [British] a loaf of bread. *Many Christians first pray and then eat the cob.* **2** short for corncoe. **3** a hazelnut or filbert. a hazel or filbert bush. **4** a powerfully built, short-legged horse. *I enjoyed riding a cob.* **5** male swan. **6** a roundish lump of coal. *We had enough cobs to keep the room hot.*

Cobalt - *(noun)* the chemical element of atomic number 27, a hard silvery-white magnetic metal. *Cobalt is used in many alloys.*

Cobby - *(adjective)* of a horse or other animal stocky. *He is strong like a cobby.*

Cobra - *(noun)* a highly venomous African or Asian snake that spreads the skin of its neck into a hood when disturbed. *We saw a cobra with its hood spread out. It looked ferocious but the snake charmer controlled it.*

Cobweb - *(noun)* a spider's web, especially an old or dusty one. *The room was dirty, untidy and full of cobwebs.*

Cocaine - *(noun)* an addictive drug derived from coca or prepared synthetically, used as an illegal stimulant and sometimes medicinally as a local anesthetic. *Cocaine is used by many youngsters.*

Coccyx - *(noun)* a small triangular hone at the base of the spinal column in humans and some apes, formed of fused vestigial vertebrae.

Cochlea - *(noun)* the spiral cavity of the inner ear containing the organ or corti, which produces nerve impulses in response to sound vibrations.

Cock - *(noun)* a small pile of hay or other material, with vertical side and a rounded top. *(verb)* [archaic] pile into a cock. *In villages you can see many cocks of hey and dung.*

Cockboat - *(noun)* a small boat towed behind a larger vessel. *My cockboat has towed by a ship as it had developed some defect.*

Cockcrow - *(noun)* [poetic/literary] dawn. *He has the habit of rising at cockcrow.*

Cockerel - *(noun)* a young domestic cock. *Our backyard is usually full of cockerel.*

Cockle - *(verb)* wrinkle or pucker.

Cockpit - *(noun)* **1** a compartment for the pilot and crew in an aircraft or spacecraft. *I when we were flying, I was very curious to see the cockpit but nobody was allowed there.* the driver's compartment in a racing car. *You can have a look at the cockpit of a racing car.* **2** a place where cockfights are held. *I chanced to see a cockfight in a cockpit.* **3** a place where a battle or other conflict takes place.

Cockroach - *(noun)* a beetle-like scavenging insect with long antennae and legs, *I don't know why, but when I look at a cockroach I feel like vomiting.*

Cockscomb - *(noun)* **1** the crest or comb of a domestic cock. *All male cocks have a cockscomb.* **2** a tropical plant with a crest of tiny yellow, orange, or red flowers, grown as a pot plant. *I bought a cockscomb plant and put it in a flowerpot to grow.* **3** a brightly coloured orchid related to the coralroots, native to southern north America.

Cocksure – *(adjective)* presumptuously or arrogantly confident. *He was cocksure to clear the interview but then nothing worked out. He failed.*

Cocky – *(noun)* austral informal a cockatoo.

Coco – *(noun)* **1** coconut. **2** [western Indian] the root of the taro.

Cocoon – *(noun)* **1** a silky case spun by the larvae of many insects for protection as pupae. something that envelops, especially in a protective or comforting way. *He found life so stressful that he sought the protective comfort of cocoon.* **2** a covering that prevents the corrosion of metal equipment. *(verb)* **1** warp in a cocoon. **2** [north American] retreat from the stressful conditions of pulbic life.

Cod – *(noun)* a large marine fish with a small barbel on the chin, important as a food fish. *My favourite fish is cod.*

Code – *(noun)* **1** a system of words, figures, or symbols used to represent others, especially for the purposes of secrecy; a sequence of numbers dialed to connect the telephone with the exchange of the telephone being called. *While in school, we had our code words for almost everything.* **2** computing program instructions. **3** a systematic collection of laws or statutes: the penal code. a set of conventions governing behaviour or activity in a particular sphere. *Every government has its set of codes.* *(verb)* **1** convert into a code. assigns a code to for purposes be the genetic code for an amino acid or protein. be the genetic determiner of a characteristic.

Codger – *(noun)* [informal, derogatory] an elderly man. *Many people become codger in old age.*

Codicil – *(noun)* an addition or supplement that explains, modifies, or revokes a will or part of one. *According to codicil, a part of the property will also go to deceased person's servant.*

Codify – *(verb)* organize into a system or code. *His full information has been codified.*

Co-education – *(noun)* the education of pupils of both sexes together. *For a healthy development students should study in co-educational institutes.*

Coefficient – *(noun)* **1** [mathematics] a numerical or constant quantity placed before and multiplying the variable in an algebraic expression. **2** [physic] a multiplier or factor that measures some property.

Co-equal – *(adjective)* having the same rank or importance. *(noun)* a person or thing equal with another. *Me and my best friends are co-equals.*

Coerce – *(verb)* persuade to do something by using force or threats. *He coerced her into marrying him.*

Coexist – *(verb)* exist at the same time or in the same place. exist in harmony. *In our society various members different families coexist.*

Coextensive – *(adjective)* extending over the same area, extent, or time. *All people living today are coextensive.*

Coffee – *(noun)* **1** a hot drink made from the roasted and ground bean-like seeds of a tropical shrub. the processed, roasted, and ground seeds used to make this drink. *My friend is so fond of a particular brand of coffee that he daily drinks four or five cups.* **2** the shrub which yields these seeds.

Coffer – *(noun)* **1** a small chest for holding valuables. the funds or financial reserves of an institution. *The coffers of our government almost seem to be empty.* **2** a decorative sunken panel in a ceiling. *(verb)* decorate with a coffer or coffers.

Coffin – *(noun)* a long, narrow box in which a dead body is buried or cremated. *His dead body was placed in a coffin and carried to the crematorium.* *(verb)* place in a coffin.

Cog – *(noun)* a broadly built medieval ship with a rounded prow and stern. *Cogs used to churn the waters in medieval times.*

Cogent – *(adjective)* clear, logical, and convincing. *His arguments were completely cogent.*

Cogitate – *(verb)* [formal] meditate or reflect. *He is given to cogitate over things.*

Cognate – *(adjective)* **1** [linguistics] having the same linguistic derivation as another. *Hindi is very much cognate to Urdu.* **2** formal related; connected. related to or descended from a common ancestor. *Me and my brother are cognate to one another.* compare with agnate. *(noun)* **1** linguistics a cognate word. **2** [law] a blood relative.

Cognition – *(noun)* the mental action or process of acquiring knowledge; through thought, experience, and the senses. a perception, sensation, or intuition resulting form this. *We gain knowledge through cognition.*

Cognizable – *(adjective)* informal perceptible; clearly identifiable. **2** [law] within the jurisdiction of court. *Your argument is perfectly cognizable.*

Cognizance – *(noun)* **1** [formal] knowledge or awareness. [law] the action of taking judicial notice. *Law has taken cognizance of this fact.* **2** [heraldry] a distinctive device or mark, especially as formerly worn by retainers of a noble house. *He is a man of keen cognizance.*

Cognizent – *(adj.)* having or showing knowledge or understanding or realization or perception. *How was cognizant of his opponent.*

Cohabit – *(verb)* **1** live together and have a sexual relationship without being married. **2** coexist.

Cohesion – *(noun)* the action or fact of forming a united whole.*The group acted in cohesion.* [physics] the sticking together of particles of the same substance. *Molecules are held together by cohesion.*

Cohesive – *(adjective)* characterized by or causing cohesion. *This is a cohesive group of workers.*

Coif – *(noun)* **1** a woman's close-fitting cap, worn under a veil by nuns. *Nuns wear a coif which is a close cap covering top back and sides.* [historical] a protective metal skullcap worn underarmour. *In old times warriors wore metal skull coif under their armour.* **2** [informal, chiefly north American] *(verb)* US also style or arrange someone's hair.

Coil – *(noun)* **1** a length of something round in a joined sequence of concentric rings. *I arranged the loose threads into a coil.* **2** an intrauterine contraceptive device in the form of a coil. *The mosquito coils do not last long.* **3** an electrical device consisting of a coiled wire, for converting the level of a voltage, producing a magnetic field, or adding inductance to a circuit. *I bought a coil of electric wire from the market.* *(verb)* arrange or form into a coil.

Coin – *(noun)* a flat disc or piece of metal with an official stamp, used as money. money in the form of coins. *I have so many coins but no notes.* **2** one of the suits in some tarot packs, corresponding metal. [British informal] earn quickly and easily. *This company is rich and coining money.* **3** invent or devise a new word or phrase. *Some writers coin new words.*

Coincide – *(verb)* occur at the same time or place. **2** correspond in nature; tally; be in agreement.

Coir – *(noun)* fibre from the outer husk of the coconut, used in potting compost and for making ropes and matting. *I have some ropes and matting made of coir.*

Coition – *(noun)* another term for coitus. *Both the lovers indulged in coition.*

Coke – *(noun)* informal term for Cocaine. *Coke or cocaine is a dangerous drug.*

Colander – *(noun)* a perforated bowl used to stain off liquid from food. *This is a strainer and you can wash vegetables in it.*

Cold – *(adjective)* **1** of or at a low or relatively low temperature. *I have caught cold.* **2** lacking affection or warmth of feeling; unemotional, not affected by emotion. *His behavior was cold to us and lacked warmth.* objective. containing pale blue or grey and giving no impression of warmth. **3** no longer fresh and easy to follow far from finding or guessing what is sought. *The police were in hot pursuit of robbers but after sometime the trail grew cold.* **4** without preparation or rehearsal; unawares. **5** [informal] unconscious. *She went out cold as a stone.* *(noun)* **1** a low temperature; cold weather; a cold environment. *Simla has a very cold weather in winters.* **2** a common infection in which the mucous membrane of the nose and throat becomes inflamed, causing running at the nose and sneezing.

Colic – *(noun)* severe pain in the abdomen caused by wind or obstruction in the intestines. *I have severe colic pain, please take me to a doctor.*

Collaborate – *(verb)* **1** work jointly on an activity or project. *Will you work in collaboration with me on this project.* **2** cooperate traitorously with an enemy. *He collaborated with another company to damage the firm where he used to work.*

Collapsible – *(adjective)* able to be folded down. *This sofa set is collapsible; it can be folded and kept in a small place.*

Collapse – *(verb)* **1** suddenly fall down or give way. fall inwards and become flat and empty. *The building suddenly collapsed.* **2** fall down as a result of physical breakdown. *He collapsed while walking in the garden.* **3** fail suddenly and completely. *The machine suddenly collapsed to work. (noun)* **1** an instance of a structure collapsing. **2** a sudden failure or breakdown.

Collar – *(noun)* **1** a band of material around the neck of a shirt or other garment, either upright or turned over. *My shirt collar is usually too dirty.* **2** a band put around the neck of a domestic animal, used to restrain or control. *Our dog has grown up now, I'll put a collar round his neck.* **3** a connecting band or pipe in a piece of machinery. **4** [British] a piece of meat rolled up and tied. a cut of bacon taken form the neck of a pig. *(verb)* informal seize or apprehend.

Collate – *(verb)* **1** collect and combine. compare and analyze. printing verify the number and order of the sheets of a book. *I worked in a book binding shop and collated there wavious books.* **2** appoint a clergyman to a benefice. *A clergyman was collated to the new office.*

Colleague – *(noun)* a person with whom one works in a profession or business. *Many colleagues work with me in the office.*

Collect – *(verb)* **1** bring or gather together. systematically seek and acquire as a hobby. *I have a collection of rare stamps, it is my favourite hobby.* **2** call for and take away; fetch. call for and receive as a right or due. **3** regain control of oneself, typically after a shock. *Somehow or the other I collected myself after the shock.* [archaic] conclude. *At the end of the meeting I collected that it was not worth attending.* infer. **4** austral collide with. *(adv. & adj.)* north Americana to be paid for by the person receiving it. *A Tax collector collects the taxes.*

Collected – *(adjective)* **1** not perturbed or distracted. *Throughout the proceeding, he remained calm and collected.* **2** brought together in one volume or edition. *The various parts of the book were collected and brought in one volume.*

Collection – *(noun)* **1** the action or process of collecting. *I have a big collection of newspaper photos regarding sport events.* a regular removal of mail for dispatch or of refuse for disposal. *His job in the office was to collect mail to dispatch.* an instance of collecting money, as in a church service. *In a church service they usually collect money.* **2** a group of things collected or accumulated. **3** [British] college examinations held at the beginning or end of a term, especially at oxford university.

Collective – *(adjective)* done by or belonging to all the members of a group. taken as a whole. *A collective effort was done to clan the old temple.* aggregate. *(noun)* a cooperative enterprise. a collective farm. *At a collective form all the farmers work as a team.*

Collector – *(noun)* **1** a person who collects things of a specified type, professionally or as a hobby. *He is a collector of rare and old books.* **2** an official who is responsible for collecting money owed. *A tax collector collects taxes.* **3** electronics the region in a bipolar transistor that absorbs charge carries.

Collet – *(noun)* **1** a segmented band put round a shaft and tightened so as to grip it. *I have got my gem set in a beautiful collet.* **2** a small collar in a clock a flange or socket for setting a gem in jewellery.

Collide – *(verb)* **1** hit by accident when moving. *He collided with a truck while crossing the rood.* **2** come into confect or opposition.

Collier - *(noun)* [chiefly British] **1** a coal miner. *He is a collier by profession.* **2** a ship carrying coal. *Colliers only carry coal and not passengers.*

Collinear - *(adjective)* [geometry] lying n the same straight line. *If point A and point B are joined by a straight line, they are collinear.*

Collision - *(noun)* an instance of colliding. *The two ships were moving on a course of collision.*

Collodion - *(noun)* a syrupy solution of nitrocellulose in a mixture of alcohol and ether, used for coating things, chiefly in surgery and in a former photographic process.

Colloquy - *(noun)* **1** a formal conference or conversation. *The colloquy between the persons did not seem to come to an end.* **2** a gathering for discussion of theological questions. *In a colloquy or gathering, religious questions are also discussed.*

Collotype - *(noun)* a process for making high-quality prints using a sheet of light-sensitive gelatin. *My friend uses the collotype process for making high quality prints.*

Collude - *(verb)* come to a secret understanding; conspire. *They colluded together to form a conspiracy to kill the king.*

Collusion - *(noun)* secret or illegal cooperation in order to cheat or deceive others. *Both the bad characters were planning for collusion.*

Collyrium - *(noun)* a kind of dark eye shadow, used especially in eastern countries. *Our women use colliyrium for eye colouring.*

Colon - *(noun)* [anatomy] the main part of the large intestine, which passes from the caecum to the rectum. *Some persons develop ulcers in their colon.*

Colonel - *(noun)* a rank of officer in the army above a lieutenant colonel and below a brigadier or brigadier general. *My father was a colonel in the army.*

Colonial - *(adjective)* **1** of, relating to, or characteristic of a colony or colonies. *The British had a big colonial empire.* **2** in the style of the period of the British colonies in America colonies. *(noun)* a person who lives in a colony.

Colonist - *(noun)* a settler in or inhabitant of a colony. *In cities people usually live in colonies and can be called colonists.*

Colonization - *(noun)* the act of coloning.*Britain had done the most colonization.*

Colonise - *(verb)* **1** establish a colony in a place. establish control over the indigenous people of a colony. *French, Dutch and Portuguese also tried to colonise India but the English beat them to it.* **2** appropriate a place or domain for one's own use. **3** [ecology] establish itself in an area.

Colonnade - *(noun)* a row of evenly spaced columns supporting a roof or other structure. *There are 12 colonnades in this hall which support the roof.*

Colophony - *(noun)* another term for rosin.

Coloration - *(noun)* **1** arrangement or scheme of colour; coluring. *There is something wrong with the coloration of this building, too bright colours.* **2** the character or tone of something, especially musical expression.

Colorific - *(adjective)* having much colour. *This mixture of colours is rather colorific.*

Colossal - *(adjective)* **1** extremely large. sculpture at least twice life size. **2** [architecture] having more than one storey of columns.

Colossus - *(noun)* a person or thing of enormous size, in particular a statue that is much bigger than life size.

Colour - *(noun)* **1** the property possessed by an object of producing different sensations on the eye as a result of the way it reflects or emits light. one, or any mixture, of the constituents into which light can be separated in a spectrum or rainbow. the use of all colours, not only black and white, in photography or television. *Almost all animals are colour blind.* **2** pigmentation of the skin, especially as an indication of someone's race. *Colours are natures great gift for us.***3**. redness of the complexion, as indicating health or an emotion such as anger. *The hot climate of Africa gives African a black colour.* **4** interest, excitement, and vitality: a town full of colour and character. *Redness of the face shows good health or anger. Different raues have different colours due to pigmentation which* *is their guard against the climate.* **5** [chiefly British] an item of a particular colour worn by a jockey or the members of sports team. a badge or cap warded to a pupil representing a school in sport. the flag of a regiment or ship. *When we blush, our complexion turns reddish.* **6** [physics] a property of quarks which can take three values designated blue, green, and red. *I first drew the picture with pencil and then gave colour to it.* **7** *Some bad experiences had coloured her whole existence.* *(verb)* **1** give a colour to. **2** show embarrassment by becoming red; blush. **3** influence, especially in negative way; distort: the experiences had coloured her whole existence.

Colouring – *(noun)* **1** the process or art of applying colour. *M.F. Hussain was a master of colouring.* **2** visual appearance with regard to colour. the natural hues of a person's skin, hair, and eyes. **3** a substance used to colour something, especially food.

Colourist – *(noun)* an artist or designer who uses colour in special or skilful way. *My friend is a famous and great colourist.*

Colter – *(noun)* US spelling of culter.

Comb – *(noun)* **1** an article with a row of narrow teeth, used for untangling or arranging the hair. *We should keep our combs clean.* a short curves comb worn by women to hold the hair in place. *Women use small combs in their hair so as to keep them in order.* **2** a device for separating and dressing textile fibers. [austral] the lower, fixed cutting piece of a sheep-shearing machine. *Combs are also used in sheep shearing machines.* **3** the red fleshy crest on the head of a domestic fowl, especially a cock. **4** a honeycomb. *(verb)* **1** untangle or arrange by drawing a comb through it. **2** prepare for manufacture with a comb. **3** search carefully and systematically. *The police combed the entire area but found nothing.*

Combat – *(noun)* fighting, especially between armed forces. *The two forces were engaged in armed combat.* *(verb)* **1** take action to reduce or prevent. **2** [archaic] engage in a fight with.

Comber – *(noun)* **1** a long curling sea wave. *I got afraid when I saw the comber coming.* **2** a person or machine that combs cotton or wool. *He is a comber who combs wool.*

Combine – *(verb)* [chemistry] unite to form a compound. *(noun)* a group of people or companies acting together for a commercial purpose. *Various companies have combined to complete this project.*

Combustible – *(adj.)* capable of ignitigng and buring. *This mixture is highly combustible.*

Combustion – *(noun)* the process of burning. [chemistry] rapid chemical combination with oxygen, involving the production of heat and light. *Chemical combustion with oxygen produces light and heat.*

Comedian – *(noun)* an entertainer whose act is designed to arouse laughter; a comic playwright. *Charlie chaplin was a great comedian.*

Comedy – *(noun)* **1** entertainment consisting of jokes and sketches intended to make an audience laugh; a film, play, or programme intended to arouse laughter. *Most people prefer comedy to tragedy.* **2** a play with a humorous or satirical tone, in which the characters ultimately triumph over adversity.

Comely – *(adjective)* **1** [archaic] typically of a woman pleasant to look at; attractive. *She is a comely women.* **2** [archaic] agreeable; suitable.

Comer – *(noun)* **1** a person who arrives. *He is a late comer.* **2** [north American, informal] a person or thing likely to succeed. *This horse is a comer.*

Comet – *(noun)* a celestial object which consists of a nucleus of ice and dust and, when near the sun, a diffuse tail, and typically follows a highly eccentric orbit around the sun. *I am so excited see a comet to tomarrou.*

Comfit – *(noun)* [archaic] a sweet consisting of a nut, seed, or other centre coated in sugar. *I like comfits a lot.*

Comfort – *(noun)* **1** a state of physical ease and freedom from pain or constraint. things that contribute to comfort. prosperity and a pleasant lifestyle. *I sat with comfort in the lounge.* **2** consolation for grief or anxiety. a person or thing that gives such consolation. *I gave comfort my friend as he had lost his father.* *(verb)* cause to feel less unhappy; console.

Comic - *(adjective)* causing or meant to cause laughter. relating to or in the style of comedy. *(noun)* a comedian. *He had a very comic face which made us often laugh.* **2** a children's periodical containing comic strips. [north American] comic strips. *American children read a lot of comic strips.*

Comity - *(noun)* **1** an association of nations for their mutual benefit; the mutual recognition by nations of the laws and customs of others. *International comity is the need of the day.* **2** formal courtesy and considerate behaviour towards others. *We shoud show comity to others.*

Comma - *(noun)* **1** a punctuation mark (,) indicating a pause between parts of a sentence or separating items in a list. *A long sentence must be separated with commas.* **2** [music] a minute interval or difference of pitch. *There was a little pause or comma is the on going music program.* **3** a widespread butterfly that has orange and brown wings and a white comma-shaped mark on the underside of the hind-wing. *Some butterflies are known as comma.*

Command - *(verb)* **1** give an authoritative or peremptory order. [military] be in charge of a unit. indicating or expressing authority; imposing. possessing or giving superior strength. *He has great command over English.* [archaic] control or restrain. **2** position from a superior height. **3** be in a position to receive. *(noun)* **1** an authoritative order. authority, especially over armed forces. a group or operation. a body of troops or a district under the control of a particular officer. **2** the ability to use or control something: his command of English. **3** computing an instruction causing a computer to perform one of its basic functions.

Commandant - *(noun)* an officer in charge of a particular force or institution. *He is a commandant of the army.*

Commander - *(noun)* **1** a person in authority, especially in a military context; a rank of naval officer, above lieutenant commander and below captain; an officer in charge of a metropolitan police district an London. *He is a commander in military.* **2** a member of a higher class in some orders of knighthood.

Commemorate - *(verb)* honour the memory of as a mark of respect, especially with a ceremony or memorial. *Mahatma Gandhi is commemorated every year on his birthday.*

Commence - *(verb)* begin. *The commonwealth games commenced at the scheduled time.*

Commend - *(verb)* **1** praise formally or officially. *He was commended for his high efficiency in the office work.* **2** present as suitable or good; recommend. **3** [archaic] entrust someone or something to; pass on someone's good wishes to.

Commensal - *(adjective)* relating to or denoting an association between two organisms in which one benefits and the other derives neither benefit nor-harm. *(noun)* a commensal organism, such as many bacteria.

Commesurable - *(adjective)* **1** measurable by the same standard. *Their performance are not commesurable.* **2** proportionate to. **3** [mathematics] in a ratio equal to a ratio of integers.

Comment - *(noun)* **1** a remark expressing an opinion or reaction; discussion, especially of a critical nature, of an issue or event; an explanatory note in a book or other written text. *He passed a comment on my nature which I did not like.* **2** [archaic] a written explanation or commentary. *(verb)* express an opinion or reaction.

Commerce - *(noun)* **1** the activity of buying and selling, especially on a large scale. *Commerce between the two countries in crease.* **2** social dalings between people. **3** [archaic] sexual intercourse.

Commiserate - *(verb)* express sympathy or pity; sympathize. *I commiserated with my friend when his relative died.*

Commissariat - *(noun)* **1** [chiefly military] a department for the supply of food and equipment. **2** a government department of the soviet union before 1946.

Commessary - *(noun)* **1** a deputy or delegate. a representative or deputy of a bishop. *He is a commissary who has come from UK to our country.* **2** [north American] a restaurant or food store in a military base or other institution. *There is commissary in the university campus, let us go and eat there.*

Commissure – *(noun)* [anatomy] **1** a seam between two bones. **2** a band of nerve tissue connecting the hemispheres of the brain, the two sides of the spinal cord, etc. **3** the line where the upper and lower lips or eyelids meet.

Commit – *(verb)* **1** perpetrate or carry out. *I am committed to serve the nation.* **2** pledge or bind to a course, policy, or use; dedicate to a cause be in a long-term emotional relationship. *He is a committed monk.* **3** transfer for safe keeping or permanent preservation. send to prison or psychiatric hospital, or for trial in a higher court. refer to a committee.

Committee – *(noun)* **1** a group of people appointed for a specific function by a larger group; a committee appointed by parliament to consider proposed legislation. the whole house of commons when sitting as a committee. *A committee appointed by a larger body does various works.* **2** [law] a person entrusted with the charge of another person or another person's property. [chiefly US] a person who has been judicially committed to the charge of another because of insanity or mental retardation.

Commodious – *(adjective)* **1** [formal] roomy and comfortable. *It is a large and commodious room.* **2** [archaic] convenient.

Commodity – *(noun)* **1** a raw material or primary agricultural product that can be bought and sold. **2** something useful or valuable. *Don't throw away this thing, it is a commodity.*

Common – *(adjective)* **1** occurring, found, or done often; not rare. without special rank or position; ordinary. of a sort to be generally expected: common decency. of the most familiar type. *We should all show common decency to one another.* **2** showing a lack of taste and refinement supposedly typical of the lower classes; vulgar. *Common people have a common purpose.* **3** shared by two or more people or things. belonging to or affecting the whole of a community. [mathematics] belonging to two or more quântities. **4** [grammar] of or denoting a noun that refers to individuals of either sex or belongs to a gender conventionally regarded as masculine or feminine. *We two friends share common interest.* **5** prosody able to be either short or long. *A park is a common land.* **6** law of lesser importance. *When we talk about all people we are talking abent common people.* **7** *A wrong kind of law can affect whole community.* **8** *A common (noun) can be both masculine or feminine.* *(noun)* **1** a piece of open land for public use. **2** [British informal] common sense. **3** a form of Christian service used for each of a group of occasions **4** English law a person's right over another's land, e.g. for pasturage or mineral extraction

Commonalty – *(noun)* [historical] people without special rank or position, usually viewed as an estate of the realm. *Gandhiji is a commonalty.*

Commoner – *(noun)* **1** one of the ordinary or common people, as opposed to the aristocracy or to royalty. *He looks gand, but he is neither an aristocrat nor a royalty, he is a commoner like us.* **2** a person who has the right of common. **3** an undergraduate without a scholarship.

Commonly – *(adverb) under normal canditions.*

Commotion – *(noun)* **1** a state of confused and noisy disturbance. *There was great commotion in crowd over the remarks of the speaker.* **2** civil insurrection.

Communal – *(adjective)* **1** shared or done by all members of a community; involving the sharing of work and property. *Communal living is sharing the work and property.* **2** between different communities, especially those having different religions or ethnic origins.

Commune – *(noun)* **1** a group of people living together and sharing possessions and responsibilities; a communal settlement in a communist country. **2** the smallest French territorial division for administrative purposes.**3** the group which seized the municipal government of Paris in the French revolution and played a leading part in the reign of terror; the municipal government organized on communalistic principles elected in Paris in 1871.

Communicable - *(adjective)* able to be communicated to others.

Communicate - *(verb)* **1** share or exchange information or ideas. *We have been communicating through letters for a long time.* convey in a non-verbal way. pass on an infectious disease. transmit heat or motion. **2** have a common connecting door. *We two friends have a common door between us. He at is communicate from one end of the iron rod to another.* **3** receive holy communion. *I have communicated my love to her.*

Communication - *(noun)* **1** the action of communicating. a letter or massage containing information or news. social contact. *There are so many means of communication. All of us make use of them.* **2** the means of sending or receiving information, such as telephone lines or computers. the means of travelling or of transporting goods, such as roads or railways.

Communion - *(noun)* **1** the sharing or exchanging of intimate thoughts and feelings. **2** the service of Christian worship at which bread and wine are consecrated and shared; the Eucharist. **3** a relationship of recognition and acceptance between Christian churches or denominations. a group of Christian churches or communities which recognize one another's ministries or that of a central authority.

Communique - *(noun)* an official announcement or statement, especially one made to the media. *A communiqué was issued to the media by a party spokesman.*

Communism - *(noun)* a theory or system of social organization in which all property is vested in the community and each person contributes and receives according to their ability and needs. a theory or system of this kind derived from Marxism and established in the soviet union, china, and elsewhere. *I believe neither in socialisan nor democracy.*

Community - *(noun)* **1** a group of people living together in one place, especially one practicing common ownership. a place considered together with its inhabitants. the people of an area or country considered collectively; society. *Some people believe in community living sharing common interest and religion.* **2** a group of people having a religion, race, or profession in common: **3** the condition of having certain attitudes and interests in common. joint ownership or liability. **4** [ecology] a group of interdependent plants or animals growing or living together.

Commutator - *(noun)* **1** an attachment, connected with the armature of a motor or dynamo, through which electrical connection is made and which ensures the current flows as direct current. *It is a device to reverse the direction of currant.* **2** a device for reversing the direction of flow of electric current.

Commute - *(verb)* **1** travel some distance between one's home and place of work on a regular basis. *We daily commute between our office and home.* **2** reduce to a less severe one. *The company has commuted my annual series of payment to a single one.* change one kind of payment or obligation for another. replace an annuity or other series of payments with a single payment. **3** [mathematics] of two operations or quantities have a commutative relation.

Compact - *(adjective)* **1** closely and neatly packed together; dense. having all the necessary components or features neatly fitted into a small space. *In the make up box, all the articles were compactly placed.* **2** [archaic] composed or made up of. *(verb)* exert force on to make more dense; compress. [archaic] form by pressing the component parts firmly together. *(noun)* a small flat case containing face powder, a mirror, and a powder puff.

Companion - *(noun)* **1** a person with whom one spends time or travels. *The railway journey was boring but luckily I found an interesting companion.* a person employed to live with and assist someone old or unwell. *He is my companion of old age.* **2** each of a pair of things intended to complement or match each other. [British] a piece of equipment containing several objects used in a particular activity. **3** a member of the lowest grade or certain orders of knighthood. *(verb)* formal accompany.

Compare – *(verb)* **1** estimate, measure, or note the similarity or dissimilarity between. *By comparison, our school is for better than that one.* point out or describe the resemblances of something with; liken to. *If you compare two things, one is bound to come out better.* be similar to or have a specified relationship with another thing or person; salaries compare favourably with those of other professions. *If we compare the salaries given by the two companies the second company gives better salary.* **2** [grammar] form the comparative and superlative degrees of an adjective or an adverb.

Comparison – *(noun)* **1** the action of comparing. the quality of being similar or equivalent. *I am making a comparison the two companies as to which to join.* **2** [grammar] the formation of the comparative and superlative forms of adjectives and adverbs.

Compass – *(noun)* **1** an instrument containing a magnetized pointer which shows the direction of magnetic north and bearings from it. *In old timers navigations was done with the help of compass.* **2** an instrument for drawing circles and arcs and measuring distances between points, consisting of two arms linked by a movable joint. **3** range or scope. *(verb)* [archaic] **1** circle or surround. **2** contrive to accomplish.

Compassion – *(noun)* sympathetic pity and concern for the sufferings or misfortunes of others. *We must have compassion for suffering of others.*

Compendious – *(adjective)* formal presenting the essential facts in a comprehensive but concise way. *His lecture was brilliant. It was so compendious that gave a long explanations in very short.*

Compendium – *(noun)* **1** a collection of concise but detailed information about a particular subject. *I just bought a compendium; I have so many friends to write to.* **2** a collection of similar items. *I have a compendium over Delhi along with its kings and queens.* **3** a package of stationery for writing letters.

Compensation – *(noun)* **1** something awarded to compensate for loss, suffering, or injury. something that compensates for an undesirable state of affairs. the action or process of compensation. *When my friend was injured in a hockey game being played at state level, he was compensated generously.* **2** [north American] money received as salary or wages.

Compete – *(verb)* strive to gain or win something by defeating or establishing superiority over others. *I competed in the race and won.*

Compentence – *(noun)* **1** the quality or extent of being competent. *His competence in playing football is excellent.* **2** [linguistics] a person's subconscious knowledge of the rules governing the formation of speech in their first language. often contrasted with PERFORMANCE. **3** dated an income large enough to live on.

Competent – *(adjective)* having the necessary ability or knowledge to do something successfully; efficient and capable. having legal authority to deal with a particular matter. *He is a competent lawyer. He is competent of sitting in the civil services examination.*

Competition – *(noun)* **1** the activity or condition of competing against others. [ecology] interaction between species or organisms which share a limited environmental resource. *Competition also takes between animals who live in a limited environment safe.* **2** an event or contest in which people compete. the person or people with whom one is competing. *There is going to be a big sports competition and my brother is going to take part is it.*

Competitive – *(adjective)* **1** relating to or characterised by competition. *He has a competitive nature; always ready to compets.* strongly desiring to be more successful than others. *He wishes to prove that he is more desirable than others.* **2** as good as or better than others of a comparable nature.

Compile – *(verb)* **1** produce by assembling material from other sources. accumulate a specified score. *He is compiling a dictionary.* **2** [computing] convert a program into a lower-level form in which the program can be executed.

Complacent – *(adjective)* smug and uncritically satisfied with oneself or one's achievements. *He is a complacent, smug and only irritatingly satisfied with himself.*

Complain – *(verb)* **1** express dissatisfaction or annoyance. *I'll complain against your behaviour to the principal.* **2** state that one is suffering from a symptom of illness. *He complained of a headache.*

Complaint – *(noun)* **1** an act or the action of complaining. a reason for dissatisfaction. [law] the plaintiff's reasons for proceeding in a civil action. an illness or medical condition, especially a relatively minor one. *I have received so many complaints against you. What have you to say?*

Complaisant – *(adjective)* willing to please others or to accept their behaviour without protest. *He is a very complaisant person. He never minds the behaviour of others.*

Complement – *(noun)* **1** a thing that contributes extra features to something else so as to enhance or improve it. *I gave her a complement on her performance on the stage.* **2** the number or quantity that makes something complete. **3** [grammar] a word, phrase, or clause governed by a verb that completes the meaning of the predicate. an (adjective) or (noun) that has the same reference as either the subject or object. **4** [physiology] protein present in blood plex to bring about the destruction of foreign cells. **5** [geometry] the amount by which a given angle is less than 90°. *(verb)* serve as a complement to.

Complete – *(adjective)* **1** having all the necessary or appropriate parts; entire. having as an additional part or feature. *I maintain complete abstinence from alcohol.* **2** having run its full course; finished. *The race was complete.* **3** to the greatest extent or degree; total: a complete surprise. *The project is entirely complete, you can rest now.* **4** skilled at every aspect of an activity; consummate. *I have written what is required on a form. These items are necessary to make the project complete.* **5** *(verb)* **1** finish making or doing. *I have completed filling my application form.* [British] conclude the sale of a property. **2** provide with the items necessary to make complete. write the required information on a form.

Complex – *(adj)* **1** consisting of many different and connected parts. *This is a complex machine.* **2** not easy to analysis or understand; complicated or intricate. *My friend suffers from abnormal behaviour. Psycho emotions analysis have revealed that some repressed are responsible for this complex problem.* **3** [mathematics] containing both a real and an imaginary part. *(noun)* **1** a group of similar buildings or facilities on the same site. an interlinked system; a network. *This complex of buildings to my creations.* **2** [psychoanalysis] a related group of repressed or partly repressed emotionally significant ideas which lead to abnormal mental states or behaviour. *He has another complex which is getting highly anxious about small things.* [informal] a feeling of disproportionate anxiety about something. **3** [chemistry] an ion or molecule in which one or more groups are linked to a metal atom by co-ordinate bonds. *(verb)* [chemistry] form or caused to form a complex with another.

Complexion – *(noun)* **1** the natural tone and texture of the skin of a person's face. *Her complexion is something to be seen to believe.* **2** the general aspect or character of something.

Complexity – *(noun)* the quality of being ritricate and compound. *He enjoyed the complexity of modern computer.*

Compliance – *(noun)* **1** the action or fact of being compliant. *Compliance is his characteristic.* **2** [physics] the capacity of a material or object of yielding when subjected to an applied force.

Compliant – *(adjective)* **1** disposed to agree with others or obey rules, especially to an excessive degree; acquiescent. *My friend is very compliant. He obeys whatever is said to him.* **2** meeting or in accordance with rules or standards. **3** [physics & medicine] having the property of compliance.

Compliment – *(noun)* a polite expression of praise or admiration, congratulations or praise expressed to someone. *My friend has the habit of paying compliment to everyone on* *some point or the other.* [formal] greetings, especially when sent as a message. *(verb)* **1** politely congratulate or praise. **2** archaic present someone with as a mark of courtesy.

Comply - *(verb)* **1** act in accordance with a wish or command. *I'll comply with your wish.* **2** meet specified standards.

Component - *(noun)* **1** a part or element of a larger whole, especially a part of a machine or vehicle. *A component of your machine is broken. It will take two hours to replace it.* **2** [physics] each of two or more forces, velocities, or other vectors acting in different directions which are together equivalent to a given vector. *(adjective)* constituting part of a larger whole; constituent.

Comport - *(noun)* another term for compote.

Compose - *(verb)* **1** write or create a work of art, especially music or poetry. order or arrange in order to form an artistic whole. *His composition of music was excellent.* **2** constitute or make up a whole. **3** clam or settle one's features or thoughts. **4** prepare for printing by setting up the characters to be printed. **5** [archaic] settle a dispute.

Composition - *(noun)* **1** the way in which a whole or mixture is made up; ingredients or constituents. a thing composed of various elements. a compound artificial substance. **2** a work of music, literature, or art. *A composition of drama is made up of many constituents.* **3** the action of composing. **4** [archaic] mental constitution; character. **5** a legal agreement to pay a sum in lieu of a larger debt or other obligation. **6** [mathematics] the successive application of functions to a variable. **7** [physics] the process of finding the resultant of a number of forces.

Compost - *(noun)* decayed organic material used as a fertilizer for growing plants; a mixture of compost with loam soil used as a growing medium. *These days farmers use compost as a fertilizer.* *(verb)* make into or treat with compost.

Composure - *(noun)* the state or feeling of being calm and composed.

Compound - *(noun)* a large open area enclosed by a fence, e.g. around a factory or within a prision. [south African] an area containing single-sex living quarters for migrant workers, especially miners. another term for pound. *The prisoners were free to move within the jail compound.*

Comprehend - *(verb)* **1** grasp mentally; understand. *I have comprehended your answer to my question.* **2** [formal] include, comprise, or encompass.

Comprehensive - *(adjective)* **1** including or dealing with all or nearly all aspects of something; of large content or scope; wide-ranging; by a large margin; providing cover for most risks, including damage to the policyholder's own vehicle. *Lecture of the professor from science academy was comprehensive.* **2** [British] denoting a system from a particular area. **3** [archaic] of or relating to understanding. *(noun)* [British] a comprehensive school.

Compress - *(verb)* flatten by pressure; squeeze into less space. [biology] having a narrow shape as if flattened, especially sideways. squeeze or press together. *(noun)* a pad of absorbent material pressed on to part of the body to relieve inflammation or stop bleeding.

Compromise - *(noun)* **1** an agreement reached by each side making concessions. an intermediate state between conflicting opinions. *Instead of fighting a long legal battle they proper compromise out of the court.* **2** the expedient acceptance of standards that are lower than is desirable. *Somehow or the other we brought the two warring parties to a compromising situation.* *(verb)* **1** settle a dispute by mutual concession. *I'll compromise if it is my mistake.* **2** expediently accept standards that are lower than is desirable. **3** bring into disrepute or danger by indiscreet or reckless behaviour revealing an embarrassing or incriminating secret.

Comptroller - *(noun)* a controller used in the title of some financial officers. *A comptroller is a financial officer.*

Compulsion - *(noun)* **1** the action or state of compelling or being compelled; constraint. *You are under no compulsion to talk to me.* **2** an irresistible urge to behave in a certain way, especially against one's conscious wishes. *Compulsion compels him to buy the drug.*

Compulsive – *(adjective)* **1** resulting from or acting on an irresistible urge or compulsion. *He is a alcoholic so it becomes compulsive for him to buy the bottle of alcohal.* **2** irresistibly interesting or exciting; compelling.

Compulsory – *(adjective)* required by law or a rule; obligatory. involving or exercising compulsion; coercive. *It is compulsory to keep to the left while driving.*

Computation – *(noun)* **1** the action of mathematical calculation. *He uses computer for the purpose of research and study.* **2** the use of computers, especially as a subject of research or study.

Compute – *(verb)* **1** reckon or calculate a figure or amount. **2** [informal] seem reasonable; make sense.

Comrade – *(noun)* a companion who shares one's activities or is a fellow member of an organization. *He is my comrade and we both belong to the some organization.*

Con – *(verb)* deceive into doing or believing something by lying to them. *(noun)* a deception of this kind.

Conation – *(noun)* [philosophy] desire or will to perform in action; volition. *He willed to go abroad and by going abroad he performed his will into action/conation.*

Concave – *(adjective)* having an outline or surface that curves inwards like the interior of a circle or sphere. compare with convex. *A concave mirror's surface curves inside like the interior of a circle.*

Conceal – *(verb)* not allow to be seen; hide. keep secret; prevent from being known. *The thief concealed his goods into a pit.*

Concede – *(verb)* **1** finally admit or agree that something is true. admit in a match or contest. *I must concede that you are speaking the truth.* **2** surrender or yield advantage, or right. fall to prevent an opponent scoring a goal or point. *I concede to your victory.*

Conceivable – *(adjective)* capable of being imagined or understood. *His wishes are conceivable.*

Conceive – *(verb)* **1** become pregnant with a child. *She has conceived and all the members of the family are very happy.* **2** devise in the mind; imagine.

Concentric – *(adjective)* of or denoting circles, arcs, or other shapes which share the same centre.

Concept – *(noun)* **1** an abstract idea. an idea to help sell or publicise a commodity. *I have a concept which will increase the sale of our commodity.* **2** [philosophy] an idea or mental picture of a group or class of objects, formed by combining all their aspects.

Concern – *(verb)* **1** relate to; be about. *I am concerned about your well being.* affect or involve. **2** worry. *(noun)* **1** worry; anxiety. **2** a matter of interest or importance. *It is a matter of our concern and we should not ignore it.* **3** a business. **4** informal, dated a complicated or awkward thing.

Concert – *(noun)* **1** a musical performance given in public, typically of several compositions. *A music concert was held in Kala Bhawan.* **2** [formal] agreement; harmony. [law] joint action, especially in committing a crime. *(verb)* [formal] arrange by mutual agreement or coordination.

Concession – *(noun)* **1** a thing that is conceded. a gesture made in recognition of a demand or prevailing standard. *The company amended 30% concession on its garments.* **2** a reduction in price for a certain category of person. **3** the right to use land or other property for a specified purpose. a commercial operation set up within the premises of a larger concern.

Conciliate – *(verb)* **1** placate; pacify. act as a mediator. [formal] reconcile. *I acted as a conciliator and conciliated the two quarreling friends.* **2** [archaic] gain.

Concise – *(adjective)* giving a lot of information clearly and in few words. *His information was concise and to the point.*

Conclave – *(noun)* **1** a private meeting. *A conclave was being held regarding the election of a pope.* **2** the assembly of cardinals for the election of a pope.

Conclude – *(verb)* **1** bring or come to an end. formally settle or arrange a treaty or agreement. *The meeting was concluded on a note of harmony.* **2** arrive at a judgment or opinion by reasoning. [US] dated decide to do. *I have concluded that I am not going to be a part of your plan.*

Conclusion – *(noun)* **1** the end or finish of something. *I have reached the right conclusion.* the summing-up of an argument or text. *This is the text of the conclusion of the meeting.* the setting of a treaty or agreement. *Let us sit and conclude as to what should be done.* **2** a judgment or decision reached by reasoning. [logic] a proposition that is reached form given premises. *No conclusion was reached till the end of the meeting.*

Conclusive – *(adjective)* decisive or convincing. *It is conclusive that I will not sell my land.*

Concomitance – *(noun)* **1** the fact of existing or occurring with something else. *Now there is concomitance between the two families.* **2** [theology] the doctrine that the body and blood of Christ are each present in the bread and wine of the eucharist.

Concord – *(noun)* **1** [formal] agreement harmony. a treaty. *A treaty was signed between the two countries.* **2** [grammar] agreement between words in gender, number, case, or person. **3** [music] a chord that is pleasing or satisfactory in itself.

Concourse – *(noun)* **1** a large open central area inside or in front of a public building. *A big crowd gathered in the concourse.* **2** [formal] a crowd or assembly. the action of coming together. *Some cars were parked in the concourse.*

Concrescence – *(noun)* [biology] the coalescence or growing together of separate parts.

Concretion – *(noun)* a hard solid mass formed by accumulation of matter.

Concubinage – *(noun)* [historical] the practice of keeping or the state of being a concubine.

Condemn – *(verb)* **1** express complete disapproval of. *I condemn your words.* **2** sentence to a punishment, especially death. *He was condemned to death.* force to endure something unpleasant. prove the guilt of. **3** officially declare to be unfit for use. *Many papers and documents lie condemned in the offices.*

Condensation – *(noun)* **1** water form humid air collecting as droplets on a cold surface. **2** the conversion of a vapour or gas to a liquid. **3** [chemistry] a reaction in which two molecules combine to form a larger molecule, producing a small molecule such as H_2O as a by-product. **4** a concise version of something. *It is a condensed version of a big volume.*

Condense – *(verb)* **1** make denser or more concentratd. thicken by heating it to reduce the water content. *The milk has thickened because all the water has condensed due to heat.* express in fewer words; make concise. *What I say will be condensed.* **2** change from a gas or vapour to a liquid.

Condole – *(verb)* express sympathy for. *I condoled him on his sickness.*

Condonation – *(noun)* a pardon by treating the offender on if the offence has not accoured.

Conduce – *(verb)* [formal] help to bring about. *I conduced my friend in getting well.*

Conduct – *(noun)* **1** the manner in which a person behaves. *He conducts himself gracefully.* **2** the directing or managing of something. *(verb)* **1** organize and carry out. *He conducted the class well.* direct the performance of a piece of music or an orchestra or choir. *He nicely conducted the orchestra.* guide to or around a place. [physics] transmit by conduction. **3** behave in a specified way.

Conduit – *(noun)* **1** a channel for conveying water or other fluid. *I bought a conduit pipe from the market.* **2** a tube or trough protecting electric wiring.

Cone – *(noun)* **1** an object which tapers form a circular or roughly circular base to a point. a plastic cone-shaped object used to separate off sections of a road. *Traffic cones are usually placed on busy roads.* a cone-shaped wafer container in which ice cream is served. the peak of a volcano. **2** the cone-shaped dry fruit of a conifer, formed of a tight array of overlapping scales on a central axis. *While in MacDonald each of us had two ice cream cones.* **3** [anatomy] one of two types of light-sensitive cell present in the retina of the eye, responding to bright light and responsible for sharpness of vision and colour perception. compare with ROD. *(verb)* [British] separate off part of a road with traffic cones.

Coney – *(noun)* **1** [British & heraldry] a rabbit. *They have gone out to hunt a coney trees produce dry conical fruit.* **2** a small grouper of the tropical western Atlantic.

Confection – *(noun)* **1** an elaborate sweet dish or delicacy. *I am very fond of confection.* **2** an elaborate article of women's dress. **3** the action of mixing or compounding something.

Confideracy – *(noun)* **1** a league or alliance, especially of confederate states. the confederate states of the US. *US is made up of confideracy.* **2** a league formed for an unlawful purpose.

Confer – *(verb)* **1** grant. *He was conferred the little of 'sir'.* **2** have discussions. *Let us go somewhere else and confer.*

Conference – *(noun)* a dessert pear of a firm-fleshed variety. *Each of us had a conference as dessert.*

Confess – *(verb)* **1** admit to a crime or wrongdoing. acknowledge reluctantly. *He admitted his crime before the judge.* **2** declare one's sins formally to a priest. hear the confession of. *I must confess*

Confidant – *(noun)* a person in whom one confides. *I always confide in my sister, she is my confidant.*

Confide – *(verb)* **1** tell someone about a secret or private matter in confidence. *Let me confide in you what I have gone through.* **2** entrust something to the care of.

Confidence – *(noun)* **1** the belief that one can have faith in or rely on someone or something. a feeling of self-assurance arising from an appreciation of one's own abilities. *He succeeded in life because he was a very confident person. I have full confidence in you.* **2** the telling of private matters or secrets with mutual trust. a secret or private matter told to someone under a condition of trust. *Let me tell you something in confidence.*

Confidential – *(adjective)* **1** intended to be kept secret. *It is a confidential file, keep it in locker.* **2** entrusted with private information. *A confidential secretary.*

Confine – *(verb)* keep or restrict someone or something within certain limits of space, scope, or time. *He was confined to four walls of jail.* be unable to leave due to illness or disability. *He has been confined to bed since long.* of a woman remain in bed for a period before, during, and after giving birth. *(noun)* limits or boundaries.

Confirm – *(verb)* **1** establish the truth or correctness of. state with assurance that something is true. reinforce someone in an opinion or feeling. *I confirmed his story to adventure.* **2** make a provisional arrangement. declare formally to be appointed to a post. *He was declared confirmed in his job.* **3** administer the religious rite of confirmation to.

Confiscate – *(verb)* take or seize with authority appropriate to the public treasury as a penalty. *His whole property was confiscated by order of magistrates.*

Conflict – *(noun)* a serious disagreement or argument. *The two friends had conflict of opinion and they separated.* a prolonged armed struggle. *The two states were since long in conflict.* an incompatibility between opinions, principles, etc. *A conflict is going on in my mind whether to go office or not.* *(verb)* be incompatible or at variance with.

Confluent – *(adj.)* flowing together.

Conflux – *(noun)* another term for confluence.

Conformity – *(noun)* **1** compliance with conventions, rules, or laws. [British, chiefly historical] compliance with the practices of the church of England. *I live in conformity with the law of land.* **2** similarity in form or type.

Confraternity – *(noun)* a brotherhood, especially with a religious or charitable purpose. *We have formed a confraternity for a charitable purpose.*

Confuse – *(verb)* **1** cause to become bewildered or perplexed. *He is a confused man who does not know what he is saying.* **2** make less easy to understand. indentify wrongly.

Confusion – *(noun)* **1** uncertainty. a situation of panic. a disorderly jumble. *There was confusion in the entire meeting.* **2** the state of being bewildered. *I am sorry, I confused you for another person.* the mistaking of one person or thing for another.

Confute – *(verb)* [formal] prove to be wrong. *I was confused about you.*

Conge – *(noun)* an unceremonious dismissal or rejection. *He had to face conge and he felt very sad.*

Congeal – *(verb)* become semi-solid, especially or rejection. *The blood flowing from his wound soon congealed.*

Congener – *(noun)* **1** a person or thing of the same kind as another. an animal or plant of the same genus as another. *Both plants are congener.* **2** a minor chemical constituent, especially one giving a distinctive character to a wine or spirit.

Congenial – *(adjective)* pleasant because of qualities or interests similar to one's own. suited to one's taste or inclination. *I find this wine very congenial.*

Congenital – *(adjective)* present for birth. having a particular trait form birth or by established habit. *He cannot walk properly, it is something congenital.*

Conglomerate – *(noun)* **1** something consisting of a number of different and distinct things. a large corporation formed by the merging of separate firms. **2** [geology] a coarse-grained sedimentary rock composed of rounded fragments cemented together. *(adjective* relating to a conglomerate. *(verb)* gather into or form a conglomerate.

Conglutinate – *(verb)* stick together.

Congratulate – *(verb)* express pleasure at the happiness or good fortune of. praise for an achievement. feel pride or satisfaction. *He congratulated my friend on his success.*

Congregate – *(verb)* gather into a crowd or mass. *A big crowd congregated in the hall.*

Congruence – *(noun)* the quality of agreing.

Congruent – *(adjective)* **1** in agreement or harmony. **2** [geometry] identical in form.

Conjoin – *(verb)* [formal] join; combine. *All of us conjoined to form a meeting.*

Conjugate – *(verb)* **1** [grammar] give the different forms of a verb. **2** [biology] of bacteria or unicellular orbanism become temporarily united in order to exchange gentic material. **3** [chemistry] be combined with or joined to reversibly. *(adjective)* **1** [chemistry] related by loss or gain of a proton. **2** [mathematics] joined in a reciprocal relation, especially having the same real parts and equal magnitudes but opposite signs of imaginary parts. **3** [geometry] adding up to 360°. *Under conjuration body gains or lose a proton.* **4** biology fused. *In mathematics it is joining reciprocal relation.* **5** *In geometry it is adding up to 360°.* **6** *I biochemistry it is a conjugated substance. (noun)* **1** [biochemistry] a conjugated substance. **2** a conjugate mathematical value or entity.

Conjunct – *(adjective)* **1** joined together, combined, or associated. **2** music of or relating to the movement of a melody between adjacent notes of the scale. *(noun)* **1** each of two or more joined or associated things. **2** [logic] each of the terms of a conjunctive proposition. **3** [grammar] an adverbial joining two sentences or clauses.

Conjunctiva – *(noun)* [anatomy] the mucous membrane that covers the front of the eye and lines the inside of the eyelids. *There was some trouble with my conjunctiva so I consulted a doctor.*

Conjunctive – *(adjective)* of, relating to, or forming a conjunction. involving the combination or co-occurrence of two or more things. *(noun)* [grammar] a conjunction. *A conjunction joins two sentences.*

Conjuncture – *(noun)* **1** a combination of events. *There is a conjuncture of the events of various companies.* **2** a state of affairs. *The conjuncture in the company is not very good.*

Conjure – *(verb)* **1** cause to appear as if by magic. call to the mind. call upon to appear by means of a magic ritual. *The magician conjure up a ghost.* **2** [archaic] implore to do something.

Connate – *(adjective)* **1** innate. **2** [biology] united so as to form a single part. **3** geology trapped in sedimentary rock during its deposition.

Connatural – *(adjective)* innate.

Connect – *(verb)* **1** bring together so as to establish a link. be related in some aspect. join together so as to provide access and communication. put into contact by vide access and communication. put into contact by telephone. *We two friends are connected together by means o chatting over computer.* **2** arrive at its destination just before another departs so that passengers can transfer. **3** [informal] hit the intended target. *The ball connected the bat and it was a hit.*

Connive – *(verb)* secretly allow a wrongdoing. conspire. *We connived against the leader of the opposition group.*

Connote – *(verb)* imply or suggest, imply as a consequence or condition.

Conquer – *(verb)* **1** overcome and take control of by military force. *Babur conquered many states of India.* **2** successfully overcome. **3** climb a mountain successfully. *Many people have conquered Everest.*

Conquest – *(noun)* **1** the action of conquering. a territory gained in such a way. *The conquest of Everest was a historial event.* **2** a person whose affection or favour has been won.

Conscience – *(noun)* a person's moral sense of right and wrong. *He is a man of high conscience.*

Conscious – *(adjective)* **1** aware of and responding to one's surroundings. *I become conscious that someone was following me.* **2** having knowledge of something concerned about a matter: security-conscious. *By nature I am very security conscious.* **3**. deliberate.

Consecrate – *(verb)* **1** make or declare sacred. make into the body and blood of Christ. **2** ordain to a sacred office, typically that of bishop. *After being consecrated he was ordained a bishop's life.*

Consecutive – *(adjective)* **1** following continuously. in sequence. **2** grammar expressing consequence or result. **3** [music] denoting intervals of the same kind occurring in succession between two parts or voices.

Consensus – *(noun)* general agreement. *A consensus was reached in the general meeting.*

Consent – *(noun)* permission. *(verb)* give permission. agree to do something.

Consentient – *(adjective)* [archaic] in agreement.

Consequent – *(adjective)* **1** following as a consequence. [archaic] logically consistent. *His consequent efforts bore result.* **2** [geology] having a direction or character determined by the original slope of the land before erosion. **4** *Imitating part in the religion song.* *(noun)* **1** [logic] the second part of a conditional proposition, whose truth is stated to be implied by that of the antecedent. **2** [music] the second or imitating voice or part in a canon.

Conservation – *(noun)* **1** preservation or restoration of the natural environment and wildlife. preservation and repair of archaeological, historical, and cultural sites and artifacts. *Conservation of wildlife and trees is the call of the day.* **2** careful use of a resource. *Preservation of archaeological, historical and cultural sites are also necessary.* **3** [physics] the principle by which the total value of a quantity remains constant in a system which is not subject to external influence.

Conservative – *(adjective)* **1** averse to change or innovation and holding traditional values. sober conventional. *My grandfather is very conservative.* **2** favouring free enterprise, private ownership, and socially conservative ideas. of or relating to a conservative party. **3** low for the sake of caution. **4** intended to control rather than eliminate a condition, and preserve existing tissue. *(noun)* **1** a conservative person. **2** a supporter or member of a conservative party.

Conservator – *(noun)* a person involved in conservation.

Conserve – *(verb)* **1** protect form harm or destruction. prevent the wasteful overuse of. preserve with sugar. *My father preserves most things.* **2** [physics] maintain at a constant overall total. *(noun)* jam.

Consideration – *(noun)* **1** careful thought. a fact taken into account when making a decision. *After much consideration I have decided to join your party.* **2** thoughtfulness towards others. **3** a payment or reward. [law] anything given or promised by one party in exchange for the promise or undertaking of another. **4** [archaic] importance.

Considering – *(prep.&conj.)* taking into consideration. ad(verb) informal taking everything into account. *Considering her wishes, I took her to a five star hotel.*

Consign – *(verb)* deliver to someone's custody. send by a public carrier. put someone or something in order to be rid of them.

Consist – *(verb)* **1** be composed of. have as an essential feature. *Tea consists of sugar milk and tea leaves.* **2** [archaic] be consistent with. *(noun)* railways the set of vehicles forming a complete train.

Consolation – *(noun)* comfort received by someone after a loss or disappointment. a source of such comfort. *My friend and many people gave their consolation me over my loss.*

Console – *(noun)* **1** a panel or unit accommodating a set of controls. a cabinet for television or radio equipment. a small machine for playing computerized video games. the cabinet or enclosure contain the keyboards, stops, etc. of an organ. **2** an ornamented bracket or corbel. *Our television needs a new console.* *(verb)* give moral or emotional strength to.

Consonance – *(noun)* **1** agreement or compatibility. **2** the recurrence of similar-sounding consonants, especially in prosody. *Now let us enter into a consonance.* **3** [music] a harmonious combination of notes. *There was great consonance in the music.*

Consonant – *(noun)* a speech sound in which the breath is at least partly obstructed and which can be combined with a vowel to form a syllable. a letter representing such a sound. *(adjective)* **1** denoting or relating to a consonant. **2** in agreement or harmony with. **3** [music] making a harmonious interval or chord. *The whole of music was in great consonant.*

Consort – *(noun)* **1** a wife, husband, or companion, in particular the spouse of a monarch. **2** a ship sailing in company with another. *(verb)* **1** habitually associate with. **2** [archaic] agree or be in harmony with.

Conspecific – *(adjective)* belonging to the same species. *(noun)* a member of the same species. *Apes and monkeys are conspecific.*

Conspectus – *(noun)* a summary or overview of a subject.

Conspicuous – *(adjective)* clearly visible. attracting notice or attention. *He was conspicuous by his absence.*

Conspiracy – *(noun)* a secret plan by a group to do something unlawful or harmful. the action of conspiring.

Conspirator – *(noun)* a member of a conspiracy. *Cassius was the main conspirator against cancer.*

Constable – *(noun)* **1** caesar a police officer. a police officer of the lowest rank. **2** the governor of a royal castle. [historical] the highest-ranking official in a royal household.

Constant – *(adjective)* **1** occurring continuously. **2** remaining the same. faithful and dependable. *(noun)* an fun changing situation. [mathematic]. a component of a relationship between variables that does not change its value. [physics] a number expressing a relation or property which remains the same in all circumstances, or for the same substance under the same conditions.

Constellation – *(noun)* **1** a group of stars forming a recognised pattern and typically named after a mythological or other figure. **2** a group of associated people or things.

Constipate – *(verb)* affect with constipation.

Constituency – *(noun)* **1** a body of voters in a specified area who elect a representative to a legislative body. [chiefly British] the area represented in this way. **2** a body of customers or supporters.

Constituent – *(adjective)* **1** being a part of a whole. **2** having the power to appoint or elect. able to make or change a political constitution. *(noun)* **1** a member of a constituency. **2** component part.

Constitute – *(verb)* **1** a body of fundamental principle or established precedents according to which a state or organisation is governed. [historical] a decree, ordinance, or law. **2** the composition or forming of something. **3** a person's physical or mental state.

Constitution – *(noun)* law determining the fundamental political principles of a government.

Constitutive – *(adjective)* **1** having the power to establish something. **2** forming a constituent of something.

Constrict – *(verb)* make or become or restriction. **2** stiffness of manner and inhibition.

Construct – *(verb)* **1** build or erect. *My friend has constructed a huge building.* **2** form various conceptual elements. **3** [grammar] form according to grammatical rules. **4** [geometry] draw or delineate a geometrical figure. *(noun)* **1** an idea or theory. **2** linguistics a group of words forming a phrase. **3** a thing constructed.

Construe – *(verb)* interpret in a particular way. dated analyse the construction of a text, sentence, or word. translate word for word.

Consul – *(noun)* **1** a state official living in a foreign city and protecting the state's citizens and interests there. *If you have any problem go consult your consul.* **2** one of the two annually elected chief magistrates who ruled the republic. any of the three chief magistrates of the first French republic (1799-1804).

Consult – *(verb)* seek information or advice from someone, especially an expert or professional. seek permission or approval from. engaged in the business of giving advice to other in the same field: a consulting engineer. *At once consult a doctor for your disease.*

Consumption – *(noun)* **1** the action or process of consuming. an amount consumed. **2** dated a wasting disease, especially tuberculosis.

Contact – *(noun)* the state or condition of physical touching. the state or condition of communicating or meeting. caused by or operating through physical touch. *I will contact you soon.* **2** a connection or relationship. a person who has associated with a patient with a contagious disease. *(verb)* get in touch or communication with. *My friend contacted a contagious disease.*

Contagion – *(noun)* the communication of disease form one person to another by close contact. a disease spread in such a way.

Contagious – *(adjective)* **1** spread by direct or indirect contact of people or organism. having a contagious disease. **2** likely to spread to and affect others.

Contain – *(verb)* **1** have or hold within. *My medicines are contained in this box.* **2** control or restrain. prevent from becoming worse. **3** be divisible by a factor without a remainder.

Contaminate – *(verb)* make impure by exposure to or addition of a hostile country or influence. *The wound became contaminate because it remain open for long in hostile atmosphere.*

Contemn – *(verb)* [archaic] treat or regard with contempt.

Contemplate – *(verb)* look at thoughtfully. think about. think profoundly and at length. have as a probable intention.

Contemporaneous – *(adjective)* existing at or occurring in the same period of time. *Lord Mohan's and Buddha were contemporaneous.*

Contemporary – *(adjective)* **1** living, occurring or originating at the same time. *Gandhiji and Vinoba Bhave were contemporaries.* **2** belonging to or occurring in the present. modern in style or design. *(noun)* a person or thing existing at the same time as another. a person of roughly the same age as another.

Contempt – *(noun)* **1** the feeling that a person or a thing is worthless or beneath consideration. *The judge said it is contempt of court and gave suitable punishment to the offender.* **2** the offence of being disobedient to or disrespectful of a court of law.

Contemptuous – *(adjective)* showing contempt. *I had nothing but contempt for him.*

Content – *(adjective)* in a state of peaceful happiness or satisfaction. *I am content with my stats of offers.* *(verb)* satisfy. accept as adequate despite wanting more or better. *(noun)* **1** a state of satisfaction. **2** a member of the British house of lords who votes for a motion.

Contention – *(noun)* **1** heated disagreement. *A contention took place between the two friends.* **2** an assertion.

Contest – *(noun)* an event in which people compete for supremacy. a dispute or conflict. *There was a boxing contest between the two boxers.* *(verb)* **1** compete to attain a position of power. take part in a competition or election. **2** challenge or dispute.

Context – *(noun)* the circumstances that form the setting for an event, statement, or idea, and in term of which it can be fully understood. the parts that immediately precede and follow a word or passage and clarify its meaning. *After the event the provident said in this context that more such friendly matches will be hold.*

Continent – *(noun)* **1** any of the world's main continuous expanses of land. *India is a big continent.* **2** the mainland of Europe as distinct from the British isles.

Contingency – *(noun)* **1** a future event or circumstance which is possible but cannot be predicted with certainty. a provision for such an event or circumstance. *You are going to face a contingency friend but it will do you good.* **2** the absence of certainly in events. **3** [philosophy] the absence of necessity.

Contingent – *(adjective)* **1** subject to chance. dependent on. *It is more or less a contingent you clear the exam.* that can be anticipated to arise if a particular event occurs. **2** [philosophy] true by virtue of the way things in fact are and not by logical necessity. *(noun)* a group of people within a larger group. a body of troops or police sent to join a larger force. *A contingent of police was sent to help a larger group.*

Continual – *(adjective)* constantly or frequently occurring. *He is continually late.*

Continue – *(verb)* **1** persist in an activity or process. remain in existence, operation, or a specified state. *I'll continue carrying on in the same direction till I find the old temple.* **2** carry on with. carry on travelling in the same direction. **3** recommence or resume. **4** US law postpone or adjourn.

Continuity – *(noun)* **1** the unbroken and consistent existence or operation of something. a connection or line of development with no sharp breaks. *The film was good but it lacked continuity.* **2** the maintenance of continuous action and self consistent detail in the scenes of a film or broadcast. *If you want to achieve something there must be continuity in your effort.* **3** the linking of broadcast items by a spoken commentary.

Continuous – *(adjective)* **1** without interruption. forming a series with no exceptions or reversals. mathematics of which the graph is a smooth unbroken curve.

Contour – *(noun)* **1** an outline, especially one representing or bounding the shape or form of something. a line on a map joining points of equal height above or below sea level. a line joining points on a diagram at which some property has the same value. *The clay was given a definite contour and it looked beautiful.* **2** a way in which something varies, especially the pitch of music or the pattern of tones in an utterance. *This clay would is full of contours.* *(verb)* **1** mould into a specific shape. **2** mark with contours. **3** follow the outline of a topographical feature.

Contraception – *(noun)* the use of artificial methods or other techniques to prevent pregnancy. *There are so many contraception's available these days.*

Contract – *(noun)* **1** a written or spoken agreement intended to be enforceable by law. *I have one year's contract with him.* **2** [informal] an arrangement for someone to be killed by a hired assassin. *A contract was given to this man to kill the girl.* **3** bridge the declarer's undertaking to win the number of tricks bid with a stated suit as trumps. *I have entered 2 years contract with it is legal and binding.* **5** *If you do not humor the contract you are liable to pay fine.* **6** *I have contracted the disease as I went to visit a sick friend of mine.* *(verb)* **1** decrease in size, number, or range. *In heat things expand in cold they contract.* **2** become shorter and tighter in order to effect movement of part of the body. **3** shorten by combination or elision. **4** enter into a formal and legally binding agreement. choose to be involved. in brutish choose to withdraw form or not become involved for work to be done by another organisation. **5** catch or develop. **6** become liable to pay.

Contradistinction – *(noun)* distinction made by contrasting the different qualities of two things.

Contrariety – *(noun)* **1** [logic] contrary opposition. **2** opposition or inconsistency between two things.

Contrariwise – *(adverb)* in the opposite way. on the other hand. *This team is good but contrariwise the batsmen of the other team are far superior.*

Contrary – *(adjective)* **1** opposite in nature, direction, or meaning. *I am contrary to his nature. So we can't become friends.* **2** opposed to one another. [logic] so related that one or neither but not both must be true. compare with contradictory. *Both logics are contrary to each other.* **3** perversely inclined to do the opposite of what is expected or desired. *(noun)* the opposite. *The contrary colours appear so beautiful.*

Contrast – *(noun)* **1** the state of being strikingly different from something else in juxtaposition or close association. *Black is in sharp contrast to white.* **2** the degree of difference between tones in a television picture, photograph, etc. *contrast is rather too much in the TV picture, reduce it.* **3** enhancement of the apparent brightness or clarity of a design provided by the juxtaposition of different colours or textures. *You can notice the great contrast between the two cricket teams.* **4** a thing or person noticeably different from another. *(verb)* differ strikingly. compare so as to emphasize differences. *If you put these colours near the bright design, it will look more bright.*

Contribute – *(verb)* give in order to help achieve or provide something. help to cause or bring about. *Others with Mahatma Gandhi contributed a lot to bring freedom.*

Contrite – *(adjective)* feeling or expressing remorse. *My friend has left for USA and I am feeling rather contrite.*

Contrivance – *(noun)* **1** the action of contriving something. *This contrivance is sure going to work.* **2** an ingenious device or scheme.

Control – *(noun)* **1** the power to influence people's behaviour or the course of events. the restriction of an activity. tendency, or phenomenon. *I have full control over events.* **2** a device by which a machine is regulated. *I know few to control this machine.* **3** the place where something is verified or from which an activity is directed. **4** bridge a high card that will prevent the opponents from establishing a particular suit. *Please don't come here it is the control room.* **5** a person or thing used as a standard of comparison for checking the results of a survey or experiment. **6** a member of an intelligence organization who personally directs the activities of a spy. *(verb)* **1** have control or command of. regulate. *By some means or other we shall control the rising prices.* **2** restricted by law in respect of use and possession. **3** take into account an extraneous factor that might affect the results of an experiment.

Controversy – *(noun)* disagreement, typically when prolonged and public. *This is a controversy going on for a long time.*

Controvert – *(verb)* deny the truth of. *I will not controvert the truth of this statement.*

Conundrum – *(noun)* an extended urban area, typically consisting of several towns merging with the suburbs of a central city. *Delhi is a conundrum city.*

Convalesce – *(verb)* gradually recover one's health after an illness or medical treatment.

Convection – *(noun)* transference of mass or heat within a fluid caused by the tendency of warmer and less dense material to rise.

Convene – *(verb)* call people together for a meeting. assemble for a common purpose. *All you people have been called to convene in the hall.*

Convenience – *(noun)* **1** freedom from effort or difficulty. a useful or helpful device or situation. **2** a public toilet. *If you are in UK and lookup for a sign 'toilet' look instead for convenience.*

Conventicle – *(noun)* [historical] a secret or unlawful religious meeting, typically of nonconformists.

Convention – *(noun)* **1** a way in which something is usually done. socially acceptable behaviour. *It is a convention in our country to touch our elders' feet.* **2** an agreement between states, especially one less formal than a treaty. **3** a large meeting, especially of members of a political party or a particular profession. [north American] an assembly of the delegates of a political party to select candidates for titular issue. [historical] a meeting of parliament without a bidding by which the bidder tries to convey specific information about the hand to their partner.

Conventual – *(adjective)* relating or belonging to a convent. relating to the less strict order of the Franciscans, living in large convents. *(noun)* a person who lives in or is a member of a convent. *My sister lives in a convent. She is a nun.*

Conversant – *(adjective)* familiar with or knowledgeable about something. *We were conversant together where he interfered.*

Conversation – *(noun)* an informal spoken exchange of news and ideas between two or more people. *A conversation between the two leaders is goings on.*

Converse – *(verb)* engage in conversation. *(noun)* [archaic] conversation. *I will converse with you after the office hours.*

Conversion – *(noun)* **1** the process or action of converting or of being converted. **2** [British] a building that has been converted to a new purpose. **3** [law] the changing of real property into personality, or of joint into separate property, or vice versa. **4** [psychiatry] the manifestation of a mental disturbance as a physical disorder or disease. **5** the action of converting a trÿ, touchdown, or down. **6** [law] the action of wrongfully dealing with goods in a manner inconsistent with the owner's rights.

Convert – *(verb)* **1** change or cause to change in form, character, or function. change into others of a different kind. adapt to make it suitable for a new purpose. *Hydrogen and Oxygen can be converted into water.* **2** change one's religious faith or other beliefs. *He is a converted Christian now.* **3** [logic] transpose the subject and predicate of according to certain rules to form a new proposition by inference. **4** [rugby score] extra points after by a successful kick at goal. [American football] make an extra score after by clicking a goal or running another play into the end zone. advance that ball far enough after to get another try for a first down.

Convex – *(adjective)* having an outline or surface curved like the exterior of a circle or sphere, compare with CONCAVE. *Convex mirrors are often used in transport vehicles.*

Convey – *(verb)* **1** transport or carry to a place. **2** communicate. **3** law transfer the title to property. *I have conveyed your message to your friend.*

Conviction – *(noun)* **1** an instance of being convicted the action or process of convicting someone. **2** a firmly held belief or opinion. the quality of showing that one is firmly convinced of something.

Convince – *(verb)* cause to believe firmly in the truth of something. persuade to do something. firm in one's belief with regard to a particular cause.

Convivial – *(adjective)* friendly, lively, and enjoyable. cheerful and sociable. *He is a convivial fellow.*

Convocation – *(noun)* **1** a representative assembly of clergy of the province of Canterbury or York. [British] a legislative or deliberative assembly of a university. [north American] a formal ceremony for the conferment of university awards. *He got the university award at convocation.* **2** the action of convoking a large formal assembly.

Convolve – *(verb)* rare roll or coil together. *He convolved the roll together into a ball.*

Convoy – *(noun)* a procession of land vehicles travelling together. *The convoy of are president has just passed.*

Cony – *(noun)* variant spelling of CONEY.

Coo – *(noun)* **1** make a soft murmuring sound. *She cooed into my ear and I loved it very much.* **2** speak in a soft gentle voice. *(noun)* a cooing sound.

Cook – *(verb)* **1** prepare by mixing, combining, and heating the ingredients. be heated so as to reach an edible state. **2** [informal] alter dishonestly. concoct a story, excuse, or plan, especially an ingenious or devious one. **3** [informal] be happening or planned. **4** [north American, informal] perform or proceed vigorously or very well. *(noun)* a person who cooks, especially as a job. *She is an expert cook and the credit goes to her for preparing some new dish also.*

Cook-house - *(noun)* a building used for cooking, especially on a ranch, military camp, etc. *let's go to cook-house to eat something.*

Cool - *(adjective)* **1** of or at a fairly low temperature. keeping one from becoming too hot. *His behaviour was cool and unenthusiastic.* **2** unfriendly or unenthusiastic. free from anxiety or excitement. **3** restrained and relaxed. *He has a cool temper, so relaxed and free from worry.* **4** [informal] fashionably attractive or impressive. *He is so cool and dressed so gracefully.* excellent. **5** restrained and relaxed. **6** [informal] fashionably attractive or impressive. excellent. **7** [informal] used to emphasize a specified large amount of money. *(noun)* a fairly low temperature, or a place, or time characterized by this. *(verb)* become or cause to become cool.

Coolie - *(noun)* **1** dated an unskilled native labourer in India, China, and some other Asian countries. *Call-that coolie, he will carry our bag and baggage.* **2** [offensive] a person form the Indian subcontinent or of Indian descent.

Coop - *(noun)* **1** a cage or pen for confining poultry. *All poultry is confined in this rather small coop.* **2** [British] a basket used in catching fish. *(verb)* confine in a small space.

Cooper - *(noun)* a maker or repairer of casks and barrels. *(verb)* make or repair.

Co-operate - *(verb)* work jointly towards the same end. assist someone or comply with their requests. *We both are going to co-operate to complete this mission.*

Co-ordinate - *(verb)* **1** bring the different elements of into a harmonious or efficient relationship. *We all shall co-ordinate with another so as to reach the desired result.* **2** negotiate with others in order to work together effectively. *We shall co-ordinate also with others so that they work with us.* **3** match or harmonize attractively. **4** [chemistry] form a coordinate bond to. *He is a jointer co-ordinate secretary equal to the rank of the other.* **5** *This blouse perfectly matches with this saree.* *(adjective)* **1** equal in rank or importance. [grammar] in rank and fulfilling identical functions. *The co-ordinate clauses in grammar are of equal strength.* **2** [chemistry] denoting a covalent bond in which one atom provides both the shared electrons. *(noun)* **1** [mathematics] each of a group of numbers used to indicate the position of a point, line, or plane. **2** matching items of clothing.

Coot - *(noun)* **1** an aquatic bird of the rail family with black plumage and a white bill that extends back on to the forehead as a horny shield. **2** [informal] a stupid or eccentric person, typically an old man.

Copal - *(noun)* resin from any of a number of tropical trees, used to make varnish.

Co-partner - *(noun)* a partner or associate, especially an equal partner in a business. *We are both co-partner partners in this firm.*

Cope - *(verb)* deal effectively with something difficult. *He coped the crisis skillfully.*

Copier - *(noun)* a machine that makes exact copies of something. *I am going to buy a photocopier machine.*

Copious - *(adj.)* **1** large in number or quantity. **2** affording an abundant supply

Copper - *(noun)* [British informal] a police officer.

Copperas - *(noun)* green crystals of hydrated ferrous sulphate, especially as an industrial product.

Coppice - *(noun)* an area of woodland in which the trees or shrubs are periodically cut back to ground level to stimulate growth and provide wood. *(verb)* cut back in this way.

Copra - *(noun)* dried coconut kernels, form which oil is obtained.

Copula - *(noun)* [logic & grammar] a connecting word, in particular a form of the *(verb)* be connecting a subject and complement.

Copulate - *(verb)* have sexual intercourse.

Copulative - *(adjective)* **1** [grammar] connecting words or clauses linked in sense. connecting a subject and predicate. **2** of or relating to sexual intercourse. *They were found in a compulative position.*

Copy - *(noun)* **1** a thing made to be similar or identical to another. *Will you please stop copying my notes?* **2** a single specimen of a particular book, record, etc. **3** matter to be printed. material for a newspaper or magazine article. *(verb)* make a copy of. imitate the behaviour or style of.

Copyhold – *(noun)* [British historical] tenure of land based on manorial records.

Copyist – *(noun)* **1** a person who makes copies. *My friend is a copyist by profession.* **2** a person who imitates the styles of others, especially in art. *He is a copyist. He imitates the art of other people.*

Coral – *(noun)* **1** a hard stony substance secreted by certain colonial marine animals as an external skeleton, typically forming large resets. precious red coral. **2** an entozoan of a large group including those that form coral reefs, secreting a calcareous, horny, or soft skeleton. **3** the edible unfertilised roe of a lobster or scallop, reddening when cooked.

Corbel – *(noun)* a projection jutting out form a wall to support a structure above it. *(verb)* support on corbels.

Cord – *(noun)* **1** long thin string or rope made from several twisted strands. a length of such material. *The pieces of wood were tied with a cord.* **2** an anatomical structure resembling a cord. **3** an electric flex. **4** corduroy. corduroy trousers. **5** a measure of cut wood. *(verb)* attach a cord to.

Cordate – *(adjective)* [botany & zoology] heart-shaped.

Cordial – *(adjective)* **1** warm and friendly. *He is a very cordial and polite man.* **2** strongly felt: cordial loathing. *(noun)* **1** [British] a sweet fruit-flavoured drink, sold as a concentrate. **2** [chiefly north American] another term for LIQUEUR. **3** a pleasant-tasting medicine.

Core – *(noun)* **1** the tough central part of various fruits, containing the seeds. *The core of coconut is very sweet.* **2** the central or most important part. the dense metallic or rocky central region of a planet. the central part of a nuclear reactor, which contains the fissile material. a piece of soft iron forming the centre of an electromagnet or an induction coil. **3** an internal mould filling a space to be left hollow in a casting. **4** [archaeology] a piece of flint form which flakes or blades have been removed. **5** a cylindrical sample of rock, ice, or other material obtained by boring with a hollow drill. *(verb)* remove the core form a fruit.

Co-religionist – *(noun)* an adherent of the same religion as another person. *We both friend belong to Hindu religion.*

Co-respondent – *(noun)* a person cited in a divorce case as having committed adultery with the respondent.

Coriander – *(noun)* an aromatic Mediterranean plant of the parsley family, the leaves and seeds of which are used as culinary herbs. *There are many types of corianders prepared in different states of India.*

Cork – *(noun)* **1** the buoyant, light brown substance obtained form the outer layer of the bark of the cork oak. *The cork was so hardly pressed into the both that it took all our efforts to take it out.* **2** a bottle stopper made of cork.. **3** a piece of cork used as a float for a fishing line or net. *We sealed the place with a cork.* **4** [botany] a protective layer of dead cells immediately below the bark of woody plants. *(verb)* **1** close or seal with a cork. spoilt by tannin from the cork. **2** baseball illicitly hollow out and fill it with cork to make it lighter.

Cormorant – *(noun)* a large diving seabird with a long neck, long hooked bill, short legs, and mainly black plumage. *Commorant is a bird worth looking at.*

Corn – *(noun)* a small, painful area of thickened skin on the foot, especially on the toes, caused by pressure.

Cornea – *(noun)* the transparent layer forming the front of the eye. *There is nothing wrong with the cornea of your eye.*

Corneous – *(adjective)* [formal] horn-like; horny.

Corner – *(noun)* **1** a place or angle where two or more sides or edges meet. a place where two streets meet. *A man was sitting in a corner of the building.* **2** [British] a triangular cut form the hind end of a side of bacon. **3** a secluded or remote region or area. *There was blind corner in the street, it was a risky place.*

4 a difficult or awarded position. *When the animal was cornered, it attacked the attacker.* 5 a position in which one dominates the supply of a particular commodity. 6 [soccer] a free kick taken by the attacking side from a corner of the field after the ball has been sent over the byline by a defender. a similar free hit in field hockey. *If the ball has been sent over the byline by a defender, then a free kick is taken by attacking side from a corner of the field.* 7 [boxing & wrestling] each of the diagonally opposite ends of the ring, where a contestant rests between rounds. a contestant's supporters or seconds. *(verb)* 1 force into a place or situation form which it is hard to escape. 2 control by dominating the supply of a particular commodity. 3 go round a bend in a road.

Cornet – *(noun)* 1 a brass instrument resembling a trumpet but shorter and wider. *He plays cornet very well.* 2 [British] a cone-shaped wafer for holding ice cream.

Cornice – *(noun)* 1 an ornamental moulding round the wall of a room just below the ceiling. a horizontal molded projection crowning a building or structure, especially the uppermost member of the entablature of an order; surmounting the frieze. 2 an overhanging mass of hardened snow at the edge of a mountain precipice.

Corollary – *(noun)* 1 [logic] a proposition that follows from one already proved. 2 a direct consequence or result. *(adjective)* 1 forming a corollary. 2 associated; supplementary.

Coronal – *(adjective)* 1 of or relating to the crown or corona of something. *The coronal ceremony was held on grand scale.* 2 [anatomy] of or in the coronal plane. 3 [phonetics] formed by raising the tip or blade of the tongue towards the hard palate. *(noun)* [phonetics] a coronal consonant.

Coronation – *(noun)* the ceremony of crowning a sovereign for a sovereigns' consort: *I had the good fortune to attend the coronation ceremony of the king.*

Coronet – *(noun)* 1 a small or simple crown, especially as worn by lesser royalty and nobles. a circular decoration for the head. 2 a ring of bone at the base of a deer's antler. 3 the band of tissue containing the horn producing cells from which a house's hoof grows.

Corporal – *(noun)* 1 a rank of non-commissioned officer in the army, above lance corporal or private first class and below sergeant. 2 [British historical] a petty officer who attended solely to police matters, under the master-at-arms.

Corporate – *(adjective)* 1 of or relating to a large company or group. 2 [law] authorized to act as a single entity and recognized as such in law. 3 of or shared by all the members of a group. *(noun)* a corporate company or group.

Corporation – *(noun)* 1 a large company or group of companies authorized to act as a single entity and recognized as such in law. 2 [British] a group of people elected to govern a city, town, or borough. 3 humorous, dated a paunch.

Corporeity – *(noun)* rare the quality of having a physical body or existence.

Corps – *(noun)* a main subdivision of an army in the field, consisting of two or more divisions. a branch of an army assigned to a particular kind of work. a body of people engaged in a particular activity.

Corpse – *(noun)* a dead body, especially of a human. *(verb)* [theatrical] slanged spoil a piece of acting by forgetting one's lines or laughing uncontrollably. *Corpses were lying all over the battle field.*

Correct – *(adjective)* 1 free from error; true; right. *My friend wrote an all correct essay.* [chiefly north American] conforming to a particular political or ideological orthodoxy: environmentally correct. 2 conforming to accepted social standards. *(verb)* put right. mark the errors in a text adjust to function accurately or accord with a standard. adjust a numerical result or reading to allow for departure from standard conditions.

Correlate – *(verb)* have a relationship or connection in which one thing affects or depends or another. establish a correlation between. *(noun)* each of two or more related or complementary things.

Correspond – *(verb)* **1** have a close similarity; match or agree almost exactly. be analogous or equivalent. **2** communicate by exchanging letters. *Each month we two friends correspond by letters.*

Corridor – *(noun)* **1** a long passage from which doors lead into rooms. [British] a passage along the side of a railway carriage giving access to compartments. *While in college, we used to spend a lot of time in the corridor.* **2** a belt of land linking two other areas or following a road or river.

Corroborate – *(verb)* confirm or give support to a statement or theory. *I corroborated his statement in the court.*

Corrode – *(verb)* destroy or damage slowly by chemical action. be destroyed or damaged in this way. gradually weaken or erode.

Corrosion – *(noun)* a state of deterioration in metals caused by oxidation or chemical reaction.

Corrosive – *(adjective)* tending to cause corrosion. *(noun)* a corrosive substance. *Wind and water are great corrosive agents.*

Corrugate – *(verb)* contract into wrinkles or folds.

Corrupt – *(adjective)* **1** willing to act dishonestly in return for money or personal gain. evil or morally depraved. *He is a very corrupt officer. He won't favour you without money.* **2** a text or a computer database or program made unreliable by errors or alternations. **3** [archaic] rotten or putrid. *(verb)* **1** cause to become corrupt. **2** debase by making errors. **3** [archaic] infect; contaminate.

Cortege – *(noun)* **1** a solemn procession, especially for a funeral. **2** a person's entourage or retinue.

Coryza – *(noun)* [medicine] catarrhal inflammation of the mucous membrane in the nose, as caused by a cold.

Cosignatory – *(noun)* a person or state signing a treaty or other document jointly with others. *Many persons and states sign a mutual treaty and other documents.*

Cosmetic – *(adjective)* **1** relating to treatment intended to improve a person's appearance. *My friend underwent cosmetic surgery of the face. Now he looks much younger and smart.* **2** affecting only the appearance of something. *(noun)* cosmetic preparations, especially for the face.

Cosmic – *(adjective)* of or relating to the universe or cosmos, especially as distinct from the earth. *Scientists have yet to know about a lot of cosmic mysteries.*

Cosmogony – *(noun)* the branch of science concerned with the origin of the universe, especially the solar system.

Cosmos – *(noun)* an ornamental plant of the daisy family, which bears single dahlia-like flowers and is native to Mexico and warm regions of America.

Cost – *(verb)* **1** require the payment of in order to be bought or obtained. cause or require the expenditure or loss of. [informal] be expensive for; it'll cost you. *Please tell me the price of this diamond.* **2** estimate the price or cost of. *(noun)* the amount that something costs. the effort or loss necessary to achieve something. legal expenses, especially those allowed in favour of the winning party or against the losing party in a suit. *It is rather costly. Will you show me another one?*

Costard – *(noun)* [British] a cooking apple of a large ribbed variety. *I didn't like the taste of this kind of apple.*

Coster – *(noun)* [British] short for costermonger.

Costive – *(adjective)* constipated. *This man appears costive.*

Costly – *(adjective)* **1** expensive. **2** causing suffering, loss, or disadvantage.

Costume – *(noun)* a set of clothes in a style typical of a particular country or historical period. *Kindly call the actors and give them their assigned costumes.* a set of clothes worn by an actor or performer for a role. *This is a special costume that belongs to 18th century.* [British] dated a woman's matching jacket and skirt. *(verb)* dress in a particular set of clothes.

Cot – *(noun)* [British] a small bed with high barred sides for a baby or very young child. a plain narrow bed. [north American] a camp bed. nautical a bed resembling a hammock hung from deck beams, formerly used by officers.

Cote – *(noun)* a shelter for mammals or birds, especially pigeons. *Pigeons live in cotes.*

Coterie – *(noun)* a small exclusive group of people with shared interests or tastes.

Cottage – *(noun)* **1** a small simple house, typically one in the country. *A monk lives in this cottage.* **2** [informal] a public toilet. *(verb)* [informal] perform homosexual acts in a public toilet.

Cotton – *(noun)* **1** a soft white fibrous substance which surrounds the seeds of the cotton plant and is used as textile fiber and thread for sewing. **2** [north American] cotton wool. **3** the tropical and subtropical plant commercially grown for this product. *(verb)* [informal] **1** begin to understand. **2** [north American] have a liking for.

Couch – *(noun)* a coarse grass with long creeping roots. *In jugle we rolled on nature made couches.*

Cough – *(verb)* **1** expel air from the lungs with a sudden sharp sound. *My friend kept on coughing loudly, so we took him to a doctor.* **2** make a sudden harsh noise, especially as a sign of malfunction. *The man was a hard customer still we made him cough some money for the doctor.* **3** [informal] give something, especially money, reluctantly. [British] reveal information; confess. (noun) an act or sound of coughing. a condition of the respiratory organs causing coughing.

Council – *(noun)* **1** a formally constituted advisory, deliberative, or administrative body. a body elected to manage the affairs of a city, county, or district. *My friend resigned from the council due to some problem.* **2** [British] denoting housing provided by a local council.

Counsellor – *(noun)* **1** a person trained to give guidance on personal, social, or psychological problems. **2** a senior officer in the diplomatic service. [US & lrish] a barrister.

Countenance – *(noun)* **1** a person's face or facial expression. *My friend has a very impressive countenance.* **2** [formal] support or approval. *(verb)* admit as acceptable or possible.

Counteract – *(verb)* act against in order to reduce its force or neutralize it. *My friend counteracted when some absurd questions were asked.*

Counterchange – *(verb)* [poetic] chequer with contrasting colours. [heraldry] interchange the tinctures of with that of a divided field. *(noun)* **1** change that is opposite in effect to a previous change. **2** patterning in which a dark motif on a light ground alternates with the same motif light on a dark ground.

Counter-claim – *(noun)* a claim made to rebut a previous claim. [law] a claim made by a defendant against the plaintiff. *(verb)* [chiefly law] make a counterclaim. *He made a counter-claim for his lost bag and baggage.*

Counterfoil – *(noun)* [chiefly British] the part of a cheque, ticket, etc., that is kept as a record by the person issuing it.

Countermand – *(verb)* revoke, declare voting invalid.

Counterpoise – *(noun)* a factor or force that balances or neutralises another. [archaic] a state of equilibrium. a counterbalancing weight. *(verb)* have an opposing and balancing effect on. bring into contrast.

Countersign – *(verb)* add a signature to a document already signed by another person. *(noun)* [archaic] a signal or password given in reply to a soldier on guard. *I didn't countersign the check.*

Countervail – *(verb)* [offset] the effect of by countering it with something of equal force.

Countless – *(adjective)* too many to be counted; very many.

Country – *(noun)* **1** a nation with its own government, occupying a particular territory. **2** districts outside large urban areas. **3** an area or region with regard to its physical features: a tract of wild country.

Coup – *(noun)* **1** a sudden violent seizure of power from a government. **2** an unexpected and notably successful act. **3** [billiards] a direct pocketing of the cure ball, which is a foul stroke. **4** [historical] an act of touching an enemy, as a deed of bravery.

Couple – *(noun)* **1** two individuals of the same sort considered together. **2** [informal] an indefinites small number. **3** two people who are married or otherwise closely associated romantically or sexually. *The two couples were married together.* **4** [mechanics] a pair of equal and paralled forces acting in opposite directions, and tending to cause rotation about an axis perpendicular to the plane containing them. *(verb)* **1** join to form a pair. combine connect to another. *Coupled together.* **2** have sexual intercourse.

Couplet – *(noun)* a pair of successive lines of verse, typically rhyming and of the same length.

Courage – *(noun)* the ability to do something that frightens one. strength in the face of pain or grief.

Courier – *(noun)* **1** a messenger who transports goods or documents. *There are many cornier agonies operating in the city.* **2** a person employed to guide and assist a group of tourists. *(verb)* send or transport by courier.

Course – *(noun)* [British] a textbook designed for use on a particular course of study. *My course of commerce consists of many text books.*

Court – *(noun)* **1** a body of people before whom judicial cases are heard. the place where they meet. *In a court of law judicial case are heard.* **2** a quadrangular area marked out for ball games such as tennis. a quadrangle surrounded by a building or group of buildings. **3** the establishment, retinue, and courtiers of a sovereign. **4** the qualified members of a company or a corporation. *(verb)* **1** be involved with romantically, typically with the intention of marrying. of male bird or other animal try to attract a mate. **2** attempt to win the support or favour of. go to great lengths to win favourable attention. *He courted me for two years.*

Courtesan – *(noun)* a prostitute, especially one with wealthy or upper-class clients. *I met a prostipute who belonged to a rather richer and upper class.*

Courtesy – *(noun)* **1** courteous behaviour. a polite speech or action, especially one required by convention. **2** [archaic] a curtsy.

Courtly – *(adjective)* very polite and refined.

Courtship – *(noun)* **1** a period of courting, especially with a view to marriage. the courting behaviour of male birds and other animals. **2** the process of courting favour or support.

Courtyard – *(noun)* an open area enclosed by walls or buildings, especially in a castle or large house. *Instead of open field, we would rather play in our courtyard.*

Covenant – *(noun)* **1** a solemn agreement. [theology] an agreement held to be the basis of a relationship of commitment with god. *My friend is a covenant member of church. He has agreed to pay by covenant.* **2** a contract by which one undertakes to make regular payments to a charity. (verb) agree or pay by covenant.

Coverlet – *(noun)* a bedspread. *It is a beautiful coverlet.*

Covert – *(adjective)* not openly acknowledged or displayed. *(noun)* **1** a thicket in which game can hide. **2** [ornithology] a feather covering the base of a main flight or tail feather of a bird. *A thick bush in which the hunted animal can hide.*

Covet – *(verb)* yearn to possess. *I covet that piece to jewellery. I wish it were mine.*

Covey – *(noun)* a small flock of birds, especially partridge. *There is a group of partridges, let's go and catch them.*

Cow – *(noun)* **1** a fully grown female animal of a domesticated breed of ox. an animal of this type which has borne more than one calf. compare with HEIFER. the female of certain other large animals, e.g. elephant, rhinoceros, or whale. *Cow is a household pet animal.* **2** [informal], derogatory a women. *Don't haggle with her, let the cow have the price she is asking for.*

Cower – *(verb)* crouch down in fear. *The dog cowered in the corner.*

Co-worker – *(noun)* an associate that one works with. *We are friends as well as co-workers.*

Cozen – *(verb)* [poetic/literary] trick or deceive.

Cozy – *(adjective)* US spelling of cosy.

Crackle – *(verb)* make a rapid succession of slight cracking noises. *(noun)* a cracking sound of this type. **2** a pattern of minute surface crackes.

Cracknel – *(noun)* **1** a light, crisp, savoury biscuit. *Cracknels are my favourites.* **2** a brittle sweet made from set melted sugar.

Cracksman – *(noun)* [informal] a safe-breaker. *Police has cought a cracksman. He has looted many people.*

Crafty – *(noun)* **1** cunning or deceitful. *He is a crafty fellow and not to be trusted at all.* **2** [informal] of or relating to the making of objects by hand.

Crambo – *(noun)* a game in which a player gives a word or line of verse to which other players must find a rhyme. *We are playing combo and it is a very exciting game.*

Crane – *(noun)* a large, tall machine used for moving heavy objects by suspending them from a projecting arm. a moving platform supporting a camera. *You see that crane operating? It has a projecting hand and with it, it can lift very heavy objects.* *(verb)* **1** stretch out in order to see something. **2** move by means of a crane.

Cranny – *(noun)* a small, narrow space or opening. *He went down the cranny and emerged at the other end.*

Crashing – *(adjective)* [informal] complete; total. *He is a crashing bore, people avoid him like anything.*

Crass – *(adjective)* showing a grossly insensitive lack of intelligence. *He is stupid and crass, not an ounce of intelligence in him.*

Crate – *(noun)* **1** a slatted wooden case used for transporting goods. a square container divided into small individual units for holding bottles. *The wooden crate is ready for transportation.* **2** informal, an old and dilapidated vehicle. *(verb)* pack in a crate for trasportation.

Crater – *(noun)* **1** large bowl-shaped cavity, especially one caused by an explosion or impact or forming the mouth of a volcano. *The volcano has a big crater.* **2** a large bowl used in ancient Greece for mixing wine. *(verb)* from a crater or craters in.

Crave – *(verb)* **1** feel a powerful desire for. *His crave for education is legendary.* **2** dated ask for. *I must crave your indulgence.*

Craw – *(noun)* the crop of a bird or insect.

Crawl – *(verb)* **1** move forward on the hands and knees or by dragging the body close to the ground. move slowly along a surface. move at an unusually slow pace. **2** [informal] behave obsequiously or ingratiatingly. **3** be unpleasantly covered or crowded with. *The place was crewing with soldiers.* feel an unpleasant sensation resembling something moving over the skin. *(noun)* **1** an act of crewing. a slow rate of movement. **2** a swimming stroke involving alternate over arm movements and rapid kicks of the legs.

Creak – *(verb)* **1** make a harsh high-pitched sound when being moved or when pressure is applied. *The bridge creaked under our weight.* **2** show weakness or fraility under strain. *(noun)* a creaking sound.

Crease – *(noun)* **1** a line or ridge produced on paper or cloth by folding, pressing, or crushing. a wrinkle or furrow in the skin, especially of the face. *He is an old man with face creased all over.* **2** [cricket] any of a number of lines marked on the pitch at specified places. *A crease is farmed when a paper is folded.* *(verb)* **1** make a crease in. **2** graze. **3** [British, informal] hit or punch hard. **4** [British, informal] burst out or cause to burst out laughing.

Creation – *(noun)* **1** the action or process of creating. a thing which has been made or invented, especially something showing artistic talent. *God created the universe.* **2** the creating of the universe, especially when regarded as an act of god. the universe.

Creative – *(adjective)* relating to or involving the use of imagination or original ideas in order to create something. *(noun)* a person engaged in creative work. *A painting is an creative task.*

Credence – *(noun)* **1** belief in or acceptance of something as true. the likelihood of something being true; plausibility. **2** a small side table, shelf, or niche in a church for holding the elements of the Eucharist before they are consecrated.

Credential – *(noun)* **1** a qualification, achievement, etc., especially when used to indicate suitability. *Excuse me sir, the principal would like to see your credentials.* **2** a letter of introduction given by a government to an ambassador before a new posting.

Credible – *(adjective)* able to be believed; convincing. *His statement sounds credible.*

Creditor - *(noun)* a person or company to whom money is owing. *I owe a lot of money to my creditors.*

Creed - *(noun)* **1** a system of religious belief; a faith. a formal statement of Christian beliefs. *Christianity is a wide spread creed.* **2** a credo.

Creek - *(noun)* a narrow, sheltered waterway such as an inlet in a shoreline or channel in a marsh. [north American & austral] a stream or minor tributary of a river.

Creep - *(verb)* **1** move slowly and carefully, especially in order to avoid being heard or noticed. move or progress very slowly and steadily. grow along the ground or other surface by extending stems or branches. **2** undergo gradual deformation under stress. **3** [informal] behave obsequiously towards. *He is a contemptible creep. (noun)* **1** [informal] a contemptible person, especially one who behaves obsequiously in the hope of advancement. **2** very slow, steady movement or progress. gradual deformation of a plastic solid under stress. **3** [British] an opening in a hedge or wall for an animal to pass through. a feeding enclosure for young animals, with a long narrow entrance.

Cremate - *(verb)* dispose of by burning it to ashes. *It is Hindu tradition to cremate dead bodies.*

Creosote - *(noun)* **1** a dark brown oil containing various phenols and other compounds distilled from coal tar, used as a wood preservative. **2** a colourless, pungent, oily liquid distilled from wood tar and used as an antiseptic. *(verb)* treat with creosote.

Crepitate - *(verb)* make a crackling sound.

Crept - past and past participle of creep. *He crept post me.*

Crest - *(noun)* **1** a comb or tuft of feathers, fur, or skin on the head of a bird or other animal. a plume of feathers on a helmet. **2** the top of a ridge, wave, etc. [anatomy] a ridge along the surface of a bone. **3** a distinctive heraldic device representing a family or corporate body, displayed above the shield of coat of arms or separately. *(verb)* reach the top of form a curling foamy top. have attached at the top.

Crew - *(noun)* **1** a group of people who work on and operate a ship, boat, aircraft, or train. such a group other than the officers. **2** [informal, often derogatory] a group of people. *(verb)* provide with a crew. act as a member of a crew.

Crib - *(noun)* **1** [north American] child's bed with barred or latticed sides; a cot. a manger. [British] a model of the nativity of Christ. **2** [informal] a translation of a text for use by students, especially in a surreptitious way. a thing that has been plagiarised. **3** [informal, north American] an apartment or house. **4** short for CRIBBAGE. the cards discarded by the players at cribbage. **5** a heavy timber framework used in foundations. **6** austral a snack. *(verb)* **1** [informal] copy illicitly or without acknowledgement. [archaic] steal. **2** [archaic] restrain. **3** [British]dated grumble.

Cricket - *(noun)* an open-air game played on a large grass field with bat and ball between teams of eleven players, the batsmen attempting to score runs by hitting the ball and running between the wickets. *Cricket is a game popular throughout the world.*

Cricoid - *(noun)* [anatomy] the ring-shaped cartilage of the larynx. *My friend underwent cricoids operation.*

Crier - *(noun)* an office who makes public announcements in a court of justice. *My name was called out in the court by a crier.*

Criminal - *(noun)* a person who has committed a crime. *(adjective)* **1** of, relating to, or constituting a crime. *He is a criminal and his spent 10 years in jail.* **2** [informal] deplorable and shocking.

Crimp - *(verb)* **1** compress into small folds or ridges. connect by squeezing together. make waves in with a hot iron. *He used hot iron to remove creases.* **2** [north American, informal] have a limiting or adverse effect on. *(noun)* **1** a curl, wave, or folded or compressed edge. **2** a small connecting piece for crimping wires or lines together.

Crimple - *(noun)* **1** a person or thing that crimps. **2** [informal] a hairdresser.

Crinoid – *(noun)* [zoology] an echinoderm of a class that comprises the sea lilies and feather stars.

Cripple – *(noun)* [archaic] or offensive a person who is unable to walk or move properly through disability or injury. *(verb)* make unable to move or walk properly. cause severe and disabling damage to.

Crisp – *(adjective)* **1** firm, dry, and brittle, especially in a way considered pleasing. having tight curls, giving an impression of rigidity. *These biscuits are fresh and crisp.* **2** cool, fresh, and invigorating. *Snacks can be made crisp by placing them into oven or grill.* **3** decisive and matter-of-fact. *(noun)* [British] a wafer-thin slice of potato fried until crisp and eaten as a snack. *(verb)* **1** give a crisp surface by placing it in an oven or grill. **2** [archaic] curl into short, stiff, wavy folds or crinkles.

Critic – *(noun)* **1** a person who expresses an unfavourable opinion of something. *He is a famous film critic.* **2** a person who judges the merits of literary, artistic, or musical works, especially one who does so professionally.

Criticism – *(noun)* **1** the expression of disapproval of some-one or something based on perceived faults or mistakes. *Criticism of a work of art carries a lot of weight with public.* **2** the critical assessment of a literary or artistic work.

Critique – *(noun)* a detailed analysis and assessment. *(verb)* evaluate in a detailed and analytical way. *A critique evaluates a work of art in a detailed and analytical way.*

Croak – *(noun)* a characteristic deep hoarse sound made by a frog or a crow. *(verb)* **1** utter a croak. **2** [informal] die. **3** [archaic prophesy] evil or misfortune.

Crocodile – *(noun)* **1** a large predatory semi aquatic retile with long jaws, long tail, short legs, and a horny textured skin. *Once I saw a live crocodile.* **2** leather made from crocodile skin, used especially to make bags and shoes. **3** [British informal] a line of schoolchildren walking in pairs.

Croesus – *(noun)* a small spring-flowering plant of the Iris family, which grows from a corm and bears bright yellow, purple, or white flowers. *I specially like the yellow purple flowers of the Croesus plinth.*

Croft – *(noun)* 1 a small rented farm, especially in Scotland, having a right of pasturage held in common with other such farms. **2** a small enclosed field, typically attached to a house. *(verb)* farm as a croft or crofts.

Crony – *(adjective)* [informal] unfit, unsound, or fraudulent. *He is cansidered a crany in society.*

Crook – *(noun)* **1** a shepherd's hooked staff. a bishop's crozier. **2** a bend, especially at the elbow in a person's arm. **3** [informal] a person who is dishonest or a criminal *(verb)* bend something, especially a finger as a signal. *(adjective)* [informal] bad, unsound, or unwell. dishonest; illegal.

Crooked – *(adjective)* **1** bent or twisted out of shape or position. **2** [informal] dishonest or illegal. **3** [austral informal] annoyed; exasperated.

Croon – *(verb)* hum, sing, or speak in a soft, low voice. *(noun)* a soft, low voice or tone.

Croquet – *(noun)* a game played on a lawn, in which wooden balls are driven through a series of square-topped hoops by means of mallets. an act of croqueting a ball. *(verb)* drive away by holding one's own ball against it and striking one's own.

Crore – [Indian] ten million; one hundred lakhs.

Crotchet – *(noun)* [music, chiefly British] a musical note having the time value of a quarter of a semibreve or half a m stem. **2** a perverse or unfounded belief or notion.

Croton – *(noun)* a strong-scented tree, shrub, or herbaceous plant, native to tropical and warm regions. **2** a small evergreen tree or shrub of the indo-pacific region, with colourful foliag.

Crouch – *(verb)* adopt a position where the knees are bent and the upper body is brought forward and down. bend over so as to be close to. *(noun)* a crouching stance or posture.

Crow - *(noun)* **1** a member of an American Indian people inhabiting eastern Montana. *Spoken by the crow .* **2** the Siouan language of this people. **3** a black bird having raucous call.

Crowd - *(noun)* a large number of people gathered together. a large audience, especially at a sporting event. [informal, often derogatory] a group of people with a common interest. *(verb)* **1** fill almost completely, leaving little or no room for movement. move or come together as a crowd. **2** move too close to don't crowd her; she needs air. **3** exclude by taking the place of someone or something.

Crown - *(noun)* **1** a circular ornamental headdress worn by a monarch as a symbol of authority. the monarchy or reigning monarch. a wreath of leaves or flowers, especially that worn as an emblem of victory in ancient Greece or Rome. **2** an award of distinction gained by a victory or achievement, especially in sport. *In a victory in sports a persona was honoured by handing over a crown to wear.* **3** the top or highest part. the top part of a person's head or a hat. the upper part of a cut gem, above the girdle. **4** the part of a tooth projecting from the gum. an artificial replacement or covering for the upper part of a tooth. **5** a British coin with a face value of five shillings or 25 pence, now minted only for commemorative purposes. **6** a paper size, 384x504mm. a book size, 186x123 mm. a book size, 246x189 mm. *(verb)* **1** ceremonially place a crown on the head a monarch. declare to be the best, especially at a sport. *He was crowned world champion.* promote to king by placing another on top of it. **2** rest on or form the top of. **3** be the triumphant culmination of an effort or endeavour. **4** fit a crown to a tooth. **5** [informal] hit on the head. **6** fully appear in the vaginal opening prior to emerging.

Crucial - *(adjective)* **1** decisive or critical, especially in the success or failure of something. *Waiting for the result was a crucial moment.* **2** [informal] excellent.

Cruciferous - *(adjective)* [botany] relating to or denoting plants of the cabbage family with four equal petals arranged in a cross.

Crucifix - *(noun)* a representation of a cross with a figure of Christ on it. *I wear a crucifix round my neck both as respect and love for Christ.*

Cruciform - *(adjective)* having the shape of a cross. *Many people wear ornaments in the form of cruciform.*

Cruel - *(adjective)* disregarding or taking pleasure in the pain or suffering of others. causing pain or suffering. *Cruel people take delight in pain or suffering of others.*

Cruet - *(noun)* **1** a small container for salt, pepper, oil, or vinegar for use at a dining table. [British] a stand holding such containers. a small container for the wine or water to be used in the celebration of the Eucharist.

Cruise - *(verb)* **1** sail, travel, or move slowly around without a smoothly at a moderate or economical speed. *I cruised round thinking something.* **2** [achieve] an objective with ease. **3** [informal] wander about in search of a sexual partner. *(noun)* an instance of crusting. a voyage on a ship taken as a holiday and usually calling in at several places. *The cruise ship sailed smoothly on gentle wares.*

Crump - *(noun)* a loud thudding sound, especially one made by an exploding bomb or shell. *There was a sudden crump and all of us ran helter-skelter.*

Crumpet - *(noun)* **1** a thick, flat, savoury cake with a soft, porous texture, made from a yeast mixture cooked on a griddle and eaten toasted and buttered. *It is one of my favourites.* **2** [British informal] women regarded as objects of sexual desire. **3** [British archaic, informal] a person's head.

Crumple - *(verb)* **1** crush or become crushed so as to become creased and wrinkled. *The piece of cloth was badly crimpled. It took me several efforts to smooth it out.* **2** suddenly lose force, effectiveness, or composure. *(noun)* a crushed fold, crease, or wrinkle.

Crusade - *(noun)* **1** any of a series of medieval military expeditions made by Europeans to recover the holy land from the Muslims. a war instigated for alleged religious ends. **2** an energetic organized campaign with a political, social, or religious aim: a crusade against crime. *(verb)* lead or take part in a crusade.

Cruse – *(noun)* [archaic] an earthenware pot or jar. *An earthen ware pot or jar.*

Crush – *(verb)* **1** deform, pulverize, or force inwards by compressing forcefully. crease or crumple. *In the accident of two cars one car was completely crushed.* **2** violently subdue opposition or a rebellion. *In medieval times many rebellious against the kings were violently crushed.* **3** cause to feel overwhelming disappointment or embarrassment. *I failed in my examination and I felt crushed.* *(noun)* **1** a crowd of people pressed closely together. **2** [informal] an intense infatuation. **3** a drink made from the juice of pressed fruit. *I drank refreshing glass of strawberry crush.* **4** a fenced passage with one narrow end used for handling cattle or sheep.

Crust – *(noun)* **1** the tough outer part of a loaf of bread. a hard, dry scrap of bread. *I cut the crust of the bread.* **2** a hardened layer, coating, or deposit on something soft. a layer of pastry covering a pie. **3** the outermost layer of rock of which a planet consists, especially the part of the earth above the mantle. *Minerals are found in the earth's crust.* **4** a deposit of tractates and other substances formed in wine aged in the bottle, especially port. *I found crust in the wine bottle.* **5** [informal] a living or livelihood. *Earning a crust.* *(verb)* form into or cover with a crust. *Crusted port.*

Crutch – *(noun)* **1** a long stick with a crosspiece at the top, used as a support by a lame person. *I saw a lame man walking with the help of crutches.* **2** something used for support or reassurance. **3** the crotch of the body or a garment.

Cryogen – *(noun)* a substance used to produce very low temperatures. *A substance used to produce very low temperature.*

Crypt – *(noun)* **1** an underground room or vault beneath a church, used as a chapel or burial place. **2**. [anatomy] a small tubular gland, pit, or recess.

Cryptography – *(noun)* the art of writing or solving codes.

Crystalline – *(adjective)* **1** having the structure and form of a crystal. *A crystalline rock* **2** [poetic/ literary] very clear. *He writes crystalline prose.*

Cub – *(noun)* **1** the young of a fox, bear, lion, or other carnivorous mammal. *She was as protective as a tiger with her cubs.* **2** a junior branch of the scout association, for boys aged about 8 to 11. a member of this organization. *(verb)* **1** give birth to cubs. **2** hunt fox cubs.

Cubeb – *(noun)* **1** a tropical shrub of the pepper family, which bears pungent berries. *A shrub of pungent berries.* **2** the dried unripe berries of this shrub, used medicinally and to flavour cigarettes.

Cubicle – *(noun)* a small partitioned-off area of a room.

Cubiform – *(adjective)* [technical] cube-shaped. *His office is in a cubiform room.*

Cukold – *(noun)* the husband of an adulterous regarded as an object of derision. *(verb)* make a married man a cuckold.

Cuckoo – *(noun)* a grey or brown bird known for the far carrying two-note call of the male and for the habit of laying its eggs in the nests of small songbirds. used in names of other birds of the same family. *(adjective)* [informal] crazy.

Cucumber – *(noun)* **1** a long, green-skinned fruit with watery flesh, eaten raw in salads. **2** the widely cultivated claiming plant of the gourd family which yields this fruit, originally native to the Chinese Himalayan region.

Cucurbit – *(noun)* [chiefly north American]a plant of the gourd family which includes melon, pumpkin, squash, and cucumber.

Cuddy – *(noun)* [chiefly Scottish] **1** a donkey. **2** a stupid person.

Cudgel – *(noun)* a short thick stick used as a weapon. *The thief bet the man with a cudgel.* *(verb)* beat with a cudgel.

Cuff – *(noun)* **1** the end-part of a sleeve, where the material of the sleeve is turned back or a separate band is sewn on. [chiefly north American] a trouser turn-up. *I asked my men to attach a cuff to the end part of my sleeve.* **2** [informal] handcuffs. *The thief was cuffed.* **3** an inflatable bag wrapped round the arm when blood pressure is measured. *(verb)* [informal] secure with handcuffs.

Cuisine – *(noun)* a style or method of cooking, especially as characteristic of a particular country or region. food cooked in a certain way.

Culinary – *(adjective)* of or for cooking. *She has great culinary skills.*

Cullet – *(noun)* recycled broken or waste glass used in glass-making.

Culminant – *(adjective)* at or forming the top or highest point.

Culminate – *(verb)* **1** reach or be a climax or point of highest development. *As the debate between the two persons culminate I began to be excited.* **2** [archaic or astrology] reach or be at the meridian.

Culpable – *(adjective)* deserving blame. *He was arrested for culpable homicide.*

Culprit – *(noun)* a person who is responsible for a crime or other misdeed. *The culprit was arrested by polices.*

Cult – *(noun)* **1** a system of religious devotion directed towards a particular figure or object. a relatively small religious group regarded by others as strange or as imposing excessive control over members. **2** something popular or fashionable among a particular section of society.

Culture – *(noun)* **1** the arts and other manifestations of human intellectual achievement regarded collectively. a refined understanding or appreciation of this. **2** the customs, institutions, and achievements of a particular nation, people, or group. **3** [biology] the cultivation of bacteria, tissue cells, etc. in an artificial medium containing nutrients. a preparation of cells obtained in such a way. the cultivation of plants. **4** denoting cultivation or husbandry: aviculture. *(verb)* [biology] maintain in conditions suitable for growth.

Culvert – *(noun)* a tunnel carrying a stream or open drain under a road or railway. *There are so many culverts in the city.*

Cuneate – *(adjective)* [chiefly anatomy & botany] wedge-shaped.

Cunning – *(adjective)* **1** skilled in achieving one's ends by deceit or evasion. **2** ingenious. *He is a cunning fellow. Don't fall under his trap.* **3** [north American] attractive; charming. *(noun)* **1** craftiness. **2** ingenuity.

Cupboard – *(noun)* a piece of furniture or small recess with a door and usually shelves, used for storage.

Cupid – *(noun)* curing is possible.

Cupidity – *(noun)* greed for money or possessions. *He suffers from cupidity he needs a lot of many and possessions.*

Curative – *(adjective)* able to cure disease. *(noun)* a curative medicine or agent.

Curcuma – *(noun)* a tropical Asian plant of a genus that includes turmeric and other species yielding spices, dyes, and medicinal products.

Curd – *(noun)* **1** a soft, white substance formed when milk coagulates, used as the basis for cheese. a fatty substance found between the flakes of poached salmon. *Curd is my favourite dish, specially when I mix sugar with it.* **2** the edible head of a cauliflower or similar plant.

Curiosa – *(plural noun)* curiosities, especially erotica or pornography.

Curl – *(verb)* **1** form or cause to form a curved or spiral shape. *He fingers curled around the microphones.* **2** move or cause to move in a spiral or curved course. **3** lift using only the hands, wrists, and forearms. *Slowly curl the barbell to shoulder height.* *(noun)* **1** something in the shape of a spiral or coil, especially a lock of hair. *Her blonde hair was a mass of tangled curls.* **2** a curling movement. **3** a weightlifting exercise involving movement of only the hands, wrists, and forearms. *I did dumb-bell curls at the gym.*

Curmudgeon – *(noun)* a bad-tempered or surly person. *He is a curmudgeon and I won't even talk to him.*

Current – *(adjective)* happening or being sued or done now. in common or general use. *(noun)* **1** a body of water or air moving in a definite direction through a surrounding body of water of air in which there is less movement. **2** a flow of electricity which result from the ordered directional movement of eclectically charged particles. *The current of water was too strong* *for me to swim.* a quantity representing the rate of flow of centric charge, usually measured in amperes.

Curricle - *(noun)* [historical] a light, open, two-wheeled carriage pulled by two horses side by side. *Curricle were very popular in 18th century.*

Currier - *(noun)* a person who curries leather. *A currier is a person who curries leather.*

Curry - *(verb)* **1** [chiefly north American] groom with a curry comb. **2** [historical] treat to improve its properties.

Curse - *(noun)* **1** a solemn appeal to a supernatural power to inflict harm on someone or something. a cause of harm or misery. **2** an offensive word or phrase used to express anger or annoyance. *(verb)* **1** use a curse against. be afflicted with. **2** utter or address with expletives. *I was so angry and felt such contempt that I cursed him with all my heart.*

Curtail - *(verb)* reduce in extent or quantity. *The powers of director were curtailed.*

Curtain - *(noun)* **1** a piece of material suspended at the top to form a screen, typically movable sideways and found as one of a pair at a window. a screen of heavy cloth or other material that can be raised or lowered at the front of a stage. a raising or lowering of such a screen at the beginning or end of an act or scene. *There was a curtain between the stage performers and audience, upside down or sideways.* **2** [informal] a disastrous outcome. *(verb)* provide with a curtain or curtains. conceal with or as with a curtain. *The play was curtained off.*

Curtilage - *(noun)* an area of land attached to a house and forming one enclosure with it.

Curvature - *(noun)* the fact of being curved or the degree to which something is curved. [geometry] the degree to which a curve deviates from a straight line, or a curved surface deviates from a plane.

Curve - *(noun)* a line or outline which gradually deviates from being straight for some or all of its length. a line on a graph whether straight or curved showing how one quantity varies with respect to another. [baseball] a delivery in which the pitcher causes the ball to deviate from a straight path by imparting spin. *(verb)* from or cause to form a curve.

Cusp - *(noun)* **1** each of the pointed ends of a crescent, especially of the moon. [architecture] a projecting point between small arcs in gothic tracery. **2** a cone-shaped prominence on the surface of a tooth, especially of a molar or premolar. **3** [mathematics] a point at which the direction of a curve is abruptly reversed. **4** astrology the initial point of an astrological sign or house. a point of transition between two different states: those on the cusp of adulthood. **5** [anatomy] a pocket or fold in the wall of the heart or a major blood vessel, forming part of a value.

Custodial - *(adj.)* providing protective supervision, watching over or safeguarding. *There are so many custodial death is India.*

Custom - *(noun)* **1** a traditional and widely accepted way of behaving or doing something that is specific to a particular society, place, or time. law established usage having the force of law or right. *It is a custom with us that we touch the feet of our elders.* **2** [chiefly British] regular dealings with a shop or business by customers.

Cutaneous - *(adjective)* of, relating to, or affecting the skin. *It is a cutaneous disease, you should be careful.*

Cutis - *(noun)* [anatomy] the true skin or dermis.

Cutlet - *(noun)* a portion of meat, especially a lamb or veal chop from just behind the neck served grilled or fried. a flat croquette of minced meat, nuts, or pulses.

Cutpurse - *(noun)* [archaic] term for pickpocket.

Cut-throat - *(noun)* **1** dated a murderer or other violent criminal. **2** a trout of western north America, with red or orange markings under the jaw. *(adjective)* ruthless and intense.

Cutting - *(noun)* **1** a piece cut off from something [British] an article or other piece cut from a newspaper. a piece cut from a plant for propagation. *I specially looked for a sports magazine, so that I could show the desired cutting to the teacher.* **2** an open passage excavated through higher ground for a railway road, or canal. *(adjective)* **1** capable of cutting. **2** hurtful.

Cuvette – *(noun)* a straight-sided container for holding liquid samples in a spectrophotometer, etc.

Cyanosis – *(noun)* [medicine] a bluish discoloration of the skin due to poor circulation or inadequate oxygenation of the blood. *Cycloid was applied on my cut because I have a poor circulation of blood.*

Cycloid – *(noun)* [mathematics] a curve traced by a point on a circle being rolled along a straight line. *A curve on a point being rolled straight.*

Cyclone – *(noun)* [meteorology] a system of winds rotating inwards to an area of low barometric pressure; a depression. another term for tropical storm. *The Daredevils actually go very near cyclone for scientific study.*

Cyclosis – *(noun)* the circulation of cytoplasm within a cell.

Cyclostyle – *(noun)* an early device for duplicating handwriting, in which a pen with a small toothed wheel makes a stencil in a sheet of waxed paper. *(verb)* cyclostyled duplicate with a cyclostyle.

Cylindrical – *(adj.)* having the form of a cylinder. *This shape is cylindrical.*

Cynic – *(noun)* **1** a person who believes that people are motivated purely by self-interest. a sceptic. a member of a school of ancient Greek philosophers founded by Antisthenes, characterized by an ostentatious contempt for wealth and pleasure. *My friend is a cynic.*

Cynosure – *(noun)* a person or thing that is the centre of attention or admiration. *Almost all film stars are cynosures.*

Cypher – *(noun)* variant spelling of cipher. *Zero or cipher.*

Cystic – *(adjective)* **1** [chiefly medicine] of, relating to, or characterized by cysts. *The doctors observed a cystic degeneration of white matter.* **2** of or relating to the urinary bladder or the gall bladder. *The cystic artery.*

Dd

D – *(noun)* **1** the fourth letter of the alphabet. **2** denoting the fourth in a set of items, categories, sized, etc. **3** music the second note of the diatonic scale of C major. **4** the roman numeral for 500. [understood as half of CI, an earlier form of M.]

Dab – *(noun)* a small, commercially important flatfish found chiefly in the north Atlantic. *Dab is considered a delicacy.*

Dabble – *(verb)* **1** move around gently in water. *They dabbled their feet in the pool.* **2** take part in an activity in a casual or superficial way. *Riya is not serious about modelling. She only dabbles in it occasionally.*

Dace – *(noun)* a freshwater fish related to the carp, typically living in running water. *The dace's beautiful blue-green body sparkled in the sunlight.*

Dacoit – *(noun)* a member of a band of armed robbers in India or Burma. *The dacoit was hiding in the bushes waiting to attack travellers passing by.*

Daft – *(adjective)* [informal, chiefly British] **1** silly; foolish. *Julian was scolded by his father for asking a very daft question.* **2** infatuated with. *He is dafit!*

Daily – *(adjective)* done, produced, or occurring every day or every weekday. *The watchman was doing his daily rounds when he noticed the burglar trying to sneak into the house.* *(adverb)* every day. *The Times of India is a daily newspaper.* *(noun)* [informal] **1** a newspaper published every day except Sunday. *The trial was reported in all the popular dalies.* **2** [British] a daily charwoman. **3** the first prints from cinematographic takes; the rushes.

Dainty – *(adjective)* **1** delicately small and pretty. delicate and graceful in build or movement. *Ballet dancers are very dainty in their movements.* **2** fastidious, typically concerning food. *The food usually consists of small amounts of fish, dressed vegetables and other dainty relishes.* *(noun)* a delicacy. *This is dainty.*

Dairy – *(noun)* a building or room for the storage processing, and distribution of milk and milk products. *John's father runs a successfu dairy business.* *(adjective)* containing or made from milk. concerned with or involved in the production of milk.*Ice-cream is a dairy product*

Dais – *(noun)* a low platform for a lectern o throne. *The professor stood on the dais while lecturing to the students.*

Daisy – *(noun)* a small grassland plant with composite flowers having a yellow disc and white rays. used in names of other plants of the same family, e.g. michaelmas daisy. *Daisie. bloom in the warm summer months.*

Dale – *(noun)* a valley, especially in northern England. *The dale is covered with flowers i the spring.*

Dally – *(verb)* **1** act or move slowly. **2** have casual romantic or sexual liaison with. show casual interest in. *She was cruelly dallying wit Jack's emotions.*

Dam – *(noun)* something that holds back water, o the body of water that is being held. *Hoover dar is built on the Colorado River in America. Ther is a need to build a dam across the river.* *(verb* to create a barrier to hold back liquid.

Dame – *(noun)* **1** given to a woman with th rank of knight commander or holder of th grand cross in the orders of chivalry. *She wa awarded the title of dame due to her aristocrati connections.* **2** [archaic or humorous] an elderl or mature woman. [north American informal] woman. *The matronly dame Mary was a ver kind woman.*

Damn – *(verb)* **1** be condemned by god to suffe eternal punishment in hell. be doomed t misfortune or failure. *I will be damned it he* *for it.* **2** condemn, especially publicly. **3** curse. [exclamatory, informal] expressing anger or frustration. *He was damned to hell for his barbarous act. (adjective)* [informal] used to emphasize one's anger or frustration: *Turn that damn thing off! I have complained about it previously and other people have complained about it too but you don't care a damn.*

Damnation – *(noun)* condemnation to eternal. punishment in hell. *He was cursed with eternal damnation for his misdeeds.* [exclamatory] expressing anger or frustration.

Damned – *(adjective)* [informal] used to emphasize one's anger or frustration. used to emphasize the surprising nature of something. *The town was better known as the town of the damned because of the misdeeds of its inhabitants.*

Damnify – *(verb)* [English law], cause injury to. *Article 86 gives rise to a cause of action at the suit of a person damnified by its contravention.*

Damming – *(adjective)* strongly suggestive of guilt or error. *His nervousness proved to be damning against him.*

Damp – *(adjective)* slightly wet, moisture in the air, on a surface, or in a solid, typically with detrimental or unpleasant effects. [archaic] damp air or atmosphere. *His clothes got damp after he was caught in the rain.* **2** [archaic] a check or discouragement. *Despite promotions, the movie turned out to be a damp squib. (verb)* **1** make damp. *Shame gave a damp to her triumph.* **2** [archaic] a check or discouragement. *Damp a small area with water.* **3** make a fire burn less strongly by reducing its air supply. *He damped down the fire for the night.* **4** reduce or stop the vibration of the strings of a musical instrument. [physics] progressively reduce the amplitude of an oscillation or vibration.

Damsel – *(noun)* [archaic or poetic/literary] a young unmarried woman. *The damsel smiled prettily and thanked the boy for his help.*

Damson – *(noun)* **1** a small purple-black plum like fruit. **2** the small tree which bears this fruit, probably derived from the bullace. *The damson tree was laden with ripe fruit.*

Dance – *(verb)* **1** move rhythmically to music, typically following a set sequence of steps. perform a particular dance or a role in a ballet. **2** move in a quick and light or lively way. of someone's eyes sparkly with pleasure or excitement. *(noun)* **1** a series of steps and movements that match the speed and rhythm of a piece of music. *She has quickly picked up the dance steps of salsa.* **2** a social gathering at which people dance. **3** music for dancing to, especially in a nightclub. *Ballet is one of the most graceful dance forms.*

Dancer – *(noun)* to move the body and feet in rhythm, ordinarily to music. *Jane is a professional dancer.*

Dandelion – *(noun)* a widely distributes weed of the daisy family, with large birth yellow flowers followed by globular heads of seeds with downy tufts. *The field was full of yellow dandelions swaying in the breeze.*

Dandiacal – *(adjective)* relating to a dandy, dandish.

Dandle – *(verb)* move a baby or young child up and down in a playful or affectionate way. *Mr. Williams was dandling his grandson and playing with him.*

Dandruff – *(noun)* small pieces of dead skin among a person's hair. *Dandruff is a disease where white pieces of dead skins accumulate on a person's head.*

Dandy – *(noun)* **1** a man unduly concerned with a stylish and fashionable appearance. **2** [informal, dated] an excellent thing of its kind. *(adjective)* [informal, chiefly north American] excellent. *Tom is quite a dandy when it comes to his appearance.*

Dane – *(noun)* a native or national of Denmark, or a person of Danish descent. *The famous writer of fairy tales, Hans Christian Anderson was a Dane.*

Danger – *(noun)* **1** the possibility of suffering harm or injury. a cause of harm or injury. *Children must be warned of the danger of playing with sharp objects.* **2** the possibility of something unwelcome or unpleasant. *There was no danger of the champagne running out.*

Dangle – *(verb)* hang or cause to hang so as to swing freely. *The bungee jumpers were dangling from the end of the rope.*

Danish – *(adjective)* of or relating to Denmark or its people or language *(noun)* the Scandinavian language spoken in Denmark. *Danish is the official language of Denmark.*

Dank – *(adjective)* damp, cold, and musty. *The house felt dank after being shut for many months.*

Dapper – *(adjective)* neat and trim in dress and appearance. *Jim looked quite dapper at the wedding in the suit.*

Dapple – *(verb)* mark with spots or rounded patches. *The sunlight dappled on the curtains creating mysterious shadows.* *(noun)* **1** a patch of colour or light. **2** an animal whose coat is dappled. *Dapple pattern that consists of a dark base colour with contrasting light areas.*

Dare – *(verb)* **1** have the courage to do something. used to express indignation. used to order someone threateningly not to do something. *How dare you challenge him for a duel?* **2** defy or challenge to do something. **3** [poetic/literary] take the risk of. *(noun)* a challenge, especially to prove courage. *Betty decided to walk on the fence on a dare.*

Daring – *(adjective)* adventurous or audaciously bold. *He is quite daring for a boy of his age.* *(noun)* adventurous courage. *At the first meeting, and scarcely daring to hope for permission, I asked if I might see the documents.*

Dark – *(adjective)* **1** with little or no light. **2** of a deep or somber colour. *One of the bandits was a tall dark ugly looking person.* brown or black. having such skin, hair, or eyes. **3** mysterious. *A dark secret.* humorous most remote, inaccessible, or uncivilized. [archaic] ignorant. **4** characterized by unhappiness or unpleasantness. *The dark days of the war.* evil; sinister: dark deeds. *(noun)* **1** the absence of light. a dark colour or shade. **2** nightfall. *It grows dark after sunset.*

Darken – *(verb)* **1** make or become dark or darker. of something unpleasant cast a shadow over; spoil. **2** make or become unhappy or angry. show anger. *Sarah's mood darkened after hearing the bad news.*

Darkish – *(adjective)* almost black. *The rug is darkish blue in colour.*

Darling – *(noun)* used as an affectionate form of address. a lovable or endearing person. a favourite of a certain group: the darling of labour's left wing. *(adjective)* beloved. pretty; charming. *Jane is her father's darling.*

Darn – *(verb)* mend by interweaving yarn across it with a needle. embroider with a large running stitch. *Sarah mended the tear in the shirt by darning it before it got bigger.* *(noun)* an area in a garment that has been darned. *It will not be noticed if you darn the hole in the garment.*

Dart – *(noun)* **1** a small pointed missile thrown of fired as a weapon. a small pointed missile with a flight, used in the game of darts. **2** an act of moving suddenly and rapidly. **3** a tapered tuck in a garment. *(verb)* **1** move suddenly or rapidly. *The thief darted through the crowd trying to escape the police.* **2** [archaic] throw or shoot.

Darter – *(noun)* **1** a long-necked bird which spears fish with its long pointed bill. *The darter was catching fish with the help of its long beak.* **2** a small north American freshwater fish. **3** a broad-bodied dragonfly which darts out to grab prey.

Darwinism – *(noun)* the theory of the evolution of species by natural selection, advanced by the English natural historian Charles Darwin (1809-82). *The followers of Darwinism refuse to accept any other theory of evolution.*

Dash – *(verb)* **1** move with sudden speed. **2** strike or fling with great force. **3** destroy or frustrate hopes or expectations. **4** write something hurriedly and without much thought. [British, informal] used to express mild annoyance. *Why would he like to dash your hope for promotion?* *(noun)* **1** an act of dashing. [chiefly north American] a sprint. **2** a small quantity of a substance, added to something else. a small amount of a particular quality adding distinctiveness to something. **3** a horizontal stroke in writing, marking a pause or to represent omitted letters or words. the longer signal of the two used in mores code. [music] a short vertical mark placed above or beneath a note to indicate that it is to be performed staccato. **4** panache. **5** short for DASHBOARD. *He made dash to the car in the rain to avoid getting wet.*

Dasher - *(noun)* **1** [informal] a flamboyant or stylish person. **2** a plunger for agitating cream in a churn. *It is important to operate the dasher properly while making cream in a churn.*

Dashing - *(adjective)* attractive in a romantic, adventurous way. stylish. *Bill looked quite dashing in his new clothes.*

Dastard - *(noun)* [dated or humorous] a dishonourable or despicable person. *He was a distard person.*

Dative - *(adjective)* denoting a case of nouns and pronouns indicating an indirect object or recipient. *(noun)* a dative noun, pronoun, etc.

Datum - *(noun)* **1** piece of information. **2** an assumption or premise from which inferences may be drawn. see SENSE DATUM. **3** a fixed starting point of a scale or operation. *Datum of a place is a position from which elevations and depths are measured in surveying.*

Daub - *(verb)* coat or smear with a thick substance carelessly or liberally. spread on a surface in such a way. *(noun)* **1** plaster, clay, etc., especially when mixed with straw and applied to laths or wattles to form a wall. *The interior chimney hood was in silver colour with brown daub finish.* **2** a patch or smear of a thick substance. **3** a painting executed without much skill. *Daub houses are perhaps the oldest remnants of the town now existing.*

Daughter - *(noun)* **1** a girl or woman in relating to her parents. a female descendant. *John and Kate have two daughters.* **2** a woman considered as the product of a particular influence or environment. **3** [physics] a nuclide formed by the radioactive decay of another.

Davit - *(noun)* a small crane on a ship, especially one of a pair for lowering a lifeboat. *The lifeboat was lowered into the water with the help of the davit when the ship was sinking.*

Dawdle - *(verb)* waste time. move slowly and idly. *Jack is very time conscious and does not dawdle.*

Dawn - *(noun)* **1** the first appearance of light in the sky before sunrise. *The rising sun appears on the horizon at dawn.* **2** the beginning of something. *It is dawn of the computer age.* *(verb)* **1** begin. **2** come into existence. become evident or understood.

Dawning - *(noun)* **1** [poetic/literary] dawn. **2** the beginning or first appearance of something. *The truth was slowly dawning upon her.*

Daze - *(verb)* make unable to think or react properly. *To daze means unable to think in an orderly way.* *(noun)* a state of stunned confusion. *Susan was shocked and in a daze after the accident.*

Dazzle - *(verb)* **1** of a bright light blind temporarily. *She came under the spell of dazzle by so many lights coming on suddenly.* **2** overwhelm with an impressive quality. *China's economic help must not dazzle us because they extract a heavy price for it in the long run.* *(noun)* blinding brightness.

Deacon - *(noun)* **1** an ordained minister of an order ranking below that of priest. in some protestant churches a lay officer assisting a minister. **2** an appointed minister of charity. *Deacon is the person who oversees church charities.* *(verb)* appoint or ordain as a deacon. *Ben was ordained as a deacon two years ago.*

Dead - *(adjective)* **1** no longer alive. *He spoke in a cold and emotionless voice as if he were dead.* devoid of living things. *One must not speak ill of the dead.* **2** numb. lacking emotion, sympathy, or sensitivity. **3** no longer relevant or important. **4** lacking activity or excitement. dull. **5** empty or no longer in use. out of play. **6** complete; absolute: dead silence. *(adverb)* absolutely. exactly. straight; directly. [British, informal] very.

Deaden - *(verb)* **1** make a noise sensation less strong or intense. make insensitive. **2** deprive of force or vitality. *The pain had deadened her sensitivity to the problems of others.*

Deal- *(noun)* an agreement. fir or pine wood as a building material. *I made a deal with her promising to finish homework each night in exchange for one hour of television.* *(verb)* to distribute.

Dealer – *(noun)* **1** a person who buys and sells goods. *Jim's father is a dealer of cotton garments.* a person who buys and sells shares or other financialassets as a principal rather than as a broker or agent. **2** a player who deals cards in a card game. *He is a dealer in a Casino.*

Dealing. *(noun)* way of acting towards others. *Dealing with customer complaints can sometimes be challenging, but there is always a solution that can be reached.*

Dean – *(noun)* variant spelling of DENE. *Mr. Harris is the dean of the college.*

Dearth – *(noun)* a scarcity or lack of something. *There is a dearth of good workers these days.*

Death – *(noun)* **1** the action or fact of dying or being killed. an instance of a person or an animal dying. **2** the state of being dead. the personification of the power that destroys life, often represented as a skeleton or an old man holding a scythe. **3** the destruction or end of something. *The death of his pet dog came as a blow to Harry.*

Debar – *(verb)* exclude or prohibit from doing something. *Having a criminal record will not debar you from doing voluntary work.*

Debase – *(verb)* **1** lower the quality, value, or character of. *I admit, I did debase myself by reading her personal letter.* **2** [historical] lower the value of by reducing the content of precious metal.

Debatable – *(adjective)* open to discussion or argument. *The benefits of the medicine were debatable.*

Debate – *(noun)* a formal discussion in a public meeting or legislative assembly. an argument, especially one involving many people. *A debate is a discussion of the opposing sides of a specific subject.* *(verb)* discuss or argue about. consider, ponder. *They came to a decision about the matter by holding a debate.*

Debauch – *(verb)* destroy the moral purity of. *(noun)* a bout of excessive indulgence in sensual pleasures. *People with traditional beliefs dislike debauchery of any kind.*

Debilitate – *(verb)* make very weak and infirm. *A virus can completely debilitate your computer and potentially cause the loss of entire information.*

Debris – *(noun)* scattered rubbish or remains. loose natural material, e.g. broken rocks. *The market site was littered with debris after the bomb blast.*

Debt – *(noun)* **1** money or services owed or due. **2** the state of owing money. *They are in debt.* a feeling of obligation or gratitude for a favour. *It is advisable to pay off one's debts on time.*

Debtor – *(noun)* a person who owes money. *Being a debtor can be a horrible experience.*

Debus – *(verb)* [British, chiefly military slang] unload or alight from a motor vehicle. *The team was asked to debus from the vehicle as soon as they reached the camp.*

Decade – *(noun)* **1** a period of ten years. **2** a set or group of ten. a range of electrical resistances or other quantities spanning from one to ten times a base value. *He ruled the movie world with his performance for more than a decade.*

Decadence – *(noun)* **1** the process, period, or manifestation of moral or cultural decline. **2** luxurious self-indulgence. *The Roman Empire came to an end due to sheer decadence of their lifestyle.*

Decagon – *(noun)* a plane figure with ten straight sides and angles. *The students were asked to create a model of a decagon.*

Decalogue – *(noun)* the ten commandments.*There were decalogue boards behind the altar.*

Decant – *(verb)* gradually pour form one container into another, typically in order to separate the liquid form the sediment. *It is time to decant the oil into another container to preserve it.*

Decapitate – *(verb)* cut off the head of. *Mercenaries don't hesitate to decapitate anyone caught spying.*

Decease – *(noun)* formal or [law] death. *(verb)* [archaic] die. *Some folklore say that the spirits of the deceased are supposed to be watching over us.*

Deceit – *(noun)* the action or practice of deceiving. a deceitful act or statement. *Lying to someone is an act of deceit.*

Deceive – *(verb)* deliberately mislead or misrepresent the truth to. *I knew she could easily deceive him.* give a mistaken impression. *The area may seem to offer nothing of interest, but don't be deceived.*

Deck – *(noun)* **1** a floor of a ship, especially the upper, open level. *There was a big thud when I hit the deck of the ship.* a similar floor or platform, as in a bus or car park. *The ship was furnished with a deck.* [informal] the ground or floor: **2** a component or unit in sound-reproduction equipment that incorporates a playing or recording mechanism for discs or tapes. **3** [chiefly north American] a pack of cards. *Deck of cards is lying there.* [north American informal] a packet of narcotics. *(verb)* **1** decorate or dress brightly or festively. *She decked up for the occassion.* **2** [informal] knock to the ground with a punch.

Declarant – *(noun)* [chiefly law] a person or party who makes a formal declaration. *A declarant is a person who signs a legal statement.*

Declaration – *(noun)* **1** a formal or explicit statement or announcement. [British] a public official announcement of the votes cast for candidates in an election. [law] a plaintiff's statement of claims in proceedings. **2** [law] an affirmation made instead of taking an oath. **3** an act or instance of declaring. *They made the declaration in front of the whole town.*

Declare – *(verb)* **1** announce solemnly or officially; make clearly known. openly align oneself for or against a party or position. *The company is about to declare a final dividend on the ordinary shares.* **2** reveal one's intentions or identity. express feelings of love to someone. **3** announce oneself as a candidate for an election. **4** acknowledge possession of taxable income or dutiable goods. **5** [cricket] close an innings voluntarily before all the wickets have fallen. announce that one holds in a card game.

Declension – *(noun)* **1** the variation of the form of a noun, pronoun, or (adjective), by which its grammatical case, number, and gender are identified. the class to which a noun or adjective is assigned according to this variation. **2** [poetic/literary] a condition of decline or moral deterioration. *Sensual and carnal worship entering the gospel temple is often an evidence of spiritual declension.*

Declination – *(noun)* **1** [astronomy] that angular distance of a point north or south of the celestial equator, north. **2** [US formal] refusal.

Declivity – *(noun)* a downward slope. *Declivity of these mountains slopes down till the sea coast.*

Decoct – *(verb)* [archaic] extract the essence from by heating or boiling it. *Please decoct by boiling if you want to extract the essence of the medicinal herb.*

Decontrol– *(verb)* release from controls or restrictions. *The government must decontrol the sale of petrol and diesel.*

Decorum – *(noun)* behaviour in keeping with good taste and propriety. prescribed behaviour; etiquette. *The children were strictly asked to maintain decorum of the house.*

Decoy – *(noun)* **1** a bird or mammal, or an imitation of one, used to lure game. *A duck used by a hunter to try to attract other ducks is an example of a decoy.* **2** a person or thing used to mislead or lure someone into a trap. *The police caught the robber by using his family as a decoy.* **3** a pond from which narrow netted channels lead, into which wild duck may be enticed for capture. *(verb)* lure by means of a decoy.

Decree – *(noun)* an official order issued by a ruler or authority that has the force of law. a judgment or decision of certain law courts. *He was retired from government service on 31 December 2011 by a presidential decree.* *(verb)* order by decree. *The school administration issued a decree banning students from bringing expensive mobile phones to school.*

Deity – *(noun)* **1** a god or goddess especially in a polytheistic religion. the creator and supreme being. **2** divine status, quality, or nature. *Krishna is worshipped as a deity by the Hindus.*

Delate – *(verb)* **1** report (an offence). **2** inform against.

Delay – *(verb)* **1** become or cause to become late or slow. **2** postpone or defer. *(noun)* a period of time by which something is late or postponed.

Unexpected problems led to delay in timely start of the function.

Delegacy – *(noun)* a body of delegates; a committee or delegation. *The Chinese delegacy is in town for the seminar.*

Delegate – *(noun)* a person sent or authorized to represent others, in particular a representative sent to a conference. a member of a committee. *He is a delegate representing Russia.* *(verb)* entrust a task or responsibility to another person. authorize to act as a representative or on one's behalf. *Arjun was asked to escort the American delegate to various meetings.*

Delete – *(verb)* **1** remove or erase. **2** remove form the catalogue of those available for purchase. *She was asked to delete all the files from the computer.*

Deliberation – *(noun)* **1** long and careful consideration. **2** slow and careful movement or thought. *The matter must be given enough deliberation before a decision is reached.*

Delicacies – *(noun)* Delicacy refers to the state of being fragile, frail, soft or subtle, or refers to a gourmet food. *That night they ate the local delicacy and stayed in a 5-star hotel.*

Delicate – *(adjective)* **1** very fine in texture or structure; of intricate workmanship or quality. of food or drink subtly and pleasantly flavoured. **2** easily broken or damaged; fragile. susceptible to illness or adverse conditions. **3** requiring sensitive or careful handling. skilful; deft. *(noun)* garments made for delicate fabric. *The vase was very delicate and on falling broke easily.*

Delicious – *(adjective)* **1** highly pleasant to the taste. *Mango is a delicious fruit.* **2** delightful: irony.

Delict – *(noun)* [law] a violation of the law; a tort.

Delight – *(verb)* please greatly. take great pleasure in. *(noun)* great pleasure. a cause or source of great pleasure. *Anne took great delight in singing.*

Delinquent – *(adjective)* **1** typically with reference to young people showing or characterized by a tendency to commit crime. *Teenage delinquency is a rapidly growing problem.* **2** formal failing in one's duty. *The programme deals with the group of aging delinquents.* **3** [chiefly north American] in arrears. *Delinquent accounts.* *(noun)* a delinquent person. *Delinquent behaviour was closely linked with a greater risk of drug use.*

Delirious – *(adjective)* **1** suffering form delirium. **2** in a state of wild excitement or ecstasy. *Delirious with happiness that I am back at home after two years.*

Dell – *(noun)* [poetic/literary] a small valley.

Delocalize – *(verb)* detach or remove form a particular location. *It was necessary to delocalize the sap before planting it in another nursery.*

Delude – *(verb)* impose a misleading belief upon. *She tried to delude him into thinking that he could trust her.*

Delusion – *(noun)* **1** an idiosyncratic belief or impression that is not in accordance with a generally accepted reality. **2** the action of deluding or being deluded. *He suffered from the delusion that he could write well.*

Demagnetize – *(verb)* remove magnetic properties from. *Research is being done on whether it is possible to demagnetize iron.*

Demagogue – *(noun)* **1** a political leader who seeks support by appealing to popular desires and prejudices rather than by using rational argument. **2** in ancient Greece and Rome an orator who espoused the cause of the common people. *Demagogues played an important role in ancient Greece and Rome.*

Demand – *(noun)* **1** an insistent and peremptory request, made as of right. pressing requirements. **2** [economics] the desire of purchasers, consumers, etc. for a particular commodity or service. *A recent slump in demand.* *(verb)* ask authoritatively or brusquely. insist on having. require; need. *The kidnappers made a ransom demand late at night.*

Demarcation – *(noun)* the action of fixing boundaries or limits. a dividing line. *The demarcation between the rich and the poor was quite obvious.*

Demerit – *(noun)* **1** a feature or fact deserving censure. **2** [north American] a mark awarded against someone for a fault or offence. *The student earned a demerit for his actions.*

Demesne - *(noun)* [historical] **1** land attached to a manor and retained by the owner for their own use. [archaic] a domain. **2** [law] possession of real property in one's own right.

Demi-lune - *(noun)* a crescent or half-circle, or a thing of this shape.

Demise - *(noun)* **1** the end or failure of something. *In a way, ideals of democracy led to the demise of soviet communism.* **2** a person's death. *Harry was very sad at his grandfather's demise.* **3** [law] the transfer of property or a title by demising. *(verb)* law convey or grant by will or lease,

Demolish - *(verb)* **1** pull or knock down. *It has been decided to demolish the old house to make way for a new apartment building.* **2** comprehensively refute or defeat. **3** humorous eat up quickly.

Demon - *(noun)* **1** an evil spirit or devil an evil or destructive person or thing. *It is usually the superstitious people who believe in demons.* **2** denoting a person forceful or skilful in a specified role. *A demon cook.* **3** another term for daemon.

Demonetize- *(verb)* deprive a coin or precious metal of its status as money. *The twenty-five paise coins have been demonetized a long time ago.*

Demonstrate - *(verb)* **1** clearly show the existence or truth or. give a practical exhibition and explanation of. **2** take part in a public demonstration. *The teacher demonstrated the experiment to the class.*

Demoralize - *(verb)* **1** cause to lose confidence or hope. **2** [archaic] corrupt the morals of. *The caustic remarks by the management may demoralize the team after their defeat.*

Demurrage - *(noun)* [law] a charge payable to the owner of a chartered ship in respect of delay in loading or discharging.*Demurrage is a fine a transporter imposes on a customer for not takin delivery of goods within stipulated time.*

Den - *(noun)* **1** a wild animal's lair or habitation. *It is dangerous to enter a lion's den.* **2** [informal] a person's private room. **3** a place where people meet secretly or illicitly. *An opium den.* *(verb)* live in or retreat to a den.

Denaturalize - *(verb)* **1** make unnatural. **2** deprive of citizenship of a country. *America threatened to denaturalize Ryan of citizenship for want to documents.*

Dendroid - *(adjective)* [biology] tree-shaped; branching. *(noun)* [palaeonlology] a graptolite of a type that formed much-branched colonies.

Dengue - *(noun)* a debilitating tropical viral disease transmitted by mosquitoes, causing sudden fever and acute pains in the joints. *The health authorities are afraid of a possible dengue outbreak.*

Denigrate - *(verb)* criticize unfairly; disparage. *Why denigrate Jill in front of everyone if it wasn't her fault?*

Denotation - *(nout)* the act of indicating or pointing out by name.

Denote - *(verb)* be a sign of; indicate. stand as a name or symbol for. *Use red ink to denote important points that need explanation.*

Dense - *(adjective)* **1** closely compacted in substance. crowded closely together. **2** [informal] of a person stupid. *The jungle is dense to the point that in places, it is almost impenetrable.*

Dent - *(noun)* a slight hollow in a hard even surface made by a blow or pressure. *From a minor dent to a full scale repair, we provide the best quality repair in the city.* *(verb)* **1** mark with a dent. *Jack noticed the dent on his car some time after the collision.* **2** have an adverse effect on.

Denture - *(noun)* a removable plate or frame holding one or more artificial teeth.

Denudation - *(noun)* the removal of covering.

Denude - *(verb)* strip of covering or possessions; make bare. *The rains washed away the soil denuding the area around the tree.*

Denunciation - *(noun)* the action of denouncing someone or something. *The denunciation of the horrible practice resulted in everyone being relieved.*

Deodorize - *(verb)* remove or conceal an unpleasant smell in. *Room freshener was used to deodorize the room.*

Deontology – *(noun)* [philosophy] the study of the nature of duty and obligation.

Depart – *(verb)* **1** leave, especially in order to start a journey. **2** deviate form a course of action. *They were supposed to depart at 5 o'clock to catch the train.*

Depasture – *(verb)* [British] put to graze on pasture.

Depauperate – *(adjective)* [biology] lacking in numbers or variety of species. imperfectly developed.

Depend – *(verb)* **1** be controlled or determined by. **2** rely on. **3** [archaic or poetic/literary] hang down. *Children depend on their parents for everything when they are young.*

Depict – *(verb)* represent by a drawing, painting, or other art form. portray in words. *The government will take action if you depict women in a derogatory manner.*

Depletion – *(noun)* erosion. loss of vegetation *The continuing depletion of the Earth's natural resources could prove very dangerous.*

Deplorable – *(adjective)* deserving strong condemnation; shockingly bad. *His actions were announced as being horribly deplorable.*

Deploy – *(verb)* bring or move into position for military action. bring into effective action. *The government will deploy military to defend its frontiers.*

Depolarize – *(verb)* [physics] reduce or remove the polarization of.

Deponent – *(adjective)* [grammar] denoting verbs which are passive or middle in form but active in meaning. *(noun)* [law] a person who makes a deposition or affidavit it under oath.

Depopulate – *(verb)* substantially reduce the population of an area. *Countries facing a huge population explosion must come up with policies to depopulate.*

Deport – *(verb)* **1** expel a foreigner or immigrant form a country. **2** [archaic] conduct oneself in a specified manner. *It was considered important for one to deport oneself with dignity in the old times.*

Deposit – *(noun)* **1** a sum of money placed in a bank or other account. *If you don't, you will forfeit the deposit.* **2** a sum payable as a first installment or as a pledge. a returnable sum paid to cover passable loss or damage. *You may also have to pay a deposit which is normally refunded at the end of your stay.* **3** a layer or body of accumulated matter. **4** the action of depositing something. *(verb)* **1** put or set down in a specific place. lay down naturally as a layer or covering. **2** store or entrust with someone for safe keeping. pay as a deposit.

Deprave – *(verb)* lead away from what is natural or right; corrupt. *To behave in such a depraved manner can only lead to disaster.*

Depreciate – *(verb)* **1** diminish in value over a period of time. reduce the recorded value of an asset over a predetermined period. **2** disparage or belittle. *Some assets only depreciate over time.*

Deprive – *(verb)* **1** deny a person or place the possession or use of something. **2** [archaic] depose someone, especially a clergyman from office. *She was deprived of the love of both her parents.*

Depth – *(noun)* **1** the distance from the top or surface to the bottom of something or to a specified point within it. distance from the front to the back of something. the apparent existence of there dimensions in a two-dimensional representation. **2** Complexity and profundity of thought. comprehensiveness of study or detail. *Third-year course go into more depth.* creditable intensity of emotion. **3** the deepest or lowest part of something. *It is important to study a subject in depth to excel in it.*

Deputation – *(noun)* a group of people who undertake a mission on behalf of a larger group. *The deputation performed the task on behalf of their seniors very well.*

Deputy – *(noun)* **1** a person appointed to undertake the duties of a superior in the superior's absence. **2** a parliamentary representative in certain countries. **3** [British] a coal mine official responsible for safety. *He was recently appointed as deputy to the minister.*

Deracinate – *(verb)* **1** tear up by the roots. **2** deracinated displaced from one's environment. *The young sap was deracinated and planted where water was in abundance.*

Derby – *(noun)* **1** an annual flat race at Epsom in surrey for three-year-old horses, founded in 1780 by the 12th earl of derby. a similar race or other important sporting contest. **2** also a sports match between two rival teams from the same area. **3** [north American] a bowler hat. **4** a boot or shoe having the eyelet tabs stitched on top of the vamp.

Derelict – *(adjective)* **1** in a very poor condition as a result of disuse and neglect. *The house has been in a derelict condition for a long time.* **2** [chiefly north American] shamefully negligent. *(noun)* **1** a destitute person. *This person is a derelict since he has no assets, home, property or job.* **2** a piece of property abandoned by its owner.

Derivation – *(noun)* **1** the deriving of something from a source or origin. **2** the fromation of a word from another word or from a root in the same or another language. *New words are derivations of old words and terms.*

Derive – *(verb)* **1** obtain something from a specified source. base something on a modification of. *Marx derived his philosophy of history form Hegel.* [Mathematics] obtain a function or equation form another, especially by differentiation. **2** have as a root or origin; originate from. *Many English words have been derived from Latin.*

Derris – *(noun)* an insecticide containing rotenone, made from the powdered roots of a tropical plant. *Derris is a woody East Indian plant whose roots are used to manufacture insecticide.*

Dervish – *(noun)* a member of a Muslim fraternity vowed to poverty and known for their wild rituals. *Whirling is one of the rituals practised by the Dervish fraternity.*

Descant – *(noun)* **1** music an independent treble melody sung or played above a basic melody. *The angels, we could say, sang the descant to creation's chorus.* [archaic or poetic/literary] a melodious song. **2** a discourse on a theme or subject. *(verb)* talk tediously or at length.

Descent – *(noun)* **1** the action of descending. a downward slope. *His descent to the bottom of the hill was full of risks.* **2** a person's origin or nationality. *The settlers were of Cornish descent.* transmission by inheritance. **3** a sudden violent attacks.

Describable – *(adjective)* to give a detailed account of. *Happiness is a describable emotion.*

Describe – *(verb)* **1** give a detailed account in words of. **2** mark out or draw a geometrical figure. *She was asked to describe her experience in a few sentences.*

Description – *(noun)* **1** a spoken or written account of a person, object, or event. the process of describing. **2** a sort, kind, or class: people of any description.

Desert – *(verb)* **1** callously or treacherously abandon. **2** leave causing it to appear empty. **3** illegally run away from military service. *The house was deserted when the police finally arrived.*

Deserve – *(verb)* do something or show qualities worthy of a reward or punishment as appropriate. *He certainly deserved the punishment for his misdeeds.*

Deshabille – *(noun)* the state of being only partly or scantily clothed. *It was not a sad thing to be caught in a state of deshabille in the old days.*

Desiccate – *(verb)* remove the moisture from. *Please desiccate a slice of banana and put in a food dehydrator.*

Desire – *(noun)* a strong feeling of wanting to have something or wishing for something to happen. *I confess that I have never had a burning desire to go to England.* strong sexual feeing or appetite. *(verb)* strongly wish for or want. want sexually. [archaic] request or entreat. *She desired the job badly and chose to work extremely hard to get it.*

Desirous. *(adjective)* desiring. *He is particularly desirous of visiting Andaman & Nicobar islands.*

Desk – *(noun)* **1** a piece of furniture with a flat or sloped surface and typically with drawers, at which one can read, write, or do other work. *The students were seated at their desks.* **2** [music] a position in an orchestra at which two players share a music stand. **3** a counter in a hotel, bank, airport, etc. *The front desk of the hotel was made of marble.* **4** a specified section of a news organization.

Desolate – *(adjective)* giving an impression of bleak and dismal emptiness. *Finally we reached a desolate place devoid of people except for some grazing sheep.* utterly wretched and unhappy. *The howling wind was adding to the desolate atmosphere.* *(verb)* make desolate.

Despair – *(noun)* the complete loss or absence of hope. *She was in deep despair six months ago.* *(verb)* lose or be without hope. *Well, don't despair, help is at hand and we will be escorted back safely.*

Desperate – *(adjective)* **1** feeling, showing, or involving despair. tried in despair or when everything else has failed. *Desperate situations may lead some people to act in a risky manner.* **2** extremely bad or serious. *A desperate shortage.* **3** having a great need or desire for something. **4** violent or dangerous. *A desperate criminal.*

Despise – *(verb)* feel contempt or repugnance for. *Due to his behaviour, he was thoroughly despised by society.*

Despite – *(preposition)* without being affected by; in spite of. *Despite poor scores, he was promoted to the next class.* *(noun)* [archaic or poetic/literary] **1** outrage; injury. **2** contempt; disdain. *Anita was determined to do well despite her handicap.*

Despond – *(verb)* [archaic] become dejected and lose confidence. *It never helps to give in to feelings of despondency.*

Destine – *(verb)* be intended or chosen for a particular purpose or end. *He was destined to become an IAS officer.*

Destiny – *(noun)* the events that will necessarily happen to a particular person in the future. the hidden power believed to control this; fate. *It is his destiny to act as saviour.*

Destroy – *(verb)* **1** put an end to the existence of something by damaging or attacking it. *The whole village was destroyed in the hurricane.* ruin emotionally or spiritually. **2** kill by humane means.

Destructibility. *(adjective)* that can be destroyed. *John had not calculated the power of destructibility of the hurricane while designing his house.*

Destruction – *(noun)* the action or process of causing so much damage to something that it no longer exists or cannot be repaired. a cause of someone's ruin. *The complete destruction of the school in the earthquake was terrible.*

Desultory – *(adjective)* lacking purpose or enthusiasm. *They were engaging in a desultory conversation unwillingly.*

Detail – *(noun)* **1** a small individual feature, fact, or item. a small part of a picture reproduced separately for close study. *The police asked her if she remembered any details of the robbery.* **2** a small detachment of troops or police officers given a special duty. a special duty assigned to such a detachment. *Please give me the detail of his business.* *(verb)* **1** a describe item by item; give the full particulars of. **2** assign to undertake a particular task.

Detain– *(verb)* **1** keep from proceeding by holding them back or making claims on their attention. **2** keep in official custody. *He was detained at the airport for more than three hours.*

Detect – *(verb)* **1** discover or identify the presence or existence of. **2** discover or investigate. **3** discern something intangible or barely perceptible. *He could detect that something was not quite right.*

Detent – *(noun)* a catch in a machine which prevents motion until released. a catch that regulates striking.

Detention – *(noun)* **1** the action or state of detaining or being detained. **2** the punishment of being kept in school after hours. *Harry was sent to detention centre after school for being naughty.*

Deter – *(verb)* discourage from doing something by instilling fear of the consequences. prevent the occurrence of. *No amount of social work was going to deter her from studying to achieve her goals.*

Deteriorate – *(verb)* become progressively worse. *Jim's condition kept deteriorating even after he was treated at the hospital.*

Deteriority *(noun)* ability to use both hands. *She has the inborn dexterity required to perform skilled knitting.*

Determinant – *(noun)* **1** a factor which determines the nature or outcome of something. **2** [biology] a gene determining the character and development of particular cells in an organism. *Y-chromosome is the determinant of the birth of a boy or girl.* **3** [mathematics] a quantity obtained by the addition of products of the elements of a square matrix according to a given rule. *Determinant of a square diagonal matrix is the product of its diagonal elements.* *(adjective)* serving to determine or decide something. *Sarah acted as a determinant in her sister's coming back home.*

Determinate – *(adjective)* **1** having exact and discernible limits or form. **2** [botany] having the main axis ending in a flower, as in a cyme.

Detonate – *(verb)* explode or cause to explode. *No one was allowed to go near the place before the bomb was detonated.*

Detrain – *(verb)* leave or cause to leave a train. *The whole family detrained as their plans got cancelled at the last moment.*

Detriment – *(noun)* the state of being harmed or damaged. *The action backfired to their detriment.*

Devil – *(noun)* **1** [Christian and Jewish] be life the supreme spirit of evil; Satan. *Some people believe that the devil exists.* an evil spirit; a demon. *He was born with the devil in him.* **2** a very wicked or cruel person. a mischievously clever or self-willed person. **3** fighting spirit; wildness. **4** deal with. **5** [informal] a person with specified characteristics. *The poor devil.* **6** expressing surprise or annoyance in various questions or exclamations. **7** an instrument or machine used for tearing or other destructive work. **8** [informal, dated] a junior assistant of a barrister or other professional. *(verb)* **1** [informal, dated] act as a junior assistant for a barrister or other professional. **2** [north American] harass or worry.

Devilish – *(adjective)* of, like, or appropriate to a devil in evil and cruelty. mischievous and rakish. very difficult to deal with or use. *He behaved in a devilish sort of way.* *(adverb)* [informal, dated] very; extremely. *Jason has such a devilish appearance sometimes.*

Devious – *(adjective)* **1** skillfully using underhand tactics to achieve goals. **2** longer and less direct than the most straightforward way. *Huma acted in a devious way to get the promotion.*

Devise – *(verb)* **1** plan or invent a complex procedure or mechanism. **2** law leave to someone by the terms of a will. *He devised a plan to bring them to our home quickly.* *(noun)* [law] a clause in a will leaving real property to someone.

Devitalize – *(verb)* deprive of strength and vigour. *The entire team was feeling devitalized after trekking for more than six hours.*

Devolution – *(noun)* **1** the devolving of power by central government to local or regional administration. **2** [formal] descent or degeneration to a lower or worse state. **3** [law] the legal transfer of property from one owner to another. **4** [biology] evolutionary degeneration. *The school authorities practiced devolution of power to make decision making more effective.*

Devolve – *(verb)* devolved, devolving to transfer or pass on (duties, responsibilities, etc. to another or others.

Devote – *(verb)* **1** give time or resources to a person or activity. **2** [archaic] invoke or pronounce a curse upon. *The teacher told Mukesh to devote more time to studies in order to score better marks.*

Devotion – *(noun)* **1** love, loyalty, or enthusiasm for a person or activity. **2** religious worship or observance. prayers or religious observances. *Scoring high marks in exams requires a lot of devotion from the student.*

Devour – *(verb)* **1** eat food or prey hungrily or quickly. consume destructively. **2** read quickly and eagerly. **3** be totally absorbed by a powerful feeling. *Anil devoured food at the restaurant like he was eating after a long time.*

Devout – *(adjective)* **1** having or showing deep religious feeling or commitment. **2** earnest; sincere. *James is a devout Christian.*

Dew – *(noun)* a liquid that condenses during the night on surfaces and plants when warm air touches a cool surface. *An example of dew is the liquid that drips off of blades of grass in the morning.*

Dexterity – *(noun)* skill in performing tasks, especially with the hands. *Mathews showed great dexterity in the fine arts competition.*

Diabetes – *(noun)* a disorder of the metabolism causing excessive thirst and the production of large amounts of urine. *Doctors say diabetes is increasing at an alarming rate.*

Diadem – *(noun)* a jewelled crown or headband worn as a symbol of sovereignty. *The diadem is a symbol of adornment.*

Diagonal – *(adjective)* denoting a straight line joining opposite corners of a rectangle, square, or other figure. straight and at an angle; slanting. mathematics denoting a matrix with non-zero elements lower right. *Do not use diagonals or right to left words. (noun)* a diagonal line.

Diagram – *(noun)* **1** a simplified drawing showing the appearance or structure of something. *The teacher asked the students to support their answers with diagrams.* **2** [British] a graphical schedule for operating railway stock to provide a desired service. *(verb)* **1** represent in graphic form. **2** [British] schedule the operations of a locomotive or train according to a diagram.

Dial – *(noun)* **1** a disc marked to show the time on a clock or indicate a reading or measurement by means of a pointer. a disc with numbered holes on a telephone, turned to make a call. a disc turned to select a setting on a radio, cooker, etc. **2** [British informal] a person's face. *This wall clock has a very large dial. (verb)* call by turning a dial or using a keypad. indicate or regulate by means of a dial. *He asked me to dial his grandfathers phone number on the telephone.*

Dialect – *(noun)* **1** a form of a language which is peculiar to a specific region or social group. **2** computing a particular version of a programming language. *I did not understand the dialect of the Bengal region.*

Dialogic – *(adjective)* relating to or in the form of dialogue.

Dialogue – *(noun)* conversation between two cession directed towards exploration of subject or resolution of a problem. *(verb)* [chiefly north American] take part in dialogue. provide a film or play with dialogue. *Smith does not want to indulge in any dialogue with Jerry.*

Diamantiferous – *(adjective)* producing or yielding diamonds.

Diana – *(noun)* goddess of the hunt (Greek Mythology); *Diana is the name of the ancient Roman goddess of moon, hunt and chastity.* female first name, a [north American] fritillary butterfly, the male of which is orange and black and the female blue and black.

Diaper – *(noun)* **1** [north American] a baby nappy. **2** a linen or cotton fabric woven in a repeating pattern of small diamonds. a repeating geometrical or floral pattern. *Diaper is an absorbent cloth worn by babies.(verb)* **1** [north American] put a nappy on a baby. **2** decorate with a repeating geometrical or floral pattern. *Maria has gone to buy diaper for her baby.*

Diarist – *(noun)* a person who writes a diary. *Anne Frank was a diarist.*

Diarrhoea – *(noun)* a condition in which faces are discharged from the bowels frequently and in a liquid form. *James missed the school trip because he was suffering from diarrhea.*

Diary – *(noun)* a book in which one keeps a daily record of events and experiences. a book with spaces for each day of the year in which to note appointments. *Writing a diary is a good habit.*

Dice – *(noun)* **1** a small cube with faces bearing from one to six spots, used in games of chance. *The player rolled the dice on the casino table.* [see also die]. a game played with dice. **2** small cubes of food. *(verb)* **1** play or gamble with dice. **2** cut food into small cubes.

Dichotomy – *(noun)* **1** a division or contrast between two things that are opposed or entirely different. **2** [botany] repeated branching into two equal parts. *The dichotomy of the situation was that though he claimed to be an artist, he was unaware of Picasso's work.*

Dictaphone – *(noun)* trademark a small cassette recorder used to record speech for transcription at a later time. *They recorded my speech on a dictaphone to play it at the function.*

Diction - *(noun)* **1** the choice and use of words in speech or writing. **2** the style of enunciation in speaking or singing. *Good diction is a pre-requisite for media persons.*

Dictum - *(noun)* a formal pronouncement from an authoritative source. *He cited Augustine's dictum in his article.* a short statement that expresses a general truth or principle. [law] short for obiter dictum.

Did - *past* of DO. *Did he go to school?*

Didactic - *(adjective)* intended to teach, in particular having moral instruction as an ulterior motive in the manner of a teacher; patronizing or hectoring. *The speech given at the assembly was supposed to be didactic.*

Diddle - *(verb)* [informal] **1** cheat or swindle. **2** [chiefly north American] pass time aimlessly or unproductively. *Mom always said not to diddle away time.* **3** vulgar stung, [chiefly north American] have sexual intercourse with.

Die - *(noun)* **1** singular form of DICE. **2** a device for cutting or moulding metal or for stamping a design on coins or medals. **3** [architecture] the cubic part of a pedestal between the base and the cornice; a dado or plinth. *James can't stand to see anyone die.*

Diehard - *(noun)* a person who strongly opposes change or who continues to support something in spite of opposition. *She is a diehard fan of Tom Hanks.*

Diet - *(noun)* **1** a legislative assembly in certain countries. [historical] a regular meeting of the states of a confederation. **2** [scoots law] a meeting or session of a court. *One should consume a balanced diet to stay healthy.* **3** a prescribed selection of food.

Difference - *(noun)* **1** a way in which people or things are different. the state or condition of being different. **2** the remainder left after subtraction of one value from another. **3** a disagreement, quarrel, or dispute. **4** [heraldry] an alteration in a coat of arms to distinguish members or branches of a family. *He couldn't explain the difference between the two portraits.*

Different - *(adjective)* **1** not the same as another or each other; unlike in nature, form, or quality. **2** [informal] novel and unusual. **3** distinct; separate. *One should understand that sex and gender are two different things.*

Differentia - *(noun)* a distinguishing mark or characteristic. [chiefly philosophy] an attribute that distinguishes a species of thing from other species of the same genus. *The birth spot is the differentia between the twins.*

Difficult - *(adjective)* **1** needing much effort or skill to accomplish, deal with, or understand. **2** not easy to please or satisfy, awkward. *The questions in final exam were very difficult.*

Diffident - *(adjective)* modest or shy because of a lack of self-confidence. *He is a very diffident person.*

Diffract - *(verb)* [physics] cause to undergo diffraction. *That effect is caused due to diffraction of light.*

Diffuse - *(verb)* spread or cause to spread over a wide area. [physics] intermingle with another substance by movement of particles. *Sugar diffuses in the tea on stirring. (adjective)* **1** spread out over a large area; not concentrated. not localized in the body. **2** lacking clarity or conciseness.

Dig - *(verb)* **1** break up and move earth with a tool or with hands, paws, etc. make by digging. Extract from the ground by digging. begin eating heartily. protect oneself by making a trench or similar ground defense. **2** poke or jab sharply. **3** search, rummage, or investigate. bring out or uncover something hidden. **4** excavate an archaeological site. **5** [informal, dated] like, appreciate, or archaeological site. **6** [informal, dated] like, appreciate, or understand. *Approximately 9 " of soil was dug out, in order to get a solid soil base. (noun)* **1** an act or spell of digging. **2** an archaeological excavation. **3** a sharp push or poke. **4** [informal] a remark intended to mock or criticize. **5** [informal, chiefly British] lodgings. *Please dig into your books and find the answer to this question. They went to dig the ground in search of dinosaur bones.*

Digest – *(verb)* **1** break down in the stomach and intestines into substances that can be used by the body. **2** [chemistry] treat with heat, enzymes, or a solvent in order to break it down. **3** understand or assimilate by reflection. **4** by reduction. *The carbohydrates present in the soup can be partially digested by your saliva.* *(noun)* **1** a compilation or summary of material or information. a methodical summary of a body of laws. the compendium of roman law compiled in the reign of Justinian. **2** [chemistry] a substance or mixture obtained by digestion.

Dight – *(adjective)* [archaic] clothed or equipped. *(verb)* **1** [poetic/literary] make ready; prepare. **2** [Scottish & north English] wipe, clean or dry. *Please dight for the competition.*

Dignify – *(verb)* make something seem worthy and impressive. give an impressive name to someone or something unworthy of it. *He felt dignified in the company of leading writers.*

Dignitary – *(noun)* a person holding high rank or office. *He is a dignitary at the office.*

Dignity – *(noun)* **1** the state or quality of being worthy of honour or respect. **2** a composed or serious manner or style. a sense of pride in oneself. *One should carry oneself with dignity and pride.*

Digress – *(verb)* leave the main subject temporarily in speech or writing. *Kindly be precise and do not digress from the topic.*

Dilapidate – *(verb)* [archaic] cause to fall into someone in power without popular consent. *The house was in a dilapidated condition.*

Dilate – *(verb)* **1** become or make wider, larger, or more open. *Capillaries were dilated to allow the excess heat to be removed by blood flow.* **2** speak or write at length on.

Dilettante – *(noun)* **1** a person who cultivates an area of interest, such as the arts, without real commitment or knowledge. **2** [archaic] a person with an amateur interest in the arts. *He is a dilettante in the field of religion.*

Diligence – *(noun)* careful and persistent work or effort. *One should show diligence towards their work.*

Dill – *(noun)* [austral informal] a naive or foolish person. *He is such a dill that everyone takes him for granted.*

Dilly-dally – *(verb)* [informal] dawdle or vacillate. *The government continues to dilly-dally on taking a decision on labour reforms.*

Dilogy – *(noun)* an ambigious speech.

Dim – abbrebation diminuendo.

Dimension – *(noun)* **1** a measurable extent, such as length, breadth, or height. *Dimension is the measurement of length, breadth and width.* physics an expression for a derived physical quantity in terms of fundamental quantities such as mass, length, or time, raised to the appropriate power. **2** an aspect or feature. *You should try to add more and more dimensions to your personality.* *(verb)* cut or shape to particular dimensions.

Dimidiate – *(verb)* [heraldry] so that only half of each is visible. having only one half depicted. *He has dimidiated the property amongst his sons.*

Diminish – *(verb)* **1** make or become less. **2** [music] denoting an interval which is one semitone less than the corresponding minor or perfect interval. *Objects appear to diminish in size as we go further away from them.*

Diminution – *(noun)* **1** a reduction. **2** [music] the shortening of the time values of notes in a melodic part.

Diminutive – *(adjective)* **1** extremely or unusually small. **2** implying smallness, either actual or as an expression of affection or scorn. **1** a shortened form of a name, typically used informally. **2** [heraldry] a charge of the same form as an ordinary but of lesser size or width.

Dimity – *(noun)* a hard-wearing cotton fabric woven with stripes or checks. *Could you buy me dimity from the market?*

Dimple – *(noun)* a small depression in the flesh, either permanent or forming in the checks when one smiles. *(verb)* produce a dimple or dimples in the surface of. form or show a dimple or dimples. *She looks very cute when she smiles because of her dimples.*

Din – *(noun)* a loud, continuous noise; confused clamour or uproar a loud. *The din created by loud speakers has made our life tough.* *(verb)* dinned, dinning, to beset with a din, to repeat insistently or noisily. *He dinned the idea into her ears by continuously speaking about it.*

Dingle – *(noun)* [poetic/literary or dated] a deep wooded valley.

Dingy – *(adjective)* gloomy and drab. *That café was poorly lit, dingy and drab so we decided to come out of it immediately.*

Dinner – *(noun)* the main meal of the day, taken either without tails, typically one in honour of a person or event. *Let's have dinner at a restaurant tonight.*

Dint – *(noun)* **1** an impression or hollow in a surface. **2** [archaic] a blow or stroke. *He succeeded in life by dint of hard study.* *(verb)* mark with dints. *He has a dint on his forehead since birth.*

Diocese – *(noun)* a district under the pastoral care of a bishop in the Christian church. *This area is the bishop's diocese.*

Dioxide – *(noun)* [chemistry] an oxide containing two atoms of oxygen in its molecule or empirical formula.*Carbon dioxide is used to extinguish fire.*

Diphtheria – *(noun)* a serious bacterial disease causing inflammation of the mucous membranes and formation of a false membrane in the throat which hinders breathing and swallowing. *He is suffering from diphtheria.*

Diplomacy – *(noun)* **1** the profession, activity, or skill of managing international relations. **2** skill and tact in dealing with people. *One should talk with diplomacy on controversial topics.*

Dipper – *(noun)* **1** a stocky, short-tailed songbird frequenting fast-flowing streams and able to dive or walk under water to feed.*Dipper is a bird found in and around Mexico.* **2** a ladle or scoop. *Truck drivers use dipper at night.* **3** [archaic, informal] a Baptist or Anabaptist.

Dipterous – *(adjective)* **1** entomology of or relating to files of the order dipteral. **2** [botany] having two wing-like appendages.

Dire – *(adjective)* **1** extremely serious or urgent. **2** [informal] of a very poor quality. *There is a dire need to improve literacy in India.*

Direct – *(adjective)* **1** going from one place to another without changing direction or stopping. *He was directed to report to the head quarters immediately.* [astronomy & astrology] proceeding from west to east in accord with actual motion. **2** straightforward; frank. clear; unambiguous. **3** without intervening factors or intermediaries. *The complications are a direct result of bacteria spreading.* proceeding in continuous succession from parent to child. soccer denoting a free kick from which a goal may be scored without another player touching the ball. **4** perpendicular to a surface. *(adverb)* in a direct way or by a direct route.*Could you direct him the way to the school*? *(verb)* **1** control the operations of. **2** aim in a particular direction. tell or show someone the way. **3** give an order or authoritative instruction to.

Direction – *(noun)* **1** a course along which someone or something moves, or which must be taken to reach a destination. a point to or from which a person or thing moves or faces. a trend or tendency. **2** the action of directing or managing people. instructions on how to reach a destination or about how to do something. *Please move in the northern direction to reach the railway station.* .

Director – *(noun)* **1** a person who is in charge of an activity, department, or organization. **2** a member of the managing board of a business. **3** a person who directs a film, play, etc. *She is the director of this prestigious organization.*

Dirge – *(noun)* **1** a lament for the dead, especially one forming part of a funeral rite. **2** a mournful song, piece of music, or sound. *The following is a dirge in rememberance of my uncle who expired yesterday.*

Dirk – *(noun)* a short dagger of king formerly carried by Scottish highlanders. *Use a dirk to fight the criminal.*

Disability – *(noun)* **1** a physical or mental condition that limits a person's movements, senses, or activaties. **2** a disadvantage or handicap, especially one imposed or recognized by the law. *He is suffering from mental and physical disability.*

Disabuse – *(verb)* persuade that an idea or belief is mistaken. *Don't disabuse innocent children.*

Disadvantage – *(noun)* an unfavourable circumstance or condition. *The disadvantage of not going on the trip is to miss out all the fun.* *(verb)* put in an unfavourable position. in socially or economically deprived circumstances.

Disaffirm – *(verb)* repudiate a settlement. *He disaffirmed that he ever signed a contract with that party.*

Disagree – *(verb)* **1** have a different opinion. **2** be inconsistent with. affect adversely *I disagree with you at this point.*

Disallow – *(verb)* refuse to declare valid. *Passengers holding ordinary tickets have been disallowed to board this coach.*

Disappear – *(verb)* cease to be visible. cease to exist or be in use. go missing or be killed. *Thieves disappeared from the house before the security could arrive.*

Disappoint – *(verb)* fail to fulfil the hopes or expectations of. prevent from being realized. *Do not disappoint your parents by indulging in bad deeds.*

Disapprobation – *(noun)* strong disapproval, especially on moral grounds. *Smoking is a disapprobated activity.*

Disapproval *(noun)* rejection, not approved. *Our request to let us in the hostel was met with stern disapproval by the warden.*

Disapprove – *(verb)* have or express an unfavourable opinion. officially refuse to agree to. *I have disapproved your leave application.*

Disarm – *(verb)* **1** take a weapon or weapons away from. a country of force give up or reduce its armed forces or weapons. remove the fuse from a bomb. **2** deprive of the power to hurt. ally the hostility or suspicions of. *The police disarmed the criminals.* *(noun)* fencing an act of disarming an opponent. *Her speech was very disarming.*

Disarrange – *(verb)* make untidy or disordered. *Why did you disarrange the crockery?*

Disarray – *(noun)* a state of disorganization or untidiness. *The entire house is in disarray.* *(verb)* make disorganized or untidy. *Cyclone left the whole town thoroughly disarrayed.*

Disaster – *(noun)* **1** a sudden accident or a natural catastrophe that causes great damage or loss of life. **2** an event or fact leading to ruin or failure. *The fire was a disaster at the wedding ceremony.*

Disastrous – *(adjective)* **1** causing great damage. **2** [informal] highly unsuccessful. *Dereliction of duty could prove to be disastrous for our aim.*

Disband – *(verb)* break up or cause to break up. *This company would be disbanded into small units for the operations.*

Disbelief – *(noun)* inability or refusal to accept that something is true or real. lack of faith. *She stared at the Taj Mahal in disbelief.*

Disburden – *(verb)* relieve of a burden or responsibility. *Please disburden yourself regarding the sale of this property.*

Disburse – *(verb)* pay out money from a fund. *The college disbursed grants to all who secured more than 75 percent marks.*

Discard – *(verb)* **1** get rid of as no longer useful or desirable. *Mom asked Ram to discard all the unwanted clothes from the wardrobe.* **2** play a card that is neither of the suit led nor a trump, when one is unable to follow suit. *Those not scoring runs would be discarded by the selectors.* *(noun)* a discarded item, especially a card in bridge or whist.

Discern – *(verb)* recognize or find out. distinguish with difficulty by sight or with the other senses. *I couldn't discern the difference between the shawls.*

Disciple – *(noun)* **1** a personal follower of Christ during his life, especially one of the twelve apostles. **2** a follower or pupil of a teacher, leader, or philosophy. *Seeta is a disciple of Gandhiji.*

Disciplinary *(adjective)* having to do with discipline. *Disciplinary action was taken against those who failed to report in time.*

Discipline – *(noun)* **1** the practice of training people to obey rules or a code of behaviour. *One must maintain discipline in their field of* *work.* controlled behaviour resulting from such training. **2** a branch of knowledge, especially one studied in higher education. *Discipline should be inculcated right from the time a child learns to speak. (verb)* **1** train in obedience or self-control by punishment or imposing rules. showing a controlled form of behaviour. **2** punish or rebuke formally for an offence.

Disclaim – *(verb)* **1** refuse to acknowledge. **2** [law] renounce a legal claim to. *Due to dispute, I disclaim his ownership of the house.*

Disclose – *(verb)* make known. expose to view. *Do not disclose this information to anyone.*

Discolour – *(verb)* become or cause to become a different, less attractive colour. *The dress I bought became discoloured after the very first wash.*

Discomfort – *(noun)* **1** slight pain. **2** slight anxiety or embarrassment. *I feel discomfort in his peresence. (verb)* cause discomfort to. *This shoe has given me a lot of discomfort.*

Discommode – *(verb)* [formal] cause trouble or inconvenience to. *Do not discommode the guests.*

Discompose – *(verb)* disturb or agitate. *With your actions you are discomposing everybody present at the gathering.*

Disconcert – *(verb)* disturb the composure of. *Do not disconcert the boss.*

Disconnect – *(verb)* break the connection of or between. put out of action by detaching it from a power supply. *Please disconnect the phone connection from my house.*

Disconsent – *(noun)* lack of contentment or satisfaction. a person who is dissatisfied. *I am disconsent with the company's performance.*

Disconsolate – *(adjective)* very unhappy and unable to be comforted. *He was very disconsolate after he heard the loss of his court case.*

Discontent – *(noun)* lack of satisfaction. *Restless desire for something more or different led her to high levels of discontent. (adjective)* discontented. *Not able to clear the papers left him a discontented man. (verb)* stop doing, providing, or making. *Please discontent this job.*

Discontinue – *(verb)* stop doing, providing, or making. *He is discontinuing the job at the firm.*

Discount – *(noun)* a deduction from the usual cost of something. [finance] a percentage deducted from the face value of a bill of exchange or promissory not when it changes hands before the due date. *Enjoy a 30 percent discount on this product during this Diwali festival. (verb)* **1** deduct a discount from the usual price of something. reduce in price. fanance buy or sell before its due date at less than its maturity value. **2** disregard as lacking credibility or significance. *That shop is offering a discount on their products.*

Discountenance – *(noun)* [finance] a method of assessing investments taking into account the expected accumulation of interest.

Discourse – *(noun)* written or spoken communication or debate. *What's your discourse on this matter?* a formal discussion of a topic in speech or writing. [linguistics] a text or conversation. *This discourse by Swami Ramdev is also available on CD. (verb)* speak or write authoritatively about a topic. engage in conversation.

Discourteous – *(adjective)* rude and lacking consideration for others. *One should not be discourteous to guests.*

Discover – *(verb)* **1** find unexpectedly or in the course of a search. become aware of a fact or situation. be the first to find or observe. **2** [archaic] divulge. display a quality or feeling. *I will discover the truth behind the robbery.*

Discovery – *(noun)* **1** the action or process of discovering or being discovered. a person or thing discovered. **2** [law] the compulsory disclosure, by a party to an action, of relevant documents referred to by the other party. *The discovery of X-rays as a means to study bones was a great discovery.*

Discredit – *(verb)* harm the good reputation of. cause to seem false or unreliable. *They have discredited him in the market by spreading false rumours. (noun)* loss or lack of reputation. *Politicians are prone to discredit opponents with all sort of allegations.*

Discreet – *(adjective)* **1** careful and prudent in one's speech or actions, especially so as to avoid giving offence or attracting attention. **2** unobtrusive. *Please be discreet about this information.*

Discrepancy – *(noun)* an illogical or surprising lack of compatibility or similarity between two or more facts. *There is no discrepancy between the findings of the two projects.*

Discrete – *(adjective)* individually separate and distinct. *please discrete this for me*

Discretion – *(noun)* **1** the quality of being discreet. **2** the freedom to decide what should be done in a particular situation. *I will reveal this information only at your discretion.*

Discriminate – *(verb)* **1** recognize a distinction. perceive or constitute the difference in or between. **2** make an unjust distinction in the treatment of different categories of people, especially on the grounds of race, sex, or age. *One must never discriminate against people as all are equals.*

Discussion – *(noun)* **1** an extended communication dealing with some particular. **2** an exchange of rings on some topic.

Disdain – *(noun)* the feeling that someone or something is unworthy of one's consideration or respect. *Her voice was choked with disdain.* *(verb)* consider or reject with disdain. *She disdain their claims.*

Disease – *(noun)* **1** a disorder of structure or function in a human, animal, or plant, especially one that produces specific symptoms or that affects a specific part. **2** a quality, habit, or disposition that adversely affects a person or group. *Cancer is a disease wherein malicious tumour develops in any part of the body.*

Disembark – *(verb)* leave a ship, aircraft, or train. *He has disembarked from the ship.*

Disembarass – *(verb)* free oneself of a burden or nuisance. *I disembarrass myself from this situation.*

Disenchant – *(verb)* make disillusioned. *He refused to promote him because he disenchanted with his performance.*

Disengage – *(verb)* **1** separate, release, or detach. emotionally detached; uninvolved. **2** remove from an area of conflict. **3** fencing pass the point of one's sword over or under the opponent's sword to change the line of attack. *(noun)* fencing a disengaging movement. *Let's disengage from this conversation before we say something we'll regret later.*

Disentangle – *(verb)* free from entanglement; untwist. remove knots or tangles from wool, rope, or hair. *Please disentangle this knot for me.*

Disesteem – *(noun)* low esteem. *(verb)* have a low opinion of.

Disfavour – *(noun)* disapproval or dislike. *He is in disfavour of the prime minister.* *(verb)* regard or treat with disfavour. *You should be fair in your decision and not disfavour anyone.*

Disfigure – *(verb)* spoil the appearance of.*Don't disfigure that statue by writing something on it.*

Disgorge – *(verb)* **1** discharge; cause to pour out. bring up or vomit. yield or give up. **2** remove the sediment form after fermentation. *The doctor gave an injection to help disgorge the food from the stomach.*

Disgrace – *(noun)* loss of reputation as the result of a dishonourable action. a person or thing regarded as shameful and unacceptable. *One mistake brought disgrace to the family.* *(verb)* bring disgrace on. cause to fall from favour or a position of power or honour.

Disguise – *(verb)* alter the appearance, sound, taste, or smell of so as to conceal the identity. conceal the nature or existence of a feeling or situation. *They disguised their faces before robbing the bank.* *(noun)* a means of disguising one's identity. the state of being disguised. *He is a master of disguise. His illness was a blessing in disguise.*

Disgust – *(noun)* strong revulsion or profound indignation. *I felt disgusted after hearing of the crime he had committed.* *(verb)* cause disgust in. *The spoilt food disgusts me.*

Dish – *(noun)* **1** a shallow, typically flat-bottomed container for cooking or serving food. all the items that have been used in the preparation, serving, and eating of a meal. a shallow, concave receptacle: a soap dish. *I need a dish washer for my house.* a bowl-shaped radio aerial. **2** a particular variety or preparation of food served as part of a meal. **3** [informal] a sexually attractive person. **4** [informal] information which is not generally known or available. **5** concavity of a spoked wheel resulting from a difference in spoke tension. *(verb)* **1** put food on to a plate or plates before a meal. dispense something in a casual or indiscriminate way. **2** [informal, chiefly British] utterly destroy or defeat. **3** [north American, informal gossip]. **4** make slightly concave.

Disharmony – *(noun)* lack of harmony. *The song is being played in disharmony.*

Dishearten – *(verb)* cause to lose determination or confidence. *Don't feel disheartened as there's always a second chance.*

Dishonest – *(adjective)* not honest, trustworthy, or sincere. *I didn't know he would turn out to be a dishonest man.*

Disinclination – *(noun)* a reluctance or unwillingness to do something. *He is disinclined towards his studies.*

Disinfect – *(verb)* make clean and free from infection, especially by the use of a chemical disinfectant. *The sanitizer will disinfect you.*

Disingenuous – *(adjective)* not candid or sincere, especially in pretending that one knows less about something than one really does. *Don't go on his looks, he is very disingenuous.*

Disintegrable – *(adjective)* capable of melting.

Disinherit – *(verb)* make less inhibited. *The father disinherited his son from his property.*

Disintegrate – *(verb)* **1** break up into small parts as a result of impact or decay. **2** lose strength or cohesion. **3** [physics] undergo or cause to undergo disintegration at a subatomic level. *In nuclear fission, the nucleus breaks into two and the process continues.*

Disinter – *(verb)* dig up something that has been buried. *Let's not disinter past secrets.*

Disinterested – *(adjective)* **1** not influenced by considerations of personal advantage; impartial. **2** having or feeling no interest or concern. *He seems absolutely disinterested in this conversation.*

Disjoint – *(verb)* **1** disturb the cohesion or organization of. **2** [dated] take apart at the joints. *(adjective)* [mathematics] having no elements in common. *Any disjointed effort will not acieve desired results.*

Disjunct – *(noun)* **1** a lack of correspondence or consistency. **2** [grammar] another term for SENTENCE ADVERB. *(adjective)* disjoined and distinct from one another. *There seems to be great disjoint in his work.*

Dislike – *(verb)* feel distaste for or hostility towards. *He disliked your brother.* *(noun)* a feeling of dislike. a thing that is disliked.

Dislocate – *(verb)* **1** disturb the normal arrangement or position of a joint in the body. **2** disturb the organization of; disrupt. *He fell while playing football and dislocated his elbow joint.*

Dislocation – *(noun)* **1** the process or state of dislocating or being dislocated. **2** [crystallography] a displacement of part of a crystal lattice structure. *Poor policies of the government may lead to social dislocations in the society.*

Disloyal – *(adjective)* not loyal or faithful. *Never be disloyal to your work.*

Dismal – *(adjective)* **1** causing or demonstrating a mood of gloom or depression; dreary. **2** [informal] pitifully or disgracefully bad: a dismal performance. *They presented a totally dismal performance at the play ground.*

Dismantle – *(verb)* take to pieces. *Please dismantle this machine before transporting it to Mumbai.*

Dismast – *(verb)* break or force down the mast or masts of a ship. *The ship has been dismasted.*

Dismember – *(verb)* **1** tear or cut the limbs from. **2** partition or divide up a territory or organization. *The train passed over and dismembered the body of the traveler.*

Disobedience *(noun)* non-compliance. *Gandhiji launched a civil disobedience movement against British administration to make India a free nation.*

Disobey - *(verb)* fail or refuse to obey. *Never disobey your parents or teachers.*

Disoblige - *(verb)* offend by not acting in accordance with their wishes. *You are disobliging your guests.*

Disorganize *(verb)* disrupt, upset, disarrange. *We had to go without food or water because the authorities were so disorganized.*

Disown - *(verb)* refuse to acknowledge or maintain any connection with. *That man disowned his daughter.*

Disparage - *(verb)* represent as being of little worth; scorn. *Don't try to pass disparaging remarks against anybody.*

Disparate - *(adjective)* essentially different in kind; not able to be compared. *(noun)* things so different that there is no basis for comparison between them. *A strong leader can motivate a geographically disparate team to achieve agreed goals.*

Dispatch - *(verb)* **1** send off promptly to destination or for purpose. **2** deal with quickly and efficiently. **3** kill. *The order was dispatched five minutes ago.* *(noun)* **1** an instance of dispatching. **2** an official report on the latest situation in state or military affairs. a report sent in from abroad by a journalist. **3** promptness and efficiency. *No dispatch rider would leave office without documents.*

Dispel - *(verb)* make doubt, feeling, or belief disappear. *The doubts he has must be dispelled.*

Dispensable - *(adjective)* **1** able to be replaced or done without. **2** able to be relaxed in special cases. *These items of my personal property are dispensable.*

Dispensation - *(noun)* **1** the action of dispensing. **2** exemption from a rule or usual requirement. *I look forward to an early dispensation of my request.* **3** a religious or political system prevailing at a particular time. **4** [archaic] an act of divine providence.

Dispense - *(verb)* **1** distribute to a number of people. supply or release a product. **2** supply according to a doctor's prescription. **3** get rid of or manage without. **4** grant an exemption from a religious obligation. *Kindly dispense these blankets among all participants.*

Dispenser *(noun)* distribute *A dispenser is a container so designed that the contents can be used in prescribed amounts.*

Disperse - *(verb)* **1** go or distribute in different directions or over a wide area. **2** thin out and eventually disappear. **3** [physics] divide into constituents of different wavelengths. *The police fired water cannon shots to disperse the crowd.* *(adjective)* [chemistry] denoting a phase dispersed in another phase, as in a colloid. *The participants may disperse after the meeting gets over.*

Dispersion - *(noun)* **1** the action, process, or state of dispersing or being dispersed. **2** another term for DIASPORA. **3** a mixture of one substance dispersed in another medium. **4** physics the separation of white light into colours or of any radiation according to wavelength. **5** statistics the extent to which values of a variable differ from a fixed value such as the mean. *With the help of a prism, we can observe the dispersion of light into seven colours.*

Dispersive - *(adjective)* spreading by diffusion.

Dispirit - *(verb)* cause to lose enthusiasm or hope. *If you keep yourself away from the meet, the participants may feel dispirited.*

Displace - *(verb)* **1** shift from its proper or usual position. **2** take the place, position, or role of; oust. **3** especially of war, persecution, or natural disaster force to leave their home: displaced persons. *Some workers have been displaced from their regular duty.*

Display - *(verb)* **1** place prominently so that it putter, television or cinema screen. **2** give a conspicuous demonstration of a quality, emotion, or skill. **3** engage in a specialized pattern of behaviour intended to attract a mate. *You are a public figure and your posture must display a positive attitude.* *(noun)* **1** an instance of displaying or being displayed. **2** a collection of objects being displayed. **3** an electronic device for the visual presentation of data. *My phone's display is not working properly.*

Displease - *(verb)* annoy or upset. *You should try not to displease any of your guests.*

Displeasure – *(noun)* a feeling of annoyance or dissatisfaction. *Never be a source of displeasure to your chairman.* *(verb)* [archaic] annoy; displease. *Please restrain him from any action that becomes a reason of displeasure for others.*

Disport – *(verb)* enjoy oneself unrestrainedly; frolic. *She disported herself thoroughly with the massage at the spa.* *(noun)* [archaic] recreation; amusement. a pastime or sport. *Going to the spa for a massage is her disport.*

Disposable – *(adjective)* **1** intended to be used once and then thrown away. able to be dispensed with; easily dismissed. **2** readily available for the owner's use as required. *I would like to be served my fruit drink in a disposable glass.* *(noun)* a disposable article. *Disposable glasses are usually made of plastic materials.*

Disposition – *(noun)* **1** a person's inherent qualities of mind and character. an inclination or tendency. **2** the action or result of arranging people or things in a particular way. the stationing of troops ready for military action. **3** [law] the action of distributing or transferring property or money to someone, in particular by bequest. **4** the power to deal with something as one pleases. [archaic] the determination of events, especially by diving power. *He can fight the lawsuit at his own disposition.*

Dispossess – *(verb)* **1** deprive of land or property. people who have been dispossessed. **2** deprive of the ball. *These people have been dispossessed of their houses.*

Dispraise – *(noun)* rare censure; criticism. *Never dispraise anybody's hard work.*

Disproof – *(noun)* action or evidence that proves something to be untrue. *I have no evidence to disproof his claims.*

Disproportion – *(noun)* a lack of proportion. *There is disproportion in the amount of water in these bottles.*

Disprove – *(verb)* prove to be false. *I can disprove her argument.*

Dispute – *(verb)* **1** argue about question whether a statement or alleged fact is true or valid. **2** contend for. **3** resist a military landing or advance. *(noun)* a disagreement or argument. a disagreement between management and employees that leads to industrial action. *There seems to be a dispute between the two brothers regarding their family property.*

Disqualify – *(verb)* pronounce ineligible for an office or activity because of an offence or infringement. make unsuitable for an office or activity. *We will disqualify any participant who fails to match up to our standards.*

Disquiet – *(noun)* a feeling of anxiety. *He is living with a sense of disquiet following his failure.* *(verb)* make anxious. *There has been disquiet within me ever since that accident.*

Disregard – *(verb)* pay no attention to; *His attitude reflects total disregard for her welfare.* *(noun)* the action or state of disregarding or being disregarded. *Don't disregard your parents.*

Disrelish – *(verb)* regard with dislike or distaste. *There is never a time when I disrelish food.*

Disrepute – *(noun)* the state of being discredited. *The fraud he committed has brought him great disrepute.*

Disrespect – *(noun)* lack of respect or courtesy. *Showing disrespect to the national flag is an offence.* *(verb)* [informal, chiefly north American] show a lack of respect for; insult. *We should never disrespect our elders.*

Disrobe – *(verb)* **1** take off one's clothes; undress. **2** take off official regalia or vestments. *To disrobe at this public place is an offence, police will haul you.*

Disrupt – *(verb)* **1** disturb or interrupt. **2** drastically alter or destroy the structure of. *Your sloppy behaviour is disrupting the normal proceedings of the day.*

Dissatisfied – *(adjective)* not content or happy. *She is more often than not dissatisfied with her marks.*

Dissatisfy – *(verb)* fail to satisfy or give pleasure to. *The poor quality of after-sales service has thoroughly dissatisfied me with the home music system.*

Dissemble – *(verb)* hide or disguise one's true motives or feelings. *He is very cunning and always dissembles his ulterior feelings to cheat.*

Disseminate – *(verb)* spread widely. *Kindly disseminate the following information among all the readers.*

Dissension – *(noun)* disagreement that leads to discord. *There has been some dissension between the family members.*

Dissent – *(verb)* express disagreement with a prevailing view or official decision. disagree with the doctrine of an established or orthodox church. *There were many dissenting voices over the selection of the chairman.* *(noun)* the holding or expression of a dissenting view. *he has expressed his dissent at the company's decision.*

Disserve – *(verb)* a harmful action. *Your selfish motives and other actions have been disserving this organization.*

Dissimulate – *(verb)* hide or disguise one's thoughts or feelings. *He should be open in his views and not dissimulate true feelings.*

Dissipate – *(verb)* **1** be dispelled or dispersed, or cause to be so. **2** waste. **3** [physics] cause to be lost through its conversion into heat. *Unnecessary discussions will only dissipate your energy.*

Dissociate – *(verb)* **1** disconnect or separate. *I dissipated myself from him.* **2** [psychiatry] cause to undergo dissociation. **3** [chemistry] undergo or cause to undergo dissociation. *The company has dissociated with a few of its clients.*

Dissolve – *(verb)* **1** become or cause to become incorporated into a liquid so as form a so as to form a solution. **2** close down, dismiss, or annul. **3** gradually blend into another. **4** subside uncontrollably into an expression of strong feeling. *The president dissolved the parliament on the recommendation of the prime minister.* *(noun)* an instance of dissolving. *Dissolve sugar in the water by stirring.*

Dissonance – *(noun)* disagreeable sounds.

Dissyllable – *(noun)* variant spelling of disyllable.

Distance – *(noun)* **1** the length of the space between two points. **2** the condition of being far off; remoteness. a far-off point or place. **3** the full length or time of a race or other contest. [British] horse racing a space of more than twenty lengths between two finishers in a race. British a length of 240 yards from the winning post on a racecourse. [north American, horse racing] the distance from the winning post which a horse must have reached when the winner interval of time or relation. **5** aloofness or reserve. *(verb)* **1** make distant. dissociate or separate. 2 [north American, horse racing] beat by a distance. *Distance between Delhi and Mumbai is more than 1400 kilometres.*

Distant – *(adjective)* **1** far away in space or time. at a specified distance. *The town lay half a mile distant.* faint or vague because far away. **2** remote or far apart in resemblance or relationship. not closely related. *A distant cousin.* **3** cool or reserved. **4** remote; abstracted: a distant look. *He is a distant cousin of my friend.*

Distemper – *(verb)* paint using whitewash. *They have decided to distemper their house before Diwali.* *(noun)* **1** a viral disease of some animals, especially dogs, causing fever, coughing, and catarrh. *My dog is suffering from a viral infection known as canine distemper.* **2** [archaic] political disorder. **3** decorative painting technique to achieve a matte surface. *The paint made by mixing the pigment with water and a binder is called distemper.*

Distend – *(verb)* swell or cause to swell because of pressure from inside. *The medical report showed the stomach to be grossly distended with a large food residue.*

Distensible – *(adjective)* capable of being distended; able to stretch and expand. *This material is distensible.*

Distinct – *(adjective)* **1** recognizably different in nature; individual or separate. **2** readily distinguishable by the senses. *The twin brothers are distinct from one another in nature.*

Distinguish – *(verb)* **1** recognize, show, or treat as different. perceive or point out a difference between. be an identifying characteristic of. **2** manage to discern. **3** change the form of during transmission or amplification. *You must learn to distinguish between right and wrong.*

Distort – *(verb)* **1** pull or twist out of shape. **2** give a misrepresentative account or impression of. **3** change the form of during transmission or amplification. *This photograph has been taken from one corner and presents a distorted picture of the show.*

Distract – *(verb)* prevent from giving their full attention to something. divert from something. *Don't distract your sister from her studies by playing with her.*

Distraught – *(adjective)* very worried and upset. *She has been very distraught about her family's well being.*

Distress – *(noun)* **1** extreme anxiety or suffering. **2** the state of a ship or aircraft when in danger or difficulty. **3** [medicine] a state of physical strain, especially difficulty in breathing. *The captain of the ship sent out distress signals upon noticing the approaching hurricane.* *(verb)* **1** cause distress to. **2** give simulated marks of age and wear. *Your actions have caused him great distress.*

Distribute – *(verb)* **1** hand or share out to a number of recipients. *Kindly distribute these sweets among all children.* **2** be spread over an area. **3** supply to retailers. **4** [logic] use to include every individual of the class to which it refers.

District – *(noun)* **1** an area or part of a town or region. *I live in the bishop's district.* **2** [British] a division of a county or region that elects its own councilors. *A district is a kind of administrative region.* *(verb)* [north American] divide into areas.

Distrust – *(noun)* lack of trust. *Distrust politicians of all stripes.* *(verb)* have little trust in; regard with suspicion. *Never give someone a chance to distrust you.*

Disusage – *(noun)* gradual cessation of use.

Disuse – *(noun)* the state of not being used; neglect. *We have purchased a new toaster and the old one is in complete disuse now.*

Ditch – *(noun)* a narrow channel dug to hold or carry water. *They started digging a six feet wide ditch around the building.* *(verb)* **1** provide with a ditch. **2** bring or come down in a forced landing on the sea. US derail. **3** informal get rid of; give up. [north American, informal] play truant from school. **4** thraw away. *You can't ditch me by dropping out of the play an hour before our show.* **5** forsake.

Diuretic – *(adjective)* causing increased passing of urine. *She has been prescribed diuretic medicines by the doctor.* *(noun)* a diuretic drug. *Thiazide diuretics can be used to reduce calcium in the urine.*

Diurnal – *(adjective)* **1** of or during the daytime. *This trend is diurnal.* **2** daily; of each day. *Diurnal rhythms.*

Divagate – *(verb)* [poetic/literary] stray; digress. *Don't divagate from the subject.*

Dive – *(verb)* **1** plunge head first and with arms outstretched into water. **2** go to a deeper level in water. swim under water using breathing equipment. **3** plunge steeply downwards through the air. move quickly or suddenly in a downward direction. or under cover. soccer deliberately fall when challenged in order to deceive the referee into when challenged in order to deceive the referee into awarding a foul. **4** drop suddenly. *He dived into the swimming pool from the 10-metre high board.* *noun* **1** an act or instance of diving. **2** [informal] a disreputable nightclub or bar. *I am learning to dive in a swimming pool.*

Diverse – *(adjective)* widely varied. *There is diverse variety of mugs available in the market.*

Diversion – *(noun)* **1** an instance of diverting. **2** [British] an alternative route for use by traffic when the usual road is temporarily closed. **3** something intended to distract someone's attention. *A raid was carried out to create a diversion.* **4** a recreation or pastime. *The construction of the mall has necessitated diversion of traffic on the roads.*

Divert – *(verb)* **1** cause to change course or take a different route. **2** reallocate to a different purpose. **3** draw the attention of; distract or entertain. *Reading self-help books can divert your mind from silly thoughts.*

Dives – *(noun)* [poetic/literary] a typical or hypothetical rich man.

Divest – *(verb)* **1** deprive or dispossess someone or something of. **2** free or rid of. *Don't divest him of his self-earned assets.*

Dividend – *(noun)* **1** a sum of money that is divided among a number of people, such as the part of a company's profits paid to its shareholders or the winnings from a football pool; an individual's share of this money. **2** a benefit from an action or policy. *The policy would pay dividends in the future.* **3** [mathematics] a number to be divided by another number. *He has not received his dividend from the company yet.*

Dividing – *(adjective)* separating *MacMohan Line is the dividing line between India and China.*

Divination – *(noun)* the practice of divining or seeking knowledge by supernatural means. *She believes in divination.*

Divine – *(adjective)* **1** of from or like god or a god. devoted to god; sacred. **2** [informal] excellent; delightful. *Only a divine grace can help me pass this examination. (noun)* **1** dated a cleric or theologian. **2** providence or god. *His face glowed as if he had some divine power.*

Divinely – *(adverb)* godly, providence. *Some fake people name claimed to possess divinely power.*

Divinity – *(noun)* **1** the state or quality of being divine. **2** a divine being; a god or goddess. **3** god. **4** the study of religion; theology. *Any super natural being worshipped is attributed with divinity.*

Divisibility – *(noun)* quality of being divided *Scientists predict the divisibility of atoms into yet more smaller particles.*

Division – *(noun)* **1** the action or process of dividing or being divided. *Division of labour is central to our way of life.* **2** the separation of members of a legislative body into groups to vote for or against a bill. **3** the action of splitting the roots of a perennial plant into parts to be replanted separately, as a means of propagation. **4** the process of dividing one number by another. [mathematics] the process of dividing a matrix, vector, or other quantity by another under specific rules to obtain a quotient. a major unit or section of an organization. a number of teams or competitors grouped together in a sport for competitive purposes. [botany] a principal taxonomic category that ranks above class and below kingdom, equivalent to the phylum in zoology. [zoology] any subsidiary category between major levels of classification. **5** a partition that divides two groups or things.

Divisor – *(noun)* [mathematic] a number by which another number is to be divided. a number that divides into another without a remainder. *In the above question, 5 is the divisor.*

Divorce – *(noun)* the legal dissolution of a marriage, a legal decree dissolving a marriage. *Divorce creates insecurity among children. (verb)* **1** legally dissolve one's marriage with. *Her parents have filed for divorce.* **2** detach or dissociate. *Religion cannot be divorced from morality.*

Dizzily – *(adverb)* in a light-hearted manner *After a few drinks, he was not steady and walked around dizzily.*

Dizzy – *(adjective)* **1** having a sensation of spinning around and losing one's balance. *She felt dizzy after going on that swing.* **2** [informal] silly but attractive. They might feel a bit dizzy or even sick. *(verb)* make feel unsteady, confused, or amazed. *The dizzying rate of change.*

Docile – *(adjective)* ready to accept control or instruction; submissive. *She seems to be a very docile girl.*

Docker – *(noun)* a person employed in a port to load and unload ships. *We need to employ a docker to speed up loading the materials into the ship.*

Docket – *(noun)* **1** [British] a document accompanying a consignment of goods that lists its contents, certifies payment of duty, or entitles the holder to delivery. *You should receive proof of purchase in the form of either a delivery docket or receipt from each of the shops you purchase from.* **2** [north American] a list of cases for trial or people having cases pending. *(verb)* **1** mark with a document listing the contents. **2** [north American] enter on to a list of those due to be heard. *Who's taking care of the docket?*

Doctrinaire – *(adjective)* seeking to impose a doctrine without questions or considerations. *Communist parties believe in the principles of doctrinaire. (noun)* a doctrinaire person. *He is a new doctrinaire of the party.*

Doctrinal – *(adjective)* relating to, involving or preoccupied with doctrine.

Doctrine – *(noun)* a set of beliefs or principles held and taught by a church, political party, or other group. *Monroe doctrine led to the formation of the League of nations.*

Document – *(noun)* a piece of written, printed, or electronic matter that provides information or evidence or that serves as an official record. *All legal documents have been sent to the lawyer. (verb)* record in written, photographic, or other form. *This is an important document, keep it safe.*

Dodder – *(verb)* be slow and unsteady. *This machine is a dodder.*

Dodge – *(verb)* **1** avoid by a sudden quick movement. *At the same time they often dodge the big decisions on things they do control.* move quickly to one side or out of the way. cunningly avoid doing or paying. **2** [photography] expose less than the rest during processing or enlarging. **3** move one place contrary to the normal sequence, and then back again in the following round. *(noun)* **1** an act or instance of dodging. **2** [informal] a cunning trick, especially one used to avoid something.

Doe – *(noun)* **1** a female roe or fallow deer or reindeer. **2** a female hare, rabbit, rat, ferret, or kangaroo.

Doer – *(adjective)* one who does. *Prove yourselves doers of the word, and not merely hearers who delude themselves.*

Doff – *(verb)* remove an item of clothing, especially a hat. *He doffed off his hat as a mark of respect for Don Bradman.*

Dogma – *(noun)* a principle or set of principles laid down by an authority as incontrovertible. *If necessary, you should discard any dogma and take practical steps to move ahead in life.*

Dogmatize – *(verb)* represent as an incontrovertible truth. *You should allow independent thinking among children and not dogmatize them with your old views.*

Doily – *(noun)* a small ornamental mat made of lace or paper, put on a plate under sweet food. *We need to buy doily for the house.*

Doing – *(noun)* **1** the activities in which someone engages. [informal chiefly British] things whose name one has forgotten. **2** [informal] excrement. **3** [informal] a beating or scolding. **4** activity or effort. *It would take some doing to claim him down.*

Doit – *(noun)* [archaic] a very small amount of money. *His fraud concerned only a doit.*

Dole – *(noun)* [archaic] or poetic sorrow; mourning. *He was definitely very dole after his wedding was called off.*

Doleful – *(adjective)* **1** sorrowful. **2** causing grief or misfortune. *The United States will not dole out any rewards to convince North Korea to live up to its existing obligations.*

Doll – *(noun)* a toy, toy in the form of a person. *A doll is a form of human being often used as a plaything for a child. (verb)* dress oneself, decorate close off with a barrier.

Dollar – *(noun)* the basic monetary unit of the US, Canada, Australia, and certain countries in the pacific, Caribbean, SE Asia, Africa, and south America. *Dollar is the most acceptable currency in the world.*

Dolly – *(noun)* **1** a child's word for a doll. **2** [informal, dated] an attractive and stylish young woman. **3** a small platform on wheels for holding heavy objects. **4** [cricket, informal] an easy catch. **5** historical a short wooden pole for stirring clothes in a washtub. *(verb)* wooden pole for stirring clothes in a washtub. be moved on a dolly. *In television and movie industry, dolly is a common means of moving a camera.*

Dolorous – *(adjective)* [poetic/literary] feeling great sorrow or distress. *I feel dolorous after failing in my test.*

Dolour – *(noun)* [poetic/literary] a state of great sorrow or distress *He is in a state of dolour after his break up with his girl friend.*

Dolphin – *(noun)* **1** a small gregarious and intelligent toothed whale with a beak-like snout and a curved fin on the back. *Dolphins are very friendly mammals living in the sea.* **2** another term for DORADO. **3** a bollard, pile, or buoy for mooring. **4** a structure protecting the pier of a bridge.

Dolt – *(noun)* a stupid person. *Sherry can't take a decision, she is a complete dolt.*

Domain – *(noun)* 1 an area owned or controlled by a ruler or government. a sphere of activity or knowledge. *Spirituality is my domain.* 2 [physics] a discrete region.

Dome – *(noun)* 1 a rounded vault forming the roof of a building or structure. the revolving openable hemispherical roof of an observatory. 2 the rounded summit of a hill or mountain. *That imposing 180-feet high dome was built in 18th century French monarch.* [geology] a rounded uplifted landform or underground structure. 3 [informal] the top of the head. 4 [poetic/literary] a stately building. *It is claimed that there are 100,000 geodesic domes in use around the world.* *(verb)* form a rounded shape; swell out.

Domestic – *(adjective)* 1 of or relating to a home or family affairs or relation. of or for use in the home. *Quarrels in the family are common domestic issues that need not be taken seriously all the time.* 2 fond of family life and running a home. 3 tame and kept by humans. *This is a domestic animal.* 4 existing or occurring within a country. *(noun)* 1 a person who is employed to do domestic tasks. *My domestic help did not come today.* 2 [informal] a violent quarrel between family members. 3 tame and kept by humans. 4 existing or occurring within a country. *(noun)* 1 a person who is employed to do domestic tasks. 2 [informal] violent quarrel between family members. 3 [north American] a product not made abroad.

Domesticate – *(verb)* 1 tame and keep it as a pet or for farm produce. humorous accustom to home life and domestic tasks. 2 cultivate for food. *Trying to domesticate wild animals should be prohibited.*

Domesticity – *(noun)* home or family life. *fights are a part of domesticity.*

Domicile – *(noun)* [formal or law] 1 the country in which a person has permanent residence. *Please mention the place of your domicile.* [chiefly north American] a person's home. 2 the place at which a company or other body is registered. *(verb)* [formal or law] treat a specified country as a permanent home.

Domiciliary – *(adjective)* concerned with or occurring in someone's home. *This is their domiciliary matter.*

Dominance – *(noun)* 1. power and influence over others. 2 [genetics] the phenomenon whereby one allelic form of a gene is expressed to the exclusion of the other. 3 [ecology] the predominance of one or more species in a plant or animal community. *One should avoid the use of dominance to keep co-workers happy.*

Dominant – *(adjective)* 1 most important, powerful, or influential. *His birthmark is very dominant on his face.* 2 overlooking others. 3 genetics relating to or denoting heritable characteristics which even when inherited from only one parent. often contrasted with RECESSIVE. 4 [ecology] denoting the predominant species in a plant or animal community. *(noun)* 1 a dominant trait or gene. 2 [ecology] a dominant species in a community. 3 [music] the fifty note of the diatonic scale of any key, considered in relation to the key of the tonic.

Dominate – *(verb)* have a commanding or controlling influence over. overlook. *There is no need for me to dominate over my workers.*

Domineer – *(verb)* behave in an arrogant and overbearing way. *The boss is such a domineering person.*

Dominical – *(adjective)* 1 of Sunday as the lord's day. 2 of JesusChrist as the lord.

Dominion – *(noun)* 1 sovereignty; control. 2 the territory of a sovereign or government. [historical] a self-governing territory of the [British] commonwealth. *Prior to independence, India was a dominion of Britain.*

Dominus – *(noun)* a clergyman; especially a settled minister or person.

Don – *(verb)* put on an item of clothing. *He donned a three-piece suit for the party.*

Donate – *(verb)* 1 give for a good cause. *Please donate blood, it may save lives.* 2 allow the removal of from one's body for transfusion or transplantation. 3 [chemistry & physics] provide or contribute.

Donation – *(noun)* something that is given to a charity, especially a sum of money. *I would like to give my property in a donation drive.*

Donative – *(adjective)* given as a donation. [historical] given directly, not presentative. *This money has been exclusively earmarked for donative purposes.*

Done – *(adjective)* **1** cooked thoroughly. **2** no longer happening or existing. **3** [informal] socially acceptable. *The done thing.* exclamatory accepted.

Donee – *(noun)* a person who receives a gift. [law] a person who is given a power of appointment. *He is the donee of this gift.*

Donkey – *(noun)* **1** a domesticated hoofed mammal of the horse family with long ears and a braying call, used as a beast of burden. **2** [informal] a foolish person **3** a low stool astride which an artist sits. **4** a children's card game.

Donor – *(noun)* **1** a person who donates something. **2** [chemistry] an atom or molecule that provides a pair of electrons in forming a coordinate bond. **3** [physics] an impurity atom in a semiconductor which contributes conductingelectrons to the material.

Don't – *(contraction)* do not. *Don't mess with the beauty products kept on the dressing table.*

Doodle – *(verb)* scribble absent-mindedly. *Don't doodle on the classroom walls.* *(noun)* a drawing made absent-mindedly. *A doodle is a drawing made by a person while his attention is somewhere else*

Doom – *(noun)* death, destruction, or another terrible fate. *The strict invigilation during examination spelled doom for many students.* [archaic] the last judgement. *(verb)* condemn to certain destruction, death, or failure.

Doomsday – *(noun)* the last day of the world's existence. the day of the last judgement. *They said 21st December 2012 would be doomsday for all living creatures on Earth.*

Door – *(noun)* a hinged, sliding, or revolving barrier at the entrance to a building, room or vehicle, or in the framework of a cupboard. used to refer to a house. *The door handle of my drawing room is broken.*

Dope – *(noun)* **1** [informal] an illegal drug, especially cannabis or heroin. a drug used to enhance the performance of an athlete, racehorse, or greyhound. *The next time I had smoked dope in a friend's garage.* **2** [informal] a stupid person. **3** [informal] information. **4** a varnish used to strengthen the fabric surface of model aircraft. a lubricant a substance added to petrol to increase its effectiveness. *(verb)* **1** administer dope. [informal] be heavily under the influence of drugs. **2** cover with varnish or other thick liquid. **3** electronics add an impurity to a semiconductor to produce a desired electrical characteristic. **4** [informal] dated work something out. *The nylon covering used on the whole model was doped.*

Doric – *(adjective)* **1** relating to or denoting a classical order of architecture characterized by a plain, sturdy column and a thick square abacus resting on a rounded molding. **2** relating to or denoting the ancient Greek dialect of the durians. **3** [archaic] broad. *(noun)* **1** the Doric order of architecture. **2** the ancient Greek dialect of the durians. **3** a broad dialect, especially that spoken in the north-east of Scotland. *Doric was a popular dialect of the ancient Greek.*

Dormant – *(adjective)* **1** in or as if in a deep sleep. heraldry lying with its head on its paws. **2** alive but not growing. **3** temporarily inactive. **4** causing no symptoms but liable to recur. *He seems to lie dormant all day long.*

Dormitory – *(noun)* **1** a bedroom for a number of people in a school or institution. *We lived in the same dormitory back in college.* [north American] a college hall of residence. **2** denoting a small town or suburb from which people travel to work in a nearby city.

Dorsal – *(adjective)* anatomy of, on or relating to the upper side or back. compare with VENTRAL. *Dorsal horn sensitisation reduces in line with tissue healing.*

Dorsum – *(noun)* [anatomy & zoology] the dorsal part of an organism or structure. *Dorsum is the back side of the humans or the upper part of animals.*

Dose - *(noun)* **1** a quantity of a medicine or radiation. time. *Please consume the medicine according to the dose prescribed.* an amount of ionizing radiation received or absorbed at one time. **2** [informal] a venereal infection. **3** [informal] a quantity of something necessary but unpleasant. *(verb)* **1** administer a dose to. **2** adulterate or blend with another.

Dot - *(noun)* [archaic] a dowry from which only the interest or annual income was available to the husband. *All that the parents gave on their daughter's wedding was a dot.*

Dotage - *(noun)* the period of life in which a person is old and weak. *Dotage means the slowing down of mental faculties of a person.*

Dotard - *(noun)* an old person, especially one who is weak or senile. *He has very old, weak and dotard and has to depend on others for even small things.*

Dote - *(verb)* **1** be extremely and uncritically fond of. *He dotes on his daughter and believes she can do no wrong.* **2** [archaic] be silly or feeble-minded, especially as a result of old age.

Double - *(adjective)* **1** consisting of two equal, identical, or similar parts or things. *This is a double-door refrigerator.* designed to be used by two people. having two different roles or interpretations. having the same number of pips on each half. **2** having twice the usual size, quantity, or strength. having more than one circle of petals. **3** music lower in pitch by an octave. predictable twice as much or as many. *(adverb)* at or to twice the amount or extent. *(noun)* **1** a thing which is twice as large as usual or is made up of two parts. *The company has made double the profit compared to last year.* **2** [British] two sporting victories or championships in the same season, event, etc.

Doubt - *(noun)* a feeling of uncertainty or lack of conviction. *I doubt if he is telling the truth.* *(verb)* **1** feel uncertain about. question the truth or fact of. disbelieve. **2** [British, archaic] be afraid. *Please have no doubt about the instructions given.*

Douceur - *(noun)* a bribe. *He offered me douseur.*

Dough - *(noun)* **1** a thick, malleable mixture of flour and liquid, for baking into bread or pastry. **2** [informal] money. *We need some dough for dinner tonight. Rotis were made out of soya dough.*

Doughty - *(adjective)* [archaic or humorous] brave and resolute. *He is a doughty person.*

Dove - *(noun)* **1** a stocky seed- or fruit-eating bird with a small head, short legs, and a cooing voice, similar to but generally smaller and more delicate than a pigeon. *Doves were seen flying around this area last year.* **2** a person who advocates peaceful or conciliatory policies. **3** [Christian art and poetry] the holy spirit.

Dowager - *(noun)* **1** a widow with a title or property derived from her late husband. *I feel sorry for the dowager.* **2** a dignified elderly woman.

Dowdily - *(adverb)* in a dowdy fashionable manner.

Dowdy - *(adjective)* unfashionable and dull in appearance. *The dress she wore at the party looked very dowdy.*

Dowery - *(noun)* money or property bought by a woman to her husband a marriage.

Down - *(noun)* **1** a gently rolling hill. ridges of undulating chalk and limestone hills in southern England. **2** a stretch of sea off the east coast of Kent. *Let's go to the park and play.*

Downeast - *(noun)* money or property brought by a woman to her husband at marriage.

Downfall - *(noun)* a loss of power, prosperity, or status. *They had a terrible downfall in business.*

Downpour - *(noun)* a heavy fall of rain. *The city has been experiencing heavy downpour since morning.*

Downright - *(adjective)* **1** utter; complete. *The rejection of application was a downright disgrace to the family.* **2** so direct in manner as to be blunt. abbreviation to an extreme degree; thoroughly. *He was downright rude.*

Downstairs - *(adjective)* on or to a lower floor. *Please go downstairs and meet your friend.* *(adjective)* situated on the ground floor or lower floors of a building. *After committing the crime, the murder ran downstairs and fled.*

Down-trodden - *(adjective)* oppressed or treated badly by people in power. *Recent government steps are addressing the concerns of the down-trodden.*

Downward - *(adjective)* moving or leading towards or lower point or level. *The spacecraft descended downwards and splashed into the sea.*

Dowry - *(noun)* property or money brought by a bride to her husband on their marriage. *Asking for dowry is an offence in the eyes of the law.*

Doxy - *(noun)* a lover or mistress. a prostitute. *They say she is his doxy.*

Doze - *(verb)* sleep lightly. *She dozed off immediately after lunch.* *(noun)* a short light sleep. *I would like to just doze off after this tiring day.*

Dozen - *(noun)* **1** a group or set of twelve. **2** a ritual exchange of insults among black Americans. *I went to buy a dozen of eggs from the grocery store.*

Dozer - *(noun)* [informal] short for Bulldozer. *A dozer is an earth moving equipment to level the surface.*

Drab - *(noun)* **1** a slovenly women. **2** a prostitute. *Don't call any woman a drab.*

Drachm - *(noun)* [historical] a unite of weight equivalent to 60 grains or one eighth of an ounce. a liquid measure equivalent to 60 minims or one eighth of a fluid ounce. *We'll need 5 drachms of water for this homeopathic medicine.*

Draff - *(noun)* dregs or refuse. *He draffed to smoke at the party.*

Draft - *(noun)* **1** a preliminary version of a piece of writing. a plan or sketch. **2** a written order to pay a specified sum. **3** compulsory recruitment for military service. a procedure whereby sports players are made available for selection or reselection by the teams in a league. *(verb)* **1** prepare a preliminary version of a text. *Could you help me draft a letter please?* **2** select and bring them somewhere for military service. *Every person above 18 is compulsorily drafted into the Israeli army.*

Draftsman - *(noun)* **1** a person who drafts legal documents. **2** variant spelling of draughtsman. *We urgently require the services of a draftsman in the office.*

Draggle- *(verb)* **1** make dirty or wet. hang untidily. **2** trail behind others. *Don't draggle the clothes.*

Dragnet - *(noun)* **1** a net drawn through water or across ground to trap fish or game. **2** a systematic search for criminals or criminal activity. *The police used a dragnet to catch the criminals.*

Dragon - *(noun)* **1** a mythical monster like a giant reptile, typically with wings and claws and able to breathe out fire. used in names of various lizards. **2** a fierce and intimidating woman.

Dragoon - *(noun)* **1** a member of any of several British cavalry regiments. a mounted infantryman armed with a carbine. *(verb)* coerce into doing something. *Don't dragoon him into doing something he doesn't like to do.*

Drail - *(verb)* to trail, daggle.

Drain - *(verb)* **1** cause the water or other liquid in to run out, leaving it empty or dry. run off or out. carry off the superfluous water from an area. become dry as liquid runs off. drink the entire contents of. **2** deprive of strength or vitality. cause to be lost or used up. **3** hole. *(noun)* **1** a channel or pipe carrying off surplus liquid, especially rainwater or liquid waste. **2** a thing that uses up a particular resource. the continuous loss of a resource. *The drains of this area are overflowing.*

Drake - *(noun)* a male duck. *Chinese restaurants prepare a variety of drake delicacies.*

Dram - *(noun)* the basic monetary unit of Armenia, equal to 100 luma.

Drama - *(noun)* **1** a play. plays as a genre or literary style. *We have planned to enact three more dramas at this theatre this week.* **2** an exciting or emotional series of events. *Let's not cause any more drama in this house.*

Drank - *past* of drink. *Socrates drank the cup of poison as soon as it was offered.*

Drape - *(verb)* arrange loosely on or round something. adorn or wrap loosely with folds of cloth. *She went to Rekha's house and taught her how to drape a sari properly.* *(noun)* **1** long curtains. **2** the way in which a garment or fabric hangs. **3** a cloth for covering a patient's body when a surgical operation is being performed.

Draper - *(noun)* a person who sells textile fabrics. *We need to go to a draper to buy curtains for our house.*

Drapery - *(noun)* cloth, curtains, or clothing hanging in loose folds. *The drapery set in this house is impeccably attractive.*

Drastic - *(adjective)* having a strong or far-reaching effect. *There has been a drastic change in her after the counselling.*

Draughtsman - *(noun)* **1** a person who makes detailed technical plans or drawings. an artist skilled in drawing. *We need to consult a draughtsman for the designs.* **2** variant spelling of draftsman.

Draughty - *(adjective)* cold and uncomfortable because of draughts of air. *The weather has become very cold and draughty for anyone to venture out.*

Drawback - *(noun)* **1** a disadvantage or problem. **2** excise or import duty remitted on goods exported. *His short height is a definite drawback in the basketball court.*

Drawee - *(noun)* the person or organization who has to pay a draft or bill. *He is the drawee of this bill.*

Drawer - *(noun)* **1** a lidless box-like storage compartment made to slid horizontally in and out of a desk or chest. *I need a drawer to keep my belongings.* **2** [dated] knickers or underpants. *I cant find my drawers.* **3** a person who draws something. the person who writes a cheque. *He is the deawer of this bill.*

Drawl - *(verb)* speak in a slow, lazy way with prolonged vowel sounds. *(noun)* a drawling accent. *In her deep South Indian drawl, she said, "thank you" but I couldn't understand.*

Drawn - *(adjective)* looking strained from illness or exhaustion: *Cathy was pale and drawn.*

Dread - *(verb)* **1** anticipate with great apprehension or fear. *I dread the prospect of receiving thousands of emails.* **2** [archaic] regard with great awe. *(noun)* **1** great fear or apprehension. **2** a sudden take-off of a flock of birds. **3** informal dreadlocks. *(adjective)* **1** greatly feared; *dreadful*. **2** [archaic] regarded with awe. *During the period of Cold War, the constant dread of nuclear war was a fact of life.*

Dreadnought - *(noun)* **1** [historical] a type of battleship of the early 20th century, equipped entirely with large-caliber guns. *In 1857, the dreadnought was replaced with a larger hulk, HMS Caledonia (renamed dreadnought) which had 120 guns.* **2** [archaic] a fearless person. **3** [archaic] a heavy overcoat for stormy weather.

Dream - *(noun)* **1** a series of thoughts, images, and sensations occurring in a person's mind during sleep. a state of mind in which someone is not fully aware of their surroundings. *He walked around in a dream.* **2** a cherished ambition or ideal; a fantasy. *It was give up her childhood dreams of becoming a writer.* [informal] someone or something perceived as wonderful or perfect. *I had a beautiful dream last night.* *(verb)* **1** experience dreams during sleep. **2** indulge in daydreams or fantasies. **3** contemplate the possibility of. *I never dreamed anyone would take offence.*

Drear - *(adjective)* [poetic] dreary. *Drear stormy days in winter when there is no transport of any kind for going to Laddakh.*

Dree - *(verb)* Scottish endure.

Dreeggy - *(noun)* sediment that has settled at the Satlam of a liquid.

Dregs - *(noun)* **1** the remnants of a liquid left in a container, together with any sediment. **2** the most worthless parts. *Criminals are the dregs of society.*

Drench - *(verb)* **1** wet thoroughly; soak. cover liberally with something. *We got drenched in the rain because we didn't have an umbrella.* **2** forcibly administer a liquid medicine to an animal. [archaic] a draught of medicine or poison.

Dress - *(verb)* **1** put on one's cloths. put clothes on someone. wear clothes in a particular way or of a particular type. *The way she dresses is very appropriate for a formal occasion.* dress in smart or formal clothes, or in a special costume. *Please dress appropriately for the occasion.* **2** clean, treat, or apply a dressing to a wound. **4** clean and prepare for cooking or eating. add a dressing to a salad. **5**. apply fertilizer to.

Drew *(verb)* to draw past of DRAW. *She drew the window shade to prevent strong sun rays peeping into the room.*

Drib *(noun)* a very small amount. *A drib is a fine mist of water evaporating before it hits the ground.*

Dribble – *(verb)* **1** fall slowly in drops or a thin stream. allow saliva to run from the mouth. **2** take forward past opponents with slight touches of the feet or the stick, or by continuous bouncing. *She dribbles the basketball very well. (noun)* **1** a thin stream of liquid. saliva running from the mouth. **2** [hockey and basketball] an act of dribbling.

Drily – *(adverb)* **1** in a matter-of-fact or ironically humorous way. **2** in a dry way or condition. *He commented drily on the text of my assignment.*

Drinker – *(noun)* **1** a person who drinks. **2** a large brownish moth, the caterpillar of which is noted for drinking dew. **3** a container from which an animal drinks. *During summer, he never fails to keep a large drinker outside his house for animals to drink clean water.*

Drinking – *(verb)* drank, drunk or [informal] drank, drinking. *He took to drinking as a way of forgetting hard blows suffered in everyday life.*

Drip – *(verb)* let fall small drops of liquid. fall in small drops. *The water was dripping from the leaves after it rained. (noun)* **1** a small drop of a liquid. *You should put a bucket underneath to catch any stray drips.* **2** [medicine] an apparatus which slowly passes fluid, nutrients, or drugs into a patient's body intravenously. **3** [informal] a weak and ineffectual person. **4** architecture a projection on a moulding or cornice, channeled to prevent rain from running down the wall below.

Drivel – *(noun)* nonsense. *Many journalists lap up any marketing drivel for want of something more interesting to write about. (verb)* **1** talk nonsense. **2** [archaic] let saliva or mucus flow from the mouth or nose. *Don't talk drivel things.*

Driver – *(noun)* **1** a person or thing that drives something. **2** a flat-faced golf club used for driving. *My chauffeur drives the car very slowly.*

Driving – *(adjective)* **1** having a strong and controlling influence. *Teachers are the driving force behind the success of their students.* **2** being blown by the wind with great force: driving rain.

Drizzle – *(noun)* **1** light rain falling in very fine drops. *It has been drizzling since morning.* **2** [cookery] a thin stream of a liquid ingredienttrickled over something. prevented me from coming *(verb)* **1** rain light. **2** [cookery] apply as a drizzle.

Droid – *(noun)* **1** a robot. **2** computing a program which automatically collects information from remote systems. *Scientists are working on the design of a droid.*

Droit – *(noun)* a legal right. *The history textbook has a chapter on droits. France was the first country to introduce droit de suite in 1920.*

Droll – *(adjective)* amusingly odd in a strange way. *He is a droll with a quiet tongue-in-cheek kind of humour. (noun)* [archaic] a jester; a buffoon. *He is such a droll that everyone around him is always laughing*

Droop – *(verb)* bend or hang downwards limply. sag down from weariness or dejection. *The clothesline was drooping significantly after the clothes were hung for drying in the sun. (noun)* act or instance of dropping.

Drop-scene – *(noun)* **1** a drop curtain used as part of stage scenery. **2** the last scene of a play. *A drop-scene is often used in the background in plays to eliminate need of actual erection of such costly scenes.*

Dropsy – *(noun)* a tip or bribe. *He offered me a dropsy to do his job.*

Dross – *(noun)* **1** rubbish. **2** scum on the surface of molten metal. *The speech chairman delivered at the farewell was rubbish and totally dross.*

Drought – *(noun)* a prolonged period of abnormally low rainfall; a shortage of water. thirst. *Gujarat is facing heavy drought this year.*

Drove – *past tense* of drive. *We drove past your house last night.*

Drown – *(verb)* **1** die or kill through submersion in water. **2** submerge or flood. **3** make inaudible by being much louder. *Michael drowned in the swimming pool.*

Drowner *(noun)* the person who drowns or the thing which drowns. *Heavy load on the boat acted as a drowner into the river.*

Drowse – *(verb)* be half asleep; doze. male sleepy. *(noun)* an instance of drowsing. a state of drowsiness. *Don't drowse in class while the teacher is teaching.*

Drowsy – *(adjective)* sleepy and lethargic. *I was feeling incredibly drowsy after a long day at work.*

Drub – *(verb)* **1** beat up, defeat, hit or beat repeatedly. **2** defeat thoroughly. *He incessantly drubbed into the pole.*

Drudge – *(noun)* a person made to do hard, menial, or dull work. *(verb)* do such work. *John was made to drudge at his previous job.*

Drug – *(noun)* a medicine or other substance which has a marked physiological effect when taken into the body. a substance with narcotic or stimulant effects. *The study of drugs results in formulation of medicines. (verb)* administer a drug to, in order to induce stupor or insensibility.

Druid – *(noun)* a priest, magician, or soothsayer in the ancient Celtic religion. a member of a present-day group claiming to be derived from this religion. *There lives a very famous druid near my house.*

Drunk – *(verb)* past participle of drink. affected by alcohol to the extent of losing control of one's faculties or behaviour. *Heavy drinking or getting drunk can damage your nerves. (noun)* **1** a person who is drunk or who habitually drinks to excess. **2** a drinking bout. *He was drunk while driving and hence met with an accident.*

Dryad – *(noun)* **1** a nymph inhabiting a tree or wood. **2** a dark brown butterfly with prominent bluish eyespots. *Dryad was a nymph that lived on a tree according to Greek mythology.*

Dual – *adjective* **1** consisting of two parts, elements, or aspects. *America has agreed to supply technology that has dual-use.* Denoting an inflection that refers to exactly two people or things. **2** related to another theorem or expression by the interchange of terms, such as 'point' and 'line'. *This is dual to another. (noun)* **1** a dual inflection. **2** a theorem or expression that is dual to another. *(verb)* convert into a dual carriageway.

Dubiety – *(noun)* uncertainty. *I have dubiety on how this machine will function.*

Dubious – *(adjective)* **1** hesitating or doubting. **2** not to be relied upon. of questionable value. *He is a very dubious man.*

Dubitation – *(noun)* doubt; hesitation. *Please do not have any dubitation in your mind.*

Duchess – *(noun)* **1** the wife or widow of a duke. a woman holding a rank equivalent to duke in her own right. **2** an affectionate form of address for a girl or woman. *She is the duchess of Norfolk in England.*

Duck – *(noun)* a bird, a batsman's score of nought. *A duck is a bird that loves swimming. Sachin returned to the pavilion out on duck.*

Ducker *(noun)* another name of duck *Ducker is a relatively small waterfowl with a flat bill, short neck and legs, and webbed feet.*

Ducking *(noun)* submersion, immersion *The culprit was tied with a chair and then ducked into water as a punishment.*

Duckling – *(noun)* a young duck. *We saw a duckling at the pond today.*

Ductile – *(adjective)* **1** able to be drawn out into a thin wire. **2** able to be deformed without losing toughness. *This connection requires the use of ductile wires.*

Ductility *(noun)* the quality of being flexible *Not every flexible material has the property of ductility.*

Dud – *(noun)* **1** a thing that fails to work properly. an ineffectual person. **2** clothes. *He is a complete dud, you can't really expect him to do a good job. (adjective)* failing to work or meet a standard. *He turned out to be a dud at the job.*

Dude – *(noun)* **1** a man. **2** a dandy. *He is quite popular among girls as a dude. (verb)* dress up elaborately. *That dude is clearly out of her mind.*

Dudgeon – *(noun)* deep resentment. *The manager walked out in deep dudgeon.*

Duet – *(noun)* a performance by two singers, instrumentalists, or dancers. a musical composition for two performers. *(verb)* perform a duet. *Chris and Jenny performed a wonderful duet.*

Duff - *(noun)* a flour pudding boiled or steamed in a cloth bag. *We were asked to prepare a duff of the vegetables.*

Dug - *past and past participle* of dig. *They dug into the history of the school.*

Dulcet - *(adjective)* sweet and soothing. *Shanon can comfort anyone for her behaviour is very dulcet.*

Dull - *(adjective)* **1** lacking interest or excitement. **2** lacking brightness or sheen. overcast. *The lighting of the room is very dull.* **3** slow to understand. slow moving. *All work and no play may make you a dull person.* **4** indistinctly felt or heard. *(verb)* make or become dull.

Duly - *(adverb)* in accordance with what is required or appropriate. as might be expected. *Please accept your payment duly sanctioned by the chief manager.*

Dumb - *(adjective)* **1** unable to speak, normally because of congenital deafness. unable to speak as a natural sate. temporally unable or unwilling to speak. **2** *She is dumb, she cant speak.* **3** having no independent processing capability. *She was so dumb, she screwed her makeup.* *(verb)* **1** [north American, informal] reduce the intellectual content of something. become less intellectually challenging. **2** [poetic/literary] silence. *The one-act play was outstanding, it left the entire audience completely dumb for some time.*

Dummy - *(noun)* **1** a model or replica of a human being. *The teacher asked for a dummy presentation before the final project.* an object designed to resemble and serve as a substitute for the real one. *Dummy objects are used by military during firing practices.* [British] a rubber or plastic teat for a baby to suck on. **2** a feigned pass or kick. **3** bridge the declarer's partner, whose cards are exposed on the table after the opening lead and played by the declarer. an imaginary fourth player. **4** [informal, chiefly north American] a stupid person. *(verb)* **1** feign a pass or kick. **2** [north American, informal] keep quiet.

Dump - *(noun)* **1** a site for depositing rubbish or waste. *A heap of rubbish left at a dump.* **2** [informal] an unpleasant or dreary place. *Why are you living in a dump like this?* *(verb)* **1** deposit or dispose of rubbish or something unwanted. put down firmly and carelessly. *Trucks dumped 900 tons of refuse here.* **2** [computing] copy to a different location, especially so as to protect against loss. print out the contents of a store. *I dumped my files to a secure folder.* **3** [north American informal] treat badly or criticize harshly. *It is advisable to dump the garbage only in dustbins.*

Dumps - *(plural noun)* [informal] depressed or unhappy. *My life is not progressing, it is totally in the dumps.*

Dumpy - *(adjective)* short and stout. *Sherry is often called dumpy because of her looks.*

Dunce - *(noun)* a person who is slow at learning. *People call Steve as dunce because he is slow to learn things.*

Dunderhead - *(noun)* [informal] a stupid person. *He didn't know the table manners and was acting like a dunderhead at the dining table.*

Dune - *(noun)* a mound or ridge of sand or other loose sediment formed by the wind, especially on the sea coast or in a desert. *During summers, the desert is covered with sand dunes.*

Dung - *(noun)* manure. *(verb)* defecate. *Cow dung is used as manure by farmers.*

Dungeon - *(noun)* **1** a strong underground prison cell, especially in a castle. **2** [archaic] term for DONJON. *It is difficult to live in that window-less poor-lit dungeon.* *(verb)* poetic imprison in a dungeon. *The criminal was sent to the dungeon as punishment.*

Duodenum - *(noun)* the first part of the small intestine immediately beyond the stomach. *The doctors said that there was an infection is his duodenum.*

Dupe - *(verb)* deceive; trick. *(noun)* a length of material worn as a head covering by woman from the Indian subcontinent. *With his smooth talks he has deceived many gullible persons.*

Duplex - *(noun)* **1** [north American] a residential building divided into two apartments. *Jenny's living room is on the ground floor and bed room on the first floor in his duplex house.* **2** [chiefly north American & austral] a semi-detached house. 3 [biochemistry] a double-stranded polynucleotide molecule. *(adjective)* **1** having two parts. **2** capable of printing on both sides of the paper. **3** lowing the transmission of two signal simultaneously in opposite directions.

Duplicate – *(adjective)* **1** exactly like something else. *A duplicate key was used to open the door.* **2** having two corresponding parts. **3** twice the number or quantity. *The stunt was done by the duplicate of Amitabh Bachchan. (noun)* one of two or more identical things. *It was proved that he produced duplicate papers to buy the house. (verb)* make or be an exact copy of. multiply by two. do again unnecessarily.

Duplicity – *(noun)* **1** deceitfulness. **2** [archaic] the quality of being double. *Duplicity of documents is an offence.*

Duramater – *(noun)* [anatomy] the tough outer most membrane enveloping the brain and spinal cord. *He hurt his duramater in the accident.*

During – *(preposition)* throughout the course or duration of. at a particular point in the course of. *There was a bomb explosion during the ceremony.*

Dust – *(noun)* **1** fine, dry powder consisting of tiny particles of earth or waste matter. any material in the form of tiny particles: coal dust. *Dust particles are a major contributor in the atmospheric pollution.* [poetic] a dead person's remains. **2** an act of dusting. *(verb)* **1** remove dust from the surface of. bring something out for use again after a long period of neglect. **2** cover lightly with a powdered substance. **3** beat up or kill. *The book case is covered in dust.*

Duster *(noun)* one that dusts. *The teacher uses a duster.*

Dusty – *(adjective)* **1** covered with or resembling dust. **2** staid and uninteresting. *The bed sheet is very dusty and needs washing.*

Dutch – *(noun)* The people of the Netherlands. *(adjective)* of or relating to the people or culture of the Netherlands. *Dutch culinary is very popular in Germany.*

Duteous – *(adjective)* [archaic] dutiful. *Cadbury has been a very duteous servant.*

Dutiable *(adjective)* subject to import duty. *All dutiable goods need to be cleared from customs department.*

Dux – *(noun)* [chiefly Scottish] the top pupil in a school or class. *Ron is the dux of his class.*

Dwindle – *(verb)* diminish gradually. *The air plane dwindled in the sky.*

Dye – *(noun)* a natural or synthetic substance used to colour something. *Synthetic dyes are not good from environment's point of view. (verb)* colour with dye. *Ron wants to dye his hair red.*

Dynamic – *(adjective)* **1** characterized by constant change or activity. full or energy and new ideas. *Only dynamic people go very far in life.* **2** [physics] of or relating to forces producing motion, often contrasted with STATIC. **3** linguistics expressing an action, activity, event, or process, contrasted with STATIVE. **4** [electronics] needing to be refreshed by the periodic application of a voltage. **5.** [music] relating to the volume of sound produced by an instrument or voice. *(noun)* **1** an energizing or motive force. **2** music another term for dynamics. *Chris has a very dynamic personality.*

Dynastics – *(plural noun)* **1** the branch of mechanics concerned with the motion of bodies under the action of forces. compare with KINEMATICS STATICS. **2** the forces which stimulate development or change within a system or process. **3** music the varying levels of volume of sound in a musical performance. *He asked me to correct the dynastics of the song. Dynastics are the forces that stimulate development inside a process.*

Dynasty – *(noun)* a line of hereditary rulers. a succession of powerful or prominent people from the same family. *The Mughal Dynasty was very autocratic in character.*

Dysentric – *(adjective)* pertaining to dysentery (intestinal disease). *Doctors describe a person as dysenteric if he is suffering from inflammatory disorder of the lower intestine.*

Dypepsia – *(noun)* indigestion. *The cause of most cases of functional dyspepsia is not known.*

Dysphagia – *(noun)* medicine difficulty in swallowing, as a symptom of disease. *Any condition that weakens or damages the muscles and nerves used for swallowing may cause dysphagia.*

Dysphonia – *(noun)* medicine difficulty in speaking due to a physical disorder of the mouth, tongue, throat, or vocal cords. *Spasmodic dysphonia may follow an infection of the respiratory tract, injury to the larynx or a period of excess voice use.*

Dysponea – *(noun)* medicine laboured breathing. *Dysponea is a disease associated with pulmonary problems that includes both obstructive and restrictive lung disease and difficulty in breathing.*

Dysuria – *(noun)* medicine painful or difficult urination. *In medicine, specifically urology, dysuria refers to pain in urination.*

Ee

E – *(noun)* **1** the fifth letter of the alphabet. **2** denoting the fifth in a set. **3** [music] the third note of the diatonic scale of C major. *It is the fifth letter in alphabet.*

Each – *(determined & pronoun)* every one of two or more people or things, regarded and identified separately. *Each battery has been kept in a separate room. They each have their own outlook. (adverb)* to, for, or by every one of a group. *Each of you students, stand up.*

Eager – *(adjective)* strongly wanting to do or have. keenly expectant or interested. *I was so very eager to see the first show of the newly released film.*

Eagle – *(noun)* **1** a large bird of prey with a massive hooked bill and long broad wings, renowned for its keen sight and powerful soaring flight. *I once had a chance to see an eagle a bird of prey. It had powerful wings and a big hooked beak.* **2** [golf] a score of two strokes under par at a hole. *She had an eagle three at the ninth.* **3** [US] a former gold coin worth ten dollars. *He has five eagle coins minted in 1940. (verb)* [golf] play in two strokes under par. *He eagled the last to share third place.*

Eaglet – *(noun)* a young eagle. *The eaglet is learining to fly.*

Eagre – *(noun)* dialect term for BORE.

Ean – *(suffix)* forming adjectives and nouns such as antipodean. *Many Europeans come to visit India.*

Ear – *(noun)* **1** the organ of hearing and balance in humans and other vertebrates, especially the external part of this. an organ sensitive to sound. *His ear drum had been perforated. So he went to an ear specialist for surgery.* **2** an ability to recognize and appreciate sounds. *he has an ear for rhyme and melody.* **3** willingness to listen and pay attention: a sympathetic ear. *I am in trouble please lend me a sympathetic ear.*

Earache – *(noun)* pain inside the ear. *I have found earache to be one of the worst aches.*

Earl – *(noun)* a [British] nobleman ranking above a viscount and below a marques. *Earl is a high ranking British nobleman.*

Early – *(adjective)* **1** before the usual or expected time. *We ate an early dinner.* **2** of, at, or near the beginning of a particular time, period, or sequence. *She is in her early twenties. The earlier chapters of the book. (noun)* **1** potatoes ready to be harvested before the main crop. *These are early potatoes.* **2** [informal] early shifts. *Her jole requires her to be on earlies. Reaching any place early is his habit.*

Earn – *(verb)* obtain in return for about or services. gain as interest or profit. gain as the reward for hard work or merit. *He has earned a lot of fame and money at such an early age.*

Earnest – *(adjective)* intensely serious. *He is an earnest police officer, never heard a complaint against him. He has been awarded for bravery as well.*

Earth – *(noun)* **1** the planet on which we live, the third planet of the solar system in order of distance from the sun. *The earth shook as the earthquake come.* **2** the substance of the land surface; soil. one of the four elements in ancient and medieval philosophy and in [astrology]. used in names of stable, dense, nonvolatile inorganic substances, e.g. fuller's earth. [poetic/literary] the substance of the human body: earth to earth, ashes to ashes. *Some plants grow best in very moist earth.* **3** [British] electrical connection to the ground, regarded as having zero electrical potential. *Please ensure that metal fittings are electrically connected to earth.* **4** the underground lair of a badger or fox. *Animals like badger and fox make their home under the earth. (verb)* [British] connect to earth. *The metalic panels must be electrically earthed to prevent shock.*

Earthen – *(adjective)* **1** made of compressed earth. *I bought an earthen pot at a high price because it looked like a relic to me.* **2** made of baked or fired clay. *Earthen pots sell like hot cakes during Diwali.*

Earthling – *(noun)* (in science fiction) a word used by aliens to describe inhabitant of the earth. *This was perfectly normal earthling behaviour.*

Earthly – *(adjective)* **1** of or relating to the earth or human life on the earth. material; worldly. *Human life on earth is millions of years old.* **2** used for emphasis: there was no earthly reason to rush. *He is a down to earth person; he does not pretend to be important. 3 There was no earthly reason for him to rush to that place.*

Earthquake – *(noun)* a sudden violent shaking of the ground as a result of movements within the earth's crust. *Suddenly the earth began to tremble and many houses collapsed. It was a severe earthquake.*

Earthwards – *(adverb)* towards the earth. *The spacecraft moved earthwards at the speed of 10,000 kmph.*

Earthworks – *(noun)* a large artificial bank of soil, especially one made as a defense in ancient times. *Earthworks used to be there in ancient times.*

Earthworm – *(noun)* a burrowing annelid worm that lives in the soil. *A lot of earthworms can be seen during the rainy season.*

Earthy – *(adjective)* **1** resembling or suggestive of soil. *His approach to every problem is very earthy.* **2** direct and uninhibited, especially about sexual subjects or bodily functions. *She is very earthly but voluptuous.*

Ease – *(noun)* absence of difficulty or effort. freedom from worries or problems. *(verb)* **1** make or become less serious or severe. facilitate. *He does everything with great ease and grace.* **2** move carefully or gradually. [nautical] slacken a rope or gently. *Take it easy man.* **3** decrease in value or amount.

Easement – *(noun)* **1** [law] a right to cross or otherwise use another's land for a specified purpose. *He leads a life of easement.* **2** [poetic/literary] comfort or peace. *Time brings easement however much the inconvenience.*

Easeful – *(adj.)* providing comfort. *Life was easeful at that time.*

Edge – *(noun)* **1** the outside limit of an object, area, or surface. an area next to a steep drop. *He sat on edge of the rock.* **2** the sharpened side of a blade. *Excitement made him sit over the edge of the chair.* **3** an intense or striking quality. a quality or factor which gives superiority over close rivals. *He has an edge over his rivals.* **4** the line along which two surfaces of a solid meet. *He edged to words him silently. (verb)* **1** provide with a border or edge. *The swimming pool is edged with metallic rods.* **2** move carefully or furtively. *he tried to edge away from her.* **3** [informal] defeat by a small margin. *Bolt won the race edging out Joyer by a whisker.* **4** give an intense or sharp quality to. *The cold edged her voice.* **5** [cricket] strike with the edge of the bat. *The batsman edged the ball to the long leg.* **6** ski with one's weight on the edges of one's skis. *To control speed you should loosen the edge of the ski.*

Edible – *(adjective)* fit to be eaten. *Don't worry, this fruit is edible.(noun)* items of food. *Delicatessen as the name suggests means delicate edibles.*

Edict – *(noun)* an official order or proclamation. *The edicts of Ashoka are famous all over the world.*

Edification – *(noun)* instruction for improvement. *A video was made for edification of fresh trainees.*

Edifice – *(noun)* **1** a building, especially a large, imposing one. *In early times, kings made a lot of edifices.* **2** a complex system of beliefs. *The concepts on which the edifice of capitalism was built exists to this day.*

Edition – *(noun)* a particular form or version of a published text, the total number of copies of a book, newspaper, etc. issued at one time. a particular version or instance of a regular programme or broadcast. **1** *This is the latest edition of the book.* **2** *The last edition of 30 thousand books was sold immediately.*

Editor – *(noun)* **1** a person who is in charge of a newspaper, magazine, or multi-author book. *An* *editor's job is a tough job. He has to look after all the aspects of the magazine or the newspaper.* **2** a person who commissions or prepares written or recorded material. *The editor has asked me to write a book on humanities.* **3** a computer program enabling the user to alter or rearrange text. *You will be able to use the editor to make any changes you want.*

Educate – *(verb)* give intellectual, moral, and social instruction to. train or give information on a particular subject. *He is a well educated man. 2 The professor educated him in ancient history.*

Education – *(noun)* **1** the process of educating or being educated. the theory and practice of teaching. information about or training in a particular subject. *Education is a most for every citizen.* **2** [informal] an enlightening experience. *He is in the profession of education. 3 Education makes a man perfect.*

Educative – *(adj.)* educational. *It is a useful educative tool.*

Educator – *(noun)* a teacher. *This is the view of a professional educator.*

Educe – *(verb)* formal **1** bring out or develop (something latent or potential). *He educed the hidden talent is him.* **2** infer from data. *More information can be educed from these statistics.*

Effable – *(adjective)* able to be described in words. *Her manner is very effable, which is what I like about her.*

Efface – *(verb)* **1** erase from a surface. *All the words from the blackboard.* **2** make oneself appear insignificant or inconspicuous. *He effaced himself by sitting in a corner.*

Effective – *(adjective)* **1** production a desired or intended result. *This rule is effective from today.* **2** operative. *The moral advice given to him proved effective.* **3** existing in fact, though not formally acknowledged as such. *Many drugs are effective against cancer.(noun)* a soldier fit and available for service. *Effectiveness of antivirus programs must be checked regularly.*

Effectual – *(adjective)* **1** effective. *The law of the land is always effectual.* **2** [law] valid or binding. *Effective discipline must be followed in schools.*

Effectuate – *(verb)* [formal] put into force or operation. *The law has been effectuated since the 1st of this month.*

Effeminate – *(adjective)* derogatory having characteristics regarded as typical of a woman. *He has an effeminate personality. People make fun of him.*

Effervesce – *(verb)* be enthusiastic. *Supervisors are supposed to effervesce with praise and encouragement.*

Effete – *(adjective)* **1** affected, over-refined, and ineffectual. *He is an effete and thus useless for action.* **2** no longer capable of effective action. *The authority of an effective manager began to dwindle.*

Efficacious – *(adjective)* formal effective. *It is an efficacious medicine.*

Efficacy – *(noun)* ability to produce results. *There is little information on the efficacy of the new programme.*

Efficient – *(adjective)* working productively with minimum wasted effort or expense. *He is an efficient worker.*

Effigy – *(noun)* a sculpture or model of a person. *The effigies of Ravan, Meghnath and Kumbhkaran are burnt on Dhssehra.*

Effloresce– *(verb)* **1** lose moisture and turn to a fine powder on exposure to air. *The atomic plant in at efflorescence.* **2** reach an optimum stage of development. *These are simple concepts that effloresce into testable conclusions.*

Effluence – *(noun)* **1** a substance that flows out. *The effluence of sewage water could be seen clearly.* **2** the action of flowing out. *While river water flows into the sea, effluence is mostly deposited at the basin.*

Efflux – *(noun)* [technical] the flowing out of a substance or particle. *The efflux of rain water was very heavy.*

Effort – *(noun)* **1** a vigorous or determined attempt. strenuous physical or mental exertion. *He put in great effort to clear the interview.* **2** [technical] a force exerted by a machine or in a process. *Greater effort is required to push a fairy when to pull it.*

Effrontery – *(noun)* insolence or impertinence. *Effrontery close not pay in the end.*

Elegy – *(noun)* **1** a mournful poem, typically a lament for the dead. *The elegy he recited was extremely mournful and moving.* **2** a poem written in elegiac couplets. *Catullus is famous for writing elegiac couplets.*

Element – *(noun)* **1** a basic constituent part. an aspect: an element of danger. a group of a particular kind within a larger group: right-wing elements. *There was an element of danger in that place.* **2** each of more than one hundred substances that cannot be chemically introverted , or broken down, each consisting of atoms with the same atomic number. *It was a hill station and there I was in my element.* **3** any of the four substances regarded as the fundamental constituents of the world in ancient and medieval philosophy. *The element of the press has burnt please put in another.* **4** the weather; especially bad weather. *The stadium has no protection against elements of nature.* **5** one's natural or preferred environment. *She was in her element.* **6** a part in an electric device consisting of a wire through which an electric current is passed to provide heat. *The element of out geyser has broken.*

Elementary – *(adjective)* **1** of or relating to the most rudimentary aspects of a subject; introductory. simple. *It is a very elementary problem, I'll solve it right away.* **2** not decomposable into elements or other primary constituents. *Anatomy is the most elementary particle capable of independent existence.*

Elemi – *(noun)* an oleoresin obtained from certain tropical trees and used in varnished, ointments, and aromatherapy. *Product of certain tropical trees used in ointments and aromatherapy.*

Elephantiasis – *(noun)* [medicine] a condition in which a limb becomes grossly enlarged due to obstruction of the lymphatic vessels, especially by nematode parasites. *He is suffering from elephantiasis. His foot has become very large and full of wounds.*

Elephantine – *(adjective)* of, resembling, or characteristic of an elephant, especially in being large or clumsy. **1** *He is large and clumsy like an elephant.* **2** *He has got an elephantine memory.*

Elevate – *(verb)* lift to a higher position. raise to a higher level or status. hold up for adoration. military raise the axis of a piece of artillery to increase its range. *He is a great scientist and enjoys an elevated position is the science academy.*

Eleven – *(cardinal number)* equivalent to the sum of six and five; one more than ten; 11. *There are eleven players in a cricket team.*

Elicit – *(verb)* evoke or draw out a response or answer. *Although he was not a brilliant student still I managed to elicit an answer from him.*

Eligibility – *(adjective)* satisfying the conditions mentioned. *His eligibility for the post cannot be questioned.*

Eligible – *(adjective)* **1** satisfying the appropriate conditions. *Many high class young men are eligible backdoors.* **2** desirable as a spouse: an eligible bachelor. *He is an eligible suitor. 3 He is eligible for this post.*

Eliminate – *(verb)* **1** completely remove or get rid of. reject or exclude from consideration or further participation. *All the anti-social elements have been eliminated prom the party.* **2** chemistry generate as a product in the course of a reaction involving larger molecules. *When acid of a molecule reacts with a base water is eliminated.*

Elision – *(noun)* the omission of a sound or syllable in speech. *The shortening of words or elision is quite popular.*

Elite – *(noun)* a group of people considered to be superior in a particular society or organization. *He belongs to the group of elite people.*

Elixir – *(noun)* a magical or medicinal potion, especially either one supposedly able to change metals into gold or supposedly able to prolong life indefinitely. *Ancient people believed in elixir which could prolong life and change base metal into gold.*

Elk – *(noun)* a large northern deer with palmate antlers and a growth of skin hanging from the neck. called moose in north America. [north American] term for wapiti. *This kind of deer or moose is found in North America.*

Ellagic acid – *(noun)* chemistry a compound extracted from oak galls and some fruits and nuts, able to retard the growth of cancer cells to some extent. *A medicine somewhat effective against cancer.*

Ellipse – *(noun)* a regular oval shape, traced by a point moving in a point moving in a plane so that the sum of its distances from two other points is constant, or resulting when a cone is cut by an oblique plane which does not intersect the base. *Ellipse is a shape in geometry.*

Ellipsis – *(noun)* the omission of words from speech or writing. a set of dots indicating such an omission. *It is rare for an ellipsis to happen without any linguistic antecedent.*

Ellipsoid – *(noun)* a three-dimensional figure sym-metrical about each of three perpendicular axes, whose plane sections normal to one axis are circles and all the other plane sections are ellipses. *A comparison in which an elliptical shape is described as ellipsoid.*

Elocution – *(noun)* the skill of clear and expressive speech, especially of distinct pronunciation and articulation. a particular style of speaking. *He has the gift of elocution, bing a leader, it makes things easy for him.*

Eloquence – *(noun)* fluent or persuasive speaking or writing. *His eloquence enables him to make things very clear. People love to hear him.*

Eloquent – *(adjective)* **1** showing eloquence. *He is eloquent and always makes things very clear, never confused, never hesitating. His selection of words in excellent.* **2** clearly expressive. *The bus journey alone is eloquent of class inequality.*

Elucidate – *(verb)* make clear; explain. '*Will you please elucidate the point?*'

Elysian – *(adjective)* of or relating to Elysium or the elysian fields, the place in Greek mythology where heroes were conveyed after death. of or like paradise. *It is the paradise of dead greek heroes.*

Emaciated – *(adjective)* abnormally thing and weak. *He is a an emaciated child, so thin and weak.*

Emanate – *(verb)* issue or spread out from a source. give out or emit. *Water emanated from a hole in the ground.*

Emancipate – *(verb)* set free, especially from legal, social, or political restrictions. free from slavery [law] set free from the authority of its father or parents. *All the negro slaves were emancipated after the civil war in America.*

Emasculate – *(verb)* **1** make weaker or less effective. *Many animals are emasculated by castration e.g. ox.* **2** make less effective. *The refusal to others to testify effectively emasculated the committee.*

Embank – *(verb)* protect or provide with an embankment. *In India many rivers cause havoc in rainy season. There should be embankment against these plods.*

Embark – *(verb)* **1** go on board a ship or aircraft. *He embarked on the ship in time.* **2** begin a new project or course of action. *He has embarked on a new project.*

Embarrass – *(verb)* cause to feel awkward, self-conscious, or ashamed. be caused financial difficulties. *I felt embarrassed when they talked of my poor economic condition in front of me.*

Embed – *(verb)* **1** fix or become fixed firmly and deeply in the surrounding mass. *The idea got embedded in my mind.* **2** implant an idea or feeling. *The plant got embedded firmly all around in the jungle.* **3** computing incorporate within the body of a file or document. *This is the way to embed data into your programme.*

Embellish – *(verb)* **1** adorn; decorate. *I embellished my bedroom.* **2** add extra details to a story or account for interest. *For the interest of children, I embellished extra characters in the story.*

Ember – *(noun)* a small piece of burning or glowing material in a dying fire. *The burning coals looked like embers.*

Emblazon – *(verb)* conspicuously display on something. depict on something. *The brand name was emblazoned on the shirt.*

Emblem – *(noun)* a heraldic device or symbolic object as a distinctive badge of a nation, organization, or family. a symbol or symbolic representation. *The three lions are the emblem of our country.*

Embodiment – *(noun)* visible form of an idea or feeling. *He seems to be living form of embodiment of vitality.*

Embower – *(verb)* [poetic/literary] surround or enclose. *His cottage was embowered by trees.*

Embroider – *(verb)* **1** sew decorative needlework patterns on. *His profession is embroidering sarees.* **2** add fictitious or exaggerated details to. *He embroidered his stories with imagined details.*

Embroil – *(verb)* involve deeply in a conflict or difficult situation. [archaic] bring into a state of confusion or disorder. *After embroiling himself, he cried for help.*

Embryology – *(noun)* the branch of [biology and medicine] concerned with the study of embryos. *His article on embryology in the medical journal was worth reading.*

Emerge – *(verb)* **1** become gradually visible or apparent. become known. *The statute emerged slowly from the receding waters.* **2** recover from or survive a difficult period. *He emerged from the disease in a short time.* **3** break out from an egg, cocoon, or pupal case.*the chicken emerged from the egg.*

Emergent – *(adjective)* **1** in the process of coming into being; emerging. *I saw a calf emerging from its mother's body.* **2** philosophy arising as an effect of complex causes and not analysable simply as the sum of their effects. *Many water plants were emergent on the surface of the water.* *(noun)* philosophy an emergent property. *Confirmed scientific knowledge is an emergent of this experiment.*

Emersion – *(noun)* the process or state of emerging, especially from water. *The emersion of a large snake from the water scared me.*

Emetic – *(adjective)* causing vomiting. *(noun)* an emetic [medicine] or other substance. *I felt emetic when I saw the rotten corpse.*

Emigrant – *(noun)* a person who leaves their own country in order to settle permanently in another. *Many foreigners are now emigrants in America.*

Eminence – *(noun)* **1** acknowledged superiority within a particular sphere. *He is an eminent scientist.* **2** an important or distinguished person a title given to a roman catholic cardinal. *He came into eminence when he gave a leture on cure of cancer.*

Eminent – *(adjective)* **1** respected; distinguished. *He is an eminent eye specialist.* **2** notable; outstanding: his eminent suitability for studio work. *He has eminent skill for making rabbets.*

Emission – *(noun)* the action of emitting something, especially heat, light, gas, or radiation. a substance which is emitted. *The emission of smoke from the engine upset me.*

Emolument – *(noun)* formal a salary, fee, or benefit from employment or office. *My total emoluments are not enough to be taxable.*

Emotion – *(noun)* a strong feeling, such as joy, anger, or sadness. instinctive or intuitive feeling as distinguished from reasoning or knowledge. *I got emotional as I met my mother after a long time.*

Empanel – *(verb)* variant spelling of impanel. *Five new members have been empanelled to the expert committee.*

Emperor – *(noun)* **1** the ruler of an empire. *Ashoka was a great emperor.* **2** in names of certain large, strikingly marked butterflies, e.g. purple emperor. *Emperor is a kind of butterfly.*

Empire – *(noun)* **1** an extensive group of states ruled over by a singly monarch, an oligarchy, or a sovereign state. *The empire of Ashoka was wide spread.* **2** supreme political power; his dream of empire in Asia minor. *Kemal Ataturk has practically converted the middle east into his empire during First World War.* **3** a large commercial organization under the control of one person or group. *(adjective)* denoting a neoclassical style of furniture and dress fashionable chiefly during the first empire in France. *Alexander dreamed of an empire in Asia minor.*

Emplane – *(verb)* go or put on board an aircraft. *He was late but he acted quickly and got emplaned for Londen.*

Employ – *(verb)* **1** give work to and pay them for it. keep occupied. *I was employed throughout the day.* **2** make use of. *(noun)* the state of being employed; employment: in employ of a wine merchant. *I have employed a driver.* *3 I am in employ of German embassy.*

Employer - *(noun)* a person that employs people. *That man over there is my employer. I drive his car.*

Empress - *(noun)* a female emperor. the wife or widow of an emperor. *There have been many famous empresses in history.*

Emptiness - *(noun)* state of containing nothing. *Through the window of an airplane you can see vast emptiness of space.*

Emulate - *(verb)* attempt to much or surpass, typically by imitation. *He tried to emulate a famous actor but failed.*

Emulsion - *(noun)* **1** a fine dispersion of minute droplets of one liquid in another in which it is not soluble or miscible. *The emulsion technique has made my house look for batter than more point.* **2** a type of paint consisting of pigment bound in a synthetic resin which forms an emulsion with water. *This room has been given three coats of pink emulsion.* **3** a light sensitive coating for photographic films and plates, containing crystals of a silver compound dispersed in a medium such as gelatin. *Emulsion comes. Off when negative films are converted into positives.*

Enable - *(verb)* **1** provide with the ability or means to do something. *My coaching enabled him to pass the exam with high marks.* **2** make possible. *The evidence enabled the court to arrive at firm conclusions.*

Enact - *(verb)* **1** make a bill or other proposal [law]. *The proposal was enacted and made a law.* **2** put into practice. *From tomorrow physical exercises will be enacted in the morning.* **3** act out a role or play. *He enacted the role of a comedian on the stage.*

Enamour - *(verb)* be filled with love or admiration for. *I was enamoured over her beauty.*

Encage - *(verb)* to confine in or as in a cage. *Four little Australian birds were encaged in a metallic cage.*

Encamp - *(verb)* settle in or establish a camp. *We encamped at a safe place in jungle.*

Encase - *(verb)* enclose or cover in a case or close-fitting surround. *Iencased the tie and sent to him as a gift.*

Encash - *(verb)* [British] convert a cheque, bond, etc. into money. *I have no money, I have to encash my cheque.*

Enchain - *(verb)* bind with as if in chains. *The buffalo was taken into custody and enchained at the police station.*

Enchant - *(verb)* **1** delight; charm. *The place is so beautiful as if it is enchanted.* **2** put under a spell: an enchanted garden. *Her enchanting beauty put me under a spell.*

Encircle - *(verb)* form a circle around; surround. *The thief was encircled by police.*

Enclose - *(verb)* **1** surround or close off on all sides. *The tree was enclosed by strobes.* **2** place in an envelope together with a letter. *I enclosed the letter in an envelope.*

Encompass - *(verb)* **1** surround and have or hold within. *The house was encompassed by a wall.* **2** include comprehensively. *No studies encompass all sections of medical care.* **3** [archaic] cause to take place. *This was an act designed to encompass the impeachment of the president.*

Encore - *(noun)* a repeated or additional performance of an item at the end of a concert, as called for by an audience. exclamatory again! as called by an audience at the end of a concert verb call for an encore. demand an encore from a performer. *Her stage performance was so nice that public demanded an encore from her.*

Encounter - *(verb)* unexpectedly meet or be faced with. *(noun)* **1** an unexpected or casual meeting. *I met a friend in a mall. It was a sudden encounter.* **2** a confrontation or unpleasant struggle. *As soon as the police encountered the dacoit, they shot him.*

Encourage - *(verb)* give support, confidence, or hope to, help or stimulate the development of. *I encouraged him to study hard.*

Encroach - *(verb)* gradually and steadily intrude on a person's territory, rights, etc. advance gradually beyond expected or acceptable limits. *The enemy encroached upon its neighbour territory and then there was a war.*

Encrust – *(verb)* encrusted cover with a hard crust. *The bread was covered with a hard crust.*

Encumber – *(verb)* impede or burden. *I felt encumbered with the huge amount of homework.*

Encumbrance – *(noun)* **1** a burden or impediment. *I am facing some encumbrance in executing my scheme.* **2** [law] a mortgage or other charge on property or assets. *The bank sought the details of encumbrance on our property.*

Encyclopedia – *(noun)* a book or set of books giving information on many subjects or on many aspects of one subject, typically arranged alphabetically. *I have a set of encyclopedia at home. I can find anything is at.*

Endanger – *(verb)* put at risk or in danger. *He endangered his life when he went very near the cubs of tiger.*

Endear – *(verb)* cause to be loved or liked. *I am endeared to you for the favour you have shown me.*

Endeavour – *(verb)* try hard to do or achieve something. *(noun)* **1** an act of endeavouring; an enterprise. *I endeavoured to climb the mountain but failed.* **2** earnest and industrious effort. *His endeavour to build a hotel succeeded after all.*

Endemic – *(adjective)* **1** regularly found among particular people or in a certain area. *Endemic a disease commonly found among people of certain area.* **2** native or restricted to a certain area. *Dengue appear to be endemic in Uttar Pradesh.*

Ending – *(noun)* an end or final part. the final part of a word, constituting a grammatical inflection or formative element. *As the film neared ending, people were almost in tears.*

Endmost – *(adjective)* nearest to the end. *The endmost part of the film was very exciting.*

Endorse – *(verb)* **1** declare one's public approval of. *I have endorsed the document.* **2** sign a cheque or bill of exchange on the back to specify another as the payee or to accept responsibility for paying it. write a comment on a document. *The manager endorsed the check.* **3** [British] enter an endorsement on a driving licence. *The police checked his driving licence for endorsement by licensing authorities.*

Endow – *(verb)* **1** give or bequeath an income or property to. establish a university pot, annual prize, etc. by donating funds. *I have endowed my property to my wife.* **2** provide with a quality, ability, or asset. *He is endowed with great ability.*

Endue – *(verb)* [poetic/literary] endow with a quality or ability. *He is endued with great ability.*

Endurance – *(noun)* the ability to endure difficult situations. *He has great endurance and can bear a lot of pain.*

Endure – *(verb)* **1** suffer and prolonged patiently. tolerate. *He endured the cancer pain for a long time.* **2** remain in existence. *The city of Dwarka is stile vibrant having endured through time.*

Endways – *(adverb)* with its end facing upwards, forwards the viewer. *The carpet covered the floor endways.*

Enema – *(noun)* a procedure in which fluid is injected into the rectum, typically to expel its contents. *He suffered from severe constipation, so the doctor gave him enema.*

Energize – *(verb)* give vitality. *The drink energized the boxers.*

Energumen – *(noun)* [archaic] a person believed to be possessed by the devil or a spirit. *That man is energumened see how wild he is acting, if possessed.*

Energy – *(noun)* **1** the strength and vitality required for sustained activity. a person's physical and mental powers as applied to a particular activity. *He has great energy and can work hard for a long time without rest.* **2** power derived from physical or chemical resources to provide light and heat or to work machines. *Machines work by light and heat derived from physical or chemical recovers.* **3** physics the property of matter and radiation which manifest as a capacity to perform work. *The process of fusion releases a lot of nuclear energy.*

Enface – *(adverb & adjective)* facing forwards. *All the famous enfaced the enemy and attacked.*

Enfeeble – *(verb)* weaken. *After the viral fever I felt very enfeebled.*

Enfold – *(verb)* surround; envelop. *I enfolded the paper and made an envelope.*

Engender – *(verb)* **1** give rise to. *The issue engendered continuing political controversy.* **2** [archaic] beget offspring. *He engendered a lot of enthusiasm.*

Engineer – *(noun)* **1** a person qualified in engineering. *My father was an engineer and he made many machines.* **2** a person who maintains or controls an engine or machine. *He is the engineer in charge of maintenance of that machine.* **3** a skilful contriver. *(verb)* **1** design and build. **2** contrive to bring about. *He is the prime engineer of this new approach.* **3** modify an organism by manipulating its genetic material.

Engorge – *(verb)* swell or cause to swell with blood, water, etc. *His stomach was engorged with water.*

Engraft – *(verb)* another term for GRAFT. *Engraft as his liver was damaged only grafting another live tissue surgically could save his life.*

Engrain – *(verb)* firmly fix, belief in a person. *He trivialized the struggle and further ingrained the long standing attitudes.*

Engrave – *(verb)* **1** cut or carve a text or design on a hard surface. cut or carve a text or design on. cut a design as lines on a metal plate for printing. *His words were engraved in my mind for ever.* **2** be permanently fixed in one's memory or mind. *He engraved a design on the metal plate for printing.* **3** *I have a strange habit of engraving my name on trees and walls.*

Enhance – *(verb)* improve the quality, value, or extent of. *As he enhanced his voice, people all over could hear him.*

Enigma – *(noun)* a mysterious or puzzling person or thing. *I could never understand that person, he is an enigma to me.*

Enjoin – *(verb)* instruct or urge to do something. [law] prohibit someone from performing an action by issuing an injunction. *He enjoined me to jump over the wall.*

Enlighten – *(verb)* give greater knowledge and understanding to. give spiritual insight to. rational, tolerant, and well-informed. *Lord Buddha enlightened many people.*

Enlist – *(verb)* enroll or be enrolled in the armed services. engage a person or their help. *He got himself enlisted in the army.*

Enmity – *(noun)* the state of being an enemy; hostility. *Now there is no enmity between us. Let us be friends.*

Ennoble – *(verb)* give a noble rank or title to. give greater dignity to; elevate. *He was ennobled to the rank of general.*

Ennui – *(noun)* listlessness and dissatisfaction arising from boredom. *Ennui got him as he felt extremely bored.*

Enormity – *(noun)* the large scale or extreme seriousness of something bad. great size or scale. *The enormity of the crime shocked me.*

Enough – *(determine & pronoun)* as much or as many as is necessary. or desirable. *(adverb)* **1** to the required degree or extent. *Enough is enough, now please be quiet.* **2** to a moderate degree. *He could get to the station easily enough.*

Enrapture – *(verb)* give intense pleasure to. *I was enraptured by the view from the hill.*

Enrich – *(verb)* **1** improve the quality or value of. *He was further enriched as his father left him all the money and property.* **2** increase the proportion of a particular isotope in an element, especially that of the fissile isotope U-235 in uranium. *Enriched uranium is converted into plutonium to make atom bombs.* **3** make wealthy or wealthier. *Politicians enrich themselves at the cost of ordinary citizens.*

Enrobe – *(verb)* formal dress in a robe or vestment. *He was dressed is a robe.*

Enroute – *(adv)* on the way while travelling. *This bus will go enroute Lady Shri Ram College, C.R. Park and Kalkaji.*

Enshroud – *(verb)* to cover something completely. *The dead body was enshrouded for burial.*

Ensign – *(noun)* flag flown on a ship to show the nationality. *An ensign flew over the naval ship.*

Enslave – *(verb)* make a slave. cause to lose freedom of choice or action. *I was enslaved by her beauty.*

Ensnare – *(verb)* catch in or as in a trap. *The tiger was ensnared in a trap.*

Ensue – *(verb)* happen or occur afterwards or as a result. *Bitterness ensued as the two friends quarreled with one another.*

Ensure – *(verb)* make certain that something will occur or be so. make sure that a problem does not occur. *I will ensure that this kind of thing does not happen again.*

Entente – *(noun)* a friendly understanding or [informal] alliance between states or factions. the understanding between Britain and France reached in 1904, forming the basis of Anglo-French cooperation in the first world war. *People hope that one day there will be entente between India and Pakistan.*

Enteric – *(adjective)* of, relating to, or occurring in the intestines. *You are suffering from an enteric disease.*

Enteritis – *(noun)* [medicine] inflammation of the intestine, especially the small intestine, usually accompanied by diarrhoea. *Enteritis medicine is given in case of inflammation of intestine.*

Enterprising – *(adjective)* showing initiative and resourcefulness. *He is an enterprising fellow and will certainly succeed.*

Entertaining – *(adj)* providing enjoyment. *An entertaining picture relieves our boredom.*

Enthrone – *(verb)* install a monarch or bishop on a throne with due ceremony. treat with honour and respect. *The king was enthroned with full pomp and show.*

Enthusiast – *(noun)* a person who is full of enthusiasm for something. *He is an enthusiast by nature. These days he is full of enthusiasm for going to USA.*

Entice – *(verb)* attract by offering pleasure or advantage. *Being enticed by her wealth, he married an elderly women.*

Entitle – *(verb)* **1** give a right to. *He was entitled to this honour.* **2** give a title to a book, play, etc. *The book was entitled 'Psychology of Crime.'*

Entity – *(noun)* a thing with distinct and independent existence. *A star is an entity.*

Entomb – *(verb)* **1** place in a tomb. *Mummified bodies were entombed in the pyramids of Egypt.* **2** bury in or under. *His dead body was entombed.*

Entomology – *(noun)* the branch of zoology concerned with the study of insects. *He is studying entomology and a lot of insects in jars can be seen in his laboratory.*

Entrails – *(plural noun)* a person's or animal's intestines or internal. organs. *His entrails were severely damaged in an accident.*

Entrain – *(verb)* board a train. *Arriving in Delhi, we entrained and travelled to Agra.*

Entrammel – *(verb)* entrammeling; US untrammeled, entrammeling [poetic/literary] entangle. *On his way home, he got entrammeled with his old enemy.*

Entrance – *(noun)* **1** an opening allowing access. *As I entered the room, I saw the panel sitting.* **2** an act of entering. **3** the right, means, or opportunity to enter. *The entrance to the show is limited to the club members only.*

Entrant – *(noun)* a person who enters something. *All the entrants were gathered together at one place.*

Entreat – *(verb)* **1** ask someone earnestly or anxiously. ask earnestly or anxiously for. *I entreat you to please pardon me.* **2** [archaic] treat in a specified manner.

Entrench – *(verb)* establish firmly. *Congress party's firmly entrenched in power in India.*

Entrust – *(verb)* assign a responsibility to. put into someone's care. *I entrusted the child to the care of the mother.*

Ensure – *(verb)* make certain that something will occur. *I ensure you that an outcome to the problem will come soon.*

Envelop – *(verb)* wrap up, cover, or surround completely. *A human figure appeared completely enveloped in a black dress.*

Envelope – *(noun)* **1** a flat paper container with a sealable flap, used to enclose a letter or document. *I bought an envelope from the post office, put the paper in it and sealed it.* **2** a covering or containing structure or layer. *Onion is enveloped in loyers of covering.*

Envisage – *(verb)* **1** regard or conceive of as a possibility. form a mental picture of. *I envisaged that I was flying in a plane.* **2** *I envisage that one day I will be free from all problem.*

Envoy - *(noun)* **1** a messenger or representative, especially one on a diplomatic mission. *The envoy from U.K. met the foreign secretary.* **2** a minister plenipotentiary, ranking below ambassador and above charge d'affaires. *The Indian envoy to Spain has been promoted as ambassador to Sweden.*

Envy - *(noun)* discontented or resentful longing aroused by another's possessions, qualities, or luck. a person or thing that inspires such a feeling. *(verb)* feel envy of. *My envy knew no bounds when I saw that my neighbor had bought a new and costly car.*

Enwrap - *(verb)* warp; envelop. *I wrapped the gift in a shining paper.*

Ephemera - *(plural noun)* items of short-lived interest or usefulness. *I do not like things that are ephemera.*

Epicycle - *(noun)* geometry a small circle whose centre moves round the circumference of a larger one. *The movement of the spring top resembles that of an epicycle.*

Epidemic - *(noun)* a widespread occurrence of an infectious disease in a community at a particular time. a sudden, widespread occurrence of an undesirable phenomenon. *(adjective)* relating to or of the nature of an epidemic. *When an epidemic like cholera spreads, lots of people die.*

Epidermal - *(adj)* related to outer covering. *This is an epidermal infection you must consult any skin specialist.*

Epigene - *(adjective)* [geology] taking place or produced on the surface of the earth. *All trees and crops are epigene.*

Epiglottis - *(noun)* a flap of cartilage at the root of the tongue, which is depressed during swallowing to cover the opening of the windpipe. *There is some trouble with my epiglottis, I am going to a docter.*

Epilepsy - *(noun)* a neurological disorder marked by sudden recurrent episodes of sensory disturbance, loss of consciousness, or convulsions. *Our neighbour has epilepsy, he often faints.*

Epilogue - *(noun)* a section or speech at the end of a book or play serving as a comment on or a conclusion to what has happened. *Epilogues of some books are so brilliant that they make the whole concept clear.*

Epiphora - *(noun)* [medicine] excessive watering of the eye. *For his watering eyes doctor diagnosed epiphora and prescribed a medicine.*

Epistaxis - *(noun)* [medicine] bleeding from the nose. *He often has epistaxis in the hot weather, he then lies down and applies ice to his nose.*

Epistle - *(noun)* formal or humorous letter. a book of the letters or literary work in the form of letters. *Just out of curiosity. I bought an epistle as I wanted to know how thoughts and emotions are expressed in the form of letters.*

Epistolary - *(adjective)* relating to or denoting the writing of letters or literary works in the form of letters. *'Mind you, this novel is epistolary.'*

Epitaph - *(noun)* words written in memory of a person who has died, especially as an inscription on a tombstone. *I read some beautiful epitaphs when I visited a graveyard.*

Epithelium - *(noun)* [anatomy] the thin tissue forming the outer layer of the body's surface and lining the alimentary canal and other hollow structures, especially that part derived from the embryonic endoderm. compare with endothelium. *The anatomy students asked the doctors many questions about epithelium.*

Epithet - *(noun)* an (adjective) or phrase expressing a quality or attribute of the person or thing mentioned. *The epithet of a 'gentleman', suited him perfectly.*

Epitome - *(noun)* a person or thing that is a perfect example of a quality or type, a summary of a written work. *She is an epitome of beauty.*

Equal - *(adjective)* **1** being the same in quantity, size, degree, value, or status. evenly or fairly balanced: an equal contest. *It was an equal contest between the two boxere.* **2** having the ability or resources to meet a challenging. *(noun)* a person or thing that is equal to another. *I am equal to my brother is height.* *(verb)* be equal or equivalent to. match or rival. *Both packets of sugar contain equal amount of sugar.*

Equality - *(noun)* **1** the state of being equal. *There is great equality of intelligence between the two brothers.* **2** [mathematics] a symbolic expression of the fact that two quantities are equal; an equation. *The sign of equality means that both sides have identical values.*

Equalize - *(verb)* make or become equal. level the score in a match by scoring a goal. *Our team scored a goal and we equalized with the rival team.*

Equator - *(noun)* a line notionally drawn on the earth equidistant from the poles, dividing the earth into northern and southern hemispheres and constituting the parallel of latitude 0°. [astronomy] short for celestial equator. *It is very hot near the equator eg. Africa.*

Equestrian - *(adjective)* **1** of or relating to horse riding. *He is an equestrian champion.* **2** depicting or representing a person on horseback. *An equestrian statue has been erected in the park.* *(noun)* a person on horseback. *Polo is a game played with sticks by equestrians.*

Equi - *combine form* equal; equally; equidistant. *The houses of both the friends are equidistant.*

Equipoise - *(noun)* balance of forces or interests. a counterbalance or balancing force. verb balance or counterbalance. *The armies of both the countries were equipoise.*

Equity - *(noun)* **1** the quality of being fair and impartial. *He is a man known for equity in treatment.* **2** [law] a branch of [law] that developed alongside common [law] in order to remedy some of its defects in fairness and justice. *If there is any conflict between principles of common law and equity, equity prevails.* **3** a trade union for professional actors. *All union members have to carry their equity cards during meeting.* **4** the value of the shares issued by a company. stocks and shares that carry no fixed interest. *Tatas own just 4% of the groups equity.* **5** the value of a mortgaged property after deduction of charges against it. *Many people have built up a large amount of equity in their homes.*

Era - *(noun)* a long and distinct period of history. [geology] a major division of time that is a subdivision of an aeon and is itself subdivided into periods. *The era of dinosaur was over enve before man evolved.*

Eradicable - *(adj)* destroyable completity. *Insurance companies accept eradicable diseases while computing premiums.*

Eradicate - *(verb)* remove or destroy completely. *The plan of Nazi government of Germany was to eradicate Jews.*

Erase - *(verb)* rub out or obliterate; remove all traces of. *The pencil drawing was erased completely by an eraser.*

Erect - *(adjective)* rigidly upright or straight. *She stood erect with her hands by her sides.* of the penis, clitoris, or nipples enlarged and rigid, especially in sexual excitement. standing up from the skin. *Some body organs become erect due to excitement.* *(verb)* construct. create or establish a theory or system. *In today's fashion some young men keep their hair erect.*

Erectile - *(adjective)* able to become erect. *The physician is trying to check the condition of erectile spies.* denoting tissues which are capable of becoming temporarily engorged with blood, particularly those of the penis or other sexual organs. relating to this process. *Many people suffer from erectile dysfinctio.*

Erection - *(noun)* **1** the action of erecting. *Erection of Taj Mahal look 22 years.* **2** a building or other upright structure. *A building with black concrete erection was visible.* **3** an erect state of this process. *There are many men who don't get complete erection.*

Eremite - *(noun)* a Christian hermit. *Many people become eremites.*

Eristic - *(adjective)* of characterized by debate or argument. aiming at winning rather than at reaching the truth. *(noun)* **1** a person given to debate or argument. the art or practice or debate or argument. *His eristic arguments were rather boring.* **2** *He is eristic and will win by some argument or the other.*

Erode - *(verb)* with reference to the action of wind, water, etc. on the land gradually wear or be worn away. *The Fords on this coast continue to be eroded by sea.* gradually destroy an abstract quality or state. *Due to public humiliation his confidence is totally eroded.* [medicine] gradually destroy. *Acids erode the enamel that protect our teeth.*

Erosion - *(noun)* **1** the process or result of eroding or being eroded. *Deserts have been formed as a result of erosion.* **2** [medicine] a place where surface tissue has been gradually destroyed. *There are any tooth parts to protect erosion of enamel of the teeth.*

Erosive - *(adjective)* erosion causing agents. *Acids have erosive qualities.*

Erotic - *(adjective)* of, relating to, or tending to arouse sexual desire or excitement. *Many ancient temples in India display erotic postures.*

Erratic - *(adjective)* not even or regular in pattern or movement. *(noun)* [geology] a large rock that differs from the surrounding rock, brought from a distance by glacial action. *The machine was defective and worked in an erratic way.*

Erratum - *(noun)* an error in printing or writing. a list of corrected errors appended to a publication. *You will find the erratum at the end of the book.*

Erroneous - *(adjective)* wrong; incorrect. *His statement is erroneous.*

Error - *(noun)* **1** a mistake. *There are lots of spelling errors in this article.* **2** the state of being wrong in conduct or judgement. *Train accident was caused by human error.* **3** [technical] a measure of the estimated difference between the observed or calculated value of a quantity and its true value. *The teacher detected an error in value in our experiment.*

Erst - *(adverb)* [archaic] long ago; formerly. *Erstwhile many big and strange animals become extinct.*

Erupt - *(verb)* **1** forcefully eject lava, rocks, ash, or gases. *Suddenly the volcano erupted.* **2** break out suddenly; fierce fighting erupted. *Due to some skin disease strange moles erupted all over his body.* **3** give vent to in a sudden and noisy way. *They erupted in fits of laughter.* **4** suddenly appear on the skin. of the suddenly develop spots, a rash, etc. *A boil has erupted behind the rack.* **5** break through the gums. *Lower incisors has erupted*

Erysipelas - *(noun)* [medicine] a skin disease caused by a streptococcus and characterized by large raised red patches on the face and legs. *He is suffering from erysipelas and has gone to see a skin specialist.*

Eschew - *(verb)* abstain from. *He eschews from drinking.*

Escort - *(noun)* **1** a person or vehicle or group of these accompanying another to provide protection or as a mark of rank. *A large escort accompanied the king.* **2** a person who is hired or formally requested to accompany a member of the opposite sex to a social event. *Celebrities are often escorted by their security staff when going out.* *(verb)* accompany as an escort. *I escorted her to the dance hall.*

Esculent - *(adjective)* fit to be eaten. *(noun)* an esculent thing. *This kind of food is not esculent.*

Esoteric - *(adjective)* intended for or understood by only a small number of people with a specialized knowledge or interest. The opposite of EXOTERIC. *This kind of meditation is esoteric.*

Espial - *(noun)* [archaic] the action or an instance of catching sight of something or of being seen. *He dicided to with drwa from his point of espial.*

Espionage - *(noun)* the practice of spying or of using spies. *Russia and America were involved in a lot of espionage work against each other during the cold war.*

Esplanade - *(noun)* a long, open, level area, typically beside the sea, along which people may promenade. an open, level space separating a fortress from a town. *There is an esplanade road in Delhi opposite the Red Fort.*

Espousal - *(noun)* the action of espousing. *His espousal of western ideas was not liked by village people.*

Espy - *(verb)* [poetic/literary] catch sight of. *I espied a rare bird in the forests of South America.*

Esquire - *(noun)* **1** [British] a polite title appended to a man's name when no other title is used, especially in a letter. *James Callaghan Esquire.*

[north American] a title appended to a lawyer's surname. *Noblemen training for knighthood were called esquires.* 2 [historical] a young nobleman who, in training for knighthood, acted as an attendant to a knight. an officer in the service of a king or nobleman. a landed proprietor or country squire. *The lord of westminster Keith Boyle.*

Essay – *(noun)* **1** a piece of writing on a particular subject. *He wrote a brilliant essay on 'Emancipation of Women.'* **2** formal an attempt or effort. *An authentic essay of politics of India.* *(verb)* attempt. *She essayed a fake smile on her face.*

Essence – *(noun)* the intrinsic nature of something the quality which determines something's character. philosophy a property or group of properties of something without which it would not exist or be what it is. *The essence of this paragraph is that man is not civilized as yet.* **2** an extract or concentrate obtained from a plant or other substance and used for flavouring or scent. *Rose scent is made from the essence of rose flower.*

Essential – *(adjective)* **1** fundamental; central. *It is essential that you catch today's flight.* **2** absolutely necessary; extremely important. *Essential things must be done first.* **3** required for normal growth but not synthesized in the body and therefore necessary in the diet. *In democracy it is essential that people should be literate.* **4** [medicine] with no known external stimulus or cause; idiopathic. *The doctor has prescribed certain essential medicines to combat stress.* *(noun)* things that are absolutely necessary. *We had only bare essential to service the extreme cold.*

Estate – *(noun)* **1** a property consisting of a large house and extensive grounds. *My father has a large estate.* **2** [British] an area of land and modern buildings developed for residential, industrial, or commercial purposes. *He cultivates coffee and rubber on his estate.* **3** a property where crops such as coffee or rubber are cultivated or where wine is produced. *He willed all his estate to his son before his death.* **4** a person's money and property in its entirety at the time of their death. *His estate has been valued at Rs. 50 crore.* **5** a class or order forming part of the body politic, in particular one of the three groups constituting parliament, now the lards spiritual the heads of the church, the lords temporal the peerage, and the commons known as the three estates. *The spiritual welfare of all estates of people is required.* **6** [archaic poetic/ literary] a particular state, period, or condition in life. *Programmes are run for improvement of everyone's estate.*

Estimable – *(adjective)* worthy of great respect. *Mahatma Gandhi was an estimable person.*

Estimate – *(noun)* **1** an approximate calculation or judgement. a written statement indicated the likely price that will be charged for specified work. *At a rough estimate the government is recycling half of the paper used.* **2** a judgement or appraisal. *(verb)* form an estimate of. *He highly estimats the quality of her poems.*

Estop – *(verb)* [law] bar or preclude by estoppel. *The firm may be estopped from denying their statement.*

Estrange – *(verb)* **1** cause to feel less close or friendly; alienate. *He no longer has any connation with his estranged wife.* **2** no longer living with their spouse. *The estranged couple are now living separately.*

Etcetra – *(adv)* used at end of a sentence to indicate that other similar items also exist. *If you are going to the market please bring some vegetables like potato, tomato, onion, cucumber etc.*

Eternity – *(noun)* infinite or unending time. theology endless life after death. [informal] an undesirably long period of time. *We shall be loving each other till eternity.*

Ethics – *(plural noun)* **1** the moral principles governing or influencing conduct. *We should follow ethics strictly.* **2** the branch of knowledge concerned with moral principles. *Neither metaphysics nor this is the home of religion.*

Ethnic – *(adjective)* **1** of or relating to a group of people having a common national or cultural tradition. *Ethnic roits sometimes take place* *because of nationality and religious differences.* **2** denoting origin by birth or descent rather than by present nationality. *This area is mostly inhabited by ethnic Indian populations.* **3** characteristic of or belonging to a non-western cultural tradition: ethnic dressed. *There ethnic jewellery belong to 1200 AD India.* *(noun)* [chiefly north American] a member of an ethnic minority.

Ethology – *(noun)* the study of the characteristics of different peoples and the differences and relationships between them. *Persons who are interested in character sticks of different people and relationships among them must sturdy ethnology.*

Ethos – *(noun)* the characteristic spirit of a culture, era, or community as manifested in its attitudes and aspirations. *The ethos of Indians has always been torching the feet of elders and worshiping natural objects.*

Ethyl – *(noun)* chemistry of or denoting the alkyl radical. C_2H_5, derived from ethane. *A chemical derived from ethane.*

Etiology – *(noun)* US spelling of AETIOLOGY.

Etiquette – *(noun)* the customary code of polite behaviour in a society. *He is a man of perfect etiquette.*

Eucalyptus – *(noun)* a fast-growing evergreen Australasian tree valued for its wood, oil, gum, and resin. the oil from eucalyptus leaves, chiefly used for its medicinal properties. *I would certainly like to have a eucalyptus tree is my garden. It is so beautiful and has so many uses.*

Eugenics – *(plural noun)* the science of using controlled breeding to increase the occurrence of desirable heritable characteristics in a population. *You should study eugenics if you want to know about controlled breeding in a population.*

Eulogist – *(noun) one who praises excessively. He is a professional praise writer.*

Eulogy – *(noun)* a speech or piece of writing that praises someone highly. *People often write eulogies about dead persons.*

Euphony – *(noun)* the quality of being pleasing to the ear. *There is great euphony in her speech.*

Euphorbia – *(noun)* a plant of a genus that comprises the spurges. *Euphorbia is a canda lebra tree.*

Eureka – *(exclamation as noun)* a cry of joy and finding something unique by chance. *I cried 'eureka' when I found a rare plant which I had been long searching for.*

European – *(adj)* relating to Europe and its inhabitants. *You can see by the colur of his skin that he is a European and not an Asian.*

Evacuant – *(adjective)* acting to induce some kind of bodily discharge. *(noun)* an evacuant [medicine]. *A laxative is an evacuant medicine.*

Evacuate – *(verb)* **1** remove from a place of danger to a safer place. leave a dangerous place. *As the flood came, the villagers were evacuated.* **2** [technical] remove air, water, or other contents from a container. empty the bowels or another bodily organ. *Water was evacuated from the tank.* ***3** His bowels were evacuated by some medicine.*

Evade – *(verb)* **1** escape or avoid, especially by guile or trickery. avoid giving a direct answer to a question. *At the party he said that he was a millionaire Industrialist and had been called specially. Thus he evaded paying anything.* **2** escape paying, especially by illegitimate presentation of one's finances. defeat the intention of especially while complying with its letter. *Although he was rich, he evaded paying any money for charity by declaring that he had gone bank rapt.*

Evaporate – *(verb)* **1** turn from liquid into vapour. *The water evaporated as it boiled for too long a time.* **2** cease to exist.

Eve – *(noun)* **1** the day or period of time immediately before an event or occasion. the evening or day before a religious festival. *There are a lot of festivals on Christmas eve.* **2** [chiefly poetic/literary] evening.

Evening – *(noun)* the period of time at the end of the day, between late afternoon and bedtime. *(adverb)* [informal] in the evening; every evening. *Most often my friend came to have tea with me in the evening.*

Event - *(noun)* **1** a thing that happens or takes place. a public or social occasion. *In event of my sudden death, please call the lawyer and have my will read.* **2** each of several contests making up a sports competition. *In commonwealth games, gymnastic event was my favourite.* **3** [physics] a single occurrence of a process, e.g. the ionization of one atom. *The ionization of an atom is known as an events in physics.*

Ever - *(adverb)* **1** at any time. used in comparisons for emphasis. *'Darling, I am ever yours.'* **2** always. *'Why did you ever go to the casino and lost such a huge amount of money.' His father cried.* **3** increasingly; constantly. *Have you ever visited kerala, if not go and see this 'city of Gods.'*

Evert - *(verb)* [biology & physiology] turn outwards or inside out. *The hyena can evert its anal pouch.*

Evidence - *(noun)* information indicating whether a belief or proposition is true or valid. [law] information used to establish facts in a legal investigation or admissible as testimony in a [law] court. signs; indications. *What is the evidence you did not commit the crime? (verb)* be or show evidence of. *Tell us where were you between 4 and 5 in the evening and you must have evidence for it.*

Evince - *(verb)* formal reveal the presence of; indicate a quality or feeling. *I evinced that I was nervous.*

Evolution - *(noun)* **1** the process by which different kinds of living organism are believed to have developed from earlier forms, especially by natural selection. *The evolution of humans took bilious of years.* **2** gradual development. *Evolution is a very slow process.* **3** [chemistry] the giving off of a gaseous product, or of heat. *The evolution of oxygen occurs quite fast in this process.* **4** a pattern of movements or manoeuvres. *Flocks of waders often perform aerial evolutions.*

Evolve - *(verb)* **1** develop gradually. *Creatures on the earth evolved very gradually.* **2** develop over successive generations by evolution. *Domestic dogs are believed to be evolved from the wolf.* **3** [chemistry] give off gas or heat. *The energy evolved during this process is transferred to water.*

Ewer - *(noun)* a large jug with a wide mouth. *He used to drink from an ewer.*

Exact - *(adjective)* not approximated in any way; precise. accurate or correct in all details: tending to be accurate and careful about minor details. *The exact details were still being worked out. (verb)* **1** demand and obtain from someone. *I exacted Rs. 500000 from him.*

Exaggerate - *(verb)* represent as being larger or better than it really is; enlarged or altered beyond normal proportions. *He exaggerated the facts and nobody came to know the real facts.*

Examine - *(verb)* **1** inspect closely to determine the nature or condition of; investigate thoroughly. *As the police examined the case thoroughly, they came to know the culprit.* **2** test the knowledge or proficiency of. *We are going to examine the candidates tomorrow.* **3** [law] formally question a defendant or witness in court. *The witness was examined in detail.*

Exasperate - *(verb)* irritate intensely. *He was exasperated by my repeated question.*

Excavate - *(verb)* **1** make by digging. extract from the ground by digging. *A lot of excavation went on in Egypt when the pyramids were discovered.* **2** carefully remove earth from an area in order to find buried remains. *Excavation had to proceed cautiously to prevent damage to buried treasures.*

Exceed - *(verb)* be greater in number or size than. go beyond what is allowed or stipulated by a set limit, especially of one's authority. surpass. *He exceeded his time limit in speaking and thus lost marks in debate.*

Excel - *(verb)* be exceptionally good at an activity or subject. perform exceptionally well. *In sports he excelled in long jump.*

Excellency - *(noun)* **1** a title or form of address for certain high officials of state, especially ambassadors, or of the roman catholic church. *His Excellency the ambassador of Britain arrived in New Delhi in today morning.*

Excellent – *(adjective)* extremely good; outstanding. *He got excellent mark in English.*

Exception – *(noun)* a person or thing that is excepted or that does not follow a rule. the action or state of excepting or being excepted. *Most people exaggerate and brag about their achievements he is an exception. He a quiet and polite man.*

Excise – *(noun)* a tax levied on certain goods and commodities and on licenses granted for certain activities. *The rate of excise duty on petrol has been lowered to 8 per cent.* *(verb)* charge excise on. goods. *He was asked to pay excise duty on certain items when he returned from abroad.*

Excitant – *(noun)* [biology] a substance which elicits an active physiological or behavioural response. *The brain could become excited if chemical excitants flood into it.*

Excite – *(verb)* **1** cause strong feelings of enthusiasm and eagerness in. arouse sexually. *I was very excited to see my favorite film star in person.* **2** give rise to a feeling or reaction. *She has the ability to execute others to play tennis.* **3** produce a state of increased energy or activity in a physical or biological system. *The every of election is sufficient to execute the atom.*

Exciter – *(noun)* a thing that excites. *Elections act as exciters in an atom.*

Exciting – *(adj)* causing enthusiasm. *It is always exciting to see the finals of one day cricket matches.*

Exclaim – *(verb)* cry out suddenly, especially in surprise, anger, or pain. *'An what a beautiful sea beach!' he exclaimed.*

Exclusion – *(noun)* **1** the process or state of excluding or being excluded. *Many players were excluded in the final selection of the team.* **2** an item or eventuality specifically not covered by an insurance policy or other contract. *Insurance Companies keep inventing exclusions to deny insurance coverage.*

Exclusive – *(adjective)* **1** excluding or not admitting other things. unable to exist or be true if something else exists or is true: mutually exclusive options. excluding all by what is specified. *This book is for exclusive sale in USA.* **2** restricted to the person, group, or area concerned. not published or broadcast elsewhere. *The whole book is to be read excluding this chapter.* **3** high-class and expensive; select. *'I have exclusively kept a beautiful diamond for you, sir.'* **4** not including. (noun) an exclusive story or broadcast. *This agenda is exclusively for the housing society it is not to be publicized.* **5** *This restaurant exclusively serves fish.*

Excogitate – *(verb)* formal thing out, plan, or devise. *I excogitated cleverly and won the chess match.*

Excrement – *(noun)* faeces. *In our villages excrement can be found lying extensively.*

Excreta – *(noun)* waste discharged from the body, especially faeces and urine. *In cities in every house there is a toilet for discharging excreta.*

Excruciate – *(verb)* rare torment physically or mentally. *He excruciated her to no end, ultimately she left him and ran away.*

Exculpate – *(verb)* formal show or declare to be not guilty of wrongdoing. *He excels pated in the court.*

Excursion – *(noun)* **1** a short journey or trip, especially one taken for leisure. *He has gone on amexcursion on his return he will visit a bird sanctuary as well.* **2** [technical] a movement along a path or through an angle. a deviation from a regular pattern, path, or level of operation. *After a brief excursion into editing he went back to his original job of writing books.*

Execrate – *(verb)* feel or express great loathing for. *He execrated over the heinous crime.*

Executive – *(adjective)* having the power to execute plans, actions, or laws. *Executive branch of the government is responsible for executing plans, actions and laws.* *(noun)* **1** a person with senior managerial responsibility in a business organization. an executive committee within an organization. *He is a junior executive engineer in DDA.* **2** the branch of a government responsible for executing plans, actions, or laws. *He is a senior manager in a big firm and head of the executive committee.*

Executor – *(noun)* [law] a person appointed by a testator to carry out the terms of their will. *Before his death, my father had already appointed on executor.*

Exemplar – *(noun)* a person or thing serving as a typical example or appropriate model. *It was exemplary show of fashion designing.*

Exequies – *(plural noun)* formal funeral rites. *When somebody dies it becomes necessary to perform exequies.*

Exhale – *(verb)* **1** breathe out. *As he exhaled his breath, I could smell alcohol.* **2** give off. *He exhaled the cigarette smoke through his nose.*

Exhilarate – *(verb)* cause to feel very happy or animated. *I was exhilarated to get first position in the class.*

Exhume – *(verb)* dig out something buried, especially a corpse from the ground. *On the orders of the judge a dead body was exhumed.*

Exigent – *(adjective)* formal pressing; demanding. *You are taking a loan from him, remember he is a very exigent person. You will have to return back all his money in time.*

Exile – *(noun)* **1** the state of being barred from one's native country. *The English exiled Mohammad Shah Zafar. He died in Burma.* **2** a person who lives in exile. *Dalai Lama had formed a government in exale in India. (verb)* expel and bar from their native country. *The party's exiled members are living in Trinidad.*

Exist – *(verb)* **1** have objective reality or being. be found: two conflicting stereotypes exist. *Truth of existence is one of the greatest truths.* **2** live, especially under adverse conditions. *Somehow or other he exists in such great poverty.*

Exit – *(noun)* **1** a way out of a building, room, or passenger vehicle. a place for traffic to leave a major road or roundabout. *'Sir, the exit gate is that.'* **2** an act of leaving. a departure of an actor from the stage. *The actor exited after playing his roll.* **3** [poetic/literary] a person's death. *Our friend has exited from this world. (verb)* **1** go out of or leave a place. leave the stage. indicating that a character leaves the stage. *The bullet entered his chest and exited through the back.* **2** computing terminate a process or program. *Upon completion of the assignment you should exit the programme.*

Exogamy – *(noun)* [anthropology] the custom of marrying outside a community, clan, or tribe, compare with endogamy. *Clan or tribal people seldom is indulge in exogamy.*

Exorbitant – *(adj)* too much high. *Despite exorbitant prices, people continue to buy onions.*

Exorcist – *(noun)* a person who makes evil spirits leave a person or place. *He is an exorcist. He drives out evil spirit from a person or place.*

Exorcise – *(verb)* drive out from a person or place. *He has exorcised the evil spirit.*

Exordium – *(noun)* [formal] the beginning or introduction of a discourse or treatise. *The exordium of the astronomer who was speaking on black holes in sky was brilliant.*

Expand – *(verb)* **1** make or become larger or more extensive. *Scientist say that our universe is ever expanding.* **2** give a fuller version or account of. *You should expond your article to 3 pages.* **3** relatively broad in shape. *Many details are missing, please expand to include them.*

Expanse – *(noun)* **1** a wide continuous area of something, typically land or sea. *The expanse of sea was vast.* **2** the distance to which something expands or can be expanded. *There exists vast expanse of farmland.*

Expansion – *(noun)* **1** the action or an instance of expanding. *Expansion of the bridge was nearing completion.* **2** the increase in the volume of fuel on combustion in the cylinder of an engine, or the piston stroke in which this occurs. *Upon heating, expansion in volume of gases is seen.*

Expansive – *(adjective)* **1** covering a wide area; extensive. *During the rainy season, rivers become expansive.* **2** relaxed, genial, and communicative. *He is an expansive man.*

Exparte – *(adjective & adverb)* [law] with respect to or in the interests of one side only. *The law gave an exparte decision.*

Expatiate – *(verb)* speak or write at length or in detail. *This time he expatiated about brain surgery.*

Expatriate – *(noun)* a person who lives outside their native country. (adjective) living outside one's native country. *He is an expatriate settled in Canada. (verb)* settle abroad.

Expect – *(verb)* **1** regard as likely to happen, do, or be the case. suppose or assume. *I expect I'll be late. I expect him to be on time.* **2** believe that will arrive soon. [informal] be pregnant. *I expect you to give me due respect.* **3** require as appropriate or rightfully due. *I expect he will top the class.* **4** *She is expecting.*

Expectorate – *(verb)* cough or spit out from the throat or lungs. *He expectorated phlegm.*

Expedite – *(verb)* cause to happen sooner or be accomplished more quickly. *Will you kindly expedite the matter.*

Expedition – *(noun)* a journey undertaken by a group of people with a particular purpose. *An expedition was sent to Himalayan mountains for the study of plants.*

Expend – *(verb)* spend or use up a resource. *He expended all his money.*

Expense – *(noun)* **1** cost incurred or required. costs incurred in the performance of a job or task. *The expenses of living in a metro city are very high.* **2** something on which money must be spent. *Can I give you something to meet your expenses.*

Expert – *(noun)* a person who is very knowledgeable about or skilful in a particular area. *(adjective)* having or involving such knowledge or skill. *He is an expert in flying helicopter.*

Expiration – *(noun)* expiry. *Before buying please check the expiration date of the medicine.*

Expire – *(verb)* **1** come to the end of the period of validity. come to an end. *This medicine has expired.* **2** die. *His grand-father expired long ago.*

Explain – *(verb)* **1** make clear by describing it in more detail. *The teacher took us to the planetarium and explained the planetary system.* **2** excuse or justify one's motives or conduct. minimize the significance of something embarrassing by giving an excuse or justification. *Please let me explain to you why I got late for the office.* **3** give a reason or justification for.

Explanatory – *(adjective)* serving to explain something. *He was asked to submit an explanatory not as to why he was absent from office for three days.*

Explicate – *(verb)* analyse and develop in detail. analyse a literary work in order to reveal its meaning. *The professor explicated a few poems of William Blake.*

Explicit – *(adjective)* **1** clear and detailed, with no room for confusion or doubt. *His lecture on the properties of medicinal plants was so explicit that there was a thunderous applause.* **2** graphically describing or representing sexual activity. *There are many websites that show explicit videos meant for adults only.*

Explode – *(verb)* **1** burst or shatter violently, especially as a result of rapid combustion or excessive internal pressure. *A bomb exploded and great damage was done.* **2** suddenly give expression to violent emotion, especially anger. *Suddenly I exploded and told him on his face what I thought of him.* **3** show to be false or unfounded. *Many decades back the population in India had suddenly exploded.* **4** increase suddenly in number or extent. *Uses of facebook has exploded in recent times.*

Exploit – *(verb)* **1** make use of and derive benefit from a resource. *He exploited his rich clients to no end.* **2** make use of unfairly; benefit unjustly from the work or actions of. *Many people exploit their influence to get their jobs done.*

Exploration – *(noun)* the act of travelling through some place. *The exploration of pyramids of Egypt brought to light many strange facts.*

Explosive – *(adjective)* **1** able or likely explode. *Police found out many explosives hidden in trash boxes.* **2** sudden and dramatic. *His explosive speech caused a lot of trouble.* **3** phonetics produced with a sharp release of air. *There are many explosive sounds in linguistics.* *(noun)* a substance which an be made to explode. *Sulphur is used as an explosive in firecrackers.*

Export – *(verb)* **1** send to another country for sale. spread or introduce to another country. **2** computing transfer in a format that can be used by other programs. *(noun)* **1** an exported commodity, article, or service. *He exports readymade garments to America.* **2** the exporting of goods or services. of a high standard suitable for export: export ales. *India exports high standard sugar, wheat and rice to many countries.*

Expositor - *(noun)* a person or thing that explains complicated ideas or theories. *He is an expositor and will explain all these theories in an explicit way.*

Expostulate - *(verb)* express strong disapproval or disagreement. *He expostulated against the plan of action.*

Exposure - *(noun)* **1** the state of being exposed to something harmful. a physical condition resulting from being exposed to severe weather conditions. *Exposure to cold made him fall sick.* **2** the action of exposing a photographic film. the quantity of light reaching a photographic film, as determined by shutter speed and lens aperture. *The photographic film was exposed and thus ruined.* **3** the revelation of something secret. the publicizing of information or an event. *His secret was ultimately exposed by his adversaries.* **4** the direction in which a building faces. *This building is exposed to east.*

Expound - *(verb)* present and explain (a theory of idea) systematically. *He expounded the theory lucidly.*

Express - *(verb)* **1** convey in words or by gestures and conduct. *He expressed his disagreement by gestures.* **2** [chiefly mathematic] represent by a figure, symbol, or formula. *Each Greek alphabet is expressed as a symbol.The mathematical formulas are often expressed by symbols.*

Expression - *(noun)* **1** the action of expressing something. *He expressed his anger by insulting his wish to travel by plane.* **2** the look on someone's face, seen as conveying a particular emotion. *The expression on his face was that of displeasure.* **3** a word or phrase expressing an idea. *The books expression of the human mind.*

Expulsion - *(noun)* the action of expelling. *His expulsion from the class was a disciplinary action taken against him.*

Expunge - *(verb)* obliterate or remove completely. *His name was expunged from the club as he frequently broke its rules and regulations.*

Expurgate - *(verb)* remove matter regarded as obscene or unsuitable from (a text or account). *A lesson was expurgated from the text book as it was historically untruly.*

Exquisite - *(adjective)* **1** of great beauty and delicacy. *She is a woman of exquisite beauty.* **2** acute: the exquisite pain of love. highly sensitive: exquisite taste. *He has exquisite tastes.*

Extant - *(adjective)* still in existence. *Some ancient animals are still extant in some form or the other.*

Extend - *(verb)* **1** make larger or longer in space or time. occupy a specified area or continue for a specified distance. *He extended the offer to him to join the party.* **2** hold out towards someone. offer. *The building extended up to hundreds of floors.* **3** be applicable to. *The railway line extended up to three thousand kilometers.*

Extensile - *(adjective)* capable of being extended. *The area around is extensile.*

Extensive - *(adjective)* **1** covering a large area. large in amount or scale. *The tea shops are extensive in this area.* **2** incuding or dealing with huge information. *Extensive research has been done into this disease.*

Extent - *(noun)* **1** the area covered by something. the size or scale of something. *He can go to any extent to fulfil his ambition.* **2** the particular degree to which something is the case: everyone has to compromise to some extent. *I can spend money only to this extent and not any further.* **3** *You must compromise to some extent.*

Extenuate - *(verb)* lessen the seriousness of guilt or an offence by reference to mitigating factor. *The lawyer tried his best to extenuate the crime.*

Exterior - *(adjective)* **1** forming, situated on, or relating to the outside. outdoor. *The exterior of this building is done very exquisitely.* **2** *His exterior is very polite. (noun)* the outer surface or structure of something. a person's apparent behaviour of demeanour. an outdoor scene. *He was seething with anger despite a cool exterior.*

Exterminate - *(verb)* destroy completely; eradicate. *The termite was exterminated from the house by spraying chemicals.*

External – *(adjective)* **1** belonging to, situated on, or forming the outside. *The building carried an attractive external appearance.* **2** coming or derived from a source outside the subject affected. coming from or relating to a country or institution other than the main subject. *The ministry of external affairs deals with matters of foreign countries.* **3** for or concerning students registered with and taking the examinations of a university but not resident there. *The external examinations of the university will take place in September.* *(noun)* examination of a university but not resident there. *(noun)* outward features.

Extinct – *(adjective)* **1** having no living members. no longer in existence. not having reputed in recorded history. *Many species of plants and animals are getting fast extinct these days.* **2** having no valid claimant. *Servants are almost extinct in in modern society.*

Extinguish – *(verb)* **1** put out a fire or light. *All the caudles were extinguished as the electricity was restored.* **2** put an end to. *I have extinguished my debts.* **3** cancel by full payment. *Claim having been paid, this policy was extinguished*

Extirpate – *(verb)* search out and destroy completely. *All the enemy hideouts were extirpated.*

Extort – *(verb)* obtain by force, threats, or other unfair means. *The mafia extorted a lot of money from shopkeepers.*

Extra– *(adjective)* added to an existing or usual amount or number. *(adverb)* **1** to a greater extent than usual. *All extra money he had was spent on his illness.* **2** in addition. *Here are some extra shirts. You can buy them at 40% discount.* *(noun)* **1** an item for which an extra charge is made. *An extra show of the film will be run in the morning from tomorrow.* **2** an extra item. *It is an imported item hence extra charge is being made.* **3** a person engaged temporarily to fill out a crowd scene in a film or play. *All the extras were paid handsome amount of money.* **4** cricket a run scored other than from a hit with the bat, credited to the batting side rather than to a batsman. *Our team got four extra runs for no balls.*

Extraordinary – *(adjective)* **1** very unusual or remarkable. *He has extra-ordinary talent for writing fiction.* **2** specially convened. specially employed: ambassador extraordinary. *An extraordinary general body meeting has been concerned tomorrow.*

Extravagance – *(noun)* the act of spending more than necessary. *He is a reasonable man and does not indulge in extravagance.*

Extravagant – *(adjective)* **1** lacking restraint in spending money or using resources. resulting from or showing this: extravagant gifts. *He is not extravagant but spends money wisely.* **2** exceeding what is reasonable or appropriate: extravagant claims. *He believes in a giving extravagant gifts.* **3** *He has made extravagant claims to the ancestral property.*

Extreme – *(adjective)* **1** very great; exceptional, very severe or serious. *He gave his studies extreme attention.* **2** far from moderate, especially politically. *He is an extremely rude person. Something very unusual.* **3** furthest from the centre or a given point. *you are extremely ill and need hospitalization.* **4** *Extreme points of earth are known as south pole and north pole.* **5** *The two brothers are extremely opposite in nature.* **6** *He was exposed to extreme defree of cold.* *(noun)* either of two abstract things that are as different from each other as possible. the most extreme degree of something. *We are in the midst of extreme of cold season.*

Extremity – *(noun)* **1** the furthest point or limit. the hands and feet. *Our hands and feet are our body's extremities.* **2** severity or seriousness. extreme adversity. *The extremity of his sons disease worried him.*

Extrinsic – *((adjective))* **1** not essential or inherent. *This theory is a complex interplay of influence and extrinsic factors.* **2** having its origin some distance from the part which it moves. *There are many reasons extrinsic to the music itself.*

Extrude – *(verb)* thrust or force out. *Ashes were being extruded from the volcano.*

Exuberance – *(verb)* full of energy. *They enjoyed the picnic with a youthful exuberance.*

Exult – *(verb)* show or feel triumphant. *Exulting in her escape, she closed the door behind her.*

Ff

F – *(noun)* **1** the sixth letter of the alphabet. **2** denoting the next after E in a set of items, categories, etc. **3** music the fourth note of the diatonic scale of C major.

Fabaceous - *(adjective)* of the pea family. *Leguminous Green-looking fabaceous plants are a good source of vitamins A, B and C.*

Fabian – *(noun)* a member or supporter of the Fabian society, an organization of socialists aiming to achieve socialism by non-revolutionary methods. *Members of the Fabian society aim to spread socialism in a gradual way. (adjective)* employing a cautiously persistent and dilatory strategy to wear out an enemy. *Most militaries employ delaying or fabian tactics to wear out the enemy before attacking them.*

Fable – *(noun)* a short story, typically with animals as characters, conveying a moral, a supernatural story incorporating elements of myth and legend. *Children like to read fables that often employs as characters animals that speak and act like humans.*

Fabricate – *(verb)* **1** invent, typically with deceitful intent. *These people have fabricated evidence.* **2** construct or manufacture especially from prepared components. *The students in practical class assembling a railway bridge is an example of fabricate.*

Fabulist – *(noun)* **1** a person who composes fables. *Book publishers look for fabulists who can compose fables that interests children.* **2** a liar. *A fabulist is a person who creates dishonest stonies.*

Fabulous - *(adjective)* **1** extraordinary, especially extraordinarily large. [informal] wonderful. *An example of fabulous is a very extravagant party.* **2** mythical. *Many fabulous creatures in mythology have no basis in reality.*

Face – *(noun)* **1** the front part of a person's head from the forehead to the chin, or the corresponding part in an animal. an aspect of something the unacceptable face of social drinking. **2** an expression on someone's face. **3** the surface of a thing, especially one that is presented to the view or has a particular function. *Face is the combination of eyes, ears, mouth and nose; Face is the part of the clock that displays the time; Happy faces of the children delighted us; we can often see the dark faces of the moon by earthshine. (verb)* **1** be positioned with the face or front towards or in a specified direction. **2** confront and deal with. have in prospect. *Students should look at and face the teacher in the class; A person must learn to face and deal with his greatest fear.*

Facetious – *(adjective)* joking, trying to joke at an inappropriate time, describes a joke made about something serious. *It is facetious trying to be humorous when the matter is serious.*

Facial – *(noun)* a beauty treatment that is designed to exfoliate, invigorate or treat the skin of the face. *A treatment done on your face that refreshes your skin is an example of a facial.*

Facile – *(adjective)* effortless. *Facile is winning a game against a team that isn't very good at that particular game.*

Facilitate – *(verb)* make easy or easier. *You must facilitate to ensure that everyone's opinions are heard.*

Facing – *(noun)* **1** a piece of material sewn on the inside of a garment, especially at the neck and armholes, to strengthen it. the cuffs, collar, and lapels of a military jacket, contrasting in colour with the rest of the garment. **2** an outer layer covering the surface of a wall. *Facing is a name given to a piece of material sewn to the edge of a garment, such as a dress or coat, as lining or decoration. Facing is an outer layer or coating applied to a surface for protection or decoration.*

Facsimile - *(noun)* an exact copy, especially of written or printed material. *An exact copy that has been made of a cheque is an example of a facsimile. (verb)* make a copy of. *When you have an exact copy of a legal document, this is an example of a facsimile copy.*

Fact - *(noun)* a thing that is indisputably the case; information used as evidence or as part of a report. [chiefly Law] the truth about events as opposed to interpretation. *In fact, he has gone to Delhi today; Even the most investigation peters out without facts; There was a question of fact as to whether they had received the letter.*

Faction - *(noun)* a small dissentient group within a larger one. *The youngsters have formed a faction within an otherwise peaceful political party.*

Factious - *(adjective)* relating or inclined to dissension. *An example of something factious is a bunch of dissatisfied elements within a class.*

Factor - *(noun)* **1** a circumstance, fact, or influence that contributes to a result. **2** mathematics a number or quantity that when multiplied with another produces a given number or expression. **3** a business agent, Scottish a land agent or steward. *An example of factor would be eye witness accounts to a news report about a crime. This skill was a factor in ensuring that so much was achieved; Two and three are factors of six; He was the chief factor for popularity of mobile phones in India. (verb)* [mathematics] another term for FACTORIZE. **2** sell to a factor. *He collected rents while she factored these forfeited estates.*

Factory - *(noun)* a building or buildings where goods are manufactured or assembled chiefly by machine. *A factory is a building or group of buildings in which goods are manufactured.*

Factotum - *(noun)* an employee who does all kinds of work. *An employee or assistant who serves in a wide range of capacities is known as factotum.*

Facula - *(noun)* [astronomy] a bright region on the surface of the sun, linked to the subsequent appearance of sunspots. *A large bright spot on the sun's photosphere is known as facula; A bright spot on the surface of a planet is known as facula.*

Fad - *(noun)* **1** a craze. **2** an idiosyncrasy or arbitrary like or dislike. *A fad is any fashion that is taken up with great enthusiasm for a brief period of time.*

Fade - *(verb)* **1** gradually grow faint and disappear. lose or cause to lose colour. become temporarily less efficient as a result of frictional heating. **2** come or cause to come gradually into or out of view, or to merge into another shot. increase or decrease in volume or merge into another recording. **3** golf deviate to the right, typically as a result of spin. **4** [north American informal] match the bet of another player. *The light had faded and dusk was advancing; Hopes of peace had faded; His hair had faded to grey she fadred near the finish. (noun)* **1** an act or instance of fading. **2** golf a shot causing the ball to fade. *When they get to the 18th the idea shot is a fade.*

Fading - *(noun)* waning; a decline: *The match had to be stopped because of fading light.*

Faeces - *(plural noun)* waste matter remaining after food has been digested, discharged from the bowels. *The body eliminates faeces through rectum.*

Fail - *(verb)* **1** be unsuccessful in an undertaking be unable to meet the standards set by a test. judge a candidate in an examination or test not to have passed. **2** neglect to do something. disappoint expectations: **3** stop working properly. become weaker or less good. go out of business. **4** desert or let down. *Her nerve failed her. (noun)* a mark which is not high enough to pass an examination or test. *He failed in his attempt to see me election; She failed in her final examination; At the last moment for nerve failed her.*

Fain - *(adjective)* pleased or willing under the circumstances. *An example of fain is a brilliant student who is eager to study with his friend who is not as sharp. (adverb)* gladly. *I am weary and would fain get a little rest.*

Faith - *(noun)* **1** complete trust or confidence. *Faith is belief in a person or thing that does not rest on logical proof or material evidence.* **2** strong belief in a religion, based on spiritual apprehension rather than proof, consideration. *Poor people show great faith in God.*

Faithful – *(adjective)* remaining loyal and steadfast. *A loyal dog that always comes to sit by your side is called faithful. (noun)* the believers in a particular religion, especially Islam. *A Muslim who adheres strictly to the tenets of the Islamic religion is faithful.*

Faithless – *(adjective)* without religious faith. *How can you have faith in a person who is so faithless, treacherous and cruel?*

Fake – *(adjective)* not genuine. *You are a fake person when you pretend to be sick when you aren't. (verb)* forage or counterfeit. pretend to feel or suffer from an emotion or illness. *One who pretends to be nice when really he is not is an example of a fake person.*

Falcate – *(adjective)* curved like a sickle; hooked. *As we moved slowly toward the deep waters in the river a big fish arched its back, showing a strongly falcate fin.*

Falchion – *(noun)* [historical] a broad, slightly curved sword with the cutting edge on the convex side. *A falchion is a short, broad sword with a curved cutting edge and a sharp point.*

Falciform – *(adjective)* curved like a sickle; hooked. *Falciform ligament is a very rare anomaly and hardly any cases are reported.*

Falcon – *(noun)* a fast-flying bird of prey with long pointed wings. [falconry] the female of such a bird, especially a peregrine, compare with TERCEL. *Falcon is a high flying bird that can spot its prey on ground from 5-6 kilometres above.*

Falderal – *(noun)* variant spelling of FOLDEROL.

Faldstool – *(noun)* **1** a folding chair used by a bishop when not occupying the throne or when officiating in a church other than his own. *Faldstool is a backless chair used by a bishop when officiating in any other church.* **2** a small movable folding desk or stool for kneeling at prayer.

Fall – *(verb)* 1move from a higher to a lower level, typically rapidly and without control, become detached and drop to the ground, hang down, slope downwards, show dismay or disappointment by appearing to droop, lose one's balance and collapse, throw oneself to the ground, collapse to the ground, decrease in number, amount, intensity, or quality, *informal* (of computer hardware or software) stop working suddenly; crash. *My purse fell out of my bag; My sunglasses fell off and broke on the pavement; Hair was allowed to fall to the shoulder; The land fell away in a steep bank; Her face fell as she thought about her life with Rajesh; She fell down at school today; She fell to her knees and began to cry; After the earthquake, part of the city fell down; Imports fell by 12 per cent last year; The programme fell over once when I clicked on the wrong control. (noun)* an act of falling or collapsing, a downward difference in height between parts of a surface, a thing which falls or has fallen, a sudden onset or arrival, a waterfall or cascade, the way in which something falls or hangs, decrease in size, number, rate, or level, defeat or downfall. *His mother had a fall as she alighted from the train; at the corner of the massif this fall is interrupted by other heights of considerable stature; In October came the first fall of snow a rock fall, You must reach home before the fall of darkness; We camped upriver from the Niagara Falls; The fall of her hair was very attractive; Increasing manufacturing brought a big fall in unemployment; Poor economy led to the fall of the government.*

Fallacious *(adjective)* containing a fallacy; erroneous: fallacious reasoning. *When you make an argument based on a mistaken belief, then the argument would be described as fallacious.*

Fallacy – *(noun)* **1** a mistaken belief. *An example of fallacy is the idea that the sun spins around the earth.* **2** logic a failure in reasoning which renders an argument invalid. *The notion that camera never lies is a fallacy.*

Fallibility *(adjective)* capable of making a mistake or being deceived, liable to be erroneous or inaccurate. *If your analysis doesn't take all factors into consideration, you only increase your chance of fallibility; The option of the parts is also subject to fallibility.*

Fallible – *(adjective)* capable of making mistakes or being erroneous. *We all human beings are fallible.*

Falling – *(noun)* a dropping, coming down; coming down suddenly from a standing position, downward direction or slope, becoming less or lower, reduction in value. *The dropping of a bird fell on his shirt; The pot fell down into a well; He was feeling unwell and fell down on the road; Be cautious while driving since the road ahead falls into a sharp decline; The value of rupee has fallen in the international market; The food prices have fallen.*

Falsification – *(noun)* any evidence that helps to establish the falsity of something. *The investigation found falsification of records.*

Falsifier – *(noun)* someone who falsifies. *The judge described him as a falsifier of records.*

Falsify – *(verb)* **1** alter so as to mislead. *He made many attempts to falsify her statement.*

Falter – *(verb)* lose strength or momentum. move or speak hesitantly. *Rapid growth of chinese economy is faltering now. When facing an interview board, you must speak clearly, never falter.*

Faltering – *(adjective)* unsteady in speech or action. *Faltering speech will not help you win top prize.*

Fame – *(noun)* the state of being famous. *By dint of sheer labour, he made a name and fame for himself within a short span of time.*

Famulus – *(noun)* [historical] an assistant or servant. *A private secretary or other close attendant, especially during medieval times, was known as famulus.*

Fanatic – *(noun)* a person filled with excessive zeal, especially for an extreme religious or political cause. *A fanatic is a person who has faith is a belief that is not supported by reason.* [informal] a person with an obsessive enthusiasm for a pastime or hobby. *He is a fitness fanatic. (adjective)* filled with or expressing excessive zeal. *His eyes had a fanatic coolness.*

Fanaticism – *(noun)* is extreme devotion or zeal. *An example of fanaticism is following a set of rules even to the extent of killing other individuals.*

Fancied – *(adjective)* imagined. *Despite knowing the opponent was a strong side, we fancied our chances of winning by scoring quick runs.*

Fanciful – *(adjective)* **1** over-imaginative and unrealistic; existing only in the imagination. *Examiners will give you marks only for knowledge, not for your fanciful writing style.* **2** highly ornamental or imaginative in design. *We went to a fanciful Jahangir Art Gallery.*

Fanion – *(noun)* a small flag used by surveyors or soldiers to mark a position. *Every army hoists a fanion to as evidence for a captured post or area.*

Farce – *(noun)* a comic dramatic work or genre using buffoonery and horseplay and typically including ludicrously improbable situations, the debate turned into a drunken farce. *The voting was farce since the supporters of the rival party were prevented from going near the polling booth.*

Farcical – *(adjective)* resembling farce, absurd or ridiculous. *When supporters of rival party are prevented from voting, the eulogy of democracy becomes totally farcical.*

Farina – *(noun)* flour or meal made of cereal grains, nuts, or starchy roots. *Farina is a wholesome meal made from different cereal grains, potatoes, nuts, etc. and eaten as a cooked cereal.*

Farm – *(noun)* an area of land and its buildings used for growing crops and rearing animals, an establishment for breeding or growing something, or devoted to a particular thing; a fish farm, a wind farm. *A farm is a place where dairy cows are raised; A farm is a place where baby fish are raised; Bangladesh has many fish forms. (verb)* **1** make one's living by growing crops or keeping livestock. breed or grow type of livestock or crop commercially. *Marshes are being drained in order to farm the land. The customs has been farmed to the collector for a fixed sum.* **2** arranging for a child to be looked after by someone. *He has farmed organically for years.* **3** [historical] allow someone to collect and keep the revenues from on payment of a fee. *The babies are farmed out for training for five years.*

Farmer – *(noun)* a person who owns or manages a farm. *A person who is primarily concerned with growing crops is called a farmer.*

Farrago – *(noun)* a confused mixture. *There was not one reasonable balanced statement in the whole farrago.*

Farrier – *(noun)* a smith who shoes horses. *Make sure that your horses feet are regularly trimmed and shod, by a competent farrier, to prevent hoof cracks.*

Farrow – *(noun)* a litter of pigs. *Piggeries have a separate farrow house for production of litters even in winter.*

Fart – *(verb)* emit wind from the anus. *Fart is the noise that gas makes when coming from the rear. (noun)* a boring or contemptible person an old fart. *Someone who constantly complains is known as a fart.*

Farthest – *(adjective & adverb)* variant form of FURTHEST. *Within the Solar system, planet Neptune is farthest from the Earth.*

Fascicle – *(noun)* **1** a separately published installment of a book. *The part of a book published prior to publication of complete book is called fascicle.* **2** [anatomy & biology] arrangement in bundles. *In botany, a bundle of stems, flowers, or leaves is called fascicle.*

Fascinate – *(verb)* **1** irresistibly attract the interest of. *With his acting ability Charlie Chaplin could fascinate a global audience for decades.* **2** [archaic] deprive of the ability to resist or escape by the power of a gaze. *The serpent fascinates its prey.*

Fascism – *(noun)* an authoritarian and nationalistic right-wing system of government.*The government led by Benito Mussolini in Italy was an example of fascism.*

Fash – *(verb)* [Scottish] feel upset or worried. *She will be coming soon don't fash anymore.*

Fast – *(verb)* abstain from food or drink, especially as a religious observance. *A fast is a period of time during which you go without food. (noun)* an act or period of fasting. *An example of fast is not eating for twelve hours.*

Fasten – *(verb)* **1** close or do up securely. fix or hold in place. *The airhostess announced to the passengers fasten the seatbelt.* **2** single out and concentrate on it obsessively. *Hold-all was fastened with a leather belt. These days traffic police will charge you if you don't fasten your seatbelt.*

Fastidious – *(adjective)* **1** very attentive to accuracy and detail. *I'm normally very fastidious about citing my sources on this blog.* **2** very concerned about cleanliness. *She is very fastidious about the cleanliness of the house.*

Fasting – *(noun)* abstaining from food.. *Iam fasting.*

Fastness – *(noun)* the ability of a dye to maintain its colour without fading or washing away. *The colour has a smooth gloss finish whilst possessing superior light fastness. Reproduced using the latest technology, these beautiful prints have a potential light fastness of over 200 years.*

Fatal – *(adjective)* causing death. leading to failure or disaster. *The shot in the head proved fatal.*

Fatalism – *(noun)* the belief that all events are predetermined and therefore inevitable. *It's time to shake off the lazy fatalism that the poor will always side with us.*

Fatalist – *(noun)* Anyone who submits to the belief that they are powerless to change their destiny. *adjetyive* of or relating to fatalism.

Fatality *(noun)* **1** an occurrence of death by accident, in war, or from disease. *70 per cent of pedestrian fatalities occur on roads.* **2** helplessness in the face of fate. *A cpital 'a' sense of fatality gripped him.*

Fathom – *(noun)* a unit of length equal to six feet. chiefly used in reference to the depth of water. *The engine shaft is sunk to a depth of 130 fathoms. (verb)* understand after much thought. *In short, scientists have not yet been able to fathom the nature of consciousness, its origins, or its role in nature.*

Fatally – *(adverb)* as determined by fate; inevitably, so as to cause death or disaster; mortally. *He was fatally wounded in the racing car accident; There were two fatal flaws in the strategy.*

Faugh – *(exclamatory)* expressing disgust. *Faugh! This place stinks.*

Fault – *(noun)* **1** a defect or mistake. a service of the ball not in accordance with the rules. *My worst fault is impatience.* **2** responsibility for an accident or misfortune. *It's nobody's fault, it's just one of those things.* **3** [geology] an extended break in a rock formation, marked by the relative displacement and discontinuity of strata. *Earthquakes occur due to fault in plates.* *(verb)* criticize for inadequacy or mistake. [archaic] do wrong.*In this the player lost a point due to double fault. A description of the problem you are having will also help to diagnose the fault. An electrical fault started the blaze, which gutted the shed.*

Faultless – *(adjective)* without any fault or defect; perfect. *She was absolutely faultless at it, never ever making a mistake.*

Faulty – *(adjective)* having or displaying faults. *If goods are deemed faulty they will either be repaired or replaced. Faulty wiring could cause fires or electric shocks, which may end in disaster.*

Favour – *(noun)* **1** approval or liking. overgenerous preferential treatment. *I have sent my request for favour of your approval.* **2** an act of kindness beyond what is due or usual. *Please do them a favour by cleaning their home.* *(verb)* regard or treat with favour. [informal] resemble in facial features. *The student receives unfair favour because he is the captain.*

Favourite – *(adjective)* preferred to all others of the same kind. *My favourite colour is blue as I like it more than any other colour.* *(noun)* **1** a favourite person or thing. *He is a favourite of the secretary.* **2** the competitor thought most likely to win. *India is favourite to win the Champions Trophy.*

Favouritism – *(noun)* the unfair favouring of one person or group at the expense of another. *Favouritism is an act of giving preferential treatment to someone or something.*

Fawn – *(verb)* give a servile display of exaggerated flattery or affection; show slavish devotion especially by rubbing against someone. *The way a young girl acts approvingly towards a boy she likes is called fawn.* *(noun)* a light yellowish brown colour. *Fawn is the name of a winter coat's colour in a catalogue.*

Fealty – *(noun)* [historical] a feudal tenant's or vassal's sworn loyalty to a lord. *I will permit you to till my land for free as long as you pledge fealty to my rule.*

Fear – *(noun)* **1** an unpleasant emotion caused by the threat of danger, pain, or harm. *Fear a feeling of anxiety and worry caused by the presence or nearness of danger, evil, pain, etc.* *(verb)* be afraid of. feel anxiety on behalf of. used to express regret or apology. *I fear the exam results. I fear I have bad news for you.*

Fearful – *(adjective)* showing or causing fear. *I am fearful of that haunted house.*

Fearless – *(adjective)* brave or not scared. *An example of fearless is a fireman's attitude when fighting a fire.*

Feasibility – *(adjective)* capable of being done or carried out. *Feasibility studies indicate that the project is worthwhile and should be executed.*

Feasible – *(adjective)* possible and practical to achieve easily or conveniently. *With deadline extended, it is now feasible to erect the plant shed.*

Feast – *(noun)* **1** a large meal, especially a celebratory one; a plentiful supply of something enjoyable. *An example of a feast is a buffet-style meal.* **2** an annual religious celebration. a day dedicated to a particular saint, [British] an annual village festival. *The feast was the highlight of village year.* *(verb)* eat and drink sumptuously. *An example of feast is to eat six courses of food at a buffet.* give a sumptuous meal to. *The concert offered a feast of classical music.*

Feat – *(noun)* an achievement requiring great courage, skill, or strength. *Sachin Tendulkar is the only cricketer to have achieved the feat of scoring one hundred international centuries.*

Feather – *(noun)* **1** any of the flat appendages growing from a bird's skin, consisting of a partly hollow horny shaft fringed with vanes of barbs. *Birds are able to fly because of feather.* *(verb)* **1** rotating the blades about their own axes in such a way as to lessen the air or water resistance. rowing turn so that it passes through the air edge ways. *The actors came of the stage, dolled* *up in ostrich feathers and pearls.* **2** covered or decorated with feathers. *He turned, feathering one our slowly. The vase can be decorated with duck or goose feather.*

Feathery – *(adjective)* **1** resembling or suggesting a feather or feathers.*The mannequin had a feathered blonde hair.* **2** Characterized by a covering of feathers. **3** Adorned with feathers or plumes

Feature – *(noun)* **1** a distinctive attribute or aspect of something. a part of the face, such as the mouth, making a significant contribution to its overall appearance. *This house has many decoration feature. Most important feature of her face is her nose.* **2** a newspaper or magazine article or a broadcast programme devoted to a particular topic. a full-light film intended as the main item in a cinema programme. *A feature is a distinct or outstanding characteristic on the editorial page.* *(verb)* have as an important actor or participant. be feature of or take an important part in. *The play featured two well-known actors from Mumbai.*

Febrile – *(adjective)* having or showing the symptoms of a fever. *Febrile describes a person who has a fever or has something caused by a fever.*

Feculent – *(adjective)* of or containing dirt, sediment, or waste matter. *The article you have written is not original, it is rubbish and feculent.*

Fecund – *(adjective)* highly fertile; able to produce offspring. *A woman who can get pregnant is an example of someone who would be described as fecund.*

Fecundate – *(verb)* [archaic] fertilize. [poetic/ literary] make fruitful. *There are no insects to fecundate flowering plants.*

Fecundity – *(noun)* The intellectual productivity of a creative imagination. The state of being fertile; capable of producing offspring. The quality of something that causes or assists healthy growth. *The property of producing offspring is known as fecundity.*

Federal – *(adjective)* having or relating to a system of government in which several states form a unity but remain independent in internal affairs. relating to or denoting the central government as distinguished from the separate units constituting a federation. *The constitution describes India as a unitary government with federal features.*

Federate – *(verb)* organize or be orgainzed on a federal basis. *To federate means to unite various parts by common agreement under a central authority.* *(adjective)* of or relating to such an arrangement. *World war II was fought primarily between two federating armies.*

Federation – *(noun)* a federal group of states. an organization within which smaller divisions have some degree of internal autonomy. *The United States is an example of federation.*

Federative *(adjective)* united under a central government. *Six colonies Australia joined together and became a federation unit in 1901.* *(verb)* unite on a federal basis or band together as a league.

Feeble – *(adjective)* lacking physical strength; lacking strength of character. falling to convince or impress. *The doctors made feeble attempts to revive the poor patient.*

Feed – *(verb)* **1** give food to, provide an adequate supply of food for. *Did you feed the cot?* **2** eat derive regular nourishment from a particular substance. *The birds feed on vegetations.* **3** supply with food material, power, water, etc. prompt with a line. *The islands agricultive could hardly feed its inhabetants.* **4** produce feedback. *I want the feed back on the tour you undertook.* *(noun)* **1** an act of feeding or of being fed, food for domestic animals. *The crops are grown for animal feed.* **2** a device or pipe for supplying material to a machine. the supply of raw material to a machine or device. *This pipe feeds the machine with paper pulp.* **3** a prompt given to an actor on stage. *The prompt given to an actor on stage is known as feed.*

Feel – *(verb)* **1** perceive, examine, or search by touch. be aware of through physical sensation. give a sensation of a particular physical quality when touched: the wool feels soft. **2** experience an emotion or sensation. consider oneself: he doesn't feel obliged to visit. **3** have a belief or impression, especially without an identifiable reason. *An example of feel is when you run your hand over a dress. An example of feel is when you make your way into your study room in the dark by touching various things in the house. The wool feels soft. (noun)* an act or feeling. the sense of touch. *Feel is the perception or sensation of something or the sense of touch.*

Feeling – *(noun)* **1** an emotional state or reaction. emotional responses or tendencies to respond. strong emotion. *Feeling is the act of sensing that the surface of something is smooth because you touched it.* **2** a belief or opinion. *Feeling is the sense of happiness.* **3** the capacity to feel. the sensation of touching or being touched. **4** a sensitivity to or intuitive understanding of. *A feeling of joy envelops you when you meet old friends me felt the justice has not been done. (adjective)* showing emotion or sensitivity. *Music can convey your feeling without the use of words.*

Feign – *(verb)* pretend to be affected by a feeling, state, or injury. *Don't feign sickness in a feeble attempt to get your sister to mop the floor.*

Felicitate – *(verb)* rare congratulate. *I felicitate you on your marriage day.*

Felicitous – *(adjective)* well chosen or appropriate, pleasing. *The author writes felicitous lines that show a genuine poetic touch.*

Felicity – *(noun)* the ability to express oneself appropriately; a felicitous feature of a work of literature or art. *Some seek their rest and happiness on earth, others eternal felicity in heaven.*

Feline – *(adjective)* or, relating to, or resembling a cat. *She is feline. (noun)* a cat or other animal of the cat family. *A feline is an animal that belongs to the cat family.*

Fell – *(verb)* To fell is to knock down. Fell is also the past tense of "fall" and means that you have fallen down. *When you are standing upright and then you fall down, this is an example of a situation where you fell.*

Felony – *(noun)* a crime, typically one involving violence, regarded in the US and other judicial systems as more serious than a misdemeanour. *An example of felony is rape.*

Felspar – *(noun)* variant spelling of felospar. *Felspar is an ore containing silicate of iron.*

Felt – *(noun)* cloth made by rolling and pressing wool or another suitable textile accompanied by the application of moisture or heat, which causes the fibres to mat together. *Felt cap as a head gear is very popular among cow boys. (verb)* means to have had a feeling. *Felt is an example of sense of feeling one gets when another person touches his arm.*

Female – *(adjective)* **1** of or denoting the sex that can bear off spring or produce egg, relating to or characteristic of woman or female animal of a plant and or flower having a pistil but no stamens. *All actors in the concert were female. Female part of a flower is knows as pisted.* **2** of a fitting manufactured hollow so that a corresponding male part can be inserted; a person, animal or a plant having reproductive structure containing eggs that can be fertilized by sperms is called the female. *Male plugs are inserted into female plugs. (noun)* a female person, animal or plant. *A herd of female deer just crossed the road.*

Feminine – *(adjective)* **1** having qualities traditionally associated with woman, especially delicacy and prettiness. female. **2** [Grammar] of or denoting a gender of nouns and adjectives, conventionally regarded as female. *Sewing and cooking are examples of hobbies that were traditionally described as feminine hobbies. Soft pink dresses are an example of clothes that would be described as feminine clothes. (noun)* (the feminine) the female sex or gender. *An example of feminine is the female sex.*

Feminize – *(verb)* make more feminine or female. *To feminize is to make or become feminine or effeminate.*

Femur – *(noun)* **1** [anatomy] the bone of the thigh or upper hind limb. *The bone in your body that goes from your pelvis to your knee is known as femur.* **2** [Zoology] the third segment of the leg in insects and some other arthropods. *Femur is the longest segment of an insect's leg.*

Fen – *(noun)* a low and marshy or frequently flooded area of land. *Low, flat, marshy and swampy land is known as fen.*

Fence – *(noun)* **1** a barrier enclosing an area, typically consisting of posts connected by wire, wood, etc. a large upright obstacle in steeplechasing, showjumping, or cross-country. *An example of a fence is a two foot wooden barrier around a person's front yard. (verb)* **1** surround or protect with a fence. enclose or separate an area with a fence. *Our garden is fully feneed.* **2** conduct a discussion or argument in an evasive way. *His arguments are never to the point always fenced.*

Fencing – *(noun)* **1** the sport of fighting with blunted swords according to a set of rules in order to score points. *Fencing is a popular sporting event at Olympic games.* **2** a series of fences. material for making fences. *A small plantation of young trees is protected with steel fencing.*

Fenestra – *(noun)* **1** [anatomy & zoology] a small hole or opening in a bone, especially either of two in the middle ear. *Fenestra is a small opening in the inner wall of the middle ear.* **2** [medicine] an artificial opening, especially one made by fenestration. *An opening made in a bandage is known as fenestra.*

Fennel – *(noun)* an aromatic yellow-flowered plant of the parsley family, with feathery leaves used as culinary herbs or eaten as a vegetable. *Fennel is a tall herb with feathery leaves and yellow flowers whose foliage and aromatic seeds are used to flavour foods.*

Feral – *(adjective)* **1** of an animal or plant in a wild state, especially after having been domesticated or cultivated, a feral snarl. *A feral is an undomesticated cat that scratches and claws if you come near it.*

Ferment – *(verb)* undergo or cause to undergo fermentation. *(noun)* **1** agitation and social unrest. **2** dated a fermenting agent or enzyme. a substance or organism causing fermentation, as yeast, bacteria, enzymes, etc. *Ferment is an agent or catalyst, such as, yeast, bacterium, mold, or enzyme that cause fermentation. Warlords often ferment choos among different communities.*

Fern – *(noun)* a flowerless vascular plant which has feathery or leafy fronds and reproduces by spores released from the undersides of the fronds. *Ferns have a system for transport of water and nutrients to the whole plant.*

Ferocious – *(adjective)* **1** savagely fierce, cruel, or violent. *While in a zoo, you must be cautious against ferocious animals.* **2** [informal] very great; extreme. *Ferocious winds uprooted many trees and electric poles.*

Ferocity – *(noun)* the state of being wild or fierce. *The extreme and wild nature of a storm is an example of the ferocity of the storm.*

Ferriage – *(noun)* charge for transportation by ferry. *What is the ferriage for crossing the river?*

Ferric – *(adjective)* [chemistry] of iron with a valence of three; of iron. *Ferric oxide is one of the chemical compounds containing iron.*

Ferrous – *(adjective)* **1** chiefly or metals containing or consisting of iron. **2** chemistry of iron with a valence of two; of iron. *Ferrous oxide is one of the chemical compounds containing iron.*

Ferrule – *(noun)* a ring or cap which strengthens the end of a handle, stick, or tube. a metal band strengthening or forming a joint. *Ferrule is a metal or plastic ring or cap put around the end of a cane, tool handle, etc. to give added strength or for tightening a joint.*

Fertilize – *(verb)* **1** cause to develop a new individual by introducing male reproductive material. *To fertilize is to make the female reproductive cell fruitful by impregnating with the male gamete.* **2** make more fertile by adding fertilizer. *Urea, phosphates and nitrates help fertilize soil for increased productivity.*

Ferule – *(noun)* -a flat ruler used for punishing children. *Ferule is an instrument, such as a cane, stick, or flat piece of wood, used in punishing children.*

Fervency – *(noun)* feelings of great warmth and intensity. *She has tremendous fervency towards old and the needy.*

Fervent – *(adjective)* intensely passionate. *It is my fervent appeal to allow me 15 days leave.*

Fervid – *(adjective)* intensely enthusiastic, especially to an excessive degree. *He is a fervid* *patriot and won't mind dying for the good of the motherland.*

Fervour - *(noun)* intense and passionate feeling. *Fervour is intense feelings or passion at a higher degree.*

Festal - *(adjective)* relating to a festival; festive. *Pudding is served on festival days after main food.*

Fester - *(verb)* **1** of a wound or sore become septic. become rotten. *When food is left out for days to rot, the food festers and becomes unfit for consumption.*

Festival - *(noun)* **1** a day or period of celebration, typically for religious reasons. *Deepawali is a festival of great pomp and show.* **2** an organized series of concerts, films etc., typically one held annually in the same place. *A major international festival of song has been organised.*

Festivity - *(noun)* joyful and exuberant celebration. celebratory activities or events. *A week or so before Deepawali, the atmosphere acquires the look of festivity everywhere.*

Fetch - *(verb)* To come or go after and take or bring back. *The puppy went to fetch the stick that we had tossed.*

Fetching - *(adjective)* attractive. *A fetching little garment.*

Fete - *(noun)* British an outdoor public function to raise funds for a charity or institution, typically involving entertainment and the sale of goods. *An example of a fete is a school carnival. (verb)* honour or entertain lavishly. *The visiting team was feted lavishly with honour, entertainment and gifts.*

Feticide - *(noun)* destruction or abortion of a fetus. *Cases of female feticide is on the rise in some parts of India.*

Fetid - *(adjective)* smelling unpleasant. *The spoiled food is an example of something that might be described as fetid.*

Fettle - *(noun)* condition. *Every jockey wants to keep his racing horse in fine fettle. She was in great fettle, bouncing all over the place.*

Fetus - *(noun)* an unborn or unhitched offspring of a mammal, in particular an unborn human more than eight weeks after conception. *A baby that has been in its mother's stomach growing for 18 weeks is an example of a fetus.*

Feudal - *(adjective)* according to, resembling, or denoting the system of feudalism. *Early developments were really about the maintenance of political power, essentially feudal in origin.*

Feudatory - *(adjective)* owing feudal allegiance to. *It is a feudatory state. (noun)* a person who held land under the feudal system. *He is a feudatory.*

Fever - *(noun)* **1** an abnormally high body temperature, usually accompanied by shivering, headache, and in severe instances, delirium. *He was running a temperature of 103 degree fahrenheit.* **2** a state of nervous excitement or agitation. *With India, Australia test series begening soon cricket fever has returned to India. (verb)* having or showing the symptoms of fever. *Health experts have known about dengue fever for more than 200 years.*

Feverish - *(adjective)* someone whose temperature is too high, or someone who is greatly excited or has high energy. *A person who has a body temperature of 102 is an example of someone who is feverish. A crowd that is shouting and yelling because their team is winning is an example of a crowd that would be described as feverish.*

Fiasco - *(noun)* a ludicrous or humiliating failure. *The party ended in a fiasco since the clown hired to entertain broke his leg and has threatened to sue the organizer.*

Fibril - *(noun)* [technical] a small or slender fibre. *Electron microscope is needed to observe the fibril formation.*

Fibrous - *(adjective)* consisting of or characterized by fibres. *When this dust is inhaled it can make the lungs gradually fibrous and lead to breathing problems.*

Fickle - *(adjective)* changeable, especially as regards one's loyalties. *Children are very fickle minded and move to new toys because of their short attention span.*

Fiction - *(noun)* prose literature, especially novels, describing imaginary events and people. *Publishers are coming out with fiction that is meant for children.*

Fictitious - *(adjective)* not real or true, being imaginary or invented. *Many authors use fictitious names instead of their original ones.*

Fiddle - *(noun)* **1** [informal], chiefly British an act of fraud or cheating. *An example of to fiddle is to pick up and rob a piece of jewellery at a jewellery store.* **2** [informal] an unnecessarily intricate or awkward task. *A major land grabbiing has fiddle has occured hene. (verb)* [informal] touch or fidget with something restlessly or nervously. *Don't fiddle with the items set out on the table.*

Fiddler *(noun)* **1** musician who plays the violin. *A person who plays violin especially in a folk music is known as fiddler.* **2** Someone who manipulates in a nervous or unconscious manner. *He is a fiddler quite likely to fudge accounts.* **3** An unskilled person who tries to fix or mend. *He is a fiddler and tries to hide this faults.*

Fidding - *(adjective)* [informal] annoyingly trivial. *Stop fidding things you don't know about.*

Fidelity - *(noun)* **1** continuing loyalty to a person, cause, or belief. **2** the degree of exactness with which something is copied or reproduced. *Fidelity is faithful devotion to duty or to one's obligations; Fidelity represents accuracy of the reproduction of sound, an image, etc transmitted electronically.*

Fidget - *(verb)* make small movements through nervousness or impatience. *He fidgeted with his notes while lecturing. (noun)* a person who fidgets. an act of fidgeting. mental or physical restlessness. *Fidget is a condition of restlessness characterized by nervous movements of body or hands.*

Fie - *(interjection)* [archaic] humour used to express disgust or outrage. *Any exclamatory expression used to denote distaste or disapproval is known as fie.*

Fiend - *(noun)* [informal] an enthusiast or devotee: a jazz fiend. *He is so obsessed with crosswords that people call him a crossword fiend.*

Fiendish - *(adjective)* extremely cruel or unpleasant, extremely difficult. *Regular expressions can get quite fiendish to read at times.*

Fierce - *(adjective)* violent or aggressive, ferocious. *Fierce fighting broke out again between India and Pakistan.*

Fiery - *(adjective)* **1** resembling or consisting of fire. **2** quick-tempered or passionate. *He was high-spirited and had a very fiery temper, which led him at times is to acts of cruelty.*

Fife - *(noun)* a kind of small shrill flute used with the drum in military bands. *A small flute with a high, piercing tone, used mainly in military bands.*

Fifteen - *(cardinal number)* equivalent to the product of three and five; one more than fourteen; 15 classified as suitable for people of 15 years and over. *Fifteen is a sum of five and ten.*

Fifth- (*cardinal number*) 1constituting number five in a sequence; *5th He was born in the fifth century BC; Her mother had just given birth to her fifth child; Venezuela is the world's fifth-largest oil exporter; The fifth of November 2012.* the fifth finisher or position in a race or competition *He finished fifth in the 100 metre race.* (in some vehicles) the fifth (and typically highest) in a sequence of gears *In my panic I changed the gear straight from third to fifth.* [Music] an interval spanning five consecutive notes in a diatonic scale. *The note which is higher by a fifth than the root of a diatonic scale.*

Fight - (*verb*) **1** take part in a violent struggle involving the exchange of physical blows or the use of weapons: *The men were fighting protesters fought with police.* engage in a war or battle: *The country is still fighting a civil war* quarrel or argue: *They were fighting over who pays the bill.* **2** struggle to overcome, eliminate, or prevent: *The Company intends to fight the decision.* strive to achieve or do something: *Doctors fought to save his life* attempt to repress a feeling or its expression): *She had to fight back tears of frustration.* (fight one's way) move forward with difficulty, especially by pushing through a crowd: She watched him fight his way across the room. (*noun*) a violent confrontation or struggle: *He'd got into a fight with some ruffians outside a club* a battle or war: *America helped Britain fight against Germany.* a vigorous struggle or campaign for or against something: *He had a long but successful fight against cancer.*

Fighter – *(noun)* **1** a person or animal that fights. *India has decided to purchase 126 Rafael fighter jets from France.* **2** a fast military aircraft designed for attacking other aircraft. *There will be months of treatment but doctors say he is a fighter.*

Fighting – *(noun)* combat, battle. *Fighting broke out between rival forces.* *(adjective)* militant, combative, warlike. *Do you think fighting in the dressing room will help good performance on the field?*

Figment – *(noun)* a thing believed to be real but existing only in the imagination. *Novels are nothing but the figment of an author's imagination.*

Figurative – *(adjective)* departing from a literal use of words; metaphorical, art representing forms that are recognizably derived from life. *We haven't taken on new artists for some years, however mainly figurative artists would be considered.*

Figurine – *(noun)* a small statue of a human form. *Figurines of a goddess have also been excavated by the archeologists.*

Filament – *(noun)* **1** a slender thread-like object or fibre, especially one found in animal or plant structures. *A type of intermediate filament found in epithelial cells have been created in the laboratory.* **2** a metal wire in an electric light bulb, made incandescent by an electric current. *A few decades ago a new design for tungsten filament lamps appeared on the scene.*

Filature – *(noun)* a place where silk thread is obtained from silkworm cocoons. *Filature is a reel of raw silk obtained from cocoons of silkworm.*

Filch – *(verb)* [informal] pilfer; steal. *The thief filched the purse and ran away into hiding.*

Filiform – *(adjective)* [Biology] thread-like. *In botany, filiform is a term used to describe leaf-shapes.*

Filling – *(noun)* **1** a quantity or place of material that fills or is used to fill something. *I have got dental fillings done for Rupees two thousand.* *(adjective)* leaving one with a pleasantly satiated feeling. *Her success filled her father with enormous satisfaction.*

Fillip – *(noun)* a stimulus or boost. *The pep talk by the coach acted as a fillip to the team's sagging morale.* *(verb)* [archaic] propel with a flick of the fingers. *Ramesh filliped his finger against my right ear.*

Filly – *(noun)* a young female horse, especially one less than four years old. *He bought a lovely 3-year old filly with a view to train her for horse racing.*

Filmy – *(adjective)* especially of fabric thin and translucent. *Filmy fern grows along the banks of the River Ravi as it runs through the hills.*

Filth – *(noun)* disgusting dirt. obscene and offensive language or printed material. *We simply didn't expect to see such filth at the family shopping store. You must stop using filthy language.*

Filthy – *(adjective)* disgustingly dirty. obscene and offensive. [British informal] very unpleasant. informal very disagreeable. *The language these college students use is pretty filthy.* *(adverb)* informal extremely: filthy rich. *He displays wealth to the point of being filthy.*

Filtrate – *(noun)* a liquid which has passed through a filter. *The liquid obtained after passing through the filter is known as filtrate.* *(verb)* rare filter. *Is this area watered out or are you producing mud filtrate?*

Fin – *(noun)* **1** a flattened appendage on the body of a fish or other aquatic animal, used for propelling, steering, and balancing. *Fin is an organ attached to a fish's body that helps them in swimming under water.* *(verb)* swim under water by means of flippers. *Divers make use of fins to swim under water.*

Final – *(adjective)* **1** coming at the end of a series. reached as the outcome of a process: *The final cost will run into six figures.* **2** allowing no further doubt or dispute. *The final chapter of the book was quite absorbing.* *(noun)* **1** the last game in a sports tournament or other competition, which will decide the winner. *India and England team reached the final of the World Cup.* **2** [music] the principal note in a mode. *The to nice note of a church mode is final.* **3** [British] a series of examinations at the end of a degree course. *She was doing her history finals.*

Finale - *(noun)* the last part of a place of music, an entertainment, or a public event. *The grand finale will end with a fabulous firework display over the stadium.*

Finance - *(noun)* the management of large amounts of money, especially by governments or large companies. monetary support for an enterprise. the monetary resources and affairs of a state, organization, or person. *Finance minister of India has imposed a severe squeeze on the Indian economy. (verb)* provide funding for. *Asian Development Bank has agreed to finance this hydro-electric project.*

Finch - *(noun)* a seed-eating songbird of a large group including the chaffinch, goldfinch, linner, etc., typically with a stout bill and colourful plumage. *Australian finches are very engaging little birds which can provide many hours of enjoyment.*

Fine - *(noun)* a sum of money dicided as a penalty by a court of [Law] or other authority. *This restaurant is renowned for fine dining, shopping and cafés. (verb)* punish by a fine. *People who do not pay fines or costs ordered by a court go to jail - there is no option.*

Finery - *(noun)* elaborate decoration (dress). *Arrive in your own finery or choose from a wide selection of our costumes.*

Fingering - *(noun)* handling with fingers, a manner or technique of using the fingers to play a musical instrument. *The main difficulty is that for a number of instruments there is no standard fingering.*

Finial - *(noun)* a distinctive section or ornament at the apex of a roof, pinnacle, or similar structure in a building. an ornament at the top, end, or corner of an object. *Attach a narrow wrought iron curtain rod with decorative finials to the wall. There were ornate curtain poles with decorative finials.*

Finical - *(adjective)* another term for PINICKY. *He is a finical person; his attitude is prone to change any moment.*

Finis - *(noun)* the end. *Hem lines are elegantly long with the subtle tailoring and immaculate finis to the skirt.*

Finite - *(adjective)* **1** limited in size or extent. *Although electricity travels fast, its speed is still finite and over a wire it is slower than in a vacuum.* **2** [Grammar] having a specific tense, number, and person. *Your sentence should couvey a finite meaning.*

Fir - *(noun)* an evergreen coniferous tree with upright cones and flat needle-shaped leaves. *Fir trees are extensively found in Kashmir.*

First - ordinal number **1** coming before all others in time or order; earliest; 1st. before doing something else specified or implied. *He came to the city for the first time.* with a specified par in a leading position: *It plunged nose first into the river.* **2** foremost in position, rank, or importance. *He is first among equals.* **3** [informal] something never previously achieved or occurring. *Sachin Tendulkar is the first person to make one hundred international centuries.* **4** British a place in the top grade in an examination for a degree. *He came first in the examination.*

Fiscal - *(adjective)* of or relating to government revenue, especially taxes. *The deficit for fiscal 2012. Fiscal tightening is needed to keep the budgetary deficit under control.*

Fish - *(noun)* **1** animal linging isn sea and used as food. **2** a flat plate fixed on a beam or across a joint to give additional strength. *You should try not to have more than two portions of oily fish a week. The girder was strengthened with the help of fish plates. (verb)* **1** strengthen or mend with a fish. **2** join with a fishplate. *Fish farming can offer a rewarding career. Railway lines are joined with fist plates.*

Fish-plate - *(noun)* a flat piece of metal used to connect adjacent rails in a railway track. *Fish-plates are used to strengthen railway tracks.*

Fission - *(noun)* the action of splitting or being split into two or more parts, a reaction in which a heavy atomic nucleus splits in two, releasing much end viding into two or more new cells or organisms. *Nuclear fission is what powers all modern day reactors. (verb)* undergo fission. *Nuclear energy is released through a process called nuclear fission.*

Fissure – *(noun)* **1** a long, narrow crack. **2** a state of division or disagreement. *Fissure sealant has been introduced to the dental market. Many fissures are created in the society by religious differences.*

Fist – *(noun)* a person's hand when the fingers are bent in towards the palm and held there tightly. *He unclenched his fist to shake hands with the visitor.*

Fisticuffs – *(plural)* fighting with the fists. *Fighting with the fists is called fisticuffs.*

Fistula – *(noun)* narrow passage, opening. *Patients who have a fistula can usually feel it "buzzing "slightly.*

Fitness – *(noun)* **1** the state of being fit. **2** [Biology] an organism's ability to survive and reproduce in a particular environment. *Running, cycling, swimming etc can all raise your body fitness. If sharp teeth increase fitness then genes causing teeth to be sharp will increase in frequency.*

Fitter – *(noun)* one who fits, tailor. *All electrical appliances should be repaired by a qualified, registered electrical fitter.*

Fittings – *(noun)* an attachment, items which are fixed in a building but can be removed when the owner moves, the action of fitting or being fitted. *This house comes with all fittings made of stainless steel. (adjective)* **1** appropriate; right or proper. **2** loose fitting trousers. *The shower fittings have been fixed very clumsily. This pair of trousers has poor fitting.*

Five – *(cardinal number)* equivalent to the sum of two and three; one more than four, or half of ten; 5 *Twenty divided by four is five.*

Fix – *(verb)* **1** attach or position securely. direct or be directed unwaveringly toward. **2** decide or settle on. **3** repair or restore. *Charges have been fixed in accordance with building regulations. Four o'clock has been fixed for the commencement of play. Please fix the attachment with epoxy adhesive to ensure they stayed on. (noun)* an act of fixing. *All fixing screws are properly concealed.*

Fixable – *(adjective)* can be fixed *All these appliances are fixable on any side of the wall.*

Fixation – *(noun)* the action or condition of fixating or being fixated, the action or process of fixing or being fixed, especially chemically or biologically. *Fixation of fractures is commonly used in many areas of trauma care.*

Fixative – *(noun)* a substance used to fix, protect, or stabilize something. *Some people find that using a denture fixative in the early stages gives them extra security. (adjective)* used in such a way. *Fixative spray is available in spray cans, or for use with mouth atomizer.*

Fixed – *(adjective)* set firmly in place, protected. *Social systems are not fixed and unchanging, even when they are relatively stable.*

Fixity – *(noun)* the state of being unchanging or permanent. *The fixity of his stave was unwavering.*

Fixture – *(noun)* **1** a piece of equipment or furniture which is fixed in position in a building or vehicle. articles attached to a house or land and considered legally part of it so that they normally remain in place when an owner moves, compare with fitting. **2** [informal] a person or thing that has become established in a particular place. *It appeared to be constructed like today's plumbing fixtures. Provisional details of the forthcoming fixtures are listed below.*

Fizzle – *(verb)* make a feeble hissing or spluttering sound. end or fail in a weak or disappointing way. *Despite a hopeful beginning, Indian batting fizzled out weakly. (noun)* an instance of fizzling. *In the end, the fire works were a fizzle.*

Flageolet – *(noun)* **1** a very small flute-like instrument resembling a recorder but with four finger holes on top and two thumb holes below. *A flageolet is a small flutelike instrument with a cylindrical mouthpiece, four finger holes, and two thumb holes.*

Flagon – *(noun)* a large container for serving or consuming drinks. a container used to hold the wine for Eucharist. a large bottle in which wine or cider is sold, typically holding 113 litres. *A flagon is a large vessel with a handle and spout and often a lid, used for holding wine or other liquors.*

Flagrant – *(adjective)* conspicuous, blatant. *The draconian order issued is a flagrant misuse of bureaucratic power.*

Flail – *(noun)* a threshing tool consisting of a wooden staff with a short heavy stick swinging from it. a similar device used as a weapon or for flogging. a machine having a similar action. *An example of a flail is a tool used to toss grain up in the air. (verb)* swing or cause to swing wildly. *Flailing about in an attempt to swim he hit his head on something hard.*

Flair – *(noun)* a natural ability or talent, stylishness. *He possesses that natural flair for journalism without which no one will succeed in the news media.*

Flam – *(noun)* music one of the basic patterns of drumming, consisting of a stroke preceded by a grace note. *Flam is a double drumbeat where first note is a short and the second a long one.*

Flame – *(noun)* **1** a hot glowing body of ignited gas that is generated by something on fire, a thing compared to a flame's ability to burn fiercely, a brilliant orange-red colour. *Flame is a zone of burning gases and fine suspended matter associated with rapid combustion. (verb)* give off flames. apply a flame to; set alight, appear suddenly and fiercely. *Only a handful of companies have flamed out in the two decades since the birth of the biotech industry.*

Flamingo – *(noun)* a tail wading bird with mainly pink or scarlet plumage, long legs and neck, and a crooked bill. *In the wild, flamingoes breed in very large numbers on salt or soda lakes.*

Flange – *(noun)* a projecting rim or piece. *I knew something was wrong when the brake drum and hub flange came off still attached to the wheel.*

Flank – *(noun)* **1** the side of a person's or animal's body between the ribs and the hip. **2** the side of something such as a building or mountain, or a gaming area. **3** the left or right side of a body of people. *Area between the ribs and hip of human or animal is known as flank. Huge trees flank the left and right side of the building. (verb)* be situated on each or on one side of. *America is doing everything to prevent the invasion of the eastern flank of the Middle East by Israel.*

Flanker – *(noun)* **1** foot ball a wing forward. *Bhutia has played number eleven as open side flanker for most of the games.*

Flannel – *(noun)* a kind of soft-woven woollen or cotton fabric that is slightly milled and raised, men's trousers made of woollen flannel. *I like to wear flannel shirts and trousers rather than expensive designer suits.*

Flannelette – *(noun)* a napped cotton fabric resembling flannel. *Flannelette is a soft cotton fabric with a nap.*

Flaring – *(adjective)* burning, curving outward *Flaring of trousers at the bottom is no longer in fashion.*

Flash – *(verb)* burst forth into or as if into flame, give off light or be lighted in sudden or intermittent bursts, appear or occur suddenly *The image flashed onto the screen. Rescue flashed on us the time we got caught in the storm. The cars flashed by while we were waiting.*

Flashy – *(adjective)* ostentatiously stylish. *I don't want anything too flashy like a Ferrari or a Bentley.*

Flask – *(noun)* a narrow-necked conical or spherical bottle, British a vacuum flask. *A thermos flask allows hot drinks to be carried.*

Flat – *(noun)* chiefly British a set of rooms comprising an individual place of residence within a larger building. *High-rise flats were to be built in the inner zone. (verb)* austral live in or share a flat. *To help her children, she moved into a self-contained flat at the top of the house.*

Flattish – *(adjective)* fairly flat. *The spinners were hammered for six and fours because of bowling a flattish deliveries.*

Flatulence – *(noun)* accumulation of gas in the stomach, emptiness *Flatulence is the expulsion of mixed gases from the body, which are the byproduct of the digestion process.*

Flatus – *(noun)* formal gas in or from the stomach or intestines. *The medical term for mixture of gases formed as a byproduct of digestion process is known as flatus.*

Flaunt – *(verb)* display ostentatiously. *There is no justification to flaunt your wealth among the poor people.*

Flavour - *(noun)* the distinctive taste of a food or drink, a quality reminiscent of something specified; a European flavour, a sample of the distinctive quality of something. *Flavoured coffees from around the world is available in this hotel.* *(verb)* give flavour to. *These foods also have the ability to enhance the flavour of our cooking.*

Flax - *(noun)* a blue-flowered herbaceous plant that is cultivated for its seed and for textile fibre made from its stalks. textile fibre obtained from this plant. *Linen is made out of the natural fibre flax.*

Flay - *(verb)* **1** strip the skin from a body of carcass, whip or beat harshly, criticize harshly. *It is demoralizing for a person to be flayed in front of many people.*

Fledge - *(verb)* develop or allow to develop wing feathers that are large enough for flight. *The now fledged chicks have to undertake the first migration on their own.*

Flee - *(verb)* run away. *They were fleeing the country in fear of persecution.*

Fleece - *(noun)* the wool coat of a sheep, a soft, warm fabric with a texture similar to sheep's wool, or a garment made from this. *Fleece lining made of long wool keeps the skin warm during winter.* *(verb)* [informal] obtain an unfair amount of money from. *There is no dearth of traders fleecing unsuspecting customers by selling inferior products.*

Fleer - *(verb)* laugh impudently or jeeringly. *Why fleer at someone who is yet to be trained for the job?* *(noun)* [archaic] an impudent or jeering look or speach. *The Fleer Company was the first to successfully manufacture bubblegum.*

Flesh - *(noun)* **1** the soft substance in the body consisting of muscle tissue and fat. **2** the edible pulpy part of a fruit or vegetable. *Future generations will scarcely believe such a person like Mahatma Gandhi ever walked in flesh and blood on this Earth. Flesh is the semi solid part of vegetables which breaks up during cooking.* *(verb)* **1** make more substantial. **2** give a hound or hawk a piece of flesh in order or stimulate it to hunt. **3** remove the flesh from a hide. **4** [poetic/literary] initiate in bloodshed or warfare. *Eating the flesh of fruits is a common practice throughout the world.*

Fletch - *(verb)* provide an arrow with feathers. *He fletched the arrow.*

Fletcher - *(noun)* chiefly historical a person who makes and sells arrows. *Fletcher is a person who sells bows and arrows.*

Flex - *(verb)* warp or bend and then revert to shape. *Exercise helps keep the muscles and joints flexed.*

Flexile - *(adjective)* [archaic] pliant and flexible. *Within these snow-beds the flexible fern occurs.*

Flexion - *(noun)* the action of bending or the condition of being bent. *This exercise involves the flexion and extension of the lower back.*

Flexor - *(noun)* anatomy a muscle whose contraction bends a limb or other part of the body. *These exercises can make only a limited contribution to strengthening the flexors.*

Flexuous - *(adjective)* full of bends and curves. *Hundreds of miles of arteries and veins adjust inside the body because of their flexuous nature.*

Flick - *(noun)* **1** a sudden smart movement with fingers. **2** [informal] a cinema film. the cinema. *He flicked some ash off his shirt me are going to see a flick.* *(verb)* **1** make or cause to make a sudden sharp movement. **2** look quickly through a volume or a collection of papers. *Flicking the ash from cigarettes is a common habit of smokers. He flecked through the book in five minutes.*

Flicker - *(verb)* shine or burn unsteadily and fitfully. *Flicker of the burning candle was finally snuffed out.* *(noun)* an instance of flickering. *We plan to have dinner in the flickering candlelight.*

Flier - *(noun)* person or thing which flies, a small advertisement *Bring your own kite or marvel at displays by the best kite fliers in the country. We have been distributing fliers all over the place.*

Flimsy - *(adjective)* weak and insubstantial, light and thin, weak; unconvincing. *Don't come out with such flimsy reasons to stay away from the college.* *(noun)* very thin paper, a copy of a document, produced on very thin paper. *He produced such an important document on a thin, flimsy paper.*

Flinch – *(verb)* make a quick, nervous movement as an instinctive reaction to fear or pain, avoid through fear or anxiety. *Never flinch from your objective in the face of any difficulties.*

Flippancy – *(noun)* quality or state of being flippant *You need to answer your absence with a little less flippancy this time.*

Flippant – *(adjective)* not showing a serious or respectful attitude. *How can you be so flippant about shattering people's lives and dreams?*

Flipper – *(noun)* **1** a broad, flat limb, without fingers, used for swimming by sea animals such as seals, whales, and turtles. **2** a flat rubber attachment worn on the foot for underwater swimming. *Seals use their front flippers for moving on land and hind limbs for swimming in water; Scuba divers use flippers while moving inside the river.*

Flit – *(verb)* move swiftly and lightly. *A butterfly was flitting nearby and disturbing me during studies.* *(noun)* [British informal] an act of leaving one's home in secrecy. *He flitted out of rented house at night noiselessly and without informing the landlord.*

Flitter – *(verb)* move quickly in a random manner. *The flittering of the butterfly around the table was disturbing my study.* *(noun)* a flittering movement. *Watching butterflies flitter is good for our eyes.*

Float – *(verb)* **1** rest or cause to rest on the surface of a liquid without sinking. **2** be suspended freely in a liquid or gas. **3** move slowly or hover in a liquid or the air. **4** make travel lightly and effortlessly through the air. **5** put forward as a suggestion or test of reactions. **6** fluctuate or allow to fluctuate freely in value. *Wooden logs can float on water. Helicopters have the capability to keep floating in the air without going forward. Floating on the surface of the water, can you reach the gems lying at the bottom of the sea? Aerial ropeways help you float through the mountains quickly. he floated his opinion to govern other reactions. Rupee is not a floating currency.* *(noun)* **1** any hollow or lightweight object or device used to achieve buoyancy in water. **2** a small floating object attached to a fishing line signalling the bait of a fish. **3** a floating device which forms part of a valve apparatus controlling a flow of water. **4** a hand tool with a rectangular blade used for smoothing plaster. *The oil rig floats in the sea while extracting crude. Buoys show where the bait for fish has been placed. A float value can close the pipe to prevent wastage of water. masows use float to smoother the surface.*

Floccule – *(noun)* a small clump of material that resembles a tuff of wool. *Floccule is a small mass of matter resembling a soft tuft of wool.*

Floe – *(noun)* a sheet of floating ice. *Was the mass of ice that sank the Titanic actually an iceberg or a floe?*

Flog – *(verb)* **1** beat with a whip or stick as a punishment. **2** [British informal] make one's way with strenuous effort. *If they are found by the police roaming suspiciously at night, they will be flogged. Despite injury, I flogged my way to the railway station.*

Flood – *(noun)* **1** an overflow of a large amount of water over dry land. **2** an outpouring of tears or emotion. **3** an overwhelming quantity of things or people appearing at once. *The town was flooded with river overflowing nearby. he face swelled with flood of tears. We were devastated by the flood of complaints that came in.* *(verb)* **1** cover or become swollen and overflow its banks. **2** arrive in or overwhelm with very large numbers. fill or suffuse completely: *Due to failure of sewerage system, whole area was flooded with dirty water. Police tried to control the flood of agitators. She flooded the room with light.*

Flooring – *(noun)* floor, *Laminated flooring has become very popular these days. Some house owners are choosing to fit laminated flooring in their homes.* *(verb)* make a floor, cover a floor *Be careful not to stain the surface of the hardwood flooring with the glue.*

Flop – *(verb)* **1** fall, hang, or collapse in a heavy, loose, and ungainly way, [informal] fail totally. **2** [informal] rest or sleep in an improvised place. *The film failed to click with the audience and flopped. He was so tired he just flipped to the* *ground and dozed off.* *(noun)* a heavy, loose, and ungainly fall, [informal] a total failure. *America's Afghan campaign has been a complete flop.*

Floral - *(adjective)* of or decorated with flowers, [botany] of flora or floras. *Floral tribute was sent on behalf of all the trust.*

Florescence - *(noun)* the process of flowering. *In the laboratory, you can use x-ray florescence to determine which metals are present in the sample.*

Floriated - *(adjective)* decorated with floral designs. *The banquet hall was floriated with colorful designs.*

Floricultural - *(adjective)* involving floriculture, flower gardening *Cultivation of flowers especially ones to be cut and sold is the business of floriculturists.*

Floriculture - *(noun)* the cultivation of flowers. *Floriculture is a growing commercial venture in India.*

Florid - *(adjective)* **1** having a red or flushed complexion. **2** elaborately or excessively intricate or complicated. **3** [medicine] occurring in a fully developed form. *The initials here are crisply engraved in a very florid style.*

Floridity - *(adjective)* flushed with red or pink; rosy; ruddy: said of the complexion *The complexion and dark eyes of the man seemed to glow with complete floridity.*

Floriferous - *(adjective)* of a plant producing many flowers. *Floriferous plants grow from early summer through to early winter and produce an abundance of flowers.*

Florin - *(noun)* a former British coin and monetary unit worth two shillings, an English gold coin of the 14th century, worth six shilling and eight old pence, a foreign coin of gold or silver, especially a Dutch guilder. *By 1550, the European trader had almost two thousand florins worth of debts. One hundred florins make a guild.*

Florist - *(noun)* a person who sells and arranges cut flowers. *Florists have a roaring business selling flowers.*

Floss - *(noun)* **1** the rough silk enveloping a silkworm's cocoon. **2** untwisted silk fibres used in embroidery. **3** a soft thread used to clean between the teeth. *Commercial silk is made from flour drawn from silkworm's cocoon. Floss between the teeth by using a gentle rocking motion.* *(verb)* clean between with dental floss. *The most common way to clean between teeth is with dental floss or thread tape.*

Flotation - *(noun)* the separation of small particles of a solid by their different capacities to float. *Froth floatation process is used to remove impurities from extracted ore.*

Flotilla - *(noun)* a small fleet of ships or boats. *Flotilla leader sent off a warning signal, to warn shipping. German torpedo flotillas attacked enemy's main fleet at night.*

Flounder - *(verb)* **1** stagger in mud of water. **2** have trouble doing or understanding. something. *The theory part seldom poses any problems but people often flounder when it comes to the numericals.*

Flourish - *(verb)* grow or develop in a healthy or vigorous way, be working or at the height of one's career during a specified period. *If you study hard you will flourish in life.Maurya Dynasty flourished during the 3rd century B.C.* *(noun)* a bold or extravagant gesture or action, an ornamental flowing curve in handwriting or scrollwork. *With a flourish, he ushed them inside the hall. She does write plainly and clearly, and avoids metaphors or stylistic flourishes.*

Flout - *(verb)* openly disregard a rule, [Law], or convention. *Those who flout the law would be dealt with severely.*

Flow - *(verb)* **1** move steadily and continuously in a current or stream. **2** move towards the land; rise, compare with ebb. **3** hang loosely in a graceful manner: a long flowing gown. **4** a permanent change of shape under stress, without melting. *From Delhi, the Yamuna River flows east. Tidal water flows towards the land. her dress was flowing graceful. A dam is built across the river to restrict the flow of water.* *(noun)* **1** the action or process of flowing. **2** the rise of a tide or a river. **3** a steady, continuous stream: the flow of traffic. *The river flows into the sea. The water flows back into the sea. There was a constant flow of visitors.*

Flower – *(noun)* **1** the seed-bearing part of a plant, consisting of reproductive organs typically surrounded by brightly coloured petals. and green sepals the calyx. **2** the state or period in which a plant's flowers have developed and opened. **3** the finest individuals out of a number of people or things. *A bunch of flowers make a bouquet. The roses were just coming into flowers. He wasted the flower of English youth on his dream of empire.* *(verb)* **1** produce flowers. **2** be in or reach an optimum stage of development. *Rafflesia is the largest known flower in the world. Sincere studies during formative years will flower into a prosperous future.*

Flowing – *(adjective)* moving along smoothly *Amid strong winds, her hair was flowing in the northerly direction.* *(verb)* move along smoothly *With the level of water rising continuously, flowing against the current of river was very difficult.*

Fluctuate – *(verb)* rise and fall irregularly in number or amount. *Sensex has been fluctuating violently in value according to bulls or bear market.*

Flue – *(noun)* a duct in a chimney for smoke and waste gases. a channel for conveying heat. *A blocked flue can lead to carbon monoxide leaking into your kitchen and home. Make sure new water heaters in a bathroom are fitted to a balanced flue.*

Fluent – *(adjective)* **1** speaking or writing easily and accurately, especially in a foreign language. used easily and accurately. **2** smoothly graceful and easy. **3** able to flow freely; fluid. *Universities in England will admit only those students who are fluent in English. His style of play was fluent. A fluent discharge from the pipe.*

Fluff – *(noun)* **1** soft fibres accumulated in small light clumps. the flur or feathers of a young mammal or bird. **2** trivial or superficial entertainment or writing. **3** [informal] a mistake, especially in speech, sport, or music. *He brushed his collar to remove the fluff. The film is a typical Bollywood fluff. She fluffed a golden job opportunity with a weak interview.* *(verb)* make something fuller and softer by shaking or patting. it. *Fluff the egg white and the yolk thoroughly if you want to make good omelettes.*

Fluid – *(noun)* a substance that has no fixed shape and yields easily to external pressure; a gas or especially a liquid. *Fluid mechanics is an important subject in engineering studies. All fluids when compressed under high pressure become solid.* *(adjective)* able to flow easily. *Paint is more fluid than grease. Her dance movements were smoothe fluid and elegant to watch.*

Fluke – *(noun)* an unlikely chance occurrence, especially a stroke of luck. *You must work hard and don't depend to pass the exam by fluke.* *(verb)* achieve by luck rather than skill. *His success was largely attributed to fluke.*

Flump – *(verb)* fall, sit, or throw down heavily. *The heavy baggage slipped from his head and flumped to the ground with a loud thud.*

Fluorine – *(noun)* the chemical element of atomic number 9, a poisonous pale yellow gas of the halogen series. *Fluorine is a fluid belonging to the Halogen family.*

Flurry – *(noun)* **1** a small swirling mass of snow, leaves, etc. moved by sudden gusts of wind. **2** a sudden short period of commotion or excitement. a number of things arriving suddenly and simultaneously. *The was a flurry of snow at Gulmarg. There was a flurry of activities in the hall. There were a flurry of articles against the governments policy.*

Fluster – *(verb)* make agitated or confused. *Aron got a bit flustered under the glare of the camera.* *(noun)* a flustered state. *Flustered, excited man was talking to them.*

Flute – *(noun)* **1** a high-pitched wind instrument consisting of a tube with holes along it, usually held horizontally so that the breath can be directed against a fixed edge. **2** a tall, narrow wine glass. *Flute is an Indian musical instrument. A flute of champagne was placed before me.* *(verb)* speak in a melodious way. [poetic/literary] play a flute or pipe. *Where are you going? She fluted.*

Flutter - (*verb*) fly unsteadily or hover by flapping the wings quickly and lightly, move with a light irregular or trembling motion, move restlessly or uncertainly. *A couple of butterflies fluttered around the rose garden; Flags of India and China fluttered in the breeze; Sita fluttered in the hall nervously.* (*noun*) an act of fluttering, a state or sensation of tremulous excitement. *There was a flutter of wings at the kitchen window; Due to hunger, her insides were in a flutter.*

Flux- (*noun*) 1 the action or process of flowing or flowing out, the total electric or magnetic field passing through a surface. 2 an abnormal discharge of blood or other matter from or within the body. 3 continuous change. *There were heavy flux of ions across the membrane; Flux is the rate of flow of a radiant energy, or particles across a given area; There is a heavy discharge of flux from the body during diarrhoea or dysentery; The whole political system of India is in a state of flux.* (*verb*) treat (a metal object) with a flux to promote melting. *Do you want to clean the board to remove left over soldering flux?*

Flying - (*adjective*) capable or engaged in flying, brief, hurried *He made a flying visit to the neighbours' house. He took a flying glance at the report. The flying time between Delhi and Mumbai is two and a half hours.*

Foal - (*noun*) a young horse or related animal. *The young of a horse is known as a foal.* (*verb*) give birth to a foal.

Fob - (*noun*) a chain attached to a watch for carrying in a waistcoat or waistband pocket. a small ornament attached to a watch chain. a small pocket for carrying a watch. a tab on a key ring. *Finally release the central locking button and press the fob to check the central locking operation. Don't fob your friends off with a sham gift!*

Focal - (*adjective*) **1** of or relating to a focus, in particular the focus of a lens. **2** occuring in one particular site in the body. *Local centres are typically also focal points for the community life of their areas.*

Focus - (*noun*) **1** the centre of interest or activity. an act of focusing on something. *Focus on these main issues of concern.* **2** geology the point of origin of an earthquake, compare with EPICENTRE. *Hindukush region was the focus of the earthquake.* **3** [medicine] the principal site of an infection or other disease. *Island of langerhans is the focus of diabetes.* **4** the state or quality of having or producing clear visual definition. *Focal point is also known as focus.* the point at which an object must be situated with respect to a lens or mirror for an image of it to be well defined. *Seeing through a lens or mirror, a well defined image will appear well defined only if situated at the point called focus.* **5** geometry one of the fixed points from which the distances to any point of an ellipse, parabola, or other curve are connected by a linear relation. *Focus is the central point in ellipse, parabola and hyperbola from which linear distances are measured.*

Fodder - (*noun*) **1** food for cattle and other livestock. *Grass and haystack are the principle fodder for cattle.* **2** a person or thing regarded only as material for a specific use; young people ending up as factory fodder. *They are the usual teen fodder who have been put to manual work like this.* (*verb*) give fodder to cattle or other livestock. *At least 60 % of the dry matter for cattle and livestock must consist of roughage, fresh or dried fodder.*

Foe - (*noun*) formal an enemy or opponent. *The sniper rifle is dead accurate and one shot in the head is enough to kill almost any foe. Pakistan has considered India as its foe number one since independence.*

Foetus - (*noun*) unborn developing child inside the mother's womb *Last year, 40,000 female foetuses were aborted in Mumbai alone.*

Foible - (*noun*) **1** a minor weakness or eccentricity. *Although Rita is very easy going person she does have a few foibles.* **2** fencing the part of a sword blade from the middle to the point. *Foible, the middle part of the sword, is the weakest point of the whole blade.*

Foist – *(verb)* impose an unwelcome or unnecessary person or thing on. *Foisting unpopular policies is always resented by people.*

Fold – *(verb)* **1** bend something over on itself so that one part of it covers another. be able to be folded into a flatter shape. *The bedsheet was neatly folded.* **2** use to cover or wrap something in. affectionately clasp in one's arms. *He folded his arms around her in an affectionate manner.* **3** [informal] cease trading as a result of financial problems. suddenly stop performing well. *For lack of vision, the company folded up within three years.* **4** mix an ingredient gently with another ingredient. *Fold in the flour, and then add enough milk to give the mixture a soft consistency.* *(noun)* **1** a form produced by the gentle draping of a garment or piece of cloth. an area of skin that sags or hangs loosely. *Sagging is more common in overweight people and people with deep skin folds.* **2** a line or crease produced by folding. *She had folds of skin on the upper eyelids and deep creases on the lower lids.*

Folder – *(noun)* **1** a folding cover or wallet for storing loose papers. *Folders made of plastic have become very popular to carry important papers.* **2** North American a leaflet or booklet made of folded sheets of paper. *The accompanying folder contains all details about the conference.* **3** computing a directory containing related files or documents. *Please note that messages in a deleted folder will also be deleted. We can create a new folder in which to save our letters.*

Foliage – *(noun)* plant leaves, collectively. *Foliage of all these trees would be collected and sent for incineration.*

Foliate – *(adjective)* foliated. *Foliate designs in linear patterns, derived from Khajuraho art were on show.* *(verb)* decorate with leaves or leaf-like motifs. *All four corners have been foliated in pencil by me.*

Folk – *(noun)* **1** [informal] people in general. *It is certainly a lovely place, populated by friendly folks.* one's family, especially one's parents. *I am going to my hometown to meet my parents and other folks.* **2** traditional music of unknown authorship transmitted orally. *Inspiration comes from folk songs passed down the generations.* **3** originating from the beliefs and customs of ordinary people: folk wisdom. *Folklores are a popular means to inculcate morality in children.*

Follower – *(noun)* **1** a person who follows. *I am a devout follower of Hindu religion.* **2** a supporter, fan, or disciple. *Followers of every cult carry a blind faith in their leader.*

Following – *(preposition)* coming after or as a result of. *Following articles matched your search criteria.* *(noun)* a body of supporters or admirers. *Shiv Sena has a devoted following among the Mumbai crowd.* *(adjective)* **1** next in time or order. about to be mentioned: the following information. *Tips to reduce fat in your diet include the following.* **2** blowing in the same direction as the course of a vessel. *The ship was following the direction of the wind.*

Fondle – *(verb)* stroke or caress lovingly or erotically. *It is indecent to fondle someone in an inappropriate way.* *(noun)* an act of fondling. *Fondling very young children lovingly makes them healthy and confident.*

Foolhardy – *(adjective)* recklessly bold or rash. *It is foolhardy not to ask for discount when you can have it.*

Foolish – *(adjective)* lacking good sense or judgment; silly or unwise. *It is foolish to ignore the guidelines regarding examination.*

Footing – *(noun)* secure placement of the feet, or something to allow stability *On a business level we are on a sound footing.*

Forage – *(verb)* search widely for food or provisions. obtain by searching. search so as to obtain food. *Cattle and livestock were foraging the plains looking for food.* *(noun)* food for horses and cattle. *Forage is the plant material, especially leaves and stems eaten by the livestock.*

Foramen – *(noun)* anatomy an opening, hole, or passage, especially in a bone. *Foramen are openings within the body which allows muscles, arteries, veins etc to connect with one another appropriately.*

Forasmuch – *(conjunction)* [archaic] because; since. *For as much as I know, he wouldn't come today.*

Foray – *(noun)* **1** a sudden attack or incursion into enemy territory. *The foray by the enemy forces was repulsed promptly.* **2** a brief but spirited attempt to become involved in a new activity. *My foray into the manufacturing is succeeding.* *(verb)* make or go on a foray. *The army sent paramilitary forces to foray into the enemy territory.*

Forbade – past of forbid. *The police forbade onlookers to go near the damaged bridge.*

Force –*(noun)***1** strength or energy as an attribute of physical action or movement *He was thrown backwards by the force of the explosion.* Physics an influence tending to, change the motion of a body or produce motion or stress in a stationary body *The magnitude of such an influence is often calculated by multiplying the mass of the body and its acceleration.* **2** coercion or compulsion, especially with the use or threat of violence *He ruled over territory by law and not by force.* **3** mental or moral strength or power *The force of popular opinion made him to modify the new law.* person or thing regarded as capable of exerting influence *He might still be a force for peace and unity in the country.* the powerful effect of something *The government accepted the force of the argument of the villagers.* **4** an organized body of military personnel or police *Indian peacekeeping force had gone to Sri Lanka. (the forces) The army, navy, and air force of India.* **5** a group of people brought together and organized for a particular activity*: The sales force of the company was taken to Goa on a two-week vacation. (verb)* **1** make a way through or into by physical strength *Break open the back door by force.* drive or push into a specified position using physical strength *Thieves tried to force open the cash register.* bring about (something) by effort *Saloni forced a smile on her face despite being disappointed at the result. He forced his way through the crowd.* **2** make (someone) do something against his will. *The schools were forced to cut unnecessary staff.*

Forceps – *(plural noun)* a pair of pincers used in surgery or in a laboratory. a large instrument of such a type with broad blades, used to assist in the delivery of a baby. *Plastic forceps are ideal for removing laboratory specimens from liquids, such as, alcohol.*

Ford – *(noun)* a shallow place in a river or stream that can be crossed on foot or in a vehicle. *Use the third ford to cross the river because water at that point is shallow. (verb)* cross at a ford. *Any person crossing this ford should take extreme care.*

Fore – *(adjective)* situated or placed in front. *Before you address the audience, please come to the fore so that they can see your face. (noun)* the front part of something, especially a ship. *Fore is the name given to the front part of the boat or ship.* exclamatory called out as a warning to people in the path of a golf ball. *Fore is the name of given to yelling that golfers make to warn spectators about the coming ball.*

Forecast – *(verb)* predict or estimate. *The meteorology department has forecasted a cold weather for the next 5 days. (noun)* a prediction or estimate, especially of the weather or a financial trend. *Produce cash flow forecasts at the beginning of each month for your business.*

Foreclose – *(verb)* take possession of a mortgaged property as a result of defaults in mortgage payments. *Banks have abolished the penalty imposed on customers if they foreclose their loan amount.*

Forefather – *(noun)* an ancestor. *Leo Tolstoy was the forefather of modern Russian literature.*

Forefinger – *(noun)* the finger next to the thumb. *You hold a pen between your thumb and forefinger.*

Forefront – *(noun)* the leading position or place. *Mahatma Gandhi was always in the forefront during India's freedom struggle against the British.*

Forehead – *(noun)* the part of the face above the eyebrows. *The old man wiped the creased lines on his forehead with the back of his wrist and sat down.*

Foreign - *(adjective)* **1** of, from, in, or characteristic of a country or language other than one's own. dealing with or relating to other countries. *All foreign nationals need to report at the immigration counter.* **2** coming or introduced from outside. *Some foreign particle has entered my eye and troubling me a great deal.* **3** unfamiliar or uncharacteristic. *I just don't understand a bit of French; it is totally foreign to me.*

Foreigner - *(noun)* a person born in or coming from a foreign country. [informal] a stranger or outsider. *To marry a foreigner, permission must be obtained from the home ministry.*

Foreland - *(noun)* an area of land in front of a particular feature. *Foreland basin near Marina beach is another area where residential construction is very active.*

Foreleg - *(noun)* either of the front legs of an animal with four legs *Kangaroos use both their forelegs and hind legs to run.*

Foreman - *(noun)* **1** a worker who supervises other workers. *The foreman in charge of maintenance unit is very strict.* **2** a person who presides over a jury and speaks on its behalf. *The court clerk will ask the jury foreman for the verdict.*

Foremast - *(noun)* the mast of a ship nearest the bow. *The foremast of the ship usually hoists the flag of the country where it is registered.*

Forenoon - *(noun)* North American or nautical the morning. *Americans call the period of time between morning and noon as forenoon.*

Forensic - *(adjective)* **1** relating to or denoting the application of scientific methods and techniques to the investigation of crime. *There is the wide difference between crime studies and a purely forensic procedure.* **2** of or relating to courts of [Law]. *The judge didn't admit the forensic report terming it as incomplete.* *(noun)* forensic tests or techniques. *Forensic psychiatry has a human face also.*

Foreordain - *(verb)* determine in advance, predetermine *He was foreordained by God to become a social leader.*

Fore-reach - *(verb)* to overtake and pass. *The boat headed into the wind in order to forereach the jetty before another sailing vessel comes about.*

Foresee - *(verb)* be aware of beforehand; predict. *The coach could foresee a test cricketer in him, even though the trainee was just seven.*

Foreshadow - *(verb)* be a warning or indication of. *The design change in this new car foreshadows the launch of latest luxury cars in 2013*

Foreshow - *(verb)* [archaic] give warning or promise of. *The tussle for one-upmanship foreshows the battle of titans for political supremacy.*

Foresight - *(noun)* **1** the ability to predict what will happen or be needed in the future *He had the foresight to check that his escape route was clear* **2** the front sight of a gun *He took aim with the foresight and shot down the bird.*

Forest - *(noun)* a large area covered chiefly with trees and undergrowth. *Gir forest is the largest sanctuary for lions in India.* *(verb)* plant with trees. *Houses have been built with forest-like environment.*

Forestall - *(verb)* prevent or obstruct by taking advance action. anticipate and prevent the action of. *Cash transfer scheme has been vigorously launched to forestall the opposition capturing power in the forthcoming general election. He would have spoken with the chief but Sanjay Forestalled him.*

Forester - *(noun)* **1** a person in charge of a forest or skilled in forestry. *Foresters are now designated as an officer under the government.* **2** a small day-flying moth with metallic green forewings. *Forester is a name given to the family of black moths.*

Forethought - *(noun)* careful consideration of what will be necessary or may happen in the future. *With a little more forethought I should have used any copper utensil.*

Foreword - *(noun)* a short introduction to a book, typically by a person other than the author. *This new edition carries a foreword by the Nobel laureate R.K.Pachauri.*

Forfeit – *(verb)* lose or be deprived of as a penalty for wrongdoing, lose or give up as a necessary consequence: *Prize winners who do not claim their prize within seven days will automatically forfeit their right to the prize.* *(noun)* a fine or penalty for wrongdoing, [Law] a forfeited item of property, right, or privilege. *Customs department will forfeit items that are not backed with proper bills.* *(adjective)* lost or surrendered as a forfeit. *The security amount would be forfeited in case of trip cancellation on your part.*

Forgave – *(verb)* past of forgive. *They talked over their misunderstanding and forgave each other.*

Forgery – *(noun)* the act or legal offense of imitating or counterfeiting documents, signatures, works of art, etc. to deceive, anything forged *Anyone who commits forgery is guilty of a criminal offense. The local police is investigating the case of document forgery.*

Forgo – *(verb)* go without something desirable. *I could happily forgo the chocolate, but not the crisp and salty snacks.*

Fork – *(noun)* **1** an implement with two or more prongs used for lifting or holding food. *The two-pronged fork is the ideal for eating fruits.* a farm or garden tool of larger but similar form used for digging or lifting. *Fork truck driver was forced to take leave off work suffering from stress.* **2** each of a pair of supports in which a bicycle or motorcycle wheel revolves. *The front fork of the bicycle gave way forcing him to carry it to the nearest mechanic.* **3** the point where something, especially a road or river, divides into two parts. either of two such parts *Keep going straight for about two kilometers and then take the right-hand fork which runs down to our house.* **4** chess a simultaneous attack on two or more pieces by one. *Queen or knight can easily fork a number of pieces in the game of chess.* *(verb)* **1** divide into two parts. take one road or the other at a fork. *To reach our house, take the right fork at the central store.* **2** [informal] pay money for something, especially reluctantly. *The police caught him for parking his bike in a 'no parking zone' and was forced to fork out money reluctantly to escape making rounds of the court.* **3** chess attack simultaneous with one. *He moved the rook into a position that forked a bishop and a knight.*

Forlorn – *(adjective)* **1** pitifully sad and lonely. *The site has been almost entirely cleared leaving just the name of the station.* **2** unlikely to succeed or be fulfilled. *She looked so forlorn, so empty like the hope had been sucked out of her.*

Formality – *(noun)* the rigid observance of rules or convention. a thing that is done simply to comply with convention, regulations, or custom. something done or happening as a matter of course. *Board members decided to observe the formality of reappointing the current auditor in order to meet the statutory mandate.*

Format – *(noun)* the way in which something is arranged or presented. computing a defined structure for the processing, storage, or display of data. *The pdf file format opens in adobe acrobat reader.* *(verb)* arrange or put into a format. prepare to receive data. *These files are in pdf format, for which you need an acrobat reader.*

Formation – *(noun)* **1** the action of forming or the process of being formed. *Magnetic fields play very significant role in formation of star. Vitamin D works with calcium to help control bone formation.* **2** a structure or arrangement. a formal arrangement of aircraft in flight or troops. *The aircrafts moved in a triangular formation during the air show.*

Formative – *(adjective)* serving to, especially having a profound influence on a person's development. *Better parental guidance is necessary during the formative years of a child.* linguistics denoting or relating to any of the smallest meaningful units that are used to form words in a language, typically combining forms and inflections. *Formative sentence is a structure that consists of a couple of words conveying some meaning.*

Former – *(adjective)* **1** having been previously. of or occurring in the past. *Sharad Pawar is the former president of BCCI.* **2** denoting the first mentioned of two people or things. *Talking of Delhi and Mumbai, the later is the capital of Maharashtra while the former is of India.*

Formica - *(noun)* trademark a hard durable plastic laminate used for worktops, cupboard doors, etc. *Formica is the trade name registered in the name of a company manufacturing plastic laminates.*

Formidable - *(adjective)* inspiring fear or respect through being impressively large, powerful, or capable. *Australia is a formidable rival of India in the game of cricket.*

Forswear - *(verb)* **1** agree to give up or do without. *He foreswore not to break the community laws before being admitted back.* **2** commit perjury. *In the northern part of Mali residents are being massacred in cold blood by the southern tribe for not forswearing the Islamic cause.*

Fort - *(noun)* a fortified building or strategic position. *Red fort was built by Moghul Emperor Jehangir in Delhi.*

Forte - *(noun)* a thing at which someone excels. *My personal secretary is Sheila whose main forte is internet research.*

Forth - *(noun)* computer language *Forth is a stack-oriented computer programming language.*

Forthwith - *(adverb)* without delay. *You must cease to operate this programme forthwith.*

Fortitude - *(noun)* courage in adversity. *We pray to God to grant you fortitude to bear this grievous loss.*

Fortnight - *(noun)* chiefly British a period of two weeks. [informal] two weeks from that day. *This magazine is published every fortnight, 24 issues each year.*

Fortress - *(noun)* a military stronghold, especially a strongly fortified town fit for a large garrison. *The Great Wall of China was primarily built to act as a fortress against marauding Mongols.*

Fortuitous - *(adjective)* happening by chance rather than design. [informal] happening by a lucky chance. *It was a fortuitous meeting with the manager at the station that has got me the job.*

Fortuitously - *(adjective)* happening by chance; accidental, bringing, or happening by, good luck; fortunate *The job I got could be attributed to my fortuitously meeting him at the club.*

Fortieth - *(noun)* the number forty in a series, fortieth part of forty equal parts *In ascending order, fortieth comes after thirty ninth.*

Forty - *cardinal number* **1** the number equivalent to the product of four and ten; ten less than fifty; 40, *Forty is the number obtained by multiplying five with eight. Forty percent of the staff has been laid off.* **2** the central north sea between Scotland and southern Norway, so called from its prevailing depth of forty fathoms or more. *Forty is a name given to an area in the sea between Scotland and Norway.*

Forum - *(noun)* **1** a meeting or medium for an exchange of views. *The decision to hold election was decided last evening at the forum.* **2** chiefly North American a court or tribunal. *The court has ordered formation of a forum for legal information exchange on line.* **3** a public square or marketplace used for judicial and other business. *We are pursuing a peaceful, diplomatic solution through a multilateral forum.*

Forwarding - *(noun)* sending, forwarding, dispatching *I am forwarding you details about the civil services examination.*

Found - *(verb)* establish, discover, create, build, melt and mould. *The physician who found the elusive particle won the Nobel Prize. She found an interesting book at the bookstore last evening.* *(adjective)* discovered. *You can report the loss of your baggage at the 'lost and found' department.*

Founder - *(noun)* a person who founds an institution or settlement. *Raja Ram Mohun Roy was the founder of Bramho Samaj.*

Foundling - *(noun)* infant that has been abandoned by its parents and is discovered and cared for by others. *The foster parents have got accustomed to foundling the infant found abandoned in the park.*

Foundry - *(noun)* a workshop or factory for casting metal. *In the brass foundry most of the work is cast from plate molded patterns.*

Fount - *(noun)* **1** a source of a desirable quality. *My idea is to reach the founts of wisdom before I turn 18.* **2** [poetic/literary] a spring or fountain.

The idea of the fountain pen perhaps came from the word fount which means spring.

Fourteen – *(cardinal number)* equivalent to the product of seven and two; one more than thirteen, or six less than twenty; 14 *Fourteen is the number we get when ten is added to four.*

Fourth – *(ordinal number)* **1** constituting number four in a sequence; 4th. *The number succeeding third is known as fourth.* **2** chiefly north American a quarter. *A quarter is a quantity that equals one fourth of any substance.* **3** music an interval spanning four consecutive notes in a diatonic scale, in particular an interval of two tones and a semitone. music the note which is higher by this interval than the tonic of a diatonic scale or root of a chord. *Fourth is the name given to the musical interval between one note and another four notes away.*

Fovea – *(noun)* anatomy a small depression in the retina of the eye where visual acuity is highest. *Fovea is any small cuplike depression or pit in the bone or organ in the body.*

Fowl – *(noun)* **1** a domesticated bird derived from a jungle fowl and kept for its eggs or flesh; a cock or hen. any domesticated bird, e.g. a turkey or duck. used in the names of birds that resemble the domestic fowl, e.g. spurfowl. *Fowl is a bird used for food. A hen is an example of fowl. Chicken is an example of fowl.* **2** birds collectively, especially as the quarry of hunters. *Any domestic or wild bird used as food is called a fowl in common parlance.*

Fowler *(noun)* a bird hunter *Fowler is a person who hunts wild birds for food.*

Fowling – *(noun)* bird hunting *Fowling is a term that includes all forms of bird catching for meat, feather or any other part.* *(verb)* hunt birds *They went to hunt fowl in the jungle.*

Fra – *(noun)* Fra, Friar, or Fray- a prefixed title. *Fra, friar or sometimes even fray is a title often used in the former Spanish colonies such as, the Philippines or Southwest America.*

Fracas – *(noun)* a noisy disturbance or quarrel. *The violent fracas between the rival factions didn't allow the function to proceed.*

Fractious – *(adjective)* **1** easily irritated. **2** difficult to control. *Fractious ethnic groups say they have little in common to oppose the enemy as a cohesive unit.*

Fracture – *(noun)* **1** the cracking or breaking of hard object or material. a crack or break, especially in a bone or a rock stratum. *Skull fracture can have serious complications for the normal functioning of the body.*

Fragile – *(adjective)* **1** easily broken or damaged. *Glass is a highly fragile material.* **2** delicate and vulnerable. *Many of these areas are environmentally fragile and forested.*

Fragment – *(noun)* a small part broken off or detached. an isolated or incomplete part. *Fragments of asteroids keep falling in one part or the other on the earth nearly every day.* *(verb)* break or cause to break into fragments. *A glass dropped on the floor breaks into several fragments.*

Fragrance – *(noun)* a pleasant, sweet, smell. a perfume or aftershave. *Now you can enjoy the calming effects of this lotion's lavender fragrance.*

Fragrant – *(adjective)* having a pleasant or sweet smell. *The delicately fragrant formula is speedily absorbed and leaves you feeling fresh.*

Frail – *(adjective)* **1** weak and delicate. *She was an old frail lady yet carrying heavy bundles in her hands.* **2** easily damaged or broken. *(noun)* US [informal], dated a woman. *Frail old lady carrying a plastic bag, was admitted to the hospital.*

Franc – *(noun)* the basic monetary unit of France, Belgium, Switzerland, Luxembourg, and several other countries, equal to 100 centimes (replaced in France, Belgium, and Luxembourg by the Euro in 2002) *Before emergence of Euro, Franc was the currency of France, Belgium and Luxemburg.*

Franchise – *(noun)* **1** an authorization granted by a government or company to an individual or group enabling them to carry out specified commercial activities, a business or service granted such authorization, leaguer to own a sports team, North American [informal] a team granted such authorization. *Whether you are an old industry professional or new, a franchise is the perfect business opportunity for you.* **2** the right to vote in public elections, especially for members of parliament. *The general election may bring the opposition party to power on the basis of a universal franchise.(verb)* grant a franchise to. grant a franchise for the sale of or the operation of a service. *The company has advertised to appoint 50 franchisees to cover the whole nation.*

Fraught – *(adjective)* **1** filled with something undesirable. *Proper care for sick and elderly remain fraught with legal uncertainty.* **2** causing or affected by anxiety or stress. *Venturing into the jungle alone is not only foolhardy but is fraught with danger to life.*

Fray – *(noun)* a situation of intense competitive activity. *With five withdrawals, only two are left in fray for leadership of the party.*

Frazil – *(noun)* North American an accumulation of ice crystals in water that is too turbulent to freeze solid. *Frazil is a name given to those tiny, round or pointed ice crystals that are formed in super cooled waters and prevented from solidifying due to turbulence.*

Freckle – *(noun)* a small light brown spot on the skin, often becoming more pronounced through exposure to the sun. *Freckles produce a sense of agedness in appearance. (verb)* cover or become covered with freckles. *To prevent appearance of freckles on the skin, use of good quality moisturizers is recommended.*

Freemason – *(noun)* a member of an international order established for mutual help and fellowship, which holds elaborate secret ceremonies. *A member of a secret fraternal society named 'Free and Accepted Mason' advocating brotherly love and mutual love is known as a freemason.*

Freezing – *(adjective)* **1** below 0°C. [informal] very cold. *Water is a freezable commodity below 0 degree Centigrade.* **2** consisting of droplets which freeze rapidly on contact with a surface. *It was so cold even the wheels had frozen to the ground. (noun)* the freezing point of water 0°C. *The freezing point of water is 0 degree Centigrade or 32 degree Fahrenheit.*

Freight – *(noun)* transport of goods in bulk, especially by truck, train, or ship. goods transported by freight. *Freight carried by rail, rather than road, produces at least 80 per cent less carbon dioxide.(verb)* transport by freight. *Road freight has grown by more than 30 per cent.*

French – *(adjective)* of or relating to France or its people or language. *Eiffel Tower is synonymous with the culture of French people. (noun)* the language of France, also used in parts of Belgium, Switerland, Canada, and certain other countries. *French wines, especially the white ones, are very popular all over the world.*

Frenetic – *(adjective)* fast and energetic in a rather wild and uncontrolled way. *Do some sincere thinking about youth force before life gets frenetic again.*

Frenzy – *(noun)* a state or period of uncontrolled excitement or wild behaviour. *Frenzy of excitement at ground since both teams were of equal standard.*

Frequency – *(noun)* **1** the rate at which something occures over a particular period or in a given sample. *Frequency of oscillations in an atom is more than nine million vibrations per second.* **2** the fact or state of being frequent. *The frequency of his coming to this place is roughly once a week.* **3** the rate per second of a vibration constituting a wave, e.g. sound, light, or radio waves. the particular waveband at which radio signals are broadcast or transmitted. *It is said that China has been using radio frequency waves to break into security systems of other countries.*

Fretful – *(adjective)* anxious or irritated. *There was little for them to eat, and the non-stop wailing of children made parents very fretful.*

Friable – *(adjective)* easily crumbled. *The property of a solid material to be broken into small pieces with little effort is known as friable.*

Friary – *(noun)* a building occupied by friars. *Friar is sometimes used in former Spanish colonies, such as, the Philippines or Southwest America as a title.*

Friction – *(noun)* **1** the resistance that one surface or object encounters when moving over another.

We can't run fast on sand desert because of very high friction. the action of one surface or object rubbing against another. *A mouse mat is normally used to reduce friction on a desk top computer.* **2** conflict or disagreement. *The agreement couldn't be signed because of friction in outlook between the two parties.*

Friday – *(noun)* the day of the week before Saturday and following Thursday. *Friday is the sixth day of the week and comes before Saturday.* *(adverb)* chiefly North American on Friday. *Islamic countries have declared each Friday as a holiday.*

Friendless – *(adjective)* without friends. *His sermon-like lectures to anyone who comes to him has left him virtually friendless.*

Friendliness – *(adjective)* not hostile. *Our new neighbour has become very popular because of his simplicity and friendliness.*

Friendly – *(adjective)* **1** kind and pleasant; of or like a friend. *We have published many child-friendly books.* **2** military of, belonging to, or allied with one's own forces. *An attack on one friendly country will be considered as an attack on all.* **3** not harmful to a specified thing: an environment-friendly policy. *Member nations must agree at the climate talks to pass the environment-friendly resolution.* *(noun)* British a game or match not forming part of a serious competition. *He is a very friendly and has no known adversaries.*

Friendship – *(noun)* the state of being friends, attachment between friends, friendly feeling or attitude; friendliness. *Through the group's social activities, you'd forge strong friendships which could last a lifetime. I have met many people during my holidays over the years, some of them having turned into lasting friendships.*

Frigate – *(noun)* a warship with a mixed armament, generally lighter than a destroyer. historical a sailing warship of a size and armament just below that of a ship of the line. *Indian Navy has built many frigates to defend the coastal waters of India.*

Fright – *(noun)* a sudden intense feeling of fear. an experience causing fright; a shock. *Stage fright has always been a major problem with me.* *(verb)* [archaic] frighten. *Then he received a letter from income tax department that gave him a great fright.*

Frighten – *(verb)* cause to be afraid. drive someone away by fear. *Being alone, the lightning and thunder at the dead of the night frightened him no end.*

Frightful – *(adjective)* **1** very unpleasant, serious, or shocking. *Frightful dreams, nonetheless they were only dreams and not a reality.* **2** [informal] terrible; awful: *Her hair was in a frightful mess.*

Frigid – *(adjective)* **1** very cold. *He described her nature as extremely frigid, cold, dry and devoid of any cheering influence.* **2** stiff or formal in behaviour or style. *Not even a number of blankets could warm us from that frigid cold.*

Frill – *(noun)* **1** a strip of gathered or pleated material sewn by one side only on to a garment or piece of material as a decorative edging or ornament. *She wore an expensive frilled shirt, pleated skirt and the long multi-coloured scarf.* **2** unnecessary extra features or embellishments: a comfortable flat with no frills. *People prefer aircrafts that offer little or no frills because of lower prices.*

Fringe – *(noun)* **1** a border of threads, tassels, or twists, used to edge clothing or material. *Fringe is the ornamental border consisting of loose hanging beads or threads in women's garments.* **2** chiefly British the front part of someone's hair, cut so as to hang over the forehead. *Fringe style hair cut is much popular among little girls.* **3** the outer or marginal part of something. not part of the mainstream. *We have decided to build a house at the fringes of the slums.* **4** a band of contrasting brightness or darkness produced by diffraction or interference of light. *Two different types of fringes can be observed in photoelasticity.* **5** North American short for fringe benefit. *When Americans say 'fringe' they actually mean 'fringe benefits'.* *(verb)* provide with or form a fringe. *Government jobs come with many fringe benefits, such as, free medical care, housing loans, group insurance, home travel concessions etc.*

Frippery – *(noun)* showy or unnecessary ornament. *Most Smartphone and mobiles are actually getting larger, sprouting LED or LCD screens, card readers and all sorts of other frippery.* *(adjective)* [archaic] frivolous and tawdry. *She is an intelligent lady; don't go by her cheap clothing, imitated jewellery or other fripperies.*

Fritter – *(verb)* waste, time, money, or energy on trifling matters. *Don't fritter away time over trivial matters.*

Frivolity – *(noun)* light heartedness, foolishness *Take this project seriously and don't spend time over frivolities.*

Frizz – *(noun)* form into a mass of small, tight curls. *Please use a conditioner to bring new shine and lustre to hair as it controls the frizz.*

Frizzle – *(verb)* form into tight curles. *To frizzle, you must shallow fry the food until it curls and becomes crisp fry.* *(noun)* a tight curl in hair. *Ms. Frizzle with curled hair was a character in 'The Magic School Bus'.*

Fro – *(adverb)* to and fro. *Why waste time shuttling between the two play grounds?*

Frock – *(noun)* **1** chiefly British a woman's or girl's dress. *Frock is one of the most comfortable dresses for girls.* **2** a loose outer garment, in particular a long gown with flowing sleeves worn by monks, priests, or clergy. *Loose outer garment, a smock is usually worn by monks.*

Frolic – *(verb)* play or move about in a cheerful and lively way. *You can expect to see festive frolics today involving our own picnic party.* *(noun)* a playful action or movement. *Frolic freely, and plenty of food, water and sunshine here for everyone.*

Frolicsome – *(adjective)* lively and playful. *Frolicsome children enjoy the thrill when it rains.*

Frond – *(noun)* the leaf or leaf-like part of a palm, fern, or similar plant. *Palm growers cut palm fronds, without harm to growing trees.*

Front – *(noun)* **1** the side or part of an object that presents itself to view or that is normally seen or used first. *The front of his house is attractively designed and decorated.* **2** the foremost line or part of an armed force; the furthest position that an army has reached. *Two enemy forces reached the front.* an organized political group: the patriotic front. *Many political parties have military fronts too to be used when needed.* **3** a particular situation or sphere of operation. *Front panel control allows you to record incoming signals.* **4** a deceptive appearance or mode of behaviour assumed by someone to conceal truth or genuine feelings. *Though a terrorist body, the outfit had a political front to hide its real identity.* **5** boldness and confidence of manner. *The front a person puts forward in an interview must be attractive and presentable.* *(adjective)* **1** of or at the tongue towards the hard palate. *The front of a chimpanzee resembles a man to a great extent.* **1** have the front facing towards. place or be placed at the front. *A mirror was placed in front of the broken window glass. The military outfit had a political front to disguise its real intent.* *(verb)* **1** have the front facing towards. place or be placed at the front of. *The façade of the fort gave an appearance of a dilapidated house.*

Frontage – *(noun)* **1** the facade of building. *The frontage of the compound gave an appearance of a bungalow.* **2** a strip or extent of land abutting on a street or waterway. *Externally there is a fully glazed frontage at ground floor level.*

Frontal – *(adjective)* **1** of or at the front. *He suffered a frontal attack.* **2** of or relating to the forehead or front part of the skull: the frontal sinuses. *The doctor detected a legion in the frontal lobe.* *(noun)* a decorative cloth for covering the front of an altar. *Frontal is a drapery that covers an alter.* Frontless *(adjective)* without a front. *He is a completely shameless and may be called a frontless person.*

Frontlet – *(noun)* another term for phylactery. *Frontlet is an ornament or band worn on the forehead.*

Froth – *(noun)* **1** a mass of small bubbles in liquid caused by agitation, fermentation, or salivating. impure matter that rises to the surface of liquid. *Froth flotation process is used to segregate impurities from the mineral ore.* **2** worthless or insubstantial talk, ideas, or activities. *(verb)* from, produce, or contain froth. *These bubbles float to the top of the glass and make froth. The aroma of fresh coffee together with the creamy milk and a rich authentic froth to top the mug.*

Frozen – past participle of freeze. *Due to very cold weather, water was frozen into ice.*

Fructification – *(noun)* **1** the process of fructifying. **2** [botany] a spore-bearing or fruiting structure, especially in a fungus. *Fructification is a name given to the structure of a fungus that is seed-bearing or spore-bearing.*

Fructify – *(verb)* **1** formal make or become fruitful. *Your sincere studies will let it fructify into good result.* **2** bear fruit. *The seeds fructified a fortnight ago.*

Fructose – *(noun)* chemistry a sugar of the hexose class found especially in honey and fruit. *Fructose is a chemical compound.*

Fructuous – *(adjective)* formal full of or producing a great deal of fruit. *His sincere studies have been very fructuous; he passed the examination with 90 per cent marks.*

Frugal – *(adjective)* sparing or economical as regards money or food. *Frugal way would be to save up and not take out a loan.*

Fruitarian – *(noun)* a person who eats only fruit. *It is difficult to stay energetic being just a fruitarian.*

Fruiterer – *(noun)* chiefly British a retailer of fruit. *Fruiterer is a person, mainly in England and Australia, who retails fruits and vegetables.*

Fruitful – *(adjective)* **1** producing much fruit; fertile. **2** producing good result; productive. *Make your ideas attractive, focus on the benefits and how you can make life more fruitful.*

Fruition – *(noun)* **1** the realization or fulfillment of a plan or project. **2** [poetic/literary] the state or action of producing fruit. *International trade negotiations take a long time to reach fruition. The tree has begun to fruition and is likely to deliver better yield than last year.*

Fruitless – *(adjective)* **1** failing to achieve the desired results; unproductive. **2** not producing fruit. *For one reason or the other, my five attempts to speak to him on phone remained fruitless.*

Fruitlet – *(noun)* an immature or small fruit. [botany] another term for drupel. *A fruitlet is a small, yet to be fully grown fruit that is part of a multiple fruit.*

Fruity – *(adjective)* **1** of, resembling, or containing fruit. *My nose was filled with the smells of fruit because a number of baskets containing assorted fruits were kept in the car.*

Frustrate – *(verb)* **1** prevent from progressing, succeeding, or being fulfilled. prevent from doing or achieving something. *Lack of money frustrated my desire to join a top ranked management school.* **2** cause to feel dissatisfied or unfulfilled. *Late running of train frustrated my chance of attending the interview. (adjective)* [archaic] frustrated. *Climbing 20 stairs in the dark because of power failure was thoroughly frustrating and tiring.*

Frustration – *(noun)* disappointment, depression, anxiety *Try to imagine the frustration, the boredom, and the anger that this desktop computer system creates.*

Frustrative – *(adjective)* preventing attainment of a desire *Constant traffic jams had been terribly frustrative in our plan to reach Delhi before night.*

Fry – *(plural noun)* young fish, especially when newly hatched, the young of other animals produced in large numbers, such as frogs. *Young of a variety of animals, including frogs and bees, are called a fry.*

Frying – *(noun)* cooking in oil. *Frying is cooking of food in oil or another fatty substance. (verb)* cook in oil, be cooked in oil. *After he quit the first company he went to one with even longer hours as if, out of the frying pan into the fire. Foods can be fried in a variety of oils, fats, rapeseed oil, vegetable or mustard oil.*

Fuddle – *(verb)* confuse or stupefy, especially with alcohol. *He is so cunning; he can befuddle you any day with his ingenuity. (noun)* a state of confusion or intoxication. *My brain is totally befuddled with the report just handed over to me.*

Fudge – *(noun)* **1** a soft crumbly or chewy sweet made from sugar, butter, and milk or cream. **2** chiefly north American rich chocolate, used as a sauce or a filling for cakes. *This as a fudge ice cream sundae with all the chocolate toppings.* **3** an attempt to fudge an issue. *We are trying to find a solution to this vexed issue whereas you are just fudging it.* [archaic] nonsense. **4** a piece of late news inserted in a newspaper page. *(verb)* present in a vague or inadequate way, especially to mislead. adjust or manipulate so as to present a desired picture . *We need to fudge on the issue to keep the coalition together. Make sure they don't fudge the truth at all.*

Fugacious – *(adjective)* [poetic/literary] tending to disappear; fleeting. *In botany, fugacious is a term used to describe withering or dropping off early.*

Fugitive – *(noun)* a person who has escaped from captivity or is in hiding. *The police is on the lookout for the fugitive who was released on bail three days back. (adjective)* quick to disappear; fleeting. *He is still the leader of an unlawful organization and a wanted fugitive.*

Fulcrum – *(noun)* the point against which a lever is placed to get a purchase, or on which it turns or is supported. *Fulcrum is the point on which a lever is balanced when a force is exerted.*

Fulgent – *(adjective)* [poetic/literary] shining brightly. *Blazing sun, blinding headlights are some of the examples of fulgent dazzle.*

Fuller – *(noun)* a grooved or rounded tool on which iron is shaped. *Fuller is a worker who cleanses wool by the process of fulling. (verb)* stamp using a fuller. *A tool used by blacksmiths to hammer grooves into iron is known as fuller.*

Fulsome – *(adjective)* **1** flattering to an excessive degree. **2** of large size or quantity. *Her stage performance received a fulsome praise from all quarters.*

Fumble – *(verb)* **1** use the hands clumsily while doing or handling something. do or handle something clumsily. move about clumsily using the hands to find one's way. fail to catch or field cleanly. *The ball was coming straight to him but he fumbled and dropped the catch.* **2** express oneself or deal with something clumsily or nervously. *Even brilliant students sometimes fumble at interviews.* an act of fumbling. [informal] an act of foundling someone for sexual pleasure. *He was fumbling with the buttons of her shirt.*

Fumigate– *(verb)* disinfect or purify with the fumes of certain chemicals. *This area is fumigated every fortnight to prevent breeding of mosquitoes.*

Fun – *(noun)* **1** light-hearted pleasure or amusement. *The picnic was a wholesome fun-filled pleasant trip.* **2** a source of this. *Merry-go-round is a great fun for children and young adults.* **3** playfulness or good humour: *She's full of fun. (adjective)* [informal] enjoyable. *(verb)* [informal, chiefly North American] joke or tease. *Children learned all the tricks of the circus trade at a family fun day.*

Fund – *(noun)* **1** a sum of money saved or made available for a particular purpose. *Funds have been earmarked to organize annual sports.* **2** financial resources. *MNCs are playing with funds to augment their hold on the market.* **3** a large stock. *(verb)* provide with a fund. *The government has set aside Rs. 5000 crore to fund implementation of 'cash transfer scheme'.*

Fundament – *(noun)* **1** the foundation or basis of something. **2** humorous a person's buttocks or anus. *The whole fundament of this argument rested on conjecture.*

Fungus – *(noun)* any of a large group of spore-producing organisms which feed on organic matter and include moulds, yeast, mushrooms, and toadstools. *The discovery of penicillin has its origin in moulds which organism like fungus feed on.*

Funicle – *(noun)* **1** [botany] a filamentous stalk attaching a seed or ovule to the placenta. *The little stalk that attaches a seed to the placenta is known as funicle.* **2** entomology a filamentous section of an insect's antenna, supporting the club. *The cord which attaches the eggs to the peridium in some species is known as funicle.*

Funicular – *(adjective)* of or relating to a rope or its tension. *A 4-star hotel on a hill with wonderful panoramic views is linked by funicular to the central station. (noun)* a funicular railways. *Funicular railroad to the top of the mountain has beautiful sceneries along the way.*

Funk – *(noun)* **1** great fear or panic. *Are you in a blue funk about running out of things to say?* state of depression. *I sat absorbed in my own blue funk.* **2** coward. *I sit shuddering, too much of a funk to fight.* *(verb)* avoid (something) out of fear. *I could have seen him this morning but I funked it.*

Furbish – *(verb)* give a fresh look to; renovate. *The hotel had furbished all rooms with new draperies and interiors for offering visitors stunning views out to the sea.*

Furcate – *(verb)* divide into two or more branches; fork. *The club has decided to furcate the entry and exit points.* *(adjective)* furcated; forked: *Entry and exit points have been furcated at the club.*

Furious – *(adjective)* **1** extremely angry. *He was furious at his staff for not completing the important project.* **2** full of energy or intensity. *Furious pace of the first half continued unabated in the second in the final of the football match.*

Furl – *(verb)* roll or fold up neatly and securely. *The flag was taken down and furled properly and neatly.*

Furlough – *(noun)* leave of absence, especially from military duty. *He has rejoined duty after remaining on furlough for six months.* *(verb)* US grant furlough to. *Furloughed employees who wish to relocate should send their applications by next week.*

Furnish – *(verb)* **1** provide with furniture and fitting. *These flats are fully furnished 3 bedroom apartment with a community swimming pool.* **2** denoting fabrics used for curtains or upholstery. *Each set has two beautifully furnished sitting rooms with soft red brick upholstery.*

Furniture – *(noun)* **1** the movable articles that are used to make a room or building suitable for living or working in, such as tables, chairs, or desks. *The hotel rooms are equipped with original antique furniture.* **2** the small accessories or fittings that are required for a particular task or function. *The fitted furniture is finished with an attractive wooden surface and trim.*

Furore – *(noun)* **1** an outbreak of public anger or excitement. *It is this photograph that caused much of the initial furore.* **2** [archaic] a craze. *Shakira's hot numbers created a furore with nearly all of her fans.*

Furrow – *(noun)* **1** a long, narrow trench made in the ground by a plough. *Each plot of land was divided from its neighbour by a deep furrow.* **2** a rut or groove. *Drill a narrow, straight furrow in the soil for sowing seeds.* **3** a deep wrinkle on a person's face. *Advanced age had produced deep furrows on his face.* *(verb)* **1** make a furrow in. *The farmer furrowed the field at right angles to his farmhouse.* **2** mark or be marked with furrows. *Determined to plow her own furrow she dug herself deeper into her opinion.*

Further – *(adverb)* **1** at, to, or by a greater distance. *The Sun lies much further from Mercury than that of Earth.* **2** over a greater expanse of space or time. beyond the point already reached. *We have to continue marching further to reach the Patni Top.* **3** at or to a more advanced, successful, or desirable stage. *Nothing he said could be further from the truth.* **4** in addition; also. *Further details of fees for all our courses can be found on our main page.* *(adjective)* **1** more distant in space. more remote from a central point. **2** additional: a further ten minutes. *Demand is expected to fall further in the next four months.* *(verb)* help the progress or development of. *Only hard work will further the interests of the company.*

Furthest – *(adjective)* situated at the greatest distance. covering the greatest area or distance. *Furthest of the planets from the Sun is a small icy rock of a planet.* *(adverb)* **1** at or by the greatest distance. *She could walk the furthest distance in the two hours.* **2** over the greatest distance or area. indicating the most distant point reached in a specified direction: *It was the furthest north I had ever travelled.* **3** to the most extreme or advanced point. *Challenger Deep is the furthest known point in the Earth's surface.*

Furtive – *(adjective)* characterized by guilty or evasive secrecy; stealthy. *Standing this side of the road, she gave a furtive look at the deserted* *shops on the opposite side of the road. Our first task as trained professional is to document what goes on in this very furtive field.*

Furuncle – *(noun)* [technical] term for boil. *There may be white patches along the body side or raised furuncles on the skin.*

Fuse – *(noun)* a length of material along which a small flame moves to explode a bomb or firework. a device in a bomb that controls the timing of the explosion. *Fuse wire was trimmed to up to the length of the explosive device.* *(verb)* fit a fuse to a bomb. *Hand grenades were exploded by igniting a fuse.*

Fusibility – *(adjective)* that can be fused or easily melted *Fusibility of a material is the property of its melting when heat is applied.*

Fusible – *(adjective)* able to be fused or melted easily. *Fusible metal plugs, which melt at known temperatures are placed across electric meters.*

Fusiform – *(adjective)* [botany & zoology] tapering at both ends; spindle-shaped. *Fusiform cells have been identified on the control plants.*

Fusion – *(noun)* **1** the process or result of fusing. *Fusion reactor a nuclear reactor in which two fuse to produce a heavier and release energy atomic nucleus.* **2** a reaction in which light atomic nuclei fuse to form a heavier nucleus, releasing much energy. *Like all stars, the sun generates its energy by a nuclear process known as thermonuclear fusion.* **3**. music that is a mixture of different styles, especially jazz and rock. *Fusion of Latin, jazz and funk music which took his audience into the early hours of the morning.* **4** referring to food or cooking which incorporates elements of both eastern and western cuisine. *We intend to have a fusion cuisine combining eastern and western foods tonight.*

Fuss – *(noun)* **1** a display of unnecessary or excessive excitement, activity, or interest. *Why this fuss over the approval over a small loan?* **2** a protest or complaint. *My mom makes a big fuss over the entry of a dog or cat in the house.* *(verb)* **1** show unnecessary or excessive concern about something. *The motion went through with minimum fuss with only a few people opposed.* **2** British disturb or bother. *Let me complete the job and not keep making a fuss about nothing.* **3** treat with excessive attention or affection. *I believe that the less fuss we make about it the better for the project.*

Futility- *(noun)* useless, worthless, triviality, vanity *We must now all accept the utter futility of trying to solve our border problems by war.*

Future – *(noun)* **1** time that is still to come. *Surf forecast websites to help you predict the future!* events or conditions occurring or existing in that time. *Future of mankind will become increasingly more sophisticated but highly individualistic.* **2** a prospect of success or happiness: *I might have a future as an artist*. **3** a tense of (verb)s expressing events that have not yet happened. *Astrologers do a good business predicting future of a person.* **4** contracts for assets bought at agreed prices but delivered and paid for later. *Futures market in commodities and crude has a great future.* *(adjective)* **1** existing or occurring a specified position. *Hopefully this will be the last increase in the foreseeable future.* **2** expressing an event yet to happen. *I think, that girl will have a bright future.*

Fuzz – *(noun)* cotton, fluff. *Fuzz is a type of short fine hair on the body of an animal. Fuzz is a fluffy hair like growth on a plant. Fuzz is an uncomplimentary term for a policeman.* *(verb)* cover with fuzz, become fuzzy *You can see a couple of rather fuzzy photographs of them here. Continuous reading makes me feel uncomfortable and my vision goes fuzzy fairly quickly.*

Fylfot – *(noun)* swastika *Fylfot is an auspicious or lucky object, especially applied to mystic science.*

Fyrd – *(noun)* the English militia before 1066. *In Anglo-Saxon times, fyrd was a name given to militia who were called upon to do service while under attack.*

Gg

G – *(noun)* **1** the seventh letter of the alphabet. **2** denoting the next after F in a set of items, categories, etc. **3** [music] the fifth note in the diatonic scale of C major.

Gab – *(verb)* **1** talk at length. *he was gabbing about his achivements at the previous job.* *(noun)* talk; chatter. *He gabbed a lot on frivolous issues and in the end I got board with him. The gabbed and ultimately I was able to understand him.*

Gabble – *(verb)* talk rapidly and unintelligibly *She gabbled in a panicky way during the interview and was disqualified.* *(noun)* rapid unintelligible talk *He wasn't very good while delivering the lectur he gabbled a lot and was not selected.*

Gabion – *(noun)* a cylindrical basket or container filled with earth, stones, or other material and used as a component of civil engineering works. *Gabion is a part and parcel of a civil engineer's work.*

Gable – *(noun)* **1** the triangular upper part of a wall at the end of a ridged roof. *He tried to put a nail in the gable but failed as it was very high and hard.* **2** a gable-shaped canopy over a window or door.

Gadfly – *(noun)* a person who annoys or criticizes others in order to provoke them into action *Always a gadfly, she attacked intellectuals and literary speakers.*

Gaff – *(noun)* **1** a stick with a hook or barbed spear, for landing large fish. *People catch fish, especially big fish, with gaff.* **2** sailing a spar to which the head of a fore-and-aft sail is bent. *(verb)* seize or impale with a gaff. *The wales are gaffed speared and knifed to death.*

Gaffer – *(noun)* **1** [British informal] an old man. *He is a gaffer and we should respect him.* **2** [informal] a boss. *He is my gaffer and a strict one.* **3** the chief electrician in a film or television production unit. *He is our gaffer on the movie sets and a very important person.*

Gag – *(noun)* **1** a piece of cloth put in or over a person's mouth to prevent him from speaking. *He is talking too much, they tied him up and putagag into his mouth.* **2** a device for keeping the patient's mouth open during a dental or surgical operation. *Dentists use gag while treating on aching tooth.* **3** a restriction on free speech. *He was gagged because he was speaking violently.* *(verb)* put a gag on. *The government is trying to gag its critics.*

Gage – *(noun)* a valued object deposited as a guarantee of good faith. *Here is a diamond ring, keep it as a gage and all your money will be returned.* *(verb)* offer as a gage. *Here is the gage pick it up and fight.*

Gaggle – *(noun)* **1** a flock of geese. *Look at the gaggle what a beautiful scene!* **2** [informal] a disorderly group of people. *Beware of this gaggle it can be violent any time, let us go.*

Gaiety – *(noun)* **1** the state or quality of being light-hearted and cheerful. *I felt great gaiety as I looked at people dancing with abandon.* **2** merrymaking; festivity. *Her gaiety in celebrating festivals always touched our heart.*

Gaily – *(adverb)* **1** in a light-hearted and cheerful manner. *I gaily participated in the group dance.* **2** without thinking of the consequences. *I gaily spent all the money in the shopping complex.* **3** with a bright appearance. *I could see him perform gaily in the play.*

Gainer – *(noun)* a person or thing that going. *The brown horse came out as a gainer in the race.*

Gainful – *(adjective)* serving to increase wealth or resources. *We should always try to indulge in gainful activities.*

Gainings – *(plural noun)* profits or earnings. *His gainings in the hardware buisness were great.*

Gainsay – *(verb)* formal deny or contradict; speak against. *The impact of good roads cannot be gainsaid. None could gainsay him.*

Gait - *(noun)* a person's manner of walking. *She has a graceful gait.*

Gaiter - *(noun)* a covering of cloth or leather for the ankle and lower leg. *Girls usually wear gaiters in US.* **2** a flexible covering for the base of a gear lever or other mechanical part. *I need a gaiter for the gear lever.*

Galactic - *(adjective)* of relating to a galaxy or galaxies. *The galactic mystries are beyond understanding of any man.*

Galea - *(noun)* [botany & zoology] a structure shaped like a helmet. *This plant looks like a galea.*

Galipot - *(noun)* hardened resin deposits formed on the stem of the maritime pine. *Galipots have stuck to the trunk of the tree.*

Gallant - *(adjective)* **1** brave; heroic. *He is a gallant officer.* **2** charming; chivalrous. *Although old, he is still gallant and ladies like his company.* *(noun)* a man who is charmingly attentive to women. *A gallant officer came and kissed her hand.* *(verb)* be charmingly attentive to a woman. *he was gallanting the British Lady.*

Galley - *(noun)* **1** [historical] a low, flat ship with one or more sails and up to three banks of oars, chiefly used for warfare or piracy and often manned by slaves or criminals. *In old times criminals or slaves used to row galleys.* **2** a large, open rowing boat kept on a warship especially for use by the captain. *The galley is at the tail end of the plane.*

Galliard - *(noun)* [historical] a lively dance in triple time for two people. *Galliards were in fashion is old times.*

Gallic - *(adjective)* of or characteristic of France or the French. *The gallic language is lovable.*

Gallipot - *(noun)* [historical] a small pot used to hold medicines or ointments. *Gallipots were used by a lot of people in early times.*

Gallium - *(noun)* the chemical element of atomic number 31. *Gallium is a soft silvery white metal.*

Gallon - *(noun)* **1** a unit of volume for liquid measure equal to eight pints: in britain, equivalent to 4.55 litres; in the US, equivalent to 3.79 litres. *He poured gallons of love on his beloved.*

Galloon - *(noun)* a narrow ornamental strip of braid, lace, etc. used as a trim. *She is very fond of galloons embroidered over her dress.*

Gallop - *(noun)* **1** the fastest pace of a horse or other quadruped, with all the feet off the ground together in each stride. *The gallop of the horses could be heard for away.* **2** a ride on a horse at a gallop. *The army horses galloped at a fast pace.* 3 British track where horses are exercised at a gallop. *He galloped through the tests and ultimately cleared the interview.* *(verb)* **1** go or cause to go at the pace of gallop. *Me galloped along the road as fast as we could.*

Galore - *(adjective)* in abundance. *There were prizes galore.*

Galoshes - *(noun)* a waterproof rubber overshoe. *He wore galoshes to protect his trousers from muddy water.*

Galvanic - *(adjective)* relating to or involving electric currents produced by chemical action. *The actor received galvanic applause from the audience.*

Galvanize - *(verb)* **1** shock or excite into action. *The adverse circumstances galvanixed him into action.* **2** coat with a protective layer of zinc. *While painting, the walls of a house are usually galvanized.*

Galvanometer - *(noun)* an instrument for detecting and measuring small electric currents. *Galvanometers are used in laboratories.*

Gamble - *(verb)* **1** play games of chance for money; bet. *He gambles a lot for money and often loses.* **2** take risky action in the hope of a desired result. *It was pure gamble that his chosen horse won the race.* *(noun)* **1** an act of gambling. **2** a risky undertaking or enterprise.

Gambler - *(noun)* a person who gambes. *He is a gambler by habit. He does not believe in working for money.*

Gambling - *(noun)* an act of taking chance. *Gambling is a bad habit one should never indulge is it. It can be the ruin of anyone.*

Gambol - *(verb)* run or jump about playfuly. *The horse gambolled around the playground.* *(noun)* an act of gambolling. *All children gambol by nature.*

Gambrel – *(noun)* a roof having a shallower slope above a steeper one on each side. *Houses in China and Japan have gambrel hind of roof.*

Game – *(noun)* **1** form of competitive activity or sport played according to rules, a meeting for sporting contests *Last Olympic Games were held in London in 2012.* athletics or sports as a lesson or activity at school *In order to be popular, you had to be good at games.* **2** an activity that one engages in for amusement *There are many computer games available for entertainment.* **3** the equipment for a game, especially a board game or a computer game *You can buy your games and software from us at a special discount till Sunday.* **4** a complete period of play, ending in a final result *The game of football is played over 120 minutes.* **5** a single portion of play forming a scoring unit in a match, especially in tennis *Then came another ace to set up game, set, and match.* **6** wild mammals or birds hunted for sport or food *Many people go and hunt game in the forest. (adjective)* eager or willing to do something new or challenging *They were game for anything as long as there was a possibility of gaining something (verb)* play at games of chance for money *The club has installed next generation of gaming consoles for members willing to take chances of winning.*

Gamma – *(noun)* **1** the third letter of the Greek alphabet. *Gamma is the third letter of the Greek alphabet.* **2** relating to gamma rays. *Many treatments are done these days by gamma knife.*

Gammer – *(noun)* [larchaic] an old woman. *She is a gammer, don't mind her talk.*

Gammon – *(noun)* ham which has been cured like bacon. *He is very fiend of eating gammon pig's bottom meat.*

Gamy – *(adjective)* having the strong flavour or smell of game, especially when it is high. *The room grew gamy as the meat cooked.*

Gander – *(noun)* **1** a male goose. *A gander usually leads a flock.* **2** [informal] a look or glance. *He gave me a mean gander.*

Gang – *(noun)* **1** an organized group of criminals or disorderly young people, [informal] a group of people who regularly associate together, *The gang of bank robbers were arrested by the police.* **2** a set of switches, sockets, or other devices grouped together. *The gang was working to mend the railway tracks. (verb)* form a group or gang. join together, typically in order to intimidate someone. *They ganged up against me and picked my pocket.*

Ganglion – *(noun)* anatomy a structure containing a number of nerve cells, often forming a swelling on a nerve fibre. a well-defined mass of grey matter within the central nervous system. *The doctor diagnosed genglion but fartunately it was benign and not cancerous.*

Gangrene – *(noun)* [medicine] localized death and decomposition of body tissue, resulting form either obstruected circulation or bacterial infection. *Gangrene set in the wound is his leg. Ultimately doctors amputed it. (verb)* become affected with gangrene. *His feet had gangrened and therefor amputed.*

Gannet – *(noun)* **1** a large seabird with mainly white plumage, catching fish by plunge-diving. *When I had my first look at a gannet I was surprised to see how cleverly it cought the fish in the sea.* **2** [British informal] a greedy person. *He is a gannet and will do anything to get money.*

Gantry – *(noun)* a bridge-like overhead structure supporting equipment such as a crane or railway signals. a tall framework supporting a space rocket prior to launching. *The rocket fired into space from the gantry.*

Gaol – *(noun)* [British] variant spelling of jail. *Jail was formerly written as gaol.*

Gap – *(noun)* **1** a break or hole in an object or between two objects. *He drove the car skilfull,y through the gap between two walls.* **2** a space, interval, or break. *I am tired. Give me a gap and I will talk to you.*

Gape – *(verb)* **1** be or become wide open. *He stared at her with a gaping mouth.* **2** stare with one's mouth open wide in amazement or wonder. *I gaped at the beautiful sunset on sea. (noun)* a wide opening. an open-mouthed stare. a widely open mouth or beak. *He jumped into the train to the gapes of commuters at the station.*

Garage - *(noun)* **1** a building for housing a motor vehicle or vehicles. *This house has the facility of garage.* **2** an establishment which sells fuel or which repairs and sells motor vehicles. *My car went out of order and I began to look for a garage.* *(verb)* put or keep in a garage. *The car should be garaged during summer days.*

Garb - *(noun)* clothing or dress, especially of a distinctive or special kind. *In the fancy dress competition he came in the garb of a beggar.* *(verb)* dress in distinctive clothes. *She came to the party garbed in Kashmiri dress.*

Garbage - *(noun)* **1** rubbish or waste, especially domestic refuse. *I put the garbage by outside. The maid will take it away.* **2** something worthless or meaningless. *This food packet his expired please throw out this garbage.*

Gargoyle - *(noun)* a grotesque carved human or animal face or figure projecting from the gutter of a building, usually as a spout to carry water clear of a wall. *I was amused to look at the gargoyle which had a jackal like face and water sprouted out of it.*

Garish - *(adjective)* obtrusively bright and showy. *His choice is weird, he wears so garish clothes.*

Garland - *(noun)* a wreath of flowers and leaves, worn on the head or hung as a decoration. *Indian people usually garland their guests.* *(verb)* adorn with a garland. *The dignitaries were garlanded with flowers on their arrival.*

Garlic - *(noun)* a strong-smelling pungent-tasting bulb, used as a flavouring in cookery. *Garlic is of great medicinal use, it also adds to the flavour of food.*

Garner - *(verb)* **1** gather or collect. *He garnered a lot of flowers from the garden.*

Garnet - *(noun)* a vitreous silicate mineral, in particular a deep red form used as a gem. *He is found of wearing rings with garnet.*

Garnish - *(verb)* decorate or embellish. *All the food centainers in the marriage feast were garnished.* *(noun)* a decoration or embellishment, especially for food. *Some flowers are edible and make attractive salad garnish.*

Garniture- *(noun)* a set of decorative vases. *I selected a garniture for giving as a gift.*

Garret - *(noun)* a top-floor or attic room, especially a small dismal one. *He lives in a garnet as he cannot afford to pay much rent.*

Garrison - *(noun)* a body of troops stationed in a fortress or town to defend it. *The king ordered that the town should be provided with a garrison.* *(verb)* provide with a garrison. *Indian troops were garrisoned at the Nathula post.*

Garron - *(noun)* a small, sturdy workhorse of a breed originating in Ireland and Scotland. *Here is a garron and it can pull heavy load.*

Garrulous - *(adjective)* excessively talkative. *He is a garrulous old man.*

Garter - *(noun)* a band worn around the leg to keep up a stocking or sock. [north American] a suspender for a sock or stocking. *She regularly wears garters to keep her stocking in place.*

Garth - *(noun)* [British] an open space surrounded by cloisters. *I have a garth at the back of my house.*

Gash - *(noun)* a long, deep slash, cut, or wound. *The gash he in the gorearm during fighting become infected.*

Gasket - *(noun)* a sheet or ring of rubber or other material sealing the junction between two surfaces in an engine or other device. *Mechanics often use gasket to seal joints.*

Gasoline - *(noun)* [north American] term for petrol. *The car needs gasoline so look out for a petrol pump.*

Gasometer - *(noun)* a large tank in which gas for use as fuel is stored before being distributed to consumers. *The petrol tanker has arrived, so open the lid of the gasometer for refillings.*

Gasp - *(verb)* **1** catch one's breath with an open mouth, owing to pain or astonishment. strain to obtain by gasping. *He gasped with pain as he sprained his ankle.* **2** [informal] be desperate to obtain or consume; crave. *I'm gasping for a drink.* *(noun)* a convulsive catching of breath. *He gasped for breath as the blow hit him in the stomach.*

Gastronomy - *(noun)* the practice or art of choosing, cooking and eating good food. *He believes that gastronomy is a great way of life.*

Gaudy - *(adjective)* extravagantly or tastelessly bright or showy. *He wears gaudy clothes.*

Gaul - *(noun)* a native or inhabitant of the ancient European region of Gaul. *Many labourers who worked in building pyramids lived in Gaul.*

Gaunt - *(adjective)* lean and haggard, especially through suffering, hunger, or age. *He is a gaunt old man.*

Gauntlet - *(noun)* a stout glove with a long loose wrist. [historical] an armoured glove. *Gladiators wore gauntlet while figliting.*

Gave - past of give. *He gave his son sufficient amount of money to start business.*

Gavel - *(noun)* a small hammer with which an auctioneer, judge, etc. hits a surface to call for attention or order. *See, this is the gavel which the judge hits on before calling order, order.* *(verb)* bring to order by use of a gavel. *The judge gavelled to quieten the court.*

Gawk - *(verb)* stare openly and stupidly. *As she approached him, he gawked at her beauty.* *(noun)* an awkward or shy person. *He is a gawking fellow.*

Gaze - *(verb)* look steadily and intently. *He could only gaze at the beauty of Taj Mahal.* *(noun)* a steady intent look. *His gaze disturbed her.* **2** *His hobby is gazing at stars.*

Gazebo - *(noun)* a small building, especially one in the garden of a house, that gives a wide view of the surrounding area. *The gardener has been taking care of the garden while staying in the gazebo.*

Gazette - *(noun)* **1** a journal or newspaper, especially the official one of an organization or institution. *The news of his appointment was published in the gazette.* *(verb)* announce or publish in an official gazette. publish the fact. *The government will need to gazette the bill when passed by legislative.*

Gazetteer - *(noun)* a geographical index or dictionary. *Look into the state gazetteer to find, this place.*

Gearing - *(noun)* the set or arrangement of gears in a machine. *Get the gearing checked by some expert mechanic.*

Gecko - *(noun)* a nocturnal lizard with adhesive pads on the feet, found in warm regions. *Look at this strange creature, slowly moving on the ceiling it is a gecko.*

Gelatin - *(noun)* a brownish baboon with a long mane and naked red rump, native to Ethiopia. *Gelatins are found in Ethiopia.*

Gelatinous - *(adjective)* having a jelly-like consistency. of or like the protein gelatin. *This food is gelatinous.*

Gelation - *(noun)* technical solidification by freezing. *The process of gelation takes place as you put water tray in the freezer.*

Gelid - *(adjective)* icy; extremely cold. *Siberia in Russia is a gelid place, very cold and defficult to live.*

Gem - *(noun)* **1** a precious or semi-precious stone, especially when cut and polished or engraved. *India is one of the largest exporters of gems and other precious stores.* **2** an outstanding person or thing. *He is gem of a person.*

Gemini - *(noun)* **1** astronomy a northern constellation the twins, said to represent the twins castor and pollex. *I am a Gemini and as such I'll do well today.* **2** astrology the third sign of the zodiac, which the sun enters about 21 May. *Geminis are people born between 21 May and 20 June.*

Gemma - *(noun)* a small cellular body or bud that can separate to form a new organism. *This gemma will fall into the earth and develop into a plant.*

Gender - *(noun)* **1**the state of being male or female (typically used with reference to social and cultural differences rather than biological ones *The entry to the Durga Pooja pandal was divided gender-wise –one for male and another for female.* the members of one or other sex (biological difference) *There is a lot of difference between the genders of male and female.*

Genealogy - *(noun)* line of descent traced continuously from an ancestor. *He is studying genealogy and willl be able to draw your family free.*

Generalissimo - *(noun)* the commander of a combined military force consisting of army, navy, and air force units. *During war he was given the post of generalissimo.*

Generality – *(noun)* **1** a statement or principle having general rather than specific validity or force. the quality or state of being general. *He confined his remarks to generalities only*. **2** the majority. *His service was better than that offered by the generality of doctors.*

Generalization – *(noun)* a general steatement. *Generalization of any commodity or rule helps people.*

Generalise – *(verb)* **1** make a general or broad statement by inferring from specific cases. *He generalizes a lot and his friends are quite amused by it.* **2** make more common or more widely applicable. *he attemped to generalise the elite school education in England.*

Generally – *(adverb)* **1** in most cases. *Generally speaking leaders do not fulfil their promises.* **2** without regard to particulars or exceptions. *Britain generally sides with America on foreign policy issues.* **3** widely. *The term of lease is generally 99 years.*

Generate – *(verb)* **1** cause to arise or come about. *He generates a lot of happiness wherever he goes.* **2** produce. *Power stations generate electricity.*

Generation – *(noun)* **1** all of the people born and living at about the same time, regarded collectively. the average period in which children grow up and have children of their own. *Old and young generations can never adjust with each other.* **2** a set of members of a family regarded as a single step or stage in descent. *Today's generation is cell phone and internet oriented.* **3** the action of producing or generating. the propagation of living organisms; procreation. *Procreation and generation is the secret of all life.*

Generator – *(noun)* **1** a person or thing that generates. *A generator creates electricity.* **2** a dynamo or similar machine for converting mechanical energy into electricity. *Miniature dynamoes comet mechanical energy and electrical one to power toys.*

Generic – *(adjective)* referring to a class or group; not specific. *These clothes are generic, not branded, but still good.* *(noun)* having no brand name. *Doctors generally prescribed branded drugs and not generic ones.*

Generosity – *(noun)* **1** the quality of being kind and generous. *I am overwhelmed by the sheer generosity of friends and neighbours.* **2** the quality or fact of being plentiful or large *Guests certainly wouldn't complain about the generosity of the host in offering superior food and comfort.*

Genet – *(noun)* a nocturnal catlike mammal with short legs and a long bushy ringed tail, found in Africa, SW Europe, and Arabia. *This zoo has received a genet. Let us go and see it.*

Genetic – *(adjective)* **1** of or relating to genes or heredity. of or relating to genetics. *This kind of superior behaviour is purely genetic.* **2** of or relating to origin, or arising from a common origin. *A strong genetic relative exist betwêen languages.*

Genetics – *(noun)* the study of heredity. *I find the science of genetics very interesting.*

Genie – *(noun)* a jinn or spirit, especially one imprisoned within a bottle or oil lamp and capable of granting wished when summoned. *The whole cosmos is like a genie you get whatever you want.*

Genius – *(noun)* **1** exceptional intellectual or creative power or other natural ability. *He is a genius, he has got 100% marks in maths.* **2** an exceptionally intelligent or able person. *He is a mathematical genius.***3** a spirit associated with a person, place, or instituation. *Many see Ravan as the man's evil genius.*

Genteel – *(adjective)* affectedly polite and refined. *He is a genteel person everybody likes him.*

Gentile – *(adjective)* not Jewish. *He is gentile and firmly believes in Christianity.* *(noun)* a person who is not Jewish. *Though a gentile he knows Hebrew language.*

Gentility – *(noun)* socially superior or genteel character or behaviour. *He has great gentility and does not believe in hurting anybody.*

Gentle – *(noun)* fishing a maggot, especially the larva of a blowfly, used as bait. *While fishing people generally use gentle as a bait.*

Gentleman – *(noun)* a courteous or honourable man. *He is a thorough gentleman you can always rely on him.*

Gently – *(adverb)* politely. *He gently asked her to go away.*

Genuine – *(adjective)* truly what it is said to be; authentic. *It is a genuine document, even the court has admitted it.*

Gendesy – *(noun)* the branch of mathematics concerned with the shape and area of the earth or large portions of it. *He is a specialist i. the study of gendesy.*

Geography – *(noun)* **1** the study of the physical features of the earth and of human activity as it relates to these. *Geography is his favourite subject.* **2** the relative arrangement of places and physical features. *You should learn the geography of your country thoroughly.*

Geomancy – *(noun)* the art of sitting buildings auspiciously. *He is an expert in geomancy.*

Geometry – *(noun)* **1** the branch of mathematics concerned with the properties and relations of points, lines, surfaces, solids, and higher dimensional analogues. *Some people find geometry very interesting.* **2** the shape and relative arrangement of the parts of something. *The geometry of an spider's was is very complicated.*

Geophagy – *(noun)* the practice in some tribal societies of eating earth. *Geophagy has no place in civilized and cultured societies.*

German – *(noun)* **1** a native or national of Germany, or a person of German descent. *I am learning German these day. (adjective)* of or relating to Germany, its people, or their language. *Germans are very proud of their culture.*

Germicide – *(noun)* a substance to or of the nature of a germ cell or embryo. *Chemical product used to kill germs.*

Germinate – *(verb)* begin to put out shoots after sometime. *Seeds germinate fast during summer season.* come into existerm. *The idea germinated slowly grew into mass following.*

Germination – *(noun)* the process of putting out shoots. *Germination is these seeds has taken place and no more water is needed.*

Gestation – *(noun)* **1** the process of carrying or being carried in the womb between conception and birth. *The gestation lasts about nine month?* **2** the development of a plan or idea over a period of time. *This painstaking work stayed longtime in gestation.*

Gesticulate – *(verb)* gesture dramatically in place of or to emphasize speech. *He gesticulate wildly to emphasize the main points of his speech.*

Gesture – *(noun)* **1** a movement of part of the body, especially a hand or the head, to express an idea or meaning. *He gestured me to follow him. (verb)* make a gesture. *A kind gesture can help us a lot.*

Getting – *(verb)* come to have, receive. *I am getting to know him better as time is passing.*

Get-up – *(noun)* [informal] a style or arrangement of dress, especially an elaborate or unusual one. *She came to the party in the get up of a princess.*

Geyser – *(noun)* **1** a hot spring in which water intermittently bolls, sending a tall column of water and steam into the air. *There are many hidden geysers in the jungles of south America.* **2** British a gas-fired water heater through which water flows as it is rapidly heated. *Modern washromms come fitted with geysers.*

Ghastly – *(adjective)* **1** causing great horror or fear, macabre. *The ghastly accident took place on highway at 3 a.m.* **2** deathly white or pallid. *Ghastly scenes of Dracula in the film frightened many people.* **3** [informal] very objectionable or unpleasant. *He had a ghastly appearance as he emerged out of the tunnel after a long time.*

Ghost – *(noun)* **1** an apparition of a dead person which is believed to appear to the living typically as a nebulous image. [larchaic] a spirit or soul. *This house is haunted by the ghost of a monk.* **2** a faint trace: the ghost of a smile. *He said that he had seen a ghost in the graveyard* **3** a faint secondary image produced by a fault in an optical system or on a cathode ray screen. *He gave me a ghost of smile and went away troubled as he was. (verb)* act as ghost writer of. *His memoirs were smoothly ghosted by a journalist.*

Giant – *(noun)* **1** an imaginary or mythical being of human form but superhuman size. *He has giant like appearance being so tall and broad* **2** an abnormally tall or large person, animal, or plant. *Amitabh Bacchan is a giant among actors.* **3** astronomy a star of relatively great size and luminosity. *There me many giant sized stars many times larger than our Sun.* **4** *Bargad is a giant of a tree. 5 He has a gigantic appearance and impresses people around. (adjective)* of very great size or force; gigantic. *The milky way is so large a galaxy that is distance measured in light years.*

Gibber – *(verb)* speak rapidly and unintelligibly, typically through fear or shock. *He was so afraid that he gibbered instead of talking.* **2** *His gibbering irritated me.*

Gibbet – *(noun)* **1** a gallows. *The murderer was gibbeted.* **2** an upright post with an arm on which the bodies of executed criminals were left hanging as a warning or deterrent to others. *Criminals are taken to gibbet and hanged.*

Gibbon – *(noun)* a small, slender tree-dwelling ape with long, powerful arms, native to the forests of SE Asia. *Gibbons can be seen in plenty in jungles of SE Asia.*

Gibe – *(noun & verb)* variant spelling of jibe. *He made a gibe against me and I was highly irritated. 2. As I gibed at him he lost his temper.*

Gibus – *(noun)* a kind of collapsible top hat. *He is fond of wearing gibus.*

Giddily – *(adverb)* disoriented. *He walked giddily and needed support.*

Giddiness – *(noun)* dizziness. *He suffers from giddiness and often falls down.*

Gift – *(noun)* **1** a thing given willingly to someone without payment; a present. *I gave her a costly gift on her birthday.* **2** a natural ability or talent. *He has a gift for acting. This opportunity is a god given gift grab it. (verb)* give as a gift, especially formally. *She received many wedding gifts.*

Gild – *(verb)* **1** cover thinly with gold. *This a gilded bracelet.* **2** wealthy and privileged: gilded youth. *He is a gilded young man belonging to wealthy persons.*

Gill – *(noun)* **1** the paired respiratory organ of fished and some amphibians, by which oxygen is extracted from water flowing over surfaces within or attached to the walls of the pharynx. *All fish have gills through which thy inhale oxygen.* **2** the vertical plates arranged radically on the underside or mushrooms and many toadstools. *The fish were caught in a gill net. (verb)* catch in a gill net. *The fish were caught in a gill net.*

Gilt – *(adjective)* covered thinly with gold leaf or gold paint. *Many artificiel jewellery is gilt edged. (noun)* **1** gold leaf or gold paint applied in a thin layer to a surface. *This dagger has a gilted handle.*

Gimlet – *(noun)* **1** a small T-shaped tool with a screw tip for boring holes. *We need a gimlet to bore holes in the wall to fix cloths hanger.*

Ginger – *(noun)* **1** a hot, fragrant spice obtained from the rhizome of a plant. *Ginger a root plant with many medicinal uses.* **2** a SE asian plant, resembling bamboo in appearance, from which ginger is taken. see also widl ginger. *I am fond of ginger in food. (verb)* **1** flavour with ginger. *Ginger flavoured cold drinks are very refreshing.* **2** stimulate or enliven someone or something. *She came and danced in a gingerly way.*

Gingerly – *(adverb)* in a careful or cautious manner. *I gingerly tonched the animal in the zoo.*

Gingham – *(noun)* lightweight plain-woven cotton cloth, typically checked. *I like to wear clathes made of gingham.*

Gingival – *(adjective)* medicine concerned with the gums. *I have bleeding gums and I need some gingival.*

Ginglymus – *(noun)* anatomy a hinge-like joint such as the elbow or knee. *There is great pain is my ginglymus.*

Girandole – *(noun)* a branched support for candles or other lights. *Please bring a girandole I have many candles to light.*

Gird – *(verb)* encircle (a person or part of the body) with a belt *A young man is to be girded with the belt of knighthood this afternoon.* secure (a garment or sword) on the body with a belt or band *He was decorated with a white robe girded with a orange coloured sash.* Surround *The ruins are girded by two deep gorges all around the area.*

Girder – *(noun)* a large metal beam used in building bridges and large buildings. *No large constructions can be done without th support of girders.*

Girdle – *(noun)* Scottish and northern English term for griddle. *She has girdled her waist by a gorgeous belt.*

Girt – *(noun)* old-fashioned term for girth. *He has a big girt as he eats too much.*

Girth – *(noun)* **1** the measurement around the middle of something, especially a person's waist. *The tailor measured his girth, it was sixty inches.* *(verb)* [larchaic] surround; encircle. *There are four seas that girth Britain.*

Gist – *(noun)* **1** the substance or essence of a speech or text. *The gist of his talk is 'never give up'.* **2** [law] real point of an action. *Claiming damage was the gist of action the lawyer suggested.*

Given – *(adjective)* **1** specified stated. *Given these hints you can find the solution to the problem.* **2** inclined or disposed to. *If given the choice, I would rather stay than go.* 3 [law, archaic] signed and dated. *preposition* taking into account. *(noun)* a known or established term for first name.

Giver – *(noun)* a person who gives something. *God is a giver of mercy.*

Glabrous – *(adjective)* technical free from hair or down; smooth. *Her skin is glabrous and glowing.*

Glace – *(adjective)* **1** having a glossy surface due to preservation in sugar. *It is a glace cherry.* **2** smooth and highly polished. *This table top is highly glaced.*

Glacial – *(adjective)* **1** relating to ice, especially in the form of glaciers or ice sheets. *The glacial mountain floated slowly on the sea.* **2** extremely cold or unfriendly; icy. *It is very difficult to take both in glacial temperatures.* *(noun)* [geology] a glacial period. *The glacial period occurred millions of years age.*

Glaciated – *(adjective)* covered or having been covered by glaciers or ice sheets. *A glaciated sea is highly dangerous for ships.*

Glacier – *(noun)* a slowly moving mass of ice formed by the accumulation and compaction of snow on mountains or near the poles. *A glacier tore apart the steel plates of the Titanic Ship.*

Glad – *(adjective)* **1** pleased; delighted. causing happiness: glad tidings. *I am glad to see you.* **2** grateful. *I am glad to see you jogging in the morning.*

Gladden – *(verb)* make glad. *He gladdens everybody he meets.*

Glade – *(noun)* an open space in a wood or forest. *Here is a glade we can fix our tents to stay overnight.*

Gladly – *(adverb)* willingly. *I will gladly do whatever you say.*

Gladness – *(adjective)* sense of happiness. *He radiates gladness wherever he goes.*

Gladstone bag – *(noun)* a bag like a briefcase having two equal compartments joined by a hinge. *He is habitual of carrying a sladstone bag.*

Glamour – *(noun)* **1** an attractive and exciting quality, especially sexual allure. *The film world is a world of glamour.* **2** [larchaic] attractive. *She is very glamorous looking.*

Gland – *(noun)* an organ of the body which secretes particular chemical substances. a lymph node. *Our body has many glands that secrete different substances.*

Glandular – *(adjective)* relating to or affecting a gland or glands. *This is a glandular disease.*

Glare – *(verb)* **1** stare in an angry or fierce way. *She glared at him with her cheeks turning red.* **2** shine with a or conspicuous. *The sun glared out of the blue sky.* *(noun)* **1** a fierce or angry stare. *She gave him a glare of contempt.* **2** strong and dazzling light. *She narrowed her eyes against the glare of the halogen light.*

Glass – *(noun)* **1** a hard, brittle, usually transparent or translucent substance made by fusing sand with soda and lime. ornaments and other articles made from glass. *The screen is made of glass. The top of this dining table is made of heavy black glass.* **2** a drinking container made of glass. *Pour the soft drink in four glasses. Bangles made of glass tend to break easily.* **3**

a lens or optical instrument, in particular a monocle or a magnifying lens. *His eyesight has become weak and he needs a reading glass.* 4 chiefly British a mirror. *Have a look at your face in the looking glass.* *(verb)* cover or enclose with glass. *Front office of most hotels is made of transparent glasses these days.*

Glaucoma – *(noun)* medicine a condition of increased pressure within the eyeball, causing gradual loss of sight. *He suffers from glaucoma and his eye sight is becoming dim.*

Glaze – *(verb)* **1** fit panes of glass into a window frame or similar structure. enclose or cover with glass. *This house has a glazed balcony.* **2** cover with a glaze. *He had all the windows newly glazed.* **3** lose brightness and animation. *The prospect of going to the village makes my eyes glaze over with boredom.* *(noun)* **1** a vitreous substance fused on to the surface of pottery to form a hard, impervious decorative coating. *The glaze of the white coffee mug was attractive.* **2** a liquid such as milk or beaten egg, used to form a smooth shiny coating on food. *Brush the cake with almond glaze.*

Glazier – *(noun)* a person whose trade is fitting glass into windows and doors. *He is a glazier by profession, call him to fix your window panes.*

Glean – *(verb)* collect gradually from various sources. *He gleaned information from the library to write a new article.*

Gleeful – *(adjective)* exuberantly or triumphantly joyful. *His gleeful talk charmed her. I'll gleefully do whatever you say.*

Gleet – *(noun)* [medicine] a watery discharge from the urethra caused by gonorrhoeal infection. *Look at the gleet, this patient apperars to have a venereal disease.*

Glen – *(noun)* a narrow valley, especially in Scotland or Ireland. *The army was attacked when it was passing through a glen.*

Glib – *(adjective)* articulate and voluble but insincere and shallow. *He is a glib fellow don't trust him too much.*

Glimmer – *(verb)* shine faintly with a wavering light. *The light glimmered and ultimately went out.* *(noun)* **1** a faint or wavering light. *I couldn't see properly in the glimmering light.* **2** a faint sign of a feeling or quality, especially a desirable one: a glimmer of hope. *Everything is not finished yet I have still a glimmer of hope.*

Glimpse – *(noun)* a momentary or partial view. *(verb)* see briefly or partially. *He had only a glimpse at the report and understood everything.* *(verb)* see briefly. *She glimpsed a figure standing behind her.*

Glint – *(verb)* give out or reflect small flashes of light. *The glasses glinted in the moonlight.* *(noun)* a small flash of light, especially a reflected one. *A glint of light told us that the tunnel was going to end.*

Glissade – *(noun)* a slide down a steep slope of snow or ice, typically on the feet with the support of an outwards from the body and then takes the weight while the second leg is brushed in to meet it. *He performed nicely with the help of glissade.* *(verb)* perform or move by means of a glissade. *The glissade here is dangerous.*

Glister – *(verb)* sparkle; glitter. *The glow worms glistered in the dark of the night.* *(noun)* a sparkle. *A glister in the switch box worried me.*

Glitter – *(verb)* **1** shine with a bright, shimmering reflected light. *All that glitters in not gold.* **2** impressively successful or glamorous: a glittering career. *Many Bollywood actresses had a glittering career.* *(noun)* **1** bright, shimmering reflected light. *A lot of glittering bulb were used in decoration.* **2** tiny pieces of sparkling material used for decoration. *The banquet hall was decorated with glittering stories.*

Gloaming – *(plural noun)* [informal] fashionable people involved in show business or some other glamorous activity. *The gloaming are a part and parcel of Bollywood life.*

Gloat – *(verb)* [poetic/literary] twilight; dusk. *He was gloating at his success in the interview.*

Globe – *(noun)* **1** a spherical or rounded object. a golden orb as an emblem of sovereignty. *Look at the globe and find out where longitude India is situated.* **2** a spherical representation of the earth with a map on the surface. *The latitude or longitude of any country can be found on the globe.* **3** the earth. *(verb)* [poetic/literary] form into a globe. *Some people have a hobby of studying globe.*

Globular – *(adjective)* globe-shaped; spherical. *Earth is globural in shape.*

Globule – *(noun)* a small round particle of a substance; a drop. *A globule of water fell down from the tree.*

Gloom – *(noun)* **1** partial or total darkness. *he strained his eyes peering into the gloom.* **2** a state of depression or despondency. *This is the year of economic gloom for car industry. (verb)* appear gloomy. *The gloom in his life persisted as he could not cope with circumstances.*

Gloomy – *(adjective)* **1** poorly lit, especially so as to cause fear or depression. *These rooms are cold and gloomy, I want to go in warm sunlight.* **2** causing or feeling depression or despondency. *His gloomy appearance saddened me.*

Glorification – *(noun)* to praise. *Her glorification made her a film star.*

Glorious – *(adjective)* worthy of bringing fame. *This is the most glorious victory of all time.*

Glossary – *(noun)* an alphabetical list of words relating to a specific subject, text, or dialect, with explanations. *Look at the glossary given at the end of the book to find out what does this word stand for.*

Glossiness – *(noun)* attractive, shiny, smooth.*The glass top of the table has lost its glossiness.*

Glossy – *(adjective)* **1** shiny and smooth. *After the paint the wall has become very glossy.* **2** superficially attractive and stylish. *The book has an attractive and glossy cover. (noun)* [informal] a magazine printed on glossy paper with many colour photographs. *This is a 32-page glossy brochure.*

Glottis – *(noun)* the part of the larynx consisting of the vocal cords and the slit-like opening between the. *There is something stuck in his glottis he can't speak.*

Glower – *(verb)* have an angry or sullen look on one's face; scowl. *She glowered at him suspiciously. (noun)* an angry or sullen look. *He glowered at me and began to quarrel.*

Glow-worm – *(noun)* a soft-bodied beetle whose larva like wingless female emits light to attract males. *It is beautiful to look at glow worm in the dark of the night.*

Glucose – *(noun)* a simple sugar which is an important energy source in living organisms and is a component of many carbohydrates. a syrup containing glucose and other sugars, made by hydrolysis of starch and used in the food industry. *Glucose is an important ingredient of diet. He is being given glucose intravenously as he grew very weak.*

Glue – *(noun)* an adhesive substance used for sticking objects or materials together. *The wood joints as being glued together. (verb)* **1** fasten or join with glue. *I was glued to his words.* **2** [informal] be paying very close attention to. *I was glued to the TV when the olympics were on.*

Glum – *(adjective)* dejected; morose. *He is a glum looking fellow who rarely breaks his silence.*

Glut .– *(noun)* an excessively abundant supply of something. *The glut of mobile phons in the market attracted the buyers. (verb)* supply or fill to excess. *He was glutted with praise.*

Gluten – *(noun)* a substance present in cereal grains, especially wheat, which is responsible for the elastic texture of dough. *Wheat possesses glutter that is why can knead it.*

Glyptography – *(noun)* the art or scientific study of gem engraving. *He is an expert in glyptography.*

Gnarl – *(noun)* a rough, knotty protuberance, especially on a tree. *Look at the gnarl of the old tree.*

Gnarled – *(adjective)* knobbly, rough, and twisted, especially with age. *The gnarled old oak tree was cut down.*

Gnat – *(noun)* a small two-winged fly resembling a mosquito, typically forming large swarms. many other species, especially in the family culicidae. *This room is infested with gnats.*

Gnaw – *(verb)* **1** bite at or nibble persistently. *he was watching the dog gnawing at the big bone.* **2** cause persistent anxiety or distress. *The doubts contirved to gnaw at him.*

Gnawing – *(adjective)* worrying distressing. *The gnawing fear made him restless.*

Gnome – *(noun)* **1** a legendary dwarfish creature supposed to guard the earth's treasures underground. *Children like to imagine and talk about gnomes.* **2** [informal] a person having secret or sinister influence, especially in financial matters. *The gnomes of Zurich influence world money market.*

Gnomic – *(adjective)* in the form of short, pithy maxims or aphorisms. *His gnomic talk disturbed me.*

Gnu – *(noun)* a large African antelope with a long head, a beard and mane, and a sloping back. *Gnu can be seen in the jungles of Africa.*

Go – *(verb)* **1** move from one place to another, travel *He went out to the shops she longs to go. We've a long way to go.* travel a specified distance *You have to go a few miles more to reach his house.* travel or move in order to engage in a specified activity *He used to go hunting quite often.* (go to) attend or visit for a particular purpose *We went to the cinema. He went to Cambridge University.* change in level, amount, or rank *Prices have gone up by 15 per cent.* [informal] said in various expressions when angrily or contemptuously dismissing someone *Go and complete all the pending jobs before you leave for home.* **2** leave, depart *I really must go home now.* (of time) pass or elapse *They had gone without talking for two weeks.* come to an end *A golden period that we enjoyed has now gone for good.* cease to exist *11,500 jobs are due to go by next year.* die (used euphemistically) *I'd like to see my grandchildren happily married before I go for good.* be lost or stolen *When she returned home minutes later her equipment had gone.* (go to) be sold or awarded to *The first prize went to a twenty-four-year-old engineering student.* **3** (be going to be/do something) intend or be likely or intended to be or do something (used to express a future tense) *I'm going to be late for work. She's going to have a baby.* **4** pass into or be in a specified state, especially an undesirable one *The food is going bad. No one ever gone hungry in our house. She has gone completely crazy.* (go to/into) enter into a specified state or course of action *He went back to the bedroom to sleep.* **5** proceed or turn out in a specified way *How did the picnic go?* **6** be harmonious, complementary, or matching *Fried rice goes with chicken. The earrings and the scarf don't really go together.* be found in the same place or situation *Cooking and eating at a picnic go together.* **7** *(of a machine or device) function No car will go without fuel.* continue in operation or existence *The committee was kept going even when its existence could no longer be justified.* **8** (go into/to/towards) contribute to or be put into (a whole) *Considerable effort had gone into making the operation successful.* **9** (of an article) be regularly kept or put in a particular place *Please try to remember which card goes into which machine slot.* **10** (of a song or account) have a specified content or wording *If you haven't heard it, the story goes like this.* **11** [informal] use a toilet; urinate or defecate *She had to go but couldn't, because he was still in the bathroom.* **12** [informal] used to emphasize the speaker's annoyance at someone's action *Don't go poking your nose where you shouldn't.* *(noun)* **1** an attempt or trial at something *Have a go at answering the questions yourself.* **2** a person's turn to use or do something *I had a go on Naresh's racing car. Come on Shyam, it's your go.* **3** spirit, animation, or energy *There's no go in me at all these days.* **4** an attack of illness *She's had this nasty go of dysentery.* *(adjective)* [informal] functioning properly *All systems are going properly.*

Goad – *(verb)* **1** a spiked stick used for driving cattle. *The cowboys goaded their catlle across the field.* **2** someone into action. *I was goaded into action by his encouraging words.* *(noun)* **1** provoke to action or reaction; urge on with a goad. *He was trying to goad him into a boxing ring for a match.*

Goal – *(noun)* **1** a pair of posts linked by a crossbar and forming a space into which the ball has to be sent in order to score. *Both the football teams scored a goal against each other.* **2** an aim or desired result. the destination of a journey. *It is my goal in life to become an administrative officer.*

Goat – *(noun)* **1** a hardy domesticated ruminant mammal that has backward-curving horns and a beard. a wild mammal related to this, such as the ibex, markhor, and tur. *The goats have a wonderful ability to climb rocky terrains.* **2** [informal] a lecherous man. *His is a goat like behaviour so far as women are concerned.* **3** british [informal] a stupid person; a fool. *He is a goat and always talks nonsense.* **4** [US informal] a scapegoat. *He was made a scapegoat for the fault of others.*

Gobbet – *(noun)* a piece or lump of flesh, food, or other matter. *This gobet looks rotten, throw it away.*

Gobble – *(verb)* eat hurriedly and noisily, use a large amount of very quickly. *He gobbled the food down as he was very hungry.*

Gobbler– *(noun)* a person who eats greedily. *He is a gobbler and makes a lot of noise while eating.*

Goblet – *(noun)* a drinking glass with a foot and a stem. [larchaic] a bowl-shaped metal or glass drinking cup. *He drank wine from a goblet.*

Goblin – *(noun)* a mischievous, ugly, dwarf-like creature of floklore. *Goblins often featured in early literature.*

Godown – *(noun)* a warehouse. *Most business house maintain a godown to stock their products.*

Goer – *(noun)* **1** a person who attends a specified place or event: a theatre-goer. *He is a thorough cinema goer.* **2** [informal] a person or thing that goes. *She is a goer and has lot of friends.*

Goggle - *(verb)* look with wide open eyes, typically in amazement *He goggled at them incomplete disbelief.* (of the eyes) open wide or protrude *They were watching the circus show with their eyes goggling and their tongues hanging out.* *(adjective)* (of the eyes) protuberant or rolling *The lights were flashing so much that it was difficult to keep eyes from goggling.* *(noun)* **1** close-fitting glasses with side shields, for protecting the eyes from glare, dust, water, etc. *She bought a pair of swimming goggles stoday.* **2** a stare with protruding eyes. *Their goggle mesmerizes even fishmongers.*

Goitre – *(noun)* a swelling of the neck resulting from enlargement of the thyroid gland. *People suffering from goitre are put on special medicine.*

Golden – *(adjective)* **1** made of, coloured like, or shining like gold. *She has wrls of glossy, golden hair.* **2** made or consisting of gold. *This is a golden crown.*

Gone - *(adjective)* **1** no longer present, departed *They were gone a long time. The bad old days are gone.* no longer in existence; dead or extinct *An aunt of mine, long since gone.* no longer available, consumed or used up *The food's all gone, I'm afraid.* in a trance or stupor, especially through exhaustion, drink, or drugs *He sat on a folding chair, half-gone.* beyond help, in a hopeless state *Spending time and effort on a gone car like old Ford.* **2** having reached a specified time in a pregnancy *She is now four months gone.* *(preposition)* (of time) past *It's gone half past eleven.* (of age) older than *He was gone seventy by then.*

Gong – *(noun)* **1** a metal disc with a turned rim, giving a resonant note when struck. *As the gong struck all courtiers stood up to receive the king.* **2** [British informal] a medal or decoration. *A music instrument in the orchestra sounded like a gong.* *(verb)* sound a gong or make a sound like that of a gong. *The old car was making a moise similar to a gong.*

Goniometer – *(noun)* an instrument for the precise measurement of angles, especially the angles between the faces of crystals. *Crystals have many faces and goniometer is used to measure the angles.*

Goose – *(noun)* **1** a large water bird with a long neck, short legs, webbed feet, and a short, broad bill, the female of such a bird. *It is a flock of geese making sounds in the garden.*

Gooseberry – *(noun)* **1** around edible yellowish-green or reddish berry with a thin translucent hairy skin. *Pick out up gooseberries from among the thorns.* **2** [British informal] a third person in the company of two people, especially lovers, who would prefer to be alone. *He is a gooseberry between the two, he should leave.*

Goosey – *(adjective)* **1** exhibiting gooseflesh. *This peace of meat is goosey.* **2** [US] sensitive to being tickled. *Don't tickle him, he is goosey.*

Gopher – *(noun)* a burrowing American rodent with fur-lined pouches on its cheeks. [informal north American] term for ground squirrel. in names of various burrowing reptiles: gopher tortoise. *In US a kind of rodents is called gopher.*

Gore – *(noun)* blood that has been shed, especially as a result of violence. *The sight of gore sickened me.*

Gorge – *(noun)* **1** a steep, narrow valley or ravine. *He fell into a gorge and had to be pulled out.* **2** the contents of the stomach. *He gorged down the food.*

Gorget – *(noun)* **1** [historical] an article of clothing a piece of amount covering the throat. a wimple. *Gorgets were in fashion in early times.* **2** a patch of colour on the throat of a bird or other animal. *Gorgets are beautiful to look at.*

Gorgon – *(noun)* **1** [Greek mythology] each of three sisters with snakes for hair, who had the power to turn anyone who looked at them to stone. *Gorgon was a frightening mythological creature.* **2** a fierce, frightening, or repulsive woman. *She is a gorgon and I would rather avoid her.*

Gorilla – *(noun)* **1** a powerfully built great ape of central Africa, the largest living primate. *Gorillas are anthropoid creatures living in Africa.* **2** [informal] a heavily built aggressive-looking man. *He is a gorilla of a man, don't mess with him.*

Gory – *(adjective)* involving or showing violence and bloodshed. *I feel horrified at such gory scenes.*

Gosling – *(noun)* a young goose. *It is a gosling let us play with it.*

Gospel – *(noun)* **1** the teaching or revelation of Christ. *It is the gospel truth.* **2** the record of Christ's life and teaching in the first four books of the New testament, each of these books. *We should study gospel if we want know about Jesus Christ.*

Gossip – *(noun)* **1** casual conversation or unsubstantiated reports about other people. *Almost all people are fond of gossip.* **2** [chiefly derogatory] a person who likes talking about other people's private lives. *Too much gossiping can turn out to be a bad habit.* *(verb)* engage in gossip. *He engaged me in gossip and I got late.*

Got - past and past participle of get. *He got past without noticing me. He got awarded for his performance on stage. He got carried away emotionally and wept. He got away with the crime as there was no evidence. He got into the classroom silently.*

Gouge - *(noun)* a chisel with a concave blade, used in carpentry, sculpture, and surgery *Gouge is an instrument carpenters use to give shape to a woodwork.* *(verb)* **1** make (a groove, hole, or indentation) with on as if with a gouge *A 6 feet wide channel had been gouged out in the field by the flowing water.* make a rough hole or indentation in (a surface), especially so as to mar or disfigure it *He had wielded the blade carelessly, gouging the grass at several places.* (gouge something out) cut or force something out roughly or brutally *One of the young man's eyes had been gouged out by the robbers.* **2** overcharge or swindle (someone) *Fake drugs sold by the unscrupulous manufacturers are gouging patients in this country.* (gouge something out) obtain money by swindling or extortion *He had gouged wads of currency notes out of Manik's pocket.*

Gourmand – *(noun)* a person who enjoys eating, sometimes to excess. *He is a gourmand and good food is his weakness.*

Gout – *(noun)* a disease in which harmful metabolism of uric acid causes arthritis, especially in the smaller bones of the feet. *His toe is inflamed because he is suffering from gout.*

Governability – *(noun)* policies, governance. *My governability was in question I had to prove that I was a good admistrator.*

Governable – *(adjective)* manageable. *It is small rebellion and therefore governable.*

Governance – *(noun)* the action or manner of governing. [archaic] control. *There are different mades of governance all over the world.*

Governess – *(noun)* a woman employed to teach children in a private household. *I have at last found a good governess for my children.*

Gowk – *(noun)* [dialect] an awkward or foolish person. *He is a gowk although he pretends to be wise.*

Gown – *(noun)* **1** a long dress worn on formal occasions. *She wore a silk gown for his cocktail party.* **2** a protective garment worn in hospital by surgical staff or patients; a loose cloak indicating one's profession or status, worn by a lawyer, teacher, academic, or university student. *Lawyers and doctors wear gowns as required by their profession. (verb)* be dressed in a gown. *She was gowned in luminous silk.*

Grab – *(noun)* **1** seize suddenly and roughly. [informal] obtain quickly or opportunistically. grip the wheel harshly or jerkily. *He grabbed the thief by the collar.* **2** [informal] impress: *He grabbed my attention. Grab the opportunity or else you will repent. (noun)* **1** a quick sudden clutch or attempt to seize. denoting a bar or strap to hold on to for clutching, lifting, and moving loads. *The crane grabs the damaged truck to place elsewhere.*

Grabble – *(verb)* [larchaic] feel or search with the hands. *The officer grabbled my luggage inside out but could find nothing objectionable.*

Graceful – *(adjective)* having or showing grace or elegance. *She is a very graceful lady.*

Gracious – *(adjective)* **1** courteous, kind, and pleasant. *Her gracious presence enchanted all people present.* **2** showing the elegance and comfort brought by wealth. *Good gracious! I didn't expect you at this hour.*

Gradation – *(noun)* **1** a scale of successive changes, stages, or degrees. *The gradation from harsh to soft tone took time.* **2** a stage in a such a scale. *The gradation from pupa to larva and adult is a slow process.* **3** a minute change form one shade, tone, or colour to another. **4** [linguistics] another term for ablaut.

Grade - *(noun)* **1** a particular level of rank, quality, proficiency, or value *Sea salt is usually available in coarse or fine grades.* a level in a salary or employment structure *Indian civil administration is structured around officers, clerical and secretarial grades.* **2** a mark indicating the quality of a student's work *She got good grades in her first semester.* (with specifying ordinal number) those pupils in a school or school system who are grouped by age or ability for teaching at a particular level for a year *She teaches first grade students in this school.* an examination, especially in music *I took grade five examination in music and got a distinction.* **3** a variety of cattle produced by crossing with a superior breed *This breed of lamb you are seeing is of superior grade stock. (verb)* **1** arrange in or allocate to grades; classify or sort The timber is graded according to its thickness. **2** [chiefly North American] give a mark to (a student or a piece of work) *Each student has to be graded according to his performance in semester exams.* **3** pass gradually from one level, especially a shade of colour, into another *The sky graded from deep blue at the top to near white on the horizon.*

Gradient – *(noun)* a sloping part of a road or railway. *Be careful the gradient is very steep here.*

Gradual – *(adjective)* **1** taking place in stages over an extended period. *The gradual introduction of new method of education is being implemented.* **2** not steep or abrupt. *Relax, the slope is gradual here.*

Graduate – *(noun)* a person who has been awarded a first academic degree, or a high-school diploma. *He is a Delhi University graduate. (verb)* **1** successfully complete a degree, course, or high school. [north American] confer a degree or other academic qualification on. *From being a draftsman he has graduated to become an engineer.* **2** move up to something more advanced. *People change gradually.*

Graduation – *(noun)* academic achievement. *He has completed his graduation from Bombay University.*

Graft – *(noun)* [informal] bribery and other corrupt measures pursued for gain in politics or business. *Graft is spread all over our country. (verb)* make money by graft. *He has made a lot of money by graft.*

Grail – *(noun)* the cup or platter used by Christ at the last supper and in which Joseph of Arimathea received Christ's blood at the cross. *In early times knights used to search for the Grail.*

Grain – *(noun)* **1** wheat or other cultivated cereal used as food, a single seed or fruit or a cereal. *The seeds of wheat or other cultivated cereals is known as grain.* **2** a small, hard particle of a substance such as sand. a discrete particle or crystal in a metal, igneous rock. etc. *Look at the grains how beautiful they are.* **3** the smallest unit or weight in the Troy and Avoirdupois systems, equal to 1/5760 of a pound troy and 1/7000 of a pound avoirdupois, the smallest possible amount. *Millions of grains make a sand hill.* **4** the longitudinal arrangement of fibres in wood, paper, etc. the texture of wood, stone, etc. *He sconed along the grain of the table with the knife.* *(verb)* **1** give a rough surface or texture to. *His fingers were grained with coal dust.* **2** from into grains. *If the sugar does grain up add more water.*

Gram – *(noun)* a metric unit of mass equal to one thousandth of a kilogram. *One thousand grams make a kilogram.*

Gram – *(noun)* chickpeas or other pulses used as food. *Gram is a cereal rich in protein.*

Grammar – *(noun)* **1** the whole system and structure of a language or of languages in general, usually taken as consisting of syntax and morphology. a particular analysis of this. *It is not easy to understand grammar of any language.* **2** a book on grammar. *Without the knowledge of grammar we cannot use a language correctly.* **3** a set of prescriptive notions about correct use of a language. *It was not bad grammar but just dialect.* **4** the basic elements of an area of knowledge of skill. *He knows the grammar of mobile repairing.*

Gramophone – *(noun)* chiefly British old-fashioned term for record player. *A gramophone or record player can be a great source of entertainment.*

Granary – *(noun)* **1** a storehouse for threshed grain. *For an agricultural state a granary is a must.* **2** a region supplying large quantities of corn: *Egypt was the granary of Rome.*

Grandee – *(noun)* a spanish or portuguese nobleman of the highest rank. a man of high rank or eminence. *A grandee commands respect.*

Grandeur – *(noun)* splendour and impressiveness. high rank or social importance. *He is a man of grandeur hence respected by all.*

Grandiloquent – *(adjective)* denoting cultivated plant varieties with large flowers. *Grandiloquent gardening is his hobby.*

Graniferous – *(adjective)* [botany] producing grain or a grain-like seed. *It is a graniferous object sow it and it will grow.*

Granite – *(noun)* a very hard, granular, crystalline igneous rock consisting mainly of quartz, mica, and feldspar. *Granite is very useful, it can be used in many ways in construction business.*

Granivorous – *(adjective)* [zoology] feeding on grain. *A lot of people are granivorous. Whose main food is cereal and not meat.*

Granny – *(noun)* [informal] one's grand-mother. *I love my granny she tells us a lot of nice stories.*

Grant – *(verb)* **1** agree to give or allow to. give a right, property, etc. formally or legally to. *Don't worry, God will grant you your wish.* **2** agree or admit to that is true. *He has'nt made much progress, I'll grant you that.* *(noun)* **1** a sum of money given by a government or public body for a particular prupose. *The government granted a big sum of money to the earthquake affected state.* **2** [law] a legal conveyance or formal conferment. *He granted all his land to charity.*

Grantable – *(adjective)* allowable. *This wish of yours is not grantable.*

Granter – *(noun)* one who allows. *God is the granter of all our wishes.*

Granular – *(adjective)* resembling or consisting of granules. *This is something granular, polish its surface to make it smooth.* **2** having a roughened surface or structure. *Anti-slip mats have granular top surface.*

Granule – *(noun)* a small compact particle. *A granule of sand can tell us a lot if studied under a microscope.*

Grape – *(noun)* a green, purple, or black berry. *He is fond of eating black grapes.*

Graphics - *(plural noun)* **1** the products of the graphic arts, especially commercial design or illustration. *Graphics have done wonders in the world of cinema.* **2** computer processing. *The use of computers to generate and manipulate visual images is known as computer graphics.*

Graphite - *(noun)* a grey, crystalline, electrically conducting form of carbon which is used as a solid lubricant, as pencil lead, and as a moderator in nuclear reactors. *Graphite is used in pencils to write.*

Grapnel - *(noun)* **1** a grappling hook. *He attacked the robber with a grapnel.* **2** a small anchor with several flukes. *He threw a grapnel down the boat.*

Grapple - *(verb)* **1** engage in a close fight or struggle without weapons. struggle to deal with. *He grappled bravely with the robbers he grappled bravely with the problem. He grappled with the thief and overpowered him. (noun)* an act of grapping. *Both wrestlers were grappling to put the other down on the mat.*

Grass - *(noun)* **1** vegetation consisting of short plants with long narrow leaves, growing wild or cultivated on lawns and pasture. ground covered with this. *The lawn has beautiful soft grass.* **2** a plant with jointed stems and spikes of small wind-pollinated flowers, predominant in such vegetation. *All the ground here is covered with wild grass.* **3** [informal] cannabis.*Smoking grass is not allowed here. (verb)* **1** cover with grass. *The railway tracks were mostly grassed over.* **2** [British informal] inform the police of criminal activity or plans. *She threatened to grass me up.*

Grassy - *(adjective)* covered with grass. *This is a barren land with grassy patches here and there.*

Grasshopper - *(noun)* a plant-eating insect with long hind legs which are used for jumping. *It is a big swarm of grasshoppers and it will eat all the crop.*

Grateful - *(adjective)* **1** feeling or showing gratitude. *I am grateful to you for the favour you have shown me.* **2** [archaic] received with gratitude. *She gave him a grateful smile.*

Gratification - *(noun)* pleasure gained from satisfaction of a desire. *I feel great gratification in serving the needy.*

Gratify - *(verb)* **1** give pleasure or satisfaction. *She was gratified to see the shock in Jim's eyes.* **2** indulge or satisfy a desire. *I gratified my desire of eating lunch in a five star hotel.*

Grating - *(adjective)* sounding harsh and unpleasant. *His grating voice upset me.*

Gratis - *(adverb & adjective)* free of charge. *The gratis entry to the function permitted many people.*

Gratitude - *(noun)* thankfulness; appreciation of kindness. *I am indebted with gratitude for this kindness of yours.*

Gratuitous - *(adjective)* **1** done without reason, uncalled for. *This rude behavior is gratuitous.* **2** free of charge. *Some lawyers provide a form of gratuitous legal advice.*

Gratuity - *(noun)* **1** [formal] a tip given to a waiter, porter, etc. *He paid 10% the fair as gratuity to the taxi driver.* **2** [British] a sum of money paid to an employee at the end of a period of employment. *He received a handsome gratuity after retirement.*

Gravely - *(adverb)* cause for alarm, seriousness. *He answered my questions gravely.*

Graveness - *(noun)* serious manner. *His graveness impressed me.*

Gravel - *(noun)* **1** a loose aggregation of small stones and coarse sand, often used for paths and roads. *The path to the garden was made of gravel. (verb)* cover with gravel. *Gate to the house the path was gravelled.*

Graver - *(noun)* **1** a burin or other engraving tool. *His name was engraved on the stone slab by a graver.*

Gravitate - *(verb)* **1** be drawn towards a place, person, or thing. *I felt gravitated to her.* **2** physics move, or tend to move, towards a centre of gravity. *All things gravitate to earth.*

Gravitation - *(noun)* movement, or a tendency to move, towards a centre of gravity. *Gravitation pulls down everything to earth.*

Gravy - *(noun)* **1** the fat and juices exuding from meat during cooking; a sauce made from these juices together with stock and other ingredients. *The gravy is very tasty.*

Grayling – *(noun)* **1** an edible silvery-grey freshwater fish with horizontal violent stripes and a long high dorsal fin. *I would like to eat a grayling very much.* **2** a mainly brown butterfly having wings with birth eyespots and grayish undersides. *Look at this grayling closely, it is seldom seen.*

Graze – *(verb)* **1** eat grass in a field; feed on grass or grassland. *Cows graze in fields.* **2** [informal] eat frequent snacks at irregular intervals. [informal, chiefly north American] casually sample something. *Grazing snacks every now and then is not good for fealth.*

Grazier – *(noun)* a person who rears or fattens cattle or sheep for market. *He is a grazier and sells fat sheep and cattle.*

Grazing – *(noun)* grassland suitable for pasturage. *This ground is good for grazing.*

Grease – *(noun)* **1** a thick oily substance, especially as used as a lubricant. *The machine is in need of grease.* **2** animal fat used or produced in cooking. *Give me some grease to cook the meat.* *(verb)* smear or lubricate with grease. *Grasing machine parts helps reduce friction.*

Greasy – *(adjective)* **1** covered with or resembling grease. producing more body oils than average. containing or cooked with too much oil or fat. *This potato vegetable is very greasy, I can't eat it.* **2** effusively polite in a repellently insincere way. *He is a greasy fellow and I don't trust him at all.*

Greatly – *(adverb)* very much. *He is greatly polite in behaviour.*

Greaves – *(noun)* [historical] a piece of armour for the shin. *The warriors used to wear greaves to protect lower body doing war.*

Greed – *(noun)* intense and selfish desire for wealth, power, or food. *Greed has been the ruin of many people.*

Greedily – *(adverb)* appetite for food or anything. *He greedily ate the food.*

Greediness – *(noun)* selfish desire. *Greediness never pays.*

Gready – *(adjective)* having or showing greed. *He is a greedy fellow hence never satisfied.*

Green – *(noun)* **1** green colour or pigment *Major roads are marked in red, yellow or green.* green clothes or material *The girls wore red and green dresses.* green foliage or vegetation *A lovely canopy of pine trees can be seen in Kashmir.* **2** a green thing, in particular, green vegetables *You must eat greens vegetables.* [informal], dated money *That's a lot of green.* **3** a piece of public grassy land, especially in the centre of a village *There is a house overlooking the green.* an area of smooth, very short grass immediately surrounding a hole on a golf course *A 60 ft putt on the last green.* 4 (usually Green) a member or supporter of an environmentalist group or party: *Green Peace members have prevented the toxic lead-laden ship from unloading its cargo at the port.* *(verb)* **1** make or become green in colour *The roof of our house was greening with lichen.* **2** make (an urban or desert area) more verdant by planting trees or other vegetation *They hope to continue greening many treeless and dusty suburbs of this town.* **3** make less harmful to the environment *I have given you all tips on how to green your home.*

Greenish – *(adjective)* resembling green.*The greenish hue in this cloth is very attractive.*

Greenness – *(noun)* freshness, refreshing. *The greenness of the valley attracted me.*

Greeny – *(adverb)* green-like. *I like greeny vegetables.*

Gregarious – *(adjective)* **1** fond of company; sociable. *He is a gregarious person.* **2** living in flocks or colonies. *Sheep is a gregarious animal.* **3** growing in clusters. *This kind of plant is gregarious.*

Grew – past of GROW. *He grew tall very fast.*

Greyish – *(adjective)* resembling grey colour. *He likes grayish colour clothes.*

Grid – *(noun)* **1** a framework of spaced bars that are parallel to or cross each other. *He got the front of his house covered with grid.* **2** a networked of lines that cross each other to form a series of squares or rectangles. a numbered grid on a map that enables a place to be precisely located. *The pwer grid broke down and there was no electricity for a long time.*

3 a pattern of lines marking the starting places on a motor-racing track. *Grid is a place where cars are repaired during car race.* *(verb)* put into or set out as a grid. *Set up a grid for flow of electricity.*

Griddle - *(noun)* a circular iron plate that is heated and used for cooking food. *She cooked chapattis on griddle.*

Grievance - *(noun)* a real of imagined cause for complain. *The officer patiently heard the grievance of the employee.*

Grieve - *(verb)* suffer grief. *The loss in business grieved him intensely.*

Grievous - *(adjective)* formal very severe or serious. *It is a grievous matter, listen carefully.*

Grill - *(noun)* variant spelling of grille. *His front door was covered with a grill.*

Grille - *(noun)* a grating or screen of metal bars or wires. *A grille encircled the whole garden.*

Grim - *(adjective)* very serious or gloomy; forbidding. black or ironic. *His grim look frightened me.*

Grime - *(noun)* dirt ingrained on a surface. *His shirt sleeves were covered with grime.* *(verb)* blacken or make dirty with grime. *Coal dusts dirties his hands with grime.*

Grimy - *(adjective)* covered with grime. *This kitchen cloth has become grimy, wash it.*

Grinder - *(noun)* a machine used for grinding something. *With this set a coffee grinder comes free.*

Grip - *(verb)* **1** take and keep a firm hold of; grasp tightly. *He gripped his hand firmly.* **2** deeply affect or afflict. compel the attention or interest of. Don't worry I have a firm grip over the problem. *(noun)* **1** a firm hold; a tight grasp or clasp. effective control. intellectual understanding. *Grief gripped him.* **2** a part or attachment by which something is held in the hand. a hairgrip. *He gripped the attention of crowd by powerful speech.* **3** a travelling bag. **4** a stage hand in a theatre. a member of a camera crew responsible for moving and setting up equipment.

Gritty - *(adjective)* **1** containing or covered with grit. *It is a rough and gritty road.* **2** showing courage and resolve. tough and uncompromising: a gritty look at urban life. *He is a gritty fellow, he will never compromise.*

Grizzle - *(verb)* [informal], chiefly British cry or whimper fretfully. *The child grizzled until its mother came.*

Groan - *(verb)* **1** make a deep inarticulate sound in response to pain or despair. *He ground in pain.* **2** make a low creaking sound when pressure or weight is applied. *The wooden bridge groaned as a truck passed over it.* **3** be oppressed by. *(noun)* a groaning sound. *The child made a groan sound because of pain.*

Groat - *(noun)* [historical] an English silver coin worth four old pence.

Groats - *(plural noun)* hulled or crushed grain, especially oats. *Groats can be a good source of nourishment.*

Grocer - *(noun)* a person who sells food and small household goods. *My uncle is a grocer and earns well.*

Grog - *(noun)* spirits mixed with water. [informal] alcoholic drink. *I want to have some grog.*

Groin - *(noun)* the area between the abdomen and the thigh on either side of the body; the region of the genitals. *The doctor prescribed him a medicine for itching in the groin.*

Groom - *(verb)* **1** brush and clean the coat of a horse or dog. give a neat and tidy appearance to. *He was grooming the horse.* **2** prepare or train played to take care of horses. *I have to be groomed in public speaking before I take part in the debate.* **3** a bridegroom. *he has employed a number of grooms to take care of his horses.* **4** British any of various officials of the royal household.

Groove - *(noun)* **1** a long, narrow cut or depression in a hard material. a spiral track cut in a gramophone record, into which the stylus fits. *There was a long groove along the hill.* **2** an established routing or habit. *He follows groove and is always punctual.* **3** [informal] a rhythmic pattern in popular or jazz music. *Groove music is very popular.* *(verb)* **1** make a groove or grooves in. **2** [informal] dance to or play popular or jazz music. enjoy oneself. *I grooved to the music.*

Grope – *(verb)* **1** feel about or search blindly or uncertainly with the hands. *He gropped for the way in complete darkness.* **2** [informal] feel or fondle for sexual pleasure, especially against their will. *A ruffian was trying to grope the lady inside the crowded bus. (noun)* [informal] an act of groping someone. *Many people have the bad habit of groping woman in the crowd.*

Grotesque – *(adjective)* **1** comically or repulsively ugly or distorted. *His grotesque appearance made all of us laugh.* **2** shockingly incongruous or inappropriate. *It was grotesque of him to behave in this way. (noun)* a grotesque figure or image. *The rods are shaped in the form of comical figures and grotesques.*

Grotto – *(noun)* a small picturesque cave, especially an artificial one in a park or garden. *All children wanted to enter the grotto.*

Ground – past and past participle of grind. *The spices have been ground in the grinder.* **2** *The plane had to be grounded as soon as it took off because of some technical fault.* **3** *This is no ground for complaint.* **4** *This is a big ground we can play cricket here.* **5** *The ship was grounded as it entered shadow waters.*

Grounding – *(noun)* basic training or instruction in a subject. *Proper grounding in necessary before you train for anything.*

Groundless – *(adjective)* not based on any good reason. *These charges are groundless.*

Groundnut – *(noun)* another term for peanut. *I am fond of eating groundnuts.*

Groundsel – *(noun)* a plant of the daisy family with small yellow rayless flowers. *I have many groundsels in my garden.*

Groundwork – *(noun)* preliminary or basic work. *Some groundwork in necessary before taking up the matter with a high official.*

Grout – *(noun)* a mortar or paste for filling crevices, especially the gaps between wall or floor tiles. *I asked the mason to fill the gap with grout. (verb)* fill in with grout. *The mason filled the crevices with grout.*

Grove – *(noun)* a small wood, orchard, or group of trees. *This a beautiful mango grove.*

Grovel – *(verb)* crouch or crawl abjectly on the ground. *Some people grovel in temples before they reach their deity.*

Grow - *(verb)* (past grew; past participle grown) **1** (of a living thing) undergo natural development by increasing in size and changing physically *She would watch her son grow to manhood.* (as adjective growing) *The need of the growing child has to be met.* (as adjective grown) *Grown up men don't act so stupidly.* (of a plant) germinate and develop *Tomatoes grow in a variety of places.* cause (plants) to germinate and develop *Scientific method is needed to increase and grow the production of food crops.* allow or cause (a part of the body) to grow or develop *She grew her hair long.* **2** come into existence and develop *A school of business was inaugurated in Delhi last month and is growing.* (of a person) come to feel or think something over time *Supposing we had grown to use nuclear power in a more safe way.* **3** become larger or greater over a period of time, increase *Turnover of our firm grew to more than Rs.100 crore within three years. (adjective) The growing concern over ozone levels is forcing scientists to think out-of-the-box methods to save the earth.* develop or expand (something, especially a business) *Banks are extending loans to entrepreneurs who are struggling to grow their businesses.*

Grower – *(noun)* a person who grows. *He is a grower of vegetables.*

Growing – *(noun)* the act of developers. *The fast growing grass had to be cut.*

Grub – *(noun)* **1** the larva of an insect, especially a beetle. a maggot or small caterpillar. *This is a grub crawling on the branch of the tree.* **2** [informal] food. *He was given some grub to eat. (verb)* **1** dig shallowly in soil. dig something up. *He was grubbing for gold.* **2** search clumsily and unmethodically; rummage. **3** do demeaning or humiliating work in order to achieve something.

Grubble – *(noun)* a person who is determined to amass something, especially in an unscrupulous manner: a money-grubber. *He is a grubble and will do anything to get money.*

Grudge - *(noun)* a persistent feeling of ill will or resentment resulting from a past insult or injury. *Although we have quarreled, I bear no grudge against you. (verb)* be resentfully unwilling to grant or allow. *I grudgingly allowed him to enter the house as I did not like him.*

Gruff - *(adjective)* rough and low in pitch. *He spoke to me in a gruff voice.*

Grumble - *(verb)* **1** complain or protest in a bad-tempered but muted way. *He grumbled before his boss.* **2** make a low rumbling sound. *The ground grumbled before the earthquake. (noun)* an instance of grumbling; a complaint. *I have many grumblings against you.*

Grumbling - *(noun)* complaint, protest. *By habit he is not given to grumbling.*

Grumpish - *(adjective)* sulking, grumpy. *He is a grumpish fellow always complaining.*

Guarantee - *(noun)* **1** a formal assurance that certain conditions will be fulfilled, especially that restitution will be made if a product is not of a specified quality. *I guarantee you the success of this project.* **2** something that gives a certainty of outcome. *Please give me the guarantee card of the fridge I have purchased. (verb)* **1** provide a guarantee. *The company guarantees to refund your money.*

Guava - *(noun)* a tropical american fruit with pink juicy flesh and a strong, sweet aroma. *Guava is a very tasty fruit.*

Guesswork - *(noun)* the process or results of guessing. *Your guesswork didn't turn out to be correct.*

Guest - *(noun)* a person who is invited to visit someone's home or take part in a function. a visiting performer invited to take part in an entertainment. *We should entertains and respect our guests.*

Guidance - *(noun)* advice or information aimed at resolving a problem or difficulty. *We should give proper guidance to our children.*

Guileful - *(adjective)* cunning, sly. *He is a guileful fellow, don't mix with him.*

Guileless - *(adjective)* innocent. *He is guileless and innocent.*

Guilt - *(noun)* the fact of having committed an offence or crime. *He has a strong sense of guilt about the wrong he has done.*

Guilty - *(adjective)* **1** culpable of a specified wrongdoing. justly chargeable with a particular fault or error. *He is feeling guilty over the crime he has committed.* **2** having or showing a feeling of guilt: a guilty conscience. *He has a guilty conscience because he has betrayed his friend.*

Guise - *(noun)* an external form, appearance, or manner of presentation. *He came to party is the guise of a waiter.*

Guitar - *(noun)* a stringed musical instrument with a fretted fingerboard and six or twelve strings, played by plucking or strumming with the fingers or a plectrum. *He plays nice guitar.*

Gular - *(adjective)* [zoology] of or relating to the throat, especially of a reptile, fish, or bird. *The gular disease of the bird in the zoo was treated by a doctor.*

Gulf - *(noun)* **1** a deep inlet of the sea almost surrounded by land, with a narrow mouth. *Iran exports oil through gulf of Persia.* **2** a deep ravine, chasm, or abyss. *The gulf between the two of us can never be bridged.*

Gullet - *(noun)* the passage by which food passes from the mouth to the stomach; the oesophagus. *Something got stuck in his gullet and a doctor had to be called.*

Gully - *(noun)* **1** a water-worn ravine. a gutter or drain. *The rain water flowed down the gully.* **2** [cricket] a fielding position on the off side between point and the slips. *In cricket, the gully position is very close to the wicketkeeper.*

Gulp - *(verb)* **1** swallow quickly or in large mouthfuls, often audibly. *He gulped down the food.* **2** make an effortful swallowing motion, typically in response to strong emotion. *He gulped as he grew tearful. (noun)* an act of gulping food or drink; a large mouthful of liquid hastily drunk. *He gulped down the drink and left for home.*

Gummy - *(adjective)* viscous; sticky. *It's a gummy object and I don't like it.*

Gunner - *(noun)* a person who operates a gun; a British artillery soldier. *He is a gunner is the navy.*

Gunnery - *(noun)* the design, manufacture, or firing of heavy guns. *He is an expert of gunnery.*

Gunny - *(noun)* [chiefly north American] coarse sacking, typically made of jute fibre. *The stolen currency notes were found is a gunny bag.*

Gush - *(verb)* **1** send out or flow in a rapid and plentiful stream. *The blood gushed out of his wound.* **2** speak or write effusively. *There is a gush of warmth in his poems.*

Gusto - *(noun)* enjoyment or vigour. *He answered my questions with gusto.*

Gusty - *(adjective)* **1** characterized by or blowing in gusts. *A gusty wind blew in the mountains.* **2** showing gusto. *His gusty songs thrilled everyone.*

Gut - *(noun)* **1** the stomach or belly. [medicine & biology] the intestine; entrails that have been removed or exposed. *He was shot in the stomach and his guts were spilled on the street.* **2** the internal parts or essence of something. *He has a lot of guts and is sure going to succeed.* **3** used in names attributing negative characteristics: greedy guts. **4** [informal] personal courage and determination. *I do not have the guts to face him.* **5** [informal] instinctive. *I have a gut feeling that something good is going to happen soon. (verb)* remove or destroy the internal parts of. *The fire gutted most of the factory.*

Gutter - *(noun)* **1** a shallow through beneath the edge of a roof, or a channel at the side of a street, for carrying off rainwater; [technical] a groove or channel for flowing liquid. *A foul smelling water flowed in the gutter.* **2** a poor or squalid environment. *The men had fought their way out of gutter. (verb)* [archaic] channel or furrow with streams, tears, etc. *My cheeks are gutted with tears.*

Guttural - *(adjective)* produced in the throat. *He made a guttural sound before he started speaking.*

Guy - *(noun)* [British informal] as a form of address. *That guy over there is my cousin.*

Guzzle - *(verb)* eat or drink greedily. *He has guzzled down many drinks.*

Guzzler - *(noun)* drinking eating greedily. *He is a guzzler of tasty food.*

Gymnastic - *(plural noun)* exercises involving physical agility, flexibility, and coordination, especially tumbling and acrobatic, feats. *She got first prize in gymnastics. (adjective)* relating to gymnastics. *Her manner of acting was a replica of gymnastic display.*

Gypsy - *(noun)* a member of a travelling people and traditionally living by itinerant trade and fortune telling. *She is a gypsy and will tell you your fortune.*

Gyrate - *(verb)* move or cause to move in a circle or spiral. *She gyrated to the tune of the song.*

Gyre - *(verb)* [poetic/literary] whirl; gyrate. *She gyred to the music.*

Gyve - *(noun)* [archaic] a fetter or shackle. *The prisoner wore gloves around his feet.*

Hh

H-the eight letter of the English alphabet. **1.** A symbol for hydrogen in Chemistry.

Ha – *(exclamatory)* expressing surprise, suspicion, triumph, etc. *Ha! I have finally learned how to make a sentence.*

Haberdasher – *(noun)* A dealer in small items of dressing. *A retail dealer in men's furnishings, such as shirts, trousers, ties, and socks is known as haberdasher.*

Habergeon – *(noun)* [historical] a sleeveless coat of mail or scale armour. *Habergeon was a sleeveless coat worn under the plated shirt during the 14th century.*

Habile – *(adjective)* skilful, dexterous, adroit. *People would call you a habile, if you can use both hands skillfully.*

Habiliment – *(noun)* [archaic] clothing. *The clothes worn in a particular profession is known as the habiliment of that profession.*

Habilitate – *(verb)* (used with object) to clothe or dress, to make fit. *Get your poorly stitched dress habilitated by a draper so that it fits you properly.*

Habitable – *(adjective)* suitable to live in. *Increasing volume of pollution each year is making the world less habitable to live than the previous year.*

Habitant – *(noun)* an early settler, less popular word for an inhabitant. *Dravidians were the original habitants of India.*

Habitat – *(noun)* the natural home or environment of an organism. *Forest is the natural habitat of wild animals.*

Habitation – *(noun)* the state or process of inhabiting, [informal] a house or home. *Wild animals prefer to live in the natural habitation of a forest.*

Habitual – *(adjective)* done constantly or as a habit, regular, usual. *Students who are habitual of getting up early for studies generally score good marks in examinations.*

Habitually – *(adjective)* according to habit or custom. *He habitually keeps his main entrance door closed.*

Habituate – *(verb)* [chiefly zoology] make or become accustomed to something. *You could harm yourself if you become habituated to self-medication.*

Habituation – *(noun)* Being abnormally tolerant to and dependent on something that is psychologically or physically habit-forming (especially alcohol or narcotic drugs). *Habituation to regular use of a particular medicine reduces its efficiency on the body.*

Hacking – *(verb)* **1** to cut or chop with repeated and irregular blows: *He hacked down the plants and saplings indiscriminately.* **2** to alter a computer programme without permission: *He hacked her computer password while she was away and read her message.*

Hackney – *(noun)* a horse-drawn vehicle kept for hire. *In the19th century London, wealthy citizens used to sit in horse-driven hackneys to go from one place to another.*

Hackneyed – *(adjective)* (of a phrase or idea) having been overused unoriginal and trite. *To write an impressive essay, avoid using hackneyed words that have become stale with overuse.*

Haddock – *(noun)* a silvery-grey bottom-dwelling fish of north Atlantic coastal waters, popular as a food fish. *Haddock is a popular north Atlantic fish, which is usually eaten baked, roasted or fried.*

Hades – *(noun)* [Greek mythology] the underworld; the abode of the spirits of the dead. *Greek mythology describes hades as a place where the spirits of the dead live.*

Haematic - *(adjective)* relating to or containing or affecting blood, having the colour of, or containing blood. *The surgeon operated upon the person to remove the haematic cyst that looked like a ball of blood.*

Haematology - *(noun)* the study of the physiology of the blood. *Doctors prescribe a number of haematological tests to determine the quality of blood of the patients.*

Haematuria - *(noun)* medicine the presence of blood in the urine. *Haematuria is a disease of the urinary tract in which blood passes along urine.*

Haemoglobin - *(noun)* [biochemistry] a red protein containing iron, responsible for transporting oxygen in the blood in most invertebrates. *The red colour of the blood is due to hemoglobin which contains iron.*

Haemorrhage - *(noun)* an escape of blood from a ruptured blood vessel. *Bleeding, medically known as haemorrhage is the loss of blood from the circulatory system. (verb)* suffer a haemorrhage. *He had begun haemorrhaging in the right.*

Haemorrhoid - *(noun)* a swollen vein or group of veins in the region of the anus. *Haemorrhoids, also known as piles are swellings that can occur in the anus and lower rectum.*

Hag - *(noun)* a witch. *The hag was walking unsteadily.*

Haggard - *(adjective)* **1** looking exhausted and unwell. *After the marathon race, he was completely exhausted and looked haggard.* **2** (of a hawk) caught and trained as an adult. *A haggard is a hawk cought as on adult for training. (noun)* a haggard hawk.

Haggle - *(verb)* dispute or bargain persistently, especially over a price. *Women are better than men at bringing down prices by haggling with sellers.*

Haggler - *(verb)* an intense bargainer. *He is a haggler by nature as he would haggle irrespective of the price quoted.*

Hagiographer - *(noun)* **1** a writer of the lives of the saints. *Any person who writes about the lives of the saints, especially Christian, is known as a hagiographer.* **2** [theology] a writer of any of the hagiographa. *A writer of any books of the Bible is known as a hagiographer.*

Hag-ridden - *(adjective)* afflicted by nightmares or anxieties. *After visiting a haunted house, his expressions have become fearful and hag-ridden.*

Ha-ha - *(noun)* a ditch with a wall on its inner side below ground level, forming a boundary to a park or garden without interrupting the view. *It is just the gap where the ha-ha is broken to allow the turn in from the road.*

Hail - *(noun)* pellets of frozen rain falling in showers from cumulonimbus clouds. *We could not go out for picnic because of torrential rains and hail storms.*

Hair - *(noun)* any of the fine thread like strained growing from the skin of mammals and other animals, or from the epidermis of a plant. such strands collectively especially those on a person's head. *I go for hair cut every month.*

Hake - *(noun)* a large-headed elongated food fish with long jaws and strong teeth. *Hake is a fish that resembles cod and found mostly in North America.*

Halberd - *(noun)* [historical] a combined spear and battleaxe. *Halberd was a weapon with axe at one end and spear at the other used during 15th and 16th centuries.*

Halcyon - *(adjective)* denoting a past time that was idyllically happy and peaceful. *Wouldn't you like to recall your halcyon days when you were happy and prosperous?*

Hale - *(adjective)* strong and healthy. *If you maintain a balanced life, you would live a hale and hearty life.*

Haliography – Description of the sea. *Haliography is a work describing the sea.*

Halliard - *(noun)* a rope that is used to hoist a sail, a flag or a yard. *In boats used for sailing, the rope used to hoist the sail is called halliard.*

Halt - *(verb)* bring or come to an abrupt stop. *The police halted the march by the agitating protestors.*

Hatting - *(noun)* A covering for the head, especially one with a shaped crown and brim. *British officers used to cover their head with a* *hatting made from coconut leaves to protect their head during Indian summer.*

Halter - *(noun)* a rope or strap placed around the head of an animal and used to lead or tether it. *The dog ran away after the leather halter tied around its neck broke.*

Halyard - *(noun)* a rope used for raising and lowering a sail, yard, or flag on a ship. *In boats used for sailing, the rope that hoists the sail is called halyard.*

Hamlet - *(noun)* a small village, especially one without a church. *Since hamlets are much smaller than villages, most people know one another.*

Hammock - *(noun)* a wide strip of canvas or rope mesh suspended by two ends, used as a bed. *Since canvas-made hammock is wide and light in weight, people use it as a swing after tying its both ends to branch of trees.*

Hamper - *(noun)* a basket with a carrying handle and a hinged lid, used for food, cutlery, etc. on a picnic. [British] a box containing food and drink for a special occasion. *Hamper is a convenient multi-purpose basket to carry food and water when going on a picnic.*

Hamshackle - *(verb)* to hobble. *Hamshakle is a method of tying a rope around the head and one of the legs of the domestic animals if they become violent.*

Hamstring - *(noun)* any of five tendons at the back of a person's knee. the great tendon at the back of a quadruped's hock. *Rafael Nadal lost in the Wimbledon tournament because his movement was severely restricted on the tennis court due to pulled hamstring.*

Hand - *(noun)* the end par of the arm beyond the wrist, including the palm fingers, adn thumb. western indian a persons' arm, including the hand. operated by or held in the hand. done or made manually. *We should wash our hands with soap before taking food. What time is it if both the small and the large hand of the watch is at two? How many hands have you employed to remove the garbage within two hours? To marry his girl friend, he met her parents asking for her hand in marriage*

Handbag - *(noun)* [British] a small bag used by a woman to carry everyday personal items. *She bought a new handbag so that her everyday personal items could be carried decently.*

Handbell - *(noun)* a small bell, especially one of a set tuned to a flange of notes and played by a group of people. *The peon rushed inside the cabin, when the officer pressed the handbell kept on his table.*

Handbill - *(noun)* a small printed advertisement or other notice distributed by hand. *A handbill is a form of paper advertisement and typically distributed within a locality.*

Hand-book - *(noun)* book giving brief information such as basic facts on a particular subject or instructions for operating a machine. *This hand-book introduces you to the rules and regulations of this club.*

Hand-cuff - *(noun)* a pair of lockable linked metal rings for securing a prisoner's wrists. *Thieves were hand-cuffed and taken to the police station.*

Handful - *(noun)* a quantity that fills the hand. a small number or amount. *Despite wide publicity, only a handful of people came to watch the game.*

Handicraft - *(noun)* a particular skill of making decorative domestic or other objects by hand. *Machine-made products have very nearly displaced the handmade handicrafts.*

Handiwork - *(noun)* something that one has made or done, the making of things by hand. *Most carpets we see in the market are the handiwork of people living in Bhadohi in Uttar Pradesh.*

Handkerchief - *(noun)* a square of cotton or other material for wiping one's nose. *Wash your hands with soap and pat it dry with a handkerchief.*

Handler - *(noun)* **1** a person who handles a particular type of article or commodity. *He is a baggage handler at the aupart.* **2** a person who trains or has charge of an animal, in particular a police officer in charge of dog. *The palice have appointed handlers to train dogs.* **3** a person who trains or manages another person, a person who trains and acts as second to a boxer. a publicity agent. *This doctor is a handler of mental patients at the hospitel.*

Handling - *(noun)*- the action of one that handles something. *Every musical instrument needs careful handling.*

Handloom - *(noun)*- A type of cloth. *Fabrics made of handloom shrink when washed and dried.*

Handmaid - *(noun)* [archaic] a female servant, a subservient partner or element. *Wealthy people use the services of handmaids for cooking, washing, cleaning etc.*

Handmill - *(noun)* - Domestic hand grinders. *These days most kitchens have a handmill to grind spices into fine powder.*

Handpress - *(noun)* to press down something by manual pressure. *Plastic granules can be converted into the shape of a glass with the help of a handpress.*

Handrail - *(noun)* a rail fixed to posts or a wall for people to hold on to for support.*Handrails fixed along the staircase help people climb floors easily.*

Handsaw - *(noun)* - woodcutting implement. *Carpenters use handsaw to cut wooden slabs to make a table.*

Handsome - *(adjective)* good-looking. striking and imposing rather than conventionally pretty, well made, imposing, and of obvious quality, substantial. *He is a handsome person. Handsome bonuses have been given to all employees.*

Handwriting - *(noun)* writing with a pen or pencil rather than by typing or printing. a person's particular style of writing. *Good handwriting will help you get good marks in examinations.*

Handy - *(adjective)* **1** convenient to handle or use; useful. *Washing machines make washing clothes very handy.* **2** skilful. *He is an alrounder and a very handy player.*

Hang - *(verb)* **1** suspend or be suspended form above with the lower part not attached, attach or be attached so as to allow free movement about the point of attachement: hangingi a door, fall or drape in a specified way. paste to a wall. *She hanged the curtains beautifully. Hanging clothes in the sun speeds up drying.* **2** kill or be killed by typing a rope attached from above around the neck and removing the support from beneath the feet. *The judge ordered the criminal to be hanged till death.*

Hangar - *(noun)* a large building with extensive floor area, typically for housing aircraft. *Aircrafts are kept in the hanger for repair or when not flying.*

Hanger - *(noun)* a shaped piece of wood, plastic, or metal with a hook at the top, for hanging clothes from a rail. *Clothes don't get crumpled or creased when hung on a hanger.*

Hanger-on - *(noun)* a person who associates sycophantically with another person. *People hanging around influential people are known as hanger-on.*

Hanging - *(noun)* the practice of hanging condemned people as a form of capital punishment. *Many countries have abolished the practice of hanging the criminals.* *(adjective)* **1** suspended in the air. **2** situated or designed so as to appear to hang down. *The Hanging Gardens of Babylon is one of the seven wonders of the world.*

Hank - *(noun)* a coil or skein of wool, hair, or other material, a measurement of the length per unit mass of cloth or yarn. *In textile industry, a hank refers to a unit that is in coiled form.*

Hanker - *(verb)* feel a strong desire for or to do something. *He is always hankering for toffees and chocolates.*

Hapless - *(adjective)* less fortunate. *The batsmen hit the hapless bowler for six boundaries in an over*

Haply - *(adjective)* by chance, possibly. *If it doesn't rain, we may haply go to the movie.*

Happen - *(verb)* **1** take place; occur. *The World Book Fair will happen every year in Delhi.* **2** come about by chance. chance to do something or come about. come across by chance. *Do you happen to know who her doctor is?* *(adv.)* perhaps; maybe. *If he reaches in time, we may be able to get movie tickets.*

Happening - *(noun)* an event or occurrence. *There is a huge crowd here. What is happening?* *(adjective)* [informal] fashionable; trendy. *Since there were few dancers in the crowd, happening a dance competition was no surprise.*

Happily – *(adjective)* gladly; joyfully. *Both of them happily went back home.*

Happiness – *(noun)* joy, glad. *Happiness is a mental state of well-being.*

Harangue – *(verb)* criticize at length in an aggressive and hectoring manner. *Dishonest politicians harangue their honest rivals by speaking against them in public.*

Harass – *(verb)* torment by subjecting to constant interference or intimidation. *With enormous power police holds, they can harass an ordinary citizen no end.*

Harbinger – *(noun)* a person or thing that announces or signals the approach of something. *Beginning of India-Pakistan cricket matches could be a harbinger of good relations between them.*

Hard – *(adjective)* **1** solid, firm, and rigid; not easily broken, bent, or pierced. not showing any signs of weakness; tough. high and stable; firm. *Iron is a very hard metal that can't be easily broken.* **2** requiring or demonstrating a great deal of endurance or effort; difficult. strict and demanding: a hard taskmaster. *You need to practice hard to become a top cricketer.* **3** concerned with precise and verifiable facts. *Solid, hard and verifiable proof is required before a hypothesis is accepted as a scientific fact.*

Harden – *(verb)* **1** make or become hard or harder. *Boiling an egg hardens and solidifies its liquid material.* **2** rise and remain steady at a higher level. *You must harden your mental state to accept the ups and downs of life graciously.*

Hardship – *(noun)* severe suffering or privation. *In addition to pay, hardship allowance is also given to soldiers posted at Siachin.*

Hare – *(noun)* a fast-running, long-eared mammal resembling a large rabbit, with very long hind legs. and other species. *Hare is a rabbit like animal mostly found in grassland.* *(verb)* run with great speed. *We all have heard the story of race between a hare and a tortoise.*

Harlot – *(noun)* [archaic] a prostitute or promiscuous woman. *Women who sell their bodies for money are known as harlots.*

Harlotry – *(noun)* prostitution. *Harlotry is one of the oldest professions where women sell their bodies for money.*

Harm – *(noun)* physical injury, especially that which is deliberately inflicted. material damage. actual or potential ill effect. *I didn't mean to cause her any harm. This oil is unlikely to do much harm to the engine. There is no harm asking her.* *(verb)* physically injure. have an adverse effect con. *You must take adequate care of your children to safeguard them from any possible harm coming their way.*

Harmful – *(adjective)* causing or likely to cause harm. *Ultra-violet rays are very harmful for our skin.*

Harmfulness – *(noun)* injuriousness, quality of being harmful. *No disease is less deadly than the other in harmfulness to the body.*

Harmless – *(adjective)* not able or likely to cause harm. *You must tell jokes that are harmless to the self-esteem of a person.*

Harmonious – *(adjective)* **1** tuneful; not discordant. *The music was very harmonious.* **2** free from conflict. *Complete peace will prevail if different communities in the society try to live harmoniously.*

Harmonium – *(noun)* a keyboard instrument in which the notes are produced by air driven through metal reeds by foot-operated bellows. *Harmonium is one of the most important musical instruments to produce melodious notes.*

Harmonization – *(noun)* bringing into agreement. *Harmonization of relations within communities is essential for peace to prevail in the society.*

Harmonize – *(verb)* **1** music provide harmony for. *You can harmonize the area around with a soothing music.* **2** make consistent. *By harmonizing rail tracks, a train can move from Istanbul in Turkey to Stockholm in Sweden*

Harmony – *(noun)* **1** the combination of simultaneously sounded musical notes to produce chords and chord progressions having a pleasing effect. *Pleasing musical notes produce peace and harmony to the mind.* **2** agreement or concord. *Man and machine should live in perfect harmony.*

Harridan – *(noun)* a strict, bossy, or belligerent old woman. *Despite belonging to the same gender, women employees resent strictness of harridans.*

Harrier – *(noun)* a hound of a breed used for hunting hares. *Harrier is a breed of hound dog used for hunting rabbits.*

Harry – *(verb)* persistently carry out attacks on an enemy. *By attacking the US forces persistently, Talibani forces are harassing and harrying them no end.*

Harsh – *(adjective)* unpleasantly rough or jarring to the senses, cruel or severe. grim and unpalatable. *Judicial courts frown upon harsh treatment by teachers to students.*

Hart – *(noun)* an adult male deer, especially a red deer over five years old. *More than five year old male deers are known as harts.*

Harum-scarum – *(noun)* a reckless irresponsible person. *If you behave irresponsibly towards your family, people would call you a complete harum-scarum.* *(adjective)* cheerfully irresponsible, reckless; impetuous. *His wealth has made him totally harum-scarum as far as throwing money is concerned.*

Harvest – *(noun)* the process or period of gathering in crops. the season's yield or crop. *Harvest time, when the crops are cut and processed, is a time of festivities in India.* *(verb)* gather as a harvest. *India has a bumper harvest of food crops this year.*

Harvester – *(noun)* one who reaps, reaping machine. *Harvesters are huge machines that are used these days to harvest the crops to save time and labour.*

Hash – *(verb)* **1** make or chop into little pieces. *Many vegetables are hashed and cooked together to prepare the bhaji of pao-bhaji dish.* **2** come to agreement after lengthy and vigorous discussion. *To prevent meeting ending in a flop, the participants managed to hash together an agreement and called it a success.*

Hasp – *(noun)* a latch, fastening. *The door could not be locked since the hasp was not there.*

Haste – *(noun)* excessive speed or urgency of action. *Any work done in haste ends up as waste.* *(verb)* [archaic] term for hasten: haste ye back! *There is no point rushing or making haste since the train will arrive at the station three hours from now.*

Hasten – *(verb)* be quick to do something move quickly, cause to happen sooner than anticipated. *The addition of a catalyst will speed up or hasten the chemical reaction.*

Hastily – *(adverb)* quickly. *Seeing the dog charging at him, he hastily retreated back to his house.*

Hatch – *(noun)* a small opening in a floor, wall, or roof allowing accesses from one area to another, in particular that in the deck of a boat leading to the cabin or lower level. a door in an aircraft, spacecraft, or submarine. *To come out of the submarine, sailors have to use the small hatch that serves both as entry or exit point.*

Hatchet – *(noun)* a small axe with a short handle for use in one hand. *Farmers often use a hatchet to make burrows in the field at the time of planting seeds.*

Hatching – *(noun)* a newly hatched young animal – bird. *These days hatching of birds from eggs takes place in modern hatcheries.*

Hate – *(verb)* feel intense dislike for or a strong aversion towards. *If you don't like another person, please try your best not to hate him.*

Hateful – *(adjective)* arousing or deserving of hatred. *Hateful attitude between two communities has never resolved any problem.*

Hater – *(noun)*- One who hates. *Don't carry such a cruel attitude towards others that people start calling you a hater.*

Hatred – *(noun)* intense dislike. *Hatred or ill-feeling towards others will not let you live in peace.*

Haughtily – *(adv.)* arrogantly, disdainfully. *He haughtily said no and didn't even bother to look at the poor man seeking alms.*

Haughty – *(adjective)* arrogantly superior and disdainful. *Haughty persons carrying an air of disdainful look are seldom liked by others.*

Haulier – *(noun)* [British] a person or company employed in the commercial transport of goods by road. *A company that transports goods, especially in Britain, is popularly called a haulier.*

Haunch - *(noun)* the buttock and thing considered together, in a human or animal. the leg and loin of an animal, as food. *The haunch of venison is a popular dish in Europe and America.*

Hautboy - *(noun)* [archaic] form of hautbois. *Hautboy is a type of strawberry found in Central Europe and Asia.*

Haven - *(noun)* a place of safety or refuge. *A place to spend the night safely in a desert is as good as a haven.*

Haversack - *(noun)* a small, stout bag carried on the back or over the shoulder, used especially by soldiers and walkers. *The kind of haversack used by soldiers has become very popular among school students to carry books and copies.*

Hawk - *(verb)* carry about and offer for sale in the street. *These days hawkers use carts to hawk vegetables in the streets and lanes.*

Hawker - *(noun)* a person who travels about selling goods. *These days hawkers use carts to hawk daily utility wares in the streets and lanes.*

Hawk-eyed - *(adjective)* having a sharp eye to see distant objects. *Hawk-eyed machines have become very popular in the game of cricket to determine whether the ball had touched the bat or not.*

Hawkish - *(adjective)* advocating aggressive policies. *Trade unions generally resort to hawkish pronouncements against the managements.*

Hazardous - *(adjective)* risky; dangerous. *All chemicals prone to catch fire or cause health problems are known as hazardous.*

Hazel - *(noun)* small tree or shrub. *Hazel is a small golden-brown coloured tree whose nuts are edible.*

Hazy - *(adjective)* covered by a haze. *The cold winter morning was misty, foggy and hazy in which nothing could be seen clearly.*

Head-ache - *(noun)* a continuous pain in the head. *I couldn't come to the office because of continuous headache since last night.*

Heading - *(noun)* **1** a title at the head of a page or section of a book. *The heading of this chapter is "Ways to sleep well'.* **2** a direction or bearing. *In which direction is our car heading now?*

Headless - *(adjective)* without a head, incapacitated, leaderless. *This organization has remained headless ever since the chairman retired six months back.*

Headlong - *(adverb&adj.)* **1** with the head foremost. *Don't recklessly headlong into doing anything without first giving sufficient thought.* **2** in a rush; with reckless haste. *It is foolish to jump headlong into doing anything without seeking sufficient advice.*

Headmaster - *(noun)* [chiefly British] a male head teacher. *The headmaster of this school is a strict disciplinarian.*

Headmost - *(adjective)* [archaic] holding a position in advance of others; foremost. *The ship behind which all ships follow is known as the headmost.*

Headstrong - *(adjective)* energetically willful and determined. *He is so headstrong that he would sidestep every comfort to complete the job.*

Headway - *(noun)* **1** Advance or progress. *Despite adequate help and support, he couldn't make any headway in finding the solution.*

Heady - *(adjective)* potent; intoxicating, having a strong or exhilarating effect. *Politicians behave in a heady and arrogant way because they have power and money in their hands.*

Heal - *(verb)* **1** make or become sound or healthy again. *The doctor's concern should be to heal sick people.* **2** correct or put right. *Psychologists and not medicines are needed to heal the mental agony.*

Healer - *(noun)* one who heals, remedy. *Anyone who can heal the sickness of mind or body is a healer.*

Healing - *(noun & adj)* curing, restoring to health. *A motherly healing touch is necessary to restore the sick child to health.*

Healthily - *adv.* in a healthy manner. *Children should be fed healthily so that they do well both in studies and games.*

Hearing - *(noun)* **1** the faculty of perceiving sounds. the range within which sounds may be heard; earshot. *I couldn't understand the discussion because they conversed at a place that was out of my hearing range. Those hard* *of hearing are known as deaf.* **2** an opportunity to state one's case. *On the next date of hearing, you will get the opportunity to state your case.*

Hearsay – *(noun)* information which cannot be adequately substantiated; rumour. *People, especially in villages, tend to easily believe in rumours or hearsays told by elders.*

Hearse – *(noun)* a vehicle for conveying the coffin at a funeral. *Hearse is a vehicle to carry the dead to hospital for post-mortem.*

Heartburn – *(noun)* a form of indigestion felt as a burning sensation in the chest, caused by acid regurgitation into the esophagus. *Heartburn is a burning sensation in the chest caused by eating too much of acidic food.*

Heartless – *(adjective)* merciless, cruel. *In the face of heartless beating by policemen, the innocent man accepted his guilt.*

Hearth – *(noun)* **1** the floor or surround of a fireplace. *They were sitting around the heart to protect themselves from freezing cold.* **2** the base or lower part of a furnace, where molten metal collects. *In a blast furnace, the molten iron is collected in the hearth.*

Heat – *(noun)* **1** the quality of being hot; high temperature. *Heat is a form of energy arising from the random motion of the molecules of bodies.* technical the amount of heat needed for or evolved in a specific process. *When heat is given to a liquied, it turns into vapour.* a source or level of heat for cooking. *The heat of the sun gives us warmth.* **2** intensity of feeling, especially of anger or excitement. [informal] intensive and unwelcome pressure. *In the heat of argument, he fired from his rifle injuring the person.* **3** a preliminary round in a race or contest. *Six successful sprinters went into the final after three rounds of heat. (verb)* make or become hot or warm. *He seemed to cool down as quickly as he had heated up.*

Heath – *(noun)* [chiefly British] an area of open uncultivated land, typically on acid sandy soil and covered with heater, gorse, and coarse grasses. *An open uncultivated land having small trees and evergreen grass is known as heath.*

Heavily – *(adv.)* in a weighty manner, clumsily. *He relied heavily on other's data to arrive at a solution.*

Heaviness – *(noun)* condition of being heavy, weightiness. *The toys were crushed due to the heaviness of the steel box.*

Heavy – *(adjective)* **1** of great weight; difficult to lift or move. *Objects that sank to the bottom of the sea quickly are quite heavy by weight.* **2** of great density; thick or substantial. *You must wear hervey woollens during winter.*hard to digest; too filling. coarse or slow-moving. *To stay healthy, we must try to avoid heavy foods.* **3** of more than the usual, size, amount, or force. *He suffered from a heavy cold.* using a lot of doing something to excess. *He is a heavy smoker.* **4** striking or falling with force. *There was heavy overnight rain.* **5** needing much physical effort. mentally oppressive; hard to endure. very important or serious. *Heavy works like road repairing have not started yet.* **6** [physics] containing atoms of an to isotope of greater than the usual mass. *India has fine heavy water reactors. (noun)* something large or heavy of its kind. [informal] a large. *I needed money to pay off heavy debts.*

Hebetate – *(adjective)* dull, blunt. *Unless the mental faculty is exercised regularly, chances are your intellectual ability will gradually hebetate.*

Hebraic – *(adjective)* of hebrew or the hebrews. *Israeli people are very proud of Hebrew language, art or anything Hebraic.*

Hebraist – *(noun)* a scholar of the Hebrew language. *Scholars of Hebrew language and literature are acknowledged as Hebraist.*

Hebrew – *(noun)* a member of an ancient people living in what is now Israel and Palestine, who established the kingdoms of Israel and judah. *Hebrew is the official language of Israel.*

Hectic – *(adjective)* full of incessant or frantic activity. *Hectic mopping of rain water became necessary in order to make the ground playable.*

Hecto – *(prep.)* one hundred; hectometre. *Hecto or hecta is a Greek word meaning one hundred.*

Hedge - *(noun)* row of bushes. *Hedge is a line of closely spaced shrubs and small trees to form a boundary or barrier.*

Hedonic - *(adjective)* pertaining to pleasure, pleasant sensations. *You are a hedonic if your soul aim is to seek sensual pleasure.*

Hedonism - *(noun)* the pursuit of pleasure; sensual self-indulgence, [philosophy] the ethical theory that pleasure is the highest good and proper aim of human life. *Hedonism is a philosophy that propagates that real pleasure comes only from sensual sensation.*

Hedonist - *(noun)* pleasure seeker. *A hedonist is a person who believes that sensual pleasure is the only real pleasure.*

Heedful - *(adjective)* careful attentive. *Unless you are heedful in the class, you would miss the main points of the lecture.*

Heedless - *(adjective)* showing a reckless lack of care or attention. *We know that heedless self-interest is bad morals for the society.*

Heehaw - *(noun)* the loud, harsh cry of a donkey or mule. *The harsh unpleasant cry of a donkey is called heehaw.*

Hefty - *(adjective)* large, heavy, and powerful. *Hefty sum of money is carried in vans secured with security guards.*

Height - *(noun)* **1** the measurement of someone or something from head to foot or from base to top. the quality of being tall or high. *To be eligible to apply for army, you must be at least 165 centimetres in height.* **2** elevation above ground or a recognized level typically sea level. a high place of area. *The height of Mount Everest is 8848 metres above the sea-level.* **3** the most intense part or period of something. an extreme instance or example of something: the height of bad manners. *The US had sent its aircraft carrier in the Bay of Bengal at the height of Indo-Pak war in 1971.*

Heighten - *(verb)* make higher, make or become more intense. *When alone, even the ticking of a wall clock heightens the perception of fear.*

Heinous - *(adjective)* utterly odious or wicked: a heinous crime. *To leave an injured person unattended is nothing short of a heinous crime.*

Heiress - *(noun)* a female heir, especially to vast wealth. *Paris Hilton is the heiress to the Empire of Hilton Hotels worldwide.*

Heirloom - *(noun)* a valuable object that has belonged to a family for several generations. *The jewelry that has been passed down the generations is popularly known as heirloom.*

Heirless - *(adjective)* lacking an heir, without successor. *The British government in India used to annexe the properties of those Maharajas who died heirless.*

Heirship - *(noun)* right to inheritance. *The state, character and priviledges of an heir is known as heirship.*

Held - *(past&past)* participle of hold. *The senate held a meeting of executive members and decided to start a new 4-year degree course from the next session.*

Helical - *(adjective)* having the shape or form of a helix; spiral. *The Universe is helical in appearance as if coiled one over the other.*

Hell - *(noun)* a place regarded in various religions as a spiritual realm of evil and suffering, often depicted as a place of perpetual fire beneath the earth to which the wicked are consigned after death, a state or place of great suffering. exclamatory used to express annoyance or surprise or for emphasis. *Being sent to the solitary cell in a jail is nothing short of living in hell.*

Hell-cat - *(noun)* a spiteful, violent woman, a witch. *Women who are spiteful and violent in nature are known in the society as hell-cats.*

Helot - *(noun)* a member of a class of serfs in ancient Sparta, intermediate in status between slaves and citizens. *Those Spartans who were not fully free as a citizen were known as helots.*

Help - *(verb)* **1** make it easier to do something. improve to, assist to move in a specified direction. *He helped me to reach Connaught Place in the shortest possible way.* **2** serve someone with food or drink. *The bartender offered help to make the right kind of cocktail.* **3** a domestic servant or employee. *We hired a new maid to help do the household shores.*

Helper – *(noun)* a person who helps someone else. *The carpenter needed five more helpers to make the complete set of furniture.*

Helpful – *(adjective)* giving or ready to give help, useful. *I found his advice very helpful in passing the examination.*

Helpless – *(adjective)* **1** unable to defend oneself or to act without help. *The cubs were born blind and helpless.* **2** uncontrollable. *She burst into helpless laughter.* laughter. *If you don't study regularly, you would find yourself helpless during exam time.*

Helpmate – *(noun)* a helpful companion or partner. *My roommate is a true helpmate in all matters of study.*

Helter-skelter – *(adj.&adv.)* in disorderly haste or confusion. *Following shooting and arson in the area, everyone started running helter-skelter to find an escape route.*

Helve – *(noun)* the handle of a weapon or tool. *A helve is a handle attached to an axe or hammer.*

Hemisphere – *(noun)* a half of a sphere. *Equator divides the earth into two halves, northern hemisphere and southern hemisphers.*

Hemlock – *(noun)* a highly poisonous plant of the parsley family, with fern-like leaves, small white flowers, and an unpleasant smell, a sedative or poisonous potion obtained from this plant. *Many allopathic medicines use hemlock as an ingredient, which otherwise is highly poisonous.*

Hemp – *(noun)* **1** the cannabis plant. the fibre of this plant, extracted from the stem and used to make rope, stout fabrics, fiberboard, and paper. · used in names of other plants that yield fibre, e.g. manila hemp. *Most 50 and 100 kg bags used for packing wheat, rice and sugar are prepared from hemp.* **2** the drug cannabis. *Hemp is used to prepare drugs that are often prescribed in the treatment of mentally disturbed patients.*

Hem-stitch – *(noun)* a decorative stitch sued especially along-side a hem, in which several adjacent threads are pulled out and the crossing threads are tied into bunches, making a row of small opening. *Skirts with hem-stitch are no longer fashionable. (verb)* incorporate such a decoration in the hem of. *We hem-stitched all table cloths.*

Hen – *(noun)* a female bird, especially of a domestic fowl, domestic fowls of either sex. used in names of various other birds, e.g. native hen. a female lobster, crab, or salmon. *The eggs laid by a hen are very popular as a breakfast item.*

Henbane – *(noun)* a poisonous plant of the nightshade family, with sticky hairy leaves and an unpleasant smell. *Also known as stinking nightshade, henbane is a poisonous plant with narcotic properties.*

Henchman – *(noun)* **1** [chiefly derogatory] a faithful follower or political supporter, especially one prepared to engage in crime or dishonest practices. *The gang leader and his henchmen creating nuisance were arrested by the police.*

Hendecagon – *(noun)* a plane figure with eleven straight sides and angles. *In geometry, a figure with eleven angles and sides is known as hendecagon.*

Henpeck – *(verb)* continually criticize and order about her husband. *His wife bullies him so much that he no longer takes any decision and has become a true henpecked.*

Hepta – *combining form* seven: having seven; heptathlon. *Hepta is a Greek word meaning seven.*

Her – *(pronoun)* **1** used as the object of a verb or preposition to refer to a female person or animal previously mentioned or easily identified. *She knew I hated her. I told Salina I would wait for her at the station.* referring to a ship, country, or other inanimate thing regarded as female. *The crew tried to sail her through a narrow gap.* used after the verb 'to be' and after 'than' or 'as'. *It must be her he was younger than her. See usage below. She will get all her wants.* **2** [archaic or North American] dialect herself. *Peevishly she flung her on her face.*

Herbarium – *(noun)* a systematically arranged collection of dried plants. *Herbarium is a room where dry plants and herbs are stored.*

Herbivorous – *adj.* plant-eaters. *All plant-eating animals are herbivorous.*

Herby – *(adjective)* of herbal. *If you want to buy herbs or herbal plants, please visit a herby dealer.*

Hereabouts – *(adv.)* near this place. *His house is hereabout Delhi railway station area.*

Hereafter – *adv.* in future. *All communications intended for the director will hereafter be addressed to the secretary.*

Hereby – *(adv.)* formal as a result of this document or utterance. *The order I sent yesterday is hereby withdrawn and you are to act as if it never existed.*

Hereditary – *(adjective)* conferred by based on, or relating to inheritance. able to be passed on from parents to their offspring or descendants. *The only qualification for membership is intellect; other distinctions, hereditary or acquired, do not count.*

Heresy – *(noun)* belief or opinion contrary to orthodox religious doctrine. *The practice of following unorthodox religious philosophy is known as heresy.*

Heretic – *(noun)* a person believing in or practicing heresy. *The person who renounces the orthodox religious doctrine is known as a heretic.*

Heritable – *(adjective)* able to be inherited. *This property is heritable among all three children.*

Heritage – *(noun)* valued things such as historic buildings that have been passed down from previous generations. of special value and worthy of preservation. *Taj Mahal is a world heritage site maintained by Archeological Society of India.*

Heritor – *(noun)* a person who inherits. *He willed his daughter as the heritor of all acquired properties after his death.*

Hermit – *(noun)* a person living in solitude as a religious discipline. a reclusive or solitary person. *Away from family members, he lives a reclusive life of a hermit as if he has renounced the worldly pleasures.*

Hermitage – *(noun)* place where hermits live. *More than 50 hermits are living in this 500 year-old hermitage.*

Heroine – *(noun)* **1** a woman admired for her courage or outstanding achievements. a woman of superhuman qualities. *It is our moral duty to praise Rani Lakshmi Bai as heroine, who fought British forces in 1857.* **2** the chief female character in a book, play, or film. *Jane Austen's heroines ore famous all over the world.*

Heroism – *(noun)* characteristics of a hero, bravery. *Perhaps this love was kindling a new heroism in him.*

Heron – *(noun)* a large fish-eating wading bird with long legs, a long s-shaped neck, and a long pointed bill. *Pelicans and flamingoes, geese and ducks, storks and herons, ibises and cranes, flew in from all directions.*

Herpes – *(noun)* a disease caused by a Herpes virus, affecting the skin or the nervous system. *Herpes is a disease badly affecting the skin and nervous system.*

Herring – *(noun)* a silvery fish which is most abundant in coastal waters and is an important food fish. *Herring is a popular edible fish mostly found in North America.*

Herself – *pro(noun)* used to refer to a thing or things belonging to or associated with a female person or animal previously mentioned. *She dressed herself with more than usual care, and came to meet visitors in her stormy beauty.*

Hesitant – *(adjective)* slow to act or speak through indecision or reluctance. *Fearing loss of job, he looked hesitant to speak the truth in front of his employer.*

Hesitating – *(adjective)* indecisive. *He was hesitating initially but finally spoke of the humiliating experience while in police lock up.*

Hesitation – *(noun)* hesitating, faltering. *After slight hesitation she sat down, burying her face in her hands.*

Hesitative – *adj.* indecisive, hesitant. *This college doesn't admit students who are indecisive or hesitative by nature.*

Hesitator – *(noun)* one who hesitates, irresolute. *Because you don't explain your position, most people consider you a hesitator.*

Hesperus – *(noun)* poetic the planet venus. *In Greek mythology, Hesperus is the evening star, the planet Venus in the evening.*

Heterodox - *(adjective)* not conforming with orthodox standards or beliefs. *A person who doesn't conform to the accepted religious beliefs is known as heterodox.*

Heugh - *(noun)* a shaft in a coal pit. *Heugh is a shaft in a coal pit through which miners and ores move between the pit and the surface outlet.*

Heuristic - *(adjective)* **1** enabling a person to discover or learn something for themselves. *Heuristic method involves finding a solution by trial and error or by rules that are only loosely defined.*

Hexa - *(combining form)* six; having six. *Hexagon is an enclosed geometric form having six sides and angles.*

Hexagon - *(noun)* a plane figure with six straight sides and angles. *Hexagon is an enclosed geometric form having six sides and angles.*

Hexameter - *(noun)* prosody a line of verse consisting of six metrical feet. *Hexameter is a verse consisting of six feet*

Hey - *exclamatory* used to attract attention or to express surprise, interest, etc. *Hey! Where had you been for such a long time?*

Heyday - *(noun)* the period of one's greatest success, activity, or vigour. *During their heyday, no team could challenge the might of Brazilian football team.*

Hiatus - *(noun)* a pause or gap in continuity, a break between two vowels coming together but not in the same syllable, as in the ear. *A small difference in pitch between two musical tones is known as hiatus.*

Hide - *(noun)* the skin of an animal, especially when tanned or dressed. *Hide of cow is considered most soft and light for footwear.*

Hideous - *(adjective)* extremely ugly. extremely unpleasant. *They had hardly finished picnic before a hideous creature came towards them.*

Hie - *(verb)* move quickly. *It is an obsolete word meaning to move quickly.*

Hiemal - *(adjective)* characteristic of or relating to winter. *Wearing an overcoat over a coat to protect one from biting cold signals the onset of hiemal.*

Hierarch - *(noun)* a chief priest, archbishop; or other leader. *Persons holding a position of authority in a church are designated an hierarch.*

Hierarchical - *(adjective)* belonging to an hierarchy. *In the hierarchical order of precedence, the prime minister stands third only behind the president and vice president of India.*

Hierachy - *(noun)* **1** a ranking system ordered according to status or authority. the upper echelons of a hierarchical system. an arrangement according to relative importance or inclusiveness. *In the hierarchy of Army, the general is the senior-most officer.*

Hiero - combing form sacred; holy. *In ancient Greece, holy shrines and temples were known as hiero.*

Higgle - *(verb)* [archaic] spelling of haggle, bargaining. *Unless you higgle hard, the vegetable seller wouldn't lower the price.*

High-born - *(adjective)* having noble parents. *This aristocratic club only admits high-born members.*

High-flier - *(noun)* racing horse. *A British thoroughbred racing horse is known as high-flier.*

High-flown - *(adjective)* pretentious, extravagant or grandiose. *The students couldn't understand the meaning of the high-flown talk on morality delivered by the speaker.*

High-handed - *(adjective)* domineering or inconsiderate. *They are your employees and shouldn't be treated in a high-handed manner.*

Highland - *(noun)* an area of high or mountainous land. *The mountainous northern part of Scotland is popularly known as highland.*

Highly - *(adv.)* to a high degree or level, favourably. *A favourable action on my application would be highly appreciated.*

High-minded - *(adjective)* having strong moral principles. *He is a high-minded person and on no account would compromise on his principles.*

High-priest - *(noun)* a chief priest of a non-christian religion, especially of historic judaism. the leader of a cult or movement. *The high-priest looked up in astonishment, as the disturbance in the church broke in on his studies.*

High-sounding - *adj*. pretentious. *The students couldn't understand the meaning of the high-sounding talk on morality delivered by the speaker.*

High-spirits - *(plural noun)* lively and cheerful behaviour or mood. *After selection into the national team, the members were in high-spirits to do their best.*

High-time - *(verb)* in a manner of warning. *To be retained in the team, it is high time you start making runs.*

High-water - *(noun)* another term for high tide. *At the time of high-water, fishermen are advised not to go out into the sea.*

Hilarity - *(noun)* cheerfulness, funniness *The attitude of hilarity can lighten the mood of any serious discussion.*

Hill - *(noun)* a naturally raised area of land, not as high or craggy as a mountain. a heap or mound. *The Aravali hills rises in the western India and merges into the plains in Delhi.*

Hillock - *(noun)* a small hill or mound. *Hillocks is a mound above the plains and lower than the hills.*

Hilly - *(adjective)* having many hills. *Shimla is an idyllic and hilly place surrounde by huge trees.*

Hilt - *(noun)* handle of a sword, dagger, weapon, tool. *The sword had a costly hilt decorated with rubies and turquoises.*

Hindmost - *(adjective)* especially of a bodily part hind. *Just then the horse stepped quickly around on his hindmost feet, and looked the professor in the face.*

Hindrance - *(noun)* a thing that hinders. *The hooligans were trying to create hindrance to prevent workers from going to the factory.*

Hindu - *(noun)* a major religious and cultural tradition of the Indian subcontinent, including belief in reincarnation and the worship of a large pantheon of deities. *Hindu religion is one of the oldest religion in the world.*

Hinny - *(noun)* the offspring of a female donkey and a male horse, compare with mule. *A hinny is an offspring of a male horse and a female donkey.*

Hippodrome - *(noun)* a theatre or concert hall. *Hippodrome is an area where chariot race takes place.*

Hippology - *(noun)* study of horses. *Hippology, the study of horses, helps one to learn how to breed thoroughbred racing horses.*

Hippopotamus - *(noun)* a large thick-skinned semiaquatic african mammal, with massive jaws. *Hippopotamus is mostly found in Africa.*

Hircine - *(adjective)* [archaic] of or resembling odour of a goat. *A strong foul smell resembling that of a goat's odour is called hircine.*

Hireable - *(adjective)* the act of hiring. *Children below 14 years are not hireable to work in any factory.*

Hireling - *(noun)* chiefly derogatory a person who is hired, especially for morally dubious or illegal work. *Mercenaries who fight on behalf of someone purely for money are called hirelings.*

Hirer - *(noun)* one who hires. *The boss hired three more men for the job.*

Hiss - *(noun)* sound like a escaping steam. *The sound made by angry snakes, cats or birds is called hiss.*

Historian - *(noun)* an expert in or student of history. *Rudrangshu Mukherjee is a famous historian of India.*

Historicity - *(noun)* [historical] authenticity. *Historicity is the quality of being a part of recorded history as opposed to myth or legend.*

Hitherto - *(adv.)* until the point in time under discussion. *Things that had hitherto seemed impossible now came true.*

Hive - *(noun)* a busy, swarming place. *The bees live in a hive. (verb)* place in a hive. *Delhi is so much populated that people live much like bees in a hive.*

Hoard - *(noun)* a store of money or valued objects. *He rushed back to rescue his hoard of gold.* an amassed store of useful information. *The police discovered a hoard of secret information about their activities. (verb)* amass and hide or store away. *Black marketers resort to hoarding large amount of food grains with a view to sell them at high prices later.*

Hoarse – *(adjective)* of a voice rough and harsh. *His face looked tired, and his voice hoarse with shouting commands for hours.*

Hoax – *(noun)* a humorous or malicious deception. *The evidence has been planted as part of elaborate hoax.* *(verb)* deceive with a hoax. *The aircraft was thoroughly searched following a hoax call about a bomb having been planted inside.*

Hobnob – *(verb)* [informal] mix socially, especially with those of higher social status. *To appear influential, he would often go to parties and hobnob with senior bureaucrats.*

Hocus-pocus – *(noun)* meaningless talk used for trickery. *Please come to the point and not indulge in hocus pocus explanation that wastes time.*

Hod – *(noun)* a builder's v-shaped tray used for carrying bricks. *These days conveyors carry bricks and mortars in building upper floors instead of hods being used on head.*

Hodman – *(noun)* a labourer carrying a hod. *A hodman carries bricks and mortars on his head during building construction.*

Hodge-podge – *(noun)* [North American] variant of hotchpotch. *Hodge-podge is a word that describes a disorderly collection of things, items etc.*

Hoe – *(noun)* a long-handled gardening tool with a thin metal blade, used mainly for weeding. *You must use a hoe to dig up earth or plants. After just two doses of the hoe in the garden, the weeds entirely disappeared.*

Hog – *(noun)* **1** a pig, especially a castrated male reared for slaughter. *Hog is a term given to the pig that is reared for consumption.*

Hoggish – *(adjective)* coarsely gluttonous or greedy. *Fat-cheeked little boy and pot-bellied father displayed pig-like manners while eating at the dining table.*

Hoist – *(verb)* raise by means of ropes and pulleys. haul up. *A white flag was hoisted.* *(noun)* an act of hoisting. *Hydraulic lifts are used for firefighting purposes. It became necessary to use a crane to hoist the goods to be stored on the terrace from the courtyard.*

Hold-all – *(noun)* [British] a large bag with handles and a shoulder strap. *Hold-all is a convenient carrying bag people use in packing sleeping materials during a train journey.*

Holding – *(noun)* gripping, to have in one's hand. *She came forward to meet him in the drawing room, holding out her hand with open-hearted frankness.*

Holdback – *(noun)* restraint, hindrance, obstacle. *Don't holdback your views when replying to psychologist's queries.*

Holdfast – *(noun)* a staple or clamp securing an object. *This staple pin will holdfast all papers in one place.*

Holland – *(noun)* a kind of smooth, hard-wearing linen, used for soft furnishings. *Cotton and linen fabric used for window and book-binding still goes by the name Holland because the manufacturing started in the country by the same name.*

Hollow - *(adjective)* **1** having a hole or empty space inside. *A hollow metal tube is required.* having a concave or sunken appearance. *Her cheeks were hollow and there were dark circles under her eyes.* **2** without real significance or value. *The result was a hollow victory for the Indian team.* insincere. *A hollow promise was made during the election speech.* *(noun)* a hole or depression in something. *There was a hollow space at the base of a tree.* an enclosed space within something. *She held them in the hollow of her hand.* a small valley. *The village is situated in a hollow on the edge of the forest.* *(verb)* form by making a hole. *A tunnel was hollowed out in a mountain range.* make a hollow in. *Sita's laugh hollowed her cheeks.*

Holly – *(noun)* an evergreen shrub, with prickly dark green leaves, small white flowers, and red berries. *Holly is an evergreen, deciduous plant with white flowers and green leaves.*

Holocaust – *(noun)* complete destruction by fire, mass killing. *Holocaust is a name that surmises the slaughter of more than six million Jews by the Nazis during the Second World War.*

Holster – *(noun)* gun pouch, case in which pistol, revolver is carried. *He placed the pistol back into the holster and sped away.*

Holt – *(noun)* grove. *Holt is a name given to an area of woodland mainly made up of grove, bushes and small trees.*

Homage – *(noun)* **1** honour or respect shown publicly. *Homage was paid by the visiting dignitary to Mahatma Gandhi, the father of the nation, at his Samadhi at Rajghat.*

Homily – *(noun)* a moralizing discourse. *Homily is a religious discourse given at a congregation for infusing morality.*

Hominy – *(noun)* US coarsely ground corn used to make grits. *Hominy is peeled and dried kernels of corn.*

Homo – *(noun)* the genus of primates of which modern humans are the present-day representatives. *Homo is the genus that is composed of modern humans and species closely related to them.*

Homologous – *(adjective)* alike, equal, similar. *The forelimbs of humans and bats are homologous in make up or structures but they are used differently.*

Homonym – *(noun)* **1** each of two or more words having the same spelling or pronunciation but different meanings and origins. *Words that have the same spelling or pronunciation but different meanings are known as homonyms.*

Honeymoon – *(noun)* **1** a holiday taken by a newly married couple. *The young couple few to Goa for honeymoon.* **2** an initial period of enthusiasm or goodwill. *The new chief ministers honeymoon period produced good results for the country's infrastructure.* *(verb)* spend a honeymoon. *The young couple in Europe on a 15-day are honeymoonig trip.*

Honk – *(noun)* the sound of a car horn. *No honking please this is a silence zone.* *(verb)* emit or cause to emit a honk. *Many drivers have a bad habit of honking even if there's no heavy traffic on the road.*

Honorific – *(adjective)* given as a mark of respect. *He was elevated to the honorific states of chairman.* *(noun)* a title or word expressing respect. *As a mark of respect, many universities offer the honorific title of doctorate to distinguished visiting dignitaries.*

Hooker – *(noun)* a prostitute, whore. *Hookers offer sensual pleasures to customers in return for money.*

Hooligan – *(noun)* a violent young troublemaker. *Curfew has been imposed in the city to prevent hooligans from inciting further violence.*

Hopple – *(verb&noun)* riding another term for bobble. *Hobble is a process of strapping the foreleg and hind leg together on each side (of a horse) in order to keep the like-sided legs moving in unison.*

Horde – *(noun)* [chiefly derogatory] a large group of people. *Until they reached the palace the hordes, so eager for booty, had completely refrained from plunder and pillage.*

Horizon – *(noun)* **1** the line at which the earth's surface and the sky appear to meet. *The sun rose above the horizon.* **2** the limit of a person's mental perception, experience, or interest. *She wanted to study abroad to broaden her horizon.*

Horizontal – *(adjective)* **1** parallel to the plane of the horizon. *Try to draw two lines parallel and horizontal to each other.*

Hormone – *(noun)* treatment with oestrogens to alleviate menopausal symptoms or osteoporosis. *The doctor has suggested hormonal treatment can reduce problem of osteoporosis.*

Horner – *(noun)* a person who blows a horn. *A horner necessarily accompanies a music party to blow the horn.*

Hornless – *(adjective)* without horns. *This cattle has no horn on its head.*

Horology – *(noun)* the study and measurement of time, the art of making clocks and watches. *Horology is the art and science of measuring time as well as of making clocks.*

Horoscope – *(noun)* a forecast of a person's future based on the relative positions of the stars and planets at the time of their birth. *Horoscope of both the boy and the girl is extensively matched before a marriage is settled in India.*

Horrible – *(adjective)* causing or likely to cause horror. [informal] very unpleasant. *She felt that another little while in this heated, horrible place would drive her mad.*

Horribly - *(adjective)* awefully, terribly. *There was a horribly deadly accident here this morning.*

Horribleness - *(noun)* awfulness, dreadfulness, repulsiveness. *This hotel is so filthy, it matches the horribleness to the previous one.*

Horrid - *(adjective* causing horror. [informal] very unpleasant. *Was she awake or was she a prey to some horrid dream?*

Horrific - *(adjective)* causing horror. *Horrific working conditions in the mining industry is simply disgusting.*

Horrify - *(verb)* fill with horror. *I was horrified at the thought of being late for my interview.*

Horror - *(noun)* an intense feeling of fear, shock, or disgust. a thing causing such a feeling. intense dismay. *For the first time since the Revolution had begun, the horror of it and the meaning of it were brought home to him.*

Horticulture - *(noun)* the art or practice of garden cultivation and management. *Horticulture is the art of garden cultivation.*

Hose - *(noun)* **1** a flexible tube conveying water, used chiefly for watering plants and in firefighting. *The firefighters were using a large hose to spray water over the building on fire.* **2** stockings, socks, and tights. [historical] breeches. *She uses garter belts to keep her house in proper fit.* *(verb)* water or spray with a hose. *He was hosing down the driveway with clean water.*

Hosier - *(noun)* a manufacture or seller of hosiery. *Jockey is one of the largest manufacturer in the world engaged in trade as a wholesale hosier.*

Hospice - *(noun)* **1** a home providing care for the sick or terminally ill. *Hospice is a name given to homes where sick travellers can stay and get treated medically.*

Hospitable - *(adjective)* showing or inclined to show hospitality. pleasant and favourable for living in. *If you want to learn the art of pleasant, ploshed and hospitable manners of treating guests, please visit a five-star hotel.*

Hospital - *(noun)* an institution providing medical and surgical treatment and nursing care for sick or injured people. *Hospital is a place where sick and injured are fully taken care of with medicine and surgery.*

Hospitality - *(noun)* the friendly and generous reception and entertainment of guests or strangers. *The poor man was received with the same hospitality by the King as that of any other rich person.*

Host - *(noun)* **1** a person who receives or entertains other people as guests. *The person you see standing there is the dinner-party host.* a person, place, or organization that holds an event to which others are invited. *London played host to the Summer Olympics in 2012.* the presenter of a television or radio programme: *The host for today's programme is Minni Mathur.* **2** an area in which particular plants or animals are found. *Australia is host to some of the world's most dangerous animals.* *(verb)* **1** act as host at (an event) or for (a television or radio programme). *Sri Lanka has been asked to host the Commonwealth heads-of-government conference in Colombo.* **2** store (a website or other data) on a server or other computer so that it can be accessed over the Internet. *Oxford University currently hosts nearly 400 websites.*

Hostage - *(noun)* a person seized or held as security for the fulfilment of a condition. *The hostage were to be released by the terrorists in exchange for five of their jailed breathen.*

Hostel - *(noun)* an establishment which provides cheap food and lodging for a specific group of people. *This private hostel is one of the best in the town to take care of food and lodging arrangements of students.*

Hostess - *(noun)* a female host. a woman employed to welcome and entertain customers at a nightclub or bar. a stewardess on an aircraft, train, etc. *Madhuri Dixit is the hostess of today's programme. Air hostesses take care of most individual needs of the flyers.*

Hostile - *(adjective)* antagonistic; opposed. of or belonging to a military enemy. opposed by the company to be bought. *A warrior had succeeded in penetrating the hostile fort of the enemy unnoticed and killed the king with a sword.*

Hostility - *(noun)* animosity. *Hostility to foreign retail trade is likely to do more harm than good to Indian cunsumers.*

Hotly - *adj.* excitedly, heatedly, angrily. *The hotly contested election went in favour of the ruling party by a thin margin.*

Hotchpotch - *(noun)* a confused mixture. *The coalition government ruling India is a hotchpotch of many political parties.*

Hotel - *(noun)* an establishment providing accommodation and meals for travellers and tourists. *Taj hotel is one of the best hotels in the world.*

Hound - *(noun)* **1** a dog of a breed used for hunting, especially one able to track by scent. *A hound is breed of dog mainly used for hunting in the jungles.*

House - *(noun)* **1** a building for human habitation. chiefly a dwelling that is one of several in a building. *The house which he had taken up for his residence was not a very large one.*

Household - *(noun)* a house and its occupants regarded as a unit. *The household was, to all appearance, asleep at the unusually early hour.*

Housewife - *(noun)* **1** a married woman whose main occupation is caring for her family and running the household. *She is a housewife and doesn't work in any office.* **2** a small case for needles, thread, and other small sewing items. *Housewife is a small case in which needles, threads and other sewing items are kept.*

Housing - *(noun)* houses and flats considered collectively. the provision of accommodation. *Housing societies are building attractive designer flats offering many options to buyers to choose.*

Hovel - *(noun)* **1** a small squalid or poorly constructed dwelling. *No bed in tent, hovel, or house was occupied; for everywhere the final packing was going on.*

Hover - *(verb)* remain in one place in the air. *Army helicopters hovered over the area.* linger close at hand in an uncertain manner. *She hovered anxiously in the background.*remain at or near a particular level. *Inflation will hover around 6 percent this month.* *(noun)* an act of hovering. *The helicopter was hovering just above the ground for sometime not knowing where to land.*

How - *(adverb)* **1** in what way or manner; by what means. *How does it work? She did not know how she ought to behave. She showed me how to adjust the focus of the camera.* **2** used to ask about the condition or quality of something. *How was your holiday? How did they play?* used to ask about someone's physical or mental state. *How are the children? I asked how he was doing.* **3** used to ask about the extent or degree of something. *How old are you? How long will it take? I wasn't sure how fast to go.* used to express a strong feeling such as surprise about the extent of something. *How I wish I had been there at the picnic!* **4** the way in which. *He told us how he had lived out of a suitcase for the last one week.* in any way in which. *I'll do business how I like.*

Howitzer - *(noun)* a short gun for firing shells on high trajectories at low velocities. *Howitzer is a short barrelled-gun armies use to fire at enemies.*

Howler - *(noun)* **1** [informal] a ludicrous mistake. *I regret my howler of throwing the banana and try to eat its skin.* **2** a fruit-eating monkey with a loud howling call, native to the forests of tropical America. *A howler is the largest monkey living in the jungles of North America.*

Howling - *(adjective)* [informal] great noise. *If you don't stop howling, I will report to the principal*

Hub - *(noun)* the central part of a wheel, rotating on or with the axle, and from which the spokes radiate, the centre of an activity, region, or network. *Colombo is the shipping hub where ships from all countries unload and reload merchandise.*

Huckaback - *(noun)* a strong linen or cotton fabric with a rough surface, used for towelling and glass cloths. *Huckaback is a strong cotton fabric used for making towels.*

Huckster - *(noun)* **1** a person who sells small items, either door-to-door or from a stall. **2** [North American] a person who uses aggressive selling techniques. *A huckster is a person who sells household items of daily use door-to-door.*

Huddle – *(verb)* **1** crowd together. *At last we reached the mouth of a ravine, and there we huddled ourselves under the streaming trees to relax.* **2** curl one's body into a small space. *She curled herself behind the sofa to hide herself from the ferocious looking person.* *(noun)* a number of people or things crowded together. a brief gathering of players during a game to receive instruction. *These days players go into a huddle for last-minute instructions before going over to their respective positions in the field.*

Hue – *(noun)* a colour or shade. technical the attribute of a colour, dependent on its dominant wavelength, by virtue of which it is discernible as red, green, etc.*There are many different hues of every colour, such as, light blue, blue, sky blue, dark blue etc.*

Huff - *(verb)* **1** blowout air loudly on account of exertion. *He was huffing under a heavy load. I was huffing and puffing to keep up with his speed.* **2** express one's feeling of petty annoyance. *'Huh!' that woman huffed no end after long journey.* **3** sniff fumes from (petrol or solvents) for a euphoric effect. *It is important to educate people about the dangers of huffing fumes, directly or indirectly.* *(noun)* a fit of petty annoyance. *He walked off in a huff.*

Hull – *(noun)* the main body of a ship or other vessel, including the bottom, sides and deck but not the superstructure, engines, and other fitting. *A hull is basically a foundation over which the ship construction takes place.*

Hullabaloo – *(noun)* [informal] a commotion or uproar. *In this hullabaloo of constant cross-talking, I can't lecture this class.*

Human – *(adjective)* of, relating to, or characteristic of human-kind. of or characteristic of people human error. *To forgive is the highest form of human life. It's a human error.* *(noun)* a human being. *Men and women belong to the human race.*

Humane – *(adjective)* compassionate or benevo- lent. inflicting the minimum of pain. *Being compassionate to feelings of others is the best humane quality*

Humanism – *(noun)* rationalistic outlook or system of thought attaching prime importance to human rather than divine or supernatural matters. *Humanism is a reflection of respectful consideration for welfare of fellow human beings*

Humanity - *(noun)* **1** human beings collectively. *Appalling crimes are being committed in Syria against humanity.* the state of being human. *No doubt our differences matter but our common humanity matters more.* **2** the quality of being humane. benevolence. *He praised the Red Cross for their standards of humanity and care.*

Humble - *(adjective)* (humbler, humblest) **1** having or showing a modest or low estimate of one's importance. *I felt very humble when meeting her.* (of an action or thought) offered with or affected by a modest estimate of one's importance. *My humble apologies for failing to attend the marriage ceremony.* **2** of low social, administrative, or political rank. *He came from a humble, unprivileged background.* **3** (of a thing) of modest pretensions or dimensions. *He built this business empire from humble beginnings.* *(verb)* cause (someone) to feel less important or proud. *He was humbled by his many ordeals.* decisively defeat (a sporting opponent previously thought to be superior). *England were humbled at the Oval cricket ground by India in the Champions Trophy final.*

Humbly – *adj.* simply, modestly, meekly. *He is very haughty but today surprisingly and very humbly he paid respect to all visitors.*

Humid – *(adjective)* marked by a relatively high level of water vapour in the atmosphere. *Due to heavy rain in this sea-resort, it has become very sultry and humid* .

Humidity – *(noun)* the state or quality of being humid. a quantity representing the amount of water vapour in the atmosphere or a gas. *Humidity is a term that define the amount of water vapour in the air.*

Humility – *(noun)* a humble view of one's own importance. *Humility is the human property of being ego-less-ness.*

Humorist – *(noun)* a humorous writer, performer, or artist. *A humorist has the innate ability to act,* *speak or write in a way that gladdens the heart of everyone.*

Humorous – *(adjective)* causing amusement. having or showing a sense of humour. *Of all the books I have read, 'Bedtime Mailbox' has been the most humorous.*

Humour – *(noun)* **1** the quality of being amusing or comic, especially as expressed in literature or speech. *His tales are full of humour.* the ability to appreciate or express humour. *The inimitable brand of humour was on show.* **2** a state of mind: *her good humour vanished.* [archaic] an inclination or whim. *He had the same quiet smile, the same quiet humour, the same calm acceptance of life.*

Hunch – *(verb)* raise and bend the top of one's body forward. sit or stand in such a position. *He sat with a forward bend in his body that looked almost like a camel.(noun)* a feeling or guess based on intuition. *He has not informed me but I have a hunch that he is coming here today.*

Hung – *(adjective)* **1** of an elected body having no political party with an overall majority. *Political pundits are predicting a hung parliament following elections.* **2** [informal] emotionally confused or disturbed. *Since we all had fled the class yesterday, suspense hung whether the principal would inform our parents.*

Hungrily – *(adjective)* in a hungry manner. *No sooner the food was served, the visitor attacked it hungrily as if he had not had a morsel for a few days.*

Hungry – *(adjective)* **1** feeling, showing, or causing hunger. *But I was not hungry any more, and did not care for food.* **2** having a strong desire. *Being hungry is a sensation when one feels the physiological need to eat food.*

Hunting – *(noun)* **1** the activity of hunting wild animals or game, especially for food or sport. *Hunting is a practice of pursuing a living wild animal for food, recreation or trade.*

Huntsman – *(noun)* a person who hunts. a hunt official in charge of hounds. *A huntsman is a person who pursues a living wildlife, especially animals for food, recreation or trade.*

Hurdle – *(noun)* **1** one of a series of upright frames which athletes in a race must jump over. a hurdle race. *Hurdles are used for handling livestock, as decorative fencing and for horse-racing.* **2** an obstacle or difficulty. *Hurdle is a movable section of light fence which must be jumped over by an athletes to complete the race. (verb)* run in a hurdle race. jump over while running. *Hurdle race is are important athletic event in any olympic games.*

Hurl – *(verb)* throw or impel with great force. utter vehemently. *Javelin throwers try to hurl by hand the long spear-like object farthest in order to win the competition.*

Hurrah – *exclamatory* used to express joy or approval. *Hurrah! Our team has won the tournament for the third time in a row.*

Hurricane – *(noun)* a storm with a violent wind, in particular a tropical cyclone in the Caribbean. *Hurricane is a name given to a tropical cyclone occurring in the Caribbean and characterized by strong winds and heavy rains.*

Hurry – *(verb)* move or act quickly or more quickly. do or finish quickly. *It was necessary to hurry this matter to a close. (noun)* great haste. a need for haste; urgency. *He was in a hurry, for preparations had to be made in the dining-hall for the reception of the distinguished guests.*

Hurtful – *(adjective)* causing mental pain or distress. *His attitude of not coming up to the door to welcome his poor friend was very hurtful.*

Hurtle – *(verb)* move or cause to move at great speed. *To enable the spacecraft escape the earth's gravitational pull, it is necessary to hurtle it at a speed more than 12 kilometres per second.*

Hush – *(verb)* make or become quiet. *In a hushed tone he said goodbye. (noun)* a silence. *No sooner the principal arrived, there was a sudden hush in the class room.*

Husk – *(noun)* the dry outer covering of some fruit or seeds. *Manufacturers are converting rice husk into edible oil. (verb)* remove the husk from. *Husk is the outer cover of food crops used mainly as fodder for animals.*

Husky - *(adjective)* **1** sounding low-pitched and slightly hoarse. *Because of cough and cold, her voice has become very husky.*

Husting - *(noun)* a meeting at which candidates in an election address potential voters. *Husting is a physical platform, usually in America, from which public representatives air their opinion to influence the voters.*

Hut - *(noun)* a small single-storey building of simple or crude construction. *A hut is a single-storey dwelling unit mostly found in villages.*

Hutch - *(noun)* a box or cage for keeping rabbits or other small domesticated animals. *Hutch is a box-like cage for keeping rabbits, guinea-pigs etc.*

Hyaena - *(noun)* variant spelling of hyena. *Hyaena is a carnivorous nocturnal animal that resembles a dog and found mostly in Africa*

Hybridize - *(verb)* cross-breed to produce hybrids. *To increase yields of food crops, only option left is to cross-breed or hybridize seeds.*

Hydrant - *(noun)* a water pipe with a nozzle to which a fire hose can be attached. *A hydrant consists of long rubber tubes attached to water support system and located at vantage point around large buildings to extinguish fires.*

Hydrate - *(verb)* cause to absorb or combine with water. *To hydrate the body, it is recommended to use a moisturising lotion over the exposed parts of the body while going out in the sun.*

Hydraulic - *(adjective)* denoting or relating to a liquid moving in a confined space under pressure. *To prevent accidents happening on the road, hydraulic brakes come attached in the vehicle in addition to the foot brakes.*

Hydric - *(adjective)* ecology containing plenty of moisture; very wet. compare with mesic and xeric.

Hydro - *(noun)* [British] a hotel or clinic originally providing hydropathic treatment. *A hydro is a shortened name for a place offering cure through hydrotherapy.*

Hydroelectric - *(adjective)* relating to or denoting the generation of electricity using flowing water to drive a turbine which powers a generator. *To increase the availability of power, stations generating hydroelectric power must be installed.*

Hydrogen - *(noun)* a gel in which the liquid component is water. *Hydrogen and oxygen when mixed produce water.*

Hydrophobia - *(noun)* extreme or irrational fear of water, especially as a symptom of rabies. *Hydrophobia is a disease in which the patient develops an abnormal fear of water.*

Hydroplane - *(noun)* **1** a light, fast motor boat. **2** a fin-like attachment which enables a moving submarine to rise or fall in the water. *A hydroplane is used for recreation on large water bodies. (verb)* [chiefly North American] another term for aquaplane. *A hydroplane is a light motorboat designed to skim over the water at high speeds with the rear part of its hull touching the water.*

Hygiene - *(noun)* conditions or practices conducive to maintaining health and preventing disease, especially cleanliness. *Hygiene is the art and practice for cleanliness, preservation of good health and prevention of illness.*

Hygrometer - *(noun)* an instrument for measuring humidity. *Hygrometer is an instrument to measure humidity in the atmosphere.*

Hymen - *(noun)* a membrane which partially closes the opening of the vagina and whose presence is traditionally taken to be a mark of virginity.

Hymn - *(noun)* a religious song of praise, typically a Christian song in praise of God. *Hymn is a song which is sung in the praise of God.*

Hypallage - *(noun)* rhetoric a transposition of the natural relations of two elements in a proposition, e.g. in the sentence *'melissa shook her doubtful curls'.*

Hyperbola - *(noun)* [mathematics] a symmetrical open curve formed by the intersection of a cone with a plane at a smaller angle with its axis than the side of the cone. *Hyperbola is one of the four kinds of conic section, the others being, parabola, ellipse and circle.*

Hyperbole - *(noun)* deliberate exaggeration not meant to be taken literally. *Hyperbole is the use of exaggeration as rhetoric to generate strong feelings and emotional bond, such as, comparing someone knowledge to Einstein.*

Hyperbolize – *(verb)* exaggerate beyond truth. *The government has chosen to hyperbolize the benefits of foreign retailers offering goods at lower prices.*

Hypercritic – *(noun)* one who is critical beyond a reason. *Most opposition parties play hypercritic to any government's move to bring in foreign retailers.*

Hypertrophy – *(noun)* [physiology] enlargement of an organ or tissue resulting from an increase in size of its cells. *Hypertrophy is the abnormal increase in the volume of an organ due to the increase in the size of cells.*

Hypothecate – *(verb)* pledge by [law] to a specific purpose. *He decided to hypothecate his property to the bank to borrow money for his son's education.*

Hypothecation – *(noun)* mortgaging. *Hypothecation is the practice where a borrower pledges a collateral as a guarantee to secure a loan.*

Hypothecator – *(noun)* one who mortgages. *A hypothecator has signed over his personal property to the bank as security for the repayment of money borrowed.*

Hypothesis – *(noun)* a supposition or proposed explanation made on the basis of limited evidence as a starting point for further investigation. [philosophy] a proposition made as a basis for reasoning. *The hypothesis that particles travel faster than light is difficult to verify on the available scientific instruments.*

Hypothetic – *(adjective)* theoretical, pertaining to hypothesis. *We have only gone as far as Moon, it is only hypothetic to calculate the possibility of going to Mars and come back to Earth.*

Hypothesize – *(verb)* create a theory, form a hypothesis. *Since that hypothesis has been scientifically proved, there is no need for him to hypothesize again.*

Hysteria – *(noun)* [psychiatry] a psychological disorder whose symptoms include selective amnesia, volatile emotions, and attention-seeking behaviour, exaggerated or uncontrollable emotion or excitement. *Hysteria is a state of mind characterized by unmanageable fear or emotional excesses.*

Hysteric – *(adjective)* another term for hysterical. *A person suffering from uncontrolled emotional outburst is known as a hysteric.*

Ii

I – *(noun)* **1** the ninth letter of the alphabet. **2** denoting the next after H in a set of items, categories, etc. **3** the roman numeral for one.

Iambic – *(adjective)* prosody of or using iambuses. *The poem is known for its use of iambic pentameter.* *(noun)* verse using iambuses. *Look carefully at the use of iambs in this poem.*

Ibex – *(noun)* a wild mountain goat with long, thick ridged horns and a beard. *Over those ice-covered mountains, we photographed an ibex on camera.*

Ibid – *(adverb)* in the same source referring to a previously cited work. *This quotation by the author is from his book on philosophy, and the next quotation, ibid.*

Ibis – *(noun)* a large wading bird with a long down curved bill, long neck and long legs. *We were amazed to see so many ibises, all at one place.*

Ice – *(noun)* **1** frozen water, a brittle transparent crystalline solid. [chiefly British] an ice cream or water ice. *Mom asked John to place all the ice cubes in the jug containing juice.* **2** [informal] diamonds. *I was jealous of the fascinating ice worn by her around her neck.* *(verb)* **1 d**ecorate with icing. *Her friend was icing the cake while she herself was entertaining the guests.* **2** north American [informal] clinch. *What that Asian country signed that day proved a lucrative ice for its development.* **3** [north American informal] kill. *The soldier got iced by a razor sharp weapon stabbed directly into his chest.*

Ichneumon – *(noun)* **1** a slender parasitic wasp with long antennae, which deposits its eggs in or on the larvae of other insects. *The biologist observed the larvae of ichneumon under microscope.* **2** the Egyptian mongoose. *It was fun to watch the movements of ichneumons from so close.*

Ichor – *(noun)* **1** greek aythology the fluid said to flow like blood in the veins of the gods. *The witch prophesied that a man with ichor in his blood will be the next ruler of the kingdom.* **2** [archaic] a watery fetid discharge from a wound. *Doctor applied antiseptic to prevent ichor flowing from the wound cause infection.*

Ichthyoid – *(adjective)* an animal that lives in water. *The aquatic animal had an ichthyoids body.*

Icicle – *(noun)* a handing, tapering piece of ice formed by the freezing of dripping water. *The icicle shaped pieces were hanging from top of the wall.*

Icon – *(noun)* **1** a devotional painting of Christ or another holy figure, typically on wood, venerated in the byzantine and other eastern churches. *The lovely icon on the wall was making the devotees go awe with respect and surprise.* **2** a person or thing regarded as a representative symbol or as worthy of veneration. *Nobody had the slightest idea that the leader would become an icon for the generations to come.* **3** computing a symbol or graphic representation on a VDU screen of a programme, option, or window. *As I clicked on the icon, the screen flickered a bit.* **4** linguistics a sign which has a characteristic in common with the thing it signifies, for example the word snarl pronounced in a snarling way. *The writer has used many iconic words to emphasize its character.*

Iconic – *(adjective)* of, relating to, or of the nature of an icon. depicting a victorious athlete in a conventional style. *His style soon became iconic in the world of fashion.*

Iconoclast – *(noun)* **1** a person who attacks cherished beliefs or institutions. *Raja Ram Mohan Roy was an iconoclast of his time as he stood against superstitions of all kind.* **2 a** person who destroys images used in religious worship, especially one belonging to a movement opposing such images in the byzaning church during the 8th and 9th century. *The Islamic ruler became a ruthless iconoclast and ordered to destroy all the sculptures placed in the temple.*

Icosahedron – *(noun)* a three-dimensional shape having twenty plane faces, in particular a regular solid figure with twenty equal triangular faces. *The chemistry teacher pointed to the icosahedrons figure on chart to explain the concept.*

Icy – *(adjective)* **1** covered with or consisting of ice. very cold. *The cave was dark and icy, so we could not enter it.* **2** very unfriendly or hostile. *It would be good if you change your icy attitude towards these people.*

Idea – *(noun)* **1** a thought or suggestion as to a possible course of action, a mental impression. a belief. *Backed by modern ideas, the country was able to bring necessary change in its social setup.* **2** the aim. *My idea is to abolish poverty in this region.* **3** [philosophy] an eternally existing pattern of which individual things in any class are imperfect copies, a concept of pure reason, not empirically based in experience. *The idea was propagated and soon, it became very popular*

Ideal – *(adjective)* **1** most suitable; perfect. *The room temperature was just ideal for doctors to perform surgery.* **2** desirable or perfect but existing only in the imagination. in an ideal world, representing an abstract or hypothetical optimum. *It is hard to create an ideal world where everything is just perfect.* *(noun)* a perfect type, a standard of perfection. *You are ideal person for a new painter like me.*

Idealistic - *(adjective)* characterized by idealism. unrealistically aiming for perfection. *An idealistic young doctor went to work for another hospital. An idealistic society is hard to conceive.*

Ideality – *(noun)* [formal] the state or quality of being ideal. *Everyone wants to go with ideality when he begins some work.*

Idealize – *(verb)* regard or represent as perfect or better than in reality. *In an idealized society, there are no crimes of any sort.*

Ideally – *(adverb)* preferably. *Ideally you should exercise for 30 minutes every day. Ideally, you should take 20 mg of each tablet in the morning.*

Ideate – *(verb)* [chiefly psychology] imagine, form ideas. *His aim was to ideate a theory that could be proved rationally.*

Ideation – *(noun)* the formation of ideas or concepts. *The scientist's ideation of psychological concept was too hard to believe.*

Idem – *(adverb)* used in citations to indicate an author or word that has just been mentioned. *Marianne Elliot, Partners in revolution,1982; idem, Wolfe Toe, 1989.*

Identical – *(adjective)* **1** exactly alike, developed from a single fertilized ovum, and therefore usually of the same sex and (usually) very similar in appearance, compare with fraternal. *Identical twins were born on July 8, to a woman in ward number 6.* **2** [logic & mathematics] expressing an identity. *These two theories are almost identical and can be applied simultaneously.*

Identifiable – *(adjective)* able to be recognized. distinguishable. *The bodies were so charred that they were no longer identifiable.*

Identification – *(noun)* **1** the action or process of identifying or the fact of being identified. *As soon as the identification process was over, we made an exit out of the office.* **2** an official document or other proof of a person's identity. *The police stopped the van and asked the driver to show his identification proof.*

Idiocy – *(noun)* extremely stupid behaviour. *He was ill-famed for his idiocy.*

Idiom – *(noun)* **1** a group of words established by usage as having a meaning not deducible from those of the individual words. *A class on idioms was arranged for us, just a week before exams.* **2** a form of expression natural to a language, person, or group. *My strength lies in my idiom, the ability to speak fluently in Spanish.* **3** a characteristic mode of expression in music or art. *Soon after his return to England, Albert took to abstract expressionistic idiom in his art.*

Idiomatic – *(adjective)* using, containing, or denoting expressions that are natural to a native speaker. *She spoke fluent, idiomatic English.*

After 10 years of my stay in France, I am now used to Idiomatic French.

Ideosyncrasy – *(noun)* **1** a mode of behaviour or way of thought peculiar to an individual, a distinctive characteristic of a thing. *I could no longer stand his idiosyncrasies, therefore, I left.* **2** [medicine] an abnormal physical reaction by an individual to a food or drug. *The doctors were tensed after the patient displayed an idiosyncrasy towards the medicine.*

Idiot – *(noun)* **1** [informal] a stupid person. *What an idiot the biker was!* **2**. [medicine, archaic] a mentally handicapped person. *Due to his senility, he was completely transformed into an idiot.*

Idiotic – *(adjective)* very stupid. *The girl rebuked the boys for their excessive idiotic behavior.*

Idleness – *(noun)* laziness. indolence. *He was punished for his idleness at school. Too much of idleness can be boring enough.*

Idler – *(noun)* **1** a person who idles. *I knew that my best friend was the biggest idler in the world.* **2** a pulley that transmits no power but guides or tensions a belt or rope. *The idler was not working, so the vehicle came to a halt.* **3** an idle wheel. *Keep an idler, in case you need it later on.*

Idly – *(adverb)* with no particular purpose, reason, or foundation. *"What are your interests?" asked my fiancée.*

Idol – *(noun)* **1** an image or representation of a god used as an object of worship. *The idols were adorned with jewels before being taken out on procession.* **2** an object of adulation. *As far as drama-writing is concerned, I take William Shakespeare as my idol.*

Idolater – *(noun)* a person who worships an idol or idols. *The things grew worse at home when I refused to be an idolater.*

Idolatrous – *(adjective)* relating to or practising idolatry, idol-worshipping, showing extreme admiration or reverence for something. *America's idolatrous worship of the cars is well known. The idolatrous behavior is seen as contempt by many societies.*

Idolatry – *(noun)* **1** worship of idols. *In Hinduism, the roots of idolatry are very deep.* **2** adulation. *Despite too much idolatry by his junior, the officer did not recommend him for the increment.*

Idolize – *(verb)* revere or love greatly or excessively. *Don't idolize me as it would be of no use.*

Idyll – *(noun)* **1** a blissful or peaceful period or situation. *For the winter-lovers, Shimla stands out as an idyll destination.* **2** a short description in verse or prose of a picturesque pastoral scene or incident. *I am keen to compile all the poet's idylls in one place.*

If – *(conjunction)* **1** introducing a conditional clause: on the condition or supposition that. introducing a hypothetical situation. *If you don't abide by rules, I would be forced to keep you out from this discussion.* **2** despite the possibility that. despite being. *Even if I study hard, I am not going to get through the exams.* **3** whether. *Tell me clearly if you will complete it or not by 2 p.m.?* **4** expressing a polite request or tentative opinion. *If you could excuse me please requested the man.* **5** expressing surprise or regret. *"Only if I could save her life!" said the doctor with a heavy heart.* *(noun)* a condition or supposition. *If the sum of two quantities is less than 50, then our problem is solved, else try it the other way.*

Igloo – *(noun)* a dome-shaped Eskimo house, typically built from blocks of solid snow. *People living in Polar areas live in the houses called igloos.*

Igneous – *(adjective)* **1** having solidified from lava or magma. *The area is all covered with igneous rocks.* **2** relating to or involving volcanic or plutonic processes. *The igneous activities that took place million of years back are responsible for the present structures.*

Ignis fatuus – *(noun)* erratic movement. *The path that he chose proved to be an ignis fatuus and he ended up doing nothing.*

Ignite – *(verb)* **1** catch fire or cause to catch fire. *As the sun set, the tribal people ignited the logs of wood.* **2** provoke or inflame an emotion or situation. *The aggressive speech by the minister ignited the violence by the mob.*

Ignition - *(noun)* **1** the action of igniting or the state of being ignited. *We kept standing there, watching the ignition of industrial waste.* **2** the process of starting the combustion of fuel in the cylinders of an internal combustion engine. *An object starts burning only when its ignition temperature is reached.*

Ignoble - *(adjective)* **1** not honourable, base. *His bad deeds are really ignoble for society.* **2** of humble origin or social status. *The peasant belonged to an ignoble family.*

Ignominious - *(adjective)* deserving or causing public disgrace or shame. *His lustful acts brought him into an ignominious situation.*

Ignoramus - *(noun)* an ignorant or stupid person. *Don't bring that ignoramus person before me.*

Ignorance - *(noun)* lack of knowledge or information. *He acted in ignorance of basic rules of the club.*

Ignorant - *(adjective)* **1** lacking knowledge or awareness in general, uninformed about or unaware of a specific subject or fact. *The students were ignorant of the changes made in their curriculum.* **2** [informal] discourteous. *The person standing before the king was displaying ignorant behavior.* **3** easily angered. *He is an ignorant man, don't mess with him.*

Ignore - *(verb)* disregard intentionally, fail to consider something significant. *In spite of all the efforts he made to approach me, I kept ignoring him.*

Iguana - *(noun)* a large lizard with a spiny crest along the back. *The guide said, "Here, you will see a number of iguanas."*

Iliad - *(noun)* a Greek epic poem in twenty-four books, traditionally ascribed to Homer, telling how Achilles killed Hector at the climax of the Trojan War. *Iliad by Homer is considered as one of the classic works of Greek literature.*

Illation - *(noun)* old-fashioned term for inference. *He could draw an illation from the facts that he had gathered.*

Illative - *(adjective)* **1** of the nature of or stating an inference. proceeding by inference. *The nature of his work is mostly illative.* **2** [grammar] relating to or denoting a case of nouns in some languages used to express motion into something. *His writing has largely been illative.*

Illegality - *(noun)* contrary to or forbidden by law, especially criminal law. Illegality in consumption of drugs can't be overemphasized. *No one could dare stop all that illegality taking place in open.*

Illegally - *(adverb)* unauthorized by law. *Bob smuggled drugs into the country and then sold them illegally.*

Illegibility - *(noun)* not clear enough to be read. *Teachers were always scolding him for not paying attention to the illegibility in his written work.*

Illegible - *(adjective)* not clear enough to be read. *The lawyer's writing was so illegible that we could not read a single thing.*

Illegitimacy - *(noun)* not in accordance with accepted social standards. *It was surprising that such illegitimacy was easily overlooked by ministers.*

Illegitimate - *(adjective)* **1** not in accordance with the law. *The lathi charge on people doing peaceful demonstration was totally illegitimate.* **2** born of parents not lawfully married to each other.*By that time, everyone knew that she was carrying an illegitimate child.*

Illiberal - *(adjective)* **1** opposed to liberal principles. *The policies of autocratic leaders were often illiberal and harsh.* **2** [archaic] illbred or unrefined. *Being born in a backward society, he acquired illiberal manners.*

Illicit - *(adjective)* forbidden by law, rules, or custom. *The two were having an illicit relationship, oblivious to everyone.*

Illimitable - *(adjective)* limitless. *A giant with illimitable powers emerged on the scene and destroyed everything.*

Illiterate - *(adjective)* **1** unable to read or write. *A majority of people living in Indian villages are still illiterate.* **2** ignorant in a particular subject or activity: politically illiterate. *He was socially illiterate, so he could not make any friends.* *(noun)* a person who is unable to read or write. *The ruffian was illiterate, so he could not read what was written about him in the newspaper.*

Illness – *(noun)* a disease or period of sickness.*His mental illness grew day by day.*

Illumination – *(noun)* **1** lighting or light. *The illumination from the bright surface was directly falling in our eyes.* **2** lights used in decorating a building or other structure. *We were awestruck to see the lovely illumination that was used to decorate the building.* **3** the action or process of illuminating. *Illuminating the room was not difficult for an expert like him.*

Illuminative – *(adjective)* helping to explain or clarify. *The illuminative setting was created by a group of experts.*

Illumine – *(verb)* [poetic/literary] light up; illuminate. *In day, all the objects get illumined by sun.*

Illusion – *(noun)* a false or unreal perception. a deceptive appearance or impression. a false idea or belief. *What he was looking at was merely an illusion, not reality.*

Illusive – *(adjective)* chiefly deceptive; illusory. *The man was trying to fool the police with his illusive looks.*

Illusory – *(adjective)* based on illusion; not real. *The film was full of illusory scenes.*

Illustrate – *(verb)* **1** provide with pictures. *"Could you illustrate your concept?" asked the student to his classmate.* **2** elucidate by using examples, charts, etc. serve as an example of. *To make us understand the theorem our teacher illustrated it with examples.*

Illustration – *(noun)* **1** a picture illustrating a book or periodical. *All the children were looking at the illustrations with surprise and interest.* **2** the action or fact of illustrating, an illustrative example. *The best illustration was given by a student of science batch.*

Illustrative – *(adjective)* serving as an example or explanation. *He gave me a few illustrative examples for my better understanding of things.*

Illustrator – *(noun)* a person who draws or creates pictures for magazines, books, advertising, etc. *The man sitting there is a famous illustrator.*

Illustrious – *(adjective)* well known and admired for past achievements. *When he looked back at his illustrious career, he felt good.*

Imagery – *(noun)* **1** figurative language, especially in a literary work, visual symbolism. *English poets have used vivid imagery to impart beauty to their work.* **2** visual images collectively. *I was surprised to see such a lovely imagery, all at one place.*

Imaginable – *(adjective)* possible to be thought of or believed. *This balcony provides most spectacular views imaginable The intensity of the pain suffered by the patients is not even imaginable.*

Imaginative – *(adjective)* having or showing creativity or inventiveness. *His imaginative thinking made him stand out of the crowd.*

Imagine – *(verb)* **1** form a mental image or concept of. believe to exist. *In these days of technology, it is hard to imagine a life without computers and mobiles.* **2** suppose or assume. *Just imagine that you are in a movie hall and watching a 3d picture.*

Imago – *(noun)* **1** [entomology] the final and fully developed adult stage of an insect. *Iamgo is the final stage of insect development cycle.* **2** [psychoanalysis] an unconscious idealized mental image of someone; which influences a person's behaviour. *The imago of his mother was quiet opposite to how she really was.*

Imbecile – *(noun)* [informal] a stupid person. *What an imbecile the person sitting on the sofa was.* *(adjective)* stupid. *His imbecile nature was the cause of woe to many.*

Imbecility – *(noun)* stupid, idiotic. *The way he handled the task clearly indicated his imbecility.*

Imbibe – *(verb)* [formal] drink, absorb. *They were imbibing far too many pitchers of beer.* [chiefly botany] absorb into ultramicroscopic spaces or pores. *The water sprinkled quickly imbibed by the leaves.*

Imbroglio – *(noun)* **1** an extremely confused or complicated situation. *Despite of his best efforts, he soon found himself caught in an imbroglio.* **2** [archaic] a confused heap. *As he opened the door, what he saw was only an imbroglio of old clothes.*

Imbrue – *(verb)* [archaic] stain, especially with blood. *As soon as I entered the basement, he imbrued me with colors.*

Imbue – *(verb)* inspire or permeate with (a feeling or quality). *His works are invariably imbued with a sense of calm and serenity.*

Imitable – *(adjective)* copy or simulate. *The singer carries a unique style that is not imitable by anyone.*

Imitate – *(verb)* **1** follow as a model. *The actor had such a good comic sense that no one could imitate him.* **2** copy a person's speech or mannerisms, especially for comic effect. copy or simulate. *He was asked to imitate his senior's way of talking, but he refused.*

Imitation – *(noun)* **1** the action of imitating. a copy. *Imitation is not everyone's cup of tea.* **2** [music] the repetition of a phrase or melody in another part or voice, usually at a different pitch. *He completed the third stanza by doing an imitation of the first one.*

Imitative – *(adjective)* **1** following a model. *Though he denies it all the time, his style is more or less imitative.* **2** reproducing a natural sound or pro(noun) ced in a way thought to correspond to the appearance or character of the object of action described. *When he produced a babble sound, everyone knew that he was being imitative.*

Immaculate – *(adjective)* **1** perfectly clean, neat, or tidy. *The saint preferred immaculate surroundings for performing meditation.* **2** free from flaws or mistakes. [catholic] free from sin. *In today's world, it is quite hard to keep an immaculate heart in every situation.* **3** [botany & zoology] uniformly colored without spots or other marks. *What we saw under the microscope was immaculate and transparent plasma.*

Immaturity – *(noun)* **1** the state of being immature. *The immaturity of the immune system in very young children makes them especially vulnerable.* **2** behaviour that is appropriate to some young person. *They were shocked by such immaturity in an adult. The seniors were expecting immaturity from my side, but I acted the opposite.*

Immeasurable – *(adjective)* too large, extensive, or extreme to measure. *The frustration that the people were facing at office had become immeasurable.*

Immediately – *(adverb)* **1** at once. *The passengers asked the drive to start the bus immediately.* **2** very close or adjacent in time or space. in direct or very close relation. *The immediate effects of pollution can be easily seen in the patients of asthma.* *(conjunction)* [chiefly British] as soon as. *As the man boarded the plane, it took off immediately.*

Immediateness – *(noun)* occurring or done at once. *The boss ordered his team to show immediateness in completing the task.*

Immedicable – *(adjective)* unable to be healed or treated, incurable. *In spite of all the efforts by the surgeons, the patient remained immedicable to the drugs.*

Immemorial – *(adjective)* very old or long past. *From the times immemorial, our culture has rooted in traditions and customs.*

Immense – *(adjective)* extremely large or great. *The sayings of the prophet had an immense effect upon my heart.*

Immensity – *(noun)* extremely large or great, especially in scale or degree. *Seeing the immensity of the situation, the President cancelled his tour to Europe.*

Immerse – *(verb)* **1** dip or submerge in a liquid. *The holy idol of the goddess was immersed by the devotees in water.* **2** involve oneself deeply in a particular activity or interest. *During exams, she gets herself completely immersed in books.*

Immersion – *(noun)* **1** the action of immersing or the state of being immersed. *The immersion ceremony was followed by chanting of hymns.* **2** [chiefly north American] a method of teaching a foreign language by the exclusive use of that language. *My tutor said, "Only by the complete immersion into the language, you can master it."* **3** [astronomy] the disappearance of a celestial body in the shadow of or behind another. *The immersion of this heavenly body behind the planet is an annual phenomena*

Immigrant – *(noun)* a person who comes to live permanently in a foreign country. *The Asian country was not willing to grant all the rights to its immigrants.*

Immigrate – *(verb)* come to live permanently in a foreign country. *As the country was constantly under war, many of its residents decided to immigrate to the neighboring land.*

Imminence – *The imminence of a clash made the ministers avoid the rally.*

Imminent – *(adjective)* **1** about to happen. *With such a support from all the parties, a powerful change is imminent.* **2** [archaic] overhanging. *It was clear that his imminent future was not going to take him anywhere.*

Immiscibility – *(noun)* (of liquids) not forming a homogeneous mixture when mixed. *The immiscibility of oil and water is the base of many chemical compounds.*

Immitigable – *(adjective)* unable to be made less severe or serious. *The pain after accident was immitigable. The sacrifices of the martyrs remain immitigable.*

Immixture – *(noun)* the process of mixing or being involved with something. *There are several ways by which an immixture of substances can be separated.*

Immobile – *(adjective)* not moving, incapable of moving or being moved. *The earthworm was crushed under his leg and had turned immobile.*

Immobility – *(noun)* incapable of moving or being moved. *In an extremely old age, a person can face the immobility of joints.*

Immoderate – *(adjective)* lacking moderation; excessive. *As per old scriptures, it is a sin to indulge in immoderate drinking and gambling.*

Immodest – *(adjective)* not humble, decent, or decorous. *His immodest behavior was a cause of disturbance to everyone.*

Immodesty – *(noun)* lacking humility or decorousness. *Client's immodesty forced the seller to put down the phone.*

Immolate – *(verb)* kill or offer as a sacrifice, especially by burning. *Sometimes, youngsters become so crazy in anger that they try to immolate themselves.*

Immolation – *(noun)* kill or offer as a sacrifice, especially by burning: *Chinese kings would often immolate vast numbers of sick or old animals. Immolation is an act of cowardice and must be avoided in every situation.*

Immolator – *(noun)* kill by burning. *The immolator's life could not be saved due to grave injuries.*

Immoral – *(adjective)* not conforming to accepted standards of morality. *The public display of affection is considered an immoral activity by many.*

Immortal – *(adjective)* **1** living forever. *As per legends, the gods drank nectar to become immortal.* **2** deserving to be remembered forever. *His bravery on the battlefield has made him immortal in our hearts.* *(noun)* **1** an immortal being, especially a god of ancient Greece or Rome. *The Roman god was considered immortal by his worshippers.* **2** a person of enduring fame. *Einstein's genius has made him an immortal being.*

Immovability – *(noun)* not able to be moved. *The immovability of the joints causes extreme pain.*

Immune – *(adjective)* **1** resistant to a particular infection owing to the presence of specific antibodies or sensitized white blood cells. biology of or relating to such resistance: the immune system. *His good health is attributed to his excellent immune system.* **2** exempt from an obligation or penalty. *The minister's son was kept immune from the penalty.* **3** not susceptible. *A balanced diet keeps the body immune from diseases.*

Immunity – *(noun)* **1** the ability of an organism to resist a particular infection or toxin by the action of specific antibodies or sensitized white blood cells. *Immunity to malaria seems to have increased spontaneously.* **2** protection or exemption from something, especially an obligation or penalty. *The rebels were assured of immunity from prosecution.*

Immunize – *(verb)* make immune to infection, typically by inoculation. *The doctor advised his patient to get immunized as soon as possible.*

Immure – *(verb)* confine or imprison. *The dacoit kept the child immured for four days.*

Immutability – *(noun)* unchanging over time or unable to be changed. *Green vegetables raise the immutability of our body.*

Imp – *(noun)* **1** mischievous child. *The old man retorted, "Why don't you keep your imp under control?"* **2** a small, mischievous devil or sprite. *The movie is based on the character of an imp who plays wicked all the time.* *(verb)* repair a damaged feather in by attaching part of a new feather. *The bird was given an imp immediately by the veterinary surgeon.*

Impact – *(noun)* **1** the action of one object coming forcibly into contact with another. *The impact was so huge that it produced a loud noise.* **2** a marked effect or influence. *Sayings of the prophet had a huge impact on my mind.* *(verb)* **1** come into forcible contact with another object. [chiefly north American]. *The bodies in parallel directions cannot impact each other directly.* **2** have a strong effect. *The decision by CEO impacted all the employees in office.* **3** press firmly. *The elephant's foot impacted man's bones so much that they were all crushed.*

Impaction – *(noun)* the condition of being or process of becoming impacted. *Under the impaction of hammer, the nail got twisted.*

Impairing – *(noun)* weaken or damage. *Keeping the mobile phone in close proximity to body can lead of impairing of cells.*

Impalpability – *(noun)* unable to be felt by touch. *The impalpability of our soul makes it all the more difficult to understand.*

Impanel – *(verb)* US enrol a jury or enrol on to a jury. *A group of five judges were impaneled for the case.*

Impart – *(verb)* communicate; bestow a quality. *As per the directions from the Principal, the teachers would be imparted technical knowledge during the training.*

Impassible – *(adjective)* incapable of feeling pain. *Years of devotion have made his heart impassable.*

Impassion – *(verb)* make passionate. *The guidance by his mentor impassioned him so much that he took the project right away.*

Impassive – *(adjective)* not feeling or showing emotion. *His impassive attitude was ridiculed by everyone.*

Impasto – *(noun)* [art] the process or technique of laying on paint or pigment thickly so that it stands out form a surface. *The beauty of the painting was aggravated by the lovely impasto work on it.*

Impatience – *(noun)* tendency of restlessness. *I want to work on my impatience. He was shifting in his seat with impatience.*

Impatient – *(adjective)* **1** having or showing a lack of patience or tolerance. *Your impatient nature is the root of all the problems.* **2** restlessly eager. *He was getting too impatient to get his passport.*

Impayable – *(adjective)* priceless. *Whatever the man did for his country is totally impayable.*

Impeccability – *(noun)* faultless highest quality. *The impeccability of the artist's work won him many applauds.*

Impedance– *(noun)* the effective resistance to an alternating electric current arising from the combined effects of holmic resistance and reactance. See also acoustic impedance. *On the blackboard was written the formula for calculating electrical impedance.*

Impending – *(noun)* about to happen. *The impending danger was the reason for the cancellation of their plans.*

Impenetrable – *(adjective)* **1** impossible to pass through or enter. impervious to new ideas or influence. *The extreme darkness had made the cave totally impenetrable.* **2** impossible to understand. *He said, "You have an erratic behavior which makes you impenetrable."* **3** [physics] incapable of occupying the same space as other matter at the same time. *The impenetrable nature of matter is indisputable.*

Imperative – *(adjective)* **1** of vital importance. *The balance in ecosystem is imperative to man's existence.* **2** giving an authoritative command. [grammar] denoting the mood of a *(verb)* that expresses a command or exhortation, as in come here! *While asking the students to pay the fine, the tone of teacher was imperative.* *(noun)* an essential or urgent thing. a factor or influence making something necessary. *Having a strong vocabulary is imperative for a good writing.*

Imperator – *(noun)* roman history commander a tile conferred under the republic on a victorious general and under the empire on the emperor. *Soon after king's death, his young son was declared an imperator.*

Imperceptible – *(adjective)* so slight, gradual, or subtle as not to be perceived. *Only an imperceptible change was noticed in the metabolic rate of the patient.*

Impercipient – *(adjective)* falling to perceive something. *His impercipient nature was attributed to his lack of experience in meta physics.*

Imperfect – *(adjective)* **1** faulty or incomplete. *All of us are born with imperfect minds.* **2** [grammar] denoting a past action in progress but not completed at the time in question. *The teacher explained in detail the use of imperfect tense.* **3** [music] ending on the dominant chord. *The last stanza of the poem is an imperfect.* **4** [law] transferred without all the necessary conditions or requirements being met. *Our law teacher explained at length the meaning of imperfect obligations.*

Imperialism – *(noun)* **1** a policy of extending a country's power and influence through colonization, use of military force, or other means. *With the start of imperialism, the developed countries started expanding their territories.* **2** [chiefly historical] rule by an emperor. *The imperialism under the ruler came to an end after his death.*

Imperialize – *(verb)* imperial influence. *As the time passed on, the tendency to imperialize Asia increased among the western nations.*

Imperil – *(verb)* put into danger. *It was not advisable to imperil the life of the child, so he was left at home.*

Impermanence – *(noun)* not permanent. *The impermanence of life makes the man grateful to God.*

Impermanent – *(adjective)* not allowing fluid to pass through. *The application of wax over a surface makes it impermanent.*

Impermissible – *(adjective)* not allowed. *It was impermissible to enter without gate-pass.*

Impersonate – *(verb)* pretend to be for entertainment or fraud. *Throughout the investigation, the man impersonated a cop.*

Impersonation – *(noun)* pretending to be someone else with intent to fraud. *He was tried on charges of impersonation and forgery*

Impersonator – *(noun)* pretending to be another person for fun or fraud. *Impersonators intending to defraud people usually end up behind bars.*

Impertinence – *(noun)* lack of respect. *My friend was punished badly for displaying impertinence to his teachers.*

Impetrate – *(verb)* request fervently; beg for. *When nothing worked for him, he tried to impetrate his parents.*

Impetration – *(noun)* requesting for something fervently. *Their impetration fell on deaf ears.*

Impetuosity – *(noun)* acting quickly and carelessly.*It is better to think before taking a step, instead of behaving with impetuosity.*

Impetus – *(noun)* the force or energy with which a body moves; a driving force. *The fear of getting public rebuke was the impetus behind quick action by the officers.*

Impiety – *(noun)* lack or piety or reverence. *In court, the peasant had to face the king's impiety and cruelty.*

Impinge – *(verb)* have an effect; come into contact; encroach. *It is inappropriate to impinge on someone's privacy.*

Impious – *(adjective)* not showing respect or reverence; wicked. *People were surprised by his impious attitude towards them.*

Impiously – *(adverb)* showing lack of respect for God or religion. *As he was behaving impiously, we left him alone.*

Impiousness – *(noun)* showing lack of respect. *It was awkward to see the saint's impiousness towards his devotees.*

Implicate – *(verb)* **1** show to be involved in a crime. bear some of the responsibility for an action or process. *As he was naïve, it was easy to implicate him.* **2** convey a meaning or intention indirectly; imply. *His answers clearly implicated that he wanted to leave the job.* *(noun)* chiefly a thing implied. *What minister* *implied was that he was going to assign the responsibility to someone else.*

Implication – *(noun)* **1** the implicit conclusion that can be drawn from something. a likely consequence. *The correspondent asked, "What are the implications of such a policy?"* **2** the action of implicating or the state of being implicated. *The result of the implication was going to affect everyone.*

Implicative – *(adjective)* show someone to be involved in crime. *Nobody knew why he was giving implicative answers.*

Implore – *(verb)* beg earnestly or desperately [archaic] beg earnestly for. *The man without the license implored before police to let him go.*

Imploringly – *(adverb)* beg someone for favour. *"Don't tell it to anyone." Said the man imploringly.*

Impolite – *(adjective)* not having or showing good manners. *"If you remain impolite to me, I shall not be able to help you", said the man to his neighbor.*

Impolitic – *(adjective)* failing to possess or display prudence. *The minister was giving all the impolitic answers to the questions raised to him.*

Imponderable – *(adjective)* **1** difficult or impossible to estimate or assess. *The time this issue takes to settle down is imponderable.* **2** [archaic] very light. *The feather was too imponderable to remain steady at one place.* *(noun)* an imponderable factor. *It is imponderable to understand every aspect of human nature.*

Import – *(verb)* **1** bring into a country from abroad. *All the goods imported into the country are of good quality.* **2** computing transfer into a file or document. *While standing there, I noticed that the files were being imported from the server.* **3** [archaic] indicate or signify. *Increase in taxes imported that the citizens' were going to face financial problems.* *(noun)* **1** an imported commodity, article, or service. the action or process of importing. *The imported packets were distributed among retailers.* **2** the implied meaning of something. *The chestnuts that my sister brought for me were all imported.*

Importable – *(adjective)* bring into a country. *All importable goods in our country carry a special customus duty.*

Importation – *(noun)* the process of importing. *The opposition was not happy with the importation process; so they walked out.*

Importance – *(noun)* the fact of being of value. *There are people that carry high importance in our lives.*

Important – *(adjective)* **1** of great significance or value. *Our company has come out with some very important policies this year.* **2** having high rank or status. *His important rank vested him with many powers.*

Importunate – *(adjective)* persistent or pressing. *His importunate habits were becoming annoying for others.*

Importune – *(verb)* **1** harass with persistent requests. *I retorted, "Don't importune me. Give me some time."* **2** approach to offer one's services as a prostitute. *As he entered the red-light area, he knew some lady would approach him to importune.*

Importunity – *(noun)* bothering to the point of annoying. *The man was always bothering us with his importunities.*

Impose – *(verb)* **1** force to be accepted, undertaken, or complied with. *As soon as the new rule was imposed, people started protesting.* **2** take advantage of someone. *It was not clear why people were imposing on her good nature.* **3** printing arrange so as to be in the correct order after printing and folding. *It was necessary to impose the characters to start printing.*

Imposing – *(adjective)* grand and impressive. *The building looked magnificent with its imposing structure.*

Imposition – *(noun)* action of imposing something or being imposed. *Tax imposition was prevalent even in ancient times.*

Imposter – *(noun)* preteading to be someone else to deceive. *After interrogation, it was clear that he was an imposter.*

Impoverish – *(verb)* **1** make poor. *The British rule impoverished Indian community to a great extent.* **2** exhaust the strength or natural fertility of. *Feeding on a poor diet impoverished him badly.*

Impracticable – *(adjective)* impossible in practice to do or carry out. *It is impracticable to listen to every employee and then take a decision.*

Imprecate – *(verb)* utter something bad. *It was his nature to imprecate everyone for all his problems.*

Imprecation – *(noun)* formal a spoken curse. *His imprecations had no affect on my mind.*

Imprecatory – *(adjective)* spoken bad or poorly. *With time, his nature became more and more imprecatory.*

Impregnation – *(noun)* saturate with a substance. *After repeated experiments, the biologists were, finally, successful in impregnation.*

Impression – *(noun)* **1** an idea, feeling, or opinion. an effect produced or someone: her quick wit made a good impression. *The interviewee was able to create good impression on everyone.* **2** an imitation of a person or thing. done to entertain. *His way of talking gave me an impression of his father.* **3** a mark impressed on a surface. [dentistry] a negative copy of the teeth or mouth made by pressing them into a soft substance. *The doctor took impression of his teeth on soap.* **4** the printing of a number of copies of a publication for issue at one time. [chiefly British] a particular printed version of a book, especially one reprinted with on or only minor alteration; a print taken from an engraving. *The publication house has planned to give at least eighty thousand impressions of the book.*

Imprison – *(verb)* put or keep in prison. *The culprit was imprisoned for five years.*

Improbability – *(noun)* unlikelihood. *The film is full of improbabilities.*

Improperly – *(adverb)* not according to acceptable standards. *Never go to an interview board improperly dressed.*

Impropriety – *(noun)* improper behaviour or character. *The lecturer said, "Such an impropriety would not be tolerated."*

Improver – *(noun)* make or become better. *He has played the role of an improver very well.*

Improvidence – *(noun)* not showing foresight, thoughtless. *Parents were worried about their children's improvidence.*

Improvisation – *(noun)* created spontaneously. *Improvisation at writing has been my greatest strength.*

Imprudence – *(noun)* not caring for consequence. *She displayed her imprudence by talking angrily to his boss.*

Impudence – *(noun)* impertinence. *The audience were shocked to see his impudence.*

Impudicity – *(noun)* formal lack of modesty. *His shouting at his juniors only showed his impudicity.*

Impugn – *(verb)* dispute the truth, validity, or honesty of a statement or motive. *The lawyer was trying to impugn the statement given by the witness.*

Impugnment – *(noun)* calling into question, honesty, validity. *The impugnment of the statement was his only motive.*

Impuissance – *(noun)* unable to take effective action. *The knight exhibited his impuissance in the battlefield.*

Impulsion – *(noun)* **1** a strong urge to do something. *His impulsion made him participate in the show.* **2** the force or motive behind an action or process. *The impulsion to earn made him search a job.*

Imputation – *(noun)* represent something undesirable. *He has always believed in imputation of failures to others.*

Impute – *(verb)* **1** attribute to someone. *He has always imputed his awkward behavior to laziness of his juniors.* **2** theology ascribe to someone by virtue of a similar quality in another. *John's dedication is imputed to his father.* **3** finance assign to something by inference from the value of the products or processes to which it contributes. *The sum was imputed from the number of sales done.*

Inability – *(noun)* the state of being unable to do something. *Her inability to perform well resulted in his expulsion from dance class.*

Inaccessible – *(adjective)* **1** unable to be reached. unable to be seen or used. *The presence of* *rugged mountains made the way to valley nearly inaccessible.* **2** difficult to understand or appreciate. *The lack of guidance is making this language inaccessible to me.* **3** not open to advances or influence; unapproachable. *His inaccessible nature is not liked by people in his company.*

Inaccessibly – *(adverb)* unable to be reached, used, unapproachable. *The jungle was located inaccessibly across the river.*

Inaccuracy – *(noun)* the state of not being accurate. *The inaccuracy in his work irked his master.*

Inaction – *(noun)* lack of action where some is expected or appropriate. *Police's inaction in the case has raised many eyebrows.*

Inactivity – *(noun)* idleness; inactive. *The inactivity of the machines in mill resulted in financial loss.*

Inadaptability – *(noun)* unable to adjust to new conditions. *The plants with inadaptability to the changing climate die early.*

Inaffable – *(adjective)* not friendly, not easy to talk to. *We could not tolerate his inaffable manners.*

Inalterable – *(adjective)* unable to be changed. *Our boss has an inalterable nature.*

Inapplicable – *(adjective)* not relevant or appropriate. *This test is inapplicable to all those who are below 20 years of age.*

Inapposite , – *(adjective)* out of place; inappropriate. *I was finding my presence at the party totally inapposite.*

Inapt – *(adjective)* not suitable or appropriate *His interference in our issues is inapt.*

Inaptly – *(adverb)* not suitable in the circumstances. *None of us could guess why she was behaving so inaptly.*

Inartistic – *(adjective)* having or showing a lack of skill or talent in art. *The poet was excellent in his work, yet he thought himself to be inartistic.*

Inattentive – *(adjective)* not paying attention. failing to attend to the comfort or wishes of others. *The inattentive students were rebuked by teachers.*

Inaudible – *(adjective)* unable to be heard. *The music was so loud that it was almost inaudible.*

Inaudibility – *(noun)* unable to be heard. *While constructing an auditorium, the inaudibility factor is to taken into account.*

Inaudibly – *(adverb)* not easy to be heard. *He was speaking in inaudibly loud manner.*

Inauguration – *(noun)* beginning of a system, policy, thing. *MLA was present at the time of inauguration of the library.*

Inauguratory – *(adverb)* introduce a system, policy or period. *The minister's inauguratory speech was praiseworthy.*

Inborn – *(adjective)* existing from birth. natural to a person or animal. *Every person carries some inborn qualities.*

Inbreathe – *While working in factory, I inbreathed some foul gas.*

Inbred – *(adjective)* **1** produced by inbreeding. *Scientists are keen to experiment on inbred animals.* **2** existing in a person or animal from birth; congenital. *All living beings are born with some inbred qualities.*

Incarnate – *(adjective)* **1** embodied in flesh; in human form. *Man has always believed in the incarnate forms of God.* **2** represented in the ultimate or most extreme form: capitalism incarnate. *People had become aggressive as they were not able to bear the burden of feudalism incarnate. (verb)* **1** embody or represent in human form. *According to the Hindu mythology, God has incarnated on earth in every era.* **2** be the living embodiment of a quality. *He incarnates truth and simplicity.*

Incarnation – *(noun)* **1** a living embodiment of a deity, spirit, or abstract quality. *Man believes in the incarnation of gods on earth.* **2** the embodiment of god the son in human flesh a Jesus Christ. *There are many stories about Jesus' incarnation.* **3** each of a series of earthly lifetimes or forms. *The disciple asked, "In which incarnation would the Lord be born again?"*

Incautious – *(adjective)* involving or guilty of incest. (Wrong meaning) (Right Meaning): *(adjective)* **1** Heedless of the potential problems. *His incautious nature brought much woe to his family.* **2** excessively close and resistant to outside influence.(Wrong meaning) (Right meaning): Carelessly failing to exercise proper caution. *Her incautious step resulted in her expulsion from office.*

Incensory – *(noun)* another term for censer. *The incensory was placed inside the temple premises.*

Incentive – *(noun)* a thing that motivates or encourages someone to do something. a payment or concession to stimulate greater output or investment. *The employees were expecting huge incentives at the end of the year.*

Inception – *(noun)* the establishment or starting point of an institution or activity. *The inception of the building took place in 1988.*

Inceptive – *(adjective)* **1** relating to or marking the beginning of something; initial. *The project is still in its inceptive stage.* **2** [grammar] expressing the beginning of an action. *The inceptive steps taken by the management were appreciable.* *(noun)* [grammar] an inceptive verb. *The teacher wrote an example of incentive verb on the board.*

Inceptor – *(noun)* undertake begin. *Many cells in body act as inceptors of signals from brain.*

Incertitude – *(noun)* a state of uncertainty or hesitation. *It was the incertitude of the situation that he was unable to take a decision.*

Incessant – *(adjective)* continuing without pause or interruption. *Over the years, the country has seen an incessant growth of population.*

Incestuous – *(adjective)* **1** involving or guilty of incest. *Their incestuous relationship continued for many years.* **2** excessively close and resistant to outside influence. *No economy can survive by being incestuous.*

Incidence – *(noun)* **1** the occurrence, rate, or frequency of a disease, crime, or other undesirable thing. *The incidence of crimes has increased manifold in last few years.* **2** physics the intersection of line, or something moving in a straight line, such as a beam of light, with a surface. *As per the first law of reflection, the angle of incidence is equal to the angle of reflection.* **3** the way in which the burden of a tax falls upon the population. *The economists were keen to know the incidence of taxes on population.*

Incinerate – *(verb)* destroy by burning. *To get rid of the excessive garbage, it was incinerated.*

Incineration – *(noun)* to destroy by burning.*The process of incineration continued for two days.*

Incinerator – *(noun)* an apparatus for incinerating waste material, especially industrial waste. *All the garbage was put into the incinerator.*

Incise – *(verb)* make a cut or cuts in a surface. *The surgeons incised patient's stomach and started operating.*

Incision – *(noun)* **1** a surgical cut made in skin or flesh. *She was quite afraid of having incision done on her belly.* **2** the action or process of cutting into something. *The doctors were engaged in the incision.*

Incisive – *(adjective)* **1** Intelligently analytical and concise. *What he wanted was an incisive report of the project.* **2** quick and direct. *Her every answer was incisive.*

Incisor – *(noun)* a narrow-edged tooth at the front of the mouth, adapted for cutting. *The incisors are meant for cutting the food bytes.*

Incite – *(verb)* encourage or stir up violent or unlawful behaviour. urge or persuade to act in a violent or unlawful way. *The crowd was incited by its leader to assemble there.*

Incivility – *(noun)* rude or unsociable speech or behaviour. *We were surprised to notice the incivility of his nature.*

Inclemency – *(noun)* unpleasantly cold or wet weather. *Our boss believes in the inclemency of punishment.*

Inclement – *(adjective)* unpleasantly cold or wet.. *The tourists were not prepared for an inclement weather.*

Inclinable – *(adjective)* favourable disposed towards something. *I am inclinable to get up late in the morning.*

Inclination – *(noun)* **1** a natural tendency or urge to act or feel in a particular way. an interest in or liking for. *The man in black trousers has inclination to the Carnatic music.* **2** a slope or slant. a dip of a magnetic needle. *A plank's inclination determines the speed of the object rolling down.* **3** the angle at which a straight line or plane is inclined to another. *The teacher* *explained about the Angle of Inclination to his students.*

Incognito - *(adjective & avberb)* having one's true identity concealed. *An incognito bar was running under the pretext of hair salon.* *(noun)* an assumed or false identity. *To avoid confrontation, he started living incognito in the foreign land.*

Incognizant - *(adjective)* [formal lacking knowledge or awareness. *We were surprised to know about his incognizant attitude towards marriage.*

Incombustibility - *While working on experiments ignition temperature, we came to know a lot about the incombustibility of substances.*

Incombustible - *(adjective)* especially of a building material not inflammable. *We are going to make a list of incombustible substances that can be used kitchen.*

Incomer - *(noun)* [chiefly British] a person who has come to live in an area in which they have not grown up. *Many writers came to India as incomers and settled here.*

Incoming - *(adjective)* in the process of coming in. being received rather than sent. *All his incoming calls were blocked by the authorities.* of an official or administration having just been elected or appointed to succeed another. *The incoming CEO has served the previous company for 15 years.* *(noun)* revenue; income. *His incoming salary was not very high.*

Incomings - *(noun)* income, revenue. *You must keep an account of all your incomings and outgoings.*

Incommensurable - *(adjective)* **1** not able to be judged or measured by the same standards; having no common standard. *The difference in their experiences makes their performances incommensurable.* **2** Mathematics in a ratio that cannot be expressed as a ratio of integers. *The incommensurable ratios in Mathematics cannot be expressed as the ratio of integers.* *(noun)* an incommensurable quantity. *He said to me, "While listing the items, you should also include incommensurable quantities into account."*

Incommensurate - *(adjective)* **1** out of keeping or proportion with. *The gravity of the situation is incommensurate with the steps taken by the government.* **2** another term for incommensurable. *The same punishment for the two convicts is incommensurate with their crimes.*

Incommutable - *(adjective)* not capable of being changed or exchanged. *The wide difference in the prices of two books makes them incommutable.*

Incompatibility - *(noun)* unable to line together harmoniously. *Incompatibility of a couple is the biggest factor responsible for a failed marriage.*

Incompatible - *(adjective)* not able to exist or be used together. unable to live together harmoniously. *Their incompatible nature was always the reason behind their clashes.*

Incompetence - *(noun)* in ability to do something successfully. *No company is willing to hire a person with incompetence to perform tasks.*

Incomprehension - *(noun)* failure to understand something. *"Can I know the reason behind your incomprehension of a simple concept?" asked the manager.*

Incomprehensive - *(adjective)* not dealing with all aspects of something. *The books recommended by teacher are incomprehensive for perfect understanding of the concept.*

Incompressibility - *(noun)* not able to be compressed. *Many uses of rubber are based on its amount of incompressibility.*

Incompressible - *(adjective)* not able to be compressed. *The tyres used in vehicles must not be incompressible.*

Incomputable - *(adjective)* rare unable to be calculated or estimated. *In spite of long hours spent, the problem remained incomputable.*

Inconceivability - *(noun)* not capable of being grasped mentally. *The complex nature of the machine is the reason behind its inconceivability.*

Inconformity - *(noun)* non-compliance with rules, laws regulations. *The new product failed to become popular, thanks to its inconformity to the quality standards.*

Incongruent - *(adjective)* **1** incongruous. *The two triangles shown in the diagram are incongruent.* **2** [chemistry] affecting the components of an alloy or other substance differently: incongruent melting. *The incongruent rise in boiling points of the two components of the alloy is due to difference in their natures.*

Incongruence – *(noun)* incompatible. *The student was asked to prove the incongruence of the two triangles.*

Inconsequent – *(adjective)* **1** not connected or following logically; irrelevant. *The experiments on artificial intelligence remained inconsequent.* **2** inconsequential. *It was no use wasting time over the inconsequential matters.*

Inconsequential – *(adjective)* not important or significant. *It was known from the beginning that the experiments were going to be inconsequential.*

Inconsequently – *(adverb)* lacking consequence. *They continued inconsequently, without bothering about results.*

Inconsiderable – *(adjective)* of small size, amount, or extent. unimportant or insignificant. *There were particles on inconsiderable size present in the atmosphere.*

Inconsonant – *(adjective)* rare not in agreement or harmony; not compatible. *As our theories were inconsonant, we could not agree with each other.*

Inconstancy – *(noun)* changing, irregular, variable. *What bothers man about life is its inconstancy.*

Inconstant – *(adjective)* frequently changing; variable or irregular. *He was trying to confuse the jury members by giving inconstant answers.*

Incontestable – *(adjective)* not able to be disputed. *The authority of the manager in financial matters is incontestable.*

Incontinence – *(noun)* lacking self-restraint uncontrolled. *The thing that he lags is the incontinence of emotions.*

Incontinent – *(adjective)* **1** lacking voluntary control over urination or defection. *The patient had the problem of having incontinent urination.* **2** lacking self-restraint; uncontrolled. *According to some saints, it is best to control our incontinent desires.*

Inconvertibility – *(noun)* not able to be changed in form, function. *The first problem that I faced in the foreign country was the inconvertibility of currencies.*

Incorrupt – *(adjective)* not having undergone decomposition. *There are only a few countries in the world that can be called incorrupt today.*

Incorruptible – *(adjective)* **1** not susceptible to corruption, especially by bribery. *The CEO was bragging about the incorruptible nature of his employees.* **2** not subject to death or decay; everlasting. *Steel is widely used in making utensils due to its incorruptible nature.*

Increasing – *(adjective)* becoming bigger in size amount or degree. *The ever increasing population has posed new threats to the society.*

Incredibly – *(adverb)* greater degree, extremely. *The man in the movie was flying at an incredibly high speed.*

Incredulity – *(noun)* unable to believe something. *As they saw a giant bird in the sky, their eyes were wide opened with incredulity.*

Increment – *(noun)* **1** an increase or addition, especially one of a series on a fixed scale. a regular increase in salary on such a scale. *I am expecting a good increment this year.* **2** mathematics a small positive or negative change in a variable quantity or function. *A small increment in the value of 'x' results in a corresponding decrease in the value of 'y'.*

Incrimination – *(noun)* make someone appear guilty or of wrong-doing. *He did not knew how to free her from the incrimination charges.*

Incrust – *(verb)* variant spelling of encrust. *The pot was incrusted with a metallic alloy.*

Inculcate – *(verb)* **1** to impress upon the mind of another by frequent instruction. *A good teacher inculcates good values in the minds of his students.* **2** to teach by frequent instruction; indoctrinate. *Their leader inculcated hatred in his followers' hearts.*

Inculcator – *(noun)* **1** an apparatus used to hatch eggs or grow micro-organisms under controlled conditions. *During our visit to the laboratory, we were allowed to see inculcators.* **2** an enclosed apparatus providing a controlled and protection environment for the care of premature babies. *As the new born was very weak, it was placed in an inculcator.*

Inculpate – *(verb)* accuse, blame, or incriminate. *It was not fair to inculpate his colleague without any concrete proof.*

Inculpation – *(noun)* accuse, blame, incriminate. *His inculpation caused a stir in the film fraternity.*

Inculpatory – *(adjective)* attitude to blame, accuse. *An inculpatory system within the office was hard to bear.*

Incumbent – *(adjective)* **1** necessary for as a duty or responsibility. *The help that we were offering them was seen as incumbent on us.* **2** currently holding office. – *(noun)* the holder of an office or post. *The incumbent was responsible for management of the entire office.*

Incur – *(verb)* become subject to as a result of one's actions. *The company incurred huge losses during the last fiscal.*

Incuriosity – *(noun)* not interested in knowing something. *The child's incuriosity to the objects around him worried his parents.*

Incurious – *(adjective)* not eager to know something; lacking curiosity. *After observing them for a long time, it was clear that they had incurious minds.*

Incursion – *(noun)* an invasion or attack, especially a sudden or brief one. *The kingdom had to face a sudden incursion from the neighboring state.*

Incurve – *(verb)* curve inwards. *The bottles were incurved to give the desired shapes.*

Incuse – *(noun)* an impression hammered or stamped on a coin. *All the old coins had incused designs on them. (verb)* mark by impressing it with a stamp. *The coins were incused with stamps of the state.*

Indecent – *(adjective)* not conforming with generally accepted standards of behavior or propriety. *One should not tolerate any indecent behavior at work place.*

Indecision – *(noun)* inability to make a decision quickly. *My sister's indecision delayed her engagement.*

Indecisive – *(adjective)* **1** not able to make decisions quickly and effectively. *The indecisive Cabinet Ministers could not reach any agreement.* **2** not settling an issue. *The outcome of the discussion remained indecisive.*

Indeclinable – *(adjective)* [grammar] having no inflections. *What we were taught in the class was the perfect example of indeclinable words.*

Indecorous – *(adjective)* not in keeping with good taste and propriety; improper. *She hated indecorous remarks from his senior.*

Indecorum – *(noun)* failure to conform to good taste, propriety, or etiquette. *The indecorum at the award function raised a few eyebrows.*

Indeed – *(avberb)* **1** used to emphasize a statement, description, or response. *He was, indeed, a good friend of mine.* **2** used to introduce a further and stronger or more surprising point. *The new hair-style allured many women and indeed men.* **3** used in a response to express interest, incredulity, or contempt. *"They are in relationship? Indeed!"*

Indefectible – *(adjective)* rare **1** not liable to fail, end, or decay. *The company has guaranteed its products to be indefectible.* **2** perfect; faultiess. *She was envied for her indefectible style.*

Indefensible – *(adjective)* **1** not justifiable by argument. *His was an indefensible case.* **2** not able to be protected against attack. *The country's security system was flawed and it made her indefensible.*

Indefinite – *(adjective)* **1** not clearly expressed or defined; vague. lasting for an unknown or unstated length of time. *The workers have gone on an indefinite strike.* **2** [grammar] not determining the person or thing referred to. *An indefinite number of people are going to reach the place.*

Indelibility – *(noun)* that cannot be removed forgotten. *The indelibility of the scars was a source of everlasting torture to her.*

Indelicate – *(adjective)* **1** lacking sensitive understanding or tact. *The mother was criticized for her indelicate behavior towards her children.* **2** slightly indecent. *Her dance was seen as a bit indelicate.*

Indemnification – *(noun)* compensate for loss or harm. *The process of indemnification was complete within a week.*

Indemnify – *(verb)* **1** compensate in respect of harm or loss. *Due to the pressure from victim's side, the authorities were forced to indemnify him.* **2** secure against legal responsibility for their actions. *The writer was asked to indemnify the community for his racist remarks.*

Indemnity – *(noun)* **1** security or protection against a loss or other financial burden. ecurity against or exemption from legal responsibility for one's actions. *We did not know whether he should be provided with indemnity or not.* **2** a sum of money paid as compensation, especially by a country defeated in war. *The war was over and the defeated China was asked to pay the indemnity.*

Indenture – *(noun)* **1** A formal agreement, contract, or list, formerly one of which copies with indented edges were made for the contracting parties. *The two parties were given indentures of mutual agreement.* **2** An agreement binding an apprentice to a master. *The employees entered into the bond by signing an indenture with the company.* **3** Historical a contract by which a person agreed to work for a set period for a colonial landowner in exchange for passage to the colony. *In ancient time, people were forced to sign the indentures that make them work for their landlords.* *(verb)* chiefly historical bind by an indenture. *During colonial period, poor people needed to be indentured to a contract to get wages.*

Independence – *(noun)* state of being free. *Some of the African countries got their independence very late.*

Independent – *(adjective)* **1** Free from outside control; not subject to another's authority. Self-governing. *The social committee set up last year works as an independent body.* **2**. Not depending on another for livelihood or subsistence. *I am proud of being an independent girl.* **3** Not connected with another; separate. *The book comprises of a number of independent stories.* **4** Historical congregational. *The independent politicians were shown the door.* *(noun)* an independent person or body. *My uncle opted to stand as an independent candidate in elections.*

Indescribable – *(adjective)* too unusual, extreme, or indefinite to be adequately described. *The incident was so shocking that it remains indescribable for me till date.*

Indestructibility – *(noun)* not able to be destroyed. *The original theory of the indestructibility of an atom was refuted by the later scientists.*

Indestructible – *(adjective)* not able to be destroyed. *The universe is indestructible.*

Indeterminable – *(adjective)* **1** Not able to be determined. *The insufficient data could only lead to indeterminable results.* **2** Law not able to be resolved. *Despite all their efforts, the infinity remained an indeterminable number.*

Indeterminate – *(adjective)* **1** Not exactly known, established, or defined. Mathematics having no definite or definable value. Medicine from which a diagnosis of the underlying cause cannot be made. *The underlying cause of his cancer remained indeterminate to doctors.* **2** Biology the axes terminating in flower buds and so potentially of indefinite length. *Some plants have shoots of indeterminate length.*

Indifferent – *(adjective)* **1** having no particular interest or sympathy; unconcerned. *The people at high positions usually have an indifferent attitude to their employees.* **2** Neither good nor bad; mediocre. *Not especially good; fairly bad. His work is indifferently mediocre.*

Indigene – *(noun)* an indigenous person. *No one can understand the nuances of his culture than an indigene.*

Indigestion – *(noun)* pain or discomfort in the stomach associated with difficulty in digesting food. *I am suffering from indigestion from past several days.*

Indigestive – *(adjective)* difficulty in digesting food. *Cellulose is indigestive to human intestines.*

Indignant – *(adjective)* anger or annoyance at something unfair, unfair treatment. *The people were indignant over the killing of a young man.*

Indignation – *(noun)* annoyance provoked by what is perceived as unfair treatment. *The residents showed their indignation over the killing incident.*

Indignity – *(noun)* treatment or circumstances that cause one to feel shame or to lose one's dignity. *No woman can tolerate any type of indignity meted out to her.*

Indirect – *(adjective)* **1** Not direct. Source denoting a free kick from which a goal may not be scored directly. *There is an indirect connection between two power grids.* **2** Derving from overhead charges or subsidiary work. *He has many sources of indirect income.* **3** Levied on goods and services rather than income or profits. *The indirect taxes are those that are levied upon goods and services.*

Indirection – *(noun)* not straightforward in action, speech. *It was due to his indirection that his team members remained confused.*

Indiscernible – *(adjective)* impossible to see or clearly distinguish. *The presence of fog was making the scenery indiscernible.*

Indiscipline – *(noun)* lack of discipline. *Principal said, "No kind of indiscipline shall be tolerated within the school premises."*

Indiscrete – *(adjective)* rare not divided into distinct parts. *This novel does not have any indiscrete chapters.*

Indiscretion – *(noun)* behaviour showing lack of good judgement. *Indiscretion has always been his weakness.*

Indiscriminate – *(adjective)* done or acting at random or without careful judgement. *He is habitual to the indiscriminate use of pills.*

Indispose – *(verb)* [archaic] make unfit for or averse to some thing. *Negative thinking can indispose a person of his sanity.*

Indisposition – *(noun)* mild illness reluctance. *My mother was admitted to hospital when she complained of indisposition.*

Indisputable – *(adjective)* unable to be challenged or denied. *He thought that only he was the indisputable heir to the property.*

Indissolubly – *(adverb)* lasting unable to be destroyed. *The unions worked indissolubly to have their demands met.*

Indistingushable – *(adjective)* not able to be identified as different or distinct. *There are animals that can change their color to make their skin indistingushable from their backgrounds.*

Indite – *(verb)* [archaic] write; compose. *The writer made it a habit to indite daily.*

Individual – *(adjective)* **1** Single; separate. *It is not possible to take care of the individual needs of all the employees.* **2** of or for a particular person. Designed for use by one person. *The rooms were designed for individual use.* **3** Striking or unusual; original. *The use of plant colors makes this painting an individual one.* *(noun)* **1** A single human being or item as distinct from a group. [informal] a person of a specified kind: a most selfish, egotistical individual. *An individual's needs are different from that of a group.* **2** A distinctive or original person. *The individual stood out from the rest of the people due to his creative instincts.*

Individually – *(adverb)* singly, are by one separately. *The parents were supposed to meet the teachers individually.*

Indivisibility – *(adjective)* unable to be divided or separated. *The indivisibility of atom was refuted by many scientists.* **2** incapable of undergoing division. *The teacher asked the students to make a list of indivisible numbers.*

Indo – *(combining form)* Indian; Indian and...... Indo-Iranian. Relating to India. *The Indo-Aryans came to settle in the country.*

Indocile – *(adjective)* difficult to teach or discipline; not submissive. *Her husband's indocile nature caused many problems.*

Indocility – *(noun)* difficulty in disciplining. *His indocility was a matter of concern to everyone.*

Indolence – *(noun)* laziness avoiding activities.*His mother said, "Your indolence will not take you anywhere."*

Indomitable – *(adjective)* impossible to subdue or defeat. *The king fortified his kingdom so well that it became indomitable by other states.*

Indubitable – *(adjective)* impossible to doubt; unquestionable. *His sincerity towards work is indubitable.*

Induce – *(verb)* **1** Succeed in persuading or leading to do something. *Workers were induced to extend their working hours.* **2** Bring about or give rise to. Produce an electric charge or current or a magnetic state by induction. *The incident induced fury among the residents.* **3** Medicine bring on artificially, typically by the use of drugs. *The drugs induced hallucinations in the patient.* **4** Logic derive by inductive reasoning. *The theory was induced after logical reasoning.*

Induct – *(verb)* **1** Admit formally to a post or organization. Formally introduce into possession of a benefice. US enlist for military service. *After an initial training for six months, the soldiers ware finally inducted into the army.* **2** [archaic] install in a seat or room. *A big heater was inducted in the room.*

Inductor – *(noun)* **1** A component in an electric or electronic circuit which possesses inductance. *We were attending a special class on inductors and their properties.* **2** A substance that promotes an equilibrium reaction by reacting with one of the substances produced. *An inductor in an equilibrium reaction gets transformed into other substance.*

Indulge – *(verb)* **1** Allow oneself to enjoy the pleasure of. Become involved in an activity that is undesirable or disapproved of. *After his exams were over, he indulged himself in partying day and night.* **2** Satisfy or yield freely to a desire or interest. Allow to enjoy a desired pleasure. *In spite of restraining himself initially, he finally indulged himself in boozing.*

Indulgence – *(noun)* **1** the action or fact of indulging, a thing that is indulged in; a luxury. *His indulgence into the luxuries of life took a toll of his bank balance.* **2** The state or attitude of being indulgent or tolerant. *Man's indulgence into drugs can play havoc on his life.* **3** An extension of the time in which a bill or debt has to be paid. *People felt relaxed upon declaration of the indulgence period.* **4** [chiefly historical] the Roman Catholic Church a grant by the people of remission of the temporal punishment in purgatory still due for sins after absolution. *The Church became famous for awarding indulgences to almost all the prisoners.*

Industrial – *(adjective)* **1** Of, used in, or characterized by industry. *There are many uses of the industrial oil.* **2** Relating to or denoting a type of harsh, uncompromising rock music incorporating sounds resembling those produced by industrial machinery. *The music was too industrial to be liked by the lovers of classical music.* *(noun)* shares in industrial companies. *We have a number of industrials in the three companies.*

Industrious – *(adjective)* tiard working, deligent. *People living in mountainous areas are known to be very industrial.*

Industry – *(noun)* **1** economic activity concerned with the processing of raw materials and manufacture of goods in factories. A particular branch of economic or commercial activity: the tourist industry. *There has been a big boom in fishery industry this year.* **2** hard work the kitchen became a hive of industry. *It became an industry to work in laboratory.*

Inebriety – *(noun)* inflected forms of inebriety. *He was carried to his home in the state of inebriety.*

Inedible – *(adjective)* not fit for eating. *Some of the mushrooms are inedible.*

Inedited – *(adjective)* not inedited. *The work by me remained inedited for a long time.*

Ineffable – *(adjective)* **1** too great or extreme to be expressed in words: the ineffable natur4al beauty of the everglades. *We were thrilled to see the ineffable beauty of the nature.* **2** too sacred to be uttered. *On seeing the cobra, we became ineffable.*

Ineffably – *(adverb)* too extreme to describe in words, difficult to utter. *We were ineffably weak to say anything.*

Ineffaceable – *(adjective)* unable to be erased or forgotten. *The bad effects of pollution are almost ineffaceable.*

Inefficacious – *(adjective)* not producing the desired effect. *The scientists' efforts had become inefficacious at that point of time.*

Inefficacy – *(noun)* not producing desired result. *The inefficacy of the old machines stalled the production rate.*

Ineffciency – *(noun)* failing to make the best use of resources. *No company wants to hire people carrying inefficiency.*

Ineffcient - *(adjective)* not achieving maximum productivity; failing to make the best use of time or resources. *As the time passed, he came to know that his team is inefficient in delivery desired results.*

Inelastic - *(adjective)* **1** no elastic. *The spring was stretched so many times that it eventually became inelastic.* **2** economics insensitive to changes in price or income. *The market is currently running inelastic.* **3** physics involving an overall loss of translational kinetic energy. *In my graduation, I learned a lot about inelastic objects.*

Inelegance - *(noun)* lacking refinement physical grace and elegance. *The tourists were roaming about in a castle that had now acquired inelegance.*

Ineptly - *(adverb)* showing no skill. *She handled the situation quiet ineptly.*

Inequality - *(noun)* **1** lack of equality. *During my visit to the foreign country, I noticed the inequality with which poor people were treated.* **2** mathematics a symbolic expression of the fact that two quantities are not equal, employing a sign such as # 'not equal to', > 'greater than', or < 'less than'. *The theorem was proved and stated in terms of inequality signs.* **3** [archaic] lack of smoothness or regularity in a surface. *Her inequality of skin color makes her depressed at times.*

Inequitable - *(adjective)* unfair; unjust. *None of us was happy with the inequitable distribution of company's profit.*

Inequity - *(noun)* lack of fairness or justice. *As a woman, she had to face the inequity of the justice.*

Inescapable - *(noun)* unable to be avoided or denied. *The presence of heavy gases was making the balloon inescapable.*

Inessential - *(adjective)* not absolutely necessary. *After having repeated discussions, the topic is now inessential to be discussed again. (noun)* an inessential thing. *The weather there is not very cold, so carrying a jacket is inessential.*

Inestimable - *(adjective)* not able to be measured; very great. *Calculating the exact age of the fossils is an inestimable thing.*

Inevitably - *(adverb)* certain to happen. *Their end was inevitably coming.*

Inexact - *(adjective)* not quite accurate. *The number of coins recovered from the site is still inexact.*

Inexecutable - *(adjective)* a programme not able to be run by computers. *There was a serious glitch that had made the programme inexecutable.*

Inexorably - *(adverb)* impossible to prevent, unrelenting. *Most of the time, things were going on inexorably.*

Inexpediency - *(noun)* not practical or advisable. *What we were worried about was the inexpediency of the project.*

Inexpendient - *(adjective)* not practical, suitable, or advisable. inexpedient *The proposal by the committee member seems to be inexpedient.*

Inexpressive - *(adjective)* showing no expression. *The model was not fit for acting as she had an inexpressive face.*

Inextricable - *(adjective)* **1** impossible to disentangle or separate. *He was trying to separate the inextricable wires.* **2** impossible to escape from. *He had kept the princess in an inextricable dungeon.*

Infallible - *(adjective)* **1** incapable of making mistakes or being wrong. *His clever mind makes him an infallible guy.* **2** never failing; always effective; infallible cures. *The herbal medicine suggested by my uncle gives infallible results.*

Infamy - *(noun)* well knwon for some bad quality. *To avoid facing infamy, he secluded himself from the society.*

Infant - *(noun)* **1** a very young child or baby. *He was still an infant when his mother passed away.* **2** [British] a schoolchild between the ages of five and seven. *A visit to a toy show was arranged for all the infants of the school.* **3** denoting something in an early stage of development: the infant universe. *Even after 10 years, the construction of the building is still in its infant stage.* **4** [law] a person who has not attained legal majority. *As far as legal matters are concerned, he is still an infant.*

Infantile – *(adjective)* **1** of or occurring among infants. *The doctor got his specialization in treating infantile diseases.* **2** [derogatory] childish. *I was irritated by their infantile behaviour.*

Infantry – *(noun)* foot soldiers collectively. *A huge infantry was prepared to take part in the war.*

Infeasible – *(adjective)* inconvenient or impracticable. *Though very useful, his plan seems to be infeasible.*

Infection – *(noun)* **1** the process of infecting or the state of being infected. *The infection was controlled by administering a set of antibiotics.* **2** an infectious disease. *Diabetes is not an infectious disease.*

Infelicitous(Wrong Word) – *(adjective)* **1** liable to be transmitted through the environment. liable to speed infection. (Right Word): Infectious: *(adjective)* **1** liable to be transmitted through the environment. liable to speed infection. *The patients were susceptible to the infectious disease.* **2** likely to spread to or influence others: *her enthusiasm is infectious. She carried an infectious smile everywhere she went.*

Infelicity – *(noun)* **1** an act or thing that is inapt or inappropriate, especially a remark or expression. *I had not expected such an infelicity from him.* **2** [archaic] unhappiness; misfortune. *The loss of hard-earned money was the beginning of his infelicity.*

Inferable – *(adjective)* deduce from evidence or reasoning. *The conclusion was inferable from the results of the experiment.*

Inference – *(noun)* **1** a conclusion reached on the basis of evidence and reasoning. *After much experimentation, the scientists, finally, reached upon an inference.* **2** the process of reaching a conclusion by inferring. *We were satisfied with the results of inference that we had worked on.*

Interiority – *(noun)* a feeling of general inadequacy caused by actual or supposed inferiority, marked by aggressive behavior or withdrawal. *After being rejected by all her friends, her interiority made her live in reclusion.*

Infernal – *(adjective)* **1** of or relating to hell or the underworld. *The place was so bad that it gave us the feeling of an infernal world.* **2** [informal] terrible; awful: *you're an infernal nuisance. I was wary of the infernal trouble that could come at any point.*

Inferno – *(noun)* **1** a large fire that is dangerously out of control. *Before the deadly inferno could be controlled, 5 shops were already gutted in it.* **2** hell with reference to Dante's divine comedy. *The devils were going to burn in the inferno.*

Infertile – *(adjective)* **1** unable to reproduce. *The infertile pigs were sent to the laboratory for some possible treatment.* **2** unable to sustain crops or vegetation. *The farmers knew that they were allotted an infertile land.*

Infinite – *(adjective)* **1** limitless in space, extent, or size. very great in amount or degree. *Today, we are going to study about the infinite space that we live in.* **2** [mathematics] greater than any assignable quantity or countable number. *Any number divided by zero is infinite and cannot be measured.*

Infinitesimal – *(adjective)* extremely small. *The infinitesimal particles cannot be seen with naked eyes.* *(noun)* [mathematics] an indefinitely small quantity; a value approaching zero. *Having solved many problems on infinitesimal quantities, we were now confident to take the test.*

Infinitive – *(noun)* the basic form of a very, without an inflection binding it to a particular subject or tense normally occurring in English with the word to, as in to see, to ask. *Tomorrow, the English teacher will take class on infinitive clauses.*

Infinitude – *(noun)* limitless. *The space is known for its infinitude.*

Infinity – *(noun)* **1** the state or quality of being infinite. a very great number or amount. *The amount of food required to feed all the poor in the world amounts to infinity.* **2** mathematics a number greater than any assignable quantity or countable number. *Infinity has always puzzled mathematicians.* **3** a point in space or time that is or seems infinitely distant: the lawns stretched into infinity. *It was all dark and cloudy till infinity.*

Infirm – *(adjective)* **1** not physically strong, especially through age. *With time, a person becomes more and more infirmed.* **2** [archaic] irresolute; weak. *It was due to his infirm nature that he could not make many friends.*

Infirmity – *(noun)* physical or mental weakness. *In old age, people have to deal with infirmity of their bodies and mind.*

Infix – *(verb)* **1** implant or insert firmly in something. *After his fracture, a rod was infixed in his leg.* **2** [grammar] insert into the body of a word. *The word 'in' was infixed at the beginning of the word.* *(noun)* [grammar] a formative element inserted in a word. *The (verb) was converted to the passive form by inserting the infix "in" at its end.*

Inflammation – *(noun)* a localized physical condition in which part of the body becomes reddened, swollen, hot, and often painful, especially as a reaction to injury or infection. *To reduce the inflammation, he was kept on antibiotics.*

Inflator – *(noun)* filling with gas or air. *An inflator was used to swell the balloons.*

Inflect – *(verb)* **1** [grammar] change or be changed by inflection. *The form of the word can be changed by inflecting it with affixes.* **2** vary the intonation or pitch of especially to express mood or feeling. *Inflecting the words is used to express change in tone.* **3** technical bend or deflect from a straight course, especially inwards. *The bottle was inflected to modify its shape.*

Inflexibility – *(noun)* not able to bend, stiff unwilling to change. *The inflexibility of hours at work place is a cause of concern for many employees.*

Inflexibly – *(adverb)* not willing to compromise hard. *He is comfortable to work inflexibly.*

Inflict – *(verb)* cause something unpleasant or painful to be suffered by someone else. *The criminals inflicted grave injuries to the victim.*

Infliction – *(noun)* inflicting painful or unpleasant. *He had no intention to cause infliction of any kind to anyone.*

Inflictor – *(noun)* causing pain to some person. *After causing serious injuries to the victim, the inflictors ran away.*

Inflow – *(noun)* **1** the action of flowing or moving in. *Many rivers have an inflow directed from west to east direction.* **2** something, such as water or money, that flows or moves in. *As long as there was an inflow of money, her parents were treating her well.*

Influence – *(noun)* **1** the capacity to have an effect on the character or behavior of someone or something, or the effect itself. *Teachings of Swami Vivekananda have had a great influence on me.* **2** the power arising out of status, contacts, or wealth. *He was rich enough to have an influence over his friends.* **3** a person or thing with such a capacity or power. *His father was a big influence over his business partners.* **4** [physics, archaic] electrical or magnetic induction. *The influence of electricity on the nearby magnetic field is an established fact.* *(verb)* have an infleuence on. *You have influenced me so much that I feel obliged.*

Inform – *(verb)* **1** give facts or information to. *Why didn't you inform me about your ill health?* **2** give incriminating information about to the police or other authority. *The person was entrusted to inform the police about any information about the criminals.* **3** give an essential or formative principle or quality to. *It is the primary function of a community to inform its future generations about its ancient culture.*

Informal – *(adjective)* **1** relaxed and unofficial; not formal. *They decided to meet for an informal meeting.* **2** of or denoting the grammatical structures, vocabulary, and idiom suitable to everyday language and conversation rather than to official or formal contexts. *The writer was asked to prepare an informal speech for the event.*

Informality – *(noun)* friendly, relaxed, easy. *It was good that they gave consent to treat each other with informality.*

Informatory – *(adjective)* information. *When everyone was gone, the CEO got engaged in an informatory talk with his manager.*

Infrequency – *(noun)* not often, rare. *One thing for which he is known is the infrequency with which he comes to college.*

Infuriate – *(verb)* make irritated or angry. *He infuriated his senior by being absent from the meeting.*

Infusion – *(noun)* **1** a drink, remedy, or extract prepared by infusing. *The hermit gave us an infusion to drink.* **2** the action or process of infusing. *The infusion of the pain-killer in his body gave him some relief.*

Ingenious – *(adjective)* clever, original, and inventive. *His ingenious ways have always surprised us.*

Ingenuity – *(noun)* the quality of being ingenious. *It is the ingenuity that makes a person stand out from the rest.*

Ingenuous – *(adjective)* innocent, artless, and unsuspecting. *The cops were surprised to see how ingenuous the suspect was.*

Ingestion – *(noun)* take food, drink into the body. *The ingestion of food takes place through the mouth.*

Ingestive – *(adjective)* taking food or other substance into the body by swallowing or absorbing it. *The ingestive process in plants takes place via roots.*

Ingoing – *(adjective)* going towards or into. *We watched the movement of the moth ingoing into its hole.*

Ingrain – *(verb)* firmly fix or establish in a person. *The moral values were ingrained in his mind since childhood.* *(adjective)* composed of fibers which have been dyed different. *The ingrained textiles were kept in a separate room.*

Ingrained – *(adjective)* **1** firmly established. *The ingrained values in a person help in shaping up his personality.* **2** deeply embedded. *It seems that men have an ingrained hypocrisy in them.*

Ingrate – *(noun)* an ungrateful person. *He, being an ingrate, did not thank me for all the help that I provided.* *(adjective)* ungrateful. *No one likes his ingrate nature.*

Ingredient – *(noun)* **1** any of the foods or substances that are combined to make a particular dish. *I used only a few ingredients to prepare the dish.* **2** a component part or element. *The main ingredient of which a curry is composed of is the chickpea flour.*

Ingress – *(noun)* the action or fact or entering or coming in: the sides are sealed against the ingress of water, arrival of the sun, moon, or a planet in a specified constellation or part of the sky. *The prevention of the ingress of the infection into the wound was the main focus of the doctors.*

Ingurgitate – *(adjective)* [poetic/literary] swallow greedily. *His habit to ingurgitate is very bad.*

Inherent – *(adjective)* **1** existing in something as a permanent or essential attribute. *There are too many traditions that are inherent in Indian culture.* **2** law vested in someone as a right or privilege. *It is our inherent right to have access to education.*

Inhospitality – *(noun)* difficult and harsh. *His inhospitality irks me.*

Inimical – *(adjective)* tending to obstruct or harm; hostile. *Why is your behavior so inimical all the time?*

Inimitable – *(adjective)* impossible to imitate; unique. *The actor is known for his inimitable style.*

Iniquitous – *(adjective)* unfair and morally wrong. *When he could not be successful in other tricks, he turned iniquitous.*

Iniquity – *(noun)* injustice or immoral behavior. *We were not bothered by his iniquity.*

Initiation – *(noun)* admitting someone into a society, usually with a ritual. *On the very first day in college, we were called for an initiation session.*

Initiative – *(noun)* **1** the ability to initiate. the power or opportunity to act before others do: we gave lost the initiative. *Who will take the initiative now?* **2** a fresh approach. *When the things became worse, my friend had to take an initiative to ameliorate the situation.*

Initiatory – *(adjective)* cause to begin. *The project is still in its initiatory phase.*

Injudicious – *(adjective)* showing poor judgment; unwise. *We were not expecting such an injudicious act from him.*

Injure – *(verb)* **1** do or undergo physical harm to; wound. *Two people were badly injured in the accident.* **2** [archaic] do injustice or wrong to. *By* *marrying someone else, she injured his fiancée's feelings.*

Injurious – *(adjective)* **1** causing or likely to cause injury. *Thriving on too much alcohol can be injurious to one's health.* **2** maliciously insulting; libelous. *It was not right to pass injurious remarks for an artist like her.*

Injustice – *(noun)* **1** lack of justice. *He had no idea how to deal with the injustice meted out to him.* **2** an unjust act or occurrence. *The injustice done to the girl is not tolerable.*

Inkling – *(noun)* a slight suspicion; a hint. *I had not the slightest inkling that she would betray me at such an hour.*

Inland – *(adjective & avberb)* **1** in or into the interior of a country. *We were thrilled to see a lovely inland there.* **2** [chiefly British] carried on within the limits of a country; domestic. *The inland rules were documented in a separate file. (noun)* the interior of a country or region. *The country's inland had a hot climate.*

Inly – *(avberb)* [poetic/literary] inwardly. *Her inly feelings had gone strong.*

Inlying – *(adjective)* within or near a centre. *The inlying island was not very large.*

Inmate – *(noun)* a person living in an institution such as a prison or hospital. *The inmates in my hospital room became life-long friends.*

Inmost – *(adjective)* innermost. *She asked, "What is your inmost desire?"*

Innervate – *(verb)* [anatomy & zoology] supply an organ or other body part with nerves. *The doctors were successful in innervating his legs.*

Innocent – *(adjective)* **1** not guilty of a crime or offence. not responsible or directly involved: an innocent bystander. *The lad's innocent behavior melted down my anger.* **2** free from moral wrong; not corrupted. *An innocent man like him could not do such a crime.* **3** not intended to cause offence; harmless. without experience or knowledge of: a man innocent of war's cruelties. without; lacking. *The man was freed from all charges as he was proved to be innocent. (noun)* an innocent person. *He is too innocent to commit such a crime.*

Innocuous – *(adjective)* not harmful or offensive. *His intentions are not as innocuous as it seems.*

Innominate – *(adjective)* not named or classified. *I was talking to an innominate man.*

Innovate – *(verb)* make changes in something already existing, as by introducing new methods, ideas, or products. *As the students of mechanical engineering, we were expected to innovate the existing models of machines.*

Innovator – *(noun)* introducer of new methods, ideas, products. *Albert Einstein was one of the best innovators of his times.*

Innumerable – *(adjective)* too many to be counted. *I had innumerable berries in my lap.*

Innutrition – *(noun)* lack of nutrition. *The child was suffering from innutrition since his birth.*

Inobservance – *(noun)* failure to notice intention. *Can't you mend your inobservance before initiating this project?*

Inodorous – *(adjective)* having no small; odourless. *An inodorous gas present in the mine killed many workers.*

Inoperative – *(adjective)* not working or taking effect. *Half of the machines in the mill are inoperative.*

Inopportune – *(adjective)* occurring at an inconvenient time. *I was irritated by his inopportune arrival to my office.*

Inpouring – *(noun)* the action of bouring something. *The water kept inpouring into the cavern.*

Inquietude – *(noun)* physical or mental unease. *My sister complaint of inquietude after a hectic day.*

Inquire – *(verb)* another term for enquire. *The police inquired the local residents about the accident.*

Inquisitor – *(noun)* a person making an inquiry or conducting an inquisition, especially when regarded as harsh or very searching. *Everyone was annoyed by the irrelevant questions asked by the inquisitor.*

Inquisitorial – *(adjective)* **1** of or like an inquisitor. *His inquisitorial behavior irked us too much.* **2** law of a trial in which the judge has an examining role. Compare with accusatorial, adversarial. *The judge was playing an inquisitorial role in that particular case.*

Inrush – *(noun)* a sudden inward rush or flow. *The sudden inrush of water in the prison created frenzy everywhere.*

Insalubrity – *(noun)* unwholesome. *His insalubrity make him leave his job.*

Insanitary – *(adjective)* so dirty or germ-ridden as to be a danger to health. *Your insanitary habits put me off.*

Insanity – *(noun)* mentally ill. *The old man had bouts of insanity all day.*

Insatiable – *(adjective)* difficult to satisfy. *I have an insatiable hunger to learn psychiatry.*

Insatiate – *(adjective)* never satisfied. *Desires of man can never be satiated.*

Inscribable – *(adjective)* write on something as record purpose. *The wooden block is inscribable.*

Inscription – *(noun)* any character written on a monument. *King Asoka's inscriptions are etched on the pillars erected by him.*

Insectarium – *(noun)* a place where insects are kept, exhibited, and studied. *It was all fun to visit the insectariums.*

Insecticide – *(noun)* a substance used for killing insects. *The farmers were using excessive insecticides to prevent their crops from diseases.*

Insectivorous – *(adjective)* feeding on insects worms etc. *The insectivorous animals play a crucial role in the biological cycle.*

Insecure – *(adjective)* **1** not confident or assured. *We were talking about our insecure futures.* **2** not firm or firmly fixed. not permanent; insecure employment. *People don't want the jobs that are insecure.* **3** easily broken into; not protected. *It was essential to keep a strict vigil over the insecure gateway.*

Insecurity – *(noun)* uncertainty on avxiety about oneself. *I have no insecurities about my career.*

Inseminate – *(verb)* introduce semen into a woman or a female animal. *She goat was inseminated by a group of veterinary doctors.*

Insensate – *(adjective)* **1** lacking physical sensation. *The patient's insensate limbs were showing a bit improvement.* **2** lacking sympathy; unfeeling. *No one could change his insensate feelings towards his tormentor.* **3** completely lacking sense or reason. *No one had idea of why he was giving such insensate answers.*

Insensible – *(adjective)* **1** without one's mental faculties; unconscious. numb; without feeling. *I met an insensible man on my way to office.* **2** unaware of; indifferent to. *Minister's insensible attitude showed his apathy towards his own people.* **3** too small or gradual to be perceived; varying by insensible degrees. *The insensible change in weather could not be perceived correctly by the meteorologists.*

Insensitive – *(adjective)* **1** showing or feeling no concern for others' feelings. *My senior's insensitive behavior towards me outs my mood off.* **2** not sensitive to physical sensation. *My body is showing insensitive response to the external stimuli.* **3** not appreciative of or able to respond to something. *No electric shock could treat his insensitive limbs.*

Insentient – *(adjective)* incapable of feeling; inanimate. *The pig's insentient response was a cause of concern.*

Inshore –*(adjective)* at sea but close to the shore; operating near the coast: an inshore lifeboat. *In this region, inshore fishing is done on a large scale.* *(avberb)* towards or closer to the shore. *They were advancing inshore.*

Insight – *(noun)* **1** the capacity to gain an accurate and deep intuitive understanding of something. an understanding of this kind. *In order to understand complex human behaviors, we need to develop an insight.* **2** [psychiatry] awareness by a mentally ill person that their mental experiences are not based in external reality. *The psychologically ill patient had developed an insight about his problem.*

Insignificant – *(adjective)* too small or unimportant to be worth consideration. *Let's ignore our insignificant problems as of now.*

Insinuate – *(verb)* **1** suggest or hint in an indirect and unpleasant way. *The dacoit was insinuated by his master to do the killing.* **2** manoeuvre oneself gradually into a favorable position. *By buttering his seniors, he insinuated his position in the company.*

Insinuatingly – *(adverb)* hint in an unpleasant way. *One of my cousins has the habit of talking insinuatingly in order to serve his means.*

Insistent – *(adjective)* **1** insisting or very demanding. *Her insistent requests to do the appraisal were ignored by the authorities.* **2** repeated and demanding attention: a telephone started ringing, loud and insistent. *Her voice was insistent and gathered everyone's attention.*

Insobriety – *(noun)* drunkenness. *It is dangerous to drive while in the state of insobriety.*

Insolence – *(noun)* rude behaviour. *Before I could tolerate more of his insolence, I left my job.*

Insolent – *(adjective)* rude and disrespectful. *Her insolent answers created a bad impression on his seniors.*

Insoluble – *(adjective)* **1** impossible to solve. *This is one of the insoluble riddles that I have ever come through.* **2** incapable of being dissolved. *The insoluble crystals settled at the bottom of the glass.*

Insolvable – *(adjective)* insoluble. *Water and oil are insolueble.*

Insolvency – *(noun)* state of being insolvent.*Even in the state of insolvency, my friend was looking forward to the luxuries of life.*

Insolvent – *(adjective)* **1** unable to pay debts owed. *The extravagancy turned the man into a pathetic insolvent.* **2** of or relating to bankruptcy. *The insolvent farmer was now on his own.* *(noun)* an insolvent person. *By the time the war ended, he had turned into an insolvent.*

Insomnia – *(noun)* habitual sleeplessness. *This girl suffers from insomnia and depression.*

Insomuch – *(avberb)* to the extent that. *We are addicted to the social networking sites insomuch that we feel pathetic without them.*

Insouciance – *(noun)* unconcern, indifference. *Insouciance on part of parents can make their children become detached.*

Inspect – *(verb)* look at closely. examine officially. *The microbiologist inspected the slide carefully.*

Inspection – *(noun)* careful examination.*The quality manager was sent on a routine inspection to the godown.*

Inspector – *(noun)* **1** an official who ensures that regulations are obeyed. [British] an official who examines bus or train tickets for validity. *An inspector was on duty the day I joined the mill.* **2** a police officer ranking below a chief inspector. *The inspector was probing into the case of abduction and killing.*

Inspectorial – *(adjective)* having to check compliance. *His inspectorial duties were assigned on the day of his joining.*

Inspirator – *(noun)* one who inspires or motivates others. *My father has been my greatest inspirator in my life.*

Inspiring – *(adjective)* having the effect of inspiring someone. *The children were listening to the inspiring stories narrated by their teacher.*

Inspirit – *(verb)* encourage and enliven. *The saint inspirited our souls.*

Inspissate – *(verb)* thicken or congeal. *The sugar solution was inspissated and added to the paste.*

Instability – *(noun)* lack of stability. *The instability of the wooden stand made me fall on the ground.*

Installation – *(noun)* **1** the action or process of installing or being installed. *The installation of electric wires took a week.* **2** a large piece of equipment installed for use. *The installation was carried on a truck.* **3** a military or industrial establishment. *The military unit was under the process of installation when we visited the area.* 4 an art exhibit constructed within a gallery. *It was the first time we were looking at the installation placed in Fine Arts room.*

Installed – *(verb)* established in a new place. *The electrician said, "I have installed the electric meter."*

Instalment – *(noun)* **1** a sum of money due as one of several equal payments for something, spread over an agreed period of time. *We have already paid this month's installment of house rent.* one of several parts of something which are published or broadcast in sequence at intervals. *The second installment of the show was withheld for some time.*

Instance – *(noun)* an example or single occurrence of something. a particular case. *It was the first instance that a child was presented as a witness to the case. (verb)* cite as an example. *A previous case was instanced to show the similarity between the two cases.*

Instancy – *(noun)* [archaic] urgency. *It was due to an instancy at office that we stayed there till midnight.*

Instantly – *(adverb)* at once, immediately. *The student replied instantly, "I have completed the project."*

Instate – *(verb)* install or establish. *After intervention of authorities, the peace was instated in our area.*

Instead – *(avberb)* as an alternative or substitute. in place of. *We were hoping promotions; instead, we were given performance bonuses.*

Instinct – *(noun)* **1** an innate pattern of behavior in animals in response to certain stimuli. a natural or intuitive way of acting or thinking. *To seek the company of others is the human's basic instinct.* **2** a natural propensity or skill. *He has a natural instinct to photography. (adjective)* formal imbued or filled with a quality. *The flowers are instinct with fragrances.*

Institutor – *(noun)* a person who introduces something. *The man in news is the institutor of Nano technology in our company.*

Instructor – *(noun)* a teacher. north American a university teacher ranking below assistant professor. *My yoga instructor has left for the U.S.A.*

Instrumentality – *(noun)* the quality of serving as an instrument. *The instrumentality of the protests in amending juvenile law is appreciable.*

Instrumentally – *(adverb)* serving as a means of pursuing an aim. *The society was instrumentally strong to bring out this law.*

Instrumentation – *(noun)* **1** the instruments used in a piece of music. the arrangement of a piece of music for particular instruments. *The instrumentation of all the pieces was yet to be decided.* **2** measuring instruments collectively. the design or use of such instruments. *The performance was about to start yet the instrumentation was not yet ready.*

Insubstantial – *(adjective)* lacking strength and solidity. imaginary. *This proposal seems to be an insubstantial to our company.*

Insufferable – *(adjective)* intolerable. unbearably arrogant or conceited. *The man's saga of insufferable tortures moved me a lot.*

Insufficiency – *(noun)* **1** the condition of being insufficient. *Many parts of the country still have the insufficiency of food grains.* **2** medicine the inability of an organ to perform normally. *My heart's insufficiency to pump enough blood has put my health in danger.*

Insufflate – *(verb)* **1** [medicine] blow or breathe into or through a body cavity. *An oxygen pump insufflated air into the mouth of the patient.* **2** [theology] breathe on to symbolize spiritual influence. *The Guru insufflated as he was blessing his disciples.*

Insulting – *(adjective)* disrespectful, abusive. *What an insulting remark he has made!*

Insuperable – *(adjective)* impossible to overcome. *The insuperable conditions forced us to leave the place.*

Insupportable – *(adjective)* **1** unable to be supported or justified. *He was banking on an insupportable theory.* **2** intolerable. *It is only recently that he has been showing insupportable behavior.*

Insurable – *(adjective)* compersation in the event of damage or loss. *The house that I purchased recently is insurable.*

Insure – *(verb)* **1** arrange for compensation in the event of damage to or loss of property, life, or a person, in exchange for regular payments to a company. secure the payment of a sum in this way. protect someone against a possible contingency. *Our company insures employees against the loss of property and life.* **2** another term for ensure. *He has insured for both his sons.*

Insurgency – *(noun)* a person or group fighting against government. *During insurgency, the government banned the use of social media sites.*

Insurgent – *(adjective)* rising in active revolt. *The insurgent attacks have turned more violent recently. (noun)* a rebel or revolutionary. *The* *insurgents from different parts of the state have joined hands.*

Insurmountable – *(adjective)* too great to be overcome. *We are facing insurmountable problems at our work place.*

Insusceptible – *(adjective)* not susceptible. *The Principal gave us an unsusceptible proposition.*

Intaglio – *(noun)* an incised or engraved design. a gem with an incised design. a printing process in which the type or design is engraved. *What we were looking at were the fascinating designs of intaglios. (verb)*engrave. *The skilled artist was intaglioing the designs over a wooden box.*

Integral – *(adjective)* **1** necessary to make a whole complete; fundamental. included as part of a whole. having all the parts necessary to be complete. *Democracy is integral to our nation.* **2** [mathematics] of or denoted by an integer or integers. *The integral mathematics is an interesting subject. (noun)* mathematics a function of which a given area under the curve of a graph of the function. *There were several questions based on integral function.*

Integrator – *(noun)* a person or a thing that integrates. *In our higher classes, we were taught about integrator functions.*

Integrity – *(noun)* **1** the quality of having strong moral principles. *He is truly a man of integrity.* **2** the state of being whole. the condition of being unified or sound in construction. internal consistency or lack of corruption in electronic data. *The integrity of our nation should not be compromised at any cost.*

Intellection – *(noun)* the action or process of understanding. *The presentation of a concept makes the intellection an easy thing.*

Intellectual – *(adjective)* of, relating to, or appealing to the intellect. having a highly developed intellect. *An interview tests your intellectual abilities along with the others qualities. (noun)* a person with a highly developed intellect. *Companies prefer to hire highly intellectual people for their jobs.*

Intellectuality – *(noun)* relating to intellect. *His intellectuality was put to test when he was asked to choose between two solutions.*

Intellectually – *(adverb)* possessing a developed intellect. *If it is to be chosen intellectually, my vote would go to my reporting manager.*

Intelligibility – *(noun)* the quality of being intelligible. *There are times where your intelligibility is put to test.*

Intemperance – *(noun)* lack of restraint excessive indulgence. *His intemperance to boozing has been his biggest weakness.*

Intend – *(verb)* **1** have as one's aim or plan. plan that something should be or act as something. plan that speech should have a particular meaning. *My sister intends to clear IAS examination this year.* **2** design or destine for a particular purpose. be meant for the use of. *The stickers were intended to be distributed among the designers.*

Intendment – *(noun)* [law] the sense in which the law understands something. *The intendment of the new law was to benefit all the citizens.*

Intensity – *(noun)* **1** the quality of being intense. *The rainfall's intensity has decreased over the years.* **2** chiefly physics the measurable amount of a property. *As the intensity of the light waves is increased, they become hotter.*

Intensive – *(adjective)* **1** very through or vigorous. *An intensive regime was suggested to him by his trainers.* **2** aiming to achieve maximum producing within a limited area. often contrasted with extensive. *The intensive agriculture depletes the soil of its nutrients.* 3 concentrating on or making much use of something: computer-intensive methods. *Our economy is agriculture-intensive.* **4** [grammar] giving force or emphasis. *Today, we shall learn about intensive (avberb) s.* **5** denoting a property measured in terms of intensity rather than extent. *The intensity of the situation was not allowing us to take any concrete steps. (noun)* [grammar] an intensifier. *We shall learn the use of intensifiers today.*

Intention – *(noun)* **1** an aim or plan. the action or fact of intending. a person's, especially a man's designs in respect to marriage. *He had no intention of marrying her.* **2** medicine the healing process of a wound. *His healing of wound took place by first intention.* **3** logic conceptions formed by directing the mind towards an object. *His intention is to become a Kung Fu master.*

Intentional – *(adjective)* deliberate. *All his flattering was intentional.*

Intently – *(adverb)* with eager attention. *We were listening to our teacher intently.*

Inter – *(verb)* place a corpse in a grave or tomb. *After all the rituals were over, he was interred.*

Interbreed – *(verb)* breed or cause to breed with an animal of a different race or species. *The scientists have been successful in interbreeding of species.*

Intercept – *(verb)* **1** obstruct and prevent from continuing to a destination. *The criminals were intercepted to enter the office.* **2** mathematics mark or cut off. *A part of the pentagon was intercepted and its area was calculated.* *(noun)* **1** an act of intercepting. *In mathematics, we got to learn the way of intercepting shapes.* **2** mathematics the point at which a given line cuts a coordinate axis. *We were asked to draw a line that could intercept the coordinate axis.*

Interception – *(noun)* obstruct to prevent something from going further. *The interception of phone calls was initiated today.*

Interceptive – *(adjective)* the system to prevent something from reacting destination. *The interceptive phone calls were the only way cops could reach him.*

Interchange – *(verb)* exchange with each other. put each of in the other's place. *Soon after the teacher ordered, the two friends interchanged their seats.* *(noun)* **1** the action of interchanging. an exchange of words. *An interchange of words was going on there.* **2** alternation: the interchange of woods and meadows. *We were enjoying the interchange of bushy trees and shrubs at regular intervals.* **3** a road junction on several levels so that traffic streams do not intersect. *We were hoping to go by the next interchange.* **4** a station where passengers may change from one railway line or bus service to another. *We alighted at the next interchange station.*

Intercolonial – *(adjective)* existing or conducted between colonies. *With intercolonial discussions going on, people had to just wait and watch.*

Intercommunion – *(noun)* participation in holy communion by members of different denominations. *The discussions were going on to decide the place for the holy intercommunion.*

Intercourse – *(noun)* **1** communication or dealings between people. *It was at the end of the intercourse that the final decision was taken place.* **2** short for sexual intercourse. *It was their first intercourse and they were enjoying it.*

Intercurrent – *(adjective)* **1** medicine occurring during the progress of another. *The doctors were worried about the intercurrent disease that too had developed in her body.* **2** rare intervening. *The intercurrent happenings are hard to ignore.*

Interdepend – *(verb)* two or more (people or things) depending on each other. *It took a while for us to understand that the two factors were interdependent.*

Interdiction – *(noun)* prohibit someone from doing something. *After the court ordered their interdiction, they could no longer carry on with their dangerous plans.*

Interdictory – *(adjective)* court order preventing someone from doing something. *The interdictory order prevented them from participating in future sacraments.*

Interested – *(adjective)* showing interest or curiosity. *Are you still interested in this work?*

Interesting – *(adjective)* arousing curiosity or interest. *The movie was an interesting combination of action and comedy.*

Interference – *(noun)* **1** the action of interfering or process of being interfered with. *His constant interference in my matters always puts me off.* **2** physics the combination of two or more waveforms to form a resultant wave in which the displacement is either reinforced or cancelled. disturbance to radio signals caused by unwanted signals from other sources. *The interference of two waveforms results in change in displacement of the resultant wave.*

Interferer – *(noun)* a person or thing preventing an activity from continuing. *What an interferer he is!*

Interfering - *(adjective)* tending to obstruct in other people's affairs. *Interfering into their discussion was not my idea at all.*

Interfuse - *(verb)* [poetic/literary] join or mix together. *The writer interfused his two articles.*

Intergrowth - *(noun)* a thing produced by intergrowth in rocks. *The microbiologist noticed a green intergrowth in the algae.*

Interim - *(noun)* the intervening time. *Today, the interim budget was presented in the parliament.* *(adjective)* **1** provisional. *In order to deal with the gravity of the situations, some interim measures were taken by the government.* **2** [chiefly British] relating to less than a full year's business activity: interim profits. *A list of interim deals was created and distributed among the employees.* *(avberb)* [archaic] meanwhile. *The politicians were busy campaigning in the interim time.*

Interior - *(adjective)* **1** situated within or inside; inner. chiefly technical situated further in or within. *A lovely interior made me buy this house.* **2** inland. *The inland of the country is quiet hot.* **3** relating to a country's internal or domestic affairs. *Currently, the country is facing some interior problems.* *(noun)* **1** the interior part of something. *The interior of the cave was very dark and cool.* **2** the internal affairs of a country. *The minister gave an eye-opener speech about the interior political conditions.*

Interject - *(verb)* say abruptly, especially as an interruption. *The man interjected and stopped us from any further discussion.*

Interjection - *(noun)* an exclamation, especially as a part of speech. *Lately, I am working on interjections.*

Interjectional - *(adjective)* an abrupt remark, especially as an interruption. *I was asked by my teacher to avoid using too much of interjectional words.*

Interlinear - *(adjective)* written between the lines of a text. *Look at the interlinear sentences and try to understand their relation to the text.*

Interlink - *(verb)* join or connect together. *The mechanic interlinked a series of small chains to form a long one.*

Interlocution - *(noun)* a person who takes part in conversation interlocution of a person is required when two people not knowing each other's language talk. *The land is an interlocation between the two islands.*

Intermeddle - *(verb)* interfere in other's matters. *One of the worst habits that one can have is to intermeddle in other's discussion.*

Intermediate - *(adjective)* **1** coming between two things in time, place, character, etc. *The best option was to stop at some intermediate place before travelling any further.* **2** having more than basic knowledge or skills but not yet advanced. *His intermediate knowledge was enough to get through the examination.* *(noun)* **1** an intermediate person or thing. *I acted as an intermediate between my two friends.* **2** a chemical compound formed by one reaction and then taking part in another. *An intermediate product is formed by such a reaction.* *(verb)* mediate. *The Vice President came there and intermediated for the two sides.*

Intermediation - *(noun)* coming between two things to sort out. *It was his maturity and experience that he was chosen for intermediation.*

Interment - *(noun)* the burial of a corpse in a grave or tomb. *As the king reached there, the interment had already taken place.*

Intermingle - *(verb)* mix or mingle together. *As time passed on, the cultures intermingled and exchanged their traditions.*

Intermission - *(noun)* a pause or break. an interval between parts of a play or film. *During the intermission, my friend went out for ordering some food for us.*

Intermittence - *(noun)* irregular, not continuous. *What bothers them is the intermittence of the money inflow.*

Intermittent - *(adjective)* occurring at irregular intervals. *The intermittent flow of money does not allow him to be extravagant.*

Intermix - *(verb)* mix together. *All the pastes were intermixed in a bowl.*

Intern - *(noun)* [chiefly north American] a recent medical graduate receiving supervised training in a hospital and acting as an assistant physician or surgeon. a student or trainee who does a job to gain work experience or for a qualification. *I am looking for a company where I can get training as an intern.* *(verb)* **1** confine as a prisoner. *The criminal was interned by the jailor.* **2** [chiefly north American] serve as an intern. *He interned in the company for a period of six months.*

Internee – *(noun)* a person who is confused as a prisoner. *See internees were released on humanitarian grounds.*

Internment – *(noun)* the process of undergoing training or studentship. *After finishing my internment, I am planning to settle abroad.*

Internal – *(adjective)* **1** of or situated on the inside. inside the body. existing within an organization. relating to affairs and activities within a country. *The internal affairs of the company are to be kept secret.* **2** experienced in one's mind. *A man's internal consciousness does not allow him to do bad deeds.* **3** intrinsic. *To get thick after freezing is the intrinsic nature of this substance.* **4** [British] attending a university as well as taking its examinations. *I am about to take the internal examinations of the university.* *(noun)* inner parts or features. *All her internals were badly damaged.*

International – *(adjective)* existing or occurring between nations. agreed on by all or many nations used by people of many nations. *The United Nations works at an international level.* **1** [British] a game or contest between teams representing different countries. a player who has taken part in such a contest. *The international series was cancelled owing to the clashes between ethnic groups.* **2** any of four associations founded to promote socialist or communist action. *The four international associations were formed between 1864 and 1936.*

Internationalize – *(verb)* **1** make international. *There was no need to internationalize this news.* **2** bring under the protection or control of two or more nations. *The country was under chaos, so it had to be internationalized under two foreign countries.*

Internecine – *(adjective)* destructive to both sides in a conflict. of or relating to conflict within a group. *For years, the countries were part of internecine wars.*

Interplay – *(noun)* the way in which two or more things affect each other. *I am trying to understand the interplay of the musical instruments.*

Interposition – *(noun)* interposing someone or something. *The interposition of senior managers within the different tiers of manager produced improved financial results.*

Interpret – *(verb)* **1** explain the meaning of words, actions, etc. translate orally the words of a person speaking a different language. *What he interpreted was not very correct.* **2** perform in a way that conveys one's understanding of the creator's ideas. understand as having a particular meaning or significance. *His signs were interpreted by the person in the form of a dance.*

Interpreter – *(noun)* **1** a person who interprets foreign speech orally. *An interpreter was hired to translate from German into English.* **2** computing a programme that can analyse and execute a programme line by line. *The role of an interpreter is to execute a computer programme.*

Interregnum – *(noun)* a period when normal government is suspended, especially between successive reigns or regimes. *The news about an interregnum in the statae was no surisre to me.*

Interrelation – *(noun)* the way two or more things are related to each other. *What is the interrelation between two concepts?*

Interrogative – *(adjective)* having the force of a question. [grammar] used in questions, contrasted with affirmative and negative. *The teacher asked us to frame an interrogative sentence.* *(noun)* an interrogative word, e.g. how or what. *We have already taken a test on interrogatives.*

Interrupt – *(verb)* **1** stop the continuous progress of. stop person who is speaking by saying or doing something. *The way he was interrupting us again and again forced us to send him away.* **2** break the continuity of a sunken fence which doesn't interrupt the view across the fields. *The programme was interrupted due to some technical problems.*

Interrupted – *(adjective)* discontinued. *The execution of the programme got interrupted due to a wrong instruction.*

Interrupter – *(noun)* **1** a person or thing that interrupts. *I had to act as an interrupter to stop their argument.* **2** a device that automatically breaks an electric circuit if a fault develops. *An interrupter is a safety device installed in homes.*

Interruption – *(noun)* the action of interupting or being interrupted. *The regular interruption of the programme has spoiled my mood.*

Interruptive – *(adjective)* the action of braking the continuity. *The interruptive ways of the person cost him dear.*

Intersect – *(verb)* divide by passing or laying across it. cross or cut each other. *A pole was erected at the place where the roads intersected each other.*

Intersection – *(noun)* a point or line common to lines or surfaces that intersect. a point at which two or more things, especially roads, interacts. *Just reach the intersection and turn left.*

Interspersion – *(noun)* the process of scattering here and there. *The farmer was busy doing interspersion of the seeds in his fields.*

Interstice – *(noun)* a small intervening space. *The dust particles were passing easily through the interstice in door.*

Interstitial – *(adjective)* of, forming, or occupying interstices. *The interstitial space was allowing the sun rays to enter the rom.*

Interwine – *(verb)* twist or twine together. *As I visited the garden again, I saw that the two branches had intertwined.*

Interval – *(noun)* **1** an intervening time or space. *We used to chat a lot during interval time.* **2** a pause or break. [British] a period of time separating parts of a theatrical or musical performance or a sports match. *The movie before the interval was not very interesting.* **3** a gap. *An interval was separating the two beams of light.* **4** the difference in pitch between two sounds. *An interval in acoustics is the difference in pitch between two sounds.*

Intervene – *(verb)* come between so as to prevent or later something. occur as a delay or obstacle to something being done. interrupt *(verb)* **1** ally. law interpose in a lawsuit as a third party. *A retired officer was asked to intervene between two parties.* **2** occur in time between events. be situated between things. *In the intervening time, I took shooting classes.*

Intervener – *(noun)* one who takes part in something so as to alter or prevent. *Despite his lack of experience, he was chosen as the intervener to settle matters.*

Intervening – *(adjective)* occur between two events, time. *In the intervening months she joined a linguistic course.*

Intervention – *(noun)* **1** the action or process of intervening. interference by a state in another's affairs. *In spite of the intervention by a third country, the two nations kept on fighting.* **2** action taken to improve a medical disorder. *A medical intervention became necessary at that point.*

Interview – *(noun)* **1** a conversation between a journalist or broadcaster and a person of *public interest. The interview of the minister continued for two hours.* **2** an oral examination of an applicant for a job or college place. a session of formal questioning of a person by the police. *My interview has gone quiet well. (verb)*hold an interview with. *The company interviewed twenty candidates on the same day.*

Interweave – *(verb)* weave or become woven together. *The old lady was interweaving threads of three different colors.*

Intestate – *(adjective)* not having made a will before one dies. *The intestate case is still under discussion. (noun)* a person who had died intestate. *It was unfortunate that his mother died intestate.*

Intimate – *(adjective)* **1** closely acquainted; familiar. having an [informal] friendly atmosphere. *An intimate atmosphere was created to welcome he guests at party.* **2** private and personal. euphemistic having a sexual relationships. *The two are quiet vocal about their intimate relationship.* **3** involving very close connection. *Only intimate friends were called for the party.* **4** detailed. (noun) a *very* close friend. *He is an intimate friend of mine.*

Intimation – *(noun)* indication, hint. *Could you give me an intimation of how to solve the problem?*

Intimidate – *(verb)* frighten or overawe. *His terrible mask was intimidating every one.*

Into – *(preposition)* **1** expressing motion or direction to a point on or within. *His entry into the room was prohibited.* **2** indicating a route to a destination. *We had to travel into the cave to reach the other side.* **3** indicating the direction towards which someone or something is turned. *We were charmed by the fresh air blowing directly into our faces.* **4** indicating an object of interest. *She loved photography so much that she was completely into it.* **5** expressing a change of state. *Soon, the droplets got changed into steam.* **6** expressing the result of an action. *The violent air turned the page into a twisted mass.* **7** expressing division. *The cake was divided into many pieces.* **8** [informal] taking a lively and active interest in. *He was listening keenly into what they were discussing.*

Intolerable – *(adjective)* unable to be endured. *Every time I meet her, she shows an intolerable behaviour.*

Intolerance – *(noun)* unwillingness to accept views beliefs opinion behaviour. *The two countries are trying to lessen the intolerance to each other.*

Intolerant – *(adjective)* not tolerant. *My uncle's intolerant behaviour keeps everyone annoyed.*

Intoxicant – *(noun)* an intoxicating substance. *He used to stupefy his victims by using intoxicants.*

Intoxicate – *(verb)* **1** cause to lose control of their faculties. *The gas intoxicated the girl and she fell on ground.* **2** poison. *To take revenge, he tried to intoxicate him by mixing drugs with alcohol.* **3** excite or exhilarate. *The smell of flowers intoxicated our senses.*

Intractable – *(adjective)* hard to control or deal with. stubborn. *That person is ill-famed for his intractable behaviour.*

Intransigent – *(adjective)* unwilling to change views. *His mother had tried persuasion but he was intransigent.*

Intricacy – *(noun)* **1** the quality of being intricate. *The intricacy of the life cycle makes it more beautiful.* **2** details. *It is very difficult to understand the intricacy of this compound.*

Introduction – *(noun)* **1** the action of introducing or being introduced. a thing, such as a product, plant, etc., newly brought in. *With the introduction of new species, scientists are hoping to raise the production.* **2** a formal presentation of one person to another, in which each is told the other's name. *Before the lecture could begin, he asked us to give our introduction.***3**. a preliminary thing, such as an explanatory section at the beginning of a book, report, etc. a preliminary section in a piece of music, often thematically different from the main section. *The introductory paragraph of the song is very hummable.* **4** a book or course of study intended to introduce a subject to a person. a person's first experience of a subject or thing. *My first introduction to botany was done through him.*

Introspection – *(noun)* the examination of one's own thoughts or feelings. *We should spare a little time to do introspection.*

Introspective – *(adjective)* given to introspection. *He was good at explaining the introspective concepts.*

Introversion – *(noun)* shy, reticent person. *Introversion is a trait of people concerned with predominantly with their own feelings.*

Introvert – *(noun)* a shy, reticent person. psychology a person predominantly concerned with their own thoughts and feelings rather than with external things. Compare with extrovert. *I am quiet introvert by nature.* *(adjective)* of, denoting, or typical of an introvert. *His introvert tendencies are worth noticing for.*

Intrude – *(verb)* **1** come into a place or situation where one is unwelcome or uninvited. introduce into or enter with adverse effect. *The thief intruded the house at midnight.* **2** geology be forced or thrust into a pre-existing formation. *The rock intruded into the nearby wall.*

Intrusion – *(noun)* the action of intruding. a thing that intrudes. *The intrusion of the army can take place at any time.*

Intrusive – *(adjective)* **1** intruding or tending to intrude. *He is known to be intrusive by nature.* **2** phonetics added between words or syllables to facilitate pronunciation, e.g. an r in saw a film. *An intrusive word facilitated the pronunciation of the word.* **3** geology relating to or formed by the intrusion of igneous rock. *Let's study how a rock is formed by an intrusive process*

Intuition – *(noun)* the ability to understand something immediately, without the need for conscious reasoning. *Recently , I have developed an intuition that our neighbors will leave their place.*

Intuitive – *(adjective)* **1** instinctive. *In many people, intuitive abilities are well formed.* **2**. easy to use and understand. *The subject's explaination has rendered it more intuitive to understand.*

Intumesce – *(verb)* rare swell up. *The raisins intumesced after they were placed in water.*

Inunction – *(noun)* chiefly medicine the rubbing of ointment or oil into the skin. *It was due to inunction that the burned part did not swell too much.*

Inundate – *(verb)* **1** flood. *During rainy season this area got completely inundated.* **2** overwhelm with things to be dealt with. *I was inundated with emotions after hearing his story.*

Inutile – *(adjective)* useless, pointless. *The mixer at home has become inutile.*

Invade – *(verb)* **1** enter as or with an army so as to subjugate or occupy it. enter in large numbers, especially intrusively. attack and spread into an organism or bodily part. *When the neighboring country invaded, our soldiers fought back with bravery.* **2** intrude on: he felt his privacy was being invaded. *He requested me not to invade his privacy.*

Invader – *(noun)* a person or group that attacks a country, place or region. *A bunch of invaders attacked from the North-West frontier.*

Invaginate – *(verb)* turned inside out or folded back to form a cavity. *The epidermis of a kangaroo is folded back to form a pouch so as to carry its young ones.*

Invalid – *(noun)* a person made weak of disabled by illness or injury. *In spite of breaking his legs, he does not consider himself an invalid.* *(verb)* remove from active service in the armed forces because of injury or illness. disable by injury or illness. *He was invalidated from his services owing to his injuries.*

Invalidate – *(verb)* deprive make or prove an argument. *His license was invalidated by the company.*

Invalidation – *(noun)* prove erroneous, deprive of legal validity. *The process of invalidation took only a week.*

Invaluable – *(adjective)* extremely useful. *I have a box of invaluable jewelry that was gifted to me by my mother.*

Invar – *(noun)* trademark an alloy of iron and nickel with a negligible coefficient of expansion. *Invar is an alloy of iron and nickel.*

Invariable – *(adjective)* never changing. *His route of going to the of see is invariable. There are both variable and invariable quantities in Physics.*

Invasion – *(noun)* an instance of invading. the action or process of being invaded. *Our country is ready to face any type of invasion.*

Invasive – *(adjective)* tending to invade or intrude. involving the introduction of instruments or other objects into the body or body cavities. *The invasive intentions of the neighboring country are well known.*

Invective – *(noun)* strongly abusive or critical language. *I want to avoid his invective talks.*

Inveigle – *(verb)* persuade by deception or flattery. *She was able to easily inveigle men.*

Invent – *(verb)* create or design a new device, process, etc. make up especially as to deceive. *Alva Edison invented electric bulb.*

Inventive – *(adjective)* having or showing creativity or original thought. *With an inventive brain like him, no one could think of winning the competition.*

Inventor – *(noun)* first made a person who a device or thing. *Our country has produced many a great inventors.*

Inventory – *(noun)* a complete list of items such as goods in stock or the contents of a building. a quantity of goods in stock. the entire stock of a business, including materials and finished product. *I was asked to prepare an inventory of the things to be used in shopping.* *(verb)* make an inventory of. *I inventoried as per the instructions.*

Inveracity – *(noun)* untruthfulness lie. *I am fed up of his inveracity.*

Inverse – *(adjective)* opposite in position, direction, order, or effect. *A ball from inverse direction was about to collide with another ball.* *(noun)* **1** a thing that is the opposite or reverse of another. *The temperature and pressure are inverse quantities.* **2** mathematics a reciprocal quantity. *The inverse of a number is calculated by dividing it by one.*

Inversion – *(noun)* **1** the action of inverting or the state of being inverted. reversal of the normal order of words, typically for rhetorical effect. music an inverted interval, chord, or phrase. *The inversion can change the state of an object.* **2** a reversal of the normal decrease of air temperature with altitude, or of water temperature with depth. *We notice an inversion of temperature with an increase in altitude.* **3** mathematics the process of finding an inverse or reciprocal quantity from a given one. *In exams, students were asked to calculate inversion of the given numbers.* **4** [chemistry] a reaction causing a change from one optically active configuration to the opposite configuration. *Inversion is a concept involving the change of optical configurations.* **5** [psychology, dated] homosexually. *He has been happy since his sexual inversion.*

Invert – *(verb)* **1** put upside down or in the opposite position, order, or arrangement. *He placed the glass in an inverted position.* **2** music modify by reversing the direction of pitch changes. alter by changing the relative position of the notes in it. *By inverting the notes, pitch of the sound can be changed.* **3** chiefly mathematics subject to inversion. *The numbers can be inverted easily.* *(noun)* **1** an inverted arch, as at the lower surface of a sewer. *What we were looking was an inverted dome.* **2** [psychology, dated] a homosexual. *The man underwent a surgery to get an inversion.* **3** a postage stamp printed with an error such that all or part of its design is upside down. *How could they not notice the blunder of printing an inverted stamp?*

Investigate – *(verb)* carry out a systematic or formal inquiry into so as to establish the truth. carry out research into a subject. make a search or systematic inquiry. *A private agency has been investigating the case since last one year.*

Investigation – *(noun)* systematic examination or research. *As long as investigation is going on, media is prohibited from interfering into the matters.*

Investiture – *(noun)* the action of formally investing a person with honours or rank. a ceremony at which this takes place. *The man was standing tall when his investiture going on.*

Investor – *(noun)* a person or body that puts in money somewhere for profit. *The builder has invited many investors for his new project.*

Inveterate – *(adjective)* having a long-standing and firmly established habit or activity. firmly established. *No one is able to change his inveterate truthfulness.*

Invigilate – *(verb)* [British] supervise candidates during an examination. *In spite of the invigilation going on, students were copying from one another.*

Inviolate – *(adjective)* free from injury or violation. *No one has the guts to disturb his inviolate state of mind.*

Invisible – *(adjective)* **1** unable to be seen, either by nature or because concealed. treated as if unable to be seen; ignored. *An invisible gas was present in the mines.* **2** [economics] relating to or denoting earnings which a country makes from the sale of services or other items not constituting tangible commodities. *There has not been any invisible growth of the country's earnings this year.* *(noun)* invisible exports and imports. *A lot has been taking in the field of invisible trading.*

Invitation – *(noun)* **1** a written or verbal request inviting someone to go somewhere or to do something. the action of inviting. *When I rejected his invitation, he got very angry.* **2** a situation or action inviting a particular outcome or response. *Their verb al duel gave invitation to new problems.*

Invitatory – *(adjective)* converting an invitation. *He sent me an invitatory message in mail.*

Involuntarily – *(adverb)* done without conscious control. *She voluntarily agreed to do the jolie.*

Involuntary – *(adjective)* **1** done without conscious control. concerned in bodily processes that are not under the control of the will. *We have no control over the involuntary actions of some of our organs.* **2** done against someone's will. *He gave involuntary consent to donate blood.*

Involution – *(noun)* **1** physiology the shrinkage of an organ in old age or when inactive. *As a man grows old, involution of his organs starts taking place.* **2** mathematics a function, transformation, or operator that is equal to its inverse. *The students were solving the involution based problems.* **3** formal the process or state of complication. *This case has reached involution.*

Invulnerable – *(adjective)* impossible to harm or damage. *No one can disturb his invulnerable state of mind.*

Inwards – *(avberb)* towards the inside. into or towards the mind, spirit, or soul. *As he used to practice meditation, his thought process was more inclined inwards.*

Inwrap – *(verb)* [archaic] spelling of enwrap. *I am about to inwrap this work.*

Iodine – *(noun)* the chemical element of atomic number 53, a halogen forming black crystals and a violet vapour. an antiseptic solution of this in alcohol. *Doctors advise to apply iodine solution over infections.*

Ion – *(noun)* an atom or molecule with a net electric charge through loss or gain of electrons, either positive or negative. *Exchange of ions takes place in a chemical reaction.*

Irascible – *(adjective)* hot-tempered; irritable. *People with irascible nature find it hard to work with colleagues.*

Ireful – *(adjective)* anger. *I am not going to bear his ireful attitude all the time.*

Iridescent – *(adjective)* showing luminous colours that seem to change when seen from different angles. *The party hall was glowing with iridescent lights.*

Iris – *(noun)* **1** a flat, coloured, ring-shaped membrane behind the cornea of the eye, with an adjustable circular opening in the centre. *Iris is an important part of our eyes.* **2** a plant with showy flowers, typically purple or yellow, and sword-shaped leaves. *The garden had many plants of iris.* **3** an adjustable diaphragm of thin overlapping plates for regulating the size of a central aperture. *Iris diaphragm has the function of controlling the pupil of eyes.* *(verb)* open or close in the manner of an iris. *The lens' aperture works the same as that of the iris of the eye.*

Irksome – *(adjective)* irritating annoying. *He was making irksome remarks on the fellow passengers.*

Iron – *(noun)* **1** a strong, hard magnetic silvery-grey metal, the chemical element of atomic number 26, used in construction and manufacturing. *Iron vessels are still used for cooking in our country.* **2** a tool or implement made of iron. fetters or handcuffs. *With iron around his wrists, he was taken to the cell.* **3** a hand-held implement with a heated flat steel base, used to smooth clothes and linen. *He sprinkled some water over the woolen cloth and started pressing it with an iron.* **4** a golf club with an angled metal head used for lofting the ball. *He reached the golf ground and picked up an iron to loft the ball.* *(verb)* **1** smooth with an iron.*Today, I ironed all my dresses on my own.* **2** settle a difficulty or problem. *With the help of her parents, she was able to iron her problems.*

Irradiate – *(verb)* **1** expose to radiation. *Some of the cancers are treated using irradiation.* **2** shine light on. *The stage was irradiated with the laser lighting.*

Irradiation – *(noun)* **1** the process or fact of irradiating or being irradiated. *The cancer patient was exposed to irradiation.* **2** optics the apparent extension of the edges of an illuminated object seen against a dark background. *We noticed the irradiation of light rays from torch as it was placed on a dark background.*

Irradicate – *(verb)* expose to radiation. *The seeds were irradicated into the soil.*

Irrational – *(adjective)* **1** not logical or reasonable. *We need to shed our irrational attitude in order to make progress.* **2** mathematics not expressible as a ratio of two integers. *An irrational number is that which cannot be expressed as a ratio of two integers.*

Irrealisable – impossible. *What an irrealisable demands they were making!*

Irreclaimable – *(adjective)* not able to be reclaimed. *They were shocked to learn that their money was irreclaimable.*

Irreconcilable – *(adjective)* **1** incompatible. *He knew from the very beginning that his nature was irreconcilable with his wife.* **2** mutually and implacably hostile. *Soon, they developed some irreconcilable differences. (noun)* any of two or more irreconcilable ideas, facts, etc. *These two statements are irreconcilables.*

Irrecoverable – *(adjective)* not able to be recovered or remedied. *My mother was suffering from an irrecoverable disease.*

Irredeemable – *(adjective)* **1** not able to be saved, improved, or corrected. *The accident has given him irredeemable injuries.* **2** on which no date is given for repayment of the capital sum. *The credits that he earned while playing were irredeemable.*

Irreducible – *(adjective)* not able to be reduced or simplified. *This complex theorem is irreducible.*

Irrefutable – *(adjective)* impossible to deny or disprove. *The actor has been facing some irrefutable charges.*

Irregularity – *(noun)* being irregular.*The Commonwealth Games saw many irregularities.*

Irregularly – *(adverb)* not conferming to usual rules. *That man is known for working irregularly.*

Irrelative – *(adjective)* rare unconnected; unrelated. *Your selection is irrelative to the fact that you have done post graduation.*

Irreligion – *(noun)* hostile to religion. *What he hates most about me is my irreligion.*

Irreligious – *(adjective)* indifferent or hostile to religion. *People who are irreligious have to face many things in society.*

Irremissible – *(adjective)* rare **1** unpardonable. *His crimes are irremissible.* **2** Of an obligation or duty (binding). *He is caught between an irremissible duty and a nagging wife.*

Irremovable – *(adjective)* incapable of being removed. *The cancer had spread to both the ovaries, thus making them irremovable.*

Irrepressible – *(adjective)* not able to be restrained. *His irrepressible desires was making him crazy.*

Irreproachable – *(adjective)* beyond criticism. *This great work is irreproachable.*

Irresolute – *(adjective)* uncertain. *In spite of his officer's faith in him, he was irresolute of his capabilities.*

Irresolution – *(noun)* uncertainty, hesitancy.*The constant irresolution on his part created a wrong impression on others.*

Irresolvable – *(adjective)* impossible to solve. *I have some irresolvable differences with my boss.*

Irrespective – *(adjective)* regardless of. *Irrespective of what I wanted, he continued doing dilly-dally.*

Irresponsible – *(adjective)* not showing a proper sense of responsibility. *Both the parents had an irresponsible attitude towards their kid.*

Irresponsive – *(adjective)* not responsive. *The newly born child was displaying an irresponsive behavior.*

Irretrievable – *(adjective)* not able to be retrieved. *The traces of the lost fossils are irretrievable.*

Irreverence – *(noun)* lack of respect for people or things that are generally respected. *He came there with irreverence in his heart.*

Irreverent – *(adjective)* disrespectful. *It was very bad on his part to display irreverent attitude towards his elders.*

Irreverential – *(adjective)* state of disrespect for things or person that are generally respected. *Over the years, he has become irreverential to everyone.*

Irreversible - *(adjective)* impossible to be reversed or altered. *Ageing is an irreversible process.*

Irrevocability - *(noun)* condition preventing any change in stand. *The main concern was irrevocability of the sale deed.*

Irrigable - *(adjective)* to supply water for irrigation. *A large part of India's land is irrigable.*

Irrigate - *(verb)* **1** supply water to by means of channels. supply with water. *The farmers use rain water to irrigate this area.* **2** [medicine] apply a flow of water or medication to an organ or wound. *The wound was irrigated with an antiseptic.*

Irrigation - *(noun)* the state of supplying water to land. *Irrigation is the main occupation of the villagers living in remote areas.*

Irrigator - *(noun)* one who supplies water to fields. *Large irrigators are used for supplying water to the fields.*

Irritable - *(adjective)* **1** easily annoyed or angered. *Would you stop doing irritable talks?* **2** medicine characterized by abnormal sensitivity. *The medicine proved to be irritable for her skin.* **3** biology able to respond actively to physical stimuli. *The insect was irritable to the external stimulus.*

Irritably - *(adverb)* tendency to become easily annoyed. *He said irritably, "Go away."*

Irritate - *(verb)* **1** make annoyed or angry. *She irritates me with her cribbing.* **2** cause inflammation in a part of the body. *The medicine irritated the affected area.* **3** [biology] stimulate an organism, cell, etc. to produce an active response. *The microbes got irritated when they were kept in hot water.*

Irritating - *(adjective)* causing annoyance, anger. *Would you stop irritating me?*

Irruption - *(noun)* enter somewhere by force.*The irruption of slang words in modern English is considered normal.*

Isagogics - *(plural noun)* introductory study, especially of the literary and external history of the bible prior to exegesis. *He was completely into isagogics.*

Islet - *(noun)* **1** a small island. *The water was surrounded by a number of islets.* **2** anatomy a portion of tissue structurally distinct from its surroundings. compare with island. *A number of islets were noticed in the sample of his anatomical organs.*

Iso - *abbreviation* **1** historical imperial service order. *ISO in the historical context stands for Imperial Service Order.* **2** international organization for standardization. *The new product has passed the ISO test.*

Isometric - *(adjective)* **1** of or having equal dimensions. *The two triangles drawn here are isometric.* **2** [physiology] in which tension is developed without contraction. *The muscles were showing isometric response to the stimuli.* **3** denoting a method of perspective drawing in which the three axes 120 apart. *The architect was looking carefully at the isometric drawing.* **4** [mathematics] without change of shape or size. *We were given lessons on isometric transformation.*

Italicise - *(verb)* write in italics. *Please italicize the important words.*

Italic - *(noun)* the branch of indo-European languages that includes Latin and the romance language. *Kindly note down the words that are printed in italics.(adjective)* relating to or denoting the italic group of languages. *The italic handwriting is quiet hard to practice.*

Itch - *(noun)* **1** an uncomfortable sensation or condition that causes a desire to scratch the skin. *The baby has developed itches on her back.* **2** [informal] an impatient desire. *His itch was prompting him to spend night with women. (verb)* 1 be the site of or experience an itch. *The cream itched me for long.* **2** [informal] feel an impatient desire to do something. *I am itching to get married.*

Itchiness - *(noun)* the condition of causing an itch. *The itchiness in summers is normal.*

Itchy - *(adjective)* having or causing an itch. *The powder was very itchy for my body.*

Item - *(noun)* an individual article or unit. a piece of news or information. an entry in an account.

Please make a list of all the items that you are going to buy. (avberb) [archaic] to introduce each item in a list. *He was writing: Item seven plates.*

Iterative – *(adjective)* **1** relating to or involving iteration, especially of a mathematical or computational process. *The program comprised of an iterative cycle.* **2** [grammar] another term for frequentative. *The iterative use of slangs is not a good idea.*

Itinerancy – *(noun)* the state of travelling from one place to another. *In ancient times, itinerancy was a common thing among traders.*

Itinerant – *(adjective)* travelling from place to place. *A number of itinerants had gathered there. (noun)* an itinerant person. *That man is an itinerant; he is very fond of doing trading.*

Itinerate – *(verb)* travel from place to place to perform one's professional duty. *He had to itinerate from place to place to do the trading.*

Itself – *(pronoun)* **1** used as the object of a verb or preposition to refer to a thing or animal previously mentioned as the subject of the clause. *The dog was so crazy that it bite itself.* **2** used to emphasize a particular thing or animal mentioned. used to emphasize what a perfect example of a particular quality someone or something is. *Software in itself is a complex thing to develop.*

Ivory – *(noun)* **1** a hard creamy white substance composing the main part of the tusks of an elephant, walrus, or narwhal. *Many jewels and handicrafts are made from ivory.* **2** the creamy-white colour of ivory. *Today, she has dressed up in an ivory coloured evening gown.* **3** [informal] the keys of a piano. *His hands were moving quickly over the ivory of the piano.* **4** [informal] a person's teeth. *His ivory-white teeth look good.*

Izard – *(noun)* a chamois. *The wild life sanctuary had many izards living in it.*

Jj

J - *(noun)* the tenth of the alphabet. *J is the tenth letter in the English alphabet.*

Jabber - *(verb)* talk rapidly and excitedly but with little sense. *He jabbered and I failed to understand him.* *(noun)* such talk. *Jabbering makes little sense.*

Jabot - *(noun)* an ornamental ruffle on the front of a shirt or blouse. *She wore a jabot which looked very attractive.*

Jacinth - *(noun)* a reddish-orange gem variety of zircon. *She wore a jacinth on her ring finger.*

Jackal - *(noun)* a slender, long-legged wild dog that often hunts or scavenges in packs, found in Africa and southern Asia. *Jackal is a wild dog and scavenger found in Asia and Africa.*

Jackass - *(noun)* **1** a stupid person. *You jackass! How dare you speak to me like that.* **2** a male ass or donkey. *The jackass brayed loudly.*

Jacket - *(noun)* **1** an outer garment extending to the waist or hips, with sleeves and a fastening down the front. *He wore a woollen grey jacket which suited him very well.* **2** an outer covering placed around something for protection or insulation. *The policemen wore bullet proof jackets.* **3** the skin of a potato. *The jacket of this pototo is very hard.*

Jacobin - *(noun)* [historical] a member of a radical democratic club established in Paris in 1789, in the wake of the French Revolution. *He was questioned for being a Jacobin.*

Jaconet - *(noun)* a lightweight cotton cloth with a smooth and slightly stiff finish. *He bought two metres of jaconet for his shirt.*

Jactitation - *(noun)* [medicine] restless tossing or twitching of the body. *He suffers from jactitation and is taking medicines.*

Jag - *(verb)* stab, pierce, or prick. *A thorn jagged his skin.* *(noun)* **1** a sharp projection. *He was wounded by jagged rocks.* **2** [chiefly Scottish] a prick or injection. *The iron rod had a jag at its end.*

Jail - *(noun)* a place for the confinement of people accused or convicted of a crime. *He was lodged in central jail.* *(verb)* put someone in jail. *He was jailed for five years.*

Jalap - *(noun)* a purgative drug obtained chiefly from the tuberous roots of a Mexican climbing plant. *You can take a dose of jalap for constipation.*

Jam - *(noun)* **1** [chiefly British] a conserve and spread made from fruit and sugar. *Children like mixed fruit jams a lot.* *(verb)* clog, congest, block. *The drain was jammed.*

Jangle - *(verb)* make or cause to make a ringing metallic sound. *The bells jangled in the temple.* *(noun)* an instance of jangling. *Jangling of bells reminded him of his home town.*

Janitor - *(noun)* [chiefly north American] a caretaker of a building. *The janitor was appointed after careful investigation.*

January - *(noun)* the first month of the year. *Visitors to Delhi found it to be a very cold January.*

Jape - *(noun)* a practical joke. *I was angry because he had played a very funny jape on me.* *(verb)* say or do something in jest or mockery. *He japed lightly and meant nothing by it.*

Jar - *(noun)* a wide-mouthed cylindrical container made of glass or pottery. *He took out some pickle form the jar.*

Jargon - *(noun)* words or expressions used by a particular profession or group that are difficult for others to understand. *He talked a lot of political jargon which left nobody wiser.*

Jasper - *(noun)* an opaque reddish-brown stone. *Jasper, being a precious stone, has many uses.*

Jaundice - *(noun)* 1 [medicine] yellowing of the skin due to an excess of bile pigments in the blood. *He has been hospitalized because of an advanced case of jaundice.* 2 bitterness or resentment. *He has a jaundiced eye and looks down at almost everybody.*

Jaunty - *(adjective)* having a lively and self-confident manner. *He is a jaunty fellow and hence liked by all.*

Jay - *(noun)* a bird of the crow family with boldly patterned plumage, typically with blue feathers in the wings or tail and a harsh chattering call. *Here is a Jay sitting over the tree, see how beautiful it looks.*

Jazz - *(noun)* a type of music of black American origin characterized by improvisation, syncopation, and a regular rhythm, and typically played on brass and woodwind instruments. *Jazz is my favourite music. (verb)* make something more lively. *Why don't you jazz up this room with more decorative flowers.*

Jealousy - *(adjective)* showing envious resentment. *Jealousy consumed her as she saw her boy friend with another girl.*

Jeer - *(verb)* make rude and mocking remarks at someone. *The crowd jeered at the speaker. (noun)* a rude and mocking remark. *His jeer upset her.*

Jejune - *(adjective)* 1 naïve and simplistic. *He is a jejune fellow.*

Jelly - *(noun)* 1 [chiefly British] a dessert consisting of a sweet, fruit-flavoured liquid set with gelatin to form a semi-solid mass. a small sweet made with gelatin. *The dinner was followed by jelly.* 2 any substance of a similar semi-solid consistency. *I found a jelly like substance in the garden. (verb)* set as or in a jelly. *Jelly sauce was served during brakfast.*

Jemmy - *(noun)* [chiefly British] a short crowbar. *The thieves forced open the door with a jimmy. (verb)* [informal] force open (a window or door) with a jimmy. *The burglar jemmied his patio doors.*

Jenny - *(noun)* 1 a female donkey or ass. *It is a jenny grazing over there.* 2 short for spinning jenny. *Jenny is an early type of spinning machine having sweral spindles.*

Jeopardize - *(verb)* put into a situation in which there is a danger arising from being on trial for a criminal offence. *He jeopardized his career by trying to bribe a clerk.*

Jeopardy - *(noun)* danger of loss, harm, or failure. *The peace process is in jeopardy.*

Jerk - *(noun)* 1 a quick, sharp, sudden movement. *A jerk near the tree attracted his attention.* 2 weightlifting the raising of a barbell above the head from shoulder level by an abrupt straightening of the arms and legs. *He lifted the weights with a jerk.* 3 [informal, chiefly north American] a contemptibly foolish person. *He is a jerk. (verb)* 1 move or cause to move with a jerk. *He jerked his shoulders for want of an answer.*

Jersey - *(noun)* 1 a knitted garment with long sleeves, worn over the upper body. *He wore a thick woolen jersey as it was bitter cold.* 2 a distinctive shirt worn by a player or competitor in certain sports. *The player wore a jersey having the teams initials on the back.* 3 small breed of light brown dairy cattle from jersey. *The jersey cattle is popular for its high butterfat content of its milk.*

Jess - *(noun)* a short leather strap that is fastened round each leg of a hawk, to which a leash may be attached. *The hawk is wearing jesses. (verb)* put a jess or jesses on a hawk. *The falcones jessed the hawks.*

Jest - *(noun)* a joke. *Forget it man, I said it in jest. (verb)* speak or act in a joking manner. *He jested most of the time in the party.*

Jester - *(noun)* [historical] a professional joker of fool at a medieval court. *There used to be court jesters in medieval times.*

Jestful - *(adjective)* entertaining. *He spoke is a jestful manner.*

Jestingly - *(adverb)* in a humorious manner. *He teased her jestingly.*

Jet - *(noun)* 1 a rapid stream of liquid or gas forced out of a small opening. *A jet of water drenched me.* 2 an aircraft powered by jet engines. *We travel long distances by jet aircrafts.*

Jetty - *(noun)* 1 a landing stage or small pier. *Let us walk over the jetty, it is beautiful to be* *surrounded with water.* **2** a bridge or staircase used by passengers boarding an aircraft. *As he stood on the jetty, someone pushed him down from behind.* **3** a construction built out into the water to protect a harbour, stretch of coast, or riverbank. *Engineers constructed jetties to control land eroseion by river.*

Jewel – *(noun)* **1** a precious stone, especially a single crystal or a cut and polished piece of a lustrous or translucent mineral. pieces of jewellery. a hard precious stone used as a bearing in a watch, compass, etc. *it is a very precious jewel and I am unable to buy it.* **2** a highly valued person or thing. *He is a jewel among writers.*

Jeweller – *(noun)* a person or company that makes or sells jewels or jewellery. *He is a jeweller by profession.*

Jezebel – *(noun)* a shameless or immoral woman. *She is a jezebel and as is out most of the nights.*

Jibe – *(noun)* an insulting or mocking remark. *Her jibes insulted him.* *(verb)* make jibes. *As he made jibes upon me, I grew angry.*

Jiffy – *(noun)* [informal] a moment. *He left in a jiffy.*

Jig – *(noun)* **1** a lively dance with leaping movements. a piece of music for jig, typically in compound time. *She jigged around him in the dance hall.* **2** a device that guides tools and holds materials or parts securely. *He is fishing with a jig.* **3** fishing a type of artificial bait that is jerked up and down through the water. *Fishing traevlers use jigs to catch big haul of fistes.* *(verb)* **1** dance a jig. **2** move up and down with a quick jerky motion. *The monkey was jigging the tree.* **3** equip with a jig or jigs. *The floor space was freshly jigged and tooled to insease production.* **4** fish with a jig. *A man jiggerd for squids.*

Jiggle – *(verb)* move or cause to move lightly and quickly from side to side or up and down. *The forest was full of jiggling monkeys.* *(noun)* an instance of jiggling. *He fell down in an instance of jiggling.*

Jill – *(noun)* variant spelling of gill. *He drank a Jill of wine.*

Jingle – *(noun)* **1** a light, loose ringing sound such as that made by metal objects being shaken together. *The jingle of bells could be heard from far.* **2** a short easily remembered slogan, verse, or tune. *The jingle of my cell phone is very catchy.* *(verb)* make or cause to make a jingle. *The faqir came to us jingling a bell.*

Jink – *(verb)* change direction suddenly and nimbly. *The truck jinked and came towards us fast.* *(noun)* a sudden quick change of direction. *A jink in the wind upset the boat.*

Jobber – *(noun)* **1** a principal or wholesaler dealing only on the stock exchange with brokers, not directly with the public. [north American] a wholesaler. *He is a jobber, and doesn't sell in retail.* **2** a person who does casual or occasional work. *He has long been a jobber and can do nothing regularly.*

Jobbery – *(noun)* the practice of using a public office or position of trust for one's own gain or advantage. *He has been accused of jobbery and an enquiry is set up against him.*

Jockey – *(noun)* a professional rider in horse races. *He is a skilful and known jockey.* *(verb)* struggle to gain or achieve something. *He jockeyed to get a job.*

Jocose – *(adjective)* formal playful or humorous. *He is a jocose fellow and liked by all.*

Jocular – *(adjective)* fond of or characterized by joking; humorous. *He is a jocular character.*

Jocund – *(adjective)* formal cheerful and light-hearted. *He is jocund by nature.*

Jogger – *(noun)* **1** a person who jogs. *He is a daily jogger in the park.* **2** tracksuit trousers worn for jogging. *I have bought a pair of joggers.*

Jogtrot – *(noun)* a slow trot. *The horse went on a jogtrot.*

Johnny – *(noun)* **1** a man. *Hey Johnny! Come here and take your money.* **2** a condom. *Use of johnnies is popular these days.*

Joinder – *(noun)* [law] the action of bringing together. *The court ordered the joinder of both witnesses.*

Joiner – *(noun)* **1** a person who constructs the wooden components of a building. *He is a joiner by profession.* **2** [informall] a person who readily joins groups. *He is quite a joiner.*

Joining – *(verb)* to link to connect. *Joining army was his main aim.*

Jointly – *(adverb)* together in association. *We jointly stood against the injustice.*

Joke – *(noun)* **1** a thing said to cause amusement. a trick played for fun. *He cut a joke and all laughed.* **2** [informal] a ridiculously inadequate person or thing. *You must be joking, how can such a thing happen? (verb)* make jokes. archaic poke fun at. *He is a joke is the office because of his strange attire.*

Joker – *(noun)* **1** a person who is fond of joking. *He is nothing but a joker, don't take him seriously.* [informal] a foolish or inept person. *Children are highly amused by jokers in the circus.* **2** a playing card with the figure of a jester, used as a wild card. *This pack of cards contains two jokers.* **3** US a clause in a bill or document affecting its operation in a way not immediately apparent. *A joker is a clause inserted in a legislative bill with the object of beating its purpose.*

Jokingly – *(adverb)* in a lighter vein. *I said it jokingly, please don't wind.*

Jollily – *(adverb)* cheerful, happy. *He jollily said all this.*

Jolliness – *(noun)* cheerfillness. *His jolliness is infectious.*

Jonquil – *(noun)* a narcissus with small fragrant yellow flowers and cylindrical leaves. *I have a few jonquils in my garden.*

Jordan – *(noun)* name of a country. *Jordan is a country situated in the middle-east.*

Josser – *(noun)* [British] a man, typically one regarded with contempt. an old josser. *He is an old josser and talks in coherently.*

Jostle – *(verb)* push or bump against roughly. struggle or compete forcefully for. *The crowd jostled to reach the famous actor. (noun)* the action of jostling. *As the bus abruptly stopped, he jostled against the door. The jostling crowd surged forward.*

Jot – *(verb)* write quickly. *He jotted down the notes. (noun)* a very small amount. *Jot is the smallest bit.*

Jotting – *(noun)* a brief note. *As he read the jotting he become upset.*

Jounce – *(verb)* jolt or bounce. *The ball jounced high.*

Journalist – *(noun)* a person who writes for newspapers or magazines or prepares news to be broadcast on radio or television. *He is a journalist by profession.*

Journalize – *(verb)* dated enter in a journal. *This article has been journalized by a famous reporter. He has journalized all the events date wise.*

Journey – *(noun)* an act of travelling from one place to another. *He has gone on a long journey. (verb)* travel. *They journeyed South India this summer.*

Jove – *(noun)* used for emphasis or to indicate surprise. *By jove! You are really a tall man!*

Jovian – *(adjective)* of or like the God Jove. *A search robot will be sent for Jovian exploration.*

Jowl – *(noun)* the lower part of a cheek, especially when fleshy or drooping. *Some people develop jowls in old age.* [north American] the dewlap of cattle or wattle of birds. *Some people prefer the jowls to other kinds of meat.*

Joyless – *(adjective)* cheerless, dismal. *He is a joyless and miserable fellow.*

Joyful – *(adjective)* feeling or causing joy. *He leads a joyful life.*

Jubilate – *(verb)* show great happiness. *It's time to sing and jubilate aloud before God.*

Jubilant – *(adjective)* happy and triumphant. *He was jubilant after having won the race.*

Jubilee – *(noun)* **1** a special anniversary, especially one celebrating twenty-five or fifty years of something. *He recently celebrated the silver jubilee of his marriage.* **2** Jewish history a year of emancipation and restoration, kept every fifty years. **3** a period of remission from the penal consequences of sin, granted by the roman catholic church under certain conditions for a year; at intervals of twenty-five years. *Jobilee yoer was proclaimed with rain-harm trompet.*

Judge – *(noun)* **1** a public officer appointed to decide cases in a law court. a person who decides the results of a competition. a personable or qualified to give an opinion: a good judge of character. *He has recently been appointed a judge.* **2** a leader having temporary authority in ancient Israel in the period between Joshua and the kings. *(verb)* form an opinion about, give a verdict on in a law court, decide the results of. *The judge decided the case in his favour.*

Judgeship – *(noun)* the person qualified and give opiniom. *To be eligible for judegeship, a lawyer must have 10 years of practise in a law court.*

Judicature – *(noun)* the administration of justice. *Our coustitution says that the legislature is separate from the judicature.*

Judicial – *(adjective)* of, by or appropriate to a law court or judge. *He has been sent to 10 days in judicial custody.*

Judiciary – *(noun)* the judicial authorities of a country. *The judiciary of a country must be impartial.*

Judicious – *(adjective)* having or done with good judgement. *It was a judicious decision.*

Jug – *(noun)* [British] a cylindrical container with a handle and a lip, for holding and pouring liquids. [north American] a large container for liquids, with a narrow mouth. *He has ordered a jug of juice.* *(verb)* **1** stew or boil in a covered container. *He is making jugged hare.* **2** [informal, chiefly north American] prosecute and imprison. *The hotel jugged him for trespassing cone wards.*

Jugful – *(noun)* contents in a jug. *She gave us jugfuls of water.*

Juggins – *(noun)* [British informal, dated] a simpleton. *You silly juggins, why did you listen to him?*

Juggle – *(verb)* continuously toss into the air and catch a number of objects so as to keep at least one in the air at any time. *He juggles balls faultlessly.* *(noun)* an act of juggling. *His juggling of bottles is worth seeing.*

Juggler – *(noun)* one who balances several activites at once. *He is a barman as well as a juggler.*

Jaguar – *(noun)* a large heavily built animal. *The jaguar is a large cat found in central and South America.*

Jugular – *(noun)* **1** of the neck or throat. *The murderer cut his jugular vein.*

Juice – *(noun)* **1** the liquid present in fruit or vegetables. a drink made from this. *He is fond of fruit juice.* **2** fluid secreted by the body, especially in the stomach. *Juice in our stomach should be in proper quantity.* **3** liquid coming from meat or other food in cooking. *The cabbage is best cooked in its own juice.* *(verb)* **1** extract the juice from. *Juice all oranges now.* **2** [informal] liven something up. *They juiced up the party.*

Juicy – *(adjective)* **1** full of juice. *It is a cent per cent juicy drink.* **2** [informal] interestingly scandalous. *You have given me a juicy news.* **3** [informal] profitable. *My investment in property has turned out to be juicy.*

Julep – *(noun)* a sweet drink made from sugar syrup, sometimes containing alcohol or medicine. *You seem to be tired, you need a drink of julep.*

July – *(noun)* the seventh month of the year. *It is hot in July in Delhi.*

Jumble – *(noun)* **1** an untidy collection of things. *Things are in a jumble in this place, sort them out.* **2** [British] articles collected for a jumble sale. *He has jumbled all the luggage.* *(verb)* mix up in a confused way. *It is a jumbled room with everything scattered.*

Jump – *(verb)* **1** push oneself off the ground using the muscles in one's legs and feet, pass over by jumping, get on or off quickly. *The cat jumped over the wall.* **2** move suddenly and quickly, make a sudden involuntary movement in surprise. *He jumped in surprise.* [informal] attack suddenly and unexpectedly. **3** pass abruptly from one subject or state to another. *The media jumped on him.* **4** rise or increase suddenly. *He jumped to her rescue.* **5** [informal] fail to stop at a red traffic light. *He jumped the traffic light.* **6** [informal] be very lively. *I am feeling very jumpy.* **7** accept eagerly. *The man jumped from a moving bus.* *(noun)* **1** an act of jumping. *The crowd jumped at the pickpocket.* **2** a sudden dramatic increase. a large or sudden change. *The sales figures of the company jumped sky high.*

Jumping - *(verb)* push oneself off a surface. *He is jumping with joy.*

Junction - *(noun)* **1** a point where two or more things, especially roads or railway lines, meet or are joined. *He was found wandering on a railway junction.* **2** [electronics] a region of transition in a semiconductor between a part where conduction is mainly by electrons and a part where it is mainly by holes. *The junction of the electric wires is here in the cavity of wall.* **3** a point where two or more things are joined. *I will meet you at the junction of the two rivers.*

Juncture - *(noun)* **1** a particular point in time. *You must start doing things at this juncture.* **2** a place where things join. *This is the juncture where all roads in the colony meet.*

Junior - *(adjective)* **1** of, for, or denoting young or younger people. [British] of, for, or denoting schoolchildren aged 7-11. *All juniors should gather here.* **2** denoting the younger of two with the same name in a family. *He is junior to me in age.* **3** low or lower in rank or status. *This matter can be handled by a junior officer.* *(noun)* **1** a person who is a specified junior. *I only teach junior classes.* **2** [British] a child at a junior school. *He is still a junior in school.* **3** [north American informal] a nickname for one's son. *Usually, sone are known as junior to the fathers name.* **4** a person with low rank or status. *Lieutent is a rank lower to a captain.*

Juniority - *(noun)* denoting young. *Juniority or seniority matters a lot corporate life.*

Junket - *(noun)* **1** a dish of sweetened and flavoured curds of milk, often served with fruit. *I like to eat junket after dinner.* **2** [informal] an extravagant trip, especially one by an official at public expense. *He often goes to junkets and spends lot of money.* *(verb)* [informal] go on such a trip.

Junta - *(noun)* a military or political group ruling a country after taking power by force. *Many countries are still ruled by the military junta.*

Jupiter - *(noun)* the largest planet in the solar system, fifth in order from the sun and one of the brightest objects in the night sky. *Astronomers are a lot interested in the planet Jupiter.*

Jural - *(adjective)* formal of or relating to the law. *It is a jural matter and advice must be sought from an expert.*

Jurisprudence - *(noun)* the theory or philosophy of law. *Jurisprudence must be fair in delivering fair openion.*

Jurist - *(noun)* an expert in law. *He is a famous jurist.*

Juror - *(noun)* a member of a jury. *He is a juror and a party to many a decision makings.*

Just - *(adjective)* morally right and fair. appropriate or deserved, well founded. *he is fair and just.* *(adverb)* **1** exactly or nearly at this or that moment. *Just a moment let me speak.* **2** hardly; by a little. *He has just reached the office.* **3** simply; *He is just an ordinary fellow.* only. *He just missed the train.* **4** expressing agreement. *He just manages to live. It is a just decision. It is a just act.*

Justice - *(noun)* **1** just behaviour or treatment. the quality of being just. *Justice must be done.* **2** the administration of the law or authority in maintaining this. *The observation was made by a justice of supreme court.* **3** a judge or magistrate. *Justices are expected to decide legal cases justly.*

Justiciable - *(adjective)* [law] subject to trail in a court of law. *We signed the agreement justicable under Indian Courts.*

Justiceship - *(noun)* just and fair treatment. *Indian justiceship is renowned for slow but fair treatment.*

Justly - *(averb)* fairly, morally. *I justly believe in the action.*

Justness - *(noun)* justifiable opinion. *The justness of the sentence is unquestionable.*

Jute - *(noun)* **1** rough fibre made from the stems of a tropical plant, used for making rope or woven into sacking. *Ropes among many other things are made from jute fibre.* **2** the plant cultivated for this fibre, with edible young shoots. *Jute is a plant which is cultivated for its fibre.*

Kk

K – *(noun)* **1** the eleventh letter of the alphabet. *The eleventh letter of alphabet.* **2** denoting the next after J in a set of items, categories, etc.

Kail – *(noun)* a vegetable. *Kail or kale is a kind of cabbage with large leaves and no compact round head.*

Kaiser – *(noun)* **1** [historical] the German emperor, the emperor of Austria, or the head of the holy Roman Empire. *Kaiser was the emperor of Austria, Germany.*

Kale – *(noun)* a hardy cabbage of a variety which produces erect stems with large leaves and no compact head. *Leaves of the kale cabbage are edible.*

Kaleidoscopical – *(adjective)* ability to change patterns. *The movement of dances was almost kaleidoscopical.*

Kalium – *(noun)* an element. *Kalium is the latin name for patassium.*

Kangaroo – *(noun)* a large plant eating marsupial with a long powerful tail and strongly developed hind limbs that enable it to travel by leaping, found only in Australia and New Guinea. *Kangaroo is the national animal of Australia.*

Kaolin – *(noun)* a fine soft white clay, used for making porcelain and china and in medicinal absorbents. *Kaolin clay is used for making china and porcelain.*

Kecks – *(plural noun)* [British informal] trousers or underpants. *He has bought a pair of kecks.*

Keenly – *(adverb)* showing eagerness or enthusiasm. *He is keenly interested in Maths.*

Keeness – *(noun)* eagerness. *She had great keenness to join dance classes.*

Keener – *(noun)* enthusiastic. *He is keener than his brother.*

Keeper – *(noun)* **1** a person who manages or looks after something or someone. *He has employed a housekeeper.* **2** short for goalkeeper. *Keepers and wicketkeepers have on important place in games.* **3** [American football] a play in which the quarterback receives the ball from the centre and runs with it. *Keeper is a kind of football in America.*

Keeping – *(noun)* the action of keeping something. *In keeping with my dad's desire, I have taken sports as my career.*

Keepsake – *(noun)* a small item kept in memory of the person who gave it or originally owned it. *This locket is a keepsake of my mother.*

Keg – *(noun)* a small barrel, especially one of less than 10 gallons or 30 gallons. *He is fond of keg beer.*

Kemp – *(noun)* a coarse hair or fibre in wool. *Please throw this bunch of kemp out.*

Ken – *(noun)* one's range of knowledge or sight. *He has great ken of this rocky terrain.*

Kennel – *(noun)* **1** a small shelter for a dog. *The dog is sleeping in its kennel.* **2** a boarding or breeding establishment for dogs. *I sent my dog to the kennel to be trained.* *(verb)* to palce or keep in kennel. *The dog has been kennelled.*

Kept – past and past participle of keep. *He has kept his promise.*

Keratose – *(adjective)* made of horny substance. *Some sponges ore composed of keratose substance.*

Kerchief – *(noun)* a piece of fabric used to cover the head. *He always carries a kerchief.*

Kernel – *(noun)* **1** a softer part of a nut, seed, or fruit stone contained within its hard shell. *The kernels of most nuts are edible.* **2** the central or most important part of something. *A grain or seed, as of a cereal grass, enclosed in a husk. This is the kernel of the problem.*

Kerosene – *(noun)* a light fuel oil obtained by distilling petroleum; paraffin oil. *Kerosene stoves are still used by people who don't have cooking gas.*

Kestrel – *(noun)* a small falcon that hunts by hovering with rapidly beating wings. *Many people living in mountains keep kestrels as pets.*

Ketchup – *(noun)* a spicy sauce made chiefly from tomatoes and vinegar, used as a relish. *Chilly tomato ketchups are quite popular.*

Kettle – *(noun)* a metal or plastic container with a lid, spout, and handle, used for boiling water. *Tea is boiling in the kettle.*

Key – *(noun)* **1** a small piece of shaped metal with incisions cut to fit the wards of a particular lick, which is inserted into the lock and rotated to open or close it or turning a screw, peg, or nut. a pin, bolt, or wedge inserted into a hole or between parts so as to lock the parts together. *I have lost my keys! How shall I open the door?* **2** a lever depressed by the finger in playing an instrument such as the organ, piano, flute, or concertina. *He pressed a few keys of the piano and a beautiful melody broke out.* **3** each of several buttons on a panel for operating a typewriter, word processor, or computer terminal. *Some keys of the computer key-board are not functioning properly.* **4** a lever operating a mechanical device for making or braking an electric circuit. *Answers to these questions are given in the key on last page.* *(verb)* to be excited or nervous. *He was all keyed up in excitement.*

Keyhole – *(noun)* a hole in a lock into which the key is inserted. *He tried to look through the keyhole.*

Keynote – *(noun)* a prevailing tone or central theme, setting out the central theme of a conference. *Read this keynote before you enter the conference room.*

Keystone – *(noun)* **1** a central stone at the summit of an arch, locking the whole together. *This is the keystone to the building.* **2** the central principle or part of a policy or system. *Social welfare remains the keystone of government's policy.*

Kibble – *(verb)* grind or chop. *The meal has been kibbled into pellets.* *(noun)* [north American] ground meat shaped into pellets, especially for pet food. *A bowl of kibble was placed before the dog*

Kibosh – *(noun)* [informal] put a decisive end to. *He decided to put the kibosh on the agreement.*

Kid – *(noun)* **1** leather made form a young goat's skin. *It is a belt of kid leather and very costly.* **2** [informal] a child or young person. *Hey kid! Don't you mess with me, you have yet to grow. Are you kidding me, how could you that?* *(verb)* give birth. *It is a kid jumping on the rocks.*

Kiddle – *(noun)* a dam or barrier in a river, with an opening fitted with nets to catch fish. *It is a kiddle here on the river with on opening to catch fish.* **2** an arrangement of fishing nets hung on stakes along the seashore. *Look at those kiddles arranged.*

Kiddy – *(noun)* a young child. *Kiddies play here.*

Kier – *(noun)* container. *This kier is of no use, it is broken.*

Kill – *(verb)* **1** cause the death of (a person animal, or other living thing). *The goat has been killed for meat.* **2** [informal] overwhelm with an emotion: the suspense is killing me. *The suspense in the film is almost killing me.* **3** pass. *The driver killed the truck engine and got down.* *(noun)* an act of killing, especially of one animal by another. *A lion has made a kill.*

Killer – *(noun)* **1** a person or thing that kills. *A serial killer is on prowl.* **2** [informal] a formidable impressive, or difficult thing. *His new novel is killer.*

Killing – *(noun)* an act of causing death. *Killing animals is forbidden in some religions.* *(adjective)* **1** causing death. *It is a killing disease.* **2** informal overwhelming or unbearable. *I have a killing schedule.*

Kiln – *(noun)* a furnace or oven for burning baking, and drying especially one for calcining lime or firing pottery. *He owns many brick kilns.*

Kilo – *(noun)* measure of weight. *Give me a kilo of potato.*

Kilogram – *(noun)* measure of weight. *A kilogram of onions will cost you 30 rupees.*

Kin – *(noun)* one's family and relations *All my kin live around here.*

Kind – *(noun)* **1** a class or type of people or things having similar characteristics. *The kind of people you mix with are not undesirable.*

2 character, nature. *He is a kind man by nature.* 3 each of the elements of the Eucharist. *His kind is rare. I am not the kind to abuse people. Will you be kind enough to let me decide the case?*

Kindliness – *(noun)* quality of being kind or gentle. *I would be much abliged for your kindliness.*

Kindling – *(noun)* 1 small sticks or twigs used for lighting fires. *It is cold and dark, kindling a fire is necessary.* 2 a process by which an event in the brain is initiated and its recurrence made more likely. *She kindled a flame of emotion in me.*

Kindly – *(adverb)* 1 in a kind manner. *He kindly asked me to have a seat.* 2 please used in a polite request. *Will you kindly sign this letter. Will you kindly call a cab.*

Kindness – *(noun)* the quality of being kind. *Kindness is a virtue.*

King – *(noun)* 1 the male ruler of an independent state, especially one who inherits the position by right of birth. *He is a king and can order anything.* 2 a person or thing regarded as the finest or most important in its sphere or group. *He is a king among actors.* 3 used in names of animals and plants that are particularly large, e.g. king cobra. *He is not rich enough but is a king by heart.* 4 the most important chess piece, which the opponent has to checkmate in order to win. *To win a game of chess one has to captive the opponent's king.* *(verb)* act in an unpleasantly superior manner. *He behaves like a king but has none of the qualition.*

Kingdom – *(noun)* 1 a country, state, or territory ruled by a king or queen. *The kingdom of Ashoka spread for and wide.* 2 a realm associated with a particular person or thing. *Kingdom of God is everywhere.* 3 the spiritual reign or authority of God, heaven as the abode of God and of the faithful after death. *Akbar ruled over vast kingdom.*

Kingless – *(adjective)* lacking a king. *The state remained kingless for some time after the death of the king.*

Kinglet – *(noun)* [chiefly derogatory] a minor king. *He is merely a kinglet ruling a small state.*

Kinglike – *(adjective)* like a king. *His behaviour is kinglike and rather irritating.*

Kingly – *(adjective)* typical of a king. *He visited his kingdom to perform his kingly duties.*

Kinless – *(adjective)* not having relative. *He is a kinless person.*

Kinsfolk – *(plural noun)* a person's blood relations, regarded collectively. *Most of his kinsfolk live abroad.*

Kinship – *(noun)* blood relationship. *In the very first meeting, I felt a strange kinship with her.*

Kirk – *(noun)* [Scottish & north English] a church, the church of Scotland. *During my stay in UK, I will visit the kirk.*

Kisser – *(noun)* a person who kisses someone. *He is a great kisser.*

Kitchen – *(noun)* a room where food is prepared and cooked. *The kitchen must be kept neat and clean.*

Kitchener – *(noun)* [historical] a range fitted with various appliances such as ovens plate warmer water heaters etc. *The new flats come equipped with modern kitchener.*

Kitsch – *(noun)* garish, tasteless, or sentimental art, objects, or design. *These are all kitsches, I never liked such works of art.*

Kloof – *(noun)* south African a wooded ravine or valley. *There are beautiful kloofs in South Africa.*

Knag – *(noun)* 1 a short dead branch. *The trunk of this tree is full of knags.* 2 a knot in wood. *Presence of kangs lower the price of a wooden log.*

Knap – *(noun)* [archaic] the crest of a hill. *There is a pathway winding around the knap of a hill.*

Knapper – *(noun)* one who shapes stones. *He is an expert knapper.*

Knapsack – *(noun)* a soldier's or hiker's bag with shoulder straps, carried on the back. *He is a tourist and always carries a knapsack.*

Knave – *(noun)* [archaic] a scoundrel. *He is a kvave and as such not to be trusted.*

Knavery – *(noun)* an act of dishonesty. *Indulging in acts of knavery may land you in jail.*

Knead – *(verb)* 1 work with the hands. *She is kneading wheat flour.* 2 massage as if kneading. *The kneading massage put her into deep sleep.*

Kneader – *(noun)* work into dough with hands. *She is an expert kneader capable of cooking 200 roties a day.*

Kneading – *(noun)* act of presing with hands. *She was kneading atta into dough.*

Knee – *(noun)* **1** the joint between the thigh and the lower leg. *He has been hurt in his knee.* **2** an angled piece of wood or metal supporting the beams of a wooded ship. *The knee work of the ship is phenomenal. (verb)* hit with the knee. *She kneed him in the groin.*

Knell – *(noun)* the sound of a bell, especially when rung solemnly for a death or funeral. something regarded as a warning of disaster. *The knell of the village bell tells us that somebody had died.*

Knew – past of know. *I knew he wasn't a thief.*

Knife – *(noun)* a cutting instrument consisting of a blade fixed into a handle. *The robber had a knife in his hand. (verb)* stab (someone) with a knife. *He was knifed to death by the robbers.*

Knighthood – *(noun)* title, rank. *He was honovred with knighthood on his birthday.*

Knit – *(verb)* **1** make by interlocking loops of yarn with knitting needles or on a machine. make in knitting. *My mother is knitting a sweater forme.* **2** unite or cause to unite. become joined. *He looked at me with knitted brows.*

Knob – *(noun)* **1** a rounded lump or ball, especially at the end or on the surface of something. *He turned the knob and opened the door.* **2** a rounded control switch or dial. *I pressed the knob and started the machine.* **3** a round button on a machine. *Press the knob.* **4** a small lump of something. *Feel the knob on my skin, is it dangerous?* **5** [chiefly north American] a prominent round hill. *Look at the knob of the hill!*

Knobble – *(noun)* [British] a small lump on something. *There is a knobble on the wall.*

Knotting – *(noun)* the action or craft of tying knots in yarn to make carpets or other decorative items. *Corpets are made by knotting the yarn.*

Knotty – *(adjective)* **1** full of knots. *It is a knotty rope.* **2** extremely difficult or intricate. *Solving India, China border issue is a knotty issue.*

Knowable – *(adjective)* becoming aware. *This idea is knowable to the core.*

Knowing – *(adjective)* being fully aware. *He looked at me with a knowing smile.*

Known – *(adjective)* **1** recognized, familiar, or within the scope of knowledge. *He is a well known person.* **2** publicly acknowledged to be. *It is a known fact.*

Knuckle – *(noun)* **1** a part of a finger at a joint where the bone is near the surface. *I bruised my knuckles. (verb)* rub or press with the knuckles. *Eyes should not be knuckled.*

Knurl – *(noun)* a small projecting knob or ridge. *It is a knurl here and a very lonely place.*

Kodak – *(noun)* a brand of camera. *Kodak has cused manufacturing cameras.*

Kraal – *(noun)* **1** a traditional African village of huts, typically enclosed by a fence. *African villages of huts are called kraaals.* **2** an animal enclosure. *They kept the animal in a kraal.*

Kymograph – *(noun) an* instrument for recording variations in pressure, e.g. in sound waves or in circulating blood. *A kymogroph is used for reording vibrations in circulating blood.*

Ll

L – *(noun)* **1** the twelfth letter of the alphabet. *L is the Roman numberal for 50.* **2** denoting the next after K in a set of items, categories. etc.

Labarum– *(noun)* a symbolic banner. *Labarum was Constantine's military symbol.*

Labefaction – *(noun)* [archaic] deterioration or downfall. *His labefaction occured soon after his business collapsed.*

Label – *(noun)* **1** a small piece of paper, fabric, etc. attached to an object and giving information about it, a piece of fabric sewn inside a garment and bearing the brand name, size, or care instructions. *The label on the shirt reads 'Peter England' 42.* **2** the name or trademark of a company, a company that produces recorded music. *Many music cassetts carry the label of T-series.* **3** a classifying name applied to a person or thing, especially inaccurately. *He was labelled the dumb kid on the class.* a word used to specify the subject area, register, or geographical origin of the word being defined. *She was describing the locations using labels.* [computing] a string of characters used to refer to a particular instruction in a program. *(verb)* **1** attach a label to. *He labelled the packet neatly with the address.* **2** assign to a category, especially inaccurately. *Many students felt they were wrongly labelled as failures.*

Labial– *(adjective)* **1** [chiefly anatomy & biology] of or relating to the lips or a labium. **2** phonetics requiring partial or complete closure of the lips requiring rounded lips. *Any thing that is in some way concerned with lips is known as labial.*

Laboratory – *(noun)* a room or building for scientific experiments, research, or teaching, or for the manufacture of drugs or chemicals. *There was a cage of white mice in the science laboratory for experimental purposes. Students were doing many tests in the chemistry laboratory.*

Laborious – *(adjective)* requiring considerable time and effort. showing obvious signs of effort. *It was a laborious job and he did it well.*

Labour – *(noun)* **1** work, especially hard physical work. *The labour was constantly working on the railway line.* **2** workers, especially manual workers, collectively. **3** the labour party. *He laboured hard but didn't earn much money.* **4** the process of childbirth from the start of uterine contractions to delivery. *Her labour pains were very intense.*

Laboured – *(adjective)* **1** done with great difficulty. *His laboured breathing could be heard form a distance.* **2** not spontaneous or fluent. *he laboured to get up to standing position.*

Labourer – *(noun)* a person doing unskilled manual work. *20 labourers were hired to clean the tank.*

Labourite – *(noun)* a member or supporter of a labour party. *He is a labourite and will not vote for any other party.*

Laburnum – *(noun)* a small hardwood tree with hanging clusters of yellow flowers followed by pods of poisonous seeds. *I have a laburnum in my garden. Don't eat its fruit.*

Labyrinth – *(noun)* a complicated irregular network of passages or paths, an intricate and confusing arrangement. *Once you enter this labyrinth underground, it will be very difficult for you to come out.*

Labyrinthine – *(adjective)* like a labyrinth, especially in being complicated or twisted. *It is labyrinthine puzzle and very difficult to solve.*

Lac – *(noun)* a resinous substance secreted as a protective covering by the lac insect, used to make varnish, shellac, etc. *Lac is an important ingredient of varnish.*

Lacerate – *(verb)* tear or deeply cut the flesh or skin. *The knife lacerated his skin.*

Laceration – *(noun)* cut or tear in skin. *He suffered lacerations to his face and hands.*

Laches – *(noun)*. [law] unreasonable delay in making an assertion or claim, which may result in refusal. *Laches resulted into refusal of his claim.*

Lacrymal – *(adjective)* **1** formal connected with weeping or tears. *He has some lachrymal problem.* **2** [physiology] concerned with the secretion of tears. *Lacrymal calls produce ters in eyes. (noun)* anatomy a small bone forming part of the eye socket. *Lacrimal bone is part of the eye socket.*

Lack – *(noun)* absence or deficiency of something. *His lack of common sense often puts his in trouble. (verb)* be without or deficient in. *he lacks confidence, that is why he doesn't succeed.*

Lackadaisical– *(adjective)* lacking enthusiasm and thoroughness. *His lackadaisical attitude was responsible for his failure in interview.*

Lackey – *(noun)* a servant, especially a liveried footman or manservant. *He looks more like a lackey the master of this mansion.*

Laconic– *(adjective)* using very few words; terse. *Laconic speech has become his habit.*

Lactation – *(noun)* **1** the secretion of milk by the mammary glands. *Lactation process starts soon after the birth of the baby.* **2** the suckling of young. *Lactation is a natural process.*

Lactic – *(adjective)* of relating to, or obtained from milk. *This is lactic powder.*

Lactometer – *(noun)* an instrument for measuring the density of milk. *A lactometer is used to find how watery is the milk.*

Lade – *(verb)* put cargo on board. *The laden ship started its journey.*

Lading – *(noun)* the action of loading a ship with cargo. *The labour were instructed to complete loading the ship in 6 hours.*

Ladle – *(noun)* **1** a large long handled spoon with a cup shaped bowl, used for serving soup or sauce. *The guests were served soup with a ladle.* **2** a container for transporting molten metal in a foundry. *Food was ladle among the poor. (verb)* serve or transfer with a ladle. *Molten metal is transported in a ladle in foundries.*

Lady– *(noun)* **1** a women. *She is a lady and as such you should respect her.* **2** a women of superior social position. *Lords and ladies were entertaened at the house.* **3** a courteous or genteel woman. *His wife is a lady with good manners.*

Laggard – *(noun)* a person who falls behind others. *(adjective)* slower than desired or expected. *He is a laggard and unlikely to succeed.*

Lagging– *(noun)* material providing heat insulation for a boiler, pipes, etc. *You can buy lagging from this shop.*

Lagoon– *(noun)* a stretch of salt water separated from the sea by a low sandbank of coral reef. *What a beautiful lagoon, let us go and swim.*

Laid – past or past participle of lay. *The hen has laid an egg. The table has been laid, please come for diner.*

Laird – *(noun)* a person who owns a large estate. *He is a laird and as such a very rich man.*

Laity– *(noun)* lay people. *He is a lay man and doesn't know much of anything. Laymen are usually employed as laborers.*

Lake – *(noun)* a large area of water surrounded by land. *Let us fish in this lake.*

Lame – *(adjective)* **1** disabled in the leg or foot. *He is a lame fellow and as such can't walk properly.* **2** unconvincingly feeble. *Don't give lame excuses for coming late.*

Lamentable – *(adjective)* deplorable or regrettable. *There was lamentable atmosphere in the house after the news of accident.*

Lamentably – *(adverb)* very bad, deplorable. *She was lamentably ignorant.*

Lamentation – *(noun)* experssion of grief, sorrow. *The accident area presentated a scene of lamentation.*

Lamenter – *(noun)* a grieving person. *Look ahead, don't be a lamenter worrying about the past.*

Laminate – *(verb)* overlay with a layer of protective material. *He got his certificates laminated. (noun)* a laminated structure or material. *Tetra packs are laminated packs.*

Lamp - *(noun)* **1** an electric, oil, or gas device for giving light. *Oil lamps are still burnt in villages without electricity.* **2** an electrical device producing ultraviolet or other radiation. *This lamp produces ultra violate rays.* *(verb)* supply with lamps; illuminate. *500 lawps have been supplied to the village.*

Lampoon - *(verb)* publicly satirize or ridicule. *He was lampooned by journalists.* *(noun)* a satirical attack. *The artist-faced lampoon from his critics.*

Lamprey - *(noun)* an eel like jawless fish, often parasitic, that has a sucker mouth with horny teeth and a rasping tongue. *The fisherman caught a lamprey in his net.*

Lance - *(noun)* a long weapon with a wooden shaft and a pointed steel head, formerly used by a horseman in charging. *The knight was hit by a lance.* **2** a similar weapon used in hunting fish or whales. *Whales are hunted with lance.* *(verb)* **1** medicine prick or cut open with a sharp instrument. *Sivgeous use steel lance to cut open the affected area.*

Lancet - *(noun)* a small, broad two-edged surgical knife or blade with a sharp point. *His skin was pricked with a lancet.*

Landau - *(noun)* a four-wheeled enclosed horse-drawn carriage with a removable front cover and a back cover that can be raised and lowered. *Royals in England used landau for fravelling even in the 20th century.*

Landed - *(adjective)* owning much land, especially through inheritance. consisting of or relating to such land. *He is lucky to have inherited huge property.*

Landing - *(noun)* **1** the process of coming to or bringing something to land. *The landing time of the plane has come.* **2** a place where people and goods can be landed from a boat. *People disembarked from the ship and were taken to the landing area.* **3** a level area tat the top of a staircase or between flights of stairs. *I stood on the landing and looked down.*

Landlady - *(noun)* a woman who leases land or property. *She is our landlady and has come to collect rent.*

Landmark - *(noun)* **1** an object or feature of a landscape or town that is easily seen and recognized from a distance. *Is there any landmark near your house whereby I can reach you easily.* **2** an event, discovery, or change marking an important stage or turning point. *The court has made a landmark decision.*

Landward - *(adverb)* towards land. *(adjective)* facing towards land as opposed to sea. *I have a house facing landwards as opposed to seawards.*

Languish - *(verb)* **1** grow weak or feeble. [archaic] pine with love or grief. *He is languishing is jail.* **2** be kept in an unpleasant place or situation. *He was languishing in jail.*

Lank - *(adjective)* long, limp, and straight. *He is a lanky fellow.*

Lantern - *(noun)* a lamp with a transparent case protecting the flame or electric bulb. the light chamber at the top of a lighthouse. *It is very dark outside take a lantern with you.*

Lap-dog - *(noun)* a person who is completely under the influence of another. *He is a lap-dog of a husband always obeying his wife blindly.*

Lapis-lazuli - *(noun)* a bright blue metamorphic rock consisting largely of laurite, used in jewellery. *Lapis-lazuli rock is used in jwellery.*

Lapse - *(noun)* **1** a brief failure of concentration, memory, or judgement. a decline from previously high standards. *He suffered from lapse of memory after the accident.* **2** an interval or time. *He returned home after a lapse of many years.* **3** [law] the termination of a right or privilege through disuse or failure to follow appropriate procedures. *My driving license has lapsed.* *(verb)* **1** become invalid because it is not used, claimed, or renewed. *He has lapsed into coma.* **2** cease to follow the rules and practices of a religion or doctrine. *Your time period for appeal in court has lapsed and there is nothing you can do about it.*

Lard - *(noun)* fat from the abdomen of a pig, rendered and clarified for use in cooking. *The meat is being cooked in lard.* *(verb)* **1** insert strips of fat or bacon in before cooking. **2** embellish excessively with esoteric or technical expressions.

Larder - *(noun)* a room or large cupboard for storing food. *All the wheat grain has been stored in the larder.*

Large - *(adjective)* **1** of considerable or relatively great size, extent, or capacity. *This medicine has a large spectrum.* **2** pursuing an occupation or activity on a significant scale. *Cloth mills produce cloth on a large scale.* **3** of wide range or scope. *He has invested large amount of money is business.* *(verb)* [British informal] go out and have a good time. *This house looks so large.* **5** *He has a large appetite for chicken meat.* **6** *He is a large hearted man and will forgive you.* **7** *He poured large amounts of love on her.*

Largely - *(adverb)* on the whole; mostly. *Largely speaking, people avoid breaking social norms.*

Larva - *(noun)* an active immature form of an insect or other animal that undergoes metamorphosis, e.g. a caterpillar or tadpole. *Larva is an immature form of insect.*

Larynx - *(noun)* [anatomy] the hollow muscular organ forming an air passage to the lungs and containing the vocal cords. *Something has gone wrong with his larynx, he is unable to speak.*

Lashing - *(noun)* **1** a whipping or beating. *He got a good lashing.* **2** a cord used to fasten something securely. *The dog is on the lash.*

Lassitude - *(noun)* physical or mental weariness; lack of energy. *He is suffering from lassitude and needs rest.*

Last - *(adjective)* **1** coming after all others in time or order; final. lowest in importance or rank. the least likely or suitable. *He came last in the race.* **2** most recent in time; latest. *You are the last man I'll believe.* **3** immediately proceeding in order, previous in a sequence or enumeration. *At last he agreed to join me in business.* *(adverb)* **1** on the last occasion before the present; previously. *The last news is that England has beaten India in cricket match.* **2** after all others in order or sequence. *These animals are the last of their species.*

Lastly - *(adverb)* in the last place; last. *Lastly, I would like to thank all who have come here.*

Latchet - *(noun)* [archaic] a narrow thong or lace for fastening a shoe or sandal. *The latchets of my shoes are worn out.*

Lately - *(adverb)* recently; not long ago. *Lately he has been behaving in a strange way.*

Lateral - *(adjective)* of, at, towards, or from the side or sides. *Lateral roots help plants take up water.* *(noun)* **1** a side part of something, especially a shoot or branch growing out from the side of a stem. *Cut back all the laterals of the plant and give it a proper shope.*

Latex - *(noun)* milky fluid found in many plants, notably the rubber tree, which coagulates on exposure to the air. *A synthetic product resembling latex is used to make paints.*

Lathe - *(noun)* a machine for shaping wood or metal by means of a rotating drive which turns the piece being worked on against changeable cutting tools. *Square pieces are being shaped on the lathe for making legs of the table.*

Lather - *(noun)* a frothy white mass of bubbles produced by soap when mixed with water. *He formed a thick layer of lather on his beard before shaving.* *(verb)* **1** form or cause to form a lather. *Soap doesn't from lather in hard water.* **2** rub with soap until a lather is produced. *He lathered himself gingerly under the showen.*

Latin - *(noun)* **1** the language of ancient Rome and its empire. *He is a Latin American.* **2** a native or inhabitant of a country whose language developed from Latin, e.g. a Latin American. *Language relating to Latin is spoken in Latin American countries.* *(adjective)* of or relating to the Latin language, relating to or denoting countries using languages that developed from Latin. *Spanish languge grew out of Latin.*

Latitude - *(noun)* **1** the angular distance of a place north or south of the equator. *That city is situated at an altitude of 50° North.* **2** regions with reference to their temperature and distance from the equator: northern latitudes. *You can find northern latitudes on the globe.* **3** scope for freedom of action of thought. *Journalists have considerable latitude in criticising government policies.*

Lattice - *(noun)* a structure or pattern consisting or strips crossing each other with square or diamond-shaped spaces left between. *I have covered the window in a lattice design.*

Laudable - *(adjective)* deserving praise and commendation. *His stage performance was laudable.*

Laudatory - *(adjective)* expressing praise and commendation. *The leader was surrounded by a laudatory crowd.*

Laughably - *(adverb)* worth laughing. *His actions on the stage where laughable pretensions.*

Laughing-stock - *(noun)* a person subjected to general mockery or ridicule. *He is a henpecked husband and hence a laughing stock among friends.*

Launderer - *(noun)* a person who washes clothes. *Your clothes are dirty, get them cleaned by a launderer.*

Laureate - *(noun)* a person given an award for outstanding creative or intellectual achievement: a nobel laureate. *Tagore was a nobel laureate.*

Lava - *(noun)* hot molten or semi-fluid rock reaped from a volcano or fissure, or solid rock resulting from cooling of this. *Lava came out of the crater of the exploding volcano.*

Lave - *(verb)* wash. *She ran cold water in the basin, laving her face and hands.*

Laver - *(noun)* an edible seaweed with thin reddish-purple and green sheet like fronds. *Some people are fond of eating laver products.*

Lawyer - *(noun)* a person who practices or studies [law], especially a solicitor or a barrister or an attorney. *As he had to appear in court he hired a lawyer.*

Lax - *(adjective)* not sufficiently strict, severe, or careful. *He is lax in attitude and will not interfere with our scheme.*

Layer - *(noun)* **1** a sheet or thickness of material, typically one of several, covering a surface or body. *A layer of white paint covered the walls of the room.* **2** a person or thing that lays something. *Hen lays eggs.* *(verb)* arrange or cut in a layer or layers. *It is the current trend for layered clothes.*

Lazar - *(noun)* [archaic] a poor and diseased person, especially a leper. *A leper used to be called lazar in old times.*

Lazy - *(adjective)* unwilling to work or use energy. *He is a lazy fellow and will keep on delaying for hours.*

Lea - *(noun)* an open area of grassy or arable land. *Let us pitch our tent here in the lea.*

Leaderless - *(adjective)* not having a person to command. *A leaderless crowd soon turns into a mob.*

Leadership - *(noun)* the action of leading a group. *We gained freedom under the leadership of Mahatma Gandhi.*

Leafage - *(noun)* plant strcture similar to leaves. *The leafage is very thick in this part of jungle.*

Leafless - *(adjective)* having no leaves. *Leafless trees have their own beauty.*

Leafy - *(adjective)* having many leaves or much foliage. *Green leafy vegetables have a lot of vitamin A.*

Leaky - *(adjective)* having a leak. *This is a leaky roof and droplets of water keep on trickling down.*

Leal - *(adjective)* [Scottish archaic] loyal and honest. *All these party men are leal.*

Leaning - *(noun)* tendency to subtend partiality to take sides. *This wall is not safe, a tree is leaning against it.*

Leanness - *(noun)* thin, little reward. *Girls tend to fallow the craze for leanness.*

Learned - *(adjective)* having or characterized by much knowledge acquired by study. *He is a highly educated and learned person.*

Learning - *(noun)* knowledge or skills acquired through experience or study or by being taught. *Learning while earning is a good scheme to follow.*

Lease-holder - *(noun)* owner of property by lease. *He is a holds a lease on this property.*

Least - *(pronoun)* smallest in amount, extent, or significance. *The least you can do is to help me unpack.* *(adjective)* used in names of very small animals and plants: least shrew. *I have been left with least amount of money.* *(adverb)* to the smallest extent or degree. *Being a drunkard, he is least bothered about his family.*

Leatherette - *(noun)* imitation leather. *It is a belt made of leatherette.*

Leathern - *(adjective)* [archaic] made of leather. *A leathern foam covered his face.*

Leathery - *(adjective)* having a tough, hard texture like leather. *This seems to be a leathery object.*

Leaved - *(adjective)* having a leaf or leaves of a particular kind or number. *It is a brown leaved plant.*

Leaven - *(noun)* a substance, typically yeast, added to dough to make it formant and rise. dough reserved from an earlier batch in order to start a later one fermenting. *Leaven is added to dough to ferment and make it rise.* *(verb)* permeate and modify or transform for the better. *The serious discussion should be leavened by humour.*

Leavings - *(plural noun)* things that have been left as worthless. *Leavings covered the entire sea beach.*

Lecher - *(noun)* a lecherous man. *He is a lecher, always running after women.*

Lechery - *(noun)* offensive sexual desire, lustfulness. *Don't indulge into lechery in this old age.*

Lecturer - *(noun)* a person who gives lectures, especially as a teacher in higher education. *He is a lecturer in English.*

Ledger - *(noun)* **1** a book or other collection of financial accounts. *Here is the ledger if you want you can check it.* **2** a flat stone slab covering a grave. *Look closely, some words are engraved on the ledger.* **3** a weight used on a fishing line to anchor the bait in a particular place. *A ledger is used for catching fish.* *(verb)* fish using a ledger. *A haul of fish was caught using a leder.*

Leech - *(noun)* **1** a parasitic or predatory annelid worm with suckers at both ends, examples of which were formerly used in medicine for bloodletting. *Formerly leeches were used in medicine for blood letting.* **2** a person who extorts profit from or lives off others. *(verb)* habitually exploit or rely on. *He is a leech who lives off others by exploiting them.*

Leer - *(verb)* look or gaze in a lascivious or unpleasant way. *He leered at her as she came is wearing shorts.* *(noun)* a lascivious or unpleasant look. *He gave her a sly leer.*

Lees - *(noun)* the sediment of wine in the barrel; dregs. *Wine barrels contain a lot of lees.*

Legacy - *(noun)* **1** an amount of money or property left to someone in a will. *He left a big legacy for his son.* **2** something handed down by a predecessor. *This poor condition of this house is a legacy of decades of neglect.* *(adjective)* denoting software or hardware that has been superseded but is difficult to replace because of its wide use. *The legacy of android has left other mobile application developers wondering what to do.*

Legal -*(adjective)* **1** of, based on, or required by the [law]. *It is a legal offence to smoke here.* **2** permitted by [law].

Legality - *(noun)* **1** the quality or state of being legal. *Legality of this rule is in question.* **2** obligations imposed by [law].

Legalization - *(verb)* to make something legal. *Legalization of something is a matter of legislature.*

Legalize - *(verb)* make legal. *It has been legalized that smoking in public places is an offence.*

Legally - *(adverb)* according to [law]. *Legally speaking same rule of law applies to everyone.*

Legatee - *(noun)* a person who receives a legacy. *He is a legatee to all his father's estate.*

Legation - *(noun)* **1** a diplomatic mission. *A legation has been sent to Pakistan.* **2** the official residence of a diplomat. *All legations are situated in diplomatic enclave.*

Legend - *(noun)* **1** a traditional story popularly regarded as historical but which is not authenticated. *There are many legends about king Dashrath.* **2** an extremely famous or notorious person: a careen legend. *Sunil Gavaskar is a cricketing legend.* **3** an inscription, caption, or key. *The Ashok Stambh with the legend 'Satyamev Jayate' is the official symbol of government of India.* *(adjective)* very well known. *Usain Bolt's' speed in 100 metres race is a living legend.*

Legendary - *(adjective)* of, described in, or based on legends. *Amitabh Bacchan is a legendary figure.*

Leghorn - *(noun)* **1** fine plaited straw. a hat made of this. *He is found of wering hats made of leghorn.* **2** a chicken of a small hardy breed. *Leghorn is a famous chicken breed in India.*

Legible – *(adjective)* clear enough to read. *It is a legible handwriting.*

Legibly – *(adverb)* readably clearly. *Try to write your notes legibly.*

Legislate – *(verb)* make or enact laws. *The legislative body legislates.*

Legitimacy – *(noun)* conferming to the [law]. *The legitimacy of this statement is doubtful.*

Legume – *(noun)* **1** a leguminous plant grown as a crop. *Legume is grown as a crop.* **2** a seed, pod, or other edible part of a leguminous plant, used as food. *The food is full of fruits vegetables and legumes.*

Leguminous – *(adjective)* botany relating to or denoting plants of the pea family typically having seed in pods, distinctive flowers, and root nodules containing nitrogen-fixing bacteria. *Many plants are leguminous bearing seeds in pods.*

Leman – *(noun)* [archaic] a lover or sweetheart. *She is my leman.*

Lemon – *(noun)* **1** a pale yellow oval citrus fruit with thick skin and fragrant, acidic juice. a drink made from or flavoured with lemon juice. *Would you like to have some lemon juice.* **2** the evergreen citrus tree which produces this fruit. *I have a lemon tree in my garden.* **3** a pale yellow colour. *I would like to buy a lemon coloured shirt.*

Lend – *(verb)* **1** grant to the use of something on the understanding that it shall be returned. *Could you lend me some money?* **2** allow the use of a sum of money under an agreement to pay it back later, typically with interest. *His business is to lend money on interest.* **3** contribute or add. *You must lend your time for the noble cause.*

Lendable – *(adjective)* allow someone to use something. *He doesn't have any lendable assets.*

Lender – *(noun)* a person or firm that lends money. *He is a money lender by profession.*

Length – *(noun)* **1** the measurement or extent of something from end; the greater or greatest of two or more dimensions of a body. *The length of this bridge is five kms.* **2** the amount of time occupied by something. *Delivery must be within a reasonable length of time.* **3** the quality of being long. *The length of these pants is not in proportion.* **4** the full distance that a thing extends for: the muscies running the length of my spine. *I can go to any length to win her love.* **5** the extent of a garment in a vertical direction when worn. *This garment is knee-length.* **6** prosody & phonetics the metrical quantity or duration of a vowel or syllable. *In English 'beat' is of greater lenth than in English 'bit'.* **7** [cricket] the distance from the batsman at which a well-bowled ball pitches. *A good bowler always pitches the ball at suitable length from the batsman.*

Lengthen – *(verb)* make or become longer. *The shadows lengthen as the sun sets.*

Lengthy – *(adjective)* of considerable or unusual duration. *We arrived at the conclusion after a lengthy discussion.*

Leniency – *(noun)* quality of being merciful. *Too much leniency with children often spoils them.*

Lenient – *(adjective)* merciful or tolerant. *He is lenient by nature.*

Lenity – *(noun)* poetic kindness; gentleness. *One of his qualities is lenity.*

Lenten – *(adjective)* of, in, or appropriate to lent. *This food without meet is appropriate to lent.*

Lentil – *(noun)* a high-protein pulse which is dried and then soaked and cooked prior to eating. *Lentil or mussur dal is full of proteins.* **2** the plant which yields this pulse, native to the Mediterranean and Africa. *The lentil plant originated in Africa.*

Lentisc – *(noun)* the mastic tree. *Lentisc is a mastic tree bearing gum.*

Leo – *(noun)* [astronomy] a large constellation said to represent the lion slain by Hercules. *Leo is a zodiacal constellation between virgo and cancer.* **2** [astrology] the fifth sign of the zodiac. *He is a leo as he was born on 25th of July.*

Leopard – *(noun)* a large solitary cat that has a fawn or brown coat with black spots, found in the forests of Africa and southern Asia. *Leopards can be seen in zoo or jungles of Asia and Africa.*

Leper – *(noun)* **1** a person suffering from leprosy. *These days there is treatment available for lepers.* **2** a person who is shunned by others. *He is treated like a leper no one wants to sit with him.*

Leprosy – *(noun)* a contagious bacterial disease that affects the skin, mucous membrane, and nerves, causing discoloration and lumps on the skin and, in severe cases, disfigurement and deformities. *Once leprosy was inerrable and was deemed as a result of evil deeds in past life.*

Lese-majesty – *(noun)* the insulting of a sovereign; treason. *Lese-majesty resulted in his being hanged on scaffold.*

Lesion – *(noun)* chiefly medicine a region in an organ or tissue which has suffered damage through injury or disease. *He suffers from lesion in right arm as a result of an accident.*

Less – *(determine & pronoun)* **1** a smaller amount of; not as much. *The class has less students today.* **2** fewer in number. *(adjective)* [archaic] of lower rank or importance: James the less. *Les of anger is always good. (adverb)* to a smaller extent; not so much. *(preposition)* minus.

Lessen – *(verb)* make or become less. *It lessened my anger when he begged pardon. Let me lessen your burden, give me those bags.*

Lest – *(conjunction)* **1** with the intention of preventing; to avoid the risk of. *Don't drive rashly lest you should have an accident.* **2** because of the possibility of.

Lethal – *(adjective)* **1** sufficient to cause death. *A lethal overdose of sleeping pills took his life.* **2** very harmful or destructive.

Lethargy – *(noun)* **1** a lack of energy and enthusiasm. *He lives a lack lustre life as a result of lethargy.* **2** medicine a pathological state of sleepiness or deep unresponsiveness. *He is in deep lethargy and needs medical treatment.*

Lettuce – *(noun)* a cultivated plant of the daisy family, with edible leaves that are eaten in salads. *Lettuce is an important part of salad.*

Leveret – *(noun)* a young hare in its first year. *I have caught a leveret and I'll make it a pet.*

Leviable – *(adjective)* possibility of being taxed, fined. *Octroi tax is leviable on out of state products.*

Leviathan – *(noun)* **1** a sea monster. a very large aquatic creature, especially a whale. something very large or powerful. *Many leviathans can be seen in this part of sea.* **2** an autocratic monlarch or state.

Levity – *(noun)* the treatment of a serious matter with humour or lack of respect. *You are a highly qualified doctor and levity doesn't behove you.*

Levy – *(noun)* **1** the imposition of a tax, fee, fine, or sub-scription. a sum of money raised by such a levy. *This year the government has collected a huge levy.* **2** an item or set of items of property seized to satisfy a legal judgment. *None of the goods were subjected to levy.* **3** [archaic] a body of enlisted troops. *He sought to levy one man from each village for military serious. (verb)* impose or seize as a levy. *A tax of 10 per cent was levied on all imported goods.*

Lewd – *(adjective)* crude and offensive in a sexual way. *His lewd remarks angered her.*

Lexicon – *(noun)* the vocabulary of a person, language, or branch of knowledge. *This shop has a number of good lexicons.*

Liability – *(noun)* **1** the state of being liable. *He is more of a liability than an asset.* **2** a thing for which someone is liable, especially a financial obligation. *Auditors are assessing the firm's assets are liabilities.* **3** a person or thing likely to cause one embarrassment or put one at a disadvantage. *Presence of drunken dancers had become a liability for the club.*

Liar – *(noun)* a person who tells lies. *Don't believe him, he is a notorious liar.*

Libel – *(noun)* [law] the publication of a false statement that is damaging to a person's reputation. compare with slider. such a statement; a written defamation. *This newspaper has published a libel and a case has been filed against its editor. (verb)* [law] defame by publishing a libel. *To court found that he was labeled by the magazine.*

Liberally– *(adverb)* in a generous way. *She liberally gifted all poor children.*

Liberate – *(verb)* **1** set free, especially from imprisonment or oppression. free from social conventions, especially with regard to sexual roles. *Many prisoners were liberated on Independence Day.* **2** chemistry & physics release as a result of chemical reaction or physical decomposition. *An educated society can afford to be liberated from narrow sexual views.*

Liberation – *(noun)* setting free from oppression. *Liberation was granted to many African colonies by the British government.*

Liberator – *(noun)* a person who liberates one from oppression. *he was seen as a liberator of persons working as bonded labourers.*

Libertine – *(noun)* a person who is freely indulgent in sensual pleasures. *He is a libertine and whole-heartedly enjoys life.*

Librate – *(verb)* oscillation of the moon. *Astrologers liberate the position at the time of birth to predict future.*

Libration – *(noun)* astronomy an apparent or real oscillation of the moon, by which parts near the edge of the disc that are often not visible from the earth sometimes come into view. *Liberation helps astrologers predict future of a person or thing or a country.*

Lid – *(noun)* **1** a removable or hinged cover for the top of a container. *One of the lids of the containers is missing.* **2** an eyelid. *Her eyes were hooded beneath heavily painted lids.*

Life – *(noun)* **1** the condition that distinguishes animals and plants from inorganic matter, including the capacity for growth, functional activity, and continual change preceding death. living things and their activity. a particular type or aspect of people's existence; school life. *Compared to plants and trees, there is apparently no life in stones.* **2** the existence of an individual human being or animal. a biography. each of a specified number of chances each player has before being put out. *Life keeps on changing till death.* **3** [informal] a sentence of imprisonment for life. *How exciting was the shoal life!* **4** vitality, vigour, or energy. *High energy food restores life to a tired person.* **5** based on a living rather than an imagined form: a life drawing. *He has been sentenced to life imprisonment. He is a person full of life. All humans and animals have life till death puts them about of existence.*

Lifelong – *(adjective)* lasting or remaining in a particular state throughout a person's life. *Lifelong habits die hard.*

Lifetime – *(noun)* **1** the duration of a person's life. the duration of a thing or its usefulness. *He didn't do even a single charitable act throughout his lifetime.* **2** [informal] a very long time. *The actor was given a lifetime achievement award.*

Liftable – *(adjective)* quality of being lifted. *Mount arteries always carry easily liftable packs.*

Lightness – *(noun)* source of illumination. *The lightness of these shoes is remarkable.*

Likeable – *(adjective)* pleasant; easy to like. *He is a likeable person welcomed by all.*

Likelihood – *(noun)* the state or fact of being likely. *In all likelihood, he will be arriving tomorrow.*

Liken – *(verb)* point out the resemblance of someone or something to. *Casteism is likened to a deadly disease.*

Likeness – *(noun)* resemblance. the semblance or outward appearance of. a portrait or representation. *Likeness between the father and son is remarkable.*

Likewise – *(adverb)* also; moreover. *He, likewise his brother is quarrelsome.*

Limitation – *(noun)* **1** a restriction. a defect or failing. *Every human being has his or her limitations.* **2** [law] a legally specified period beyond which an action may be defeated or a property right is not to continue. *As regards property a limitations of two years has been imposed on him.*

Limited – *(adjective)* **1** restricted in size, amount, or extent. not great in ability. *It is a private limited company and not a government concern.* **2** exercised under limitations of power prescribed by a constitution. *He has limited abilities.* **3** [British] denoting a limited company. *He was given limited amount of facilities in the hospital.*

Limitations – *(noun)* restriction. *All government officials have limitations to their discretionary powers.*

Limn – *(verb)* poetic depict or describe in paining or words. suffuse or highlight with bright colour or light. *The painting was limned to attract customers.*

Limner – *(noun)* a painter of portraits. *He is a renowned limner having painted many portraits.*

Limp – *(verb)* walk with difficulty. *He walked limpingly.*

Limpness – *(noun)* state of walking with great difficulty. *His limpness caused him to walk slowly.*

Lineage – *(noun)* **1** ancestry or pedigree. *His lineage is royal.* **2** [biology] a sequence of species each of which is considered to have evolved from its predecessor. *The lineage of humans goes back to great apes.*

Lineal – *(adjective)* in a direct line of descent or ancestry. *The lineal crawl of ants is remarkable.*

Linger – *(verb)* be slow or reluctant to leave. spend a long time over. be slow to disappear or die. *He lingered on till he was firmly asked to leave. Life linger on till death. He lingered in the club till 2 a.m.*

Lingerer – *(noun)* one who is reluctant to leave. *He is a lingerer and want go easily.*

Lingering – *(adjective)* lesting for a long time, slow to end. *His lingering figure caused disturbance to us.*

Linguist – *(noun)* a person skilled in foreign languages. *He is a well known linguist.*

Link – *(noun)* relationship between two things or situations. *Police have found his name linked to a terrorist outfit.*

Linn – *(noun)* [Scottish archaic] a waterfall. the pool below a waterfall. a steep precipice. *Let's take bath in this linn.*

Liny – *(adjective)* [informal] marked with lines. *It is a liny piece of paper.*

Lion – *(noun)* **1** a large tawny-coloured cat of Africa and NW India, of which the male has a shaggy mane. *He fought like a lion in the battle.* **2** a brave, strong, or fierce person. dated a celebrity. *His is a lion among men.*

Lip – *(noun)* **1** either of the two fleshy parts forming the edges of the mouth opening. another term for labium. *Beautiful lips make a face attractive.* **2** the edge of a hollow container or an opening. *The lip of this cup is a little rough.* *(verb)* lap against. *Beaches were lipped by the sea water.*

Liquefaction – *(noun)* process to make liquid. *Liquefaction is the process to convert gas into liquids.*

Liquefier – *(noun)* means to make liquid. *Use of liquefier is necessary to change gases into liquids.*

Liquescent – *(adjective)* poetic becoming or apt to become liquid. *Ice is liquescent.*

Liquidity – *(noun)* finance the availability of liquid assets to a market or company. liquid assets. *How much your liquid assets are worth?*

Liquidation – *(noun)* process of liquidating a business. *The firm went into liquidation last year.*

Liquorice – *(noun)* a sweet, chewy, aromatic black substance made from the juice of a root and used as a sweet and in medicine. *Liquourice has a sweet taste and is used in medicine.*

Listener – *(noun)* a person who listens. *I like him as he is a patient listener.*

Listless – *(adjective)* lacking energy or enthusiasm. *I found him listless and lying in bed.*

Literacy – *(noun)* the ability to read and write. *A literacy drive has been launched in the village.*

Literally – *(adverb)* **1** taking words in their usual or most basic sense without metaphor or allegory. free from distortion. [informal] absolute. *Literally speaking, the matter is closed, no more discussion.* **2** representing the exact words of the original text. *The article was literally copied.*

Litigation – *(noun)* the process of taking legal action. *No firm wishes to go into litigation.*

Litigious – *(adjective)* tending to go to [law] to settle disputes. concerned with or disputable by litigation. *He is a litigious fellow always quarreling and raising disputes.*

Liturgics – *(plural noun)* the study of liturgies. *Liturgies are often perfumed in set places e.g. mosques or temples.*

Liven – *(verb)* make or become more lively or interesting. *The atmosphere became livened as she sang melodiously.*

Livid - *(adjective)* [informal] furiously angry. *He was livid with anger.*

Living - *(noun)* an income sufficient to live on, or the means of earning it. *He earns his living by working as a labourer. (adjective)* alive. still spoken and used. perennially flowing. *There is a lot of difference between the living and non-living. He is a living example of politeness.*

Lizard - *(noun)* a reptile that typically has a long body and tail, four legs, movable eyelids, and a rough, scaly, or spiny skin. *I find lizards very repulsive.*

Lo - *(exclamatory)* [archaic] used to draw attention to an interesting event. *Lo! here comes our esteemed guest.*

Load - *(noun)* **1** a heavy or bulky thing that is being carried or is about to be carried. the total number or amount that can be carried in a vehicle or container: a carload of people. *The load is about to be moved in a truck.* **2** a weight or source of pressure. the amount of work to be done by a person or machine. a burden of responsibility, worry, or grief. *The actor was loaded with complements. Only 1,000 kg of load can be carried in this vehicle.* **3** [informal] a lot of. plenty. *The work load is prouing quite costly to my health.* **4** the amount of power supplied by a source. the resistance of moving parts to be overcome by a motor. electronics an impedance or circuit that receives or develops the output of a transistor or other device. *This factory has a sanctioned load of 100 KV. (verb)* **1** put a load on or in a vehicle, ship, etc. take on a load. *He has loads of money.* **2** make carry or hold a large amount of heavy things. supply someone or something in overwhelming abundance or to excess with. *He has been granted two KW of load by the electricity supplying authority.* **3** bias towards a particular outcome. *After having taken a heavy load the cargo ship started its journey.*

Loader - *(noun)* **1** a machine or person that loads something. *About fifteen persons worked round the clock as loaders to load the cargo ship.* **2** a gun, machine, or truck which is loaded in a specified way: a front-loader. *This front-loader is used to shrift heavy materials within the factory area.*

Loan - *(noun)* a thing that is borrowed, especially a sum of money that is expected to be paid back with interest. the action of lending. short for loanword. *The bank gave him a loan of one lakh rupees. (verb)* give as a loan. *He offered to buy her a dinner set in exchange for a movie.*

Loath - *(adjective)* reluctant; unwilling: I was loath to leave. *I was loath to leave the party.*

Loathe - *(verb)* feel hatred or disgust for. *She loathed his presence.*

Loathing - *(noun)* feeling of dislike. *He felt nothing but loathing for her.*

Loathsome - *(adjective)* causing hatred or disgust. *I find centipedes loathsome.*

Lobelia - *(noun)* a plant of the bellflower family, typically with blue or scariest flowers. *I have just bought a lobelia for my garden.*

Local - *(adjective)* relating or restricted to a particular area or one's neighbourhood. relating to a particular region or part, or to each of any number of these. *A local infection.* computing only available for use in one part of a programme. *(noun)* a local person or things. [British informal] a pub convenient to a person's home. [north American] a local branch of a trade union. *The local post office is quite near my house. It is a local infection on and can be treated in the dispensary. A local person told me your address.*

Locality - *(noun)* the position or site of something. an area or neighbourhood. *Is there any cinema house in your locality?*

Locate - *(verb)* **1** discover the exact place or position of. *I located his address with much difficulty.* **2** be situated in a particular place. [north American] establish oneself or one's business in a specified place. *Will you look into the map to find where this city is located?*

Location - *(noun)* **1** a particular place or position. the action or process of locating. *The director was on look out for a suitable location to shoot his film.* **2** an actual place in which a film or broadcast is made, as distinct from a simulation in a studio. *It took him time to locate the building.*

Lockage – *(noun)* the construction or use of locks on waterways. the amount of rise and fall of water levels resulting from the use of locks. *This lockage system is quite difficult to operate.*

Locket – *(noun)* a small ornamental case worn round a persons' neck on a chain and used to hold things of sentimental value. *He wears a locket which has his wife's photo.*

Lock-stitch – *(noun)* a stitch made by a sewing machine by firmly linking together two threads or stitches. *These stitches are made by a lock-stitch machine.*

Lock-up – *(noun)* **1** a jail, especially a temporary one. *He was put is lock-up for a hit and run case.* **2** British non-residential premises that can be locked up, typically a garage. *This is a typical lock-up garage.* **3** an investment in assets which cannot readily be realized or sold on in the short term. *Don't invest in poorly managed companies your investment may get locked up.*

Locomotor – *(adjective)* [chiefly biology] of or relating to locomotion. *Locomotor modes of all creatures are different.*

Locust – *(noun)* a large, mainly tropical grasshopper which migrates in vast swarms and is very destructive to vegetation. *A big swarm of locust descended on the fields.*

Locution – *(noun)* a word or phrase, especially with regard to style or idiom. a person's style of speech. *His locution is unique.*

Lofty – *(adjective)* **1** of imposing height. *It is a lofty building.* **2** noble; elevated. haughty and aloof. *He is a high class officer and very lofty.*

Loftiness – *(noun)* state of being noble. *His loftiness know no bounds.*

Logarithm – *(noun)* a quantity representing the power to which a fixed number must be raised to produce a given number. *Logarithms simplifies calculations.*

Logger – *(noun)* a person who fells trees for timber. *He is a lagger whose profession is to cut trees for tember.*

Logician – *(noun)* one who justifies with logic. *He does good reasoning, he is a fine logician.*

Loiter – *(verb)* stand around or move without apparent purpose. *He loitered round the place.*

Loiterer – *(noun)* waiting around without any reason. *He is a loiterer and does no work.*

Loitering – *(noun)* state of waiting without reason. *He was found loitering and police questioned him.*

Lollop – *(verb)* move in an ungainly way in a series of clumsy bounds. *Some animals lollop.*

Lone – *(adjective)* having no companions; solitary. lacking the support of others. poetic unfrequented and remote. *He is a lone wolf, mixing with nobody.*

Loneliness – *(noun)* without companion. *He began to suffer as loneliness surrounded him.*

Longevity – *(noun)* long life. *Longevity has been a matter of study for scientists since long.*

Longevous – *(adjective)* rare. *Tortoise is a longevous specie.*

Longish – *(adjective)* great distance. *The railway platform was quite longish.*

Longitude – *(noun)* the angular distance of a place east or west of a standard meridian, especially the Greenwich meridian. *Longitude lines are drawn on a map or globe for mearwing the distance of a place form Greenwich meridian.*

Looker-on – *(noun)* a person who behaves more like a spectator than a participant. *The lookers-on stared at the two filleting persons in a public place.*

Looking – *(noun)* attention towards a particular direction. *Looking down I saw a man climbing stairs.*

Loom – *(verb)* appear as a vague form, especially one that is threatening. seem about to happen. *(noun)* a vague first appearance of an object seen in darkness or fog, especially at sea. *An iceberg loomed large over the ship.*

Loon – *(noun)* [informal] a silly or foolish person. *He is a loon and talks nonsense.*

Loophole – *(noun)* an ambiguity or inadequacy in the [law] or a set of rules. *Lawyers are smart enough to find loopholes in the law.*

Loosely – *(adverb)* frivolous. *People avoid him as he is in the habit of talking loosely.*

Looseness – *(noun* not fitting properly. *I couldn't wear the pants because of their looseness.*

Loosen – *(verb)* make or become loose. make more lax. warm up in preparation for an activity. *I got my trousers loosened by a tailor as they were very tight.*

Lore – *(noun)* a body of traditions and knowledge on a subject: farming lore. *Lore is an important part of any social culture.*

Loser – *(noun)* a person or thing that loses or has lost. [informal] a person who fails frequently. *He is a loser and will never amount to anything.*

Lotus – *(noun)* a large water lily, now or formerly regarded as sacred. *Lotus is regarded as a sacred flower in India.*

Lounger – *(noun)* **1** a comfortable chair, especially an outdoor chair that reclines. *I intend to buy a lounger and relax on it.* **2** a person spending their time lazily or in a relaxed way. *He is a lounger and can be seen relaxing in his easy-chair.*

Lout – *(noun)* an uncouth or aggressive man. *He is a lout and sure to quarrel with you sooner or later.*

Loutish – *(adjective)* rude and aggressive person. *He is a loutish fellow. Don't mix with him.*

Love – *(noun)* **1** an intense feeling of deep affection. a deep romantic or sexual attachment to someone. a great interest and pleasure in something. affectionate greetings. *I love my granddaughter a lot.* **2** a person or thing that one loves. *I love playing chess.* [British informal] a friendly form of address. *He loves his wife with.* **3** a score of zero. *he couldn't play properly and lost the game six love.* *(verb)* feel a deep romantic or sexual attachment to. like very much. showing love or great care. *Kam Dev is our god of love.*

Loveliness – *(noun)* state of being attractive. *Her loveliness is to be seen to be believed.*

Lovely – *(adjective)* exquisitely beautiful. [informal] very pleasant. *She is a lovely woman.* *(noun)* [informal] a beautiful woman or girl. *The rising sun over the sea is a lovely sight.*

Lowermost – *(adjective)* at the bottom. *Our body's lowermost parts are feet. He stooped to his lowermost to gain success.*

Lowliness – *(noun)* low manner, low status. *His lowliness almost reduced him to zero.*

Lowly – *(adjective)* **1** low in status or importance. *He is a lowly employee of the company.* **2** primitive or simple. *(adverb)* to a low degree: lowly paid workers. *These are lowly paid workers.*

Loyal – *(adjective)* showing firm and constant support or allegiance to a person or institution. *He is a loyal worker of the party.*

Loyalist – *(noun)* a person who remains loyal to the established ruler or government, especially in the face of a revolt. a supporter of union between great Britain and northern Ireland. *Congress loyalists keep attacking the opposition parties.*

Lozenge – *(noun)* a rhombus or diamond shape. heraldry a charge in the shape of a solid diamond. *Take this lozenge, it will melt in your mouth and soothe your throat.*

Lubber – *(noun)* [archaic] or dialect a big, clumsy person. *He is a lubber and not smart enough to do this job.*

Lucent – *(adjective)* poetic shining. *This is a lucent piece of writing.*

Lucidly – *(adverb)* in a simple manner. *The tough vocabulary of the text was lucidly explained by the teacher.*

Luckily – *(adverb)* fortunate. *Luckily I won the lottery.*

Luckless – *(adjective)* unfortunate. *The luckless fellow passed through many difficulties in life.*

Lucre – *(noun)* poetic money, especially when gained dishonourably. *He is a miser and loves to hoard lucre.*

Luculent – *(adjective)* rare, clearly expressed. *The luculent moon was a sight to see.*

Lues – *(noun)* dated syphilis. *He suffers from lues.*

Lumbago – *(noun)* pain in the lower back. *He has been diagnosed as suffering from lumbago.*

Luminary – *(noun)* **1** a person who inspires or influence others. *He is a luminary who does a lot of inspirational talking.* **2** poetic a natural light giving body, especially the sun or moon. *Sun is a luminary heavenly body.*

Lumpish - *(adjective)* **1** roughly or clumsily formed. *It is a lumpish pointing.* **2** stupid and lethargic. *He is a lumpish person.*

Lumpishness - *(noun)* to behave in a rough manner. *Lumpishness is not a desirable trait.*

Lunacy - *(noun)* insanity. *He suffers from lunacy.*

Lupin - *(noun)* a plant of the pea family, with deeply divided leaves and tall colourful tapering spikes of flowers. *Lupin is an edible plant of the pea family.*

Lurcher - *(noun)* [British] a crow-bred dog, typically a retriever, collie, or sheepdog crossed with a greyhound originally used for hunting and by poachers. *A lurcher is a born hunter.*

Lustful - *(adjective)* having strong feelings of sexual desire. *He is a lustful person, throws lustful glance at women.*

Lustiness - *(noun)* state of casting lewd glances. *Our society does not consider lustiness a desirable trait.*

Luteous - *(adjective)* [biology] of a deep orange-yellow or greenish yellow colour. *He is interested in the luteaous study of yellow colour.*

Luxuriant - *(adjective)* rich and profuse in growth. *The true has luxuriant foliage.*

Luxuriate - *(verb)* enjoy as a luxury. *He luxuriated in a five star hotel.*

Luxury - *(noun)* **1** the state of great comfort and extravagant living. *He is a rich man and lives in great luxury.* **2** an inessential but desirable item. *Buying a plane is a luxury which not many people can afford.* *(adjective)* of the nature of a luxury. *This is a luxury yacht.*

Lydian - *(noun)* a native or inhabitant of the ancient region of Lydia in western Asia minor. *Lydians were proved people who lived during 7th century.* *(adjective)* of or relating to the lydians or their language. *Lydians were the first to use coined money.*

Lying - *(adjective)* not telling the truth. *I can see very clearly that right now you are lying.*

Lymph - *(noun)* [physiology] a colourless fluid containing white blood cells, which bathes the tissues and drains through the lymphatic system into the bloodstream. *This is the micro graph a lymph node.* [literary] pure water. *He drank lymph from the holy up.*

Lynch - *(noun)* kill for an alleged offence without a legal trial, especially by hanging. *The thief was lynched by the mob.*

Lynx - *(noun)* a wild cat with a short tail and tufted ears. *We saw a lynx in the zoo.*

Lyre - *(noun)* a stringed instrument like a small Unshaped harp with strings fixed to a crossbar, used especially in ancient Greece. *Ancient Greeks used to play the lyre.*

Lyric - *(noun)* the words of a song. *The poet wrote a beautiful lyric.* *(adjective)* **1** expressing the writer's emotions, usually briefly and in stanzas or recognized forms. *His lyric poems are of extraordinary beauty.* **2** using a light register. *A lyric soprano with a light, clear timbre.*

Mm

M – *(noun)* **1** the thirteenth letter the alphabet. **2** denoting the next after L in a set of items, categories. etc. **3** the Roman numeral for 1000. *About 1M people participated in the protests.*

Ma – *(noun)* [informal] one's mother. *Priyanka's Ma runs her own construction business.*

Ma'am – *(noun)* a respectful form of address for a woman, in particular for female royalty or any woman. *Nigar ma'am is an excellent teacher.*

Mab – *(noun)* a fairy queen said to create and control men's dreams. *Sonya played the character of Queen Mab perfectly at the carnival yesterday.*

Mac – *(noun)* [informal, chiefly north American] a form of address for man whose name is unknown to the speaker. *Hey there, brother Mac, could you please tell me the way to Sandy Street?*

Macaque – *(noun)* a medium-sized monkey with a long face and cheek pouches for holding food. *To study the habits of macaque monkeys, one needs to live close to their habitat.*

Macaroni – *(noun)* **1** a variety of pasta formed in narrow tubes. *I remember my childhood days over a bowl full of macaroni and cheese that I often have for breakfast.* **2** an 18th century [British] dandy affecting continental fashions. *Sam resembled the figure of Macaroni in his tailcoat and hat at a summer pool party.*

Macaronic – *(adjective)* denoting languages, especially burlesque verse, containing words or inflections from one language introduced into the context of another. *English is becoming macaronic by incorporating words from other languages.* *(noun)* acaronic verse. *Ted's macaronic words and manner of speaking confused his wife.*

Macaroon – *(noun)* a light biscuit made with egg white, sugar, and ground almonds or coconut. *Strawberry macaroons are Tom's favourite evening refreshment.*

Macassar – *(noun)* a kind of oil fomerly used by men to give shine to their hair. *Ved explained the benefits of Macassar oil at the workshop.*

Macaw – *(noun)* a longtailed parrot with bright plummage. *Its colourful plumage characterizes the Macaw species.*

Mace – *(noun)* **1** [historical] a heavy club with a metal head and spikes. *The robber used a mace to attack his victim.* **2** a staff of office, especially that which lies on the table in the house of commons when the speaker is in the chair. *The mace stayed intact despite the sudden political upheaval at the meeting.*

Machiavelli – *(noun)* a person who is prepared to use unethical means to gain power.*Machiavelli was a great political writer.*

Machinate – *(verb)* engage in plots and intrigues; scheme. *The police found out that Sandy's own brother machinated his murder.*

Machination – *(noun)* a plot or scheme. *Nefertiti's political machinations brought her to control the whole of Egypt.*

Machine – *(noun)* **1** an apparatus using or applying mechanical power and having several parts, each with a definite function and together performing a particular task. technical any device that transmits a force or directs its application. *A pulley is a simple machine.* **2** an efficient and well-organized group of powerful people: the party machine. *The party machine led to the success of the election agenda.* **3** a person who acts with the mechanical efficiency of a machine. *Rob is a man-machine when he is at work, as he is absolutely perfect at what he does.* *(verb)* make or operate on with a machine. *The team machined a new process in no time.*

Machinery - *(noun)* 1 machines collectively, or the components of a machine. *Mining requires the use of some heavy machinery.* 2 the organization or structure of something: the machinery of the state. *The party machinery swing into action no sooner the election dates were announced.*

Mackerel - *(noun)* a surface-dwelling marine fish with a greenish-blue back, commercially important as a food fish. *Mackerel is a delicacy in some parts of the world.*

Mackintosh - *(noun)* [British] a full-length waterproof coat. *Sam put his mackintosh on to shelter himself from the heavy snowfall that came suddenly.*

Macrame - *(noun)* the craft of knotting cord or string in patterns to make decorative articles. *Tina surprised everyone with her talent of macramé at the summer camp.*

Macrocosm - *(noun)* 1 the universe, the cosmos. *Our solar system is just a small part of the macrocosm, which is a collection of several such solar systems.* 2 the whole of a complex structure, especially as represented or epitomized in a small part of itself a microcosm. *The economy of India can be understood both at the microcosmic as well as the macrocosmic level.*

Macron - *(noun)* a written or printed mark used to indicate a long vowel in some languages and phonetic transcription systems, or a stressed vowel in verse. *Tina learnt the importance of macrons in her phonetics class at the university today.*

Macula - *(noun)* [anatomy] an oval yellowish area surrounding the fovea near the centre of the retina in the eye, which is the region of greatest visual acuity. *Rob hurt the macula of his eyes in an accident.*

Maculate - *(adjective)* spotted or stained. *The maculated cloth revealed the secret behind the murder crime. (verb)* mark with a spot or spots; stain. *The farmer moved swiftly around his farm maculating his cattle with black paint.*

Maculation - *(noun)* mark of spot. *Maculation on a leopard's body is a natural phenomenon.*

Mad - *(adjective)* 1 mentally ill; insane. extremely foolish or ill advised. *To challenge the authority and expecting it to bend its rules is a mad idea.* 2 [informal] frenzied. very enthusiastic about something: he's football-mad. *Trevor is absolutely mad about playing baseball.* 3 [informal] very angry. *Mom was mad at me yesterday for ruining her new tablecloth. (verb)* [archaic] make mad or insane. *The noise makes me mad.*

Madden - *(verb)* 1 drive insane. *His love for her maddened him.* 2 irritate or annoy greatly. *The argument over the shoes maddened everyone and led to no definite consequence.*

Madder - *(noun)* a plant related to the bedstraws, with roots that yield a red dye. a red dye or pigment obtained from this plant. *The madder plant is known for the red dye that it yields.*

Mademoiselle - *(noun)* 1 a title or form of address for an unmarried French-speaking woman. *Monsieur Heathcliff requested Mademoiselle Emma for a drink in the bar.* 2 a young Frenchwoman. dated a French governess. *Mademoiselle Jane is a strict teacher when it comes to dealing with noisy children.*

Madhouse - *(noun)* 1 [historical] a mental institution. [informal] a psychiatric hospital. *The state government employs the inmates of the Boston madhouse.* 2 [informal] a scene of extreme confusion or uproar. *The fish market in the evening resembles a madhouse.*

Madly - *(adverb)* extreme intensity. *Tom is madly in love with Rita.*

Madness - *(noun)* foolish behaviour, mental illness. *Playing with fire is an act of sheer madness.*

Madrigal - *(noun)* a 16th or 17th century part song for several voices, typically unaccompanied and arranged in elaborate counterpoint. *The Madrigal is an interesting form of music that involves of people singing together or individually.*

Magazine - *(noun)* 1 a periodical publication containing articles and illustrations. a regular television or radio programme comprising a variety of items. *Elle Décor is a good magazine* *to learn about the current trends in the market.* 2 a chamber for holding a supply of cartridges to be fed automatically to the breech of a gun. *The general emptied the entire magazine on the civilians during the civil war.* 3 a store for arms, ammunition, and explosives. *The thief entered a room and was shocked when he realized that it was a magazine of dangerous explosives.*

Mage - *(noun)* [archaic] or poetic a magician or learned person. *Sita knew that the heavily bearded man was a mage the moment she saw him meditating in the Himalayas.*

Maggot - *(noun)* 1 a soft-bodied legless larva, especially that of a fly or other insect and found in decaying matter. *The meat dish was infested with maggots.* 2 [archaic] a whimsical fancy. *Darla's dream to marry John was nothing but a maggot.*

Maggoty - *(adjective)* full of maggots. *The rice dish turned maggoty after two days.*

Magi - *(plural noun))* the three wise men from the east who brought gifts to the infant Jesus. *Karen told her son about the Magi who brought gifts for the infant Jesus on the eve of Christmas.*

Magical - *(adjective)* containing magic. *Preeti says that her trip to Venice was absolutely magical.*

Magician - *(noun)* a person with magical powers. a conjuror. *Tory invited a magician to delight the kids attending her son's birthday party.*

Magnanimity - *(noun)* generosity. *Monty's donations to the children's fund reflect his magnanimity.*

Magnate - *(noun)* a wealthy and influential person, especially in business. *Lalit Mohan is a business magnet in the steel industry.*

Magnet - *(noun)* 1 a piece of iron or other material, typically in the form of a bar or horseshoe, that has the property of attracting similar objects or aligning itself in an external magnetic field. *A magnet attracts all objects made out of iron.* 2 a person or thing that has a powerful attraction. *Sam is a magnet when it comes to impressing the ladies.*

Magnetism - *(noun)* 1 a physical phenomenon produced by the motion of electric charge, which results in attractive and repulsive forces between objects. *Leela and Sam share a strong aura of magnetism that is not easily understood by others.* 2 the ability to attract and charm people. *People are often attracted to Tara because of her intelligence and magnetism.*

Magnetization - *(noun)* property of attraction. *The iron ore under the Earth's surface leads to its magnetization.*

Magnifiable - *(adverb)* make something appear bigger than it actually is. *Virus and bacteria are easily magnifiable with the help of a microscope.*

Magnification - *(noun)* look larger and begerr. *Viruses are visible only under high magnification.*

Magnificence - *(noun)* 1 the quality of being magnificent. *Nefertiti, the Egyptian queen, prided herself over the magnificence of her empire.* 2 a title or form of address for a monarch or other distinguished person. *Nobody dared to contest the law set down by His Magnificence, Julius Ceaser.*

Magnifico - *(noun)* nent, powerful, or illustrious person. *The jury facilitated the illustrious magnificoes of the Bollywood industry.*

Magnifier - *(noun)* an equipment that used to to look things begger. *Biologists study microorganisms with the help of a magnifier.*

Magniloquence - *(noun)* use of flwery language. *The dowager Queen was known for her magniloquence throughout the kingdom.*

Magpie - *(noun)* 1 a long-tailed bird of the crow family, typically with pied plumage and a raucous voice. a black-and-white Australian butcher-bird with musical calls. *We saw a beautiful magpie at the bird sanctuary yesterday.* 2 a person who obsessively collects things or who chatters idly. *Looking at Rita's collection of thimbles, I was suddenly reminded of a magpie.*

Mahogany - *(noun)* 1 hard reddish-brown wood from a tropical tree, used for furniture. *Ben ordered new mahogany wood furniture for his new office.* 2 the tree which produces this wood. *Will treasures the mahogany tree in his backyard.* 3 a rich reddish -brown colour. *Naina gifted her mother a beautiful mahogany jewellery box.*

Maiden – *(noun)* **1** archic or poetic a girl or young woman. a virgin. *The fair maiden loved her village and never wanted to leave it.* **2** cricket an over in which no runs are scored. *The maiden over sent down by Razzak to the Indian cricket team led to their victory. (adjective)* **1** unmarried. *Only maidens below 25 years can apply for the job .* **2** being or involving the first attempt or act of its kind: the titanic's maiden voyage. *The Carpathia sailed in April on its maiden voyage.* **3** denoting a horse that has never won a race, or a race intended for such horses. *The bookies arranged a race at the racecourse for all their maiden participants.*

Mailable – *(adjective)* letter and mails that can be sent by mail. *Betty sent all the mailable documents to Veronica as soon as possible.*

Maintenance – *(noun)* **1** the process or state of maintaining or being maintained. *The government of Goa has ensured strict compliance over the maintenance of school timings.* **2** a husband's or wife's provision of livelihood for a spouse after separation or divorce. *Ram will have to pay his estranged wife maintenance after the divorce.* **3** [law, historical] the former offence of aiding a party in a legal action without lawful cause. *The parents' of the accused offered to pay maintenance to the victim's family, hoping to close the case.*

Maize – *(noun)* [chiefly British] a cereal plant originating in central America and yielding large grains set in rows on a cob. *Maize forms an integral part of breakfast in the West.*

Major – *(adjective)* **1** important, serious, or significant, greater or more important, main. *Financial inadequacy is a major problem in developing nations.* **2** [music] having intervals of a semitone between the third and fourth, and seventh and eighth degrees, contrasted with minor. equivalent to that between the tonic and another note of a major scale, and greater by a semitone than the corresponding minor interval. *Priya plays the piano in adept fashion, majoring all the intervals perfectly.* **3** [British] indicating the eider of two brothers. *Sam and Ben are brothers, with Sam being the major one.* 4 logic occurring as the predicate in the conclusion of a categorical syllogism. containing of a categorical syllogism. containing the major term in a categorical syllogism. *(noun)* **1** a rank of officer in the army and the US air force, above captain and below lieutenant colonel. an officer in charge of a section of band instruments: a trumpet major. *Harmeek is a Major in the Indian Army now.* **2** music a major key, interval, or scale. **3** a major organization, company, or competition. *Sam is a Piano player with major scales being his area of expertise.* **4** [North Amreican] a student's principal subject or course. a student specializing in a specified subject: a math major. *Preeti is an English major from the University of California. (verb)* [north American] specialize in at college or university. *Tiya is currently majoring in Mathematics from the University of North Carolina.*

Make-believe – *(noun)* the action of pretending or imagining. *All the characters in the play are make-believe. (adjective)* imitating something real. *Sam lives in a make-believe world. (verb)* pretend, imagine. *Her trick is to make-believe the entire story.*

Maker – *(noun)* **1** a person or thing that makes or produces something. *The maker of this chair is Sam.* **2** god. *The maker created this world with a lot of love.*

Makeshift – *(adjective)* interim and temporary. *Our accommodation in this house is a makeshift arrangement. (noun)* a temporary substitute or device. *The makeshift bed was as comfortable as the regular one.*

Makeweight – *(noun)* **1** something put on a scale to make up the required weight. *The makeweight added by the vegetable vendor was faulty.* **2** an extra person or thing needed to complete something. *Tina was the makeweight at Tora's wedding.*

Making – *(noun)* **1** the process of making or producing something. *The making of a cake requires patience and precision.* **2** [informal] earnings or profit. *His failure in life is due to his own corrupt makings.* **3** the necessary qualities: *She had the makings of a great teacher. Tom has* *the makings of a great leader.* **4** [north American & austral informal] paper and tobacco for rolling a cigarette. *Will always keeps a good supply of makings while travelling abroad.*

Maladjustment – *(noun)* failure to adjust to the conditions. *Rex is a maladjusted boy in his school.*

Malady – *(noun)* a disease or ailment. *Depression is one of the most widespread maladies in the world.*

Malaise – *(noun)* a general feeling of discomfort, illness, or unease. *Rita often experiences a sense of malaise at her workplace.*

Malapropos – *(adverb)* inopportunely; inappropriately. *He commented on his fellow colleagues were malapropos. (adjective)* inopportune; inappropriate. *No one appreciated his malapropos comments. (noun)* something inappropriately said or done. *These strict rules applied only to the malapropos.*

Malcontent – *(noun)* a discontented person. *The malcontents are the first ones to create problems in a happy environment. (adjective)* discontented; complaining. *The malcontent carpenter refused to fix the leg of the bed in spite of repeated requests from the owner.*

Malefaction – *(noun)* a person who commits a crime or some wrong. *Unfortunately, politicians are allowed to commit crimes such as financial corruption and other such malefactions by the state apparatus.*

Malefactor – *(noun)* formal a person who commits a crime or some other wrong. *The malefactor involved in the murder is still at large.*

Malefic – *(adjective)* **1** poetic causing harm. *His malefic attitude made the supervisor exercise control over all the workers.* **2** astrology relating to the planets Satwrn and Mars traditionally considered to have an unfavourable influence. *In astrology, bad luck is often attributed to the malefic stars that control our destiny.*

Maleficence – *(noun)* most black magic originate out of male ficence. *Maleficence often leads to forced agreement in a given situation.*

Maleficent – *(adjective)* state of cusing harm. *His maleficent eyes often led to the undoing of women.*

Malevolence – *(noun)* state of hostility. *Tina's eyes reflect her malevolence towards Rob.*

Malformation – *(noun)* abnormality of shape or form in a part of the body. *Warts are a malformation by birth and need to be removed surgically.*

Malice – *(noun)* **1** the desire to do harm to someone; ill will. *Rita experiences unbearable malice towards men who molested her last year and seeks revenge.* **2** [law] wrongful intention, especially as increasing the guilt of certain offences. *One need not bear any malice towards the juvenile delinquents in society.*

Malicious – *(adjective)* characterized by malice; intending or intended to do harm. *His malicious nature is the cause of his unethical behaviour.*

Malign – *(adjective)* harmful or evil in native or effect. *(verb)* speak ill of. *Tom's nature to malign colleagves led to his dismissal from his workplace yesterday.*

Malignancy – *(noun)* **1** the state or presence of a malignant tumour; cancer. a cancerous growth. a form of cancer. *The biopsy revealed the nature of the malignancy.* **2** the quality of being malign or malevolent. *Her actions are reflective of natural malignancy.*

Malignity – *(noun)* speaking in a spiteful manner. *Criminals often show signs of heinous malignity.*

Malignly – *(adveb)* attitude of speaking ill of others. *All of Iago's dialogues with Othello are malignly planned.*

Malison – *(noun)* [archaic] a curse. *The onlookers screamed several malisons at the murderers.*

Mall – *(noun)* **1** a large enclosed shopping area from which traffic is excluded. *Rob likes grocery shopping at the mall on Sundays.* **2** a sheltered walk or promenade. *The lovers walked through the mall after a romantic drink at a bar.* **3** [historical] another term for the game pall-mall. an alley used for this. *The Pharaoh walked swiftly through the mall after levying heavy taxes on the temples.*

Mallard – *(noun)* the commonest duck of the northern hemisphere, the male having a dark green head and white collar. *Mallard is a delicacy in some parts of the world.*

Mallet – *(noun)* **1** a hammer with a large wooden head. *She murdered her abusive husband using only a mallet.* **2** a long-handled wooden stick with a head like a hammer, used for hitting a croquet or polo ball. *A mallet is used to hit the ball while playing polo.*

Malodorous – *(adjective)* smelling very unpleasant. *She walked through malodorous alleys to reach the post office.*

Malpractice – *(noun)* improper, illegal, or negligent professional activity or treatment. *The doctor lost his license to practice medicine because of his malpractice.*

Malt – *(noun)* **1** barely or other grain that has been steeped, germinated, and dried, used especially for brewing or distilling and vinegar-making. *Malt beer is a refreshing drink, especially during summers.* **2** chiefly short for malt whisky. *A glass of malt whiskey can enliven your spirits anytime.* **3** [north American] short for malted milk. *Malted milk is good for babies when consumed regularly.* *(verb)* **1** convert into malt. *Barley is malted to make beer.* **2** become malt when germination is checked by drought. *Seeds start malting due to lack of proper irrigation of the crops.*

Maltreat – *(verb)* treat cruelly or with violence. *Sam had been maltreating his wife since the day they got married.*

Mammary – *(adjective)* denoting or relating to the human female breasts or the milk secreting organs of other mammals. *Rita realized that her mammary tumour had spread throughout her chest area.* *(noun)* [informal] a breast. *She had to get rid of her mammary glands to avoid the risk of cancer.*

Mammon – *(noun)* wealth regarded as an evil influence or false object of worship. *Greeks worshipped Mammon for greater wealth.*

Mammoth – *(noun)* a large extinct elephant of the Pleistocene epoch, typically hairy and with long curved tusks. *The Mammoth is an extinct animal.* *(adjective)* huge. *He looked at the mammoth project with anticipation.*

Manacle – *(noun)* a metal band, chain, or shackle for fastening someone's hands or ankles. *Patients who have severe mental illness are often kept in manacles.* *(verb)* fetter with a manacle or manacles. *The robber's hands were manacled while being taken to prison.*

Manage – *(verb)* **1** be in charge of; run. *She managed the entire fashion show on her own.* **2** supervise. *Rita manages the entire office single handedly.* **3** be the manager of a sports team or a performer. *Ted manages the cricket team at this club.* **4** administer and regular resources under one's control. *Tom manages the company's finances in New York.* **5** maintain control or influence over a person or animal. *Beth manages her dog's training with great expertise.* **6** control the use or exploitation of land. *The owner managed to fleece his customers for several years.* **7** succeed in surviving or in attaining one's aims; cope. *Riya managed to survive despite all odds after her car accident.*

Manageability – *(noun)* ability to control or deal without difficulty. *A person's ability to work in a stressful environment depends the manageability of various tasks.*

Manageable – *(adjective)* able to control without difficulty. *All things are manageable once planned in an organized fashion.*

Management – *(noun)* **1** the process of managing. *The management of any company depends on its team.* **2** the people managing an organization. *The Management decided to fire Tom after checking his previous records.* **3** [medicine & psychiatry] the treatment or control of diseases or disorders, or the care of patients who suffer them. *Proper management of a diseased patient can led to a speedy recovery.* **4** [archaic] trickily; deceit. *Cleopatra's management led to her controlling the entire Egyptian empire.*

Manager – *(noun)* **1** a person who manages an organization or group of staff. *My Manager is a strict disciplinarian.* **2** a person who controls the professional activities of a performer, sports player, etc. *Jerry Macguire is a Hollywood movie that shows the protagonist playing the part of a celebrity manager to a boxer.* **3** a person in charge of the activities, tactics and training of a sports team. *Every cricket team ought to* *have a competent manager.* **4** computing a program or system that controls or organizes a peripheral device or process. *The company created a mechanical manager for its core teams to help increase efficiency.* **5** [British] a member of either house of parliament appointed with others for some duty in which both housed are concerned. *Each manager in the parliament gets a fair chance to put forward the case of his house before any debate.*

Manageress – *(noun)* a female manager. *Deepika makes an intelligent and a competent mangeress.*

Managerial – *(adjective)* relating to management. *Preeti fulfills her managerial duties in perfect order.*

Mandate – *(noun)* **1** an official order or commission to do something. *All drivers are said to follow the state mandate of safe and slow driving.* **2** [law] a commission by which a party is entrusted to perform a service, especially without payment and with indemnity against loss by that party. *The culprit was issued a mandate to serve in the old-age home for 6 months.* **3** a written authority enabling someone to carry out transactions on another's bank account. *The bank allowed Rita to carry out the transaction once she produced the required mandate.* **4** [historical] a commission from the league of nations to a member state to administer a territory. *1947 saw the end of the British mandate in India.* **5** the authority to carry out a policy or course of action, regarded as given by the electorate to a party or candidate that wins an election. *The MLA misused his mandate.* *(verb)* **1** give authority to act in a certain way. *The mall mandated the security people to frisk the customers.* **2** make mandatory. *The government mandated getting an identification card for all citizens.* **3** [historical] assigns under a mandate of the league of nations. *The chairperson mandated all participating nations to sign a peace treaty in order to avoid any future wars.*

Mandatory – *(adjective)* required by [law] or mandate. *Mandatory rules enforced by the government ought to be followed by all the citizens on a nation.* compulsory. *Wearing a vermilion mark on the forehead is mandatory for all married Hindu women.* *(noun)* variant spelling of mandatary.

Manes – *(plural noun)* the defined souls of dead ancestors. *Some tribes still pray to their manes hoping that they would be rid of any diseases or misfortunes.*

Mangle – *(noun)* **1** [chiefly British] a machine having two or more cylinders turned by a handle, between which wet laundry is squeezed and pressed. *Mangles are used to dry and iron out clothes in large numbers.* **2** US a large machine for ironing sheets or other fabrics, using heated rollers. *During the World War mangles were used to iron our creases from the uniforms of the soldiers.* *(verb)* press with a mangle. *All the pages of the report lay mangled beyond repair in the storeroom.*

Mango – *(noun)* **1** a fleshy yellowish red tropical fruit which is eaten ripe or used green for pickles or chutneys. the evergreen Indian tree which bears this fruit. *Mango is the king of fruits.* **2** a tropical American hummingbird that typically has green plumage with purple feathers on the wings, tail, or head. *A mango can be spotted in the tropical region of North America, humming amongst the flowers.*

Mangy – *(adjective)* **1** having mange. *The mangy dog was sent to the veterinarian.* **2** in poor condition; shabby. *Rita wore a particularly mangy old dress to the wedding.*

Mania – *(noun)* **1** mental illness marked by periods of excitement, delusions, and overactivity. *Patients suffering from mania are often unable to control their anger.* **2** an obsession. *Ram's mother often complains about his cricket mania that makes him neglect his studies.*

Maniac – *(noun)* **1** a person exhibiting extremely wild or violent behavior. *Ginger is a maniac and is very aggressive.* **2** [informal] an obsessive enthusiast. *Siya a Hannah Montana Maniac.* **3** [psychiatry archaic] a person suffering from mania. *Mental depression is a symptom displayed by most maniacs.*

Manikin – *(noun)* **1** a very small person. *Dicken's fictional character or Uncle Scrooge is depicted* *as a manikin.* **2** a jointed model of the human body. *Fashion stores display their new collection on manikins.*

Manipulation – *(noun)* the action of manipulating something in skillful manner. *Rob is a manipulative boss.*

Manner – *(noun)* **1** a way in which something is done or happens. *Clive gives orders to his team in an unstoppable manner.* **2** a style in literature or art. *Ben Jonson wrote plays following the tradition of the Comedy of Manners.* **3** poetic a kind or sort. *Leonard professed his love for Tiya in a unique manner.* **4** a person's outward bearing or way of behaving towards others. *Sam is popular with the girls due to his perfect manners.* **5** polite or well-bred social behavior. social behavior or habits. *Every child should be taught good manners.*

Manse – *(noun)* the house occupied by a minister of a Scottish Presbyterian church. *Civilians visit the manse on Sunday.*

Mansion – *(noun)* **1** a large, impressive house. *Raman lives in a mansion in Mumbai.* **2** [British] a large block of flats. *Fiona walked across the mansion just to take a look at the Victorian windows again.* **3** a terrace or mansion block: Carlyle mansions. *Gia sits on the mansion often, especially when she wants to pen down her thoughts.*

Mansuetude – *(noun)* [archaic] meekness; gentleness. *His wife takes advantage of his mansuetude.*

Mantelet – *(noun)* variant spelling of mantlet. *Tia gave the poor beggar her mantelet on Christmas eve.*

Mantis – *(noun)* a slender predatory insect with a triangular head, typically waiting motionless for prey with its forelegs folded like hands in prayer. *Ned saw a Mantis on his way back home from work.*

Manually – *(adverb)* by human labour. *Some machinery ought to be operated manually.*

Manufactory – *(noun)* [archaic] a factory. *The carpenter's wife worked at the manufactory to earn a little extra.*

Manufacture – *(verb)* **1** make on a large scale using machinery. *Steel factories manufacture utensils.* **2** produce naturally. *Plants manufacture food using sunlight.* **3** make or produce something abstract in a merely mechanical way. *The Grub street writers manufactured stories in the 19th century.* **4** invent or fabricate. *The lady manufactured an alibi to save herself from being imprisoned.* *(noun)* the process of manufacturing. *The manufacture turned out to be faulty.*

Mar – abbreviation march. *Spring season lasts from Mar-May.*

Marasmic – *(adjective)* undernourished children. *Nancy felt sorry for her marasmic child.*

Marasmus – *(noun)* medicine undernourishment causing a child's weight to be significantly low for their age. *Vicky's son suffers from Marasmus.*

Maraud – *(verb)* attack and steal; raid. *The invading army marauded the village.*

Marcescence – *(noun)* property of with ering low remaining attached to the stem. *With the advent of winter, the crops in the village had started to marcescence.*

Marcescent – *(noun)* botany withering but remaining attached to the stem. *The China Rose had marcescent but had not lost its beauty.*

Mare – *(noun)* the female of a horse or other equine animal. *Ruth loved to ride her mare during vacations.*

Margosa – *(noun)* neem tree. *Margosa has healing and antiseptic properties.*

Marigold – *(noun)* a plant of the daisy family with yellow, orange, or copper-brown flowers, cultivated as an ornamental. used in names of other plants with yellow flowers, e.g. marsh marigold. *Marigold garlands are used to beautify the bride in Indian weddings.*

Marine – *(adjective)* **1** of, relating to, or produced by the sea. *Vinit is a botonist who specializes in marine plants.* **2** of or relating to shipping or navel matters. *The marine laws forbade them from entering the port.* *(noun)* a member of a body of troops trained to serve on land or sea, in particular a member of the royal marines or a member of the marine corps. *The marine talked about his adventures on the sea.*

Mariner - *(noun)* formal or poetic a sailor. *Fawaz wants to become a mariner when he grows up.*

Maritime - *(adjective)* **1** connected with the sea, especially in relation to seafaring commercial or military activity. *Cindy knows all the rules of maritime sailing.* **2** living or found in or near the sea. *Jellyfish is a maritime aquatic animal.* **3** moist and temperate owing to the influence of the sea. *Aquatic plants flourish in moist maritime conditions.*

Marked - *(adjective)* **1** having a visible mark. having distinctive marks on their backs to assist cheating. *All the victims of the holocaust were marked on their skin.* **2** linguistics distinguished by a particular feature. *Semantics is marked by different literary rules, as is Phonetics.* **3** clearly noticeable. *Veronica has marked eyebrows.* **4** singled out, especially as a target for attack: a marked man. *Jesse was marked out during the terror attack and was killed in the same.*

Marker - *(noun)* **1** an object used to indicate a position, place, or route. a thing serving as a standard of comparison. *Promotion acts as a marker of success.* **2** a felt-tip pen with a broad tip. *Children had their names written out using a marker.* **3** a player who marks an opponent. *Rudolph marked out Fred as his strongest competitor in the first round itself.* **4** a person who marks a test or examination a person who records the score in a game, especially in snooker or billiards. *Danny often acts as a marker while his friends play snooker in the evenings.* **5** [north American informal] a promissory note; an IOU. *The American government sent the Indian President a marker as a sign of solidarity and friendship.*

Market - *(noun)* **1** a regular gathering of people for the purchase and sale of provisions, livestock, and other commodities. an open space or covered building where vendors convene to sell their goods. *I go to the market in the morning to buy fresh vegetables.* **2** an area or arean in which commercial dealings are conducted: the labour market. *Dickens portrays the working conditions of the labour market in his novels.* **3** a demand for a particular commodity or service. the free market; the operation of supply and demand: market forces. *The supply and demand forces rule the market in any given society.* **4** a stock market. *Evan earned a lot of profit when the market fell.* *(verb)* **1** advertise or promote. *Every celebrity ought to market his talent to become famous.* **2** dated buy or sell goods in a market. *Goods marketed regularly are often the highest in demand.*

Marketable - *(adjective)* **1** able or fit to be sold or marketed. *Marketable goods often enjoy huge popularity.* **2** in demand. *Marketable goods sold once are seldom taken back.*

Marking - *(noun)* an identification mark. a pattern of marks on an animal's fur, feathers, or skin. *The markings on a leopard are unique.*

Marksman - *(noun)* a person skilled in shooting. *Sam is an excellent marksman.*

Marmoreal - *(adjective)* poetic made of or likened to marble.b*Rita has Marmoreal flooring in her attic.*

Maroon - *(noun)* a member of a group of black people living in parts of Surinam and the West Indies, descended from runaway slaves. *Ben's ancestors belonged to the Maroon community.*

Marriageable - *(adjective)* fit or suitable for marriage, especially in being wealthy or of the right age. *Geeta wants to be married to her lover once she attains the marriageable age.*

Mars - *(noun)* a small planet of the solar system which is fourth in order from the sun and the nearest to the earth. *Mars is the fourth planet in our solar system.*

Marsh - *(noun)* an area of low-lying land which is flooded in wet seasons or at high tide, and typically remains waterlogged at all times. *Lotus plant grows in abundance in marshlands.*

Marshiness - *(noun)* proneness to water logging. *Tropical American land is known for its marshiness.*

Marshy - *(adjective)* resembling a marsh. *Marshy areas are usually accident prone.*

Mart - *(noun)* a trade centre or market. *Heena bought a new pair of shoes from the Mart yesterday.*

Martian – *(adjective)* of or relating to the planet mars or its supposed inhabitants. *The Martian rock was being studied by the scientists. (noun)* a hypothetical or fictional inhabitant of mars. *The martian fled the scene after the crash.*

Martinet – *(noun)* a strict disciplinarian, especially in the armed forces. *George was an excellent Martinet in the American army.*

Martingale – *(noun)* **1** a strap or set of straps running form the noseband or reins to the girth of a horse, used to prevent the horse from raising its head too high. *Gia fell from her horse when the martingale broke.* **2** a gambling system that involves a continual doubling of the stakes. *Martingale is a popular trick with gamblers.*

Martyr – *(noun)* **1** a person who is killed because of their religious or other beliefs. *Shaheed Bhagat Singh was a martyr.* **2** a person who displays or exaggerates their suffering or discomfort in order to obtain sympathy or admiration. *Ria pretends to be the martyr in her house all the time. (verb)* kill as a martyr; make a martyr of. *The people martyred Dan after he was tortured to death by the police.*

Masher – *(noun)* a utensil for mashering food. *I want to buy a potato masher.*

Masked – *(adjective)* cover with a mask. *Both the robbers were masked in order to hide their identities.*

Masker – *(noun)* a thing used to conceal something. *Grub Street writers were great maskers of good literature.*

Mason – *(noun)* **1** a builder and worker in stone. *Fred's father is a mason.* **2** a freemason. *Masons are known to have secret societies. (verb)* build from or strengthen with stone. *Sam masoned the entire building with his bare hands.*

Masonry – *(noun)* **1** stonework. the work of a mason. *Dany says his talent lies in masonry.* **2** freemasonry. *Harold is actively involved in the acts depicting the influence of masonry.*

Masque – *(noun)* a form of amateur dramatic entertainment, popular in 16th and 17th century England, which consisted of dancing and acting performed by masked players. *Several women writers such as Aphra Behn wrote plays that were dramatized as masques in the 18th century.*

Massacre – *(noun)* **1** an indiscriminate and brutal slaughter of people. *The Jallianwala massacre continues to haunt people till date.* **2** [informal] a very heavy defeat. *The riots were a massacre of innocence. (verb)* **1** deliberately and violently kill a large number of people. *Enemy soldiers were massacred mercilessly during the war.* **2** [informal] inflict a heavy defeat on. *Their pride was massacred when Beth ran away from the house.*

Massage – *(noun)* the rubbing and kneading of muscles and joints of the body with the hands, especially to relieve tension or pain. *A good massage is a great way to relieve stress. (verb)* **1** give a massage to rub a substance into the skin or hairy. *Gia massaged her mother's legs to relieve her of the joint pain.* **2** manipulate to give a more acceptable result. *Cindy massaged Beth's vanity to manipulate her into going to the masquerade with her.* **3** gently flatter. *Dan massaged his boss's ego in order to ensure a promotion..*

Masseur – *(noun)* a person who provides massage professionally. *Michel hired a masseur for his wife after she fell from the stairs.*

Massy – *(adjective)* massive. *I need to buy a massy bed for the kids.*

Mast – *(noun)* **1** a tall upright post, spar, or other structure on a boat, in sailing vessels generally carrying a sail or sails. *The sailor fixed the mast before the ship sailed.* **2** any tall upright post, especially a flagpole or a television or radio transmitter. *The wires were broken near the mast.*

Masterly – *(adjective)* performed or performing very skillfully. *Naved's masterly act made him a popular favourite with all his superiors at his workplace.*

Mastership – *(noun)* through knowledge. *A man's mastership is judged by his manners in front of his juniors.*

Mastery – *(noun)* **1** comprehensive knowledge or skill in a particular field. *Fred has mastery understanding over all of Dickens novels.* **2** the mastering of a subject or skill. *Ned has mastery in Physics.* **3** control or superiority over someone or something. *The lion has mastery over all the others animals in the jungle.*

Mastic – *(noun)* **1** an aromatic gum or resin exuded from the bark of a Mediterranean tree, used in making varnish and chewing gun and as a flavouring. *Mastic has no side effects in the long run.* **2** the bushy evergreen Mediterranean tree which yields mastic, closely related to the pistachio. used in names of similar or related trees, e.g. American mastic. *Mastics can be found only in the Mediterranean region.* **3** a putty-like waterproof filler and sealant used in building. *Fred fixed the hole in the pipes using mastic.*

Mastication – *(noun)* state of chewing. *The mastication of food depends on the bacteria in the human gut.*

Masticate – *(verb)* chew food. *George's mother bit her tongue while masticating her meal.*

Mastitis – *(noun)* inflammation of the mammary giand in the breast or udder. *Mastitis is often seen as an early symptom of cancer.*

Matchable – *(adjective)* equal to one another in quality. *The matchable characteristics of aquatic plants are of great importance to marine biologists.*

Matchless – *(adjective)* unequalled; incomparable. *Cleopatra's matchless beauty is talked about even today.*

Materialism – *(noun)* **1** a tendency to consider material possessions and physical comfort as more important than spiritual values. *Materialism is a distinct characteristic of selfish individualism.* **2** [philosophy] the doctrine that nothing exists except matter and its movements and modifications. *Spiritualism is devoid of any form of materialism.*

Materialize – *(verb)* **1** become actual fact; happen. appear or be present: the train failed to materialize. *The driver failed to materialize despite constant phone calls.* **2** appear in bodily form. *Sagar swore he saw a mermaid materialize in front of him at the beach.*

Maternity – *(noun)* **1** motherhood. *Karen is on her maternity leave till September.* **2** the period during pregnancy and shortly after childbirth: maternity clothes. *Her maternity clothes do not fit her anymore.*

Mathematician – *(noun)* expert in mathematic. *Anurag was a well-known mathematician in the University of Delhi.*

Mathematics – *(plural noun)* the branch of science concerned with number, quantity, and space, either as abstract concepts or as applied to physics, engineering, and other subjects. *Mathematics plays an important part in the study of planetary shifts in space.*

Matricidal – *(adjective)* showing tendency to kill one's mother. *Tom is suspected to have matricidal tendencies after his mental illness.*

Matricide – *(noun)* the killing of one's mother. a person who kills their mother. *Matricide is a heinous crime.*

Matrimonial – *(adjective)* relating to marriage. *Sagar got his matrimonial pictures clicked by a professional photographer.*

Matrimony – *(noun)* the state or ceremony of being married; marriage. *Guneet and Avreen are enjoying a healthy state of holy matrimony as on date.*

Matting – *(noun)* material used for mats, especially coarse fabric woven from a natural fibre. *Matting is a common practice in the villages of India.*

Mattock – *(noun)* an agricultural tool similar to a pickaxe, but with one arm of the head curved like an adze and the other like a chisel edge, used for breaking up hard ground, digging up roots, etc. *The farmer's daughter gifted him a mattock with her first salary.*

Mattress – *(noun)* **1** a fabric case filled with soft, firm, or springy material used for sleeping on. *Prisoners are just given a mattress to sleep on in jail.* **2** engineering a flat structure of brushwood, concrete, or other material used as strengthening for foundations, embankments, etc. *The government allows heavy funds to civil engineers to create a strong mattress for dams in order to avoids any mishaps.*

Maturate – *(verb)* form pus. *The soldier's wounds maturated despite the timely medication.*

Maturity – *(noun)* **1** the state, fact, or period of being mature. *The farmers wait a long time for the maturity of their crops.* **2** the time when an insurance policy, security, etc. matures. *Do not forget to pay your premiums in order to avoid any hassles after the maturity of your insurance policy.*

Maudlin – *(adjective)* self-pityingly or tearfully sentimental. *Betty is prone to sudden bouts of maudlin reactions.*

Maund – *(noun)* a measeve of weight equal to 8 kilogram. *The Zamindar promised a maund of rice to every villager in his village.*

Maunder – *(verb)* move, talk, or act in a rambling or aimless manner. *Sam is often seen maundering the streets after losing his job.*

Mausoleum – *(noun)* a building, especially a large and stately one, housing a tomb or tombs. *Shahjahan is a renowned Mughal emperor for building mausoleums in and around his territory.*

Mauve – *(noun)* a pale purple colour. *Mauve is my favourite colour.*

Maw – *(noun)* the jaws or throat, especially of a voracious animal. *The canine caught the neck of the mongoose in his maw.*

Maximize – *(verb)* **1** make as large or great as possible. *The key to a successful business is to minimize time taken and maximize profits.* **2** make the best use of. *Ben wanted to maximize his pleasure in the given time at the spa.*

Maze – *(noun)* **1** a network of paths and hedges designed as a puzzle through which one has to find a way. *The maze at the theme park is the most popular form of entertainment for people in Disneyland.* **2** a confusing mass of information. *I need to sort out the facts from this maze of information. (verb)* [archaic] or dialect be dazed and confused. *Tim was absolutely mazed at Rita's aggressive reaction following the dinner date.*

Mead – *(noun)* an alcoholic drink of fermented honey and water. *The men were drunk on mead.*

Meagre – *(adjective)* **1** lacking in quantity or quality. *These meagre offerings won't help the children.* **2** lean; thin. *The meagre boy was happy to get some food.*

Mean – *(verb)* **1** intend to convey or refer to. have as its signification in the same language or its equivalent in another language. be of a specified degree of importance to. *I mean that I will see you in two hours.* **2** intend to occur or be the case. design or destine for a particular purpose. have as a motive or excuse in explanation. *I mean what I say.* **3** have as a consequence or result. *The mean of this entire situation is that we need to start again.*

Meander – *(verb)* **1** follow a winding course. *The river meandered through the forest.* **2** wander aimlessly. *The drunk man meandered through the streets. (noun)* **1** a winding curve or bend of a river or road. *The meander made the drive challenging.* **2** a circuitous journey. *The meander made me feel sick.* 3 an ornamental pattern of winding or interlocking lines, e.g. in a mosaic. *The pattern had some beautiful meanders.*

Meaning – *(noun)* **1** what is meant by a word, text, concept, or action. *What is the meaning of this poem?* **2** worthwhile quality; purpose. *Your idea has given a meaning to my life. (adjective)* expressive: she gave him a meaning look. *The mother gave the naughty child a meaning look.*

Meaningly – *(adverb)* inttnded to communicate something. *He looked at her meaningly.*

Measles – *(plural noun)* **1** an infectious viral disease causing fever and a red rash, typically occurring in childhood. *Each child must be vaccinated against measles.* **2** a disease of pigs caused by encysted larvae of the human tapeworm. *His pigs were sick because of measles.*

Measurable – *(adjective)* able or large enough to be measured. *Please give me a measurable quantity of milk.*

Measureless – *(adjective)* having no limits. *My love for my parents is measureless.*

Measurement – *(noun)* the action of measuring. an amount, size, or extent as established by measuring. a unit or system of measuring. *The designer worked on incorrect measurements.*

Meat – *(noun)* flesh of an animal. *The lion pounced upon the meat.*

Mechanical - *(adjective)* **1** working or produced by machines or machinery. of or relating to machines or machinery. *The engine being demonstrated is mechanical.* **2** lacking thought or spontaneity. *He is very mechanical when it comes to work.* **3** relating to physical forces or motion. explaining phenomena in terms only of physical processes. *The mechanical force made the engine move.* *(noun)* **1** the working parts of a machine, especially a car. *I do not understand the mechanicals of any machine.* **2** [archaic] a manual worker. *They do not pay the mechanicals well.*

Mechanism - *(noun)* **1** a piece of machinery. *A very complex mechanism runs this car.* **2** a process by which something takes place or is brought about. *This is a very fascinating mechanism of producing electricity.* **3** [philosophy] the doctrine that all natural phenomena allow mechanical explanation by [physics and chemistry]. *I don't subscribe to Mechanism.*

Meconium - *(noun)* the dark green substance forming the first faeces of a newborn infant. *The meconium had a bad smell.*

Meddler - *(noun)* one who interferes. *He is such a meddler in everyone's business.*

Medial - *(adjective)* **1** situated in the middle. *The medial line was a little slanted.* **2** pro(noun) ced in the middle of the mouth. *"Ye" is a medial sound.*

Median - *(adjective)* **1** situated in the middle, especially of the body. *Median depth of the river is six feet.* **2** denoting or relating to a value or quantity lying at the mid point of a frequency distribution of observed values or quantities, such that there is an equal probability of falling above or below it. *The median duration for this diseese is three months.* *(noun)* **1** a median value. *The median of the heights is 52 in this group.* **2** [north American] term for central reservation. *The truck crashed into the median of the road.* **3** a straight line drawn from any vertex of a triangle to the middle of the opposite side. *The median the child drew wasn't straight.*

Medical - *(adjective)* of or relating to the science or practice of medicine. *He is a medical practitioner.* *(noun)* an examination to assess a person's state of physical health or fitness. *The boss has gone for his annual medical.*

Medicinal - *(adjective)* having healing properties. relating to medicines or drugs. *The herb has medicinal use.* *(noun)* a medicinal substance. *The medicinals were misplaced by the hospital staff.*

Medicine - *(noun)* **1** the science or practice of the diagnosis, treatment, and prevention of disease. *The child wants to study medicine when he grows up.* **2** a drug or other preparation for the treatment or prevention of disease. *Have you taken your medicines today?* **3** a spell, charm, or fetish believed to have healing or magical power. *A smile can be a medicine to stress.*

Mediocre - *(adjective)* of only moderate or average quality. *His mediocre performance failed to impress the critics.*

Mediocrity - *(noun)* the quality of being just average. *I am tired of all the mediocrity.*

Meditate - *(verb)* **1** focus one's mind for a period of time for spiritual purposes or as a method of relaxation. *I meditate for a few minutes every day.* **2** think carefully about. *Please meditate about this for some time.*

Meditation - *(noun)* **1** the action or practice of meditating. *Meditation gives you peace.* **2** a discourse expressing considered thoughts on a subject. *The meditation was very interesting.*

Meditative - *(adjective)* absorbed in deeper thorghts. *His stance was very meditative.*

Mediterranean - *(adjective)* of or characteristic of the Mediterranean sea, the countries bordering it, or their inhabitants. *The Mediterranean climate does not suit me.* *(noun)* a native of a Mediterranean country. *I was pleased to meet the Mediterranean.*

Meed - *(noun)* [archaic] a deserved share or reward. *He was happy to have reserved his meed.*

Meek - *(adjective)* quiet, gentle, and submissive. *At times, his meek demeanor looks quite fake.*

Meeting - *(noun)* **1** an assembly of people for a particular purpose, especially for formal discussion. an organized event at which a number of races or other sporting contests are held. *The meeting failed to cause any breakthroughs.* **2** an instance of two or more people meeting. *I am looking forward to the meeting with my potential boss.*

Meetness – *(noun)* suitable or proper. *In spite of his meetness for the job, his profile was rejected.*

Megrim – *(noun)* [archaic] **1** low spirits. *Snap out of your megrim.* **2** a whim or fancy. *It isn't always prudent to act upon your megrim.*

Melancholia – *(noun)* melancholy. [dated] a mental condition marked by persistent depression and ill-founded fears. *Her melancholia threatened to turn into something serious.*

Melancholic – *(adjective)* sadness. *The melancholic poem touched many a solitary hearts.*

Melancholy – *(noun)* **1** a deep and long lasting sadness. another term for melancholia condition. *I wish my friend would get out of the melancholy.* **2** [historical] another term for black bile. *He is suffering from melancholy.* *(adjective)* depressed or depressing. *The melancholy lyrics brought tears to my eyes.*

Melee – *(noun)* a confused crowd or scuffle. *I was dying to get out of the melee.*

Meliferous – *(adjective)* yielding or producing honey. *Bee is a meliferous insect.*

Mellifluence – *(noun)* pleasing to listen. *The mellifluence of the beautiful music touched my heart.*

Melodic – *(adjective)* of, having, or producing melody. pleasant sounding. *His melodic voice won him a nomination.*

Melodious – *(adjective)* pleasant sounding tuneful. relating to melody. *The melodious music echoed in the church.*

Melodist – *(noun)* **1** a composer of melodies. *The melodist has done a wonderful job.* **2** [archaic] a singer. *The melodist sang beautifully.*

Melody – *(noun)* a sequence of single notes that is musically satisfying. the principal part in harmonized music. *The Melody was beautiful.*

Melon – *(noun)* **1** the large round fruit of a plant of the gourd family, with sweet pulpy flesh and many seeds. *I love melons.* **2** the plant which yields this fruit. *The melon took a lot of space in the garden.* **3** a waxy mass in the head of some toothed whales, thought to focus acoustic signals. *The whale seems to use its melon to communicate.*

Membrane – *(noun)* **1** a pliable sheet like structure acting as a boundary, lining, or partition in an organism or cell. *He had hurt his tympanic membrane.* **2** a thin pliable sheet of material. *The membrane was torn.* **3** a double layer of lipids and proteins forming the boundary of a cell or organelle. *Membranes only let some substances pass.*

Memorize – *(verb)* learn by heart. *The child has memorized the entire poem.*

Memory – *(noun)* **1** the faculty by which the mind stores and remembers information. *He has a very sharp memory.* **2** something remembered. the remembering or commemoration of a dead person. the length of time over which a person or event continues to be remembered. *I have very pleasant memories of her.* **3** a computer's equipment or capacity for storing data or program instructions for retrieval. *My computer's memory needs to be upgraded.*

Menace – *(noun)* a threat or danger. a threatening quality. He is a menace to the society. *(verb)* threaten. *You cannot menace me.*

Mend – *(verb)* **1** restore to a sound condition. return to health. *The cobbler mended my shoes.* **2** add fuel to. *Do not mend the fire.* *(noun)* a repair in a material. *The mend in her dress was clearly visible.*

Mendacious – *(adjective)* untruthful. *He is a mendacious person.*

Mendacity – *(noun)* untruthfulness. *I am tired of your mendacity.*

Mendicancy – *(adjective)* depending on alone for a living. *The family was reduce to mendicancy.*

Mendicant – *(adjective)* given to begging. of or denoting a religious order originally dependent on alms. *The mendicant sage roamed the streets.* *(noun)* a beggar. a member of a mendicant order. *The mendicant collected enough food for the day.*

Menial – *(adjective)* requiring little skill and lacking prestige. domestic. *He started his career with menial jobs.* *(noun)* a person with a menial job. *The menial worked hard all his life.*

Meniscus - *(noun)* **1** the curved upper surface of a liquid in a tube. *The meniscus was turbulent.* **2** a thin lens convex on one side and concave on the other. *The meniscus is very useful in optics.* **3** a thin fibrous cartilage between the surfaces of some joints. *He hurt his meniscus.*

Mensal - *(adjective)* monthly. *This is a mensal occurrence.*

Menses - *(noun)* **1** blood and other matter discharged from the uterus at menstruation. *She went to the doctor to consult regarding the heavy menses.* **2** the time of menstruation. *It is important to be conscious of hygiene during menses.*

Menstruate - *(verb)* discharge blood and other material from the lining of the uterus at intervals of about one lunar mouth. *One can get stomach ache during menstruation.*

Mensurable - *(adjective)* able to be measured. *The results should be mensurable.*

Mensuration - *(noun)* measurement. the part of geometry concerned with ascertaining lengths, areas, and volumes. *He scored full marks in mensuration.*

Mental - *(adjective)* **1** of, done by, or occurring in the mind. *The child performs mental calculations quickly.* **2** of or relating to disorders or illnesses of the mind. mad. *He has a family history of mental illnesses.*

Mention - *(verb)* refer to briefly. refer to by name. *Yes, she did mention you to me. (noun)* a reference to someone or something. a formal acknowledgement of something noteworthy. *I was surprised by the mention of my name during the discussion.*

Mentioned - past tense of mention. *I mentioned you to my boss.*

Mentor - *(noun)* an experienced and trusted adviser. an experienced person in an institution who trains and counsels new employees or students. *I consider him as my friend and mentor.* *(verb)* be a mentor to. *She mentored the new employee very well.*

Mercantile - *(adjective)* **1** of or relating to trade or commerce. *His mercantile interests led him to to take up business studies.* **2** of or relating to mercantilism. *The mercantile discussion was very informative.*

Mercenary - *(adjective)* motivated primarily by the desire for gain. *The company entered India with apparent mercenary interests. (noun)* a professional soldier hired to serve in a foreign army. *The mercenary fought valiantly.*

Merchandise - *(noun)* goods for sale. products used to promote a film, pop group, etc. *The store sold good quality merchandise. (verb)* promote the sale of. advertise or publicize. trade or traffic in. *The company merchandized the product well.*

Mercurial - *(adjective)* **1** subject to sudden changes of mood or mind. *I am vary of his mercurial temper.* **2** of or containing the element mercury. *The mercurial compound was very unstable.* **3** of the planet mercury. *The mercurial conditions aren't suitable to life similar to that on the Earth. (noun)* a drug containing mercury. *A mercurial drug may help this condition.*

Mercury - *(noun)* a small planet that is the closest to the sun in the solar system. *There is no atmosphere on Mercury.*

Mercy - *(noun)* **1** compassion or forgiveness shown towards an enemy or offender in one's power. *The government showed mercy towards the captured soldier.* **2** something to be grateful for. *It is a mercy that we have a doctor in our household.* **3** motivated by compassion. used to express surprise or fear. *Oh Mercy! What a sight?*

Mere - *(adjective)* **1** that is solely or no more or better than what is specified: mere mortals. *We are mere mortals, not Gods!* **2** the smallest or slightest:the merest hint. *If you had given me a mere hint, I would have brought my laptop along.*

Meretricious - *(adjective)* **1** showily but falsely attractive. *The marriage party was full of meretricious people.* **2** characteristic of a prostitute. *She has a meretricious way of speaking.*

Merge - *(verb)* combine or be combined to form one. blend or cause to blend gradually into something else. absorb in another. *Please merge the two sentences.*

Marino - *(noun)* **1** a sheep of a breed with long, fine wool. *The marino was very healthy.* **2** a soft woolen or wool and cotton material, originally of merino wool. *The sweater is made of marino.*

Merit - *(noun)* **1** excellence; worth. an examination grade denoting above average performance. *I completed my course with a merit.* **2** a good point or feature. good deeds entitling someone to a future reward. the intrinsic rights and wrongs of a case. *Marketability is one of the merits of this product.* *(verb)* deserve or be worthy of. *He merited an award.*

Merle - *(noun)* a blackbird. *The two Merles were fighting for territory.*

Merman - *(noun)* male equivalment of a mermaid. *Mermen are mythical creatures.*

Merriness - *(noun)* cheerfullness, festivity. *We invited our neighbours to be a part of the merriment.*

Mesdames - plural form of madame. *Mesdames, what will you have for lunch?*

Mesentery - *(noun)* a fold of the peritoneum attaching the stomach, small intestine, and other organs to the posterior wall of the abdomen. *The professor pointed out the mesentery to the students during dissection.*

Mesmerist - *(noun)* one who hypnotises. *The mesmerist amazed the audience with his performance.*

Mesmerization - *(noun)* state of mesmerising. *The thief claimed that he was under the effect of mesmerization when he committed the crime.*

Message - *(noun)* **1** a verbal, written, or recorded communication sent by one person to another. *I sent a message to all my friends to wish them a happy new year.* **2** a significant point or central theme. a divinely inspired communication. *I could not understand the message the play was trying to convey.* **3** an errand. things brought; shopping. *I dumped the message on the floor and crashed on the sofa.* *(verb)* send a message to, especially by email. *I have messaged my team members to be on time for the meeting.*

Messenger - *(noun)* a person who carries a message. *The messenger handed me the envelope and rushed back.* *(verb)* send by messenger. *I messengered the invitation to all.*

Messieurs - plural form of monsieur. *Messieurs, what would you like to order for lunch?*

Messuage - *(noun)* a house with outbuildings and land. *The messuage was huge.*

Metabolism - *(noun)* the chemical processes that occur within a living organism to maintain life. *She has a high rate of metabolism.*

Metabolize - *(verb)* process or undergo processing by metabolism. *The stomach metabolizes some types of food easily.*

Metacarpus - *(noun)* the group of five bones of the hand between the wrist and the fingers. *He hurt his metacarpus.*

Metallic - *(adjective)* of relating to, or resembling mental. sharp and ringing. having the sheen or lustre of metal. *I like the metallic jewellery box.* *(noun)* a thing that is made of, contains, or resembles metal. *The metallics usually have a shine.*

Metallography - *(noun)* the descriptive science of the structure and properties of metals. *She is a student of metallography.*

Metallurgy - *(noun)* the branch of science concerned with the properties, production, and purification of metals. *He was interested in metallurgy.*

Metamorphose - *(verb)* **1** undergo metamorphosis. *The tadpole metamorphosed into a frog.* **2** change or cause to change completely. *You have metamorphosed the system.* **3** subject to metamorphoism. *The new chief of the police metamorphosed all his juniors.*

Metamorphosis - *(noun)* **1** zoology the process of transformation from an immature form to an adult form in two or more distinct stages. *I am fascinated by the process of metamorphosis.* **2** a change in form or nature. *The entire system underwent a metamorphosis under the new chief.*

Metaphor - *(noun)* a figure of speech in which a word or phrase in applied to something to which it is not literally applicable. a thing regarded as symbolic of something else. *The young poet did not like using metaphors.*

Metaphysical - *(adjective)* **1** of or relating to metaphysics. based on abstract reasoning.

transcending physical matter or the laws of nature. *I love metaphysical poems.* **2** denoting certain 17th century English poets known for their subtlety of thought and complex imagery. *The metaphysical poets wrote some interesting poems.* *(noun)* the metaphysical poets. *The metaphysicals used complex imagery.*

Metaphysics – *(plural noun)* **1** the branch of [philosophy] concerned with the first principles of things, including abstract concepts such as being and knowing. *He likes discussing the concepts of metaphysics.* **2** [informal] abstract talk; mere theory. *This discussion is nothing but metaphysics.*

Mete – *(verb)* **1** dispense or allot justice, punishment, etc. *The jury meted out an appropriate punishment to the culprit.* **2** measure out. *The cloth merchant meted out the correct length of fabric.*

Meteor – *(noun)* a small body of matter from outer space that becomes incandescent as a result of friction with the earth's atmosphere and appears as a streak of light. *I love watching meteors falling from the outer space.*

Meteoroid – *(noun)* astronomy a small body in the solar system that would become a meteor if it entered the earth's atmosphere. *The students discovered a new meteoroid.*

Meteorology – *(noun)* **1** the study of the processes and phenomena of the atmosphere, especially as a means of weather forecasting. *With the introduction of new satellites, there have been considerable advances in meteorology.* **2** the climate and weather of a region. *This region has unpredictable meteorology.*

Meter – *(noun)* a device that measures and records the quantity, degree, or rate of something. *The meter was faulty.* *(verb)* measure with a meter. *They metered the usage of electricity.*

Method – *(noun)* **1** a particular procedure for accomplishing or approaching something. *The method to solve this mathematical problem is quite simple.* **2** orderliness of thought or behavior. *He often loses his method when he is angry.*

Methodical – *(adjective)* characterized by method or order. *He is very methodical in his approach.*

Methodize – *(verb)* arrange in an orderly or systematic manner. *Please methodize the slides.*

Metrical – *(adjective)* **1** or, relating to, or composed in poetic meter. *The poet writes metrical poems.* **2** of or involving measurement. *The process of stitching clothes is metrical.*

Mica – *(noun)* a silicate mineral found as minute shiny scales in granite and other rocks. *Little bits of mica shone through the sand.*

Mice – *plural* form of mouse.*The house is infested with mice.*

Microbe – *(noun)* a micro-organism, especially a bacterium causing disease or fermentation. *Many microbes are helpful to human beings.*

Microscope – *(noun)* an optical instrument for viewing very small objects, typically magnifying by several hundred times. *The doctors studied the sample under a microscope.*

Mid – *(adjective)* **1** of or in the middle part or position of a range. *The population of this state is in the mid of the range of populations of various states of the country.* **2** phonetics pro(noun) ced with the tongue neither high nor low. *Because of the wound in his mouth, he has problems pronoun cing mids.*

Middle – *(adjective)* **1** at an equal distance from the extremities of something; central. placed so as to have the same number of members on each side. intermediate in rank, quality, or ability. *The chair in the middle is slightly misaligned.* **2** [grammar] denoting a voice of verb s in some languages, such as Greek, which expresses reciprocal or reflexive action. *The actor's pronunciation of the middle words needs work.* *(noun)* **1** a middle point or position. *Let's move to the middle.* **2** [informal] a person's waist and abdomen. *He needs to lose weight off his middle.* **3** [grammar] a middle form or voice of a verb. *The middle is very rarely used nowadays.* *(verb)* strike with the middle of the bat, racket, or club. *The batsman middled the ball.*

Midget – *(noun)* an extremely small person. extremely small. *The midget entertained the crowd.*

Mien - *(noun)* a person's look or manner. *We weren't comfortable with his mien.*

Miff - *(verb)* [informal] offend or irritate. *I think I miffed him by my silence.*

Migration - *(noun)* movement animals, birds or people to new places. *The wildebeest are about to start their annual migration.*

Migratory - *(adjective)* animal or birds that move from one place to another. *Geese are migratory birds.*

Mike - *(noun)* a microphone. *The mike stopped working while he was speaking. (verb)* place a microphone close to or in. *Please mike the stage.*

Milch - *(adjective)* denoting a domestic mammal giving or kept for milk. *This milch cow is very docile.*

Mild - *(adjective)* **1** gentle and not easily provoked. *He has very mild manners.* **2** of only moderate severity. not keenly felt: mild surprise. acting gently. not sharp or strong in flavor. *You gave me a mild shock.* **3** moderately warm; less cold than expected. *I want to stay at home and enjoy this mild day.(noun)* [British] a kind of dark beer not strongly flavoured with hops. *Please give me a pint of mild.*

Mile - *(noun)* **1** a unit of measure equal to 1,760 yards. *I have travelled 7 miles today.* **2** [historical] a Roman measure of 1,000 paces. *The warrior charged for 2 miles before stopping.* **3** [informal] a very long way or a very great amount. *The beach is miles away from our hotel. (adverb)* [informal] by a great amount or a long way: it is miles better. *This presentation was miles more interesting than the previous one.*

Mileage - *(noun)* **1** a number of miles travelled or covered. *The car has good mileage.* **2** [informal] actual or potential benefit or advantage: he was getting a lot of mileage out of the mix-up. *She tried to get mileage out of the corporate status.*

Milfoil - *(noun)* **1** the common yarrow. *The milfoil is an abundant plant.* **2** an aquatic plant with whorls of fine submerged leaves and wind-pollinated flowers. *The milfoil is an invasive plant.*

Militancy - *(noun)* adopting violent methods for some cause. *Militancy needs to be curbed at any cost.*

Militant - *(adjective)* favouring confrontational methods in support of a cause. *The militant organization was banned in several countries. (noun)* a militant person. *The militant was arrested before he could strike.*

Militarism - *(noun)* the belief that a country should maintain and readily draw on a strong military capability for the defence or promotion of national inferests. *Confrontations are common when two neighbouring countries favour militarism.*

Military - *(adjective)* of, relating to, or characteristic of soldiers or armed forces. *The military ways of life are very fascinating. (noun)* the armed forces of a country. *The military was called in to control the situation.*

Militia - *(noun)* a military force that is raised from that civil population to supplement a regular army in an emergency. a rebel force acting in opposition to a regular army. all able-bodied civilians eligible by [law] for military service. *Some countries consider it important to have a strong militia.*

Milk - *(noun)* an opaque white fluid rich in fat and protein, secreted by female mammals for the nourishment of their young. the milk of cows as a food and drink for humans. the milk-like juice of certain plants, such as the coconut. a milk-like liquid with a particular ingredient or use: cleansing milk. *Milk is an important source of calcium for children. (verb)* **1** draw milk from a cow or other animal. extract sap, venom, or other substances from. *Please milk the bad-tempered cow.* **2** exploit or defraud by taking small amounts of their money over a period of time. *The servant milked his employer for years.*

Milkiness - *(noun)* resembling milk in colour or quality. *The milkiness of her skin got her many admirers.*

Milky - *(adjective)* **1** containing milk. *The chocolate is too milky for my liking.* **2** reassembling milk; of a soft white colour or clouded appearance. *The advertisement claimed* *that you can get a milky complexion if you use the product.*

Mill – *(noun)* **1** a building equipped with machinery for grinding grain into flour. a piece of machinery for grinding grain. *The mill runs for four hours every day.* **2** a domestic device for grinding a solid substance to powder or pulp: a pepper mill. *I bought a new pepper mill.* **3** a building fitted with machinery for a manufacturing process: a steel mill. a piece of manufacturing machinery. *The mill was shut because of a strike.* *(verb)* 1 grind in a mill. *Please mill this sack of grains.* **2** cur or shape with a rotating tool. *I brought a sheet of steel to get it milled.*

Millepede – *(noun)* very small invertebrates that live in socil and under stones. *I found a millipede in my bathroom.*

Millet – *(noun)* a cereal which bears a large crop of small seeds, used to make flour or alcoholic drinks. *She bought a sack of millet.*

Million – *(cardinal number)* **1** the number equivalent to the product of a thousand and a thousand; 1,000,000 or 10^6 *She needs to save 3 million dollars to buy the house she likes.* **2** [informal] a very large number or amount. *There are millions of reasons why you should do this.*

Milionaire – *(noun)* a person whose assets are worth one million pounds or dollars or more. *Her parents wanted her to marry a millionaire but she fell in love with me.*

Milt – *(noun)* the semen or sperm-filled reproductive gland of a male fish. *The fish stores its sperm in the milt.*

Mimicry – *(noun)* skill of imitating something for entertainment or ridicule. *She is very good at mimicry.*

Minacious – *(adjective)* menacing, threatening. *The students ran to the classroom when they saw the minacious principal coming.*

Minaret – *(noun)* a slender tower, especially that of a mosque, with a balcony from which a muezzin calls Muslims to prayer. *The mosque has beautiful minaret.*

Mince – *(verb)* **1** cut up or shred into very small pieces. *I went to get the meat minced.* **2** walk in an affected manner with short, quick steps and swinging hips. *She minced across the street.* *(noun)* [chiefly British] minced meat. *They stuffed the turkey with mince.*

Mind – *(noun)* **1** the faculty of consciousness and thought. *At times, it is prudent to follow your mind.* **2** the source of a person's thoughts; the intellect. a person's memory. a person identified with their intellectual faculties: he was one of the greatest minds of his time. *This book is a great way to exercise our mind.* **3** a person's attention. a person's will or determination. *He has a good mind to take up the challenge.* *(verb)* **1** be distressed or annoyed by; object to. *Please don't mind my saying so.* **2** remember or take care to do something: mind you look after the children. give attention to; watch out for: mind your head! *Mind you, don't make any noise in the class while I am gone.* **3** take care of temporarily. *The farmer asked his son to mind the cattle.*

Minded – *(adjective)* inclined to think in a particular way: liberal-minded scholars. *I love to spend time with like-minded people.*

Mindful – *(adjective)* conscious or aware or responses planned for their psychological effect on another. *They are very mindful of the way they speak to each other in the presence of their children.*

Mine – *(possessive pronoun)* referring to a thing or things belonging to or associated with the speaker. possessive determine [archaic] used before a vowel my. *This pencil box is mine.*

Minerva – *(noun)* Roman goddess. *She wanted to name her baby girl Minerva.*

Mingle – *(verb)* **1** mix or cause to mix together. *The two liquids mingled well.* **2** move around and engage with others at a social function. *Let us all mingle with the crowd.*

Minimal – *(adjective)* **1** of a minimum amount, quantity, or degree. *My expenditure on cosmetics is minimal.* **2** art characterized by the use of simple or primary forms or structures. music characterized by the repetition and gradual alteration of short phrases. *He specializes in minimal paintings.*

Minion - *(noun)* a follower or underling of a powerful person, especially a servile or unimportant one. *He is but a minion in the party.*

Ministerial - *(adjective)* relating to a government menister. *The ministerial convoy has just passed this way.*

Ministry - *(noun)* **1** a government department headed by a minister. *The ministry approved his proposal.* **2** a period of government under one prime minister. *The ministry has almost completed its term.* **3** the work, vocation, or office of a minister of religion. spiritual service to others provided by the Christian church. *The ministry was in service.* **4** the action of ministering to someone. *The priest's powerful ministry prevented the disciple from committing the crime.*

Minor - *(adjective)* **1** having little importance, seriousness, or significance. *This is a minor issue.* **2** [music] having intervals of a semitone between the second and third degrees, and the fifty and sixth, and the seventh and eighth. contrasted with major. characteristic of a minor scale and less by a semitone than the equivalent major interval. based on a minor scale: concerto in a minor. *The minor tones made the entire melody beautiful.* *(noun)* **1** a person under the age of full legal responsibility. *The minor got away with relatively lenient punishment.* **2** music a minor key, interval, or scale. *The musician uses minors with expertise.* **3** bell-ringing a system of change-ringing using of American football. **4** [north American] a student's subsidiary subject or course. *She took up philosophy as her minor.* **5** [logic] a minor term or premise. *She based her argument with a minor.* **6** a small drab moth which has purplish caterpillars that feed on grass. *The garden was infested by minors.*

Minotaur - *(noun)* Greek mythology a creature who was half-man and half-bull, kept in a labyrinth on Crete by King Minos and killed by Theseus. *The movie had an excellent depiction of a minotaur.*

Minster - *(noun)* a large or important church, typically one of cathedral status in the north of England that was built as part of monastery. *I visit the Minster every sunday.*

Minstrel - *(noun)* a medieval singer or musician. *The minstrel was famous for his melodious voice.*

Mint - *(noun)* **1** an aromatic plant with two-lipped, typically lilac flowers, several kinds of which are used as culinary herbs. the flavor of mint, especially peppermint. *Mint grows very easily.* **2** a peppermint sweet. *Can you give me a mint please?*

Mintage - *(noun)* menting of coins. *The mintage of coins is a complicated process.*

Minute - *(noun)* **1** a period of time equal in sixty seconds or sixtieth of an hour. *It will take me 5 minutes to complete this task.* **2** [informal] a very short time. *This is a matter of minutes.* **3** a sixtieth of a degree of angular measurement. *The ship was at 400 minutes from the wreck.*

Miracle - *(noun)* **1** an extraordinary and welcome event that is not explicable by natural or scientific laws, attributed to a diving agency. a remarkable and very welcome occurrence. *Her recovery is nothing less than a miracle.* **2** an amazing product or achievement, or an outstanding example of something: a miracle of design. *This building is a miracle of design.*

Miraculous - *(adjective)* having the character of a miracle. *The new medicine has produced miraculous results.*

Mire - *(noun)* **1** a stretch of swampy or boggy ground. soft mud or drill. [ecology] a wetland area or ecosystem based on peat. *The children keep away from the mire.* **2** a state of difficulty from which it is hard to extricate oneself. *The government was in mire because of its policies.* *(verb)* cause to become stuck in mud. cover or spatter with mud. *The children mired each other.*

Mirror - *(noun)* **1** a surface, typically of glass coated with a metal amalgam which reflects a clear image. *I bought an ornate mirror for my house.* **2** something regarded as accurately representing something else. *Her thoughts were a mirror of her experiences.* **3**]]contents copied from another site. *I want to create a mirror of my website.* *(verb)* **1** show a reflection of. *The clear lake mirrored the landscape around.* **2**

correspond to. *My views mirror my experience with your company.* **3** [computing] copy the contents of a network site and store at another site. sorted copies of data in two or more hard disk. *I called a technical consultant to mirror my website.*

Mirth – *(noun)* amusement; laughter. *The party was full of mirth.*

Mirthless – *(adjective)* lacking real smile or laugh. *She had a mirthless face.*

Misadvised – *(adjective)* wrong recommendation. *Children should never be misadvised.*

Misalliance – *(noun)* an unsuitable or unhappy alliance or marriage. *Their marriage was a misalliance from the very beginning.*

Misbegotten – *(adjective)* **1** badly conceived, designed, or planned. contemptible. *This is a misbegotten building.* **2** [archaic] of a child illegitimate. *The teacher told a painful story of a misbegotten child.*

Misbehave – *(verb)* behave badly. *The bus conductor was fired because he misbehaved with children.*

Misbehaviour – *(noun)* bad behaviour. *The child was reprimanded for his misbehavior.*

Misbelief – *(noun)* **1** a wrong or false belief or opinion. *The misbelief led to a wrong decision.* **2** less common term for disbelief. *His misbelief was written all over his face.*

Miscarriage – *(noun)* the spontaneous or unplanned expulsion of a fetus from the womb before it is able to survive independently. *She was upset after her miscarriage.*

Miscarry – *(verb)* **1** have a miscarriage. *She was admitted in the hospital when she miscarried.* **2** fail. *Their plans miscarried.* **3** dated fail to reach its destination. *The ship miscarried.*

Miseallaneous – *(adjective)* of various types. composed of members or elements of different kinds. *The boy had a huge collection of miscellaneous stamps.*

Miscellany – *(noun)* a mixture. a collection of pieces of writing by different authors. *The miscellany was published by a reputed publisher.*

Mischief – *(noun)* **1** playful misbehavior or troublemaking. *The children's faces were full of mischief.* **2** harm or injury caused by someone or something. [archaic] a person responsible for this. *Their mischief landed them in the prison.* **3** [law] a wrong or hardship which it is the object of a statute to remove or for which the common [law] affords a remedy. *Mischiefs committed by juvenile are dealt with differently than crimes committed by adults.*

Mischievous – *(adjective)* **1** causing or disposed to mischief. *The mischievous children were scolded every day.* **2** intended to cause harm or trouble. *The mischievous act wasn't forgiven easily.*

Misconceive – *(verb)* **1**fail to understand correctly. *You misconceived what I was saying.* **2** judge or plan badly. *The company's plans for expansion were misconceived.*

Misconception – *(noun)* a false or mistaken view or opinion. *I want to remove this misconception.*

Miscount – *(verb)* count incorrectly. *I miscounted the number of pages that I had to read.* *(noun)* an incorrect count. *The miscount led to the incorrect balance sheet.*

Miscreant – *(noun)* **1** a person who behaves badly or unlawfully. *The police caught the miscreant.* **2** [archaic] a heretic. *The church boycotted the miscreant.* *(adjective)* *1* behaving badly or unlawfully. *The miscreant player was suspended from the team.* **2** [archaic] heretical. *The miscreant villager was boycotted by everyone.*

Miscreated – *(adjective)* created wrongly misshappen. *The miscreated cow attracted a crowd.*

Misdemeanour – *(noun)* a minor wrongdoing. [law] a not-indictable offence, regarded in the US as less serious than a felony. *The judge let him go with just a warning as this was his first misdemeanour.*

Misdoing – *(noun)* a misdeed. *His mother reported his misdoing to his father.*

Misdoubt – *(verb)* chiefly [archaic] have doubts about the truth or existence of. be suspicious about. *I have my misdoubts about the existence of the so-called monster.*

Miser – *(noun)* a person who hoards wealth and spends very little. *My uncle is a miser.*

Miserable – *(adjective)* **1** wretchedly unhappy or uncomfortable. causing unhappiness or discomfort. habitually morose. *My brother was miserable for days after losing his new ball.* **2** pitiably small or inadequate. contemptible. austral miserly. *Don't offer me such miserable amount of food.*

Miserliness – *(noun)* extreme desire to same money. *My father was tired of his boss's miserliness.*

Misfire – *(verb)* **1** fail to fire properly. fail to ignite that fuel correctly or at all. *The rocket misfired.* **2** fall to produce the intended result. *His plans misfired. (noun)* an instance of misfiring. *The misfire of his plans cost him his job.*

Misfortune – *(noun)* bad luck. an unfortunate event. *We condoled him for his misfortune.*

Misgiving – *(noun)* a feeling of doubt of apprehension about something. *I have my misgivings about this itinerary.*

Misguide – *(verb)* rare mislead. *The ignorant man misguided the tourists.*

Mishap – *(noun)* an unlucky accident. *It was nothing but a mishap.*

Mishmash – *(noun)* a confused mixture. *The platter looked more like a mishmash than edible food.*

Misjudge – *(verb)* form an incorrect opinion of. judge wrongly. *I misjudged the situation.*

Mislead – *(verb)* cause to have a wrong impression about someone or something. *Don't mislead the students.*

Mislike – *(verb & noun)* [archaic] dislike. *(noun) His mislike for her was written all across his face. (verb) - I mislike this place.*

Mismanage – *(verb)* manage badly or wrongly. *The event management company mismanaged the birthday party.*

Misogamy – *(noun)* rare hatred of marriage. *His misogamy was the reason that he never married.*

Misplace – *(verb)* put in the wrong place. *I misplaced my trust in you.*

Misprize – *(verb)* rare undervalue. *The antique dealer misprized the cutlery collection.*

Misquotation – *(noun)* in accurate quote. *The misquotation became a subject of mockery.*

Misquote – *(verb)* quote inaccurately. *The news channel misquoted the politician. (noun)* an inaccurate quote. *The misquote by the news channel led to a controversy.*

Misread – *(verb)* read or interpret wrongly. *I misread the email and sent a wrong reply.*

Misreport – *(verb)* give a false or inaccurate report of. *The audit company was penalized for its misreport.*

Misrule – *(noun)* unfair or inefficient government. disorder. *The government's misrule plunged the country into turmoil. (verb)* govern badly. *The government misruled the country for several years.*

Miss – *(verb)* fail to hit. *He shot at the robber but missed. (noun)* form of addressing an unmarried woman. *Miss Tate, can you please come here?*

Misshapen – *(adjective)* not having the normal or natural shape. *No one bought the misshapen box.*

Missile – *(noun)* **1** an object which is forcibly propelled at a target. *The missile was very big.* **2** a weapon that is self-propelled or directed by remote control. *The missile was test fired yesterday.*

Mission – *(noun)* **1** an important assignment, typically involving travel abroad. a group of people sent on a mission. an organization or institution involved in a long-term assignment abroad. a military or scientific expedition. *The spies were on a mission to save the country.* **2** the vocation of a religious organization to spread its faith. a strongly felt aim or calling. *The mission did many charity works.*

Mis-spend – *(verb)* spend time or money foolishly or wastefully. *I mis-spent my life's saving on useless investments.*

Mist – *(noun)* a cloud of tiny water droplets in the atmosphere at or near the earth's surface, limiting visibility to. a lesser extent than fog. a condensed vapour settling on a surface. a blurring of the sight, especially caused by tears. *The mist swirled across the landscape. (verb)* cover or become covered with mist. *My eyes misted when I was speaking to my father.*

Mistake - *(noun)* a thing which is not correct. an error of judgement. *This entire idea was a mistake. (verb)* be wrong about. wrongly identify someone or something as. *I mistook you to be someone else.*

Mistaken - *(adjective)* wrong. based on a misunderstanding or faulty judgement. *It was a case of mistaken identity.*

Mister - *(noun)* variant form of Mr., often used humorously. [informal] a form of address to a man. *Now look here Mister, you cannot get away with this.*

Mistress - *(noun)* **1** a woman in a position of authority or control. [chiefly British] a female schoolteacher. the female owner of a dog, cat, etc. [archaic] a female head of a household. *The children respected the mistress.* **2** a woman skilled in a particular subject or activity: a mistress of the sound bite. *She is a mistress of piano.* **3** a woman having a sexual relationship with a married man, [archaic] or poetic a woman loved and courted by a man. *His wife slapped a divorce case on him as soon as she found out about his mistress.* **4** [archaic] Mrs. *Mistress Braithwaite, please give me some cake.*

Mistrust - *(verb)* have no trust in. *The teacher mistrusted the students. (noun)* lack of trust. *I am tired of your mistrust.*

Misusage - *(noun)* [archaic] unjust treatment. *The public was protesting against the misusage of the victim.*

Mite - *(noun)* a minute arachnid with four pairs of legs, several kinds of which are parasitic. *The house is infested with mites.*

Mitigable - *(adjective)* making less severe, painful. *The situation is still mitigable.*

Mitigate - *(verb)* make less server, serious, or painful. *He mitigated the argument between the neighbours.*

Mitigation - *(noun)* the action of reducing seriousness of something. *They had to go to the court for mitigation.*

Mitigatory - *(adjective)* action of making pain less severe. *Their mitigatory moves were welcome.*

Mix - *(verb)* **1** combine or be able to be combined to form a whole. make by mixing ingredient's combine into one to produce a recording. *Please mix this powder in the milk.* **2** spoil the order or arrangement of something. confuse someone or something with another. *Don't mix up the order of the speakers.* **3** associate with others socially. *Let us go out and mix with people.* **4** [informal] be belligerent. *The belligerent nation steeped up the forces on the border. (noun)* a mixture of two or more different people or things the proportion of different people or things constitution a mixture. a version of a recording mixed in a different way from the original. *This mix is rich in proteins.*

Mixture - *(noun)* a substance made by mixing other substances together. the process of mixing or being mixed. a combination of different things in which the components are individually distinct. the charge of gas or vapour mixed with air admitted to the cylinder of an internal-combustion engine. *The mixture was very tasty and nutritious.*

Mizzle - *(noun)* light rain; drizzle. *The mizzle at this time of the year is beneficial for the crops. (verb)* rain lightly. *It mizzled a bit yesterday.*

Moan - *(noun)* **1** a long, low sound expressing suffering or sexual pleasure. a low sound made by the wind. *The little boy moaned because of pain.* **2** a trivial complaint. *I am tired of your moans. (verb)* **1** utter or make a moan. lament. *The doctors rushed to the patient when he moaned.* **2** complain or grumble. *The professor doubled the homework when the students moaned.*

Moat - *(noun)* a deep, wide defensive ditch surrounding a castle or town, typically filled with water. *The moat was full of crocodiles. (verb)* surround with a moat. *The workers moated the castle in no time.*

Mobile - *(adjective)* able to move or be moved freely or easily. accommodated in a vehicle so as to travel around. able or willing to move between occupations, places of residence, or social classes. *I love the concept of mobile libraries. (noun)* **1** a decorative structure suspended so as to turn freely in the air. *The mobile was very attractive.* **2** a mobile phone. *I need a new mobile.*

Mobility – *(noun)* the ability to move or be moved easily. *The injury impacted his mobility.*

Mobilizable – *(adjective)* one taht can be moved impressed. *This plan sounds mobilizable.*

Mocha – *(noun)* **1** a fine quality coffee. a drink or flavouring made with this, typically with chocolate added. *I like having a mocha with my breakfast.* **2** a soft leather made from sheepskin. *The sofa was made of mocha.*

Mock – *(verb)* tease scornfully; ridicule. mimic scornfully or contemptuously. *The grow-up boys mocked the younger ones.* *(adjective)* **1** not authentic or real. *The mock television failed to please the children.* **2** undertaken for training or practice. *The mock drill was a spectacle in itself.* *(noun)* **1** mock examinations. *He did brilliantly in his mocks.* **2** an object of derision. *He was a mock in his school days.*

Mode – *(noun)* **1** a way in which something occurs or is done. a way of operating a system. any of the kinds or patterns of vibration of an oscillating system. the character of a modal proposition. another term for mood. *I like this mode of working.* **2** a style in clothes, art, etc. *He liked to dress up in street mode.* **3** the value that occurs most frequently in a given data set. *Looking at the mode, it looked as if people hadn't been too honest while answering the survey.* **4** a set of notes forming a scale, from which melodies and harmonies are constructed. *They started with a solid mode but the ultimate melody fizzled.*

Model – *(noun)* **1** a three dimensional representation of a person or thing, typically on a smaller scale. a figure in clay or wax, to be reproduced in a more durable material. *The investors were impressed by the model of the new car.* **2** something used as an example. a simplified description, especially a mathematical one, of a system or process, to assist calculations and predictions. a person or things that is an excellent example of a quality: she was a model of self control. *He is a model of professional conduct.* 3 a person employed to display clothes by wearing them. a person employed to pose for an artist, sculptor, etc. *The models did excellent job on the ran...* product. a garment o... well known designer. *Whic... the two?* *(verb)* **1** fashion or shap... etc. cause to appear three dimensional. mathematical model of. *I modeled a nice c... pot for my nephew.* **2** use as an example for something. *Please model the problem for me.* **3** display by wearing them. work as a model. *The supermodel agreed to model the new designer's clothes.*

Moderate – *(adjective)* **1** average in amount, intensity, or degree. *The moderate intensity storm is expected to hit the shore today.* **2** not radical or excessively right or left wing. *He is of moderate opinions.* *(noun)* a person with moderate views. *The moderate convened a meeting.* *(verb)* **1** make or become less extreme, intense, or violent. *Please moderate the flame.* **2** review so as to ensure consistency of marking. *The experts were called to moderate the checking of the papers.* **3** preside over or at. *He wants to moderate the conference.* **4** retard with a moderator. *Please moderate so that the students can understand the concepts.*

Moderation – *(noun)* **1** the avoidance of excess or extremes, especially in one's behavior or political opinions. *Everything should be practiced in moderation.* **2** the process of moderating examination papers or results. the first public examination in some faculties for the BA degree at oxford university. *The moderation at the examination was full of flaws.* **3** the retardation of neutrons by a moderator. *The professor demonstrated the moderation to the students.*

Moderator – *(noun)* **1** an arbitrator or mediator. a presiding officer, especially a chairman of a debate. a Presbyterian minister presiding over an ecclesiastical body. *The moderator did his job well.* **2** a person who moderates examination papers. *The moderator didn't tolerate any nonsense.* **3** a substance used in a nuclear reactor to retard neutrons. *It is important to keep the moderator safe.*

Modern – *(adjective)* of or relating to the present or recent times. characterized by or using the most up to date techniques, equipment, etc. denoting a recent style in art, architecture, etc. marked by a departure from traditional styles and values. *The modern mobile phones are much more sophisticated than the older ones.* *(noun)* a person who advocates a departure from traditional styles or values. *The modern was a huge influence on the masses.*

Modernization – *(noun)* adoption of modern ideas, habits, equipments, methods. *Modernization has his benefits as well as drawbacks.*

Modest – *(adjective)* **1** unassuming in the estimation of one's abilities. *He is a modest player.* **2** relatively moderate, limited, or small. *He made modest offerings to the priests.* **3** decent; decorous. *She is a modest girl.*

Modesty – *(noun)* quality of being unassuming. *I was humbled by his modesty.*

Modifable – *(adjective)* make partial changes. *The plan is still modifiable.*

Modification – *(noun)* the action of modifying a change made. *The modification of the plan led to its failure.*

Modulate – *(verb)* **1** exert a modifying influence on; regulate. *The new manager modulated the processes the team had been following.* **2** vary the strength, tone, or pitch of. alter the amplitude or frequency of in accordance with the variations of a second signal. *He modulates his voice very well.* **3** change from one key to another. *The musician expertly modulated the music.*

Modulator – *(noun)* one who exerts a madifying inflvence. *The modulator malfunctioned.*

Modulus – *(noun)* **1** another term for. the position square root of the sum of the squares of the real and imaginary parts of a complex number. *I have always found calculating the modulus tiresome.* **2** a constant factor or ratio, especially one relating a physical effect to the force producing it. **3** a number used as a divisor for considering numbers in sets, numbers being considered congruent when giving the same remainder when divided by it. *Please use the correct modulus.*

Moist – *(adjective)* **1** slightly wet; damp or humid. rainy. *The clothes were all moist in the morning.* **2** marked by a fluid discharge. *The dog had moist eyes.*

Moisten – *(verb)* wet slightly. *The fumes moistened my eyes.*

Moistness – *(noun)* slightly wet. *The moistness of her eyes made her look as if she'd been crying.*

Moisture – *(noun)* water or other liquid diffused in a small quantity as vapour, within a solid, or condensed on a surface. *The moisture in the air encouraged moulding.*

Molar – *(noun)* a grinding tooth at the back of a mammal's mouth. *The dentist filled the cavity in her molar.*

Molasses – *(noun)* **1** thick, dark brown juice obtained from raw sugar during the refining process. *Molasses is very useful in yeast production.* **2** golden syrup. *The molasses wasn't as tasty as it looked.*

Mole – *(noun)* **1** a small burrowing mammal with dark velvety fur, a long muzzle, and very small eyes, feeding mainly on worms and grubs. *I saw a mole in my garden.* **2** a spy who gradually achieves an important position within the security defences of a country. a betrayer of confidential information. *The mole was caught by the state intelligence.*

Molecule – *(noun)* a group of atoms bonded together, representing the smallest fundamental unit of a compound that can take part in a chemical reaction. *It is possible to see molecules under the microscope.*

Molest – *(verb)* pester or harass in a hostile way. assault or abuse sexually. *The culprits who molested the girl were sentenced to the harshest punishment.*

Mollification – *(noun)* appeasement of anger or anxiety. *He is always successful in his mollification attempts.*

Mollify – *(verb)* appease the anger or anxiety of. reduce the severity of; soften. *The government's attempts to mollify the indignant youth backfired.*

Molly – *(noun)* a small live bearing killifish which has been bred for aquaria in many colours, especially black. *I have many mollies in my aquarium.*

Molten – *(adjective)* liquefied by heat. *The molten lava flowed into the river.*

Moment – *(noun)* **1** a brief period of time. an exact point in time. *Wait a moment! I forgot something.* **2** importance. *This was his moment.* **3** a turning effect produced by a force on an object, expressed as the product of the force and the distance from its line of action to a given point. *The moment reversed the direction of the motion.*

Momentarily – *(adverb)* **1** for a very short time. *I was momentarily nervous before the speech.* **2** very soon. *Help will be there momentarily.*

Momentariness – *(noun)* lasting for a very short time. *The celestial event was missed because of its momentariness.*

Momentary – *(adjective)* brief. *There was a momentary interruption in the telecast.*

Momentum – *(noun)* **1** the quantity of motion of a moving body, equal to the product of its mass and velocity. *The vehicle's momentum kept it going for a bit.* **2** impetus gained by movement or progress: the investigation gathered momentum. *The reforms gathered momentum after the new policies were adopted.*

Monad – *(noun)* **1** a single unit; the number one. *The number 1 is called a Monad.* **2** an indivisible and hence ultimately simple entity, e.g. an atom or a person. *It is possible to see monads under a microscope.* **3** a single celled organism or a single cell. *Some monads also cause disease.*

Monarch – *(noun)* **1** a sovereign head of state, especially a king, queen, or emperor. *The monarch was generous and just.* **2** a large migratory orange and black butterfly, [chiefly north American], whose caterpillars feed on milkweed. *The Monarch is a beautiful butterfly.*

Monarchy – *(noun)* government by a monarch. a state with a monarch. *A monarchy functions in a different way than a democracy.*

Monastic – *(adjective)* of or relating to monks, nuns, etc. or the buildings in which they live. resembling monks or their way of life. *The monastic way of life is very difficult.* *(noun)* a monk or other follower of a monastic rule. *The monastic was curious about the city.*

Monetary – *(adjective)* of or relating to money or currency. *Will there be any monetary benefit for me out of this work?*

Money – *(noun)* a medium of exchange in the form of coins and banknotes. formal sums of money. wealth. payment or financial gain. *Everyone wants to earn money.*

Mongrel – *(noun)* **1** a dog of no definable type or breed. The mongrel was dirty but cute. **2** offensive a person of mixed descent. *They were very rude to the homeless person and called him a mongrel.*

Monism – *(noun)* [philosophy & theology]. **1** a theory or doctrine that denies the existence of a distinction or duality, such as that between matter and mind, or god and the world. *He subscribes to the philosophy of Monism.* **2** the doctrine that only one supreme being exists. compare with pluralism. *Some people believe in monism while the others in pluralism.*

Monk – *(noun)* a member of a religious community of men typically living under vows of poverty, chastity, and obedience. *The monk spent his life studying theology.*

Monkey – *(noun)* **1** a small to medium-sized primate typically having a long tail and living in trees in tropical countries. *Monkeys can be very destructive.* **2** a mischievous person, especially a child. *He is such a monkey!* **3** [British] a sum of 500. *Give me a monkey.* **4** a pile driving machine consisting of a heavy hammer or ram, working vertically in a groove. *He knows how to work a monkey.* *(verb)* behave in a silly or playful way. *Children were all monkeying around.*

Monological – *(adjective)* a long speech by one actor. *Monological sequences depend a lot upon the acting skills of the actor.*

Monotonous – *(adjective)* **1** dull, tedious, and repetitions. *I want to change my monotonous schedule.* **2** lacking in variation of tone or pitch. *He has a monotonous voice.*

Monseiur – *(noun)* a title or form of address for a French speaking man, corresponding to Mr or sir. *Monsieur, what would you like to order?*

Monsoon – *(noun)* **1** a seasonal prevailing wind in the region of the Indian subcontinent and SE Asia, bringing rain when blowing from the south-west. *We wait eagerly for monsoon every year.* **2** the rainy season accompanying the SW monsoon. *Plants grow a lot during monsoon.*

Monstrosity – *(noun)* **1** something very large and unsightly. a grossly malformed animal, plant, or person. *Some people showcase deformities in animals as monstrosities to earn money.* **2** something which is outrageously or offensively wrong. *This crime is such a monstrosity.*

Monstrous – *(noun)* **1** very large and ugly or frightening. *The monstrous tree was centuries old.* **2** inhumanly or outrageously evil or wrong. *The monstrous crime shocked the nation.*

Monticle – *(noun)* a hill or a small mountain. *The Church stood on the monocle.*

Monument – *(noun)* **1** a statue, building, or other structure erected to commemorate a notable person or event. *The monument is a popular tourist spot.* **2** a structure or site of [historical] importance or interest. *The archeological team is set to start digging inside the monument today.* **3** an enduring and memorable example or reminder: the house was a monument to untutored taste. *The school is a monument to progress.*

Mood – *(noun)* **1** a state of mind or feeling. an angry, irritable, or sullen state of mind. *I am in a good mood today.* **2** the atmosphere or pervading tone of a work of art. *The critics were discussing the contemplative mood of the painting.* **3** inducing or suggestive of a particular mood: mood music. *The mood music appeals to me when I am feeling sentimental.*

Moon – *(noun)* **1** the natural satellite of the earth, visible by reflected light from the sun. a natural satellite of any planet. *The Moon looks exceptionally bright today.* **2** a month: many moons ago. *Many moons ago, I bought a site dress.* *(verb)* **1** behave or move in a listless or dreamy manner. *Don't moon around.* **2** [informal] expose one's buttocks to someone in order to insult or amuse them. *The drunkard mooned a whole group of people.*

Moor – *(noun)* a member of a NW unaware of one's surroundings, especially through being in love. *The moor was completely in love with the actress.*

Mop – *(noun)* **1** an implement consisting of a bundle of thick loose strings or a sponge attached to a handle, used for wiping floors. an act of wiping with a mop. *The mop was very dirty and needed to be washed.* **2** a thick mass of disordered hair. *He had a curly mop of hair.* *(verb)* **1** clean or soak up liquid by wiping. *Please mop the floor.* **2** put an end to or dispose of something. *Let us mop this dispute.*

Mopish – *(adjective)* feel dijected. *Why are you in such a mopish mood?*

Moquette – *(noun)* a thick pile fabric used for carpets and upholstery. *The moquette used in making this carpet is of a very good quality.*

Moralist – *(noun)* **1** a person who moralizes, or who teaches or promotes morality. *Our class teacher is a moralist.* **2** a person who behaves morally. *Prison transformed the criminal into a moralist.*

Morality – *(noun)* **1** principles concerning the distinction between right and wrong or good and bad behaviour. a system of values and moral principles. *Some people need lessons in morality.* **2** the extent to which an action is right or wrong. *The panelists questioned the morality of government's actions.*

Moralization – *(noun)* comment on issues of right and wrong. *Moralization of some issues is simply uncalled for.*

Moralize – *(verb)* **1** comment on issues of right and wrong, typically with an unfounded air of superiority. *The panel was attempting to moralize the crime.* **2** interpret or explain as giving moral lessons. *The priest was moralizing at the wedding ceremony.* **3** improve the morals of. *The ideal of the juvenile home was to moralize the young wrong-doers.*

Morally – *(adverb)* principles of right or wrong behaviour. *Your argument is morally wrong.*

Morbid – *(adjective)* **1** characterized by or appealing to an abnormal and unhealthy interest in unpleasant subjects, especially death and disease. *Some writers enjoy writing morbid stories.* 2 medicine of the nature of or indicative disease. *Sometimes morbid medicines can be very useful.*

Mordacious – *(adjective)* formal 1 bitingly sarcastic or vituperative. *The mordacious article hurt many egos.* 2 given to biting. *The mordacious dog had to wear a muzzle at times.*

Mordant – *(adjective)* sharp or critical; biting. *His mordant comments earned him many enemies.* *(noun)* a substance that combines with a dye or stain and thereby fixed it in a material. an adhesive compound for fixing gold leaf. a corrosive liquid used to etch the lines on a printing plate. *The mordant used in drying this piece of cloth is very strong.* *(verb)* impregnate or treat with a mordant. *Please mordant the dye.*

Moreover – *(adjective)* as a further matter; besides. *Moreover, you also owe me a treat.*

Morgue – *(noun)* 1 a mortuary. *The student felt scared when he was in the morgue.* 2 [informal] a newspaper's collection of miscellaneous information for use in future obituaries. *Please go and scan the morgue for the right dates.*

Moribund – *(adjective)* 1 at the point of death. *The moribund man asked for his lawyer.* 2 in terminal decline; lacking vitality or vigour. *The moribund business needs to be closed.*

Morning – *(noun)* the period of time between midnight and noon, especially from sunrise to noon. sunrise. *I like waking up early in the morning.* *(adverb)* [informal] every morning. *You should brush your teeth morning.*

Moron – *(noun)* [informal] a stupid person. *Don't brave like a moron.*

Morphia – *(noun)* dated morphine. *The patient was administered morphia before the surgery.*

Morrow – *(noun)* [archaic] the following day. *I will contact my friend the first thing morrow.*

Mortgage – *(noun)* 1 the charging of property by a debtor to a creditor as security for a debt, on the condition that it shall be returned on payment of the debt within a certain period. *The poor farmer offered his land as a mortgage to educate his children.* 2 a loan obtained through the conveyance of property as security. *The mortgage helped the family build a new house.* *(verb)* convey to a creditor as security on a loan. *I mortgaged my jewellery to be able to study further.*

Mosque – *(noun)* a muslim place of worship. *The mosque has beautiful minarets.*

Mosquito – *(noun & adjective)* variant spelling of miskito. *The mosquito buzzed around my ear all night.*

Mostly – *(adverb)* 1 as regards the greater part or number. *The results are mostly positive.* 2 usually. *Mostly, I reach office before everyone else.*

Mot – *(noun)* a compulsory annual test for safety and exhaust emissions of motor vehicles of more than a specified age. *My car failed the mot.*

Mote – *(noun)* a speck. *The plane was no bigger than a mote.*

Moth – *(noun)* a chiefly nocturnal insect having tow pairs of broad wings covered in microscopic scales, typically drably coloured and held felt when at rest, and lacking the clubbed antennae of butterflies. *The moth fluttered around the lamp.*

Mother – *(noun)* 1 a woman in relation to a child or children to whom she has given birth. a woman who has care of a child through adoption. a female animal in relation to its offspring. *A mother's love is unconditional.* 2 the head of a female religious community. *Mother Teresa was a noble soul.* 3 [informal] an extreme example or very large specimen: the mother of all traffic jams. *Necessity is the mother of all inventions.* *(verb)* 1 bring up with care and affection. *Elephants mother their children for a long time.* 2 look after kindly and protectively, sometimes excessively so. *The hostel's warden mothers the hostel inmates.* 3 dated give birth to. *She mothered triplets.*

Motile – *(adjective)* 1 [zoology & botany] capable of motion. *Protozoans are motile microbes.* 2 [physchlogy] of, relating to, or characterized by responses that involve muscular rather than audio-visual sensations. *The upper airway has motile sensory receptors.*

Motion – *(noun)* **1** the action or process of moving or being moved. *Moving things remain in motion for a while before stopping.* **2** a movement or gesture. *His motion towards the enemies showed his aggression.* **3** a piece of moving mechanism. *The motion malfunctioned and the vehicle broke down.* **4** a formal proposal put to a legislature or committee. *The motion was passed without any objections.* **5** [law] an application for a rule or order of court. *The lawyer raised an objection to the motion.* **6** [British] an evacuation of the bowels. a portion of excrement. *He was suffering from loose motions.* *(verb)* direct with a gesture. *The policeman motioned the traffic to pass.*

Motive – *(noun)* **1** a factor inducting a person to act in a particular way. *One should be focussed in working towards a motive.* **2** a motif. *Some of the motives in the book are beautiful.* *(adjective)* **1** producing physical or mechanical motion. *The motive force moved the vehicle.* **2** acting as a motive. *The motive for quick money turned him into a thief.*

Motley – *(adjective)* varied in appearance or character; disparate. *Her motley dress didn't suit the professional working atmosphere.* *(noun)* **1** a varied mixture. *The motley of movies was playing on TV.* **2** [historical] the particoloured costume of a jester. *The jester's motley tore during the performance.*

Motor – *(noun)* **1** a machine, especially one powered by electricity or internal combustion, that supplies motive power for a vehicle or other device. *A large capacity generator needs a powerful motor.* **2** [British informal] a car. *Tom has a red coloured motor car.* *(adjective)* **1** giving imparting, or producing motion or action. *The motor power set the vehicle in motion.* **2** [physiology] relating to muscular movement or the nerves activating it. *The two types of nerve fibres are sensory and motor fibres.* *(verb)* [informal, chiefly British] travel in a car. *The boy motors in a car to his work place.*

Motto – *(noun)* **1** a short sentence or phrase encapsulating a belief or ideal. *In order to be successful, everyone should have a clear motto.* **2** [music] a symbolically significant phrase which recurs throughout a musical work. *That poet has a distinctive use of motto in his poems.*

Mould – *(noun)* **1** a hollow container used to give shape to molten or hot liquid material when it cools and hardens. *The bakery shop near the market has lovely cake moulds.* **2** something made in this way, especially a dish such as a jelly or mousse. *The mould turned out in perfect shape.* **3** a distinctive form, style, or character: a superb striker in the same mould as linker. *The actors from the academy have distinctive mould.* **4** a frame or template for producing. *The moulds for making the posters are available in the market.*

Moulder – *(verb)* slowly decay. *Food was mouldering due to breakdown of refrigerator.*

Mound – *(noun)* **1** a raised mass of earth or other compacted material, especially one created for purposes of defence or burial. baseball a slight elevation form with for pitcher delivers the ball. *Soldiers hid behind the mound during attack from enemies.* **2** a small hill. *There is a beautiful lake at the foot of the mound.* **3** a heap or pile. *Teacher had a mound of test paper to assess.* **4** large quantity. *Mounds of hands are required to meet the deadline.* *(verb)* **1** heap up into a mound. *Librarian was asked to mound up the books for transportation.* **2** [archaic] enclose or fortify with an embankment. *The workers mounded the fort.*

Mount – *(verb)* **1** climb up or on to; ascend. *Stock prices mounted steadily.* **2** get up on in order to ride it set on horseback: provide with a horse. *In order to go for riding, one has to mount the horse first.* **3** get on for the purpose of copulation. *In the breeding period, dogs look for a mate to mount.* **4** grow larger, more numerous, or more intense. *The costs mount up when you buy a home. Officer's anger mounted when the subordinates failed to give a valid reason for the mistake.* **5** organize and initiate. *Scientific team got together to mount for the upcoming conference.* *(noun)* **1** a backing on which a picture or photograph is set for display. *When the photograph fell down,* *its glass broke while the sturdy mount remained intact.* **2** a support for a pieced of equipment. *The mount for the precious telescope could be dismantled.* **3** a microscope slide. *For re-evaluation of the disease, the doctor asked to send the histopathology mounts of the patients for second opinion.* **4** a stamp hinge. *The mount was very beautifully engraved.* **5** a horse used for riding. *He was a beautiful mount.*

Mountable – *(adjective)* ability of being climbed up. *He bought a set of mountable band pads.*

Mountebank – *(noun)* **1** a swindler. *The mountebank was exposed.* **2** [historical] a person who sold patent medicines in public places. *He bought the medicines from a mountebank.*

Mounted – *(adjective)* riding an animal, typically a horse. *Mounted riders were dressed in traditional gear.*

Mourn – *(verb)* feel deep sorrow following the death or loss of. express this sorrow through conventions such as the wearing or black clothes. *She mourned the loss of her pet.*

Mournful – *(adjective)* feeling, expressive, or inducing sadness, regret, or grief. *He played a mournful melody.*

Mouse – *(noun)* **1** a small rodent that typically has a pointed snout, relatively large ears and eyes, and a long tail. *She has a pet mouse.* **2** a timid and quiet person. *He is a mouse but is very intelligent.* **3** computing a small hand-held device which is dragged across a flat surface to move the cursor on a computer screen, having buttons which or bruise to control computer functions. *He couldn't complete his presentation as he broke his mouse yesterday.* **4** [informal] a lump or bruise on or near the eye. *He tried to hide the mouse under his eye.* *(verb)* **1** hunt for or catch mice. *His cat is very efficient in mousing.* **2** prowl about. *He moused around in the lawn.*

Mouth – *(noun)* **1** the opening and cavity in the lower part of the human face, surrounded by the lips, through which food and air are taken and vocal sounds are emitted. the corresponding opening through which an animal takes in food. *He filled his mouth with sweets.* **2** [informal] talkativeness; impudence. *he has a bad mouth on him.* **3** an opening or entrance to a structure that is hollow, concave, or almost completely enclosed. *The mouth of the bottle was blocked with a marble.* *(verb)* **1** say in an insincere or pompous way. [informal] talk in an opinionated or abusive way. *He mouthed back to all the officials.* **2** move the lips as if to form: she mouthed a silent farewell. *The little boy mouthed his complaints immediately.* **3** take in or touch with the mouth. *He mouthed the entire fruit at once.* **4** train the mouth of so that it responds to a bit. *Her horse was mouther for the first time this weekend.*

Mouthless – *(adjective)* the opening through which food is taken or words spoken. *The box is mouthless.*

Movability – *(noun)* ability to be moved. *They were concerned about the movability of the display case.*

Movable – *(adjective)* **1** capable of being moved. *They kept the costumes in an easily movable cupboard.* **2** denoting a religious feast day that is variable in date from year to year. *He made a calendar of all movable religious days of the year.* **3** [law] of the nature of a chattel, as distinct from land or buildings. *He made a significant amount of movable property.* *(noun)* **1** property or possessions not including land or buildings. *They removed all the movables from the old house before the monsoon.*

Move – *(verb)* **1** go or cause to go in a specified direction or manner. *He moved left to catch the ball.* **2** change or cause to change position. adjust one's position to be nearer to or make room for someone else. *He moved a little to make room for the old lady.* **3** change one's place of residence. start living or working in a place. *She moved back to her hometown.* **4** take a new job. *He moved to the sales team last month.* **5** change or cause to change from one state, opinion, sphere, or activity to another. *She moved the guests' attention to the performers.* **6** take or cause to take action. *They moved against the new rule.* *(noun)* **1** an instance of moving. *Her move was very subtle.* **2** a change or state or opinion. *Her* career move was successful. **3** an action that initiates or advances a process or plan. *The group's next move is to gain more support.* **4** a manoeuvre in a sport or game. *His wining move was excellent.*

Movement – *(noun)* **1** an act of moving. *The dancers' movement was reflected in the mirror.* **2** a person's activities during a particular period of time. *His movements during the play were observed very carefully by everyone.* **3** a group of people working together to advance a shared cause. a cause of this type. *They discussed the labour movement.* **4** a change or development. *The movement towards stronger laws.* **5** music, a principal division of a musical work, that is self-sufficient in terms of key, tempo, and structure. *He beautifully captured the slow movement of the musical piece.* **6** the moving parts of a mechanism, especially a clock or watch. *The clocks movements were broken.*

Mower – *(noun)* an equipment to cut grass. *He bought a new mower.*

Mowing – *(noun)* **1** loose mown grass. *The mowings were kept neatly in a corner.* **2** US a field plutonium oxides.

Muchness – *(noun)* [informal] very similar. *The performances appeared much of muchness.*

Mucid – *The planter was mucid.*

Mucous – *(adjective)* mouldy, musty festering. *The mucous wound took a long time to heal.*

Mud – *(noun)* **1** soft, sticky matter consisting of mixed earth and water. *The kids are playing with mud.* **2** damaging information or allegations. *The opposition threw mud at the leaders.*

Muddle – *(verb)* **1** bring into a disordered or confusing state. confuse two or more things with each other. *The muddled up the piles.* **2** confuse. *The muddled the audience.* **3** busy oneself in a confused and ineffective way. cope more or less satisfactorily. *They muddled through the tests.* **4** US, mix or stir into a drink. *He muddled the lemon perfectly in the drink.* *(noun)* a muddied state. *The papers were in a muddle.*

Muff – *(noun)* **1** a short tube made of fur or other warm material into which the hands are placed for warmth. *She lost her muff.* **2** vulgar slang a woman's genitals. *She's got an infection in the muff.*

Muffler – *(noun)* **1** a wrap or scarf worn around the neck and face for warmth. *The red muffler is his favourite.* **2** a device used to deaden the sound of a drum, bell, piano, or other instrument. *He bought a muffler for his friend's drums.* **3** [north American], a silencer for a motor vehicle exhaust. *His bike's muffler is damaged.*

Mug – *(noun)* **1** a large cup, typically cylindrical and with a handle and used without a saucer. *The tea mug was empty.* **2** [informal], a person's face. *His mug was really funny.* **3** [British informal] a stupid or gullible person. *He acts like a mug.* **4** US [informal] a hoodlum or thug. *She was cautious of the mugs on the road.* *(verb)* **1** attack and rob in a public place. *He was mugged on the train.* **2** make faces before an audience or a camera. *He mugged for the audience.*

Mugginess – *(noun)* unpleasantly humid. *It was a warm and humid, full of mugginess.*

Muggy – *(adjective)* unpleasantly warm and humid. *It's very muggy today.*

Mulberry – *(noun)* small deciduous tree with broad leaves. *There is a mulberry tree in our yard.*

Mulet – *(noun)* male mule. *He bought a young mulet for his barn.*

Mulish – *(adjective)* stubborn like a mule. *He irritated everyone with his mulish behaviour.*

Muller – *(noun)* a stone used for grinding materials such as artists pigment. *The cat broke my muller.*

Mullock – *(noun)* **1** rubbish or nonsense. *Everyone avoids his mullock.* **2** austral rock which contains no gold or form which gold has been extracted. *He has a small collection of mullocks.*

Multangular – *(adjective)* having many angles. *He drew a multangular.*

Multifarious – *(adjective)* having great variety and diversity. many and various. *The stall has a multifarious display.*

Multiform –. existing in many forms or kinds. *They offer a multiform programme.*

Multilateral – *(adjective)* agreed upon or participated in by three or move parties. *They took multilateral decision.*

Multinomial – *(adjective) & (noun)* mathematics another term for polynomial. *They did an exercise on multinominals.*

Multiplex – *(adjective)* **1** consisting of many elements in a complex relationship. *They have a multiplex relation.* **2** involving simultaneous transmission of several message along a single channel of communication. *The multiplex line was distrupted.* **3** having several separate screens within one building. *The new mrket has a multiplex cinema also. (noun)* **1** a multiplex system or signal. **2** a multiplex cinema. *The new multiplex is very grand. (verb)* 1 incorporate into a multiplex signal or system. *The signals from the building were multiplexed.*

Multiplicable – *(adjective)* able to be multiplied. *The numbers were multiplicable.*

Multiplicand – *(noun)* a quantity which is to be multiplied by another the multiplier. *The multiplicand was written in blue.*

Multiplication – *(noun)* **1** the process of multiplying. *He used a calculator for multiplication.* **2** mathematics the process of combining matrices, vectors, or other quantities under specific rules to obtain their product. *The question required a number of multiplications.*

Multiplier – *(noun)* **1** a quantity by which a given number is to be multiplied. *He copied the multiplier wrongly.* **2** [economics], a factor by which an increment of income exceeds the resulting increment of saving or investment. *He was happy with his multiplier.* **3** a device for increasing by repetition the intensity of an electric current, force, etc. to a measurable level.

Multiply – *(noun)* **1** obtain form another which contains the first number a specified number of times. **2** increase or cause to increase in number or quantity. *They multiplied the snack and drinks to accommodate the large number of guests.* **3** increase in number by reproducing. *The number of bugs in the area has multiplied in the recent years.* **4** propagate. *They multiplied the issue.*

Multitude – *(noun)* large number of people or things. *A multitude of people supported the cause.*

Mumble – *(verb)* **1** say something indistinctly and quietly. *He only mumbled his protest.* **2** bite or chew with toothless gums. *He mumbled the sweets. (noun)* a quiest and indistinct utterance. *Her mumbles seemed loud in the library.*

Mummy – *(noun)* a body that has been preserved for burial by embalming and wrapping in bandages. *We saw Tutankhamen's mummy in the museum.*

Mundane – *(adjective)* **1** lacking interest or excitement. *His teaching method was very mundane.* **2** of this earthly world rather than a heavenly or spiritual one. *They spent their vacations in the hills to take a break from their mundane routine.*

Munificence – *(noun)* quality of being very generous. *They thanked him for his munificence.*

Munificent – *(adjective)* very generous. *She is very munificent to her employees.*

Monuments – *(plural noun)* [chiefly law] title deeds or other documents proving a person's title to land. *He kept the monuments safely in the drawer.*

Munition – *(noun)* military weapons, ammunition, equipment, and stores. *The lost because of shortage of munitions. (verb)* supply with munitions. *They were able to munition the force despite the bad routes to the field.*

Mural – *(noun)* a paining executed directly on wall. *The murals on the temple walls are almost perfectly preserved. (adjective)* **1** of, like, or relating to a wall. *They made a mural quadrant.* **2** medicine of or relating to the wall of a body cavity or blood vessel. *He was issued a mural medicine.*

Murderer – *(noun)* a person who commits murder. *He was wrongly suspected to be a murderer.*

Murderous – *(adjective)* **1** capable of, intending, or involving murder or extreme violence. *He was a murderous person.* **2** [informal] extremely violence. *The fight was murderous.* **3** [informal] extremely arduous or unpleasant. *It was a murderous sight.*

Mure – *(verb)* [archaic] confine in or as in a prison. *They were murred in because of heavy storm.*

Murk – *(noun)* darkness or fog causing poor visibility. *The murk was making it difficult to drive. (adjective)* [archaic] dark or gloomy. *His room was murky.*

Murmur – *(noun)* **1** a low continuous backgroung noise. *The murmur of the class was very distracting.* **2** a quietly spoken utterance. the quiet or subdued expression of a feeling. *There was a murmur of agreement.* **3** [medicine] a recurring sound heard in the heart through a stethoscope that is usually a sing of disease or damage. *The doctor detected no murmur. (verb)* **1** say something in a murmur. *He murmured the name of the artist.* **2** make a low continuous sound. *He was murmuring while studying.*

Murrain – *(noun)* **1** dewater fever or a nature, to the infectious disease affecting cattle or other animals. *His cow is suffering from murrain.* **2** [archaic], a plague or crop blight. *He described last year's murrain year in his article.*

Murrey – *(noun)* [archaic], the deep purple-red colour of a mulberry. *She bought a murrey scarf.* Heraldry, another term for sanguine. *He felt murrey.*

Muscle – *(noun)* **1** a band of fibrous tissue in the body that has the ability to contract, producing movement in or maintaining the position of a part of the body. *He pulled a muscle while running.* **2** physical power. *He has a lot of muscle.* **3** political or economic power. *They used muscle to stop the protest. (verb)* **1** [informal north American], move by use of physical strength. *They muscled away the luggage.* **2** force one's way into. *They muscled their way into the venue.*

Museum – *(noun)* a building in which objects of [historical], scientific, artistic, or cultural interest are stored and exhibited. *The museum was reopened after major renovations.*

Mush – *(noun)* **1** a soft, wet, pulpy mass. *There was a mush outside the door.* **2** [north American] thick maize porridge. *He eat mush on Saturdays.* **3** cloying sentimentality. *He was acting mush.* **4** [British informal] a person's mouth or face *His mush was swollen. (verb)* reduce to mush. *She mushed the fruits for filling.*

Mushroom – *(noun)* **1** a spore producing fungal growth, often edible and typically having a domed cap with gills on the underside. *He loves mushrooms on his pizza.* **2** a pale pinkish brown colour. *It has a mushroom colour. (verb)* **1** increase or develop rapidly. *The resentment mushroomed in the state.* **2** form a shape resembling that of a mushroom. *The blast mushroomed into a white cloud.* **3** gather mushrooms. *She went mushrooming in the morning.*

Mushy – *(adjective)* soft and fulffy. *She gifted the baby a mushy toy.*

Music – *(noun)* **1** the art or science of combining vocal or instrumental sounds to produce beauty of form, harmony, and expression of emotion. the sound so produced. *They play soothing music in the evening.* **2** the written or printed signs representing such sound. *She is learning to read music.*

Musician – *(noun)* a person who plays a musical instrument or is otherwise musically gifted. *She is a brilliant musician.*

Musk – *(noun)* **1** a strong smelling reddish brown substance secreted by the male musk deer, used as an ingredient in perfumery. *The display showed raw musk along with the processed perfume.* **2** a musk scented plant related to the monkey flower. *The nursery has a musk plant too.*

Musket – *(noun)* an infantryman's light gun with a long barrel, typically smooth bored and fired from the shoulder. *The musket broke after it fell from the cliff.*

Muslin – *(noun)* lightweight cotton cloth in a plain weave. *He hung the curd in a muslin cloth.*

Muss – *(verb)* make untidy or messy. *He mussed the sketch. (noun)* a mess or muddle. *The room was a muss.*

Must – *(verb)* **1** be obliged to; should. expressing insistence. *The seal must be broken before trying to open the can.* **2** expressing an opinion about something that is very likely. *They must have started the decorationing last evening. (noun)* something that should not be overlooked or missed. *A visit to the forts is must if you go to Jaipur.*

Mustard - *(noun)* **1** a hot tasting yellow or brown paste made from the crushed seeds of certain plants, eaten with meat or used as a cooking ingredient. *I loved mustard in sandwich.* **2** a plant of the cabbage family whose seeds are used to make this paste. *I have a mustard plant in my kitchen garden.* **3** a brownish yellow colour. *He dyed the cloth in mustard colour.*

Musty - *(adjective)* **1** having a stale or mouldy smell or taste. *He found a musty cloak in the store room.* **2** unoriginal or outdated. *All the story ideas were rejected as the editor found them musty.*

Mutable - *(adjective)* liable to change. inconstant in one's affections. *The audience response is very mutable.*

Mutation - *(noun)* **1** the action or process of changing. a change. *The mutation of the structure was too rapid.* **2** a change in the structures of a gene resulting in a variant form which may be transmitted to subsequent generations. a distinct form resulting from such a change. *His new novel is based around a new mutant variety of humans.* **3** change of an initial consonant in a word caused by the preceding word. umlaut.

Mute - *(adjective)* **1** refraining from speech or temporarily speechless. *They were so shocked that they stayed mute for a minute.* **2** lacking the faculty of speech. *The baby was born mute.* **3** not giving tongue while hunting. **4** not pro(noun) ced. *He often misspells words with mute letters in them.* *(noun)* **1** a person without the power of speech. a servant who was deprived of the power of speech. *The workers were mute in face of the owner's cruelty.* **2** a professional attendant or mourner at a funeral. *The mute was late to the service.* **3** a clamp placed over the bridge of a stringed instrument to deaden the resonance without affecting the vibration of the strings. *He went to buy a new mute.* **4** a pad or cone placed in the opening of a brass or other wind instrument. *She spent a long time cleaning the mute of her instrument.* *(verb)* **1**deaden or muffle the sound of. *They muted the TV when the phone rang.* **2** reduce the strength or intensity of. not bright; subdued. *He muted the lights after dinner.*

Mutilate - *(verb)* injure or damage severely, typically so as to disfigure. *The doll was mutilated.*

Mutter - *(verb)* say in a barely audible voice. talk or grumble in secret or in private. *He muttered his unhappiness with the arrangements.* *(noun)* a barely audible utterance. *His muttering was ignored.*

Mutual - *(adjective)* **1** experienced or done by each of two or more parties towards the other or others: mutual respect. having the same specified relationship to each other. *They had a mutual respect for each other's ritual.* **2** held in common by two or more parties: a mutual friend. *They got the news from a mutual friend.* **3** denoting a building society or insurance company owed by its members and dividing some or all its profits between them. *The new company is mutual.*

Muzzle - *(noun)* **1** the projecting part of the face, including the nose and mouth, of an animals such as a dog or horse. a guard fitted over an animal's muzzle to stop it biting or feeding. *The child coloured crocodile's muzzle yellow!* **2** the open end of the barrel of a firearm. *The jammed the gun's muzzle with tiny stones.* *(verb)* **1** put a muzzle on. *The muzzled the horse in the afternoon.* **2** prevent from freedom of expression. *The government muzzled the press on the new case.*

Muzzy - *(adjective)* **1** confused. *He felt muzzy as he didn't get proper sleep the previous night.* **2** blurred. indistinct. *The vision was muzzy because of the water on the lense.*

My- *(possess. det.)* **1** belonging to or associated with the speaker. used with forms of address in affectionate, sympathetic, humorous, or patronizing contexrs. *My mother baked a cake for me.* **2** used in various expressions of surprise. *Oh my! It's such beautiful sunset.*

Myalgia - *(noun)* pain in a muscle or group of muscles. *He is taking medicines to treat myalgia.*

Myalism - *(noun)* a Jamaican folk religion focused on the power of ancestors, typically involving drumming, dancing, spirit possession, ritual sacrifice, and herbalism. *They spent the night discussing myalism beliefs.*

Myopia - *(noun)* **1** short sightedness. *She suffers from myopia.* **2** lack of foresight or intellectual insight. *Their myopia caused a lot of delay in completing the project.*

Myriad - *(noun)* **1** an indefinitely great number. *A myriad of colours were created by the glass work.* **2** a unit of ten thousand. *A group of myriad, or 10,000, officers gathered in the ground to practice for the parade. (adjective)* innumerable elements: the myriad political scene. [phrase already provided]

Myriapod - *(noun)* a centipede, millipede, or other arthropod having an elongated body with numerous leg bearing segments. *They studied a myriapod sample in the lab today.*

Myrobalan - *(noun)* **1** another term for cherry plum. *They were asked to bring leaves of a cherry plum or myrobalan.* **2** a tropical tree of a characteristic pagoda shape. the fruit of this tree, used in tanning. *She collected many myrobalan tree in the orchard today.*

Myrrh - *(noun)* a fragrant gum resin obtained from certain trees and used, especially in the near east, in perfumery, medicines, and incense. *Ancient Egyptians were very fond of myrrh.*

Myrtle - *(noun)* **1** an evergreen shrub with glossy aromatic foliage and white flowers followed by purple black oval berries. *The gardener planted four new myrtle in the garden today.* **2** the lesser periwinkle. *She drew a myrtle on the greeting card.*

Mysterious - *(adjective)* difficult to understand. *He disappeared under mysterious circums- tances.*

Mystic - *(noun)* **1** a person who seeks by contemplation and self surrender to attain unity with the deity or the absolute, and so reach truths beyond human understanding. *He is self-proclaimed mystic. (adjective)* another term for mystical. *She narrated a mystic tale after dinner.*

Mysticism - *(noun)* **1** the belief or state of mind characteristic of mystics. *The discussed the popular ancient mysticism of the area.* **2** vague or ill defined religious or spiritual belief, especially as associated with a belief in the occult. *The theory was rejected as it was based on mysticism.*

Mystify - *(verb)* **1** utterly bewilder. *The audience was mystified by his performance.* **2** make obscure or mysterious. *They mystified the system to fool ignorant people.*

Myth - *(noun)* **1** a traditional story concerning the early history of a people or explaining a natural or social phenomenon, and typically involving supernatural being or events. *Despite his education, he firmly believes in the hindu myth of creation.* **2** a widely held but false belief. *Shop owners and customers often believe in many myths about each other.* a fictitious person or thing. an exaggerated or idealized conception of a person or thing. *She gave a lecture on myth of Sisyphus.*

Mythical - *(adjective)* occurring in myths or fock tales. *She made a project on mythical monsters.*

Mythologer - *(noun)* one having a collection of myths. *He is famous mythologer.*

Mythology - *(noun)* **1** a collection of myths, especially one belonging to a particular religious or cultural tradition. *Indian mythology is very vast and varied.* **2** a set of widely held but exaggerated of fictitious stories or beliefs. *His new book describes the famous mythology from his hometown.* **3** the study of myths. *He is a teacher of mythology.*

Mythus - *(noun)* a myth or mythos. *He narrated a mythus.*

Nn

N– *(noun)* **1** the fourteenth letter of the alphabet. *N is the fourteenth letter of the alphabet.* **2** denoting the next after M in a set of items, categories, etc.

Nab– *(verb)* **1** catch doing something wrong. *The police nabbed the thief.* **2** take or grab suddenly. *I nabbed him.*

Nacelle– *(noun)* **1** the outer casing of an aircraft engine. *The passengers were carried to the airship in a nacelle.* **2** the car of an airship.

Nag– *(verb)* **1** harass constantly to do something to which they are averse. *Disturbing nagged him day and night.* **2** be persistently painful or worrying to. *A nagging worry got hold of me.* *(noun)* **1** a person who nags. *A nag doubt haunted me.* **2** a persistent feeling of anxiety. *He felt a little nag of doubt.*

Naiad– *(noun)* a nymph inhabiting a river, spring, or waterfall. *In Greek mythology Naids were female spirits who presided over water bodies.*

Nail – *(noun)* **1** a small metal spike with a broadened flat head, driven typically into join things together or to serve as a hook. *He drove nail in the wall.* **2** a horny covering on the upper surface of the tip of the finger and toe in humans and other primates. a hard growth on the upper mandible of some soft billed birds. *She has long nails.* **3** a former measure of length for clot, equal to $2^1/_4$ inches. *The carpenter fixed the joint with nails.* **4** a former measure of wool, beef, or other commodity, roughly equal to 7 or 8 pounds. *He was nailed in a false case of murder (verb)* **1** fasten with a nail or nails. *Decorative strips have been nailed to the wall.* **2** detect or catch. *The police promptly nailed the robber.* **3** strike forcefully and successfully. *Federer nailed the opponent with backhand serves.* **4 4** defeat or outwit. *The bowler tried to nail the batsman with inswingers.*

Naive– *(adjective)* lacking experience, wisdom, or judgment. *Please forgive him, he is a naïve fellow.*

Name – *(noun)* **1** a word or set of words by which someone or something is known, addressed, or referred to. *His name is famous among novelists.* **2** a famous person. a reputation, especially a good one. *Among friends, he is known by the name of puppy.* **3** an insurance underwriter belonging to a Lloyd's syndicate. *He is a name known for social work. (verb)* **1** give a name to. indentify or mention by name. call someone or something by the same name as. [chiefly British] mention by name as disobedient to the chair and thereby subject to a ban from the house. *Do you know a building named Laxmi Niwas.* **2** specify a sum, time, or place. *(adjective)* having a well-known name. *the kidnappers named a sum of 5 lakh rupees.*

Namkeen – *(noun)* indian salty snack. *Indians usually serve guests namkeen and tea as refreshment.*

Nanny – *(noun)* **1** a person, typically a woman, employed to look after a child in its own home. *He hired a nanny for his baby.* **2** a person or institution regarded as interfering and overprotective. *His mother acts like a nanny even for the grown up son.* **3** a female goat. *Female of a goat is known as nanny. (verb)* be overprotective towards. *Nannies have a tendency to be extra caring towards their grand children.*

Nape – *(noun)* the back of a person's neck. *The hair stood on his nape as he watched the horror film.*

Napery – *(noun)* archaic household linen, especially tablecloths and napkins. *I am going to wash the napery today.*

Naphtha – *(noun)* [chemistry] a flammable oil containing various hydrocarbons, obtained by the dry distillation of organic substances such as coal, shale, or petroleum. *Naphtha is a dangerous petroleum product.*

Napkin – *(noun)* **1** a square piece of cloth or paper used at a meal to wipe the fingers or lips and to protect garments. *Please wipe your fingers on a napkin.* **2** [British] a baby's nappy. *Mothers tie a napkin around toddler's neck before feeding.*

Napoleonic – *(adjective)* of, relating to, or characteristic of napoleon I or his time. *It is a Napoleonic hat.*

Narcissus – *(noun)* a daffodil with a flower that has white or pale outer petals and a shallow orange or yellow centre. *I have a narcissus in my garden.*

Narcosis – *(noun)* medicine a state of stupor, drowsiness, or unconsciousness produced by drugs. *He has taken a strange drug and is under narcosis.*

Narcotic – *(noun)* an addictive drug, especially an illegal one, affecting mood or behaviour. *He is a narcotic.* [medicine] a drug which induces drowsiness, stupor, or insensibility, and relieves pain. *He is under the influence of narcotic.* *(adjective)* relating to narcotics. *This drug belongs to a group of narcotics.*

Narcotize – *(verb)* affect with or as if with narcotic drug. *The robbers wanted to narcotize the family to rob without fear.*

Nard – *(noun)* a himalayan plant. *Some Ayurvedic medicines use nards during preparation.*

Narrate – *(verb)* give a spoken or written account of. provide a commentary to accompany. *He narrated the incident very clearly.*

Narrative – *(noun)* a spoken or written account of connected events; a story. the narrated part of a literary work, as distinct from dialogue. the practice or art of narration. *It was a brilliant piece of narrative.* *(adjective)* in the form of or concerned with narration. *Narrative by the witness confused the police.*

Narrowly – *(adverb)* by a small margin. *It was a bad accident. He narrowly escaped death.*

Narrowness – *(noun)* limited in space, amount or scope. *Narrowness of mind is responsible for many foolish acts.*

Nasal – *(adjective)* **1** of or relating to the nose. *He sings in a nasal voice.* **2** pronounced by the breath resonating in the nose, e.g. m, n, ng, or French en, un. the letter 'm' is characterized by the nasal. *He has got a helmet which has a nasal piece.* *(noun)* **1** a nasal speech sound. **2** [historical] a nosepiece on a helmet. *He speaks with a nasal tone.*

Nascency – *(noun)* state of just coming into existence. *Indian space industry is 40 years old and is completely out of nascency.*

Nascent – *(adjective)* **1** just coming into existence and beginning to display sings of future potential. *It is a nascent bud.* **2** [chemistry] freshly generated in a reactive form. *Nascent hydrochloric acid is very dangerous.*

Nasturtium – *(noun)* a south American trailing plant with round leaves and bright orange, yellow, or red flowers, widely grown as an ornamental. *I have just purchased a nasturtium.*

Nasty – *(adjective)* **1** highly unpleasant or repugnant. *There was a nasty smell in the kitchen.* **2** unpleasant or spiteful in behavior. annoying or unwelcome. *Don't mess with him, he is a nasty person.*

Natal – *(adjective)* of or relating to the place or time of one's birth. *His natal sign is Gemini.*

Natation – *(noun)* swimming. *The frogs train tadpoles the art of natation.*

Nates – *(plural noun)* [anatomy] the buttocks. *She has well-rounded nates.*

Nation – *(noun)* a large aggregate of people united by common descent, culture, or language, inhabiting a particular state or territory. *India is a multi-lingual and multi-cultural nation.*

National – *(adjective)* **1** of, relating to, or characteristic of nation. *Crimes against women have become a national issue.* **2** owned, controlled, or financially supported by the state. *He is a French national.* *(noun)* **1** a citizen of a particular country. *Saina Nehwal is the national champion in badminton.* **2** a national newspaper as opposed to a local one. *The Times of India is a national newspaper.*

Nationalism – *(noun)* patriotic feeling, principles, or efforts; an extreme form of this marked by a feeling of superiority over other countries. *Uncontrolled nationalism sometimes leads to dictatorship and war.*

Nationalize - *(verb)* **1** transfer a major branch of industry or commerce from private to state ownership or control. *Big private companies are often nationalized in socialist countries.* **2** make distinctively national. *He is a nationalized foreigner.*

Native - *(noun)* **1** a person born in a specified place or associated with a place by birth. a local inhabitant. *He is a native of Australia.* **2** indigenous to a place. *Neem is our native plant.* **3** dated, chiefly offensive a non-whit original inhabitant of a country as regarded by European colonists or travelers. *Natives of India speak many languages and follow many religions.* *(adjective)* **1** associated with the place or circumstances of a person's birth. of the indigenous inhabitants of a place. *His native place is Jaipur, Rajsthan.* **2** of indigenous origin or growth. *Akbar Birapal stories show the native wit of India.* **3** innate; in a person's character. *Native wit.*

Nativity - *(noun)* the occasion of a person's birth. *The nativity of Jams Christ is celebrated as festival of Christmas.*

Natron - *(noun)* a mineral salt found in dried lake beds, consisting of hydrated sodium carbonate. *Natron is a useful mineral.*

Nattily - *(adverb)* smartly. *She turned out at the reception dresses nattily.*

Nattiness - *(noun)* state of smartness. *She is well mannered and so is her nattiness with dress.*

Natty- *(adjective)* small and fashionable. *Because of her fashionable style; she is known as the most natty girl in the college.*

Natural - *(adjective)* **1** existing in or derived from nature; not made, caused by, or processed by humankind. unbleached and undyed; off-white. *Oceans, mountains, trees rivers etc. are natural objects.* **2** in accordance with nature; normal relaxed and unaffected. inevitable the natural choice. based on innate moral sense. *Natural state of mind is peaceful which is often disturbed by over ambition and spirit of competition.* **3** related by blood. *It was but natural that he should beg her pardon after his misbehaviour.* **4** music not sharpened or flattened. having no valves and able to play only the notes of the harmonic series above a fundamental note. of or relating to the notes and intervals of the harmonic series. *He is my natural brother.* **5** Christian theology relating to human or physical nature as distinct form the spiritual or supernatural realm. *He has a natural ability for solving tough mathematical sums.* *(noun)* **1** a person with an innate gift or talent for a particular task or activity. *The colour of this sweater is natural.* **2** music a natural note, or a sing denoting one when a previous sign or the key signature would otherwise demand a sharp or a flat. *Nature-wise, he is a kind man.* **3** an off-white colour. *Natural selection led to the evolutionary growth of species.*

Naturalism - *(noun)* **1** a style and theory of representation based on the accurate depiction of detail. *His writings have a lot of naturalism.* **2** a philosophical viewpoint according to which everything arises from natural properties and causes, and supernatural or spiritual explanations are excluded or discounted. the theory that ethical statements can be derived from non-ethical ones. *He is a follower of the theory of naturalism and has no belief in supernatural.*

Naturalist - *(noun)* an expert in or student of natural history. *My brother is a naturalist and studies how certain animals and plants developed into present form.*

Naturalize - *(verb)* admit a foreigner to the citizenship of a country. alter so that it conforms more closely to the phonology or orthography of the adopting language. *He is a naturalized citizen of India and not so by birth.*

Naturally - *(adverb)* **1** in a natural manner. *Naturally we don't feel at case with strangers.* **2** of course. *A wife is not naturally allowed to travel on officeal trips of her husband.*

Naturalness - *(noun)* quality of being natural. *He demonstrates naturalness that many others try hard to project on the stage.*

Naught - *(noun pronoun)* [archaic] nothing. *All his efforts were brought to naught.*

Nausea – *(noun)* a feeling of sickness with an inclination to vomit. *He had nausea in the foul smelling place.*

Nauseate – *(verb)* affect with nausea; offensive to the taste or smell. *He felt nauseated after eating the food.*

Nautical – *(adjective)* of or concerning sailors or navigation; maritime. *A nautical mile covered by ship is about 2,025 yards.*

Naval – *(adjective)* of, in, or relating to a navy or navies. *He is a high ranking naval officer.*

Nave – *(noun)* the central part of a church building usually separated from the chancel by a step or rail and from adjacent aisles by pillars. *There were a lot of people present in the nave.*

Navel – *(noun)* a rounded knotty depression in the centre of a person's belly caused by the detachment of the umbilical cord after birth; the umbilicus. *She wears a diamond in her navel.*

Navicular – *(adjective)* chiefly archaic boat-shaped. *He had a navicular bone fracture in on accident.*

Navigable – *(adjective)* of a waterway or sea able to be sailed on by ships or boats. *It is a stormy sea and not navigable at this time.*

Navigate – *(verb)* **1** plan and direct the route or course of a ship, aircraft, or other form of transport, especially by using instruments or maps. *The captain navigated the ship safely through ice bergs.* **2** sail or travel over a stretchy or water or terrain. guide a vessel or vehicle over a specified route or terrain. *Bhagirathi river is being desilted to make ships navigate.*

Navigation – *(noun)* **1** the process or activity of navigating the passage of ships. *He has finished his training in navigation.* **2** [chiefly dialect] a navigable inland waterway, especially a canal. *The canal has been opened for navigation by small boats.*

Navigator – *(noun)* a person who navigates a ship, aircraft, etc. *He is an expert navigator and trusted by the captain.*

Navvy – *(noun)* [British dated] a labourer employed in the excavation and construction of a road, railway, or canal. *A navvy is usually hired on daily wages.*

Navy – *(noun)* **1** the branch of a state's armed services which conducts military operations at sea. poetic a fleet of ships. *The British navy is very powerful.* **2** a dark blue colour. *He is wearing a navy coloured shirt.*

Nawab – *(noun)* [Indian] **1** a native governor during the time of the Mogul Empire. *He lives lavishly like a nawab.* **2** a Muslim nobleman or person of high status. *Mansur Ali Khan was the Nawab of Pataudi.*

Nay – *(adverb)* or rather; and more than that. *He is foolish, nay ill-mannered as well.*

Nazi – *(noun)* **1** historical a member of the national socialist German worker's party. *He is called a nazi because of his super racial views.* **2** [derogatory] a person with extreme racist or authoritarian views. *People with feelings of extreme hatred are known as Nazis.*

Neap – *(noun)* a tide just after the first or third quarters of the moon when there is least difference between high and low water. *Trapped in a neap tide, the ship ran aground.*

Near – *(adverb)* **1** at or to a short distance away. *My house is near a big super market.* **2** a short time away in the future. *He is going to be rich in the near future.* **3** almost. *He nearly fainted during the 400 m race. (preposition)* **1** at or to a short distance away from a place. *He is nearer to his mother than to his father.* **2** a short period of time from. *I had nearly reached the station when the train left.* **3** almost. *He nearly lost his temper.* **4** similar to. *This glass in the ring nearly resembles a diamond. (adjective)* **1** located a short distance away. *We need the help of our nears and dears in times of trouble.* **2** only a short time ahead. *The thief stood near my car.* **3** similar, close to being the thing mentioned. *This shirt is nearly the same as the one I brought last week. (verb)* approach. *He slipped near the finish line of 400 metre race.*

Nearness – *(noun)* proximity. *Too much nearness in any relation is not good.*

Neat – *(adjective)* **1** in good order; tidy or carefully arranged. *The room was neat and clean.* **2** done with or demonstrating skill of efficiency. *He drank neat whisky neatly.*

Neath – *(preposition)* chiefly beneath. *There is a cat sitting beneath the table.*

Neb – *(noun)* [Scottish] a nose, snout, or bird's beak. *The neb of an eagle looks frightening.*

Nebula – *(noun)* [astronomy] a visible cloud of gas or dust in outer space. old-fashioned term for galaxy. *You can see the nebula shining over there in the sky.*

Necessary – *(adjective)* **1** required to be done, achieved, or present; needed. *It is something necessary, so do it.* **2** inevitable: a necessary consequence. [philosophy] inevitable resulting from the nature of things, so that the contrary is impossible. philosophy having no independent volition. *Necessary consequences of a bad action are always bad.* *(noun)* **1** the basic requirements of life, such as food and warmth. *Basic necessities of life must be met.*

Necessitate – *(verb)* make necessary as a result or consequence, force or compel to do something. *He was necessitated into selling his property.*

Necesitous – *(adjective)* of a person poor, needy. *He is a necessitous person give him some money.*

Necessity – *(noun)* **1** the state or fact of being necessary. *Necessity is the mother of invention.* **2** an indispensable thing.

Neck – *(noun)* **1** the part of a person's or animal's body connecting the head to the rest of the body. *She has a slim round neck.* **2** a narrow connecting or end part. the part of a bottle or other container near the mouth. *The neck of the bottle was rather narrow. I caught the thief by the neck.* **3** the part of a violin, guitar, or other instrument that bears the fingerboard. *The string of a guitar is situated at the neck.* *(verb)* [informal] kiss and caress amorously. *The couple was necking amorously in the park.*

Necrology – *(noun)* an obituary notice. *His name does not appear in necrology.*

Necromancy – *(noun)* the supposed practice of communicating with the dead, especially in order to predict the future. witchcraft, sorcery, or black magic in general. *He practices black magic and is supposed to be indulged in necromancy.*

Necrophobia – *(noun)* extreme or irrational fear of death or dead bodies. *He suffers from necrophobia and won't enter the mortuary.*

Necrosis – *(noun)* medicine the death of most or all of the cells in an organ or tissue due to disease, injury, or failure of the blood supply. *The old man had an accident and died of necrosis.*

Nectar – *(noun)* **1** a sugary fluid secreted within flowers to encourage pollination by insects, collected by bees to make into honey. *Bees and insects collect nectar from flowers.* **2** the drink of the Gods, a delicious drink. *The drink he offered me was so delicious that it tasted like nectar.*

Neddy – *(noun)* [British] a child's word for a donkey. *He is a fine neddy and will certainly win the race.*

Need – *(verb)* **1** requirement, because it is essential or very important rather than just desirable. *If need be, I'll come to your house.* **2** expressing necessity. or obligation. *Need I say more?* **3** [archaic] be necessary. *Enough for today need I practice more?* *(noun)* **1** circumstances in which something is necessary; necessity. *You need not come to see me tomorrow.* **2** a thing that is wanted or required. *All of us need a certain amount of money to fulfil the basic necessities of life.*

Needful – *(adjective)* [formal] necessary: requisite. *The needful must be done urgently to help the flood incites.*

Neediness – *(noun)* lacking necessities of life. *Their look and clothes showed neediness for financial wealth.*

Needle – *(noun)* **1** a very fine slender piece of metal with a point at one end and a hole or eye for thread at the other, used in sewing. a similar, larger instrument used in crochet, knitting, etc. *give me a needle and some black thread; I have to darn the torn packet of my shirt.* **2** the pointed hollow end of a hypodermic syringe. *The needle of this syringes is broken.* **3** a stylus used to play records. *He played on his instrument very well indeed with his needle.*

Needless – *(adjective)* unnecessary; avoidable. *It is needless to observe these formalities here.*

Needs – *(adverb)* of necessity. *Let your needs be limited.*

Needy – *(adjective)* lacking the necessities of life; very poor. *He is needy, so let us help him.*

Never – *(adverb)* at no time in the past or future. *Never use such abusive language again.*

Nefarious – *(adjective)* criminal or antisocial. *He is a nefarious fellow and had been in jail many times, His nefarious activities brought bad name to the family.*

Negative – *(adjective)* **1** consisting in or characterized by the absence rather than the presence of distinguishing features. expressing or implying denial, disagreement, or refusal. grammar & logic stating that something is not the case. contrasted with affirmative and interrogative. *Don't talk to him, he is in a negative state of mind.* **2** pessimistic, undesirable, or unwelcome. *Negative thoughts cause a lot of harm.* **3** less than zero. *She replied in negative to my proposal.* **4** of containing, producing, or denoting the kind of electric charge carried by electrons. *Give me the negatives of my photo. (noun)* **1** a word or statement expressing denial, refusal, or negation. a bad or unwelcome quality or aspect. *Check the negative and positive ends of the battery cells before you fit them in the remote.* **2** a negative photographic image form which positive prints may be made. *Photographs trere days are not developed from the negatives. (verb)* **1** reject, veto, or contradict. **2** render ineffective; neutralize. *Parliament negatived the bill by 300 to 250.*

Neglect – *(verb)* fail to give proper care or attention to. fail to do something. *He spent a negative childhood. (noun)* the state or process of neglecting or being neglected. failure to do something. *He neglected his studies and failed in the class.*

Neglectful – *(adjective)* not giving proper attention. *He is a neglectful parent.*

Negligence – *(noun)* failure to take proper care over something. *Negligence on the part of guard cost him his job.* [law] breach of a duty of care which results in damage. *Negligence in duty is not pardonable.*

Negilgent – *(adjecitive)* failing to take proper care. *He is a negligent worker and hence cannot be relied upon.*

Negligible – *(adjective)* so small or unimportant as to be not worth considering; insignificant. *He passed the exam with negligible margin.*

Negotiable – *(adjective)* open to discussion or modification. *This flat is for sale and the price is negotiable.*

Negro – *(noun)* a member of a dark-skinned group of peoples originally native to Africa south of the Sahara. *Many negroes were enslaved by European colonizers.*

Negus – *(noun)* [historical] a ruler, or the supreme ruler, of Ethiopia. *He was the negus of a big African tribe.*

Neigh – *(noun)* a characteristic high whinnying sound made by a horse. *The horse was disturbed and neighed as the stranger approached him. (verb)* utter a neigh. *The horse neighed several times to draw the owner's attention.*

Neighbour – *(noun)* a person living next door to or very near to another. *My neighbor is a mice fellow. (verb)* be situated next to or very near another. *Lets go to air neighboring place.*

Nemesis – *(noun)* the inescapable agent of someone's downfall, especially when deserved a downfall caused by such an agent. *His wife proved to be his nemesis.*

Neo – *(combining form)* **1** new: neonate. *Neoclassical paintings are a lot attractive to look at.* **2** a new or revived form of: neo-Darwinian.

Neologist – *(noun)* coining of new words. *Lexicographers use the services of neologist to introduce new words to dictionary.*

Neon – *(noun)* **1** the chemical element of atomic number 10, an inert gaseous element of the noble gas group. *Neon lights are spread all over metro cities.* **2** fluorescent lighting and signs using neon or another gas. *Advertisers use neon lights to advertise products in market place.*

Neophyte – *(noun)* a person who is new to a subject, skill, or belief. *He is a neophyie and it will take him some time to adjust.*

Neoteric – *(adjective)* recent; new; modern. *His neoteric views on religion are worth reading.*

Nephew – *(noun)* a son o one's brother or sister, or of one's brother-in-law or sister-in-law. *This young man is my nephew.*

Nephology – *(noun)* the study or contemplation of clouds. *Nephology interests me a lot.*

Nephritic – *(adjective)* [renal] of or relating to nephritis. *He has a nephritic disease, take him to a hospital.*

Nepotism – *(noun)* the favouring of relations or friends, especially by giving them jobs. *Almost all political leaders practice nepotism.*

Neptune – *(noun)* a planet of the solar system, eighth in order from the sun. *Neptune is a very distant planet.*

Nerve – *(noun)* **1** a whitish fiber or bundle of fibers in the body that transmits impulses of sensation between the brain or spinal cord and other parts of the body. *He sure had nerve to face the challenge.* **2** bravery; assurance. one's steadiness and courage. *Have you the nerve to speak to me like that?* **3** nervousness. *Nervousness overpowered him as he approached the girl.* **4** [informal] cheek. *Many of his nerves were damaged in the accident.* *(verb)* brace oneself for a demanding situation. *You should have the nerve of steel to face South African fast bowlers.*

Nerveless – *(adjective)* **1** lacking vigour or feeling. *He is nerveless in the face of danger.* **2** confident not nervous. *Being nerveless, he leads a lovely life.*

Nervous – *(adjective)* **1** easily agitated or alarmed, apprehensive, resulting form anxiety or anticipation. *He is a very nervous fellow and gets frightened easily.* **2** relating to or affecting the nerves. *His nervous system broke down and he wept bitterly.*

Nest – *(noun)* **1** a structure or place made or chosen by a bird for laying eggs and sheltering its young. a place where an animal or insect breeds or shelters. a snug or secluded retreat. a bowl-shaped object likened to a bird's nest. *This large tree has many nests in its branches.* **2** a place filled with undesirable people or things: a nest of spies. *This cottage is my nest.* *(verb)* **1** use or build a nest. *This cluster of houses is a nest of goons.*

Nestle – *(verb)* **1** settle comfortably within or against something. *She nestled against me.* **2** lie in a sheltered position. *The town nestled at the foot of the hell.*

Nestling – *(noun)* a bird that is too young to leave the nest. *She is a nestling and isn't ready to fly yet.*

Net – *(noun)* **1** a length of open-meshed material of twine, cord, etc. used typically for catching fish. a net supported by a frame at the end of a handle, used for catching fish or insects. *Many fish were caught in the net.* **2** a structure with a net used in various games, e.g. as a goal in football, to divide a tennis court, or to enclose a cricket practice area. *The team scored a goal as the ball entered the net.* **3** a fine fabric with a very open weave. [British informal] net curtains. *Net curtains hung in the house.* **4** a trap. a system for selecting or recruiting someone. *The tennis ball struck against the net.* **5** a communications or broadcasting network. a network of interconnected computers. the internet. *TV network is the most important part of media.* *(verb)* **1** catch or obtain with or as with a net. *Internet system has proved very useful.* **2** into the net; score. *Food plates were covered with net.* **3** cover with a net. *He caught many in sects in the net.* **4** *Once a network of spies existed in many communist countries.*

Nether – *(adjective)* lower in position. *He is nether in position to many employees.*

Nettle – *(noun)* a herbaceous plant having jagged leaves covered with stinging hairs, also used in names of plants of a similar appearance. *Don't touch this plant. It is a nettle.*

Neural – *(adjective)* of or relating to a nerve or the nervous system. *He underwent a neural surgery.*

Neuritis – *(noun)* [medicine] inflammation of a peripheral nerve or nerves. *He is suffering from neuritis.*

Neurosis – *(noun)* medicine a relatively mild mental illness not caused by organic disease, involving depression, anxiety, obsessive behavior, etc. but not with a radical loss of touch with reality. *He has neurosis and is consulting a psychologist.*

Neurotic – *(adjective)* **1** [medicine] having, caused by, or relating to neurosis. *His neurotic* *behaviour upset all. (noun)* abnormally sensitive and obsessive, a neurotic person. *He is a neurotic and at times wouldn't listen to anyone.*

Neuter – *(adjective)* **1** of or denoting a gender of nouns typically contrasting with masculine and feminine or common. *'It' is a neuter gender.* **2** lacking developed sexual organs; castrated or spayed. having neither functional pistils nor stamens. *An ox is a neuter bull. (noun)* **1** [grammar] a neuter word. *A worker bee or ant is a neuter insect.* **2** a non-fertile caste of social insect, especially a worker bee or ant. a castrated or spayed domestic animal. *(verb)* **1** castrate or spay. *Bull quite often are made neuter to conserve energy for farming.* **2** render ineffective. *The bomb squad neutered the bomb.*

Neutral – *(adjective)* **1** impartial, belonging to an impartial state or group, unbiased. *He is a neutral person, you can go and seek his advice.* **2** having no strongly marked characteristics. *He remained neutral during the argument between two parties.* **3** [chemistry] neither acid nor alkaline. *Neutral is defined as a substance with a pH of. (noun)* **1** an impartial or unbiased state or person. *He is a neutral person.* **2** a neutral colour or shade. *Brown is a neutral shade.* **3** a disengaged position of gears. *We left the car in neutral.* **4** an electrically neutral point, terminal etc. *Third point in a plug is a neutral to prevent electrical shock.*

Never – *(adverb)* **1** not ever. *Never before did he speak in such a way.* **2** not at all. [British informal] definitely or surely not. *He went abroad and never came back.*

Nevertheless – *(adverb)* in spite of that. *He is foolish, nevertheless honest.*

New – *(adjective)* **1** not existing before; made, introduced, or discovered recently or now for the first time. not previously used or owned. *He has bought a new car.* **2** harvested early in the season. *As the locality was new to me, I felt ill at ease.* **3** seen, experienced, or acquired recently or now for the first time. unfamiliar or strange to. inexperienced at or unaccustomed to. discovered or founded later than and named after. *I am new to these customs.* **4** reinvigorated, restored, or reformed. superseding and more advanced than others of the same kind: the new architecture. *Columbus and many other sailors discovered new countries. (adverb)* newly. *New trains run at a very fest speed. The newly born baby looked very healthy.*

News – *(noun)* **1** newly received or noteworthy information, especially about recent events. *This is the latest news you are hearing.* **2** a broadcast or published news report. *A special news bulletin will be telecast just now.* **3** [informal] information not previously known to. *This is news to me.*

Nexus – *(noun)* **1** a connection a connected group or series. *The nexus between politicos and mafia is something highly undesirable.* **2** the central and most important point. *You have talked extravagantly, completely missing the nexus.*

Nib – *(noun)* the pointed end part of a pen, which distributes the ink, a pointed or projecting part of an object. *The nib of pen is broken.*

Nibble – *(verb)* **1** take small bites out of. eat in small amounts. gently bite at. *Rats have nibbled the piece of bread.* **2** gradually erode. *The rabbit was nibbling at the carrot.* **3** show cautious interest in a project. *(noun)* **1** an instance of nibbling. **2** a small piece of food bitten off. [informal] small savoury snacks. *Do you want a nibble.*

Nice – *(adjective)* **1** pleasant; agreeable; satisfactory. good-natured; kind. *He is a nice man by nature.* **2** fine or subtle. requiring careful attention. *This is a nice piece of silk.* **3** [archaic] fastidious. *It was nice of you to come here.*

Nicely – *(adverb)* in a pleasant manner. *The Job was nicely done.*

Niceness – *(noun)* the quality of being nice. *The niceness of his behavior impressed all.*

Niceties – *(noun)* manners and etiquette.*He observed all the niceties of behavior.*

Nicety – *(noun)* a fine detail or distinction. accuracy. a detail of etiquette. *His drawings had great nicety.*

Niche – *(noun)* **1** a shallow recess, especially one in a wall to display an ornament. *The golden statue was placed in a niche.* **2** a comfortable or suitable position in life. *He has found his niche in life.* **3** a specialized but profitable corner of the market. **4** ecology a role taken by a type of organism within its community. *(verb)* place or position in a niche. *Usually niche markets are visited by rich people.*

Nicknacks – *(noun)* variant spelling of knick-knack. *She is fond of wearing knickknacks.*

Nicotiana – *(noun)* an ornamental plant related to tobacco, with tubular flowers that are particularly fragrant at night. *The plant of nicotiana smells fragrant at night.*

Nicotine – *(noun)* a toxic oily liquid which is the chief active constituent of tobacco. *He is addicted to nicotine.*

Niece – *(noun)* a daughter of one's brother or sister, or of one's brother-in-law or siter-in-law. *Meet her, she is my niece.*

Nifty – *(adjective)* [informal] particularly good, skilful, or effective. stylish. *It is a nifty piece of art.*

Niggard – *(noun)* a mean or stingy person. *He is a niggard, keep away from him.*

Niggardliness – *(noun)* mean and meagre. *The niggardliness of the government's budget angered voters.*

Niggardly – *(adjective)* ungenerous. meager. *he gave me a niggardly amount of money. (adverb)* archaic in a mean or meager manner. *He talked to me in a very niggardly way.*

Nigger – *(noun)* [offensive] a black person. *To call a black person nigger is to insult him.*

Niggle – *(verb)* **1** cause slight but persistent annoyance, discomfort, or anxiety. *She is quarrelsome and niggles her husband daily.* **2** find fault with in a petty way. *You always find niggles in my work. (noun)* a trifling worry, dispute, or criticism. *It is a niggle and will pass away in a short while.*

Night – *(noun)* **1**the time from sunset to sunrise. this as the interval between tow days. *It grew pitch dark at night.* **2** the darkness of night, poetic nightfall. *He returned from club late in night.* **3** an evening. *The clock struck at midnight. (adverb)* [informal] at night. *The house looked haunted in the night.*

Night-bird – *(noun)* another term for night owl. *Owl keeps awake at night and hence is called a night-bird.*

Night-blindness – *(noun)* less technical term for nyctalopia. *He suffers from night-blindness, as the night descends, he loses his vision.*

Night-fall – *(noun)* dusk. *It is night-fall now and he hasn't returned as yet.*

Night-hawk – *(noun)* **1** an American night-hawk with pointed wings. *Owl is a bird of prey and is also called night-hawk.* **2** [north American] term for night owl. *Look! Its a nigth-hawk!*

Nightlong – *(adjective)* throughout the night. *After the nightlong vigil, the police caught the culprit.*

Nightsoil – *(noun)* human excrement collected at night from cesspools and privies, sometimes used as manure. *These persons collect the nightsoil.*

Nigrescent – *(adjective)* rare blackish. *These negroes are nigrescent.*

Nil – *(noun)* nothing; zero. *They beat us three-nil. (adjective)* non-existent. *So far, his achievement is nil.*

Nimble – *(adjective)* quick and light in movement or action. *Small birds are usually very nimble.*

Nimbly – *(adverb)* in a nimble way. *The monkey leapt nimbly from one tree to another.*

Nimbus – *(noun)* **1** a large grey rain cloud. *Do you see that nimbus in the sky, it is going to rain.* **2** a luminous cloud or a halo surrounding a supernatural being or saint. *The photos of saints have a nimbus around their heads.*

Nimrod – *(noun)* a skilful hunter. *The ancient man was a nimrod.*

Nincompoop – *(noun)* a stupid person. *What a nincompoop he is!*

Nine – *(cardinal number)* **1** equivalent to the product of three and three; one less than ten. *There are nine muses in Greek mythology*

Nineteen – *(cardinal number)* one more than eighteen; nine more than ten; 19. *He is only nineteen years old.*

Ninety – *(cardinal number)* equivalent to the product of nine and ten; ten less than one hundred; 90. *Ninety is the word for the digit 90.*

Ninny – *(noun)* [informal] a foolish and weak person. *He is a ninny, don't expect anything wise from him.*

Niobium – *(noun)* the chemical element of atomic number 41, a silver-grey metal used in superconducting alloys. *Wires made with niobium as a constituent lowers the resistance to electricity.*

Nip – *(noun)* [informal, offensive] a Japanese person. *He is a nip, you can't understand his language.*

Nippers – *(noun)* **1** [informal] a child. **2** pliers, pincers, or a similar too. *Please bring me a pair of nippers.* **3** a creature that nips. *A rat is a nipper.* the claw of a crab or lobster. *Fishermen use nippers to catch fish.*

Nipple – *(noun)* **1** the small projection in which the mannary ducts of female mammals terminate and from which milk can be secreted. the corresponding vestigial structure in a male, *The baby sucked at the nipple of her mother.* **2** a small projection on a machine, especially one from which oil or other fluid is dispensed. a short section of pimple with a screw thread at each end for coupling. *All feeding bottles have nipples.* *(verb)* provide with a projection like a nipple. *Nipples are provided as projections in male joints for coupling with female joints.*

Nisi – *(adjective)* [law] valid or taking effect only after certain conditions are met. *(adjective)* (of a decree, order or rule) that takes effect or is valid only after certain. *Conditions are met "an order nisi".*

Nit – *(noun)* [informal] **1** the egg or young form of a louse or other parasitic insect, especially the egg of a human head louse. *There are many nits in her hair.* **2** [British] a stupid person. *He is a nit.*

Nitre – *(noun)* potassium nitrate; saltpeter. *He brought a vial of nitre for some experiment.*

Nitric – *(adjective)* containing nitrogen with a valency of five. *Nitric acid is used in chemical experiments.*

Nitrify – *(verb)* [chemistry] an organic compound containing a cyanide group CN bound to an alkyl group. *To nitrify means to convert ammonia into nitrates or nitrites.*

Nix – *(exclamatory)* expressing denial or refusal. *The government nixed the proposal to organise indo-pak cricket series.*

No – *(abbreviation)* [US] short for number. *The no.7 horse will win.*

Nob – *(noun)* [austral, informal] a shark. *I have just seen a nob near our boat.*

Nobble – *(verb)* [British informal] **1** try to influence or thwart by underhand or unfair methods. tamper with to prevent it from winning a race. *Being at am influential post, he nobbled a lot of money.* **2** accost. *He nobbled his way through the interview.*

Nobility – *(noun)* **1** the quality of being noble. *He belongs to nobility and is a much respected man.*

Noble – *(adjective)* **1** belonging by rank, title, or birth to the aristocracy. *He is a noble man by birth and manners.* **2** having fine personal qualities or high moral principles. **3** imposing; magnificent. *(noun)* a person of noble rank or birth. *Tax was imposed on both nobles and commoners.*

Nock – *(noun)* archery a notch at either end of a bow or at the end of an arrow, for receiving the bowstring. *Every arrow has a nock at its end to fit the bow-string.* *(verb)* fit to the bowstring.

Noctambulist – *(noun)* sleepwalker. *She is a noctambulist capable of making tea while a sleep.*

Nocturnal – *(adjective)* done, occurring, or active at night. *Owl is a nocturnal bird.*

Nocturne – *(noun)* music a short composition of a romantic nature. *I saw a nocturne in an art exhibition and bought it at quite a high price.*

Noddle – *(noun)* [informal, dated] a person's head. *There was a holo around the holy person's noddle.*

Noddy – *(noun)* dated a silly or foolish person. *Sometimes he acts noddy but otherwise is quite intelligent.*

Node – *(noun)* a point in a network at which lines intersect or branch. a piece of equipment, such as a computer or peripheral, attached to a network. mathematics a point at which a curve intersects itself. astronomy either of the tow points at which a planet's orbit intersects the plane of the ecliptic or the celestial equator. *New leaves are growing form the node.*

Nodose – *(adjective)* technical characterized by hard or tight lumps; knotty. *The tree was quite old and had a nodose trunk.*

Nodule – *(noun)* a small swelling or aggregation of cells, especially an abnormal one. *The doctor noticed a nodule on his hand.*

Nogging – *(noun)* brickwork in a timber frame. *The mason finished noggin in the wooden frame.*

Noise – *(noun)* **1** a sound, especially one that is loud, unpleasant, or disturbing. continuous or repeated loud, confused sounds. *I can no longer stand this loud noise.* **2** conventional remarks expressing some emotion or purpose: the government made tough noises about defending sterling. *The noise created by loudspeakers is a menace.* **3** technical irregular fluctuations accompanying and tending to obscure an electrical signal or other significant phenomenon. *Students were waking a lot of noise in the classroom.* *(verb)* **1** dated talk about or make known publicly. *The speaker confronted a noisy crowd.* **2** poetic make much noise. *Birds are noising loudly.*

Noiseless – *(adjective)* silent very quiet. *The house was noiseless as nobody lived there. He entered the room noiselessly.*

Noisy – *(adjective)* **1** full of or making a lot of noise. *It was a noisy classroom.* **2** technical accompanied by random fluctuations that obscure information. *The noisy crowd soon became uncontrolled.*

Nomad – *(noun)* a member of a people continually moving to find fresh pasture for its animals and having no permanent home. a wanderer. *These are nomads and won't stay here for long.*

Nomadic – *(adjective) living a life of a nomad.He is nomadic by nature, always wondering.*

Nominal – *(adjective)* **1** existing in name only. relating to or consisting of names. *It is an outdated law and has only a nominal value.* **2** grammar headed by or having the function of a noun. *This club has a nominal fee.*

Nominally – *(adverb)* existing in name only. *He resigned the membership, nominally on health grounds.*

Nominate – *(verb)* **1** put forward as a candidate for election or for an honour or award. appoint to a job or position. *Party has nominated him as a candidate for the coming election.* **2** specify formally. *These four actors have been nominated for the best actor award.* *(adjective)* zoology denoting a race or subspecies having the same epitet as the species to which it belongs, e.g. homo sapiens sapiens. *In zoology man has been nominated as homo sapiens.*

Nominative – *(adjective)* **1** grammar denoting a case of nouns, pronouns, and adjectives expressing the subject of a verb. *He is a nominative case in grammar.* **2** of or appointed by nomination as distinct from election. *He has not been elected to the part, his selection is nominative.*

Nominator – *(noun)* one who nominates. *The only president has the power as numerator to fill two seats.*

Nominee – *(noun)* **1** a person who is nominated. *He is a nominee to the leadership of the party.* **2** a person or company, not the owner, in whose name a company, stock, etc. is registered. *He is only a nominees in the company.*

Non – *(prefix)* expressing negation or absence: non-recognition. not of the kind or class described: non-believer. expressing a neutral negative sense where in or un has a special connotation. *He is a non-believer in God. Certain species of insects have become non-existent.*

Nonagon – *(noun)* a plane figure with nine straight sides and angles. *Nonagon is a geometrical figure with nine sides and angles.*

Nondescript – *(adjective)* lacking distinctive or interesting characteristics. *He is a nondescript person, nobody takes interest in him.* *(noun)* a nondescript person or thing.

Nonentity – *(noun)* an unimportant person or thing. *People hardly notice a nonentity.*

Non-existence – *(noun)* not real or present. *Non-existence of police led to riots.*

Non-plus – *(verb)* surprise and confuse, flummox. *He became nonplussed as he saw the horrible accident.* *(noun)* a state of being nonplussed. *She was non-plussed at his eagerness to help her.*

Non-resident – *(adjective)* not living in a particular country or a place of work. not requiring residence at the place of work or instruction. *There are many non-resident Indians.* *(noun)* a person not living in a particular place. *Non-resident indians can retain their indian passport.*

Nonsense – *(noun)* **1** words that make no sense. *What nonsense! You shouldn't have behaved like that.* **2** foolish or unacceptable behavior. an absurd or unthinkable scheme, situation, etc. *You are talking nonsense, shout up.*

Nonsensical – *(adjective)* having no meaning. *You must stop reading nonsensical books.*

Non-sequitur – *(noun)* a conclusion or statement that does not logically follow from the previous argument or statement. *His non-sequitur did not impress anybody.*

Nonsuit – *(verb)* subject to the stoppage of their suit on the grounds of failure to make a legal case or bring sufficient evidence. *His case was declared to be nonsuited.* *(noun)* the stoppage of a suit on such grounds. *The lack of efficient evidence resulted in nonsuit.*

Noodle – *(noun)* a very thin, long strip of pasta or a similar flour paste. *He is fond of eating noodles.*

Nook – *(noun)* a corner or recess, especially one offering seclusion or security. *Many insects lived in the nooks of the deserted house.*

Noon – *(noun)* twelve o'clock in the day; midday. *His much awaited call came at noon.*

Noose – *(noun)* a loop with a running knot which tightens as the rope or wire is pulled, used especially to hang offenders or trap animals. *The noose tightened around the criminal's neck,* *(verb)* apply a noose to; catch with a noose. form into a noose. *Stray cows were being noosed.*

Nor – *(conjunction & adverb)* **1** and not; and not either: they were neither cheap nor convenient. neither: nor can I . *he cannot use such abusive language, nor can I.* **2** [archaic] or dated than. *This car is neither cheap nor impressive.* *(noun)* **1** a logical operation which gives the value one if and only if all the operands have a value of zero, and otherwise has a value of zero. *OR, NOR and NAND are different types of gates to make electrons flow in a desired direction.*

Norm – *(noun)* the usual, typical, or standard thing. a required or acceptable standard. *He observes all norms of good behaviour.*

Normal – *(adjective)* **1** conforming to a standard; usual, typical, or expected. *Once his anger subsided he will behave normal.* **2** [technical] intersecting a given line or surface at right angles. *"A single plane of symmetry with a diad axis normal to it".* *(noun)* **1** the normal state or condition. *Her temperature was above normal.* **2** [technical] a line at right angles to a given line or surface. *The rays are reflected normal to the incident rays.*

Normalcy – *(noun)* condition of being usual or typical. *He regained normalcy of behavior after the psychiatric treatment.*

Normality – *(noun)* the state of being normal. *Normality in every sphere of life is something desirable.*

Normalize – *(verb)* **1** bring to a normal or standard state. *His behavior became normalized after a long time after accident.* **2** [mathematics] multiply by a factor that makes the norm equal to a desired value. *Both sets of date a have been normalized such that the lowest value is equal to.*

Normally – *(noun)* **1** in a normal manner; in the usual way. *Although angry, he behaved normally.* **2** as a rule. *Normally speaking please avoid walking alone at night.*

Norman – *(noun)* **1** a member of a people of mixed Frankish and Scandinavian origin who settled in Normandy in the 10th century; in particular, any of the Normans who conquered England in 1066 or their descendants. a native or inhabitant of modern Normandy. *He lives in Normandy and is called a Norman.* **2** the northern form of old French spoken by the Normans. the French dialect of modern Normandy. *Britain, was conquered by the Normans.* *(adjective)* of or relating to the Normans of Normandy. denoting the style of Romanesque architecture used in Britain under the Normans. *Normans conquered England in the 10th century.*

Norse – *(noun)* **1** an ancient or medieval form of Norwegian or a related Scandinavian language. *Ancient Norwegians spoke Norse language.* **2** Norwegians or Scandinavian language. **3** Norwegians adjective of or relating to Norway or Scandinavia, or their inhabitants or language. *Norse are used to living in a very cold climate.*

North – *(noun)* **1** the direction in which a compass meddle normally points, towards the horizon on the left-hand side of a person facing east. *Delhi is situated in the north of India.* **2** the northern part of a country, region, or town. the NE states of the United States. *Northern parts of India grow very cold in winters. (adjective)* **1** lying towards, near, or facing the north. *Needle of compass normally points to north.* **2** blowing from the north. *(adverb)* to or towards the north. *North-western winds bring rain to the western part of India.*

Northing – *(noun)* **1** distance travelled or measured northward, especially at sea. *By convention, everything above 80 nothing is considered as positive.*

North-star – *(noun)* the pole star. *North-star is also called pole star.*

Northward – *(adjective)* in a northerly direction. *The wrrent that runs northward up this coast. (adverb)* towards the north. *The treasure chest lies northward. (noun)* the direction or region to the north. *The ship had hardly gone a few miles northward when a storm overtook it.*

Northwest – *(noun)* **1** the point of the horizon midway between north and west. *Many cities are situated in the northwest of India.* **2** the north western part of a country, region, or town. *(adjective)* **1** lying towards, near, or facing the north-west. **2** blowing from the north-west. *(adverb)* to or towards the north-west. *Winds blowing narthwest bring heavy rains.*

Nose – *(noun)* **1** the part projecting above the mouth on the face of a person or animal, containing the nostrils and used in breathing and smelling. *He has a long and prominent nose.* **2** the sense of smell. the aroma of a particular substance, especially wine. *The nose of the car was smashed in an accident.* **3** the front end of an aircraft, car, or other vehicle. a projecting part. *Don't poke your nose in my personal affairs.* **4** an instinctive talent for detecting something: he has a nose for a good script. *He has a nose for a good story. (verb)* thrust its nose against or into something. smell or sniff. *He nosed the car slowly through the heavy traffic.*

Nosebag – *(noun)* a bag containing fodder, hung from a horse's head and into which it can reach to eat. *The horse was eating from the nosebag.*

Nosed – *(adverb)* to interfere. *The nose into their domestic affairs uninvited.*

Nose-pin – *(noun)* wearing a pin on nose. *Indian women like to wear a gold nose pin.*

Nose-ring – *(noun)* metallic ring worn by women. *Most Indian women wear nose-ring.*

Nosing – *(noun)* rounded edge of a step or moulding. a metal shield for such an edge. *He put his foot on the nosing.*

Nostalgia – *(noun)* sentimental longing or wistful affection for a period in the past. *When idle he usually has nostalgia.*

Nostril – *(noun)* either of two external openings of the nasal cavity in vertebrates that admit air to the lungs and smells to the olfactory nerves. *We breathe through our nostrils.*

Nosy – *(adjective)* [informal] showing too much curiosity about other people's affaris. *As he was too nosy, I asked him to mind his own business.*

Not – *(adverb)* **1** used chiefly with an auxiliary verb or be to form the negative. *He does not want to go to school.* **2** used as a short substitute for a negative clause. *Light in this room in not sufficient to read.* **3** a quantifier to exclude a person or part of a group. less than. *There is not enough food for all of us. (noun)* **1** a logical operation which gives the value zero if the operand is one, and vice versa. **2** denoting a gate circuit which produces an output only when there is no input signal. *Not is a circuit that produces an output when there is no input signal. (adjective)* [art] not hot pressed, and having a slightly textured surface. *Any art paper with slightly rough surface is known as not paper.*

Notability - *(noun)* a famous or important person. *He is a notability among writers.*

Notable - *(adjective)* worthy of attention or notice. *This is the only notable part of an otherwise long speech.* *(noun)* a famous or important person. *Don Bradman is notable for his contribution to the game of cricket.*

Notably - *(adverb)* **1** in particular. *This guide-book is very informative, notably in the third chapter.* **2** in a notable way. *Warning of disciplinary action has been issued to all late comes notably the repeaters.*

Notarial - *(adjective)* something related to notaries. *To perform notarial works, you must be a law graduate.*

Notary - *(noun)* a person authorized to perform certain legal formalities, especially to draw up or certify contracts, deeds, etc. *This deed is to be certified by a notary.*

Notation - *(noun)* a system of written symbols used to represent numbers, amounts, or elements in a field such as music or mathematics. *Look carefully at the notation of this mathematical sum.*

Notch - *(noun)* **1** an indentation or incision on an edge or surface. each of a series of holes for the tongue of a buckle. a nick made on something to keep a record. a point or degree in a scale. *There are only four notches on this belt, I need at least two more.* **2** [north American] a deep, narrow mountain pass. *He notched his name in the trunk of the tree.* *(verb)* **1** make notches in. secure or insert by means of notches. *He notched his belt a little more tighter.* **2** score or achieve. *He notched up 25 years of series with the company.*

Notelet - *(noun)* a small folded sheet of paper with a decorative design on the front, for an [informal] letter. *He sent me a note, inviting me on his birthday.*

Notepaper - *(noun)* paper for writing letters on. *Please bring me pad of notepapers I have some letters to write.*

Noteworthy - *It is something noteworthy that throughout the meeting he kept quiet.*

Nothing - *(pronoun)* not anything, something of no importance or concern, naught. *There is nothing good I see in him.* *(adjective)* [informal] of no value or significance. *Right now, I want nothing, please go.* *(adverb)* not at all. used to contradict something emphatically. *There was nothing of importance in his speech. There is nothing I can do about this problem.*

Nothingness - *(noun)* **1** the absence or cessation of existence. *The nothingness of many things can be seen clearly in old age.* **2** worthlessness; insignificance. *There is only a dark nothingness after death. Nothingness surrounded the lonely man at night.*

Noticeable - *(adjective)* easily seen or noticed; clear. *The politeness of his behavior was noticeable.*

Notifiable - *(adjective)* denoting something, especially a serious infectious disease, that must be reported to the appropriate authorities. *Outbreak of AIDS became a notifiable serious disease in early 1980s.*

Notification - *(noun)* the action of notifying something. *A notification has been issued to the effect that everyone must be present in the office by 10 a.m. tomorrow.*

Notify - *(verb)* inform, typically in a formal or official manner; report formally or officially. *All employees have been notified that no short leave will be given.*

Notion - *(noun)* **1** a concept or belief. a vague awareness or understanding. *I have a notion that we shall soon find a solution to the problem.* **2** an impulse or desire. *She had a notion to ring her friend at work.*

Notional -*(adjective)* hypothetical or imaginary. *It is only a national problem and hence no concrete answer is available.*

Notoriety - *(noun)* the state of being known for some bad deeds. *He soon gained notoriety as a gangster.*

Notorious - *(adjective)* famous for some bad quality or deed. *He was a notorious smuggler.*

Nought - *(noun)* the digit 0. *All his efforts were brought to nought.* *(pronoun)* variant spelling of naught nothing. *He is naught but a worthless fool.*

Noun – *(noun)* a word used to identify any of a class of people, places, or things, or to name a particular one if these. *The Taj Mahal is a monument worth seeing.*

Nourish – *(verb)* **1** provide with the food or other substances necessary for growth and health, enhance the fertility of. *I nourished the sapling and it fast grew into a tree.* **2** keep in one's mind for a long time. *He nourishes a grudge against me.*

Nourishment – *(noun)* the food necessary for growth, health and well-being. *Proper nourishment helps children grow fast and healthy.*

Novel – *(noun)* a fictitious prose narrative of book length. *He is a famous novel writer.*

Novelette – *(noun)* a short novel, typically a light romantic one. *I finished reading the novelette in an hour.*

Novelist – *(noun)* a writer of novels. *Charles Dickens was a famous novelist.*

Novelty – *(noun)* the quality of being novel; a new or unfamiliar thing or experience; denoting something intended to be amusing as a result of its originality or unusualness. *Exploring the ancient caves was a novelty.*

Novice – *(noun)* **1** a person new to and inexperienced in a job or situation. *He is a novice and as such to be pardoned for the lapse.* **2** a person who has entered a religious order and is under probation, before taking vows. *He is a vovice.* **3** a racehorse that has not yet won a major prize or reached a level of performance to qualify for important events. *Very few are willing to bet on a novice.*

Novitiate – *(noun)* the period or state of being a novice; especially in a religious order. *During his entire novitiate he kept aloof.*

Now – *(adverb)* **1** at the present time. at or from this precise moment. under the present circumstances. *It is late, I should leave now.* **2** used especially in conversation, to draw attention to something. *'Now and here' should be our motto.* **3** used in a request, instruction, or question. conjunction as a consequence of the fact. *We should disperse now.* *(adjective)* fashionable or up to date. *See more of what's now during our autumn catwalk show.*

Nowhere – *(adverb)* not in or to any place. *"Plants and animals found nowhere else in the world".* *(pronoun)* **1** no place. *He is nowhere to be seen.* **2** a place that is remote or uninteresting. *This road gees nowhere.* *(adjective)* having no prospect of progress or success. *There is nowhere else I can go.*

Noxious – *(adjective)* harmful, poisonous, or very unpleasant. *The smoke arising here is noxious.*

Nozzle – *(noun)* a spout at the end of a pipe, hose, or tube used to control a jet of liquid or gas. *The nozzle of the hose was blocked.*

Nuance – *(noun)* a subtle difference in or shade of meaning, expression, colour, etc.*the newspaper published his views but with a nuance.* *(verb)* give nuances to. *She wrote a book on nuances of Hindustani classical music.*

Nubile – *(adjective)* youthful but sexually mature and attractive. *He prefers to appoint nubile young staff.*

Nubility – *(noun)* girl old enough to be married. *Many lecherous employers try to take advantage of nubility of young secretaries.*

Nudge – *(verb)* **1** prod gently with one's elbow to attract attention. *He nudged her in the crowd.* **2** touch or push gently or gradually. *He nudged his son to go on stage.* **3** give gentle encouragement to. *(noun)* a light touch or push. *A gentle peptalk by Sachin Tendulkar nudged young boys to perform better on the field.*

Nugatory – *(adjective)* **1** worthless. *The committee came was passed a nugatory and pointless observation.*

Nugget – *(noun)* **1** a small lump of gold or other precious metal found ready formed in the earth. *He found a number of nuggets while digging the earth.* **2** a small but valuable fact. *This is a true nugget among most books available on health.*

Null – *(adjective)* **1** having no legal force; invalid. *The archaic law was declared null and void.* **2** having or associated with the value zero; having no elements or only zeros as elements. *His is a null statement.* **3** having no positive substance. *(noun)* **1** a dummy letter in a cipher. **2** a condition in which no signal is generated;

something generating no signal. *Something is wrong with this circuit despite sending input signals, it is null at the output.*

Nullification – *(noun)* to invalidate. *Those seeking nullification of the admission list name filed an appealing the court.*

Numb – *(adjective)* deprived of the power of sensation. *His fingers grew numb with cold. (verb)* make numb. *He became numb with grief.*

Numbly – *(adverb)* deprive of feeling or responsiveness. *He numbly nodded his head.*

Numeral – *(noun)* a figure, word, or group of figures denoting a number. *I understand this numeral very well. (adjective)* of or denoting a number. *We are studying numerals.*

Numeration – *(noun)* the action or process of numbering or calculating; a method of numbering or computing. *Numeration requires knowledge of arithmetic.*

Numeric – *(adjective)* relating to numbers. *The list has been prepared in numeric order.*

Numerical – *(adjective)* of, relating to, or expressed as a number or numbers. *Remember the symbol of this numerical.*

Numerous – *(adjective)* many. consisting of many members. *Numerous members attended the club meeting.*

Numismatic – *(adjective)* of or relating to coins or medals. *He is deeply interested in numismatics, you should show him this old coin.*

Numskull – *(noun)* variant spelling of numbskull. *The numbskull didn't understand me and began to quarrel.*

Nuncio – *(noun)* a papal ambassador to a foreign government or court. *The nuncio met bishops and visited churches.*

Nunnery – *(noun)* a religious house of nuns. *She being a nun, lives over there in the nunnery.*

Nuptial – *(adjective)* **1** of or relating to marriage or weddings. *Nuptial bells rung in the church. (noun)* a wedding. *The forth coming nuptials between Richard and Maulene.*

Nutriment – *(noun)* nourishment; sustenance. *Bees reprocess the food and extract the last particle of nutriment from it.*

Nutrition – *(noun)* **1** the process of ingesting and assimilating nutrients. food; nourishment.. *The hungry man was immediately provided nutrition.* **2** the branch of science concerned with nutrients and their ingestion. *She has a post graduate diploma in Nutrition sciences.*

Nutritious – *(adjective)* full of nutrients; nourishing. *A pomegranate is a nutritious fruit.*

Nutritive – *(adjective)* **1** of or relating to nutrition. *The food served was high in nutritive value.* **2** nutritious. *The hotel serves organic food of good nutritive value.*

Nuzzle – *(verb)* rub or push against gently with the nose and mouth. *The child nuzzled against his mother.*

Nyctalopia – *(noun)* a condition marked by inability to see in dim light or at night. *He suffers from nyctalopia and con't see at night.*

Nymph – *(noun)* a mythological spirit of nature imagined as a beautiful maiden; a beautiful young woman. *She is almost a nymph, I love her very much.* **2** an immature form of a dragonfly or other insect that does not undergo complete metamorphosis. *He made a fishing fly that resembled the aquatic nymph of an insect.*

Oo

O – *(noun)* **1** the fifteenth letter of the alphabet. **2** denoting the next after N in a set of items, categories, etc. **3** a human blood type lacking both the A and B antigens. *My blood group is O.* **4** zero in a sequence of numerals, especially when spoken. *My telephone nubmer is six 0 tripple five (60555).*

Oh – *(noun)* exlamation. *Oh! such a lovely place.*

Oaf – *(noun)* a stupid, boorish, or clumsy man. *He is considered an oaf among his friends.*

Oak – *(noun)* **1** a large tree which bears acorns and typically has lobed leaves and hard durable wood. used in names of other trees or plants resembling this, e.g. poison oak. *Oak trees are generally found in temperate forests.* **2** a smoky flavour or nose characteristic of wine aged in oak barrels. *The place had a nice oak smell.*

Oaken – *(adjective)* resembling properties of an oak tree. *The oaken smell indicated that there was some winery around.*

Oakum – *(noun)* [chiefly historical] loose fibre obtained by untwisting old rope, used especially in caulking wooden ships. *Oakum is used for caulking purposes in ships.*

Oar – *(noun)* a pole with a flat blade, used to row or steer a boat through the water. a rower. *We steered the boat to safety despite two of our oars damaged.*

Oarless – *(adjective)* lack of oars. *You can't take a rowing boat out to sea of being totally oarless.*

Oarsman – *(noun)* a rower. *A new oarsman was hired for the boat that we were going to sit in.*

Oasis – *(noun)* **1** a fertile spot in a desert where the water table rises to ground level. *It was pleasant to see an oasis after spending hours in desert.* **2** an area or period of calm in the midst of a difficult or hectic place or situation. *The cool ambience of room seemed to be an oasis after spending hours in scorching heat.*

Oast – *(noun)* a kiln for drying hops. *A woman was placing hops in an oast.*

Oat – *(noun)* a cereal plant with a loose branched cluster of florets, cultivated in cool climates. *Oat plants are generally used for feeding animals.*

Oath – *(noun)* **1** a solemn promise, often invoking a divine whiteness, as to the truth of something or as a commitment to future action. *The President is going to take his oath today.* **2** a profane or offensive expression of anger or other strong emotions. *The man, in an inebriated state, was throwing oaths to everyone around.*

Oatmeal – *(noun)* **1** meal made from ground oats and chiefly used in porridge or oatcakes. *Oatmeal was the primary food for the tribes living in that area.* **2** a grayish-fawn colour flecked with brown. *She was wearing a lovely gown of the oatmeal colour.*

Obduracy – *(noun)* stubborn unyielding. *My brother's obduracy had made him unpopular in his friend circle.*

Obdurate – *(adjective)* stubbornly refusing to change one's opinion or course of action. *The leader was so obdurate that he refused to listen to anyone.*

Obeah – *(noun)* a kind of sorcery practiced especially in the Caribbean. *The lady was an expert in practicing obeah.*

Obedience – *(noun)* **1** compliance with an order or law or submission to another's authority. *The student who were lacking in obedience were rusticated.* **2** observance of a monastic rule. *The monks are expected to show obedience to all the rules of monastery.*

Obedient – *(adjective)* willing to comply with order. *As a student, I was quite obedient to my teachers.*

Obedientiary – *(noun)* holder of an authoritative position in a monastery. *Two monks were made obedientiaries by their seniors.*

Obeisance – *(noun)* differential respect. *Every religion teaches us the lessons of obeisance and truthfulness.*

Obelisk – *(noun)* a tapering stone pillar of square or rectangular cross section, set up as a monument or landmark. *Beside the pyramid was standing a tall obelisk.*

Obelus – *(noun)* **1** a symbol used as a reference mark in printed matter, or to indicate that a person is deceased. *An obelus in the article indicated the man was no longer alive.* **2** a mark used in ancient manuscripts to mark a word or passage as spurious or doubtful. *Earlier, an obelus was widely used to indicate the unreliable facts in a text.*

Obese – *(adjective)* grossly fat or overweight. *His seven year old child was quite obese.*

Obesity – *(noun)* the state of being grossly overweight. *Obesity gives rise to a number of health problems.*

Obey – *(verb)* submit to the authority of. carry out a command or instruction. behave in accordance with a general principle, natural law, etc. *All the royal ministers were expected to obey to the command of the king.*

Obfuscate – *(verb)* **1** make unclear or unintelligible. *His action further obfuscated the situation.* **2** bewilder. *The lady was so obfuscated by her employer's remarks that she left the office immediately.*

Obi – *(noun)* variant form of obeah. *Japanese women used to wear an obi over their kimonos.*

Obituarist – *(noun)* one who writes and releases in newspapers brief sketch of a departed soul. *That man has been an obituarist for many years.*

Obituary – *(noun)* a notice of a person's death in a newspaper or periodical, typically including a brief biography. *After a day of his death, we saw his obituary in the newspaper.*

Objectify – *(verb)* **1** express in a concrete form. *His strength as a writer was to objectify emotions in words.* **2** degrade to the status of an object: a sexist attitude that objectifies women. *The women organizations blamed the director that he has objectified women in his latest movie.*

Objection – *(noun)* the action of challenging or disagreeing with something. an expression of disapproval or opposition. *People raised an objection to the way voting was done in our area.*

Objectionable – *(adjective)* arousing distaste or opposition. *The movie had many objectionable scenes in it.*

Objectivity – *(noun)* the quality of being objective. *Editor said to author, "While creating this piece, you should employ objectivity."*

Objectless – *(adjective)* an object that can't be seen or imagined. *His idea was rejected for being objectless.*

Objector – *(noun)* one who objects to something. *No one had the slightest idea that the man would turn out to be an objector.*

Objurgation – *(noun)* to rebuke severely. *The party member could not bear the objurgation and left immediately.*

Objurgatory – *(adjective)* to scold severely. *We were shocked by the objurgatory remarks that he made that day.*

Oblate – *(noun)* a person dedicated to a religious life, but typically not having taken full monastic vows. *The wife had no qualms about her husband being an oblate.*

Obligate – *(verb)* **1** compel legally or morally. *As per the law, the criminal was obligated to sign the documents.* **2** commit as security. *Having taken the bank loan, I was obligated to return the sum within 10 years.* *(adjective)* restricted to a particular function or mode of life: an obligate parasite. *It has been many years that he has been living the life of an obligate man.*

Obligatory – *(adjective)* compulsory. having binding force. *It was his obligatory duty to keep a check on the number of crimes in his area.*

Oblige – *(verb)* **1** compel legally or morally. *The teacher asked to make notes and the students obliged.* **2** perform a service or favour for. be indebted or grateful. *The lady felt obliged to do all the social work on her own.*

Obligee – *(noun)* a person to whom another is bound by contract or other legal procedure. compare with obligor. *In that case, I was an obligee and the man had to comply with my terms.*

Obliging – *(adjective)* willing to do a service or kindness; helpful. *His obliging ways earned him popularity among his mentors.*

Obligor – *(noun)* a person who is bound to another by contract or other legal procedure. compare with obligee. *The obligor had no choice but wait for the contract to end.*

Oblique – *(adjective)* **1** neither parallel nor at right an gles; slanting. *The sun rays fall obliquely on earth's surface.* **2** not explicit or direct. *He always followed an oblique approach to get the things done.* **3** inclined at other than a right angle. acute or obtuse. with an axis not perpendicular to the plane of its base. *An oblique line is intersecting the plane.* **4** neither parallel nor perpendicular to the long axis of a body or limb. *He was getting treated for the numbness in his oblique muscle.* **5** denoting any case other than the nominative or vocative. *"She slapped me!" is an example of an oblique case in English grammar.* (*noun*) **1** another term for slash. *The sign for slash (/) is also known as an oblique in English.* **2** an oblique muscle. *The oblique muscles of his body are well developed.*

Obliquely – *(adverb)* not being done in a direct way. *The sunrays fall on earth obliquely.*

Obliquity – *(noun)* slanting. *The obliquity of the light rays determines their degree of hotness.*

Obliterate – *(verb)* **1** destroy utterly; wipe out. *An entire species of turtles got obliterated after the landslide.* **2** blot out; erase. *As the time passed, his memories got obliterated from her mind.*

Obliteration – *(noun)* destructing or being destructed. *The obliteration of the entire army came as a shock to the king.*

Oblivious – *(adjective)* not aware of what is happening around one. *While doing work, I become oblivious of all the things happening around.*

Oblong – *(adjective)* having a rectangular shape. *The lady has an oblong face.* *(noun)* an oblong object or flat figure. *The students were asked to calculate the area of the oblong figure.*

Obloquy – *(noun)* strong public condemnation. *The minister is trying to become popular by using obloquy as a tool.*

Obmutescence – *(noun)* persistent silence. *His obmutescence was an indication that he was not interested in our discussion.*

Obnoxious – *(adjective)* extremely unpleasant. *The obnoxious presence of the criminal in the victim's family was angering many.*

Obnubilate – *(verb)* darken as if covered with something. *Soon, the dark clouds obnubilated the entire sky.*

Obnubilation – *(noun)* making obscure, covering. *His act of obnubilation to hide his crime soon came to light.*

Oboe – *(noun)* a woodwind instrument of treble pitch, played with a double reed and having an incisive tone. *As we reached the hut, some natives were playing oboes.*

Obscene – *(adjective)* **1** offensive or disgusting by accepted standards of morality and decency. *I objected to the obscene remarks made by the man.* **2** repugnant. *What the juvenile did to the girl was totally obscene.*

Obscurant – *(noun & adjective)* the act of deliberately preventing the facts. *We did not have the slightest idea of his obscurant activities.*

Obscuration – *(noun)* keeping from being seen, conceal. *The lady's obscuration of the facts was taken in the bad light.*

Obsecrate – *(verb)* earnest pleading. *The man obsecrated for getting pardon.*

Obsequies – *(pl. noun)* funeral rites. *Her mother's obsequies were performed in wee hours.*

Obsequious – *(adjective)* obedient or attentive to an excessive or servile degree. *The employee's obsequious attitude gave him no benefits at the time of appraisals.*

Observable – *(adjective)* able to be noticed. *Despite being very far, the island was still observable from our ship.*

Observance – *(noun)* **1** the practice of observing the requirements of law, morality, or ritual. *Our Principal expected from the students a thorough observance of rules.* **2** an act performed for religious or ceremonial reasons. a rule to be followed by a religious order. *The yagna was followed by the observance of the rites.* **3** respect; deference. *The son paid observance to his father's last remains.*

Observant – *(adjective)* **1** quick to notice things. *His observant eyes were able to locate the lost* *keys.* 2 observing the rules of a religion. *He has been an observant Christian throughout his life.* *(noun)* a member of a branch of the Franciscan order that followed a strict rule. *He was included as an observant of the Franciscan order.*

Observation – *(noun)* **1** the action or process of closely observing or monitoring. *The mentally unstable man was kept under a strict observation.* **2** the ability to notice significant details. *It was due to his keen observation that Alexander Fleming was able to discover Penicillin.* **3** the taking of the sun's or another celestial body's altitude to find a latitude or longitude. *The astronomers made an observation of the planet's altitude.* **4** a comment based on something one has seen, heard, or noticed. *The lady wrote down her keen observation about the city that she had visited recently.*

Observationally – *(adverb)* the process of observing something or someone. *In order to get details of an object, it is required to notice them observationally.*

Observe – *(verb)* **1** notice; perceive. watch attentively. detect in the course of a scientific study. *I was observing the petridish with full concentration.* **2** say; remark: *He observed, "The girl played a significant part in the play."* **3** fulfil or comply with. *The company observes compliance with quality standards.*

Observer – *(noun)* a person who watches something. *What a keen observer he is!*

Observing – *(adjective)* a person watching something. *Observing from far, he said, "The land is now not very far."*

Obsess – *(verb)* **1** preoccupy continually or to a troubling extent. *He is obsessed with social media networking.* **2** be preoccupied in this way. *The way she was obsessing about her reimbursement was hardly surprising.*

Obsession – *(noun)* **1** the state of being obsessed. *His obsession with food never seems to end.* **2** an idea or thought that obsesses someone. *He is obsessed with flute playing.*

Obsolescence – *(noun)* becoming out of date, out of fashion. *The obsolescence of this technology is attributed to the new developments in the field.*

Obsolescent – *(adjective)* becoming obsolete. *The introduction of electric engine rendered the steam locomotives obsolescent.*

Obsolete – *(adjective)* **1** no longer produced or used; out of date. *The water clocks have now become obsolete.* **2** less developed than formerly or in a related species; rudimentary; vestigial. *With the evolution of mankind, many organs became obsolete.* verb cause to become obsolete by replacing it with something new. *The introduction of personal computers rendered the typewriters obsolete.*

Obstacle – *(noun)* a thing that blocks one's way or hinders progress. *He was not deterred by the obstacles coming his way.*

Obstetrics – *(noun)* of or relating to childbirth and the processes associated with it. *My sister is keen to study obstetrics as her field of specialization.*

Obstetrician – *(noun)* a physician or surgeon qualified to practice in obstetrics. *He recommended my wife to join the hospital as a qualified obstetrician in the city.*

Obstinate – *(adjective)* **1** stubbornly refusing to change one's opinion or chosen course of action. *Her obstinate nature did not allow her to do idol worship.* **2** unyielding. *The man kept on showing his obstinate behavior in front of officials.*

Obstreperous – *(adjective)* noisy and difficult to control. *In spite of being a jury member, he could not control his obstreperous ways.*

Obstruction – *(noun)* **1** the action of obstructing or the state of being obstructed. *Many obstructions were placed in his way, yet he did not succumb to them.* **2** a thing that obstructs. *An obstruction in her arteries resulted in a massive heart attack.*

Obstructive – *(adjective)* causing a blockage or obstruction. *The path was too obstructive to drive a vehicle smoothly.*

Obtain – *(verb)* **1** acquire or secure. *The students obtained their teacher's permission to visit the library.* **2** be prevalent, customary, or established. *There is no need to comply with the standards that no longer obtain.*

Obtrude – *(verb)* **1** become obtrusive. *We were annoyed as he obtruded on us.* **2** impose or force on someone. *He obtruded his thinking on all of us.*

Obtruncate - *(verb)* (to deprive of a limb). *In a feat of anger, the villager obtruncated his brother.*

Obtrusive – *(adjective)* noticeable or prominent in an unwelcome or intrusive way. *We loathed him due to his obtrusive way of behaving.*

Obtund – *(verb)* deaden the sensitivity, blunt. *In summers, the monsoon rain obtunds hotness in air.*

Obturate – *(verb)* to block, obstruct. *The rust on the surface obturated the machine from running smoothly.*

Obtuse – *(adjective)* **1** annoyingly insensitive or slow to understand. *The student was so obtuse that he could not get the concept even after three hours of lecture.* **2** more than 90 degree and less than 180 degree. *We were asked to draw an obtuse angled triangle.* **3** not sharp pointed or sharp edged; blunt. *The knife had turned obtuse, so I bought a new one.*

Obtusion – *(adjective)* the blunting, dulling or weakening of normal sensation. *Too much of disturbance resulted in obtusion of my mind.*

Obverse – *(noun)* **1** the side of a coin or medal bearing the head or principal design. *The archeologist remarked, "Look at the obverse of this coin; there is a unique symbol on it."* **2** the opposite or counterpart of a fact or truth. *The obverse to the presence of fast track courts is that trial in them is too slow.* adjective **1** of or denoting the obverse of a coin or medal. *On the obverse side of the medal, I noticed some words etched.* **2** corresponding to something as its opposite or counterpart. *To know the truth, look at the obverse state of affairs.*

Obvert – *(verb)* so as to infer another proposition with a contradictory predicate or to turn something so as to present another side or aspect of the view. *He obverted the plank and saw a cobweb in the corner.*

Obversion – *(noun)* alter a preposition so as to infer another preposition with an entirely different meaning. *The obversion of vision will help you with the other aspects of the story.*

Obviate – *(verb)* **1** remove. *She, very cleverly, obviated all the evidences related to the crime.* **2** avoid; prevent. *Her presence of mind obviated the accident to happen.*

Obvious – *(adjective)* **1** easily perceived or understood; clear. *What he was trying to say was indicated from his obvious speech.* **2** predictable and lacking in subtlety. *Our team leader left the company for the obvious reasons.*

Ocarina – *(noun)* a small wind instrument with holes for the fingers, typically having the shape of a bird. *The lovely lady in the room was playing very well at ocarina.*

Occasion – *(noun)* **1** a particular event, or the time at which it takes place. a suitable or opportune time. *He knew that this was the only occasion he could convey his feelings to her.* **2** a special event or celebration. *On the occasion of Diwali, we were invited for a party by our boss.* **3** reason; cause: we have occasion to rejoice. *It was an occasion when no one was in a mood to celebrate.* *(verb)* cause. *The arrival of the unexpected guests occasioned us to make the necessary arrangements.*

Occasioned – *(adverb)* particular time when something happened. *The resignation of the CEO occasioned the company to choose the senior most person to occupy the vacant place.*

Occipital – *(adjective)* relating to the back of the head. *The technician took an X-ray of the patient's occipital view.*

Occiput – *(noun)* the back of the head. *The doctor examined his occiput and wrote remarks on the prescription.*

Occlude – *(verb)* **1** stop, close up, or obstruct. *His gigantic body was occluding the light from behind.* **2** [chemistry] absorb and retain. *The sponge immersed in the liquid soon occluded it.* **3** come into contact with another in the opposite jaw. *The dentist noticed that incisors of my lower jaw did not occlude with that of upper jaw.*

Occulsion – *(noun)* **1** medicine for the blockage or closing of a blood vessel or hollow organ. *An occlusion in her heart became the cause of her untimely death.* **2** meteorology a process by which the cold front of a rotating low-pressure system catches up the warm front, so that the warm air between them is forced upwards. *The occlusion of the warm front is overtaken by the cold front in a cyclone.* **3** dentistry the position of the teeth when the jaws are closed. *The artificial teeth that the dentist had developed did not align with the occlusion of the jaws.*

Occultation – *(noun)* mystical powers, practice, phenomene. *In astronomy, the process of occultation is used to determine the presence of asteroids.*

Occultism – *(noun)* practice of mystical powers. *Occultism is related to the study of supernatural phenomena.*

Occultist – *(noun)* one who practices mystical supernatural powers. *The lady hired an occultist to know about her future.*

Occultly – *(adverb)* in a manner of mystical supernatural powers. *Their occultly talk continued for hours.*

Occultness – *(noun)* in a manner of mystical powers without scientific explanation. *We could not ignore the factor of occultness while discussing astrology.*

Occupancy – *(noun)* **1** the action or fact of occupying a place. *The allotment of houses depends upon their current state of occupancy.* **2** the proportion of hotel or office accommodation occupied or used. *We reached the hotel and inquired about the occupancy of the deluxe rooms.*

Occupant – *(noun)* **1** a person who occupies a place at a given time. law a person holding property, especially land, in actual possession. *The occupants of this house are out on a tour.* **2** the action, state, or period of occupied or used. *Where have the occupants of high moral ground gone?*

Occupation – *(noun)* **1** the action, state, or period of occupying or being occupied. *His occupation with his job left him with no spare time.* **2** job or profession. *In spite of being confused initially, he finally took dentistry as his occupation.* **3** a way of spending time. *Watching movies at night had become his occupation.*

Occupy – *(verb)* **1** reside or have one's place of business in. take control of by military conquest or settlement. enter and stay in without authority, especially as a form of protest. *On reaching there, we saw that the room was already occupied by a couple.* **2** fill or take up. *Who is ready to occupy the vacant seat?* **3** hold. *The Vice President occupied the position soon after.* **4** keep busy, active, or preoccupied. *He occupies himself by writing novels.*

Occur – *(verb)* **1** happen; take place. *When the incident occurred, the family was out of town.* **2** exist or be found to be present in a place or under a particular set of conditions. *The coal in India mostly occurs in the states of Jharkhand and Orissa.* **3** come into the mind of. *It occurred to me that the team was not following the guidelines of the project.*

Occurrence – *(noun)* **1** the fact or frequency of something occurring. *The rare occurrence of the event makes it all the more interesting.* **2** a thing that occurs; an incident or event. *The presence of coal mines in the area is attributed to huge deposits of coal there.*

Occurrent – *(adjective)* actually occurring or observable. *The long words are quiet occurrent in this article.*

Ocean – *(noun)* a very large expanse of sea; in particular, each of the Atlantic, Pacific, Indian, Arctic, and Antarctic oceans. [chiefly north American] the sea. *The Pacific Ocean is the biggest ocean in the world.*

Oceanic – *(adjective)* **1** of or relating to the ocean. *There are a number of oceanic activities that keep on taking place from time to time.* **2** another term for oceanian. *'Oceanic' is the another term for 'oceanian'.*

Ochlocracy – *(noun)* formal government by the populace; mob rule. *The movement to establish ochlocracy was crushed very badly.*

Ochlocrat – *(noun)* government by popular, mob rule. *He refused to admit that he was an ochlocrat.*

Ochre – *(noun)* an earthy pigment containing ferric oxide, varying from light yellow to brown or red. *In party, a lady was wearing an ochre colored dress.*

O'clock – *(adverb)* used to specify the hour when telling the time. *My sister reached the airport exactly at 5 o' clock in the evening.*

Octad – *(noun)* a group or set of eight. *In the practical test, We were shown an octad compound and were asked to write about its properties.*

Octagon – *(noun)* a plane figure with eight straight sides and eight angles. *It is easy to calculate area of an octagon.*

Octahedron – *(noun)* a three-dimensional shape having eight plane faces, in particular a regular solid figure with eight equal triangular faces. *The compound that we were asked to test was an octahedron.*

Octangular – *(adjective)* having eight angles. *An octangular shape is defined by the presence of eight angles.*

Octant – *(noun)* **1** an arc of a circle equal to one eighth of its circumference, or the area enclosed by such an arc with two radii of the circle. *Our mathematics teacher explained the method of calculating the area of an octant.* **2** each of eight parts into which a space or solid body is divided by three planes which intersect at a single point. *An octant is one of the eighth part into which a solid body is divided.* **3** an obsolete instrument in the form of a graduated eighth of a circle, used in astronomy and navigation. *In ancient times, astronomers used to rely on octants to calculate the position of celestial bodies.*

Octave – *(noun)* **1** music a series of eight notes occupying the interval between two notes, one having twice or half the frequency of vibration of the other. the interval between threes two notes. each of the two notes at the extremes of this interval. these two notes sounding together. *Our music teacher gave us good lessons on octave.* **2** a group or stanza of eight lines. *The poet has written the verse in the form of octaves.* **3** the seventh day after a church festival. a period of eight days beginning with the day of such a festival. *The first day of an Easter octave is the feast day.* **4** fencing the last of eight parrying positions. *Octave in fencing is last of the parries.* **5** [British] a wine cask holding an eight of a pipe. *An octave is one eighth amount of the pipe of wine.*

Octavo – *(noun)* a size of book page that results from folding each printed sheet into eight leaves. *An octavo is the size of the pages resulting from folding a printed page into eight leaves.*

Octennial – *(adjective)* lasting for or recurring every eight years. *Through our telescope, we were looking at an octennial star in the sky.*

October – *(noun)* the tenth month of the year. *My sister's birthday falls on eighteenth of October.*

Octopod – *(noun)* an octopus. *Octopods are short animals with eight arms.*

Octroi – *(noun)* a duty levied in some countries on various goods entering a town or city. *The truck carrying the freight had to pay an octroi before entering the neighboring city.*

Octuple – *(adjective)* **1** consisting of eight parts or things. *In college, our octuple group was famous for giving musical performances.* **2** eight times as many or as much. *We needed an octuple amount of food for our guests. (verb)* make or become eight times as numerous or as large. *Soon, the mollusk octupled to its original size.*

Oddish – *(adjective)* different from what is normal. *He was doing everything in an oddish way.*

Oddly – *(adverb)* different to what is usual. *Of late, he is behaving in an oddly manner.*

Odds – *(plural noun)* **1** the ratio between the amounts staked by the parties to a bet, based on the expected probability either way. *The odds on horse race are 14 to 3.* **2** the chances of something happening or being the case. *The odds that India would win the match are very low.* **3** the balance of advantage; superiority in strength, power, or resources: the clung to the lead against all the odds. *In this fight, the old wrestler is at odds.*

Odious – *(adjective)* extremely unpleasant; repulsive. *What an odious remark was passed by him!*

Odium – *(noun)* general or widespread hatred or disgust. *The recent killing of a girl has created odium among masses.*

Odontalgia – *(noun)* toothache. *The development of plaque was giving her an odontalgia.*

Odontoid – *(noun)* anatomy a projection from the second cervical vertebra on which the first can pivot. *He was feeling pain in his odontoid joint.*

Odontology – *(noun)* the scientific study of the structure and diseases of teeth. *His avid interest in odontology made him go abroad and do specialization in it.*

Odorous – *(adjective)* having or giving off odour. *The fish tank was giving an odorous smell.*

Odour – *(noun)* a distinctive smell. a lingering quality or impression. *In order to avoid the bad odour, she sprayed room freshener.*

Oecology – *(noun)* a less common spelling of ecology *All the elements in an ecology should be in balance with one another.*

Oedipus – *(noun)* a person in Greek mythology. *As per the legend, Oedipus was the son of Laius and Jocasta.*

O'er – *(adverb & preposition)* [archaic] or poetic form of over. *O'er that hill, he met the princess of her heart.*

Oesophagus – *(noun)* the part of the alimentary canal which connects the throat to the stomach. *Any constriction in oesophagus does not let the food to pass to the stomach easily.*

Of – *(preposition)* **1** expressing the relationship between a part and a whole. *Of all the coaches in train, only three had passengers in them.* **2** expressing the relationship between a scale or measure and a value. expressing an age. *After completing a year in office, he got an increase of 30%.* **3** indicating an association between two entities, typically one of belonging. *The youngest son of the king was dexterous in archery.* **4** expressing the relationship between a direction and a point of reference. *As we walked a few steps to the west of the university, we saw a pool.* **5** expressing the relationship between a general category and something which belongs to such a category. *The city of Paris is one of the most sought-after places for tourism.* **6** expressing the relationship between an abstract concept and a (noun) denoting the subject or object of the underlying verb. *The opinion of the managers was not taken in this case.* **7** indicating the relationship between a verb and an indirect object. *He died of hypertension.* **8** indicating the material constituting something. *The walls of the mosque are made up of red sandstone.*

Off – *(abbreviation)* **1** office. *His off is not very far from his house.* **2** officer. *The off on duty was to be blamed for the incident.*

Offal – *(noun)* **1** the entrails sand internal organs of an animal used as food. *As the girl saw the man eating offal, she vomited at once.* **2** decaying or waste matter. *The sanitary officer ordered to bury the offal underground.*

Offence – *(noun)* **1** an act or instance of offending. *Man's offence was too much to be given any kind of pardon.* **2** resentment or hurt. *Despite being treated badly, he took no offence.* **3** the action of making a military attack. *The military offense was the first cue that the country did not believe in peace talk.* **4** [north American] the attacking team in a sport. *The team in blue was playing offense.*

Offend – *(verb)* **1** cause to feel hurt or resentful. *By not succumbing to the demands of his master, he had offended him.* **2** be displeasing to. *Walking through a smelly street offended us.* **3** commit an illegal act. break a commonly accepted rule or principle. *He smuggled goods into the country, thus offending the law.*

Offensiveness – *(noun)* acting aggressively *When he could not find any other way to gather attention, he stooped to offensiveness.*

Offer – *(verb)* **1** present or proffer. *He offered me job immediately after going through my curriculum vitae.* **2** express readiness to do something for or on behalf of someone. *He offered his services to complete the pending project.* **3** provide access or opportunity. *The boom in private sector has offered new job opportunities to people.* **4** present to a deity. *The people visiting the temple offer oil and fruits to the deities.* **5** place something in juxtaposition with something else. *A glass jug has been offered along with a pack of five dishes.* (noun) **1** an expression of readiness to do or give something. *He expressed eagerness to offer me a seat in the auditorium.* **2** an amount of money that someone is willing to pay for something.

found her offer to pay me money in cash instead of cheque very pleasing. **3** a specially reduced price. *The portal's offer to sell the machine at 20% discount is garnering attention.* **4** a proposal of marriage. *On noticing his discreet philandering ways, the lady rejected his offer.*

Offerer – *(noun)* one who offers something or some proposal. *The offerer presented us with new plans.*

Offering – *(noun)* a thing offered, especially as a gift or contribution. something offered as a religious sacrifice or token of devotion. *As soon as he entered the temple premises, we knew that he had come with some offering.*

Office – *(noun)* **1** a room, set of rooms or building used as a place of business for non-manual work. *Recently, we have been shifted to a brand new office.* **2** a position of authority or service. tenure of an official position. *As soon as he took office, he sacked three employees.* **3** a service done for others. *Through his good offices of the Secretary, he gained immense popularity.* **4** Christian church the services of prayers and psalms said daily by catholic priests or other clergy. *The Church was always crowded during morning hours.*

Officer – *(noun)* **1** a person holding a position of authority, especially a member of the armed forces who holds a commission or a member of the police, civil, or ecclesiastical office. *The officer on duty did not pay any attention to the ongoing protests.* **2** a member of a certain grade in some honorary orders, such as the grade next below commander in the order of the [British] empire. *Seeing his dedication, the officer was promoted to the position of lieutenant commander.* *(verb)* provide with an officer or officers. *CEO was provided with an officer to fill the vacant position.*

Official – *(adjective)* **1** of or relating to an authority or public body and its activities and responsibilities. *As per the official notice, the employees submitted their income tax forms.* **2** having the approval or authorization of such a body. *The employees were waiting for the order to become official.* *(noun)* a person holding public office or having official duties. *The official was entrusted with a number of duties.*

Officially – *(adverb)* in a formal way. *It is now known officially that some of the projects would be kept on hold till next announcement.*

Officiant – *(noun)* a priest or minister who performs a religious service or ceremony. *The ceremony was concluded with the officiant offering 'prasadam' to the devotees.*

Officiate – *(verb)* **1** act as an official. *The manager officiated for the time COO was out of town.* **2** perform a religious service or ceremony. *The priest officiated at my brother's wedding.*

Officinal – *(adjective)* used in medicine. *We were not aware of the herb's officinal properties.*

Officious – *(adjective)* asserting authority or interfering in an annoyingly domineering way. *There was no other option but to sack him in order to get rid of his officious ways.*

Offing – *(noun)* the more distant part of the sea in view. *We were looking at a ship in the offing.*

Offish – *(adjective)* [informal] aloof or distant in manner. *I abhorred his offish attitude towards me.*

Offset – *(noun)* **1** a consideration or amount that diminishes or balances the effect of a contrary one. *The family of the victim was given monetary assistance as an offset against the job offer.* **2** the amount by which something is out of line. *While calculating, we kept an offset of 5%.* **3** surveying a short distance measured perpendicularity form the main line of measurement. *The students drew an offset in order to measure the given area.* **4** a side shoot from a plant serving for propagation. *The offsets of the plant were cut and planted separately.* **5** a spur in a mountain range. *The offset of the mountain was looking very fascinating, so we photographed it.* *(verb)* **1** counterbalance; compensate for. *We were given a week's leave to offset our double shifts.* **2** place out of line. *At many places, the road was offset to its length.*

Offside – *(adjective)* & *(adverb)* occupying a position on the field where playing the ball or puck is not allowed, generally through being between the ball and the opponent's goal. *The* *coach was explaining to him the offside rule of the game.* *(noun)* **1** the fact of being offside. *The player could not play offside.* **2** chiefly [British] the side of a vehicle furthest from the kerb. compare with nearside. the right side of a horse. *The offside wheel of the rear side had to be replaced immediately.*

Offspring – *(noun)* a person's child or children, or the young of an animal. *The offspring of the mammal were too small and were kept under veterinary observation.*

Oft – *(adverb)* [archaic] or poetic often. *It would be oft that she crossed the barrier and go across the river.*

Ogive – *(noun)* architecture **1** a pointed or gothic arch. *It was clear that some skilled craftsmen were involved in the construction of the ogive.* **2** one of the diagonal groins or ribs of a vault. *The wall near one of the ogives had cracked.*

Ogle – *(verb)* stare at lecherously. *The shabby man used to ogle the ladies waiting for the train.* *(noun)* a lecherous look. *The girl was getting harassed by the continuous ogle of the man in the coach.*

Oh – *(exclamatory)* **1** expressing surprise disappointment, joy, or other emotion. *The girl exclaimed, "Oh! The poor man has not eaten since yesterday."* **2** used when responding to something that has just been said. *After listening to her entire story, he responded, "Oh!!"*

Ohm – *(noun)* the SI unit of electrical resistance, transmitting a current of one ampere when subjected to a potential difference of one volt. *The correct answer to the question was 4 ohms.*

Oil – *(noun)* **1** a viscous liquid derived from petroleum, used especially as a fuel or lubricant. petroleum. *The driver thought it would be better to fill the oil tank before he could run out of it.* **2** any of various viscous liquids which are insoluble in water but soluble in organic solvents and are obtained from animals or plants. *The extracts of the vegetable oil are used for industrial purposes.* **3** [chemistry] any of a group of natural esters of glycerol and various fatty acids, which are liquid at room temperature. compare with fat. *It is healthier to cook food in oil rather than ghee.* verb **1** lubricate, coat or impregnate with oil. *The sewing machine had to be oiled before it could work properly.* **2** supply with oil as fuel. *It was necessary to oi[l] the substance before it could be burned.*

Ointment – *(noun)* a smooth oily substance tha[t] is rubbed on the skin for medicinal purpose[s] or as a cosmetic. *Apply some ointment over th[e] infected area.*

Olden – *(adjective)* of a former age: the olde[n] days. *In olden days, people used to travel a lo[t] by boats.*

Oldish – *(adjective)* of or belonging to the pas[t]. *Retorted the manager, "This idea is a b[it] oldish."*

Oldness – *(noun)* of a certain age. *The oldness o[f] the building is evident from its withered look.*

Oldster – *(noun)* [informal chiefly nor[th] American] an older person. *The child was to[o] happy to see the same oldster walking down th[e] street.*

Oleaginous – *(adjective)* **1** oily or greasy. *Wat[er] had almost no effect over the oleaginous woo[d].* **2** exaggeratedly complimentary; obsequious. *[In] order to please his boss, he made an oleagino[us] speech.*

Oleander – *(noun)* a poisonous evergreen shr[ub] grown in warm countries for its clusters [of] white, pink, or red flowers. *The oleanders we[re] all laden with lovely flowers.*

Oleic – *(noun)* [chemistry] name of an acid. *Ole[ic] acid is used in the manufacture of soaps.*

Oligarch – *(noun)* a ruler in an oligarchy. *It w[as] the high time that an oligarch had to be select[ed] from among the group members.*

Olivary – *(adjective)* anatomy relating to denoting the nucleus situated in the olive the medulla oblongata in the brain. *The olive bodies are present in medulla oblongata.*

Olive – *(noun)* **1** a small oval fruit with a ha[rd] stone and bitter flesh, green when unripe a[nd] blusih black when ripe, used as food and as [a] source of oil. *Olives were given to the patient [in] order to have his speedy recovery.* **2** the sm[all] evergreen tree which yields this fruit, nati[ve] to warm regions of the old world. *The a[...]*

remains populated with olives in all the seasons. **3** a grayish-green colour like that of an unripe olive. yellowish brown; sallow. *The olive colour dress was making her all the more pretty.* **4** a slice of beef or veal made into a roll with stuffing inside and stewed. *On our way to the market, we gobbled some olives.*

Olympian – *(adjective)* **1** associated with mount Olympus in NE Greece, traditional home of the Greek gods. resembling or appropriate to a god, especially in superiority and aloofness. *The prince's olympian looks caught everybody's attention.* **2** relating to the ancient or modern Olympic games. *This year, a new Olympian sport has been introduced.* *(noun)* **1** any of the twelve Greek gods regarded as living on Olympus. a very superior or exalted person. *According to Greek mythology, Hades is one of the Olympians that are venerated by people.* **2** a competitor in the Olympic games. *The Olympian had the fortitude to endure his failures and strike back again.*

Omega – *(noun)* **1** the last letter of the greek alphabet, transliterated as 'O'. *Omega is the last letter of the Greek alphabet.* **2** the last of a series; the final development. symbolic ohm(s). *The unit of resistance, ohm, is represented symbolically by the omega sign.*

Omen – *(noun)* an event regarded as a portent of good or evil. *Setting out on the journey was considered a bad omen that time.*

Ominous – *(adjective)* giving the worrying impression that something bad is going to happen. *I had the ominous feeling about her going out, so I did not let her do so.*

Omissible – *(adjective)* leave out or exclude. *Before working on the project again, he got rid of all the omissible data.*

Omission – *(noun)* someone or something that has been left out. *The omission of data took about an hour.*

Omissive – *(adjective)* less important. *He had no idea that he was wasting his time on the omissive details.*

Omit – *(verb)* leave out or exclude. fail to do. *As our syllabus was still pending, the teacher omitted two chapters from it.*

Omni – *(combining form)* all; of all things: omnifarious. in all ways or places: omnipresent. *The omnipotent gods were challenged by the demons for war.*

Omnifarious – *(adjective)* formal comprising or relating to all sorts or varieties. *The book had omnifarious details about the growth and evolution of species.*

Omnipotence – *(noun)* the quality of having great power. *The demon had grown arrogant over his omnipotence.*

Omnipotent – *(adjective)* formal comprising or relating to all sorts or varieties. *The book depicted the giant to have omnipotent powers.*

Omnipresence – *(noun)* to be present everywhere. *Every religious text talks about the omnipresence of God.*

Omnipresent – *(adjective)* **1** present everywhere at the same time. *The priest said, "We should pay our reverence to the omnipresent Almighty."* **2** widely or constantly encountered. *The omnipresent warming of climate is a cause of concern.*

Omniscience – *(noun)* knowledge of everything. *He tried to convince of his omniscience, but no one believed him.*

Omniscient – *(adjective)* knowing everything. *None of our deeds is hidden from the omniscient God.*

Omnivorous – *(adjective)* **1** feeding on a variety of food of both plant and animal origin. *The birds are known to be omnivorous creatures.* **2** indiscriminate in taking in or using whatever is available. *Our poor financial condition forced us to be an omnivorous buyer of the property.*

Omoplate – *(noun)* shoulder blade. *After the accident, he had to undergo surgery of his omoplate.*

Onagar – *(noun)* an animal of a race of the Asian wild ass native to northern Iran. *Onagars are known to inhabit regions of northern Iran.*

Once – *(adverb)* **1** on one occasion or for one time only. at all; on even one occasion. *We were allowed to talk to the minister only once.* **2** formerly. *Once upon a time, a hunter used to live in a deep dark cavern.* **3** multiplied by one.

conjunction as soon as; when. *Once he got all the details, he started working on the project.*

Oncoming – *(adjective)* approaching from the front; moving towards one. *The driver could not notice the oncoming bus and hence, met an accident. (noun)* the approach or onset of something. *With the oncoming of the winters, we started making all the necessary arrangements.*

One – *(cardinal number)* **1** the lowest cardinal number; half of two; 1, *We ordered only one plate of the main course menu.* **2** single, or a single person or thing. denoting a particular item of a pair or number of items. a certain. [informal chiefly] a noteworthy example of. identical; the same. *I needed to repair only one of the shoes, as the other one was working fine.* **3** [informal] a joke or story. *We were anxious to hear the one about item numbers. (pronoun)* **1** used to refer to a person or thing previously mentioned or easily indentified. *We were getting to that one anytime soon.* **2** a person of a specified kind. *He is one of those kinds who hesitate to speak to anyone.* **3** used to refer to the speaker, or any person, as representing people in general. *One must appreciate his leadership qualities.*

Oneness – *(noun)* **1** the state of being unified, whole, or in harmony. *Only by the oneness of the nation, we can expect to thwart our enemies.* **2** the state of being one in number. *My oneness has been bothering my family members.*

Onerous – *(adjective)* involving a great deal of effort. *I was pretty sure that hurdle race was going to be onerous job. (noun)* something done, made, or happening only once. a unique or remarkable person. *He is the only one who can do the task.*

Oneself – *(pronoun)* **1** used as the object of a verb or preposition when this is the same as the subject of the clause and the subject is one. *How to neglect the promises that one is making to oneself?* **2** used to emphasize that one does something individually or unaided. *Doing all the things oneself is not possible.* **3** in one's normal and individual state of body or mind. *To assert oneself is man's basic tendency.*

Onflow – *(adverb)* the action of moving steadily. *Initially, the onflow was high, but later, it slowed down.*

Onion – *(noun)* **1** an edible bulb used as a vegetable, having a pungent taste and smell and composed of several concentric layers. *There are many antimicrobial properties in onion.* **2** the plant that produces this bulb, with spherical heads of greenish-white flowers. *The onion belongs to the Liliaceae family.*

Onlooker – *(noun)* a non-participating observer; a spectator. *The onlookers were just standing there, without bothering to do anything for the victims.*

Onset – *(noun)* **1** the beginning of something, especially something unpleasant. *With the onset of monsoons, the water-borne diseases become common.* **2** [archaic] a military attack. *The onset was so sudden that the enemy did not find chance to retaliate.*

Onslaught – *(noun)* a fierce or destructive attack. an overwhelmingly large quantity of people or things. *The onslaught took lives of many innocent people.*

Ontological – *(adjective)* study of native of being. *More research is required in the field of ontological studies.*

Ontologist – *(noun)* one who studies the nature of being. *An ontologist deals with the study of metaphysics.*

Ontology – *(noun)* the branch of metaphysics concerned with the nature of being. *His inclination towards philosophy made him opt for a course on ontology.*

Onus – *(noun)* a burden, duty, or responsibility. *As we were not ready to take the onus, another eligible person was chosen for the post.*

Onward – *(adverb)* **1** in a containing forward direction; ahead. forward in time. *From that time onward, the two companies decided to work together.* **2** so as to make progress or become more successful. *Since independence, the financial sector has moved onward. (adjective)* moving forward. *On its way onward, the river crossed many ridges and valleys.*

Onymous - (bearing in author's name) *The site did not allow the authors to post onymous articles.*

Onyx - *(noun)* a semi-precious variety of agate with different colours in layers. *Onyx is used as an ornamental stone.*

Oogenesis - *(noun)* biology the production or development of an ovum. *During oogenesis, female's body produces an ovum.*

Oology - *(noun)* the study or collecting of birds' eggs. *I have an avid interest in oology.*

Ooze - *(verb)* **1** slowly trickle or seep out. slowly exude or discharge. *Water was oozing out of the pore at the bottom of the pot.* **2** give a powerful impression of: the oozes sex appeal. *Her fashion oozes both seduction and style.* *(noun)* **1** the sluggish flow of a fluid. *As she squeezed the bottle, she saw the ooze of gel.* **2** an infusion of oak bark or other vegetable matter, used in tanning. *The ooze from the oak bark was collected and sent for testing.*

Oozy - *(adjective)* slowly trickling out of something. *A hole in the gum bottle had rendered it oozy.*

Opacity - *(noun)* the condition of being opaque. *In Photoshop, to see the underlying layer, the opacity of the upper layer needs to be decreased.*

Opalescent - *(adjective)* showing many small points of shifting colour against a pale or dark gound. *With light shining directly over oil, its surface had turned opalescent.*

Opaline - *(adjective)* opalescent. *What we were looking at was a beautiful opaline sky.* *(noun)* translucent or semi-translucent glass such as milk-glass. *The milk-glass is also termed opaline.*

Opaque - *(adjective)* **1** not able to be seen through; not transparent. *An opaque object does not allow light to pass through its surface.* **2** difficult or impossible to understand. *The concept was too opaque to be grasped.* *(noun)* an opaque thing. photography a substance for producing opaque areas on negatives. *The opaque is used in the process of photography.*

Ope - *(adjective & verb)* [poetic or archaic] form of open. *Cool breeze was coming in the room through ope window.*

Openable - *(adjective)* allowing access. *As the bottle was placed in freezer for many days, its cap was no longer openable.*

Opener - *(noun)* **1** a device for opening something. *To open the soda bottles, I needed an opener.* **2** a person or thing that opens or begins, in particular the first goal in a match or a cricketer, who opens the batting. *In a match against Australia, an Indian player with ICC ranking 3 became the opener.*

Openly - *(adverb)* without concealment, deception, or prevarication; frankly or honestly. *The model had no qualms to talk openly about her relationships.*

Openness - *(noun)* unlock, to allow access. *It required a great deal of effort on leader's part to bring openness in the attitude of his workers.*

Opera - *(noun)* a dramatic work in one or more acts that is set to music for singers and instrumentalists. a building for the performance of opera. *All of us were given the passes to the Opera, but two of us could not attend it.*

Opera-glasses - *(plural noun)* small binoculars for use at the opera or theatre. *Sitting on rear seats, we had to put on the opera-glasses to see the happenings on the stage clearly.*

Operant - *(adjective)* involving the modification of behavior by the reinforcing or inhibiting effect of its own consequences. *The operant conditioning is based on the fact that the behavior is based on the type of stimulus applied.* *(noun)* an item of behavior that is not a response to a prior stimulus but something which is initially spontaneous. *An operant is an element of the behaviour which is initially independent of the stimulus.*

Operate - *(verb)* **1** function or control the functioning of. *As soon as the machine started operating, it developed some hitches.* **2** manage or be managed and run. conduct military activities. *During war, the Indian army was operating from Siachin glacier.* **3** be in effect. *At the time of war, all the recently passed acts were operated.* **4** perform a surgical operation. *The doctors operated on man's limbs and he was, soon, discharged.*

Operatic - *(adjective)* of, relating to, or characteristic of opera. extravagantly theatrical. *Their operatic performances were worth applauding.*

Operative - *(adjective)* **1** functioning; having effect. having the most relevance or significance in a phrase. *The machine guns were put to test during their operative phase.* **2** of or relating to surgery. *In a surgery, it becomes necessary to follow the operative precautions.* *(noun)* **1** a worker, especially a skilled one. *The operatives were not on duty on that very night.* **2** a private detective or secret agent. *An operative was hired to spy over the proceedings of the private conference.*

Operator - *(noun)* **1** a person who operates equipment or a machine. a person who works at the switchboard of a telephone exchange. *The operator just put down the receiver without saying a word.* **2** a person or company that runs a business or enterprise: a tour operator. *The textile operator had opened three new mills in the city.* **3** [informal] a person who acts in a specified, especially manipulative, way: smooth operator. *He being the manipulative operator had lured the company for doing business with him.* **4** mathematics a symbol or function denoting an operation. *The 'greater than' operator in Mathematics is represented by the symbol '>'.*

Operetta - *(noun)* a short opera, usually on a light or humours theme and having spoken dialogue. *The group members were thrilled when they were handed over the tickets of the operetta.*

Operose - *(adjecitve)* involving much effort. *They could not allow their operose efforts to go in vain.*

Ophidion - *(adjective & noun)* relating to reptile group, snake. *The fish belonged to the ophidion genus.*

Ophiology - (study of snakes) *Would you like to opt for Ophiology as your field of specialization.*

Ophite - *(noun)* a green rock with spots or markings. *The place was abundant in ophite structures that had built over millions of years.*

Ophthalmia - *(noun)* medicine inflammation of the eye, especially conjunctivitis. *The eye surgeon had many cases of opthalmia that day.*

Ophthalmology - *(noun)* the branch of medicine concerned with the study and treatment of disorders and diseases of the eye. *His son is keen to go abroad and study ophthalmology.*

Opine - *(verb)* formal hold and state as one's opinion. *She opined on the country's poor security system for women.*

Opinion - *(noun)* **1** a view or judgement not necessary based on fact or knowledge. the beliefs or views of a large number of people: the changing climate of opinion. an estimation of quality or worth: he had a high opinion of himself. *Would you mind giving your opinion in this case?* **2** law a formal statement of reasons for a judgement given. a barrister's advice on the merits of a case. *The judge's opinion on the rape case was acceptable to everyone.*

Opium - *(noun)* **1** an addictive drug prepared from the juice of a poppy used illicitly as a narcotic and occasionally in medicine as an analgesic. *The illegal trading of opium from China into other Asian countries still continues.* **2** something inducing a false and unrealistic sense of contentment. *Morphine, prepared from opium, had stupefying effect on his body.*

Opossum - *(noun)* **1** an American marsupial which has a naked prehensile tail and hind feet with an opposable thumb. *The zoology chapter was entirely focused on the study of Opossums.* **2** Australian a possum. *An opossum is informally called a possum.*

Opponent - *(noun)* a person who opposes. *In the tournament, she was going to face a strong opponent.*

Opportunism - *(noun)* taking advantage of opportunities without regard for the consequences for others. *Sometimes, it becomes necessary to employ opportunism to further one's case.*

Opportunist - *(noun)* a person who takes advantage of opportunities as and when they arise, regardless of planning or principle. *What an opportunist he is!* *(adjective)*opportunistic.

The man was too naïve to employ any opportunistic tactics.

Opportunity – *(noun)* a favourable time or set of circumstances for doing something. *An opportunity never comes twice.*

Opposable – *(adjective)* zoology capable of facing and touching the other digits on the same hand. *Our opposable thumb has rendered us with many capabilities.*

Oppose – *(verb)* **1** disapprove of, resist, or be hostile to. compete with or fight. *When my turn came, I vehemently opposed the barbaric act.* **2** contrasting or conflicting. *The two opposing issues came into picture while discussing the solution to the problem.* **3** opposite. *Both the opposite parties came to clash during the demonstrations.*

Opposer – *(noun)* disagree with, actively resist. *Our own team member turned out to be our opposer.*

Opposing – *(adjective)* different from or in conflict with each other. *The two opposing forces clashed and the result was disastrous.*

Oppositely – *(adverb)* situated on the other side. *The two tables were placed oppositely.*

Opposition – *(noun)* **1** resistance or dissent. a group of opponents. [British] the principal parliamentary party opposed to that in office. *The opposition is raising its voice against the recommendations proposed by the ruling party.* **2** a contrast or antithesis. *A new policy needs to be framed, in opposition to the existing one.* **3** astronomy the apparent position of two celestial objects that are directly opposite each other in the sky, especially the position of a planet when opposite the sun. *The astronomers are on their way to find the two stars in opposition.*

Oppositional – *(adjective)* expressing dissent. *Their oppositional behavior came in the way of coming out with a resolution.*

Oppression – *(noun)* cruel, unjust treatment. *The peasants raised their voice against the oppression of landlords.*

Oppressive – *(adjective)* **1** harsh and authoritarian. *In order to get rid of his oppressive ways, I just ran away.* **2** Weighing heavily on the mind or spirits. *The saint was able to feel an oppressive aura in the room.* **3** close and sultry. *We had no idea that we were going to live in an oppressive climate there.*

Oppressor – *(noun)* a person who oppresses people. *A time came when the oppressor had to succumb to the demands of the peasants.*

Opprobrious – *(adjective)* highly scornful. *He was staring at me with opprobrious looks.*

Oppugn – *(verb)* [archaic] dispute the truth or validity of. *In spite of giving assurance about positive results, his team mates oppugned the new strategy.*

Oppugner – *(noun)* question the validity of. *In contrast to our expectations, he turned out to be an oppugner.*

Opsonic – *(adjective)* an antibody or other substance that binds with foreign their organisms inside the body. *An opsonic reaction became active as soon the foreign bodies entered the surface.*

Opsonin – *(noun)* biochemistry an antibody or other substance which binds to foreign micro-organisms or cells making them more susceptible to phagocytosis. *The body had not enough opsonins to fight against the attack of microorganisms.*

Optative – *(adjective)* grammar relating to or denoting a mood of verbs in Greek and certain other languages, expressing a wish, equivalent in meaning to English let's or if only. *She was talking in an optative mood that day.*

Optic – *(adjective)* of or relating to the eye or vision. *An operation needed to be done on his optic nerve.* *(noun)* **1** a lens or other optical component in an optical instrument. *The experiment could be carried out only with the help of two optic lenses.* **2** [archaic] the eye. *The experiment on optic was going on in the laboratory.* **3** [British] trademark a device fastened to the neck of an inverted bottle for measuring out spirits. *The lab technician was dispensing the liquid by taking measurement from the optic.*

Optical – *(adjective)* **1** of or relating to vision, light, or optics. *The lecture was based on the use of optical devices.* **2** of or using visible light. *The optical telescopes are widely used for experimentation.*

Optician – *(noun)* a person qualified to prescribe and dispense glasses and contact lenses, and to detect eye diseases, or to make and supply glasses and contact lenses. *I went to the optician and he advised to use glasses as soon as possible.*

Optics – *(plural noun)* the branch of science concerned with vision and the behavior of light. *Optics was a mandatory subject in our graduation course.*

Optimist –*(noun)* person who expects good things to happen. *He was such an optimist that even during worst period of his life, he did not get discourage.*

Option – *(noun)* **1** a thing that is or may be chosen. the freedom or right to choose. *After hopping from job to job, I didn't have any options left.* **2** a right to buy or sell a particular thing at a specified price within a set time. *The European country had an option on the 3D movie. (verb)* buy or sell an option on. *The crop was optioned by the country before anyone could give a thought to it.*

Optional – *(adjective)* available to be chosen but not obligatory: optional extras. *I did no preparation of the optional subject, yet passed it with flying colors.*

Opulence – *(noun)* using expensive materials. *We lived in opulence and spent extravagantly.*

Opulent – *(adjective)* ostentatiously rich and luxurious wealthy. *The child was born into an opulent family.*

Or – *(noun)* a logical operator. *We were asked to write the truth-table of the logical operator 'OR'.*

Oracular – *(adjective)* **1** hard to interpret. *The problem had become oracular, so left it for the time being.* **2** holding or claiming the authority of an oracle. *He sits at the top in oracular designing.*

Oral – *(adjective)* **1** spoken rather than written. *One must take care of his oral hygiene.* **2** of or relating to the mouth. done or taken by the mouth. psychoanalysis relating to or denoting a stage of infantile psychosexual development in which the mouth is the main source of sensuous experience. *He opened his oral cavity to the maximum so that the dentist could remove the plaque easily. (noun)* a spoken examination or test. *I am very bad at taking oral exams.*

Orange – *(adjective)* of or relating to Orangemen or their order. *The Orange organization is based in Ireland.*

Orangery – *(noun)* a building like a large conservatory where orange trees are grown. *An orangery was constructed within the botanical institute.*

Orator – *(noun)* a proficient public speaker. an official speaking for a university on ceremonial occasions. *Being an orator, she was always encouraged to participate in discussions.*

Oratory – *(noun)* **1** a small chapel for private worship. *Only priest was allowed to enter the oratory.* **2** a religious society of secular priests founded to provide plain preaching and popular services. *The oratory was working fine and there were many priests in it.*

Orb – *(noun)* a spherical object or shape. a golden globe surmounted by a cross, forming part of the regalia of monarch. *The orb present on king's crown was shimmering with light.*

Orbicular – *(adjective)* **1** technical having the shape of a flat ring or disc. *I could not understand what that orbicular object was.* **2** poetic spherical or rounded. *The orbicular moon was shining in the sky.* **3** geology containing spherical igneous inclusions. *The geologists are working on an orbicular rock to determine its age.*

Orbit – *(noun & verb)* path an object takes to circle another object. *Every planet revolves in its own orbit.*

Orchard – *(noun)* a piece of enclosed land planted with fruit trees. *We were fascinated by the presence of a lovely orchard near our new house.*

Orchestra – *(noun)* **1 a** group of instrumentalists, especially one combining string, woodwind, brass, and percussion sections. *Before orchestra could begin, one of the singers fell on the stage.* **2** the part of a theatre where the orchestra plays, typically in front of the stage and on a lower level. *While constructing the theater, only a little space was allotted to the orchestra.* **3** [north American] the stalls in a theatre. *I was looking at my friend who was sitting and playing in orchestra.* **4** the semicircular space in front of an ancient Greek theatre stage where the chorus danced and sang. *In Greece, orchestra was reserved for the performances by the chorus.*

Orchid - *(noun)* a plant of a large family distinguished by complex showy flowers with a labellum and frequently a spur. *I am thinking of buying a banquet of orchid flowers.*

Orchitis - *(noun)* medicine inflammation of one or both of the testicles. *The man got irritated by the constant orchitis, so he consulted a sexologist.*

Ordain - *(verb)* **1** confer holy orders on. *The clergyman was ordained under the administration of a bishop.* **2** order officially. decide in advance. *The minister was ordained to submit all his credentials.*

Ordainer - *(noun)* one who passes orders. *The cleric was the ordainer in the holy ceremony.*

Ordainment - *(noun)* official order. *The ceremony of ordainment had to be interrupted in between.*

Ordeal - *(noun)* **1** a prolonged painful or horrific experience. *I have been facing this ordeal from a very long time.* **2** an ancient test of guilt or innocence by subjection of the accused to severe pain, survival of which was taken as divine proof of innocence. *In order to check his innocence in crime, the man was subjected to a horrifying ordeal.*

Orderliness - *(noun)* in a heat and methodical way. *The man vouched to bring orderliness in his institute.*

Orderless - *(adjective)* lacking organisation or order. *She had no idea that she would have to teach an orderless class.*

Orderly - *(adjective)* **1** neatly and methodically arranged. *Everyone was impressed with the orderly way he used to do things.* **2** well behaved. *The girl charmed us with her orderly manners.* **3** military charged with the conveyance or execution of orders. *The orderly cop conveyed the message to his subordinates.* *(noun)* **1** an attendant in a hospital responsible for cleaning and other non-medical tasks. *The orderly on duty was sitting idle.* **2 a** soldier who carries orders or performs minor task for an officer. *The officer instructed the orderly to load the gun for him.*

Ordinal - *(noun)* Christian church, a service book, especially one with the forms of service used at ordinations. *We were expected to follow the orders of Cardinal.* *(adjective)* **1** of or relating to order in a powers of ten. *Depending upon its value, the number was given the ordinal ranking.* **2** size or quantity. *The students could now use ordinal numbers easily.*

Ordinance - *(noun)* formal. **1** an authoritative order. [north American] a by-law. *The government, recently, passed an ordinance regarding vehicle parking.* **2 a** religious rite. *The priest completed the religious ordinance with all the rites and the rituals.* **3** [archaic] term for ordonnance. *'Ordinance' is another term for the word 'ordonnance'.*

Ordinarily - *(adverb)* usually. *The Mathematics genius could solve all the problems ordinarily.*

Ordinariness - *(noun)* no special or distinctive features. *We were surprised to see the ordinariness of his dress at the party.*

Ordinary - *(adjective)* **1** with no distinctive features; normal or usual. *In spite of her ordinary looks, she was able to garner the attention of boys.* **2** Exercising authority by virtue of office and not by deputation. *He was exercising his powers through ordinary authority.* *(noun)* **1** [British] a law a judge exercising authority by virtue of office and not by deputation. *An ordinary judge was presiding over the proceedings* **2** an ecclesiastic, such as an archbishop in a province, with ordinary jurisdiction. *We were going to meet the bishop who had ordinary jurisdiction over the area.* **3** a rule or book laying down the order of divine service. *We were going through the ordinary to know more about the divine service.* **4** heraldry any of the simplest principal charges used in coats of arms. *His coat of arms was bearing only ordinaries.* **5** [British archaic] a meal provided at a fixed time and price at an inn. *What they were looking forward to was an ordinary at the inn.*

Ordinate – *(noun)* mathematics a straight line from a point on a graph drawn parallel to the vertical axis and meeting the other; the y-coordinate, compare with abscissa. *The class on ordinate and abscissa was an interesting one.*

Ordination – *(noun)* the action of ordaining someone in holy orders. *The man was too adamant to follow the ordination.*

Ordinance – *(noun)* **1** mounted guns; cannon. US munitions. *The army ordered for a whole new ordinance.* **2** a government department dealing especially with military stores and materials. *On our way, we saw an ordinance depot.*

Ordure – *(noun)* excrement; dung. *The street had a stench of ordure.*

Ore – *(noun)* a naturally occurring solid material from which a metal or valuable mineral can be extracted profitably. *In our Chemistry class, we learned the process of extracting iron from its ore.*

Oread – *(noun)* Greek a nymph believed to inhabit mountains. *Oread is a Greek mythological character.*

Orectic – *(adjective)* technical, rare of or concerning desire or appetite. *His orectic manners clearly indicate that he had fetish for food.*

Organ – *(noun)* **1** a large musical instrument having rows of pipes supplied with air form bellows and arranged in ranks, each controlled by a stop, and played using a keyboard or by an automatic mechanism. a smaller instrument without pipes, producing similar sounds electronically. *He is dexterous at playing organ pipe.* **2 a** part of an organism which is typically self-contained and has a specific vital function. *Most of her internal organs had stopped working; this led to her death.* **3 a** department or organization that performs a specified function. *Finance is the main organ of this company*

Organdie – *(noun)* a fine, translucent, stiff cotton muslin, used chiefly for dresses. *She was looking pretty in her dress made of organdie.*

Organic – *(adjective)* **1** relating to or derived from living matter. [chemistry] relating to or denoting compounds containing carbon and chiefly or ultimately of biological origin. compare with inorganic. *The organic matter is biodegradable.* **2** physiology of or relating to a bodily organ or organs. *The organic processes in man are quiet complex.* **3** produced or involving production without the use of chemical fertilizers or other artificial chemicals. *The farmers are encouraged to use organic manure for their crops.* **4** denoting a harmonious relationship between the elements of a whole. characterized by natural development. *A good literary work has an organic unity among its different elements.*

Organization – *(noun)* **1** the action of organizing. Systematic arrangement of elements. a systematic approach to tasks. *We work in an organization that works for social welfare.* **2** an organized body of people with a particular purpose, such as a business or government department. *Recently, my friend found a job in a financial organization.*

Organize – *(verb)* **1** arrange systematically, order. *As she saw the things scattered here and there, she started organizing them.* **2** [British] make arrangement or preparations for. *A huge party was organized to welcome the guests.* **3** form into a trade union or other political group. *A group of ten people organized to form a separate party.*

Orgasm – *(noun)* the climax of sexual excitement, characterized by intensely pleasurable sensations canted in the genitals. *It was the first time that he was not able to fully enjoy the orgasm.* *(verb)* have an orgasm *The man was having orgasm immediately after the lady touched his genitals.*

Orgastic – *(adjective)* relating to orgasm. *He could not hold his joy that he experienced during the orgastic activity.*

Orgy – *(noun)* **1** a wild party characterized by excessive drinking and indiscriminate sexual activity. *Orgies are usually organized secretly.* **2** excessive indulgence in a specified activity. *They used to indulge in drinking orgies.* **3** secret rites used particularly in the worship of Bacchus and Dionysus, celebrated with dancing, drunkenness, and singing. *Divine orgies were organized to worship Greek gods.*

Orient – *(noun)* **1** poetic the countries of the east, especially east Asia. *The Orient is blamed for aping the West.* **2** the special luster of a pearl of the fines quality. *It was the orient of the pearls that we were tempted to buy them.* adjective oriental. *What the zoologist was looking for was the oriental species of animals. (verb)* **1** align or position relative to the points of a compass or other specified positions. find one's position in relation to unfamiliar surroundings. *On their first day to college, the students were oriented about different courses.* **2** tailor to specified circumstances. *The services of the institution are oriented towards underprivileged class.*

Oriental – *(adjective)* relating to Asians. *There is no doubt about the oriental origin of the gibbons.*

Orientally – *(adverb)* characteristic of people of Asia. *It was clear that their mannerism was driven orientally.*

Orientate – *(verb)* orient orientate is another term for orient. *It was her lack of her knowledge about Indian culture that she requested me to orientate her.*

Origanum – *(noun)* an aromatic plant of a genus that includes marjoram and oregano. *The aromatic properties of origanum are used for various purposes.*

Origin – *(noun)* **1** the point where something begins or arises. anatomy the more fixed end or attachment of a muscle. *The origin of mankind has always remained a puzzle.* **2** a person's social background or ancestry. *Their peasant origin remained a taboo throughout their lives.* **3** mathematics a fixed point from which coordinates are measured. *Teacher asked students to calculate the distance of the coordinate points from the origin.*

Original – *(adjective)* **1** existing from the beginning; first or earliest. *The original species of human had a close resemblance to the modern man.* **2** produced first-hand, not a copy. *We went out to buy the original DVD of the movie.* **3** inventive or novel. *He is known to have all the original ideas. (noun)* **1** the earliest form of something, form language in which something was first written. *Sanskrit is known to be the original language.* **2** an eccentric or unusual person. *It is due to his weirdness that he is called an original by his friends.*

Originality – *(noun)* ability to think orginally.*The director was looking for originality in acting.*

Originally – *(adverb)* from or in the beginning. *Originally, there were no wireless technology in the field of communication.*

Originate – *(verb)* have a specified beginning. create or initiate. *A few varieties of jute originated in India.*

Origination – *(noun)* some of beginning. *India is attributed to be the origination place of many spices.*

Originatives – *(adjective)* creating or initiating something new. *My son is gifted with an originative mind.*

Originator – *(noun)* a person who creates something new. *Man is considered the originator of many innovations.*

Orion – *(noun)* a constellation on the equator to the east of Taurus; contains Betelgeuse and Rigel. *Orion is a constellation that can be seen during winter season.*

Orison – *(noun)* a prayer or plea to deity. *The devotees paid their reverence by saying an orison.*

Orleans – *(noun)* a city in France. *Orleans is a city in France where Joan of Arc led French against battle against England.*

Orlop – *(noun)* the lowest deck of a wooden sailing ship with three or more decks. *We saw captain sitting on an orlop.*

Ornament – *(noun)* **1** an object designed to add beauty to something. decorative items collectively; decoration. music embellishments made to a melody. *Ornaments have been recovered from the excavation sites of Harappa civilization.* **2** Christian church the accessories of worship, such as the chalice. *In medieval times, the use of gold and silver ornaments for Church rituals was in vogue. (verb)* beautify. *The palace was ornamented with the delicate ivory work.*

Ornamental – *(adjective)* serving or intended as an ornament. *The ornamental vessels have* *always been a part of Indian aestheticism.* *(noun)* a plant grown for its attractive appearance. *The indoors of my house have been decorated with ornamental plants.*

Ornamentalism – *(noun)* intended to be decorative item. *The fetish for ornamnetalism never ceases to exist.*

Ornamentalist – *(noun)* user of ornament as a decoration piece. *Today, I am going to meet a renowned ornamentalist from Israel.*

Ornamentally – *(noun)* in the manner of decoration. *The king's room was looking ornamentally beautiful.*

Ornate – *(adjective)* **1** elaborately or highly decorated. *The elephant was ornate with gold jewellery.* **2** using unusual words and complex constructions. *It is not advisable to use too much of ornate words in your writing.*

Ornithology – *(noun)* the scientific study of birds. *Dr. Salim Ali did an excellent job in ornithology.*

Orphan – *(noun)* **1** a child whose parents are dead. *The business was keen to donate money for educating orphans in his society.* **2** printing the first line of a paragraph set as the last line of a page or column, considered undesirable. *You are currently reading an orphan.* *(verb)* make an orphans. *Your task is to utilize the pages by making orphans.*

Orphanage – *(noun)* residential utilities for care of orphans. *This orphanage takes care of 50 abandoned children.*

Orphic – *(adjective)* **1** of or concerning Orpheus, a legendary Greece, said to have been based on poems by Orpheus, characterized by rites of purification, death, and rebirth. *The orphic rites and rituals were common in ancient Greece.* **2** a short-lived art movement within cubism, characterized by a more lyrical use of colour than is found in other cubist works. *The orphic practices of art emphasized on lyrical use of colors.*

Ort – *(noun)* remainder of food from meal. *After eating he ort it to his cat.*

Orthodox – *(adjective)* **1** conforming with traditional or generally accepted beliefs. *She belongs to an orthodox family.* **2** conventional; normal. *Some of the orthodox conventions are still in practice.* **3** of or relating to orthodox Judaism or the orthodox church. *One of my friends is an orthodox Jew.*

Orthoepy – *(noun)* the study of correct or accepted pronunciation. *Only a few people are interested in orthoepy.*

Orthogonal – *(adjective)* **1** of or involving right angles; at right angles to each other. *The students were asked to calculate the area of the given orthogonal shape.* **2** statistics statistically independent. *The two phenomena are orthogonal in nature and occurrence.*

Ortolan – *(noun)* a small songbird formerly eaten as a delicacy, the male having an olive-green head and yellow throat. *A male ortolan was sitting over a tree branch.*

Oscillate – *(verb)* **1** move or swing back and forth at a regular speed. waver between extremes of opinion or emotion. *The pendulum of the clock oscillates back and forth repeatedly.* **2** [physics] move or vary with periodic regularity. cause an electric current or voltage to behave thus. *In a transverse wave, the particles oscillate at right angle to the direction of propagation of the wave.*

Oscillation – *(noun)* back and forth movement in a regular rhythm. *Electro mechanical oscillations take place in a microphone.*

Oscillating – *(adjective)* moving back and forth steadily. *The government is still oscillating over the decision to pass Jan Lokpal bill.*

Oscitant – *(adjective)* yawning. *The students were usually oscitant during the boring History lecture.*

Oscular – *(adjective)* **1** *humorous* of mouth or relating to kissing. *The doctor was going to operate oscular bone.* **2** zoology of or relating to an osculum. *We are going to read a chapter on oscular excretion.*

Osculation – *(noun)* humorous kiss. *The two were lost in their act of osculation.*

Osmium – *(noun)* the chemical element of atomic number 76, a hard, dense silvery-white metal. *Osmium is used in applications where durability of material is required.*

Ossicle – *(noun)* **1** anatomy & zoology a very small bone, especially one of those in the middle ear. *Ossicle is a bone in man's middle ear.* **2** zoology a small piece of calcified material forming part of the skeleton of an invertebrate animal such as an echinoderm. *The skeleton of echinoderms comprises of a calcified material called ossicle.*

Ossification – *(noun)* cease developing, became stony, stagnant. *As the time progressed, the society saw an ossification of the traditional beliefs.*

Ossify – *(verb)* **1** turn into bone or bony tissue. *Osteoclasts are specialized cells that ossify and help in bone formation.* **2** cease developing; become inflexible. *After a few months, his fractured arm ossified and became completely immovable.*

Ostensible – *(adjective)* apparently true, but not necessarily so. *No one could doubt his ostensible purpose of charity.*

Ostensive – *(adjective)* linguistics denoting a way of defining by direct demonstration, e.g. pointing. *Teacher's ostensive way of teaching appealed all the students.*

Ostracism – *(noun)* exclusion form a group or society. *The couple's ostracism from the society has raised a few eyebrows.*

Ostrich – *(noun)* **1** a large flightless swift-running African bird with a long neck, long legs, and two toes on each foot. *An ostrich lays the biggest eggs in the world.* **2** a person who refuses to accept facts. *His being in the denial mode makes him an ostrich.*

Otalgia – *(noun)* medicine earache. *My doctor has prescribed Otalgia for my earache.*

Other – *(adjective & pronoun)* **1** used to refer to a person or thing that is different from one already mentioned or known. alternative of two. those not already mentioned. *The other criminal is still out of the reach.* **2** additional. *An additional dose of 20 mg is required to be taken on daily basis.* **3** [informal] sexual intercourse. *At that time, he wanted to have a bit of the other* **4** philosophy & sociology that which is distinct from, different from, or opposite to something or oneself. *She is looking forward to know more about the other.*

Otherness – *(noun)* the quality of fact of being different. *She had some sort of otherness in her and this made him fall in love with her.*

Otherwise – *(adverb)* **1** in different circumstances; or else. *Do it now, otherwise I would report it to your manager.* **2** in other respects. *The article has a few grammatical errors, otherwise its content is quite good.* **3** in a different way. alternatively. *Though we were told a way of solving the mathematical problem, there is a method to do it otherwise.* adjective in a different state or situation. *We were into solving a lengthy but otherwise simple numerical.*

Otiosly *(adverb)* leisure. *I do not appreciate his way of living otiosely.*

Otitis – *(noun)* medicine inflammation of part of the ear, especially the middle ear. *Why don't you get your otitis get treated.*

Otology – *(noun)* the study of the anatomy and diseases of the ear. *I am going to take a course in Otology.*

Otter – *(noun)* **1** a semi aquatic fish-eating mammal of the weasel family, with an elongated body, dense fur, and webbed feet. *What we were looking at was a large otter.* **2** a piece of board used to carry fishing bait in water. *Don't forget to carry that otter with you.*

Otto – *(noun)* another term for attar. *The sweet smell of otto had an intoxicating smell on me.*

Oubliette – *(noun)* a secret dungeon with access only through a trapdoor in its ceiling. *The prince was hooked to a chain in the dark oubliette.*

Ought – *(modal verb)* **1** used to indicate duty or correctness. used to indicate a desirable or expected state. used to give or ask advice. *You ought to carry this responsibility on your shoulders.* **2** used to indicate something that is probable. *He is ought to be on time.*

Our – *(possession determine)* **1** belonging to or associated with the speaker and one or more others previously mentioned or easily indentified. belonging to or associated with people in general. *Our culture has many flaws that need to be corrected.* **2** used in formal contexts by a royal person or a writer to refer to something belonging to himself or herself.

The king said, "We expect the war to end very soon." **3** [informal] used with a name to refer to a relative or friend of the speaker. *Our own John is out on a tour with his friends.*

Ousel – *(noun)* variant spelling of ouzel. *An ousel resembles a blackbird.*

Oust – *(verb)* **1** drive out or expel from a position or place. *We could no longer take his rubbish attitude, so he was ousted.* **2** law deprive of or exclude form possession of something. take away in a matter. *The prisoners were ousted from getting any form of bail.*

Ouster – *(noun)* **1** law ejection form a freehold or other possession; deprivation of an inheritance. removal from the jurisdiction of the courts. a clause that is or is claimed to be outside the jurisdiction of the courts. *His ouster from family business came as no surprise to us.* **2** [chiefly north American] dismissal from a position. *The chief's ouster from office was predictable.*

Outbalance – *(verb)* be more valuable or important than. *I have no idea of why the party is outbalancing the issue over other things.*

Outburn – *The flames were so high that the entire building got outburned.*

Outburst – *(noun)* a sudden violent occurrence or release of something, especially angry words. *No one was amused to see her sudden outburst as soon as she had occupied her seat.*

Outcast – *(noun)* one that has been excluded from a society or system *The Panchayat declared the dalit an outcast.*

Outcaste – *(noun)* a person with no caste, or one expelled from their caste. *He was declared an outcaste after he confessed his love for the dalit woman.* *(verb)* cause to lose their caste. *The lady purposely did an objectionable thing in order to outcaste herself.*

Outclass – *(verb)* be far superior to. *She outclassed her friends in her choice of sophisticated things.*

Outcry – *(noun)* a strong expression of public disapproval. an exclamation or shout. *After the public outcry, the case was reopened.*

Outdistance – *(verb)* leave a competitor or pursuer far behind. *After only a mile was left, I outdistanced the person running in front of me.*

Outdoor – *(adjective)* done, situated, or used outdoors. liking the outdoors. *We should encourage our children to pursue outdoor activities.*

Outer – *(adjective)* **1** outside; external. further from the centre or the inside. *A line was drawn from the center of the inner circle to the half of radius of outer one.* **2** objective or physical. *The outer surface of the earth is not as hot as the inner one.* *(noun)* **1** [British] the division of a target furthest from the bulls eye. *Almost every shot of mine was hitting the outer part* **2** [British] an outer garment or part of one. *To give layering effect to my style, I bought an outer from the market.* **3** [British] a container for transport for display of packaged items. *Don't remove the outer as the items need to be transported over a long distance.* **4** austral [informal] the part of a racecourse outside the enclosure. *A man was standing at the outer of the racecourse.*

Outermost – *(adjective)* furthest from the centre. *The outermost region of a candle flame is the coldest.*

Outfall – *(noun)* the place where a river, drain, etc. empties into the sea, a river, or a lake. *The tourists were allowed to have the view of the outfall.*

Outfit – *(noun)* **1** a set of clothes worn together. *His outfit was apt for the occasion.* **2** a group of people undertaking a particular activity together. *A band of jazz outfit was going to present its show on the occasion.* **3** a complete set of equipment needed for a particular purpose. *The mechanic required a mechanical outfit to do the assigned task.* *(verb)* provide with an outfit of clothes or equipment. *The dance troupe was outfitted with sequin dresses.*

Outfitter – *(noun)* **1** a shop selling men's clothing. *Why don't you visit a good outfitter in your area?* **2** a shop selling equipment, typically for outdoor pursuits. *Before going to trip, we had to buy some outdoor essentials from some outfitter.*

Outfly – *(verb)* more agility. *It was thrilling to see how the jet aircraft was able to outfly its older counterparts.*

Outgoing – *(adjective)* **1** friendly and confident. *I wish I were a bit more outgoing.* **2** leaving an office or position. going out or away from a place. *The outgoing chairman could not hold his tears.* *(noun)* **1** one's regular expenditure. *In spite of the average earnings, his outgoings are too high.* **2** an instance of going out. *The outgoing of money was the main concern for the company.*

Outgrow – *(verb)* **1** grow too big for. *My son has outgrown of his teenage clothes.* **2** leave behind as one matures. *We were outgrown in our relationship.* **3** the faster or taller than. *The lion's male cubs had outgrown their female counterparts.*

Outgrowth – *(noun)* **1** something that grow out of something else. *We noticed some green outgrowths on potatoes.* **2** a natural development or result. *The outgrowth of imagination is attributed to the complexity of the problem.* **3** the process of growing out. *The slow outgrowth of the plants is attributed to lack of nutrients in soil.*

Outhouse – *(noun)* a smaller building built on to or in the grounds of a house. an outside toilet. *The guests had to be kept in the outhouse.* *(verb)* store away from the main storage area. *Some of the spices were outhoused for dealing with inflation.*

Outlaw – *(noun)* **1** a fugitive from the law. *His being an outlaw can create problems for him.* **2** a person deprived of the benefit and protection of the law. *The lady was declared an outlaw, thanks to her heinous crime.* *(verb)* **1** ban. *The selling of tobacco in public places has been outlawed.* **2** deprive of the benefit and protection of the law. *The criminal was outlawed, thanks to his unruly behavior in court.*

Outlay – *(noun)* an amount of money spent. *Kindly give me an account of the outlay on arranging tours.*

Outlet – *(noun)* **1** a pipe or hole through which water or gas may escape. *I forgot to close the gas outlet.* **2** the mouth of a river. *The river's outlet was not very wide.* **3** an output socket in an electrical device. *Please plug-in the device in this outlet.* **4** a point from which goods are sold or distributed. *You can buy all the grocery items from the outlet.* **5** a means of expressing one's talents, energy, or emotions. *Writing was like an outlet for releasing her emotions.*

Outline – *(noun)* **1** a line or lines enclosing or indicating the shape of an object in a sketch or diagram. the contours or bounds of an object. *The teacher drew an outline of human heart and asked us to draw its parts.* **2** a word in shorthand. *An outline is the representation of a word in shorthand.* **3** a general plan showing essential features but no detail. the main features of something. *The team had already discussed the outline of the coming project.* *(verb)* **1** draw or define the outer edge or shape of. *The teacher outlined the shape and asked the students to fill it with colors.* **2** give a summary of. *Can you outline the main points once again?*

Outlive – *(verb)* **1** live longer than. survive or last beyond. *The husband outlived her wife by several years.* **2** live through. *He outlived all the ordeals that came his way.*

Outlook – *(noun)* **1** a person's point of view or attitude to life. *You should change your negative outlook of life.* **2** a view. *The outlook was serene and gave us pleasure.* **3** the prospect for the future. *What is the outlook for a content writer in this company?*

Outlying – *(adjective)* remote. *The doctor had no qualms about working in an outlying village.*

Outmeasure – *(verb)* exceed in quantity or extent. *The imported rice outmeasured our needs.*

Outmost – *(adjective)* furthest away. *Pluto is the outmost planet of our solar system.*

Outnumber – *(verb)* be more numerous than. *The number of articles contributed by her has outnumbered the total articles written by anyone else.*

Outpace – *(verb)* go faster than. *My sister walks slow and can never outpace me.*

Outplay – *(verb)* play better than. *The continuous practice on her part made her outplay other girls.*

Outpost – *(noun)* a small military camp at a distance from the main army. a remote part of a country or empire. an isolated or remote branch of something. *After some time, he was stationed at the outpost.*

Output – *(noun)* **1** the amount of something produced by a person, machine, or industry. the process of producing something. the power, energy, etc. supplied by a device or system. *The farmers are expecting more output of grains this year.* **2** a place where power or information leaves a system. *The output gate of the logic circuit had disconnected from the system. (verb)* produce or supply. *The new machine can output 10 kg of processed sugar at a time.*

Outrage – *(noun)* an extremely strong reaction of anger or indignation. a cause of outrage. *The delay in the murder case created an outrage in public. (verb)* **1** arouse outrage in. *The hiking of prices has outraged common people.* **2** violate or infringe flagrantly. *He outraged all the legalities of the system.*

Outrageous – *(adjective)* **1** shockingly bad or excessive. *The minister was criticized for his outrageous comment on communalism.* **2** very bold and unusual. *She had chosen an outrageous outfit for the occasion.*

Outreach – *(verb)* reach further than. reach out. *There was no doubt that our team shall outreach theirs. (noun)* **1** the extent or length of reaching out. *The number of literate people in an area depends on the outreach of literacy there.* **2** an organization's involvement with or influence in the community. *The literary society has not been able to outreach its area.*

Outride – *(verb)* **1** ride better, faster, or further than. *With regular practice, he could outride everyone else.* **2** come safely through. *The team could outride the communal riots in the foreign country.*

Outrun – *(verb)* **1** run or travel faster or further than. escape from. *Can you outrun me?* **2** exceed. *Due to a high demand, the gas supply soon outran.*

Outset – *(noun)* the start or beginning. *It was clear from the outset that he was unwilling to take the case in his hand.*

Outshine – *(verb)* **1** shine more brightly than. *One of the vases in the shop was outshining others.* **2** be much better than. *The girls outshined boys in the board exam results.*

Outsider – *(noun)* **1** a person who does not belong to a particular group. a person not accepted by or isolating themselves from society. *They were not willing to accept an outsider like him in their group.* **2** a competitor thought to have little chance of success. *Being new to the game, he is considered an outsider.*

Outsize – *(adjective)* exceptionally large. *His outsized body required specially tailored clothes. (noun)* an outsize person or thing. *We were surprised to know that our friend was going to fight against an outsized man.*

Outskirts – *(plural noun)* the outer parts of a town or city. *He stopped the car on the outskirts of the city.*

Outspoken – *(adjective)* frank in stating one's opinions. *She is always condemned for her outspoken nature.*

Outspread – *(adjective)* fully extended or expanded. *His outspread arms showed that he wanted to hug her. (verb)* spread out. *The disease was outspread by then.*

Outstanding – *(adjective)* **1** exceptionally good. *Her performance in the exams was outstanding.* **2** clearly noticeable. *Her short figure hardly made her outstanding in class.* **3** not yet done. unpaid. *The payment for editing of the last fifty pages is still outstanding.*

Outstep – *(verb)* exceed. *Don't outstep the limits imposed on you.*

Outstretch – *(verb)* **1** extend or stretch out. *To grab the handle, he outstretched his arm.* **2** go beyond the limit of. *This matter has outstretched due to the laidback attitude of authorities.*

Outstrip – *(verb)* move faster than and overtake. exceed. *The leopard outstripped the hyena and grabbed it.*

Outturn – *(noun)* **1** the amount of something produced. *The outturn of the mill has exceeded the expectation.* **2** a result or consequence. *An outturn of the event was that more people started enrolling for the course.*

Outvalue – *(verb)* to be of greater value than. *That the character outvalues all other virtues in man is a fact.*

Outvote – *(verb)* defeat by gaining more votes. *The independent candidate surprised everyone by outvoting his rival.*

Outwalk – *(verb)* walk faster. *No matter how fast I walk, I cannot outwalk my friend.*

Outward – *(adjective)* **1** of, on, or from the outside. relating to the external appearance of something rather than its true nature. outer. *Don't get deceived by his outward appearance.* **2** going out or away from a place. *On applying an outward force, the shape of the object changed.* *(adverb)* outwards. *In a tornado, the wind flows from the center to outwards.*

Outwatch – *(verb)* watch until it disappears. keep awake beyond the end of. *The child kept outwatching the train till it became invisible.*

Outweigh – *(verb)* be heavier, greater, or more significant than. *Being a highly experienced man, his decision outweighs many others.*

Outwit – *(verb)* deceive by greater ingenuity. *It was due to his sharp mind that he outwitted everyone in the discussion round.*

Outwork – *(noun)* **1** an outer section of a fortification or system of defence. *The security level at the outwork is unsatisfactory.* **2** work done outside the factory or office which provides it. *No one seemed interested in completing the outwork.*

Ova – plural form of ovum. *The fertilization takes place when one of the ova fuses with one or more sperms.*

Oval – *(adjective)* having a rounded and slightly elongated outline; egg shaped. *Her oval face makes her wear any type of makeup.* *(noun)* an oval body, object, or design. an oval sports field or track. a ground for Australian rules football. *She was filling colors in an oval.*

Ovarian – *(adjective)* of or relating to an ovary or the ovaries. *The risk of the ovarian cancer is higher in women who smoke heavily.*

Ovary – *(noun)* **1** a female reproductive organ in which ova or eggs are produced. *Her left ovary has a cyst.* **2** the base of the carpel of a flower, containing one or more ovules. *An ovary of a flower contains ovules reserved for fertilization.*

Ovate – *(adjective)* oval; egg shaped. *Yesterday, I bought an ovate lantern.*

Oven – *(noun)* **1** an enclosed compartment, usually part of a cooker, for cooking food. *Why don't you purchase an oven?* **2** a small furnace or kiln. *It took hardly ten minutes to get the food cooked in oven.*

Overact – *(verb)* act a role in an exaggerated manner. *She overacted for that situation.*

Overall – *(adjective)* total. taking everything into account. *The overall result of the discussion is that project should be completed by May this year.* *(adverb)* taken as a whole. *Overall, the meeting was quite fruitful.* *(noun)* **1 a** loosefitting coat or pair of dungarees worn over ordinary clothes for protection. *The cowboy had been wearing overalls.* **2** close fitting trousers worn as part of an army uniform on formal occasions. *Every soldier had to wear overalls on the formal occasions.*

Overawe – *(verb)* subdue or inhibit with a sense of awe. *The speaker overawed the crowd by his inspiring speech.*

Overbalance – *(verb)* **1** fall or cause to fall due to loss of balance. *Being drunk, she overbalanced and fell on ground.* **2** outweigh. *The support of millions has overbalanced the voice of a few leaders.* *(noun)* excess of weight, value, or amount. *Her overbalance has given rise to many diseases.*

Overbear – *(verb)* overcome by emotional pressure or physical force. *The traumatic incident was too much for her to overbear.*

Overbearing – *(adjective)* unpleasantly overpowering. *The overbearing lad badly needs a lesson.*

Overboard – *(adverb)* from a ship into the water. *It was due to deadly waves that he was thrown overboard.*

Overbuild – *(verb)* **1** put up too many buildings in. build too many of. build elaborately. *This city is overbuild and needs a revamp.* **2** build on top of. *Overbuilding a small structure is the first step that the architects are going to take.*

Overburden – *(verb)* burden excessively. *The rearing of four children has overburdened her.* *(noun)* **1** rock or soil overlying a mineral deposit, archaeological site, etc. *When the overburden was removed, some clues of the ancient civilization came into light.* **2** an excessive burden. *The overburden of running two states is taking a toll on the minister's health.*

Overbusy – *(adjective)* excessively busy. *Where are you overbusy these days?*

Overcareful – *(adjective)* excessively careful. *Her overcareful attitude has been the subject of mockery among her colleagues.*

Overcast – *(adjective)* **1** cloudy; dull. *The overcast sky looks so pleasing.* **2** edged with stitching to prevent fraying. *His clothes are all overcast with stitches.* *(noun)* cloud covering a large part of the sky. *The plane was flying above overcast.* *(verb)* **1** cover with clouds or shade. *All of a sudden, the dark clouds had overcast the entire sky.* **2** stitch over to prevent fraying. *She was busy overcasting her clothes.*

Overcharge – *(verb)* **1** charge too high a price. *I rebuked the seller for overcharging.* **2** put too much electric charge into. *Keeping a device plugged-in for a long time overcharges it.*

Overcoat – *(noun)* **1** a long warm coat. *Before setting out, don't forget to wear an overcoat.* **2** a top, final layer of paint or varnish. *An overcoat of paint gave an everlasting shine to the wall.*

Overcrowd – *(verb)* fill beyond what is usual or comfortable. *Getting in of more passengers overcrowded the bus.*

Overdose – *(noun)* an excessive and dangerous dose of a drug. *Overdose of any pill can be dangerous.* *(verb)* take an overdose. give an overdose to. *She overdosed herself to death.*

Overestimate – *(verb)* form too high an estimate of. *The minister had overestimated his victory in the coming elections.* *(noun)* an excessively high estimate. *An overestimate of the things is never advisable.*

Overestimation – *(verb)* approximate usage. *His overestimation of the things cost him dear.*

Overfeed – *(verb)* feed too much. *Overfeeding the cattle can make them ill.*

Overfill – *(verb)* fill to excess. *Our department is overfilled with employees.*

Overgrown – *(adjective)* **1** grown over with vegetation. *Farmer was busy plucking out the overgrown grass.* **2** grown too large. used in likening an adult to a child. *A baby with an overgrown brain died soon after.*

Overhang – *(verb)* **1** hang over. *The branches of this tree are overhanging.* **2** loom over. *A pall of gloom could be seen overhanging there.* *(noun)* an overhanging part. *The obese man had the overhanging mass everywhere on his body.*

Overhaul – *(verb)* **1** examine and repair it if necessary. *The driver stopped his jeep and overhauled the tyres.* **2** overtake. *It was due to his hard work that he was able to overhaul his rival in match.* (noun) an act of overhauling. *My car needs a thorough overhauling.*

Overhead – *(adverb)* above one's head; in the sky. *At that time, the sun was shining overhead.* *(adjective)* **1** situated overhead. *We were on our way to the restaurant overhead.* **2** above the object driven. *An overhead valve engine has many advantages.* **3** incurred in the upkeep or running of premises or a business. *The maintenance overhead for the new car is not much.* *(noun)* **1** an overhead cost or expense. *The accounts manager was responsible for taking care of the overhead involved.* **2 a** transparency for use with an overhead projector. *He had neatly written all the points in the overhead to be seen in the projector.*

Overhear – *(verb)* hear accidentally or secretly. *He was overhearing to the secret conversion.*

Overheat – *(verb)* **1** make or become too hot. *The cylinder overheated and then exploded.* **2** show marked inflation when increased demand results in rising prices. *The market has overheated, thanks to the increase in demand.*

Overissue – *(verb)* issue beyond the authorized amount or the issuer's ability to pay. *An inadvertent error in software made the bank* *overissue the man.* *(noun)* the action of overissuing. *Overissuing of the amount was not taken into consideration.*

Overjoy – *(verb)* much too happy. *I was overjoyed on getting through the bank exam.*

Overlaying – *(verb)* to lay or spread over or on. *The skin overlaying was ruptured at many places.*

Overlie – *(verb)* lie on top of. *The cucumbers were grated and made to overlay the lower piece of bread.*

Overload – *(verb)* **1** load excessively. *Don't overload your taxi with the unnecessary things.* **2** put too great a demand on. *The server was overloaded with download requests.* *(noun)* an excessive amount. *He was not able to face the overload of projects.*

Overlong – *(adjective & adverb)* too long. *This overlong street bends to the right.*

Overlook – *(verb)* **1** fail to notice. ignore or disregard. pass over in favour of another. *All my requests to redevelop the site were overlooked.* **2** have a view of from above. *The plateau overlooked the vegetation below.* **3** supervise. *An attendant was overlooking the things.* **4** bewitch with the evil eye. *We had a superstitious belief that overlooking by a cursed man can spoil everything.* *(noun)* a commanding position or view. *The overlook from there was very enticing.*

Overlooker – *(noun)* a supervisor. *The company badly needs an overlooker for its godowns.*

Overlord – *(noun)* a ruler, especially a feudal lord. *The farmer requested his overlord to lower the rent.*

Overmaster – *(verb)* overcome. *With patience and dedication, you can overmaster any difficulty.*

Overmeasure – *(noun)* an amount beyond what is proper. *The shopkeeper was in a habit of overmeasuring the commodities.*

Overmuch – *(adverb determine & pronoun)* too much. *The man has been practicing overmuch.*

Overnice – *(adjective)* dated excessively fussy or fastidious. *Don't try to be overnice with your boss.*

Overnight – *(adverb)* **1** for the duration of a night. during the course of a night. *Only an overnight and the government had lost its majority.* **2** suddenly. *The things changed drastically overnight.* *(adjective)* **1** for use overnight. done or happening overnight. *Our overnight journey was full of fun.* **2** sudden. *The overnight change of the weather came as a surprise to us.* *(verb)* stay overnight. [north American] convey overnight. *My friends decided to stay in the place overnight.* *(noun)* a stop or stay lasting one night. *Nothing could thrill us more than going to an overnight trip.*

Overpass – *(noun)* a bridge by which a road or railway line passes over another. *As the train reached the overpass, we heard some noise.* *(verb)* **1** rare surpass. *The girls have overpassed boys in the yearly exams.* **2** [archaic] come to the end of. *Our bus had already overpassed the tunnel.*

Overpower – *(verb)* defeat with superior strength. overwhelm. *The king's huge army easily overpowered their enemy.*

Overproduction – *(noun)* more than normal. *With the overproduction of wheat, the prices have gone down.*

Overrate – *(verb)* rate more highly than is deserved. *This movie by Shyam Bengal is overrated.*

Overreach – *(verb)* **1** reach too far. try to do more than is possible. *I have no idea of why he is trying to overreach his goal.* **2** bring the hind feet so far forward that they fall alongside or strike the forefeet. *The horse was running so fast that it almost overreached.* **3** outwit. *The man's intellect helped him in overreaching others.* *(noun)* an injury to a horse's forefoot due to overreaching. *Overreaching made the horse hurt itself.*

Override – *(verb)* **1** use one's authority to reject or cancel. *With his power and influence, he could override any decision made by the community members.* **2** interrupt the action of an automatic function. *By pressing off the power button,* *you can override the function of the shut down command.* **3** be more important than. *The demand for resuming water supply overrode everything else.* **4** overlap. *The external rendering should not override the damp-proof membrane.* **5** travel or move over. *It is not advisable for vehicles to override. (noun)* **1** the action or process of overriding. *Overriding on roads should be avoided in all situations.* **2** a device on a machine for overriding an automatic function. *An override switch can be used to interrupt the flow of current.* **3** an excess or increase on a budget, salary, or cost. *An override of salaries was never expected at this time.*

Overrule - *(verb)* reject or disallow by exercising one's superior authority. *The judge overruled the objection raised by the lawyer.*

Overseas - *(adverb)* in or to a foreign country. *His business has seen a huge growth overseas. (adjective)* form, to, or relating to a foreign country. *The overseas treaty was signed by the two countries. (noun)* foreign countries regarded collectively. *Overseas, the per capita income is much higher than in India.*

Oversee - *(verb)* to supervise: *The inspector came to oversee the quality of the manufactured goods.*

Overseer - *(noun)* a person who supervises others. *He, being an overseer, was assigned the job of supervision.*

Oversell - *(verb)* **1** sell more of than exists or can be delivered. *He used to dupe people by overselling their shares.* **2** exaggerate the merits of. *These days, overselling of movies has become common.*

Overset - *(verb)* **1** upset emotionally. *The son's rude behavior has overset his mother.* **2** [archaic] overturn. *The vehicle collided with a nearby tree before oversetting.*

Overshadow - *(verb)* **1** tower above and cast a shadow over. *The tall building has overshadowed the small house.* **2** cast a gloom over. *The incident has overshadowed the celebrations.* **3** appear more prominent or important than. *The aura of the actor easily overshadowed the presence of others at the award function.* **4** be more impressive or successful than. *By his sheer talent, the old man was able to overshadow his younger counterparts.*

Overshoot - *(verb)* **1** go past unintentionally. *As she remained utterly confused, she easily overshot her destination.* **2** exceed a financial target or limit. *As against the expectation, the financial target has overshot. (noun)* an act of overshooting. *The overshoot of prices needs to be controlled.*

Oversight - *(noun)* **1** an unintentional failure to notice or do something. *Oversight should not be made an excuse every time.* **2** the action of overseeing. *Whenever he is asked about the mail, he excuses of overseeing it.*

Overspent - *(noun past partiple)* spent more than expected. *After shopping was done, he realized that his savings have been overspent.*

Overstate - *(verb)* state too emphatically; exaggerate. *My friend has the habit of overstating any incident or happening in the company.*

Overstay - *(verb)* stay longer than the duration or limits of. *The hotel is charging more money for overstay.*

Overstep - *(verb)* go beyond a prescribed or generally accepted limit. *Don't overstep or I will have to register complain against you.*

Overstock - *(verb)* stock with more than is necessary or required. put more animals in than it is capable of supporting in terms of food or space. *Most of the godowns are overstocked this year. (noun)* chiefly a supply or quantity in excess of demand. *The authorities are facing the problems that come with the overstock of food grains.*

Overtax - *(verb)* tax excessively. *In India, an average man is overtaxed.*

Overtly - *(adverb)* done openly. *This man is prone to talk with an overtly bold way.*

Overtone - *(noun)* **1** a musical tone which is a part of the harmonic series above a fundamental note, and may be heard with it. *Overtone is a* *frequency that is more than the fundamental frequency.* **2** a subtle or subsidiary quality, implication, or connotation. *The religious overtones in his article have been criticized.* **3** [physics] a component of any oscillation whose frequency is an integral multiple of the fundamental frequency. *The overtones in a high quality instrument are harmonious.*

Overtrade – *(verb)* engage in more trade than that can be supported by market or resources. *The businessman is inclined to overtrade to get more profits.*

Overturn – *(verb)* **1** turn over or cause to turn over and come to rest upside down. *The driver hit the pole and his car overturned.* **2** abolish, invalidate, or reverse. *The policy of getting the testimonials signed by a clerical has been overturned in our company.* *(noun)* **1** an act of overturning. *The overturning of the vehicle and then catching fire was an unfortunate event.* **2** ecology the occasional mixing of the water of a thermally stratified lake. *Overturning of water in a thermally stratified lake is an example of maintaining ecological balance by nature.*

Overvaluation – *(noun)* overestimate the importance of. *Overvaluation of anything or anyone does no good, so it should be avoided.*

Overvalue – *(verb)* **1** overestimate the importance of. *Don't overvalue them too much.* **2** fix the value of at too high a level. *Why is he overvaluing the commodities at his shop?*

Overwatch – *(verb)* to watch through or throughout. *He was assigned the duty to overwatch the activities of his neighbors.*

Overweight – *(adjective)* above a normal, desirable, or permitted weight. *The overweight lady was finding it difficult to climb the stairs.* *(noun)* excessive or extra weight. *Being overweight makes one lethargic.* *(verb)* overload. *The bag was overweighing than the prescribed limit, so it could not be checked-in.*

Overzeal – *(noun)* too zealons. *She was overzealed to go abroad.*

Ovine – *(adjective)* of, relating to, affecting, or resembling sheep. *She was made fun due to her ovine facial features.*

Oviparous – *(adjective)* producing young by means of eggs which are hatched after they have been laid by the parent, as in birds. compare with viviparous and ovoviviparous. *Snake is an oviparous animal.*

Oviposit – *(verb)* zoology lay an egg or eggs. *The hen was ovipositing at the time it was shifted to another cell.*

Owing – *(adjective)* yet to be paid or supplied. *Please pay the owing amount.*

Owl – *(noun)* nocturnal bird of prey with large eyes, a hooked beak, and typically a loud hooting call. *An owl is a nocturnal bird.*

Owlery – *(noun)* characteristics of an owe. *An owlery is where owls habitate.*

Own – *(adjective & pronoun)* belonging or relating to the person specified. done or produced by the person specified. particular to the person or thing specified; individual. *All the property that he has rented is his own.* *(verb)* **1** possess. *He owns five flats in his name.* **2** formal admit to having done something wrong or embarrassing. *On pressing hard, the criminal owned up.*

Owner – *(noun)* a person who owns somethings. *The owner of this building lives in Canada.*

Ox – *(noun)* a domesticated bovine animal kept for milk or meat; a cow or bull, see also cattle. used in names of wild animals related to or resembling this, e.g. musk ox. a castrated bull, especially as a draught animal. *The farmer has kept an ox that he uses as a draught animal.*

Oxford – *(noun)* a type of lace-up shoe with a low heel. *He preferred wearing oxford on every occasion.*

Oxonian – *(adjective)* of or relating to oxford or oxford university. *The Oxonian degree keeps a high value.* *(noun)* **1** a native or inhabitant of oxford. *One of my close friends is an Oxonian.* **2** a member of oxford university. *He was happy being an Oxonian.*

Oxygen – *(noun)* the chemical element of atomic number 8, a colouriess, odourless reactive gas that forms about 20 percent of the earth's atmosphere and is essential to plant and animal life. *All living beings require oxygen to live.*

Oxygenate – *(verb)* supply, treat, charge, or enrich with oxygen. *The dying plants in room need to be oxygenated.*

Oxygon – *(noun)* mathematics a figure with three acute angles. *An oxygon is a triangle with three acute angles.*

Oxyphonia – *(adjective)* an unusually sharp quality or pitch of sound or voice. *She used to sing with an irritating oxyphonia.*

Oyster – *(noun)* **1** a bivalve marine mollusk with a rough, flattened, irregularly oval shell, several kinds of which are farmed for food or pearls. *She is very fond of eating oysters.* **2** a shade of grayish white. *The painting had excess of the oyster shade.* **3** an oval morsel of meat on each side of the backbone in poultry. *The market had many shops selling oyster-shaped meat morsels.*

Ozone – *(noun)* **1** an unstable, pungent, toxic form of oxygen with three atoms in its molecule, formed in electrical discharges or by ultraviolet light. *The ozone layer developed a hole as it got exposed to the ultra-violet rays.* **2** [informal] fresh invigorating air. *A cool ozone was blowing from sea to the shore.*

Pp

P – *(noun)* **1** the sixteenth letter of the alphabet. **2** denoting the next after O in a set of items, categories, etc.

Pace – *(noun)* **1** a single step taken when walking or running. *With each pace, we were nearing the gates of the haunted house.* **2** a gait of a horse, especially one of the recognized trained gaits. *He is bound to win thanks to his tremendous pace.* **3** speed or rate of motion, development, or change. *My weightloss plan is moving at snails's pace.* **4** the state of a wicket as affecting the speed of the ball. *His pace can leave the best batsmen dumbstruck.* *(verb)* **1** measure by walking it and counting the number of steps taken. *He walked ten paces and sat down for a drink.* **2** walk at a steady speed, especially without a particular destination and as an expression of anxiety. *Your pacing up and down the room is not going to get you solutions.* **3** move with a distinctive lateral gait in which both legs on the same side are lifted together. *The camel's pace and its widened feet help it to move without sinking its feet into the sand.* **4** lead in order to establish a competitive speed. *Don't run at a wild pace, lest you lose control.* **5** do something at a restrained and steady rate or speed. *We were able to drive on the newly laid road at a leisurely pace.* **6** move or develop at a particular rate or speed. *The new reforms were a pace-setter for India and it was noticed by the rest of the world.*

Pacific – *(adjective)* peaceful in character or intent. *The pacific nature of the leaders is the reason behind justice prevailing in the State.* *(noun)* the pacific ocean. *The states around the Northern Pacific Ocean were the only ones invited for the international conference.*

Pacify– *(verb)* **1** quell the anger or agitation of. *Somehow we managed to pacify the angry crowd that had collected at his shop.* **2** bring peace to. *Pacifying the infuriated nation was not an easy task after they ousted the corrupt minister.*

Pack – *(noun)* **1** a cardboard or paper container and the items contained within it. *The toys were rattling inside the pack noisily.* **2** a collection of related documents. *I had kept my certificates in a pack on the table.* **3** a set of playing cards. *A pack would do for a game of rummy for three people.* **4** a rucksack. *All your travel needs have been neatly arranged in your backpack.* **5** a quantity of foods packed or canned in a particular season. *Pack the coffee beans in the container for at least a week.* **6** a group of wild animals, especially wolves, living and hunting together. a group of hounds kept for hunting. *A pack of wolves killed a deer.* **7** an organized group of cub scouts or brownies. *The pack of scouts did an excellent job at the Scouts Parade.* **8** a team's forwards considered as a group. *The aggressive pack scored a brace in the league match.* **9** the main body of competitors following the leader in a race or competition. *There was not much choice when we had to pack a jury.* **10** a group or set of similar things or people: a pack of lies. *A pack of chocolates was kept on the table.* **11** a hot or cold pad of absorbent material, used for treating an injury. *The best way to reduce the swelling is to apply an ice pack on the wound.* *(verb)* **1** fill with clothes and other items needed for travel. *Pack your bags quickly!* **2** place in a container for transport or storage. be capable of being folded up for transport. or storage. *It was not an easy task to pack all the belongings into a single bag.* **3** carry. *The children were packed* *off to bed.* **4** cram a large number of things into. crowd and fill. *Thousands of people packed into the temple.* **5** cover, surround, or fill. *She asked us to pack the box up to its edge.* **6** form a scrum. *The kids in the attacking side formed a pack as soon as the bell was rung.*

Package – *(noun)* **1** an object or group of objects wrapped in paper or packed in a box. a packet. *The package was nicely covered so no one could guess what was inside.* **2** a set of proposals or terms offered or agreed as a whole. *The board was quite impressed with the package agreed upon.* **3** a package holiday. *The company had a wonderful holiday package planned for the employees.* **4** a collection of programs or subroutines with related functionality. *We are eager to see how the market responds to the new package.* *(verb)* **1** put into a box or wrapping. *The chocolates are to be packaged for sale.* **2** present in a particular and advantageous way. *The proposal has to be packaged in an attractive way for it to work in the market.* **3** combine for sale as one unit. *The board combined two of its products into an attractive package.* **4** commission and produce to sell as a complete product to publishers. *The publisher took a long time to respond to the author's package.*

Packet – *(noun)* **1** a paper or cardboard container. *They were trying to pack all the groceries into one packet.* **2** a block of data transmitted across a network. *They received the transmitted packet late because of the distance between the two networks.* **3** a large sum of money. *We saw the agent handing over quite a packet to the officer.* **4** a boat travelling at regular intervals between two ports, originally for the conveyance of mail. *The postmen were waiting at the port for the packet to arrive.* *(verb)*, wrap up in a packet. *We quickly wrapped the gift in a packet and rushed for the party.*

Packing – *(noun)* **1** material used to protect fragile goods in transit. *The instrument was covered with safe packing so it would reach safely.* **2** material used to seal a join or assist in lubricating an axle. *What kind of packing was used here, I wondered, as it was breaking quite easily.*

Pact – *(noun)* a formal agreement between individuals or parties. *The countries drew a pact to work towards saving and nurturing the environment.*

Pad – *(noun)* **1** a thick piece of soft or absorbent material. *We covered the wound with a pad so it would heal fast.* **2** the fleshy underpart of an animal's foot or of a human finger. *We could see that the animal was quite heavy thanks to the prints of its pads on the sand.* **3** a protective guard worn over a part of the body by a sports player. *The cricketer kept adjusting his shoulder pad much to the bowler's distraction.* **4** a number of sheets of blank paper fastened together at one edge. *She wrote down the recipes in her notepad.* **5** a flat topped structure or area used for helicopter take off and landing or for rocket launching. *The crew asked us to clear the pad as the helicopter could land any moment.* **6** a flat area on a track of a printed circuit or on the edge of an integrated circuit to which wires or component leads can be attached to make an electrical connection. *The electrician was ready with all the wires when he realized that the pad was missing!* **7** a person's home. *I went to visit him in his temporary bachelor pad.* *(verb)* **1** fill or cover with a pad. *The carpenter padded up the cushion of the seats.* **2** put on protective pads. use one's pads to block a ball. *The coach added some extra pads to the player's elbows as they were still healing.* **3** lengthen a speech or piece of writing with unnecessary material. *The enthusiastic teacher kept padding out his speech, much to the student's chagrin.* **4** defraud by adding false items to. *I was irritated at the way he had padded out the program cunningly.*

Paddle – *(noun)* **1** a short pole with a broad blade at one or both ends, used to move a small boat or canoe through the water. *We were terrified when the paddles fell from our hands into the water.* **2** a short handled bat such as that used in table tennis. *He hit the ball so hard his grip on the paddle slipped.* **3** any of various paddle shaped instruments used for stirring or mixing. *Paddles were distributed in the kitchen to quicken the cooking.* **4** a paddle shaped instrument used for administering corporal punishment. *The teacher warned the disobedient children not to force her to use the paddle to discipline them.* **5** each of the boards fitted round the circumference of a paddle wheel or mill wheel. *When you visit the farm, do not miss the paddle wheels; they are a rare sight these days.* 6 the fin or flipper of an aquatic mammal or bird. *The seal could not swim with it's injured paddle.* **7** a flat array of solar cells projecting from a spacecraft. *The astronaut was shifting the paddles with the switches inside as the rocket changed its direction.* **8** a plastic covered electrode used in cardiac stimulation. *The surgeons quickly brought out the paddles to resuscitate the patient.* **9** an act of paddling. *The guides taught the five people how to paddle in the raft.* *(verb)* **1** propel with a paddle or paddles. *The guide was shouting and asking us to start paddling fast as the raft neared the rapid.* **2** swim with short fast strokes. *As the shark came nearer, he panicked and started paddling faster.* **3** beat with a paddle as a punishment. *Disobedient children will be punished with a paddle to discipline them.*

Paddy – *(noun)* an Irishman. *Calling him Paddy is what led to the fight and even took him to the local sheriff's office.*

Padlock– *(noun)* a detachable lock hanging by a pivoted hook on the object fastened. *We returned back after seeing padlock on the front door of the house.* *(verb)* secure with a padlock. *Ever since the thieves struck, we have been extra careful to lock the main doors with padlocks.*

Paediatrician – *(noun)* medical practitioner specialishing in children another disease. *She took her baby to the paediatrician when the fever did not come down with a tablet.*

Pagan – *(noun)* a person holding religious beliefs other than those of the main world religions. *The Church declared him an atheist when he told them he was a pagan.* *(adjective)* of or relating to pagans or their beliefs. *The Church asked him to stop spreading his pagan views among the public and corrupting them.*

Page – *(noun)* **1** one side of a leaf of a book, magazine, or newspaper, or the material written or printed on it. *He folded page after page though he understood nothing of what was written there.* **2** both sides of such a leaf considered as a single unit. *The computer kept instructing him to insert a new page in order to be able to type further.* **3** a section of stored data, especially that which can be displayed on a screen at one time. *We found several webpages on diverse topics saved on his laptop.* **4** a particular episode considered as part of a longer history. *The end of the war implied the end of a significant page in the history of the country.* *(verb)* **1** leaf through. move through and display one page at a time. *He was carefully browsing through each page of the book.* **2** divide into sections, keeping the most frequently accessed in main memory and storing the rest in virtual memory. *Performance of a computer would improve if optimum memory paging techniques are used.* **3** paginate. *Its easier to read and review if you pag your manuscript.*

Pageant – *(noun)* **1** an entertainment consisting of a procession of people in elaborate costumes, or an outdoor performance of a [historical] scene. *The group organized pageants in the villages to educate them about the history of their country.* **2** a beauty contest. *It took a lot of hard work for her to win the Miss India beauty pageant.* **3** a scene erected on a fixed stage or moving vehiçle as a public show. *The city was witness to a spectacular pageant that started at the stadium and went around the city.*

Pail – *(noun)* a bucket. *Jack and Jill went up the hill to fetch a pail of water.*

Pain – *(noun)* **1** a strongly unpleasant bodily sensation such as is caused by illness or injury. *She was already in immense pain by the time the doctor arrived.* **2** mental suffering or distress. *Watching the beggars crying for food was indeed a pain.* **3**.an annoying or tedious person or thing. *The irritating employee proved quite a pain for her to bear with.* **4** careful effort. *She took great pains to come out successful in the reality show.* *(verb)* cause mental or physical pain to. hurt. *It pained to see her going through such a tough period in her life.*

Painful – *(adjective)* **1** affected with or causing pain. *She was a painful character to associate with.* **2** very bad. *She was injured and had a rather painful wound on her knee.*

Painless – *(adjective)* **1** not causing physical pain. *There is now a painless war in Iraq.* **2** involving little effect or stress. *The doctor explained that the surgery is minor and would involve a painless procedure.*

Paint – *(noun)* **1** a substance which is spread over a surface and dries to leave a thin decorative or protective coating. *The fence required at least two coats of paint.* **2** an act of painting. *Michaelangelo's act of painting is a widely researched topic even today.* **3** informal cosmetic make-up. *Some dancers need extensive face paint to look perfect.* **4** basketball a rectangular area marked near the basket at each end of a court. *He dominates play in the paint.* **5** [north American] a piebald horse. *The American Paint Horse is a unique breed of horse that has prints of dark and white patches all over it.* *(verb)* **1** apply paint to. apply to a surface with a brush. efface something with paint. *The father taught his son the basics of how to paint.* **2** depict or produce with paint. give a description of something. *He was painting a bad character sketch of his friend.* **3** computing create using a paint program.. *Animation enthusiasts can easily draw characters using the paint program in Windows.*

Painter – *(noun)* **1** an artist who paints pictures. *Though he is an engineer by profession, he is also an excellent painter.* **2** a person who paints buildings. *Now that the building was ready, he decided to call the painter for a final coating of paint.*

Painting – *(noun)* **1** the action or process of painting. *He sat in the garden all day painting the trees and birds around.* **2** a painted picture. *We saw several prominent paintings in the Arts Museum yesterday.*

Pal – *(noun)* a friend. *Dhanya was my best pal in school.* *(verb)* form a friendship. *I was looking forward to making more pals in high school.*

Palace – *(noun)* a large, impressive building forming the official residence of a sovereign, president, archbishop, etc. *The Buckingham Palace is indeed one of the greatest tourist attractions in UK.*

Palatable – *(adjective)* **1** pleasant to taste. *I suggested that she should add some more salt to her curry to make it palatable.* **2** acceptable. *After a brief meeting, we arrived at a palatable solution to the problem.*

Palate – *(noun)* **1** the roof of the mouth, separating the cavities of the mouth and nose in vertebrates. *Cleft palate is a common disability where the nose or lips do not form properly.* **2** a person's ability to distinguish between and appreciate different flavours. *The chef designed the menu to tempt the most discerning palate, complemented with a wonderful mocktail from the bar.* **3** the flavor of a wine or beer. *He has a good palate for wine.*

Palatial – *(adjective)* resembling a palace, especially in being spacious or grand. *She owns a palatial house in Beverly Hills.*

Pale – *(adjective)* **1** containing little colour or pigment; light in colour or shade. having little colour, typically as a result of shock, fear, or ill health. *She was pale with fever when the doctor came to see her.* **2** unimpressive or inferior: a pale imitation. *Your work is a pale imitation of the original painting.* *(verb)* **1** become pale in one's face. *She paled at the sight of the principal walking towards her.* **2** seem or become less important. *My work pales before hers as she is the best employee in the office.*

Pall – *(noun)* **1** a cloth spread over a coffin, hearse, or tomb. *The unappealing sight of his death seemed to have been turned into a beauty thanks to the exquisiteness of the pall spread on his coffin.* **2** a dark cloud of smoke, dust, etc. *The city was covered in a pall of sand when the herd of bulls left.* **3** an enveloping air of gloom or fear. *The pall of gloom enveloping the room was somewhat lifted with her arrival.* **4** an ecclesiastical pallium. heraldry a Y-shaped charge representing the front of an ecclesiastical pallium. *The pall of the sixth century was a long,* *white, moderately wide piece of wool with a red or black cross on the ends.*

Pallid – *(adjective)* **1** pale, especially because of poor health. *The pallid face of the invalid tore my heart.* **2** feeble or insipid. *She gave a rather pallid performance today in comparison to her usual expertise.*

Pallor – *(noun)* an unhealthy pale appearance. *She stood in the driveway of our garage with swollen eyes, mangled hair and an eerie pallor on her face.*

Palm – *(noun)* **1** an unbranched evergreen tree with a crown of very long feathered or fan-shaped leaves, growing in tropical and warm regions. *The beach was lined with beautiful palms.* **2** a leaf of a palm awarded as a prize or viewed as a symbol of victory. *The image of the palm flashed in her mind as she stood at the starting line of the race.*

Palmist – *(noun)* Fortuneteller who predicts your future by the lines on your palms. *Desperate to know if the astrologer's predictions were believable, we decided to take a second opinion from the palmist who lived across the street.*

Palpable – *(adjective)* **1** able to be touched or felt. *The liver, spleen and kidneys are not palpable, said the doctor.* **2** plain to see or comprehend: a palpable sense of loss. *When the star arrived, the excitement in the air was palpable.*

Palpitate – *(verb)* **1** beat rapidly, strongly, or irregularly. *The air in the room seemed to palpitate with the deep fear that inflicted the children trapped there.* **2** shake; tremble. *The realization made her heart palpitate with fear and excitement!*

Palsy – *(noun)* **1** dated paralysis, especially when accompanied by involuntary tremors. *He could not finish the painting as his actions were frequently disturbed by his palsy.* **2** [archaic] a condition of incapacity or helplessness. *She jumped with a little palsy of indignation. (verb)* be affected with palsy. *The doctors knew she was affected with palsy the moment they saw her fits.*

Paltry – *(adjective)* **1** very small or meager. *Sadly, what she received as a reward was a paltry sum in comparison to the amount her rival received.* **2** petty; trivial. *The prize was too paltry for the lives it must have cost.*

Pamper – *(verb)* indulge with a great deal of attention and comfort; spoil. *The younger sibling is always more pampered.*

Pamphlet – *(noun)* a small booklet or leaflet containing information or arguments about a single subject. *We had kept several pamphlets talking about the features of the product, at the counter. (verb)* distribute pamphlets to. *The company asked us to distribute the prepared pamphlets among the people, only at its instructions.*

Pamphleteer – *(noun)* a native or inhabitant of the ancient region of pamphylia in southern Asia Minor. *The people of Pamphylia are called Pamphylians, and not Pamphleteers.*

Pan – *(noun)* **1** a metal container for cooking food in. *She made the curry in a beautiful non-stick pan.* **2** a bowl fitted at either end of a pair of scales. *One of the pans of the fruit-seller had definitely been tampered with, the officer realized.* **3** a shallow bowl in which gravel and mud is shaken and washed by people seeking gold. *The miners will head to the East now to pan for gold.* **4** British the bowl of a toilet. *The lavatory pan had cracked and was in desperate need of being changed.* **5** a hollow in the ground in which water collects or in which a deposit of salt remains after evaporation. *There was a natural pan near the farm, dry though.* **6** a part of the lock that held the priming in old types of gun. *He accidentally inserted the gunpowder in the pan instead!* **7** a hard stratum of compacted soil. *The geography teacher drew the different levels of soil on the board and asked the students to identify the pan from them.*

Panacea – *(noun)* a solution or remedy for all difficulties or disease. *Eating chocolates is no panacea for your mental issues.*

Pancake – *(noun)* **1** a thin, flat cake of batter, fried and turned in a pan and typically rolled up with a sweet or savoury filling. *My aunt made chocolate and banana pancakes for tea.* **2** theatrical make-up consisting of a flat solid layer of compressed powder. *The make-up artist* *spread a pancake on her face to hide her acne.* *(verb)* 1 make a pancake landing. *The crew made a pancake landing as instructed by the chief, as the last resort.* **2** informal flatten or become flattened. *You should take back your words or I will flatten you like a pancake, he warned.*

Panda – *(noun)* **1** a large bear-like black-and-white mammal native to bamboo forests in china. *There was a time when China was the land of pandas.* **2** a Himalayan raccoon-like mammal with thick reddish-brown fur and bushy tail. *In my trip to the mountains, one of the striking sights I came across was the Himalayan Panda!*

Pandemonium – *(noun)* wild and noisy disorder or confusion; uproar. *The sisters had created such a pandemonium, their neighbours were worried.*

Pander – *(verb)* gratify or indulge. *I will not pander to your demands and requests and spoil you.* *(noun)* **1** dated a pimp. *The newspaper report revealed how some petty politicians pandered to pimps for a living before turning into politics.* **2** [archaic] a person who panders to the desires of another. *The government refused to pander to the desires of the terrorists.*

Pane – *(noun)* **1** a single sheet of glass in a window or door. *He hit a flying sixer and the next moment we heard the crash of the window pane!* **2** a sheet or page of stamps. *I requested the postman to hand me a pane.*

Panel – *(noun)* **1** a distinct section, typically rectangular, forming part of or set into a door, vehicle, garment, etc. a decorated area within a larger design containing a separate subject. *I suggested that the architect consider a separate panel on the wall to place the telephone and other accessories.* **2** a flat board in which instruments or controls are fixed. *The electronics panel is always overflowing with his adapters and chargers.* **3** a small group of people brought together or investigate or decide upon a particular matter. [British] a list of medical practitioners registered as accepting patients under the national health service. *A panel of the best doctors had been arranged for the queen's treatment.* *(verb)* cover a wall or other surface with panels. *The walls of the electronics shop was covered with panels of all kinds.*

Pang – *(noun)* a sudden sharp pain or painful emotion. *I felt a sudden pang of guilt and pain in my heart when I heard her confession.*

Panic – *(noun)* sudden uncontrollable fear or anxiety. informal frenzied hurry to do something. *She panicked when the tremors started.* *(verb)* be affected by or cause to feel panic. drive someone through panic into hasty or rash action. *The car swerved and narrowly missed the bike as the driver jumped at her panic stricken shriek.*

Panorama – *(noun)* **1** an unbroken view of a surrounding region. *These days comverse come equipped with options to get a panorama shot.* **2** a complete survey of a subject or sequence of events. *She gave a broad panorama of what lay ahead in the following year.*

Pansy – *(noun)* **1** a viola with flowers in rich colours, especially of a cultivated variety. *The garden was blooming with pansies of all kinds and colours.* **2** [informal] an effeminate or homosexual man. *He was a bully alright but his friend was quite a pansy.*

Pant – *(verb)* **1** breathe with short, quick breaths, typically from exertion or excitement. long for or to do something. *She came up the stairs, panting in excitement and stress, eager to see her brother waiting at the door.* **2** poetic throb violently from strong emotions. *They left the crowd panting for more.*

Panther – *(noun)* a leopard, especially a black one. *Bagheera is the name of the panther in The Jungle Book.* **2** [north American]a a puma or a jaguar. *The panthers in North America are bigger than the Asian variety.*

Panties – *(plural noun)* [informal] legless underpants worn by women and girls; knickers. *She had folded and kept her panties neatly in a pile in the drawer.*

Pantomime – *(noun)* **1** [British] a theatrical entertainment involving music, topical jokes, and slapstick comedy, usually produced around Christmas. *The students organized* *a pantomime for their Annual School Day celebrations around Christmas.* **2** a dramatic entertainment in which performers express meaning through gestures accompanied by music. *The theatre company is known for its colorful, award-winning pantomimes organized during this time of the year.* **3** [informal] a ridiculous or confused action or satiation. *When the family gets together, it's a perfect scene for a traditional pantomime. (verb)* express or represent by extravagant and exaggerated mime. *My dramatic reactions drew flak from my family and my mother asked me to quit my pantomime and get to the point!*

Pantry - *(noun)* a small room or cupboard in which food, crockery, and cutlery are kept. *My father's hunger grew stronger at the mere sight of the delicious food being cooked in the pantry car next to his coach.*

Pants - *(plural noun)* **1** [British] underpants or knickers. *The kid's mother took him to the lavatory and instructed him to take off his pants on his own without her help.* **2** [chiefly north American] trousers. *They had found a good tailor to stitch his pants.* **3** [British informal] rubbish; nonsense. *The soldier charmed the pants off the girls at the party.*

Papa - *(noun)* **1** [north American]a or dated one's father. *We wanted to wait for Papa to arrive, before we started dinner.* **2** a code word representing the letter P, used in radio communication. *The radio message said, "papa july one, this is papa july two speaking, message over!"*

Papaya - *(noun)* **1** a fruit shaped like an elongated melon, with edible orange flesh and small black seeds. *The doctor advised her to stick to a papaya diet to have a detox effect.* **2** the fast-growing tree which bears this fruit, native to warm regions of America. *I had a notion that certain diseases were rare among Americans because they eat a lot of papaya.*

Paper - *(noun)* **1** material manufactured in thin sheets from the pulp of wood or other fibrous substance, used for writing or printing on or as wrapping material. sheets of paper covered with writing or printing; documents. officially documented but having no real existence or use: a paper profit. *When the document did not print, I checked the printer and realized that the printing paper had finished.* **2** a news-paper. *All the leading newspapers carried the news of the death of the Minister.* **3** a government report or policy document. *It was only evident now that all those policies and reforms were only on paper and not in execution.* **4** an essay or dissertation read at a seminar or published in a journal. *The professor asked me to present a paper on my thesis.* **5** a set of examination questions to be answered at one session. the written answers to such questions. *The teacher took the answer paper from under her hands without even waiting for her response. (verb)* **1** cover with wallpaper. disguise instead of resolving it. *We decided to cover the gaping hole in the wall with a wallpaper.* **2** theatrical slang fill by giving out free tickets. *I was glad I got a paper for the show!*

Par - *(noun)* **1** golf the number of strokes a first-class player should normally require for a particular hole or course. a score of this number of strokes at a hole. *They were late again, but that's par for the course.* **2** the usual or expected level or amount. *Her performance was at par with the exceedingly impressive performance of her brother.* **3** stock exchange the face value of a share or other security, as distinct from its market value. the recognized value of one country's currency in terms of another's. *My CA explained that par value implies the value imprinted on the face of a share certificate or bond. (verb)* golf play in par. *To score* **5**-*under par in a championship golf course is no mean task.*

Parable - *(noun)* a simple story used to illustrate a moral or spiritual lesson. *We were all asked to narrate a parable each at the storytelling session.*

Parachute - *(noun)* a cloth canopy which fills with air and allows a person or heavy object attached to it to descend slowly when dropped from a high position, especially in an aircraft.

We saw a parachute descending from a distance and realized it was a sky diver. (verb) drop or cause to drop by parachute. *The senior officer directed us that we should jump by parachute at his signal.*

Parade – *(noun)* **1** a public procession, especially one celebrating a special day or event. *The city was lit up and the colourful parade made its way from Central Park to the farthest corner of the city where it ends.* **2** a formal march or gathering of troops for inspection or display. *People came from several states to the capital to catch the famous Republic Day Parade.* **3** a series or succession: a parade of celebrities trooped on to his show. *A parade of celebrities trooped on to his show that day.* **4** a boastful or ostentatious display. *His display of emotions seemed like a parade of the different potentialities of his talent.* British a public square, promenade, or row of shops. *The tourists had gathered at the parade ground. (verb)* **1** walk, march, or display in a parade. *The different dance forms displayed in the parade forced the people to get up on their feet.* **2** display publicly in order to impress or attract attention: he paraded his knowledge. *She was embarrassed to be paraded around in her new designation.*

Paradise – *(noun)* **1** heaven as the ultimate abode of the just. the garden of Eden. *The Father said there was a place for all of us in paradise.* **2** an ideal or idyllic place or state. *The vacation was like paradise and we never wanted to return.*

Paradox – *(noun)* **1** a seemingly absurd or self-contradictory statement or proposition that may in fact be true. an apparently sound statement or proposition which leads to a logically unacceptable conclusion. *He presented a paradoxical situation for us to evaluate, so we would know both extremes.* **2** a person or thing that combines contradictory features or qualities. *His mere existence seemed like a paradox.*

Paraffin – *(noun)* **1** a flammable waxy solid obtained by distilling petroleum or shale and used for sealing and waterproofing and in candles. *In the candle-making class, we were taught to work with paraffin wax.* **2** [British] a liquid fuel made similarly, especially kerosene. *We may find an alternate source of energy in paraffin.* **3** [chemistry] old-fashioned term for alkane. *I lost marks in the exam because I used the term paraffin instead of the latest terminology.*

Paragon – *(noun)* **1** a person or thing regarded as a model of excellence or of a particular quality. *He is a paragon of excellence for all of us to follow.* **2** a perfect diamond of 100 carats of more. *What he gifted me for my wedding anniversary was a paragon!*

Paragraph – *(noun)* a distinct section of a piece of writing. indicated by a new line, indentation, or numbering. *There were too many paragraphs in her prose. (verb)* arrange in paragraphs. *The teacher asked us to arrange our write-ups in different paragraphs to make a single story.*

Parallel – *(adjective)* **1** side by side and having the same distance continuously between them. *The roads were parallel to one another and hence reached simultaneously.* **2** occurring or existing at the same time or in a similar way; corresponding. computing involving the simultaneous performance of operations. *The officer instructed both the teams to function in parallel as a better defense strategy.* **3** of or denoting electrical components connected in parallel. *LED lights need to be connected in a parallel circuit for it to function. (noun)* **1** a person or thing that is similar or analogous to another. *Little did the twins know that their lives were actually moving parallel to each other.* **2** a similarity or comparison. *The two sisters were so similar that even their shopping patterns seemed parallel.* **3** each of the imaginary parallel circles of constant latitude on the earth's surface. *The geography teacher explained how important the parallel latitudes were.* **4** printing two parallel lines as a reference mark. *The parallel signs indicated a reference mark, I knew, though I did not know which one. (verb)* **1** run or lie parallel to. *The trains were running parallel to one another's routes.* **2** be similar or corresponding to. *Her performance paralleled her mother's.*

Parallelogram – *(noun)* a four-sided plane rectilinear figure with opposite sides parallel. *The mathematics teacher explained how to construct a parallelogram to the class.*

Paralyse – *(verb)* **1** cause to become incapable of movement. *The accident caused her to be paralysed below the waist.* **2** bring to a standstill by causing disruption. *The accident also paralysed her life, and not just her body.*

Paralysis – *(noun)* **1** the loss of the ability to move part or most of the body. *Her paralysis, after the accident, brought down her self esteem.* **2** inability to act or function. *The shock of the accident was as if she was struck by paralysis.*

Paramilitary – *(adjective)* organized on similar lines to a military force. *The government ordered the paramilitary forces to act as a last resort attack against the terrorists.* *(noun)* a member of a paramilitary organization. *We were told that the late officer had served as a chivalrous soldier in the paramilitary during the 26/11 attacks.*

Paramount – *(adjective)* **1** more important than anything else; supreme. *Taking over the prime minister's seat was of paramount importance to him.* **2** having supreme power. *The President was the paramount power in the Indian Army.*

Paranoia – *(noun)* **1** a mental condition characterized by delusions of persecution, unwarranted jealousy, or exaggerated self-importance. *Post the accident, she had paranoia for a long time especially when she sat in a car.* **2** unjustified suspicion and mistrust of others. *The husband was getting sick of his wife's paranoia.*

Parapet – *(noun)* **1** a low protective wall along the edge of a roof, bridge, or balcony. *The thief hid on the parapet all night which is why he could not be caught.* **2** a protective wall or earth defense along the top of a military trench. *The soldiers hid in the parapet during a break in the war.*

Paraphernalia – *(noun)* miscellaneous articles, especially the equipment needed for a particular activity. *The photographers gathered their paraphernalia and moved to the next location.*

Paraphrase – *(verb)* express the meaning of using different words, especially to achieve greater clarity. *The editor asked me to paraphrase the poem to suit the author's tastes.* *(noun)* a rewording of a passage. *The write-up was actually a paraphrased version of a famous poem.*

Parasite – *(noun)* **1** an organism which lives in or on another organism and benefits by deriving nutrients at the other's expense. *The disease is caused by single-celled parasites that multiply in the human blood stream.* **2** derogatory a person who habitually relies on or exploits others and gives noting in return. *I asked my roommate to stop being a parasite and move out in a week.*

Paratroops – *(plural noun)* troops equipped to be dropped by parachute from aircraft. *The army instructed the paratroops to be released into the building slowly.*

Parcel – *(noun)* **1** an object or collection of objects wrapped in paper in order to be carried or sent by post. *I received a parcel by courier this morning.* **2** a quantity or amount of something, in particular post. *Parcels heading overseas were sent by airmail.* **3** a quantity or amount of something, in particular land. *Parcels of land can be found in the modern landscape.* *(verb)* **1** make into a parcel by wrapping it. *We asked the waiter to parcel the leftover food.* **2** divide something into portions and then distribute it. *The mother kept the parcels ready for distribution.* **3** nautical wrap with strips of tarred canvas to reduce chafing. *We parceled the bonds tightly so it won't give away.*

Parch – *(verb)* **1** make or become dry through intense heat. roast lightly. *The earth was parched and so were we.* **2** extremely thirsty. *We were parched as we had been walking in the desert for hours.*

Parchment – *(noun)* **1** a stiff material made from the prepared skin of a sheep or goat, formerly used as a writing surface. *The sage had written a message on a parchment.* **2** stiff translucent paper treated to resemble parchment. *We decided to use a parchment* *instead in the play rehearsals.* **3** [informal] a diploma or other form document. *I realized that I had to collect the parchment from the college office.*

Pardon – *(noun)* **1** the action of forgiving or being forgiven for an error of offence. *The jury agreed in unison that the criminal should not be given pardon.* **2** a remission of the legal consequences of an offence or conviction. *Her offence was pardonable in court.* **3** Christian church, [historical] an indulgence. *The Pope will grant you pardon, the bishop assured his colleague.* *(verb)* **1** forgive or excuse. *She begged to be pardoned for her error in judgment.* **2** release from the legal consequences of an offence or conviction. exclamatory used to ask a speaker to repeat something because one did not hear or understand it. *She knew her crime will not be pardoned by the court.*

Parent – *(noun)* **1** a father or mother. an animal or plant form which younger ones are derived. *All the students were asked to inform their parents about the meeting.* **2** an organization or company which owns or controls a number of subsidiaries. *SAP is the parent company of Business Objects.* **3** [archaic] a forefather or ancestor. *My grandfather is the parent of the entire Mohan family.* *(verb)* be or act as a parent to. *Parenting is not the most comfortable responsibilities.*

Parenthesis – *(noun)* **1** a word or phrase inserted as an explanation or after-thought, in writing usually marked off by brackets, dashes, or commas. *We had to memorize the parenthesis along with the formulae for the exam.* **2** a pair of round brackets () used to include such a word phrase. *She asked me to enter the actual meaning in parenthesis, beside the pun.*

Pariah – *(noun)* **1** an outcast. *As I left the village, I came across a group of pariahs waiting to see me.* **2** [historical] a member of a low caste or of no caste in southern India. *One of Gandhiji's best initiatives was to remove the divisions between pariahs and other general castes.*

Parish – *(noun)* **1** a small administrative district with its own church and clergy. *All the members of the parish had gathered at the Church for the baptism ritual.* **2** British the smallest unit of local government in rural areas. *Elections happened in the parish as well.* **3** [US] a territorial division corresponding to a country in other states. *What are the chances of attacks on local parish?*

Parity – *(noun)* **1** equality or equivalence, especially as regards status, pay, or value. *The target to achieve parity could not be reached.* **2** [mathematics] the fact of being an even or an odd number. *One can test if the equality is likely to be correct by testing the parity of each side.* **3** [physics] the property of a spatial wave equation that either remains the same or changes sign under a given transformation. *Performing a parity inversion transforms a phenomenon into its mirror image.*

Park – *(noun)* **1** a large public garden in a town, used for recreation. *The kids love playing in the park every evening.* **2** a large enclosed area, typically with woodland and pasture, attached to a country house. *Every apartment complex must have a park for general recreation and maintaining eco balance.* **3** an area devoted to a specified purpose: a wildlife park. *We were considering visiting the biological park this weekend.* **4** an area in which vehicles may be parked: a coach park. *There was parking space available for visitors in the new apartment complex.* *(verb)* **1** bring to a halt and leave it temporarily, typically in a car park or by the side of the road. *Vehicles were to be parked on the left side of the road this week.* **2** [informal] deposit and leave in a convenient place until required. *We decided to park the trolley behind the building till we returned.* **3** [informal] sit down. *We found everyone parked at the garden and rushed there.*

Parka – *(noun)* **1** a large windproof hooded jacket for use in cold weather. *She ensured that we were all wearing our parkas before skiing.* **2** a hooded jacket made of animal skin, worn by Eskimos. *We came across Eskimos clad in their traditional Parkas.*

Parley – *(noun)* a conference between opposing sides in a dispute, especially regarding an armistice. *Unfortunately, the parley yielded little results.* *(verb)* hold a parley. *The ministers finally decided to hold a parley to discuss all the issues.*

Parliament – *(noun)* **1** the highest legislature, consisting of the sovereign, the house of lords, and the house of commons. the members of this legislature for the period between dissolutions. *The Parliament is in a constant state of chaos in our country.* **2** a similar body in other nations and states. *The bill will be brought up in the Parliament today.*

Parlour – *(noun)* **1** dated a sitting room in a private house. *We were asked to wait in the parlour for the VIP to arrive.* **2** a room in a public building, hotel, monastery, etc. for receiving guests or private conversation. *The guests were asked to meet the monk one at a time in the parlour, to take the interviews.* **3** a shop or business providing specified goods or services: an ice-cream parlour. *A new ice cream parlour had opened down the street.* **4** a room or building equipped for milking cows. *The parlour in Australia was well equipped with all the modern facilities for milking the cows.* *(adjective)* dated denoting a person who professes but doses not actively support a particular political view: a parlour socialist. *Being a parlour socialist will not save the country.*

Parochial – *(adjective)* **1** of or relating to a church parish. *The parochial clergy was to be elected soon.* **2** having a narrow outlook or scope: parochial attitudes. *He had a parochial attitude towards the party's activities.* .

Parody – *(noun)* **1**.an imitation of the style of a particular writer, artist, or genre with deliberate exaggeration for comic effect. *The children had prepared a parody of the latest movie for the Annual Day function.* **2** a travesty: a parody of a smile. *The final product came out as a parody of the original act.* *(verb)* produce a parody of. *We were producing a parody of the famous movie.*

Parole – *(noun)* **1** the temporary or permanent release of a prisoner before the expiry of a sentence, on the promise of good behavior. *The town was living in fear ever since the news broke out of the criminal being out on parole.* **2** [historical] a prisoner of war's word of honour to return or act as a non-belligerent if released. *John was released on parole, much to this gang's relief.* **3** linguistics the actual language used by people. contrasted with langue. *The distinction between the two linguistic elements, langue and parole, was defined by Ferdinand de Saussere.* *(verb)* release on parole. *Minor offenders of the law will be released on parole, we heard.*

Parsimony – *(noun)* extreme unwillingness to spend money or use resources. *Such parsimony may help you cross this stage of financial crisis.*

Parsley – *(noun)* a plant with white flowers and crinkly or flat leaves used as a culinary herb and garnish. *You may garnish the pasta with some chopped parsley.*

Parsnip – *(noun)* **1** long tapering cream-coloured root with a sweet flavour. *We wanted mother to make something with parsnip for dinner today.* **2** the plant of the parsley family which yields this root. *We grew parsley hoping to get parsnip as well, but later realized we were wrong.*

Parson – *(noun)* a beneficed member of the Anglican clergy; a rector or vicar. [informal] any clergyman, especially a protestant one. *The parson was called to fix the date of the engagement and decide the availability of the Chapel.*

Part – *(noun)* **1** a piece or segment of something which combined with others makes up the whole. a component of a machine: aircraft parts. *All the parts combined make a whole document.* **2** a measure allowing comparison between the amounts of different ingredients used in a mixture. a specified fraction of a whole. *For a 1 kg cake, you would need one part of flour and two parts of sugar.* **3** some but not all of something. *Part of the fault lay with her sister too.* **4** [informal] a region, especially one not clearly specified or delimited. *Part of the company was under scanner.* **5** a role played by an actor or actress. music a melody or other constituent of harmony assigned to a particular voice or instrument, the contribution made by someone to an action or situation. *She* *got a greater part to play in the school play.* **6** [archaic] abilities. *She had better parts than her sister.* *(verb)* **1** move apart or divide to leave a central space. leave someone's company. leave the company of someone. *We parted ways much before his marriage to my best friend.* **2** give up possession of; hand over. *I had to part with my favourite toys when we moved out of Delhi.* **3** separate with a comb. *The hair stylist suggested I make a side parting to change my current look.* *(adverb)* partly : *part jazz, part blues. The music was innovative and different as it was part jazz, part blues.*

Partial – *(adjective)* **1** existing only in part; incomplete. *A partial solar eclipse was visible in India.* **2** favouring one side in a dispute above the other; biased. *The teacher was always partial towards the best student.* **3** having a liking for. *I couldn't make up my mind as I was partial towards my best friend though I liked her too.* *(noun)* music an overtone or harmonic. *He had a keen ear and so he could detect the partial overtone.*

Participate – *(verb)* **1** take part. *Everybody had a chance to participate in the function.* **2** [archaic] partake of a quality. *She did participate in her success.*

Participle – *(noun)* [grammar] a word formed from a verb and used as an adjective or noun or used to make compound verb forms. *We were asked to identify the participle in the given sentences in the exam.*

Particle – *(noun)* **1** a minute portion of matter. *The tiny particles floating in the air in the room made us sneeze constantly.* **2** [physics] a subatomic constituent of the physical world, e.g. an electron, proton, neutrino, or photon. *His thesis was a study in particle physics.* **3** [grammar] a minor function word that has comparatively little meaning and does not inflect, e.g. in, up, off, or over used with verbs to make phrasal verbs. *The statement had too many particles for us to understand it.*

Particular – *(adjective)* **1** denoting an individual member of a specified group or class. *It was a particular child in the class that she had been talking about for the past one hour, I finally realized.* **2** especially great or intense. *We were asked to pay particular attention to some of the diving instructions given by the guide.* **3** fastidious about something. *He was very particular about the cleanliness of his room.* **4** logic denoting a proposition in which something is asserted of some but not all of a class. contrasted with universal. *There is a particular line of the series that needs to be highlighted.* *(noun)* **1** a detail. *We were browsing through the particulars presented by the manager.* **2** [philosophy] an individual item, as contrasted with a universal quality. *Try and universalize your situation instead of particularizing it, in order to arrive at a solution.*

Parting – *(noun)* **1** the action of moving away or being separated from someone. *To see the couple parting was a painful sight.* **2** the action of dividing something into parts. *Through a parting in the bushes, we saw the man slowly pulling out the thing hidden in his pocket.* **3** [British] a line of scalp revealed in a person's hair by combing the hair away in opposite direction on either side. *The hairstylist gave a zig zag parting to the model's hair.*

Partition – *(noun)* **1** the action or state of dividing or being divided into parts. *The country's partition was the most tragic event in its history.* **2** a structure dividing a space into two parts, especially a light interior wall. *The room was huge so it definitely needed a false partition.* **3** [chemistry] the distribution of a solute between two immiscible solvents in contact with one another: in accordance with its differing solubility in each. *The partition between the two chemicals was to be recorded in this experiment.* **4** computing each of a number of portions into which some operating systems divide memory or storage. *The new computers have invisible partitions inside the CPU.* *(verb)* **1** divide into parts. *The house was later partitioned just like the family.* **2** divide or separate by erecting a partition. *Post the family feud a partition was erected between the two segments.*

Partner – *(noun)* **1** a person who takes part in an undertaking with another or others, especially in a business or firm with shared risks and profits. *Both the husband and wife were equal partners in their family business.* **2** either or two people doing something as a couple or pair. *My sister was my partner in crime.* **3** either member of a married couple or of an established unmarried couple. *He asked the lady if he could have her daughter as a partner for life.* **4** dated friendly form of address by one man to another. *"Whats Up, partner!" he asked.* *(verb)* **1** be the partner of. *She was my partner throughout school and college and now at work as well.* **2** [north American] associate as partners. *The world had associated us as partners in this business.*

Partridge – *(noun)* a short-tailed game bird with mainly brown plumage. *I was surprised to see so many partridges in the farm.*

Party – *(noun)* **1** a social gathering of invited guests, typically involving eating, drinking, and entertainment *We decided to organize a surprise birthday party for our father.* **2** a formally constituted political group that contests elections and attempts to take part in government. *During elections, it is as if all the parties are at war with each other.* **3** a trip. *The tourists were headed towards a party.* **4** a person or group forming one side in an agreement or dispute. *I could not make up my mind which party was right in the dispute.* **5** [informal] a person, especially one with specified characteristics. *He was the guilty party in the dispute.* *(verb)* [informal] enjoy oneself at a party or other lively gathering. *After work, we decided to party at the club.*

Pass – *(noun)* a route over or through mountains. *The pass was closed owing to incessant snowing in the mountains.*

Passable – *(adjective)* **1** good enough to be acceptable. *The last of the ten points she kept was the only passable one.* **2** clear of obstacles and able to be travelled along or on. *The route between points A and B is passable.*

Passage – *(noun)* a riding movement in which a horse executes a slow elevated trot, giving the impression of dancing. *Black Beauty was known for performing the most superior passage in the whole series.*

Passbook – *(noun)* **1** a book issued by a bank or building society to an account holder, recording transactions. *My passbook was overflowing with entries, so the officer issued another one.* **2** [historical] a black person's identity book, used to control travel and residence. *The immigration officer requested the black man to show his passbook for reviewing.*

Passenger – *(noun)* **1** a traveler on a public or private conveyance other than the driver, pilot, or crew. *The passengers beat up the eve-teaser and kicked him out of the bus.* **2** a member of a team who does very little effective work. *The others in the team were extremely efficient, while he was just a passenger.*

Passing – *(adjective)* **1** going past. *The band was passing by the crowd and everybody cheered.* **2** going by. *We were passing by the temple the other day, when I was reminded of a pending task.* **3** carried out quickly and lightly: a passing glance. *A passing glance between the two was enough for them to click.* **4** slight. *She mentioned him in passing in her speech.* *(noun)* **1** the passage of something, especially time. *Time was passing by, but no action was being taken.* **2** the action of kicking, hitting, or throwing a ball to another team member during a sports match. *Certain games only allow backward passing.* **3** the end of something. euphemistic a person's death. *His passing away left a void in our lives.*

Passion – *(noun)* **1** strong and barely controllable emotion. an outburst of such emotion. *He screamed at her passionately.* **2** intense sexual love. *The love between them was driven more by passion than emotion.* **3** an intense enthusiasm for something. *Cooking was her passion, and not just a hobby.* 4 the suffering and death of Jesus. a musical setting of this. *The theatre company was presenting The Passion of the Christ next month.*

Passionate – *(adjective)* showing or caused by passion. *She was very passionate about travelling.*

Passive – *(adjective)* **1** accepting or allowing what happens or what others do, without active response or resistance. *We were urged to rise from our passive state and start acting!* **2** [grammar] denoting a voice of (verb)s in which the subject undergoes the action of the (verb) the opposite of active. *I understood active voice, but passive voice was a bit difficult to comprehend.* **3** denoting a circuit or device containing no source of energy or electromotive force. receiving or reflecting radiation rather than generating its own signal. *All the elements of a passive circuit had been laid out on each table in the lab.* **4** [chemistry] uncreative because of a thin inert surface layer of oxide. *Grit is often used in passive physical surface treatment method.* *(noun)* [grammar] a passive form of a verb. *I bought an English Grammar book focusing on passive verbs.*

Passport – *(noun)* an official document issued by a government, certifying the holder's identity and citizenship and entitling them to travel abroad under its protection. *I showed the officer my passport so that I could board the flight fast.*

Password – *(noun)* a secret word or phrase used to gain admission to something. *I had written the password somewhere so that I do not forget it but I think I should have revealed it to my mother at least.*

Past – *(adjective)* **1** gone by in time and no longer existing. recently elapsed: the past twelve months. *I had been waiting for the past two hours.* **2** [grammar] expressing a past action or state. *It was long past the scheduled time of arrival.* *(noun)* **1** a past period or the events in it. a person's or thing's history or earlier life: the country's colourful past. *Our country had a colourful past.* **2** [grammar] a past tense or form of a verb. *We had to identify the past tense in the statements given in the exam.* *(preposition)* **1** to or on the further side of. *He said my friend stayed in the house just past the Church.* **2** in front of or from one side to the other of. *As I stood at the bus station, he walked past me.* **3** beyond in time; later than. *Its past midnight, he said, so we should sleep now.* **4** no longer capable of. *After the accident, her legs were past recognition. beyond.* **5** the scope of. *Her marriage is past the stage intervention.* *(adverb)* **1** so as to pass from one side of something to the other. *The troops marched past.* **2** used to indicate the passage of time: a week went past. *A week went past and I did not even realize.*

Pasta – *(noun)* dough extruded or stamped into various shapes. for cooking in boiling water and eating, typically with a savoury sauce. *The chef prepared the best pasta I had ever had.*

Paste – *(noun)* **1** a thick, soft, moist substance, typically produced by mixing dry ingredients with a liquid. *We made a loose paste before adding coconut to it.* **2** an adhesive of this kind. *I tried to stick the paper with paste.* **3** a mixture of kaolin and water of low plasticity, used for making porcelain. *We got the paste ready for making the plates.* **4** a hard vitreous composition used in making imitation gems. *I had to prepare paste in bulk as I had too many orders for the gems.* *(verb)* **1** coat or stick with paste. *We were pasting stars on the paper.* **2** computing insert into a documents. *All I had to do was to copy-paste the para from the internet to the document.* **3** [informal] beat or defeat severely. *The feud was bloody and he was pasted.*

Pasteboard – *(noun)* thin board made by pasting together sheets of paper. *The pasteboard was full, so we needed another board.*

Pastel – *(noun)* **1** a crayon made of powdered pigments bound with gum or resin. a work of art created using pastels. *I bought her a packet of pastel colours as she loved art and colouring.* **2** a soft and delicate shade of a colour. *She bought me a pastel sari.* *(adjective)* of or denoting such a shade: *We were looking for pastel pink bedspreads.*

Pasteurize – *(verb)* subject to a process of partial sterilization, especially by heating. *I have started ordering pasteurized milk.*

Pastime – *(noun)* an activity that someone does regularly for enjoyment; a hobby. *Television is not the best pastime for a child.*

Pastor – *(noun)* a minister in charge of a Christian church or congregation, especially in some non-Episcopal churches. *We felt blessed as our neighbor was a pastor! (verb)* be the pastor of. *He became the pastor of St Francis' Church shortly.*

Pastry – *(noun)* **1** a dough of flour, fat, and water, used as a base and covering in baked dishes such as pies. *Ma taught me how to bake the pastry-base for pie.* **2** an item of food consisting of sweet pastry with a cream, jam, or fruit filling. *There was chocolate pastry for dessert.*

Pasture – *(noun)* **1** land covered mainly with grass, suitable for grazing cattle or sheep. *The cows and buffaloes were having the time of their life in the pasture.* **2** grass and herbage growing on such land. *It was once a park but now it is like a pasture. (verb)* put to graze in a pasture. *The farmer put the cows in the pasture to graze.*

Pasty – *(noun)* [chiefly British] a folded pastry case filled with seasoned meat and vegetables. *I loved the beef pasty she made for tea the other day.*

Pat – *(verb)* **1** touch quickly and gently with the flat of the hand. *Dogs always love being patted the head.* **2** mould or position with gentle taps. *We had to pat the moulds lightly to give it a final shape. (noun)* **1** a light stroke with the hand. *She gave me a pat on the back for my efforts.* **2** a compact mass of soft material. *The pat of butter was kept on the table outside the refrigerator.*

Patch – *(noun)* **1** a piece of material used to cover a torn or weak point. a shield worn over a sightless or injured eye. a piece of cloth sewn on to clothing as a badge. an adhesive piece of drug impregnated material worn on the skin so that the drug may be gradually absorbed. [historical] a small black silk disc worn on the face, especially by woman in the 17th and 18th centuries. *She covered the injured eye with a patch of cloth.* **2** a small area differently coloured or otherwise distinct. *The whole cloth looked like a patch-work.* **3** a small piece of ground especially one used for gardening. *She grew a vegetable garden in a patch outside her kitchen.* [British informal] an area for which someone is responsible or in which they operate. *The sixth regiment was posted in the patch beyond Kensington Street.* **4** [British informal] a period of time regarded as distinct: a bad patch. *Everybody has to go through a bad patch in their lives.* **5** a temporary electrical or telephone connection. *We were connected with a patch for so long.* **6** computing a small piece of code or telephone connection. *The township was initially connected in patches.*

Patchwork – *(noun)* **1** needlework in which small pieces of cloth in different designs are sewn together. *She made a patchwork bag and it looked quite cool.* **2** a thing composed of many different elements so as to appear variegated. *Her entire project work actually looked like a patchwork.*

Patchy – *(adjective)* **1** existing or happening in small, isolated areas. *She had sewn me patchy trousers.* **2** not of the same quality throughout; inconsistent. *Their work is patchy at best.*

Patent – *(noun)* a government license to an individual or body conferring a right or title for a set period, especially the sole right to make, use, or sell an invention. *She was an acclaimed scientist who had patents on six discoveries. (adjective)* **1** easily recognizable; obvious. [medicine] showing detectable parasites in the tissues or faces. *Their scorn was patent to everyone.* **2** [medicine] open and unobstructed. *The cancer was spreading out widely patent branches in the rest of the body.* **3** made and marketed under a patent. *The new concept car was patented under the designer's label. (verb)* obtain a patent for an invention. *She received six patents for her inventions.*

Paternal – *(adjective)* **1** of or appropriate to a father. *His paternal instincts were aroused when he saw his child walking on the wrong track.* **2** related through the father: his paternal grandfather. *She resembled her paternal grandfather more than her own father.*

Paternity – *(noun)* the state of being someone's father. *He did not accept claims of his paternity easily.* **2** paternal origin. *She went searching the entire state for her paternity.*

Path - *(noun)* **1** a way or track laid down for walking or made by continual treading. *There was a well laid out walking path in the park.* **2** the direction in which a person or thing moves. *Was she walking on the wrong path, her mother questioned herself.* **3** a course of action or conduct. *There was a definite path ahead of her in her life.*

Pathetic - *(adjective)* **1** arousing pity, especially through vulnerability or sadness. *The pathetic state of existence of the tramp brought tears to her eyes.* **2** [informal] miserably inadequate. *The politics of our country is in a pathetic state.* **3** [archaic] relating to the emotions. *She cried pathetically when she saw the accident.*

Pathological - *(adjective)* **1** involving, caused by, or of the nature of a disease. *Her disease was diagnosed as pathologicaly caused by bacteria.* **2** [informal] compulsive: a pathological gambler. *He was a pathological gambler, beyond treatment.* **3** of or relating to pathology. *She was taken to the pathology lab immediately.*

Pathology - *(noun)* the branch of [medicine] concerned with the causes and effects of disease. *The head of the pathology department is now voted to take over as the dean of the university.*

Pathos - *(noun)* a quality that evokes pity or sadness. *Khalil Gibran's writings involve a lot of pathos.*

Patience - *(noun)* **1** the capacity to tolerate delay, trouble, or suffering without becoming angry or upset. *Living in those terrible conditions was testing my patience.* **2** [chiefly British] a card game for one player, the object of which is to use up all one's cards by forming particular arrangements and sequences. *She could pick up a card game easily, so I taught her the game of patience.*

Patient - *(adjective)* having or showing patience. *She has always been extremely patient with her son.* *(noun)* a person receiving or registered to receive medical treatment. *She has been a patient in this hospital for the last two weeks.*

Patriarch - *(noun)* **1** the male head of a family or treble. an older man who is powerful within a family or organization. a founder. *He was the undefiable patriarch of the royal family.* **2** a biblical figure regarded as a father of the human race, especially Abraham, Isaac, and Jacob, and their forefathers, or the sons of Jacob. *There are groups in the Church who disapprove of certain decisions made by the patriarchs.* **3** a bishop of one of the most ancient Christian sees. the head of an autocephalous orthodox church. a roman catholic bishop ranking above primates and metropolitans and immediately below the pope. *The party patriarch's statements are not to be defied by any member.*

Patriot - *(noun)* a person who vigorously supports their country and is prepared to defend it. *Shaheed Bhagat Singh was a patriot who laid down his life for the country.*

Patriotic - *(adverb)* one who is filled with sense of nationalism. *The patriotic song that my friend sang in the school assembly aroused tears in everyone's eyes.*

Patrol - *(noun)* **1** a person or group sent to keep watch over an area, especially a detachment of guards or police. *The patrol kept watch over the hotel that was under hijack.* **2** the action of patrolling an area. *The thief's plan was foiled as there was a police van on patrol there.* **3** an expedition to carry our reconnaissance. *A special patrol had been arranged for the minister's security.* **4** a routine operational voyage of a ship or aircraft. *An airborne patrol was closely watching the developments in the building under siege.* *(verb)* keep watch over by regularly walking or travelling around it. *The navy regularly patrols our seas.*

Patron - *(noun)* **1** a person who gives financial or other support to a person, organization, cause, etc. *My brother has been a patron of our organization for several years.* **2** a distinguished person, organization, cause, etc. *Her organization has been our patron for several years.* **2** a distinguished person who takes an honorary position in a charity. *We felicitated him in the annual function as the chief patron of the organization.* **3** a customer of a restaurant, hotel, etc., especially a regular one. *I am a regular patron of this restaurant.* **4** a patrician in relation to a client. *In Ancient Rome, patrons were held in high respect by the clients.* **5** the former owner of freed slave. *Tom looked up to his patron as it was the latter who had initiated the whole freedom movement of the slaves.* **6** British, chiefly [historical] a person or institution with the right to grant a benefice to a member of the clergy. *The Church had a patron saint they never talked about.*

Patronage - *(noun)* **1** the support given by a patron. *We thanked the president and the trustee for their patronage to our institution.* **2** the power to control appointments to office or the right to privileges. *The king had all the rights of patronage in the kingdom.* **3** a patronizing manner. *Though I was grateful to his patronage, I was a bit irritated at his condescending attitude.* **4** the regular customer attracted by a restaurant, hotel, etc. *I provided a lot of patronage to the hotel thanks to my regular official trips.* **5** the position of a patron. *His patronage was indeed a boon to the institution.*

Patronize - *(verb)* **1** treat with an apparent kindness which betrays a feeling of superiority. *Though I was grateful for his contribution to our institution, I detested his patronizing attitude.* **2** frequent as a customer. *I would patronize this restaurant any day.* **3** act as a patron towards. *We asked him politely if he would like to patronize our institute.*

Pattern - *(noun)* **1** a repeated decorative design. an arrangement or sequence regularly found in comparable objects or events. *The sheriff recognized a definite pattern in the series of crimes that had been occuring in the town of late.* **2** a model or design used as a guide in needlework and other crafts. *The teacher taught her different patterns of stitching that she could try out.*

Paucity - *(noun)* the presence of something in only small or insufficient amounts. *There was a paucity of resources in the city which is why they were demanding help from the Centre.*

Paunch - *(noun)* **1** a large or protruding abdomen or stomach. *Mother asked us to start exercising else we will soon have a paunch.* **2** nautical, [archaic] a thick strong mat used to give protection from chafing on a mast or spar. *She spread a layer of paunch on the mat.* *(verb)* disembowel. *He wanted the paunch to disappear.*

Pave - *(verb)* cover with flat stones or bricks. *It was as if the path had been paved for her to walk on.*

Pavement - *(noun)* **1** [British] a raised paved or asphalted path for pedestrians at the side of a road. *If we do not walk on the pavement, there is a risk we will get hit by a vehicle.* **2** [north American] the hard surface of a road or street. *The employees had made space for themselves on the pavement to resume their strike.* **3** geology a horizontal expanse of bare rock with cracks or joints: a limestone pavement.*The archeologists came across a medieval pavement at the excavation site.*

Pavillion - *(noun)* **1** [British] a building at a cricket ground or other sports ground used for changing and taking refreshments. *The sportsmen made their way to the pavillion to freshen up during the break.* **2** a summer house or other decorative shelter in a park or large garden. *The farmhouse had huge lawns, complete with pavillions and green house cabins.* **3** a detached or semi-detached block at a hospital or other building complex. *They decided to convert the pavilion into a staff room with various amenities for the nurses.* **4** a marquee with a pack and crenellated decorations, used at a show or fair. *The fair was bubbling with games, rides and colourful pavillions of all kinds.* **5** a temporary stand or other structure in which items are displayed at a trade exhibition. *There were several pavillions representing books from every state of the country at the book fair.*

Paw - *(noun)* **1** an animal's foot having claws and pads. *We found paw prints in the garden, probably belonging to some wild animal.* **2** [informal] a person's hand. *The teacher asked us to stretch our paws to the maximum limit.* *(verb)* **1** feel or scrape with a paw or hoof. *I heard Blacky pawing at the door.* **2** [informal] touch or handle clumsily or lasciviously. *Mother* *was angry and asked me to stop pawing at the items on the mantlepiece.*

Pawn – *(noun)* **1** a chess piece of the smallest size and value. *Moving the pawn near his bishop was the only way out for her in the game.* **2** a person used by others for their own purposes. *He was only a pawn in the game, while the core of the plan was the gangster's own.*

Pea – *(noun)* **1** a spherical green seed eaten as a vegetable. *Peas masala was my favourite curry.* **2** the hardy climbing leguminous plant which yields pods containing peas. *There were huge crops of green peas in his farm.* **3** used in names of similar or related plants or seeds. *We decided to grow peas in the farm.*

Peace – *(noun)* **1** freedom from disturbance, tranquility. *I went to the mountains in search of peace.* **2** freedom from or the cessation of war. *After a long battle, finally there was peace.* **3** Christian church an action such as a handshake taking the place or the kiss of peace. *The warring communities decided to dissolve their differences and declare their peace with a handshake.*

Peaceable – *(adjective)* **1** inclined to avoid war. *We should look for a peacable solution than resorting to war.* **2** free from conflict; peaceful. *Ashoka's kingdom was defined by a peaceable ruler.*

Peaceful – *(adjective)* **1** free from disturbance; calm. *Her 11th storey balcony was indeed very peaceful.* **2** not involving war or violence. *The crowd dispersed in a peaceful manner.* **3** inclined to avoid conflict. *His rule established a peaceful environment in the province.*

Peach – *(noun)* **1** a round stone fruit with juicy yellow flesh and downy yellow skin flushed with red. *We decided to try and bake a peach cake.* **2** the Chinese tree which bears this fruit. *The peach was a rare tree in our country.* **3** a pinkish orange colour like that of a peach. *She wore a peach sari for her best friend's wedding.* **4** [informal] an exceptionally good or attractive person or thing. *Her complexion was like peach.*

Peacock – *(noun)* a male peafowl, having very long tail feathers with eye-like markings that can be erected and fanned out in display. *There were almost twenty peacocks dancing in the rain in all their glory at the zoo.*

Peak – *(noun)* **1** the pointed top of a mountain. a mountain with a peak. *The peak of that mountain cannot be conquered.* **2** a stiff brim at the front of a cap. *He adjusted the peak of his cap and hit a six that had everyone up on their feet to give him a standing ovation.* **3** a point in a curve or on a graph, or a value of a physical quantity, which is higher than those around it. the point of highest activity or achievement. *He showed in the presentation the time period when the sales of the company were at their peak.* **4** the upper, outer corner of a sail extended by a gaff. *The peak of the sail was painted a bright blue so it could be seen from far.* *(verb)* reach a highest point. *She had reached the peak of her career at 30.*

Peal – *(noun)* **1** a loud riming of a bell or bells. bell-ringing a series of changes rung on a set of bells. a set of bells. *There was a peal of bells when the priest came out of the sanctum sanctorum.* **2** a loud repeated or reverberating sound of thunder of laughter. *I could hear peals of laughter coming from the room.* *(verb)* **1** ring loudly or in a peal. *A peal of bells resounded from the temple.* **2** sound in a peal. *People were left in peals of laughter at the comedian's jokes.*

Peanut – *(noun)* **1** the oval seed of a south American plant, eaten as a snack or used for making oil or animal feed. *Having too many peanuts at a time came make you put on weight.* **2** the leguminous plant that bears these seeds, which develop in underground pods. *Peanuts were numerous in number at the farm.*

Pear – *(noun)* **1** a yellowish or brownish green edible fruit, narrow at the stalk and wider towards the tip. *We decided to add some pears to the dessert.* **2** the tree which bears this fruit. *The pear is all that's left of her fruit garden.*

Pearl – *(noun)* **1** a hard, lustrous spherical mass, typically white or bluish-grey, formed within the shell of an oyster or other bivalve mollusc and highly prized as a gem. an artificial imitation of this. *He bought me a pearl necklace for our* *wedding anniversary.* **2** a thing of great worth: pearls of wisdom. *His words were pearls of wisdom that I just had to note down.* **3** a very pale bluish grey or white colour. *Her necklace was a pearl colour. (verb)* **1** poetic form pearl like drops. *Tears dropped from her eyes like pearls.* **2** dive or fish for pearl oysters. *The jeweller had actually employed divers to fish for pearl oyesters.*

Peasant – *(noun)* **1** a poor smallholder or agricultural laborer of low social status. *The peasants were discussing a revolt against the capitalists who were trespassing into their area.* **2** [informal] an ignorant, rude, or unsophisticated person. *He was a thorough peasant in his mannerisms.*

Peasantry – *(noun)* poor agricultural labourer. *The whole peasantry was revolting against the capitalists.*

Peat – *(noun)* partly decomposed vegetable matter forming a deposit on acidic, boggy ground, dried for use in gardening and as fuel. *The agriculturist advised the farmers to use peat as a form of fuel.*

Pebble – *(noun)* small stone made smooth and round by the action of water or sand. *I love sitting quietly at the riverside, throwing an occassional pebble into the water. (adjective)* [informal] very thick and convex. *It was a pebble that could not be crushed.*

Peck – *(noun)* **1** a measure of capacity for dry goods, equal to a quarter of a bushel. *A peck of those items would be worthless for the price I was being offered.* **2** [archaic] a large number or amount of something. *He threw me a peck of onions and I almost fell under its weight.*

Peculiar – *(adjective)* **1** strange or odd. *She had a peculiar smile on her face that I would never forget.* **2** belonging exclusively to. *The leaves were peculiar to this tree.* **3** [formal] particular. *This was a symptom peculiar to his condition. (noun)* chiefly a parish or church exempt from the jurisdiction of the diocese in which it lies, though subject to the jurisdiction or the monarch or an archbishop. *People often discuss the peculiar jurisdiction of the Archbishop of Canterbury.*

Pedagogue – *(noun)* [formal] a teacher, especially a strict or pedantic one. *The pedagogues of yore have all been laid to rest.*

Pedal – *(noun)* **1** each of a pair of foot-operated levers for powering a bicycle or other vehicle propelled by leg power. *The bike had colourful blue pedals.* **2** a foot-operated throttle, brake, or clutch control in a motor vehicle. *The pedals of his bicycle were giving away in the middle of the race.* **3** each of a set of two or three foot-operated levers on a piano, for sustaining or softening the tone. a foot-operated lever on other musical instruments, such as a harp or organ. *She had oiled the pedals well for a soft movement of the music. (verb)* **1** move by working the pedals. *She pedalled faster and faster up the mountain.* **2** use the pedals of a piano, organ, etc. *The teacher taught her how to use the pedals of the piano.*

Pedantic – *(adjective)* excessively concerned with minor details. *It was a rather pedantic effort.*

Pedestal – *(noun)* **1** the base or support on which a statue, obelisk, or column is mounted. a position in which one is greatly or uncritically admired: you shouldn't put him on a pedestal. *My friend asked me not to put her up on a pedestal.* **2** each of the two supports of a kneehole desk or table. *She sat on the table with her feet up on the pedestal.* **3** the supporting column or base of a washbasin or toilet pan. *The pedestal of the toilet pan was on the verge of giving away.*

Pedestrian – *(noun)* a person walking rather than travelling in a vehicle. *The pedestrians had crowded around the accident site. (adjective)* dull; uninspired. *What a pedestrian attitude she had.*

Pedigree – *(noun)* **1** the record of descent of an animal, showing it to be pure-bred. *She did not like the idea of keeping strays pets, so she bought a pedigree.* **2** a person's lineage or ancestry. a genealogical table. *She asked her grandmother to explain her pedigree.* **3** the history or provenance of a person or thing. *She belonged to a royal pedigree.*

Pedlar – *(noun)* **1** an itinerant, trader in small goods. *He had been unsuccessful in big businesses and eventually became a pedlar* *of small articles.* **2** a person who sells illegal drugs or stolen goods. *There were drug pedlars haunting the whole street at midnight.* **3** a person who peddles an idea or view. *She was a pedlar of strong views.*

Pee – *(verb)* urinate. *She hurried to find a place to pee.* *(noun)* **1** an act of urinating. *The gastroenterologist asked her to pee in a bottle for a urine test.* **2** urine. *Her pee was a bright yellow colour, the doctor noted.*

Peek – *(verb)* **1** look quickly or furtively. *She was peeking from the corner of the tree.* **2** protrude slightly so as to be just visible. *She caught a peek of the actor's costly shoes.* *(noun)* a quick or furtive look. *The sight was definitely worth a peek.*

Peel – *(noun)* a small square defensive tower of a kind built in the 16th century in the border countries of England and Scotland. *There were peels of all kinds in the countryside.*

Peep – *(verb)* **1** look quickly and furtively. *She peeped from the hole in the wall.* **2** come slowly or partially into view. *She was asked to peep through peep-hole.* *(noun)* **1** a quick or furtive look. *I caught a peep from the hole in the door.* **2** a momentary or partial view of something. *Peep shows are common in the US.*

Peer – *(verb)* **1** look with difficulty or concentration. *She was peering at the man who stood at a distance.* **2** be just visible. *To peer at someone is impolite, my mother instructed.*

Peerless – *(adjective)* unequalled. *The princess's beauty was peerless.*

Peeved – *(adjective)* annoyed irritated. *She was a bit peeved at him for his carelessness.*

Peevish – *(adjective)* irritable. *On reviewing the conduct of the culprit, and examining his somewhat peevish and whimsical correspondence, the judge finally drew the sentence in the favour of the victim.*

Peg – *(noun)* **1** a short projecting pin or bolt used for hanging things on, securing something in place, or marking a position. a clip for holding things together or hanging up clothes. *The clothes peg came off by itself a few days ago.* **2** [chiefly Indian] a measure of spirits. *We had downed a few pegs before taking the cab.* **3** a point or limit on a scale, especially a exchange rates. *The weak currency was pegged to the US dollar.* **4** a strong throw. *He pegged a throw at the striker and there goes the ball!* **5** [informal] a person's leg. *He fastened the peg with a string and ran after the pirate.* **6** a place marked by a peg and allotted to a competitor to fish or shoot from. *A fishing station was allotted to an angler in a competition, marked by a peg in the ground.* *(verb)* **1** fix attach, or mark with a peg or pegs. *We decided to peg the tents near the river.* **2** fix. *I pegged the last string of the tent on a stone nearby.* **3** [north American informal] form a fixed opinion of. *The officer probably has us pegged as anarchists.* **4** [chiefly baseball] throw hard and low. *He pegged a throw at the striker and there goes the ball!*

Pelican – *(noun)* a large gregarious water bird with a long bill and an extensible throat pouch for scooping up fish. *The zoo has several seasonal birds including pelicans.*

Pellet – *(noun)* **1** a small, rounded, compressed mass of a substance. *A beetle was rolling a pellet of dung up a hill.* **2** a piece of small shot or other lightweight bullet. *He emptied the gun of all its pellets.* **3** [ornithology] a small mass of bones and feathers regurgitated by a bird of prey. *I found pellets lying near the eagle and I knew he did not like what I had left for him today.* *(verb)* **1** form into pellets. *I came to a factory where they make pellets.* **2** hit with or as if with pellets. *Pellets of bullets were showered at him.*

Pelt – *(verb)* **1** hurl missiles at. *The enemies were being pelted with missiles non stop.* **2** fall very heavily. *Its pelting down with rain there.* **3** run very quickly. *She pelted down the stairs in her nightgown.* *(noun)* [archaic] an act of pelting. *The children were asked not to pelt stones at the poor animal.*

Pen – *(noun)* **1** an instrument for writing or drawing with ink, typically consisting of a metal nib or ball, or a nylon tip, fitted into a metal or plastic holder. writing as an occupation. an electronic device used in conjunction with a writing surface to enter commands or data into a computer. *My handwriting was most beautiful when I wrote with a fountain pen.* **2** [zoology] the tapering cartilaginous internal shell of a squid. *The chef finally cut through the pen of the squid and went on to finish the dish. (verb)* write or compose. *It gave her the greatest pleasure to pen down her thoughts every night in her diary.*

Penal – *(adjective)* **1** of, relating to, or prescribing the punishment of offenders under the legal system. punishable by law. *I was told that her crime was punishable under the penal code.* **2** extremely severe. *I wanted his sentence to be penal, so he would know what pain his victims went through.*

Penalty – *(noun)* **1** a punishment imposed for breaking a law, rule, or contract. *Breaking traffic rules will invite a penalty you can easily avoid.* **2** a handicap imposed on a player or team for infringement of rules, especially a penalty kick. bridge points won by the defenders when the declarer fails to make the contract. *His only chance in the game was the penalty kick.*

Penance – *(noun)* **1** voluntary self-punishment as an open expression of repentance for wrongdoing. *The sage was known to have been through a lot of penance to attain this state.* **2** a sacrament in which a member of the church confesses sins to a priest and is given absolution. a religious observance or other duty imposed as part of this sacrament. *I confessed my sin and was ready to accept penance for the same. (verb)* [archaic] impose a penance on. *The Church imposed a penance on me for the sin I had confessed there.*

Pence – plural form of penny. *The small magnet cost just a few pence.*

Pencil – *(noun)* **1** an instrument for writing or drawing, typically consisting of a thin stick of graphite enclosed in a long thin piece of wood or fixed in a thin cylindrical case. *She bought different kinds of pencils for her daughter's first day at school.* **2** [physics] a set of light rays, lines, etc. converging to or diverging narrowly from a point. *I saw a pencil of rays just as the teacher had mentioned in the lab. (verb)* **1** write, draw, or colour with a pencil. *He pencilled an outline of the house.* **2** arrange or note down something provisionally. *I pencilled his name for a meeting next week.*

Pendant – *(noun)* **1** a piece of jewellery that hangs from a necklace chain. *I gifted her a pendant on her birthday.* **2** a light designed to hang from the ceiling. *There were several hanging pendants in her newly designed house.* **3** the part of a pocket watch by which it is suspended. *I found the pendant of the pocket watch hanging from his pocket.* **4** a short rope hanging from the head of a ship's mast, yardarm, or clew of a sail, used for attaching tackles. *We tightened the pendant and set sail!* **5** nautical a tapering flag. *The pendant flapped in the air.* **6** complementary of matching artistic, literary, or musical work. *What a pendant piece of work.* (adjective) pendent. *She bought a pendent bunch of grapes from the market.*

Pendulum – *(noun)* **1** a weight hung from a fixed point so that it can swing freely, especially a rod with a weighted end that regulates the mechanism of a clock. *She bought a grandfather clock from the antique shop with a modified pendulum.* **2** the tendency of a situation to oscillate between extremes: the pendulum of fashion. *The pendulum of fashion always swings between extremes.*

Penetrate – *(verb)* **1** force a way into or through. other sounds. *We tried hard to penetrate into the hole in the tree, but got stuck.* **2** infiltrate. *Terrorists managed to penetrate into the guarded area with no qualms at all.* **3** understand or gain insight into something complex or mysteries. *The psychotherapist was tired of trying to penetrate into her mind.* **4** the penis into the vagina or anus of a sexual partner. *The sex education teacher taught us the science of penetraiton.*

Penguin – *(noun)* a flightless black and white seabird of the southern hemisphere, with wings used as flippers. *The advocates resemble penguins in their attire.*

Penicillin – *(noun)* an antibiotic produced naturally by certain blue moulds, now usually prepared synthetically. *We had to procure a* *certain dosage of penicillin as soon as possible to cure the patient.*

Peninsula - *(noun)* a long, narrow piece of land projecting out into a sea or lake. *Our geography teacher explained the concept of peninsula.*

Penitent - *(adjective)* feeling or showing sorrow and regret for having done wrong. *What is the point of being penitent after making a mistake?* *(noun)* a person who repents his sins. a person who confesses his sins to a priest and submits to the penance that he imposes. *She made mistakes and was penitent at the end of the whole episode.*

Penitentiary - *(noun)* **1** [north American] a prison for people convicted of serious crime. *There was no other option but to send the criminal to a penitentiary institution.* **2** a priest appointed to administer penance. an office in the papal court deciding questions relating to penance, dispensations, etc. *We decided to approach the penitentiary in search of a solution.*

Penknife - *(noun)* a small knife with a blade which folds into the handle. *I tried cutting the fruits with my penknife.*

Penniless - *(adjective)* without money; destitute. *After the grand party, she was left penniless.*

Penny - *(noun)* **1** a British bronze coin and monetary unit equal to one hundredth of a pound. *We were taught by the British Academy how to exchage pennies and pounds at the Exchange Office.* **2** a former British coin and monetary unit equal to one twelfth of a shilling and 240th of a pound. *I had more pennies than pounds in my wallet, I realized.* **3** [informal] a one-cent coin. *I need a penny to buy a toffee at the tea shop.* **4** no money at all. *They were paying us in pennies than pounds.* **5**. a denarius. *All the pennies were of the same denomination.*

Pension - *(noun)* a small hotel or boarding house in France and other European countries.*A pension had somewhat lesser to offer than a hotel.*

Pensive - *(adjective)* engaged in deep thought. *Don't disturb you father when he is in a pensive mood.*

Pentagon - *(noun)* **1** a plane figure with five straight sides and five angles. *The geometry teacher taught us to draw a pentagon.* **2** the headquarters of the US Department of defense, near Washington DC.*The package tour includes a visit to the Pentagon.*

Penthouse - *(noun)* **1** a flat on the top floor of a tall building. typically luxuriously fitted and offering fine views. *The executive bought a plush penthouse in a posh locality downtown.* **2** [archaic] an outhouse with a sloping roof, built on the side of a building.*We were given a penthouse service appartment to stay in.*

Penultimate - *(adjective)* last but one.*The penultimate line of the chemical series was difficult to learn.*

Penury - *(noun)* extreme poverty.*Unknown to the world, she lived in a state of penury.*

People - *(plural noun)* **1** human beings in general or considered collectively. the mass of citizens in a country; the populace.*The people of the country were getting ready to revolt against the dictator.* **2** one's parents or relatives.*I did invite my people for my wedding.* **3** one's employees or supporters.*Our people are our strength and we should protect them.* **4** the members of a particular nation, community, or ethnic group: the native peoples of Canada. *The native people of Canada rejoiced at the declaration of independence.* *(verb)* **1** particular group of people inhabit. fill or be present in. *Stalin wanted people the empty steppes.* **2** fill with a particular group of inhabitants. *People lived in Africa several years ago.*

Pepper - *(noun)* **1** a pungent, hot-tasting powder prepared from dried and ground peppercorns, used to flavor food. *I was growing pepper in my kitchen garden.* **2** a climbing vine with berries that are dried as black or white peppercorns. used in names of related plants having hot-tasting leaves, or fruits used as pungent spice, e.g. Jamaica pepper, water pepper. *I was instructed to add white pepper to the curry.* **3** a capsicum, especially a sweet pepper. a reddish and typically hot-tasting spice prepared from various forms of capsicum. *I love red bell peppers in salad.* **4** [baseball] a practice game in which a fielder throws at close range to a batter who hits back to the fielder. *I noticed his hits had improved in the pepper.* *(verb)* **1** sprinkle or season with pepper. *Add pepper to the salad to make it spicy.* **2** scatter liberally over or through. *Season with pepper to make it spicy.* **3** hit repeatedly with small missiles or gunshot. *The enemies were being peppered with shots.*

Peppermint – *(noun)* **1** the aromatic leaves of a plant of the mint family, or an oil obtained from them, used as a flavouring in food. *Peppermint is a nice mouthfreshner to have after dinner.* **2** the plant which yields these leaves or oil. *I bought some peppermint oil from the station.* **3** a sweet flavoured with peppermint oil. *Peppermint is one of my favourite sweets.* **4** austral, a eucalyptus or myrtle with peppermint-scented foliage.*A eucalyptus oil with peppermint flavour would drive away my headache anyday.*

Per – *(preposition)* **1** for each: **2** per square yard. *We bought the land for Rs 3000 per square feet.* **2** by means of. *As per the manual, we had to twist the wires in the opposite direction.* **3** in accordance with.*The author was charged as per his instructions.* **4** heraldry divided by a line in the direction of.*We had divided the land at the rate of 40 per cent distribution.*

Perceive – *(verb)* **1** become aware or conscious of.*How we perceive the world is how the world perceives us.* **2** regard as.*I perceived the problem as much bigger than it actually was.*

Percent – *(adverb)* **1** by a specified amount in or for every hundred.*We got 30 percent of the total distribution of the land.* *(noun)* one part in every hundred. the rate, number, or amount in each hundred.*The land was being distributed at 30 percent of its actual landspace.*

Percentage – *(noun)* **1** a rate, number, or amount in each hundred. *She scored a bad percentage in the internal exams.* **2** a proportion of a larger sum of money granted as an allowance or commission. *Half of the earned money makes for the broker's percentage.* **3** any proportion or share in relation to a whole. *What percentage of share do you hold in the company?*

Perceptible – *(adjective)* able to be perceived. *Only 10 percent of space lies in the perceptible limit.*

Perception – *(noun)* **1** the ability to see, hear, or become aware of something through the sense. the state of being or process of becoming aware of something in such a way. *She was amazed at the level of perception of the baby.* **2** a way of regarding, understanding, or interpreting something. intuitive understanding and insight. *You must have a deeper perception of things in order to grow spiritually.* **3** [psychology] the neurophysiological processes, including memory, by which an organism becomes aware of and interprets external stimuli.*It is after the age of* **4** *years that perception develops properly in a child.*

Perceptive – *(adjective)* having or showing acute insight.*She was more perceptive and receptive as a student than others.*

Perch – *(noun)* **1** a thing on which a bird alights or roosts. *The bird fluttered for a while and then settled itself precariously on a perch high above.* **2** a high or narrow seat or resting place. *He sat himself on a perch high above.* *(verb)* **1** alight, sit, or rest on a perch. *The birds were perched high above the others on the only banyan tree.* **2** be situated above or on the edge of something. *I told my friend that it was not really a pleasure to be perched up on an inaccessible point of a treehouse.* **3** set or balance someone or something on.*She was perched up on the highest point of the house.*

Percolate – *(verb)* **1** filter through a porous surface or substance. *The liquid was percolating through the filter cloth.* **2** spread gradually through a group of people. *It was amazing how the terrorists had managed to percolate through the crowd into their positions.* **3** prepare or be prepared in a percolator.*I prepared the decoction coffee in the percolator and now it was ready.* **4** [US] be or become full of lively activity or excitement.*She percolated with happiness.*

Percussion – *(noun)* **1** the action of playing a musical instrument by striking or shaking it. denoting musical instruments played in this way. percussion instruments forming a band or section of an orchestra. *The percussion team was the star of the evening's performance.* **2** the striking of one solid object with or against another with some degree of force. *The sound of the percussion instruments stood out in the orchestra.* **3** [medicine] the action of percussing a part of the body.*The doctors were considering an immediate percussion to revive the body.*

Peremptory – *(adjective)* **1** insisting on immediate attention or obedience; brusque and imperious. *The teacher spoke in a peremptory tone.* **2** law not open to appeal or challenge; final.*The sentence was given in a swaggering, peremptory manner.*

Perennial – *(adjective)* **1** lasting through a year or several years. *This condition is a perennial occurance.* **2** living for several year. Compare with annual, biennial. *That perennial definicit was a hardy one.* **3** lasting for a long time: enduring or continually recurring. continually engaged in a specified activity: a perennial student.*We were aiming at achieiving perennial happiness.(noun)* a perennial plant.*We had sown a perennial plant, we realized later.*

Perfect – *(adjective)* **1** having all the required elements, qualities, or characteristics. *When the batter had reached that perfect consistency, we poured it into a tin and baked it.* **2** free from any flaw; faultless. *She was a perfect beauty.* **3** complete; absolute *It made perfect sense.* **4** [mathematics] equal to the sum of its positive divisors, e.g. the number 6, whose divisors also add up to 6. *The easiest question in the exam was to find the perfect integer.* **5** [grammar] denoting a completed action or a state or habitual action which began in the past, formed in English with have or has and the past participle, as in they have eaten. *In the english test, I had some trouble finding the past perfect tense of the given words.* **6** having both stamens and carpals present and functional. *We were taking practical classes on how to identify perfect flowers.* **7** [botany] denoting the stage or state of a fungus in which the sexually produced spores are formed. *The fungus I was trying to grow for my botany test seemed to be in a perfect state. (verb)* **1** make perfect. *He is busy perfecting his bowling technique.* **2** bring to completion. *If urged, she will definitely perfect her work. (noun)* [grammar] the perfect tense. *I had to find the perfect tense in the statement.*

Perfection – *(noun)* **1** the action, process, or condition of perfecting or being perfect. *Perfection of the invention took years.* **2** a perfect person or thing. *She seems to be perfection herself.*

Perforate – *(verb)* pierce and make a hole or holes in. *We placed it in a tin perforated with round holes. (adjective)* [biology & medicine] perforated. *The paper needs to be perforated to make it easier to tear.*

Perform – *(verb)* **1** carry out, accomplish, or fulfill. *She knew she had to perform in this exam.* **2** work, function, or do something to a specified standard. *The car performs well at low speeds.* **3** yield a profitable return. *If we perform well, we will be rewarded.* **4** present to an audience. *She had to perform best in the whole lot today.*

Performance – *(noun)* **1** an act of performing a play, concert, or other form of entertainment. *There was a performance scheduled for the weekend.* **2** a person's rendering of a dramatic role, song, or piece of music. *She gave a stellar performance in the music festival.* **3** [informal] a display of exaggerated behavior; an elaborate fuss. *Seeing my excitement, my mother asked me to stop my performance.* **4** the action or process of performing a task or function. *Experience generally improves performance.* 5 the capabilities of a machine or product. *The car's performance has been impressive in spite of its age.* **6** the extent to which an investment is profitable. *The performance generally improves by the end of the year.*

Perfume – *(noun)* **1** a fragrant liquid typically made from essential oils, used to impart a pleasant smell to one's body or clothes. *Her clothes smell really good because of the perfume she uses.* **2** a pleasant smell. *A sweet perfume* *was spreading in the room as soon as she entered.* **3** impregnate with perfume or a sweet-smelling ingredient.*Orange blossoms perfumed the air in the garden.* **4** apply perfume to. *She perfumes herself everyday.*

Perhaps – *(adjective)* **1** expressing uncertainty or possibility. *Perhaps it was this way or perhaps it was that.* **2** used when making a polite request or suggestion. *Perhaps she will call tomorrow.*

Peri – *(noun)* a genie or fairy. *She was divine, a peri indeed!*

Perimeter – *(noun)* **1** the continuous line forming the boundary of a closed geometrical figure. *I was trying to calculate the perimeter of the circle in the paper.* **2** the outermost parts or boundary of an area or object. *The enemies had covered the perimeter of the city* **3** baseball an area away from the basket, beyond the reach of the defensive team. *I asked him to cross the perimeter and initiate defense.* **4** an instrument for measuring the extent and characteristics of a person's field of vision. *She examined using a perimeter.*

Period – *(noun)* **1** a length or portion of time. *The country was going through a period of economic prosperity.* **2** a portion of time characterized by the same prevalent features or conditions. *She saved the artifacts of the pre-colonial period in a shelf.* **3** a major division of geological time that is a subdivision of an era and is itself subdivided into epochs. *Picasso's early career is divided into his blue period and rose period.* **4** each of the set divisions of the day in a school. *As we went from fourth standard to fifth, our number of periods increased as well.* **5** a monthly flow of blood and other material from the lining of the uterus, occurring in women of child-bearing age when not pregnant.*Women are advised to take rest and avoid strain during their period.* **6** chiefly a full stop.*You will not go to the movies tonight, period!* **7** [physics] the interval of time between successive occurrences of the same state in an oscillatory or cycle phenomenon.*The pendulum oscillates during different periods of interval.* **8** [mathematics] the interval between successive equal values of a periodic function *The teacher explained the significance of the concept of period in mathematics to the class today.*

Periodic – *(adjective)* **1** appearing or occurring at intervals. *The meteors appeared at periodic intervals.* **2** [chemistry] relating to the elements or the pattern of chemical properties which underlies it.*The periodic table in chemistry actually made the subject even more interesting.* **3** of or relating to a rhetorical period. *She had periodic feelings of anxiety.*

Periodical – *(adjective)* occurring or appearing at intervals, published at regular intervals.*She had periodical fits of depression.* *(noun)* a periodical magazine or newspaper. *She had published in several periodicals.*

Periphery – *(noun)* **1** the outer limits or edge of an area or object. *The enemies had reached the periphery of the region.* **2** a marginal or secondary position, part, or aspect. *The preliminary research did not take me beyond the periphery of my problem.*

Periscope – *(noun)* an oppartus consisting of a tube attached to a set of mirrors or prisms, by which an observer typically in a submerged submarine or behind a high obstacle can see things that are otherwise out of sight. *Suddenly he saw a periscope rising from the water at a distance.*

Perish – *(verb)* **1** die, especially in large numbers. *Thousands had perished in the fire accident.* **2** suffer complete ruin or destruction. *His entire business had perished.* **3** rot or decay. *All the vegetables had perished by the time we returned from the trip.* **4** [British] be suffering from extreme cold. *It is believed that the dinosaurs perished when the cold wave hit earth.*

Perjure – *(verb)* law commit perjury.*The witness perjured herself when she denied knowing the defendant.*

Perk – *(verb)* make or become more cheerful or lively. *She perked up as soon as she was shown a chocolate.* *(adjective)* dialect perky; pert. *You're in a perky mood.*

Perm – *(noun)* a method of setting the hair in waves or curls and treating it with chemicals so that the style lasts for several months. *The hollywood actress's perm was back.* *(verb)* treat in such a way. *She had her hair permed.*

Permanence – *(noun)* the state of remaining unchanged in definitely. *There is no permanence to anything in this world.*

Permanent – *(adjective)* lasting or remaining unchanged indefinitely, or intended to be so; not temporary. *Nothing in this world is permanent.* *(noun)* a perm for the hair. *Her hair colour was permanent.*

Permeate – *(verb)* spread throughout; pervade. *A thinker once said, our thinking is permeated by our historical myths.*

Permissible – *(adjective)* allowable; permitted. *The minerals in our tap water were beyond the permissible limit.*

Permission – *(noun)* authorization. *She asked for permission to leave at noon.*

Permissive – *(adjective)* **1** allowing or characterized by freedom of behavior. *You are lucky to have permissive parents.* **2** law allowed but not obligatory; optional. denoting a path available for public use by the landowner's consent, not as a legal right of way. *Direct primary legislation is more permissive than prescriptive.*

Permit – *(verb)* **1** give permission to or for something. *They were denied permit to sell alcoholic beverages.* **2** make possible. *This permits the water to rush in.* **3** [formal] allow for; admit of. *She permitted her son to meet her estranged husband.* *(noun)* an official document giving permission to do something. *She had to get written permit in order to open a shop there.*

Perpendicular – *(adjective)* **1** at an angle of 90 to a given line, plane, or surface. *The axes are perpendicular to each other.* **2** at an angle of 90 to the ground; vertical. *The tree stood perpendicular to the ground.* **3** denoting the latest stage of English gothic church architecture, prevalent from the late *14th* to mid *16th* entries, characterized by broad arches and elaborate fan vaulting. *She wanted a perpendicular style while designing her palace.* *(noun)* a perpendicular line. *The perpendicular and steep stairs led to the attic.*

Perpetrate – *(verb)* carry out or commit. *The perpetrators of the crime will be punished.*

Perpetual – *(adjective)* **1** never ending or changing. denoting or having a position or trophy held for life rather than a limited period. having no fixed maturity date. *She had opened a perpetual fixed deposit in the bank.* **2** occurring repeatedly. *A father had two sons who were perpetually quarrelling.* **3** blooming or fruiting several times in one season. *The tree was in perpetual bloom.*

Perpetuate – *(verb)* cause to continue indefinitely. *The new library will perpetuate its founder's great love of learning.*

Perplex – *(verb)* cause to feel baffled. *She looked perplexed when I asked her about her project.*

Perquisite – *(noun)* **1** [formal] a special right or privilege enjoyed as a result of one's position. *Politics is the perquisite of the upper class.* **2** [historical] a thing which has served its primary use and to which a subordinate or employee has a customary right. *Long distance calls at discount rates was one of the perquisites of the job.*

Persecute – *(verb)* **1** subject to prolonged hostility and ill-treatment. *Jews were mercilessly persecuted in the former Soviet Union.* **2** persistently harass or annoy. *He described his first wife as constantly persecuting him.*

Persevere – *(verb)* continue in a course of action in spite of difficulty or with little or no indication of success. *To persevere is the only way to success.*

Persist – *(verb)* **1** continue firmly or obstinately in an opinion or a course of action in spite of difficulty or opposition. *Though I refused to buy her a chocolate, she continued to persist.* **2** continue to exist. *The legend of Rama persists till date.*

Person – *(noun)* **1** a human being regarded as an individual. *Each one of us is an individual person whose rights ought to be guarded and respected.* **2** an individual characterized by a preference or liking for a specified thing.

She's not a cat person. **3** an individual's body. *The bomb was concealed on his person.* **4** a character in a play or story. *She played the character of a person in distress.* **5** [grammar] a category used in the classification of pronouns, possessive determiners, and verb forms, according to whether they indicate the speaker, the addressee, or a third party. *We were asked to give a third person description of the given dialogue.* **6** Christian theology each of the three modes of being of god, namely the father, the son, and the Holy ghost. *A christian is a person who believes in Christianity.*

Personal – *(adjective)* **1** of, affecting, or belonging to a particular person. involving the presence or action of a particular individual. *You have to take personal initiative to get this project done.* **2** of or concerning a person's private rather than professional life. *In office, it is always best to keep your personal life away from the professional sphere.* **3** making inappropriate or offensive reference to a person's character or appearance: personal remarks. *One must refrain from making personal remarks about an individual.* **4** of or relating to a person's body: personal hygiene. *One must always try and maintain personal hygiene.*

Personality – *(noun)* **1** the combination of characteristics or qualities that from an individual's distinctive character. *She had a charming personality.* **2** the qualities that make someone interesting or popular. *He had an extremely charismatic personality.* **3** a celebrity. *He was always a public personality.*

Personalize – *(verb)* **1** design or produce to meet someone's individual requirements. *The designer offered to get a personalized version of his product designed especially for the queen.* **2** make identifiable as belonging to a particular person. *I had to personalize the design so people do not mess with it or copy it.* **3** cause to become concerned with personalities or feelings rather than with general or abstract matters. *When your parents advise you, try not to personalize matters.* **4** personify. *She wanted to personalize her wedding card.*

Personify – *(verb)* **1** represent by a figure in human form. *She was happiness personified.* **2** attribute a personal nature or human characteristics to. *She personifies happiness.* **3** represent or embody in physical form. *To make history more interesting, I personify it.*

Personnel – *(plural noun)* people employed in an organization or engaged in an organized undertaking. *Thousands of personnel had been employed at several points to make the fair a success.*

Perspective – *(noun)* **1** the art of representing three-dimensional objects on a two-dimensional surface, so as to convey the impression of height, width, depth, and relative distance. *These drawings are difficult to comprehend from a certain perspective.* **2** a view or prospect. *My perspective might differ from yours.* **3** a particular way of regarding something. *You have to view your problems from a larger perspective to be able to deal with them.* **4** understanding of the relative importance of things. *We must keep a sense of perspective about what he's done.* **5** an apparent spatial distribution in perceived sound. *Medieval constructions lack perspective.*

Perspire – *(verb)* give out sweat through the pores of the skin as a result of heat, physical exertion, or stress. *She was perspiring heavily at the gym.*

Persuade – *(verb)* **1** cause to do something through reasoning or argument. *I tried my best to persuade her about the benefits of the scheme.* **2** cause to believe something. *We have to persuade children to learn the code of conduct expected in an apartment complex.* **3** provide a sound reason for to do something. *Nothing could persuade her to change her mind.*

Persuasion – *(noun)* the action of persuading someone to do or believe in something. *Three foremost aids of persuasion, according to me, are humility, concentration and gusto.*

Persuasive – *(adjective)* **1** good at persuading someone to do or believe something. *She was quite persuasive in her beliefs.* **2** providing sound reasoning or argument. *She gave a persuasive case for the day.*

Pert – *(adjective)* **1** attractively lively or cheeky. *She was pert in her conduct, smart and spontaneous.* **2** neat and jaunty. *She appeared rather pert at the interview.*

Pertain – *(verb)* **1** be appropriate, related, or applicable. *The evidence that pertains to the accident was collected and saved.* **2** [chiefly law] belong to something as a part, appendage, or accessory. *These pages don't pertain to the book you're suggesting.* **3** be in effect or existence in specified place or at a specified time. *None of these circumstances pertained during the Jurassic.*

Pertinent – *(adjective)* relevant; appropriate. *Her advice was quite pertinent to his situation.*

Perturb – *(verb)* **1** make anxious or unsettled. *She was perturbed by his carelessness as it could lead to an accident some day.* **2** alter the normal or regular state or path of a system, moving object, or process. *Scientists found that symmetrical ions perturb bulk water asymmterically.*

Peruse – *(verb)* formal read or examine thoroughly or carefully. *I sent the employer my project report for his perusal.*

Pervade – *(verb)* spread or be present throughout; suffuse. *Corruption is like cancer that pervades every corner of society.*

Pervasive – *(adjective)* widespread. *The pervasive odour of garlic was irritating me.*

Perverse – *(adjective)* **1** showing a deliberate and obstinate desire to behave unacceptably. sexually perverted. *He took perverse satisfaction in foiling her plans.* **2** contrary to that which is accepted or expected. law of against the weight of evidence or the direction of the judge. *He had a perverse sense of loyalty.*

Perversion – *(noun)* the action of perverting. abnormal or unacceptable sexual behavior. *His perversion was met with strong repercussions.*

Pervert – *(verb)* **1** alter from its original meaning or state to a corruption of what was first intended. *It is an analysis that perverts the meaning of the poem.* **2** lead away from what is right, natural, or acceptable. *Socrates was accused of perverting young men.* *(noun)* a person with abnormal or unacceptable sexual behavior. *The criminal turned out to be not just a murderer but a pervert as well.*

Pessimism – *(noun)* **1** lack of hope or confidence in the future. *Do not lie in a state of pessimism if you are unable to face your problems.* **2** [philosophy] a belief that this world is as bad as it could be or that evil will ultimately prevail over good. *Pessimism does not bring out the best in man.*

Pessimist – *(noun)* a tendency to see the worst aspect of things. *Do not be a pessimist and run from your problems.*

Pest – *(noun)* **1** a destructive insect or other animal that attacks crops, food, or livestock. *The crop was infested with pests this season.* **2** [informal] an annoying person or thing. *He is such a pest!* **3** [archaic] bubonic plague. *The government was struggling to keep away pests from spreading to the humans.*

Pester – *(verb)* trouble or annoy with persistent requests or interruptions. *Do not pester your parents for sweets when they have just had a fight.*

Pesticide – *(noun)* a substance for destroying insects or other pests of plants or animals. *Thanks to the new pesticides, our crops were saved this year.*

Pestilence– *(noun)* [archaic] a fatal, epidemic disease, especially bubonic plague. *The government had planned strict actions against the pestilence.*

Pet – *(noun)* **1** a domestic or tamed animal or bird kept for companionship or pleasure. *I love animals and have always wanted to own a pet.* **2** a person treated with special favour. *She has always been the teacher's pet.* **3** fused as an affectionate form of address. *"Would you like some ice cream, pet?"* *(adjective)* **1** of, relative to, or kept as a pet. *He kept a cat as a pet.* **2** favourite or particular. *My pet hate is woodwork.* *(verb)* **1** stroke or pat. *She pet me with love.* **2** caress sexually. *Her petting was going overboard.*

Petal – *(noun)* each of the segments of the corolla of a flower. *I took out the petals of the rose and spread them in the water.*

Peter - *(verb)* diminish or come to an end gradually. *The water that was gushing was now reduced to a peter.*

Petite - *(adjective)* attractively small and dainty. *She had a petite figure.*

Petition - *(noun)* **1** a formal written request, typically signed by many people, appealing to authority in respect of a cause. an appeal or request. *I signed a petition in favour of the bill that was currently being discussed in the Parliament.* **2** law an application to a court for a writ, judicial action in a suit, etc. *His petition was rejected by the court. (verb)* make or present a petition to. *He filed a mercy petition in the Supreme Court.*

Petrify - *(verb)* **1** paralyse with fear. *She was petrified at the sight of the thief in the house.* **2** change into stone by encrusting or replacing its original substance with a mineral deposit. *We were taught how to petrify the rock in the mining class.* **3** deprive or become deprived of vitality. *He sought help from a doctor as he was petrified.*

Petrol - *(noun)* [British] refined petroleum used as fuel in motor vehicles. *We had to fill petrol in the car before we went on the road trip.*

Petroleum - *(noun)* a hydrocarbon oil found in suitable rock strata and extracted and refined to produce fuels including petrol, paraffin, and diesel oil; oil. *The different countries were fighting over petroleum extraction.*

Petticoat - *(noun)* **1** a woman's light, loose undergarment in the form of a skirt of dress. *Her petticoat seemed longer than her sari.* **2** [informal] often derogatory associated with women: petticoat government. *The minister revolted at the charges of running a petticoat government against her.*

Petty - *(adjective)* **1** trivial. *The children were fighting over petty issues.* **2** mean; small minded. *He seemed very petty from his conversation.* **3** minor. law of lesser importance compare with grand. *It is these petty laws that were actually stopping the growth of our country's economy.*

Pew - *(noun)* a long bench with a back, placed in rows in churches for the congregation. [British informal] a seat. *The VIPs were seated in the front pews while the commoners behind.*

Phantom - *(noun)* chiefly [archaic] variant spelling of fantast. *She was paranoid and thought there was a phantom in the house.*

Pharmaceutical - *(adjective)* of or relating to medicinal drugs, or their preparation, use or sale. *The drugs she was buying were purely for pharmaceutical use. (noun)* a compound manufactured for use as a medicinal drug. *I had to resort to pharmaceuticals as yoga was not yielding any results.*

Pharmacy - *(noun)* **1** a place where medicinal drugs are prepared or sold. *I rushed to the pharmacy to buy the medicines.* **2** the science or proactive of preparing and dispensing medicinal drugs. *She wanted to pursue a course in pharmacy for graduation.*

Phase - *(noun)* **1** a distinct period or stage in a process of change or development. each of the aspects of the moon or a planet, according to the amount of its illumination. *We were asked to stay away from the sea when the moon's phase changes.* **2** [zoology] a genetic or seasonal variety of an animal's coloration. *The white colour phase of a weasel takes months to change.* **3** [chemistry] a distinct and homogeneous form of matter separated by its surface from other forms. *The reaction occurs in the liquid phase of the system.* **4** [physics] the relationship in mite between the cycles of an oscillating or repeating system and a fixed reference point of a different system. *The concept of phase was explained in physics class. (verb)* **1** carry out in gradual states. introduce something into use in gradual stages. *The plan was to gradually phase out blue line buses from the city.* **2** [physics] adjust the phase of especially so as to synchronize it with something else. *I tried adjusting the phases to see if electricity comes on.*

Pheasant - *(noun)* a large long-tailed game bird native to Asia, the male of which typically has showy plumage. *There were lots of pheasants in the jungle.*

Phenomenal - *(adjective)* **1** extraordinary. *It was a phenomenal achievement to cross that border.* **2** perceptible by the senses or through immediate experience. *Conquering the kingdom was a phenomenal experience.*

Phenomenon – *(noun)* **1** a fact or situation that is observed to exist or happen, especially one whose cause is in question. *We decided to study the phenomenon as it was a rare occurrence.* **2** [philosophy] the object of a person's perception. *We were asked to analyse the phenomenon from the perspective of the subject in question.* **3** a remarkable person or thing. *The new model is quite a phenomenon!*

Phew – *(exclamatory)* [informal] expressing relief. *Phew! Finally we are there!*

Phial – *(noun)* a small cylindrical glass bottle, typically for medical samples or [medicines]. *She poured the tonic into a phial and handed it over to the customer.*

Philanthrope – *(noun)* [archaic] a philanthropist. *Bill Gates is known for being quite a philanthrope in his circle.*

Philately – *(noun)* the collection and study of postage stamps. *He had an active interest in philately.*

Philology – *(noun)* **1** the study of the structure, [historical] development, and relationships of a language or language. *She decided to major in philology.* **2** [chiefly north American] literary or classical scholarship. *As for the philology of them, that is but a circle of tales and therefore not fit for the writing.*

Philosopher – *(noun)* a person engaged or learned in [philosophy]. *India is known for its share of philosophers and spiritual gurus.*

Philosophy – *(noun)* **1** the study of the fundamental nature of knowledge, reality, and existence. a set of theories of a particular philosopher. *I wanted to take up philosophy in my post graduation.* **2** the study of the theoretical basis of a branch of knowledge or experience. *After majoring in psychology, she went on to study philosophy.* **3** a theory or attitude that guides one's behaviour. *Learning philosophy can help you broaden your perspective towards life.*

Phlegm – *(noun)* **1** the thick viscous substance secreted by the mucous membranes of the reparatory passages, especially when produced in excessive quantities during a cold. *The doctor realized that his patient's lungs were filled with phlegm.* **2** one of the four bodily humours, believed to be associated with a calm or apathetic temperament. calmness of temperament. *Ayurveda refers to phlegm as kapha, related to a bodily condition.*

Phlegmatic – *(adjective)* unemotional and stolidly clam. *He had a phlegmatic attitude.*

Phobia – *(noun)* an extreme or irrational fear of something. *He had a phobia of small insects.*

Phone – *(noun)* phonetics a speech sound. *I could hear different phones of music.*

Phonetic – *(adjective)* phonetics of or relating to speech sounds. having a direct correspondence between symbols and sounds. of or relating to phonetics. *We were trying to analyse the phonetics of the musical note.*

Phoney – *(adjective)* not genuine. *It was a phoney affair.* *(noun)* a fraudulent person or thing. *He turned out to be a phoney guy.*

Phosphorus – *(noun)* the chemical element of atomic number 15, a poisonous, combustible non-metal which exists as a yellowish waxy solid which ignites spontaneously in air and glows in the dark and as a less reactive form used in making matches. *One can modify the lights in their house and use phosphorus lamps.*

Photocopy – *(noun)* a photographic copy of something produced by a process involving the action of light on a specially prepared surface. *Ever since I bought a photocopy machine, all the college students have been flocking to my shop.* *(verb)* a photocopy of. *To photocopy her notes was the only way I could make up for the classes I missed.*

Photograph – *(noun)* a picture made with a camera, in which an image is focused on to film and then made visible and permanent by chemical treatment. *She has lots of photographs of our school days.* *(verb)* take a photograph of. *I wanted to take a photograph of my favourite actor with me.*

Phrase – *(noun)* **1** a small group of words standing together as a conceptual unit. an idiomatic or short pithy expression. *I had trouble understanding the phrases she used in her essay.* **2** [music] a group of notes forming a distinct unit within a longer passage. *The phrases in her passage made the whole tune sound ridiculously off tune. (verb)* **1** put into a particular form of words. *We can make new phrases if we know the language well.* **2** divide into phrases in a particular way. *We had to divide the whole passage into phrases.*

Physical – *(adjective)* **1** of or relating to the body as opposed to the mind. involving bodily contact or activity: a physical relationship. *He shared a physical relationship with the girl next door.* **2** of or relating to things perceived through the senses as opposed to the mind; tangible or concrete. *It may not be a physical evidence before you, but it exists for sure.* **3** of or relating to [physics] or the operation of natural forces generally. *Physical sciences have always fascinated me. (noun)* **1** a medical examination to determine a person's bodily fitness. *His physical examination was scheduled for the first week of next month.* **2** stock exchange stocks held in actual commodities for immediate exchange, as opposed, for example, to futures. *A friend inherited some physical shares from his father.*

Physician – *(noun)* a person qualified to practice [medicine], especially one how specializes in diagnosis and medical treatment as distinct from surgery. *We decided to approach a general physician to get a diagnosis.*

Physics – *(noun)* the branch of science that studies nature and properties of matter. *She did a bachelors honours course in physics before going on to astronomy.*

Physiognomy – *(noun)* a person's facial features or expression, especially when regarded as indicative of character or ethnic origin. *His physiognomy seemed different from the actual description the witness gave.* **2** the supposed art of judging character from facial characteristics. *He was an expert at physiognomy.*

Physiology – *(noun)* the branch of biology concerned with the normal functions of living organisms and their parts. the way in which a living organism or bodily part functions. *We were studying the physiology of aquatic animals.*

Physiotherapy – *(noun)* the treatment of disease, injury, or deformity by physical methods such as massage and exercise rather than by drugs or surgery. *The doctor advised three months of physiotherapy for the patient to recover completely.*

Physique – *(noun)* the form, size, and development of a person's body. *His powerful physique attracted quite a few proposals.*

Piano – *(noun)* a large keyboard musical instrument with a wooden case enclosing a soundboard and metal strings, which are struck by hammers when the keys are depressed. *The piano was the star in the entire orchestra.*

Pick – *(noun)* **1** a tool headed by a curved bar with a point at one end and chisel edge or point at the other, used for breaking up hard ground or rock. *He owned a factory that makes picks.* **2** an instrument for picking [informal] a plectrum. *He used a toothpick to clean his teeth.*

Picket – *(noun)* **1** a person or group of people standing outside a workplace trying to persuade others not to enter during a strike. *Let's go and picket the shop.* **2** a soldier or small body of troops sent out to watch for the enemy. *The outlying sonar picket was to detect, localize and engage any submarine trying to close the convoy.* **3** a pointed wooden stake driven into the ground to form a fence or palisade or to tether a horse: a picket fence. *She had put up a picket fence around her garden. (verb)* act as a picket outside. *The miners went on strike and picketed the power station.*

Pickle – *(noun)* **1** a relish consisting of vegetable or fruit preserved in vinegar, brine, or mustard. [north American] a cucumber preserved in this way. liquid used to preserve food or other perishable items. *Pickle with curd rice is a delicious combination.* **2** [informal] a difficult situation. *He was caught in quite a pickle.* **3** an acid solution for cleaning metal objects. *She asked me to clean the bowls using pickle solution. (verb)* **1** preserve in pickle. *I decided to preserve all the leftover mangoes in pickle.* **2** immerse in an acid solution for cleaning. *She pickled the bowls so they may come out clean.*

Picnic – *(noun)* a packed meal eaten outdoors, or an occasion when such a meal is eaten. *The school had planned a picnic for the children.* *(verb)* have or take part in a picnic. *The children were excited about participating in the picnic.*

Pictorial – *(adjective)* of or expressed in pictures; illustrated. *The album was a pictorial description of the whole event.* *(noun)* a newspaper or periodical with pictures as a main feature. *She bought a pictorial often sold at the newspaper shop.*

Picture – *(noun)* **1** a painting, drawing, or photograph. a portrait. an image on a television screen. *The pictures spoke for themselves.* **2** an impression formed from an account or description. [informal] a state of being fully informed about or involved in something. *A full picture of the disaster had not yet emerged.* **3** a cinema film. the cinema. *We decided to go to the local movie hall to catch a picture.* **4** [archaic] a person or thing resembling another closely. *She was a perfect picture of her mother.* *(verb)* **1** represent in a picture. *She drew a picture of her experience at the hill station.* **2** form a mental image of. *She tried to picture what the actual scene must have been like.*

Picturesque – *(adjective)* visually attractive in a quaint or charming manner. unusual and vivid. *The hill station was picturesque and a photographer's paradise.*

Pie – *(noun)* a baked dish of savory or sweet ingredients encased in or topped with pastry. *I asked mother to bake an apple pie for tea.*

Piece – *(noun)* **1** a portion of an object or of material produced by cutting, tearing, or breaking the whole. *I asked my friend to pass me a piece of her bread to taste.* **2** an item used in constructing something or forming part of a set; a component. an instance or example: a crucial piece of evidence. *The detectives had laid their hands on a crucial piece of evidence.* **3** a musical or written work: a piece of music. *This particular piece of music has always been a hit with the crowd.* **4** a figure or token used to make moves in a board game. *I asked her not to hide my pieces and strike when I am not looking.*

Piecemeal – *(adjective & adverb)* characterized by unsystematic partial measures taken over a period of time. *It was a piecemeal effort she made.*

Pierce – *(verb)* **1** make a hole in or through with a sharp pointed object. *The thorn had pierced through her skin.* **2** force or cut a way through. *A shrill voice pierced the air.* **3** very sharp, cold, or high-pitched. *The silence was disturbed by a piercing shriek.* *(verb)* astute or intelligent. *Her words pierced through the students.*

Piety – *(noun)* the quality of being pious or reverent. a belief accepted with unthinking conventional reverence. *He impressed the Gods with his piety.*

Pig – *(noun)* **1** an omnivorous domesticated hoofed mammal with sparse bristly hair and a flat snout, kept for its meat. a wild animal related to this, a hog. *The pig sty had not been cleaned in weeks.* **2** [informal] a greedy, dirty, or unpleasant person. [British informal] officer. *When he saw me eating he asked me not to be a pig!* **4** an oblong mass of iron or lead from a smelting furnace. *I had a chance to see pig iron when I visited the factory.* **5** a device which fits snugly inside an oil or gas pipeline and is sent through it to clean or test the inside. *Practice of using pigs to perform maintenance operations on a pipeline is termed pigging.*

Piggery – *(noun)* a farm where pigs are bred. *The stench came from the piggery nearby.*

Pigeon – *(noun)* **1** a stout seed or fruit-eating bird with a small head, short legs, and a cooing voice, similar to but generally larger than a dove. *Two pigeons had built a nest in my terrace.* **2** [informal] a gullible person, especially the victim of a confidence trick. *He is a pigeon so it should not be a task to trick him.*

Piggy bank – *(noun)* a money box especially one shaped like a pig. *I got a piggy bank as a gift on my ninth birthday.*

Pig headed – *(adjective)* stupidly obstinate. *When I insisted stubbornly, mother asked me to stop being so pig headed.*

Piglet – *(noun)* a young pig. *The pigs in the sty had given birth to cute little piglets.*

Pigment – *(noun)* **1** the natural colouring matter of animal or plant tissue. *The leaves were unique as they had different pigments.* **2** a substance used for colouring or painting, especially a dry powder which constitutes a paint or ink when mixed with oil or water. *We decided to use a different combination of pigment for the rest of the painting.* *(verb)* colour with or as if with pigment. *The leaf had pigmented.*

Pigtail – *(noun)* **1** a plaited lock of hair worn singly at the back or on each side of the head. *I like the girl with pigtails who sits at the back of the class.* **2** a short length of braided wire connecting a stationary part to a moving part in an electrical device. *The pigtails were twisted and had to be repaired.* **3** a twist of tobacco. *I begged for at least one pigtail.*

Pile – *(noun)* **1** a heavy stake or post driven into the ground to support the foundations of a superstructure. *Pile is a form of deep foundation typically found in high rise buildings.* **2** heraldry a triangular charge or ordinary formed by two lines meeting at an acute angle, usually pointing down from the top of the shield. *A standard pile issues from the chief (upper edge) by default.* *(verb)* strengthen or support with piles. *Piling as opposed to drilling shafts is advantageous because the soil displaced by pile compresses the surrounding soil.*

Piles – *(plural noun)* hemorrhoids. *The doctor advised the piles patient to avoid eating spicy food.*

Pilgrim – *(noun)* a person who journeys to a sacred place for religious reasons. *The facilities for pilgrims in our country need to improve dramatically.* *(verb)* [archaic] travel or wander like a pilgrim. *I came across several people wandering like pilgrims on my road trip.*

Pilgrimage – *(noun)* a pilgrim's journey. *Mecca is one of the most crowded and famous pilgrimage points in the world.* *(verb)* go on a pilgrimage. *My mother wants to go on a pilgrimage after retirement.*

Pill – *(noun)* **1** a small round mass of solid [medicine] for swallowing whole. a contraceptive pill. *The doctor prescribed sleeping pills to the insomniac.* **2** [informal] a tedious person. *His competitor's success was a bitter pill to take.* *(verb)* form small balls of fluff on its surface. *Pilling is a surface defect of textiles caused by wear and is considered unsightly.*

Pillage – *(verb)* rob or steal with violence, especially in wartime. *Pillage by a victorious army during war has been a common practice throughout recorded history.* *(noun)* the action of pillaging. *A bitter pillage followed the war.*

Pillar – *(noun)* **1** a tall vertical structure, usually of stone, used as a support for a building or as an ornament or monument. *The pillars in the palace had been ornately designed.* **2** a person or thing providing reliable support. *He was a pillar of his local community.*

Pillion – *(noun)* **1** a seat for a passenger behind a motorcyclist. *The pillion rider also needs to wear a helmet.* **2** [historical] a woman's light saddle. a cushion attached to the back of a saddle for an additional passenger. *The horse nearly threw the rider and the pillion off its back.*

Pillow – *(noun)* **1** a rectangular cloth bag stuffed with feathers, wadding, or other soft materials, used to support the head when lying or sleeping. *He went hunting around the city for the best pillows to sleep on.* **2** short for lace pillow. *Pillows add colour and style to the living room.* *(verb)* rest as if on a pillow. *My mother's lap is the best pillow I could sleep on.*

Pilot – *(noun)* **1** a person who operates the flying controls of an aircraft. *Its alarming to know some of the pilots sleep over the 'controls during a flight.* 2 a person with expert local knowledge qualified to take charge of a ship entering or leaving a harbor. a navigational handbook for use at sea. [archaic] a guide or leader. *He has been a pilot for this project.* **3** something done or produced as an experiment or test before wider introduction: a pilot scheme. *A pilot project helps discover all the shortcomings before the main project.* **4** telecommunications an unmediated reference signal transmitted with another signal for the purposes of control or synchronization. *In FM Stereo broadcasting, a pilot tone of 19khz* *indicates there is stereophonic information.* *(verb)* **1** act as a pilot of an aircraft or ship. guide; steer. *The first person to pilot an aircraft across the Pacific was Amelia Earhart.* **2** test scheme, project, etc. before introducing it more widely. *We are piloting the scheme through Parliament.*

Pimple – *(noun)* a small hard inflamed spot on the skin. *Getting pimples may also be a sign of attaining puberty.*

Pin – *(noun)* a thin price of metal with a sharp point at ore end to fasten papers, cloth etc. *The girl used a safety pin to secure her handkerchief to the uniform.*

Pinafore – *(noun)* a collarless, sleeveless dress worn over a blouse or jumper. *The children wore pinafores at nursery school.* [British] a woman's loose sleeveless garment worn over clothes to keep them clean. *A bright pinafore to go with garment is what Maria is shopping for.*

Pincer – *(noun)* **1** a tool made of two pieces of metal bearing blunt concave jaws arranged like the blades of scissors, used for gripping and pulling things. *I screamed when the dentist brought an instrument that looked like a pincer close to my mouth.* **2** a front claw of a lobster, crab, or similar crustacean. *When in danger, the crab uses it's pincers as a deadly weapon.*

Pinch – *(verb)* **1** grip tightly and sharply between finger and thumb. hurt by being too tight. tighten the lips or a part of the face, especially with worry or tension. *Pinching nerves in the neck can be very painful.* **2** live in a frugal way. *You're bound to feel the pinch a little when you're a student.* **3** [informal] steal. *Alex tried to pinch off with his colleague's new pen.* **4** [informal] arrest. *The cops pinched Max for driving without a license.* **5** remove to encourage bushy growth. *Pinch the buds off the lower branches so the one at the top will bloom.* *(noun)* **1** an act of pinching. an amount of an ingredient that can be held between fingers and thumb. *This dish requires no more than a pinch of salt.* **2** baseball a critical point in the game. *A pinch hitter is the need of the hour now.*

Pine – *(noun)* **1** an evergreen coniferous tree having clusters of long meddle-shaped leaves, grown for its soft wood or for tar and turpentine. used in names of coniferous trees of other families, e.g. Chile pine. *Natural stands of scots pine can also be found in the heath lands of southern england.* **2** used in names of unrelated plants that resemble the pines in some way, e.g. screw pine. *Our pine furniture is made from solid pine which comes from the sustainable forests of Brazil.*

Pineapple – *(noun)* **1** a larg juicy tropical fruit consisting of aromatic edible yellow flesh surrounded by a tough segmented skin and topped with a tuft of stiff leaves. *A diet based on pineapple fruit is said to work wonders for weight reduction.* **2** the tropical American plant the bears this fruit, with a spiral of spiny sword-shaped leaves on a thick stem. *Ananas, the native American pineapple plant has an edible plum shaped fruit.*

Ping-pong – *(noun)* [informal] term for table tennis. *The Asian teams tend to dominate Ping-Pong games at the Olympics.*

Pinnacle – *(noun)* **1** a high pointed piece of rock. *The islands are known to have a number of shallow reefs and coral pinnacles.* **2** a small pointed turret built as an ornament on a roof. *Between the lofty windows are tall walls surmounted by small pinnacles that gives the front a handsome appearance.* **3** the most successful point: the pinnacle of his career. *A sense of satisfaction prevails when one reaches the pinnacle of his career.*

Pinpoint – *(noun)* a tiny dot or point. (adjective) absolutely precise. *The new imaging software can pinpoint the area of impact to within a few millimeters.*

Pinprick – *(noun)* **1** a prick caused by a pin. *The tire of the bike had a small puncture much like a pinprick.* **2** a very small dot or amount. *Here is our little community, a pinprick on the map of the five great continents of the world.*

Pint – *(noun)* a unit of liquid or dry capacity equal to one eighth of a gallon, in Britain equal to 0.568 litre and in the US equal to 0.473 litre.

[British informal] a pint of beer. *Mix extracts, pour into a clean pan and boiling until the mixture measures 2 pint.*

Pioneer – *(noun)* **1** a person who is the first to explore or settle a new country or area. *American pioneers in history who migrated west to join in settling and developing new areas are still revered.* 2 an innovator or developer of new ideas or techniques. *There is an exhibition in town that explains the work of the famous Yorkshire aviation pioneer, Robert Blackburn.* **3** a member of an infantry group preparing roads or terrain for the main body of troops. *A pioneer from the Mid West Infantry was sent to perform engineering tasks, form roads, and dig trenches as the troop advances towards the border. (verb)* **1** be a pioneer. *The American business man's idea is a pioneering venture, unique in Asia and most other parts of the world* **2** open up a road or terrain as a pioneer. *Pioneering new roads using modern machines has helped conquer new terrains.*

Pious – *(adjective)* **1** devoutly religious. *He was revered by many as a saint because he was so pious.* **2** making a hypocritical display of virtue. *The so called miracles enacted by many 'god' men in today's world need to be studied in detail before terming them as pious fraud.* **3** sincere but unlikely to be fulfilled. *He spent his last days in pious hope that God would appear before him.*

Pip – *(noun)* a small hard seed in a fruit. *The fibroid detected is as miniscule as a pip of an orange.*

Pipe – *(noun)* **1** a tube used to convey water, gas, oil, or other fluids. a cavity in cast metal. *The pipe in my bathroom needs to be replaced.* **2** a device used for smoking tobacco, consisting of a narrow tube with a bowl at one end in which the tobacco is burned, the smoke from which is then drawn into the mouth. *Cinema has often shown actors smoking a pipe on screen quite stylishly.* **3** a wind instrument consisting of a single table with holes along its weight that are covered by the fingers to produce different notes. bagpipes. a set of musical pipes joined together, as in pan pipes. any of the cylindrical tubes by which notes are produced in an organ, a boatswain's whistle. *Jack was the leader of his city's pipe band that won the mayor's medal.*

Pipeline – *(noun)* **1** a long pipe for conveying oil, gas, etc. over long distances. *The proposed pipeline for gas between the two countries would run below the sea.* **2** the hollow formed by the breaking of a large wave. *The Banzai pipeline is a surf reek break located in Hawaii.* **3** computing a linear sequence of specialized modules used for pipelining. *The number of pipeline stages that a processor has can speed up performance of a unit. (verb)* convey by a pipeline. *The project's objective is to pipeline oil from the far north to ports that are free from ice.* **1** computing design or excite using the technique of pipelining. *Pipelining of instructions through sub units is a technique used in modern CPUs.*

Piping – *(noun)* **1** lengths of pipe. *A frequent failure of piping in air conditioning units is a concern that needs to be addressed.* **2** thin lines of icing or cream, used to decorate cakes and desserts. *One has to learn modern piping techniques to make elegant and artistic decorations on the cake.* **3** thin cord covered in fabric, used for decoration and to reinforce seams. *Piping is common on upholstery and decorative pillows.* **4** the action or art of playing a pipe or pipes. *The piping festival held every year in the town brings together artists from across the country.*

Pirate – *(noun)* **1** a person who attacks and robs ships at sea. *The threat of pirates in the Indian Ocean has brought the South Asian countries together to weed them out.* **2** a person who appropriates or reproduces the work of another for profit without permission: pirate recordings. a person or organization broadcasting without official authorization: a pirate radio station. *The once popular radio station, Bollystudio, was made to close down after being labeled as a pirate station by the lower court. (verb)* **1** dated rob or plunder. *Those who engage in piracy are dealt with strongly by the military personnel.* **2** use or reproduce for profit without permission. *Copyright infringement in the world of movies* *and publishing is often associated with piracy and theft.*

Pisces – *(noun)* **1** astronomy a large constellation said to represent a pair of fishes tied together by their tails. *Pisces is a constellation lying between Aquarius and Aries.* **2** [astrology] the twelfth sign of the zodiac, which the sun enters about 20 February. *Pisces is the twelfth sign of the zodiac and is considered a mutable water sign.*

Pistol – *(noun)* a small firearm designed to be held in one hand. *The policeman ordered the robber to throw his pistol towards the door.*

Piston – *(noun)* **1** A disc or short cylinder fitting closely within a tube in which it moves up an down against a liquid or gas, used in an internal-combustion engine to derive motion, or in a pump to impart motion. *The mechanic realized that the car was not functioning as the piston in its engine was stuck.* **2** A valve in a brass instrument, depressed to alter the pitch of a note. *The composer asked the musician to not press the piston too much else the music would turn to cacophony.*

Pit – *(noun)* the stone of a fruit. *You should remove the pit and eat the pulp of any fruit. (verb)* remove the pit from fruit. *The fruit is eaten after removing the pit.*

Pitch – *(noun)* a sticky resinous black or dark brown substance which hardens on cooling, obtained by distilling tar or turpentine and used for waterproofing. *The pitch was used to lay down new roads. (verb)* chiefly [archaic] cover or coat with pitch. *Applying pitch on the roof helped Anna keep her hut safe during the rains.*

Pitcher – *(noun)* a large jug. *As the afternoon got on, the mother brought out a large pitcher of lemonade for the children playing outside.*

Pitchfork – *(noun)* a farm tool with a long handle and two sharp metal prongs, used for lifting hay. *The pitchfork is used to lift hay in farms. (verb)* **1** lift with a pitchfork. *The police suspect that the murder was committed using the pitchfork they found lying near the body.* **2** thrust suddenly into an unexpected and difficult situation: an ordinary intellect pitch forked into power. *The sudden turn of events pitch forked Tom to the forefront of things.*

Piteous – *(adjective)* deserving or arousing pity. *As the moon rose in the sky, the wolf let out a piteous cry.*

Pitfall – *(noun)* **1** a hidden or unsuspected danger or difficulty. *The company's new CEO has a hard task of resurrecting the firm from the recent economic pitfall.* **2** A covered pit for use as a trap. *The poachers led the unsuspecting elephants to the dug up pitfalls.*

Pith – *(noun)* **1** spongy white tissue lining the rind of citrus fruits. [botany] the spongy cellular tissue in the stems and braches of many higher plants. [archaic] spinal marrow. *The pith of the orange acts as a protective cover to the soft fruit within.* **2** the true nature or essence: the pith and care of socialism. *Do not beat around the bush and just explain the pith of the matter.* **3** vigorous and concise expression. *A catch-22 situation is a pith expression for someone in trouble. (verb)* **1** remove the pith from. kill or immobilize by piercing or severing the spinal cord. *Removing the pith of the matter does not change the situation at hand.*

Pitiable – *(adjective)* **1** deserving or arousing pity. *Mary wanted to help the man who seemed to be in a pitiable condition.* **2** contemptibly poor or small. *There is no chivalry in declaring oneself to be in a pitiable state.*

Pitiful – *(adjective)* **1** deserving or arousing pity. [archaic] compassionate. *The baby let out a pitiful moan on seeing his mother.* **2** very small or poor; inadequate: a pitiful attempt. *Saying that you do not get time to exercise is a pitiful excuse for escaping from the punishment.*

Pitiless – *(adjective)* showing no pity; harsh or cruel. *The warden at the hostel is a pitiless man.*

Pittance – *(noun)* **1** a very small or inadequate amount of money. *Despite working hard for an entire year, he was given a pittance as salary.* **2** [historical] a pious bequest to a religious house to provide extra food and wine at particular festivals or other occasions. *The association made a pittance to the church during Christmas.*

Pity – *(noun)* **1** the feeling of sorrow and compassion caused by the sufferings of others. *One feels great pity for the people who have* *no shelter of their own.* **2** a cause of regret or disappointment: what a pity. *(verb)* feel pity for. *It is a pity that despite earning well you hardly save any money.*

Pivot - *(noun)* **1** the central point, pin, or shaft on which a mechanism turns or oscillates. *You just need to adjust the pivot and the wheel will function effortlessly.* **2** a person or thing playing a central part in an activity or organization. chiefly a player in a central position in a team sport. *How could the actor miss the show? He was the pivot in the story.* **3** the person or position from which a body of troops takes its reference point when moving or changing course. *We won the war because of our commanding officer. He was indeed the pivot who guided us well.* *(verb)* **1** turn on or as if on a pivot. provide with or fix on a pivot. *The car spun around as if it was rotating on a pivot.* **2** depend on. *The grandfather was the pivot of the family.*

Pixie - *(noun)* [electronics] a minute area of illumination on a display screen, one of many from which an image is composed. *The farther the object, you need smaller pixie to get a clearer image.*

Pizza - *(noun)* a dish or Italian origin, consisting of a flat, round base of dough of Italian origin, consisting of a flat, round base of dough baked with a topping of tomatoes, cheese, and other ingredients. *There are more than a dozen chains of this pizza making firm spread all across the country.*

Placard - *(noun)* a sign for public display, either posted on a wall or carried during a demonstration. *To bring the point to the notice of the authorities, it is best to cover the topic with placards.* *(verb)* cover with placards. *The angry crowd outside the palace was holding placards against the royal family.*

Placate - *(verb)* calm, pacify or appease. *It is not an easy task to placate a crying toddler.*

Place - *(noun)* **1** a particular position or point in space; a location. [informal] a person's home. a point in a book reached by a reader at a particular time. *If you are searching for this place, you need to go straight and turn right at the intersection.* **2** a portion of space available or designated for someone. a vacancy or available position: a place at university. the regular or proper position of something: lay each slab in place. *The manager always sits in his designated place at the table during important meetings.* **3** a position in a sequence or hierarchy. a person's rank or status. a specific role or position: *It is not my place to ask.* [British] any of the first three or sometimes four positions in a race. [north American] the second position, especially in a horse race. *Remember your place in the family before arguing with your father.* **4** the position of a figure in a series indicated in decimal notation: calculate the ratios to one decimal place. *Solve this numerical and find the answer up to two decimal places.* **5** a square or short street. *This is the place next to the house.* *(verb)* **1** put in a particular position. *It was sensible of you to put him to place.* **2** find an appropriate place or role for. arrange for the implementation of an order, bet, etc. order or obtain a connection for a telephone call. dispose of something, especially shares by selling. *Would you help me find an appropriate place for my nephew in your organization?*

Placid - *(adjective)* not easily upset or excited; calm. *A strong individual is always placid in his heart.*

Plagiarize - *(verb)* take the work or an idea of someone else and pass it off as one's own. *Imitation may be the best form of flattery but plagiarism is not appreciated by anyone.*

Plague - *(noun)* **1** a contagious bacterial disease characterized by fever and delirium, typically with the formation of bosons and sometimes infection of the lungs. *The best way to avoid a plague epidemic is to keep the surroundings clean.* **2** an unusually large number of insects or animals infesting and causing damage to a place: a plague of locusts. *The wheat crops were affected this season by a plague of insects.* *(verb)* cause continual trouble or distress to. pester of harass continually. *Stop plaguing the seniors and try to understand their intentions.*

Plain – *(adjective)* **1** not decorated or elaborate; simple or ordinary. without a pattern; in only one colour. unmarked; without identification: a plain envelope. *I love the combination of a floral top with a plain skirt.* **2** easy to perceive or understand; clear. not using concealment or deception; frank: he recalled her plain speaking. *Explaining the problem in plain words would avoid any confusion.* **3** of a person having no pretension; not remarkable or special. not marked by any particular beauty; ordinary looking. *She may be a plain looking person but her resolve is made of steel.* **4** sheer; simple used for meddle through the front of the stitch form left to right. compare with purl. *This embroidery is based on plain stitch and a little bit of cross stitch on the borders.* *(adverb)* [informal] **1** used for emphasis: that's just plain stupid. *Raising prices seem to be plain robbery on the part of the monopolists.* **2** clearly; unequivocally. *This is a plain demand by the workers. There is no hidden meaning to it.*

Plaintiff – *(noun)* [law] a person who brings a case against another in a court of law. compare with defendant. *The plaintiff and the judge seem to be known to each other.*

Plaintive – *(adjective)* sounding sad and mournful. *Why are you sounding so plaintive after receiving the phone call?*

Plait – *(noun)* **1** a single length of hair, rope, or other material made up of three or more interlaced strands. *The rope has been plaited strongly around the box.* **2** [archaic] term for pleat. *Plait the ends of the cloth and stitch accordingly to form a pocket.* *(verb)* form into a plait or plaits. *Plait your hair as this is a kitchen and I will not allow people to move around with their hair open.*

Plan – *(noun)* **1** a detailed proposal for doing or achieving something. a scheme for the regular payment of contributions towards a pension, insurance policy, etc, a personal pension plan. *What is your plan for the future of your children?* **2** an intention or decision about what one is going to do. *Have you made any plans for this weekend?* **3** a map or diagram: a street plan. a scale drawing of a horizontal section showing the layout of a given level of a building. *One should have a clear plan of the layout before beginning the construction.* *(verb)* **1** decide on and arrange in advance. make preparations for an anticipated event or time. *Please plan a trip to the countryside next week.* **2** make a plan of. *Why don't you make a plan of visiting us during winters.*

Plane – *(noun)* a tool consisting of a plank with a projecting street blade, used to smooth a wooden surface by paring shavings from it. *I cannot finish the varnish today as the plane is broken.* *(verb)* smooth with a plane. *The best and smoothest finish will be achieved only after we plane the surface.*

Planet – *(noun)* a celestial body moving in an elliptical orbit round a star. the earth. [chiefly astrology & historical] a celestial body distinguished from the fixed stars by having an apparent motion of its own. *The hunt for planets outside the solar system has been on for centuries.*

Plank – *(noun)* **1** a long, thin, flat piece of timber, used in building and flooring. *If you do not place the plank properly, the entire work will fail.* **2** a fundamental part of a political or other programme. *The chief minister's address was the plank of this evening's ceremony.* *(verb)* **1** make, provide, or cover with planks. **2** [informal, chiefly] set down forcefully or abruptly. *He planked down the cup in anger.*

Plant – *(noun)* **1** a living organism of the kind exemplified by trees, shrubs, grasses, ferns, and mosses, typical growing in a permanent site, absorbing water and inorganic substances though the roots, and synthesizing nutrients in the leaves by photosynthesis using the green pigment chlorophyll. a small plant, as distinct from a shrub or tree. *Plants help maintain a balance in nature.* **2** a place where an industrial or manufacturing process takes place. machinery used in an industrial or manufacturing process. *There is a leather manufacturing plant in the neighbourhood.* **3** a person placed in a group as a spy or informer. a thing put among someone's belongings to incriminate or discredit them. *The bug was planted in the victim's mobile phone.* **4** snooker a shot in which the cue ball is made to strike on of two touching or nearly touching balls with the result that the second is potted. *He is an excellent snooker player as most of his plants hit the target well. (verb)* **1** place in the ground so that it can grow. place a plant in the ground out of doors. *Plant the trees at equal distance.* **2** place or fix in a specified position. stock a river or lake with young fish, spawn, oysters, etc. secretly place. *Plant the rock next to the gate.* **3** establish in someone's mind. *Once the idea is planted among the group, you just need to wait for the result.*

Plantation - *(noun)* **1** a large estate on which crops such as coffee, sugar, and tobacco are grown. *The bride comes from an family that owns several coffee plantations.* **2** an area in which trees have been planted, especially for commercial purposes. *All the raw materials for making sugar comes from the nearby sugarcane plantations.* **3** [historical] a colony. *Up till the last century, this entire area was covered with plantations.*

Plaque - *(noun)* **1** an ornamental tablet fixed to a wall in commemoration of a person or event. *He always placed his victory plaques on the walls of his study.* **2** a sticky deposit on teeth in which bacteria proliferate. *The dentist noticed that the patient's teeth were yellowish due to plaque.* **3** [medicine] a small, distinct, typically raised path on or within the body, caused by local damage or depositon fo material. [microbiology] a clear area in a cell culture caused by the inhibition of growth or destruction of cells. *The researcher observed plaque in the cell culture.* **4** a flat counter used in gambling. *As the rivals sat down, the manager of the club placed the plaque between them.*

Plaster - *(noun)* **1** a soft mixture of lime with sand or cement and water for spreading on walls and ceilings to form a smooth hard surface when dried. *Plaster was applied on the walls of the house.* **2** a hard white substance made by the addition of water to powdered gypsum, used for holding broken bones in place and making sculptures and casts. *Robert's broken hand was placed in a plaster by the attending nurse.* **3** an adhesive strip of material for covering cuts and wounds. dated a bandage on which a poultice is spread for application. *My wound is not too deep, a simple band aid plaster should do to cover it up. (verb)* **1** cover with plaster; apply plaster to. *The old mansion needed a new look; it was time to apply a layer of plaster and have it painted again.* **2** coat or cover all over with something, especially to an extent considered excessive: a face plastered in heavy make-up. display widely and conspicuously: her story was plastered all over the papers. *The sporting hero was shocked at how details of his personal life were plastered all over yesterday's newspaper.*

Plastic - *(noun)* **1** a synthetic material made from a wide range of organic polymers such as polyethylene, PVC, nylon, etc., that can be moulded into shape while soft, and then set into a rigid or slightly elastic form. *We need to reduce the use of plastic as much as possible to save planet earth from further poisoning.* **2** [informal] credit cards or other plastic cards that can be used as money. *I don't carry cash in my wallet anymore, why bother when there is plastic? (adjective)* **1** made of plastic. *Majority of the toys available in this shop are made of plastic.* **2** [biology] exhibiting adaptability to change in the environment. *The plastic forces of nature always add variety to the environment of the place.* **3** of or relating to moulding or modeling in three dimensions, or to produce three-dimensional effects. *Plastic figures made out of clay can be used as items of dĕcor in the house.*

Plate - *(noun)* **1** a flat dish, typically circular, form which food is eaten or served. [north American] a main course of a meal, austral a plate of food contributed by a guest to a social gathering. *Please clean your own plates after you have eaten your meals.* 2 any shallow dish, especially one used for collecting donations in a church. [biology] a shallow glass dish on which a culture may be grown. *The students are expected to keep their plates in a temperature controlled* *environment inside the biology lab.* **3** bowls, cups, and other utensils made of gold or silver. a silver or gold dish or trophy awarded as a prize. *The runner up at Wimbledon was presented with a silver plate for her efforts.* **4** a thin, flat sheet or trip of metal or other material, typically one used to join or strengthen or forming part of a machine. a small, flat piece of metal bearing a name or inscription, designed to be fixed to a wall or door. *The kid underwent surgery to have a steel plate put into his leg. (verb)* **1** cover with a thin coating of a different metal. cover with plates of metal for decoration or protection. *She had already taken the ring to a jeweler to be plated.* **2** serve or arrange on a plate. *Overcooked meat won't look appetizing irrespective of how they are plated.* **3** [baseball] score or cause to score. *Home plate in the game of baseball is an irregular pentagon with two parallel sides, each perpendicular to a base*

Plateau – *(noun)* **1** an area of fairly level high ground. *The Deccan plateau is one of the largest plateaus in Asia.* **2** a state or period of little or no change following a period activity or progress. *The manager of the retail company is deeply concerned about the plateau in the sales graph over the last few months. (verb)* reach a plateau. *The IT industry's problems seem to have plateaued out.*

Platform – *(noun)* **1** a raised level surface on which people or things can stand. *A platform was raised for the political leader to address the big gathering.* 2 a raised structure along the side of a railway track where passengers get on and off trains. *Many of the railway platforms are still not disabled person friendly.* **3** a raised structure standing in the sea from which oil or gas wells can be drilled. *One needs to take a boat from the jetty to reach the raised platform at the oil rigs.* **4** computing a standard for the hardware of a computer system, which determines the kinds of software it can run. *The software that we are building now is independent of any platform; it works across the spectrum.*

Platinum – *(noun)* **1** a precious silvery white metal, the chemical element of atomic number 78. used in jewellery, electrical contacts, laboratory equipment, and industrial catalysts. *Platinum wedding rings are in vogue today.* **2** grayish-white or silvery like platinum. *My friend has got himself a platinum colored car.*

Platonic – *(adjective)* **1** of or associated with the Greek philosopher Plato or his ideas. *Many of the platonic ideas are so very relevant in today's world too.* **2** intimate and affectionate but not sexual. *My relationship with Rani is purely platonic in nature; nothing more than that.*

Platoon – *(noun)* **1** a subdivision of a company of soldiers, usually commanded by a subaltern or lieutenant and divided into three sections. *The platoon serving in the East boasts of highly decorated soldiers amongst them.* **2** engaged in of alternating in a specified field position in successive games. *The defensive platoon of the football team was the reason behind the defeat.*

Plausible – *(adjective)* apparently reasonable or probable, without necessarily being so. *The story narrated by the apprehended thief sounded plausible to the cops.*

Play – *(verb)* **1** engage in games or other activities for enjoyment rather than for a serious or practical purpose. amuse oneself by engaging in imaginative pretence. treat inconsiderately for one's own amusement: *She likes to play with people's emotions.* tamper with something so as to damage it: *Has somebody been playing with these taps?* **2** take part in a sport or contest. compete against. take a specified position in a sports team: *I play cricket in a professional club.* **3** be cooperative. *I have decided to play along.* **4** represent in a play or film. give a performance at a particular venue. pretend to be. *The skipper played the innocent.* **5** perform on a musical instrument. produce form a musical instrument; perform a piece of music. make produce sounds. accompany with music in a ceremony or procession. *It has always been my desire to play the flute.***6**. move lightly and quickly; flicker. *A smile played about her lips.*

Player – *(noun)* **1** a person taking part in a sport or game. *She got the best player's award at the Sports Day function.* **2** a person that is involved and influential in an activity. *He was the most efficient player in the team.* **3** a person who plays musical instrument. a device for playing compact discs, cassettes, etc. *I bought a DVD player from Croma the other day.* **4** an actor. *He is the chief player in the plot.*

Playful – *(adjective)* **1** found of games and amusement. *Children are best in their playful age.* **2** intended for amusement; light-hearted. *A playful puppy followed her home.*

Playmate – *(noun)* **1** a friend with whom a child plays. *She is my playmate and I have grown up with her.* **2** euphemistic a person's lover. *That he is a ladies' man is evident from the number of playmates he has.*

Plaything – *(noun)* **1** a toy. *The child asked her father to find her a plaything as she was bored.* **2** a person treated as amusing but unimportant. *He asked his girlfriend not to reduce him to a plaything.*

Plea – *(noun)* **1** a request made in an urgent and emotional manner. *Her plea fell on deaf ears.* **2** [law] a formal statement by or on behalf of a defendant or prisoner, stating guilt or innocence in response to a charge, offering an allegation of fact, or claiming that a point of law should apply. an excuse or claim of mitigating circumstances. *The criminal wanted to file a plea for mercy to save himself from the noose.*

Plead – *(verb)* **1** make an emotional appeal. *He pleaded forgiveness.* **2** present and argue for a position, especially in court or in another public context. [law] address a court as an advocate on behalf of a party. [law] state formally in court whether one is guilty or not guilty of the offence with which one is charged. law invoke as an accusation or defense. offer or present as an excuse for doing or not doing something. *She pleaded self-defense.*

Pleasant – *(adjective)* giving a sense of happy satisfaction or enjoyment. and considerate; likeable. *He had a pleasant nature and was easily lovable.*

Please – *(verb)* **1** cause to feel happy and satisfied. *He was pleased at her social etiquettes.* **2** take only one's own wishes into consideration in deciding how to act or proceed. wish or desire to do something. used in polite requests or to express indignation. *Feel free to wander around as you please.* *(adverb)* used in polite requests or questions, or to agree to a request or accept an offer. used to add urgency and emotion to a request. *I asked her if she could please finish my work faster.*

Pleasure – *(noun)* **1** a feeling of happy satisfaction and enjoyment. enjoyment and entertainment, as opposed to necessity. an event or activity from which one derives enjoyment. intended for entertainment rather than business: pleasure boats. sensual gratification. *She derives great pleasure from feeding others.* **2** [formal] one's wish or desire. *The landlord could terminate the agreement at his pleasure.* *(verb)* **1** give sexual enjoyment or satisfaction to. *He seems to have had the relationship to derive sexual pleasure alone.* **2** [archaic] derive enjoyment from. *Talking to you is a pleasure.*

Pleat – *(noun)* **1** a double or multiple fold in a garment or other item made of cloth, held by stitching the tip or side. *The pleats on her skirt had to be rearranged.* **2** a plait. *Her hair had been neatly pleated.* *(verb)* fold or form into pleats. *The pleated skirt looked lovely on her.*

Plebiscite – *(noun)* direct vote by all ectorates on any specific issue. *After the plebiscite, the state was left in a pathetic condition.*

Pledge – *(noun)* **1** a solemn promise or undertaking. a promise of a donation to charity. a solemn undertaking to abstain from alcohol. *The amount pledged for the child had actually increased after the advertisement.* **2** law a thing that is given as security for the fulfillment of a contract or the payment of a debt and is liable to forfeiture in the event of failure. a thing given as a token of love, favour, or loyalty. *She pledged a huge amount to the charitable institution.* **3** [archaic] the drinking of a person's health; a toast. *"A pledge to his health, wealth and a joyful life ahead!"* *(verb)* **1** solemnly undertake to do or give something. *He pledged to never drink again.* **2** [law] give as security on a loan. *He pledged his house against the bank loan.*

Plenty – *(pronoun)* a large or sufficient amount or quantity; more than enough. *There was plenty of food left for the others. (noun)* a situation in which food and other necessities are available in sufficiently large quantities. *Food was available in plenty. (adverb)* [informal] fully; sufficiently. *She had plenty of clothes to give away.*

Pliable– *(adjective)* **1** easily bent; flexible. *The wires were pliable and therefore could be adjusted easily.* **2** easily influenced or swayed. *To be pliable has its own disadvantages.*

Pliant – *(adjective)* pliable. *The tool kit was rather fancy as it even had a pliant with the plier for a sample.*

Pliers – *(plural noun)* pincers with parallel, flat, serrated jaws, used for gripping small objects or bending wire. *I bought him a new plier for his tool kit.*

Plight – *(noun)* a dangerous, difficult, or otherwise unfortunate situation. *You must consider the plight of the needy when you walk past them.*

Plinth – *(noun)* **1** a heavy base supporting a stature or vase. *When the plinth started cracking, we knew the tremors had started.* **2** [architecture] the lower square slab at the base of a column. *The plinth was built of strong granite.*

Plod – *(verb)* walk doggedly and slowly with heavy steps. work slowly and perseveringly at a dull. task. *We were plodding through the task to get the best results. (noun)* **1** a slow, heavy walk. *After running across half the city, we were now plodding through the street near his house.* **2** [British informal] a police officer. *We decided to approach the plod to lodge our complaint.*

Plop – *(noun)* a short sound as of a small, solid object dropping into water without a splash. *The snail fell into the puddle with a plop. (verb)* fall or drop with such a sound. *There was a plop when it landed.*

Plot – *(noun)* **1**.a plan made in secret by a group of people to do something illegal or harmful. *They had devised a sinister plot to kill the minister.* **2** the main sequence of events in a play, novel, or film. *The plot had an interesting twist that captivated the audience.* **3** a small piece of ground marked out for building, gardening, etc. *I had a plot that I had inherited from my father.* **4** a graph showing the relation between two variables. [chiefly US] a diagram, chart, or map. *We were all given plots to draw graphs on in the exam. (verb)* **1** secretly make plans to carry out. *We were plotting to trick the girl out of the event.* **2** devise the plot of a play, novel, film. *We were devising the plot for the play.* **3** make on a chart. mark out or allocate on a graph make by marking out a number of such points. illustrate by use of a graph. *We had to plot the graph in a certain way.*

Plough – *(noun)* **1** a large farming implement with one or more blades fixed in a frame, drawn over soil to turn it over and cut furrows in preparation for the planting of seeds. *The land that has been ploughed will give a better crop.* **2** a prominent formation of seven stars in the constellation Ursa major. *My father taught me to spot the plough in the constellation every night. (verb)* **1** turn up with a plough. clear snow from using a snow plough. *We could not move out unless the snow was cleared with a snow plough.* **2** move in a fast and uncontrolled manner. *We ploughed through the forest wildly.* **3** travel through. *We ploughed through the countryside at an alarming speed.*

Ploy – *(noun)* a cunning plan or action designed to turn a situation to one's own advantage. *He had devised a cunning ploy to rob the bank.*

Pluck – *(verb)* **1** take hold of and quickly remove if from its place. catch hold of and pull quickly. *She plucked her eyebrows before setting out for the party.* **2** pull the feathers from to prepare it for cooking. pull some of the hairs from to make them look neater. *She plucked out the few feathers that were left on the chicken.* **3** sound in summon up to do something frightening. *She plucked up courage and ran for her life! (noun)* **1** spirited and determined courage. *Hey, show some pluck!* **2** the heart, liver, and lungs of an animal as food. *The pluck tastes better than any other part of an animal.*

Plug - *(noun)* **1** a piece of solid material fitting tightly into a hole and blocking it up. a mass of solidified lava filling the neck of a volcano. *I put the plug into the hole so it won't leak any more.* **2** a device consisting of an insulated casing with metal pins that fit into holes in a socket to make an electrical connection. [informal] an electrical socket. *The plug was loose, which was why the lamp wasn't working.* **3** [informal] a piece of publicity promoting a product or event. *The editor asked me to get a plug of the event that was being sponsored by our news agency.* **4** a piece of tobacco cut from a larger cake for chewing. tobacco in large cakes designed to be cut for chewing. *Plugs of tobacco were being distributed among the masses.* **5** fishing a lure with one or more hooks attached. *I had lined several plugs on the line so we the catch may be more.* **6** [north American informal] a tired or old horse. *He is a plug, not fit for the race.* *(verb)* **1** block or fill in a hole or cavity. *I plugged the hole with a pebble.* **2** connect an electrical appliance to the mains by means of a socket. have or gain access to an information system or area of activity. *I asked the electrician if the wires have been plugged into the right socket.* **3** informal promote by mentioning it publicly. *I decided to cover the plug sponsored by my company myself.* **4** [informal] shoot or hit. *He plugged the right shot.*

Plumb - *(verb)* install a bath, washing machine, etc. and connect it to water and drainage pipes. install and connect pipes in a building or room. *It was a new house so we had a lot of plumbs to fix.*

Plumber - *(noun)* a person who fits and repairs the pipes and fitting of water supply, sanitation, or heating systems. *The plumber came to fix the pipes in our house.*

Plumb line - *(noun)* a line with a plumb attached to it. *The leak was found to have started from the plumb below the sink.*

Plume - *(noun)* **1** a long, soft feather or arrangement of feathers used by a bird for display or worn on a hat or helmet as decoration. *The bird's plumes were shining in the sun's rays.* **2** a long spreading cloud of smoke or vapour. *Plumes of smoke were spreading in the sky.* **3** geology a column of magma rising by convection in the earth's mantle. *The geologists were flying over the volcano to capture the plumes in their camera.* *(verb)* **1** [chiefly archaic] preen itself. *The bird shuffled its plumes and danced in the rain.* **2** chiefly feel a great sense of self-satisfaction. *She plumed herself in front of the mirror and set out for the party.*

Plummet - *(verb)* fall or drop straight down at high speed. decrease rapidly in value or amount. *The value of the shares was plummeting.* *(noun)* **1** a steep and rapid fall or drop. *What she feared the most was the status of her life plummeting.* **2** a plumb or plumb line. *"He stopped his horse, raised the trap, and dropped his phonographic voice, like a lead plummet, through the aperture."*

Plump - *(adjective)* full and rounded in shape. rather fat. *I was meeting her after a long time and realized she had grown plump.* *(verb)* make or become full and round. *She had turned plump over the years.*

Plunder - *(verb)* forcibly steal goods from, especially in time of war or civil disorder. *The enemies had plundered the whole state.* *(noun)* the action of plundering. property acquired in this way. *Property acquired by plundering will not yield profits for a long time.*

Plunge - *(verb)* **1** fall or move suddenly and uncontrollably. jump or dive quickly and energetically. *With a deep breath, he plunged into the water.* **2** embark impetuously on a speech or course of action. *He asked me when I intend to take the plunge.* **3** push or thrust quickly. *He plunged the stick into the hole.* **4** suddenly bring someone or something into a specified condition or state. *He plunged into the scene too quickly.* *(noun)* an act of plunging. *Do not take the plunge without thinking twice.*

Plural - *(adjective)* move than one in number. [grammar] denoting more than one, or more than two. *Unfortunately, you may not have to* *consider the number of students appearing for the blood donation camp in plural. (noun)* [grammar] a plural word or form. the plural number.*The teacher asked the students the list out the plural forms of the given words.*

Plus – *(preparation)* with the addition of. [informal] together with. *When you make icing, chocolates are indeed a plus. (adjective)* **1** at least: $500,000 plus. *The cheque amounts to $500,000 plus.* **2** above zero; positive. *Integers above zero are written with a plus suffixes such as* +2 3. **3** having a positive electric charge. *Place a battery in the torch in such a way that the plus signs are aligned together. (noun)* **1** short for plus sign. a mathematical operation of addition. *The teachers taught the children how to add using the plus sign.* **2** [informal] an advantage. conjunction [informal] furthermore; also. *I would like to order a plate of salad plus some juice.*

Plush – *(noun)* a rich fabric of silk, cotton, or wool, with a long, soft nap. *Let us not live a plush life when we cannot afford it. (adjective)* [informal] richly luxurious and expensive. *I bought her a plush cushion to sleep on.*

Pluto – *(noun)* the most remote known planet of the solar system, ninth in order from the sun. *Pluto is no longer considered a planet belonging to the solar system.*

Plutonium – *(noun)* the chemical element of atomic number 94, a dense silvery radioactive metal of the actinide series, used as a fuel in nuclear reactors and as an explosive in nuclear fission weapons. *Every since they discovered plutonium in the land behind his ancestral house, several government agencies have been flocking the place.*

Ply – *(noun)* **1** a thickness or layer of a folded or laminated material. *There were several layers of ply spread on the carpenter's table.* **2** each of a number of multiple layers or strands of which something is made: four-ply. *The table had a four-ply structure.*

Pneumatic – *(adjective)* containing or operated by air or gas under pressure. *We realized that the instrument he bought was not working because it was pneumatic.*

Pneumonia – *(noun)* a lung infection in which the air sacs is fulled with pus. *Unlike the earlier times, today there is a positive treatment available for pneumonia.*

Poach – *(verb)* cook by simmering in a small amount of liquid. cook without its shell in or over building water. *Poached egg is extremely healthy and a good option for losing weight.*

Pocket – *(noun)* **1** a small bag sewn into or on clothing so as to form part of it, used for carrying small articles. a pouch like compartment providing separate storage space. [informal] one's financial resources. *I bought her a bag with several pockets so she could keep it neat and organized.* **2** a small, isolated patch, group, or area. *The grass had grown in pockets.* **3** an opening at the corner or on the side of a billiard table into which balls are struck. *He signaled with his eyes the pocket where I should aim the ball.* **4** [American] a protected area behind the line of scrimmage, from which the quarterback throws a pass. *The fielders had covered all the pockets so it was difficult to hit there.* **5** [baseball] a hollow in a baseball mitt in which the ball is caught and held. *He ran to the pocket and caught the ball. (adjective)* of a suitable size for carrying in a pocket: a pocket dictionary. *I bought her a pocket dictionary for her birthday. (verb)* **1** put into one's pocket. *I asked her to put the coins into her pocket.* **2** take for one self, especially dishonestly. *Do not try to pocket the money that does not belong to you.*

Pod – *(noun)* a small herd or school of marine animals, especially whales. *The friends were like peas in a pod.*

Podium – *(noun)* **1** a small platform on which a person may stand to be seen by an audience. [north American] a lectern. *The chief guest was invited to the podium to say a few words to the audience.* **2** a continuous projecting base or pedestal under a building. a raised platform surrounding the arena in an ancient amphitheatre. *The podium was waiting for next star to arrive.*

Poem – *(noun)* a literary composition that is given intensity by particular attention to diction rhythm, and imagery. *Her diary was full of poems.*

Poet – *(noun)* a person who writes poems. a person possessing special powers of imagination or expression. *Her beauty could turn anyone into a poet.*

Poetic – *(adjective)* relating to or of the nature of poetry. *The prose he wrote was more poetic than an actual prose.*

Poetry – *(noun)* poems collectively or as a genre of literature. a quality of beauty and intensity of emotion regarded as characteristic of poetry. *She wanted to attend the poetry convention that would start soon.*

Poignant – *(adjective)* **1** evoking a keen sense of sadness or regret. *It was a poignant theme to write a play on.* **2** [archaic] sharp or pungent in taste or small. *The taste was poignant and stayed in everybody's minds for a long time.*

Point – *(noun)* **1** the tapered, sharp end of a tool, weapon, or other object. [archaeology] a pointed flake or blade. ballet another term for Pointe. boxing the tip of a person's chin as a spot for a blow. the prong of a deer's antler. *The spear was shining at its point so much that it would make any man shiver.* **2** a dot or other punctuation mark, in particular a full stop. a decimal point. a dot or small stroke used in Semitic languages to indicate vowels or distinguish particular consonants. a very small dot or mark on a surface. *Twenty two point three was the end result of the whole algorithm.* **3** a particular spot, place, or moment. the verge or brink of. something having position but not spatial extent, magnitude, dimension, or direction. *We had reached the point of satiation.* **4** a single item or detail in an extended discussion, list, or text. an argument or idea. the significant or essential element: come to the point. advantage or purpose. relevance. a distinctive feature or characteristic, typically a good one. *The teacher asked the student to stop beating around the bush and come to the point.* **5** a mark or unit of scoring awarded for success or performance. a unit used in measuring value, achievement, or extent. the longest suit in a player's hand, containing a specified number of up to eight cards. a unit of weight for diamonds. *At halftime the opposing team had scored more points than us.*

Point-blank – *(adjective & adverb)* **1** fired from very close to its target. *The shots were fired at point blank range.* **2** without explanation or qualification. *He refuses point-blank to give interviews.*

Pointer – *(noun)* **1** a long, thin piece of metal on a scale or dial which moves to give a reading. a rod used for pointing to features on a map or chart. computing a link. *Do not depend on the pointer too much to get your results.* **2** a hint as to what might happen in the future. a small piece of advice, a tip. *I gave her several pointers on how to succeed at work.* **3** a dog of a breed that on scenting game stands rigid looking towards it. *The pointer stood erect the moment the cat turned round the corner.*

Pointless – *(adjective)* **1** having little or no sense purpose. *It is pointless shedding tears before my father told me.* **2** having scored no points. *Even at halftime, the team was pointless.*

Poise – *(noun)* [physics] a unit of dynamic viscosity, such dignity of manner. *He was somehow precariously poised at a 45 degree angle.* **2** [archaic] balance; equilibrium. *She tried to maintain her poise even in the face of adversity.* *(verb)* **1** be or cause to be balanced or suspended. *Poised boulders can be passed to a hanging ledge beneath a vast hanging choke.* **2** composed and elegant or self-assured. *He was an embodiment of poise and grace.* **3** be ready and prepared to do something. *We were poised to raise the lance.*

Poison – *(noun)* **1** a substance that causes death or harm when introduced into or aborted by a living organism. *The poison was gradually spreading in the rest of his body.* **2** something that has a destructive or corrupting influence. *What is tasty to the tongue may be poison to the body.* **3** [chemistry] a substance that reduces the activity of a catalyst. *They introduced the poison to reduce the activity of the catalyst quickly.*

4 [physics] an impurity that retards nuclear fission by absorbing neutrons. *Poison reduces the speed of nuclear fission.* *(verb)* **1** administer poison to or contaminate with poison. *Socrates was poisoned by the State.* **2** corrupt or harm. *Socrates was blamed for poisoning the minds of the youth.*

Poke – *(noun)* a bag or small sack. [north American informal] a purse of wallet. *He stole the neighbour's poke.*

Poker – *(noun)* a metal rod with a handle, used for prodding and stirring an open fire. *She took the poker out of the fire and shoved it at the boy as if to scare him away.*

Polar – *(adjective)* **1** of or relating to a pole or poles, in particular, of the north or south pole or their adjacent area. *News has been doing the rounds that the polar ice caps are melting.* **2** [physics & chemistry] having an electrical or magnetic field. *Sodium chloride makes polar crystals.* **3** directly opposite in character tendency. *Often in marriages you come across couples who are polar opposites to one another.* *(noun)* [geometry] the straight line joining the two points at which tangents from a fixed point touch a conic section. *The angular coordinate is often called the polar angle.*

Polaroid – *(noun)* trademark a composite material with the property of polarizing light, produced in thin plastic sheets. sunglasses a finished print rapidly after each exposure. a photograph taken with such a camera. *Father bought me a polaroid camera this birthday.*

Pole – *(noun)* a native or national of Poland, or a person of polish descent. *There were people from several countries in our boat, including an American, two Indians, a Chinese couple and a Pole.*

Police – *(noun)* a civil force responsible for the prevention and detection of crime and the maintenance of public order. members of such a force. *Right from childhood, he has dreamt of joining the police force.* *(verb)* control and maintain law and order in an area, with or as with a police force. *The guards were asked to police the area for a few days.*

Policy – *(noun)* **1** course or principle of action adopted or proposed by an organization or individual. *The government introduced several policies in the agricultural sector this year.* **2** [archaic] prudent or expedient conduct or action. *Honesty is the best policy.*

Polio – *(noun)* short for poliomyelitis. *He had polio when he was an infant.*

Polish – *(noun)* the western Slavic language of Poland. *Initially I mistook his language for French but later I realized it was Polish.* *(adjective)* of or relating to Poland, its inhabitants, or their language. *He made a typical polish gruel for dinner.*

Polite – *(adjective)* respectful and considerate of other people. cultured and refined: polite society. *I had met her only once but she always came out as extremely polite.*

Political – *(adjective)* **1** of or relating to the government or public affairs of a country. interested in or active in politics. *That he had political ambitions was evident from the message he conveys in all his movies.* **2** [chiefly] done or acting in the interests of status within an organization rather than on principle. *It was an open secret that the change in the board was more a political development than anything else.*

Politician – *(noun)* **1** a person who is professionally involved in politics, especially as a holder of an elected office. *He made an excellent politician for the country.* **2** [chiefly US] a person who acts in a manipulative and devious way, typically to gain advancement. *He is an amazingly cunning politician of.*

Politics – *(plural noun)* **1** the activities associated with the governance of a country or area. a particular set of political beliefs or principles. *The politics of our country are beyond my understanding.* **2** activities aimed at improving someone's status within an organization; office politics. *With a few months of our Director's demise, the politics in the office had gone from good to bad.* **3** the principles relating to or inherent in a sphere or activity, especially when concerned with power and status: the politics of gender. *She wanted to write a book on the* *politics of gender that have been troubling our society from time immemorial.*

Poll – *(noun)* **1** the process of voting in an election. a record of the number of votes cast in an election. an opinion poll. *The results of the opinion poll were in favour of the Democrats.* **2** [dialect] a person's head or scalp. *He applied some of the dandruff oil on his poll as well.* **3** a hornless animal, especially one of a breed of hornless cattle. *Scores of polls had been left stranded on the road.* *(verb)* **1** record the opinion or vote of. receive a specified number of votes. *He had polled enough votes to force a second ballot.* 2 cut the horns off an animal, especially a young cow. lacking horns. [archaic] cut off the top of pollard. *The hunter cut off the top of the pollard in one blow.* **3** check the status of a device, especially as part of a repeated cycle. *More than 18,000 people were polled.*

Pollen – *(noun)* a powdery substance discharged from the male gamete that can fertilize the female ovule. *There is a heavy concentration of pollen grains in the air here.*

Pollute – *(verb)* **1** contaminate water; the air, etc. with harmful or poisonous substances. *We were asked to get used to waste segregation and stop polluting the environment.* **2** corrupt. *Socrates was arrested by the State for polluting the minds of the youth.*

Polo – *(noun)* a game of eastern origin with rules similar to hockey, played on horseback with a long-handled mallet. *My cousin is a State level Polo player.*

Poly – *(noun)* **1** polyester. *She had found a rare sari made of polyester fabric.* **2** polythene. *Polythene bags are banned in our state.* **3** [British] a polytechnic. *After school, she applied at a polytechnic college for higher studies.*

Polyandry – *(noun)* where a woman has more than one husband. Compare with polygyny. *There are several instances of polyandry in our scriptures.*

Polyester – *(noun)* a synthetic resin in which the polymer units are linked by ester groups, used chiefly to make textile fibers. *She wore a lovely polyester sari for her friend's wedding.*

Polygamy – *(noun)* **1** practice or custom of having more than one wife or husband at the same time. *In the ancient times, polygamy was actually forgiven.* **2** [zoology] a pattern of mating in which an animal has more than one mate. *Today, it seems animals are less polygamous than men.* **3** botany the condition of bearing some flowers with stamens only, some with pistils only, and some with both, on the same or different plants. *The teacher showed us how polygamy works in plants.*

Polygon – *(noun)* geometry a plane figure with at least three straight sides and angles, and typically five or more. *I can never draw a perfect polygon!*

Polytechnic – *(noun)* an institution offering higher education in vocationed subjects. *She has taken admission in civil engineering in government polytechnic.* *(adjective)* **1** having many sounds or voices. *She bought a phone that had polyphonic ringtones.* **2** music in two or more parts each having a melody of its own; contrapuntal. music capable of producing more than one note at a time. *He bought an instrument that played polyphonic tones.*

Polythene – *(noun)* [chiefly British] a tough, light, flexible synthetic resin made by polymerizing ethylene, chiefly used for packaging. *The poor cow died because of the polythene bag that it accidentally ate and that got stuck in its throat.*

Pomp – *(noun)* **1** ceremony and splendid display. *The wedding will be celebrated with great pomp and show.* **2** [archaic] vain and boastful display. *The Queen arrived with great pomp and ceremony.*

Pompous – *(adjective)* **1** affectedly grand, solemn, or self-important. *He read it out in a pompous voice.* **2** [archaic] characterized by pomp or splendor. *The Headmaster is inclined to be a bit pompous.*

Pond – *(noun)* **1** a fairly small body of still water. *I asked the horticulturist to design a small pond for our garden.* **2** humorous the Atlantic ocean. *Calling the Atlantic a 'pond' is just like calling the Americas 'the colonies'.* *(verb)* hold back or dam up to form a pond. *This little puddle had formed into a pond over the years.*

Ponder – *(verb)* consider carefully. *The notices were passed to all of us to ponder over.*

Ponderous – *(adjective)* **1** slow and clumsy because of great weight. *He strolled about with a ponderous heavy gait.* **2** dull or laborious. *He had a dense ponderous writing style.*

Pony – *(noun)* **1** a horse of a small breed, especially one below 15 hands or 14 hands 2 inches. *The hill station had ponies at every nook and corner.* **2** [informal] a small glass or measure of liquor. *When they offered me some beer I said I'll have just a pony.* **3** [British, informal] twenty five pounds sterling. *What would you do in a city like London if you earn just a pony! (verb)* [north American informal] hand over a sum of money, especially to settle an account. *Pony up all your money now!*

Pooh – *(exclamatory)* **1** expressing disgust at an unpleasant smell. *"Pooh Pooh!" said Richard Parker, "and how could I know who did it?"* **2** expressing impatience or contempt. *"Pooh! How much time do you take to get ready!" (noun)* excrement. an act of defecting. *The child's pooh made the whole plane stink. (verb)* defecate. *"Ma'am, he poohed in his pants today!"*

Pool – *(noun)* **1** a small area of still water, typically one formed naturally. a deep place in a river. an artificial pool for swimming in. *We had a pool in our ancestral house where we all learnt swimming as kids.* **2** a small, shallow patch of liquid lying on a surface. *The hotel where we stayed also had a small pool. (verb)* **1** form a pool. *The receding tide pooled in hollows along the shores.* **2** accumulate in parts of the venous system. *The surgeons were trying to prevent the blood from pooling in the limbs.*

Poor – *(adjective)* **1** lacking sufficient money to live at a standard considered comfortable or normal. *Studies say that there are more poor people in our country than in any other country in the world.* **2** of a low or inferior standard or quality. lacking in. *Never buy poor quality of pulses from the market as it could be adulterated.* **3** deserving of pity or sympathy. *Poor Sam has been lonely ever since his wife left him.*

Poorly – *(adverb)* in a poor manner. *She did poorly in the exams once again. (adjective)* chiefly unwell. *I have been feeling poorly ever since we had dinner at that Dhaba the other day.*

Pop – *(noun)* commercial popular music, in particular accessible, tuneful music of a kind popular since the 1950. *Michael Jackson is known as the king of pop music. (adjective)* **1** of or relating to pop music. *She wanted to grow up to become a pop singer.* 2 often derogatory made accessible to the general public. *The pop culture that dominated society for several years did not do it any good.*

Popcorn – *(noun)* maize of a variety with hard kernels that swell up and burst open when heated and are then eaten as a snack. *She could never imagine watching a movie without popcorn.*

Pope – *(noun)* **1** the bishop of Rome as head of the roman catholic church. *Everyone hoped that the next pope would be a great peacemaker.* **2** the head of the Coptic church, the patriarch of Alexandria. *For a while, the whole Church was torn by the question of the rival popes.* **3** another term for ruffe. *I could spot several popes in the aquarium as well.*

Poplin – *(noun)* a plain woven fabric, typically a very light-weight cotton, with a corded surface. *She was prettily dressed in gray poplin, trimmed with gray velvet and a deep red sash around her trim waist.*

Poppy – *(noun)* a plant having showy flowers, typically red or yellow, and rounded seed capsules. *Bengalis use a lot of poppy seeds in their cooking.*

Populace – *(noun)* the general public. *A large proportion of the populace was against the idea of breaking down the structure.*

Popular – *(adjective)* **1** liked or admired by many or by a particular person or group. *She was easily the most popular girl in school.* **2** intended for or suited to the taste or means of the general public. widely held among the general public. *We decided on a popular resort as a venue for our wedding.* **3** of or carried on by the people as a whole. *The popular vote went to the Republicans this year.*

Populate - *(verb)* form the population of a place. cause people to settle in a place. *North America was largely populated by Europeans.*

Population - *(noun)* **1** all the inhabitants of a particular place. a particular group within this. the action of populating an area. *The population of our country has doubled over the last few years.* **2** [biology] a community of interbreeding organisms. *They hired hunters to reduce the deer population in the area.* **3** [statistics] a finite or infinite collection of items under consideration. *It is an estimate of the population of the area.*

Porcelain - *(noun)* a white vitrified translucent ceramic; china. soft-paste. articles made of this. *Porcelain cutlery makes for some of the most beautiful and affordable cutlery.*

Porch - *(noun)* **1** a covered shelter projecting in front of the entrance of a building. *Every villa in the complex had a designer car porch.* **2** [north American] a veranda. *They had lawns near the porch where they would sit down for a high tea with friends and relatives or just a simple get together.*

Porcupine - *(noun)* a large rodent with defensive spines or quills on the body and tail. *The population of porcupines had reduced over the years.*

Pore - *(noun)* a minute opening in the skin or other surface through which gases, liquids, or microscope particles may pass. *The dermatologist advised me to wash my face frequently so the pores of my skin would not be closed.*

Pork - *(noun)* **1** the flesh of a pig used as food, especially when uncured. *Home cooked pork vindaloo was his favourite dish whenever he was at home.* **2** short for pork barrel. *However much the people may distrust the party and dislike pork, the advantages of being represented by an incumbent with seniority are hard to deny.*

Pornography - *(noun)* printed or visual material intended to stimulate sexual excitement. *The government was intending to put a censor on pornography in the internet as well.*

Porous - *(adjective)* of a rock or other material having minute interstices through which liquid or air may pass. *Local limestone is extremely porous.*

Porpoise - *(noun)* a small toothed whale with a low triangular dorsal fin and a blunt rounded snout. *The island was known for an occasional sighting of the porpoise.*

Porridge - *(noun)* **1** a dish consisting of oatmeal or another cereal boiled with water or milk. *My parents prefer having porridge for breakfast since its easy to cook.* **2** [British informal] time spent in prison. *I realized that "doing porridge" is a slang for serving a prison sentence.*

Port - *(noun)* a town a city with a harbor or access to navigable water where ships load or unload. *Tuesday morning was a typical day at the port with all the hustle bustle and chaos of the fishermen, sailors and travelers.*

Portable - *(adjective)* **1** able to be easily carried or moved. *I bought her a portable music player that she could take with her wherever she travels.* **2** a loan or pension capable of being transferred or adapted in altered circumstances. *The bank gave him some portable cash.* **3** computing able to be ported. *Everybody needs portable cash these days.* *(noun)* a portable object. *Her portable music player was of great help when she was travelling.*

Porter - *(noun)* [British] an employee in charge of the entrance of a hotel, block of flats, or other large building. *The manager signaled to the porter to take the customer's luggage to his room.*

Portfolio - *(noun)* **1** large, thin, flat case for carrying drawings, maps, etc. *He had a portfolio in the almirah in which he keeps all his pictures and drawings.* **2** a set of pieces of creative work intended to demonstrate a person's ability to a potential employer. *She posted her portfolio to the modeling agency and prayed she get selected soon.* **3** a range of investments held by a person or organization. *They were disappointed by the poor returns on their stock portfolio.* **4** the position and duties of a minister of secretary of state. *He holds the portfolio of foreign affairs.*

Porthole - *(noun)* a small window on the outside of a ship or an aircraft. *He clung to the frame of the porthole as the airship swung and swayed in all directions.*

Portion – *(noun)* **1** a part or a share. an amount of food suitable for or served to one person. [law] the part or share of an estate given or descending by law to an heir. *The dietician advised us to take only one portion of meal at a time.* **2** [archaic] a person's destiny or lot. *Whatever his portion may be he deserved a better death.* **3** [archaic] a dowry. *He demanded his portion in cash.* *(verb)* **1** divide into portions and share out. *The money was portioned out among the three children.* **2** [archaic] give a dowry to. *They had demanded a portion for the brothers of the groom well before the wedding.*

Portly – *(adjective)* **1** rather fat. *Men are portly and women are stout.* **2** [archaic] stately or dignified. *I turned and found a portly old gentleman smiling at me.*

Portrait – *(noun)* **1** an artistic representation of a person, especially one depicting only the face or head and shoulders. *I asked the painter to paint my portrait.* **2** a description in language or on film or television. *The book was a beautifully written and sensitive portrait of a great woman.* **3** denoting a format of printed matter which is higher than it is wide. Compare with landscape. *The picture looked better in portrait format than landscape.*

Portray – *(verb)* **1** depict in a work of art or literature. *The actress's life was portrayed in a beautiful manner in the movie.* **2** describe in a particular way. *The actor portrays an elderly lonely man.* **3** play the part of.*The father is portrayed as a good-looking man in the painting.*

Pose – *(verb)* [archaic] perplex with a question or problem. *The teacher was dumbfound at the question the student posed.*

Posh – *(adjective)* **1** elegant or stylishly luxurious. *He always had a tendency to live a posh life.* **2** [chiefly British] upper-class. *While he was a poor trader, she belonged to the posh elite.* *(adverb)* [British] in an upper-class way. *I was used to hearing her posh talk.* *(verb)* [British] smarten something up. *I took her with me to posh things up at the club.*

Position – *(noun)* **1** a place where someone or something is located or has been put. the correct place. a place where part of a military force is posted for strategic purposes: *The paratroops had been given positions in such a way that the terrorists could not see where they were being attacked from.* **2** a way in which someone or something is placed or arranged. the configuration of the pieces and pawns on the board at any point in a game of chess. *He was new to chess, so he did not know what position each piece stood in.* **3** a situation or set of circumstances. the state of being advantageously placed in a competitive situation. a person's place or rank in relation to others. high rank or social standing. *I told her that she wouldn't know what I was going through since she was in a more advantageous position in the hierarchy.* **4** a job. *She was given the position of the manager soon after she cleared the exams.* **5** a point of view or attitude. *He was right from his position, but so was she.* *(verb)* **1** put or arrange in a particular position. *The troops were positioned in a way that they could strike right at the enemy's bunker itself.* **2** promote within a particular sector of a market. *We decided to position the sales in a way that the entire market would turn around.*

Positive – *(adjective)* **1** consisting in or characterized by the presence rather than the absence of distinguishing features. expressing or implying affirmation, agreement, or permission. *I look forward to a positive reply from you.* **2** constructive, optimistic, or confident. *I am positive he is right.* **3** with no possibility of doubt; certain. *We had positive proof of his criminal activities.* **4** greater than zero. *I liked working on positive numbers than negative since it was easier.* **5** of, containing, producing, or denoting the kind of electric charge opposite to that carried by electrons. *The teacher taught us how to distinguish between positive and negative ions.* **6** showing light and shade or colours true to the original. *The film would have been more helpful if it was positive.* *(noun)* **1** a positive quality or attribute. *She is a positive darling!* **2** a positive photographic image, especially one printed from a negative. *The positive of the film revealed some details that the negative did not.*

Possess – *(verb)* **1** have as belonging to one. [law] have possession of as distinct from ownership. *He is said to possess a huge forturne.* **2** have as an ability, quality, or characteristic. in possession of. *He possesses great knowledge about the Middle East.* **3** dominate the mind of. "What possessed you to buy this house?" **4** [poetic] have sexual intercourse with a woman. *To possess you would be a dream come true for me.*

Possession – *(noun)* **1** the state of possessing something. law visible power or control, as distinct from lawful ownership. temporary control of the ball by a player or team. *The home team was in possession during most of the fourth quarter.* **2** a thing owned or possessed. a territory or country controlled or governed by another. *History is replete with stories of the Queen's colonial possessions.* **3** the state of being possessed by a demon, emotion, etc. *It was as if the devil had taken possession over his mind.*

Possessive – *(adjective)* **1** demanding someone's total attention and love. *She had a tendency to be extremely possessive of her loved ones.* **2** showing an unwillingness to share one's possessions. *His possessive attitude towards his wife is what strained their marriage.* **3** [grammar] relating to or denoting the case of nouns and pronouns expressing possession. *We tried making sentences in possessive case since we couldn't make sense of the others.*

Possibility – *(noun)* **1** a thing that is possible. *There is a good possibility it may rain today.* **2** the state or fact of being possible. *There is a possibility his hearing may be impaired.* **3** unspecified qualities of a promising nature. *This room has great possibilities.*

Possible – *(adjective)* capable of existing, happening, or being achieved. that may be so, but that is not certain or portable. *It is not possible to finish this in two weeks.* *(noun)* **1** a possible candidate for a job or member of a team. *The list of possible candidates was more this week.* **2** that which is likely or achievable. *The idea is a possible money-spinner.* **3** the highest possible score, especially in a shooting competition. *She got the highest possible score in the shooting.*

Post – *(noun)* **1** a job. *She had applied for an interview for the post of manager.* **2** a place where someone is on duty or where an activity is carried out. [north American] a force stationed at a permanent position or camp. *A soldier manned the entrance post.* **3** [historical] the status or rank of full-grade captain in the royal navy. *Sir Peter held several senior military posts.* *(verb)* send to a place to take up an appointment. station in a particular place. *He is currently posted in Jammu.*

Postage – *(noun)* the sending of letters and parcels by post. the amount required to send something by post. *I bought a dozen postage stamps so I don't need to run to the post office every time I need one.*

Postal – *(adjective)* **1** of or relating to the post. *The one postal delivery in our locality was in the morning.* **2** [chiefly British] carried out by post: a postal vote. *He did a postal vote since he was not in town that entire week.* *(noun)* [US informal] a postcard. *She was going away for so long, so I asked her to send me a postal once in a while.*

Postdate – *(verb)* **1** affix or assign a date later than the actual one to a document or event. *I gave her a postdated cheque.* 2 occur or come at a later date than. *In Alaska, the most recent fossil remains of mammoths postdate the arrival of humans around the Bering ice land.*

Poster – *(noun)* **1** a large printed picture or notice used for decoration or advertisement. *The police arrested the goons for pasting posters on the wall in spite of the warning not to.* **2** computing someone who sends a message to a newsgroup. *Can't find a meaning corresponding to this. Kindly check and revise.*

Posterity – *(noun)* all future generation. *A photographer recorded the scene for posterity.*

Postgraduate – *(adjective)* relating to or denoting a course of study undertaken after completing a first degree. *She did her Post graduation in Applied Operation Analysis.* *(noun)* a person engaged in postgraduate study. *He is a post graduate so he could be allowed for seminar.*

Posthumous – *(adjective)* occurring awarded, or appearing after the death of the originator. *He was given a posthumous award and title for his bravery.*

Post-mortem – *(noun)* **1** an examination of a dead body to determine the cause of death. *They took the body from the accident site for a post mortem.* **2** an analysis of an event made after it has occurred. *We have a post mortem meeting everyday to analyze the errors of the previous day's print. (adjective)* **1** of or relating to a post-mortem. *What is the point of a post mortem after the error has been made?* **2** happening after death. *We had to do a post mortem to ascertain the real cause of the accident.*

Postpone – *(verb)* arrange for to take place at a time later than that first scheduled. *Never postpone for tomorrow the work that you can finish today.*

Postscript – *(noun)* 1 an additional remark at the end of a letter, following the signature. *He had added a note as postscript in his mail saying the balance money is attached.* **2** a sequel. *He gave his signature as a postscript at the end of the note.*

Postulate – *(verb)* **1** suggest or assume the existence, fact, or truth of as a basis for reasoning, discussion, or belief. *He postulated several theories in his lifetime.* **2** nominate or elect to an ecclesiastical office subject to the sanction of a higher authority. *I postulate Richard Parker for the post of the chief. (noun)* a thing postulated. *Freud's postulate that we all have a death instinct was challenged by several philosophers.*

Posture – *(noun)* **1** a particular position of the body. the way in which a person holds their body. *You must sit upright on a chair in order to have a good posture.* **2** [zoology] a particular pose adopted by a bird or other animal, signaling a specific pattern of behavior. *When the deer stands in a certain posture, all the others become alert and ready to flee.* **3** an approach or attitude towards something. *She assumed a posture of angry defiance. (verb)* behave in a way that is intended to impress or mislead others. *She postured and made a total fool of herself.*

Pot – *(noun)* an attempt to score a goal with kick *He took a pot-shot at the bird on the fence. (verb)* score a goal. *"What a pot he scored!"*

Potable – *(adjective)* drinkable. *Wine and other potables were kept in a different bunker.*

Potato – *(noun)* **1** a starchy plant tuber which is one of the most important food crops, cooked and eaten as a vegetable. *Boiled potatoes with cheese and ham are a common dish Europeans eat for breakfast.* **2** the plant of the nightshade family which produces these tubers on underground runners. *My friend has a huge potato farm in the countryside.*

Potent – *(adjective)* **1** having great power; influence, or effect. *The drug is extremely potent but can have extreme side effects.* **2** able to achieve an erection or to reach an orgasm. *The boy was pleased to know he was potent.*

Potential – *(adjective)* having the capacity to develop into something in the future. *Your ideas have potential, I have to admit. (noun)* **1** latent qualities or abilities that may be developed and lead to future success or useful ability of something happening or of someone doing something in the future. *He has a huge potential to become someone great when he grows up.* **2** [physics] the quantity determining the energy of mass in a gravitational field or of charge in an electric field. *It was the first time I was answering a question on kinetic and potential energy in an exam.*

Pothole – *(noun)* **1** a deep natural underground cave formed by the eroding action of water. a deep circular hole in a river bed formed by the eroding action of stones in an eddy. *Warnings were issued as the rain had caused several pot holes on the roads.* **2** a depression or hollow in a road surface caused by wear or subsidence. *He fell into a pot hole in the rain as the road was waterlogged and he could not see it.* **3** [north American] a lake formed by a natural hollow in the ground in which water has collected. *It started as a pot hole and all these years later it is now a lake.*

Potter – *(verb)* **1** occupy oneself in a desultory but pleasant manner. *She was pottering around the whole place all day.* **2** move or go in a casual, unhurried way. *(noun)* a spell of pottering. *I spent the afternoon pottering.*

Potty – *(adjective)* **1** foolish, crazy. *"Are you going potty?"* **2** extremely enthusiastic about someone or something. *He was going potty with excitement.*

Pouch – *(noun)* **1** a small flexible bag. a able bag for mail or dispatches. *I carried all my junk jewellery in a pouch.* **2** a pocket-like abdominal receptacle in which marsupials carry their young during lactation. *The kangaroo had a baby in its pouch.* **3** any of a number of similar animal structures, such as those in the cheeks of rodents. a baggy area of skin underneath a person's eyes. *He was developing pouches indicating the amount of stress he has been taking over the months.* *(verb)* **1** put into a pouch. *The kangaroo carefully put its baby in its pouch.* **2** [informal] take possession of. *Don't try to pouch my belongings.* **3** cricket catch. *What a pouch it was!* **4** make or form into a pouch. *She made a pouch of her belongings.*

Poultry – *(noun)* chickens, turkeys, ducks, and geese; domestic fowl. *Most of the poultry was being culled because of the rumours of bird flu.*

Pounce – *(verb)* **1** spring or swoop suddenly to catch or as if to catch prey. *The tiger ran after the deer and pounced on its neck.* **2** notice and take swift advantage of a mistake or sing of weakness. *He only had to get a whiff of it and he would have pounced on the opportunity.* *(noun)* an act of pouncing. *The cat made a pounce on the bird.*

Pound – *(noun)* **1** a place where strays may officially be taken and kept until claimed. a place where illegally parked motor vehicles removed by the police are kept until the owner pays a fine. *I visited the pound down the street to buy a pet.* **2** [archaic] a trap or prison. *The thief was sent to the pound.* *(verb)* [archaic] shut in a pound. *The dog was whining as it was shut in the pound.*

Pour – *(verb)* **1** flow or cause to flow in a steady stream. fall heavily. prepare and serve. *Pour the curry into the serving bowl.* **2** come or go in a steady stream. *The rain was pouring.* **3** express one's feelings in an unknown origin. *She poured out her feelings throughout the bus journey.*

Pout – *(verb)* push one's lips or bottom lip forward as an expression of petulant annoyance or in order to make one-self look sexually attractive. *The actress tried pouting during the photo shoot but it didn't help her at all.* *(noun)* a pouting expression. *Her pout was not really of much help.*

Poverty – *(noun)* the state of being extremely poor. the renunciation of the right to individual ownership of property as part of a religious vow. *The leaders of our country dreamt of achieving a state of no poverty in the country.* **2** the state of being insufficient in amount. *They lived in a state of utter poverty.*

Powder – *(noun)* **1** fine dry particles produced by the grinding, crushing, or disintegration of a solid substance. *Coffee beans need to be powdered to make instant coffee.* **2** a cosmetic in this form applied to a person's face. *The make up man had applied a thicker pack of powder on her face than she needed.* **3** dated a [medicine] in this form. *She applied the powder needed to dry her wound.* **4** loose, dry, newly fallen snow. *The snow was loose and powdery and perfect for skiing.* **5** short for gunpowder. *Gunpowder is also called black powder.* *(verb)* **1** apply powder to; sprinkle or cover with powder. *Her face was packed with powder.* **2** reduce to a powder. *You must powder the whole spices to make a spice powder.*

Power – *(noun)* the ability to do something or act in a particular way. *The power of his love saved her.* **2** the capacity to influence the behavious of others, the emotions, or the course of events. *Her words had the power to influence the crowd.* **3** a right or authority given or delegated to a person or body. political authority or control. *Danger heightened his powers of discrimination.* **4** a country viewed in terms of its international influence and military strength: a world power. *The United States was growing into a super* *power.* **5** physical strength or force. capacity or performance of an engine or other device. the magnifying capacity of a lens. *The car has a powerful engine. (verb)* **1** supply with power. switch an electrically powered device on or off. *Switch off the power of the batteries before closing the bonnet.* **2** move or cause to move with speed or force. *He powered round a bend.*

Powerful – *(adjective)* having power. *The ruling party is one of the most powerful we have ever had till date. (adverb)* chiefly dialect very. *It was powerful humid.*

Powerless – *(adjective)* without ability, inflvence, power. *The cat was left powerless in front of the dog.*

Practicable – *(adjective)* **1** able to be done or put into practice successfully. *Teachers can only be expected to do what is practicable.* **2** useful. *The minister gave a practicable solution to the problem his party has been facing.*

Practical – *(adjective)* **1** of or concerned with practice. *He gained practical experience of sailing as a deck hand.* **2** likely to be effective in real circumstances; feasible. suitable for a particular purpose. *She gave us practical suggestions on how to improve our diet.* **3** realistic in approach. skilled at manual tasks. *She was always so practical and full of common sense.* **4** so nearly the case that it can be regarded as so; virtual. *It was practically the edge of the cliff. (noun)* [British] an examination or lesson involving the practical application of theories and procedures. *There are still no practical cures for cancer.*

Practice – *(noun)* **1** the actual application or use of a plan or method, as opposed to the theories relating to it. *We tried putting the diet into practice but it was very difficult.* **2** the customary or expected procedure or way of doing something. *Certain practices and rituals are not to be thrashed or done away with.* **3** the practicing of a profession. the business or premises of a doctor or lawyer. *He is a practicing doctor.* **4** the action or process of practicing. *He has been a practicing law for the last ten years.*

Practise – *(verb)* **1** perform or exercise repeatedly or regularly in order to acquire, maintain, or improve proficiency in it. *Only constant practise can help you master mathematics.* **2** carry out or perform habitually or regularly. *You must practise courtesy in social situations.* **3** be engaged in a particular profession. *He set up practise as a lawyer.* **4** observe the teaching and rules of a particular religion. *He has been practising his religion piously.* **5** [archaic] scheme or plot for an evil purpose. *The IT department caught his illegal practises before they could go out of hand.*

Practitioner – *(noun)* a person actively engaged in an art, discipline, or profession, especially [medicine]. *He has been a practitioner of ayurvedic medicine for the last ten years.*

Pragmatic – *(adjective)* **1** dealing with things in a way that is based on practical rather than theoretical considerations. *He gave a pragmatic perspective to the problem at hand.* **2** relating to philosophical or political pragmatism. *Pierce's pragmatism was criticized by several philosophers of his age.* **3** [linguistics] of or relating to pragmatics. *In linguistics, pragmatics studies the way context contributes to meaning.*

Prairie – *(noun)* a large open area of grassland. *With global warming, even the prairies were disappearing.*

Praise – *(verb)* **1** express warm approval of or admiration for. *She received lots of praise from her peers and teachers for being an all rounder.* **2** express respect and gratitude towards. *She praised the hard work and sincerity her seniors had put into the whole event. (noun)* the expression of approval or admiration. *The principal praised the efforts put in by everyone in making the festival a success.* **2** the expression of respect and gratitude as an act of worship. *She asked the congregation to praise God.*

Pram – *(noun)* [British] a four-wheeled carriage for a baby. pushed by a person on foot. *He was so excited about the baby coming home, he bought five different kinds of prams.*

Prance – *(verb)* **1** move with high springy steps. *She was prancing around like a rooster in a hen* *house.* **2** walk or move around with ostentatious, exaggerated movements. *The cheerleaders pranced on the far side of the pitch.* *(noun)* an act of prancing. *He made a prancing movement and for a second I thought he would fall off the stage.*

Prank – *(noun)* a practical joke or mischievous act. *The actor was known for the pranks he would play on the sets.*

Prattle – *(verb)* talk at length in a foolish or inconsequential way. *She prattled on till I wanted to scream.* *(noun)* foolish or inconsequential talk. *I had had enough of his mindless prattle.*

Prawn – *(noun)* a marine crustacean which resembles a large shrimp. *Prawn sandwiches are her favourite indeed.*

Pray – *(verb)* **1** address a prayer to god or another deity. *I have been taught from childhood to pray before I sleep at night.* **2** wish or hope earnestly for a particular outcome. *I prayed incessantly for his speedy recovery.* *(adverb)* formal used in polite requests or questions. *"Pray continue."*

Prayer – *(noun)* **1** a solemn request for help or expression of thanks addressed to god or another deity. *The doctor told us that only prayer could save her now.* **2** a religious service at which people gather to pray together. *We had to hurry and clean up the place before people started arriving for the prayer.* **3** an earnest hope or wish. *I sent out an earnest prayer for your exam.*

Pre – *(prefix)* before in time, place, order, degree, or importance: pre-adolescent. *She has entered her pre-adolescent years now.*

Preach – *(verb)* **1** deliver a religious address to an assembled group of people. publicly proclaim. *The father preached the gospel.* **2** earnestly advocate. give moral advice to in a self-righteous way. *My parents always preached tolerance.*

Preamble – *(noun)* a preliminary statement; an introduction. *The Preamble of our Constitution contains the Directive Principles of State Authority.*

Precarious – *(adjective)* **1** not securely held or in position; likely to fall. *He was standing in a precarious position, and I feared anyone could easily catch him.* **2** dependent on chance; uncertain. *You have to admit it was a precarious solution to a tough problem.*

Precaution – *(noun)* **1** a measure taken in advance to prevent something undesirable from happening. *You must take proper precautions before you go for the adventure trip.* **2** [informal] contraception. *My gynaecologist advised precaution for a while till my ovaries have healed.*

Precede – *(verb)* come or go before in time, order, or position. preface something with. *Stone tools precede bronze tools.*

Precedence – *(noun)* the condition of preceding others in importance, order, or rank. an acknowledged or legally determined right to such precedence. *Recipients of military honour were called in order of precedence—higher ranking officers first.*

Precedent – *(noun)* an earlier event or action serving as an example or guide. law a previous case or legal decision that may be or must be followed in subsequent similar cases. *The trial could set an important precedent for similar cases.* *(adjective)* preceding in time, order, or importance. *The President followed historical precedent in forming the Cabinet.*

Precept – *(noun)* **1** a general rule regulating behavior or thought. *He believed and followed all the precepts of Buddhism.* **2** a writ or warrant. *This violates every precept of English law as well as natural justice.* **3** [British] an order issued by one local authority to another specifying the rate of tax to be charged on its behalf. [British] this rate, or the tax itself. *The local council tax precept for policing is the second lowest in the country.*

Precinct – *(noun)* **1** the area within the walls or perceived boundaries of a particular place. an enclosed or clearly defined area of ground around a cathedral, church, or college. [British] an area in a town designated for specific or restricted use, especially one closed to traffic. *Hunting is not allowed within the precincts of the estate.* **2** a district of a city or town as defined for policing or electoral purposes. *Precincts usually do not have separate government authorities.*

Precious – *(adjective)* 1 having great value. *She has kept all her precious jewels safely in the locker.* 2 greatly loved or treasured by someone. *My daughter is most precious to me.* 3 [informal, chiefly] considerable: a precious lot you know!. *These kittens are a precious lot, you know!* 4 derogatory affectedly concerned with elegant or refined language or manners. *"You can keep your elite and precious mannerisms to yourself!" (noun)* a term of address to a beloved person. *"You are my precious precious, aren't you?"*

Precipice – *(noun)* a tall and very steep rock face or cliff. *The path had sheer rock on one side and a precipice on the other.*

Precipitate – *(verb)* 1 cause to happen unexpectedly or prematurely. *The killings in the city have precipitated the worst crisis ever.* 2 cause to move suddenly and with force. send someone or something without warning into a particular state or condition. *The finest bridge in all Peru broke and precipitated five travelers into the gulf below.* 3 [chemistry] cause to be deposited in solid form from a solution. cause to be deposited from the atmosphere or from a vapour or suspension. *Dust was precipitated into the air. (adjective)* done, acting, or occurring suddenly or without careful consideration. *We should not make any precipitate decisions. (noun)* [chemistry] a substance precipitated from a solution. *In chemistry class today, we had a look at the precipitate produced by sewage treatment.*

Precis – *(noun)* a summary of a text or speech. *We were asked to present a précis before the actual presentation. (verb)* make a précis of. *His précis invited a huge applause, so I won't be surprised if his presentation was a runaway success.*

Precise – *(adjective)* marked by exactness and accuracy of expression or detail. very attentive to detail; careful in the expression of detail. exact; particular. *I want the precise details of the project that the rival company is taking up.*

Precision – *(noun)* 1 the quality, condition, or fact of being precise. *He handled it with the precision of an automated machine.* 2 marked by or designed for accuracy and exactness: a precision instrument. *You must use a precision tool so you won't make a mistake in the calculations.* 3 refinement in a measurement or specification, especially as represented by the number of digits given. *What is the precise number of balls in this bowl?*

Precocious – *(adjective)* 1 having developed certain abilities or inclinations at an earlier age than usual. *Radhika has always been a precocious child.* 2 flowering or fruiting earlier than usual. *Precocious flowers appear before the leaves as in some species of magnolias.*

Preconceived – *(adjective)* formed prior to having evidence for its truth or usefulness. *Do not enter into the experiment with any preconceived notions in your mind.*

Preconception – *(noun)* a preconceived idea or prejudice. *He did not even try to confirm his preconceptions before he passed the news.*

Predator – *(noun)* 1 an animal that preys on others. *Life in the jungle follows the prey-predator format.* 2 a person who exploits others. a company that tries to take over another. *Walmart is like a predator in the market that can gobble up anything in its way.*

Predecessor – *(noun)* 1 a person who held a job or office before the current holder. *The new manager should learn a thing or two about management from his predecessor.* 2 a thing that has been followed or replaced by another. *The new building is more spacious and larger than its predecessor.*

Predicament – *(noun)* 1 a difficult situation. *You would definitely never understand my predicament unless you were in my shoes.* 2 [philosophy] each of the ent categories in Aristotelian logic. *Aristotle's Categories is divided into three parts: Pre Predicamenta, Predicamenta, and the Post Predicamenta.*

Predicate – *(noun)* 1 [grammar] the part of a sentence or clause containing a very and stating something about the subject. *The question was: Identify the predicate in "The child is very sleepy".* 2 logic something which is affirmed or denied concerning an argument of a proposition. *"Socrates is a man' predicates 'manhood of*

Socrates". (verb) **1** [grammar & logic] state, affirm, or assert about the subject of a sentence or an argument of proposition. *Solving the problem is predicated on understanding it well.* **2** found or base something on. *I predicated my arguments on facts.*

Predicative – *(adjective)* **1** [grammar] forming or contained in the predicate, as old in the dog is old. contrasted with attributive. denoting a use of the (verb) to be to assert something about the subject. *Identify the predicate in : Jane opened the door.* **2** logic acting as a predicate. *The sermon predicated the perfectibility of mankind.*

Predict – *(verb)* state that a specified event will happen in the future. *Nostradamous predicted the world to come to an end in 2012.*

Predictable – *(adjective)* able to be predicted. derogatory always behaving or occurring in the way expected. *She has a predictable nature.*

Predominant – *(adjective)* present as the strongest or main element. having or exerting the greatest control or power. *He played a predominant role in shaping the constitution of our country.*

Predominance – *(noun)* state or condition of being greater in number. *An interesting note was the predominance of London club players.*

Predominate – *(verb)* be the strongest or main element. have or exert control or power.*Good predominates over evil in most of our scriptural epics.*

Preeminent – *(adjective)* surpassing all others. *We were honoured to have a preeminent scholar amongst us.*

Preen – *(verb)* **1** tidy and clean its feathers with its beak. *The birds were preening themselves in the sun.* **2** devote effort to making oneself look attractive. *She spent half an hour preening in front of the mirror.* **3** congratulate or pride oneself. *The desire to brag and preen himself on is abilities is what brought him down in the end.*

Preface – *(noun)* **1** an introduction to a book, typically stating its subject, scope, or aims. *The preface explains how to use a dictionary.* **2** [church] the introduction to the central part of the Eucharist. *The father's rendition of the preface was spectacular. (verb)* provide with a preface. *I requested my professor to write a preface for my book.* 2 introduce or begin a speech or event with or by doing something.*He prefaced his lecture with a few critical comments on the book.*

Prefect – *(noun)* **1** [chiefly British] a senior pupil authorized to enforce discipline in a school. *Right from primary school, I dreamt of being a prefect when I reached High School.* **2** chief officer, magistrate, or regional governor in certain countries. a senior magistrate or governor in the ancient roman world. *The Centurian gave the Prefect the right to arrest and execute the culprit.*

Prefer – *(verb)* **1** like better than another or others; tend to choose. *I prefer gravy over a dry curry.* **2** formal submit for consideration. *The college asked us to submit our preferences in subsidiary subjects by the end of the day.* **3** [archaic] promote to a prestigious position.*John was preferred over Smith for the post for which a replacement was sought.*

Preference – *(noun)* **1** a greater liking for one alternative over another or others. a thing preferred. favour shown to one person over another or others. *She has a greater preference for literature.* **2** [law] a prior right, especially in connection with the payment of debts. *Preference in paying off debts can lead you to legal troubles since it is prohibited by law.*

Preferential– *(adjective)* of or involving preference or partiality. *The employer was given an earful by the Chief for giving preferential treatment to his secretary.* **2** having a claim for repayment which will be met before those of other creditors. *Giving preferential treatment to your creditor in a bankruptsy situation can land you in trouble since it is against the law.*

Prefix – *(noun)* a word, letter, or number placed before another. an element placed at the beginning of a word to adjust or qualify its meaning as an inflection. a title placed before a name. *A numerical prefix implies how many places to rotate the text. (verb)* add as a prefix or introduction. add a prefix or introduction to. *I thought it agreeable to prefix your name before them in both English and Latin.*

Pregnant – *(adjective)* **1** of a woman or female animal having a child or young developing in the uterus. *I gave the pregnant woman my seat as she looked very tired.* **2** full of meaning or significance. *There was a conversation occasionally punctuated by pregnant pauses.*

Prehistoric – *(adjective)* of or relating to prehistory. [informal] very old or out of date. *I wanted to sell of my mother's prehistoric cooker which she held on to for so long.*

Prejudice – *(noun)* **1** preconceived opinion that is not based on reason or actual experience. unjust behavior formed on such a basis. *Her unjust prejudice towards children with better marks was leading to a rebellious attitude developing among other children.* **2** [chiefly law] harm or injury that results or any result from some action or judgement. *I think it can be done without prejudice to anybody's principles. (verb)* **1** give rise to prejudice in make biased. *I think your upbringing has prejudiced you.* **2** [chiefly law] cause harm to a state of affairs. *He claimed that the media coverage had prejudiced his chances of a fair trial.*

Preliminary – *(adjective)* preceding or done in preparation for something fuller or more important. *Preliminary talks began yesterday. (noun)* **1** a preliminary action or event. *Today's survey is a preliminary to a more detailed one.* **2** a preliminary round in a sporting competition. *This is the last match of the preliminary round.* **3** fuller form of prelims. *She cleared her preliminaries and now she is preparing for the mains.*

Prelude – *(noun)* **1** an action or event serving as an introduction to something more important. *Training is a necessary prelude to employment.* **2** a piece of music serving as an introduction, e.g. to an act of an opera or to a suite or a fugue. *The pianist had the audience captivated right from the prelude.* **3** the introductory part of a poem or other literary work. *The little boy was the only one to give a prelude before reciting the poem.(verb)* serve as a prelude or introduction to. *The protests are now seen as a prelude to last year's uprising.*

Premature – *(adjective)* **1** occurring or done before the proper time. *A 24-year old man was suffering from premature balding.* **2** born before the end of the full term of gestation, especially three or move weeks before. *She gave birth to premature twins.*

Premeditate – *(verb)* think out or plan beforehand. *The murder was definitely premeditated.*

Premiere – *(noun)* the first performance of a musical or theatrical work or the first showing of a film. *The premiere of the film was a gala event attended by the who's-who of the industry. (verb)* give the premiere of. *He is organizing a special premiere of our movie specially for me.*

Premise – *(noun)* **1** logic a previous statement from which another is inferred. an underlying assumption. *The judgment was based on the premise that men and women share equal space in society. (verb)* **1** base an argument, theory, etc. on. *The plan is premised on continuing abundant tax returns.* **2** state or presuppose as a premise. *He premised these remarks so that his readers might understand.*

Premises – *(plural noun)* a house or building, together with its land and outbuildings, occupied by a business or considered in an official context. *Smoking is not allowed within the office premises.*

Premium – *(noun)* **1** an amount paid for a contract of insurance. *This month my account balance is low as I had to fill in a premium of an insurance I had applied for last year.* **2** a sum added to an ordinary price, charge, or other payment. superior and more expensive. *Customers are not willing to pay a premium.* **3** something given as a reward or incentive. *Shareholders did not receive a premium on the price of their shares.*

Premonition – *(noun)* a strong feeling that something is about to happen. *I had a strong premonition that one of us would die.*

Preoccupation – *(noun)* the state of being preoccupied. a matter that preoccupies someone. *Post retirement men ought to find some or the other preoccupation to keep their mind busy.*

Preoccupy – *(verb)* dominate or engross the mind of to the exclusion of other thoughts. *I had asked my son to study but he was preoccupied with something else.*

Preparation – *(noun)* **1** the action or process of preparing or being prepared. something done to get ready for an event of undertaking. *Behind any successful event lies several months of preparation.* **2** a specially made up substance, especially a [medicine] or food. *She was using a specially formulated natural skin preparation.* **3** [music] the sounding of the discordant note in a chord in the preceding chord where it is not discordant, lessening the effect of the discord. *The resolution of one dissonance is often the preparation for another dissonance.*

Preparatory – *(adjective)* serving as or carrying out preparation. [British] relating to education in a preparatory school. *Now that she has turned four, her parents wanted to send her to preparatory school.*

Prepare – *(verb)* **1** make ready for use of consideration. make ready for cooking or eating. *What are you preparing for dinner tonight?* **2** make or get ready to do or deal with something. be willing to do something. *Are you done and prepared for the wedding?* **3** make by chemical reaction. *The crew has been preparing the ship for storage.* **4** [music] lead up to be means of preparation. *The instruments were not prepared to repair the dissonant note.*

Prepay – *(verb)* pay for in advance. *I applied for a prepaid connection for my mobile phone.*

Preposition – *(noun)* [grammar] a word governing, and usually preceding, a noun or pronounand expressing a relation to another word or element, as in she arrived after dinner and what did you do it for. *We were being given a class on how to use prepositions effectively in essays.*

Preposterous – *(adjective)* utterly absurd or ridiculous. *The idea she gave was more preposterous than obnoxious.*

Prerequisite – *(adjective)* required as a prior condition. *Competence is prerequisite to promotion. (noun)* a prerequisite thing. *Crossing the age bar of 18 years is a prerequisite to vote.*

Prerogative – *(noun)* **1** a right or privilege exclusive to a particular individual or class. *It was the prinicipal's prerogative to suspend a student.* **2** the right of the sovereign, theoretically unrestricted but usually delegated to government or the judiciary. *Suffrage was the prerogative of white adult males. (adjective)* arising from or relating to the royal prerogative. *It is totally her prerogative to make the decision.*

Prescribe – *(verb)* **1** advise and authorize the use of especially in writing. *The doctor prescribed antibiotics for her lung infection.* **2** recommend as something beneficial. state authoritatively that should be carried out. *The judge said that he was passing the sentence prescribed by law.*

Prescription – *(noun)* **1** an instruction written by a medical practitioner that authorizes a patient to be issued with a [medicine] or treatment. *She took the doctor's prescription to another doctor to seek a second opinion.* **2** the action of prescribing. *I tried to follow her prescription for success.* **3** an authoritative recommendation or ruling. *The party tried using the leader's prescription for electoral success, but failed.* **4** [law] the establishment of a claim founded on the basis of long usage or custom. *One must try to follow only the positive prescriptions for law and order in society.*

Presence – *(noun)* **1** the state or fact of being present. a person or thing that is present but not seen. *Her presence was missed greatly during the family get-togethers.* **2** the impressive manner or appearance of a person. *He still has the presence, mental and physical, of a young man.*

Present – *(noun)* a thing given to someone as a gift. *I thought it bad etiquette to arrive at the party without a present for the host.*

Presentable – *(adjective)* clean, smart, or decent enough to be seen in public. *I asked Ram if I was looking presentable enough for the party.*

Presentation – *(noun)* **1** the action or an instance of presenting or being presented. the manner or style in which something is presented. a formal introduction. *The presentation was grand but the content was poor.* **2** [medicine] the position of a fetus at the time of delivery. *The most common form of cephalic presentation is the vertex presentation where the occiput is the leading part.* **3** another term for candlemas. *The Candlemas feast was a grand presentation indeed this year.*

Presently - *(adjective)* **1** after a short time; soon. *The emcee announced that the flautist will arrive presently.* **2** at the present time; now. *He is presently staying with us.*

Preservation - *(noun)* a legal obligation laid on an owner to preserve a historic building, valuable natural habitat, etc. *Our school taught us the importance of preservation of natural resources.*

Preside - *(verb)* be in a position of authority in a meeting, court, etc. be in charge of a situation. *The Prime Minister presided over the meeting.*

Presidency - *(noun)* the office or status of president, the period of this. *Things were peaceful during the Eisenhower presidency.*

President - *(noun)* **1** the elected head of a republican state. the head of a society, council, college, or other organization. *The President likes to go for a jog every morning.* **2** [Christian church] the celebrant at a Eucharist. *Prophet, seer and revelator is an ecclesiastical title used for the Assistant President of the Church.*

Press - *(verb)* **1** put to a specified use, especially as a temporary or makeshift measure. *This is a pressing problem.* **2** [historical] force to enlist in the army or navy. *He was pressed to join the armed forces.* *(noun)* [historical] a forcible enlistment of men, especially for the navy. *No amount of pressing would make him change his mind about not joining the navy.*

Pressure - *(noun)* **1** the continuous physical force exerted on or against an object by something in contact with it. the force per unit area exerted by a fluid against a surface. *The pressure of his fingers had relaxed.* **2** the use of persuasion, intimidation, etc. to make someone do something. a feeling of stressful urgency. *He may be putting pressure on her to agree.* *(verb)* attempt to persuade or coerce into doing something. *He claimed the police pressured him to change his testimony.*

Pressurize - *(verb)* **1** produce or maintain raised pressure artificially in. *The airplane cabin is pressurized.* **2** attempt to persuade or coerce into doing something. *He thought she was trying to pressurize him into marriage.*

Prestige - *(noun)* widespread respect and admiration attracted through a perception of high achievements or quality. *His work gained him international prestige.*

Prestigious - *(adjective)* having high status. *He was given a prestigious award by the Prime Minister last year.*

Presumably - *(adverb)* as may reasonably be presumed. *Presumably, the culprit was one of the millions that died in the blast.*

Presume - *(verb)* **1** suppose that something is the case on the impertinent enough to do something. unjustifiably regard as entitling one to privileges. *I presume that you would have done some preliminary research before taking on the project.*

Presumption - *(noun)* **1** an act or instance of presuming something to be the case. an idea that is presumed to be true. [chiefly law] an attitude adopted towards something in the absence of contrary factors. *He prepared a rough analysis after going through the various presumptions.* **2** presumptuous behavior. *He had the presumption to answer me back.*

Presumptuous - *(adjective)* failing to observe the limits of what is permitted or appropriate. *Your presumptuous behavior is not going too well with your friends, I can see.*

Presuppose - *(verb)* require as a precondition of possibility or coherence. tacitly assume to be the case. *All your arguments presuppose that he is a rational man.*

Pretence - *(noun)* **1** an act of pretending. *He betrayed him under the pretence of friendship.* **2** pretentious behavior. *Anyone could tell that her behaviour was a mere pretence while the actual characteristics were being carefully hidden within.* **3** a claim, especially a false or ambitious one. *His conformity was only pretence.*

Pretend - *(verb)* **1** act so as to make it appear that something is the case when in fact it is not. engage in an imaginative game or fantasy. simulate an emotion or quality. *I cannot pretend to say that you are wrong.* **2** lay claim to a quality or title. *She doesn't pretend to be an expert.* *(adjective)* [informal] imaginary; make-believe. *Many children have a pretend playmate.*

Pretension - *(noun)* **1** a claim or aspiration to something. *One of the few designers who doesn't have the pretensions to be an artist.* **2** pretentiousness. *We liked him for his honesty and lack of pretension.*

Pretentious - *(adjective)* attempting to impress by affecting greater importance or merit than is actually possessed. *He talked a lot of pretentious twaddle about modern art.*

Pretext - *(noun)* an ostensible or false reason used to justify an action. *He excused himself on the pretext of a stomachache.*

Pretty - *(adjective)* **1** attractive in a delicate way without being truly beautiful. *She is a charming and pretty girl.* **2** [informal] used ironically to express displeasure. *He led me a pretty dance.* *(adverb)* [informal] to a moderately high degree; fairly. *I had a pretty good idea what she was going to do.* *(noun)* [informal] a pretty thing; a trinket. an attractive person. *The sofas were covered with a pretty floral print cover.* *(verb)* make pretty or attractive. *The credit for making her pretty on her wedding goes to the beautician.*

Prevail - *(verb)* **1** prove more powerful; be victorious. be widespread or current. *We hoped that common sense would prevail.* **2** persuade to do something. *Do you think she can be prevailed upon to do this?*

Prevalent - *(adjective)* widespread in a particular area at a particular time. [archaic] predominant; powerful. *Smoking is becoming increasingly prevalent among younger women.*

Prevent - *(verb)* **1** keep from happening or arising. make unable to do something. *The state took several steps to prevent the strike.* **2** [archaic] go before with spiritual guidance and help. *The surest way to prevent war is to not fear it.*

Preventable - *(adjective)* keep something form happenig. *It is sad that preventable diseases kill half of our population.*

Prevention - *(noun)* keep somethig from occurring. *Prevention is better than cure.*

Preventive - *(adjective)* designed to prevent something from occurring. *They accused the police of failing to take enough preventive measures.* *(noun)* a preventive [medicine] or other treatment. *Cabbage is a preventive against stomach ulcers.*

Preview - *(noun)* a viewing or display of something before it is acquired or becomes generally available. a publicity article, review, or trailer of a forthcoming film, book, etc. *They were releasing previews of the forthcoming movie before show in the movie hall.* *(verb)* provide or have a preview of a product, film, etc. *We will preview this season's collection from Paris.*

Previous - *(adjective)* **1** existing or occurring before in time or order. *She had two children from a previous marriage.* 2 [informal] over-hasty. *They should have told their parents before they published it in the mewspaper.*

Prey - *(noun)* an animal hunted and killed by another for food. a victim or quarry. [archaic] plunder or a prize. *The muggers recognized their prey.* *(verb)* **1** hunt and kill or for food. *The larvae preyed on small aphids.* **2** exploit or injure; cause trouble to. *The problem had begun to prey on my mind.*

Price - *(noun)* the amount of money expected, required, or given in payment for something. something expended or endured in order to achieve an objective. the odds in betting. [archaic] value; worth. *Rice is sold at a lower price in the kirana store near my house.* *(verb)* decide the price of. *I spent the day pricing dresses.*

Prick- *(verb)* **1** press briefly or puncture with a sharp point. draw or decorate by making small holes in a surface. *She gave a prick and the ball burst.* **2** feel a sensation as though a sharp point were sticking into one. cause mental or emotional discomfort to. *My conscience has been pricking me for a long time, so I decided I had to confess.* **3** make stand erect when on the alert. *She pricked for the slightest sound and* *readied herself for the attack.* **4** plant in small holes made in the earth. *She made a hole in the ground, no bigger than a pin prick. (noun)* **1** an act of pricking something. a small hole or mark made by pricking. *The hole in the ground was no bigger than a pin prick.* **2** a sharp pain caused by being pierced with a fine point. a sudden feeling of distress, anxiety, etc. [archaic] a goad for oxen. *She felt a sharp prick at the back of her neck.* **3** vulgar slang a man's penis. a man regarded as stupid, unpleasant, or contemptible. *He is such a prick!*

Prickle – *(noun)* **1** a short spine or pointed outgrowth on the surface of a plant or on the skin of an animal. *A hedgehog is covered with prickles.* **2** a tingling or mildly painful sensation on the skin. *I felt a prickle of fear when I saw the shadow. (verb)* **1** experience or produce a prickle. cause such a sensation in. *His scalp prickled under his wig.* **2** react defensively or angrily. *The prickle at the nape of my neck reminded me of my fears.*

Prickly – *(adjective)* **1** covered in or resembling prickles. having or causing a prickling sensation. *I had a prickly sensation in my foot.* **2** ready to take offence. liable to cause someone to take offence: a prickly subject. *It was a rather prickly situation.*

Pride – *(noun)* **1** a feeling of deep pleasure or satisfaction derived from achievements, qualities, or possessions that speciousness of one's own dignity. the quality of having an excessively high opinion of oneself. poetic the prime of something. *She felt a sense of pride rising in her when she saw her project report.* **2** a group of lions forming a social unit. *The state was furious as the pride of lions that were sent to the neighbouring state had reached dead. (verb)* be especially proud of a quality or skil. *He prides himself on making it to law school.*

Priest – *(noun)* **1** an ordained minister of the catholic, orthodox;s or Anglican church, authorized to perform certain rise and administer certain sacraments. a person who performs ceremonies in a non-Christian religion. *He became a priest after dropping out of school.* **2** a mallet used to kill fish caught when angling. *Anglers often use priests to quickly kill fish. (verb)* formal ordain to the priesthood. *He was trained into priesthood by the Church.*

Prim – *(adjective)* feeling or showing disapproval of anything improper; stiffly correct. *The new teacher was prim and proper in her attire. (verb)* purse into a prim expression. *She primed her lips after every bite of food.*

Primafacie – *(adjective & adverb)* law at first sight; accepted as so until proved otherwise. *Primafacie evidence showed the culprit trying to flee from the scene of crime.*

Primary – *(adjective)* **1** of chief importance; principal. *Your health is primary to dieting.* **2** earliest in time or order. not caused by or based on anything else. *The manager stated the primary goals for the following year in the year-end meeting.* **3** relating to or denoting education for children between the ages of about five and eleven. *The government passed the bill for ensuring primary education of every child.* **4** of or denoting the input side of a transformer or other inductive device. *Current through the primary coil induces current in the secondary coil.* **5** [chemistry] having its functional group on a carbon atom bonded to no more than one other carbon atom. derived from ammonia by replacement of one hydrogen atom by an organic group. *Primary pH standard values are determined using a concentration cell with transference.* **6** producing current by an irreversible chemical reaction. *Current through the primary coil induces current in the secondary coil. (noun)* **1** a preliminary election to appoint delegates to a party conference or to select the candidates for a principal, especially presidential, election. *She won the primary elections and is now looking ahead towards winning.* **2** [astronomy] the body orbited by a smaller body. *The sun is the primary of the earth.*

Prime – *(adjective)* **1** of first importance; main; primary. *Political stability was of prime concern.* **2** of the best possible quality; excellent. having all the expected characteristics.

most suitable or likely. *It was one of the city's prime localities.* **3** divisible only by itself and one. *I thought for a long time and realized these were prime numbers. (noun)* **1** a state or time of greatest vigour or success in a person's life. [archaic] the beginning or earliest period. *She was at the prime of her youth.* **2** a prime number. *There was something wrong in the teacher's list of prime numbers.* **3** printing a symbol (') written as a distinguishing mark or to denote minutes or feet. *The programme will be aired at prime time.* **4** fencing the first of the eight parrying positions. *When the blade points down and the edge faces away from the fencer, it is a prime position.* **5** a special section in a cycle race. *Strangely she wanted to stay as away from the prime as she could.* **6** [Christian church] a service traditionally said at the first hour of the day but now little used. *Did I just hear the prime?*

Primer – *(noun)* **1** a substance painted on wood, metal, etc. as a preparatory coat. *I put a coating of primer on the walls before applying the paint.* **2** a cap or cylinder containing a compound which ignites the charge in a cartridge or explosive. *She pried the primer, from the shell, and laid it on the rock in the midst of the scattered powder.* **3** a small pump for priming an engine. *The primer had rusted, so we had to buy another one from the wholesale market.*

Primitive – *(adjective)* **1** of, relating to, or denoting the earliest times in history or stages in evolution or development. of or denoting a preliterate, noun-industrial society of simple organization. biology undeveloped; rudimentary. *All credits go to primitive man for discovering fire, for all the technological development that followed.* **2** offering an extremely basic level of comfort, convenience, or efficiency. *You have to admit, primitive tools must have been the easiest to handle.* **3** instinctive and unreasoning. *Living among primitive societies will not be easy for your thesis.* **4** of or denoting a deliberately simple and direct artistic style. *She specializes in primitive art forms. (noun)* **1** a person belonging to a primitive society. *He was primitive in his mannerisms and choices.* **2** a pre-renaissance painter, or one employing a primitive style. *He has a primitive style of sculpting.*

Primrose – *(noun)* **1** a woodland and hedgerow plant which produces pale yellow flowers in early spring. *She had primroses in her garden, in full bloom.* **2** a pale yellow colour. *I want a primrose dress to go with my new stilettos.*

Prince – *(noun)* **1** a son, grandson, or other close male relative of a monarch. a male monarch of a small state, actually or nominally subject to a king or emperor: a nobleman, usually ranking next below a duke. *The kingdom rejoiced as the prince was born.* **2** a man or thing preeminent in a particular sphere or group. *He is the prince in the whole lot.*

Principal – *(adjective)* **1** first in order of importance; main. *Their principal concern is of winning the election.* **2** denoting an original sum of money invested or lent. *Nowadays they have even introduced a loan on the principal amount. (noun)* **1** the most important or senior person in an organization or group. the head of a school or college. a fully qualified practitioner. *I fondly remember the principal of our school.* **2** a sum of money lent or invested, on which interest is paid. *Use the higher premiums to pay the interest and principal on the debt.* **3** a person for whom another acts as an agent or representative. law a person directly responsible for a crime. *He is the principal schemer in the entire plot.* 4 a main rafter supporting purlins. *He was the oldest and strongest in the rafters' group so we chose him as the principal.* **5** an organ stop sounding a set of pipes typically an octave above the diapason. *We should reduce the sound of the principal a bit.*

Principle– *(noun)* **1** a fundamental truth or proposition serving as the foundation for belief or action a rule or belief governing one's personal behavior. morally correct behavior and attitudes: a man of principle. *He is known for being a man of principle.* **2** a general scientific theorem or natural law. *I was shocked at the number of principles I had to memorize for the test.* **3** a fundamental source or basis of something. a fundamental quality or attribute. *The basic principle you should live on is to never hurt or be a pain to another person.* **4** [chemistry] an active or characteristic constituent of a substance. *What are the principle constituents and features of the acid?*

Print – *(verb)* **1** produce by a mechanical process involving the transfer of text or designs to paper. produce in such a way, publish. produce in such a way. publish. produce a paper copy of information stored on a computer. *This news should not be printed.* **2** produce a photographic print from a negative. *The boss asked me to get him the prints of the negative he gave me yesterday.* **3** write clearly without joining the letters. *Her handwriting was as if printed.* **4** mark with a coloured design or pattern. make a mark or indentation by pressing something on a surface or soft substance. *Their pet dog had made paw prints on her art book.* **5** fix firmly or indelibly in someone's mind. *The accident was indelibly printed on his mind.* *(noun)* **1** the text appearing in a book, newspaper, etc. the state of being avaible in published form. of or relating to the printing industry or the printed media. [informal] a newspaper. *The newspaper was sent to print at 2am.* **2** an indentation of mark left on a surface or soft substance by pressure. fingerprints. *There were visible fingerprints on the door knob.* **3** a printed picture or design. a photograph printed on paper from a negative or transparency. a copy of a motion picture on film. *She got five prints of the design.*

Prior – *(adjective)* existing or coming before in time, order or importance. *The promotion came prior to his taking on the project.* *(noun)* [north American informal] a previous criminal conviction. *Prior to joining the new job and marriage, he had been convicted and had spent a few years in jail.*

Priority – *(noun)* **1** the fact or condition of being regarded as more important. a thing regarded as more important than others. *She gave priority to her home over her job.* **2** the right to proceed before other traffic. *The VIP was given priority exit at the traffic signal.*

Prison – *(noun)* a building for the confinement of criminals or those awaiting trial. *She was born in a prison.* *(verb)* poetic imprison. *He was imprisoned for his crime.*

Prisoner – *(noun)* a person legally committed to prison. a person captured and kept confined. a person trapped by a situation or circumstances. *The princess was kept prisoner in a tower far far away.*

Pristine – *(adjective)* in its original condition. spotless. *At the hill staton, we saw nature in its pristine glory.*

Privacy – *(noun)* a state in which one is not observed or disturbed by others. freedom form public attention. *The employer instructed the secretary not to disturb him as he wanted some privacy for the next few hours.*

Private – *(adjective)* **1** for or belonging to one particular person or group only. not to be shared or revealed. not choosing to share their thoughts and feelings. secluded. alone and undisturbed by others. *The actor was known for being a very private person.* **2** having no official or public position. not connected with one's work or official position. *He was working privately.* **3** provided or owned by an individual or commercial company rather than the stat. of or relating to a system of education or medical treatment conducted outside the state system and charging fees. *His was a private company with a turnover of more than six million dollars per annum.* **4** relating to or denoting a transaction between individuals. *I think we should discuss this in private.*

Privatize – *(verb)* transfer from public to private ownership. *Several public sector organizations are being privatized these days.*

Privilege – *(noun)* **1** a special right, advantage, or immunity for a particular person. a special benefit or honour. *Shareholders have several privileges in the company.* **2** the right to say or write something without the risk of punishment. *Every citizen of the country has as many privileges as he has duties towards the country.* **3** the right of a lawyer or official to refuse to divulge confidential information. *He will use* *parliamentary privilege to make this information public.* 4 [historical] a grant of special rights or immunities, especially in the form of a franchise or monopoly. *She would be entitled to executive privileges after her promotion. (verb)* formal grant a privilege or privileges to. exempt from a liability or obligation. *They are privileging a select few for the disadvantage of all.*

Privy - *(adjective)* **1** sharing in the knowledge of something secret. *His wife was privy to his official confidential information.* **2** [archaic] hidden; secret. *I needed a privy place to rest and think. (noun)* **1** a toilet in a small shed outside a house. *The house had an outside privy.* **2** law a person having a part or interest in any action or matter. *He was privy to the fraud that had been practiced on his friend.*

Prize - *(noun)* **1** a thing given as a reward to a winner or in recognition of an outstanding achievement. something won in a game of chance. something of great value that is worth struggling to achieve. *The winners were awarded a prize of Rs 2000.* 2 chiefly [historical] an enemy ship captured during warfare. *(adjective) At the end of the fierce battle, the prize went to the pirates.* **1** having been or likely to be awarded a prize. *A settlement of the dispute would be a great prize.* **2** outstanding of its kind. *A single winner is in line for a jackpot prize of $ 8 million. (verb)* value highly. *These items are greatly prized by collectors.*

Pro - *(noun)* an advantage or argument in favour of something. *Those who were against and pro the motion were grouped separately. (preposition & adverb)* in favour of. *He was always pro-reforms.*

Probability - *(noun)* the extent of which something is probable. a probable or most probable event. *There is a probability she may take voluntary retirement from her service.*

Probable - *(adjective)* likely to happen or be the case. *War seemed probable in 1938. (noun)* person likely to become or do something. *Chances of her promotion are highly probable.*

Probation - *(noun)* **1** [law] the release of an offender from detention, subject to a period of good behavior under supervision. *He was kept under probation until his crime was proved.* **2** the process of testing the character or abilities of a person in a certain role. *She is under probation for six months after which she will be made permanent.*

Probationary - *(adjective)* a process of testing and observing the abilities of a new person.*She joined the bank as a probationary officer.*

Probe - *(noun)* **1** a blunt-ended surgical instrument for exploring a wound or part of the body. *The probe helped to bring out the shrapnel stuck deep in his shoulder.* **2** a small measuring or testing device, especially an electrode. *A pH probe is the entire assembly that is used for measuring pH.* **3** a projecting device on an aircraft for in-flight refueling or on a space-craft for docking with another craft. *The total air temperature is measured by a temperature probe mounted on the surface of the aircraft.* **4** an unmanned exploratory spacecraft. *The Mars probe was sent to the planet to bring information about the planet.* **5** an investigation. *Another probe was started into the second aspect that the murder had just revealed. (verb)* physically explore or example. enquire into closely. *I should not have gone probing into the haunted house.*

Problem - *(noun)* **1** an unwelcome or harmful matter needing to be dealt with and overcome. a thing that is difficult to achieve. *We need an urgent solution for the problem at hand.* **2** [physics] an inquiry starting from given conditions to investigate or demonstrate something. *Starting from the given conditions, we had to first clarify the problem and then find the solution.* **3** an arrangement of pieces in which the solver has to achieve a specified result. *Life is full of problems.*

Procedure - *(noun)* **1** an established or official way of doing something. a series of actions conducted in a certain order or manner. *Stick to the procedure and you will surely arrive at the solution.* **2** computing a subroutine. *Computation is the procedure of calculating and determining something by mathematical methods.*

Proceed – *(verb)* **1** begin a course of action go on to do something. carry on or continue. *Please proceed with your work without a break.* **2** move forward. *The guides asked us to proceed in a queue.* **3** [law] start a lawsuit against someone. *The judge proceeded against the defaulting debtor.* **4** originate from. *Evil proceeds from the heart.*

Proceedings – *(plural noun)* **1** an event or a series of activities with a set procedure. *The monkey perched up on the tree watched the fishermen below and their proceedings.* **2** [law] action taken in a court to settle a dispute. *I just could not get a hang of the legal proceedings.* **3** a report of a set of meetings or a conference. *Go ahead with the proceedings after lunch and then have a meeting with me.*

Proceeds – *(plural noun)* money obtained from an event or activity. *The proceeds of the show will go to charity.*

Process – *(verb)* walk in procession. *Leaves and plants follow the process of photosynthesis to breathe and live.*

Procession – *(noun)* **1** a number of people or vehicles moving forward in an orderly fashion, especially as part of a ceremony. the action of moving in such a way. a relentless succession of people or things. *Processions should be forbidden during peak traffic hours.* **2** [theology] the emanation of the holy spirit. *I have studied the doctrine of the procession of the Holy Spirit from the Father and the son.*

Proclaim – *(verb)* announce officially or publicly. declare to be. indicate clearly. *He was a proclaimed king.*

Procrastinate – *(verb)* delay or postpone action. *You should stop procrastinating and start acting.*

Procure – *(verb)* **1** obtain. as a prostitute for someone else. *The minister asked the pimp to procure a woman for him the following night.* **2** law persuade or cause to do something. [archaic] cause to happen. *We were trying to procure a solution to a knotty problem.*

Procurement – *(noun)* the action of obtaining something. *He was waiting for his procurement to arrive.*

Prod – *(verb)* **1** poke with a finger pointed object, etc. *Her ceaseless prodding got on his nerves.* **2** stimulate or persuade to do something. *He prodded her into action.* *(noun)* **1** a poke. *She gave the donkey a prod on its backside.* **2** a stimulus or reminder. *She won't do it without a prod from you.* **3** a pointed implement, typically discharging an electric current and used as a goad. *He bought a cattle prod from the market.*

Prodigal – *(adjective)* **1** wastefully extravagant. *His prodigal habits will lead him to his own doom.* **2** lavish. *You are prodigal of both your toil and your talent.* *(noun)* a prodigal person. a person who leaves home to lead a prodigal life but returns repentant. *The prodigal son made a living of his own.*

Prodigy – *(noun)* a person, especially a young one, with exceptional abilities. an outstanding example of a quality. an amazing or unusual thing. *The child was growing into a prodigy.*

Produce – *(verb)* **1** make, manufacture, or create. or form as part of a physical, biological, or chemical process. *The yield produced a huge profit this year.* **2** cause to happen or exist. *She produced a delicious dinner for us tonight.* **3** provide for consideration, inspection, or use. *We had to somehow produce the evidence the next day.* **4** administer the financial and managerial aspects of or the staging of a play. supervise the making of a musical recording. *He produced two plays and a movie last year.* **5** extend or continue . *The company produces circuitry for communications systems.* *(noun)* things that have been produce or grown. the result of work or effects. *I buy organic produce whenever possible.*

Producer – *(noun)* a person, firm or country that makes goods for sale. *They are producers of high quality wine.*

Product – *(noun)* **1** an article or substance manufactured or refined for sale. a substance produced during a natural, chemical, or manufacturing process. a result of an action or process. *Try to get the best products at the lowest price.* **2** a person whose character has been formed by a particular period or situation.

He is a product of partition. **3** [mathematics] a quantity obtained by multiplying quantities together, or form an analogous algebraic operation. *What is the product of two and two?*

Production – *(noun)* **1** the action or process of producing or being produced. the amount of something produced. denoting a vehicle manufactured in large numbers, as opposed to a prototype or other special version. *Production and manufacture at the factory had reduced by at least three times ever since the company went bankrupt.* **2** a film, record, or play, viewed in terms of its making or staging. *Having been a successful actor, she was now venturing into production.*

Productive – *(adjective)* **1** producing or able to produce large amounts of goods, crops, etc. relating to or engaged in the production of goods, crops, etc. *The crop has been highly productive ever since we started using the new fertilizers.* **2** achieving or producing a significant amount or result. *They had a highly productive collaboration.* **3** producing. *The soil there was highly fertile and productive.* **4** currently used in forming new words or expressions. *He is a highly productive writer of fiction.* **5** [medicine] raising mucus from the respiratory tract. *He had caught a productive cough.*

Productivity – *(noun)* **1** the state or quality of producing something. *Productivity had increased five times this year.* **2** the effectiveness of productive effort. *Your productivity increases when you are with this team.* **3** [ecology] the fertility or capacity of a given habitat or area. *The soil has a high rate of productivity here.*

Profane – *(adjective)* **1** secular rather than religious. not initiated into religious rites. *I encouraged her to listen to more sacred and profane music.* **2** not respectful of religious practice. blasphemous or obscene. *Churches should not be used for secular or profane purposes.* *(verb)* treat with irreverence. *They have profaned the traditions of the Church.*

Profess – *(verb)* **1** claim that one has a quality or feeling. *She professes peace but her actions prove otherwise.* **2** affirm one's faith in or allegiance to a religion. be received into a religious order under vows. *The terrorists professed allegiance to their country.* **3** dated teach as a professor. *She professes organic chemistry.* **4** [archaic] have or claim knowledge or skill in. *He professes innocence.*

Profession – *(noun)* **1** a paid occupation, especially one involving training and a formal qualification a body of people engaged in a profession. *She has taken up stitching for a profession.* **2** an open but typically false claim *She is a profession of allegiance.* **3** a declaration of belief in a religion. the vows made on entering a religious order. the fact of being professed in a religious order. *He has a profession of Christianity.*

Professional – *(adjective)* **1** of, relating to, or belonging to a profession. worthy of or appropriate to a professional person. *The event was attended by several professionals such as doctors, engineers, lawyers, and the like.* **2** engaged in an activity as a paid occupation rather than as an amateur. *She is a now a professional astrologer.* **3** [informal] habitually engaged in a particular activity. *His mother calls him a professional timewaster.* *(noun)* a professional person. a person having impressive competence in a particular activity. *She has always been very professional at work.*

Professor – *(noun)* **1** a university academic of the highest rank; the holder of a university chair. [north American] a university teacher. *She works as a professor of English literature at the University now.* **2** a person who affirms a faith in or allegiance to something. *He is a professor of peace and love.*

Proficient – *(adjective)* competent; skilled. *She is proficient in Spanish language.*

Proficiency – *(noun)* a high degree of skill or expertise. *She has established her proficiency in the language.*

Profile – *(noun)* **1** an outline of something, especially a face, as seen from one side. *She asked the photographer to click a side profile.* **2** a vertical cross section of something. a flat outline piece of scenery on stage. *The geologist was trying to analyse the profile to see if he* *could get clues about the soil.* **3** a graphical or other representation of information recorded in quantified form. *The profile was well made but the content was rotten.* **4** a short descriptive article about someone. *We were asked to submit a profile about ourselves along with our portfolio.* **5** the extent to which a person or organization attracts public notice. *He has always maintained a low profile. (verb)* **1** describe in a short article. *She was trying to profile the debut actor.* **2** appear in outline. *He was profiled in a TV documentary about talented children.*

Profit – *(noun)* **1** financial gain, especially the difference between an initial outlay and the subsequent amount earned. *The company had made a profit of US$ 200,000000 this year.* **2** advantage; benefit. *They saw little profit in risking their lives to capture the militants. (verb)* benefit, especially financially. be beneficial to. *The dealers profited shamelessly at my family's cost.*

Profitable – *(adjective)* yielding profit or financial gain. *Drug manufacturing is the most profitable business in the US.*

Profound – *(adjective)* **1** very great or intense: profound social changes. severe. *The book was indeed profound.* **2** showing great knowledge or insight. demanding deep study or thought. *There was a profound silence after his talk.* **3** [archaic] very deep. *He gave a profound sigh. (noun)* poetic profound things; great depths. *The depth in the lyrics of the song was profound.*

Profundity – *(noun)* great depth of knowledge. *The profundity of this book had me baffled.*

Profuse – *(adjective)* **1** plentiful; abundant. *He was bleeding profusely by the time the doctor arrived.* **2** [archaic] extravagant. *They were profuse in their compliments.*

Profusion – *(noun)* an abundance or large quantity of something. *We came across a delightful river with a profusion of flowers growing along its banks.*

Progeny – *(noun)* offspring. *They set aside funds for the welfare of their progeny.*

Programme – *(noun)* **1** a planned series of events. a set of related measures or activities with a long-term aim. *He was admitted to a new programme at the university.* **2** a sheet or booklet detailing items or performers at an event. *You can't tell the players without a programme.* **3** a radio or television broadcast. *Did you catch his programme on TV last night?* **4** a series of coded software instructions to control the operation of a computer or other machine. *The programme required several hundred lines of code. (verb)* **1** provide with a program. input into a computer or other machine. *I can programme a new code for the software.* **2** cause to behave in a predetermined way. *Most VCRs can be programmed using a remote control.* **3** arrange according to a plan or schedule. plan; schedule. *His homework is more manageable because it has been programmed into his schedule.*

Progress – *(noun)* **1** forward or onward movement towards a destination. *The road was too rough to make any progress in the car.* **2** development towards a better, more complete, or more modern condition. *She is making progress in maths.* **3** [British archaic] a state journey or official tour. *The two states made little progress towards any dialogue. (verb)* **1** move or develop towards a destination or an improved or advanced condition. cause to make regular progress. *He progressed gradually along the coast.* **2** [astrology] calculate the position of all the planets and coordinates of a chart. *There are many ways in which astrologers 'progress' a chart.*

Progression – *(noun)* **1** a gradual movement or development towards a destination or a more advanced state. a succession. music a passage or movement from one note or chord to another. *Both the drugs slow the progression of the virus.* 2 a sequence of numbers following a mathematical rule. *We had to complete the arithmetic progression of the sequence given in the test paper.* **3** [astrology] a predictive technique in which the daily movement of the planets represents a year in the subject's life. *The astrologer mentioned the progression of Mars into her central square.*

Progressive – *(adjective)* **1** proceeding gradually or in stages: a progressive decline in popularity. increasing in severity. increasing as a proportion of the sum taxed as that sum increases. *He has been experiencing a progressive decline in popularity in the last few months.* **2** involving a series of sections for which participants successively change place. [archaic] engaging in or constituting forward motion. *The parties have been working towards progressive change.* **3** favouring social reform. favouring change or innovation. *He is a progressive politician.* **4** [grammar] denoting an aspect or tense of a verb expressing an action in progress, e.g. am writing. *The progressive form of the verb 'to walk' is 'is walking'.* *(noun)* a person advocating social reform. *The Republicans were split between progressives and conservatives.*

Prohibit – *(verb)* **1** formally forbid by law, rule, etc. *She was prohibited from leaving the country till a judgment was passed.* **2** prevent. *Smoking is prohibited within the office premises.*

Prohibitive – *(adjective)* **1** serving to forbid, restrict, or prevent. *Prohibitive regulations were set up for the welfare of the animals.* 2 excessively high. *The price was prohibitive.*

Project – *(noun)* **1** an enterprise carefully planned to achieve a particular aim. a proposed or planned undertaking. *The children were working on a community clean-up project.* **2** a piece of research work by a school or college student. *Students complete their projects at their own pace.* **3** [north American] a government -subsidized estate or block of homes. *The project plan by the government would have almost 300 apartments.* *(verb)* **1** estimate or forecast on the basis of present trends. *Africa's population is projected to double by 2015.* **2** protrude. *A piece of metal projected out of the side.* **3** throw or cause to move forward or outward. cause to fall on surface. cause to be heard at a distance. imagine as having moved to a different place or time. *The hardware can be used for projecting missiles.* **4** present or promote. display in one's behavior. *He projects his own ideas onto her.* **5** attribute an emotion to especially unconsciously. *I tried to project an idea about him into her mind.*

Projectile – *(noun)* a missile fired or thrown at a target. *At the museum we saw an ancient enormous artillery gun used to fire a huge projectile.* *(adjective)* **1** of or relating to a projectile. *The army museum had displayed several kinds of projectile weapons.* **2** propelled with great force. *The baby on the roller coaster let out a projectile vomit.*

Projection – *(noun)* **1** an estimate or forecast based on present trends. *The meeting involved a presentation on the company's sales projections for the next year.* 2 the projecting of an image, sound, etc. *3D movies require a special type of projection.* **3** the presentation or promotion of someone or something in a particular way. a mental image viewed as reality. *The philosopher insists that mental projections of reality are what actually form reality for every individual.* **4** the unconscious transfer of one's own desires or emotions to another person. *Even trained anthropologists have been guilty of unconscious projection during the time of experiment.* **5** a protruding thing. *There were spiky projections on top of the fence.* **6** a map or diagram made by projecting a given figure, area, etc. *The satellite map showed a new projection of land across the coast.*

Projector – *(noun)* **1** a device used to project rays of light, especially an apparatus for projecting slides or film on to a screen. *My colleague showed me how to use the projector for the presentation scheduled for the next day.* 2 [archaic] a person who plans and sets up a project. a promoter of a dubious enterprise. *He pictured to himself the anxious projector of the enterprise.*

Proletariat – *(noun)* **1** workers or working-class people often used with reference to Marxism. *Karl Marx's philosophy led to a war between the bourgeoisie and the proletariat.* **2** the lowest class of citizens in ancient Rome. *There is a shortage of skilled proletariat in this field.*

Proleferate – *(verb)* reproduce rapidly; increase rapidly in number. *A certain section of the population fears that nuclear weapons might proliferate.*

Prolific – *(adjective)* **1** producing much fruit or foliage or many offspring. *Closer planting will give you a more prolific crop.* **2** producing many works. *He is a prolific writer.* **3** plentiful. *We had a prolific pear tree near our house.*

Prologue – *(noun)* **1** a separate introductory section of a literary or musical work. an introductory scene in a play. *The prologue of the book was written in the form of a newspaper account.* **2** an event or action leading to another. *This is just the prologue, he threatened; the movie follows.*

Prolong – *(verb)* **1** extend the duration of. *We should not prolong the appointment with the doctor any more.* **2** [technical] extend in spatial length. *The foreign military aid was prolonging the war.*

Prominent – *(adjective)* **1** important; famous. *We had to invite a prominent personality as a chief guest for the event.* 2 protuberant. *A new theory is the most prominent feature in the book.* **3** particularly noticeable. *Your bushy eyebrows are quite prominent in the picture.* *(noun)* a drab-coloured moth with tufts on the forewings which stick up while it is at rest. *The prominents belong to the Notodontidae family of moths.*

Promise – *(noun)* **1** assurance that one will do something or that something will happen. an indication that something is likely to occur: the promise of spring. *I promise never to hurt you again.* **2** potential excellence. *He shows great promise in this field.* *(verb)* **1** make a promise. [archaic] be pledged to marry. *Promise that this will be done by tomorrow morning.* **2** give good grounds for expecting. *Promise to help her with the work.* **3** firmly intend. *She promised to see this till the end.*

Promote – *(verb)* **1** further the progress of; support or encourage. publicized. attempt to ensure the passing of a private act of parliament. *He wishes to promote this appeal.* **2** raise to a higher position or rank. *The boss announced that he will promote the boy in a month's time.* **3** [chemistry] increase the activity of a catalyst. *This chemical works to promote the production of that drug.*

Promotion – *(noun)* **1** activity that supports or encourages. *The actors were present for the promotion of their movie.* **2** the publicizing of a product or venture so as to increase sales or public awareness; a publicity campaign. the activity or business of organizing such publicity. *We need to keep an amount separately for promotions.* **3** the action of raising someone to a higher position or rank or the fact of being so raised. the transfer of a sports team to a higher division of a league. *His promotion is due since a year.*

Prompt – *(verb)* **1** cause or bring about. cause someone to take a course of action. *I wonder what prompted her to reply so caustically.* **2** assist or encourage supply a forgotten word or line to an actor. *My job is to prompt the lines during the play.* *(noun)* **1** an act of prompting a hesitating speaker. a word of phrase used in prompting a hesitating speaker. a word or phrase used in prompting an actor. a prompter. *The teacher prompted Phil when he forgot his lines.* **2** computing a word or symbol on a VDU screen to show that input is required. *When you click this button you will see the prompt jump two lines on the computer screen.* **3** the time limit for the payment of an account, stated on a prompt note. *The billing goes according to the prompt mentioned.*

Promulgate – *(verb)* promote or make widely known. put into effect by official proclamation. *The decree was promulgated across the town.*

Prone – *(adjective)* **1** likely or liable to suffer from, do, or experience. *She has always been prone to accidents.* **2** lying flat, especially face downwards. with the palm of the hand facing downwards. *The body lay prone on the bed.* **3** [archaic] with a downward slope or direction. *The sales are looking prone since the last couple of months.*

Prong – *(noun)* **1** each of two or more projecting pointed parts on a fork or other device. *I think she will need to use prongs here.* **2** each of the separate parts of an attack or operation. *This is not a diversion but a prong.* *(verb)* pierce or stab with a fork. *Why did you prong the sleeping man?*

Pronoun - *(noun)* a word used instead of a noun to indicate someone or something already mentioned or known, e.g. I, she, this. *Translate this sentence and underline any pronouns it might contain.*

Pronounce - *(verb)* **1** make the sound of a word or part of a word. *The kid can now pronounce some basic words.* **2** declare or announce. pass judgement or make a decision on. *I pronounce you knight to the royal family.*

Pronunciation - *(noun)* the way in which a word is pronounced. *She is good at writing but her pronunciation is really bad.*

Proof - *(noun)* **1** evidence establishing a fact or the truth of a statement. [law] the evidence in a trial. the proving of the truth of a statement. [archaic] a test or trial. a trial or a civil case before a judge without a jury. *I cannot believe all this without seeing any proof.* **2** a series of stages in the resolution of a mathematical or philosophical problem. *This is the umpteenth proof that got rejected by the council.* *(verb)* **1** make waterproof. *Proof the terrace with this paint.* **2** make a proof of printed work, engraving, etc. proofread. *I can only print the article after you proofread it.* **3** [north American] activate. knead until light and smooth. prove. *Prove the dough to a soft and spongy consistency.*

Prop - *(noun)* a portable object used on the set of a play or film. *This was supposed to be an important prop for tonight's show.* **2** [informal, dated] a property man or mistress. *He thinks that prop would reciprocate his feelings.*

Propaganda - *(noun)* information, especially of a biased or misleading nature, used to promote a political cause or point of view. the dissemination of such information. *The people opposed such shocking propaganda by the leaders.* **2** a committee of roman catholic cardinals responsible for foreign missions. *The pope wishes to meet the propaganda tomorrow.*

Propagate - *(verb)* **1** breed by natural processes from the parent stock. cause to increase in number or amount. *The new species could propagate without the drug.* **2** promote widely. *She always propagated her views on widow remarriages.* **3** transmit or/be transmitted in a particular direction. *The shuttle was propagated in the northern direction.*

Propel - *(verb)* drive or push for wards. drive into a particular situation. *Be careful not to propel the decision into the opposite direction.*

Propensity - *(noun)* an inclination or tendency. *As the temperature increases, the propensity to multiply also increases in the bacterial strain.*

Proper - *(adjective)* **1** truly what something is said or regarded to be; genuine: she's never had a proper job. strictly so called: the world cup proper. *He is exhibiting proper depression tendencies.* **2** suitable or appropriate; correct. respectable. *This is the proper etiquette.* **3** belonging or relating exclusively. *He is a proper idiot.* *(adverb)* [British informal] correctly. thoroughly noun the part of a church service that varies with the season or feast. *I wish to have a proper ceremony.*

Property - *(noun)* **1** a thing or things belonging to someone. *Do not eye another's property.* **2** a building and the land belonging to it. ownership. *He owns atleast four properties across the country.* **3** a characteristic of something. *List the properties of this element.* **4** old fashioned term for prop. *The play requires some innovative properties.*

Prophecy - *(noun)* a prediction the faculty or practice of prophesying. *The Mayan prophesy dictates that the Earth will perish in less than a month from today.*

Prophet - *(noun)* **1** an inspired teacher or proclaimed of the will of god. Muhammad. Joseph smith or one of his successors. *They read the teachings of the Prophet every morning.* **2** a person who predicts the future. a person who advocates a new belief or theory. *You think you are some prophet.* **3** the prophetic writings of the old testament. one of the three canonical divisions of the Hebrew bible. *She asked me to follow the teachings of the prophet regularly.*

Prophetic - *(adjective)* **1** accurately predicting the future. *Sometimes she seems so prophetic.* **2** of, relating to, or characteristic of a prophet or prophecy. *They believe he shows prophetic behavior at times.*

Propitiate - *(verb)* appease. *The tribes believed their dance would propitiate their Gods.*

Proponent - *(noun)* a person who ad vacates a theory, proposal, or project. *He is the proponent of this principle.*

Proportion - *(noun)* **1** a part, share, or number considered in relation to a whole. the ratio of one thin to another. the correct or pleasing relation of things or between the parts of a whole. *Take only in proportion to what others should take.* **2** dimensions; size. *Give me the room's proportions. (verb)* formal adjust so as to have a particular or suitable relationship to something else. *The quantity of colors bought should be in proportion to the canvas.*

Proportional - *(adjective)* **1** corresponding in size or amount to something else. *Keep the weights on one side, proportional to the weight of goods required.* **2** [mathematics] having a constant ratio to another quantity. *First step in the calculations is to find the proportional values and then we add them.*

Proportionate - *(adjective)* another term for proportional. *If the bricks are placed proportionate to the height, they will hold on for a longer period of time.*

Proposal - *(noun)* a plan or suggestion. the action of proposing something. *There have been many proposals for this construction site in the past few months.* 2 an offer of marriage. *At this rate he might never think of marriage proposals.*

Propose - *(noun)* **1** put forward an idea or plan for consideration by others. nominate for an office or position. put forward to a legislature or committee. *I propose we meet after you complete your exams.* **2** make an offer o marriage to someone. *We feel he would propose her any day now.*

Proposition - *(noun)* **1** a statement expressing a judgement or opinion. logic a statement expressing a concept that can be true or false. mathematic a formal statement of a theorem or problem. *This proposition needs to be proved using the right formulae.* **2** a proposed scheme or plan. US a constitutional proposal. *This law emerged from last year's propositions in the constitutional amendment.* **3** [informal] an offer of sexual intercourse. *He wanted to go for a formal proposition but she saw him right through it.* **4** a mater or person to be dealt with, with reference to the likelihood of a successful outcome. *He thinks she is a sensible proposition.* (verb) [informal] make an offer, especially of sexual intercourse, to. *I do not believe in proposition after the first date itself.*

Propound - *(verb)* put forward an idea, theory, etc. for consideration. *He wishes to propound a new plan of action.*

Proprietor - *(noun)* **1** the owner of a business. *I wish to have a meeting with the proprietor.* **2** a holder of property. *Who is the proprietor of this society?*

Propriety - *(noun)* correctness concerning standards of behavior or morals. the details or rules of conventionally accepted behavior. appropriateness; rightness. *She believes in maintaining propriety.*

Propulsion - *(noun)* the action of driving or pushing forward. *The right amount of propulsion will help the rocket take off in to the sky.*

Prosaic - *(adjective)* **1** having the style or diction of prose. *That poet had a prosaic style of writing.* **2** commonplace; unromantic. *The woman complained her husband was quite prosaic in public.*

Prose - *(noun)* **1** ordinary written or spoken language, without metrical structure. *He loved speaking in prose.* **2** another term for sequence *The dialogues should all be in prose. (verb)* **1** talk tediously. *He went on in prose while the back benchers dozed.* **2** dated compose in or convert into prose. *This is a copy of the play where the lines have been converted in to prose*

Prosecute - *(verb)* **1** institute legal proceedings against, institute legal proceedings in respect of a claim or focused or sued in a lawsuit *Trespassers will be legally prosecuted.* **2** continue with a view to completion. [archaic] carry on a trade or pursuit. *Do not prosecute that party before checking all details.*

Prosecution - *(noun)* **1** the prosecuting of someone in respect of a criminal charge. th party prosecuting someone in a lawsuit. *The prosecuting party walked up to the defendant.* **2** the continuation of a course of action with a view to its completion. *Prosecution of the current job will decide the course of future events.*

Prospect – *(noun)* **1** the possibility or likelihood of some future event occurring. a mental picture of a future or anticipated event. chances or opportunities for success. *What are her prospects are at winning tournament.* **2** a person regarded as a potential customer or as likely to be successful. *The boss considers him to have good prospects in the company.* **3** an extensive view of landscape. *Come on to the terrace to get a better prospect of the surroundings.* **4** a place likely to yield mineral deposits. *The government believes this area will be a good prospect. (verb)* search for mineral deposits, especially by means of drilling and excavation. *I suggest you look up prospects here before heading to the next town.*

Prospective – *(adjective)* expected or likely to happen or be in the future. *He looks like a prospective son – in – law.*

Prospectus – *(noun)* a printed booklet advertising a school or university or giving details of a share offer. *The application form will be provided along with the college prospectus.*

Prosper – *(verb)* succeed or flourish, especially financially, thrive. make successful. *I want you to prosper beyond anyone's imagination.*

Prosperity – *(noun)* the condition of being prosperous. *Wishing you prosperity and happiness as you embark upon the journey.*

Prosperous – *(adjective)* bringing wealth and success. *It is a joy to see him become so prosperous today.*

Prostitute *(noun)* a person, typically a woman, who engages in sexual activity for payment. offer as a prostitute. *Being a prostitute is considered to be unlawful in this country.*

Protagonist – *(noun)* **1** the leading character in a drama, film, or novel. a prominent figure in real situation. *You can never guess who the actual protagonist turns out to be.* **2** an advocate or champion of a cause or idea. *He is the main protagonist that led to the abolishing of the tyrant's rule.*

Protect – *(verb)* **1** keep safe from harm or injury. aim to preserve by legislating against collecting or hunting. *Wear woolens to protect yourself from the harsh winds.* 2 economics shield from competition by imposing import duties on foreign goods. *These fall under the protected goods category.* **3** provide funds to meet. *I wish to invest here to protect my children.*

Protection – *(noun)* **1** the action or state of protecting or being protected. a person or thing that protects. a document guaranteeing safety to the person specified in it. *She left me under their protection.* **2** the payment of money to criminals to prevent them from attacking oneself or one's property. *The thugs demanded protection from the poor shopkeepers.*

Protective – *(adjective)* **1** serving, intended, or wishing to protect. *I feel very protective of her.* **2** economics relating to protectionism. *(noun)* [British] a thing that protects. dated a condom. *Use the protective shield at all times.*

Protector – *(noun)* **1** a person or thing that protects. *I have always seen my father as my protector.* **2** [historical] a regent in charge of a kingdom during the minority, absence, or incapacity of the sovereign. the tile of Oliver Cromwell and his son Richard as heads of state in England 1653-9. *He willingly forsake all rights of being the protector in the absence of his brother.*

Protein – *(noun)* any of a class of nitrogenous organic compounds forming structural components of body tissues and constituting an important part of the diet. *You should include less proteins and more carbohydrate in your diet for the next few months.*

Protest – *(noun)* **1** a statement or action expressing disproval of or objection to something. an organized public demonstration objecting to an official policy or course of action. law a written declaration, typically by a notary public, that bill has been presented and payment or acceptance refuse. *The streets are filled with people who want to protest against the new law.* (verb) **1** express an objection to what someone has said or done. engage in public protest. *Better brace yourself for protests in the near future.*

Protestant - *(noun)* a member of follower of any of the western Christian churches that are separate from the roman catholic church in accordance with the principles of the information. *The protestant Christians of this town have always been a tolerant group. (adjective)* of, relating to, or belonging to any of the protestant churches. *Why should you hate the protestants?*

Protocol - *(noun)* **1** the official procedure or system of rules governing affairs of state or diplomatic occasions. the accepted code of procedure or behavior in a particular situation. *I cannot breach the protocol followed in such situations.* **2** the original draft of a diplomatic document, especially of the terms of a treaty agreed to in conference and signed by the parties. an amendment to a treaty of convention. *Do read the entire protocol before signing.* **3** a formal record of scientific experimental observations. a procedure for carrying out a scientific experiment or a course of medical treatment. *This is the basic protocol for this procedure.* **4** computing a set of rules governing the exchange or transmission of data between devices. *The problem seems to be in the protocol, so do make the necessary changes and try again.*

Prototype - *(noun)* **1** a first or preliminary form from which other forms are developed or copied. *Bacteria is considered to be a prototype to all animal forms.* **2** a typical example of something. *This is the prototype of the robots made by this firm. (verb)* make a prototype of. *Make a prototype of this experiment and include it in the presentation.*

Protracted - *(adjective)* lasting for a period longer than expected. *They just ended a much protracted divorce.*

Protrude - *(verb)* extend beyond or above a surface. cause to do this. *The broken log protruded out of the top floor window.*

Proud - *(adjective)* **1** feeling pride or satisfaction in one's own or another's achievements. poetic imposing; splendid. *He made us all proud of him today.* **2** having or showing a high opinion of oneself. conscious of one's own dignity. *The peacock is considered to be a proud bird.* **3** slightly projecting from a surface. overgrown round a healing wound. *The rash seems to proud after itching.*

Prove - *(verb)* **1** demonstrate by evidence or argument the truth or existence of. [law] establish the genuineness and validity of a will. *I will believe only if you can prove this.* **2** be seen or found to be: the scheme has proved a great success. demonstrate to be. demonstrate one's abilities or courage. *That proved to be the last straw to break the camel's back.* **3** subject to a testing process. *I have to prove this to my family.* **4** become aerated by the action of yeast; rise. *The dough proved by morning.*

Proven - *(verb & adjective)* demostrate the existence of a thing. *He will be treated as a convict until proven otherwise.*

Proverb - *(noun)* a short pithy saying in general use, stating a general truth or piece of advice. *"Making hay while the sun shines" is a very popular proverb.*

Proverbial - *(adjective)* **1** referred to in a proverb or idiom. *This feels like the proverbial catch-22 situation.* **2** well known, especially so as to be stereotypical. *She behaves like the proverbial albatross hanging on his neck.*

Provide - *(verb)* **1** make available for use; supply. equip or supply someone with. *Please provide me with the raw materials.* **2** make adequate preparation or arrangements for. enable or allow something to be done. *I order you to provide for this family.* **3** stipulate in a will or other legal document. *The old man provided enough and more for each of his children before he died.* **4** Christians church appoint an incumbent to a benefice. *The church has decided to provide him with an assistant.*

Provided - *(conjunction)* on the condition or understanding that. *She will listen to you provided you let her have her say afterwards.*

Providence - *(noun)* **1** the protective care of god or of nature as a spiritual power. god or nature as providing such care. *I certainly believe providence to be the reason for his success.* **2** timely preparation for future eventualities. *One should always adhere to providence.*

Provident - *(adjective)* making or inductive of timely preparation for the future. *He prefers to invest in provident funds.*

Providential - *(adjective)* **1** occurring at a favorable time; opportune. *Your appearing in the morning seem to be providential.* **2** involving divine foresight or interference. *It almost seems providential that they both received the same command.*

Province - *(noun)* **1** a principal administrative division of a country or empire. [British northern Ireland]. Christian church a district under an archbishop or a metropolitan. a territory outside Italy under a roman governor. *I do not recognize which province he belongs to.* **2** an area in which one has special knowledge, interest, or responsibility. *His province is mathematics and physics but he is weak in English.* **3** the whole of a country outside the capital, especially when regarded as lacking in sophistication or culture. *Your act seems to suggest you belong to the province.*

Provincial - *(adjective)* **1** of or concerning a province of a country or empire. *This battalion belongs to the provincial army.* **2** of or concerning the regions outside the capital city of a country, especially when regarded as unsophisticated or narrow minded. *He certainly seems to live in a provincial area.* *(noun)* **1** an inhabitant of a province of country or empire. *Let the provincial people solve this situation.* **2** an inhabitant of the regions outside the capital city of a country. *All her friends seem to be provincial.*

Provision - *(noun)* **1** the action of providing or supplying something supplied or provided. arrangements for future eventualities or requirements. *Please make the necessary provisions for their stay.* **2** supplies of food, drink, or requirements, especially for a journey. *I hope you have packed all the needed provisions for the trip.* **3** a condition or requirement in a legal document. *He has made provision to include your opinion.* **4** an amount set aside out of profits in the accounts of an organization for a known liability. *Ten percent will be kept aside for any provisions arising during the month.* *(verb)* **1** supply with provisions. *Phil wanted to supply him with all the necessary provisions.* **2** set aside a provision for a known liability. *Why do you set aside such a provision?*

Provisional - *(adjective)* arranged or existing for the present, possibly to be changed later. *This is just a provisional certificate and you will get the final document soon.* *(noun)* a member of the provisional wings of the IRA or sinn fein. *I never knew he worked under the provisional office of the secret service.*

Proviso - *(noun)* a condition attached to an agreement. *This has been clearly mentioned in the proviso I sent in the morning.*

Provocation - *(noun)* **1** the action of provoking. action or speech that provokes. law action or speech held to be likely to prompt physical retaliation. *Provocation would be my last resort.* **2** [medicine] testing to elicit a particular response or reflex. *Will provocation solve the matter?*

Provocative - *(adjective)* **1** causing annoyance, anger, or another strong reaction, especially deliberately. *Everyone avoids the provocative neighbor on the street.* **2** arousing sexual desire or interest, especially deliberately. *She signaled provocatively to the waiting policeman.*

Provoke - *(verb)* **1** stimulate in someone. *Do not provoke unnecessarily or the dog will bite you.* **2** deliberately annoy or anger. incite to do or feel something, especially by arousing anger. *I know you are trying to provoke me into fighting.*

Prow - *(noun)* the pointed front part of a ship; the bow. *The prow was the last bit to be seen slowly drowning into the waters.*

Prowess - *(noun)* **1** skill or expertise in a particular activity of field. *He not only plays the piano, but his prowess is also in writing stories.* **2** bravery in battle. *The prowess of the country's armies was well known throughout the world.*

Proximity - *(noun)* nearness in space, time, or relationship. *The rumbling sound assured us that the vehicle was in our proximity.*

Proxy - *(noun)* **1** the authority to represent someone else, especially in voting. a person authorized to act on behalf of another. *John* *would like to give proxy for his father William.* **2** figure used to represent the value of something in a calculations. *Just find the value to the proxy.*

Prude – *(noun)* a person who is easily shocked by matters relating to sex or nudity. *He is just pretending to be prude..*

Prudent – *(adjective)* acting with or showing care and thought for the future. *He is a prudent and miserly fellow.*

Prune – *(noun)* **1** a plum preserved by drying and having a black, winkled appearance. *She stared at the giant prunes strewn all over the backyard.* **2** [informal] a disagreeable person. *She is such a prune.*

Pry – *(verb)* enquire too intrusively into a person's private affairs. *I do not intend to pry, but if ever you need anything please let me know.*

Psalm – *(noun)* a sacred song or hymn, in particular any of those contained in the biblical book of psalms. a book of the bible comprising a collection of religious verses, sung or recited in both Jewish and Christian worship. *We have to memorize five psalms for the function on Sunday.*

Pseudo – *(adjective)* not genuine; fake, pretentious, or insincere. *I fired him as he was a pseudo at work. (noun)* a pretentious or insincere person. *I will not stand to tolerate any pseudo workers at my firm.*

Pseudonym – *(noun)* a fictitious name, especially one used by an author. *Many letters are sent to the editors under pseudonyms.*

Psych – *(verb)* **1** [informal] mentally prepare for a testing takes or occasion. intimidate an opponent or rival by appearing very confident or aggressive. *His confidence sometimes looks like a plan to psych the opponent before the duel.* **2** [informal] subject to psychological investigation or psychotherapy. *He thinks she is a psych and needs help.* **3** make a psychic bid. *Do not psych that old man. (noun)* **1** [informal] a psychiatrist or psychologist. *He is the best psych in town.* **2** bridge a psychic bid. *Matt thinks you are trying to psych him out.*

Psyche – *(noun)* the human soul, mind, or spirit. *Tom loves to study the psyche of his fellow team mates.*

Psychiatry – *(noun)* the branch of medicine concerned with the study and treatment of mental illness, emotional disturbance, and abnormal behavior. *Psychiatry is a never ending study.*

Psychiatrist – *(noun)* a medical practitioner specializing in the diagnosis and treatment of mental illness. *Please show her to a good psychiatrist soon.*

Psychic – *(adjective)* **1** relating to or denoting facilities or phenomena that are apparently inexplicable by natural laws, especially involving telepathy or clairvoyance. appearing or considered to be telepathic or clairvoyant. *Ever since she has been meditating, she has become increasingly psychic.* **2** of or relating to the soul or mind. *I do not believe in all this psychic talk.* **3** bridge denoting a bid that deliberately misrepresents the bidder's hand, in order to mislead the opponents. *He tried to be psychic to confuse the opponent. (noun)* **1** a person considered or claiming to have psychic powers; a medium. *The priest is widely known to be a psychic.* **2** the study of psychic phenomena. *He has been researching on psychic phenomena since the past few years.*

Psychoanalysis – *(noun)* a system of psychological theory and therapy which aims to treat mental disorders by investigating the interaction of conscious and unconscious elements in the mind and bringing repressed fears and conflicts into the conscious mind. *The company policies call for a psychoanalysis of each new recruit.*

Psychology – *(noun)* **1** the scientific study of the human mind and its functions, especially those affecting behavior in a given context. *A parent always understands the psychology of the child.* **2** the mental characteristics or attitude of a person. the mental factors governing a situation or activity. *I cannot understand the psychology of the individual who commits a crime and feels proud about it.*

Psychopath – *(noun)* a person suffering from chronic mental disorder with abnormal or violent social behavior. *The police declared the man a psychopath and warned his friends to be careful around him.*

Psychotherapy - *(noun)* the treatment of mental disorder by psychological rather tan medical means. *She has trained in psychotherapy treatment under the guidance of this professor.*

Pub - *(noun)* **1** an establishment for the sale and consumption of beer and other drinks, often also serving food. *He often heads to the nearest pub after work.* **2** austral a hotel. *I would like to meet them at that popular pub in town. (verb)* [informal] frequent pubs. *Let us go pub out.*

Puberty - *(noun)* the period during which adolescents reach sexual maturity and become capable of reproduction. *Most of the female chimpanzees seem to have crossed their puberty years.*

Public - *(adjective)* **1** of, concerning, or open to the people as a whole. involved in the affairs of the community, especially in government or entertainment: a public figure. *This is her first public performance in two years.* **2** done, perceived, or existing in open view. *I only state the public opinion here.* **3** of or provided by the state rather than an independent, commercial company. *He works in the public sector domain.* (noun) ordinary people in general; the community. *You really believe that you can fool the public easily.*

Publication - *(noun)* **1** the action or process of publishing something. *Which publication house have you approached?* 2 a book o journal that is published. *The professor has nearly a dozen publications to his credit.*

Publicity - *(noun)* notice or attention given to someone or something by the media. the giving out of information for advertising or promotional purposes. material or information used for such a purpose. *He attributed his popularity to all the publicity he does for his books.*

Publicize - *(verb)* **1** make widely known. *Be careful not to publicize the issue any further.* **2** give out publicity about; advertise or promote. *I need your help in order to publicize my work on a national level.*

Publish - *(verb)* **1** prepare and issue for public sale. print in a book or journal so as to make generally known. *How many copies have been published so far?* **2** formally announce or read. *The final judgement was published in all leading newspapers.* **3** [law] communicate to a third party. *You need to publish your case.*

Pucker - *(verb)* tightly gather or contract into wrinkles or small folds. *The child puckered under his mother's angry eyes. (noun)* a wrinkle origin. *Her skin seems to never pucker.*

Pudding - *(noun)* **1** a cooked sweet dish served after the main course of a meal. chiefly the dessert course of a meal. [north American] a dessert with a soft or creamy consistency. *My favorite dessert is chocolate pudding.* **2** a sweet or savoury steamed dish made with suet and flour. *She wants to have pudding after lunch today.* **3** the intestines of a pig or sheep stuffed with oatmeal, spices, and meat and boiled. *She doesn't like pudding with potatoes.* **4** [informal] a fat, dumpy, or stupid person. *Her friend is quite a pudding when it comes to studies.*

Puddle - *(noun)* **1** a small pool of liquid, especially of rainwater on the ground. *The children loved sailing their paper boats in the puddle.* **2** clay and sand mixed with water and used as a watertight covering for embankments. *The strength of these embankments is due to the quality of puddle used.* **3** rowing a circular patch of disturbed water made by the blade of an oar at each stroke. *As the oarsmen kept paddling in synchronization, we observed similar puddles in the waters. (verb)* **1** cover with or form puddles. *Do not puddle the entrance.* **2** dabble or wallow in mud or shallow water. informal occupy oneself in disorganized or unproductive way. *She has puddle away most of her year.* **3** line with puddle. knead into puddle. work water and clay to separate gold or opal. *The goldsmith uses a puddle when he has to separate the gold.*

Puff - *(noun)* **1** a short burst of breath or wind. a small quantity of vapour or smoke emitted in one blast. an act of drawing quickly on a pipe, cigarette, or cigar. [informal] berth. *The man huffed and puffed as he walked up the alley.* **2** a light pastry case containing a sweet or savour filling. *The gild waited for the guests to leave* *and then opened the puff box slowly.* **3** [informal] a complimentary review of a book, play, etc. British an advertisement. *I think we need to puff this article well.* **4** a gathered mass of material in a dress or other garment. *Puffed sleeves are the latest fashion trend.* **5** a rolled protuberant mass of hair. *The puffed hairstyle is a thing of the past.* **6** [north American] an eiderdown. *The children loved curling into their favorite orange colored puffs at night.*

Puffin – *(noun)* a hole-nesting northern auk with a large head and a massive brightly coloured triangular bill. *My friend sent me this photograph of a beautiful puffin stuttering around in their yard.*

Puke – *(verb & noun)* [informal] vomit. *This stench makes me want to puke.*

Pull – *(verb)* **1** exert force on so as to cause movement towards oneself or the origin of the force. be attached to the front and be the source of forward movement of a vehicle. remove by pulling. [informal] bring out for use. British - draw from a barrel to serve. inhale deeply while drawing on a cigarette. damage by abnormal strain. *Try pulling the door knob towards you.* **2** move steadily: the bus pulled away. move one's body against resistance. *She pulled the thread off the present.* **3** attract as a customer; cause to show interest. *They pulled us in to their conversation.* **4** [informal] cancel or withdraw an entertainment or advertisement. arrest. check the speed of especially so as make it lose a race. *Due to an accident he had to pull out of the race in the last minute.*

Pulley – *(noun)* a wheel with a grooved rim around which a cord passes, used to raise heavy weights. a wheel or drum fixed on a shaft and turned by a belt, used to increase speed or power. *I can haul this rock to the upper landing with the pulley.* *(verb)* hoist with a pulley. *The minister hoisted the national flag with the help of a pulley.*

Pulp – *(noun)* **1** a soft, wet, shapeless, mass of material. the soft fleshy part of a fruit. a soft wet mass of fibers derived from rags or wood, used in papermaking. *The pulp is kept out in the sun to harden up.* **2** vascular tissue filling the interior cavity and root canals of a tooth. *The pain was primarily due to an infection in the pulp.* **3** mining pulverized ore mixed with water. *The miners wanted the expert to check the ingredients of the pulp obtained.* *(verb)* **1** crush into a pulp. *The huge truck crushed the car into a pulp.* **2** withdraw from the market and recycle the paper. *Is this where you form the pulp?*

Pulpit – *(noun)* **1** a raised enclosed platform in a church or chapel from which the preacher delivers a sermon. *The churchgoers waited patiently for the Bishop to step on to the pulpit.* **2** raised platform in the bows of a fishing boat or whaler, a guard rail enclosing a small area at the bow of a yacht. *The entire catch for the day was spread out on the pulpit.*

Pulsate – *(verb)* **1** expand and contract with strong regular movements. *The doctor exclaimed that the body still pulsated feebly.* **2** produce a regular throbbing sensation or sound. *The gong pulsated over the countryside.*

Pulse – *(noun)* the edible seeds of various leguminous plants, e.g. lentils. the plant or plants producing such seeds. *Pulses are a rich source of proteins in our diet.*

Pulverize – *(verb)* **1** reduce to fine particles. *The aliens pulverised the entire building into a huge heap of rubble.* **2** [informal] defeat utterly. *Do not attack once you have pulverized the enemy.*

Pump – *(noun)* **1** [chiefly north English] a plimsoll. *He refused to come jogging with us as he couldn't find his pumps.* **2** a light shoe for dancing. *The dancer looked graceful in her gown and complementing pumps.* **3** [north American] a court shoe. *Do you get these pumps in any other color?*

Pumpkin – *(noun)* **1** a large rounded orange-yellow fruit with a thick rind and edible flesh. *We have a pumpkin farm in the backyard.* **2** a plant of the gourd family bearing this fruit, native to warm regions of America. *She loves the sweetness of ripe pumpkins.* **3** [British] another term for squash. *She made delicious pumpkin pie for dissect.*

Pun – *(noun)* a joke exploiting the different meanings of a word or the fact that there are words of he same sound and different meanings. *He loves to include pun in his speech. (verb)* make a pun. *It was hilarious to note that she could not note the pun intended.*

Punch – *(verb)* **1** strike with the fist. *Stop immediately or else I will punch you hard.* **2** press a button or key on a machine. [north American] clock in or out. *We are planning to install a punching machine at the entrance.* **3** [north American] drive by prodding them with a stick. *Why did you punch that old beggar on the street? (noun)* **1** a blow with the fist. *Please do not punch him.* **2** [informal] effectiveness; impact. *The entire audience erupted as the hero delivered one punch dialogue after another for nearly 10 minutes.*

Punctual – *(adjective)* **1** happening or doing something at the appointed time. *She believes in being punctual to the last second.* **2** [grammar] of or denoting action that takes place at a particular point in time. contrasted with durative. *His christmas parties are a punctual affair for the whole town.*

Punctuate – *(verb)* **1** occur at intervals throughout. interrupt an activity with. *His rhythmic snoring seemed to punctuate the silence of the night.* **2** insert punctuation marks in. *He carefully punctuated his phrases so as to not offend the listener.*

Punctuation – *(noun)* the marks, such as full stop, comma, and brackets, used in writing to separate sentences and their elements and to clarify meaning. the use of such marks. *I wish you write this sentence by changing the punctuation marks.*

Puncture – *(noun)* a small hole caused by a sharp object, especially one in tyre. *Where can I get my punctured tyre mended? (verb)* **1** make a puncture in. *Puncture into the snow to let the animal out.* **2** cause a sudden collapse of a mood, feeling, etc. *What did you say to puncture her mood?*

Pungent – *(adjective)* **1** having a sharply strong taste or small. *The kitchen had a pungent smell of rotten eggs.* **2** sharp and caustic. *They tricked him to tasting the pungent liquid.*

Punish – *(verb)* **1** inflict a penalty on as retribution for an offence. inflict a penalty on someone for an offence. *His father would certainly punish him today.* **2** treat harshly. *Why do you punish the poor child?*

Punishable – *(adjective)* subject to punishment. *Littering the streets is a punishable offence.*

Punishment – *(noun)* **1** the action of punishing or the state of being punished. the penalty inflicted. *He deserves the harshest punishment possible for this crime.* **2** [informal] rough treatment. *It is a punishment in itself to talk sense into you.*

Punitive – *(adjective)* inflicting or intended as punishment. *This is such a punitive remark from you.*

Punk – *(noun)* **1** a loud, fast-moving, and aggressive form of rock music, popular in the late 1970s. an admirer or player of such music. *My parents loved punk during their college days.* **2** [informal chiefly] a worthless person; a thug or criminal. *Do not believe hid his punk as he will surely trick you.* **3** US [informal] a passive male homosexual. *He his his punk characteristic from his family.* **4** [chiefly north American] soft crumbly wood that has been attached by fungus, used as tinder. *The carpenter asked us to beware of punk wood. (adjective)* **1** [north American] [informal] bad; worthless. *I feel so punk and depressed.* **2** of or relating to punk rock and its associated subculture. *He wishes to know more about the punk music culture of the previous decade.*

Puny – *(adjective)* **1** small and weak. *I am not affected by your puny threats.* **2** meager. *After a whole day's work, they are paid a puny wage.*

Pupil – *(noun)* **1** a person who is taught by another, especially a schoolchild. *The teacher observed the pupil sleeping in the last row.* **2** [British] a trainee barrister. *You need to apprentice as a pupil before practicing on your own in court.*

Puppet – *(noun)* **1** a movable model of a person or animal, typically moved either by strings or by a hand inside it. used to entertain. *The charlatan pretended to belong to the puppet show party.* **2** a person under the control of another. *He is a puppet in her hands.*

Puppetry – *(noun)* a movable model by strings of a person or animal used for entertainment.*She is holding a workshop on traditional puppetry this Saturday.*

Puppy – *(noun)* **1** a young dog. *The children promised to take good care of the puppy.* **2** [informal, date] a conceited or arrogant young man. *Stop being such a puppy and behave maturely.*

Purchase – *(verb)* **1** buy. *He just purchased the painting to gift his wife.* **2** nautical haul up by means of a pulley or lever. *The captain ordered a purchase as the wind changed course. (noun)* **1** the action of buying. a thing bought. law the acquisition of property by one's personal action and not by inheritance. *I would like to purchase a house in this neighbourhood.* **2** firm contact or grip. *His purchase left her grimacing in pain.* **3** a pulley or similar device for moving heavy objects. *The workmen needed a purchase to move the heavy boulder from the road.* **4** [archaic] the annual rent or return from land. *It is smart to invest here as the purchase is much higher as compared to the town.*

Pure – *(adjective)* **1** not mixed or adulterated with any other substance or material. *This is pure gold.* of unmixed origin or descent. **2** innocent or morally good. *He is a pure soul.* **3** perfectly in tune and with a clear tone. *This is pure music to ones ears.* **4** theoretical rather than practical. compare with applied. *His thesis is based on pure sciences as opposed to applied sciences.* **5** complete; nothing but. *This is purely blasphemous.* **6** phonetic not joined with another to form a diphthong. *This is the pure thing.*

Purge – *(verb)* **1** rid of an unwanted feeling or condition. *I wish to purge myself of this emotional baggage.* **2** remove from an organization or place. *It is best to purge him from this organization.* **3** remove by a cleansing process. *The hospital needs to be purged regularly.* **4** evacuate one's bowels, especially as a result of taking a laxative. *The doctor asked the patient to purge himself before the operation.* **5** [law] atone for or wipe out contempt of court. *The victim was purged of his charges. (noun)* an act of purging people from an organization or place. *The dictator purged all those from their jobs, who dared raise their voice against him.*

Purify – *(verb)* remove contaminants from; make pure. *Camphor is considered to purify the surroundings.*

Purification – *(noun)* remove contaminants from. *The temple priests demanded a purification ceremony.*

Puritan – *(noun)* **1** a member of a group of English protestants who regarded the reformation of the church under Elizabeth I as incomplete and sought to simplify and regulate forms of worship. *The puritans always were a bane to the church.* **2** a person with censorious moral beliefs, especially about self-indulgence and sex. *His ideas mark him to be a sure puritan. (adjective)* **1** or relating to the puritans. *Puritans across the world will reunite soon.* **2** characteristic of a puritan. *Do not mingle with him as he is a puritan by thought.*

Purity – *(noun)* the state of being pure. *The goldsmith rubbed the ring on his stone to check for its purity.*

Purl – *(adjective)* made by putting the needle. *The cloth has a purl stitch.* through the front of the stitch from right to left. compare with plain. *(verb)* knit with a purl stitch. *The new sewing machine has facilities of doing the purl stitch.*

Purple – *(noun)* **1** a colour intermediate between red and blue. *The sky turned a dark shade of purple in the setting sun.* **2** a crimson dye obtained form some mollusks, formerly used for fabric worn by an emperor or senior magistrate in ancient Rome or Byzantium. a position of rank, authority, or privilege. *Purple is considered to be a favourite colour of the royals.* **3** the scarlet official dress of a cardinal. *The absent minded servant spilled milk on the purple garment of his cardinal. (adjective)* of a colour intermediate between red and blue. *I need a purple scarf to match my skirt. (verb)* become or make purple in colour. *As she blushed, her cheeks turned purple.*

Purpose – *(noun)* **1** the reason for which something is done of for which something exists. *What is the purpose of studying all night if you* *end up sleeping during the exam.* **2** resolve or determination. *Once you decide the purpose of the experiment, half your job is done. (verb)* formal have as one's objective. *What is your purpose in attempting to malign her reputation?*

Purr – *(verb)* **1** make a low continuous vibratory sound expressing contentment. *The cat purred contentedly as she lazed around in the winter sun.* **2** move or run smoothly while making a similar sound. *The car purred silently into the night. (noun)* a purring sound. *The stillness of the mountain was disturbed by a strange purring sound.*

Purse – *(noun)* **1** a small pouch of leather of plastic used for carrying money. *The lady let out a scream as the thief ran off with her purse.* **2** [north American] a handbag. *I think I would like a small purse as a wedding present.* **3** an amount of money available; funds. a sum of money given as a prize in a sporting contest. *The king allotted a generous purse to the winner. (verb)* pucker or contract. *She tried to purse her lips in pain as the doctor gave her an injection.*

Pursue – *(verb)* **1** follow in order to catch or attack. *Do not try to pursue him or you might get hurt.* **2** seek to attain. *The sage wished to pursue mental peace and stability.* **3** proceed along. *Let bygones be bygones and do not pursue the matter any further.* **4** follow or continue with a course of action. continue to investigate or discuss. *I think the case is not solved and that the police need to pursue the suspects.*

Pursuit – *(noun)* **1** the action of pursuing. *The police gave pursuit to the escaping convicts.* **2** a recreational or sporting activity. *Why don't you take up a hobby to pursuit in your free time?* **3** a cycling race in which competitors set off from different parts of a track and attempt to overtake one another. *This was his first attempt at a track pursuit.*

Purview – *(noun)* **1** the scope of the influence or concerns of something. *What is the purview of this brand on the market?* **2** a range of experience or thought. *I always have faith in my teacher's purview regarding all matters.*

Push – *(verb)* **1** exert, force on in order to move them away from oneself. hold and exert force on so as to cause it to move in front of one. move one's body or a part of it forcefully into a specified position. exert pressure with an oar etc. so as to move a boat out form a bank. *Push the table back into the corner.* **2** move forward by using force. go in front of people who are already queuing. proceed with or continue a course of action. [British informal] go away; depart. *Keep pushing the water and you will soon move on.* **3** urge to greater effort. demand persistently. *Do not try to push your luck this far.* **4** [informal] promote the use, sale, or acceptance of. sell illegally. *His ideas gave a good push to the sales figures.* **5** [informal] have very little of something, especially time. *Take your own sweet time and do not push yourself too much.* **6** informal be nearly. *Do not push me into believing all that he says. (noun)* **1** an act of pushing. *Why do you have to push your way through every argument.* **2** a vigorous effort. forcefulness and enterprise. *The doctor asked the pregnant lady to push hard.* **3** [informal] something that is hard to achieve. *You need to push yourself initially but then soon the journey feels easy.*

Pushy – *(adjective)* excessively self-assertive or ambitious. *No one likes the pushy kid in her class.*

Put – *(verb)* **1** move to or place in a particular position. proceed in a particular direction: the boat put out to sea. *Please put the books back in the right order.* **2** bring into a particular state or condition: they tried to put me at ease. express in a particular way: to put it bluntly, he was not really divorced. *Why don't you put your expertise to this case?* **3** cause to carry or be subject to something: commentators put the blame on congress. assign a particular value, figure, or limit to. *Did you put out the fire?* **4** throw as an athletic sport. *He threw short put really far. (noun)* a throw of the shot or weight. *Put the plate on the table.*

Putrefy – *(verb)* decay or rot and produce a fetid smell. *The abandoned flat had a putrefied odour to it.*

Putty - *(noun)* **1** a malleable paste, made from whiting and raw linseed oil, that gradually hardens and is used chiefly for sealing glass in window frames. a malleable substance used as a filler, modeling material, etc. *The architect suggested using the latest brand of putty instead of the usual brand.* **2** a polishing powder, usually made from tin oxide, used in jewellery work. *Applying the putty is the last work before you have the finished jewellery in your hand.* *(verb)* seal or cover with putty. *You can trust me with your secrets. I can cover them with putty.*

Puzzle - *(verb)* **1** confuse because difficult to understand. *Do not try to puzzle me with your riddled speech.* **2** think hard about something difficult to understand. *The whole story was such a puzzle.* *(noun)* knowledge. *If you think you are smart enough then try solving this puzzle.* **2** a puzzling person or thing. *Matt believes in speaking the truth and not being so puzzling to others.*

Puzzled - *(adjective)* unable to understand. *He looked puzzled as the police asked him to show his license.*

Pygmy - *(noun)* **1** a member of certain peoples of very short stature in equatorial Africa or parts or SE asia. *Consider yourself lucky that you were not caught by the indigenous pygmy clan in the jungle.* **2** chiefly derogatory a very small person or thing. *Be careful before calling anyone a pygmy.* **3** a person who is deficient in a particular respect: an intellectual pygmy. *She is behaving like an intellectual pygmy.* *(adjective)* very small; dwarf. *She isn't a pygmy but as compared to her 7 foot tall husband she looks the part.*

Pyjamas - *(plural noun)* **1** a jacket and loose trousers for sleeping in. *Whatever I may forget, I can never forget to carry my pyjamas during any trip.* **2** loose trousers with a drawstring waist, worn by both sexes in some Asian countries. *The thief was caught as he tried jumping from the height and his pyjamas got stuck on a low pole.*

Pylon - *(noun)* **1** a tall tower-like structure for carrying electricity cables. *The electrician needed a pylon to carry all the cables.* **2** a pillar-like structure on the wing of an aircraft used for carrying an engine or other load. *The detective suspects that the pylon got burnt which led to the accident.* **3** a tower, or post marking a path for light aircraft, cars, or other vehicles, especially in racing. *The driver of the racing car swept past the last pylon to claim his victory.* **4** a monumental gateway to an ancient Egyptian temple, formed by two truncated pyramidal towers. *The structure excavated looks like a pylon of an ancient Egyptian temple.*

Pyramid - *(noun)* **1** a monumental stone structure with a square or triangular base and sloping sides that meet in a point at the top, especially one built as a royal tomb in ancient Egypt. *Who build the pyramids in Egypt is still a mystery waiting to be solved.* **2** [geometry] a polyhedron of which one face is a polygon and the other faces are triangles with a common vertex. *The meditation hall is the structure which looks like a giant pyramid.* **3** [anatomy] a pyramid-shaped structure, especially in the brain. *The children formed a human pyramid to reach the top.* **4** a system of financial growth achieved by a small initial investment. *The tax planner suggested some investments that would guarantee a pyramid like growth in the future.* **5** a game played on a billiard table with fifteen coloured balls arranged in a triangle and a cue ball. *The boys have gone to the club to have a game of pyramid.* *(verb)* [chiefly north American] heap or stack in a pyramidal shape. *The shopkeeper stacked the goods in a pyramidal pattern for the customers to choose easily.*

Pyre - *(noun)* a heap of combustible material, especially one for burning a corpse as part of funeral ceremony. *Matt was inconsolable as he lit his father's pyre.*

Python - *(noun)* a large non-venomous snake which kills prey by constriction. *The highlight of our safari trip was a python we found lying on the side of the road.*

Qq

Q – *(noun)* **1** the seventeenth letter of the alphabet. *Eleventh letter of the alphabet.* **2** denoting the next after P in a set of items, categories, etc.

Q-boat – *(noun)* a boat used by Germany during WWII. *Germany had used q-boats to chase boats and ships of allied forces.*

Qua – *(conjunction)* in the capacity of. *equity holders qua members must attend the meeting called by the company.*

Quack – *(noun)* the characteristic harsh sound made by a duck. *Ducks make the sound of quack, quack! (verb)* make this sound.

Quackery – *(noun)* a person who claims to have special skills but is not. *Quackery is the cause of many deaths.*

Quackish – *(adjective)* in the manner of aquack. *Quackish treatment leads to medical complications.*

Quadragesimal – *(adjective)* belonging or appropriate to the period of Lent. *During lent, many Christians observe fast to repent for wrong doving they may have committed.*

Quadrangle – *(noun)* a four sided geometrical figure, especially a square or rectangle. *He has a quadrangle courtyard at the back of his house.*

Quadrangular – *(adjective)* having four sides. *Quadrangular teams were playing against one another in a big playground.*

Quadrant – *(noun)* **1** each of four parts of a circle, plane, body, etc. divided by two lines or planes at right angles. *A quadrant is used for measuring angles.* **2** an instrument for taking angular measurements, consisting of a graduated quarter circle and a sighting mechanism. *A quadrant is an instument used to measure angles upto 90°.*

Quadrate – *(noun)* a squarish bone in the skull of a bird or reptile, with which the jaw articulates. *The upper connects to the lower jaw by the quadrate bone. (adjective)* roughly square or rectangular. *This plot seems quadrate.*

Quadrennial – *(adjective)* lasting for or recurring every four years. *The term of my computer course is quadrennial.*

Quadrilateral – *(noun)* a four sided figure. *I want to buy a quadrilateral plot. (adjective)* having four straight sides. *Humans have few quadrilateral muscles.*

Quadruple – *(adjective)* **1** consisting of four parts or elements. *Four teams formed a quadruple alliance.* **2** consisting of four times as much or as many. *Eight is the quadruple of digit two. (noun)* a quadruple thing, number, or amount. *The trapeze artist performed a quadruple.*

Quadruplicate – *(adjective)* consisting of four parts or elements. *Please make quadruplicate copies of this document.*

Quag – *(noun)* a marshy or boggy place. *The animal fell in a quag.*

Quagmire – *(noun)* a soft boggy area of land that gives way underfoot. *His downfall was to get trapped in the quagmire of dirty politics.*

Quail – *(noun)* a small short tailed game bird. *While in jungle, he shot some quails.*

Quaint – *(adjective)* attractively unusual or old fashioned. *It is a quaint little piece of art.*

Quake – *(verb)* **1** shake or tremble. *His legs quaked with fear as a violent crowd confronted him.* **2** shudder with fear. *The rumbling vibrations felt by the people made administration search for safety measures. (noun)* an earthquake. *Many describe earthquake as a quake.*

Qualifiable – *(adjective)* minimum acceptable level. *Qualifiable speeds for 100 metres race have been announced.*

Qualified – *(adjective)* certified as being trained to perform a job. *He is fully qualified for this job.*

Qualifier - *(noun)* a person or a team that qualifies for a competition. *He was the sixth and the last qualifier for one-mile race.*

Qualitative - *(adjective)* of, concerned with, or measured by quality. often contrasted with quantitative. *The difference is qualitative and not quantitated.* **2** describing the quality of something in size, appearance, etc. *His qualitative talk was impressing.*

Quality - *(noun)* **1** the standard of something as measured against other things of a similar kind. general excellence. high social standing. *Although rude, he has many qualities.* **2** a distinctive attribute or characteristic. *He has high quality social standing. The quality of these goods is simply superb.*

Quandary - *(noun)* a state of uncertainty over what to do in a difficult situation. *He was in a quandary as he found no place in the hostel.*

Quantitative - *(adjective)* of, concerned with, or measured by quantity. often contrasted with qualitative. *It is not the qualitative put the quantitative value of these things that counts.*

Quantity - *(noun)* **1** a considerable number or amount. *Our success depends upon the quantity of goods that we produce.* **2** the property of something that is measurable: wages depended on quantity of output, regardless of quality. *I can't handle such huge quantity of assignments.*

Quarrel - *(noun)* **1** an angry argument or disagreement. *He picked up a quarrel with his neighbour.* **2** a reason for disagreement. *He quarreled against the injustice done to him.*

Quarry - *(noun)* a place, typically a large pit, from which stone or other materials may be extracted. *The mining mafia is extracting lots of minerals from illegally dug quarries.* *(verb)* extract from a quarry. cut into to obtain stone or other materials. *Limestone is quarried for use in blast furnaces.*

Quart - *(noun)* a unit of liquid capacity equal to a quarter of a gallon or two pints, equivalent in Britain to approximately 113 litres and in US to approximately 0.94 litre. a unit of dry capacity equivalent to approximately 110 litres. *I bought two quarts of milk.*

Quarterage - *(noun)* a sun paid or received quarterly. *The quarterage sum is only rupees four thousand.*

Quarterly - *(adjective)* **1** produced or occurring once every quarter of a year. *The installments are quarterly payable.* **2** divided into quarters. *(adverb)* **1** once every quarter of a year. **2** in the four, or in two diagonally opposite, quarters of a shield. *(noun)* a publication produced four times a year. *Many health magazines are published quarterly.*

Quartern - *(noun)* a fourth part as a unit of measurement. *A quartern loaf is used for mating sandwich.*

Quartz - *(noun)* a hard mineral consisting of silica, typically occurring as colourless or white hexagonal prisms. *Quartz watches are quite popular.*

Quasi - *(comb. form)* seemingly: quasi scientific. *I think this statement is quasi scientific.*

Quaternary - *(adjective)* **1** fourth in order or rank. *He is a quaternary officer.* **2** relating to or denoting the most recent period in the Cenozoic era, following the tertiary period. *The quaternary period comprises of pleistocene and holocene epochs.*

Quaternion - *(noun)* a complex number of the form w + xi + yj + zk, where w, x, y, z are real numbers and I, j, k are imaginary units that satisfy certain conditions. *Quaternion is a theory in identities in algebra.*

Quatrain - *(noun)* a stanza of four lines, typically with alternate rhymes. *This quatrain belongs to a famous poem.*

Quatre-foil - *(noun)* an ornamental design of four lobes or leaves, resembling a flower or clover leaf. *The flowers were arranged in quatre-foil for the design of carrings.*

Quaver - *(verb)* tremble. *He quavered as he ran.* *(noun)* a tremble in a voice. *He spoke with a quaver.*

Quean - *(noun)* an impudent girl or woman. *She is a quean and as such not worth talking to.*

Queasiness - *(noun)* in the manner of feeling sick. *Queasiness overwhelmed me and I threw up.*

Queasy – *(adjective)* **1** nauseous. inducing nausea. *The smell in the kitchen was queasy.* **2** slightly nervous or worried. *He appears queasy.*

Queer – *(adjective)* **1** strange; odd. slightly ill. *I feel queer may be because I am running a temperature.* **2** homosexual. *He is a queer and as such shunned by society.* *(verb)* spoil or ruin. *He queered our plans by spreading rumours about our night long trip.*

Quench – *(verb)* **1** satisfy by drinking. *He quenched his thirst by drinking a few glasses of water.* **2** satisfy. *The fire was quenched in time.* **3** extinguish. rapidly cool. *The cries of the animal quenched as it was set free.* **4** stifle. reduce to silence. *Anger rose in him but he quenched it.* *(noun)* an act of quenching something very hot. *The red hot metal was quenched by dropping in cold water.*

Quenelle – *(noun)* a small seasoned ball of fish or meat. *Quenelle is being cooked.*

Querist – *(noun)* a questioner. *Here is a querist for you to answer.*

Quern – *(noun)* a simple hand mill for grinding grain, typically consisting of two circular stones. *Querns may still be in use in villages.*

Querulous – *(adjective)* complaining in a petulant or whining manner. *She became querulous as her husband rebuked her.*

Quest – *(noun)* **1** a long or arduous search. *Quest for pyramids had begun in early twentieth century.* **2** an expedition by a knight to accomplish a prescribed task. *Indian kings found the quest of finding lost treasury fascinating.* *(verb)* search for something. *David Levingstone toured Southern Africa in quest of finding the source of River Zembezi.*

Questionable – *(adjective)* **1** open to doubt. *Your behaviour is questionable.* **2** of suspect morality, honesty, value, etc. *The police arrested hem due to his questionable movements.*

Questionnaire – *(noun)* a set of printed questions, usually with a choice of answers, devised for a survey or statistical study. *Kindly fill this questionnaire, a survey is going on.*

Quibble – *(noun)* **1** a slight objection or criticism. *Quibble started after his talk to the press.* **2** a pun. *He quibbled over a very small matter.* *(verb)* argue about a trivial matter. *Stop quibbling about matters of little significance.*

Quick – *(adjective)* **1** moving fast or doing something in a short time. lasting a shot time. prompt. *He is a quick fellow and acts immediately.* **2** intelligent. alert. *Quick and appropriate action saved his life.*

Quicken – *(verb)* **1** make or become quicker. *As she approached me, my heart beat quickened.* **2** stimulate or be stimulated. give or restore life to. make burn brighter. *His pulse quickened after he received intensive treatment.*

Quicklime – *(noun)* a white caustic alkaline substance consisting of calcium oxide, obtained by heating limestone. *Quicklime is obtained from limestone.*

Quickly – *(adjective)* promptly. *He quickly jumped into water to save her from drowning.*

Quicksand – *(noun)* loose wet sand that sucks in anything resting on it. *He was pulled out timely from being sucked into quicksand.*

Quickset – *(noun)* hedging, especially of hawthorn, grown from slips or cuttings. *Quickset was thick and nobody could enter.*

Quick-silver – *(noun)* liquid mercury. *His moods change rapidly like quick-silver.*

Quick-witted – *(adjective)* showing an ability to think or respond quickly. *Birbal was a quick-witted courtier of Akbar.*

Quid – *(noun)* one pound sterling. *He used to save one quid every day.*

Quiddity – *(noun)* the inherent nature or essence of a person or thing. *Quiddity of a person hardly changes.*

Quiescent – *(adjective)* in a state or period of inactivity. *He is quiescent these days, recovering from illness.*

Quiet – *(adjective)* **1** making little or no noise. free from activity, disturbance, or excitement. undisturbed; uninterrupted. *I like this quiet place.* **2** discreet, moderate, or restrained. tranquil and reserved. unobtrusive. *(noun)* silence; calm. *It was a quiet and peaceful prayer.* *(verb)* make or become quiet. *He is a quiet and peaceful man.*

Quietus - *(noun)* 1 death or a cause of death, regarded as a release from life. *The man is dead, we have to find the quietus.* 2 something calming or soothing. *The night in the mountain village was very quietus.*

Quinate - *(noun)* a salt in chemistry. *Easter of quinic acid is known as quinate.*

Quince - *(noun)* 1 a hard, acid, pear shaped fruit used in preserves or as flavouring. *Quince a fruit, grows on shrubs in Asia and is used for flavoring.* 2 the Asian shrub or small tree which bears this fruit. *Quinine is a shrub from which medicines is made.*

Quinine - *(noun)* a bitter crystalline compound present in cinchona bark, used as a tonic and formerly as an antimalarial drug. *Quinine used to be taken against malaria.*

Quin-quennium - *(noun)* a period of five years. *It is a quin-quennium course of computer training.*

Quinsy - *(noun)* inflammation of the throat, especially an abscess near the tonsils. *He had pain in throat as he suffered from quinsy.*

Quintal - *(noun)* 1 a unit of weight equal to a hundredweight or, formerly, 100 IB. *He purchased a quintal of wheat grain.* 2 a unit of weight equal to 100 kg. *Ten quintals make a metric ton.*

Quintessential - *(adjective)* representing the most perfect or typical example. *She is a quintessential of beauty.*

Quintet - *(noun)* a group of five people playing music or singing together. a composition for such a group. *The band was played by a quintet.*

Quintuple - *(adjective)* consisting of five parts or elements. *Ten is the quintuple of two.* *(verb)* increase or be increased fivefold. *His business has quintupled in last five years.*

Quintuplicate - *(adjective)* fivefold. *You need to have quintuplicate copies of this document.* *(verb)* multiply by five. *He got quintuplicate copies made of his original certificate.*

Quintuply - *(adverb)* increase five times. *The company's profits quintuplied last year.*

Quip - *(noun)* a witty remark. *A quip is usually on his lips.* *(verb)* make a quip. *She usually quips.*

Quirk - *(noun)* 1 a peculiar behavioural habit. *A quirk of fate destroyed his career.* 2 a strange chance occurrence. *He has a quirk of non-stop talking.* 3 a sudden twist, turn, or curve. *The bus quirked and he almost fell down.*

Quit - *(verb)* 1 leave, especially permanently. *He has quit smoking.* 2 resign from. *'Quit India' movement gained strength in forties.* 3 stop or discontinue. *I want to quit somking.* *(adjective)* rid of. *She wants to be quit of him.*

Quite - *(adverb)* 1 absolutely; completely. US very; really. *You are quite right in saying this.* 2 fairly; moderately. *He was quite nice throughout the talks.*

Quitter - *(noun)* a person who gives up easily. *He is a quitter and never stays in one job.*

Quits - *(adjective)* two people disagreeing to work together. *We are quits now, there should be no longer any grudge.*

Quiver - *(noun)* an archer's portable case for arrows. *All archers carry quivers on their back.*

Quivevingly - *(adverb)* trembling with a visible rapid motion. *He quiveringly told us about his horror dream.*

Quivive - *(noun)* on the alert or lookout. *Every soldier has to be very quivive on border.*

Quixotic - *(adjective)* impractically idealistic or fanciful. *His quixotic behaviour amused her.*

Quixotism - *(noun)* being extremely idealistic. *Sometimes his quixotism is very upsetting.*

Quixotry - *(noun)* attitude of being unrealistic. *We are tired of his quixotism in seaching for cleen hotels.*

Quiz - *(noun)* a test of knowledge, especially as a competition for entertainment. *Can you solve this quiz?* *(verb)* 1 question. 2 give an informal written test to. *He was quizzed about his behaviour*

Quizzically - *(adverb)* amusingly strangle. *He answered all my questions quizzically.*

Quod - *(noun)* prison. *He spent five years in quod.*

Quoin - *(noun)* an external angle of a wall or building. *Most building in the hills were made with coloured quoins.* *(verb)* provide with quoins. *The yellow coloured walls were quoined with red sandstone blocks.*

Quoit – *(noun)* a ring of iron, rope, or rubber thrown in a game to encircle or land as near as possible to an upright peg. a game of aiming and throwing quoits. *He won many prizes in the game of quoit.*

Quota – *(noun)* **1** a limited quantity of a product which may be produced, exported, or imported. *There is only 30 per cent quota fixed for the export of these goods.* **2** a share of something that one is entitle to receive or bound to contribute. *My quota is 10 per cent profit in these sales.* **3** a fixed number of a group allowed to do something, e.g. immigrants entering a country. *This month's quota for immigrants is 500.* **4** the minimum number of votes required to elect a candidate. *Some communities are demanding 10 per cent of reservation quota.*

Quotable – *(adjective)* suitable for or worth quoting. *There are many quotable words in his speech. It is a quotable quote.*

Quotation – *(noun)* **1** a group of words from a text or speech repeated by someone other than the originator. a short musical passage or visual image taken from one piece of music or work of art and used in another. the action of quoting from a text, work of art, etc. *Let us buy this book of famous quotations.* **2** a formal statement of the estimated cost of a job or service. a price offered by a market maker for the sale or purchase of a stock. *The quotation of the firm providing such services is Rs. 5 lakh.* **3** a registration granted to a company enabling their shares to be officially listed and traded. *The quotation from the text reads "There are no short cuts to success."*

Quote – *(verb)* **1** repeat or copy out. repeat a passage or statement from. *He quoted Gandhiji many times in his speech.* **2** put forward or describe someone or something as being. *The actual group of words of the originator is presented in quotation marks.* **3** give someone. name someone or something at. *The railway spoken was quoted as saying that all trains are running on time now.* *(noun)* **1** a quotation. *This is a quote from Napoleon Hill.* **2** quotation marks. *Double quotes are used to emphasize actual words said by the speaker.*

Quotient – *(noun)* a result obtained by dividing one quantity by another. *Four divide by two has the quotient two.*

Rr

R – *(noun)* **1** the eighteenth letter of the alphabet. **2** denoting the next after Q in a set of items, categories, etc.

Rabbi - *(noun)* **1** a Jewish scholar or teacher, especially of Jewish [law]. *There was a Rabbi among the rebels who were against anti-abortion laws in Ireland.* **2** a Jewish religious leader. *We arranged for a Rabbi to come just in time for her last minutes.*

Rabbit - *(noun)* **1** a burrowing gregarious plant-eating mammal, with long ears, long hind legs, and a short tail. the fur of the rabbit. [north American] a hare. *There were cute little rabbits running around in the farm.* **2** [informal] a poor performer in a sport or game. *He was a total rabbit on the field.* **3** [US] a runner acting as pacesetter. *They had a rabbit in their team too, just to set the pace.* **4** [British informal] a conversation. *We had a fun rabbit about it!* *(verb)* **1** hunt rabbits. *We were hunting for places where we could go rabbiting.* **2** [British informal] chatter. *The warden shouted at us to stop rabbiting and go to sleep!*

Rabble - *(noun)* **1** a disorderly crowd. *A rabble of uncouth young men greeted the minister outside the court.* **2** ordinary people regarded as socially inferior or uncouth. *The British had no qualms about favouring the aristocracy and rejecting the pleas of the rabble.*

Rabid - *(adjective)* **1** extreme; fanatical. *She is a rabid feminist, known for her scathing remarks to the ministers and politicians.* **2** of, relating to, or affected with rabies. *He got bitten by a rabid dog.*

Race - *(noun)* **1** each of the major divisions of humankind, having distinct physical characteristics. racial origin or distinction. an ethnic group. a group descended from a common feature. *People of all races, colour and creed are welcome to our country.* **2** [biology] a distinct population within a species; a subspecies. *Almost two of the races of tigers are extinct due to extensive poaching.*

Racial - *(adjective)* **1** of or relating to a race. *Racial minority is a one of the reasons why the Blacks are still suffering today.* **2** relating to relations or differences between races. *Racial oppression is still rampant in our society.*

Racism - *(noun)* **1** the belief that there are characteristics, abilities, or qualities specific to each race. *We were taught theories of racism in Sociology class today.* **2** discrimination against or antagonism towards other races. *Racism is still rampant in the US society today.*

Rack - *(noun)* a horse's gait between a trot and a canter. *The horse's rack had everyone smiling.* *(verb)* move with such a gait. *Rack up, mate! You're getting late.*

Racket - *(noun)* **1** a bat with a round or oval frame strung with catgut, nylon, etc., use especially in tennis, badminton, and squash. *The rackets are out and the players are ready!* **2** [chiefly north American] a snowshoe resembling this. *He wore a weird looking show, something like a racket.*

Radar - *(noun)* a system for detecting the presence, direction, and speed of aircraft, ships, etc. by sending out pulses of radio waves which are reflected back of the object. *The ship was frantically sending radar messages hoping someone will respond.*

Radial - *(adjective)* **1** of or arranged like rays or the radial of a circle; diverging in lines from a common centre. running form a town centre to an outlying district. *Four mosaics having a radial arrangement were placed on a mat.* **2** denoting a tyre in which the layers of fabric have their cords running at right angles to the circumference of the tyre. *We need radial tyres for better performance of the vehicle.* **3** denoting an internal combustion engine with its cylinders fixed like the spokes of a wheel around a rotating crankshaft. *The radial was repaired and the aircraft had no more complaints.* **4** [anatomy & zoology] of or relating to the radius. *The teacher explained the concept of radials in the class today. (noun)* **1** a radial tyre. *We bought radial tyres for the vehicle today.* **2** [zoology] a supporting ray in a fish's fin. *The fish's radials had been torn.*

Radiant - *(adjective)* **1** shining or glowing brightly. emanating great joy, love, or health. emanating powerfully. *We met a radiant sage at the hermitage in the forest today.* **2** transmitted by electromagnetic radiation, rather than conduction or convection. emitting radiant energy for cooking or heating. *The teacher taught us how plants convert radiant energy of the sun into chemical energy. (noun)* **1** a point or object from which light or heat radiates. *One of the radiants of my gas fire was missing.* **2** [astronomy] the apparent focal point of a meteor shower. *Staring at the radiant won't give you the best view of the meteor shower.*

Radiate - *(verb)* **1** emit in the form of rays or waves. be emitted in such a way. emanate a strong feeling or quality. *The stars radiate energy.* **2** diverge from or as if from a central point. used in names of animals with markings arranged like rays. *The radiated tortoise stood staring at the grills.* **3** [biology] evolve into a variety of forms. *Plants radiate easily. (adjective)* rare radial. *A radiate was found in the attic.*

Radiation - *(noun)* **1** the action or process of radiating. *The boy suffering from cancer has been exposed to high level radiation.* **2** [physics] energy emitted as electromagnetic waves or subatomic particles. *Background radiation should help the scene.*

Radical - *(adjective)* **1** of, relating to, or affecting the fundamental nature of something. innovative or progressive. *We need a radical transformation of the existing legal system.* **2** thorough and intended to be completely curative. *The treatment will be radical and quite helpful for you.* **3** advocating thorough political or social reform; politically extreme. [British historical] belonging to an extreme section of the liberal party in the 19th century. *He is known for being a radical right wing activist.* **4** [mathematics] of the root of a number or quantity. *Check the sequence of the radicals here.* **5** denoting or relating to the roots of a word. *Mention the radicals of the given words here.* **6** [music] belonging to the root of a chord. *The music manager corrected our radicals.* **7** [botany] of or coming from the root or stem base of a plant. *The botany teacher showed us radicals of the plants in the lab. (noun)* **1** an advocate of radical political or social reform. *He is a right wing radical.* **2** [chemistry] a group of atoms behaving as a unit in a number of compounds. *Calculate the radicals for the given compounds.* **3** [mathematics] a quantity forming or expressed as the root of another. *Calculate the radicals of the given numbers.*

Radio - *(noun)* **1** the transmission and reception of radio waves, especially those carrying audio messages. *Radio stations were demanding the eviction of the RJ from the Big Brother show.* **2** broadcasting sound. a broadcasting station or channel. *All the radio stations in the city were being vandalized by the right wing group.* **3** an apparatus for receiving radio programme. an apparatus capable of receiving and transmitting radio messages. *Dad bought his first radio when he was thirty. (verb)* send a message by radio. communicate with,by radio. *We radioed for help immediately.*

Radioactive - *(adjective)* emitting or relating to the emission of ionizing radiation or particles. *The water was radioactive.* [radiography] *He worked in the radiography department of the hospital.*

Radish - *(noun)* **1** a pungent-tasting edible root, typically small, spherical, and red, and eaten raw. *There were radishes of all kinds in the farm.* **2** the plant of the cabbage family which yields this root. *We decided to plant radishes in our kitchen garden.*

Radium – *(noun)* the chemical element of atomic number 88, a radioactive metal of the alkaline earth series. *Radium was used on clocks to make dials.*

Radius – *(noun)* **1** a straight line from the centre to the circumference of a circle or sphere. a radial line from the focus to any point of a curve. *The radius of a circle is half its circumference.* **2** a specified distance from a centre in all directions. *There are several pubs within a two mile radius.* **3** anatomy a bone of the forearm or forelimb, in humans the thicker and shorter of two. *His radius had cracked in the accident.* **4** [zoology] a radially symmetric feature in an echinoderm or coelenterate, e.g. an arm of a starfish. *The radius of the insect was delicate and transparent.* **5** [entomology] a main vein in an insect's wing. *The butterfly was delicate and its radius was visible.* *(verb)* make a corner or edge rounded. *Try radiusing the paper mould.*

Raffle – *(noun)* a lottery with goods as prized. *I bought a raffle ticket at the mall.* *(verb)* offer as a prize in a raffle. *A toy was to be raffled for the appeal tomorrow.*

Raft – *(noun)* **1** a flat buoyant structure of timber or other materials fastened together, used as a boat or floating platform. a small inflatable boat. *Pi was stranded on a raft in the middle of the sea for 200 days.* **2** a floating mass of fallen trees, ice, etc. *They decided to collect the raft materials and save themselves.* **3** a foundation of reinforced concrete for a building. *The raft is ready, the building is on its way.* *(verb)* **1** travel or transport on or as if on a raft. *Pi rafted across the ocean for 200 days.* **2** make into or transport as a raft. *The stores were rafted ashore.*

Rafter – *(noun)* a beam forming part of the internal frame-work of a roof. *The rafters above the bed were falling off.*

Rag – *(noun)* **1** a piece of old cloth, especially one torn from a larger piece. old or tattered clothes. *I wiped my hands on a rag after cleaning the walls.* **2** the remnants of something. *Her fancy dress was reduced to rags.* **3** [informal] a low quality newspaper. *The local rag reported the affair of the actor.* *(verb)* give a decorative effect to by applying paint with a rag. *The background walls have been ragged below.*

Rage – *(noun)* **1** violent uncontrollable anger. violent anger associated with conflict arising form a particular context: air rage. the violent action of a natural agency. *Her face was distorted with rage.* **2** a vehement desire or passion. poetic prophetic, poetic, or martial enthusiasm or ardour. *A rage of emotions filled her heart.* **3** [austral] a lively party. *The campus was resounding with the sound of the rage.* *(verb)* **1** feel or express range. continue violently or with great force. *We raged at the futility of the police's action.* **2** [austral] enjoy oneself socially. *Let's get ready to rage!*

Ragged – *(adjective)* **1** old and torn, wearing such clothes. *The tramp wore ragged clothes on his body and a radiant smile on his face.* **2** rough or irregular. having a rough, shaggy coat. lacking finish, smoothness, or uniformity. printing uneven. *We noticed a ragged coastline nearby.* **3** suffering from exhaustion or stress. *She looked a bit ragged from the game.*

Raid – *(noun)* **1** a rapid surprise attack on people or premises. *A bombing raid was carried out in the desert.* **2** a surprise visit by police to arrest suspects or seize illicit goods. *There was a police raid at his home.* **3** stock exchange a hostile attempt to buy a controlling interest in the shares of a company. *There has been a raid on his company now.* *(verb)* **1** conduct a raid on. *His office and house were both raided by the IT Department.* **2** quickly and illicitly take something from a place. *Stealthily she stepped downstairs to steal the iPhone.*

Rail – *(verb)* complain or protest strongly. *She railed at the police inefficacy in the high profile murder case.*

Railing – *(noun)* a fence or barrier made of rails. *The thief jumped over the railing and escaped.*

Railway – *(noun)* [chiefly British] **1** a track made of rails along which trains run. *The railway tracks badly needed maintenance.* **2** a system of such tracks with the trains, organization, and personnel required for its working. *The freight carriage on the railways was lying in the shed.*

Rain - *(noun)* **1** the condensed moisture of the atmosphere falling visibly in separate drops. falls of rain. *I love dancing in the rain!* **2** a large quantity of things falling or descending. *A rain of blows descended on the thief.* *(verb)* **1** rain falls. poetic send down rain. *It's going to rain this evening.* **2** be terminated or cancelled because of rain. *She told me that raining on someone's event was the worst thing you could do to them.* **3** fall or cause to fall in large quantities. *It was just raining dust following volcanic eruption.*

Rainbow - *(noun)* **1** an arch of colours visible in the sky. caused by the refracting and dispersion of the sun's light by water droplets in the atmosphere. *There was a beautiful rainbow visible from my window.* **2** a wide range of things of different colours or kinds. *There was a rainbow of colours in my wardrobe.*

Rainy - *(adjective)* having or characterized by considerable rainfall. *It is going to be a rainy month now.*

Raise - *(verb)* **1** lift or move to a higher position or level. set upright. *Raise the curtain rod a bit higher.* **2** construct or build. *The building was raised last year.* **3** increase the amount, level, or strength of. promote to a higher rank. *She has been demanding a raised salary for some time now.* **4** [mathematics] multiply a quantity to a specified power. *3 raised to the 7th power is 2187.* **5** bet more than another player. higher bid in the same suit as that bid by one's partner. *I'll raise the bid by another fifty dollars.* **6** cause to be heard, felt, or considered. *Doubts have been raised.* **7** generate an invoice or other document. *I have raised an invoice for the document.* **8** collect or levy money or resources. *We hope the event will raise at least Rs 5,000.* **9** bring up a child. *She was born and raised in New Delhi.* *(noun)* **1** [chiefly north American] an increase in salary. *He has been demanding a raise and some perks too.* **2** an act of raising a stake or bid. *His raise was a bluff.* **3** weightlifting an act of lifting or raising a part of the body while holding a weight. *He has been working on his raise so he can ensure at least one medal.*

Raisin - *(noun)* a partially dried grape. *I bought raisins for the cake.*

Rake - *(noun)* a fashionable or wealthy man of dissolute habits. *He is known for being a merry restoration rake.*

Rally - *(verb)* [archaic] tease. *I've been rallied throughout high school for my funny hair.*

Ram - *(noun)* **1** an uncastrated male sheep. *There were scores of rams on the farm.* **2** short for battering ram. *Obelix threw the ram on to the unsuspecting Roman.* **3** the falling weight of a pile-driving machine. *The ram was ready to fall.* **4** a hydraulic water-raising or lifting machine. the piston of a hydrostatic press. the plunger of a force pump. *The piston of the ram seemed to be loose.* **5** [historical] a projecting part of the bow of a warship, for piercing the sides of other ships. a warship with such a bow. *The ram of the ship was glowing in the distance.* *(verb)* **1** roughly force into place. *He rammed the stick into the hole in the ground.* **2** be driven violently into. *The naval ship rammed into the pirate ship and crashed.* **3** crash violently against. *The van rammed into the post.* **4** beat with a heavy implement to make it hard and firm. *The walls are made of rammed earth.*

Ramble - *(verb)* **1** walk for pleasure in the countryside. *I wanted a vacation where I can ramble aimlessly among trees in the woods.* **2** grow over walls, fences, etc. *There were climbers rambling over the walls.* **3** talk or write at length in a confused or inconsequential way. *She has been rambling for some time now.* *(noun)* a walk taken for pleasure in the countryside. *They are out on a ramble.*

Ramification - *(noun)* **1** the action or state of ramifying or being ramified. *His angiogram showed a ramification of the right coronary artery.* **2** a complex consequence of an action or event. *Your action is bound to have legal ramifications.* **3** a subdivision of a complex structure or process. *We have an extended family with its ramifications of neighbouring in-laws.*

Ramp - *(noun)* **1** a sloping surface joining two different levels. *They had built a wheelchair ramp to make the hospital disabled-friendly.*

2 a movable set of steps for entering or leaving an aircraft. *We were waiting for the ramp to be set so we could get out of the flight.* **3** [British] a transverse ridge in a road to control the speed of vehicles *The ramp was almost ready to be used.* **4** [north American] an inclined slip road leading to or from a main road or motorway. *There is an exit ramp that you should follow while going out.* **5** an upward bend in a stair rail. *People had started using the ramp more frequently now.* **6** an electrical waveform in which the voltage increases or decreases linearly with time. *The voltage ramp was damaged.* **7** [British, informal] a swindle involving a fraudulent increase of the price of a share. *The police is investigating the fraudulent share ramps.* *(verb)* **1** provide with a ramp. *The place has been ramped now to make it disabled-friendly.* **2** increase or decrease in voltage linearly with time. *The circuit's voltage ramps negatively.* **3** [British] purchase shares or other securities in order to raise their price fraudulently. *The rule against share price ramping has finally been passed.* **4** especially in reference to the production of goods increase or cause something to increase in amount. *Production has been ramped up, thus benefiting the company.*

Rampage – *(verb)* rush around in a violent and uncontrollable manner. *The protestors rampaged around the whole city.* *(noun)* an instance of rampaging. *Thieves went on a rampage in the house.*

Rampant – *(adjective)* **1** flourishing or spreading unchecked. *Corruption is rampant in our country.* **2** unrestrained in action or performance. *The rampant corruption in governmental offices needs to be checked.* **3** lush in growth. *Police has controlled the rampant chain snatching incidents in this area.* **4** [heraldry] represented standing on its left hind foot with its forefeet in the air. *They had a lion rampant drawn on the flag.*

Ramshackle – *(adjective)* in a state of severe disrepair. *I was shocked to see the ramshackle cottage he lived in.*

Ranch – *(noun)* **1** a large farm, especially in the western US and Canada, where cattle or other animals are bred. *She has been living in a ranch for several years now.* **2** [north American] a single-storey house. *I bought a ranch in the countryside.* **3** [north American] a type of thick white salad dressing made with sour cream. *Get the ranch for the salad ready before the guests arrive.* *(verb)* run a ranch. breed on a ranch. use as a ranch. *She has been breeding on a ranch and even bought some more animals.*

Rancid – *(adjective)* smelling or tasting unpleasant as a result of being stale. *We could smell the rancid meat from outside.*

Rancour – *(noun)* bitterness; resentment. *He spoke without rancour.*

Random – *(adjective)* **1** made, done, or happening without method or conscious decision. *It was evident from the result that she had made a random decision.* **2** [statistics] governed by or involving equal chances for each item. *A random sample of 50 families was taken for the survey.* **3** of masonry or something similarly constructed with stones or components of irregular size and shape. *Random stones lay around at the work site.*

Range – *(noun)* **1** the area of variation between limits on a particular scale. *The cost for this house will range between Rs 25 lakh to Rs 35 lakh.* **2** a set of different things of the same general type. *Revlon offers a range of products.* **3** the scope or extent of a person's or thing's abilities or capacity. *The film shows some range of his skills.* **4** the distance within which a sense, detector, transmitter, etc. is effective. the distance that can be covered by a vehicle or aircraft without refueling. the distance attained or attainable by a gun, projectile, etc. the distance between a camera and the subject to be photographed. *Hand held photos taken at extreme ranges can be a shaky affair.* **5** a line or series of mountains or hills. *We learnt to identify the Himalayan Range on the global map.* **6** a large area of open land for grazing or hunting. *The tourists were ready to survey the range.* *(verb)* **1** vary or extend between specified limits. *There were vehicles with prices ranging from Rs 15 lakh to 25 lakh.* **2** run or extend in a line in a particular direction. *He is often seen on the benches ranging along the path.* **3** place or arrange in a row or rows or in a specified order or manner. *The benches were ranged along the path.* **4** place oneself or be placed in opposition to. *The Japanese ranged themselves against the British.* **5** [British] printing align or be aligned at the ends of successive line. *Please range these in the correct alignment.* **6** travel or wander over a wide area. *Patrols ranged along the international border area.*

Rangefinder – *(noun)* an instrument for estimating the distance of an object, especially for use with a camera or gun. *She bought a new fancy rangefinder to be attached to her camera.*

Rank – *(adjective)* **1** growing too thickly. *There were clumps of rank grass in her garden.* **2** having a foul smell. *Breathing rank air is no mean task.* **3** conspicuously undesirable; flagrant. *Presence of criminals is rank outside this Solemn gathering.*

Rankle – *(verb)* **1** cause annoyance or resentment. [chiefly] annoy or irritate. *His mannerisms still rankle.* **2** [archaic] continue to be painful; fester. *The wound still rankles somewhere below.*

Ransack – *(verb)* **1** go hurriedly through sterling things and causing damage. *The thieves had ransacked every house in the whole village.* **2** thoroughly search. *He had ransacked the company for his benefit.*

Ransom – *(noun)* a sum of money demanded or paid for the release of a captive. *The kidnappers had demanded a ransom of Rs 15 lakh.* *(verb)* obtain the release of by paying a ransom. detain and demand a ransom for their release. release after receiving a ransom. *The kid had to be ransomed.*

Rant – *(verb)* speak or shout at length in a wild, impassioned way. *The politician was ranting about the opposition's demonstrations outside his house.* *(noun)* a spell of ranting. *She opened her mouth and out came a spell of ranting!*

Rap – *(noun)* the smallest amount. *He doesn't care a rap.*

Rapacious – *(adjective)* aggressively greedy. *Rapacious landlords are ruling the countryside to this day!*

Rape – a plant of the cabbage family with bright yellow flowers, especially a variety grown for its oil-rich seed and as stock feed. *There were rape seeds in the nursery.*

Rapid – *(adjective)* happening in a short time or at great speed. *The rapid economic decline of the country brought huge changes in its people's lifestyles.* *(noun)* a fast-flowing and turbulent part of the course of a river. *The raft was jumping in and around the rapid.* *(noun)* [geography] the part of river where flow of water is very turbulent and fast. *The raft was stuck in one of the rapids.*

Rapport – *(noun)* a close and harmonious relationship in which there is common understanding. *I share a good rapport with my colleagues and employer.*

Rapt – *(adjective)* **1** fully absorbed and intend; fascinate. *The therapist had a rapt teenage audience at his introduction speech.* **2** enraptured. *The kids listened with rapt attention.* **3** austral, [informal] another term for wrapped. *The new minister was rapt with his new portfolio.* **4** [archaic] transported bodily. *He was rapt on high.*

Rapture – *(noun)* **1** a feeling of intense pleasure or joy. *My daughter listened to my stories with rapture.* **2** the expression of intense pleasure or enthusiasm. *The paparazzi went into raptures about her.* **3** [north American] the transporting of believers to haven at the second coming of Christ. *Thousands of Christians had gathered, awaiting the Rapture.*

Rare – *(adjective)* **1** occurring very infrequently. *The bird is rarely seen during this time of the year.* **2** remarkable: a player of rare skill. *He is a player of rare skill.*

Rarefied – *(adjective)* **1** of lower pressure than usual; thin. *Trudging uphill in rarefied air can turn out to be the most difficult task.* **2** very esoteric or refined. *He has rarefied scholarly pursuits planned.*

Raring – *(adjective)* [informal] very eager to do something. *She was raring to go.*

Rarity – *(noun)* **1** the state or quality of being rare. *Honesty and integrity are a rarity in people today.* **2** a rare thing. *To take the morning off is indeed a rarity.*

Rascal – *(noun)* a mischievous or cheeky person, especially a child. *Dennis is such a rascal!*

Rash – *(adjective)* acting or done impetuously, without careful consideration. *Please refrain from making a rash assumption.*

Rasher – *(noun)* a thin slice of bacon. *She placed two rashers on his plate.*

Rasp – *(noun)* **1** a coarse file for use on metal, wood, or other hard material. *She tried rubbing on the table with a rasp.* **2** a harsh, grating noise. *The rasp of the engine was a source of worry. (verb)* **1** file with a rasp. *The horse needs to have his teeth rasped.* **2** scrape in a painful or unpleasant way. *The bark was rasping her fingers.* **3** make a harsh, grating noise. *My breath was rasping in my throat.*

Raspberry – *(noun)* **1** an edible soft fruit related to the blackberry, consisting of a cluster of reddish-pink drupes. *I bought a kilo of raspberries from the fruit market.* **2** the prickly shrub which yields this fruit. *They were growing raspberry shrubs in the farm as well.* **3** [informal] a sound made with the tongue and lips, expressing derision or contempt. *She blew a raspberry.*

Rat – *(noun)* **1** a rodent resembling a large, long-tailed mouse, typically considered a serious pest. *There has been a rat menace in the colony of late.* **2** [informal] a despicable person. *He is a rat, no one likes his behaviour.* **3** [informal] an informer. *He was the biggest rat in political history.* **4** [north American] a person who is associated with or frequents a specified place: a wharf rat. [informal] expressing mild annoyance. *Mall rats need to be caught and dealt with. (verb)* **1** hunt or kill rats. *Ratting is his second nature.* **2** [informal] desert one's party, side, or cause. *Several of his followers ratted and joined the Opposition.* **3** [informal] on someone. *I will never rat on my buddies.* **4** [informal] break. *The government has ratted on their earlier pledge.*

Rate – *(verb)* [archaic] scold angrily. *She berated her daughter for forgetting her values.*

Rather – *(adverb)* **1** indicating one's preference in a particular matter. *Would you like chocolate or would you rather stick to a sugar-free sweet?* **2** to a certain or significant extent or degree. *She has been behaving rather strangely.* **3** on the contrary. *There is no shortage of resources, rather the problem is with execution of policies.* **4** more precisely. *I walked, or rather dragged myself, for almost four miles.* **5** instead of; as opposed to. *She seemed indifferent, rather than stoic. (exclamatory)* [British] dated expressing emphatic affirmation, agreement, or acceptance. *I would rather go with you than anybody else.*

Ratify – *(verb)* give formal consent to; make officially valid. *Both the parties have to ratify the treaty in a few days.*

Rating – *(noun)* **1** a classification or ranking based on quality, standard, or performance. *The company retained its five star rating.* **2** the value of a property or condition which is claimed to be standard, optimal, or limiting for a material, device, etc. *It is a fuel with a low octane rating.* **3** the estimated audience size of a particular television or radio programme. *The TRP ratings of the programme have been falling rapidly in the last few weeks.* **4** any of the classes into which racing yachts are assigned according to dimensions. *He bought a masthead boat of similar rating as his opponent's.* **5** [British] a noncommissioned sailor in the navy. *The crew was made up of naval ratings.*

Ratio – *(noun)* the quantitative relation between tow amounts showing the number of times one value contains or is contained within the other. *The sex ratio in the state has dipped in favour of males.*

Ration – *(noun)* **1** a fixed amount of a commodity officially allowed to each person during a time of shortage, as in wartime. *The bread ration had reduced during battle times.* **2** an amount of food supplied on a regular basis to members of the armed forces during a war. *Battle rations had improved over the years.* **3** food; provisions. *I was running out of emergency rations. (verb)* **1**

limit the supply of to fixed rations. *The party is for those who can surisece on rationed food.*

Rational - *(adjective)* **1** based on or in accordance with reason or logic. *There has to be a rational explanation to your action.* **2** able to think sensibly or logically. *Stop being emotional and try being rational in your decisions.* **3** endowed with the capacity or reason. *Man is a rational being.* **4** [mathematics] expressible, or containing quantities which are expressible, as a ratio of whole numbers. *We learnt rational numbers today in maths class.*

Rationalism - *(noun)* **1** the practice of principle of basing opinions and actions on reason and knowledge rather than one religious belief or emotional response. *Scientific rationalism has its own limitations.* **2** [philosophy] the theory that reason rather than experience is the foundation of certainty in knowledge. *Rationalism has more supporters in philosophy than faith.*

Rationalize - *(verb)* **1** attempt to justify with logical reasoning. *You cannot rationalize your urge to eat sweets.* **2** recognize in such a way as to make it more logical and consistent. *Law makers should try to rationalize the country's legal procedures.* **3** make a more efficient by dispensing with superfluous personnel or equipment. *Rationalizing production may not lead to redundancies.* **4** [mathematics] convert to a rational form. *Convert the given fractions into rational numbers.*

Rattle - *(verb)* **1** make or cause to make a rapid succession of short, sharp knocking or clinking sounds. *The tiles on the roof were rattling in the strong wind.* **2** move or travel somewhere while making such sounds. *Trains rattled past.* **3** be in or occupy. *We just rattled around in the big house.* **4** [informal] cause to feel nervous, worried, or irritated. *She was visibly rattled by his presence.* *(noun)* **1** a rattling sound. *Everyone heard the rattle of the tea cups on the tray.* **2** a thing that makes a rattling sound, in particular a baby's toy consisting of a container filled with small pellets. *I bought a fancy rattle for her baby.* **3** a gurgling sound in the throat. *Only a choking rattle escaped his throat and he died.* **4** [archaic] a person who talks incessantly in a lively or inane way. *He is such a rattle!* **5** the set of horny rings at the end of a rattlesnake's tail. *I saw the rattles and knew what snake it was.*

Ravage - *(verb)* cause extensive damage to; devastate. *The town was ravaged by the tornado.* *(noun)* the destructive effects of something. *He had withstood the ravages of life.*

Rave - *(noun)* a framework added to the sides of a cart to increase its capacity. *The raves were bending under the weight of the load.*

Raven - *(noun)* a large heavily built black crow. *The farm had more ravens than common crows.* *(adjective)* especially of hair of a glossy black colour. *She had thick raven hair.*

Ravenous - *(adjective)* voracious; rapacious. *He had a ravenous appetite.*

Ravine - *(noun)* a deep, narrow gorge with steep sides. *The car plunged into the deep ravine.*

Ravishing - *(adjective)* causing intense delight; entrancing. *She was a ravishing beauty.*

Ray - *(noun)* a broad flat cartilaginous fish with wing like pectoral fins and a long slender tail. *The marine researcher died when he was stung by a ray.*

Raze - *(verb)* tear down and destroy. *Villages were razed to the ground.*

Razor - *(noun)* an instrument with a sharp blade, used to shave unwanted hair from the face or body. *I bought an electric razor from the shop.* *(verb)* cut with a razor. *His hair had to be razored for a close cut.*

Reach - *(verb)* **1** stretch out an arm in a specified direction in order to touch or grasp something. stretch out one's hand or arm. stretch upwards to pick something up and bring it down to a lower level. hand to. *I tried to reach up to the loft to take out the suitcase.* **2** be able to touch with an outstretched arm or leg. *I reached out my hand and pulled her pigtail.* **3** arrive at or attain; extend to. *She bid adieu as she reached the door.* **4** succeed in achieving. *The conference reached its ending with a signed treaty between the two countries.* **5** make contact with. *You can reach out to me at my email id.* **6** be received by. *The television has reached every nook and corner of* *the country today.* **7** succeed in influencing or having an effect on. *He intends to reach out to viewers without any journalistic intervention.* **8** sailing sail with the wind blowing from the side. *The Patriot white-sail reached while Goldstone came nearer. (noun)* **1** an act of reaching. *She tried a reach for him.* **2** the distance to which someone can stretch out their hand. *He was huge with a height of six feet and a reach of 18 inches.* **3** the extent or range of something's application. effect, or influence. *The film gives an idea about the reach of his fame.* **4** a continuous extend of land or water, especially a stretch of river between two bends. *It was the upper reaches of the river that had been affected by constant industrial pollution.*

React – *(verb)* **1** respond to something in a particular way or with particular behaviour. *She reacted angrily at the news of the break up.* **2** respond with hostility or a contrary cause of action to. *They reacted against the elite groupism that was being maintained in the society.* **3** suffer from adverse physiological effects after ingesting, from adverse physiological effects after ingesting, breathing, or touching a substance. *Many people have skin that reacts to sun and dust.* **4** [chemistry] interact and undergo a chemical or physical change. *During combustion, sulphur reacts with the limestone.* **5** stock exchange fall after rising. *Shares reacted to 111 points before rising to 150 pints.*

Reaction – *(noun)* **1** an instance of reacting to or against something. *My immediate reaction was to throw something at him.* **2** a person's ability to respond physically and mentally to external stimuli. *He was a skilled surgeon with quick response.* **3** opposition to political or social progress or reform. *The opposition is under threat from forces of reaction.* **4** a process in which substances interact causing chemical or physical change. *The mixing of certain acids causes harmful chemical reactions.* **5** [physics] a force exerted in opposition to an applied force. *The law of action and reaction was one of my favourite topics.*

Reactor – *(noun)* **1** an apparatus or structure in which fissile material can be mad to undergo a controlled, self-sustaining nuclear reaction releasing energy. *The nuclear reactor is under threat.* **2** a container or apparatus in which substances are made to react chemically. *There is a proposal to set up a nuclear reactor there.* **3** [medicine] a person who reacts to a drug, antigen, etc. *He offered his body for a reactor for the pharma industry.* **4** [physics] a coil or other who component which provides reactance in a circuit. *We saw a reactor in the mechanical lab today.*

Read – *(verb)* **1** habitually read. *I like to read before I sleep.* **2** discover by reading it in a written or printed source. having a specified level of knowledge as a result of reading. *She was well read.* **3** understand or interpret the nature or significance of. convey a specified impression to the reader. *She watched her reactions so they won't be read as a sign of weakness.* **4** proofread. *I want you to read and point out errors before passing it on to the typesetter.* **5** present a bill or other measure before a legislative assembly. *The bill was read a second time.* **6** inspect and record the figure indicated on a measuring instrument. indicate a specified measurement or figure. *The manager came to read the gas meter.* **7** [chiefly British] study an academic subject at a university. *She reads at the University. (noun)* **1** [chiefly] a period or act of reading. *I was having a quiet read in the sun.* **2** [informal] a book considered in terms of its readability. *Your book is a thoroughly entertaining read.* readable *Your work is readable is all I can say to qualify it.*

Reader – *(noun)* **1** a person who reads. *She is a voracious reader.* **2** a person who reports to a publisher on the merits of manuscripts submitted for publication. [British] a university lecturer of the highest grade below professor. *She is a reader at the university.* **4** short for lay reader. *There is good chance that the reader may misinterpret the sayings.* **5** a book containing extracts of a text or texts for teaching purposes. *The teacher asked the students to take out their readers.* **6** a device that produce on a screen a readable image from a microfiche or microfilm. *The reader needed maintenance.*

Readership – *(noun)* **1** the readers of a newspaper or magazine regarded collectively. *The readership of the daily had gone down.* **2** [British] the position of reader at a university. *I would love to take up readership at the University.*

Reading – *(noun)* **1** the action or skill of reading. *It was time for reading the will.* **2** an instance of something being read to an audience. *I am going for a poetry reading at the book shop at the mall.* **3** an interpretation of a text. *Feminist readings of Freud are very popular.* **4** a figure recorded ability expressed with reference to an average age at which a comparable ability is found. *His reading age will never be more than 8 or 9.*

Ready – *(adjective)* **1** in a suitable state for an activity or situation; fully prepared. *Get ready for the party quickly.* **2** made suitable and available for immediate use. *Please have the list ready before I come home from office.* **3** easily available or obtained; within reach. *There was ready supply of food and water in the house.* **4** willing to do something. *She is ready to take up the responsibility.* **5** immediate, quick, or prompt. *I want to marry a girl with a ready smile.* **6** in such a condition as to be likely to do something. *By the time he scaled the peak, he was ready to drop.* *(noun)* [British informal] available money; cash. *Is the cash ready?* *(verb)* make ready. *The suitcase was readied for shipping.*

Real – *(noun)* **1** the basic monetary unit of Brazil since 1994, equal to 100 centavos. *His salary in Brazil was 10,000 Real.* **2** a former coin and monetary unit of various Spanish-speaking countries. *I had a collection of old reals.*

Realism – *(noun)* **1** the practice of accepting a situation as it is and dealing with it accordingly. *Try and ground yourself in realism instead of getting deluded.* **2** the representation of things in a way that is accurate and true to life. *British soaps are known for their gritty realism.* **3** [philosophy] the doctrine that universals or abstract concepts have an objective or absolute existence. Often contrasted with nominalism. the doctrine that matter as the object or perception has real existence. *The professor was here for a lecture on Platonic realism.*

Reality – *(noun)* **1** the state of things as they actually exist, as opposed to an idealistic or notional idea of them. *Try and face the reality now.* **2** a thing that is actually experienced or seen. *The show gave them a taste of reality that they would have never experienced.* **3** the quality of being lifelike. *The reality of the show was wonderful.* **4** the state or quality of having existence or substance. *Death has a reality that nothing else has.* **5** [philosophy] existing that is absolute, self-sufficient, or objective, and not subject to human decisions or conventions. *She followed reality as a philosophy and way of life.*

Realize – *(verb)* **1** become fully aware of as a fact; understand clearly. *He realized his mistake when I pointed out.* **2** cause to happen. *Her worst fears were realized.* **3** achieve fulfil. *She has now begun to realize her potential.* **4** give actual or physical form to a concept or work. *Your decorations have been aesthetically realized.* **5** [music] add to or complete a piece of music left sparsely notated by the composer. *Realizing short score into full score I finally got the full composition ready.* **6** sell for or make a profit of. *He realized a profit of Rs 10 lakh in the business.* **7** convert an asset into cash. *I realized all my mutual funds into cash.*

Really – *(adverb)* **1** in reality; in actual fact. *The pie is really good.* **2** very; thoroughly. *It is a really cold day.* *exclamatory* **1** expressing interest, surprise, doubt, or protest. *You made it? Really?* **2** [chiefly US] expressing agreement. *Oh Yeah, really!*

Realm – *(noun)* **1** [archaic, poetic] a kingdom. *He was banished from the realm.* **2** a field or domain of activity or interest. *These topics are beyond the realm of my interest.*

Ream – *(noun)* **1** 500 sheets of paper. *She bought several reams of paper for her business.* **2** a large quantity of something, especially paper. *Reams of paper were lying at the press.*

Reap – *(verb)* **1** cut or gather a crop or harvest the crop from land. *We've been reaping a rich crop this year.* **2** receive as a consequence of one's own or others actions. *As you sow, so you reap.*

Reappear – *(verb)* appear again. *Where did you just reappear from?*

Rear – *(noun)* **1** the back or hindmost part of something. *I will be waiting at the rear side of the building.* **2** a person's buttocks. *I had a good mind to give him a kick on his rear. (adjective)* at the back. *The thief broke open the car's rear window and ran away with my wallet.*

Rearrange – *(verb)* arrange again in a different way. *I was in a mood to rearrange our furniture.*

Reason – *(noun)* **1** a cause, explanation, or justification. good or obvious cause to do something. logic a premise of an argument in support of a belief, especially a minor premise given after the conclusion. *She didn't give a reason for her decision.* **2** the power of the mind to think, understand, and form judgements logically. one's sanity. *Have you lost your reason that you made such a hasty decision?* **3** what is right, practical, or possible. *You must permit the action, within reason of course. (verb)* **1** think, understand, and form judgements logically. find a solution to a problem by considering possible options. *It is not possible to reason entirely from facts.* **2** persuade with rational argument. *Its very difficult to reason with her.*

Reasonable – *(adjective)* **1** fair and sensible. *It is only reasonable to allow him to present his side of the argument.* **2** [archaic] able to reason logically. *The policeman was quite reasonable.* **3** as much as is appropriate or fair; moderate. fairly good. relatively inexpensive. *It was reasonably inexpensive.*

Reassure – *(verb)* allay the doubts and fears of. *She gave me a reassuring smile.*

Rebate – *(noun)* **1** a partial refund to someone who has paid too much for tax, rent, or a utility. *Rebates will be given in the first year alone.* **2** a deduction or discount on a sum due. *The offer gives 20% rebate on all the products. (verb)* pay back as a rebate. *You will be given rebates by the government for your NI contributions.*

Rebel – *(noun)* a person who rebels. *She has been a rebel ever since her teenage days. (verb)* rise in opposition or armed resistance to an established government or ruler. resist authority, control, or convention. show or feel repugnance. *The youth has started rebelling against the government's corruption.*

Rebellion – *(noun)* **1** armed resistance to an established government or ruler. *The army took the rebellion to the streets to rebel against the ruling government.* **2** defiance of authority or control. *The rebellion had begun and was building up.*

Rebound – *(verb)* **1** bounce back after hitting a hard surface. *The ball hit the post and rebounded right on to his face.* **2** recover in value, amount, or strength. *The share has rebounded to a nine time high.* **3** have an unexpected adverse consequence for. *Your tricks will rebound on you!* **4** [basketball] gain possession of a missed shot after it bounces off the backboard or basket rim. *He can rebound as well as the top players. (noun)* **1** a ball or shot that rebounds. basketball a recovery of possession of a missed shot. *The rebound blasted into the net.* **2** an instance of recovering in value, amount, or strength. *The rebound in profits last year was quite a motivation for this year.* **3** [medicine] recurrence of a condition after withdrawal of treatment. *He has been having rebound hypertension.*

Rebuff – *(verb)* reject in an abrupt or ungracious manner. *She rebuffed my offer in no mean terms. (noun)* an abrupt rejection. *Please don't misunderstand my non-reaction to your comments as a rebuff.*

Rebuild – *(verb)* build again. *The house will be rebuilt in the same way. (noun)* **1** an instance of rebuilding. *The school commended the initiative of all who were involved in the rebuild.* **2** a thing that has been rebuilt. *The rebuilds include a house, a farm and a bridge.*

Rebuke – *(verb)* criticize or reprimand sharply. *She was rebuked for sporting the wrong look at the theme party. (noun)* a sharp criticism. *I didn't intend my comments to be a rebuke.*

Recall – *(verb)* **1** remember. cause one to remember or think of. bring back the memory of someone or something to. *I do recall meeting your friends long back.* **2** call up storied computer data. *Can you recall the last restore point?* **3** officially order to return. request the return of faulty products. *The faulty cars were being recalled by the manufacturer.* **4** reselect a sports player as a member of a team. *The player was recalled for the crucial match.* **5** bring out of a state of inattention. *I was recalled from my unconscious state.* **6** [archaic] revoke or annul. *I sent the employee another note recalling the previous one.* *(noun)* **1** the action or faculty of remembering. *People's recall of their experiences make interesting stories.* **2** an act of officially recalling someone or something. *A recall of Parliament was announced.* **3** [north American] the removal of an elected government official from office by voting. *The minister's recall was sharply objected by the opposition.*

Recapitulate – *(verb)* **1** summarize and state again the main points of. *He was trying to recapitulate his arguments before stepping into the courtroom.* **2** [biology] repeat an evolutionary or other process during development and growth. *Several features of our body point at recapitulation during development.*

Recede – *(verb)* **1** move back or further away. *The sea had receded after the tsunami.* **2** gradually diminish. *The possibility of a promotion receded even more.* **3** cease to grow at the temples and above the forehead. *He has a receding hairline.* **4** slope backwards. *She has a slightly receding chin.* **5** [archaic] withdraw from an undertaking, agreement, etc. *I will not recede from our deal.*

Receipt – *(noun)* **1** the action of receiving something or the fact of its being received. a written acknowledgement of this. an amount of money received over a period by an organization. *I requested the shop keeper to give a receipt of the commodities bought.* **2** [archaic] a recipe. *Can you give me a receipt of this dish?* *(verb)* mark a bill as paid. *I got a receipt after paying the bill at the restaurant.*

Receive – *(verb)* **1** be given, presented with, or paid. take delivery of. buy or accept. *She received an advance of Rs 10,000 for her project.* **2** detect or pick up. *The system's work depends on the signals received from the satellite.* **3** from an experience. *The impression she received was to just let things go when things are out of your hands.* **4** be the player to whom the server serves. *The coach showed the little girl how to receive the serve.* **5** consent to hear. *I couldn't find a magistrate to receive my oath.* **6** serve as a receptacle for. *Please remove the basin that receives the water.* **7** suffer, experience, or be subject to. respond to in a specified way. meet with a specified reaction. widely accepted as authoritative or true. *The function received wide coverage.* **8** great or welcome formally. be visited by. admit as a member. *The tourists were received warmly at the hotel.* **9** accommodate. *You will be received at the airport.*

Receiver – *(noun)* **1** a person or thing that receives something. *Did you check the receiver before mailing the courier?* **2** a piece of radio or television apparatus converting broadcast singles into sound or images. a telephone handset, in particular the part that converts electrical signals into sounds. *The receiver was placed off hook which is why we were not receiving calls for so long.* **3** a person appointed to manage the financial affairs of a bankrupt business. *Her company is in the hands of receivers now.* **4** [American football] a player who specializes in catching passes. *He is a receiver for the team.*

Recent – *(adjective)* having happened or been done. *She is the most recent employee to have joined the company.*

Receptacle – *(noun)* **1** an object or space used to contain something. *We got the food packed in the receptacle.* **2** [chiefly zoology] an organ or structure which receives a secretion, eggs, etc. *The receptacle had been damaged severely.* **3** botany the base of a flower, flower head, or other sexual organ. *The botany teacher helped us identify the receptacle of the flowers.*

Reception – *(noun)* **1** the action or process of receiving someone or something. the way in which something is received. *She received a warm reception at the event.* **2** a formal social occasion organized to welcome someone or celebrate an event. *The groom's family organized a large reception party.* **3** the area in a hotel, office, etc. where visitors are greeted. *I was waiting for her at the reception.* **4** [British] the first class in an infant school. *She was admitted in Reception class.* **5** the quality with which broadcast signals are received. *The radio reception is terrible here.*

Receptive – *(adjective)* **1** able or willing to receive something. willing to consider new suggestion and ideas. *My appraisal says I am quite receptive to criticism.* **2** ready to mate. *The animal was receptive.*

Recess – *(noun)* **1** a small space set back in a wall. a hollow in something. remote, secluded, or secret places. *The table has a recess in its base.* **2** a period when the proceedings of a parliament, [law] court, etc. are temporarily suspended. suspend its proceedings temporarily. *Talks resumed after the recess.*

Recession – *(noun)* **1** a temporary economic decline during which trade and industrial activity are reduced. *It was IT that was least affected in the recession.* **2** [chiefly astronomy] the action of receding. *Recession has affected people's lives in a huge way.*

Recipe – *(noun)* **1** a set of instructions for preparing a dish. *I learnt the typical South Indian recipe for pancakes.* **2** something likely to lead to a particular outcome; a recipe for disaster. *Your strategy is a perfect recipe for disaster.* **3** [archaic] a medical prescription. *You don't need to describe the drugs and their recipes for application.*

Recipient – *(noun)* a receiver of something. *She was the recipient of my gift.*

Reciprocal – *(adjective)* **1** given, felt, or done in return. *I was hoping for some reciprocal action from him.* **2** bearing on or binding two parties equally. *The treaty declared a reciprocal relationship between the two countries.* **3** [grammar] expressing mutual action or relationship. *Give the reciprocal versions of the given sentences.* **4** opposite in direction. *She gave a reciprocal reaction to my action.* *(noun)* **1** [mathematics] the quantity obtained by dividing the number one by a given quantity. *The mathematics teacher explained reciprocal numbers.* **2** [grammar] a reciprocal pronoun or verb. *'Each other' is an example of a reciprocal pro(noun).*

Recital – *(noun)* **1** the performance of a programme of music by a soloist or small group. *I bought passes for the sitar recital this weekend.* **2** the enumeration of connected names, facts, or elements. *She went into a recital of her adventures at the work site.* **3** [law] the part of a legal document giving factual information. *Council directive 56/85 contains detailed extracts from the Social Charter in its recitals.* recitation *She has enrolled for the poetry recitation competition.*

Reckless – *(adjective)* without thought or care for the consequences of an action. *He was a reckless driver.*

Reckon – *(verb)* **1** calculate. *Her bank balance was reckoned to be around 5 crore.* **2** [informal] be of the opinion. *I reckon you should follow the opposite route.* **3** regard in a specified way. include someone or something in a group. [informal] have a specified view or opinion of. *What do you reckon on this place?* **4** rely on or be sure of. [informal] expect. *They had reckoned on a day or two more of privacy.* **5** take into account. *They hadn't reckoned with a visit from her.* **6** [archaic] settle accounts with. *God will reckon with us when we die.*

Reckoning – *(noun)* **1** the action of calculating or estimating something. *By my reckoning, we are at least 5 miles away.* **2** an opinion or judgement. *By his reckoning we were all fools while he knew best.* **3** [archaic] a bill or account, or its settlement. *It's time for reckoning before we close down for the day.* **4** the working out to consequences or retribution for one's actions. *A terrible reckoning will haunt you if you trust people often.*

Reclaim - *(verb)* **1** retrieve or recover. *You must reclaim your lost money.* **2** redeem from a state of vice. *Societies should be commended for reclaiming its lower elements.* **3** bring under cultivation. recycle. *The wasteland was being reclaimed. (noun)* the action of reclaiming or being reclaimed. *He is working on his VAT reclaims.*

Recline - *(verb)* **1** lean or lie back in a relaxed position. *She was reclining on her beach chair.* **2** have a back able to move into a sloping position. *I bought a reclining arm chair from the furniture fair.*

Recluse - *(noun)* a person who avoids others and lives a solitary life. *The actress became a recluse after the death of her husband. (adjective)* favouring a solitary life. *She wishes to lead a reclusive life.*

Recognition - *(noun)* the action or process of recognizing or being recognized. *He has been working towards a recognition from his workplace.*

Recognize - *(verb)* **1** identify as already known; know again. identify and respond correctly to a sound, character, etc. *I recognized her at the market.* **2** acknowledge the existence, validity, or legality of. formally acknowledge that a country or government is eligible to be dealt with as a member of the international community. *Your papers will be recognized by the court.* **3** reward formally. *His efforts were recognized by the office.* **4** call on someone to speak. *He was recognized for the speech.*

Recoil - *(verb)* **1** suddenly spring back or flinch in fear, horror, or disgust. feel such emotions at the thought of something. *She recoiled at the memories of that accident.* **2** move abruptly backwards as a reaction on firing. spring back through force of impact or elasticity. *The gun recoiled for a moment and fired again.* **3** have an adverse consequence for the originator. *If you don't do your duties properly, it will recoil upon you. (noun)* the action or recoiling. *He jerked at the recoil of the rifle.*

Recollect - *(verb)* remember. *I do recollect certain episodes of that soap.*

Recollection - *(noun)* **1** the action or faculty of remembering. *To my recollection, he has never given a reason to complain.* **2** a memory. *We're working on a book on her recollections of her interactions with the famous actor.*

Recommend - *(verb)* **1** put forward with approval as being suitable for a purpose or role. advise as a course of action. advise to do something. *She recommended me for the post.* **2** make appealing or desirable. *This shampoo is highly recommended.* **3** [archaic] commend or entrust someone or something to. *I recommended my spirit to its creator.* recommendation *I would rather not get a job on her recommendation.*

Recompense - *(verb)* **1** compensate. pay or reward for effort or work. make amends to or reward someone for loss, harm, or effort. *Victims should be recompensed by their culprits.* **2** [archaic] punish or reward appropriately. *Your efforts will be recompensed. (noun)* **1** compensation or reward. *Workers need adequate recompense.* **2** [archaic] restitution made or punishment inflicted for a wrong or injury. *He received recompense for his crime.*

Reconcile - *(verb)* **1** restore friendly relations between, settle a quarrel. *The two warring actors had reconciled.* **2** make or show to be compatible. *The team had to be reconciled with the existing policies.* **3** make someone accept a disagreeable thing. *She reconciled to his demands.*

Recondition - *(verb)* **1** condition again. *The car needs to be reconditioned.* **2** [British] overhaul or renovate. *The house was being reconditioned.*

Reconsider - *(verb)* consider again. *Would you like to reconsider your decision?*

Reconstruct - *(verb)* **1** construct again. *The ship was being reconstructed.* **2** form an impression, model, or re-enactment of something from evidence. *The CIDs were trying to reconstruct the scene of crime.*

Record - *(noun)* **1** a piece of evidence about the past, especially a written or other permanent account of something. [law] an official report of the proceeding and judgements in a court. *They had a record of the proceedings of the* court. **2** a person or thing's previous conduct or performance. a criminal record. *He is known for his criminal record.* **3** the best performance or most remarkable event of its kind on record. *It's the best dance on record.* **4** a thin plastic disc carrying recorded sound in grooves on each surface, for reproduction by a record player. a piece or collection of music reproduced on such a disc or on another medium. *I have records of her music.*

Recorder – *(noun)* **1** an apparatus for recording sound, pictures, or data. *I bought a recorder from the market.* **2** a person who keeps records. *His work in the team was as a recorder of rural data.* **3** a barrister appointed to serve as a part-time judge. [British historical] a judge in certain courts. *He is a recorder in the court.* **4** a simple woodwind instrument without keys, played by blowing air through a shaped mouthpiece. *I bought a recorder from the antique shop.* recording *I am going to the studio for my recording.*

Recount – *(verb)* give an account of something. *The police asked her to recount the sequence of events.*

Recoup – *(verb)* regain. reimburse or compensate for money spent or lost. regain recover. *The companies are trying to recoup the money they lost in the recession.* **2** [law] deduct or keep back part of a sum due. *Law allows them to recoup the money they lost in the natural disaster.*

Recourse – *(noun)* **1** a source of help in a difficult situation, demand compensation or payment. *A surgery may be the only recourse.*

Recover – *(verb)* **1** return to a normal state of health, mind or strength. *She has recovered well from her trauma.* **2** find or regain possession of. regain control of oneself or a physical or mental state. regain or secure. *She has recovered all the loss she incurred in the accident.* **3** remove or extract for use, reuse, or waste treatment. *Only 13% of chemicals were being recovered from domestic recycling.*

Recovery – *(noun)* **1** an act or the process of recovering. the action of taking a vehicle that has broken down or crashed for repair. *I phoned a recovery vehicle to come and help immediately.* **2** [golf] a stroke bringing the ball out of the rough of a bunker. *He finished the season with two recoveries.* **3** the action of returning the paddle, leg, or arm to its initial position for a new stroke. *My heel is above the pedal before the recovery.*

Recreation – *(noun)* enjoyable leisure activity. *There are few options for recreation here.*

Recruit – *(verb)* enlist in the armed forces. enroll as a member or worker in an organization. [informal] persuade to do or help with something. *Our toughest soldiers are recruited from the desert.* *(noun)* a newly recruited person. *He is our new recruit.*

Rectangle – *(noun)* a plane figure with four straight sides and four right angles, especially one with unequal adjacent sides. *She bought me a curio that was a rectangular marble piece.*

Rectify – *(verb)* **1** put right; correct. convert to direct current. *Statements made now cannot be rectified later.* **2** find a straight line equal in length to a curve. *The teachers were not in favour of his methods of rectifying the cycloid.*

Rector – *(noun)* **1** the incumbent of a parish where all tithes formerly passed to the incumbent. a member of the clergy in charge of a parish. a priest in charge of a church or a religious institution. *He is a rector at the parish nearby.* **2** the head of certain universities, colleges, and schools. an elected student representative on a university's governing body. *He was appointed the rector of the university body.*

Rectum – *(noun)* the final section of the large intestine, terminating at the anus. *The doctor broke the news to the patient that he had been diagnosed with rectum cancer.*

Recuperate – *(verb)* **1** recover from illness or exertion. *She is still recuperating from her illness.* **2** regain something lost. *They are trying to recuperate the losses incurred during the recession.*

Recur – *(verb)* occur again. come back to one's mind. go back to in thought or speech. *This phenomenon has been seen to be recurring in her body ever few years.*

Recurrence - *(noun)* occur again. *The recurrence of this phenomenon can be a source of worry.*

Recycle - *(verb)* **1** convert into reusable material, use again. *Water recycling is a good option to follow in our future.* **2** return to a previous stage in a cyclic process. *During the synthesis of other proteins, amino acids are recycled.*

Red - *(adjective)* **1** of a colour at the end of the spectrum next to orange and opposite violet, as of blood, fire, or rubies. of a reddish-brown colour. red due to embarrassment, anger, or heat. dated or offensive having reddish skin. *She was bright red with embarrassment as soon as she saw her boyfriend entering the show.* **2** made from dark grapes and coloured by their skins. *I only need a glass of red wine.* **3** of or denoting a red light or flag used as a signal to stop. *He desperately waved the red flag, hoping the train driver will see him.* **4** of the second-highest level of difficulty. *The one standing on the red mark was indeed the toughest.* *(noun)* **1** red colour or pigment. *The teacher marked all the wrong answers in red.* **2** [informal], chiefly a communist or socialist. *He is a Red.* **3** the situation of having spent more than is in one's bank account. *He was Rs 5 crore in the red.*

Redden - *(verb)* **1** make or become red. *She was reddened and tanned after the whole week she spent at the beach.* **2** blush. *She reddened as soon as she saw her fiancé entering the show.*

Redeem - *(verb)* **1** compensate for the faults or bad aspects of. make up for one's poor past performance or behaviour. save from sin, error, or evil. *It was a disappointing competition redeemed only by the exceptional performance of the winner.* **2** gain or regain possession of in exchange for payment. finance repay at the maturity date. exchange for goods or money. *The peasants could now redeem their lands.*

Redemption - *(noun)* **1** the action of redeeming someone or something, or of being redeemed. *The terms of redemption were not very attractive.* **2** a thing that saves someone from error or evil. *One must seek redemption from evil.*

Red-handed - *(adjective)* in or just after the act of doing something wrong. *We hatched a plan to catch the thief red-handed.*

Redistribute - *(verb)* distribute again or differently. *The products were redistributed among the teammates.*

Redouble - *(verb)* make or become much greater, more intense, or more numerous. *I thought it was over, but it was back redoubled!* *(noun)* bridge a call that redoubles a bid. *If you're redoubling, you're asking your opponent to bid something.*

Redress - *(verb)* **1** remedy or set right. *The onus was on the government now to set policies to redress racist issues.* **2** [archaic] set upright again. *An architect was called to redress the leaning wall.* *(noun)* remedy or compensation for a wrong or grievance. *Those seeking redress of their problems should approach this lawyer.*

Reduce - *(verb)* **1** make or become smaller or less in amount, degree, or size. boil so that it becomes thicker and more concentrated. chiefly lose weight. photography make less dense. *They reduced the workforce by 10,000.* **2** bring someone or something by force or necessity to an undesirable state or action. *The temple was reduced to rubble in the earthquake.* **3** change something to. convert a fraction to the form with the lowest terms. *Reduce the fraction to its lowest common denominator.* **4** [archaic] conquer a place. *The team was reduced last year.* **5** [chemistry] cause to combine chemically with hydrogen. undergo or cause to undergo a reaction in which electrons are gained from another substance or molecule. the opposite of oxidize. *Hydrogen reduces the carbon dioxide.* **6** restore to its proper position. *He reduced his dislocated thumb.*

Reduction - *(noun)* **1** the action of reducing something. the amount by which something is reduced. *Talks on arms reduction have resumed.* **2** an arrangement of an orchestral score for piano or a smaller group of performers. *I have a reduction ready for the smaller group.* **3** a smaller copy of a picture or photograph. *Can you get me a reduction of the pictures we took today?* **4** a thick and concentrated liquid or sauce. *A reduction was flowing from the tap.*

Redundant – *(adjective)* **1** no longer needed or useful; superfluous. able to be omitted without loss of meaning or function. [engineering] not strictly necessary but included in case another component fails. *Microsoft Windows 2 is redundant.* **2** [chiefly] unemployed. *He is redundant and needs a job.*

Reed – *(noun)* a tall, slender-leaved plant, of the grass family, growing in water or one marshy ground. *Reeds had grown and spread all around the pond.*

Reef – *(noun)* **1** a ridge of jagged rock, coral, or sand just above or below the surface of the sea. *The coral reef off the Australian coast is endangered.* **2** a vein of gold or other ore. *They have discovered a reef somewhere beyond the desert.*

Reek – *(verb)* **1** have a foul smell. [archaic] give off smoke, steam, or fumes. *He was reeking, so I knew where he was coming from.* **2** be suggestive of something unpleasant. *His speech reeked of anti-communism.* *(noun)* **1** a foul smell. *The reek of cattle dung was unbearable here.* **2** [chiefly Scottish] smoke. *He was trying to peer through the reek.*

Reel – *(noun)* **1** a cylinder on which film, wire, thread, etc. can be wound. a length of something wound on a reel. *I bought a cotton reel from the thread shop.* **2** a part of a film. *It was the last reel that got burnt in the fire.* **3** a lively Scottish or Irish folk dance. a piece of music for a reel, typically in simple or duple time. *Everybody had begun dancing reels the moment the music was played.* *(verb)* **1** wind a line on to a reel by turning the reel. bring something attached to a line, especially a fish, towards one by turning a reel. *He reeled in a good perch.*

Refectory – *(noun)* a room used for communal meals, especially in an educational or religious institution. *The monk took his bowl of gruel and made his way towards the refectory.*

Refer – *(verb)* **1** mention or allude to. direct the attention of someone to. *She never referred to him again.* **2** pass a matter to for a decision. send to a medical specialist. consult a source of information. *I wanted to refer my case to the appellate.* **3** [archaic] trace or attribute something to as a cause or source. *She prayed to the god to whom she refers her highest aspirations.* **4** fail a candidate in an examination.. *More than 25 of her students were referred.*

Referee – *(noun)* **1** an official who watches a game or match closely to ensure that the rules are adhered to. *The referee showed the red card ti the player.* **2** a person willing to testify in writing about the character or ability of a job applicant. *I could sue the referee for libel.* **3** a person appointed to examine and assess an academic work for publication (verb) officiate as referee at or over. *The referee's reports were sent to the authors.*

Reference – *(noun)* **1** the action of mentioning something. a mention or citation of a source of information in a book or article. *Please use the Chicago style of reference in the bibliography.* **2** the action of referring to a source of information or higher authority. *He made reference of the higher authority.* **3** a letter from a previous employer testifying to someone's ability or reliability. *I requested my employer to provide a reference to the future company.* *(verb)* provide with references. *Each chapter in this book is referenced.*

Referendum – *(noun)* a general vote by the electorate on a single political question which has been referred to them for a direct decision. *The parliament was discussing a referendum.*

Refill – *(verb)* act of refilling or a glass that is refilled. *Could you please refill my glass?*

Refine – *(verb)* **1** remove impurities or unwanted elements from. *Please refine the liquid twice before consuming it.* **2** make minor changes so as to improve a theory or method. *The final thesis needs just a little bit of refining.* **3** elegant and cultured. *He belongs to a refined family.* refinement *His refinement reflects in his tastes.*

Refit – *(verb)* replace or repair machinery, equipment, and fittings in a ship, building, etc. *I am taking up a contract to refit the factory equipment.* *(noun)* an act of refitting. *After the extensive refit, the plumber is back in action.*

Reflect – *(verb)* **1** throw back without absorbing it. show an image of. *The light was reflected off the box's surface.* **2** embody or represent pacts of his life. bring about a good or bad impression of. *Your values should be reflected in your actions.* **3** think deeply or carefully about. *Can you reflect on what you just said?*

Reflection – *(noun)* **1** the fact or phenomenon of light, heat, sound, etc. being reflected. something reflected or an image so formed. *The teacher showed us how reflection of light occurs.* **2** a thing bringing discredit. *The crime was a sad reflection on society.* **3** serious thought or consideration. a considered idea, expressed in writing or speech. *She decided to put her reflections into words.* **4** [mathematics] the symmetry operation of inverting something with respect to a plane. *The mathematics teacher taught us how reflection works.*

Reflective – *(adjective)* **1** providing or capable of providing a reflection. produced by reflection. *She bought some reflective clothing.* **2** thoughtful. *He is a quite reflective man.*

Reflex – *(noun)* **1** an action performed without conscious thought as a response to a stimulus. a response in a part of the body to stimulation of a corresponding point on the feet, hands, or head. *I thought you would have basic reflexes.* **2** a thing that reproduces the essential features or qualities of something else. *Politics is a reflex of economics.* **3** a word formed by development from an earlier stage of a language. *Reflexes of language have been extensively researched.* **4** [archaic] a reflected source of light. *Her face lit up with the reflex of the light from the window.* *(adjective)* **1** performed as a reflex. *Sneezing is a reflex action.* **2** exceeding 180. *Its reflex time now!* **3** [archaic] reflected. *Light reflexes on the glass.* **4** [archaic] bent of turned backwards. *He reflexed under the pressure.*

Reform – *(verb)* **1** make changes in to relinquish an immoral or criminal lifestyle. *We need to reform this society.* **2** [chemistry] subject to a catalytic process in which straight-chain molecules are converted to branched forms. *We learnt reforms today in chemistry lab.* *(noun)* the action or process of reforming. *We need a reform of existing rape laws in the country.*

Reformation – *(noun)* **1** the action or process of reforming. *The philosopher is responsible for the reformation that has taken the society by surprise.* **2** a 16th-century movement for the reform of abuses in the roman church, ending in the establishment of the reformed and protestant churches. *Reformation is an interesting chapter in History.*

Reformer – *(noun)* a disputant who advocates reform. *Our country has produced some of the greatest reformers.*

Refrain – *(verb)* stop oneself from doing something. *Please refrain from taking a hasty decision.*

Refresh – *(verb)* **1** give new strength or energy to. *The old lady brought out some lemonade to refresh the spirits of the construction workers.* jog by going over previous information. *He refreshed his memory by going through his class notes.* **2** revise or update. *Please click on the green button to refresh this webpage.*

Refreshing – *(adjective)* **1** serving to refresh. *A refreshing shower helps out tremendously on a hot sweaty day.* **2** welcome or stimulating because new or different. *It is refreshing to hear good news on the television.*

Refreshment – *(noun)* **1** a light snack or drink. *The refreshments at the party were delicious.* **2** the giving of fresh strength or energy. *Yoga is another way to find refreshment for the mind and soul.*

Refrigerate – *(verb)* subject food or drink to cold in order to chill or preserve it. *Please refrigerate the chicken until further use.*

Refrigerator – *(noun)* an appliance or compartment which is artificially kept cool and used to store food and drink. *Cold meat straight from the refrigerator should not be put into a hot pan.*

Refuge – *(noun)* a place or state of safety from danger or trouble. *A number of people took refuge from the storm in their basements.* [British] a traffic island. *Refuges are necessary to provide safety for pedestrians.*

Refugee – *(noun)* a person who has been forced to leave their country in order to escape war, persecution, or natural disaster. *A large percentage of refugees suffer from dispersion.*

Refund – *(verb)* pay back money to. *Customers will be refunded if the device is found faulty.* *(noun)* a refunded sum of money. *No refunds are allowed here.*

Refusal – *(noun)* act of refuseing something. *My request for more chocolate was met with outright refusal.*

Refuse – *(verb)* indicate unwillingness. indicate unwillingness to accept or grant something offered or requested. decline to jump a fence or other obstacle. *The dessert was too good to refuse.*

Refute – *(verb)* prove a statement or the person advancing it to be wrong. *He refutes any hint that he behaved badly.* **2** deny a statement or accusation. *The finance department refutes the contractor's claim.*

Regain – *(verb)* **1** obtain possession or use of something again after losing it. *She regained her strength after a week of rest.* **2** get back to. *The boys regained their place in the nationals after much practice.*

Regal – *(adjective)* of, resembling, or fit for a monarch, especially in being magnificent or dignified. *The regal gesture of the queen left the commoners in awe.*

Regale – *(verb)* **1** entertain with conversation. *The sailor regaled the boys with stories of his old days.* **2** lavishly supply with food or drink. *The lodge regales its guests with seven-course meals every fortnight.*

Regard – *(verb)* **1** consider in a particular way. *She regards herself as a dog lover.* **2** gaze at in a specified fashion. . [archaic] pay attention to. *He regarded the dirty boys distrustfully.* *(noun)* **1** heed or concern. *She rescued him without regard for herself.* **2** high opinion; esteem. best wishes used especially at the end of letters. *She held her husband in high regard.* **3** a steady look. *The teacher fixed the same stern regard on all the students.*

Regency – *(noun)* the office or period of government by a regent. a commission acting as regent. the period of a particular regency, especially from 1811 to 1820 and from 1715 to 1723 adjective relating to or denoting a broadly neoclassical style of [British] architecture, clothing, and furniture of the late 18th and early 19th centuries. *The wealth of the kingdom was restored during his regency.*

Regenerate – *(verb)* **1** regrow new tissue. regrow. *Salamanders are remarkable for their ability to regenerate limbs.* **2** bring new and more vigorous life to an area or institution. *Bank management partnerships aim to regenerate banks' commercial papers.* **3** give a new and higher spiritual nature to. *Regenerative powers of nature can be found in herbs.* **4** [chemistry] precipitate as fibres following chemical processing. *Cellulose can be regenerated from ionic liquids.* *(adjective)* reborn, especially in a spiritual or moral sense. *Yoga helps us to spiritually regenerate.*

Regent – *(noun)* **1** a person appointed to administer a state because the monarch is a minor or is absent or incapacitated. *The regent represented the King of Denmark as sovereign of Iceland until the country became a republic.* **2** [north American] a member of the governing body of a university or other academic institution. (adjective) acting as regent; prince regent. *The colonized state was ruled by a regent.*

Regime – *(noun)* **1** a government, especially an authoritarian one. *Hitler's regime showed early signs of army fascism.* **2** a systematic or ordered way of doing something. *The school follows a rigorous education regime.* **3** the conditions under which a scientific or industrial process occurs. *Zimbabwe is not in favour of the diamond-control regime.*

Regimen – *(noun)* **1** a therapeutic course of medical treatment, often including recommendations as to diet and exercise. *The new regimen will surely make her lose weight.* **2** [archaic] a system of government. *A lot of people have prayed for the party to have regimen over the nation.*

Regiment – *(noun)* **1** a permanent unit of an army, typically divided into several smaller units and often into two battalions. *The British army has an armoured regiment.* **2** a large number of people or things. *The speaker rose to face the regiment of boys and girls.* **3** [archaic] rule or government. *The 14th century saw the French regiment in power. (verb)* **1** organize according to a strict system. *She cautiously regiments her own diet.* **2** rare form into a regiment or regiments. *The school regiments its students by having strict rules.*

Region – *(noun)* **1** an area of a country or the world having definable characteristics but not always fixed boundaries. an administrative district of a city or country. *The river flows downstream along the northern region of the city.* **2** a part of the body, especially around or near an organ. *She faced severe pain in the pelvic region of her body.*

Regional – *(adjective)* characteristic of a region. *His accent has a regional. (noun)* a thing produced in a particular region. *Cotton textiles are produced with regional imprints in Bangladesh*

Register – *(noun)* **1** an official list or record. a record of attendance, for example of pupils in a class. *The teacher always carried her attendance register.* **2** a particular par to the range of a voice or instrument. *Various writers state that there are from anywhere from one to seven registers present.* **3** [linguistics] a variety of language determined by degree of formality and choice of vocabulary, pronunciation, and syntax. *The choice of register is affected by the setting and topic of speech.* **4** printing the exact correspondence of the position of colour components in a printed positive. printing the exact correspondence of the position of printed mater on the two sides of a leaf. *The photograph was regrettably out of register.* **5** a location in a store of data, used for a specific purpose and with quick access time. *The inn's register lies on the table.* **6** a sliding device controlling a set of organ pipes which share a tonal quality. a set of organ pipes so controlled. *The organ is controlled by several registers.*

Registrar – *(noun)* **1** an official responsible for keeping a register of official records. *The Commissioner is the registrar of births and deaths in some corporations.* **2** the chief administrative officer in a university. *The position of a registrar constitutes the hub around which the management of a university revolves.* **3** the judicial and administrative officer of the high court. *The registrar has the power to reject or direct amendments.* **4** [British] a middle-ranking hospital doctor undergoing training as a specialist. *He is an orthopaedic registrar at the hospital.*

Registration – *(noun)* **1** the action or process of registering or of being registered. *The newly-married couple are eager for their marriage registration.* **2** [British] the series of letters and figures identifying a motor vehicle, displayed on a number plate. *The number of public vehicle registrations has decreased.* **3** the action or process of acquiring full [British] citizenship by a commonwealth resident or a person of [British] descent. *It is possible to become a British citizen by naturalisation or registration.*

Registry – *(noun)* **1** a place where registers are kept. *Windows maintains a hefty registry of files.* **2** registration. *She needs a registry form to book a place.*

Regret – *(verb)* feel or express sorrow, repentance, or disappointment over. *I regret not reaching the venue on time. (noun)* a feeling of sorrow, repentance, or disappointment. used in polite formulas to express apology or sadness. *Sorrow and regret go hand in hand.* regretful. *He is regretful of his action.*

Regular – *(adjective)* **1** arranged in a constant of definite pattern, especially with the some space between individual instances. recurring at short uniform intervals. *The plants in the lawn were placed at regular intervals.* **2** doing the same thing often or at uniform intervals: regular worshippers. done or happening frequently. *Regular exercise is the key to good health.* **3** conforming to or governed by an accepted standard of procedure or convention. of or belonging to the permanent professional armed forces of a country. properly trained or qualified and pursuing a full-time occupation. Christian church subject to or bound by religious rule. contrasted with secular. *A regular job is not her cup of tea.* **4** usual or customary. [chiefly north American] of an ordinary kind. denoting merchandise of average size. *The customers usually order regular fries.* **5** [grammar] following the normal pattern of inflection. *There are thousands of regular (verb)s in English.* **6** [geometry] having all sides and all angles equal. bounded by a number of equal figures. *The teacher drew a regular octagon on the board.* regularize. *The garment industry agreed to regularize women's clothing sizes.*

Regulate – *(verb)* **1** control or maintain the rate or speed of a machine or process. *The green button regulates the tension in the sewing machine.* **2** control or supervise by means of rules and regulations. *The new principal regulated the school with strict discipline.*

Regulation – *(noun)* **1** a rule or directive made and maintained by an authority. in accordance with regulations. [informal] of a familiar or predictable type. *The new regulations were too tough.* **2** the action or process of regulating or being regulated. *The king's regulation was kind and considerate.*

Rehabilitate – *(verb)* **1** restore to health or normal life by training and therapy after imprisonment, addiction, or illness. *The sensible doctor successfully rehabilitated the alcoholic.* **2** restore the standing or reputation of. *The quick actions rehabilitated the Governor's reputation.* **3** restore to a former condition. *The archaeological department rehabilitated the monument.*

Rehearse – *(verb)* **1** practice for later public performance. *The dance troupe rehearsed their act many times.* **2** state a list of points that have been made many times before. *The lawyer rehearsed the points in the accuses defence.*

Reign – *(verb)* **1** rule as monarch. *The cruel king reigned for decades.* **2** sports player or team currently holding a particular title. *Our football team reigned over the title last year.* **3** prevail: confusion reigned. *Confusion reigned the entire session of parliament.* *(noun)* **1** the period of rule of a monarch. *The king took good care of his subject during his reign.* **2** the period during which someone or something is predominant or pre-eminent. *During the reign of terror, people barely stepped out of their houses.*

Reimburse – *(verb)* repay a person who has spent or lost money. repay a sum of money that has been spent of lost. *My company reimburses my travel expenses.*

Rein – *(noun)* **1** a long, narrow strap attached at one end to a horse's bit, typically used in Paris to guide or check a horse in riding or driving. a similar device used to restrain a young child. *The new rider pulled the reins too hard.* **2** the power to direct and control: a new chairperson will soon take over the reins. *Law and order conditions improved as soon as the new Government took over the reins.* *(verb)* **1** check or guide by pulling on its reins. *The rider reined the horse expertly.* **2** restrain. *Please rein your horses.*

Reindeer – *(noun)* a deer with large branching antlers, native to the northern tundra and subarctic and domesticated in parts of Eurasia. *The herd of reindeers grazed on the sparse grasses.*

Reinforce – *(verb)* **1** strengthen with additional personnel or material. *After the threat, the government reinforced the security at crowded places.* **2** give added strength to. *We reinforced the boundary walls around our house.*

Reinstate – *(verb)* restore to a former position or state. *The law and order situation was reinstated with some tough actions.*

Reiterate – *(verb)* say something again or repeatedly. *The principal reiterated her points regarding importance of discipline.*

Reject – *(verb)* **1** dismiss as inadequate or faulty. refuse to consider or agree to. *The manufactured goods were rejected by the inspection department.* **2** fail to show due affection or concern for. *The pigeon rejected her eggs.* **3** [medicine] show a damaging immune response to a transplanted organ or tissue. *His body rejected the transplanted kidney.* *(noun)* a rejected person or thing. *The store sold the rejects at discounted prices.*

Rejoice – *(verb)* feel or show great joy. [archaic] cause joy to. *The children rejoiced upon hearing about the unexpected holidays.*

Rejuvenate – *(verb)* **1** make or cause to appear younger or more vital. *The morning walks have rejuvenated me.* **2** restore a river or stream to a condition characteristic of a younger landscape. *The project rejuvenated the polluted river.*

Relapse – *(verb)* deteriorate after a period of improvement. *The conditions of the patient relapsed.* **2** return to a worse of less active state. *The discipline of the school relapsed as soon as the principal left.* *(noun)* a deterioration in health after a temporary improvement. *The chances of his survival were minimal after the relapse.*

Relate – *(verb)* **1** give an account of. *The child related the details of the family vacations to all his friends.* **2** be connected by blood or marriage. *I was glad to relate to the man I loved.* **3** establish a causal connection between. concern. *I don't relate to her at all.* **4** feel sympathy with. *I can relate to her situation.*

Relation – *(noun)* **1** the way in which two or more people or things are connected or related. the way in which two or more people or groups feel about and behave towards each other. *The relation between them demanded respect.* **2** a relative. *I was thrilled to discover that the famous painter was a relation.* **3** the action of telling a story. *The master storyteller's vivid relation thrilled the children.* **4** formal sexual intercourse. *Their relation spoiled the friendship they shared.*

Relationship – *(noun)* **1** the way in which two or more people or things are connected, or the state of being connected. the way in which two or more people or groups regard and behave towards each other. *The relationship between hard work and success cannot be denied.* **2** an emotional and sexual association between two people. *Their relationship was founded on love and trust.*

Relative – *(adjective)* **1** considered in relation or in proportion to something else. existing or possessing a characteristic only in comparison to something else. *He admired his elder brother for his relative success in the sad economic environment.* **2** [grammar] denoting a pronoun, determiner, or adverb that refers to an expressed to implied antecedent and attaches a subordinate clause to it. e.g. which. attached to an antecedent by a relative word. *The child had a lot of trouble understanding the concept of relative words.* **3** [music] having the same key signature. *They started with relative notes.* **4** corresponding in grade to another in a different service. *The armyman was glad to find an officer of relative position in the Navy.* *(noun)* **1** a person connected by blood or marriage. a species related to another by common origin. *She turned out to be my relative.* **2** [philosophy] a term or concept which a dependent on something else. *It is difficult to understand this philosophy without understanding the relative concept.*

Relax – *(verb)* **1** make or become less tense or anxious. cause to become less rigid. *Her face relaxed and broke into a smile.* **2** rest from work or engage in a recreational activity. *She wants to relax after the hectic travel.* **3** make a rule or restriction less strict. *The police relaxed the curfew after two days of peace.*

Relay – *(verb)* lay again or differently. *She relayed the foundations for her company.*

Release – *(verb)* **1** set free. *The policeman released the little pickpocket.* **2** allow information to be generally available. make a film or recording available to the public. *They will release the brochure today.* **3** allow to move or flow freely. remove from a fixed position, allowing something else to move or function. *The water was released from the dam to avoid flood.* **4** [law] remit or discharge a debt. surrender a right. make over to another. *The bank released the debt yesterday.* *(noun)* **1** the action or process of releasing or being released. a film or other product released to the public. *The film release was highly successful.* **2** a handle or catch that releases part of a mechanism. *The release* *of the engine was stuck.* **3** [law] the action of releasing property, money, or a right to another. a document effecting this. *The release order was signed today.*

Relegate – *(verb)* **1** assign an inferior rank or position to. *The general relegated the officer.* **2** [British] transfer a sports team to a lower division of a league. *Our team was relegated in the tournament.*

Relent – *(verb)* **1** abandon or mitigate a harsh intention or cruel treatment. *The teacher relented when the student told her the reason.* **2** become less intense. *The storm relented in the evening.*

Relentless – *(adjective)* **1** oppressively constant. *The relentless winds damaged the seaside houses.* **2** harsh or inflexible. *The principal is pretty relentless in purging the bad students from the school.*

Relevant – *(adjective)* closely connected or appropriate to the matter in hand. *The audience asked all the relevant questions.*

Reliable – *(adjective)* able to be relied on. *My car is pretty reliable.*

Reliance – *(noun)* dependence on or trust in someone or something. *It was a question of reliance.*

Relic – *(noun)* **1** an object of interest surviving from an earlier time. a surviving but outdated object, custom, or belief. *The archaeologists were thrilled to find the relic.* **2** a part of a deceased holy person's body or belongings kept as an object of reverence. *The relic was centuries old.*

Relief – *(noun)* **1** the alleviation or removal of pain, anxiety, or distress. a feeling or cause of relief. a temporary break in a generally tense or tedious situation. *She felt some relief after taking the painkillers.* **2** financial or practical assistance given to those in special need or difficulty. *The relief helped the family of the deceased.* **3** a person or group of people replacing others who have been on duty. [British] an extra vehicle providing supplementary public transport at peak times or in emergencies. *The relief arrived late.* **4** distinctness due to being accentuated. *The relief was beautiful.* **5** a method of moulding, craving, or stamping in which the design stands out from the surface, to a greater or lesser extent. a representation of relief given by an arrangement of line, colour, etc. *The artist decorated the vase with traditional reliefs.*

Relieve – *(verb)* **1** alleviate or remove cause to stop duty by taking their place. *The morning guard relieved the night guard late today.* **2** take from someone. *She relieved her friend of some of the weight she was carrying.* **3** bring military support for a besieged place. *The friendly nation relieved their troubled neighbour.* **4** make less tedious or monotonous. *The energetic professor relieved the class.* **5** formal urinate or defecate. *He relieved himself in the woods.* **6** [archaic] make stand out. *His energy relieved him in the group.*

Religion – *(noun)* **1** the belief in and worship of a superhuman controlling power, especially a personal God or gods. a particular system of faith and worship. *There are many religions in the world.* **2** a pursuit or interest followed with devotion. *My work is my religion.*

Religious – *(adjective)* **1** of, concerned with, or believing in a religion. belonging or relating to a monastic order or other group united by their practice of religion. *This is a congregation of religious people.* **2** treated or regarded with a devotion and scrupulousness appropriate to worship. *The religious tree stood right in the middle of the road.* *(noun)* a person bound by monastic vows. *The religious teacher spent most of his time reading.*

Relinquish – *(verb)* voluntarily cease to keep or claim; give up. *I relinquished my claim on the property.*

Relish – *(noun)* **1** great enjoyment. pleasurable anticipation. *I wish the relish lasts forever.* **2** a piquant sauce or pickle eaten with plain food to add flavour. *I love the relish you make.* **3** [archaic] an appetizing flavour. a distinctive taste or tinge. *Please comment about the relish.* *(verb)* **1** enjoy greatly;. anticipate with pleasure. *I relished the food tonight.* **2** [archaic] make pleasant to the taste. *Please relish the turkey.*

Relive – *(verb)* live through an experience or feeling again in one's imagination. *I relived my college life during the reunion.*

Reluctant – *(adjective)* unwilling and hesitant. *I took my reluctant dog to the vet.*

Rely – *(verb)* **1** depend on with full trust. *I rely upon you for quality work.* **2** be dependent on. *I rely upon my agent for work.*

Remain – *(verb)* **1** be in the same place or condition during further time. continue to be: he remained alert. *She remained in her seat even after all the students had left.* **2** be left over after others or other parts have been completed, used, or dealt with. *Only few more pages remain.*

Remainder – *(noun)* **1** a part, number, or quantity that is left over. the number which is left over in a division in which one quanity does not exactly divide another. *She calculated the remainder wrong.* **2** a part that is still to come. *The remainder of the series is bound to be interesting.* **3** a copy of a book left unsold when demand has fallen. *The huge remainder sealed the fate of the book.* **4** [law] an interest in an estate that becomes effective in possession only when a prior interest ends. *There will be a long remainder for this property.* *(verb)* dispose of a book left unsold at a reduced price. *The publisher remaindered the book.*

Remains – *(plural noun)* **1** things remaining. *The remains of the fight still make me angry.* **2** [historical] or archaeological relics. *The remains of the ancient civilization gave great insights into the way of life for the people.* **3** a person's body after death. *His remains were buried near the church.*

Remand – *(verb)* place a defendant on bail or in custody, especially when a trial is adjourned. *The court remanded the suspect.* *(noun)* a committal to custody. *The suspect was put into remand.*

Remark – *(verb)* **1** say as a comment; mention. *He remarked about the quality of the thesis.* **2** regard with attention; notice. *The police remarked the woman who fidgeted with her pencil.* *(noun)* a comment. notice or comment. *His remarks upset me a great deal.*

Remedy – *(noun)* **1** a medicine or treatment for a disease or injury. *It was an effective remedy.* **2** a means of counteracting or eliminating something undesirable. *The remedy was successful in reinstating peace.* **3** a means of legal reparation. *The remedy wasn't acceptable to any of the parties.* **4** the margin within which coins as minted may differ from the standard fineness and weight. *The fake coins were identified based on the remedy put in place.* *(verb)* rectify an undesirable situation. *His sensibility remedied an ugly argument.*

Remember – *(verb)* **1** have in or be able to bring to one's mind someone or something form the past. bear in mind by making them a gift, making provision for them, or mentioning them in prayer. recover one's manners after a lapse. *Do you remember our first meeting?* **2** keep in mind. *Please remember me.* **3** convey greetings from one person to another. *Please remember me to your father.*

Remembrance – *(noun)* the action of remembering a memory. a thing kept or given as a reminder or in commemoration of someone. *Please keep this ring as a remembrance of our relationship.*

Remind – *(verb)* cause to remember something or to do something. cause someone to think of something because of a resemblance. *It was good of you to remind me of this association.*

Reminder – *(noun)* a thing that causes someone to remember something. a letter sent to remind someone to pay a bill. *Did you get a reminder from the company?*

Reminiscent – *(adjective)* **1** tending to remind one of something. *Your voice is reminiscent of someone I knew.* **2** absorbed in memories. *I am reminiscent today of happy school days.*

Remiss – *(adjective)* lacking care or attention to duty. *It would be remiss of me not to convey this information to students.*

Remission – *(noun)* **1** the cancellation of a debt, charge, or penalty. [British] the reduction of a prison sentence, especially as a reward for good behavious. *The poor family was glad to have received a remission.* **2** a temporary diminution of the severity of disease or pain. *She is currently* *in remission.* **3** formal forgiveness of sins. *A visit to the shrine is said to cause remission.*

Remit – *(verb)* **1** refrain from exacting or inflicting. theology pardon a sin. *Will God remit my sin?* **2** send in payment, especially by post. *I have remitted the money.* **3** refer a matter for decision to an authority. [law] send back to a lower court. [law] send for one tribunal to another for a trial or hearing. *The high court remitted the matter to the local courts.* **4** [archaic] diminish. *The crime remitted his reputation. (noun)* **1** the task or area of activity officially assigned to an individual or organization. *The remit was well handled.* **2** an item referred for consideration. *The remit was very expensive.*

Remittance – *(noun)* a sum of money remitted. the action of remitting money. *Have you received the notification about the remittance?*

Remnant – *(noun)* **1** a small remaining quantity. a piece of cloth left when the greater part has been used or sold. *Please keep the remnants safe.* **2** a surviving trace. *One can still see the remnants of traditions in some rituals.* **3** [Christian theology] a small minority of people who will remain faithful to god and so be saved. *The Remnants have nothing to worry about.* (adjective) remaining. *The remnant fabric can be used to create new designs.*

Remonstrate – *(verb)* make a forcefully reproachful protest. *The students remonstrated against the new rules.*

Remorse – *(noun)* deep regret or guilt for a wrong committed. *I was touched by his genuine feelings of remorse.*

Remote – *(adjective)* **1** far away in space or time. situated far from the main centres of population. *The remote village didn't have any electricity supply.* **2** distantly related. having very little connection with. *I barely know my remote relations.* **3** unlikely to occur. *There is a remote possibility that I will complete this task today.* **4** aloof and unfriendly in manner. *His remote behaviour cost him many friends.* **5** operating or operated by mains of radio or infrared signals. *Please use the remote control to turn up the volume.*

Remove – *(verb)* **1** take off or away from the position occupied. abolish or get rid of. dismiss from a psot. dated relocate to another place. *The guard was removed after he was found sleeping.* **2** be very different from. *The unique design of her dress removed her from the rest of the crowd.* **3** separated by a particular number of steps of descent: his second cousin once removed. *She turned out to be his second cousin once removed. (noun)* a degree of remoteness or separation. *It was difficult to estimate the remove of the village from the city.*

Remunerate – *(verb)* pay for services rendered or work done. *The company promised to remunerate him well for his services.*

Remuneration – *(noun)* money paid for some work. *Diana agreed to work overtime if her firm promised to pay her extra remuneration.*

Renaissance – *(noun)* **1** the revival of art and literature under the influence of classical models in the 14th-16th centuries. *Shakespeare and Ben Jonson are writers that belonged to the Renaissance age.* **2** a revival of or renewed interest in something. *The art of enacting folktales has become something of a renaissance with the younger generation.*

Render – *(verb)* **1** provide or give a service, help, etc. submit for inspection, consideration, or payment. poetic hand over; surrender. *Sheela wished to be adequately paid for the services rendered by her.* **2** cause to be or become. *Gita was rendered helpless after the car accident.* **3** represent or depict artistically. music perform a piece. *Gia's piano piece was exceptionally well rendered.* **4** translate. *The President's speech was rendered into Japanese for the civilians present at the meeting.* **5** melt down typically in order to extract proteins, fats and other usable parts. *The milk was being whipped to be rendered into cheese and cream.* **6** cover with a coat of plaster. *The palace walls were rendered to protect them from detrimental environmental factors. (noun)* a first coat of plaster applied to a brick or stone surface. *The rendered walls were essential to protect the house during monsoon.*

Renew - *(verb)* **1** resume or re-establish after an interruption. *The sisters renewed their love and affection for each other after the fight.* **2** give fresh life or strength to. *Cindy resumed her work with renewed determination to excel.* **3** extend the period of validity of a licence, subscription, or contract. *Tom's contract with the company was renewed this evening.* **4** replace or restore something broken or worn out. *The licence was renewed yesterday.*

Renounce - *(verb)* **1** formally declare one's abandonment of a claim, right, or possession. [law] refuse or resign a right or position, especially one as an heir or trustee. *The priest renounced all his worldly possessions for a life of piety.* **2** refuse to recognize any longer. *Sia renounced her relationship with her husband once she was made aware of his affair with another woman.* **3** abandon. *Xen renounced his mother and sister for his lady love.*

Renovate - *(verb)* **1** restore something old to a good state of repair. *The old house was renovated last month.* **2** [archaic] reinvigorate. *Chaucer resumed writing about social pressures with renovated exuberance after his argument with the priest.*

Renown - *(noun)* the state of being famous. *Dancers of great renown were present at the party last night.*

Renowned - *(adjective)* famous. *Vineet has renowned the world over for his talent of tap dancing.*

Rent - *(noun)* **1** a tenant's regular payment to a landlord for the use of property or land. *Fiona was ready to pay the exorbitant monthly rent for the seaside apartment.* **2** a sum paid for the hire of equipment. *Diana decided to rent out her apartment to the campers for the summer.* *(verb)* pay someone for the use of. let someone use in return for payment. [chiefly north American] be let or hired out at a specified rate. *The campers had to pay Diana for renting her apartment for the summer.*

Renunciation - *(noun)* **1** the action of renouncing. *The promise to celibacy demands the renunciation of marriage.* **2** [law] a document expressing renunciation. *The lawyer presented the documents enlisting the renunciation of all heritage property by the state government.*

Reorganize - *(verb)* **1** order again. *The General reorganized the ranks to suit the interest of the army.* **2** arrange again. *Stacy reorganized her desk after her promotion.* *(noun)* a renewed or repeated order for goods. *The reorganized produce was transferred from the farm to the market yesterday.*

Repair - *(verb)* **1** restore something damaged, worn, or faulty to a good condition. *Cindy repaired her bike for the new year at college.* **2** set right a rift in relations. *Gia's mother settled all the arguments between her children and effectively repaired their relations.* *(noun)* **1** the action of repairing. a result of this. *Breaking the moulds was part of the repair.* **2** the relative physical condition of an object. *Wear and tear of tyres is an effective step in the process of repair.*

Repartee - *(noun)* conversation or speech characterized by quick, witty comments or replies. *Seema is popular all over the college campus for the witty repartee.*

Repast - *(noun)* formal a meal. *We had a sumptous repast during the marning celebration last evening.*

Repatriate - *(verb)* send back to their own country. *After the war ended, trucks were repatriating the enemy soldiers to their country.* *(noun)* a person who has been repatriated. *Tim is a war repatriate.*

Repay - *(verb)* **1** pay back a loan. pay back money owed to someone. *Fiona repaid her car loan in just about six months time.* **2** do or give something as recompense for a favour or kindness received. *Sera repaid the favour that Beth had done to her by gifting her a watch.* **3** be worth subjecting to a specified action. *The social networking site will repay more detailed information.*

Repeal - *(verb)* revoke or annul a [law] or act of parliament. *The law was repealed after the mass murder.* *(noun)* the action of repealing. *The entire jury voted in favour of repeal.*

Repeat – *(verb)* **1** say or do again. say or do the same thing again. *Ben decided to repeat himself in order to get his point through to the audience at the workshop.* **2** be tasted after being swallowed, as a result of indigestion. *Danny repeated his dish just to check if it was alright or had gone bad.* *(noun)* **1** an instance of repeating or being repeated. occurring, done, or used more than once: a repeat prescription. *The dentist prescribed a repeat of the same medication to Ned.* **2** a repeated broadcast of a television or radio programme. *Ned was eager to watch the repeats of the show as he had nothing better to do on the weekend.* **3** a consignment of goods similar to one already received. *The smugglers noticed a repeat consignment on their ship and were taken aback.* **4** a decorative pattern which is repeated uniformly over a surface. *The embroidery on the doily was a beautiful repeat pattern done up in several colours.* **5** [music] a passage intended to be repeated. a mark indicating this. *The piano player played the repeat again at the request of the audience.*

Repel – *(verb)* **1** drive or force back or away. *Oil and water repel each other.* **2** be repulsive or distasteful to. *Tina repelled Jim and was adamant on refusing all his favours.* **3** formal refuse to accept; reject. *The jury repelled all pleas of the guilty.* **4** force something similarly magnetized or charged away. *The mercury on the floor was instantly repelled by the damp surface.* **5** resist mixing with or be impervious to. *Gia made it clear that she disliked Jim by consciously repelling all his friendly gestures towards her.*

Repent – *(verb)* feel or express sincere regret or remorse. [archaic] feel regret or penitence about. *It is futile to repent one's actions after the damage has been done.* repentance. *The capacity of repentance is impossible in the heart of an egotist.*

Repercussion – *(noun)* **1** a consequence of an event or action. *The political agenda can have multiple repercussions.* **2** [archaic] the recoil of something after impact. *The bend in the stick was a natural repercussion to the force applied to it.* **3** [archaic] an echo or reverberation. *Jim's untimely death was nothing but a repercussion of his evil actions.*

Repertoire – *(noun)* the body of pieces known or regularly performed by a performer push back. *Jim is renowned all over the city for his performances and impeccable repertoire.*

Repetition – *(noun)* the act or an instance of repeating or being repeated. a thing that repeats another. *Any concept can be learned and internalized by the process of repetition.*

Replace – *(verb)* **1** take the place of. *Diana's sister could never replace Nina's mother no matter how hard she tried.* **2** provide a substitute for. *Daily sugar intake can be replaced with glucose for energy and strength.* **3** put back in a previous place or position. *Fiona replaced Dina's jewellery that she had borrowed, at its original position after the prom night.*

Replacement – *(noun)* replacing something or someone. *Ted found a suitable replacement for his secretary who has gone on a maternity leave.*

Replay – *(verb)* **1** play back a recording. *Danny requested his wife to replay the song on the recorder at the party.* **2** play a match again. *The school team replayed the cricket match once it stopped raining.* *(noun)* **1** the act or an instance of replaying. *The replay of movie was refrishing.* **2** a replayed match. *The match on shown on television today was a replay.*

Replenish – *(verb)* fill up again. *Europe turns to India in order to replenish all their resources.*

Replete – *(adjective)* **1** filled or well-supplied with something. *Our trip to Egypt was replete with incidents that reminded us of the yester years.* **2** very full with food; sated. *Tim left the party yesterday replete and satisfied.*

Replica – *(noun)* an exact copy or model of something, especially. *The museum of Madame Tussaud has on display exact replicas of famous personalities from all over the world.*

Reply – *(verb)* say or write something in response to something said or written. *I hope my mother replied to the Principal's letter.* *(noun)* **1** the action of replying. *Jenny's letter to the landlord was more of an informal replay.* **2** a spoken or written response. [law] a plain-tiff's response to the defendant's plea. *The guilty party sent a legal reply to the victim's family as directed by the court.*

Report – *(verb)* **1** give a spoken or written account of something. convey information about an event or situation. *All the new cadets reported their daily schedules to the manager on duty.* **2** make a formal complaint about. *Fiona went and reported her abusive husband to the police.* **3** present oneself as having arrived at a particular place or as ready to do something. *All new candidates were asked to report for the interview at noon.* **4** be responsible to a supervisor or manager. *Sheena reports to her Editor directly.* **5** [British formally] announce that a parliamentary committee has dealt with a bill. US return a bill to the legislative body for action. *The British government officially reported the extinction of the law of abortion today.* *(noun)* **1** an account given of a matter after investigation or consideration. *Wendy was asked to make a detailed report about the monthly expenditure by her lawyer.* **2** a piece of information about an event or situation. talk; rumour. *Cindy asked Tina to give her a detailed report of the party last night.* **3** [British] a teacher's written assessment of a pupil's work and progress. *All parents were summoned by the teacher so that she could hand over the progress reports of the kids in her class.* **4** [law] a detailed formal account of a case heard in a court. *The jury ordered the lawyer to prepare a detailed report of the case.* **6** an employee who reports to another employee. *All copy editors were asked to report directly to the manager.*

Repose – *(verb)* place something, especially one's confidence or trust, in. *Tina succumbed to her fate of loneliness with quiet repose.*

Represent – *(verb)* **1** be entitled or appointed to act or speak for. be an elected member of parliament of member of a legislature for. act as a substitute for. *Dan surprised the judge when he chose to represent the guilty party.* **2** constitute; amount to. be a specimen or example of, typify. be present to a particular degree: abstraction is well represented in this exhibition. *The study group in the library represents the intellectual quotient of the university.* **3** depict in a work of art. portray in a particular way: they were represented as being in need of protection. signify; symbolize, or embody. *The poetry written by children represents a distinct form of creativity in them.* **4** formal state or point out. *I am representing the Indian population in Australia at the rally.*

Representation – *(noun)* **1** the action or an instance of representing or being represented. *The theatre group was present at the court for representation purpose only.* **2** an image, model, or other depiction of something. *The clay model is a representation of the space shuttle.* **3** statements made to an authority to communicate an opinion or register a protest. *All the society members made a representation at the court hearing to fight for justice.*

Representative – *(adjective)* **1** typical of a class or group. containing typical examples of many or all types. *Anna Hazare is a proper representative of the working class in India.* **2** a legislative or deliberative assembly consisting of people chosen to act and speak on behalf of a wider group. based on such representation of the people. *The Indian government boasts a well defined representative assembly.* **3** serving as portrayal of something. *The book is a representative of the socio-economic conditions prevalent in India.* *(noun)* **1** a person chosen or appointed to act or speak for another or others. *Tom stood as a people's representative in the elections.* **2** an agent of a firm who travels to potential clients to sell its products. *Sid works as a sales representative for the plastic company.* **3** an example of a class or group. *Fiona is a representative of the lower middle working class in Africa.*

Repress – *(verb)* **1** subdue by force. *Celibacy demands the repressing of all sexual desires.* **2** restrain, prevent, or inhibit. suppress a thought, feeling, or desire. in oneself of that it becomes or remains unconscious. *One needs to repress* *individual desires for the greater good of society.* **3** [biology] prevent the transcription of a gen. *The X-chromosome is repressed by the Y-chromosome in males.*

Reprieve – *(verb)* cancel or postpone the punishment or demise of. *The new policy allowed the punishment of all wrong doers to be reprieved. (noun)* such a cancellation or postponement. *Tim was so guilty of his actions that he refused to ask for his punishment to be reprieved.*

Reprimand – *(noun)* a formal expression of disapproval. *To reprimand is to teach control and manners. (verb)* address a reprimand to. *Jenna was reprimanded for her work in public by her boss.*

Reprisal – *(noun)* **1** an act of retaliation. *The British government was shocked by the Indian reprisal.* **2** [historical] the forcible seizure of a foreign subject or their goods as an act of retaliation. *The Indian government denied any laxity in punishing the culprits guilty of the reprisal.*

Reproach – *(verb)* **1** express to someone one's disapproval of or disappointment in their actions. *Tina was strongly reproached by her mother for her indecent behaviour.* **2** accuse someone of. *Gia was reproached by all her classmates for breaking Zen's heart. (noun)* **1** an expression of disapproval or disappointment. *Reproach is the strongest kind of criticism.*

Reproachful – *(adjective)* expresseing disapproval disappoitment. *Tia was reproachful of her husband's behaviour towards her relatives.*

Reproduce – *(verb)* **1** produce a copy or representation of. create something in a different medium or context that is very similar to. *The play was a reproduction of the original art form.* **2** produce offspring. *Mammals reproduce once a year, unlike reptiles.*

Reproof – *(noun)* a rebuke or reprimand. *Tim strongly disapproved of his public reproof by his boss.*

Reprove – *(verb)* rebuke or reprimand. *Tina was strongly reproved by her husband at the party last night.*

Reptile – *(noun)* **1** a cold-blooded vertebrate animal of a class that includes snakes, lizards, crocodiles, turtles, and tortoises, typically having a dry scaly skin and laying soft-shelled eggs on land. *Lizard is a reptile.* **2** [informal] a person regarded with loathing and contempt. *Vineet is nothing but a reptile and I absolutely loath him.*

Republic – *(noun)* a state in which supreme power is held by the people and their elected representatives, and which has an elected or nominated president rather than a monarch. *He was unanimously elected president of the Republic of Kenya.*

Republican – *(adjective)* **1** belonging to or characteristic of a republic. *Every nation ought to have democratic as well as republican attributes.* **2** advocating republican government. *America is a republican nation.* **3** supporting the republican party. *The opposition is the Republican party. (noun)* **1** a person advocating republican government. *The present President belongs to the Republican Party.* **2** republican party. *The present President belongs to the Republican Party.*

Repudiate – *(verb)* **1** refuse to accept or be associated with. *Tina repudiated the gender sensitization policies of the firm that she was working with.* **2** deny the truth or validly of. *The judge repudiated the allegations of child sexual abuse.* **3** [chiefly law] refuse to fulfil or discharge. *Flouting of rules gives the opposition party the power to repudiate the constitution.* **4** [archaic] disown or divorce one's wife. *Tina was disowned by her parents because she repudiated her siblings.*

Repugnant – *(adjective)* **1** extremely distasteful; unacceptable. *Domestic violence is a repugnant act.* **2** in conflict with; incompatible with. *Every outlaw seems repugnant to society as a whole.* **3** [archaic] given to stubborn resistance. *His repugnant behaviour led to his excommunication from society.*

Repulse – *(verb)* **1** drive back by force. rebuff or refuse to accept. *Ned's repulsive behaviour was the main cause of his banishment from* *the Sunday meet group.* **2** cause to feel intense distaste or disgust. *The garbage strewn all over the house was a repulsive sight. (noun)* the action or an instant of repulsing or being repulsed. *The utter repulsiveness of the divorce proceedings forced Gia to let go of her kid's custody.*

Repulsion – *(noun)* a feeling of intense distaste or disgust. *The estranged husband and wife shared a mutual feeling of repulsion towards each other.* **2** [physics] a force under the influence of which objects tend to move away form each other. *The lack of a magnetic field led to the repulsion of objects instantly.* **3** of or relating to repulsion between physical objects. *The car and trolley experienced a repulsive force separating them constantly.*

Repulsive – *(adjective)* **1** arousing intense distaste or disgust. *A repulsive odour emanated from the cupboard.*

Reputable – *(adjective)* having a good reputation. *The company can bank upon its reputable owners.*

Reputation – *(noun)* the beliefs or opinions that are generally held about someone or something. a widespread belief that someone or something has a particular characteristic. *The company's reputation depends upon its employees as well as its employers.*

Repute – *(noun)* **1** the opinion generally held of someone or something. *Lack of public safety can lead to a bad repute for the government.* **2** the state of being highly regarded; chefs of international repute. *Chef Vinod Khanna enjoys great repute in the entire culinary world. (verb)* be generally regarded as having done something or as having particular characteristics. being generally believed to exist. *Naved is reputed in his family for having made the best house.*

Request – *(noun)* an act of asking politely or formally for something. a thing that is asked for in such a way. *Tim's plea to his father regarding the mowing down of their family home was more of a humble request. (verb)* politely or formally ask for politely or formally ask to do something. *Diana requested her teacher to let her off a little early due to a family emergency.*

Require – *(verb)* **1** need or depend on. wish to have. *The orphanage required a great amount of donation to provide proper education for its inmates.* **2** strict or expect to do something. regard an action or quality as due from. specify as compulsory: required by [law]. *It is required by law to file a petition in the court before taking any action against state offenders.*

Requisite – *(adjective)* made necessary by particular circumstances or regulations. *The divorce proceedings will not be forwarded until the requisite fee is paid. (noun)* a thing that is necessary for the achievement of a specified end. *My mother believed a good maid to be a requisite for good home management.*

Requisition – *(noun)* **1** an official order laying claim to the use of property or materials. *Heidi was required to make various requisitions to hire the office area.* **2** the appropriation of goods for military or public use. *Requisition at gun point was a means of extracting food items during war.* **3** a formal written demand that something should be performed or put into operation. *Requisitions for a meeting with the head of the company are required to carry a defined purpose of visit. (verb)* demand the use, supply, or performance of through the issue of requisition. *Hitler had assumed the power to requisition property in the name of justice.*

Rescue – *(verb)* save from a dangerous or distressing situation. *The stray dogs were rescued by the shop keepers. (noun)* an act of rescuing or being rescued. *The soldiers decided to launch a rescue mission to look for the President's daughter who was kidnapped by a group of terrorists.*

Research – *(noun)* the systematic investigation into and study of materials and sources in order to establish facts and reach new conclusion. *Field work is an important part of any scientific research. (verb)* carry out research into. use research to discover or verify information presented in a book, programme, etc. *Tina found numerous interesting facts while researching for her new book.*

Researcher - *(noun)* one who conducts research. *Tim is employed as a researcher at the University of California.*

Resemble - *(verb)* to look alike or similar in appearance. *John greatly resembles his grandfather.*

Resemblance - *(noun)* the state of resembling. a way in which two or more things resemble each other. *The resemblance between Tim and his father is uncanny.*

Resent - *(verb)* feel bitterness or indignation at. *Sam resents having betrayed his girlfriend for another woman.*

Resentment - *(noun)* bitterness; indignation. *The resentment that Gill has towards her estranged husband is very visible.*

Reservation - *(noun)* **1** the action of reserving. an arrangement whereby something has been reserved. *Tim made reservations in a popular restaurant to surprise his wife on her birthday.* **2** an area of land set aside for occupation by [north American] Indians or Australian aboriginals. *The crime rate has reportedly increased in the Australian reservation area.* **3** [law] a right or interest retained in an estate being conveyed. *The urge to annex the property of a deceased relative will be a reservation.* **4** a qualification or expression of doubt attached to a statement or claim. *Tina expressed her reservation regarding the pre-nuptial agreement.* **5** the action of a superior of reserving the power of absolution. a right reserved to the pope of nomination to a vacant benefice. *The pope has the right to reservation where baptism is concerned.*

Reserve - *(verb)* **1** retain for future use. *Tina believes in reserving her money for the rainy day.* **2** arrange for to be kept for the use of a particular person. *Denny reserved his car for his wife.* **3** retain or hold a right or entitlement. *Sheena reserved the right to her organs to her husband in case of her untimely demise.* **4** refrain from delivering without due consideration or evidence. *Cindy reserved her comments regarding the divorce in front of her family members.* *(noun)* **1** a reserved supply of a commodity. funds kept available by a bank, company, or government. a part of a company's profiles added to capital rather than paid as a divided. *Veena decided to spend her reserve money cautiously after she lost her job.* **2** a force or body of troops withheld from action to reinforce or protect others, or additional to the regular forces and available in an emergency. *The Indian government deployed its reserve troops in the Kashmir region to restore peace.* **3** an extra player in a team, serving as a possible substitute. the second-choice team. *Satiago was excited that he had at least made it to the reserve football team.* **4** an area designated as a habitat for a native people. *Andaman & Nicobar Islands maintains the tribal reserve with great care as it is an essential part of cultural heritage.* **5** a protected area for wildlife. *The entire family planned a trip to the wildlife reserve sanctuary in Florida.* **6** a lack of warmth or openness. *Diana has very few friends owing to her reserved nature.* **8** an area in which the original material or background colour remains visible. *The old photograph exposed the reserve area in the background.*

Reserved - *(adjective)* slow to reveal emotion or opinions. *Tina's reserved nature is her only drawback.*

Reservoir - *(noun)* **1** a large natural or artificial lake used as a source of water supply. a supply or source of something. *Fiona's mother is a reservoir of information where their family history is concerned.* **2** a place where fluid collects, especially in rock strata or in the body. *All the muddy water collected in the reservoir near the village.* **3** a receptacle or part of a machine designed to hold fluid. *The engineer took no time to identify the broken reservoir that had led to the leakage.*

Reshuffle - *(verb)* **1** interchange the positions of members of a team, especially government ministers. *Coach Ned decided to reshuffle the team for better productivity.* **2** rearrange. *(noun)* an act of reshuffling. *Priya reshuffled all items in her handbag to kill some time while waiting for her boyfriend.*

Reside – *(verb)* **1** have one's permanent home in a particular place. *The family has been residing in the same locality for over five decades now.* **2** belong to a person or body. *All emotions, good or bad reside within the human self.* **3** be present or inherent in something. *The potential of being good or evil resides within the human mind.*

Residence – *(noun)* **1** the fact of residing somewhere. *The company owner needed a residence in the city to open an office.* **2** a person's home. *Can you please give me your residence address?* **3** the official house of a government minister or other official figure. *The Rashtrapati Bhavan is the residence of the President of India.*

Resident – *(noun)* **1** a person who lives somewhere on a long-term basis. a bird, butterfly, or other animal of a species that does not migrate. [British] a guest in a hotel who stays for one or more nights. [US] a pupil who boards at a boarding school. *American residents are investing in property in india.* **2** [north American] a medical graduate engaged in specialized practice under supervision in a hospital. *Ben is a resident at the hospital in Florida.* **3** an intelligence agent in a foreign country. *Vineet is stationed as a diplomat in Iraq by the Government of India.* **4** [historical a British] government agent in any semi-independent state, especially the governor general's representative at the court of an Indian state. *Danny enjoys a dual residency, both as an American as well as an Indian.* *(adjective)* **1** living somewhere on a long-term basis. having quarters on the premises of one's work. attached to and working regularly for a particular institution. non-migratory. *Ben has been a resident in Britain for a really long time.* **2** immediately available in computer memory, rather than having to be loaded from elsewhere. *The computer programmes are resident inside the hard disk by default.*

Residential – *(adjective)* **1** designed for people to live in. providing accommodation in addition to other services. occupied by private houses. *John was given a residential apartment by his company upon relocation to another city.* **2** concerning or relating to residence. *Ben forgot to give John his residential address despite his having reminded Ben twice.*

Residue – *(noun)* **1** a small amount of something that remains after the main part has gone or been taken or sued a substance that remains after a process such as combustion or evaporation. *Seers often read futures depending upon the residue left after drinking the cup of tea offered to the customer.* **2** [law] the part of an estate that is left after the payment of charges, debts, and bequests. *After their mother's death, the residue of her belongings was equally distributed amongst all her children.*

Resign – *(verb)* **1** voluntarily leave a job or position of office. *Tina's improper behaviour with her co-workers forced her to resign from her job.* **2** accept that something undesirable cannot be avoided. *After realizing that she had lost the battle with life, Diana resigned to her fate and finally succumbed to the disease.* **3** [archaic] surrender oneself to another's guidance. *The villagers resigned in from of the priest's advice.*

Resignation – *(noun)* **1** an act of resigning. a document conveying an intention to resign. *Fiona made her resignation public after being accused of being unethical.* **2** acceptance of something undesirable but inevitable. *Tim realized that Sheena had made up her mind when he noticed the sad look of resignation written all over her face.*

Resilient – *(adjective)* **1** able to recoil or spring back into shape after bending, stretching, or being compressed. *She won accolades all over campus for her resilient behaviour and forbearance.* **2** able to withstand or recover quickly from difficult conditions. *Being resilient is a virtue.*

Resist – *(verb)* **1** withstand the action or effect of. *She strongly resisted his favours.* **2** try to prevent by action or argument. *India resisted Pakistan's attack aggressively.* **3** refrain from something tempting. *She resisted having the chocolate fudge.* **4** struggle against. *She resisted all her husband's abuses with grit and strength* *of character. (noun)* a resistant substance applied as a coating to protect a surface during some process, for example to prevent dye or glaze adhering. *Oil and water resist mixing with each other.*

Resistance – *(noun)* **1** the action of resisting. *The boys showed resistance when confronted by the school authorities.* **2** armed or violent opposition. *The Naxals showed resistance when confronted by the army.* **3** a secret organization resisting political authority. the underground movement formed in France during the second world war to fight the German occupying forces and the Vichy government. *The French troops showed resistance towards the German ships.* **4** the impeding effect exerted by one material thing on another. **5** the ability not to be affected by something. [medicine & biology] lack of sensitivity to a drug, insecticide, etc. especially as a result of continued exposure or genetic change. *HIV-virus shows resistance towards all antibiotics.* **6** the degree to which a material or device opposes the passage of an electric current, causing energy dissipation. a resistor. *The window pane cleaner is water resistant.*

Resolute – *(adjective)* determined; unwavering. *Nina's resolute behaviour is her greatest strength.*

Resolution – *(noun)* **1** the quality of being resolute. *Tina listed her New Year resolutions on a piece of paper.* **2** a firm decision. a formal expression of opinion or intention agreed on by a legislative body. *She took a firm resolution to control her anger.* **3** the action of solving a problem or dispute. *My father came up with a suitable resolution for my problem.* **4** [music] the passing of a discord into a concord during the course of changing harmony. *The piano player wanted to work on the resolution of his piano.* **5** the process of reducing or separating something into components. *The chemist decided to inspect the resolution for gold particles.* **6** the smallest interval measurable by a telescope or other scientific instrument. *The scientist decided to check the resolution of his instruments before commencing work.* **7** the degree of detail visible in a photographic or television image. *I want to buy a high resolution camera.*

Resolve – *(verb)* **1** settle or find a solution to. medicine cause to heal or disappear. *The medicine is said to resolve my problem in a month.* **2** decide firmly on a course of action take a decision by a formal vote. *I resolved to get justice for the downtrodden.* **3** [music] cause to pass into a concord during the course of harmonic change. *Music resolves disharmony by overlapping notes.* **4** reduce a subject or statement by mental analysis into separate elements or a more elementary form. [chiefly chemistry] separate into constituent parts or components. *The chemist resolved the solution to distinguish between its components.* **5** turn into a different form when seen more clearly. separate of distinguish between closely adjacent objects. technical separately distinguish. *As we went nearer, the image resolved into a clearer one.* **6** [physics] analyse into components acting in particular directions. *The scientist checked the resolution power of the lens. (noun)* **1** firm determination. *The judge resolved to punish the murderer.* **2** [US] a formal resolution by a legislative body or public meeting. *The resolve to save the girl child is a major part of the election campaign.*

Resonant – *(adjective)* **1** deep; clear, and continuing to sound or ring. tending to reinforce or prolong sounds especially by synchronous vibration. filled or resounding with a sound. *His resonant voice charmed the ladies.* **2** having the ability to evoke or suggest enduring images, memories, or emotions. *The memory had a clear resonance to itself.* **3** enhancing another or others by contrast. *The resonance of the echo was even greater on the cliff.* **4** technical relating to or bringing about resonance in a circuit, atom, or other object. *The chemist strived to bring about resonance in the atomic structure of his model.*

Resonance – *(noun)* the quality of sound being clear and continuing for a long time. *The audience was mighty impressed with the resonance of the speaker's voice.*

Resort – *(noun)* the place where a lot of people for vacation. *The bride and groom decided to book the entire resort for their honeymoon.*

Resound – *(verb)* to fill a place with voice sound. *The palace resounded with a distinct echo of the yester year charm that the place once enjoyed.*

Resource – *(noun)* **1** a stock or supply of materials or assets. *Sheena wanted to take full advantage of her estranged husband's resources even after their divorce.* **2** an action or strategy adopted in adverse circumstances. personal attributes and capabilities that sustain one in adverse circumstances. a teaching aid. *Cindy decided to employ all her resources to the best of her ability to help her get a decent job in the new city.* *(verb)* provide with resources. *Sheena wanted to marry a resourceful man who would help her advance in her career.*

Respect – *(noun)* **1** a feeling of deep admiration for someone elicited by their qualities or achievements. polite greetings. *We should respect our elders.* **2** due regard for the feelings or rights of others. *We should respect other's feelings.* **3** a particular aspect, point, or detail. *Respecting the condition of the house, we decided to sit outside.* *(verb)* **1** feel or have respect for. *Ben respected his mother a lot.* **2** avoid harming or interfering with. *We should respect all religions.*

Respectable – *(adjective)* **1** regarded by society as being proper, correct, and good. *Ria wanted to be married into a respectable family.* **2** of some merit or importance. adequate or acceptable in number, size, or amount. *Mike wanted a job that would fetch him a respectable income.*

Respectful – *(adjective)* showing respect. *Children should be taught to be respectful of elders.*

Respective – *(adjective)* belonging or relating separately to each of two or more people or things. *All the candidates were requested to talk about their respective personal lives as part of the interview process.*

Respiration – *(noun)* **1** the action of breathing. a single breath. *The doctors decided to monitor the patient's respiration for a day or so.* **2** [biology] a process in living organisms involving the production of energy, typically with the intake of oxygen and the release of carbon dioxide from the oxidation of complex organic substances. *The biology teacher taught her students about the process of respiration in class today.*

Respire – *(verb)* breathe. carry out respiration. *Plants respire throughout the day.*

Respite – *(noun)* a short period of rest or relief from something difficult or unpleasant. *The prisoners of war sought respite from the Pakistan government.*

Resplendent – *(adjective)* attractive and impressive through being richly colourful or sumptuous. *The peacock's resplendent plumage is a sight to behold.*

Respond – *(verb)* say or do something *in* reply or as a reaction. *The court responded to her pleas.* *(noun)* **1** [architecture] a half-pillar or half-pier attached to a wall to support an arch. **2** a responsory; a response to a versicles.

Response – *(noun)* **1** an instance of responding; an answer or reaction. *It is impossible to elicit a positive response from an intolerant person.* **2** an excitation of a nerve impulse. *His pupil responded to the sudden light impact.*

Responsibility – *(noun)* **1** the state or fact of being responsible. *It is the responsibility of children to take care of their parents.* **2** the opportunity or ability to act independently and take decisions without authorization. often responsibilities a thing which one is required to do as part of a job, role, or legal obligation. *She was given the responsibility of the entire office because of her good work ethic.*

Responsible – *(adjective)* **1** having an obligation to do something, or having control over or care for someone. *Diana relies a lot on her responsible son.* **2** being the primary cause of something and so able to be blamed or credited for it. responsible to reporting to; answerable to. morally accountable for one's behaviour. *She is responsible for his success.* **3** of a hob or position involving important duties or decisions or control over others. *He is responsible for the functioning of the entire office.* **4** capable of being trusted. *Tim is a responsible boy.*

Responsive - *(adjective)* **1** responding readily and positively. *A well defined organization is responsive to any misdemeanours in society.* **2** in response; answering. *She is responsive of the treatment.*

Rest - *(noun)* **1** the remaining party of something. the remaining people or things; the others. *He was unable to convince the rest of the group.* **2** a small, detached portion of an organ or tissue. *The doctors were unable to save the rest of the leg.* *(verb)* remain or be left in a specified condition: rest assured we will do everything we can. *You can rest assured that all your needs will be taken care of at the hotel.*

Restaurant - *(noun)* a place where people pay to sit and eat meals that are cooked and served on the premises. *He made reservations at the restaurant for lunch.*

Restitution - *(noun)* **1** the restoration of something lost or stolen to its proper owner. *Restitution of the documents was vital for the reputation of the institution.* **2** recompense for injury or loss. *The wife demanded adequate restitution from her estranged husband.* **3** the restoration of something to its original state. the resumption of an object's original shape or position through elastic recoil. *Restitution of our culture is in our hands.*

Restive - *(adjective)* **1** unable to keep still or silent; restless. *A restive wife causes strife.* **2** of a horse refusing to advance; stubbornly standing still or moving backwards or sideways. *The restive horse caused his owner a great deal of trouble.*

Restless - *(adjective)* unable to stay calm or be happy where you are because a feeling of boredom. *She was feeling rather restless after lunch.*

Restoration - *(noun)* **1** the action or process of restoring. a model or drawing representing the supposed original form of an extinct animal, ruined building, etc. *Restoration is definitely needed in our building.* **2** the return of a monarch to a throne, a head of state to government, or a regime to power. the restoration the re establishment of Charles II as king of England in 1660, or the period following this. *Charles II was restored to his former glory after the fall of Cromwell.*

Restore - *(verb)* **1** bring back a previous right, practice, or situation; reinstate. return to a former condition or position. *The government restored peace in the war struck area.* **2** repair or renovate. *The heritage structure was restored by the state government.* **3** give something stolen or removed back to the original owner. *The artefacts were restored to the museum by the community.*

Restrain - *(verb)* **1** prevent from doing something; keep within limits. deprive of freedom of movement or personal liberty. *The child had to be restained from walking out of the house.* **2** repress a strong emotion. *We must exercise restraint.*

Restrict - *(verb)* **1** put a limit on; keep under control. *Entry to the museum was restricted.* **2** deprive of freedom of movement or action. *During war the civilan rights are restricted.*

Result - *(noun)* **1** a consequence, effect, or outcome. a satisfactory outcome: persistence guarantees results. *His poverty was result of his carelessness.* **2** an item of information or a quantity or formula obtained by experiment or calculation. *The chemist was happy to achieve the desired result.* **3** a final score, mark, or placing in a sporting event or examination. *I am awaiting my exam results.* **4** the outcome of a business's trading over a given period, expressed as a statement of profit or loss. *(verb)* occur or follow as a result. *Monetary profit is a result of smart investments.*

Resume - *(verb)* begin again or continue after a pause or interruption. take or put on again. *We shall resume our work after a short break.*

Resurgent - *(adjective)* increasing or reviving after a period of little activity; popularity, or occurrence. *Resurgent communalism is a result of intolerant religious factions of society.*

Resurrect - *(verb)* **1** restore to life. *The mummy was resurrected from his sarcophagus.* **2** revive the practice, use, or memory of. *The art of Dastangoi was resurrected by folk artists of Lucknow.*

Resuscitate – *(verb)* **1** revive from unconsciousness. *The man tried to resuscitate his wife using his mouth to blow air directly into her mouth.* **2** make active or vigorous again. *Measures to resuscitate the ailing Indian economy have time and again proved futile.*

Retail – *(noun)* the sale of goods to the public for use or consumption rather than for resale. *(adverb)* being sold in such a way. *He has done a course in retail management.* *(verb)* **1** sell goods in such a way. be sold in this way for a specified price. *The difficulties in retailing Indian products in the market are due to the influx of foreign brands.*

Retailer – *(noun)* a person or business that sells goods to public. *My brother is a retailer of sports goods.*

Retain – *(verb)* **1** continue to have; keep possession of, not abolish, discard, or alter. keep in one's memory. *Katherine decided to retain her mother's jewellery.* **2** absorb and continue to hold a substance. *Cotton has the capacity to retain water double its weight.* **3** keep in place; hold fixed. *Nails help retain the object at its original place.* **4** keep engaged in one's service. secure the services of a barrister with a preliminary payment. *The lawyer decided to retain the services of his secretary.*

Retaliate – *(verb)* make an attack or assault in return for a similar attack. *Tina retaliated violently to her husband's accusations.*

Retard – *(verb)* delay or hold back in terms of development or progress. *Bad weather conditions retard the growth of plants.* *(noun)* a mentally handicapped person. *My brother is a retard.*

Retarded – *(adjective)* less advanced in mental, physical, or social development than is usual for one's age. *The progress of the Indian economy is retarded owing to slow implementation of laws.*

Retention – *(noun)* **1** the act of retaining or state of being retained. *The state government ordered the retention of all landed property even after the buyout by the multinational company.* **2** failure to eliminate a substance from the body. *Sia suffers from the problem of water retention in her body.*

Rethink – *(verb)* assess or consider a policy or course of action again. *I am rethinking my decision of buying a sedan car.* *(noun)* an instance of rethinking. *She was asked to rethink her decision by her parents.*

Reticent – *(adjective)* not revealing one's thoughts or feelings readily. *His reticence adds to his charming personality.*

Retina – *(noun)* a layer at the back of the eyeball that contains cells sensitive to light, which trigger nerve impulse that pass via the optic nerve to the brain, where a visual image is formed. *The optician informed her that her blurred vision was a result of her torn retina.*

Retinue – *(noun)* a group of advisers or assistants accompanying an important person. *The judge always travels with his retinue of lawyers.*

Retire – *(verb)* **1** leave one's job and cease to work, especially because one has reached a particular age. of a sports player cease to play competitively. *My father retired from job last year.* **2** withdraw from a race or match because of accident or injury. baseball put out a batter; cause a side to end a turn at bat. *Irfan Pathan retired hurt in yesterday's cricket match.* **3** withdraw to or from a particular place. leave the courtroom to decide the verdict of a trial. retreat. *She retired to her country house to relieve herself of all tensions.* **4** go to bed. *I will retire to bed in an hour from now.*

Retirement – *(noun)* **1** the action or fact of retiring. *He was given a farewell party post retirement by his office people.* **2** the period of one's life after retiring from work. *He decided to inculcate good hobbies during his retirement period.* **3** seclusion. [archaic] a secluded or private place. *His retirement to a far away country was a sort of a self imposed exile.*

Retort – *(verb)* **1** say something sharp, angry, or witty in answer to a remark or accusation. *She retorted to her sister's accusatory tone.* **2** [archaic] return or repay an insult to injury. *He always taught his kids to retort in kind on being insulted by anyone.* *(noun)* a sharp, angry, or witty reply. *The ability to retort with agility is sometimes a virtue.*

Retouch – *(verb)* improve or repair a painting, photograph, etc. by making slight additions or alternations. *The marble sculptures needed a retouch before being reinstalled to the hotel lobby.*

Retrace – *(verb)* **1** go back over the same route that one has just taken. discover and follow a route or course taken by someone else. *She retraced her footsteps to get out of the jungle safely.* **2** trace something back to its source or beginning. *Using old photographs, Tina managed to retrace her entire family history.*

Retract – *(verb)* **1** draw or be drawn back or back in. *The snail retracted into its shell on being disturbed.* **2** withdraw as untrue or unjustified. withdraw or go back on an undertaking or promise. *He retracted his accusations after being confronted by her wife in court.*

Retreat – *(verb)* withdraw from confrontation with enemy forces. move back from a difficult or uncomfortable situation. withdraw to a quiet or secluded place. *The lion retreated back to his cave after having ravished his prey. (noun)* **1** an act of retreating. a signal for a military force to withdraw. *Both the warring armies decided to retreat after the 100th day of war.* **2** a quiet or secluded place. a period or place of seclusion for the purposes of prayer and meditation. *His country house is his retreat where he finds peace and tranquillity.* **3** a military musical ceremony carried out at sunset. *The ceremony of Beating Retreat is scheduled to take place on the 29th of January.*

Retrench – *(verb)* **1** reduce costs or spending in response to economic difficulty. chiefly make redundant in order to reduce costs. *Several people lost their jobs because their companies retrenched.* **2** formal reduce or diminish. *The mountains retrenched after the earthquake.*

Retrenchment – *(noun)* to reduce costs or work force. *Numerous companies were forced to undergo retrenchment following the global economic slowdown.*

Retribution – *(noun)* punishment inflicted in the spirit of moral outrage or personal vengeance. *The thieves were pelted to death by the public as retribution for their heinous crime.*

Retrieve – *(verb)* **1** get or bring back. find and bring back. *The emperor sent his general to retrieve his imperial sword.* **2** find or extract information stored in a computer. *It was difficult to retrieve the files after my hard disk crashed.* **3** rescue from a state of difficulty or collapse. (noun) an act of retrieving. *The invaders attacked the retrieving army.*

Retrograde – *(adjective)* **1** directed or moving backwards. the order of something reversed; inverse. *To act negatively would be a retrograde step.* **2** reverting to an earlier and inferior condition. *Refusal to take medicines has left her in a retrograde state.* **3** [geology] of a metamorphic change resulting from a decrease in temperature or pressure. *The retrograde state of the earth's surface is a result of various forms of pollution.* **4** [astronomy] in a reverse direction form normal, resulting from the relative orbital progress of the earth and the planet. the opposite of protrude. astronomy in a reverse direction from that normal in the solar system. *To understand the dynamics behind astronomy one has to see it as both a retrograde as well as a prograde science.*

Retrospect – *(noun)* a survey or review of a past course of events or period of time. *In retrospect, war can be considered a mass murder.*

Retrospective – *(adjective)* **1** looking back on or dealing with past events or situations. of an exhibition or compilation showing the development of an artist's work over a period of time. *His paintings were retrospective in nature.* **2** of a statute or legal decision taking effect from a date in the past. *The punishment was announced taking the retrospective in consideration. (noun)* a retrospective exhibition or compilation. *The theme of his art exhibition was retrospective.*

Return – *(verb)* **1** come or go back to a place. go back to a particular state or activity. come back after a period of absence. golf play the last nine holes in round of eighteen holes. give or send back or put back in place. *He promised to return after his project.* **2** feel, say, or do in response. back to an opponent. American football intercept and run unfiled with the ball. *The Indian cricketer returned the Australian cricketer's sledging in kind.* **3** state or present a verdict. **4** yield or make a profit. *Smart investments yield profitable returns.*

Reunion – *(noun)* **1** the process or an instance of reuniting. *All classmates decided to meet at the school reunion.* **2** a social gathering attended by members of a group of people who have not seen each other for some time. *All classmates reunited at the school reunion.*

Reunite – *(verb)* come together or cause to come together again after a period of separation or disunity. *The refugee camp ensured that all refugees were reunited with their family members.*

Revalue – *(verb)* **1** value again. *He revalued his property before the final sell off.* **2** [economics] adjust the value of a currency in relation to other currencies. *The heritage property was scheduled for a revaluation by the government.*

Reveal – *(noun)* disclose previously known or secret information. make known to humans by divine or supernatural means. *Jesus revealed his presence to his followers on the 40th day.* **2** cause or allow to be seen. *The diamond was revealed to the public yesterday.*

Revel – *(verb)* engage in lively and noisy festivities. *They revelled themselves eating and dacing at the picnic yesterday.* *(noun)* lively and noisy festivities. *The youngsters plan to revel themselves by going on a picnic the coming sunday.*

Revelry – *(noun)* noisy fun involving eating dancing drinking. *Carnival ensures a night of revelry and joy.*

Revelation – *(noun)* **1** a surprising disclosure. the revealing of something previously unknown. a surprising or remarkable thing. *Suddenly, he had a revelation that life was not just about monetary benefits, but also about love and brotherhood.* **2** a divine or supernatural disclosure to humans. the last book of the new testament, recounting a divine revelation of the future to st john. *Moses had a revelation that God was omnipresent.*

Revenge – *(noun)* retaliation for an injury or wrong. the desire to inflict this. *Revenge is a vice that ought to be avoided under all circumstances.* *(verb)* chiefly inflict revenge for an injury or wrong done to oneself. inflict revenge on behalf of someone else. inflict revenge for a wrong or injury. *Zen promised his mother to take revenge from his brother's killers.*

Revenue – *(noun)* income, especially when of a company and which public expenses are met. items or amounts constituting revenue. the department of the civil service collecting revenue. *The government body in villages is responsible for collecting revenue from the villages every year.*

Reverberate – *(verb)* **1** of a loud noise be repeated as an echo. [archaic] return or re-echo a sound. *Diana's screaming reverberated through the entire hall and took everyone by surprise.* **2** have continuing serious effects. *Mental abuse often reverberates through a series of generations.*

Revere – *(verb)* respect or admire deeply. *Good teachers are always revered by their students.*

Reverence – *(noun)* **1** deep respect. *Everybody stood up as the retired teacher entered the classroom as a mark of reverence.* **2** [archaic] a bow or crusty. *People bow in front of the Pope as a mark of reverence.* **3** a title given to a member of the clergy, especially a priest in Ireland. *Reverend Smith was requested to atıend the sermon.* *(verb)* regard or treat with reverence. *He treated his mother with reverence irrespective of the place and time.*

Reverend – *(adjective)* a title or form of address to members of the clergy. *The reverend jury members were requested to attend the court hearing.* *(noun)* [informal] a clergyman. *Reverend Jacob was present at the sermon today.*

Reverent – *(adjective)* showing reverence. *The students were taught the importance of being reverent in class today.*

Reverie – *(noun)* **1** a daydream. [archaic] a fanciful idea or theory. *Leela pinched Tim on the arm in order to snap him out of his reverie.* **2** music an instrumental piece suggesting a dreamy or musing state. *Norah Jones delivered an outstanding reverie at the concert last night.*

Reversal – *(noun)* **1** a change to an opposite direction, position, or course of action. [law] an annulment of judgement made by a lower court or authority. an adverse change of fortune. *The judge ordered a reversal of the court proceedings in order to ensure justice.* **2** [photography] direct production of a positive image from an espoused film or plate.

Revert – *(verb)* **1** return to a pervious state, condition, etc. [biology] return to a former or ancestral type. *The teacher reverted back with the results within a day.* **2** [law] return or pass to by reversion. *The judge reverted back his decision after the pleas of the affected party.* **3** [archaic] turn back. *She wished he would revert back her feelings back with the same intensity.*

Review – *(noun)* **1** a formal assessment of something with the intention of instituting change if necessary. [law] a reconsideration of a judgement or sentence by a higher court or authority. *The government plans to review certain laws for the betterment of society.* **2** a critical appraisal of a book, play, or other work. a periodical with critical articles on comport. *The Theatre Review is a venerable magazine.* **3** a ceremonial display and formal inspection of military or naval forces. *The review of military forces is an important occassion.* **4** a facility for playing a tape recording during a fast wind. *The review button of my music player has broken.* *(verb)* **1** carry out or write a review of. *Sheena was asked to review the play.* **2** view or inspect again. *I was told to review my decision to resign.*

Reviewer – (noun) a person who writes reviews of books, films etc. *The student hired two reviewers to review her paper.*

Revile – *(verb)* criticize abusively. *The teacher reviled the student who had abused his classmate.*

Revise – *(verb)* **1** examine and improve or amend something, especially written matter. reconsider and later an opinion or judgement. *I want to read the revised version of this play.* **2** [British] reread work done previously to improve one's knowledge, typically for an examination. *He revised his paper once again before leaving the examination hall.* *(noun)* printing a proof including corrections made in an earlier proof. *Print the revised document for final corrections.*

Revision – *(noun)* the action or revising. a revised edition or form. *Preeti is a travel editor who heads the revisions team.*

Revival – *(noun)* **1** an improvement in the condition or strength of something. *The Celtic revival is a defining moment in the history of English Literature.* **2** an instance of something becoming popular, active, or important again. a reawakening of religious fervor, especially by means of evangelistic meetings. *The New Year saw the revival of Jazz music amongst the youth of the nation.* **3** a new production of an old play. *The theatre is showing a revival of Shakespear's comedies.*

Revive – *(verb)* restore to or regain life, consciousness, or strength. restore interest in or the popularity of. restore or improve the position or condition of. *The doctor managed to revive the patient by injecting coramin.*

Revoke – *(verb)* end the validity or operation of a decree, decision, or promise. *I am revoking all your powers.*

Revolt – *(verb)* **1** rise in rebellion. refuse to acknowledge someone or something as having authority. [archaic] having rebelled. *The Indian Army revolted on realizing what the British troops had done.* **2** cause to feel disgust. *I revolted at the sight of that beggar.* *(noun)* an attempt to end the authority of a person or body by rebelling. a refusal to obey or conform. *The revolt led to the overthrowing of the monarch.*

Revolting – *(adjective)* causing intense disgust. *The filth strewn all over the house was a revolting sight.*

Revolution – *(noun)* **1** a forcible overthrow of a government or social order, in favour of a new system. the class struggle expected to lead to political change and the triumph of communism. *The Marxist leaders demanded a revolution to* *change the existing order.* **2** a dramatic and wide-reaching change. *In order to ascertain women's safety, India will need a revolution.* **3** an instance of revolving. motion in orbit or in a circular cause or round an axis or centre. the single completion of an orbit or rotation. *The Earth's revolution is recorded by the satellite.*

Revolutionary – *(adjective)* **1** involving or causing dramatic change or innovation. *His revolutionary spirit can land him into trouble with the authorities.* **2** engaged in, promoting, or relating to political revolution. *His revolutionary activities do not go unnoticed and often win him laurels.* *(noun)* a person who revolts or advocates revolution. *Mahatma Gandhi was a revolutionary.*

Revolutionize – *(verb)* change radically or fundamentally. *Liberal thinking leads to a revolutionized society.*

Revolve – *(verb)* **1** move in a circle on a central axis. move in a circular orbit around. **2** treat as the most important point or element. *The earth revolves around its own axis.* **3** consider repeatedly and form different angles. *The entire concept revolves around one basic fact.*

Revolver – *(noun)* **1** a pistol with revolving chambers enabling several shots to be fired without reloading. *Sam carries a licensed revolver for his personal safety.* **2** an agreement to provide revolving credit. *The bank issued a revolver for the villagers.*

Revulsion – *(noun)* **1** a sense of disgust and loathing. *Gia felt a sense of revulsion after meeting her sister's husband.* **2** [medicine, chiefly historical] the drawing of disease or blood congestion from one part of the body to another, e.g. by counter irritation. *I often get a feeling of revulsion whenever it is time to take my medicine.*

Reward – *(noun)* **1** a thing given in recognition of service, effort, or achievement. a fair return for good or bad behaviour. a sum offered for the detection of a criminal, the restoration, of lost property, etc. *A reward acts as motivation to perform better.* *(verb)* give a reward to. show one's appreciation of an action or quality by making a gift. receive what one deserves. *Tina was rewarded by her employers for impeccable work quality.*

Rewarding – *(adjective)* providing satisfaction. *Sid's rewarding work brought him laurels at his workplace.*

Rewind – *(verb)* wind back to the beginning. *Sitting on the beach, Cindy sat rewinding her life.* *(noun)* a mechanism for rewinding a film or tape. *Tim pressed the rewind button on the tape recorder.*

Rewrite – *(verb)* write again in an altered or improved form. *Mandy was asked to rewrite the essay by his teacher.* *(noun)* an instance of rewriting something. a text that has been rewritten. *Rewritten text has undergone extensive editing and proofreading processes.*

Rhetoric – *(noun)* the art of effective or persuasive speaking or writing. language with a persuasive or impressive effect, but often lacking sincerity or meaningful content. *Rhetoric and prosody is an essential subject in literature.*

Rheumatic – *(adjective)* of, relating to, caused by, or suffering from rheumatism. *Sid's rheumatic legs made it tough for him to run swiftly.* *(noun)* a rheumatic person. *All rheumatic patients experience pain and uneasiness.*

Rheumatism – *(noun)* any disease marked by inflammation and pain in the joints, muscles, or fibrous tissue, especially rheumatoid arthritis. *Rheumatism is an affliction of the bones.*

Rhinoceros – *(noun)* a large, heavily built plant-eating mammal with one or two horns on the nose and thick folded skin, native to Africa and south Asia. *Rhinoceros is one of the endangered species.*

Rhombus – *(noun)* geometry a parallelogram with oblique angles and equal sides. *Tom learned about geometrical shapes such as the rhombus today.*

Rhyme – *(noun)* **1** correspondence of sound between words or the endings of words, especially when used in poetry. a word with the same sound as another. *It is easier to remember songs that have words that rhyme.* **2** a short poem with rhyming line.s rhyming poetry or verse. *Haiku poetry does not follow a rhyme scheme.* *(verb)* a word, syllable, or line have or end with a sound that corresponds to another. treat a word as rhyming with another. of a poem or song be composed in rhyme. *His entire novel followed a rhyme scheme.* **2** poetic compose verse or poetry. *Poetry is best enjoyed when it follows a rhyme scheme.*

Rhythm – *(noun)* **1** a strong, regular, repeated pattern of movement or sound. the systematic arrangement of musical sounds, according to duration and periodical stress. a type of pattern formed by this. *Tim's tutor realized that his pupil's music was in perfect rhythm and that he was nothing short of a prodigy.* **2** a person's natural feeling for rhythm. *There is a rhythm to all our daily activities.* **3** the measured flow of words and phrases in verse or prose as determined by the length of and stress on syllables. *His verse was in perfect rhythm.* **4** a regularly recurring sequence of events or actions. *The rhythmtic flow of classes was disrupted due to the school emergency.* **5** art a harmonious sequence or correlation of colours or elements. *Cubist paintings are characterized by a distinct lack of rhythm.*

Rib – *(noun)* **1** each of a series of slender curved bones articulated in pairs to the spine, protecting the thoracic cavity and its organs. an animal rib with meat adhering to it used as food. *Eve is said to have been created from Adam's rib.* **2** [architecture] a curved member supporting a vault or defining its form. *Once the rib of the building broke, the entire structure collapsed.* **3** a curved transverse strut of metal or timber in a ship, forming part of the framework of the hull. *The ship started malfunctioning once its rib was destroyed during the storm.* **4** each of the curved pieces of wood forming the body of a lute or violin. *The efficiency of a violin also depends on the quality of the ribs used to create its structure.* **5** each of the hinged rods supporting the fabric of an umbrella. *My umbrella was rendered useless after its ribs broke.* **6** [aeronautics] a structural member in an aerofoil. *The aeronautical engineers were lectured on the importance of the ribs in an aerofoil.* **7** a vein of a leaf or an insect's wing. *The ribbed veins of a leaf are clearly visible when you hold it against sunlight.* *(verb)* **1** mark with or form into raised bands or ridges. **2** [informal] tease good-naturedly. *Tom often ribbed at his younger brother to lighten a tense moment.*

Ribbon – *(noun)* **1** a long, narrow strip of fabric, used for tying something or for decoration. a ribbon of a special colour or design awarded as a prize or worn to indicate the holding of an honour. *Sia ties a pretty red ribbon to her plait.* **2** a long, narrow strip of something. *Please brings the tape ribbon to the desk.* **3** a narrow band of impregnated material wound on a spool and forming the inking agent in some typewriters and computer printers. *(verb)* extend or move in a long narrow strip. *Xen ribboned through the entire marshy stretch.*

Rice – *(noun)* a swamp grass which is cultivated as a source of food, especially in Asia. the grains of this cereal used as food. *Rice is the staple food in India.*

Rich – *(adjective)* **1** having a great deal of money or assets having valuable natural resources or a successful economy. of expensive materials or workmanship. *Tom's rich relative offered to finance his university education.* **2** plentiful; abundant. having in large amounts. containing much fat, spice, etc. containing a high proportion of fuel. *Pregnant women are advised to eat food rich in vitamins and minerals.* **3** colour, sound, or smell pleasantly deep and strong. *The coffee beans were rich in odour.* **4** full of interesting diversity or complexity. *India is renowned for its rich cultural heritage.* **5** producing or yielding a large quantity of something. fertile. *The soil around the Tapti river is nutrient rich.*

Riches – *(plural noun)* material wealth valuable natural resources. *He lost of all his riches due to his incompetence and misdemeanour.*

Rickety – *(adjective)* **1** poorly made and likely to collapse. *The rickety bullock cart was unable to pull through the course of the entire journey.* **2** suffering from rickets. *Jim's rickety legs are unable to support him anymore.*

Ricochet – *(verb)* rebound off a surface. move or appear to move in such a way. *The ball ricocheted across the room due to the forceful impact of the thump. (noun)* a shot or hit that ricochets. the ricocheting action of a bullet or other projectile. *The ricocheting bullet hit the cop instead of the thief.*

Rid – *(verb)* make someone or something free of an unwanted person or thing. be freed or relieved of. *Tina wished to be rid of all her financial troubles by Christmas.*

Riddance – *(noun)* the action of getting rid of someone of something. *Doing away with meaningless superstitions is good riddance.*

Ridden – past participle of ride. *Nightmares are often ridden with mental imbalance.*

Riddle – *(noun)* a question or statement phrased so as to require ingenuity in ascertaining its answer or meaning. a person or thing that is difficult to understand. *This is complex riddle. (verb)* [archaic] speak in or pose riddles. explain a riddle to. *The jester riddled the court.*

Ride – *(verb)* **1** sit on and control the movement of a horse, bicycle, or motorcycle. travel in or on a vehicle or horse. compete in on a horse, bicycle, or motorcycle. [north American] travel in a lift or vehicle. *He rides his bicycle to work.* **2** be carried or supported by something with great momentum. sail or float. come safely come safely through something. so as to reduce its impact. *She rode the waves with a lot of style.* **3** project or overlap. gradually move upwards out of its proper position. *Her dress rode up every few minutes.* **4** depend on. *I rode the suggested approach for some time.* **5** be full of or dominated by: crime-ridden streets. *The crime-ridden streets of the city were dangerous at night.* **6** vulgar slang have sexual inter course with. *He rode her.* **7** [north American] annoy or tease. *Stop riding me. (noun)* **1** an act of riding. *The ride was exciting.* **2** [north American] a person giving a lift in a vehicle. *My ride was a pleasant companion.* **3** US [informal] motor vehicle. *The car ride shortened my journey time.* **4** a path for horse riding. *The ride needed some maintenance.* **5** a roller coaster, roundabout, etc. ridden at a fir or amusement park. *Children were happy to see the circular rides.* **6** a cymbal keeping up a continuous rhythm. *The ride made the tune pleasant.*

Rider – *(noun)* **1** a person who rides a horse, bicycle, motorcycle, etc. *She is an expert rider.* **2** an added condition or proviso. [British] an addition or amendment to a bill at its third reading. [British] a recommendation or comment added by the jury to a judicial verdict. a supplementary clause in a performer's contract specifying food, drink. etc. *The policy had many riders.* **3** a small weight on the beam of a balance for fine adjustment. *Please use the rider to correct the balance.*

Ridge – *(noun)* **1** a long narrow hilltop, mountain range, or watershed. *I am going to the ridge.* **2** the edge formed where the two sloping sides of a roof meet at the top. *He stood at ridge to fix the chimney.* **3** meteorology an elongated region of high barometric pressure. *The boat is moving through a ridge.* **4** a narrow raised band on a surface. *The ridges formed an attractive pattern.* **5** a raised strip of arable land, especially one of a set separated by furrows. *The farmer planted the crops in the ridge. (verb)* with or form into ridges. *The geological forces have over the years ridged the mountains.*

Ridicule – *(noun)* mockery or derision. *Your ridicule doesn't help anyone. (verb)* subject to ridicule. *Don't ridicule my efforts.*

Ridiculous – *(adjective)* inviting ridicule; absurd. *Your ridiculous idea spoilt everything.*

Rife – *(adjective)* wide spread. rife with full of. *The rife violence was a cause of worry.*

Rifle – *(noun)* **1** a gun, especially one fired from shoulder level having a long spirally grooved barrel to make a bullet spin and thereby increase accuracy over a long distance. *The hunter carried a rifle on his shoulder.* **2** rifles troops armed with rifles. *The Gorkha rifles marched in the parade. (verb)* **1** make spiral grooves in. *The man rifled the sand.* **2** hit or kick hard and straight. *She rifled him on his nose.*

Rift - *(noun)* **1** a crack, split, or break in something. *The rift in the rock was dangerous.* **2** a serious break in friendly relations. *One could clearly see the rift between the two friends.* **3** a rift valley. *We are going for a trip to the rift.* (verb) move or force to move apart. *The earthquake rifted the two rocks.*

Rig - *(verb)* manage or conduct fraudulently so as to gain an advantage. *He rigged the records to his benefit.* *(noun)* a trick or swindle. *The rig was clever.*

Rigging - *(noun)* **1** the system of ropes or chains supporting a ship's masts and controlling or setting the yards and sails. *The rigging was old and needed to be replaced.* **2** the ropes and wires supporting the structure of an airship, biplane, hang-glider, or parachute. the cables and fittings controlling the flight surfaces and engines of an aircraft. *The rigging needs to be very reliable.*

Right - *(adjective)* **1** morally good, justified, or acceptable. *She says that my views are right.* **2** factually correct. most appropriate. socially fashionable or important. *You have arrived at the right figure.* **3** in a satisfactory, sound, or normal state or condition. *She said this is the right condition.* **4** on, towards, or relating to the side of a human body or of a thing which is to the east when the person or thing is facing north. *Look towards your right.* **5** complete; absolute. *Please mix the ingredients in the right proportion.* **6** of or relating to a right wing person or group. *I don't agree with your right views.* *(adverb)* **1** to the furthest or most complete extent or degree. exactly; directly. immediately. very. *Open the book right away.* **2** correctly. satisfactorily. *You say it right.* **3** on or to the right side. *Move right.* *(noun)* **1** that which is morally right. *The priest talked about the virtues of right.* **2** a moral or legal entitlement to have or do something. the authority to perform, publish, or film a particular work or event. *They have the rights to the story.* **3** the right hand part, side, or direction. a right turn. a person's right fist, or a blow given with it. *She gave him left and right.* **4** a group or political party favoring conservative views. *The right are more likely to win these elections.* *(verb)* **1** restore to a normal or upright position. restore to a normal or correct condition. *Please right the sails to prevent boat from sinking into the ocean.* **2** rectify. compensate. *The organization righted the situation.*

Righteous - *(adjective)* morally right or justifiable. *I sometimes find your righteous approach tiresome.*

Rightful - *(adjective)* having a legitimate right to something legitimately claimed; fitting. *You are the rightful owner of the estate.*

Rightfully - *(verb)* in the manner of ownership. *This estate is rightfully yours.*

Rigid - *(adjective)* **1** unable to bend or be forced out of shape. of a person stiff and unmoving. *You have a rigid personality.* **2** not able to be changed or adapted. *The rigid laws of the caste system will hold us back.* (noun) a truck which is not articulated.

Rigidity - *(noun)* the physical property of being stiff and resisting bending. *Your rigidity will cause problems for you in your life.*

Rigmarole - *(noun)* a lengthy and complicated procedure. a long, rambling story. *When will this rigmarole end!*

Rigor - *(noun)* **1** a sudden feeling of cold accompanied by shivering and a rise in temperature, especially at the onset or height of a fever. *The rigor lasted only a few minutes.* **2** short for rigor mortis. *The corpse had started showing signs of rigor.*

Rigorous - *(adjective)* **1** extremely thorough, exhaustive, or accurate. *He hurt his back while doing some rigorous exercise.* **2** of a rule, system, etc. strictly applied or adhered to. adhering strictly to a belief, opinion, or system. *Caste system was once a rigorous belief in this country.* **3** of weather harsh. *The rigorous storm only lasted a few minutes.*

Rim - *(noun)* **1** the upper or outer edge of something, typically something circular. the outer edge of a wheel, on which the tyre is fitted. the part of a spectacle frame surrounding the lenses. *The rim of the spectacle was bent.* **2** the limit or boundary of something. an encircling stain or deposit. *The rim of the sleeves were dirty.* (verb) provide with a rim. *The tailor rimmed the sleeves.*

Rind – *(noun)* a tough outer layer or covering, especially of fruit, cheese, or bacon. the bark of a tree. *Some people consume the rind of an orange.* *(verb)* strip the bark from a tree. *Children rinded the tree.*

Ring – *(noun)* **1** a small circular band, typically of precious metal, worn on a finger as an ornament or as a token of marriage or engagement. *He gave her a ring.* **2** a circular band, article, or mark. a thin band of rock and ice particles round a planet. a flat circular heating device forming part of a gas or electric hob. a circular prehistoric earthwork, typically consisting of a bank and ditch. *Saturn has several rings.* **3** an enclosed space in which a sport, performance, or show takes place. *The boxers entered the ring.* **4** a circle of people or things. a group of people with a shared interest or goal, especially one involving illegal activity. *It is important to bust the ring.* **5** a number of atoms bonded together to form a closed loop in a molecule. *The atoms in a molecule are present in a ring.* **6** a set of elements with two binary operations, addition and multiplication, the second being distributive over the first and associative. *Children were struggling to understand the concept of a ring.* *(verb)* **1** surround. draw a circle round. *She ringed her sand castle.* **2** put an identifying strip around the leg of a bird. *The rare bird was ringed.* **3** put a circular band through the nose of a bull, pig, etc. to lead or control it. *It was a tough bull to ring.* **4** fraudulently change the identity of a motor vehicle. *The stolen car had been ringed.*

Rinse – *(verb)* wash with clean water to remove soap or dirt. remove by rinsing. *Please rinse this bottle properly.* *(noun)* **1** an act of rinsing. *The rinse was not thorough enough.* **2** an antiseptic solution for cleansing the mouth. *I bought a new rinse.* **3** a preparation for conditioning or tinting the hair. *The rinse smelled awful.*

Riot – *(noun)* **1** a violent disturbance of the peace by a crowd. rowdy behaviour. *The riots went out of control.* **2** a confused or lavish combination or display: a riot of colour. *The bag was a riot of colour.* **3** a highly amusing or entertaining person or thing. *He is such a riot.* *(verb)* **1** take part in a riot. *The crowd rioted throughout the day.* **2** behave in an unrestrained way. *The child rioted in the store.* **3** act in a dissipated way. *He rioted after drinking.*

Rip – *(verb)* **1** tear or pull forcibly away from something or someone. tear something into small pieces. *The bully ripped the toy away from the child.* **2** move forcefully and rapidly. *The player ripped through the field.* **3** [informal] make a vehement vertical attack on. *She ripped him.* **4** [informal] cheat someone, especially financially. [informal] steal plagiarize something. *The robbers ripped them of money.* **5** computing such a program to copy on to a computer's hard drive. *I ripped the CD contents.* *(noun)* **1** a long tear or cut. *The rip in her dress was clearly visible.* **2** [north American] a fraud or swindle. *The rip was soon discovered.*

Ripe – *(adjective)* **1** ready for harvesting and eating. fully matured. *The fruit was ripe.* **2** arrived at a fitting time for. *The time was ripe for a decision.* **3** advanced. *It was a ripe system.* **4** full of. *The fruit was ripe with juice.* **5** ready to lay eggs or spawn. *The frog looks ripe.*

Ripen – *(verb)* become or make ripe. *The fruits ripen by February.*

Ripple – *(noun)* **1** a small wave or series of waves. [physics] a small wave in which the dominant force is surface tension rather than gravity. *Ripple look beautiful on the surface of water.* **2** a gentle rising and failing sound that spreads through a group of people. a feeling that spreads through someone or something. *A ripple of joy ran through the crowds.* **3** a small periodic voltage variation superposed on a direct voltage or low-frequency alternating voltage. *The ripples needed to be regulated.* **4** a type of ice cream with wavy lines of coloured flavoured syrup running through it. *I want to have a ripple.* *(verb)* **1** form or cause to form ripples. *The water rippled.* **2** spread through a person or place. *Joy rippled through me.*

Rise - *(verb)* **1** come or go up reach a higher social or professional position. succeed in not being constrained by. *He rose up the corporate ladder.* **2** get up from lying, sitting, or kneeling. chiefly adjourn. *Please rise.* **3** incline upwards be much taller than the surrounding landscape. *The building rose up into the sky.* **4** appear above the horizon. *The sun rises in the morning.* **5** increase in number, size, intensity, or quality. *The rise in quality led to a rise in sales.* **6** respond adequately to a challenging situation. *He rose up to the challenge.* **7** cease to be submissive or peaceful. *The masses rose up against the dictator.* **8** have its source: the Euphrates rises in turkey. *Hinduism rises in India.* **9** be restored to life. *The messiah rose.* *(noun)* **1** an act or instance of rising. *The rise changed the direction of his career.* **2** an upward slope or hill. *She cycled up the rise.* **3** [British] an increase in salary or wages. *She got a good rise.* **4** the source of a river. *The explorers hiked up to the rise.* **5** the vertical height of a step, arch, or incline. another term for riser. *The slope had a steep rise.*

Risk - *(noun)* **1** a situation involving exposure to danger. the possibility that something unpleasant will happen. *This investment is a huge risk.* **2** a person or thing causing a risk or regarded in relation to risk: a fire risk. *He is such a risk to the company.* *(verb)* expose to danger or loss. act in such a way as to incur the risk of. incur risk by engaging in an action. *He risked his job to help her.*

Rite - *(noun)* a religious or other solemn ceremony or event, e.g. marriage, marking an important stage in someone's life. *They left as soon as all the rites completed.*

Ritual - *(noun)* **1** a religious or solemn ceremony involving a series of actions performed according to a prescribed order. a prescribed order of performing such a ceremony. *Hindu marriages involve many rituals.* **2** a series of actions habitually and invariably followed by someone. *He has a very strict morning ritual.* *(adjective)* of, relating to, or done as ritual. *He went for his ritual walk even when he was ill.*

Rival - *(noun)* a person or thing competing with another for superiority or the same objective. a person or thing equal to another in quality. *The two rivals fought a bitter battle.* *(verb)* [US] be comparable to. *She rivalled the world's top chess player.*

Rivalry - *(noun)* competition between people, groups, etc. *There was a lot of rivalry between the sisters.*

River - *(noun)* **1** a large natural flow of water travelling along a channel to the sea, a lake, or another river. used in names of animals and plants living in or associated with rivers, e.g. river dolphin. *The river has carved a passage for itself across the centuries.* **2** a large quantity of a flowing substance. *Rivers of milk were flowing on the auspicious day.*

Rivet - *(noun)* a short metal pin or bolt for holding together two metal plates, its headless end being beaten out or pressed down when in place. *Watch out for the rivet.* *(verb)* **1** join or fasten with a rivet or rivets. *Please rivet the two plates.* **2** completely engross. direct intently. *Her attention was riveted in her child.*

Rivulet - *(noun)* a very small stream. *Several rivulet flow into the river.*

Road - *(noun)* **1** a wide way between places, especially one surfaced for use by vehicles. *The road was wide and smooth.* **2** a way to achieving a particular outcome. *Hard work is a road to success.* **3** a partly sheltered stretch of water near the shore in which ships can ride at anchor: Boston roads. *The ship sailed through the road slowly.* **4** [north American] a railroad. [British] a railway track, especially as clear for a train to proceed. *The road is clear.* **5** an underground passage or gallery in a mine. *The miners crowded in the road.*

Roam - *(verb)* travel aimlessly over a wide area. wander over, through, or about. pas lightly over. *He roamed all across the world when he was young.* *(noun)* an aimless walk. *His roam wasn't leading him anywhere.*

Roar - *(noun)* a full, deep, prolonged sound as made by a lion, natural force, or engine. a loud, deep sound uttered by a person, especially as an expression of pain, anger, or great amusement. *The lion's roar could be heard miles away.* *(verb)* **1** make or utter a roar. express in a roar. laugh loudly. make a loud noise in breathing as a symptom of disease of the larynx. *The lion roared loudly.* **2** move at high speed making a roar. act or happen fast and decisively. *The car roared away at a very high speed.*

Roast – *(verb)* **1** cook or be cooked by prolonged exposure to heat in an oven or over a fire. process by subjecting it to intense heat. *Please roast the meat.* **2** make or become very warm. *I roasted in a sweater.* **3** criticize or reprimand severely. *The boss roasted me over the mistake.* *(adjective)* having been roasted. *I like roast meat.* *(noun)* **1** a joint of meat that ahs been roasted or that is intended for roasting. a dish or meal of roasted food. *The roast was well done.* **2** the process of roasting something, especially coffee. a particular type of roasted coffee. *The roast had a strong flavour.*

Rob – *(verb)* **1** take property unlawfully from a person or place by force or threat of force. [informal] overcharge. *She robbed the man at gunpoint.* **2** deprive of something needed, deserved, or significant. *The university robbed him of his award.*

Robbery – *(noun)* the action of robbing a person or place. [informal] unashamed swindling or overcharging *The police were able to crack the case of robbery.*

Robe – *(noun)* **1** a long, loose outer garment reaching to the ankles. such a garment worn, especially on formal or ceremonial occasions, as an indication of the wearer's rank, office, or profession. *She wore a beautiful robe over her dress.* **2** [north American] a lap robe. *The airhostess handed out the lap robes.* *(verb)* clothe in or put on a robe or robes. *She robed herself and went out in the cold.*

Robin – *(noun)* **1** a small European songbird of the thrush family with a red breast and brown back and wings. *Robins flitted around in the sky.* **2** a large [north American] thrush with an orange-red breast. *A couple of robins were building a nest.* **3** used in names of numerous similar or related birds, e.g. pekin robin. *I saw a pekin robbin the other day.*

Robot – *(noun)* **1** a machine capable of carrying out a complex series of actions automatically, especially one programmable by a computer. *My sister gifted me a robot for my birthday.* **2** South African a set of automatic traffic lights. *The robot malfunctioned, causing a huge traffic jam.*

Robust – *(adjective)* **1** sturdy or resilient. strong and healthy. *The robust laptop didn't need any repairs for many years.* **2** not perturbed by or attending to subtleties. *He had a robust confidence.* **3** strong and rich in flavor or smell. *This is a robust whiskey.*

Rock – *(noun)* **1** the hard mineral material of the earth's crust, exposed on the surface or underlying the soil. a mass of this projecting out of the ground of water. a boulder. [north American] a stone of any size. *The rock from moon was placed in a museum.* **2** geology any natural material with a distinctive mineral composition. *I found a beautiful rock in my backyard.* **3** [British] a kind of hard confectionery in the form of cylindrical peppermint-flavoured sticks. *My nephew loves rocks.* **4** [informal] a diamond or other precious stone. *Her fiancé gave her a huge rock.* **5** [informal] a small piece of crack cocaine. *The policeman caught them with the rock.* **6** vulgar slang a man's testicles. *The ball hit him in the rocks.*

Rocket – *(noun)* **1** a cylindrical projectile that can be propelled to a great height or distance by the combustion of its contents. a missile or spacecraft propelled by an engine providing thrust on the same principle. *We saw the rocket launch.* **2** [British] [informal] a severe reprimand. *She gave him a rocket.* *(verb)* **1** increase very rapidly and suddenly. *The prices rocketed.* **2** move or progress very rapidly. *He rocketed up the corporate ladder.* **3** attack with rocket propelled missiles. *The country contemplated rocketing the enemy.*

Rod – *(noun)* **1** a thin straight bar, especially of wood or metal. *Rods of iron were used to give strength to the structure.* **2** a fishing rod.

The fisherman dropped the rod. **3** a slender straight stick or shoot growing on or cut from a tree or bush. the use of stick for caning or flogging. *Teachers were asked to spare the rod.* **4** [historical] another term for perch. *The king rod on the throne.* **5** [US informal] a pistol or revolver. *He pulled out the rod from the holster and fired at the robber.* **6** [anatomy] one of two types of light-sensitive cell present in the retina of the eye, responsible mainly for monochrome vision in poor light. compare with cone. *He had a problem in the rod.*

Rodent – *(noun)* a mammal of an order that includes rats, mice, squirrels, and porcupines, distinguished by strong constantly growing incisors and no canine teeth. *I don't think rodents make good pets.*

Roe – *(noun)* **1** the mass of eggs contained in the ovaries of a female fish or shellfish, especially when ripe and used as food. *Roe is a delicacy in many parts of the world.* **2** the ripe testes of male fish, especially when used as food. *I don't like the taste of roe.*

Rogue – *(noun)* **1** a dishonest or unprincipled man. a mischievous but likeable person. *He is such a rogue.* **2** an elephant or other large wild animal with destructive tendencies driven away or living apart from the herd: a rogue elephant. a person or thing that is defective, aberrant, or unpredictable a seedling or plant deviating from the standard variety. *The rogue climber refused to climb the wall. (verb)* remove rogue plants or seedlings from a crop. *Please rogue the plant area of seedlings.*

Role – *(noun)* **1** an actor's part in a play, film, etc. *Can you tell me more about your role in the movie?* **2** a person's or thing's function in a particular situation. *What was your role in the film?*

Roll – *(verb)* **1** move by turning over and over on an axis, ship, aircraft, or vehicle sway on an axis parallel to the direction of motion. *The ship rolled towards the port.* **2** move or cause to move along. move or flow forward with an undulating motion. flow. elapse steadily: the years rolled by. steady and continuous: a rolling programme of reforms. extend in gentle undulations be displayed as if moving on a roller up the screen. begin or cause to begin operating. *The years rolled by.* **3** turn over and over on itself to form a cylindrical or spherical shape. curl up tightly. *Farmers rolled up the hay.* **4** flatten by passing a roller over it or by passing it between rollers. *They rolled the cotton.* **5** reverberate. pronounce with a trill. flow mellifluously: the names rolled off his lips. *His name rolled off her lips.* **6** [informal] rob. *They rolled the poor student. (noun)* **1** a cylinder formed by rolling flexible material. a cylindrical shape. an item of food made by wrapping a flat sheet of pastry, cake, meat, or fish round a filling. [north American] a quantity of banknotes rolled together. *Please give me some egg rolls.* **2** a rolling movement. a gymnastic exercise in which the body is rolled into a trucked position and turned in a forward or backward or backward circle. *She performed the front roll with perfection.*

Roller – *(noun)* **1** a cylinder that rotates about a central axis and is used in various machines and devices to move, flatten, or spread something. *Use a roller to roll the cotton.* **2** a small cylinder on which hair is rolled in order to produce curls. *She used rollers for those beautiful curls.* **3** a long surgical bandage rolled up for convenient application. *Please bring the roller.* **4** a long swelling wave that appears to roll steadily towards the shore. *The surfer rode the roller.* **5** a brightly coloured crow sized bird, predominantly blue and having a characteristic tumbling display flight. *The roller flew away.* **6** a breed of tumbler pigeon. *The rollers fornicate endlessly.* **7** a breed of canary with a trilling song. *She bought a roller for her child.*

Romance – *(noun)* the group of Indo-European language descended from Latin, principally French, Spanish, Portuguese, Italian, Catalan, Occitan. and Romanian. *I know several romances. (adjective)* relating to or denoting this group of languages. *It is a pleasure to hear a romance language.*

Romantic – *(adjective)* **1** inclined towards or suggestive of romance. relating to love, especially in a sentimental or idealized way.

This is a romantic poem. **2** characterized by an idealized view of reality. *He had some romantic views of life.* **3** relating to romanticism. *The romantic poet is very popular. (noun)* **1** a person with romantic beliefs or attitudes. *The romantic shared his views.* **2** a writer or artist of the romantic movement. *The romantic writer wrote many poems.*

Romp – *(verb)* **1** play about roughly and energetically. *The children romped around.* **2** achieve something easily. finish as the easy winner of a race or other contest. *He romped the race.* **3** engage in sexual activity, especially illicitly. *They romped in the car. (noun)* **1** a spell of romping. *The romp seemed to last for hours.* **2** a light hearted film or other work. *This movie was a romp.* **3** an easy victory. *The team was proud of their romp.*

Roof – *(noun)* **1** the structure forming the upper covering of a building or vehicle. the top inner surface of a covered area or space. *The ladder almost touched the roof.* **2** the upper limit or level of prices or wages. *The prices shot up to the roof after the assignment. (verb)* cover with a roof. function as the roof of. *The workmen roofed the cottage.*

Rook – *(noun)* a gregarious crow with black plumage and a bare face, nesting in colonies in treetops. *A rook was making a lot of noise around the tree. (verb)* defraud, swindle, or overcharge. *The shopkeeper rooked the visitors.*

Room – *(noun)* **1** space viewed in terms of its capacity to accommodate contents or allow action: she was trapped without room to move. *There was no room to move.* **2** a part of a building enclosed by walls, floor, and ceiling. a set of rooms rented out to lodgers. *This is my room.* **3** opportunity or scope: room for improvement. *(verb)* share lodgings, especially at a college or similar institution. *The police gave him no room to escape.*

Roomy – *(adjective)* having plenty of room; spacious. *This is a roomy house.*

Roost – *(noun)* a tidal race. *These waters are risky because of the tidal race.*

Rooster – *(noun)* a male domestic fowl. *I bought a rooster yesterday.*

Root – *(verb)* **1** turn up the ground with its snout on search of food. rummage. *The antelopes rooted around.* **2** support enthusiastically. cheer or urge someone on. *I will be rooting for Newcastle United. (noun)* an act of rooting. *I was glad to see the root for our team.*

Rope – *(noun)* **1** a length of stout cord made by twisting together strands of hemp, sisal, nylon, etc. the ropes enclosing a boxing or wrestling ring. execution by hanging. *The rope was very strong.* **2** a quantity of roughly spherical objects strung together. *The rope looked very beautiful.* **3** the established procedures in an organization or area of activity: I showed her the ropes. *The manager showed me the ropes.* (verb) **1** catch, fasten, or secure with rope. connect each other together with a rope. *They roped the fails together.* **2** persuade someone, despite reluctance, to take part in. *They roped all the children into the organizing activities.*

Rosary – *(noun)* **1** in the Roman catholic church a form of devotion in which five or fifteen decades of hail marys are repeated, each decade preceded by an our father and followed by those assembled there. *I love the sound of rosary.* **2** a string of beads for keeping count in such a devotion or in the devotions of some other religions. *My father uses a rosary at the congregation.*

Rose – *(noun)* **1** a prickly bush or shrub that typically bears red, pink, yellow, or white fragrant flowers, native to north temperate regions and widely grown as an ornamental. used on names of other plants with similar flowers, e.g. a stylized representation of a rose in heraldry or decoration. *I planted a rose in my garden.* **2** a perforated cap attached to a shower, the spout of a watering can, or the end of a hose to produce a spray. *Several holes of the rose were blocked.* **3** a warm pink or light crimson colour. a rosy complexion. *The rose on her cheeks made her look very attractive.* **4** favourable circumstances or ease of success: everything was coming up roses. *The opportunities were bringing up roses. (verb)* make rosy. *The rosy cheeks reflected her immense pleasure.*

Rostrum – *(noun)* **1** a raised platform on which a person stands to make a public speech, play music, or conduct an orchestra. a similar platform for supporting a film or television camera. *The rostrum had been set up well.* **2** a beak like projection. *She hit him on the rostrum.*

Rosy – *(adjective)* **1** rose red or pink, typically as an indication of health or youthfulness: rosy cheeks. *She is very proud of her rosy cheeks.* **2** promising or suggesting good fortune; hopeful. *He is certain of a rosy future.*

Rot – *(verb)* **1** decompose by the action of bacteria and fungi; decay. *The vegetables had started rotting.* **2** gradually deteriorate or decline. *The empire rotted gradually.* *(noun)* **1** the process of decaying. rotten or decayed matter. *The rot will destroy this building in no time.* **2** a process of deteriorate or decline in standards: there is enough talent to stop the rot. *The quality of your product is in rot.* **3** any of a number of fungal or bacterial diseases that cause tissue deterioration, especially in plants. liver rot in sheep. *The vet has diagnosed rot.* **4** rubbish: don't talk rot. *Many programmes on TV only talk rot.*

Rota – *(noun)* **1** a list showing times and names for people to take their turn to undertake certain duties. *No one seems to be following the rota.* **2** the supreme ecclesiastical and secular court of the Roman Catholic Church. *The Rota will decide this matter.*

Rotate – *(verb)* **1** move or cause to move in a circle round an axis. *The ball rotated for quite some time.* **2** pass to each member of a group on a regularly recurring order. *Please rotate the brochure.* **3** grow in succession on a particular piece of land. *The farmers rotated the crops for better yield.*

Rote – *(noun)* mechanical or habitual repetition: a poem learnt by rote. *I am trying to break out of my rote.*

Rotor – *(noun)* **1** the rotating part of a turbine, electric motor, or other device. *The rotor needs cleaning.* **2** a hub with a number of radiating blades that is rotated to provide the lift for a helicopter. *The helicopter's rotor slowly gathered speed.* **3** a large eddy in which the air circulates about a horizontal axis. *The rotor caused some wind.*

Rotten – *(adjective)* **1** suffering from decay. *The tomato is rotten.* **2** corrupt. *The system is rotten.* **3** very bad or unpleasant. *You have rotten breath.* *(adverb)* very much: your mother spoiled you rotten. *Don't spoil your child rotten.*

Rotund – *(adjective)* large and plump. round; spherical. *The rotund man went to the dietician for advice.*

Rouble – *(noun)* the basic monetary unit of Russia and some other former republics of the USSR, equal to 100 kopeks. *This costs 100 Roubles.*

Rouge – *(noun)* a red powder or cream used as a cosmetic for colouring the cheeks or lips. *She applied rouge with perfection.* *(verb)* colour with rouge. *Please rouge the actor's cheeks a little.*

Rough – *(adjective)* **1** having an uneven or irregular surface; not smooth or level. having many obstacles; difficult or cross. *The rough terrain is making the ride uncomfortable.* **2** harsh and rasping. sharp or harsh in taste. *You have a rough voice.* **3** not gentle; violent or boisterous: rough treatment. wild and stormy. *Please stop rough treatment of the prisoners.* **4** difficult and unpleasant. *She is a rough person to live with.* **5** not finished tidily; plain and basic. not worked out or correct in every detail; approximate: a rough draft a rough guess. lacking sophistication or refinement. *This looks like rough work.* *(noun)* **1** a disreputable and violent person. *The rough was put behind the bars.* **2** the area of longer grass around the fairway and the green. *The car slid into the rough.* **3** a preliminary sketch. *This is just a rough of the ultimate sketch.* **4** an uncut precious stone. *I found some roughs on the footpath.* *(verb)* **1** work or shape in a rough, preliminary fashion. *Please rough the design.* **2** make uneven. *He roughed up the road.* **3** live in discomfort with only basic necessities. *He roughed it up.* **4** beat someone up. *The ruffians roughed him up.*

Roughly – *(adverb)* **1** in a rough or harsh manner. *He was punished for handling the patient roughly.* **2** approximately. *This will roughly take 10 hours.*

Roughage – *(noun)* fibrous indigestible material in vegetable foodstuffs which aids the passage of food and waste products through the gut. coarse, fibrous fodder. *You need to increase the amount of roughage in your diet.*

Roughen – *(verb)* make or become rough. *The ride roughened as the quality of the roads went down.*

Roulette – *(noun)* **1** a gambling game in which a ball is dropped on to a revolving wheel with numbered compartments, the players betting on the number at which the ball comes to rest. *She was delighted to have won the roulette.* **2** a tool or machine with a revolving toothed wheel, used in engraving of for making perforations. between postage stamps. *The man operated the roulette with perfection.* *(verb)* use a roulette to make perforations in. *Please roulette these sheets of paper.*

Round – *(adjective)* **1** shaped like a circle or cylinders. *I liked the round logo better than the square one.* **2** shaped like a sphere. having a curved surface with no sharp projections. *A cricket ball is round.* **3** bent forward. **4** rich and mellow. *The round old man was jolly.* **5** expressed in convenient units rather than exactly, for example to the nearest whole number. used to show that a figure has been completely and exactly reached: the batsman made a round 100. considerable. *I earn a round money of Rupees 40,000 per month.* *(noun)* **1** a circular piece or section. *Please place the round on this page.* **2** an act of visiting a number of people or places in turn, especially in a fixed order as part of one's duties: a newspaper round, a regularly recurring sequence of activities. *The doctor is on his round right now.* **3** each of a sequence of sessions kin a process, especially in a sports contest. a single division of a game or contest, especially in a boxing or wrestling match. an act of playing all the holes in a golf course once. *One round of the match is already over.* *(adverb)* **1** so as to rotate or cause rotation. so as to cover the whole area surrounding a particular centre. *Turn the chair a round.* **2** so as to rotate and face in the opposite direction. used in describing the relative position of something : it's the wrong way round. *You are going the wrong way round.* **3** so as to surround. so as to give support. *We will round you if there is a need.* **4** so as to reach a new place or position. *I will go round.* **5** used to suggest idle and purposeless motion or activity. *You are going round cape of Good hope and reach South Africa.* *(preposition)* **1** on every side of. *It was a bad idea all round.* **2** so as to encircle. *Let's gather round the table.* *(verb)* **1** pass and go round. *Let us round it up.* **2** make less exact but more convenient for calculations: we'll round the weight up to the nearest kilo. *Round the distance and let us know.* **3** become or cause to become round in shape. *Round the dough.*

Roundabout – *(noun)* **1** a road junction at which traffic moves in one direction round a central island to reach one of the roads converging on it. *There was an accident on the roundabout.* **2** a large revolving device in a playground for children to ride on. a merry go round. *Children made merry on the roundabout.* *(adjective)* **1** not following a short direct route; circuitous. *He suggested me a roundabout way.* **2** not clear and direct; circumlocutory. *Don't talk in a roundabout language.*

Rouse – *(verb)* **1** bring out of sleep; awaken. cease to sleep; wake up. *The noise of the boxes falling roused the sleeping family.* **2** bring out of inactivity. *The ghastly crime roused the nation.* **3** excite; provoke: his evasiveness roused my curiosity. *His suspicious actions roused the dog's curiosity.* **4** stir. *The speech roused the masses.*

Rout – *(noun)* **1** a disorderly retreat of defeated troops. a decisive defeat. *The rout was intercepted by the enemy.* **2** an assembly of people who have made a move towards committing an illegal act which would constitute an offence of riot. *Policemen were deployed in large numbers to control the shouting and disorderly rout.* **3** a disorderly or tumultuous crowd of people. *The rout at the fair spoiled the fun.* *(verb)* defeat utterly and force to retreat. *Our army routed the enemy.*

Route – *(noun)* **1** a way or course taken in getting from a starting point to a destination. the line of a road, path, railway, etc. *What route should I take to the railway station?* **2** a round travelled in delivering, selling, or collecting goods. *This is my daily route. (verb)* send or direct along a specified course. *Please route your queries through the information desk.*

Routine – *(noun)* **1** a sequence of actions regularly followed; a fixed unvarying programme. *I finished my daily routine well in time. (adjective)* **1** performed as part of a regular procedure: a routing inspection. *This is just a routine procedure.* **2** characteristic of routine; without variety. *I am bored of routine life.*

Rove – *(verb)* **1** travel constantly without a fixed destination; wander. travel for one's work, having no fixed base: a roving reporter. *She roves around the world.* **2** look around in al directions. *He roved around to make sure no one was watching. (noun)* an act of roving. *The rove was tiring her out now.*

Row – *(noun)* a number of people or things in a more or less straight line. *I sat in the third row.*

Royal – *(adjective)* **1** of, relating to, or having the status of a king or queen or a member of their family. *The royal family travelled to the hills for vacations.* **2** of a quality or size suitable for a king or queen; splendid. *This is a royal dress.* (noun) **1** a member of the royal family. *The royal strutted towards the throne.* **2** a paper size, 636*480 mm. a book size, 234*156mm. a book size, 312*237mm. *Please print it on royal.*

Royalty – *(noun)* **1** people of royal blood or status. an individual member of a royal family. the status or power of a king or queen. *The royalty does a lot of charity in this country.* **2** a sum paid for the use of a patent or to an author or composer for each copy of a book sold or for each public performance of a work. *The company landed itself in trouble by not paying the royalty.* **3** a royal right granted by the sovereign. a payment made by a producer of minerals, oil, or natural gas to the owner of the site. *He was delighted by the royalty he received.*

Rub – *(verb)* **1** apply firm pressure against the surface of, using a repeated back and forth motion. move to and fro against a surface. apply with a rubbing action: she rubbed some cream on her nose. blend or mix ingredients together using a rubbing action: rub in the fat. dry, smooth, or clean something by rubbing. erase pencil marks with a rubber. be transferred by contact or association. *He rubbed her back to ease her backache.* **2** cope or get along without undue difficulty. *They rubbed well together.* **3** reproduce the design of by rubbing paper laid on it with pencil or chalk. *The child rubbed the design.* **4** be slowed or diverted by the unevenness of the ground. *My car rubbed away from the path.* (noun) **1** an act of rubbing. *He gave her back a soft rub.* **2** an ointment designed to be rubbed on the skin. *I have bought a rub for my face.* **3** the central or most important difficulty. *The rub of the matter is that we do not have enough money.*

Rubber – *(noun)* **1** a tough elastic polymeric substance made from the latex of a tropical plants or synthetically. *This unusual dress is made of rubber.* **2** a piece of such material used for erasing pencil marks. *The child forgot to carry his rubber to school.* **3** a condom. *They used a rubber to have safe sex.* **4** rubber boots; galoshes. *My rubbers are very comfortable.*

Rubbish – *(noun)* **1** waste material; refuse or litter. *There was rubbish everywhere.* **2** material that is considered unimportant or valueless. nonsense; worthless talk or ideas. *Don't give me rubbish. (verb)* criticize and reject as worthless. *He rubbished my idea. (adjective)* very bad. *His rubbish language made him a very unpleasant person to stay with.*

Rubble – *(noun)* waste or rough fragments of stone, brick, concrete, etc. especially as the debris from the demolition of buildings. *Some people rummaged through the rubble.*

Ruby – *(noun)* **1** a precious stone consisting of corundum in colour varieties varying from deep crimson or purple to pale rose. *I like wearing rubies.* **2** an intense deep red colour. *The ruby of her dress stood out in the crowd.* **3** an old type size equal to 5*1/2 points. *Not many people use ruby anymore.*

Rucksack – *(noun)* a bag with two shoulder straps which allow it to be carried on the back, used by hikers. *My rucksack is too heavy.*

Rudder – *(noun)* a flat piece hinged vertically near the stern of a boat for steering. a vertical aerofoil pivoted from the tailplane of an aircraft, for controlling movement about the vertical axis. application of the rudder in steering a boat or aircraft. *The rudder can be used to decide the direction of the boat.*

Ruddy – *(adjective)* **1** having a healthy red colour. *She has a ruddy complexion.* **2** used as a euphemism for bloody. *It was a ruddy fight. (verb)* make ruddy in colour. *The makeup man ruddied the actor's cheeks.*

Rude – *(adjective)* **1** offensively impolite or ill mannered. referring to sex in a way considered improper and offensive. *His rude language made him very unpleasant to work with.* **2** very abrupt: a rude awakening. *The crime was a rude awakening for the society.* **3** vigorous or hearty. *I had some rude food at the party.* **4** roughly made or done; lacking sophistication. ignorant and uneducated. *The finishing of this vase is quite rude.*

Rudiments – *(noun)* **1** the first principles of a subject. an elementary or primitive form of something. *You don't even seem to know the rudiments.* **2** an undeveloped or immature part of organ. *There was no way of correcting the rudiments.* **3** a basic pattern used by drummers, such as the roll, the flam, and the paradiddle. *The drummers practiced the rudiments.*

Rudimentary – *(adjective)* **1** involving or limited to basic principles. *It is important to follow the rudimentary practices.* **2** of or relating to an immature, undeveloped, or basic form. *These are all rudimentary arguments.*

Ruffian – *(noun)* a violent or lawless person. *The ruffian turned out to be the king in disguise.*

Rug – *(noun)* **1** a small carpet. a thick woolen blanket. *The rug had gathered dust.* **2** a toupee or wig. *She pulled the rug off his head.*

Rugged – *(adjective)* **1** having a rocky and uneven surface. *The terrain is rugged.* **2** having or requiring toughness and determination. having attractively masculine, rough hewn features. *His rugged features suited the role well.*

Ruin – *(noun)* **1** physical destruction or collapse. *No one knows what led to the ruin of the civilization.* **2** a building that has suffered much damage. *The ruins are centuries old.* **3** a dramatic decline; a downfall. *Corruption led to the ruin of the empire. (verb)* **1** damage irreparably; reduce to a state of ruin. reduce to poverty or bankruptcy. *You have ruined my work.* **2** fall headlong. *The traitor ruined the empire.*

Ruinous – *(adjective)* **1** disastrous or destructive. *His ruinous tendencies are bound to land him in trouble.* **2** in ruins; dilapidated. *The ruinous house needed repairs.*

Rule – *(noun)* **1** a regulation or principle governing conduct or procedure within a particular sphere. *The new rule wasn't acceptable to the students.* **2** control or government: an end to [British] rule. *The current government's rule has been questioned many times.* **3** a code of practice and discipline for a religious community: the rule of St Benedict. *He lived during the rule of St Benedict.* **4** the normal or customary state of things. *It is pretty much a rule that one has to switch off the mobile phone during a class.* **5** a straight strip of rigid material used for measuring; a ruler. *Please draw a line using a rule.* **6** a thin printed line or dash. *The rule made it easy to align the text. (verb)* **1** exercise ultimate power over. exert a powerful and restricting influence on. be prevalent; be the norm. *The dictator ruled for years before democracy was restored.* **2** pronounce authoritatively and legally to be the case. *The judge ruled in favour of the victim.* **3** make parallel lines on. make with a ruler. *Rule the notebook so that you can write on it.* **4** exclude something as a possibility. *The committee ruled out treason.*

Ruler - *(noun)* **1** a person or agent exercising government or dominion. *The ruler of this country is tough but unjust.* **2** a straight edged strip of rigid material, marked at regular intervals and used to draw straight lines or measure distances. *Please use a ruler to draw a line in your notebooks.*

Ruling - *(noun)* an authoritative decision or pronouncement. *The court issued the ruling without any delay.* *(adjective)* exercising rule. *The ruling party was fighting to resolve some internal issues.*

Rum - *(noun)* an alcoholic spirit distilled from sugar cane residues or molasses. any intoxicating liquor. *He drank rum with water.*

Rumble - *(verb)* **1** make a continuous deep, resonant sound. move with such a sound. *The thunder rumbled throughout the night.* **2** continue in a persistent but low key way. *The speaker rumbled on.* **3** discover: it wouldn't need a genius to rumble his little game. *I rumbled upon a strange looking mushroom.* **4** take part in a street fight. *The mob rumbled in the streets.* *(noun)* **1** a continuous deep, resonant sound like distant thunder. *The rumble of the thunder shook the earth.* **2** a street fight between rival gangs. *Police intercepted the rumble.*

Ruminate - *(verb)* **1** think deeply about something. *I would like to ruminate over this matter for some time.* **2** chew the cud. *The cow ruminated for a long time.*

Rummage - *(verb)* search unsystematically and untidily for something. make a thorough search of a vessel. *They rummaged through the cabinets.* *(noun)* an act of rummaging. *Their rummage left the room very disorganized.*

Rumour - *(noun)* a currently circulating story or report of unverified or doubtful truth. *Rumour has it that they are going to marry soon.* *(verb)* be circulated as a rumour. *It is rumoured that she will soon act in her first film.*

Run - *(verb)* **1** move at a speed faster than a walk, never having both or all feet on the ground at the same time. enter or be entered in a race. chase or hunt their quarry. sail straight and fast directly before the wind. go upriver from the sea in order to spawn. *The thief ran as soon as he saw the police.* **2** move about in a hurried and hectic way. *Stop running around.* **3** pass or cause to pass: Helen ran her fingers through her hair. move or cause to move forcefully: the tanker ran aground. fail to stop at a red traffic light. navigate in a boat. *The ship ran aground.* **4** flow or cause to flow. cause water to flow over. emit or exude a liquid: her nose was running. dissolve and spread when wet. *Turn the tap to let the water run.* **5** make a regular journey on a particular route. transport in a car: I'll run you home. *The bus runs the same route every day.* **6** be in charge of; manage or organize. continue, operate, or proceed: everything's running according to plan. own, maintain, and use a vehicle. *She runs her enterprise well.* **7** be in or cause to be in operation; function or cause to function. *Please run the show.* **8** be common or inherent in. *Diabetes runs in their family.* **9** stand as a candidate. *He is running for the chief minister's post this year.* **10.** pass into or reach a specified state or level. *The ship has run its course.* *(noun)* **1** an act or spell of running. a running pace. *He broke into a run.* **2** a journey or route. a short excursion made in a car. *It is a long run to Jaisalmer.* **3** a unit of scoring achieved by hitting the ball so that both batsmen are able to run between the wickets. a point scored by the batter returning to the home plate after touching the bases. *They managed to secure three runs.* **4** a spell of producing, proceeding, or operating: a run of bad luck. a continuous stretch or length of something . a rapid series of musical notes. a sequence of cards of the same suit. *He has been having a run of bad luck.* **5** a widespread and sudden demand: a big run on nostalgia toys. *There is a big run on heavy jackets this year.* **6** a course or track made or regularly used: a ski run. *She is on a ski run* *nowadays*. 7 the average or usual type: she stood out from the general run of tory women. *The tall tree stood out from the general run of the trees in the locality.* **8** an enclosed area in which animals or birds may run freely in the open. free and unrestricted use of or access to somewhere. a large open stretch of land used for pasture or livestock. *Put the fowl in the run.* **9** a ladder in stockings or tights. *I was horrified to note the run in my stockings.* **10.** a downward trickle of liquid. *The run of water stopped as soon as I plugged the hole.*

Rung – *(noun)* **1** a horizontal support on a ladder for a person's foot. a strengthening crosspiece in the structure of a chair. *The rung broke as I was climbing up the ladder.* **2** a level in a hierarchical structure. *I sit at the lowest rung in my company.*

Runner – *(noun)* **1** a person or animal that runs. a horse that runs in a particular race. a messenger, collector, or agent for a bank, bookmaker, or similar. an orderly in the army. *He is a fast runner.* **2** a vehicle or machine that runs in a satisfactory or specified way. *The car is a smooth runner.* **3** an idea that has a chance if being accepted. *This idea is a runner.* **4** a rod, groove, or blade on which something slides. a roller for moving a heavy article. a ring capable of sliding or being drawn along a strap or rod. *The runner gave way while the stuntman was performing.* **5** a shoot which grows along the ground and can take root at points along its length. a climbing plant, or one that spreads by means of runners. *The runner that has covered our boundary wall makes it look so pretty.* **6** a long, narrow rug or strip of carpet. *We got the runner laid throughout the length of the corridor.*

Running – *(noun)* **1** the activity or movement of a runner. *The running in the race today was exceptional.* **2** the action or business of managing or operating. *The running of this business is flawless.* *(adjective)* **1** flowing naturally or supplied through pipes and taps. exuding liquid or pus: a running sore. *The running water was clean.* **2** continuous or recurring: a running joke. *It was a running joke in the company for a long time.* **3** done while running. *It is a running activity.* **4** consecutive; in succession: he failed to turn up for the third week running. *She delivered successful speeches for three weeks running.*

Runny – *(adjective)* **1** more liquid in consistency than is usual or expected. *The cake batter is too runny.* **2** producing or discharging mucus. *She was tired of her runny nose.*

Runway – *(noun)* **1** a strip of hard ground along which aircraft take off and land. *A deer strolled on to the runway.* **2** a raised gangway extending into an auditorium, especially as used for fashion shows. *The models catwalked down the runway.* **3** an animal run. **4** a chute down which logs are slid. *The runway is blocked.*

Rupee – *(noun)* the basic monetary unit of India, Pakistan, Sri Lanka, Nepal, Mauritius, and the Seychelles, equal to 100 paisa in India, Pakistan, and Nepal, and 100 cents un Sri Lanka, Mauritius, and the Seychelles. *I spent Rupees 300 on this dress.*

Rupture – *(verb)* **1** break or burst suddenly. cause to break or burst suddenly. suffer an abdominal hernia. *She had to be operated upon immediately when her appendix ruptured.* **2** breach or disturb. *You have ruptured the peace of the class.* *(noun)* an instance of rupturing. *The rupture needed to be operated upon.*

Rural – *(adjective)* in, relating to, or characteristic of the country. side rather than the town. *I am very fascinated by the rural lifestyle.*

Ruse – *(noun)* a stratagem or trick. *The ruse was very clever.*

Rush – *(noun)* **1** a marsh or waterside plant with slender stem like pith filled leaves, some kinds of which are used for matting, baskets, etc. *This basket is made of rush.* **2** used in names if similar plants, e.g. flowering rush. *I was delighted to find a flowering rush.*

Russet – *(adjective)* **1** reddish brown. *The russet dress is my favourite.* **2** rustic; homely. *The russet girl manages her house very well.* *(noun)* **1** a reddish brown colour. *I don't like russet much.* **2** a dessert apple of a variety with a slightly rough greenish brown skin. *Do you want a russet?* **3** a coarse homespun reddish brown or grey cloth. *The russet was very useful.*

Rust – *(noun)* **1** a reddish or yellowish brown flaking coating of iron oxide that is formed on iron or steel by oxidation, especially in the presence of moisture. *The rust made the rod unusable.* **2** a fungal disease of plants which results in reddish or brownish patches. *I got a spray medicine for rust.* **3** a reddish brown colour. *I bought a dress in rust colour.* *(verb)* be affected with rust. *The rods rusted over the years.*

Rustic – *(adjective)* **1** of or characteristic of life in the country. having a simplicity and charm that is considered typical of the countryside. *He had a rustic home.* **2** made of rough branches or timber. *The rustic cottage couldn't survive the storm.* *(noun)* **1** an unsophisticated country person. *The rustic managed to impress everyone.* **2** a small brownish European moth. *The rustic fluttered near the lamp.*

Rustle – *(verb)* **1** make a soft, muffled crackling sound like that caused by the movement of dry leaves or paper. move with such a sound. *Her dress rustled in the wind.* **2** round up and steal. *The robbers rustled them up.* **3** produce something quickly. *Please rustle a response.* **4** move or act quickly or energetically. *She rustled through the bushes.* *(noun)* a rustling sound. *I was started by the rustle in my backyard.*

Ss

S-the nineteenth letter of the English alphabet. **1** Any object shaped like S. **2** Roman numeral for 70 or 70,000.

Sabbath - *(noun)* **1** a day of religious observance and abstinence from work, kept by Jews from Friday evening to Saturday evening, and by most Christians or Sunday. *I will visit my grandmother on Sabbath.* **2** a supposed annual midnight meeting of witches with the devil. *Sabbath isn't really the safest time to be out on the streets.*

Sable - *(noun)* a marten with a short tail and dark brown fur, native to Japan and Siberia. *I believe I saw a sable take a flight at dawn.*

Sabotage - *(verb)* deliberately destroy. or obstruct, especially for political or military advantage. *The athlete who had sabotaged the practice session was suspended. (noun)* the action of certain gambling games. *He planned the sabotage on the slot machine in the casino.*

Sabre - *(noun)* **1** a heavy cavalry sword with a curved blade and a single cutting edge. historically a cavalry soldier and horse. *Even though the sabre was old, it was still sharp.* **2** a light fencing sword with a tapering, typically curved blade. *He pointed the rusted sabre at the dummy. (verb)* **1** [archaic] cut down or wound with a sabre. *The witness saw the two men sabre the king.*

Saccharin - *(noun)* a sweet-testing synthetic compound used as a substitute for sugar.*She added saccharin to her porridge.*

Sachet - *(noun)* [chiefly British] a small sealed bag or packet containing a small quantity of something. *Companies use sachets to promote their consumer products.*

Sack - *(noun)* **1** a large bag made of a material such as hessian or thick paper, used for storing and carrying goods. *The social workers gathered the garbage in sacks.* **2** [informal] dismissal from employment. *She was given a sack when she failed to meet the performance targets.* **3** [informal chiefly north American] bed. *I wish I could hit the sack right now.* **4** baseball, [informal] a base. *The new player was asked to play at the 2nd sack.* **5** [American football] a tickly of a quarterback behind the line of scrimmage. *After the sack, a cheer arose from the spectators. (verb)* **1** [informal] dismiss from employment. *The board of directors sacked the CEO of the company.* **2** [informal] go to sleep or bed. *I will hit the sack early tonight.* **3** American football tackle with a sack. *After the opponents sacked them, our team discussed the next strategy.* **4** put into a sack or sacks. *I sacked all my old toys and gave them to charity.*

Sacrament - *(noun)* **1** a religious ceremony or ritual regarded as imparting diving grace, such as baptism, the Eucharist, and penance and the anointing of the sick. *During the sacrament, everyone's face was lit with joy.* **2** the consecrated elements of the Eucharist, especially the bread or host. *When the sacraments were distributed, everyone felt the love of God.* **3** a thing of mysterious or sacred significance; a religious symbol. *The archaeologists found the ancient sacrament buried behind the old church.*

Sacred - *(adjective)* **1** connected with a deity and so deserving veneration; holy. embodying the doctrines of a religion. sacrosanct. *All sacred objects were collected from the antique dealer and installed in the temple.* **2** religious rather than secular. *I think the priest was able to feel my son's sacred thoughts.*

Sacrifice - *(noun)* **1** the practice or an act of killing an animal or person or surrendering a possession as an offering to a deity. an animal, person, or object offered in this way. *She offered all her* *jewellery as a sacrifice for her husband's health.* **2** an act of giving up something of value for the sake of something that is of greater value or importance. *The independence of India was a result of many sacrifices.* **3** [baseball] a bunted or fly ball which puts the batter out but allows a base-runner to advance. *The spectators half-heartedly cheered the sacrifice. (verb)* offer or give up as a sacrifice. *She sacrificed her life of comfort to help the needy.*

Sacrilege – *(noun)* violation or misuse of something regarded as sacred or as having great value. *He was punished severely for the sacrilege he had committed.*

Sad – *(adjective)* **1** feeling sorrow; unhappy. causing or characterized by sorrow or regret. *She felt very sad when her cousin had to go back home after vacations.* **2** [informal] pathetically inadequate or unfashionable. *The man was clearly uncomfortable because of his sad clothes.*

Sadden – *(verb)* cause to feel sad. *The news of the delay in his parents arrival saddened him.*

Sadness – *(noun)* the feeling of sorrow. *However hard she tried, she couldn't explain the sadness in her heart.*

Saddle – *(noun)* **1** a seat with a raised ridge at the front and back, fastened on the back of a horse for riding. *The saddle was made of pure leather.* **2** a seat on a bicycle or motorcycle. *The hard saddle made cycling very uncomfortable.* **3** a low part of a ridge between two higher points or peaks. *As the sun rose from the saddle, the lovely scenery was revealed.* **4** a shaped support for a cable, pipe, or other object. *When the saddle broke, the whole network of pipes came crashing down.* **5** [mathematics] a low region of a curve between two high points. *The analysts weren't worried about the saddle in the growth.* **6** the lower part of the back in a mammal or fowl, especially when distinct in shape or marking. *The strange bird's saddle was red.* **7** a joint of meat consisting of the two loins. *He cooked the entire saddle and ate it all by himself. (verb)* **1** put a saddle on a horse. *The horse grew restless as soon as the rider saddled it.* **2** burden with an onerous responsibility or task. *When my colleague went on unexpected vacation, I was saddled with his work.* **3** enter a horse for a race. *He was worried as well as excited when he saddled the new horse.*

Safari – *(noun)* an expedition to observe or hunt animals in their natural habitat, especially in east Africa. *The science students were very excited about going on a safari.*

Safe – *(adjective)* **1** protected from or not exposed to danger or risk; not likely to be harmed or lsot. not causing or leading to harm or injury. affording security or protection. *He believed that he was at a safe place.* **2** often derogatory cautious and unenterprising. *He has always been a safe player.* **3** law based on wrong. *The safe law saved him from imprisonment.* **4** uninjured; with no harm done. *I was glad to know that my uncle was found safe after the accident.* **5** [informal] excellent. *He was in a safe shape. (noun)* **1** a strong fireproof cabinet with a complex lock, used for the storage or valuables. *She bought a safe for her jewellery when she moved into the new colony.* **2** [north American informal] a condom. *It is better to use a safe than risk catching AIDS.*

Safeguard – *(noun)* a measure taken to protect or prevent something. *Construction of the new fence around the house proves to be an effective safeguard. (verb)* protect with a safeguard. *He promised his wife that he will do anything to safeguard the house.*

Safe-keeping – *(noun)* preservation in a safe place. *My father left his car with his brother for safe-keeping.*

Safety – *(noun)* **1** the condition of being safe. denoting something designed to prevent injury or damage: a safety barrier. *They stayed indoors for safety.* **2** US [informal] a condom. *It is better to use safety than risk spoiling your future.* **3** [American football] a defensive back who plays in a deep position. *The safety did his best to prevent the goal.* **4** [American football] a play in which the ball is downed by the offence in their own end zone, scoring two points to the defence. *The team had to pay a price for the safety of players.*

Safety pin - *(noun)* small pin to tie two things together. *She used a safety pin to secure the ribbon to her dress.*

Safety net - *(noun)* **1** a net placed to catch an acrobat in case of a fall. *It was fortunate that the trapeze artist fell on the safety net.* **2** a safeguard against adversity. *The health insurance she had bought for her parents proved to be a valuable safety net.*

Saffron - *(noun)* **1** an orange-yellow spice used for falvouring and colouring food, made from the dried stigmas of a crocus. *The flavour of the saffron overwhelmed the other flavours of the dish.* **2** an autumn-flowering crocus with reddish-purple flowers that yields this spice. *The fields of saffron stretched as far as I could see.*

Sag - *(verb)* sink, subside, or bulge downwards gradually under weight or pressure or through lack of strength. hang down loosely or unevenly. *The roof of the house sagged dangerously.* *(noun)* **1** an instance of sagging. *It was getting difficult to ignore the sag in the roof.* **2** [geometry] the amount of a downward curve, measured as the perpendicular distance from the middle of the curve to the straight line between the two supporting points. *I lost one mark because I miscalculated the sag.*

Saga - *(noun)* **1** a long story of heroic achievement, especially a medieval prose narrative in old Norse or old Icelandic. *I was touched by the sheer courage of the hero of the medical saga.* **2** a long, involved account or series of incidents. *As he narrated his saga, many listeners were moved to tears.*

Sage - *(noun)* an aromatic plant with grayish-green leaves used as a culinary herb, native to southern Europe and the Mediterranean. used in names of similar aromatic plants, e.g. wood sage. *I love the fragrance of sage.*

Sagittarius - *(noun)* **1** [astronomy] a large constellation said to represent a centaur carrying a bow and arrow. *The students tried but weren't able to locate Sagittarius.* **2** [astrology] the ninth sign of the zodiac, which the sun enters about 22 November. *Her zodiac sign is Sagittarius.*

Sail - *(noun)* **1** a piece of material extended on a mast to catch the wind and propel a boat or ship. a wind-catching apparatus attached to the arm of a windmill. the broad fin on the back of a sailfish or of some prehistoric reptiles. a structure by which an animal is propelled across the surface of water by the wind, e.g. the float of a Portuguese man-of-war. *The boat could be identified easily by its bright sails.* **2** voyage or excursion in a sailing boat or ship. *The crew was excited at the idea of going on a sail.* *(verb)* **1** travel in a sailing boat as a sport or for recreation. travel in ship or boat using sails or engine power. begin a voyage; leave a harbor. travel by ship on or across or on a route. navigate or control a boat or ship. *I would love to sail in this single scull boat.* **2** move smoothly and rapidly or in a stately or confident manner. *She sailed confidently through the English channel alone.*

Sailor - *(noun)* a person who works as a member of the crew of a commercial or naval ship or boat, especially one who is below the rank of officer. a person who sails as a sport or recreation. a person who rarely becomes sick at sea in rough weather. *The actress was smitten by the handsome sailor.*

Saint - *(noun)* **1** a person who is acknowledged as holy or virtuous and regarded in Christian faith as being in heaven after death. a person of exalted virture who is canonized by the church after death and who may be the object of veneration and prayers for intercession. [informal] a very virtuous person. *There is no doubt that he was a saint.* **2** a member of the church of Jesus Christ of latter-day saints; a Mormon. *The students were inspired by the lives of the saints.* *(verb)* **1** formally recognize as a saint; canonize. *The great missionary was sainted after he died.* **2** worthy of being a saint; very virtuous: his sainted sister. *The sainted teacher taught her students really well.*

Sake - *(noun)* a Japanese alcoholic drink made from fermented rice. *The boss shamed his company by getting drunk on Sake.*

Salad – *(noun)* a dish consisting of a mixture of raw vegetables or other cold ingredients, typically served with a dressing. *Her diet consisted mostly of salads.*

Salary – *(noun)* a fixed regular payment made usually on a monthly basis by an employer to an employee, especially a professional or white-collar worker. *The employees were overjoyed to receive bonus with their salary. (verb)* pay a salary to. *Our company pays salary to its staff on first day of the month.*

Sale – *(noun)* **1** the exchange of a commodity for money; the process of selling something. a quantity or amount sold. *The family is very happy with the sale of the flat.* **2** the activity or profession of selling. *The sale took care of their financial needs.* **3** a period in which goods are disposed of at reduced prices. *There was a long queue outside the store because of the sale.* **4** a public or charitable event at which goods are sold. a public auction. *The sale was expected to collect sufficient funds for the treatment of the sick child.*

Saleable – *(adjective)* fit or able to be sold. *The mirror was very old but saleable.*

Salesman – *(noun)* a person whose job involves selling or promoting commercial products. *The door-to-door salesman managed do good business.*

Salesmanship – *(noun)* **1** the technique of selling a product. *The experienced businessman delivered a valuable lecture on salesmanship.* **2** erest in new ideas, products, methods,etc. *The new sales manager impressed everyone with her salesmanship.*

Saleswoman – *(noun)* a woman whose job involves selling or promoting commercial products. *The saleswoman made a very strong sales pitch to sell her product.*

Salient – *(adjective)* **1** most noticeable or important. *Her shapely nose was the salient feature of her face.* **2** pointing outwards. the opposite of reentrant. *She held her arms salient.* **3** [heraldry] standing on its hind legs with the forepaws raised, as if leaping. *The statue of the salient lion dominated the scenes. (noun)* a piece of land or section of fortification that juts out to form an angle. *The top of the salient offered a good view of the sea.*

Saline – *(adjective)* **1** containing or impregnated with salt. *The saline solution tasted horrible.* **2** [chiefly medicine] containing sodium chloride and a or salts of magnesium or another alkali metal. *The saline liquid was horrible but very effective. (noun)* a saline solution. *Saline was intravenously introduced into the patient.*

Saliva – *(noun)* a watery liquid secreted into the mouth by glands, providing lubrication for chewing and swallowing, and aiding digestion. *He swallowed his own saliva because he was thirsty.*

Sallow – *(adjective)* of a yellowish or pale brown colour. *The student's sallow skin was a reminder of her long illness. (verb)* make sallow. *The horrible words of the dictator sallowed the faces of his people.*

Salmon – *(noun)* **1** a large edible fish that matures in the sea and migrates to freshwater streams to spawn. any of various unrelated marine fish resembling this. the flesh of such a fish as food. *I enjoyed watching the salmon jump.* **2** a pale pink colour like that of the flesh of a salmon. *The salmon of her dress was very pleasing to the eyes.*

Saloon – *(noun)* **1** a public room or building used for a specified purpose. *They entered the saloon expecting splendour.* **2** [British] another term for a ship. *The saloon was in no shape to go sailing.* **3** [north American historical] a place where alcoholic drinks may be bought and drunk. *The group entered a saloon after the baseball match.* **4** [British] a car having a closed body and separate bot. *The grand saloon looked out of place in the crowded streets.* **5** [British] a luxurious railway carriage used as a lounge or restaurant or as private accommodation. *The saloon was attached near the pantry car of the train.*

Salt – *(noun)* **1** sodium chloride, a white crystalline substance which gives seawater its characteristic taste and is used for seasoning or preserving food. poetic something which adds freshness or piquancy. *I added salt to my bland salad.* **2** [chemistry] any with a base, with the hydrogen of the acid replaced by a metal or other cation. *The salts in the test tubes had a strong smell.* **3** [informal] an experienced sailor. *The old salts gathered around the fire and discussed their experiences. (adjective)* **1** impregnated with salt. *The salt water made me feel even more thirsty.* **2** growing on the coast or in salt marshes. *The salt weeds lay strewn across the beach. (verb)* **1** season or preserve with salt. make piquant or more interesting. sprinkle a road or path with salt in order to melt snow or ice. *They salted the streets yesterday.* **2** [informal] fraudulently make appear to be paying one by placing rich ore into it. *The team salted the archaeological site to get more funds.* **3** [informal] secretly store or put by something, especially money. *She regularly salted money for difficult times.* **4** having developed a resistance to disease by surviving it. *The child salted the deadly condition.*

Salty – *(adjective)* **1** tasting of, containing, or preserved with salt. *The fish was salty.* **2** down-to-earth; coarse. *Even though the businessman was rich, his thinking was quite salty.*

Salubrious – *(adjective)* **1** health-giving; healthy. *My mother's salubrious potion has always worked for me.* **2** pleasant; not run-down. *The salubrious old book was fun to read.*

Salutary – *(adjective)* **1** beneficial in providing an opportunity for learning from experience. *The salutary interview will prove to be very helpful for the new gradates.* **2** [archaic] health-giving. *The salutary herbal drink was quite popular in historic times.*

Salute – *(noun)* **1** a gesture of respect and recognition. *The children offered salutes to everyone who passed them that day.* **2** a prescribed or specified movement, typically a raising of a hand to the head, made as a salute by a member of a military or similar force. *I watched my son with pride as he responded to the salutes from his battalion.* **3** the discharge of a gun or guns as a formal or ceremonial sign of respect or celebration. *All cannons were fired together as a salute to the popular leader.* **4** fencing the formal performance of certain guards or other movements by fencers before engaging. *Everyone watched with baited breaths as the fencers offered salutes to each other. (verb)* **1** make a formal salute to. greet. *The soldiers saluted the president.* **2** show or express admiration and respect for. *I salute the brave soldiers.*

Salvage – *(verb)* **1** rescue from loss at sea. *The rescue team salvaged the precious jewel just before the ship sank.* **2** retrieve or preserve from loss or destruction. *Residents of the colony salvaged the old building from demolition. (noun)* **1** the process or an instance of salvaging. *Everyone was glad that the salvage was successful.* **2** the cargo saved from a wrecked or sunken ship. *The salvage remained unattended in the office for days.* **3** [law] payment made or due to a person who has saved a ship or its cargo. *The brave sailor got the salvage he deserved.*

Salvation – *(noun)* **1** [theology] deliverance from sin and its consequences, believed by Christians to be brought about by faith in Christ. *My grandfather prays for salvation every day.* **2** preservation or deliverance from harm, ruin, or loss. a source or means of being saved in this way. *The old businessman was thankful for the salvation.*

Same – *(noun)* **1** identical; uncharged. *The twins had the same taste in food.* **2** referring to a person or thing just mentioned. *The man tore open the envelope, though he carefully avoided the stamps on the same. (pronoun)* **1** the same thing as previously mentioned. identical people or things. *She wore the glamorous dress, though she hadn't worn the same ever before.* **2** the person or thing just mentioned. *My mother broke her spectacles. She had got the same made just a week back. (adverb)* in the same way. *The tailor designed my dress beautifully. He had done the same with my other dress too.*

Sample – *(noun)* **1** a small part or quantity intended to show what the whole is like. *The artist showcased a sample of his work.* **2**

[statistics] a portion of a population, serving as a basis for estimates of the attributes of the whole population. *The sample the survey agency had selected did not represent the whole population.* **3** a specimen taken for scientific testing or analysis. *The sample wasn't stored properly.* **4** a sound created by sampling. *The sample was very pleasing to the ears.* *(verb)* **1** take a sample or samples of. *The pest control sampled the infestation in my house.* **2** get a representative experience of. *I want to sample your delicious cake.* **3** [electronics] ascertain the momentary value of many times a second so as to convert the signal to digital form. *The sampling produced excellent results.*

Sanatorium – *(noun)* **1** an establishment for the treatment of people who are convalescing or have a chronic illness. *The family sent the woman to a sanatorium to recover.* **2** [British] a place in a boarding school for children who are unwell. *She missed her class today because she was in the sanatorium.*

Sanctify – *(verb)* **1** consecrate. *The priests sanctified the piece of land.* **2** make legitimate or binding by religious sanction. *The minister sanctified the couple's marriage.* **3** free from sin. *They sanctified the little orphan.* **4** give the appearance of being right or good. *The regressive law does not sanctify marriage between a girl and a boy of the same caste.*

Sanctimonious – *(adjective)* derogatory making a show of being morally superior. *Her sanctimonious attitude is the reason why no one wants to talk to her.*

Sanction – *(noun)* **1** a threatened penalty for disobeying a law or rule. measures taken by a state to coerce another to conform to an international agreement or norms of conduct. [ethics] a consideration operating to enforce obedience to any rule of conduct. *The community imposed sanctions against the family for disobeying the law.* **2** official permission or approval for an action. official confirmation or ratification of a law. *The preparations for the festival commenced as soon as the sanctions were received.* *(verb)* **1** give official sanction for. *The manager sanctioned the budget for the party.* **2** impose a sanction or penalty on. *The judge sanctioned the accused for indiscipline in the court.*

Sanctity – *(noun)* **1** holiness; saintliness. *No one can question his sanctity.* **2** ultimate importance and inviolability. *The head often took advantage if his sanctity.*

Sanctuary – *(noun)* **1** a place of refuge or safety. immunity form arrest. *Even though the criminal was in the sanctuary, he never felt secure.* **2** a nature reserve. a place where injured or unwanted animals are cared for. *The injured tiger cub recovered quickly in the sanctuary.* **3** a holy place. the innermost recess or hoist part of a temple. the part o the chancel of a church containing the high altar. *Not many people have been fortunate enough to see the sanctuary of the church.*

Sand – *(noun)* **1** loose granular substance, typically pale yellowish brown, resulting from the erosion of siliceous and other rocks and forming a major constituent of beaches, river beds, the seabed, and deserts. an expanse of sand. technical sediment whose particles are larger than silt. *The sand sparkled in the sun.* **2** [north American informal] firmness of purpose. *The sand in her words impressed me a lot.* **3** a pale yellow-brown colour. *He applied some extra strokes of sand to his painting.* *(verb)* **1** smooth with sandpaper or a sander. *They were sanding the plaster when I checked last.* **2** sprinkle or overlay with sand. *The construction workers sanded the damp site.*

Sandal – *(noun)* a light shoe with an openwork upper or straps attaching the sole to the foot. *I prefer sandals over the other types of footwear.*

Sandpaper – *(noun)* paper with sand or another abrasive stuck to it, used for smoothing wooden or other surfaces. *It was good that I had the sandpaper handy.* *(verb)* smooth with sandpaper. *I sandpapered the rough plaster.*

Sandstone – *(noun)* sedimentary rock consisting of sand or quartz grains cemented together, typically red, yellow, or brown in colour. *The spectacular formations of sandstone mesmerized the onlookers.*

Sandwich – *(noun)* an item of food. *Usually, one sandwich is enough for me.*

Sandy – *(adjective)* **1** covered in or consisting of sand. *The sandy beach was abandoned during the day.* **2** light yellowish-brown. *The sandy dress was very ugly.*

Sane – *(adjective)* **1** of sound mind; not mad. *The lawyer proved in the court that the accused was a sane person.* **2** reasonable; sensible. *He gave sane arguments to prove his point.*

Sanguine – *(adjective)* **1** cheerfully optimistic. *The naughty boy remained sanguine even when he was on his way to the principal's office.* **2** medieval [medicine] having a predominance of blood among the bodily humours, supposedly marked by a ruddy complexion and an optimistic disposition. [archaic] of the complexion ruddy. *He was sanguine, and, therefore would most likely lead a long, healthy life.* **3** [archaic] bloody or bloodthirsty. *The dog's sanguine eyes scared the lone pedestrian.* *(noun)* a blood-red colour. *She looked like a rose in her sanguine dress.*

Sanitary – *(adjective)* **1** of or relating to conditions affecting hygiene and health. *The sanitary conditions of the market were horrible.* **2** hygienic. *The cook's sanitary habits are appalling.*

Sanitation – *(noun)* conditions relating to public health. *At last, the department woke up to the sanitation.*

Sanity – *(noun)* the condition of being sane. reasonable and rational behaviour. *I was thankful of my sanity through the tough times.*

Sap – *(noun)* **1** the fluid, [chiefly] water with dissolved sugars and mineral salts, circulating in the vascular system of a plant. *The sap of the tree was sweet.* **2** vigour or energy. *He used all his sap to convince the investors.* *(verb)* gradually weaken a person's strength or power. drain someone of strength or power. *His work in the mines gradually sapped his strength.*

Sapling – *(noun)* **1** a young, slender tree. *The sapling looked healthy.* **2** poetic a young and slender or inexperienced person. *The young man was a sapling when compared to the veteran artist.* **3** a greyhound in its first year. *The grey hound sapling is cute, but he will become ferocious as he grows up.*

Sapphire – *(noun)* **1** a transparent precious stone, typically blue, which is a form of corundum. *The large sapphire on her engagement finger confused everyone.* **2** a bright blue colour. *The sapphire in the girl's eyes mesmerized everyone.* **3** a hummingbird with shining blue or violet plumage. *The sapphire was easily visible from a distance even though the bird was tiny.*

Sarcasm – *(noun)* the use of irony to mock or convey contempt. *His sarcasm irritated me during our fight.*

Sardine – *(noun)* **1** a young pilchard or other young or small herring-like fish. *The preserved sardines tasted nice.* **2** [British] a children's game in which one child hides and the other children, as they find the hider, join him or her in the hiding place. *The children were looking forward to their daily game of sardine.* *(verb)* [informal] pack closely together. *The scared children sardined together as the teacher shouted at them.*

Sash – *(noun)* a long strip or loop of cloth worn over one shoulder or round the waist. *She wore her sash with pride.*

Satan – *(noun)* the devil; Lucifer. *The family was accused of worshipping Satan.*

Satanic – *(adjective)* **1** of or characteristic of Satan. *His satanic ideas were rejected by his friends.* **2** connected with Satanism. *The Satanic family were banished by the villagers.*

Satchel – *(noun)* a shoulder bag with a long strap, used especially for school books. *He picked his satchel reluctantly and started walking towards the school.*

Satellite – *(noun)* **1** an artificial body placed in orbit round the earth or another planet to collect information or for technology. satellite television. *The satellite was visible to naked eyes on clear nights.* **2** [astronomy] a celestial body orbiting a planet. *Some planets have many satellites.* **3** a thing separate from something else but dependent on or controlled by it. a small town, country, etc. dependent on another. *The* *satellite town was very different from the city.* **4** [biology] a portion of DNA with repeating base sequences and of different density from the main sequence. *The scientists were surprised to find the satellite when they were trying to identify the strange organism.*

Satiate – *(verb)* another term for sate. *The generous helping satiated the poor man's hunger. (adjective)* [archaic] fully satisfied. *The girl's satiated curiosity was apparent on her face.*

Satin – *(noun)* **1** a smooth, glossy fabric, usually of silk, produced by a weave in which the threads of the warp are caught and looped by the weft only at certain intervals. *She planned to wear satin for the awards ceremony.* **2** denoting or having a smooth, glossy surface or finish. *The table top was like satin. (verb)* give a satin surface to. *They satined the staircase in preparation of the arrival of the CEO.*

Satire – *(noun)* **1** the use of humour, irony, exaggeration, or ridicule to expose and criticize people's stupidity or vices. *The satire managed to move many people.* **2** a play, novel, etc. using satire. a literary miscellany, especially a poem ridiculing prevalent vices or follies. *The famous satire was a part of our curriculum.*

Satisfaction – *(noun)* **1** the state of being satisfied. *Satisfaction made his life peaceful.* **2** [law] the payment of a debt or fulfillment of an obligation or claim. *Peace returned to their home after the satisfaction of the huge debt.* **3** what is felt to be owed or due to one. *The satisfaction kept him awake at nights.* **4** [Christian theology] Christ's atonement for sin. *The stories of the satisfaction have inspired many.* **5** [historical] the chance to defend one's honour in a duel. *He was glad to be granted satisfaction.*

Satisfactory – *(adjective)* fulfilling expectations or needs; acceptable. *His work was satisfactory.*

Satisfy – *(verb)* **1** meet the expectations, needs, or desires of. fulfil a desire or need. *The quality of the student's work satisfied the teachers.* **2** provide with adequate information about or proof of something. *The lawyer satisfied the jury about the innocence of the accused.* **3** comply with a condition, obligation, or demand. pay off debt or creditor. *They satisfied all conditions of the contract.* **4** [mathematics] of a quantity make an equation true. *The student managed to satisfy the equation on the black board.*

Saturate – *(verb)* **1** soak thoroughly with water or other liquid. *The sponge was saturated and therefore left a trail of water when used for wiping.* **2** cause to combine with, dissolve, or hold the greatest possible quantity of another substance. full until no more can be held or absorbed. *The dessert was saturated with sugar.* **3** magnetize or charge a substance or device fully. *The phone battery was saturated and would have lasted long.* **4** supply a market beyond the point at which the demand for a product is satisfied. *The market is saturated with toothpastes.* **5** overwhelm by concentrated bombing. *The town was saturated in the war. (noun)* a saturated fat. *The saturate made the dish tasty by unhealthy.*

Saturday – *(noun)* the day of the week before Sunday and following Friday. *I promise I will complete the work by this Saturday. (adverb)* [chiefly north American] on Saturday. on Saturdays; each Saturday.*The biker likes to go to the hills saturdays.*

Saturn – *(noun)* a planet of the solar system, sixth in order from the sun and circled by broad flat rings. *Saturn has several rings of different colours.*

Satyr – *(noun)* **1** [Greek] one of a class of lustful, drunken woodland gods, represented as a man with a horse's ears and tail or in roman representations with a goat's ears, tail, legs, and horns. *The image of the Satyr frightened my son.* **2** a man with strong sexual desires. *He watched her like a Satyr.* **3** a butterfly with chiefly dark brown wings. *The satyr fluttered amongst the flowers.*

Sauce – *(noun)* **1** thick liquid served with food to add moistness and flavour. *He ate pizza with sauce.* **2** [north American] stewed fruit, especially apples. *They served a tasty sauce as an accompaniment.* **3** [informal, chiefly] alcoholic drink. *The sauce intoxicated a lot of men that night.* **4** impertinence. *I could hear the sauce in my daughter's voice. (verb)* **1** season with a sauce. *I sauced the dish generously.* **2** make more interesting and exciting. *The script writer sauced the story with a lot of humour.* 3 [informal] be impudent to. *Don't sauce me.*

Saucepan – *(noun)* a deep cooking pan, typically round, made of metal, and with one long handle and a lid. *My saucepan broke when it fell from the stove.*

Saucer – *(noun)* a shallow dish, typically with a central circular indentation, on which a cup is placed. *The saucer looked more beautiful than the cup.*

Sauna – *(noun)* **1** a small room used as a hot-air or steam bath for cleaning and refreshing the body. *I enjoyed being in the sauna.* **2** a session in a sauna. *The sauna rejuvenated me.*

Saunter – *(verb)* walk in a slow, relaxed manner. *The doctor leisurely sauntered through the wards. (noun)* a leisurely stroll. *My saunter transformed into a run when I heard the dog bark.*

Sausage – *(noun)* **1** a short cylindrical tube of minced pork, beef, etc. encased in a skin, typically sold raw and grilled or fried before eating. a cylindrical tube of minced meat seasoned and cooked or preserved, sold mainly to be eaten cold in slices. *The sausages were excellently cooked.* **2** a sausage-shaped object. *The sausage in his bag turned out to be a banana.*

Savage – *(adjective)* **1** fierce, violent, and uncontrolled. cruel and vicious. *The savage eyes of the accused convinced the jury that he could have committed the crime.* **2** primitive; uncivilized. *His savage hair made him look like a caveman.* **3** wild; uncultivated. *The savage land lay barren for years. (noun)* **1** a member of a people regarded as primitive and uncivilized. *The savages attacked the village in the night.* **2** a brutal or vicious person. *The savage turned out to be a gentleman in disguise.* **3** heraldry a representation of a bearded and semi-naked man with a wreath of leaves. *The savages were the star attraction of the museum. (verb)* **1** attack ferociously. *He savaged the fridge after the long run.* **2** criticize brutally. *The teacher savaged the children's attempts.*

Save – *(preposition & conjunction)* formal except; other than. *They were all average students save Akhil, who was a genius.*

Saving – *(noun)* **1** an economy of or reduction in money, time, etc. *The saving proved to be timely.* **2** money saved, especially through a bank or official scheme. *My savings helped me in my time of need.* **3** a reservation; an exception. *A saving in the rules of the boarding school was that the students could stay out late on the days the market was on. (adjective)* preventing waste of a particular resource. *The old man's saving attitude towards money proved to be good for his future. (preposition)* **1** except. *Saving movies, he hardly watched television.* **2** with due respect to. *Saving the headmaster, the students need to play at times.*

Saviour – *(noun)* **1** a person who saves someone or something from danger or harm. *My boss proved to be my saviour when I made a mistake in the presentation.* **2** God or Jesus Christ. *We remember the Saviour at every opportunity.*

Savor – *(verb & noun)* US spelling of savour. *I savored cardamom-flavoured cookies.*

Savoury – *(adjective)* **1** salty or spicy rather than sweet. *I prefer savoury dishes to sweet ones.* **2** morally wholesome or acceptable. *My father is proud of his savoury past. (noun)* a savoury snack. *The savoury left me with a very nice taste in my mouth.*

Saw – past tense of see. *I saw several animals in the zoo.*

Saxophone – *(noun)* a member of a family of metal wind instruments with a reed like a clarinet, used especially in jazz and dance music. *He played saxophone like an expert.*

Say – *(verb)* **1** utter words so as to convey information, an opinion, an instruction, etc. convey information or instructions. of a clock or watch indicate a time. be asserted or reported. recite a speech or formula. *Please do as I say.* **2**

present a consideration in favour of or excusing. *If you say something about this issue, it is going to make a difference.* **3** assume as a hypothesis. exclamatory [north American informal] used to express surprise or to draw attention to a remark or question. *Say! That girl looked a lot like my cousin.* *(noun)* an opportunity to stare one's opinion or feelings. an opportunity to influence events. *He wanted to have his say in the business.*

Saying - *(noun)* a short, commonly known expression containing advice or wisdom; an adage or maxim. *The little girl is well versed with many common sayings.*

Scab - *(noun)* **1** a dry, rough protective crust that forms over a cut or wound during healing. *The little boy kept scratching his scab.* **2** mange or a similar skin disease in animals. any of a number of fungal diseases of plants in which rough patches develop, especially on apples and potatoes. *The poor sheep was miserable because of scab.* **3** [informal] a person or thing regarded with contempt. a person who refuses to strike or who takes the place of a striking worker. *He was a scab in the entire team.* *(verb)* **1** become encrusted with a scab or scabs. *The wound had already scabbed all over before the child was taken to the doctor.* **2** act or work as a scab. *Your words scab my worries.* **3** [British informal] scrounge. *I saw the drunk person scab for money.*

Scabbard - *(noun)* a sheath for the blade of a sword or dagger. a sheath for a gun or other weapon or tool. *The museum only had the sheath, not the sword.*

Scabies - *(noun)* a contagious skin disease marked by itching and small raised red spots, caused by the itch mite. *He had a bad case of scabies.*

Scaffold - *(noun)* **1** a raised wooden platform used formerly for public executions. *The crowd was relieved when the execution was called off and the scaffold dismantled.* **2** a structure made using scaffolding. *The construction was delayed for so long that even the scaffold was in ruins.* *(verb)* attach scaffolding to. *The scaffold was dismantled in no time.*

Scald - *(verb)* **1** injure with very hot liquid or steam. *The hot water scalded my hand.* **2** heat to near boiling point. immerse briefly in boiling water. [archaic] clean by rinsing with boiling water. *I scalded the dirty clothes to clean them.* **3** cause to feel a searing sensation like that of boiling water on skin. *The drop of acid scalded her hand.* *(noun)* **1** a burn or other injury caused by hot liquid or steam. *The scald on his palm itched constantly.* **2** any of a number of plant disease which produce a similar effect to that of scalding, especially a disease of fruit marked by browning and caused by excessive sunlight, bad storage conditions, or atmospheric pollution. *The scald on the apples made them look unappetizing.*

Scale - *(noun)* an instrument for weighting, originally a simple balance but now usually a device with an electronic or other internal weighting mechanism. either of the dishes on a simple balance. *The vegetable vendor's scale didn't give correct results.* *(verb)* have a weight of. *The stone scaled 400 grams.*

Scalp - *(noun)* **1** the skin covering the tip and back of the head. *His hair had thinned so much that his scalp was visible through them.* **2** [historical] the scalp with the hair cut away from an enemy's head as a battle trophy, a former practice among amreican Indians. *The tribe was overjoyed when the warrior brought back the scalp.* **3** [Scottish] a bare rock projecting above surrounding water or vegetation. *The scalp was shaped like an old man.* *(verb)* **1** take the scalp of an enemy. [informal] punish severely. *The furious warrior scalped his opponent after defeating him.* **2** [informal] resell at a large or quick profit. *They scalped the unfinished house.*

Scalpel - *(noun)* a knife with a small sharp blade, as used by a surgeon. *I was petrified by the sight of the surgeon holding the scalpel.*

Scam - *(noun)* [informal] a dishonest scheme; a fraud. *The rich businessman lost a lot of respect after the scam came to light.* *(verb)* swindle. *The clever robbers scammed lakhs of Rupees from the rich businessman.*

Scamp – *(noun)* [informal] a mischievous person, especially a child. *The teacher scolded the scamp after he was caught trying to jump the school gate.*

Scamper – *(verb)* run with quick light steps, especially through fear or excitement. *The children scampered away as soon as the gate of the haunted house opened. (noun)* an act of scampering. *There scamper gave their fear away.*

Scan – *(verb)* **1** look at quickly in order to identify relevant features or information. *My brother scanned the store and saw the laptop he would like to buy.* **2** traverse with a detector or an electromagnetic beam, especially to obtain an image. cause a beam to traverse across a surface or object. resolve into its elements of light and shade in a pre-arranged pattern for the purposes of television transmission. convert into digital form for storage or processing on a computer. *If she wasn't hiding anything illegal in her bag, why was she so reluctant to let the machine scan it.* **3** analyse the metre of a line of verse by reading with appropriate intonation or by examining the pattern of feet or syllables. conform to metrical principles. *The poem was good to listen to when scanned properly. (noun)* **1** an act of scanning. *The scan did not reveal anything illegal.* **2** a medical examination using a scanner. an image obtained by scanning or with a scanner. *The scan revealed a broken bone.*

Scandal – *(noun)* an action or event regarded as morally or legally wrong and causing general public outrage. outrage, rumour, or gossip arising from this. *The coalgate scam was a scandal that people talked about for months.*

Scant – *(adjective)* barely sufficient or adequate. barely amounting to the amount specified: a scant two pounds. *The scant food barely satisfied anyone's hunger. (verb)* [chiefly north American] provide grudgingly or in insufficient amounts. deal with inadequately; neglect. *The naughty girl constantly scanted her homework.*

Scanty – *(adjective)* small or insufficient in quantity or amount. revealing; skimpy. *The beggar's scanty clothes hardly protected him from cold.*

Scapegoat – *(noun)* **1** a person who is blamed for the wrongdoing or mistakes of others. *The employee was made a scapegoat when the scam came to light.* **2** a goat sent into the wilderness after the Jewish chief priest had symbolically laid the sins of the people upon it. *The scapegoat wandered off into the woods, taking everyone's sins with it. (verb)* make a scapegoat of. *Several employees of the company feared being scapegoated by the boss.*

Scar – *(noun)* **1** a mark left on the skin or within body tissue after the healing of a wound or burn. a mark left at the point of separation of a leaf, frond, or other part from a plant. *Even though the burn had healed, the scars would take some time to go.* **2** a lasting effect left following an unpleasant experience. *The scars of the bitter experience would take years to heal.* **3** a steep high cliff or rock outcrop. *The philosopher stood on the scar and contemplated about life. (verb)* mark or be marked with a scar or scars. *The experience has scarred him permanently.*

Scarce – *(adjective)* of a resource insufficient for the demand. *The scarce vegetables worried everyone. (adverb)* [archaic] scarcely. *He scarcely displayed discipline in his work.*

Scare – *(verb)* **1** cause great fear or nervousness in; frighten. drive or keep someone away by fear. become scared. *The old man scared the children with his stories of ghosts.* **2** [informal] find or obtain something. *I scared a beautiful ring from the antique shop. (noun)* a sudden attack of fright. a period of general anxiety or alarm about something: a bomb scare. *The scare caused the shops to close down.*

Scarecrow – *(noun)* a figure made to look and dressed like a person to frighten birds away. *The scarecrow looked like a man from a distance.*

Scarf – *(verb)* join the ends of by beveling or notching them so that they fit together. make an incision in the blubber of a whale. *I scarfed the strip of leather. (noun)* an instance of scarfing. *The scarf was already coming undone by the time I started working on the decorations.*

Scarlet – *(noun)* a brilliant red colour. *Her scarlet dress complemented her fair complexion.*

Scathing – *(adjective)* witheringly scornful; severely critical. *His mother-in-law often gave him scathing looks.*

Scatter – *(verb)* throw in various random directions. separate or cause to separate and move off in different directions. occur or be found at various places rather than all together. physics deflect or diffuse. *The decorators scattered the rose petals on the carpet. (noun)* **1** a small, dispersed amount of something. *The scatter of traffic on the roads was a pleasant sight.* **2** [statistics] the degree to which repeated measurements or observations of a quantity differ. *Even though the observations indicated that the study was successful, the scatter worried the scientists.*

Scavenge – *(verb)* **1** search for and collect from discarded waste. search for as food. *The hungry dog scavenged for food in the garbage.* **2** remove from an internal-combustion engine cylinder on the return stroke of the piston. *The scavenge caused an unpleasant odour.* **3** [chemistry] combine with and remove from a particular medium. *The scientists scavenged the mineral after the chemical reaction was over.*

Scenario – *(noun)* **1** a written outline of a film, novel, or stage work giving details of the plot and individual scenes. a setting, in particular for a work of art of literature. *The scenario the writer had presented interested the publisher.* **2** a postulated sequence or development of events. *The scenario seems very grim right now.*

Scenery – *(noun)* **1** the natural features of a landscape considered in terms of their appearance, especially when picturesque. *The scenery took my breath away.* **2** the painted background used to represent the fictional surroundings on a stage or film set. *The scenery appeared authentic on the camera.*

Scenic – *(adjective)* **1** of or relating to impressive or beautiful natural scenery: the scenic route. *I am so glad we took the long but scenic route to the desert.* **2** of or relating to theatrical scenery. *The scenic representation was very impressive.* **3** representing an incident. *The scenic representation was true to life.*

Scent – *(noun)* **1** a distinctive smell, especially one that is pleasant. *The scent of the roses attracted bees to the garden.* **2** pleasant-smelling liquid worn on the skin; perfume. *She wore a pleasant scent.* **3** a trail indicated by the characteristic smell of an animal. a trail of evidence assisting someone in a search or investigation. *The lioness was on the deer's trail.* **4** [archaic] the faculty or sense of smell. *She lost her scent in an accident. (verb)* **1** impart a pleasant scent to. *I scented my house to welcome the guests.* **2** discern by the sense of smell. sense the presence or imminence of: the premier scented victory last night. *The antelopes scented the cheetah and became alert.*

Sceptic – *(noun)* a person inclined to question or doubt accepted opinions. a person who doubts the [philosophy] a philosopher who denies the possibility of knowledge, or even rational belief, in certain spheres. *I am a sceptic by nature.*

Sceptre – *(noun)* a staff carried by rules on ceremonial occasions as a symbol of sovereignty. *The king carried a beautifully ornated sceptre.*

Schedule – *(noun)* **1** a plan for carrying out a process or procedure, giving lists of intended events and time. a timetable. *The secretary couldn't find even one empty slot in the boss's schedule.* **2** [chiefly] law an appendix to a formal document or statute, especially as a list, table, or inventory. *The schedule alone was more informative than the rest of the document.* **3** any of the forms issued relating to various classes of taxable income. *The schedules made the filing of return easy. (verb)* **1** arrange or plan to take place at a particular time. *I scheduled the meeting for tomorrow.* **2** include in a schedule. *The secretary managed to schedule a discussion about the goals in the meeting agenda.* **3** [British] include in a list for legal preservation or protection. *The officer scheduled the forest because it had several rare plants and trees.*

Scheme – *(noun)* **1** a systematic plan or arrangement for attaining some particular object or putting a particular idea into effect. a particular ordered system or arrangement: a classical rhyme scheme. *We were interested in the scheme as it seemed to offer considerable profit.* **2** a secret or underhand plan; a plot. *He went into hiding when his scheme came to light. (verb)* **1** form a scheme, especially a devious one or with intent to do something wrong. *All the time, while living in their house, he schemed against them.* **2** arrange according to a colour scheme. *Please scheme these paint cans.*

Schizophrenia – *(noun)* a long-term mental disorder of a type involving a breakdown in the relation disorder of a type involving a breakdown in the relation between thought, emotion, and behaviour, leading to faulty perception, inappropriate actions and feelings, and withdrawal from reality into fantasy and delusion. *Several members of his family were suffering from schizophrenia.*

Scholar – *(noun)* **1** a specialist in a particular branch of study, especially the humanities; a distinguished academic. [chiefly] a person who is highly educated or has an aptitude for study. *The students were highly impressed by the knowledge of the history scholar.* **2** a university student holding a scholarship. *Scholars have a big advantage because they do not have to spend as much money on the course fee.* **3** [archaic] a student or pupil. *The teacher took the scholars out for a history tour.*

Scholarly – *(adjective)* spending a lot of time studying and having a lot of knowledge about academic subject. *The boy's scholarly approach to everything has enabled him to learn a lot from life.*

Scholarship – *(noun)* **1** academic achievement; learning of a high level. *The learned man has a series of scholarships to his credit.* **2** a grant made to support a student's education, awarded on the basis of achievement. *The poor student was delighted when he received the scholarship.*

Scholastic – *(adjective)* **1** of or concerning schools and education. *The organizations concerns were mostly scholastic.* **2** relating to medieval scholasticism. typical of scholasticism in being pedantic or overly subtle. *At times, professors scholastic references were too difficult to understand. (noun)* **1** [philosophy] an adherent of scholasticism; a schoolman. *The orator's speech revealed him as a scholastic.* **2** a member of a religious order, especially the society of jesus, who is between the novitiate and the priesthood. *The scholastic's voice was calm and his face serene.*

School – *(noun)* a large group of fish or sea mammals. *The school swam quickly and hid behind the rocks. (verb)* of fish or sea mammals form a school. *The fish of the same colour schooled together.*

Science – *(noun)* **1** the intellectual and practical activity encompassing the systematic study of the structure and behaviour of the physical and natural world through observation and experiment. *The young scientist revealed that she had become interested in science when she was very young.* **2** a systematically organized body of knowledge on any subject. *The science of microbiology intrigues me.* **3** [archaic] knowledge. *Everyone listened with respect when the old man shared his science.*

Scientist – *(noun)* a person who is studying or has expert knowledge of one or more of the natural or physical sciences. *The scientist changed the world by his new discovery.*

Scientific – *(noun)* involving science. *We need to be more scientific in agriculture production.*

Scissors – *(plural noun)* **1** an instrument used for cutting cloth and paper, consisting of two crowing blades pivoted in the middle and operated by thumb and fingers inserted in rings at each end. *The children's mother took the scissors away from them.* **2** denoting an action in which two things cross each other or open and close like a pair of scissors: a scissor kick. *The gymnast performed an excellent act of scissors in the air.*

Scoff – *(verb)* speak about something in a scornfully derisive way. *His friends scoffed at his new hairstyle. (noun)* an expression of scornful derision. [archaic] an object of ridicule. *Everyone noticed his scoff.*

Scold – *(verb)* angrily remonstrate with or rebuke. *My mother often scolds me for not* *studying*. *(noun)* [archaic] a woman who nags or grumbles constantly. *Everyone thought that my grandmother was a huge scold.*

Scone – *(noun)* a small unsweetened or lightly sweetened cake made from flour, fat, and milk. *I had a scone with my tea.*

Scoop – *(noun)* **1** a utensil resembling a spoon, having a short handle and deep bowl, used for extracting liquids or substances from a container. the bowl-shaped part of a digging machine or dredger. a long-handled spoon-like surgical instrument. *The ice-cream vendor used the scoop with perfection.* **2** [informal] a piece of news published or broadcast in advance of being released by other newspaper or broadcast stations. [north American] the latest news. *The scoop caught everyone's attention.* **3** an exaggerated upward slide or portamento in singing. *Some listeners thought that the scoop was out of tune.* *(verb)* **1** pick up with a scoop. create with or as if with a scoop. pick or gather up a swift, fluid movement: he laughed and scooped her up in his arms. *The ice-cream vendor scooped out the delicious ice cream.* **2** [informal] publish a scoop. *The newspaper scooped the story before everyone else.* **3** win. *She easily scooped the contest.*

Scooter – *(noun)* **1** a light tow-wheeled motorcycle. *He loved his new scooter.* **2** any small light vehicle able to travel quickly across water or snow. *The scooter crossed the lake in no time.* **3** a child's toy consisting of a footboard mounted on two wheels and a long steering ground. *The little girl thoroughly enjoyed her new scooter.* *(verb)* travel or ride on a scooter. *The entire team scootered away after the amazing performance.*

Scope – *(noun)* **1** the extent of the area or subject matter that something deals with or to which it is relevant: these complex matters are beyond the scope of this book. *This topic is beyond the scope of this discussion.* **2** the opportunity or possibility for doing something. [archaic] a purpose or intention. *There is a huge scope of research in this field.* **3** nautical the length of cable extended when a ship rides at anchor. *It is important to keep the scope in mind when anchoring the ship.*

Scorch – *(verb)* **1** become burnt or cause to become burnt on the surface or edges. cause to become dried out and withered as a result of extreme heat. *The extreme heat scorched all the leaves of the tree.* **2** [informal] move very fast. *The racer scorched the track.* *(noun)* the burning of charring of the surface of something. *The scorch on the leaves made them appear spotted.* **2** [botany] a form of plant necrosis marked by browning of leaf margins. *The plant needed to be treated for scorch.*

Score – *(noun)* **1** the number of points, goals, runs, etc. achieved in a game or by an individual. a mark or grade. *Everyone was eagerly watching the score.* **2** [informal] the state of affairs; the real facts. *The score was that the company wasn't doing too good.* **3** a group or set of twenty. a large amount or number : he sent scores of letters to friends. *I always send scores of greeting cards to my friends and relatives on Diwali.* **4** a written representation of a musical composition showing all the vocal and instrumental parts. *The musicians followed the score perfectly.* **5** a notch or line cut or scratched into a surface. [historical] a running account kept by marks against a customers' name, typically in a public house. *The score was barely visible because the wall was dusty.* **6** [informal] an act of buying illegal drugs. [informal] the proceeds of a crime. *The police caught them with the score.* *(verb)* **1** gain in a competitive game. be worth a number of points. record the score during a game. baseball cause to score. *The team in blue scored easily against the team in red.* **2** orchestrate or arrange a piece of music. compose the music for a film or play. *The listeners went into a trance as the musician scored.* **3** cut of scratch a mark or notch on a surface. delete text by drawing a line through it. *The editor scored two whole paragraphs of the short story.* **4** [informal] secure a success of an advantage. be successful. succeed in obtaining illegal drugs. succeed in attracting a sexual prater. *They were sure that they would score on the night of the party.* **5.**

[Birtish informal] outdo or humiliate, especially in an argument. *The girl scored the boy in the argument.*

Scorn – *(noun)* **1** contempt or disdain expressed openly. *No one could ignore the persistent scorn she expressed throughout the party.* **2** [archaic] a statement or gesture showing contempt. *The principal's scorn for the children made him unpopular.* *(verb)* **1** express scorn for. *She scorned unhygienic snack joints.* **2** reject in a contemptuous way. *The family scorned her offer of letting them stay in her outhouse for the night.*

Scorpio – *(noun)* [astrology] the eighth sign of the zodiac which the sun enters about 23 October. *I have many good friends whose zodiac sign is Scorpio.*

Scorpion – *(noun)* **1** an arachnid with lobster-like pincers and a poisonous sting at the end of its tail. used in names of similar arachnids and insects, e.g. false scorpion. *A poisonous scorpion was hiding in the bathroom.* **2** [poetic] a whip with metal points. *The guards brandished the scorpions at the hapless peasants.*

Scot-free – *(adverb)* without suffering any punishment or injury. *He went scot-free even though he had committed the crime.*

Scoundrel – *(noun)* a dishonest or unscrupulous person; a rogue. *The scoundrel ran away after cheating all of his neighbours.*

Scour – *(verb)* **1** clean or brighten by vigorous rubbing, typically with an abrasive or detergent. remove by rubbing in such a way. *I watched with amazement as the man scoured age-old dust off the antique tray.* **2** erode a channel or pool. *The workers scoured but weren't able to clean the grime.* **3** suffer from diarrhea. *The calf scoured the entire night.* *(noun)* **1** the action of scouring or the state of being scoured. *Though he didn't say it but it was apparent he thoroughly enjoyed the scour.* **2** diarrhea in livestock, especially cattle and pigs. *The farmer despaired as his cattle became thinner because of scour.*

Scourge – *(noun)* **1** [historical] a whip used as an instrument of punishment. *I can't imagine from where he found the old scourge.* **2** a person or thing causing great treble or suffering. *He was such a scourge to his partners.* *(verb)* **1** [historical] whip with a scourge. *Several innocent peasants were scourged during .the king's reign.* **2** cause great suffering to. *He scourged his neighbours by his loud parties.*

Scout – *(noun)* [chiefly US] a fast armoured vehicle used for military reconnaissance and liaison. *People were amazed to see the scouts on the streets.*

Scowl – *(noun)* an angry or bad-tempered expression. *The teacher's scowl made him think that he had said something wrong.* *(verb)* frown in an angry or bad-tempered way. *He has very few friends because he scowls throughout the day.*

Scrabble – *(verb)* **1** scratch or grope around with one's fingers to find, collect, or hold on to something. *She scrabbled inside her purse for money.* **2** move quickly and in a disorderly manner; scramble. *The children scrabbled instead of moving in queues.* *(noun)* **1** an act of scrabbling. *The scrabble was very difficult to manage.* **2** a disorderly struggle or fight. *Both friends felt terrible after the scrabble.* **3** trademark a board game in which players build up words from small lettered squares or tiles. *They thoroughly enjoyed their daily game of scrabble.*

Scraggy – *(adjective)* **1** scrawny. *The little boy was scraggy as compared to the rest of his classmates.* **2** [north American] ragged or untidy in form or appearance. *They donated some of their clothes to the scraggy beggar.*

Scramble – *(verb)* **1** move or make one's way quickly and awkwardly, typically by using one's hands as well as one's feet. [informal] act in a hurried, disorderly, or undignified manner: firms scrambled to win public-sector contracts. *All of them scrambled out of the room as soon as the angry teacher looked at them.* **2** take off or cause to take off immediately in an emergency or for action. *The hospital staff scrambled towards their stations as soon as they heard of the minister's arrival.* **3** make or become jumbled or muddled. in a pan. *I scrambled some eggs* *for breakfast today.* **4** make unintelligible unless received by an appropriate decoding device. *The detective agency scrambled their messages before sending.* **5** [American football] run with the ball behind the line of scrimmage, avoiding tackles. *The player scrambled away leaving the others too awestruck to stop him. (noun)* **1** an act of scrambling. *The scramble led to a lot of confusion.* **2** a walk up steep terrain involving the use of one's hands. *I scrambled up the hill when I spotted the black bear in a distance.* **3** [British] a motorcycle race over rough and hilly ground. *The scramble was very exciting for the first-time racer.* **4** a disordered mixture. *The scramble lay scattered for days in her room.*

Scrap – *(noun)* **1** a small piece or amount of something, especially one that is left over after the greater part has been used. bits of uneaten food left after a meal. *The scraps were all they had to give the beggar.* **2** material, especially metal, discarded for reprocessing. *The scrap lay outside their complex unused for days. (verb)* **1** remove from use or service, especially so as to convert it to scrap metal. *The jeep was scrapped after years of use.* **2** abolish or cancel a plan, policy, or law. *The policy was scrapped because it wasn't yielding the desired results.*

Scrape – *(verb)* **1** drag or pull a hard or sharp implement across. use a sharp or hard implement to remove. *The cupboard was scraped across the room.* **2** rub or cause to rub against a rough or hard surface. humorous play a violin tunelessly. *I scraped the deposit with a metal strip.* **3** just manage to achieve, succeed, or pass. collect or accumulate something with difficulty. try to manage to live with difficulty.. *My friend just managed to scrape through her university exams. (noun)* **1** an act or sound of scraping an injury or mark caused by scraping. *The scrape was hard to remove.* **2** [British] a thinly applied layer of butter or margarine on bread. *The scrape was too thin to add any flavour to the toast.* **2** [informal] an embarrassing or difficult predicament. *After I spilled my drink all over my dress, I rushed to the bathroom to escape the scrape.***3**. [archaic] an obsequious bow in which one foot is drawn backwards along the ground. *The court jester scraped in front of the king.*

Scratch – *(verb)* **1** score or mark with a sharp or pointed object make a long, narrow superficial wound in the skin of. rub with one's fingernails to relieve itching. rake the ground with the beak or claws in search of food. make a living of find resources with difficulty. *I scratched my skin with the hard wooden board.* **2** cancel or strike out with a pen or pencil. withdraw form a competition. cancel or abandon an undertaking or project. *The child scratched out a lot of words in his notebook.* **3** play a record using the scratch technique. *The DJ scratched the song to everyone's delight. (noun)* **1** a mark or wound made by scratching. [informal] a slight or insignificant wound or injury. an act or spell of scratching. *The scratch took a long time to heal.* **2** the starting point in a handicap of zero, indicating that a player is good enough to achieve par on a course. *He started from a scratch.* **3** a technique, used especially in rap music, of stopping a record by and an moving it back and forwards to give a rhythmic scratching. effect. *The scratch was very appealing to the ears.*

Scrawl – *(verb)* write in a hurried, careless way. *The students scrawled the notes as the professor spoke. (noun)* an example of hurried, careless writing. *Can you read the doctor's scrawl?*

Scream – *(verb)* **1** make a long, loud, piercing cry or sound, especially expressing extreme emotion or pain. *My mother screamed when she saw the fat rat.* **2** move very rapidly with or as if with such a sound. *The students screamed through the corridors.* **3** [informal, dated] turn informer. *He was punished because he screamed. (noun)* **1** a screaming cry or sound. *Her scream rang through the empty corridors.* **2** [informal] an irresistibly funny person or thing. *The new comedian is such a scream!*

Screech – *(noun)* a loud, harsh, piercing cry or sound. *The screech startled me out of my sleep. (verb)* **1** make a screech. *The teacher asked the student to stop screeching.* **2** move rapidly with a screech. *The bike screeched to a stop.*

Screen – *(noun)* **1** an upright partition used to divide a room, give shelter, or provide concealment. a windscreen of a motor vehicle. a frame with fine wire netting used to keep out flying insects. *The screen effectively divided the huge room into two.* **2** the surface of a cathode ray tube or similar electronic device, especially that of a television, VDU, or monitor, on which images and data are displayed. a blank surface on which a photographic image is projected. films or television. photography a falt piece of ground glass on which the image formed by a camera lens is focused. *The impact shattered the screen of the television.* **3** printing a transparent. *The image was printed on a screen.* **4** a system or act of screening for the presence or absence of something. *The screen returned negative result.* **5** a large sieve or riddle. *The flour passed through the screen with ease.* **6** military a detachment of troops or ships detailed to cover the movements of the main body. *The screen's efficient tactics made the operation a success.* **7** a part of an electrical or other instrument which protects it from or prevents it causing electromagnetic interference. electronics a grid placed between the control grid and the anode of a valve to reduce the capacitance between these electrodes. *The screen was too damaged to protect the expensive instrument.* *(verb)* **1** conceal, protect, or shelter with a screen. protect from something dangerous or unpleasant. *Her parents screened her from their poverty.* **2** show a film or video or broadcast. *The film was screened in their school.* **3** test for the presence or absence of a disease. investigate typically to ascertain suitability for a job. *They screened out most of the candidates based on the experience.* **4** pass through a large sieve or screen, especially so as to sort it into different sizes. *The scientists screened the samples.*

Screw – *(noun)* **1** a short, slender, sharp-pointed metal pin with a raised helical thread running around it and a slotted head, used to join things together by being rotated in under pressure. a cylinder with a helical ridge or thread running round the outside that can be turned to seal an opening, apply pressure, adjust position, etc. historical an instrument of torture acting in this way. *The screws held the dilapidated cupboard together.* **2** an act of turning a screw. [British] a small twisted-up piece of paper containing a substance such as salt or tobacco. *The man watched the screwing of the mirror into the wall.* **3** a ship's or aircraft's propeller. *They had to call for help because their ship's screw got caught in the weeds.* **4** [informal] a prison warder. *The screw didn't allow the prisoners to keep their lights on at night.* **5** vulgar slang an act of sexual intercourse. *They enjoyed the casual screw after the party.* **6** [British informal, dated] an amount of salary or wages. *The workers' screw wasn't enough for their needs.* *(verb)* **1** fasten or tighten with a screw. rotate so as to attach or remove it by means of a spiral thread. impart spin or curl to a ball or shot. turn one's head or body round sharply. *The workmen screwed the bathroom fittings tight.* **2** [informal] cheat or swindle. [informal] ruin or render ineffective. *The hacker screwed the security system of the website.*

Scribble – *(verb)* **1** write or draw carelessly or hurriedly. *I like to scribble important information when I am talking on the phone.* **2** [informal] write for a living or as a hobby. *I scribble stories and poems whenever I get some time.* *(noun)* a piece of writing or a picture produced carelessly or hurriedly. *The story was nothing but a scribble compared to his other works.*

Scribe – *(noun)* **1** [historical] a person who copied out documents. [informal] a writer, especially a journalist. *The scribe maintained the records very diligently.* **2** professional theologian and jurist. *The scribe advised them against their actions.* **3** a pointed instrument used for making marks to guide a saw or in sign writing. *The scribe needed sharpening.* *(verb)* [chiefly] poetic write. *She scribed a few lines as soon as she saw the pretty flowers.* **2** mark with a pointed instrument. *The workers scribed carelessly and therefore the measurements were all wrong.*

Scrip – *(noun)* **1** a provisional certificate of money subscribed to a bank or company, entitling the holder to a formal electively. finance an issue of additional of this type collectively. [finance] an issue of additional shares to shareholders in proportion to the shares already held. *The shareholders were pleasantly surprised to receive the scrip.* **2** [north American] a certificate entitling the holder to acquire possession of certain portions of public land. *The land belonged to his family as per the scrip.***3.** [north American historical] paper money in amounts of less than a dollar. *Little children played around with the scrip.*

Script – *(noun)* **1** handwriting as distinct from print: written characters. writing using a particular alphabet: Russian script. *Hindi has a script different from English.* **2** the written text of a play, film, or broadcast. *The play was so good because of its powerful script.* **3** [British] a candidate's written answers in an examination. *He lost a lot of marks because of his illegible script.* **4** computing a program or sequence of instructions that in carried out by another program rather than by the computer processor. *The computer crashed as soon as the engineer ran the script. (verb)* write a script for. *Whoever scripted the play did a brilliant job.*

Scriptures – *(noun)* the sacred writings Christianity contained in the bible. the sacred writings of another religion. *My mother likes to read scriptures of all religions.*

Scroll – *(noun)* **1** a roll of parchment or paper for writing or painting on. an ancient book or document on such a roll. *The scroll was so fragile that it looked as if it will crumble at the slightest touch.* **2** an ornamental design or carving resembling a partly unrolled scroll of parchment. *The scroll was shining even though it was very old. (verb)* **1** move displayed text or graphics on a computer screen in order to view different parts of them. *The teacher scrolled down the screen to show the complete document to the students.* **2** cause to move like paper rolling or unrolling. *I scrolled the starched cloth.*

Scrub – *(noun)* **1** vegetation consisting mainly of brushwood or stunted forest growth. land covered with such vegetation. *The scrub was vast and deserted.* **2** denoting a shrubby or small form of a plant. [north American] denoting an animal of inferior breed or physique. *The little scrub was thorny.* **3** [informal] an insignificant or contemptible person. [north American] a mediocre sports team or player. *The baseball player was so obnoxious that people called him a scrub.*

Scruff – *(noun)* the back of a person's or animal's neck. *The magician held the rabbit by its scruff.*

Scruple – *(noun)* **1** a feeling of doubt or hesitation with regard to the morality or propriety of an action. *He has no scruples against stealing.* **2** a unit of weight equal to 20 grains used by apothecaries. a very small amount. *The gold only weighed a few scruples. (verb)* hesitate or be reluctant to do something that one thinks may be wrong. *The policeman scrupled for a few minutes before accepting the bribe.*

Scrupulous – *(adjective)* **1** diligent, thorough, and attentive to details. *I need a very scrupulous person for this job.* **2** very concerned to avoid doing wrong. *You need to be scrupulous to be a part of this society.*

Scrutinize – *(verb)* examine or inspect closely and thoroughly. *You need to scrutinize all evidences thoroughly before the court case.*

Scrutiny – *(noun)* critical observation or examination. *There was no cheating in the examination hall because of the scrutiny.*

Scuffle – *(noun)* **1** a short, confused fight or struggle at close quarters. *I came running out of my room when I heard the scuffle.* **2** an act or sound of moving in a scuffing manner. *The scuffle upstairs turned out to be some rats. (verb)* **1** engage in a scuffle. *The school children were scuffling over a new pencil.* **2** move in a hurried, confused, or shuffling way. *The suspicious man scuffled away as soon as he heard the police siren.*

Scull – *(noun)* each of a pair of small oars used by a single rower. an oar placed over the stern of a boat to propel it with a side to side motion a light, narrow boat propelled with a scull or a pair of sculls. a race between boats in which each participant uses a pair of oars. *A pair of sculls was kept beside the boat. (verb)* propel a boat with sculls. *The rower felt so weak that he wasn't even able to hold the sculls.*

Scullery – *(noun)* a small kitchen or room at the back of a house used for washing dishes and other dirty household work. *The maid worked in the scullery after clearing the table.*

Sculptor – *(noun)* an artist who makes sculptures. *I couldn't believe I was meeting the famous sculptor in person.*

Sculpture – *(noun)* **1** the art of making three-dimensional representative or abstract forms, especially by carving stone or wood or by casting metal or plaster. a work of such a kind. *The sculpture was true to life.* **2** raised or sunken patterns on a shell, pollen grain, etc. *The sculptures on the shell were shaped like sand dunes. (verb)* make or represent by sculpture. form or shape as if by sculpture, especially with strong, smooth curves. *They sculptured the new prime minister almost immediately after he was elected.*

Scum – *(noun)* **1** a layer of dirt or froth on the surface of a liquid. *They cleared the scum off the surface of the lake.* **2** [informal] a worthless or contemptible person or group of people. *Those rogues were nothing but scum. (verb)* cover or become covered with a layer of scum. *The lake has scummed over years.*

Scurrilous – *(adjective)* making scandalous claims about someone with the intention of damaging their reputation. humorously insulting. *When I joined my job, my father warned me of scurrilous colleagues.*

Scurry – *(verb)* move hurriedly with short quick steps. *The little man scurried to take cover as soon as the rain started. (noun)* **1** a situation of hurried and confused movement. *The canvas almost fell in the scurry.* **2** a flurry of rain or snow. *This is the first scurry of the season.*

Scurvy – *(noun)* a disease caused by a deficiency of vitamin C, characterized by swollen bleeding gums and the opening of previously healed wounds. *Many people are suffering from scurvy and they don't even know it. (adjective)* [archaic] worthless or contemptible. *The scurvy workers were fired from the construction site.*

Scuttle – *(noun)* **1** a metal container with a sloping hinged lid and a handle, used to fetch and store coal for a domestic fire. *Mother noticed just in time that the scuttle was almost empty.* **2** [British] the part of a car's bodywork between the windscreen and the bonnet. *There were several scratches on the scuttle.*

Scythe – *(noun)* a tool used for cutting crops such as grass or corn, with a long curved blade at the end of a long pole attached to one or two short handles. *The old scythe was rusty and blunt. (verb)* **1** cut with a scythe. *The farmer's hands moved expertly while scything.* **2** move through or penetrate rapidly and forcefully. *The army scythed through the forest and cleansed it of all the dacoits.*

Sea – *(noun)* **1** the expanse of water that covers most of the earth's surface and surrounds its land masses. a roughly definable area of this: the black sea. waves as opposed to calm sea. *The sunset at the sea was mesmerizing.* **2** a vast expanse or quantity: a sea of faces. *A sea of eager faces was waiting for the orator when he arrived.*

Seal – *(noun)* a fish-eating aquatic mammal with a streamlined body and feet developed as flippers. *The young seal was barely able to swim. (verb)* hunt for seals. *The family hunted for seals everyday.*

Seam – *(noun)* **1** a line where two pieces of fabric are sewn together in a garment or other article. a line where the edges of two pieces of wood or other material touch each other. *I was about to leave for office when I noticed that my dress was torn at the seam.* **2** an underground layer of a mineral such as coal or gold. *A seam of gold was discovered beneath his farmhouse.* **3** a long thin indentation or scar. *The deep seam of the wound was still visible on his face. (verb)* **1** join with a seam. *I seamed the sleeve to my sleeveless dress.* **2**. make a long narrow indentation in. *I seamed the soap bar.*

Search – *(verb)* **1** try to find something by looking or otherwise seeking carefully and thoroughly. examine thoroughly in order to find something. *I searched through my bag to find my keys.* **2** scrutinizing thoroughly, especially in a disconcerting way. *The policeman searched the suspect's face for guilt.* *(noun)* an act of searching. law an investigation of public records to find if a property is subject to any liabilities or encumbrances. *The team of detectives has just gone in search of clues.*

Searchlight – *(noun)* a powerful outdoor eclectic light with a concentrated beam that can be turned in the required direction. *The rescue services were using searchlights to look for the ship.*

Season – *(noun)* **1** each of the four divisions of the year marked by particular weather patterns and daylight hours. the time of year when a particular fruit, vegetable, etc. is plentiful and in good condition. *This is not the season for mango trees to produce fruit.* **2** a period of the year characterized by an activity or event, especially a particular sport: the football season. the time of year traditionally marked by fashionable upper-class social events. *The football fans desperately waited for the football season to start.* **3** a period when a female mammal is ready to mate. *The male lion was seen wandering around the female in season.* **4** [archaic] a proper or suitable time: to everything there is a season. an indefinite or unspecified period of time; a while. *There's a suitable season for romance.* *(verb)* **1** add salt, herbs, or spices to food. *She seasoned the salad well.* **2** add an enlivening quality or feature to. *The piano player's lovely performance seasoned the evening.* **3** keep so as to dry if for use as timber. *The villagers seasoned the wood before use.* **4** accustomed to particular conditions; experienced. *That man is a seasoned cricket player.*

Seasonal – *(adjective)* relating to or characteristic of a particular season of the year. fluctuating according to the season. *Apple is a seasonal fruit.*

Seasoned – *(adjective)* having lot of experience in a particular field. *She has become a seasoned lawyer over time.*

Seat – *(noun)* **1** a thing made or used for sitting on, such as a chair or stool. the roughly horizontal part of a chair. a sitting place for a passenger in a vehicle or for a member of an audience. *It was uncomfortable sitting there because the seats were hard.* **2** a person's buttocks. a manner of sitting on a horse. *His seat started hurting after riding the horse.* **3** [chiefly British] a place in an elected parliament or council. [British] a parliamentary constituency. *Her good work ensured a seat for him in the parliament.* **4** a sit or location a large country house and estate belonging to an aristocratic family: a country seat. *The seat of the king was empty because there was no heir to occupy it.* **5** a part of a machine that supports or guides another part. *The seat of the crane showed signs of disrepair.* *(verb)* arrange for to sit somewhere. sit down have sufficient seats for. fit in position. *Please seat the guests while the food gets ready.*

Secede – *(verb)* withdraw formally from membership of a federal union or a political or religious organization. *After giving it a good thought, I seceded my membership in the union.*

Seclude – *(verb)* keep away from other people. *The family secluded themselves from everyone.*

Secluded – *(adjective)* not seen or visited by many people; sheltered and private. *Not many people enter the secluded part of the forest.*

Second – *(noun)* **1** a sixtieth of a minute of time, which as the SI unit of time is defined in terms of the natural periodicity of the radiation of a casesium-133 atom. [informal] a very short time. *He was up and ready to go in seconds.* **2** a sixtieth of a minute of angular distance. *The ship was located at 2 seconds from the landmark.*

Secondary – *(adjective)* **1** coming after, less important than, or resulting from something primary. *Studies were secondary to the tennis player.* **2** of or relating to education for children from the age of eleven to sixteen or eighteen. *My daughter has just complete her secondary school.* **3** of or denoting the output side of a transformer or other inductive device. *I could see some deposits at the secondary side of the transformer.* **4** chemistry having its functional group on a carbon atom bonded to two other carbon atoms. derived from ammonia by replacement of two hydrogen atoms by organic groups. *The secondary compound turned out to be harmful to some humans.* **5** geology former term for Mesozoic. *Many important geological changes took place during the Mesozoic.* **6** having a reversible chemical reaction and therefore able to store energy. *Lead acid batteries use secondary compounds to store energy.*

Secrecy – *(noun)* the fact of making sore nothing gets leaked about something. *I can't understand the secrecy around this issue.*

Secret – *(adjective)* not known or seen or not meant to be known or seen by others. fond of having or keeping secrets; secretive. *I formed a secret society with my friends when I was young.* *(noun)* **1** something kept or meant to be kept secret. something not properly understood; a mystery: the secrets of the universe. *My parents wanted to keep the plans for my birthday party a secret.* **2** a valid but not commonly known method of achieving something: the secret of a happy marriage is compromise. *The secret of a fulfilling relationship is trust.* **3** a prayer said quietly by the priest after the offertory in a roman catholic mass. *Everyone kept their eyes closed as the priest said the secret.*

Secretive – *(adjective)* inclined to conceal feelings and intentions or not to disclose information. *The actress was very secretive about her real identity.*

Sect – *(noun)* **1** a religious group or faction regarded as heretical or as deviating from orthodox tradition. often a group that has separated from an established church; a nonconformist church. *They helped form a new sect of the religion.* **2** a group with extreme or dangerous philosophical or political ideas. *Several sects were banned during the war.*

Sectarian – *(adjective)* denoting, concerning, or deriving from a sect or sects. carried out on the grounds of membership of a sect, denomination, or other group: sectarian killings. *They passed a sectarian judgment for the man's sins.* *(noun)* a member of follower of a sect. *She has been a sectarian for long.*

Section – *(noun)* **1** any of the more or less distinct parts into which something is or may be divided or from which it is made up. [north American] a measure of land, equal to one square mile, [chiefly north American] a particular district of a town. a building plot. *You need to fill all sections of the form.* **2** a distinct group within a larger body of people or things. a subdivision of an army platoon. [biology] a secondary taxonomic category, especially a subgenus. *The two sections of the class were allocated different class teachers.* **3** the cutting of a solid by or along a plane. the shape resulting from cutting a solid along a plane. a representation of the internal structure of something cutting. *The vertical section of the plane revealed roomy seats.* **4** [biology] a thin slice of plant or animal tissue prepared for microscopic examination. *The pathologist took a section of the human tissue for examination.* *(verb)* **1** divide into sections. *She sectioned the cake neatly.* **2** surgery divide by cutting. *The surgeon sectioned the tissue.* **3** [British] commit compulsorily to a psychiatric hospital in accordance with a section of a mental health act. *The politician was sectioned because of his bizarre behavior.*

Sector – *(noun)* **1** an area or portion that is distinct from others. a distinct part of an economy, society, or sphere of activity. a subdivision of an area for military operations. *Our sector mostly has apartments.* **2** the plane figure enclosed by tow radial of a circle or ellipse and the are between them. *The circle was divided into equal sectors.* **3** a mathematical instrument consisting to two arms hinged at one end and marked with sines, tangents, etc. for making diagrams. *She used a sector to draw the diagram.*

Secular – *(adjective)* **1** not religious, sacred, or spiritual. *India is a secular country.* **2** [Christian church] not subject to or bound by religious rule. contrasted with regular. *His* *churchmen considered him too secular for their church.* **3** [astronomy] of or denoting slow changes in the motion of the sun or planets. *The secular change in Earth's rotation will have big impact on the climate.* **4** economics occurring or persisting over an indefinitely long period. *The secular slowdown has impacted the small-scale industries the most.* **5** occurring once every century or similarly long period. *People who were able to view the secular cosmic event were very lucky.* *(noun)* a secular priest. *The secular was an inspiration for the younger members of the society.*

Secure – *(adjective)* **1** fixed or fastened so as not to give way. become loose, or be lost. *The door was secured properly.* **2** certain to remain safe and unthreatened. protected against attack or other criminal activity. *The house was very secure despite its deserted surroundings.* **3** feeling no double about anxiety. dated feeling no double about attaining. *I feel very secure when I am with my parents.* **4** having provisions against the escape of inmates. *The jail was made very secure to keep the inmates in.* *(verb)* **1** make secure; fix or fasten securely. *I secured the lock at night.* **2** protect against threats. *The fire alarm secured the house against disaster.* **3** succeed in obtaining. seek to guarantee repayment of by having a right to take possession of an asset in the event of non-payment. *I secured the permission to stay out late at night.* **4** [surgery] compress to prevent bleeding. *The nurse secured the wound.*

Security – *(noun)* **1** the state of being or feeling secure. *Security made him very generous.* **2** the safety of a state or organization against criminal activity such as terrorism. measures taken to ensure such safety. *Doubts were being raised about the country's security.* **3** a thing deposited or pledged as a guarantee of the fulfillment of an undertaking or the repayment of a loan, to be forfeited in case of default. *I deposited my property documents as security against the loan.* **4** a certificate attesting credit, the ownership of stocks or bonds, or the right to ownership connected with tradable derivatives. *I was afraid that I had lost the securities.*

Sedate – *(adjective)* **1** calm and unhurried. *The sedate congressman had a huge fan following.* **2** staid and rather dull. *The sedate cow showed no excitement when I went to feed her.*

Sedative – *(adjective)* promoting calm or inducing sleep. *The sedative properties of the medicine kept me from taking it during office hours.* *(noun)* a sedative drug. *The sedative was fast and effective.*

Sediment – *(noun)* **1** matter that settles to the bottom of a liquid. *The sediment was a proof of the dirtiness of water.* **2** [geology] particular matter carried by water or wind and deposited on the land surface or seabed. *The sediment made the land very fertile.* *(verb)* settle or deposit as sediment. *I looked at the sand slowly sediment at the bottom of the glass container.*

Sedimentary – *(adjective)* of or relating to sediment. [geology] that has formed from sediment deposited by water or wind. *The sedimentary rock formations were breathtaking.*

Sedition – *(noun)* conduct or speech inciting rebellion against the authority of a state or monarch. *Even though he was punished for sedition, his speech inspired many.*

Seduce – *(verb)* **1** persuade to do something inadvisable. *Allegedly the broker seduced the firm to cheat the investors.* **2** entice into sexual activity. *The man seduced the young girl but managed to escape the law.*

Seduction – *(noun)* the act of persuading someone to have sex with you. *Several people fell prey to her seduction.*

Seductive – *(adjective)* tempting and attractive. *People often tell her that she has a very seductive voice.*

Seductiveness – *(noun)* attractiveness shown to someone in a way that makes you want to do or have something. *People often compliment her on the seductiveness of her eyes.*

See – *(noun)* the place in which a cathedral church stands, identified as the seat of authority of a bishop or archbishop. *The see was surrounded by dense forest.*

Seed – *(noun)* **1** a flowering plant's unit of reproduction, capable of developing into another such plant. a quantity of these. *The seed sprouted almost immediately.* **2** the beginning of a feeling, process or condition. *The seed of the change was laid long back.* **3** [archaic] a man's semen. *His friend advised him not to waste his seed.* **4** [archaic] offspring or descendants. *Their seed went on to create a big name for themselves.* **5** a small crystal introduced into a liquid to act as a nucleus for crystallization. *The seed produced lovely, blue crystals.* **6** a small container of radiotherapy. *Everyone was asked to keep clear of the seed.* **7** any of a number of stronger competitors in a sports tournament who have been assigned a position in an ordered list to ensure they don not play each other in the early rounds. *All the seeds got into the quarterfinals as planned. (verb)* **1** sow with seeds from. *I seeded the pansies as soon as the season arrived.* **2** initiate the development or growth of. *The learned graduate seeded the idea of paperless office in his organization.* **3** place a crystalline substance in order to cause condensation or crystallization. *I seeded the blue crystal into the solution.* **4** give the status of seed in a tournament. *He was proud when the organizers seeded him for the first time.*

Seedy – *(adjective)* **1** sordid or squalid. *The place looked very seedy.* **2** dated unwell. *The seedy man was afraid that he would never get better.*

Seek – *(verb)* **1** attempt to find. search for and find someone or something. *I seek a good friend in you.* **2** attempt of obtain or do. *He seeks success in his career.* **3** ask for. *She seeks her parent's approval for her marriage.* **4** [archaic] go to a place. *The holymen seek the banks of Ganga.*

Seem – *(verb)* **1** give the impression of being. *He made it seem so simple.* **2** be unable to do something, despite having tried. *He did not seem to understand concept even after leaving for a long time.*

Seemly – *(adjective)* conforming to propriety or good taste. *Her dress was quite seemly.*

Seep – *(verb)* flow or leak slowly through porous material or small holes. *Water seeped in through the concrete. (noun)* [north American] a place where petroleum or water seeps out of the ground. *The farmer was delighted to find the seep in his land.*

Seer – *(noun)* **1** a person of supposed supernatural insight who sees visions of the future. *The seer foretold that the businessman would do very well.* **2** [chiefly archaic] a person who sees something specified. *He was such a seer when it came to acting talent.*

See-saw – *(noun)* **1** a long plank balanced on a fixed support, on each end of which children sit and move up and down by pushing the ground alternately with their feet. *My nephew was desperate to go to the see-saw but there was no other child to play with him.* **2** a situation characterized by rapid, repeated changes from one state or position to another. *The see-saw in the merger deal continued for a while. (verb)* change rapidly and repeatedly from one state or position to another and back again. *He see-sawed in between the two choices many times.*

Seethe – *(verb)* **1** boil or be turbulent as if boiling. [archaic] cook by boiling. *I seethed the vegetables so that they could be cooked in a short time.* **2** be filled with intense but unexpressed anger. *The security guard seethed under his pleasant demeanor.* **3** be crowded with people or things moving about in a rapid or hectic way. *The ground seethed with people.*

Segment – *(noun)* **1** each of the parts into which something is or may be divided. *That segment of the crowd is much more disciplined than this segment.* **2** [geometry] a part of a circle cut off by a chord, or a part of a sphere cut off by a plane not passing through the centre. *The child divided the circle into unequal segments.* **3** [phonetics] the smallest distinct part of a spoken utterance, especially with regard to similar anatomical units of which the body and appendages of some animals are composed. *The body of the insect was divided in two segments. (verb)* **1** divide into segments. *The construction worker segmented the rope into equal parts.* **2** undergo cleavage. *The large plain was gradually segmenting into two huge land masses.*

Segregate – *(verb)* **1** set apart from or relating to the division of speech into segments. *The teacher segregated the children into two groups based on their heights.* **2** separate along racial, sexual, or religious lines. *The survey segregated the populace according to their religions.* **3** [genetics] be separated at meiosis and transmitted independently via separate garmetes. *Through the microscope, I watched the two cells segregate.*

Segregation – *(noun)* the act of setting something apart from others. *The teacher does not believe in any kind of segregation.*

Seismic – *(adjective)* **1** of or relating to earthquakes or other vibrations of the earth and its crust. relating to or denoting geological surveying methods involving vibrations produced artificially by explosions. *The geologists predicted heavy seismic activities during the day.* **2** of enormouns proportions or effect. *The President walked off after delivering a seismic speech.*

Seize – *(verb)* **1** take hold of suddenly and forcibly. take forcible possession of by warrant or legal right. *The thugs seized my uncle's property.* **2** take eagerly and decisively. take eager advantage of. *I seized the opportunity as soon as I saw it.* **3** affect suddenly or acutely. *Panic seized the guard when he saw the shadow lurking in the corner.* **4** of a machine with moving parts or a moving part in a machine become jammed. *The arms of the robot seized without warning.* **5** [English law] be in legal possession of. historical have or receive freehold possession of property. be aware or informed of. *The government seized the land.* **6** nautical, fasten or attach by binding with turns of rope. *The sailor seized the liferaft to the boat.*

Seizure – *(noun)* **1** the action of seizing. *They called the police after the unauthorized seizure.* **2** a sudden attack of illness, especially a stroke or an epileptic fit. *His seizure was very frightening and left him feeling exhausted.*

Seldom – *(adverb)* not often. *I seldom visit the city park.* *(adjective)* dated infrequent. *The father's seldom visits left the child confused.*

Select – *(verb)* **1** carefully chose as being the best or most suitable. *The teacher selected the tallest students for the dance.* **2** [biology] determine whether will survive. *Nature selects only the strongest.* *(adjective)* **1** carefully chosen from a larger number as being the best. *Only a select few will be asked to join the session.* **2** used by or consisting of a wealthy or sophisticated elite. *The shop sells select clothes, especially for the elite.*

Selection – *(noun)* **1** the action of fact of selecting. a number of selected things. a range of things from which a choice may be made. a horse or horses tipped as worth bets in a race or meeting. *Even though the selection appeared random, it had an unseen logic to it.* **2** [biology] the evolutionary process which determines which types of organism thrive; natural selection. *Natural selection has been the most powerful process in determining the progress of the life on the Earth.*

Selective – *(adjective)* **1** relating to or involving selection. tending to choose carefully. *The film star claims that he is very selective about his roles.* **2** affecting some things and not others. *The tornado was very selective about the houses it destroyed.*

Self – *(noun)* a person's essential being that distinguishes them from others, especially considered as the object of introspection or reflexive action. a person's particular nature or personality. one's own interests or pleasure. *He doesn't understand the concept of self.* *(pronoun)* **1** used ironically to refer in specified favourable terms to oneself or someone else: a picture of my good self. *The politician's honest self was disgusted by the policeman who accepted the bribe.* **2** used on counterfoils, cheques, and other papers to refer to the holder or person who has signed. *The businessman often issued cheques to self.* *(adjective)* of the same material or colour as the rest. *The self-embroidery on the fabric was exquisite.* *(verb)* self pollinate; self fertilize. *The plant stayed healthy even when no one took care of it because it self fertilized.*

Self-centred – *(adjective)* preoccupied with oneself and one's affairs. *The man was very self-centred.*

Self-conscious – *(adjective)* **1** nervous or awkward because unduly aware of oneself or one's actions. *The self-conscious student forgot his lines during the play.* **2** deliberate and with full awareness. *His action was very self-conscious.* **3** [philosophy & psychology] having knowledge of one's existence, especially the knowledge of oneself as a conscious being. *The self-conscious professor was very approachable.*

Self-control – *(noun)* the ability to control one's emotions or behaviour, especially in difficult situation. *Everyone commended his self-control in the face of loss.*

Self-defence – *(noun)* the defence of one's person or interests, especially through the use of physical force, which is permitted in certain cases as an answer to a charge of violent crime. *The crime was committed in self-defence.*

Selfish – *(adjective)* concerned chiefly with one's own personal profit or pleasure at the expense of consideration for others. *His actions appeared selfish to the others.*

Selfishly – *(adverb)* [chiefly] concerned with one's own pleasure. *He selfishly ate all the food.*

Selfless – *(adjective)* concerned more with the needs and wished of others than with one's own. *No one can question a mother's selfless love.*

Self-made – *(adjective)* **1** having become successful or rich by one's own efforts. *My father is a self-made man.* **2** made by oneself. *Her self-made pizza tasted much better than the shop-bought one.*

Self-respect – *(noun)* pride and confidence in oneself. *The matter became a question of self-respect for her.*

Self-sufficient – *(adjective)* **1** able to satisfy one's basic needs without outside help, especially with regard to the production of food. *The island dwellers were self-sufficient in their agricultural needs.* **2** emotionally and intellectually independent. *The students soon became self-sufficient in their assignments.*

Self-willed – *(adjective)* obstinately pursuing one's own wishes. *At times, he regretted his self-willed attitude.*

Sell – *(verb)* **1** hand over in exchange for money. be subject to a specified demeand on the market: the book didn't sell well. sell all of one's stock of something. have sex in exchange for money. *I sold my painting for good money.* **2** persuade someone of the merits of. make enthusiastic about. *The young employee sold his idea to his bosses successfully.* **3** betray someone for one's own financial or material benefit. abandon one's principle for reasons of expedience. *The policeman sold his family's trust for a little money.* **4** [archaic] trick or deceive. *The magician sold his audience by his swiftness.* *(noun)* [informal] **1** an act of selling or attempting to sell. *The sell was successful.* **2** a disappointment. *The workshop was such a sell.*

Seller – *(noun)* **1** a person who sells. *The vegetable seller lived a honest life.* **2** a product that sells in a specified way. *The software was a fast seller.*

Selvedge – *(noun)* **1** an edge produced on woven fabric during manufacture that prevents it from unraveling. *The selvedge of the fabric was very ornate.* **2** [geology] a zone of altered rock at the edge of a rock mass.*The pattern on the selvedge was different from rest of the rock.*

Semantic – *(adjective)* relating to meaning in language or logic. *I have never understood the semantic behind the usage of some words.*

Semblance – *(noun)* **1** the outward appearance or apparent form of something. *The friendship they shared had the semblance of love.* **2** [archaic] resemblance. *The semblance between the two twins was unbelievable.*

Semi – *(noun)* **1** [British] a semi-detached house. *The boy and his father lived in a semi.* **2** a semi-final. *The duo made it to the semi.* **3** [north American] a semi-trailer. *They bought themselves a semi.*

Semicolon – *(noun)* a punctuation mark (;) indicating a more pronounced pause than that indicated by a comma. *I asked the teacher to explain me the usage of a semicolon.*

Semifinal – *(noun)* a match or round immediately preceding the final. *The semifinal was very exciting.*

Seminar – *(noun)* **1** a conference or other meeting for discussion or training. *Some very relevant topics were covered in the seminar.* **2** a small group of students at university, meeting to discuss topics with a teacher. *The teacher couldn't make it to the seminar today.*

Senate – *(noun)* **1** the smaller upper assembly in the US, US states, France, and other countries. the governing body of a university or college. *The senate is meeting tonight to discuss the bilateral ties between the two countries.* **2** the state council of the ancient roman republic and empire. *The senate took some very tough decisions.*

Send – *(verb)* **1** cause to go or be taken or delivered to a particular destination. arrange for someone to attend. *I requested my father to send me some books.* **2** cause to move sharply or quickly; propel. *The force sent the ball to the other end of the ground.* **3** cause to be in a specified state: it nearly sent me crazy. *The noise sent me crazy.* **4** [informal] cause to feel ecstasy or elation. *The reunion sent me.*

Senior – *(adjective)* **1** of a more advanced age. [British] of, for, or denoting schoolchildren above a certain age, typically eleven. [US] of the final year at a university or high school. denoting the elder of two with the same name in a family. *Show respect to senior people.* **2** high or higher in rank or status. *The senior people were forced to take some tough decisions.* *(noun)* **1** a person who is a specified number of years older than someone else: she was two years his senior. *My father is 6 years senior to my mother.* **2** a student in one of the higher forms of a senior school. *The senior was a good guide to the younger students.* **3** a competitor of above a certain age or of the highest status. *He was delighted to have defeated the senior.* **4** an elderly person, especially an old age pensioner. *Please vacate the seat for a senior.*

Seniority – *(noun)* the state of being higher or older in rank or status than someone else. *He never took advantage of his seniority.*

Sensation – *(noun)* **1** a physical feeling. or perception resulting from something that happens to or comes into contact with the body. the capacity to have such feeling or perceptions. *I had a sensation of pain in my arm.* **2** an inexplicable awareness or impression. *She was scared by the sensation of someone's presence in her room.* **3** a widespread reaction of interest and excitement. a person or thing that arouses such interest and excitement. *The band's music was a sensation amongst the teenagers.*

Sense – *(noun)* **1** a faculty by which the body perceives an external stimulus; one of the faculties of sight, smell, hearing, taste, and touch. one's sanity. *Dogs have a powerful sense of smell.* **2** an awareness of something or feeling that something is the case. *I had a sense of being followed.* **3** a sane and realistic attitude to situations and problems. a reasonable or comprehensible rationable. *The little child demonstrated a lot of sense while dealing with the adults.* **4** a way in which an expression or situation can be interpreted; a meaning. *What he said made no sense.* **5** [chiefly] the property distinguishing. two opposite but otherwise identical things, e.g. motion in opposite directions. *The sense of their natures was quite apparent.* **6** [genetics] relating to or denoting a coding sequence of nucleotides, complementary to an antisense sequence. *The scientists were delighted to discover the sense in the DNA they were studying.* *(verb)* **1** perceive by a sense a senses. be vaguely or indefinably aware of. *The blind man sensed the faraway movement.* **2** detect. *I sensed a motion behind the bushes.*

Senseless – *(adjective)* **1** unconscious or incapable of sensation. *The drunkard lay senseless on the footpath.* **2** without discernible meaning or purpose. lacking common sense; wildly foolish. *His senseless quest for money made his family worried for him.*

Sensibility – *(noun)* **1** the ability to appreciate and respond to complex emotional or aesthetic influences; sensitivity. a person's tendency to be offended or shocked. *The artist had the sensibility to judge a good work of art.* **2**

[zoology, dated] sensitivity to sensory stimuli. *The bear's sensibilities were very sharp.*

Sensible – *(adjective)* **1** wise and prudent; having or showing common sense. practical and functional rather than decorative. *My father is a very sensible man.* **2** [archaic] readily perceived; appreciable. able to notice or appreciate. *It is very difficult to be sensible to someone else's goodness.*

Sensitive – *(adjective)* **1** quick to detect, respond to, or be affected by slight changes, signals, or influences. photographic materials responding rapidly to the action of light. *The blind man is very sensitive to the changes in the intensity of light.* **2** quickly and delicately appreciating the feelings of others. *My mother is very sensitive towards me.* **3** easily offended or upset. *You are too sensitive.* **4** kept secret or with restrictions on disclosure. *The sensitive information was leaked by some careless employees.* *(noun)* a person supposedly able to respond to paranormal influences. *The sensitive person appeared startled by something no one else could see in the room.*

Sensual – *(adjective)* **1** of or relating to the physical senses, especially as a source of pleasure. *The artist was very proud of his sensual paintings.* **2** arousing sexual or other physical gratification. *The men found the movie very sensual.*

Sensuous – *(adjective)* **1** relating to or affecting the senses rather than the intellect. *The movie was very sensuous.* **2** attractive or gratifying physically, especially sexually. *Their relationship was very sensuous.*

Sentence – *(noun)* **1** a set of words that is complete in itself conveying a statement, question, exclamation, or command and typically containing a subject and predicate. logic a series of signs or symbols expressing a proposition in an artificial or logical language. *The child has started talking in complete sentences.* **2** the punishment assigned to a defendant found guilty by a court. *His sentence was appropriate for his crime.* *(verb)* declare the punishment decided for an offender. *The judge sentenced the criminal to spend 10 years in the jail.*

Sentiment – *(noun)* **1** a view, opinion, or feeling. general feeling or opinion. *I express my sentiments very openly.* **2** exaggerated and self-indulgent feelings of tenderness, sadness, or nostalgia. *He was overcome by his sentiments.*

Sentimental – *(adjective)* deriving from feelings of tenderness, sadness, or nostalgia. having or arousing such feelings in an exaggerated and self-indulgent way. *The sentimental actress started crying for real during the scene.*

Sentinel – *(noun)* **1** a soldier or guard whose job is to stand and keep watch. *The sentinel came running to announce the approach of the enemy.* **2** [medicine] a thing that acts as an indicator of the presence of disease. *The pain in his stomach was the sentinel for the stone in his kidney.* *(verb)* station a sentinel to keep watch over. *The chief sentineled the tallest man.*

Sentry – *(noun)* a soldier stationed to keep guard or to control access to a place. *The sentry was doing his job well.*

Separable – *(adjective)* **1** able to be separated or treated separately. *The hair-dryer has separable attachments.* **2** [grammar] having a prefix that is written as a separate word in some circumstances. *The word counterclockwise has a separable prefix.*

Separate – *(adjective)* forming or viewed as a unit apart or by itself; not joined or united with others. different; distinct. *Both friends run separate businesses.* *(verb)* **1** move or come apart; make or become detached or disconnected. stop living together as a couple. [US] discharge or dismiss from service or employment. *No one knows why they separated.* **2** divide into constituent or distinct elements. extract or remove for use or rejection. distinguish between or from another, consider individually. *I separated the yolk from rest of the egg.* **3** form a distinction or boundary between. *They separated the land with barbed-wire fencing.* *(noun)* things forming units by themselves, in particular individual items of clothing suitable for wearing in different combinations. *I find separates very convenient as I don't buy too many clothes.*

Separation – *(noun)* **1** the action or state of separating or being separated. the state in which a husband and wife remain married but live apart: a trial separation. *Their separation was very traumatic for their children.* **2** distinction between the signals carried by the two channels of a stereophonic system. *The separation wasn't clearly indicated on the display of the system.*

September – *(noun)* the ninth month of the year. *My niece was born in September.*

Septic – *(adjective)* **1** infected with bacteria. *The septic wound needed to be treated immediately.* **2** denoting a drainage system incorporating a septic tank. *The septic was not functioning properly.*

Sepulchre – *(noun)* a small room, cut in store in which a dead person is buried. *The children were scared to go near the Sepulchre.*

Sequel – *(noun)* **1** a published, broadcast, or recorded work that continues the story or develops the theme of an earlier one. *I loved the movie so much that I was desperately waiting for the sequel.* **2** something that takes place after or as a result of an earlier event.*The sacking of the players was a sequel to their horrible performance in the game.*

Sequence – *(noun)* **1** a particular order in which related events, movements, etc. follow each other. [music] a repetition of a phrase or melody at a higher or lower pitch. biochemistry the order in which amino-acid or nucleotide residues are arranged in a protein, DNA, etc. *The piano sequence in the musical left everyone in awe.* **2** a set of related events, movements, etc. that follow each other in a particular order. A set of three or more playing cards of the same suit next to each other in value. *He won the last hand at the card game a he had the highest colour sequence.* **3** a part of a film dealing with one particular event or topic. *In the film, the sequence where the leading lady lost her luggage was very comic.* **4** a hymn said or sung after the gradual or alleluia that precedes the gospel. *Sequence hymns are sung in church during Easter Day celebrations.* *(verb)* **1** arrange in a sequence. *I put the marbles in a sequence of blue followed by green.* **2** play or record with a sequencer. *Jim was asked to record his last piece on a sequencer.* **3** [biochemistry] ascertain the sequence of amino-acid or nucleotide residues in a protein, DNA, etc. *It is important to understand how the DNA is sequenced in our bodies.*

Seraph – *(noun)* an angelic being associated with light, ardour, and purity. *The seraphs floating around in her dream made a beautiful picture.*

Serene – *(adjective)* calm, peaceful, and untroubled; tranquil. *The serene look on the saint's face was worth noticing.* *(noun)* [archaic] clear sky or calm sea. *The serene inspired many poets.*

Serenely - *(adverb)* calmly, peacefully. *My mother listened to my problem serenely before giving me advice.*

Serf – *(noun)* an agricultural labourer who was tied to working on a particular estate. *In earlier times serfs were made to work without wages.*

Sergeant – *(noun)* **1** a rank of noncommissioned officer in the army or air force, above corporal and below staff sergeant. *The sergeant ordered his platoon to gather in the grounds for a warm-up.* **2** [British] a police officer ranking below an inspector. *The sergeant was sent to investigate the scene of crime.* **3** [US] a police officer ranking below a lieutenant. *Sergeant Greene prepared the report that was to be submitted to the lieutenant.*

Serial – *(adjective)* **1** consisting of, forming part of, or taking place in a series. *The class was asked to stand according to their serial numbers.* **2** repeatedly committing the same offence or following a characteristic behaviour pattern: a serial killer. *The police were unable to catch the serial killer.* **3** [music] relating to or using serialism. *The serial pattern of drums in his music makes it sound very dramatic.* **4.** computing involving the transfer of data as a single sequence of bits. *Data transfer in computers occurs in a serial order made up of 0s and 1s.* *(noun)* **1** a published or broadcast story or play appearing in regular installments. *Nowadays there are a lot of serials that one can watch on the television.* **2**. a periodical. *The* *third serial publication of the monthly magazine was a sell-out.*

Series – *(noun)* **1** a number of similar or related things coming one after another. a set of books, periodicals, etc. published in a common format. a set of stamps, banknotes, or coins issued at a particular time. *The kidnapper was caught with the series of banknotes that had been marked out by the police.* **2** a sequence of related television or radio programmes. *The "Discover India" series aired on the Travel channel is very informative.* **3**. [music] another term for tone row. *Music is generated by putting together a series of high and low notes.* **4** having or denoting electrical components connected in series. *House wiring is usually done in parallel and not in series.* **5** [mathematics] a set of quantities constituting a progression or having values determined by a common relation. *The infinite series is a sum of infinitely many numbers.*

Serious – *(adjective)* **1** demanding or characterized by careful consideration or application. solemn or thoughtful. *The problem of water not reaching the field in time for cultivation needed serious consideration.* **2** sincere and in earnest, rather than joking or halfhearted. *He was serious when he spoke of putting together a fund for the homeless.* **3** significant or worrying in terms of danger or risk: serious injury. *The accident could have caused serious injury.* **4** [informal] substantial in terms of size, number, or quality: serious money. *His business idea had a lot of risk as there was serious money involved.*

Seriously – *(adverb)* in a serious manner or to a serious extent. *We need to seriously think about the problem of beggars in our country.*

Sermon – *(noun)* **1** a talk on a religious or moral subject, especially one given during a church service and based on a passage from the bible. *During the Sunday church service the sermon lasts for over an hour.* **2** [informal] a long or tedious piece of admonition or reproof. *The teacher is known to give a sermon to her students each time she finds them loitering around.*

Sermonise – *(verb)* deliver an opinionated lecture to someone. *Nowadays children feel that every time their parents tell them something, they are sermonizing.*

Serpent – *(noun)* **1** [chiefly] a large snake. a dragon or other mythical snake-like reptile. a biblical name for satan. a sly or treacherious person. *The serpent had made its nest in the large tree trunk.* **2** [historical] a bass wind instrument made of leather-covered wood in three U-shaped turns, with a cup-shaped mouthpiece and few keys. *The serpent was played in military bands during the 17th century.*

Serpentine – *(adjective)* of or like a serpent or snake. winding and twisting. complex, cunning, or treacherous. *Many people suffer from motion sickness while travelling to the hills due to the serpentine roads.* *(noun)* **1** dark green mineral consisting of hydrated magnesium silicate, sometimes mottled or spotted like a snake's skin. *Serpentine is found in various shades of green and is used as an ornamental stone.* **2** a riding exercise consisting of a series of half-circles made alternately to right and left. *Young horses are trained with serpentines.* **3** historical a kind of cannon. *The serpentine was so named because its slender barrel resembled a snake.* *(verb)* move or lie in a winding path or line. *The river serpentines through the mountains before moving to the plains.*

Serrated – *(adjective)* having or denoting a jagged edge; saw like. *The serrated blade of the knife was very sharp.*

Servant – *(noun)* a person employed to perform duties for others, especially in a house on domestic duties or as a personal attendant. a person employed in the service of a government. a devoted and helpful follower or supporter. *Guru Nanak looked upon himself as a servant of God.*

Server – *(noun)* **1** a person or thing that serves. [north American] a waiter or waitress. *The server was asked to put down the food and get some water.* **2** a computer or computer program which manages access to a centralized resource or service in an network. *All office work came to a halt due to a problem in the server.*

Service – *(noun)* **1** the action of process of serving. an act of assistance. a period of employment with a company or organization: he retired after 40 year's service. pose. employment as a servant. *He was in government service for 21 years.* **2** a system supplying a public need such as transport, or utilities such as electricity and water. a public department or organization run by the state: the probation service. the armed forces. [chiefly British] a motorway service area. *The state bus service has undergone a complete facelift in the last couple of years.* **3** a ceremony of religious worship according to a prescribed form. *All my Christian friends make it a point to attend the church service on Sundays.* **4** a set of matching crockery used for serving a particular meal. *The dinner service was attended by a large number of people.* **5** a serve. *After the badminton player dropped his shot, the service went to his opponent.* **6** a periodic routine inspection and maintenance of a vehicle or other machine. *My car's service is due next month.* *(verb)* **1** perform routine maintenance or repair work on a vehicle or machine. provide a service or services for. *The workshop staff will service my car.* **2** pay interest on a debt. *The bank asked him to service his loan in time.* **3** mate with a female animal. *Stud farms use high breed stallions to service mares.*

Serviette – *(noun)* [British] a table napkin. *I asked the waiter for a serviette.*

Servile – *(adjective)* **1** excessively willing to serve or please others. *Sam has a servile attitude when interacting with his boss.* **2** of or characteristic of a slave or slaves. *It is not right to expect domestic help to stand in servile obedience in front of their employers.*

Sesame – *(noun)* a tall annual herbaceous plant of tropical and subtropical areas of the old world, cultivated for its oil-rich seeds. *My uncle grows sesame in his fields.*

Session – *(noun)* **1** a period devoted to a particular activity: a training session. [informal] a period of heavy or sustained drinking. a period of recording music in a studio. *I had a session with the dietician today.* **2** a meeting of a deliberative or judicial body to conduct its business. *The court is now in session.* **3** a period during year. the period during which a school has classes. *The session has just begun.* **4** the governing body of a Presbyterian church. *The session presided over the gathering.*

Set – *(verb)* **1** put, lay, or stand in a specified place or position. be situated in a specified place or position. represent as happening at a specified time or in a specified place. mount a precious stone in a piece of jewellery. printing arrange as required. prepare for a meal by placing cutlery, crockery, etc., on it. add to a written work. sailing put up in position to catch the wind. *The stage was set for the play.* **2** put, bring, or place into a specified state: the hostages were set free. instruct to do something. give someone a task: the problem we have been set. establish as an example or record. decide on or fix a time, value, or limit. *We have set a time for the meeting.* **3** adjust a device as required. *We set the radio to the frequency of our favorite channel.* **4** into the required style. put a broken or dislocated bone or limb into the correct position for healing. adopt, a rigid attitude indicating the presence of game. *The doctor set his dislocated shoulder.* **5** take or have a specified direction or course. *We set the boat in the direction of the land.* **6** [chiefly north American] start a fire. *The hooligans set the forest on fire.* **7** form into or produce fruit. *It was nice to see the fower set.* **8** [informal] sit. *They set together on Friday.* **9** acknowledge one's partner using the steps prescribed. *The male dancer set to his partner beautifully.* **10** give the teeth of an alternate outward inclination. *The wood cutter set the saw.*

Settee – *(noun)* a long upholstered seat for more than one person, typically with a back and arms. *Most of the guests preferred to sit on the settee.*

Setting – *(noun)* **1** the surroundings of a place or the location where an event happens. the place and time at which a story is represented as happening. *The author used the town of his* *birth as the setting.* **2** a piece of metal in which a precious stone or gem is fixed to form a piece of jewellery. *Platinum is commonly used as a setting for diamonds.* **3** a piece of vocal or choral music composed for particular words. *The setting brought out the beauty of the song.* **4** a complete set of crockery and cutlery for one person at a meal. *She believed in a perfect setting when it came to feeding the guests.* **5** a level at which a machine or device can be adjusted to operate. *The setting of the washing machine seemed to be unsuitable for woollen clothes.*

Settle – *(noun)* a wooden bench with a high back and arms. typically incorporating a box under the seat. *The settle has broken down because of disrepair.*

Settlement – *(noun)* **1** the action or process of setting. *The settlement was taking a long time.* **2** an official agreement intended to resolve a dispute or conflict. *The terms of the settlement were suitable to everyone.* **3** a place where people establish a community. *The settlement flourished in no time at all.* **4** [law] an arrangement whereby property passes to a person or succession of people as dictated by the settler. *They got a fair share of property as per the agreement.*

Settler – *(noun)* a person who settles in an area, especially one with no or few previous inhabitants. *The settlers soon began to cultivate crops.*

Seven – *(cardinal number)* **1** equivalent to the sum of three and four; one more than six, or three less than ten; 7. *There were seven children in the balcony.* **2** seven-a-side rugby. *The team got together to play sevens.*

Seventh – *(ordinal number)* **1** constituting number seven in a sequence; 7th. *He stood seventh in the queue.* **2** each of seven equal parts into which something is or may be divided. *I ate a seventh of the pizza.* **3** [music] an interval spanning seven consecutive notes in a diatonic scale. the note which is higher by this interval than the tonic of a diatonic scale or root of a chord. a chord in which the seventh note of the scale forms an important component. *As soon as the music hit the seventh, the audience erupted in cheer.*

Seventeen – *(noun)* a number. *There were a total of seventeen pigeons in the tree.*

Seventy – *(cardinal number)* the number equivalent to the product of seven and ten; ten less than eighty; 70. *The class had 70 students.*

Sever – *(verb)* **1** divide by cutting or slicing. *The workmen severed the ropes.* **2** put an end to a connection or relationship. *We severed our ties years ago.*

Several – *(determined & pronoun)* more than two but not many. *Several of the guests left very early.* *(adjective)* **1** separate or respective. *Everyone left for their several homes.* **2** [law] applied or regarded separately. contrasted with joint. *The judge instructed the jury to consider their several crimes.*

Severe – *(adjective)* **1** very great; intense. *I had a severe headache.* **2** strict or harsh. *The principal is a very severe woman.* **3** very plain in style or appearance. *The supermodel was very severe off the ramp.*

Sew – *(verb)* **1** join, fasten, or repair by making stitches with a needle and thread or a sewing machine. *I sewed the torn rim of my skirt.* **2** [informal] bring something to a favourable state or conclusion. *The families sewed their ties.*

Sewing – *(noun)* the action or activity of sewing. *My mom loves sewing.*

Sewage – *(noun)* waste water and excrement conveyed in sewers. *The smell of the sewage made it difficult to stand there.*

Sewer – *(noun)* an underground conduit for carrying off drainage water and waste matter. *The road was dug up because the sewer was being laid.*

Sex – *(noun)* **1** either of the two main categories into which humans and most other living things are divided on the basis of their reproductive functions. the fact of belonging to one of these categories. the group of all members of either sex. *The lion cub belonged to female sex.* **2** sexual activity, specifically sexual intercourse. euphemistic a person's genitals. *It is important to educate students about sex.* *(verb)* **1** determine the sex of. *It is illegal to determine the sex of foetus.* **2** [informal] arouse or attempt to arouse someone sexually. *The movie aroused the feeling of sex in both of them.*

Sexism - *(noun)* prejudice, stereotyping, or discrimination, typically against women, on the basis of sex. *Sexism isn't healthy in workplaces.*

Sexual - *(adjective)* **1** relating to the instincts, physiological processes, and activities connected with physical attraction or intimate physical contact between individuals. *The photographer was working on a documentary about the sexual behaviour of tigers.* **2** involving the fusion of gametes. biology being of one sex or the other; capable of sexual reproduction. *Mammals are sexual animals.*

Shabby - *(noun)* **1** worn out or dilapidated. dressed in old or worn clothes. *The shabby man roamed around in the streets late at night.* **2** mean and unfair. *Your behaviour towards your younger sister was very shabby.*

Shack - *(noun)* a roughly built hut of cabin. *We were glad to find the shack when we got lost in the forest. (verb)* [informal] live with someone as a lover. *The man shacked with the girl he loved.*

Shackle - *(noun)* **1** a pair of fetters connected by a chain, used to fasten a prisoner's wrists or ankles together. restraints or impediments. *The man in the shackles was very menacing.* **2** a metal link, typically U-shaped, closed by a bolt and used to secure a chain or rope to something. *The door was closed with a shackle. (verb)* **1** chain with shackles. *The policeman shackled the accused.* **2** restrain; limit. *The dog-owner shackled the ferocious dog.*

Shade - *(noun)* **1** comparative darkeness and coolness caused by shelter from direct sunlight. *The shade was such a relief in the blazing sun.* **2** a position of relative inferiority of obscurity. *The manager felt frustrated because he thought that he was still in shade.* **3** a colour, especially with regard to how light or dark it is. a slight degree of difference between colours. *The yellow on my wall was only a shade lighter than my curtains.* **4** a slightly differing variety: all shades of opinion. *It was nice to listen to all shades of opinion in the conference.* **5** a slight amount. *Can you share with me a shade of your knowledge?* **6** a lampshade. *My parents have gone to the market to buy shades for the house.* **7** [north American] a screen or blind on a window. *Please lower the shades as it is too sunny outside.* **8** [informal] sunglasses. *The shades suited the shape of his face.* **9** [poetic] a ghost. the underworld. *The man became a hero after his interaction with the shade. (verb)* **1** screen from direct light. cover, moderate, or exclude the light of. *The mother shaded her baby from the sun.* **2** darken or colour with parallel pencil lines or a block of colour. *The children shaded their drawings.* **3** [informal] narrowly win. *The visiting team shaded the close match.* **4** reduce or decline in amount, rate, or price. *The value of the car shaded over the years.*

Shadow - *(noun)* **1** the dark area or shape produced by a body coming between light rays and a surface. partial or complete darkness. a dark patch or area. *The dog chased its shadow.* **2** an air or expression of sadness and gloom. *As soon as he heard the news, a shadow descended upon his face.* **3** a position of relative inferiority or obscurity. *Employees who weren't performing well were put in the shadow.* **4** the slightest trace. *The competitor didn't display even a shadow of fear.* **5** a weak or inferior remnant or version of something. *He is but a shadow of his former self.* **6** an inseparable attendant or companion. a person secretly following and observing another. *The detective shadowed the man to his home.* **7** [British] denoting the opposition counterpart of a government insister. *The shadow of the chancellor was a powerful person. (verb)* **1** envelop in shadow; cast a shadow over. *His personality shadows that of everyone around him.* **2** follow and observe secretly. accompany in their daily activities for experience of or insight into a job. *The new recruit shadowed his mentor to learn the tricks of the trait.*

Shady - *(adjective)* **1** situated in or full of shade. *Let us move to a shady part of the park.* **2** giving shade. *The shady tree was everyone's favorite.* **3** [informal] of doubtful honesty or legality. *The residents called the police because of the shady activities going around the locality.*

Shaft - *(noun)* **1** a long, narrow part of section forming the handle of a toll or club, the body of a spear or arrow, or similar. an arrow or spear. a column, especially the part between the base and capital. a long cylindrical rotating rod for the transmission of motive power in a machine. each of the pair of poles between which a horse is harnessed to a vehicle. *He was hit by the shaft of the spear.* **2** a ray of light or bolt of lightning. *The shaft illuminated the entire sky.* **3** a sudden flash of a quality or feeling. a witty, wounding, or provoking remark. *I felt a sudden shaft of happiness.* **4** vulgar slang a man's penis. *He tucked his shaft in his trousers.* **5** [north American] harsh or unfair treatment. *His shaft made many employees leave the country. (verb)* **1** shine in beams. *The light shafted through the window.* **2** vulgar slang have sexual intercourse with. *They shafted in the car.* **3** [informal] treat harshly or unfairly. *He shafted his subordinates at every opportunity.*

Shaggy - *(adjective)* long, thick, and unkempt. having shaggy hair or fur. of or having a covering resembling shaggy hair. *The dog had shaggy hair.*

Shake - *(verb)* **1** tremble or vibrate or cause to do so. tremble uncontrollably with strong emotion. *The entire building shook with the impact.* **2** move forcefully or quickly up and down or to and fro. remove from something by shaking. brandish in anger or as a warning. *The furious man shook his fists at the noisy children.***3**. [informal] get rid of or put an end to. *It is important to shake your fear away.* **4** shock or astonish. cause a change of mood by shocking or disturbing. weaken or impair. *You have shaken me up. (noun)* **1** an act of shaking. an amount sprinkled from a container. *I gave the glass of milk a good shake.* **2** [informal] a milkshake. *I would love to have a chocolate shake with the burger.* **3** [informal] a fit or trembling or shivering. *He suffered from shakes during the fever.* **4** music a trill. *The musician used the shake well in the sequence.*

Shaky - *(adjective)* **1** shaking or trembling. *The shaky man narrated his horrible tale of fear.* **2** unstable. *The shaky cabinet came crashing down on the floor.*

Shall - *(modal verb)* **1** expression the future tense. *I shall complete this assignment by tomorrow.* **2** expressing a strong assertion or intention. *I shall get the work done.* **3** expressing an instruction or command. *You shall come for the class in time.* **4** used in questions indicating offers or suggestions. *Shall I come to your house to talk to you?*

Shallow - *(adjective)* **1** of little depth. *The lake was shallow but dangerous.* **2** not showing, requiring, or capable of serious thought. *The girl appeared shallow but was actually very thoughtful. (noun)* a shallow area of water. *Let us go to the shallows to relax. (verb)* become shallow. *The lake has shallowed over the years.*

Sham - *(noun)* **1** a person or thing that is not what they are purported to be. *His love was just a sham.* **2** pretence. *She tried sham to get approval of her parents. (adjective)* bogus; false. *I don't need your sham sympathy. (verb)* **1** falsely present something as the truth. *He shammed his marriage.* **2** pretend to be or to be experiencing. *She shammed happiness in marriage.*

Shambles - *(noun)* **1** [informal] a chaotic state. *No one wanted to visit the shambles.* **2** [archaic] a butcher's slaughterhouse. *The shamble always smelled putrid.* **3** a scene of carnage. *A visit to the shambles was always enough to make me feel afraid.*

Shame - *(noun)* **1** a feeling of humiliation or distress caused by the consciousness of wrong of foolish behaviour. *He experienced a lot of shame when he was caught cheating.* **2** dishonor. a person or thing bringing dishonor. *You have brought shame upon the family.* **3** a regrettable or unfortunate thing. *It is such a shame that you have to go back home tonight. (verb)* cause to feel ashamed. *The professor shamed the students for their pathetic performance in the exams.*

Shameful - *(adjective)* worthy of or causing shame. *Her actions were seen as shameful by her relatives.*

Shameless - *(adjective)* showing a lack of shame. *The thief was absolutely shameless even when he was caught by the police.*

Shampoo – *(noun)* **1** a liquid preparation for washing the hair. a similar substance for cleaning a carpet, car, etc. *I prefer using a herbal shampoo.* **2** an act of washing with shampoo. *Her shaggy hair became soft and shiny after the shampoo. (verb)* wash or clean with shampoo. *I shampoo my hair once every two days.*

Shape – *(noun)* **1** the external form or appearance of someone or something; the outline of an area or figure. a specific form or guise assumed by someone or something. a piece of material, paper, etc. made or cut in a particular form. *I could see the shape of a man behind the curtains.* **2** the condition or state of someone or something. the distinctive nature or qualities of something. *The athlete was in a good shape.* **3** definite or orderly arrangement. *Let us all shape the seats and prepare the venue for the guests. (verb)* **1** give a particular shape or form to. make fit the form of something else. *This course will help you shape your future as per your desire.* **2** determine the nature of. *Let us see the shape of things first.* **3** develop in a particular way. *It is important to shape the personality of a child in a positive way.* **4** become physically fit. [informal] improve something. *I am trying to shape up a bit before my sister's marriage.* **5** form or produce a sound or words. *They celebrated when the child started shaping the first words.*

Shapeless – *(adjective)* lacking definite or attractive shape. *The dress is decidedly shapeless.*

Shapely – *(adjective)* having an attractive or well-proportioned shape. *It is important for a model to have a shapely body.*

Share – *(noun)* **1** a part of portion of a larger amount which is divided among or contributed by a number of people. any of the equal parts into which a company's capital is divided. part-ownership of property. *Everyone was happy with their share in the property.* **2** the allotted or due amount of something expected to be had or done. a contribution of something. *I paid my share as soon as I received the request. (verb)* **1** have a share of with another or others. give a share of to another or others. possess in common with others. have a part in an activity. *I shared my ice cream with my sister.* **2** tell someone about. *I shared my problem with my teacher.*

Shavings – *(noun)* **1** a thin strip cut off a surface. *My friend collected pencil shavings.* **2** used when shaving. *My father carried his shaving kit wherever he went.*

Shawl – *(noun)* a piece of fabric worn by women over the shoulders or head or wrapped round a baby. *I loved her pashmina shawl.*

She – *(pronoun)* **1** used to refer to a woman, girl, of female animal previously mentioned or easily indentified. *Ruby is the only daughter of her parents, and she is her father's favorite.* **2** used to refer to a ship, country, or other inanimate thing regarded as female. *The boat's sails flapped as she sailed in the calm weather.* **3** any female person in modern use, now largely replaced by 'anyone' or the person. *She who wants to win will need to cook faster and better.* **4** austral [informal] it; the state of affairs. *She'll be alright. (noun)* a female; a woman. *Is this baby a she or a he?*

Sheaf – *(noun)* **1** a bundle of grain stalks laid lengthways and tied together after reaping. *The farmer's wife carried the sheaf of wheat on her head.* **2** a bundle of objects, especially papers. *A new sheaf of papers was put into the printer. (verb)* bundle into sheaves. *The farmer sheafed the wheat stalks.*

Shear – *(verb)* **1** cut the wool off a sheep or other animal. cut off with scissors or shears. have something cut off. *The men sheared the unwilling sheep.* **2** break off or cause to break off, owing to a structural strain. *The window sheared because of the load of ceiling. (noun)* a strain produced by pressure in the structure of a substance, when its layers are laterally shifted in relation to each other. *The shear caused the building to lose shape.*

Shears – *(plural noun)* cutting instrument in which two blades move past each other, like very large scissors. *The shears were very sharp and dangerous.*

Sheath – *(noun)* **1** a cover for the blade of a knife or sword. *The sheath was very ornate.* **2** a structure in living tissue which closely envelops another. *The nerve-fibres are protected by a sheath.* **3** a protective covering around an electric cable. *The cable was risky because its sheath had started fraying.* **4** a condom. *They threw the used sheath in the garbage.* **5** a close-fitting dress. *The sheath was uncomfortable.*

Sheathe – *(verb)* **1** put a knife or sword into a sheath. *I saw the warrior sheathe the sword.* **2** encase in a close-fitting or protective covering. *The dress-maker sheathed the bride-to-be.*

Shed – *(noun)* **1** a simple roofed structure, typically of wood and used for storage or to shelter animals. a larger structure, typically with one or more sides open, for storing vehicles or machinery. *The tractor rolled out of the shed.* **2** [austral] an open-sided building for shearing sheep or milking cattle. *The cattle were mooing in the shed.* *(verb)* part a vehicle in a depot. *The driver sheds the bus.*

Sheen – *(noun)* a soft luster on a surface. *The new car had a beautiful sheen.* *(verb)* [poetic] shine or cause to shine softly. *The little boy worked hard to sheen his father's car.*

Sheep – *(noun)* **1** a domesticated ruminant mammal with a thick woolly coat, kept, in flocks for its wool or meat. a wild mammal related to this, e.g. a bighorn. *I love to see the sheep on the rolling green hills.* **2** a person who is too easily influenced or led. *She is a sheep when it comes to making a decision.* **3** a member of a minister's congregation. *The sheep followed the minister everywhere.*

Sheepish – *(adjective)* showing embarrassment from shame. *The boy was caught because he was acting sheepish.*

Sheer – *(adjective)* **1** nothing other than; unmitigated: sheer hard work. *He owed his success to sheer hard work.* **2** perpendicular or nearly so. *The sheer rock jutting out of the hills presented a spectacular sight.* **3** very thin. *The sheer strip of metal was very dangerous for a child to hold.* *(adverb)* **1** perpendicularly. *The rock rose sheer out of the mountain.* **2** [archaic] completely; right. *I sheer agree with him.*

Sheet – *(noun)* a rope attached to the lower corner of a sail. *The sailor desperately pulled the sheet.* the space at the bow or stern of an open boat. *They kept some luggage in the sheet.* *(verb)* make a sail more or less taut. set a sail as flat as possible. *The skipper asked the crew to sheet the mainsail.*

Shelf – *(noun)* **1** a flat length of wood or rigid material attached to a wall or forming part of a piece of furniture, providing a surface for the storage or display of objects. *All my books are displayed on the shelf.* **2** a ledge of rock or protruding strip of land. a submarine bank, or a part of the continental shelf. *Several seagulls perched on the shelf.*

Shetter – *(noun)* **1** a place giving protection from bad weather or danger. *The storm shelter proved to be very helpful when the tornado hit.* **2** a place providing food and accommodation for the homeless. *The rich businessman got the shelter constructed for the poor.* **3** an animal sanctuary. *The animal shelter hired a new veterinarian.* **4** a shielded condition; protection. *The children were used to shelter.* *(verb)* **1** provide with shelter. find refuge or take cover. *The rich man sheltered many homeless people.* **2** prevent from having to do or face something difficult. *My parents have sheltered me throughout my life.* **3** protect from taxation. *Good thinking by my financial advisor sheltered my income.*

Shelve – *(verb)* **1** place on a shelf. *I shelved my old books.* **2** abandon or defer a plan or project. *Our project was shelved after the product manager declared that the product will not sell.* **3** fit with shelves. *He shelved his room to create more space for his clothes.*

Shepherd – *(noun)* **1** a person who tends sheep. *The shepherd sat near the sheep and played his flute.* **2** a member of the clergy providing spiritual care and guidance for a congregation. *The shepherd guided his people well.* *(verb)* **1** tend. *The farmer shepherded his cattle throughout his life.* **2** guide or direct somewhere. *The teacher shepherded the school children towards the main attraction of the museum.* **3** give spiritual or other guidance to. *The guru shepherded his disciples.*

Sheriff - *(noun)* **1** the chief executive officer of the crown in a country, having administrative and judicial functions. an honorary officer elected annually in some English towns. *The sheriff ordered the men to be arrested immediately.* **2** a judge. *The sheriff pronounced the two thieves guilty.* **3** [US] an elected officer in a country, responsible for keeping the peace. *The sheriff felt that the country needed a new law for owning guns.*

Shield - *(noun)* **1** a broad piece of armour held by straps or a handle on one side, used for protection against blows or missiles. hardly a stylized representation of a shield used for displaying a coat of arms. *His shield protected him from the enemies sword.* **2** a sporting trophy consisting of an engraved metal plate mounted on a piece of wood. *He displayed his shield proudly.* **3** a US police officer's badge. *The crowd became quiet when they saw the cop's shield.* **4** [geology] a large rigid area of Precambrian plate, screen, or other structure. *The geologists discovered a shield beneath the surface.* *(verb)* **1** protect from a danger, risk, etc. enclose or screen to protect the user. *The army shields the country from the enemies.* **2** prevent from being seen. *The curtain shielded the thief from the police.* **3** prevent or reduce the escape of sound, light, or other radiation. from. *The metal shielded the workers from the radiation.*

Shift - *(verb)* **1** move or change or cause to move or change from one position to another. move one's body slightly due to discomfort. *The passengers shifted themselves slightly to accommodate the old man.* **2** [Birtish informal] move quickly. [British informal] move or rouse oneself. *The police shifted from the street to the market area in search of the suspected criminals.* **3** [British] in large quantities. *The market saw a shift in sales.* **4** [British informal] eat or drink hastily or in large amounts. *The excited crowd shifted in the pub.* **5** change gear. *I shifted to the fifth gear for the first time in my life.* **6** [archaic] be evasive. *He shifted constantly from his stand.* *(noun)* **1** a slight change in position, direction, or tendency. *The shift in the market impacted the economy.* **2** a key used to switch between two sets of characters or functions on a keyboard. *The shift key is often used to type capital letters.* **3** [north American] a gear lever or gear-changing mechanism. *They stopped the car because the shift got stuck.* **4** building the positioning of successive rows of bricks so that their ends do not coincide. *The brick-layers were laying the shift.* **5**. each of two or more periods in which different groups of workers do the same jobs in relay. a group of people who work in this way. *In this company, the employees work in shifts.* **6** a straight untwisted dress. historical a long, loose undergarment. *She hung the shift to dry.*

Shifty- *(adjective)* **1** deceitful or evasive. *I did not trust the man because he looked shifty.* **2**. constantly changing. *If he wasn't so shifty in his beliefs, he would have established his company by now.*

Shilling - *(noun)* **1** a former British coin and monetary unit equal to one twentieth of a pound or twelve pence. *The child had a huge collection of shillings.* **2** the basic monetary unit of Kenya, Tanzania, and Uganda, equal to 100 cents. *The movie tickets cost many shillings.*

Shimmer - *(verb)* shine with a soft tremulous light. *Her dress shimmered in the bright light.* *(noun)* a light with such qualities. *A shimmer lampshade was installed in the drawing room.*

Shin - *(noun)* the front of the leg below the knee. a cut of beef from the lower part of a cow's leg. *Her dress came down to the middle of her shins.* *(verb)* climb quickly up or down by gripping with one's arms and legs. *He shinnied up the drain pipe to avoid his professor.*

Shine - *(verb)* **1** give out a bright light; glow with reflected light. direct somewhere. be bright with the expression of emotion. *Her eyes seemed to shine with excitement.* **2** be clearly evident. *The fact that he would be the topper shone through.* **4** polish. *The man was busy shining his car.* *(noun)* **1** a quality of brightness, especially through reflecting light. *The shine from the surface of the lake was blinding even at the distance.* **2** an act of polishing. *The shine had changed the entire look of the car.*

Shingle – *(noun)* **1** a rectangular wooden tile used on walls or roofs. *Several shingles fell from the roof.* **2** dated a woman's short haircut, tapering from the back of the head to the nape of the neck. *The shingle suited the shape of her face.* **3** [north American] a small signboard, especially one outside an office. *Birds say on top of our office's shingle.* *(verb)* roof or clad with shingles. *The workers shingled the roof.* **2** dated cut in a shingle. *The factory shingled the blocks of wood.*

Ship – *(noun)* **1** a large seagoing boat. a sailing vessel with a bowsprit and three or more square-rigged masts. *The ship was huge but didn't have enough lifeboats.* **2** a spaceship. *The residents of the town thought they saw the lights of a ship in the sky.* **3** [north American] an aircraft. *I am boarding the ship for New York tonight.* *(verb)* **1** transport on a ship. transport by other means. take service on a ship. *The items I had ordered were shipped today.* **2** make available for purchase. *The books I ordered were ready to be shipped a month back.* **3** take in over the side. *The crew was worried when high waters started shipping.* **4** take from the rowlocks and lay them inside a boat. fix a rudder, mast, etc. in place on a ship. *The rudder was shipped today.*

Shipmate – *(noun)* a fellow member of a ship's crew. *The young sailor got along well with his shipmates.*

Shipment – *(noun)* **1** the action of shipping goods. *The shipment has happened an hour back.* **2** a consignment of goods shipped. *The shipment arrived yesterday.*

Shipshape – *(adjective)* orderly and neat. *The shipshape cabin was such a relief.*

Shipwreck – *(noun)* the destruction of a ship at sea by sinking or breaking up. a ship so destroyed. *The shipwreck happened miles from the shore.* *(verb)* suffer a shipwreck. *The shipwrecked passengers held on to the lifeboats.*

Shipyard – *(noun)* enclosed area where ships are made or repaired. *The shipyard was full so we had to move ahead.*

Shirk – *(verb)* avoid or neglect a duty or responsibility. *Only irresponsible people shirk their responsibilities.* *(noun)* [archaic] a person who shirks. *The shirk did not have too many friends.*

Shirker – *(noun)* neglecting responsibility. *The shirker got scolded by his boss regularly.*

Shirt – *(noun)* a garment for the upper body, with a collar and sleeves and buttons down the front. a similar garment of stretchable material without full fastenings, worn for sports. *The pattern of his shirt was very tropical.*

Shiver – *(verb)* shake slightly an uncontrollably as a result of being cold, frightened, or excited. *I shivered because of fear.* *(noun)* a momentary trembling movement. a spell or attack of shivering. *In spite of layers and layers of warm clothes, the shivers refused to stop.*

Shoal – *(noun)* **1** large number of fish swimming together. *The shoal was getting bigger and bigger.* **2** [informal] a large number of people. *The shoal headed from the stadium to the pub.* *(verb)* from shoals. *Little fish all shoaled together.*

Shock – *(noun)* a group of twelve sheaves of grain placed upright an supporting each other to allow the grain to dry and ripen. *The shock is a very effective arrangement.* *(verb)* arrange in shocks. *The farmer whistled as he shocked the grain.*

Shoddy – *(noun)* **1** badly made or done. *The sticking was very shoddy.* **2** lacking moral principle; sordid. *The neighbourhood was teeming with shoddy people.* *(noun)* an inferior yarn of fabric made from shredded woolen waste. *The farmer's wife used shoddy to make sweaters for use at home.*

Shoe – *(noun)* **1** a covering for the foot having a sturdy sole and not reaching above the ankle. a horseshoe. *He likes leather shoes.* **2** a drag for a wheel. *The shoe could not slow the vehicle.* **3** a socket on a camera for fitting a flash unit. *The shoe of the camera was broken.* **4** a metal rim or ferrule, especially on the runner of a sledge. *The shoe of the sledge needed some repair.* **5** a step for a mast. *The shoe looked too risky to climb.* **6** a box from which cards are dealt at baccarat or some other card games. *There were very few cards left in the shoe.* *(verb)* **1** fit with a shoe or shoes. *The blacksmith shoed the horse.* **2** be wearing shoes of a specified kind. *I like to shoe sneakers when running.* **3** protect with a metal shoe. *They shoed the poor animal's leg.*

Shoelace – *(noun)* a cord or leather strip passes through eyelets or hooks on opposite sides of a shoe and pulled tight and fastened. *His shoelaces had come undone.*

Shoot – *(verb)* **1** kill or wound with a bullet or arrow. cause to fire. hunt game with a gun. bring down an aircraft or person by shooting. *He shot the dummy thrice.* **2** move suddenly and rapidly. sudden and piercing. direct at someone. *The students shoot through the corridors as soon as the school gets over.* **3** kick, hit, or throw the ball or puck in an attempt to score a goal. [informal] make for a round of golf. [north American informal] play a game of pool, dice, or cards. *The player shot with all his might.* **4** film or photograph a scene, film, etc. *The director wanted to shoot the scene as soon as possible.* **5** send out buds or shoots; germinate. *The rose plant was shooting in spite of the cold weather.* **6** [informal] inject oneself with a narcotic drug. *The drug abuser shot himself.* **7** sweep swiftly down or under rapids, a waterfall, or a bridge. [informal] drive past. move a door bolt to fasten or unfasten a door. *The little birds shot under the bridge playfully.* *(noun)* **1** a young branch or sucker springing from the main stock of a tree or other plant. *The shoot is very delicate.* **2** an occasion when a group of people hunt and shoot game for sport. [British] land used for shooting game. *The young men decided to go out for a shoot.* **3** an occasion of taking photographs professionally or making a film or video: a fashion shoot. *The shoot was over in no time.*

Shop – *(noun)* **1** a building or part of a building where goods or services are sold. [informal] an act of going shopping. *The shop is closed today.* **2** a place where things are manufactured or repaired; a workshop. *We took our old car to the shop.* **3** matters concerning one's work, especially when discussed at an inappropriate time. *The retailer chose to talk shop at a funeral.* *(verb)* **1** go to a shop or shops to buy goods. look for the best available price or rate for something. *I shop on the weekends.* **2** [informal, chiefly] inform on someone. *The informer's shopping helped the police a great deal.*

Shopping – *(noun)* the purchasing of goods from shops. *Shopping is my favourite activity.*

Shore – *(noun)* a prop or beam set obliquely against something weak or unstable as a support. *Workers were worried because the shore had started splintering.* *(verb)* support or hold up with shores. *We shored the damaged door and called the carpenter for repairs.*

Short – *(adjective)* **1** of a small length or duration. travelling only a small distance before bouncing. *We took the short journey home.* **2** relatively small in extent. *He learnt the tricks of the trait in a relatively short span of time.* **3** small in height. *The short girl stood first in the queue.* **4** not having enough of lacking or deficient in. in insufficient supply. *The milkman couldn't deliver the milk because the supply was short.* **5** terse; uncivil. *At times she is short with her friends.* **6** [phonetics] categorized as short with regard to quality and length. prosody having the lesser of the two recognized durations. *The sound of 'm' in "maple" is short.* **7** stock sold in advance of being acquired. maturing at a relatively early date. *The short stock did not get too much profits for the seller.* **8** containing a high proportion of fat to flour and therefore crumbly. having poor plasticity. *I love short bread.* *(adverb)* at, to, or over a short distance. not as far as the point aimed at. *He stopped short of the destination.* *(noun)* **1** [British informal] a strong alcoholic drink, especially spirits, served in small measures. *The short was enough to get him drunk.* **2** a short film as opposed to a feature film. a short sound, vowel, or syllable. a short circuit. *The short got the attention of the critics.* **3** stock exchange a person who sells short. short-dated stocks. *The shorts did not get too much of profit.* **4** a mixture of bran and coarse flour. *My grandmother uses short in most of her recipes.* *(verb)* short-circuit. *The water heater shorted and had to be repaired.*

Shortage – *(noun)* a state of situation in which something needed cannot be obtained in sufficient amounts. *The shortage of water caused a lot of worry amongst the residents.*

Shorten – *(verb)* **1** make or become shorter. *The orator shortened his speech as the time was running out.* **2** sailing reduce the amount of sail spread. *The crew shortened the sail.*

Shortly – *(adverb)* **1** in a short time, soon. *I will be there shortly.* **2** in a few words; briefly. abruptly, sharply, or curly. *She was very upset when her husband spoke to her shortly.*

Shorts – *(plural noun)* **1** short trousers that reach only to the knees or thighs. *No one was allowed to wear shorts at the workplace.* **2** [north American] men's underpants. *He hung his shorts to dry.*

Shot – *(adjective)* **1** woven with a warp and weft of different colours, giving a contrasting effect when looked at from different angles. interspersed with a different colour. *The shot fabric brought out the beauty of the dress.* **2** [informal] ruined or worn out. US & austral drunk. *The man was shot after the party.*

Should – *(modal verb)* **1** used to indicate obligation, duty, or correctness. used to give or ask advice or suggestions. *You should make a schedule for your studies.* **2** used to indicate what is probable. *The storm should not affect this area.* **3** [formal] expressing the conditional mood. indicating the consequence of an imagined event. referring to a possible event or situation. *If things work out well, I should be off for vacations soon.* **4** used in a clause with that after a main clause describing feelings. *If my parents were to visit me, I should be very happy.* **5** used in a clause with that expressing purpose. *If I want good grades, I should study harder.* **6** the first person expressing a polite request or acceptance.*I should be able to help you with your work.* **7** expressing a conjecture or hope. *The country should get over the economic slowdown soon.*

Shoulder – *(noun)* **1** the joint between the upper arm or fore-limb and the main part of the body. the part of a bird or insect at which the wing is attached. *My shoulder started aching when I lifted the heavy suitcase.* **2** a part of something resembling a shoulder, in particular a point at which a steep slope descends from a plateau or highland area. *The shoulder offered some beautiful views of the valleys.* **3** short for hard shoulder. *We stopped the car at the shoulder.* *(verb)* **1** put over one's shoulder or shoulders to carry. *He shouldered the sack and walked away.* **2** take on a burden or responsibility. *The little girl shouldered her family's responsibilities.* **3** push out of one's way with one's shoulder. *The player shouldered his way through the crowd to get back to the dressing room.*

Shout – *(verb)* **1** speak or call out very loudly. reprimand loudly. prevent someone form speaking or being heard by shouting. *The teacher shouted at the students.* **2** [austral] treat to something, especially a drink. *The man who got the promotion shouted his colleagues to drinks.* *(noun)* **1** loud cry or call. *The watchman heard the shout.* **2** [British informal] one's turn to buy a round of drinks. *It was my shout now.*

Shove – *(verb)* **1** push roughly. *The girl shoved her friend away.* **2** [informal] put some-where carelessly or roughly. used to express angry dismissal. *I shoved the phone away.* *(noun)* a strong push. *His shove sent his friend crashing on the floor.*

Shovel – *(noun)* a tool resembling a spade with a broad blade and upturned sides, used for moving coal, earth, snow, etc. *They bought a shovel to prepare for the winters.* *(verb)* **1** move with a shovel. *The child shovelled the snow to clear the driveway.* **2** [informal] eat food quickly and in large quantities. *His mother asked him not to shovel the food inside his mouth.*

Show – *(verb)* **1** be, allow, or cause to be visible. exhibit or produce for inspection. present on a screen for viewing. represent or depict in art. allow oneself to be seen; appear in public. [informal] arrive for an appointment or at a gathering. *He showed the film in his home theatre.* **2** display or allow to be perceived. accord or treat someone with a specified quality. *She liked to show her paintings to friends.* **3**

demonstrate or prove. explain or demonstrate something to. conduct or lead: show them in, please. *The teacher showed to the principal that students can be disciplined without punishments.* **4** [north American] finish third or in the first three in a race. *The athlete was happy that he was allowed to show up in the 100 metres race.* **5** [informal] be visibly pregnant. *She was clearly showing by then. (noun)* **1** a spectacle or display. *The show was worth the money.* **2** a play or other stage performance, especially a musical. a light entertainment programme on television or radio. an event or competition involving the public display of animals, plants, or products. [informal] an undertaking, project, or organization: I run the show. *I have booked tickets for the show.* **3** an outward appearance or display of a quality or feeling. an outward display intend to give a false impression. *It was easy to see through his show.* **4** [medicine] a discharge of blood and mucus from the vagina at the onset of labour or menstruation. *The show made her feel very uncomfortable.* **5** US & austral [informal] an opportunity or chance. *They could not let go of the show at any cost.*

Shower – *(noun)* **1** a brief and usually light fall of rain or snow. *The shower lasted for barely a few minutes.* **2** a mass of small things falling or moving at once. a large number of things happening or given at the same time: a shower of awards. a group of particles produced by a comic-ray particle in the earth's atmosphere. *The meteor shower was a spectacular sight.* **3** a cubicle or bath in which a person stands under shower. *The shower was slippery.* **4** [north American] a party at which presents are given to a woman who is about to get married or have a baby. *Everyone had fun at her shower.* **5** [British informal] an incompetent or worthless group of people. *The company fired the shower at the first opportunity. (verb)* **1** fall, throw, or be thrown in a shower: broken glass showered down. *Sand showered down from the building under construction.* **2** or give a great number of things to someone. *My parents showered me with gifts on my birthday.* **3** wash oneself in a shower. *I showered before going out.*

Shred – *(noun)* **1** a strip of material that has been torn, cut, or scraped from something larger. *The shred was too small to be used as a patch.* **2** a very small amount. *I want a shred of chicken with rice. (verb)* tear or cut into shreds. *The machine shredded the papers into countless pieces.*

Shrewd – *(adjective)* **1** having or showing sharp powers of judgement; astute. *Her shrewd observations were very helpful for the company.* **2** [archaic] piercingly cold. severe. mischievous; malicious. *His shrewd approach put everyone on their guard.*

Shriek – *(verb)* utter a high-pitched piercing sound, cry, or words. *She shrieked when she saw the shadow. (noun)* **1** a high-pitched piercing cry or sound. *The hungry baby's shriek awakened its parents.* **2** [informal] an exclamation mark. *Replace the full stop with a shriek.*

Shrill – *(adjective)* high-pitched and piercing. derogatory loud and forceful. *Stop the shrill sound immediately. (verb)* make a shrill noise. *"Close the door behind you," she shrilled.*

Shrimp – *(noun)* **1** a small free-swimming edible crustacean with ten legs, mainly marine. *The shrimps swam away.* **2** derogatory a small, physically weak person. *It is rude to call someone a shrimp. (verb)* fish for shrimps. *The fisherman shrimps the whole day.*

Shrine – *(noun)* **1** a place regarded as holy because of its associations with a divinity or a sacred person. *The shrine received millions of visitors each year.* **2** a casket containing sacred relics; a reliquary. a niche or enclosure containing a religious stature or other object. *Don't take the shrine away from the temple. (verb)* [poetic] enshrine. *He shrined the house of his beloved.*

Shrink – *(verb)* **1** become or make smaller in size or amount; contract. become smaller as a result of being immersed in water. *The t-shirt shrank considerably after the first wash.* **2** move back or away in fear or disgust. be averse to or unwilling to do something. *The dog shrinked away seeing a man advancing towards it. (noun)* [informal] a psychiatrist. *The dog shrank away from the man with the stick.*

Shrivel – *(verb)* [US] wrinkle and contract, or cause to wrinkle and contract, through loss of moisture. *The long exposure to water shrivelled her hands.*

Shroud – *(noun)* **1** a length of cloth or an enveloping garment in which a dead person is wrapped for burial. *The holy man was wrapped in a saffron shroud.* **2** a thing that envelops or obscures: a shroud of mist. *The ship was soon lost in the shroud of mist.* **3** [technical] a protective casing or cover. *The shroud remained undamaged by the explosion.* **4** a set of ropes forming part of the standing rigging of a sailing boat and supporting the mast or top mast. each of the lines joining the canopy of a parachute to the harness. *The shroud was strong and reliable.* *(verb)* **1** wrap or dress in a shroud. *He was shrouded in pure white gown.* **2** cover or envelop so as to conceal from view. *The clouds soon shrouded the view.*

Shrub – *(noun)* a woody plant which is smaller than a tree and has several main stems arising at or near the ground. *The thorny shrub had to be removed.*

Shrug – *(verb)* raise slightly and momentarily to express doubt, ignorance, or indifference. dismiss something as unimportant. *He shrugged away the opinions of his subordinates.* *(noun)* **1** an act of shrugging one's shoulders. *He was irritated by her shrug.* **2** a woman's close-fitting cardigan or jacket cut short at the front and back so that only the arms and shoulders are covered. *I bought a beautiful shrug from the shop.*

Shudder – *(verb)* tremble or shake convulsively, especially from fear or repugnance. *She shuddered with fear when she saw a shadow.* *(noun)* act of shuddering. *I shudder at the memory of those tough times.*

Shuffle – *(verb)* **1** walk by dragging one's feet along or without lifting fully from the ground. restlessly shift one's position. get out of or avoid a responsibility or obligation. *The lazy boy shuffled away.* **2** rearrange by sliding them over each other quickly. sort or look through a number of thins hurriedly. *He shuffled through the papers.* 3 move around into different positions or a different order. *The seats of the employees were shuffled to increase interaction.* *(noun)* **1** a shuffling movement, walk, or sound. a quick dragging or scraping movement of the feet in dancing. a dance performed with such steps. *The shuffle upstairs alarmed everyone.* **2** an act of shuffling a pack of cards. *The shuffle was very effective.* 3 a change of order or relative positions; a reshuffle. *The organizational shuffle was aimed at increasing the productivity.* 4 a facility on CD player for playing tracks in an arbitrary order. *I turned on the shuffle on my CD player.* **5** [archaic] a piece of equivocation or subterfuge. *His shuffle was easy to see.*

Shun – *(verb)* persistently avoid, ignore, or reject. *I shunned his views on traditional education.*

Shunt – *(verb)* **1** slowly push or pull so as to make up or remove from a train. push or shove direct or divert to a less important place or through which some of the current may be diverted. *The extra carriages were shunted to another route.* *(noun)* **1** an act of shunting. *The shunt improved the performance of the train.* **2** [British informal] a motor accident, especially a collision of vehicles travelling one close behind the other. *The shunt did not cause any major damages.* **3** an electrical conductor joining two points of a circuit. *There was a fault in the shunt.* **4** [surgery] an alternative path created for the passage of blood or other fluid. *The doctors installed a shunt in his heart.*

Shut – *(verb)* **1** move or cause to move into position to block an opening. confine or exclude by closing something such as a door. prevent an opponent from scoring in a game. [informal] stop or cause someone to stop talking. *I shut the door as it was very windy outside.* **2** fold or bring together the sides or parts of. *I shut the book because I was sleepy.* **3** [chiefly British] make or become unavailable for business or service. cease or cause something to cease business or operation. *The shop has been shut for several months now.* 4 stop or cause something to stop flowing or working. *The sewage shut the drains.*

Shutter – *(noun)* **1** each of a pair of hinged panels fixed inside or outside a window that can be closed for security or privacy or to keep out the light. *The shutter was opened by the helper.* **2** [photography] a device that opens and closes to expose the film in a camera. *The shutter of the camera is dysfunctional.* **3** [music] the blind enclosing the swell box in an organ, used for controlling the volume of sound. *The shutter of the organ was found torn.* *(verb)* close the shutters of a window or building. *The shop owner shuttered the shop.*

Shuttle – *(noun)* **1** a form of transport that travels regularly between two places. *The shuttle from the office to the train station isn't running today.* **2** a bobbin with two pointed ends used for carrying the weft thread across between the warp threads in weaving. a boddin carrying the lower thread in a sewing machine. *The shuttle of the sewing machine needed to be replaced.* **3** short for shuttlecock. *The shuttle went straight into the net.* *(verb)* travel regularly between two or more places. transport in a shuttle. *I regularly shuttle between Delhi and Bangalore.*

Shy – *(verb)* fling or throw at a target. *He shied his shoe at the rat.* *(noun)* an act of shying. *His shy missed its target.*

Sibling – *(noun)* each of two or more children or offspring having one or both parents in common; a brother or sister. *I have one sibling.*

Sick – *(adjective)* affected by illness. *Half of my staff were sick.* *(noun)* **1** relating to those was are ill. *She went to the hospital to visit the sick children.* **2** suffering from serious problems. *The British economy continues to remain sick.* **3** wanting to vomit. *She was starting to feel sick.* **4** feel unwell emotionally. *She had a sick fear of returning to the hostel.* **5** intensely annoyed. *I am completely sick of your changing moods.* **6** abnormal tendencies. *He is a deeply sick man from whom children need to be protected.*

Sicken – *(verb)* **1** become disgusted or appalled. [informal] very irritating or annoying. [archaic] disgust or horror. *The stench in the abandoned house sickened me.* **2** become ill. begin to show symptoms of a particular illness. *The old man sickened as the temperature dropped.*

Sickle – *(noun)* a short-handled farming tool with a semicircular blade, used for cutting corn, lopping, or trimming. *We needed to buy a new sickle as the old one was broken.*

Sickly – *(adjective)* **1** often ill; in poor health. causing, characterized by, or indicative of poor health. *She was a sickly child.* **2** inducing discomfort or nausea: a sickly green. excessively sentimental or mawkish. *The sickly green shade of the dish made it very unappetizing.*

Sickness – *(noun)* **1** the state of being ill. a particular type of illness or disease. *Doctors are yet to diagnose my aunt's sickness.* **2** nausea or vomiting. *He was overcome by mountain sickness.*

Side – *(noun)* **1** a position to the left or right of an object, place, or central point. *Please move to the other side.* **2** either of the two halves of something regarded as divided by an imaginary central line. *The left side of the globe looked more blue when compared to the right.* **3** an upright or sloping surface of a structure or object that is not the tip or bottom and generally not the front or back. each of the flat surfaces of a solid object. each of the lines forming the boundary of a plane rectilinear figure. each of the two surfaces of something flat and thin, e.g. paper. each of the two faces of a record or of the two separate tracks on a cassette tape. *Please print on the smooth side of the paper.* **4** a part or region near the edge and away from the middle of something. subsidiary or less important: a side dish. *Please bring the side dish along with the mains.* **5** a person or group opposing another or others in a dispute or contest. the cause, interest, or attitude of tone person or group. a particular aspect: the had a disagreeable side. a person's kinship or line of descent as traced through either their father or mother: Richard was of French descent on his mother's side. *The visiting side won the debate.* **6** a sports team. *Our side won the match.*

Sidle – *(verb)* **1** walk in a furtive or stealthy manner, especially sideways or obliquely. *She sidled up to her to surprise her.* *(noun)* an instance of sidling. *His sidle was noticed by everyone.*

Siege – *(noun)* **1** a military operation in which enemy forces surround a town or building, cutting off essential supplies, with the aim of compelling the surrender of those inside. *The siege was successful after seven days.* **2** a similar operation by a police team to compel the surrender of an armed person. *The pictures of the siege were show on the news channel.*

Sieve– *(noun)* a utensil consisting of a wire or plastic mesh held in a frame, used for straining solids, from liquids, for separating coarser from finer particles, or for reducing soft solids to a pulp. *I bought a new sieve today.* *(verb)* **1** put through a sieve. *He sieves the juice before keeping it in the fridge.* **2** examine in detail. *They sieved the sample from the site.*

Sift – *(verb)* **1** put through a sieve so as to remove lumps or large particles. *He sifted the beach sand to look for small snails.* **2** cause to flow or pass as through a sieve. *He spilled soup while sifting it.* **3** descend lightly or sparsely as if having passed through a sieve. *The water sifted down the wall.* **4** examine thoroughly so as to isolate that which is important or useful. *He sifted through the papers.* *(noun)* **1** an act of sifting. *The sifted sample was kept in a box.*

Sigh – *(noun)* **1** a long, deep, audible exhalation expressing sadness, tiredness, relief, etc. *She repressed a sigh at the sight.* **2** a sound resembling this. *The sigh was audible in the otherwise silent room.* *(verb)* **1** emit a sigh. *He sighed at the loss of sleep.* **2** [poetic] yearn for. *He was sighing for freedom.*

Sight – *(noun)* **1** the faculty or power of seeing. *Her sight is perfect.* **2** the action or fact of seeing someone or something. *She was depressed at the sight of destruction.* **3** the area or distance within which someone can see or that can be seen. *It was a beautiful sight.* **4** places of interest to tourists and other visitors. *It is a famous religious sight.* **5** [informal], a person or thing having a ridiculous or unattractive appearance. *He presented an awful sight.* **6** a device on a gun or optical instrument used for assisting in precise aim or observation. *The sight of the gun was broken.* *(verb)* **1** manage to see or briefly observe. *Several bears have been sighted in the area.* **2** take aim by looking through the sights of a gun. *He took a long time sighting down the rifle.* **3** take a detailed visual measurement with or as with a sight. *He sighted the path before carpeting.* **4** adjust the sight of a gun or optical instrument. *He needs to sight his binoculars.*

Signal – *(adjective)* striking; outstanding. *The article describes the signal historical events of the city.*

Signature – *(noun)* **1** a person's name written in a distinctive way as a form of identification or authorization. *The papers were cancelled as her signatures were missing.* **2** the action of applying one's signature. *He waited an hour for her signature on the papers.* **3** a distinctive product or characteristic by which someone or something can be identified. *She made her signature dish on Sunday.* **4** music, short for key signature. *The signature of the song was brilliant.* **5** printing a letter or figure printed at the foot of one of more pages of each sheet of a book as a guide in binding. *The binding had to be redone as the signature was not put properly.* **6** a printed sheet after being folded to form a group of pages. *She prepared three signatures.* **7** [north American], the part of a medical prescription that gives instructions about the use of the [medicine] or drug prescribed. *She went to get another prescription as the signature was blurred by water on the first one.*

Significance – *(noun)* **1** the quality of being significant; importance. *The significance of her contribution was recognized by everyone.* **2** the unstated meaning to be found in words or events. *The significance of the speech was lost on many.* **3** the extent to which a result deviates from that expected to arise simply from random variation or errors in sampling. *She calculated the statistical significance wrongly.*

Significant – *(adjective)* **1** having an unstated meaning; indicative of something. *She gave her a significant glance.* **2** extensive or important enough to merit attention. *Significant percentage voted for her.* **3** [statistics] of, relating to, or having significance. *It is a significant part of the process.*

Signify – *(verb)* **1** be an indication of. *The gathering signified the importance of the event.* **2** be a symbol of; have as meaning. *The seal signifies the association's approval.* **3** indicate or declare. *The happy workers signify the company's success.* **4** be of importance. *Whether everyone agree or not do not signify.*

Silence – *(noun)* **1** complete absence of sound. *She likes to study in silence.* **2** the fact or state of abstaining from speech. *The class was asked to remain in silence.* **3** the avoidance of mentioning or discussing something. *He maintained silence on the issue.* *(verb)* **1** make silent. *He could not silence the crowd.* **2** fit with a silencer. *He repaired and silenced the old bike.*

Silent – *(adjective)* **1** not making or accompanied by any sound. without an accompanying soundtrack. *They presented a silent act.* **2** not speaking or not spoken aloud. not prone to speak much. *He is silent since yesterday.* **3** written but not pronounced, e.g. be in doubt. *She often misspell spellings with silent letters.* **4** saying or recording nothing on a particular subject. *They were silent on the subject of a raise.*

Silhouette – *(noun)* **1** the dark shape and outline of someone or something visible in restricted light against a brighter background. *She identified them from their silhouette only.* **2** a representation of someone or something showing the shape and outline only, typically coloured in solid black. *Their symbol is a silhouette of a lighthouse.* *(verb)* **1** cast or show as a silhouette: the caste was silhouetted against the sky. *The hands were silhouetted against the screen.*

Silicon – *(noun)* **1** the chemical element of atomic number 14, a shiny grey crystalline non-metal with semiconducting properties, used in making electronic circuits. *She presented a paper on the different uses of silicon.*

Silk – *(noun)* **1** a fine, strong, soft lustrous fibre produced by silkworms in making cocoons. *Silk fibre is quite expensive.* **2** thread or fabric made from this fibre. *She used silk thread to decorate the invitation.* **3** garments made from silk, especially as worn by a jockey in the colours of a particular horse owner. *He wore a red silk.* **4** [British, informal] a queen's counsel. *He is a member of silk.* **5** the silky styles of the female maize flower. *He removed the silks before boiling the cob.*

Silky – *(adjective)* **1** of or resembling silk. *The fabric was silky soft.* **2** suave and smooth: a silky, seductive voice. *He has a silky voice.*

Sill – *(noun)* **1** a shelf or slab of stone, wood, or metal at the foot of a window or doorway. *She kept the flowers on the window sill.* **2** a strong horizontal member at the base of any structure, e.g. in the frame of a motor or rail vehicle. *He scrapped his hand by the sill of the motor.* **3** [geology] a tabular sheet of igneous rock intruded between and parallel with the existing strata. compare with dyke. *He examined the sill.* **4** an underwater ridge or rock extending across the bed of a body of water. *He took many pictures of the growth along the sill.*

Silver – *(noun)* **1** a precious shiny grayish-white metal, the chemical element of atomic number 47. *She gifted her friend a silver pendant.* **2** a shiny grey-white colour or appearance like that of siliver. *She drives a silver car.* **3** silver dishes, containers, or cutlery. household cutlery of any material. *The hotel's silver was stolen by the guests.* **4** coins made from silver or from a metal that resembles silver. *In past, its cost was four silvers.* *(verb)* **1** coat or plate with silver. *She silvered the board.* **2** provide with a backing of a silver-coloured material in order to make it reflective. *He silvered this glass himself.* **3** [poetic] give a silvery appearance. *They silvered the stage with lights.* **4** turn or cause to turn grey or white. *Her hair silvered a long time ago.*

Similar – *(adjective)* **1** of the same kind in appearance, character, or quantity, without being identical. *She bought similar gifts for all the kids.* **2** [geometry] having the same angles and proportions, though of different sizes. *He successfully calculated the angles of similar triangles.* *(noun)* **1** [chiefly] a person or thing similar to another. *I met his similar last night.* **2** a substance that produces effects resembling the symptoms of a disease the basis of homeopathic treatment. *He was cured by the treatment of similars.*

Similarity – *(noun)* the state or fact of being similar. *They were asked to list the similarities.*

Simile – *(noun)* a figure of speech involving the comparison of one thing with another thing of a different kind. *He used too many similes in his essay.*

Simmer – *(verb)* **1** stay or cause to stay just below boiling point while bubbling gently. *The soup smelled wonderful after it started simmering.* **2** be in a state of suppressed anger or excitement. become calmer and quieter. *The crowd was simmering at the injustice. (noun)* **1** a state or temperature just below boiling point. *The dish should be kept at simmer.*

Simple – *(adjective)* **1** easily, understood or done. *She taught them simple calculations.* **2** plain and uncomplicated in form, nature, or design. humble and unpretentious. *He is a simple man.* **3** composed of a single element; not compound. not divided or branched. consisting of a single lens or component. *He bought simple lens binoculars.* **4** of very low intelligence. *He is simple minded.* **5** denoting a tense formed without an auxiliary. *We did an exercise on simple present tense.* **6** payable on the sum loaned only. compare with compound. *He paid back the simple interest. (noun)* a medicinal herb, or a [medicine] made from one. *He stored the simple in glass bottles.*

Simplicity – *(noun)* **1** the quality or condition of being simple. *Everyone was impressed by his simplicity.* **2** a thing that is simple. *He prefers the simplicity of the village life.*

Simplify – *(verb)* make more simple. *She simplified the problem for him.*

Simulate – *(verb)* imitate or reproduce the appearance, character, or conditions of. *They were asked to simulate the experiment.*

Simultaneous – *(adjective)* occurring, operating, or done at the same time. *Both of them were burning crackers simultaneously.*

Sin – *(noun)* **1** an immoral act considered to be a transgression against divine law. *Immortality is considered a sin.* **2** an act regarded as a serious offence. *His betrayal was a sin against the family. (verb)* commit a sin. cause offence or harm to. *He was pardoned as he sinned unknowingly.*

Sinful – *(adjective)* immoral, committing sins.*His actions were sinful.*

Sinfully – *(adverb)* activity sinful. *It was sinfully delicious.*

Sinfulness – *(noun)* in the manner of committing sins. *The sinfulness of their act is unforgiveable.*

Since – *(preposition)* in the intervening period between and the time under consideration. *They have been fighting since morning. (conjunction)* **1** during or in the time after. *She has stopped eating potatoes since she visited her dietician.* **2** for the reason that; because. *He didn't eat the pizza since he has allergic to its toppings. (adverb)* from the time mentioned until the present or the time under consideration. *I met her in school but haven't seen her since.* **2** ago. *Since long the ritual was discontinued.*

Sincere – *(adjective)* proceeding from or characterized by genuine feelings; free from pretence or deceit. *Their sincere work won them the first prize.*

Sincerity – *(noun)* the absence of pretence, deceit or high procrisy. *Her sincerity was recognized by the administration.*

Sing – *(verb)* **1** make musical sounds with the voice, especially words with a set tune. perform in this way. sing in accompaniment to a song or piece of music. *All gathered to hear her sing.* **2** make characteristic melodious whistling and twittering sounds. *I can hear the sparrows singing.* **3** make a high-pitched sound. *The kettle is singing.* **4** [informal] act as an informer to the police. *After a minor threat, he started singing.* **5** recount or celebrate, especially in poetry: sing someone's praises. [archaic] compose poetry. *He always sing his teacher's praises. (noun)* [informal] an act or spell of singing. *They are meeting tonight for a bit of sing.*

Singer – *(noun)* a person who sings, especially professionally. *She's my favourite singer.*

Singe – *(verb)* **1** burn or be burnt lightly or superficially. *He singed his hair in the lab.* **2**

burn the bristles or down off to prepare it for cooking. *He signed it perfectly before cooking.* *(noun)* a light or superficial burn. *She got a singe from the hot pot.*

Single – *(adjective)* **1** only one; not one of several. regarded as distinct from others in a group. even one use for emphasis: they didn't receive a single reply. designed or suitable for one person. *He didn't eat a single cookie.* **2** not involved in a stable romantic or sexual relationship. *He is single.* **3** consisting of one part. having only one whorl of petals. *It is one single piece work.* **4** [British] valid for an outward journey only. *It's a single pass.* **5** [archaic] free from duplicity or deceit: a pure and single heat. *No one can doubt the single nature of children.* *(noun)* **1** a single person or thing. *The singles are having their own party.* **2** a short record with one song on each side. *Her single was a major hit.* **3** [US informal] a one-dollar note. *You owe me a single.* **4** [cricket] a hit for one run. baseball a hit which allows the batter to proceed safely to first base. *They just need a single to win.* **5** a game or competition for individual players. *She won the single's championship.* **6** bell ringing a system of changeringing in which one pair of bells changes places at each round. *All bells in the single sounded the same.* *(verb)* **1** choose someone or something from a group for special treatment. *The hotel singled him out because of his popularity.* **2** thin out. *They have singled the pile.* **3** reduce to a single line. *The queue singled after lunch.* **4** [baseball] hit a single. cause to be scored by hitting a single. advance by hitting a single. *He singled at a crucial point.*

Singly – *(adverb)* one at a time; separately or individually. *The teacher talked to each student singly.*

Singular – *(adjective)* **1** exceptionally good or great; remarkable strange or eccentric in some respect. *He is a singular performer.* **2** single; unique. grammar denoting or referring to just one person or thing. *The test was to write singular form of the given words.* **3** [mathematics] having a zero determinant. *The answer was singular.* **4** [physics] relating to or of the nature of a singularity. *He studied singular atom.* *(noun)* [grammar] the singular form of word. *Singular of men is man.*

Sinister – *(adjective)* suggestive of evil or harm. *He acted out his sinister ideas.*

Sink – *(noun)* **1** a fixed basin with a water supply and outflow pipe. *The sink broke yesterday.* **2** short for sinkhole. *The concrete constructions have reduced the number of sinks.* **3** a pool or marsh in which a river's water disappears by evaporation or percolation. *He fell in the sink.* **4** [technical] a body or process which absorbs or removes energy or a particular component from a system. the opposite of source. *It acts as a heat sink.* **5** denoting a school or estate situated in a socially deprived area: a sink school. *She teaches in a sink school.*

Sinner – *(noun)* a person who sins. *He was termed a sinner by the society.*

Sinus – *(noun)* **1** [anatomy & zoology] a cavity within a bone or other tissue, especially one in the bones of the face or skull connecting with the nasal cavities. *His sinus troubles him in the winters.* **2** [anatomy] an irregular venous or lymphatic cavity, reservoir, or dilated vessel. *The doctors took care not to damage the sinus during the operation.* **3** [medicine] an infected tract leading from a deep-seated infection and discharging pus to the surface. *He had to be operated to remove the sinus.* **4** [botany] a rounded notch between two lobes on the margin of a leaf or petal. *He studied the sinus under a microscope.*

Sip – *(verb)* drink by taking small mouthfuls. *He sipped the tea slowly.* *(noun)* a small mouthful of liquid. *Just a sip of milk is left.*

Siphon – *(noun)* **1** a tube used to convey liquid upwards from a container and then down to a lower level, the flow being forced initially by suction and maintained by atmospheric pressure. *It worked as a siphon.* **2** [zoology] a tubular organ in an aquatic animal through which water is drawn in or expelled. *This creature uses the siphon to survive underwater.* *(verb)* **1** draw off convey by means of a siphon. *The store owner siphoned oil in their container.* **2** draw off over a period of time, especially illicitly: *He's been siphoning money off the firm.*

Sir – *(noun)* **1** a polite or respectful form of address to a man. *They all call him 'sir'.* **2** used to address a man at the beginning of a formal or business letter. *He couldn't write anything in his letter after 'Dear sir'.* **3** used as a title before the forename or a knight or baronet. *He was proud to have earned the title of 'sir'.*

Siren – *(noun)* **1** a device that makes a loud prolonged signal or warning sound. *The siren woke him up.* **2** [Greek] each of a number of women or winged creatures whose singing lured unwary sailors on to rocks. *She sang like a siren.* **3** a woman who is considered to be alluring but also dangerous in some way. *She is considered a siren.* **4** an eel-like American amphibian, typically living in muddy pools. *He caught a siren and immediately throw it way.*

Sissy – *(noun)* a person regarded as feeble or effeminate. *He was angry when they called him sissy.* *(adjective)* feeble or effeminate. *It was a sissy effort.*

Sister – *(noun)* **1** a woman or girl in relation to other daughters and sons of her parents. *He has two sisters.* **2** a female friend or associate. [north American] a fellow black woman. *Her sisters from work stood up for her.* **3** denoting an organization or a place which bears a relationship to another of common origin or allegiance. *It is a sister organization of a successful brand.* **4** a member of religious order of woman. *The church sister is very polite.* **5** [British] a senior female nurse. *He asked the sister for first aid.*

Sister-in-law – *(noun)* **1** the sister of one's wife or husband. *He hates his sister-in-law.* **2** the wife of one's brother or brother-in-law. *His sister-in-law cooks very well.*

Sit – *(verb)* **1** be or cause to be in a position in which one's weight is supported by one's buttocks rather than one's feet and one's back is upright. rest with the hind legs bent and the body close to the ground. *He sat down immediately after the race.* **2** remain on its nest to incubate its egg. *I saw a sitting pigeon.* **3** pose for an artist or photographer. *He sits for artists on weekends.* **4** be or remain in a particular position or state. be harmonious with. *They were sitting in a state of peace.* **5** be engaged in its business. serve as a member of a council, jury, or other official body. [British] take an examination. *She will sit for the entrance test next month.* **6** have enough seats for. *The room can sit 20 people.* **7** look after children, pets, or a house while the parents or owners are away: the want me to house-sit for them. *She often baby-sit to earn extra money.* 8 [north American] not use in a game. *He was asked to sit the second half of the game.* *(noun)* a period of sitting. *He paused for while to a sit in the shade.*

Site – *(noun)* **1** an area of ground an which something is constructed. *This is the site for proposed metro station.* **2** denoting a protest in which demonstrators occupy their workplace or sit down on the ground in a public place, refusing to leave until their demands are met. *The workers sat at the factory site demanding raise in salaries.*

Sitting– *(noun)* **1** a period or spell of sitting. *He was bored in the sitting.* **2** a period of time when a group of people are served a meal. *She was absent from the afternoon sitting.* *(adjective)* **1** in a seated position. *Wrong sitting posture can be very harmful in the long run.* **2** currently present or in office. *The doctor is sitting for another hour.*

Situate – *(verb)* **1** place in a particular location or context. *He situated the new comers in perfect roles.* **2** be in a specified financial or marital position. *They are situated perfectly in their marriage.* *(adjective)* law or [archaic] situated. *People often situate themselves in trouble.*

Situation – *(noun)* **1** a set of circumstances in which one finds oneself. *He got caught in a bad situation.* **2** the location and surroundings of a place. *The situation of her new home is great.* **3** a job. *The situation is vacant for the last five months.*

Six – *(cardinal number)* **1** equivalent to the product of two and three; one more than five, or four less than ten; 6. *I have six pens in my bag.* **2** [cricket] a hit that reached the boundary without first striking the ground, scoring six runs. *He scored a six.* **3** a group of six brownies or cubs. *They became friend in their Six Cubs group.*

Sixteen – *(cardinal number)* equivalent to the product of four and four; one more than fifteen, or six more than ten; 16. *She has won 16 races so far.*

Sixty – *(cardinal number)* the number equivalent to the product of six and ten; ten more than fifty; 60. *There are 60 chairs in that room.*

Size – *(noun)* **1** a thing's overall dimension. *Russia is six times the size of India.* **2** magnitude. *She was overawed by the size of the building. (verb)* sort out in terms of how large they are. *I hardly find any shirt in my size.*

Sizzle – *(verb)* **1** make a hissing sound when frying or roasting. *The meat is sizzling on the grill.* **2** [informal] be very hot. *The music was sizzling.* **3** [informal] be very exciting or passionate, especially sexually. *They are a sizzling pair. (noun)* an instance or the sound of sizzling. *The sizzle of the grill could be heard in the other room.*

Sizzling – *(adjective)* very hot. *The chemistry between the couple is sizzling.*

Skate – *(noun)* an edible marine fish of the ray family with a diamond-shaped body. *I cooked skate last night.*

Skeleton – *(noun)* framework of bone cartilage supports the body or other structure. *I saw skeletons of dinosaurs in the museum.*

Sketch – *(noun)* **1** a rough or unfinished drawing or painting. *He drew an impressive sketch of the couple.* **2** a brief written or spoken account or description. *She has provided a character sketch of the new officer.* **3** a short humorous play, scene, or performance. *They presented an interesting sketch.* **4** [informal], dated a comical or amusing person or thing. *The sketch entertained everyone at the party. (verb)* make a sketch of give a brief account or general outline of. *He sketched the plan of action for the next term.*

Skewer – *(noun)* a long piece of wood or metal used for holding pieces of food together during cooking. *She poked him with a skewer. (verb)* fasten together or pierce with a pin or skewer. *My little niece likes to skewer the marshmallows herself.*

Ski – *(noun)* each of a pair of long, narrow pieces of hard flexible material fastened under the fee for travelling over snow. a similar device attached beneath a vehicle or aircraft. *My brother gifted me a new pair of skis. (verb)* **1** travel over snow on skis. *We have been skiing in the evening everyday for the last one week.*

Skid – *(verb)* **1** slide, typically sideways, on slippery ground or as a result of stopping or turning too quickly. slip; slide. *He skidded on the ice.* **2** fasten a skid to as a brake. *He skidded his car to avoid collision. (noun)* **1** an act of skidding. *The skid was heard by everyone.* **2** a runner attached to the underside of an aircraft for use when landing on snow or grass. [north American] each of a set of wooden rollers for moving a log or other heavy object. *It didn't stop on time as the skids were worn.* **3** a breaking device consisting of a wooden or metal shoe that prevents a wheel from revolving. *He used the skid at the perfect moment.* **4** a beam or plank of wood used to support a ship under construction or repair. *They used double skids to support the heavy ship.*

Skill– *(noun)* the ability to do something well; expertise or dexterity. *She has the skill to drive heavy trucks. (verb)* train to do a particular task. *The training made him skilled in carpentry.*

Skim – *(verb)* **1** remove from the surface of liquid. *He skimmed the milk.* **2** move quickly and lightly over or on a surface or through the air. throw so that it bounces several times on the surface of water. *She skimmed the stones over the lake water.* **3** read quickly, noting only the important points. deal with or treat briefly or superficially. *He skimmed through the news report.* **4** [informal] steal or embezzle in small amounts over a period of time. *He has been skimming the organization's funds over the last year. (noun)* **1** a thin layer of a substance on the surface of a liquid. *There was a skim of oil over the water.* **2** an act of reading something quickly or superficially. *It was a quick skim through the book.*

Skimp – *(verb)* expend fewer resources on something than are necessary in an attempt to economize. *They skimped the farewell lunch.*

Skin – *(noun)* **1** the thin layer of tissue forming the natural outer covering of the body of a person or animal. the skin of a dead animal used as material for clothing or other items. a container made fro the skin of an animal, used for holding liquids. *She used moisturizer to soften her dry skin.* **2** the peel or outer layer of a fruit or vegetable. the outermost layer of a structure such as an aircraft. the thin outer covering of a sausage. a thin layer forming on the surface of a hot liquid as it cools. *I eat apples with their skins.* **3** [British informal] a skinhead. *The skin did not have too many friends.* **4** [informal] a drum or drum head. *The drummer beat the skin with the drumstick.* **5** [informal] relating to or denoting pornography; the skin trade. *They earned money off the skin.* **6** [US] a card game in which each player has one card which they bet will not be the first to be matched by a card which they bet will not be the first to be matched by a card dealt from the pack. *They played a game of skin.* **7** [informal] a cigarette paper. *He rolled the skin around the tobacco.* *(verb)* **1** remove the skin from graze a part of one's body. *I skinned my arm against the wall.* 2 [archaic] cover with or form skin. *The surgeons skinned the wound.* **3** [informal] take money form or swindle. *The thieves skinned the poor students.* **4** [informal] take the ball past with ease. *The player skinned across the field.* **5** [British] [informal] make a cannabis cigarette. *They skinned after the class.*

Skip – *(noun)* **1** [British] a large transportable open-topped container for bulky refuse. *The skip needed to be emptied.* **2** a cage or bucket in which workers or materials are lowered and raised in mines and quarries. *The skip was being repaired.* **3** variant spelling of skep. *Not too many bees took to the skep.*

Skipper – *(noun)* the captain of a ship, boat, or aircraft. the captain of a side in a game or sport. *The skipper is down with fever.* *(verb)* act as captain of. *She knows how to skipper small yatchs.*

Skirmish – *(noun)* an episode of irregular of unpremeditated fighting, especially between small or outlying parts of armies. *The skirmishes were tiring and fruitless.* *(verb)* engage in a skirmish. *They skirmished with the king's army.*

Skirt – *(noun)* **1** a woman's outer garment fastened around the waist and hanging down around the legs. the part of a coat or dress that hangs below the waist. *She wore a black skirt.* **2** a surface that conceals or protects the wheels or underside of a vehicle or aircraft. the curtain that hangs round the base of a hovercraft to contain the air cushion. *The skirt was very dirty.* **3** an animal's diaphragm and other membranes as food. a cut of meat from the lower flank. *She gave him the skirt from the dish.* **4** a small flap on a saddle covering the bar from which the stirrup hangs. *The skirt broke as it was very old.* **5** an edge, border, or extreme part. *The tree is on the skirts of the estate.* *(verb)* go round or past the edge of. avoid dealing with. *They both have been skirting around the main issue.*

Skittle – *(noun)* **1** a game played with wooden pins, typically nine in number, set up at the end of an alley to be bowled down with a wooden ball or disc. a game played with similar pins set up on a board to be knocked down by swinging a suspended ball. *He didn't win even a single game of skittles.* **2** a pin used in the game of skittles. *He bought a skittle-shaped eraser.* **3** chess that is not played seriously. *People often play skittles game at the coffee shop.* *(verb)* knock over as if in a game of skittles. get out in rapid succession. *In his hurry he skittled the display.*

Skulk – *(verb)* hide or move around secretly, typically with a sinister or cowardly motive. *The spy skulked around the colony.* *(noun)* a group of foxes. *The skulk only came out at night.*

Skull – *(noun)* a bone framework enclosing the brain of a vertebrate. a person's head or brain. *I bought a model of a skull.* *(verb)* hit on the head. *She skulled him.*

Sky – *(noun)* **1** the region of the atmosphere and outer space seen from the earth. *The sky is clear today.* **2** heaven; heavenly power. *He asked the* *skies for help. (verb)* hit high into the air. *He skied the last ball.*

Skyline – *(noun)* an outline of land and buildings defined against the sky. *It's a beautiful skyline.*

Slab – *(noun)* **1** a large, thick, flat piece of solid material, in particular stone, concrete, or heavy food. *The slab fell down and broke.* **2** a flat, heavy table top or counter used for food preparation. a table used for laying a body on in a mortuary. *She asked the maid to clean the slab properly.* **3** an outer piece of timber sawn from a log. *The slab was used to make the table.* **4** a large, smooth body of rock lying at a sharp angle to the horizontal. *The slab jutted out from the side of the cliff. (verb)* remove slabs from to prepare it for sawing into planks. *They slabbed the log.*

Slack – *(noun)* coal dust or small pieces of coal. *He cleaned the slack off the floor.*

Slacken – *(verb)* reduce or decrease in intensity. *The children slackened their pace to let others catch up.*

Slacks – *(noun)* casual trousers. *She had outgrown her pair of slacks.*

Slake – *(verb)* **1** quench. satisfy. *The athletes slaked their thirst after the long run.* **2** combine with water to produce calcium hydroxide. *They slaked water and calcium in the lab.*

Slam – *(noun)* a grand slam or small slam, for which bonus points are scored if bid and made. *He won the slam.*

Slander – *(noun)* the action or crime of making a false spoken statement damaging to a person's reputation. compare with libel. a false and malicious spoken statement. *He sued the company for slander. (verb)* make such statements about. *He slandered the government.*

Slang – *(noun)* [informal] language that is more common in speech than in writing and is typically restricted to a particular context or group. *He has learned the language but still faces problem with local slang. (verb)* attack using abusive language. *He slanged the other driver.*

Slant – *(verb)* **1** diverge from the vertical or horizontal; slope or lean. *The building slanted dangerously.* **2** present or view from a particular angle, especially in a biased or unfair way. *The manager slanted the appraisal to benefit some employees. (noun)* **1** a sloping position. *The slant was a popular play area for the children.* **2** a point of view. *Not everyone agreed with his slant. (adjective)* sloping. *The slant building needed to be repaired immediately.*

Slap – *(verb)* **1** hit or strike with the palm of one's hand or a flat object. hit against with athe sound of such an action. reprimand someone forcefully. *The older child slapped the younger one.* **2** apply something quickly, carelessly, or forcefully. impose a fine or other penalty on. *The police officer slapped a penalty on the reckless driver. (noun)* **1** an act or sound of slapping. *The slap was heard outside the house.* **2** make up. *The slap was visible clearly. (adverb)* suddenly and directly, especially with great force. exactly; right. *The chimpanzee jumped slap at the man.*

Slapdash – *(adjective & adverb)* done too hurriedly and carelessly. *It was a slapdashed project.*

Slapstick – *(noun)* **1** comedy based on deliberately clumsy actions and humorously embarrassing events. *He enjoys slapstick humour.* **2** a device consisting of two flexible pieces of wood joined together at one end, used by clowns and in pantomime to produce a loud slapping noise. *The children loved the slapstick act at the circus.*

Slash – *(verb)* **1** cut with a violent sweeping movement. *The tiger slashed the sheet with its claws.* **2** reduce greatly. vigorously incisive or effective. *The workforce was slashed considerably to deal with the losses.* **3** lash, whip, or thrash severely. criticize severely. *The horseman slashed the whip at the rearing horse. (noun)* **1** a cut made with a wide, sweeping stroke. *The slash needed to be treated immediately.* **2** a bright patch or flash of colour or light. *The slash of yellow light blinded me for a few seconds.* **3** an oblique stroke used between alternatives, in fractions and ratios, or between separate elements of a text. *The slash was not clearly legible, leading to considerable confusion.* **4** an act of urinating. *The man was* *caught taking a slash against the tree.* **5** debris resulting from the felling or destruction of trees. *The slash was a proof that the environment was under threat.*

Slat – *(noun)* a thin, narrow piece of wood or other material, especially one of a series which overlap or fit into each other, as in a venetian blind. *The slats were left piled up on the wet floor.*

Slate – *(noun)* **1** a fine grained grey, green, or bluish purple metamorphic rock easily split into smooth, flat plates. a flat plate of such rock used as roofing material. *The slate formed spectacular scenery in the hills.* **2** a plate of slate formerly used in school for writing on. *She wrote with a piece of chalk on the slate.* **3** a bluish grey colour. *The slate suited the décor.* **4** a list of candidates of election to a post or office. a record of a person's debt or credit: put it on the slate. a range of something on offer. *It was difficult to select the most suitable candidate from the slate.* **5** a board showing the identifying details of a take of a film, held in front of the camera at the beginning and end of the take. *The slate showed take 24. (verb)* **1** cover with slates. *They slated the exteriors of the house.* **2** criticize severely. *The teacher slated the students for their bad behaviour.* **3** schedule; plan. nominate as a candidate for an office or post. *The party slated their best worker for the post.*

Slaughter – *(noun)* **1** the killing of farm animals for food. *The slaughter was a grisly sight to see.* **2** the killing of a large number of people in a cruel or violent way. *There is no justification for the slaughter.* **3** a thorough defeat. *The team needed to introspect after suffering the slaughter. (verb)* **1** kill for food. *He slaughtered the goat to feed his family.* **2** kill in a cruel or violent way. *People stopped the criminal in time from slaughtering the family.* **3** defeat thoroughly. *The visiting team slaughtered the hosts on their home turf.*

Slave – *(noun)* **1** a person who is the legal property of another and is forced to obey them. a person who is excessively dependent upon or controlled by something: a slave to fashion. *She was but a slave to fitness.* **2** a device, or part of one, directly controlled by another. compare with master. *The slave hard disk has crashed. (verb)* **1** work excessively hard. *I slaved at work for two years before realizing that I was ignoring my family.* **2** the action or process of enslaving people. *You cannot slave anyone now.* **3** subject to control by another. *He was slaved by his commitment to his work.*

Slavish – *(adjective)* **1** showing no attempt at originality. *The slavish writer churned out manuscript after manuscript of unsuccessful writing.* **2** servile or submissive. *His slavish attitude put everyone off.*

Slay – *(verb)* **1** kill in a violent way. murder someone. *The criminal slayed the victim mercilessly.* **2** greatly impress or amuse. *The comedian slayed the audience.*

Sleazy – *(adjective)* **1** sordid, corrupt, or immoral. squalid and seedy. *His sleazy actions are bound to land him in trouble one day.* **2** flimsy. *It is too cold to wear sleazy clothes.*

Sledge – *(noun)* a vehicle on runners for travelling over snow or ice, either pushed, pulled, or allowed to slide downhill. a toboggan. *My father bought me a new sledge. (verb)* ride or carry on a sledge. *I sledged down the snow-covered hill.*

Sledge-hammer – *(noun)* **1** a large, heavy hammer used for breaking rocks, driving in posts, etc. *The sledge-hammer was too heavy for me to carry.* **2** very powerful, forceful, or unsubtle: sledgehammer blows. *The sledge-hammer went on pounding the crowd with his terrible words.*

Sleek – *(adjective)* **1** smooth, glossy, and healthy looking. *She has sleek hair.* **2** wealthy and well groomed in appearance. elegant and streamlined: a sleek car. *They bought a sleek car for their anniversary. (verb)* make sleek by applying pressure or moisture. *The hair-dresser sleeked her hair.*

Sleep – *(noun)* **1** a regularly recurring condition of body and mind in which the nervous system is inactive, the eyes closed, the postural muscles relaxed, and consciousness practically suspended. *I went to sleep really late in the night.* **2** a gummy secretion found in the corners of the eyes after sleep. *He cleaned the sleep and got up to brush his teeth.* *(verb)* **1** rest in such a condition. recover from something by going to sleep. remain asleep or in bed later than usual in the morning. *I slept really late last night.* **2** provide with beds or bedrooms. *I will sleep my friends in my house if they are too tired to go home.* **3** have sexual intercourse or be involved in a sexual relationship. have many casual sexual partners. *The man sleeps with many women.*

Sleepless – *(adjective)* experiencing lack of sleep. *I spent many sleepless nights worrying about my exam results.*

Sleeper – *(noun)* **1** a sleeping car or a train carrying sleeping cars. *The sleeper was very comfortable.* **2** a sleep suit for a baby or small child. *The sleeper was too small for the baby.* **3** a sofa or chair that converts into a bed. *The sleeper did not take too much space.* **4** a film, book, play, etc. that suddenly achieves success after initially attracting little attention. *The writer was thrilled when his book turned out to be a sleeper.* **5** a secret agent who remains inactive for a long period while establishing a secure position. *The intelligence confirmed that there were several sleepers in the department.* **6** a ring or bar worn in a pierced ear to keep the hole from closing. *The sleeper she wore was very pretty.* **7** a wooden or concrete beam laid transversely under railway track to support it. *The sleepers were made of sturdy wood.* **8** a stocky fish with mottled coloration. *The sleeper swam around lazily.*

Sleepy – *(adjective)* **1** needing or ready for sleep. *I am very sleepy.* **2** without much activity. not dynamic or able to respond to change. *He knew he couldn't get anywhere unless he stopped being so sleepy about his work.*

Sleet – *(noun)* rain containing some ice, or snow melting as it falls. [US] a thin coating of ice formed by sleet or rain freezing on coming into contact with a cold surface. *The sleet made the roads slippery.* *(verb)* sleet falls. *It sleeted in the morning.*

Sleeve – *(noun)* **1** the part of a garment that wholly or partly covers a person's arm. *The sleeves of his pullover were too tight.* **2** a protective paper or cardboard cover for a record. a protective or connecting tube fitting over a rod, spindle, or smaller tube. *Please put the record in the sleeve.* **3** a windsock. a drogue towed by an aircraft. *The sleeve of the aircraft was damaged.*

Sleigh – *(noun)* a sledge drawn by horses or reindeer. *The sleigh was heavy but the horses drew it without any problems.* *(verb)* ride on a sleigh. *The farmer sleighed the entire distance to the town.*

Sleight – *(noun)* the use of dexterity or cunning, especially so as to deceive. *He managed to fool everyone with his sleight.*

Slender – *(adjective)* **1** gracefully thin. *The athletic girl was very slender.* **2** barely sufficient: people of slender means. *The slender villagers chose to move to cities for work.*

Slice – *(noun)* **1** a thin, broad piece of food cut from a larger portion. a portion or share. *I would love to have a slice of cake.* **2** a utensil with a broad, flat blade for lifting foods such as cake and fish. *The fish slid off the slice.* **3** a sliced stroke or shot. *The batsman delighted the crowd with his elegant slice.* *(verb)* **1** cut into slices. cut with or as if with a sharp implement. *She slices the cakes very easily.* **2** move easily and quickly. *The beautiful race car sliced through the other cars to take the lead.* **3** strike so that it curves away to the right for a left handed player, the left. propel with a glancing contact so that it travels for ward spinning. *The batsman sliced the ball through to the boundary.*

Slick – *(adjective)* **1** done or operating in an impressively smooth and efficient way. glibly assured. *His slick operating the computer impressed the interviewer.* **2** smooth and glossy. smooth, wet, and slippery. *One could see their reflection in the slick floor.* *(noun)* **1** an oil slick. *The slick was disastrous for marine life.* **2** a racing car or bicycle tyre without a tread, for use in dry weather conditions. *The slicks helped him race ahead of his competitors.* 3 a glossy magazine. *I can never tire of flipping through a slick.* **4** a glibly assured person. *The slick managed to* *impress his supervisor but not his peers. (verb)* **1** make flat and slick with water, oil, or cream. cover with a film of liquid. *The hairdresser slicked her hair with oil.* **2** make someone or something smart, tidy, or stylish. *Her mom slicked her for the party.*

Slide – *(verb)* **1** move along a smooth surface, especially downwards, while maintaining continuous contact with it. *Children slid down the slides.* **2** change gradually to a worse condition or lower level. *Board members helplessly watched as the stock prices slid. (noun)* **1** a structure with a smooth sloping surface for children to slide down. a smooth stretch of ice or packed snow for sliding or tobogganing on. *Children didn't play on the dirty slides.* **2** an act of sliding. a part of a machine or instrument that slides. *The slide was fun for the children.* **3** a rectangular piece for glass on which an object is mounted or placed for examination under a microscope. *The slides had all been prepared and mounted by the technician.* **4** a mounted transparency, especially one placed in a projector for viewing on a screen. *The slides prepared by the presenter were very informative.* **5** a hairslide. *She fastened her hair with a red hairslide.*

Slight – *(adjective)* **1** small in degree; inconsiderable. not profound or substantial. *Even a slight drop in the temperature now will make it uncomfortably cold.* **2** not sturdy and strongly built. *He was often ridiculed by his friends for his slight built. (verb)* **1** insult by treating them without proper respect or attention. *The director slighted the actors for their shoddy acting.* **2** raze or destroy. *The army slighted the village. (noun)* an insult caused by a failure to show someone proper respect or attention. *The slight hurt her a lot.*

Slim – *(adjective)* **1** gracefully thin; slenderly built. small in width and long and narrow in shape. *The slim girl looked like a model.* **2** very small: a slim chance. *There's a slim chance that the actor will attend the party tonight.* crafty or unscrupulous. *(verb)* make or become thinner, especially by dieting and sometimes exercising. reduce to a smaller size to make it more efficient. *He has slimmed down considerably. (noun)* **1** a course or period of slimming. *The slim helped her improve her health.* **2** African term for aids. *He was distressed to discover that he had slim.*

Slime – *(noun)* an unpleasantly moist, soft, and slippery substance. *I slipped on the slime. (verb)* cover with slime. *They slimed each other.*

Sling – *(noun)* a sweetened drink of spirits, especially gin, and water. *A good sling is enough to make him happy.*

Slink – *(verb)* move quietly with gliding steps, in a stealthy or sensuous manner. come or go unobtrusively or furtively. (noun) an act of slinking. *The thief slinked through the kitchen door and headed towards the safe.*

Slip – *(noun)* **1** a small piece of paper for writing on or that gives printed information. *He gave the waiter a slip, instructing him to bring the surprise birthday cake.* **2** a long, thin, narrow strip of wood or other material. *The slip was risky as it had splintered.* **3** a small, slim young person: a slip of a girl. *She is such a slip of a girl and yet she wants to lose more weight.* **4** a printer's proof on a long piece of paper; a galley proof. *The slip was approved without too many issues.* **5** a cutting taken from a plant for grafting or planting; a scion. *The slip shooted early.*

Slipper – *(noun)* a comfortable slip on shoe that is worn indoors. a light slip on shoe, especially one used for dancing. *I like to rubber slippers at home. (verb)* beat with a slipper. *I don't mind wearing my slippers even when I am stepping out.*

Slippery – *(adjective)* **1** difficult to hold firmly or stand on through being smooth, wet, or slimy. *The surface was slippery because of the rain.* **2** evasive and unpredictable. changing in meaning according to context or point of view. *She had some slippery moods.*

Slipshod – *(adjective)* **1** lacking in care, thought, or organization. *She had a slipshod way of working.* **2** worn down at the heel. *His slipshod trousers gave his poverty away.*

Slit – *(noun)* a long, narrow cut or opening. *The slit was getting longer by the minute. (verb)* **1** make a slit in. cut into strips. *The magician* *slit the cloth into ribbons.* **2** form into slits. *The magician slit the cloth.*

Slither – *(verb)* move smoothly over a surface with a twisting or oscillating motion. slide or slip unsteadily on a loose or slippery surface. *The snake slithered around in the enclosure. (noun)* **1** a slithering movement. *The slither of the snake creeped everyone out.* **2** a sliver. *The slither can hurt your finger.*

Slob – *(noun)* **1** a lazy and slovenly person. *He was such a slob when it came to keeping his workplace clean.* **2** muddy land. *My shoes got dirty in the slob. (verb)* behave in a lazy and slovenly manner. *Don't slob around the house.*

Slog – *(verb)* **1** work hard over a period of time. walk or move with difficulty or effort. *I slogged the entire last year.* **2** hit or strike forcefully. fight or compete fiercely. *The boxer slogged the opponent. (noun)* **1** a spell of difficult, tiring work or travelling. *The slog appeared to be the longest period of her life.* **2** a forceful hit or strike. *The slog gave him a black eye.*

Slogan – *(noun)* **1** a short, memorable phrase used in advertising or associated with a political party or group. *The brand had a catchy slogan.* **2** a Scottish highland war cry. *The slogan instilled energy in each warrior.*

Slop – *(noun)* **1** a workman's loose outer garment. *The slop was so dirty by the end of the day that it had to be discarded.* **2** wide, baggy trousers, especially as worn by sailors. clothes and bedding supplied to sailors by the navy. readymade or cheap clothing. *The slops were full of mud.*

Slope – *(noun)* **1** a surface of which one end or side is at a higher level than another. a difference in level or sideways position between two ends or sides. a part of the side of a hill or mountain, especially as a place for skiing. *The skiers skied down the slope.* **2** an oriental person, especially a Vietnamese. *The slope worked hard. (verb)* **1** be inclined from a horizontal or vertical line; slant up or down. *The rope sloped down towards the town centre.* **2** move in an idle or aimless manner. leave unobtrusively, typically in order to evade work or duty. *Don't slope around, do some work.*

Sloppy – *(adjective)* **1** containing too much liquid; watery. *The sloppy curry was tasteless.* **2** careless and unsystematic; excessively casual. *He is a sloppy worker.* **3** casual and loose fitting. *She hides herself beneath sloppy clothes.* **4** weakly or foolishly sentimental. *At times, she suffers because of her sloppy nature.*

Slot – *(noun)* the track of a deer, visible as slotted footprints in soft ground. *The curious child followed the slot.*

Sloth – *(noun)* **1** reluctance to work or make an effort; laziness. *He is such a sloth when it comes to work.* **2** a slow moving tropical American mammal that hangs upside down from branches using its long limbs and hooked claws. *The child was excited to see the sloth.*

Slovenly – *(adjective)* **1** untidy and dirty. *Her slovenly hair needed washing.* **2** careless; excessively casual. *His slovenly manners cost him the job.*

Slow – *(adjective)* **1** moving or capable of moving only at a low speed. lasting or taking a long time. *My car was stuck behind the slow bullock cart.* **2** showing a time earlier than the correct time. *The slow watch made me late for office.* **3** not prompt to understand, think, or learn. *Even though he was thought to be slow, he was very generous.* **4** uneventful and rather dull. with little activity; slack. *The slow evening bored my nephew.* **5** needing long exposure. *The slow light was such a pain for the cameraman.* **6** burning or giving off heat gently. *The slow fire died down in the middle of the night. (verb)* reduce one's speed or the speed of a vehicle or process. live or work less actively or intensely. *Please slow down as it is not safe to drive fast.*

Sludge – *(noun)* **1** thick, soft, wet mud or a similar viscous mixture. dirty oil or industrial waste. *The sludge spoiled the entire scenery.* **2** sea ice newly formed in small pieces. *The sludge couldn't hold the weight of the polar bear.* **3** an unattractive muddy shade of brown or green. *The sludge made the city unsightly.*

Slug – *(verb)* strike with a hard blow. settle a dispute or contest by fighting or competing fiercely. *The wrestler slugged the opponent.*

(noun) a hard blow. *The slug made him fall down.*

Sluggish – *(adjective)* slow moving or inactive. lacking energy or alertness. *The sluggish movement of the traffic was very frustrating.*

Slum – *(noun)* a squalid and overcrowded urban area inhabited by very poor people. a house in such a place. *My maid lives in a slum near the bus stand.* *(verb)* voluntarily spend time in uncomfortable conditions or at a lower social level than one's own. *Several plans were formulated for the betterment of the slum dwellers.*

Slumber – *(noun)* a sleep. *The deep slumber refreshed me.* *(verb)* sleep. *The woodcutter slumbered beneath the tree he was planning to cut.*

Slump – *(verb)* **1** sit, lean, or fall heavily and limply. *Don't slump. Sit straight.* **2** fail or decline substantially or over a prolonged period. *The economy slumped considerably over the years.* *(noun)* **1** an instance of slumping. *His slump made him look lazy.* **2** a prolonged period of abnormally low economic activity. *The slump caused a lot of people to lose their jobs.*

Slur – *(verb)* **1** articulate or be articulated indistinctly. *He slurred under anesthesia.* **2** pass over so as to conceal or minimize it. *The manager slurred over the concerns of his team.* **3** perform legato. mark with a slur. *The music composer slurred over the notes.* make insinuations or allegations about. *The employee slurred against the organization.* *(noun)* **1** an insinuation or allegation. *His slur landed him in trouble.* **2** an indistinct utterance. *The teacher asked him to speak clearly when she heard his slur.* **3** a curved line indicating that notes are to be slurred. *The musicians did not follow the slur.*

Slurp – *(verb)* eat or drink with a loud sucking sound. *He slurped his tea.* *(noun)* an act or sound of slurping. *His slurp was very distracting.*

Slush – *(noun)* **1** partially melted snow or ice. *The slush made walking around very inconvenient.* watery mud. *His trousers got dirty when he walked through the slush.* **2** excessive sentiment.*His slush looked fake.* *(verb)* make a soft splashing sound. *Children merrily slushed through the muddy water.*

Slut – *(noun)* a slovenly or promiscuous woman. *She played the role of a slut in the movie.*

Sly – *(adjective)* **1** having a conning and deceitful nature. *She is a sly woman.* **2** insinuating. *He is a sly man.* **3** surreptitious. *Their sly conversation was soon out in open.*

Smack – *(noun)* a single masted sailing boat used for coasting or fishing. *His smack is in urgent need of repair.*

Small – *(adjective)* **1** of a size that is less than normal or usual. *The clown was a small person.* **2** not great in amount, number, strength, or power. *She repaid her loan in small installments.* **3** not fully grown or developed; young. *The small child tried to behave like a grown-up person.* **4** insignificant; unimportant. *I just need a small favour.* **5** low or inferior in rank or position. *He is a small businessman when compared to his friend.* **6** operating on a modest scale. *It is a small enterprise.* *(noun)* underwear. *He hung his small for drying.* *(adverb)* **1** into small pieces. *Cut the fruit small.* **2** in a small manner or size. *Don't act so small.*

Smallpox – *(noun)* an acute contagious viral disease, with fever and pustules usually leaving permanent scars. *They claim that smallpox has been eradicated.*

Smart – *(adjective)* **1** clean, tidy, and stylish. *Her room is smart.* **2** bright and fresh in appearance. *His smart personality impressed the interviewer.* **3** fashionable and up market. *She has a smart sense of dress.* **4** having a quick intelligence. capable of independent and seemingly intelligent action. impertinently clever or sarcastic. *His smart responses made everyone smile.* **5** quick; brisk. *The fireman's smart movements saved many lives.* *(verb)* **1** present a sharp, stinging pain. *The bump on my head smarted.* **2** feel upset and annoyed. *He was still smarting about the argument with his friend.* *(noun)* **1** intelligence; acumen. *The child with the smarts topped the class.* **2** a smarting pain. *Even after applying the medicine, his smart didn't go away.* *(adverb)* in a quick or brisk manner. *He walked smartly.*

Smash - *(verb)* **1** break or cause to break violently into pieces. violently knock down. *The mirror smashed into a hundred pieces.* **2** crash and severely damage. hit or collide with forcefully. *The car smashed into the tree.* **3** strike or score with great force. strike downwards with a hard over arm stroke. *The player smashed the ball with all his strength.* **4** completely defeat, destroy, or foil. fail financially. *His partner smashed the business.* *(noun)* an act, instance, or sound of smashing. *The smash rang through the building.* **2** a very successful song, film, or show. *The music director knew the song was a smash as soon as he heard it.* **3** a mixture of spirits with flavoured water and ice. *The smash wasn't tasty.* *(adverb)* with a sudden smash. *The mirror broke with a smash.*

Smattering - *(noun)* **1** a small amount. *A smattering of raindrops was enough to make the children happy.* **2** a slight knowledge of a language or subject. *I only know a smattering of French.*

Smear - *(verb)* **1** coat or mark with a greasy or sticky substance. *The smear didn't go away even after getting the dress dry-cleaned.* **2** spread over a surface. *She smeared paint over her sister's face.* **3** blur or smudge. *She smeared her eye make-up.* **4** damage the reputation of by false or unwarranted accusations. *His friends didn't intend to smear him.* *(noun)* **1** a greasy or sticky mark. *The smear is stubborn.* **2** a false or unwarranted accusation. *He fought the smear well.* **3** a sample thinly spread on a microscopic slide. short for smear test. *The smear seemed contaminated.* **4** an insecure foothold. *Be careful on the smear.*

Smell - *(noun)* **1** the faculty of perceiving odours by means of the organs in the nose. *She lost her sense of smell in the accident.* **2** a quality in something that is perceived by this faculty; an odour. an unpleasant odour. *The smell made it difficult to sit there.* **3** an act of inhaling in order to ascertain an odour. *The dog just used the smell to uncover the evidence.* *(verb)* **1** perceive or detect the odour of. sniff at in order to ascertain its odour. *The dog smelled my feet and started wagging its tail.* **2** detect or discover something by the faculty of smell. *My friend smelled out the dead rat.* **3** detect or suspect by means of instinct or intuition. *He smelled something fishy in the business.* **4** emit an odour of a specified kind. have a strong or unpleasant odour. *The entire house smelled of fish.* **5** be suggestive of something. *The dish smelled of burnt onions.*

Smelt - *(noun)* a small silvery fish of both marine and fresh water. *The smelt quickly swam away.*

Smile - *(verb)* **1** form one's features into a pleased, friendly, or amused expression, with the corners of the mouth turned up. *They smiled at each other.* **2** regard favourably or indulgently. *Good fortune smiled upon us.* *(noun)* an act of smiling; a smiling expression. *He has a warm smile.*

Smirk - *(verb)* smile in an irritatingly smug or silly way. *He smirked at our low marks.* *(noun)* a smug or silly smile. *He was offended by my smirk.*

Smith - *(noun)* a worker in metal. short for blacksmith. *The smith repaired the spade.* *(verb)* treat by heating, hammering, and forging it. *Please smith the misshapen iron sheet.*

Smock - *(noun)* **1** a loose dress or blouse having the upper part closely gathered in smocking. *She wore a blue smock.* **2** a loose overall worn to protect one's clothes. a smocked linen overgarment worn by an agricultural worker. *She was glad to have worn the smock before starting painting.* *(verb)* decorate with smocking. *She smocked herself before she started to paint.*

Smooth - *(adjective)* **1** having an even and regular surface; free from projections or indentations. having an even consistency; without lumps. *The smooth batter will rise beautifully when baked.* **2** without jerks. *It was a smooth ride to the hills.* **3** without problems or difficulties. *Life has been smooth so far.* **4** without harshness or bitterness. *We have a smooth partnership.* **5** suavely or unctuously charming. *His smooth language appeals to everyone.* *(verb)* in a way that is without difficulties. *Please smooth the wrinkles off the shirt.*

Smother – *(verb)* **1** suffocate by covering the nose and mouth. *The thief tried to smother the servant but failed.* **2** extinguish by covering it. *I smothered the candle.* **3** cover someone or something entirely with. *He smothered his car with flowers.* **4** cause to feel trapped and oppressed. *He was always cautious not to smother his children.* **5** suppress. stop the motion of the ball or a shot. *The player smothered the ball. (noun)* a mass of something that stifles or obscures. *The smother was removed and the drain cleaned.*

Smoulder – *(verb)* **1** burn slowly with smoke but no flame. *The coal smouldered for a long time.* **2** express or be expressed in a barely suppressed state. *The man smouldered in front of the jury. (noun)* an instance of smouldering. *The smoulder kept the room warm for a bit.*

Smudge – *(verb)* cause to become messy, smeared. *She dabbed her eyes carefully not to smudge the makeup. (noun)* a blurred view. *We could see the low smudge of the mountain during winter nights.*

Smug – *(adjective)* irritatingly pleased with oneself; self satisfied. *The student's smug attitude irritated everyone else.*

Smuggle – *(verb)* **1** move illegally into or out of a country. *The smugglers smuggled many paintings and artifacts out of the country.* **2** convey secretly and illicitly. *The spies smuggled the confidential information out of the office.*

Snack – *(noun)* **1** a small quantity of food or a light meal, eaten between meals or in place of a meal. *We just had snacks at the party.* **2** a thing that is easy to accomplish. *The task was a snack when compared to the upcoming project. (verb)* eat a snack. *Don't snack too much between the meals.*

Snag – *(noun)* a sausage. *The snag tasted stale.*

Snail – *(noun)* a slow moving mollusc with a spiral shell into which the whole body can be withdrawn. *I saw several snakes in my garden.*

Snake – *(noun)* **1** a predatory reptile with a long slender limbless supple body, many kinds of which have a venomous bite. *My brother was excited to see the snake in the zoo.* **2** a treacherous or deceitful person. *My boss threw the snake out of the company.* **3** a long flexible wire for clearing obstacles in piping. *The snake cleared the pipe. (verb)* move or extend with the twisting motion of a snake. *The reporters snaked through the crowd.*

Snap – *(verb)* **1** break or cause to break with a sharp cracking sound. *The stick snapped.* **2** make a sudden audible bite. quickly secure something that is in short supply. *The dog snapped at the cat.* **3** open or close with a brisk movement or sharp sound. *The purse snapped shut.* **4** suddenly lose one's self control. say something quickly and irritably. *The teacher snapped at the student.* **5** get out of by a sudden effort. *Please snap out of this.* **6** take a snapshot of. *The photographer snapped the moment. (noun)* **1** an act of snapping; a sudden snapping sound or movement. *They turned around when they heard the snap.* **2** a brief spell of cold or otherwise distinctive weather. *I wore my sweater because of the snap.* **3** vigour; liveliness. *He was the life of the party because of his snap.* **4** a snapshot. *The snap came out really well.* **5** a card game in which players compete to call 'snap' as soon as two cards of the same type are exposed. *They played snap till late at night. (adjective)* done on the spur of the moment: a snap decision. *He paid dearly for the snap judgment.*

Snare – *(noun)* **1** a trap for catching small animals, consisting of a loop of wire or cord that pulls tight. a wire loop for severing polyps or other growths. *The snare failed to catch anything.* **2** a length of wire, gut, or hide stretched across a drumhead to produce a rattling sound. another term for side drum. *The snare produced a horrible sound. (verb)* catch in a snare. *The hunters managed to snare the deer.*

Snarl – *(verb)* **1** growl with bared teeth. *The dog snarled at me.* **2** say something aggressively. *My father snarled at me when I missed school. (noun)* an act or sound of snarling. *The dog's snarl was very threatening.*

Snatch – *(verb)* seize quickly and deftly. [informal] steal or kidnap by seizing suddenly. quickly secure or obtain. *The child snatched my pencil. (noun)* **1** an act of snatching. *The* *snatch was caught on the camera.* **2** a fragment of music or talk. *I want to listen to the snatch at least.* weightlifting the rapid raising of a weight from the floor to above the head in one movement. *He sprained his back during the snatch.* **4** [vulgar slang] a woman's genitals. *It is rude to say snatch.*

Sneak – *(verb)* **1** move, go, or convey in a furtive or stealthy manner. stealthily acquire or obtain: she sneaked a glance at her watch. *She sneaked into the house late at night.* **2** [Birtish informal] someone in authority of a person's misdeeds. *He sneaked on his colleague.* *(noun)* [informal] **1** a furtive person. *The sneak was very self-centred.* **2** [British] a telltale. *The sneak didn't have too many friends in the office.* **3** [north American] short for sneaker. *Wear your sneaks for practice tomorrow.* *(adjective)* acting or done surreptitiously: a sneak preview. *This is just a sneak preview of the movie.*

Sneer – *(noun)* a contemptuous or mocking smile, remark, or tone. *Her sneer was quite unnecessary.* *(verb)* smile or speak in a contemptuous or mocking manner. *The senior sneered at the juniors.*

Sneeze – *(verb)* make a sudden involuntary expulsion of air from the nose and mouth due to irritation of one's nostrils. *He sneezed loudly.* *(noun)* an act or the sound of sneezing. *His loud sneeze alarmed the entire class.*

Snide – *(adjective)* **1** derogatory or mocking in an indirect way. *This is no time for making snide remarks.* **2** [chiefly north American] devious and underhand. *His partner's snide tricks warned him of the risk.* counterfeit; inferior. *The snide currency should be reported immediately.* *(noun)* a snide person or remark. *The wife's snide failed to hurt the husband.*

Sniff – *(verb)* **1** draw air audibly through the nose. *My friend sniffed the air.* **2** show contempt or dislike for: the price is not to be sniffed at. *Do not sniff at me.* **3** [informal] investigate something covertly. [informal] discover something by covert investigation. *The detective sniffed the criminal out.* *(noun)* **1** an act or sound of sniffing. *The sniffs of the child worried the mother.* **2**. [informal] a hint or sign. *I have given him a sniff.*

Sniffle – *(verb)* sniff slightly or repeatedly, typically because of a cold or fit of crying. *He was sniffling by the time he reached home.* *(noun)* an act of sniffling. *He caught everyone's attention because of his sniffles.* **2** a slight head cold. *I think I have sniffles.*

Snigger – *(noun)* a smothered or half-suppressed laugh. *The girls didn't know that everyone could hear their sniggers.* *(verb)* give such a laugh. *If you snigger again, you can go stand outside the class.*

Snip – *(verb)* cut with scissors or shears, with small, quick strokes. *The barber snipped the locks off.* *(noun)* **1** an act of snipping. *The rope was cut into half with one quick snip.* **2** a small piece that has been cut off. *One snip of cloth is enough to patch this hole up.* **3** [British informal] a bargain. *This t-shirt was a good snip.* **4** shears for cutting metal. *I am off to the market to purchase a snip.* [north American informal] a small or insignificant person. *You may feel that you are a snip, but you are not.*

Snipe – *(noun)* a wading bird with brown camouflaged plumage and long straight bill. *I saw a snipe near the pond.* *(verb)* **1** shoot at someone from a hiding place at long range. *The soldier sniped at the enemy.* **2** make a sly or petty (verb)al attack. *The two friends sniped at each other.*

Snippet – *(noun)* a small piece or brief extract. *This is a snippet from the story she wrote.*

Snivel – *(verb)* **1** cry and sniffle. *She snivelled after the fall.* **2** complain in a whining or tearful way. *After the fight, she snivelled to her husband.* *(noun)* a spell of snivelling. *Please stop the snivel.*

Snob – *(noun)* a person who has an exaggerated respect for high social position or wealth and who looks down on those regarded as socially inferior. a person with a similar respect for tastes considered superior in a particular area: a wine snob. *At times, you sound like a snob.*

Snooker – *(noun)* **1** a game played with cues on a billiard table in which the players use a white cue ball to pocket the other balls in a set order. *She is a good player of snooker.* **2** a position make a direct shot at any permitted ball. *The snooker hit the target.* *(verb)* subject to a snooker. [informal] be ruined or placed in an impossible position. *His business was snookered.*

Snoop - *(verb)* investigate or look around furtively in an attempt to find out something. *The detective snooped around the crime scene for clues.* *(noun)* **1** an act of snooping. *Her snooping in her husband's cupboard yielded no results.* **2** a person who snoops. *The snoop had collected all the evidence he needed.*

Snooty - *(adjective)* [informal] showing disapproval of or contempt towards others, especially those considered to be socially inferior. *She is such a snooty employer.*

Snooze - *(noun)* a short, light sleep. *I took a snooze in the afternoon.* *(verb)* have a snooze. *She snoozed in the class.*

Snore - *(noun)* a snorting or grunting sound in a person's breathing while they are asleep. *His snores made it difficult for me to sleep.* *(verb)* make such a sound while asleep. *She snores at times.*

Snorkel - *(noun)* a tube for a swimmer to breathe through while under water. *He forgot to carry his snorkel.* *(verb)* swim using a snorkel. *They snorkelled during their vacations.*

Snort - *(noun)* **1** an explosive sound made by the sudden forcing of breath through the nose. *He laughed with a snort.* **2** [informal] an inhaled dose of cocaine. *The drug addict was forcefully stopped from taking a snort.* **3** [informal] a measure of an alcoholic drink. *He took a snort of vodka.* *(verb)* **1** make a snort. express indignation or derision by making a snort. *My friend snorted at my accusations.* **2** [informal] inhale. *He snorted loudly.*

Snot - *(noun)* [informal] **1** nasal mucus. *Please wipe the snot off your face.* **2** a contemptible person. *My friend introduced me to the snot.*

Snout - *(noun)* **1** the projecting nose and mouth of an animal, especially a mammal. the projecting front or end of something such as a pistol. *The alligator hurt its snout.* **2** [British informal] a cigarette. tobacco. *Do you have some snout?* **3** [British informal] a police informer. *The snout provided some valuable information regarding the crime.*

Snow - *(noun)* **1** atmospheric water vapour frozen into ice crystals and falling in light white flakes or lying on the ground as a white layer. falls of snow. *Pure white sheet of snow covered the landscape.* **2** a mass of flickering white spost on a television or radar screen, caused by interference or a poor signal. *The television only has snow on all channels.* *(verb)* **1** snow falls quantity of snow. *It snowed yesterday.* **2** arrive in overwhelming quantities: in the last week it had snowed letters. be overwhelmed with a large quantity of something, especially work. *Letters snowed in yesterday.* **3** [informal chiefly] mislead or charm with elaborate and insincere words. *The student tried to snow the teacher when she asked him why he hadn't completed the homework.*

Snub - *(verb)* **1** ignore or spurn disdainfully. *She snubbed me in the party.* **2** restrict the movement of by means of a rope wound round a post. *The mahouts snubbed the white elephant.* *(noun)* an act of snubbing. *Everyone noticed his snub.* *(adjective)* short and turned up at the end. *She wore snubbed shoes.*

Snuff - *(verb)* **1** extinguish a candle. *Please snuff the candles.* **2** abruptly put an end to. *He snuffed the life out of the victim.* **3** trim the charred wick from a candle. *The butler snuffed the candle.* *(noun)* the charred part of a candle wick. *The snuff of the candle needed to be trimmed.*

Snug - *(noun)* **1** warm and cosy. *I felt very snug in my duvet.* **2** [archaic] allowing one to live in comfort. *She has a snug flat.* **3** very tight or close-fitting. *He wore a snug t-shirt.* *(noun)* [British] a small, cosy public room in a pub or small hotel. *Does your pub have any snugs available.* *(verb)* [chiefly north American] place or settle safely or costly. *The family soon snugged in their new home.*

Snuggle - *(verb)* settle into a warm, comfortable position. *The puppies snuggled together to keep warm.*

So – *(noun)* variant spelling of soh. *The audience erupted as soon as the musician hit the so.*

Soak – *(verb)* **1** make or become thoroughly wet by immersion in liquid. *I soaked my clothes overnight.* **2** make extremely wet: the rain soaked their hair. *The rain soaked their clothes.* **3** absorb a liquid. expose oneself to something beneficial or enjoyable. *I soaked in the spiritual energy.* **4** immerse oneself in a particular experience. *I soaked in all the positive energy.* **5** [informal] impose heavy charges or taxation on. *The government soaked the salaried people.* **6** [archaic], [informal] drink heavily. *The football players soaked after the win.* *(noun)* **1** an act or spell of soaking. *I felt very cold after the soak.* **2** [informal] a heavy drinker. *The soak had to be sent to the rehabilitation.* **3** [austral] a hollow where rainwater collects. *The soak was full of water.*

Soap – *(noun)* **1** a substance used with water for washing and cleaning, made of a compound of natural oils or fats with sodium hydroxide or another strong alkali, and typically perfumed. *I ran to the market as I had run out of soap.* **2** [informal] a soap opera. *I watched the soap with my mother.* *(verb)* wash with soap. *Please soap your face.*

Soar – *(verb)* **1** fly or rise high into the air. glide high in the air. *The eagle soared through the sky.* **2** increase rapidly above the usual level. *The noise soared after the hit.*

Sob – *(verb)* cry making loud, convulsive gasps. say while sobbing. *The little girl sobbed when she thought she was lost.* *(noun)* an act or sound of sobbing. *His sobs were heard by some men passing by.*

Sober – *(adjective)* **1** not affected by alcohol; not drunk. *The drunk was sober today.* **2** serious; thoughtful. *The teacher was sober after punishing the class.* **3** muted in colour. *People usually wear sober clothes to funerals.* *(verb)* **1** make or become sober after drinking alcohol. *He sobered up considerably when he saw the police.* **2** make or become serious. *The worry about finances sobered him up.*

Sobriety – *(noun)* the state of being sober. *Everyone was curious about his sobriety.*

Soccer – *(noun)* a form of football played by two teams of eleven players with a round ball which may not be handled during play except by the goalkeepers, the object of the game being to score goals by kicking or heading the ball into the opponents goal. *The game of soccer was very exciting.*

Sociable – *(adjective)* engaging readily with other people. marked by friendliness. *She is a sociable person.* *(noun)* **1** [historical] an open carriage with facing side seats. *They rode the sociable to the concert.* **2** [historical] a tricycle with two seats side by side. *The sociable took them everywhere.* **3** [chiefly British] an S-shaped couch for two people who sit partially facing each other. *The red sociable looked very regal.* **4** [informal] social gathering. *The sociable was a great success.*

Social – *(adjective)* **1** of or relating to society or its organization. of or relating to rank and status in society: a woman of high social standing. *This is a social gathering.* **2** needing companionship; suited to living in communities. *She is a social person.* **3** relating to or designed for activities in which people meet each other for pleasure. *Let's go to a social place.* **4** [zoology] breeding or living in colonies or organized communities. *Elephants are social animals.* *(noun)* an [informal] social gathering organized by the members of a particular club or group. *I am going to the social.*

Socialism – *(noun)* a political and economic theory of social organization which advocates that the means of production, distribution, and exchange should be owned or regulated by the community as a whole. a transitional social state between the overthrow of capitalism and the realization of communism. *He believed in socialism.*

Society – *(noun)* **1** the aggregate of people living together in a more or less ordered community. a particular community of people. who are fashionable. wealthy, and influential, regarded as forming a distinct group. *They were very protective about their society.* **2** a plant or animal community. *The society of buffalos thrived.* **3** an organization or club formed for a particular purpose or activity. *I joined the society to be able to enjoy canoeing.* **4** the situation of being in the company of other people: she shunned the society of others. *She loved the society of her friends.*

Sociology – *(noun)* the study of the development, structure, and functioning of human society. the study of social problems. *He took up sociology in college.*

Sock – *(noun)* **1** a knitted garment for the foot and lower part of the leg. *The sock was torn.* **2** an insole. *The sock of the shoe was comfortable.* **3** a white marking on the lower part of a horse's leg. *The socks made the horse recognizable.* **4** [informal] a hard blow. [US] force or emphasis. *They gave him a sock on the eye.* *(verb)* [informal] **1** hit forcefully. *They socked his eye.* **2** [north American] save up money. *Please sock up for rainy day.* **3** [north American] envelop or make impassable by inhospitable weather conditions: the beach was socked in with fog. *The fog socked the road.*

Socket – *(noun)* **1** a hollow in which something fits or revolves. the part of the head of a golf club into which the shaft is fitted. *The socket was too tight for the shaft.* **2** an electrical device receiving a plug or light bulb to make a connection. *The socket wasn't working.* *(verb)* **1** place in or fit with a socket. *I socketed the lamp's plug.* **2** [golf] shank a ball. *I saw the player socket the ball.*

Soda – *(noun)* **1** carbonated water. [chiefly north American] a sweet carbonated drink. *I want to have a soda with my pizza.* **2** sodium carbonate. sodium in chemical combination: nitrate of soda. *Soda is used in making a cake.*

Sofa – *(noun)* a long upholstered seat with a back and arms, for two or more people. *She sat on the sofa.*

Soften – *(verb)* **1** make or become soft or softer. *My mom softened the dough.* **2** undermine the resistance of. *They softened their stand.*

Software – *(noun)* programs and other operating information used by a computer. compare with hardware. *Software are usually very expensive.*

Softy – *(noun)* variant spelling of softie. *I want to eat a softy after dinner.*

Soggy – *(adjective)* very wet and soft. *The bread was soggy.*

Soil – *(noun)* **1** the upper layer of earth in which plants grow, a black or dark brown material typically consisting of organic remains, clay, and rock particles. *The soil was very fertile.* **2** the territory of a particular nation. *The Prime Minister warned the neighbouring country not to step on the soil of his country.*

Sojourn – *(noun)* a temporary stay. *His stay is sojourn.* *(verb)* stay temporarily. *I loved my little sojourn to the hills.*

Solace – *(noun)* comfort or consolation in time of distress. *Her solace really helped me in my grief.* *(verb)* give solace to. *I solaced my friend.*

Solar – *(adjective)* of, relating to, or determined by the sun or its rays. *Solar energy is green energy.*

Solder – *(noun)* a low-melting alloy, especially one based on lead and tin, used for joining less fusible metals. *The electrician forgot to bring the solder with himself.* *(verb)* join with solder. *The electrician soldered two ends of the wire together.*

Soldier – *(noun)* **1** a person who serves in an army. a private in an army. *The soldier was very brave.* **2** [entomology] a wingless caste of ant or termite with a large modified head and jaws, involved [chiefly] in defence. *The soldiers marched on to protect their colony.* **3** [British informal] a strip of bread or toast, dipped into a soft-boiled egg. *I ate soldiers for breakfast.* **4** an upright brick, timber, or other building element. *The soldiers lay on the floor for days before being used.* *(verb)* **1** serve as a solder. *I soldiered for my country.* **2** [informal] persevere. *I soldiered on the job without any hindrance.*

Sole – *(noun)* **1** the underside of a person's foot. the section forming the underside of a piece of footwear. the underside of a tool or implement, e.g. a plane or the head of a golf club. *His soles hurt after the long run.* **2** the floor of a ship's cabin or cockpit. *The sole needed to be painted.*

(verb) put a new sole on a shoe. *The cobbler soled the shoe.*

Solemn – *(adjective)* **1** formal and dignified: a solemn procession. *The funeral was a solemn procession.* **2** not cheerful; serious deeply sincere. *His solemn tone conveyed his sincerity.*

Solemnity – *(noun)* **1** the state of quality of being solemn. *Her solemnity was noticed by everyone.* **2** a solemn rite or ceremony. *The solemnity continued the entire day.*

Solemnize – *(verb)* duly perform a ceremony, especially that of marriage. mark with a formal ceremony. *Their marriage was solemnized in a church.*

Solicit – *(verb)* **1** ask for or try to obtain from someone ask for something from. *I solicited his advice.* **2** accost someone and offer one's or someone else's services as a prostitute. *They were caught soliciting customers.*

Solicitor – *(noun)* **1** [British] a member of the legal profession qualified to deal with conveyancing, draw up wills, advise clients and instruct barristers, and represent clients in lower courts. compare with barrister. [north American] the chief law officer of a city, town, or government department. *They called a solicitor for advice.* **2** [north American] a canvasser. *The solicitor made the arrangements to get the required number of votes.*

Solicitous – *(adjective)* showing interest or concern. [archaic] eager or anxious to do something. *She was very solicitous about his situation.*

Solicitude – *(noun)* care or concern. *His solicitude was very evident.*

Solid – *(noun)* **1** firm and stable in shape: solid fuel. strongly built or made. *He had a solid body.* **2** [geometry] three dimensional. relating to three-dimensional objects. *A sphere is a solid shape.* **3** not hollow or having spaces or gaps. consisting of the same substance throughout. continuous. *The planet was thought to be solid.* **4** dependable; reliable. sound but without special qualities. *He was a solid friend.* **5** US [informal] on good terms with. *They were solid with their neighbours.* **6** [austral] severe; unfair. *The teacher was solid at times.* **7** a solid substance or object. food that is not liquid. *He was asked not to eat solids for some days.* **8** [geometry] a three dimensional body or geometric figure. *The solids were all coloured with different colours.*

Solidarity – *(noun)* unity or agreement of feeling or action, especially among individuals with a common interest. *Their solidarity was quite evident.*

Solidify – *(verb)* make or become hard or solid. *The liquid solidified under certain conditions.*

Soliloquy – *(noun)* an act of speaking one's thoughts aloud when alone or regardless of hearers, especially by a character in a play. *The soliloquy was very touching.*

Solitary – *(adjective)* **1** done or existing alone. not social or colonial. *She was a solitary person.* **2** secluded or isolated. *The solitary hut was the main attraction of the landscape.* **3** single; only. *He was the solitary participant of the quiz.* **4** borne singly. *It was a solitary gem.* *(noun)* **1** a recluse or hermit. *The solitary made a hut in the wilderness.* **2** [informal] solitary confinement. *He was banished to the solitary after his misbehaviour.*

Solitude – *(noun)* the state of being alone. a lonely or uninhabited place. *He loved his solitude.*

Solo – *(noun)* **1** a piece of music, song, or dance for one performer. *His solo was touching.* **2.** an unaccompanied flight by a pilot. *He found his first solo very thrilling.* **3** a card game resembling whist in which the players make bids and the highest bidder plays against the others. a bid by which a player undertakes to win five tricks in this game. *The friends played Solo.* **4** a motorbike without a sidecar. *I like a solo better.* *(adjective & adverb)* for or done by one person. *He played solo.* *(verb)* **1** perform a solo. *The actor soloed for half-an-hour.* **2** fly an aircraft unaccompanied. *The pilot soloed for the first time.*

Soluble – *(adjective)* **1** able to be dissolved, especially in water. *The substance was soluble.* **2** able to be solved. *The puzzle was soluble.*

Solution – *(noun)* **1** a means of solving a problem. the correct answer to a puzzle. *Can you tell me* *the solution to this problem?* **2** a liquid mixture in which the minor component is uniformly distributed within the major component the solvent. the process or state of being dissolved. *The solution was blue.* **3** [archaic] dissolution. *The solution of salt changed the taste of the water.*

Solve – *(verb)* find an answer to, explanation for, or way of dealing with a problem or mystery. *I was able to solve the puzzle.*

Sombre – *(adjective)* **1** dark or dull. *The movie was very sombre.* **2** oppressively solemn or sober. *His sombre attitude depressed everyone.*

Some – *(determine)* **1** an unspecified amount or number of. *Some people were talking.* **2** denoting an unknown or unspecified person or thing. *Your attitude can appear offensive to some people.* **3** used with a number approximately. *Some 100 people participated in the show.* **4** a considerable amount or number of. *Some employees will turn up for the party.* **5** at least a small amount or number of. *At least some people will perform tonight.* **6** expressing admiration: that was some goal. used ironically to express disapproval or disbelief. *That was some song. (pronoun)* **1** an unspecified number or amount of people or things. *His attitude may hurt some.* **2** at least a small number or amount of people or things. *Some liked his performance. (adverb)* [informal] to some extent. *They liked his performance some.*

Somebody – *(pronoun)* someone. *Somebody needs to do this work.*

Someday – *(adverb)* in some way. for an unknown or unspecified reason. *I will do this someday.*

Somehow – *(adverb)* in some way. for an unknown or unspecified reason. *I will complete this somehow.*

Somersault – *(noun)* **1** an acrobatic movement in which a person turns head over heels in the air or on the ground and finishes on their feet. *The somersault was perfect.* **2** a dramatic upset or reversal of policy or opinion. *The government's somersault was not appreciated by the public. (verb)* perform a somersault. *He somersaulted across the stage.*

Something – *(pronoun)* **1** an unspecified or unknown thing. *Something is moving upstairs.* **2** an unspecified or unknown amount or degree. *We know something about the kind of problems that one may face. (adverb)* **1** [informal] used for emphasis with a following adjective: my back hurts something terrible. *Her head ached something terrible.* **2** [archaic] or dialect somewhat. *The statement was something incorrect.*

Sometime – *(adverb)* at some unspecified or unknown time. [archaic] formerly. *I will do this sometime. (adjective)* **1** former. *The sometime star still had a charming personality.* **2** [north American] occasional. *The sometime showers can be disastrous to the crops.*

Somewhat – *(adverb)* to some extent. *I find this somewhat disturbing.*

Somewhere – *(adverb)* **1** in or to some place. *I am going somewhere.* **2** used to indicate an approximate amount. *He scored somewhere close to 100. (pronoun)* some unspecified place. *Somewhere will be better than here.*

Somnolent – *(adjective)* sleepy; drowsy. inducing drowsiness. *I was somnolent after the sleepless night.*

Son – *(noun)* **1** a boy or man in relation to his parents. a male descendant. a man regarded as the product of a particular influence or environment. *They are very proud of their son.* **2** the second person of the trinity; Christ. *The Son was the saviour.* **3** used as a form of address for a boy or younger man. *"Son, come here."*

Sonata – *(noun)* a classical composition for an instrumental soloist, often with a piano accompaniment. *The audience enjoyed the sonata.*

Song – *(noun)* **1** a short poem or other set of words set to music. singing or vocal music. a musical composition suggestive of a song. *The song was very beautifully composed.* **2** the musical phrases uttered by some birds, whales, and insects, used [chiefly] for territorial defence or for attracting mates. *The song of the nightingale touched everyone.* **3** a poem, especially one in rhymed stanzas. [archaic] poetry. *He recited his song.*

Sonic – *(adjective)* **1** relating to or using sound waves. *The sonic waves carried the sound far.* **2** denoting or having a speed equal to that of sound. *He travelled with sonic speed.*

Son-in-law – *(noun)* the husband of one's daughter. *She invited her daughter and son-in-law for dinner.*

Sonnet – *(noun)* a poem of fourteen lines using any of a number of formal rhyme schemes, in English typically having ten syllables per line. *The sonnets were beautifully written. (verb)* [archaic] compose sonnets. celebrate in a sonnet. *I heard him sonnet his thoughts.*

Soon – *(adverb)* **1** in or after a short time. early. *I will work on this soon.* **2** readily used to indicate a preference. *I would go their soon.*

Soot – *(noun)* a black powdery or flaky substance consisting largely of amorphous carbon, produced by the incomplete burning of organic matter. *The young boy was covered with soot. (verb)* cover or clog with soot. *The chimney was sooted.*

Soothe – *(verb)* gently calm. reduce pain or discomfort, in. relieve pain. *His mom's hand on his head soothed his headache.*

Sooty – *(adjective)* covered with or coloured like soot. *The sooty chimney needed to be cleaned.*

Sop – *(noun)* **1** a thing given or done to appease or bribe someone. *It was sop for the cop.* **2**. a piece of bread dipped in gravy, soup, or sauce. *The hungry man ate the sop. (verb)* soak up liquid. [archaic] soak. *The mop sopped the water.*

Sophisticated – *(adjective)* **1** highly complex. aware of and able to interpret complex issues. *It was a sophisticated piece of machinery.* **2** showing sorely experience and knowledge of fashion and culture. appealing to sophisticated people. *The sophisticated man impressed the crowds.*

Soppy – *(adjective)* **1** self-indulgently sentimental. *Her soppy behaviour often irritated her friends.* **2** feeble. *The support wire was very soppy.*

Soprano – *(noun)* **1** the highest singing voice. a singer with such a voice. *The soprano's voice was very soothing.* **2** an instrument of a high or the highest pitch in its family. *I would like to buy a wind soprano.*

Sorcerer – *(noun)* a person believed to have magic powers. *Everyone thought that he was a sorcerer.*

Sordid – *(adjective)* **1** involving ignoble actions and motives. *It was a sordid affair.* **2** dirty or squalid. *The sordid house could not be sold.*

Sore– *(adjective)* **1** painful or aching. suffering pain. *I have a sore throat.* **2** [informal chiefly] upset and angry. *She was often a sore person in the morning.* **3** severe; urgent. *It was a sore punishment. (noun)* **1** a raw or painful place on the body. *The sore hurt.* 2 a source of distress or annoyance. *Please let go of the sore. (adverb)* [archaic] extremely; severely. *I will sorely miss you.*

Sorrow – *(noun)* a feeling of deep distress caused by loss or disappointment. a cause of sorrow. the outward expression of grief. *His sorrow was written all over his face. (verb)* feel sorrow. *He sorrowed over his failure.*

Sorry – *(adjective)* **1** feeling distress, especially through sympathy with someone else's misfortune. filled with compassion for. *I was sorry for her.* **2** feeling regret pitiful state. unpleasant and regrettable. *Her house was in a sorry state.*

Sort – *(noun)* **1** a category of people or things with a common feature. [informal] a person with a specified nature. *He is the sort of person who plays to win.* **2** [archaic] a manner or way. *His sort was unfair.* **3** computing the arrangement of data in a prescribed sequence. *What is the sort of the data? (verb)* **1** arrange systematically in groups. separate from a mixed group. look at in succession for classification or to make a selection. *I sorted my papers.* **2** resolve a problem or difficulty. [informal] deal with a troublesome person. *The teacher sorted the issue very easily.*

SOS – *(noun)* an international coded signal of extreme distress, used especially by ships at sea. an urgent appeal for help. [British] a message broadcast to an untraceable person in an emergency. *The ship sent out an SOS.*

Soul – *(noun)* **1** the spiritual or immaterial part of a human, regarded as immortal.

one's moral or emotional nature or sense of identity. emotional or intellectual energy or intensity. *The solitude appealed to my soul.* **2** short for soul music. *I love soul.* **3** a person regarded as the embodiment of some quality: he was the soul of discretion. an individual. a person regarded with affection or pity. *He was the very soul of honesty.*

Soulful – *(adjective)* expressing deep and typically sorrowful feeling. *His soulful voice mesmerized the audience.*

Sound – *(noun)* a narrow stretch of water forming an inlet or connecting two larger bodies of water. *I love visiting the sound when I want to be alone.*

Soundproof – *(adjective)* preventing the passage of sound. *The room is soundproof. (verb)* make soundproof. *We soundproofed the conference room.*

Soup – *(noun)* **1** a savoury liquid dish made by boiling meat, fish, or vegetables in stock or water. *The soup was very tasty.* **2** [US informal] nitroglycerine or gelignite, especially as used of safe breaking. *The thieves carried soup to break the safe.* [informal] the chemicals in which film is developed. *The photo studio ran out of soup. (verb)* increase the power and efficiency of an engine. make something more elaborate or impressive. *They souped up the stage.*

Sour – *(adjective)* **1** having an acid taste like lemon or vinegar. *The sour orange was very difficult to eat.* **2** having gone bad because of fermentation. having a rancid smell. *The sour grapes had to be thrown away.* **3** showing resentment, disappointment, or anger. *He was sour after the exam results.* **4** deficient in lime. *The sour soup wasn't such a hit.* **5** containing a high proportion of sulphur. *The sour water was supposed to be good for health. (noun)* a cocktail made by mixing a spirit with lemon or lime juice. *He loves sour cocktail. (verb)* make or become sour. *Their relationship had soured over the years.*

Source – *(noun)* **1** a place, person, or thing from which something originates. a spring or fountain head from which a river or stream issues. *He was a source of inspiration for many youngsters.* **2** a person who provides information. a book or document providing evidence for research. *The source was very informative.* **3** [technical] a body or process by which energy or a component enters a system. the opposite of sink. *His mind was the source of all his positivism. (verb)* obtain from a particular source. find out where to obtain. *I sourced the money from a friend.*

South – *(noun)* **1** the direction towards the point of the horizon 90 degree clockwise from east. *There is a park towards the south.* **2** the southern part of a country, region, or town. the southern states of the united states. *I am headed to the south. (adjective)* **1** lying towards, near, or facing the south. *The south pool was very peaceful.* **2** blowing from the south. *The wind is blowing south ways. (adverb)* to or towards the south. *The south wind is very humid.*

Southwards – *(adverb)* towards the south. *The train was southwards bound. (noun)* the direction or region to the south. *The colony stood southwards to the park.*

Southern – *(adjective)* situated in the south or directed towards south. *The southern hemisphere has more water.*

Souvenir – *(noun)* a thing that is kept as a reminder of a person, place, or event. *She kept the ticket as a souvenir.*

Sovereign – *(noun)* **1** a supreme, ruler, especially a monarch. *He was a well-loved sovereign.* **2** a former [British] gold coin worth one pound sterling, now only minted for commemorative purpose. *I have a collection of sovereigns. (adjective)* **1**possessing supreme or ultimate power. possessing royal power and status. *The sovereign king ruled justly.* **2** acting or done independently and without outside interference. *The country is sovereign.* **3** very good or effective. *The system is sovereign for development.*

Sow – *(verb)* **1** plant by scattering it on or in the earth. plant with seed. *They sowed tomato seeds.* **2** disseminate or introduce: the new policy has sown confusion an doubt. *His words have sown discontent amongst people.*

Spa – *(noun)* a mineral spring considered to have health giving properties. a place or resort with such a spring. a commercial establishment offering health and beauty treatment. *I would love to visit a spa.*

Space – *(noun)* **1** a continuous area or expanse which is free or unoccupied. a gap between printed or written words or characters. pages in a newspaper, or time between broadcast programmes, available for advertising. the freedom and scope to live and develop as one wishes. one of two possible states of a signal on certain systems. the opposite of mark. *The space was empty for a long time.* **2** an interval of time: both cars were stolen in the space of a few hours. *They had two major fights in the space of a few hours.* **3** the dimensions of height, depth, and width within which all things exist and move. the physical universe beyond the earth's atmosphere. the near vacuum extending between the planets and stars. *It is impossible to estimate the size of space.* *(verb)* **1** position at a distance from one another. insert spaces between. *He spaced his deliveries.* **2** be or become euphoric or disorientated, especially from taking drugs. *He spaced out in the party.*

Spacecraft – *(noun)* a vehicle used for travelling in space. *The spacecraft started its journey today.*

Spaceman – *(noun)* a male astronaut. *The spaceman described his adventures.*

Spacious – *(adjective)* having plenty of space. *They had a spacious house.*

Spade – *(noun)* **1** a tool with a sharp edged, rectangular metal blade and a long handle, used for digging. *The spade was broken.* **2** shaped like a spade: a spade bit. *It is difficult to find shoes for my spade feet.* *(verb)* dig over with a spade. move or lift with a spade. *He spaded the earth in his garden.*

Spadework – *(noun)* hard for routine preparatory work. *Do some spadework before the presentation.*

Spaghetti – *(plural noun)* pasta made in solid strings, between macaroni and vermicelli in thickness. *I love spaghetti.*

Span – *(noun)* **1** a rope with its ends fastened at different points in order to provide a purchase. *The span was broken.* **2** a team of people or animals, especially a matched pair of horses or oxen. *The span of oxen worked hard all day.* *(verb)* yoke an animal. *The farmer spanned the oxen.*

Spank – *(verb)* slap with one's open hand or a flat object, especially on the buttocks as a punishment. *His mother spanked him.* *(noun)* a slap or series of slaps of this type. *He still remembered the spanking.*

Spanner – *(noun)* a tool with a shaped opening or jaws for gripping and turning a nut or bolt. *The spanner was missing from his toolkit.*

Spare – *(adjective)* **1** additional to what is required for ordinary use. not currently in use or occupied. *The spare tyre was flat.* **2** with no excess fat; thin. *His spare body needed some nourishment.* **3** elegantly simple. *Her spare look was different from others.* *(noun)* **1** an item kept in case another item of the same type is lost, broken, or worn out. *The spare was lost too.* **2** an act of knocking down all the pins with two balls. *The spare won them the game.* *(verb)* **1** give something of which one has enough to. make free or available. *Do you have a spare pencil?* **2** refrain form killing or harming. refrain from inflicting on: they have been spared the violence. *He spared the beautiful deer.* **3** be frugal. *He spared very little money.*

Spark – *(noun)* a lively person. *He was the spark of the party.* *(verb)* engage in courtship. *They sparked together.*

Sparkle – *(verb)* **1** shine brightly with flashes of light. *The stage sparkled.* **2** be vivacious and witty. *He sparkled in the party.* **3** effervescent. *The metal sparkled.* *(noun)* **1** a glittering flash of light. *The sparkle blinded everyone.* **2** vivacity and wit. *She won a lot of admirers with her sparkle.*

Sparrow – *(noun)* a small, typically brown and grey finch like bird related to the weaver birds. used in names of many other birds which resemble this, especially American birds of the bunting family, e.g. java sparrow, song sparrow. *Sparrows chirped outside my house.*

Sparse– *(adjective)* thinly dispersed. *He had sparse hair on his head.*

Spartan – *(noun)* a Canadian apple dessert of a variety with crisp white flesh and maroon flushed yellow skin. *I ate a spartan after lunch.*

Spasm – *(noun)* **1** a sudden involuntary muscular contraction or convulsive movement. *His body went into spasms during the fit.* **2** a sudden brief spell of activity or sensation. *I felt a spasm in my arm.*

Spate – *(noun)* **1** a large number of similar things or events coming in quick succession. *Children were overwhelmed with a spate of tests.* **2** a sudden flood in a river. *The spate took only a few hours to subside.*

Spatial – *(adjective)* of or relating to space. *I find the spatial discussions very interesting.*

Spatter – *(verb)* cover with drops or spots. splash or be splashed over a surface. *The child spattered the table with milk.* *(noun)* **1** a spray or splash. *I enjoyed getting wet in the spatter.* **2** a short outburst of sound. *The sudden spatter echoed through the halls.*

Spawn – *(verb)* **1** release or deposit eggs. produce off spring. *The frog spawned in the pond.* **2** produce or generate; give rise to. *The company spawned several products.* *(noun)* **1** the eggs of fish, frogs, etc. *The frogs' spawn will turn into tadpoles.* **2** offspring. *The dog licked its spawn.* **3** the mycelium of a fungus, especially a cultivated mushroom. *The spawn is very useful for mushroom cultivation.*

Speak – *(verb)* **1** say something. make a speech. communicate in or be able to communicate in a specified language. express the views or position of. express one's opinions frankly and publicly. speak more loudly. hail and hold communication with at sea. *I was glad I heard him speak.* **2** talk to in order to advise, pass on information, etc. appeal or relate to. *I speak for the benefit of the society.* **3** serve as evidence for something. show or manifest to be. *The door bolted from inside speaks of the maid's innocence.* **4** make a sound. bark. *All organisms speak in one language or the other.*

Spear – *(noun)* **1** a metal weapon with a pointed tip and a long shaft, used for thrusting or throwing. *The ancient spear was very valuable.* **2** a plant shoot, especially a pointed stem of asparagus or broccoli. *The monkeys broke the spears of the plant.* **3** denoting the male side or members of a family. compare with distaff. *There were a lot of spears on the family tree.* *(verb)* pierce or strike with a spear or other pointed object. *They speared the target.*

Spearhead – *(noun)* **1** the point of a spear. *Archaeologists found several spearheads on the site of the ancient battle.* **2** an individual or group leading an attack or movement. *The spearhead penetrated the advancing enemy.* *(verb)* lead an attack or movement. *The warrior effectively spearheaded the attack.*

Special – *(adjective)* **1** better, greater, or otherwise different from what is usual. *The special occasion deserves to be celebrated.* **2** designed for or belonging to a particular person, place, or event. studied in particular depth. *This ring is very special to me.* **3** used to denote education for children with particular needs. *Several children attend special schools.* *(noun)* **1** something designed or organized for a particular occasion or purpose. a dish not on the regular menu but served on a particular day. *What is today's special?* **2** a person assigned to a special duty. *Everyone waited for the special to arrive with the news.*

Speciality – *(noun)* **1** a pursuit, area of study, or skill to which someone has devoted themselves and in which they are expert. a product for which a person or region is famous. *Chicken curry was the chef's speciality.* **2** a branch of medicine or surgery. *Renal pathology is his specialty.*

Specialize – *(verb)* concentrate on and become expert in a particular skill or area. make a habit of engaging in. adapt or set apart to serve a special function. *I specialize in growing flowering plants.*

Species – *(noun)* **1** a group of living organisms consisting of similar individuals capable of exchanging genes or interbreeding, considered as the basic unit of taxonomy and denoted by a

Latin binomial, e.g. homo sapiens. *New species are being discovered every day.* **2** denoting a plant belonging to a distinct species rather than to one of the many varieties produced by hybridization: a species rose. *This tomato species were big and red.* **3** a kind or sort. *Flowers of a species look alike.* **4** the visible form of each of the elements of consecrated bread and wine in the Eucharist. *The Eucharistic species belong to the essence of sacrament.*

Specific – *(adjective)* **1** clearly defined or identified. precise and clear: when ordering goods be specific. of or relating uniquely to a particular subject. *Her instructions were quite specific.* **2** of, relating to, or connected with species or a species. *The long ears are a specific traits.* **3** levied at a fixed rate per physical unit of the thing taxed, regardless of its price. *The import duties are specific.* **4** of or denoting a physical quantity expressed in terms of a unit mass, volume, or other measure, or calculated as a ratio to the corresponding value for a substance used as a reference. *The specific mass of the compound has to be calculated.* *(noun)* **1** a medicine or remedy effective in treating a particular disease or part of the body. *The doctor prescribed a specific to my friend.* **2** a precise detail. *Let us deal with the specifics.*

Specification – *(noun)* **1** the action of specifying. a detailed description of the design and materials used to make something. a description of an invention accompanying an application for a patent. *I have brought the specifications of design for the meeting.* **2** a standard of workmanship, materials, etc. required to be met in a piece of work. *Let us aim to meet the specifications for the raw material exactly.*

Specify – *(verb)* **1** identify clearly and definitely. *They specified their choice of the dish clearly.* **2** include in an architect's or engineer's specifications. *I specified my requirements clearly to the builder.*

Specimen – *(noun)* **1** an individual animal, plant, object, etc. used as an example of its species or type for scientific study or display. an example of something regarded as typical of its class or group: a specimen signature. used to refer humorously to a person or animal. *He is a fine specimen of human species.* **2** a sample for medical testing, especially of urine. *Please deposit the specimen at the lab.*

Speck – *(noun)* a tiny spot. a small particle. *Don't worry it is just a speck.* *(verb)* mark with small spots. *The child specked the wall with paint.*

Spectacle – *(noun)* a visually striking performance or display. *The ballet was a spectacle.*

Spectacles – *(plural noun)* [British] a pair of glasses. *The spectacles suited him very well.*

Spectacular – *(adjective)* **1** very impressive, striking, or dramatic. *The spectacular fireworks show is about to begin.* **2** strikingly large; marked. *The building was spectacular in dimensions.* *(noun)* a performance or event produced on a large scale and with striking effects. *Let's all go and watch the spectacular.*

Spectator – *(noun)* a person who watches at a show, game, or other event. *The spectators applauded his performance.*

Specter – *(noun)* US spelling of spectre. *The specter floated around in the old building.*

Spectrum – *(noun)* **1** a band of colours produced by separation of the components of light by their different degrees of refraction according to wavelength, e.g. in a rainbow. the entire range of wavelengths of electromagnetic radiation. a characteristic series of frequencies of electromagnetic radiation emitted or absorbed by a substance. the components of a sound or other phenomenon arranged according to frequency, energy, etc. *The whole spectrum of colours was visible in the rainbow.* **2** a scale extending between two points; a range: the political spectrum. *The wide spectrum denoted the huge impact of the change.*

Speculate – *(verb)* **1** from a theory or conjecture without firm evidence. *The team was speculating the change.* **2** invest in stocks, property, or other ventures in the hope of gain but with the risk of loss. *He speculated blindly.*

Speculation – *(noun)* theory or conjecture without firm evidence. *His speculation proved to be accurate.*

Speech – *(noun)* **1** the expression of or the ability to express thoughts and feelings by articulate sounds. *The child developed speech very early.* **2** a formal address delivered to an audience. a sequence of lines written for one character in a play. *The President's speech motivated many young minds.*

Speechless – *(adjective)* unable to speak, especially as the temporary result of shock or strong emotion. *The teacher's response left me speechless.*

Speed – *(noun)* **1** the rate at which someone or something moves or operates or is able to move or operate. rapidity of movement or action. *They were moving at a high speed.* **2** each of the possible gear rations of a bicycle. *The bicycle had seven possible speeds.* **3** the light gathering power or number of a camera lens. the duration of a photographic exposure. the sensitivity of photographic film to light. *The photographer used a lens with a high speed.* **4** an amphetamine drug, especially methamphetamine. *They were caught using speed.* **5** success; prosperity. *He flaunted his speed at every opportunity.* *(verb)* **1** move quickly. move or work more quickly. *Please speed up if you want to catch your flight.* **2** travel at a speed greater than the legal limit. *The vehicle was speeding.* **3** take or be under the influence of an amphetamine drug. *The athlete speeded and was caught.* **4** make prosperous or successful: may god speed you. *Hope you speed soon.*

Speedy – *(adjective)* **1** done or occurring quickly. *That was a speedy recovery.* **2** moving quickly. *The speedy vehicle was stopped by the police.*

Spell – *(noun)* **1** a short period of time. a period of rest from work. *There was a short spell of silence.* **2** a series of overs in which a particular bowler bowls. *The fast bowler's spell was over.* *(verb)* take someone's place in order to allow them to rest briefly. take a brief rest. *The 12th man spelled for the injured fielder.*

Spellbound – *(verb)* hold the complete attention as if by magic. *The little girl left the crowd spellbound with her poetry.*

Spend – *(verb)* **1** pay out in buying or hiring goods or services. *He spends a lot of money in buying clothes.* **2** use or use up; exhaust. pass in a specified way. *His energy was spent.* *(noun)* an amount of money paid out. *What was your spend for the day?*

Spendthrift – *(noun)* a person who spends money in an extravagant, irresponsible way. *She was a spendthrift.*

Spew – *(verb)* **1** expel or be expelled in large quantities rapidly and forcibly. *The volcano spewed ash.* **2** [informal] vomit. *He spewed all over the place.* *(noun)* [informal] vomit. *The spew smelled horrible.*

Sphere – *(noun)* **1** a round solid figure, with every point on its surface equidistant from its centre. *The sphere of light became bigger by the day.* **2** each of a series of revolving concentrically arranged spherical shells in which celestial bodies were formerly thought to be set in a fixed relationship. a celestial body. the sky perceived as a vault upon or in which celestial bodies are represented as lying. a globe representing the earth. *The sphere revolved around the star.* **3** an area of activity, interest, or expertise; a group or section distinguished and unified by a particular characteristic. *The sphere of writers is an interesting group to be in.* *(verb)* enclose in or form into a sphere. *I sphered the dough.*

Spherical – *(adjective)* shaped like a sphere. of or relating to the properties of spheres. formed inside or on the surface of a sphere. *The scientists discovered a spherical asteroid heading towards the comet.*

Sphinx – *(noun)* **1** an ancient Egyptian stone figure having a lion's body and a human or animal head. *The Sphinx is located near the pyramids.* **2** an enigmatic or inscrutable person. *The manager was a sphinx.* **3** [north American] term for hawkmoth. *The sphinx hovered over the flowers.*

Spice – *(noun)* **1** an aromatic or pungent vegetable substance used to flavor food, e.g. pepper. *The dish had all the spices in the correct proportion.* **2** an element providing interest and excitement. *Action is the main spice in the movie.* **3** confectionery. *Honey* *was the spice of the cake. (verb)* **1** flavor with spice. *My grandmother spiced up the dish.* **2** make more exciting or interesting. *The art classes spiced up my life.*

Spider - *(noun)* **1** an eight legged predatory arachnid with an unsegmented body consisting of a fused head and thorax and a rounded abdomen, most kinds of which spin webs in which to capture insects. used in names of other arachnids, e.g. sea spider. *I am afraid of spiders.* **2** a long legged rest for a billiard cue that can be placed over a ball without touching it. *The organizers could not find any spiders for the tournament.* **3** [British] a set of radiating elastic ties used to hold a load in place on a vehicle. *The spider looked as if it would break under the load.* **4** another term for crawler. *The spider crawled out of side. (verb)* **1** move in a scuttling manner. *The insects spidered across the floor.* **2** form a pattern suggestive of a spider or its web. *The colourful spider in the painting was very artistic.*

Spike - *(noun)* [botany] a flower cluster formed of many flower heads attached directly to a long stem. *The colourful spikes made the garden beautiful.*

Spill - *(noun)* a thin strip of wood or paper used for lighting a fire, pipe, etc. *The campers used a spill to light a fire.*

Spin - *(verb)* **1** turn or cause to turn round quickly. give a sensation of dizziness. move or cause to move through the air with a revolving motion. shape by pressure applied during rotation on a lathe. *All planets spin on their axes.* **2** draw out and convert it into threads. make in this way. *They were spinning the yarn.* **3** produce or construct by extruding a fine viscous thread from a special gland. *The spider spins a web.* **4** make something last as long as possible. *He kept on spinning the tale till his friends fell asleep.* **5** lose control in a skid. *The skater spinned out of control. (noun)* **1** a spinning motion. a fast revolving motion of an aircraft as it descends rapidly. the intrinsic angular momentum of a subatomic particle. *The spin lasted for a full two minutes.* **2** a brief trip in a vehicle for pleasure. *Let's go for a spin to take our mind off work.* **3** a favourable bias or slant given to a news story. *The news reporter gave the story a good spin.* **4** a piece of good or bad luck. *The spin wasn't in her favour.*

Spinach - *(noun)* an edible Asian plant of the goosefoot family, with large dark green leaves which are eaten as a vegetable. *Spinach is good for health.*

Spinal - *(adjective)* of or relating to the spine. *Her spinal injury took a long time to heal.*

Spine - *(noun)* **1** a series of vertebrae extending from the skull to the small of the back, enclosing the spinal cord and providing support for the thorax and abdomen; the backbone. *It is important to sit with your spine in the correct position.* **2** a central feature or main source of strength. *She is the spine of the team.* **3** the part of a book's jacket or cover that encloses the inner edges of the pages. *The spine was strong enough to hold the 1000 pages of the book.* **4** a prickle or other hard pointed projection or structure. *The spines on the board pointed up.* **5** a linear pay scale operated by some large organizations that allows flexibility for local and specific conditions. *The spine was convenient for the employees.*

Spinster - *(noun)* an unmarried woman, typically an older woman beyond the usual age for marriage. *The spinster didn't want to get married.*

Spiral - *(adjective)* winding in a continuous and gradually widening curve around a central point or axis. winding in a continuous curve of constant diameter about a central axis, as though along a cylinder; helical. denoting galaxies in which the stars and gas clouds are concentrated mainly in spiral arms. *The spiral staircase was very risky. (noun)* **1** a spiral curve, shape, or pattern. *The spiral of the pasta wasn't even.* **2** a progressive rise or fall of prices, wages, etc. each responding to an upward or downward stimulus provided by a previous one. a process of progressive deterioration. *The spiral in prices of the fuel has made travelling very expensive. (verb)* **1** take or cause to follow a spiral course. *They* *spiralled down the slide.* **2** show a continuous and dramatic increase. decrease continuously. *The spiralling prices were a cause for worry.*

Spire – *(noun)* [zoology] the upper tapering part of the spiral shell of a gastropod mollusc. *The snail had a beautiful spire.*

Spirit – *(noun)* **1** the non physical part of a person which is the seat of emotions and character. this regarded as surviving after the death of the body, often manifested as a ghost. a supernatural being. *People say his spirit still haunts the building.* **2** the prevailing or typical quality or mood: the nation's egalitarian spirit. a person identified with their role or most prominent quality: he was a leading spirit in the conference. a person's mood. *The spirit of a revolution brought around a transformation in the nation.* **3** courage, energy, and determination. *Show some spirit young man.* **4** the real meaning or intention of something as opposed to its strict verbal interpretation. *You missed the spirit of the conversation.* **5** strong distilled liquor such as rum. a volatile liquid, especially a fuel, prepared by distillation: aviation spirit. a solution of volatile components extracted from something: spirits of turpentine. *Stay away from spirits for some days.* *(verb)* **1** convey rapidly and secretly. *The messengers spirited the news to the king.* **2** animate or cheer up someone. *We need to spirit him up.*

Spiritual – *(adjective)* **1** of, relating to, or affecting the human spirit as opposed to material or physical things. *My sister enjoys spiritual discussions.* **2** of or relating to religion or religious belief. *My mother enjoys spiritual ceremonies.* *(noun)* a religious song of a kind associated with black Christians of the southern US. *They all sang spiritual together.*

Spit – *(noun)* **1** a long, thin metal rod pushed through meat in order to hold and turn it while it is roasted over an open fire. *The spit was too hot to touch.* **2** a narrow point of land projecting into the sea. *The spit was a popular picnic spot.* *(verb)* put a spit through meat. *Spit the lamb and put it on the fire to roast.*

Spite – *(noun)* a desire to hurt, annoy, or offend. *She let go of her spite against her opponent.* *(verb)* deliberately hurt, annoy, or offend. *She felt guilty after spiting her friend.*

Spiteful – *(adjective)* showing or caused by malice. *She is very spiteful.*

Splash – *(verb)* **1** make strike or fall on something in drops. strike or move around in water, causing it to fly about. land on water. *Children splashed around in water.* **2** display in a prominent place in a newspaper or magazine. *The newspaper splashed the story on the front page.* **3** spend money freely. *They splashed to celebrate their special day.* **4** be decorated with scattered patches of. *The sheet was splashed by children.* *(noun)* **1** an instance of splashing or the sound made by this. a small quantity of liquid that has splashed on to a surface. a small quantity of liquid added to a drink. *The child fell into the puddle with a loud splash.* **2** a bright patch of colour. *The splash of yellow brightened the sheet.* **3** a prominent news feature or story. *The splash was the talk of the town for days.*

Splashdown – *(noun)* alighting of a returning spacecraft on the sea. *The splashdown was successful and the crew were all fine.*

Splatter – *(verb)* splash with a sticky or viscous liquid. splash. *The child splattered the glue over the sheet.* *(noun)* **1** a splash of a sticky or viscous liquid. *The splatter of colour was difficult to wash.* **2** denoting or referring to films featuring many violent and gruesome deaths. *I would not go and watch a splash with my family.*

Splay – *(verb)* **1** spread or be spread out or further apart. *They splayed the dummy's arms.* **2** construct so that it is wider at one side of the wall than the other. *The staircase was splayed intentionally.* *(noun)* **1** a tapered widening of a road at an intersection to increase visibility. *The driver stopped at the splay to take stock of things.* **2** a surface making an oblique angle with another, especially a splayed window or other aperture. *The splayed window was an attractive feature of the house.* *(adjective)* turned outward or widened: the girl sat splay legged. *The dummy stood splay armed.*

Spleen – *(noun)* **1** an abdominal organ involved in the production and removal of blood cells and forming part of the immune system. *I had a pain in my spleen.* **2** bad temper; spite. *He displayed a lot of spleen.*

Splendid –* *(adjective)* **1** magnificent; very impressive. *The valley was a splendid sight.* **2** [informal] excellent. *This is a splendid news.*

Splendour – *(noun)* splendid appearance. *The audience were blinded by all the splendour.*

Splice – *(verb)* join by interweaving the strands at the ends. join at the ends. join or insert. *The sailors spliced the rope ends.* *(noun)* a spliced join. the wedge shaped tang of a cricket bat handle, forming a joint with the blade. *The splice was secure and difficult to undo.*

Splint – *(noun)* **1** a strip of rigid material for supporting a broken bone when it has been set. *He had to get a splint for his broken arm.* **2** a long, thin strip of wood used in basketwork or to light a fire. *The armymen practiced using splints to light a fire.* **3** a bony enlargement on the inside of a horse's leg, on the splint bone. *The race horse hurt its splint.* *(verb)* secure with a splint or splints. *The doctors splinted his arm.*

Splinter – *(noun)* a small, thin, sharp piece of wood, glass, etc. broken off from a larger piece. *A splinter pierced my skin.* *(verb)* break or cause to break into splinters. *The blow splintered the log of wood.*

Split – *(verb)* **1** break or cause to break forcibly into parts. cause the fission of. *The cell split into two.* **2** divide or cause to divide into parts or groups. end a marriage or other relationship. *They are splitting up.* **3** suffer great pain from a headache. *My head is splitting.* **4** betray the secrets of or inform on someone. *The informer split on his friends.* **5** leave, especially suddenly. *I think I need to split.* *(noun)* **1** a tear, crack, or fissure. *The split was getting wider.* **2** an instance of splitting or being split. *The split was painful for the family.* **3** an act of leaping in the air or sitting down with the legs straight and at right angles to the body, one in front and the other behind, or one at each side. *The split performed by the dancers was very graceful.* **4** a split osier used in basketwork. *The split used to make the basket was very flexible.* **5** a single thickness of split hide. *The split has started to decay.*

Sprit – *(noun)* a small spar reaching diagonally from a mast to the upper outer carner of the sail. *The sprit broke in the rough weather.*

Spoke – *(noun)* **1** each of the bars or wire rods connecting the centre of a wheel to its rim.*The spokes of the wheel were broken.* **2** each of a set of radial handle projecting from a ship's wheel. *The spokes provided a good grip.* **3** each of the metal rods in an umbrella to which the material is attached. *The spokes of the umbrella were very fragile.*

Spokesman – *(noun)* a person who makes statements on behalf of a group. *He was born to be a spokesman.*

Sponge – *(noun)* **1** a sedentary aquatic invertebrate with a soft porous body supported by a framework of fibres or sickles. *The wreck was covered with sponges.* **2** a piece of a soft, light, porous, absorbent substance originally consisting of the fibrous skeleton of a sponge but now usually made of synthetic material, used for washing, as padding, etc. a piece of sponge impregnated with spermicide and inserted into a woman's vagina as a form of barrier contraceptive. *After spilling the milk, the child wiped it off the floor with a sponge.* **3** a very light cake made with eggs, sugar, and flour but little or no fat. *The sponge had risen very well in the oven.* **4** [informal] a person who lives at someone else's expense. *She told him clearly that he was being a sponge.* **5** [informal] a heavy drinker. *He used to be a sponge before he gave up drinking.* **6** metal in a porous form. *The sponge was heavy.* *(verb)* wipe or clean with a wet sponge or cloth. *Please sponge the table top.* **2** obtain money or food from others without giving anything in return. *He sponged others' money.* **3** give a decorative effect to by applying paint with a sponge. decorate using a sponge. *The painters sponged the wall to create a lovely pattern.*

Spongy – *(adjective)* **1** like a sponge, especially in being porous, compressible, or absorbent. *The creature had a spongy feel to it.* **2** having an open, porous structure. *The cloth is very spongy.* **3** lacking firmness. *Spongy material won't work here.*

Sponsor – *(noun)* **1** a person or organization that pays for or contributes to the costs of a sporting or artistic event or a radio or television programme in return for advertising. *The sponsors wanted their product to be featured at a prominent place.* **2** a person who pledges a certain amount of money to a charity after another person has participated in a fundraising event. *The sponsors contributed double the amount raised by the fundraiser.* **3** a person who introduces and supports a proposal for legislation. *The sponsor felt that the new legislation would make a difference.* **4** a person taking official responsibility for the actions of another. a godparent at a child's baptism. a person presenting a candidate for confirmation. *The stranger offered to become a sponsor for the abandoned child.* *(verb)* be a sponsor for. *The successful businessman sponsored the charity event.*

Spontaneous – *(adjective)* **1** performed or occurring as a result of an unpremeditated inner impulse and without external stimulus. occurring without apparent external cause. instinctive or involuntary. *His spontaneous help was well appreciated.* **2** open, natural, and uninhibited. *He is a very spontaneous person.* **3** growing naturally and without being tended or cultivated. *The spontaneous growth of plants in the garden needed trimming.*

Spooky – *(adjective)* **1** sinister or ghostly. *The spooky mansion has always been an attraction for the children.* **2** easily frightened. *She is such a spooky person.*

Spoon – *(noun)* **1** an implement consisting of a small, shallow oval or round bowl on a long handle, used for eating, stirring, and serving food. a pair of spoons held in the hand and beaten together rhythmically as a percussion instrument. *The man used a spoon to eat rice.* **2** a fishing lure designed to wobble when pulled through the water. *The spoon helped us catch many fish today.* **3** an oar with a broad curved blade. *The spoon was lost in the water.* *(verb)* **1** transfer with a spoon. *He spooned the rice into a bowl.* **2** behave in an amorous way. *He spooned with the actress.* **3** hit up into the air with a soft or weak stroke. *The tired athlete spooned the ball into the air.*

Spoonful – *(noun)* the contents in a spoon. *The child ate only a spoonful of rice.*

Sporadic – *(adjective)* occurring at irregular intervals or only in a few places. *The city was under curfew because of reports of sporadic violence.*

Sport – *(noun)* **1** an activity involving physical exertion and skill in which an individual or team competes against another or others for entertainment. success or pleasure derived from an activity such as hunting. *I love sports.* **2** a person who behaves in a good or specified way in response to teasing, defeat, etc. *He is usually a sport.* **3** a friendly form of address, especially between unacquainted men. *"Hey sport, how are you doing?"* *(verb)* **1** wear or display. *She sported an expensive watch.* **2** amuse oneself or play in a lively, energetic way. *The children sported throughout the day.*

Sportsmen – *(noun)* men who take part in a sport, especially as a professional. *The sportsmen gathered to discuss the improvements in the stadium.*

Sporty – *(adjective)* **1** fond of or good at sport. *The athlete was sporty even when he was a child.* **2** suitable for wearing for sport or for casual use. *She wore smart, sporty shoes.* **3** compact and with fast acceleration. *The sporty car was stopped by the policeman for zigzagging through the street.*

Spot – *(noun)* **1** a small round or roundish mark, differing in colour or texture from the surface around it. a pip on a domino, playing card, or dice. *The spots on one cheetah were darker than the spots on the others.* **2** a pimple. *She was worried about the spot on her face.* **3** a particular place, point, or position. a small feature or part with a particular quality: his bald spot. a place for an individual item within a show. *Please decide the spot of the meeting.* **4** a small amount of something: a spot of lunch. *I only had a spot of lunch.* **5** denoting a system of trading in which commodities or currencies are delivered and paid for immediately after a sale. *They organized a spot to support the charity.* *(verb)* **1** see, notice, or recognize that is difficult to detect or sought after. locate an enemy's position, typically from the air. *I spotted my friend in the crowd.* **2** mark or become marked with spots. *The children spotted the sketch of the leopard.* **3** rain slightly. *It was spotting when I woke up in the morning.* **4** place on its designated starting point on a billiard table. *The balls were spotted and the game began.* **5** give or lend to. allow to in a game or sport. *They spotted an exception in the match.*

Spotless – *(adjective)* absolutely clean or pure. *His spotless white shirt was visible amongst the crowd.*

Spotlight – *(noun)* **1** a lamp projecting a narrow, intense beam of light directly on to a place or person. *She couldn't believe it when the spotlight fell on her.* **2** intense public attention. *He enjoyed being in the spotlight.* *(verb)* **1** illuminate with a spotlight. *The organizers spotlighted the winner.* **2** direct attention to. *He spotlighted the defect.*

Spouse – *(noun)* a husband or wife. *He introduced his spouse in the party.*

Spout – *(noun)* **1** a projecting tube or lip through or over which liquid can be poured from a container. *The spout of the kettle was dirty.* **2** a stream of liquid issuing with great force. *I got out of the way of the spout.* **3** a pipe, trough, or chute for conveying liquid, grain, etc. a lift in a pawnshop used to convey pawned items up for storage. *The spout was already full.* *(verb)* **1** send out or issue forcibly in a stream. *The geyser spouted at regular intervals.* **2** express in a lengthy or declamatory way. *She spouted for a long time, ignoring the yawns of her friends.*

Sprain – *(verb)* wrench the ligaments of violently so as to cause pain and swelling but not dislocation. *I sprained my arm.* *(noun)* the result of such a wrench. *The sprain in my arm was very painful.*

Sprawl – *(verb)* **1** sit, lie, or fall with one's limbs spread out in an ungainly way. *My father scolded me when he found my friends sprawled all over the drawing room.* **2** spread out irregularly over a large area. *The disease sprawled across the city.* *(noun)* **1** a sprawling position or movement. *His sprawl made him look lazy.* **2** a sprawling group or mass. the disorganized expansion of an urban or industrial area into the adjoining countryside. *The sprawling city threatened to swallow the forest cover.*

Spray – *(noun)* **1** a stem or small branch of a tree or plant, bearing flowers and foliage. *The sprays were weighed down by the flowers.* **2** a bunch of cut flowers arranged in an attractive way. a brooch in the form of a bouquet. *The spray was very beautiful.*

Spread – *(verb)* **1** open out so as to increase in surface area, width, or length. stretch out so that they are far apart. *The spilt milk spread out all over the floor.* **2** extend or distribute over a wide area or a specified period of time. move apart so as to cover a wider area. gradually reach or cause to reach a wider area or more people. *We have to spread awareness everywhere.* **3** apply in an even layer. cover with a substance in such a way. be able to be applied in such a way. *She spread the butter on her toast.* *(noun)* **1** the fact or action of spreading. *The spread of education was beneficial to the country.* **2** the extent, width, or area something. the difference between on bread. *The environmentalists set out to measure the spread of the forest.* **5** an article or advertisement covering several columns or pages of a newspaper or magazine. *The spread was colourful but left very less space for anything else.* **6** [north American], a large farm or ranch. *He was the owner of the spread.* **7**. [informal] a large and elaborate meal. *She couldn't wait to get started with the spread.*

Spree – *(noun)* a spell of unrestrained activity of a particular kind. *I went on a shopping spree after receiving my salary. (verb)* dated take part in a spree. *I spreed with rest of the participants.*

Sprightly – *(adjective)* lively; energetic. *She is a sprightly young lady.*

Spring – *(verb)* **1** move suddenly or rapidly upwards or forwards. cause to rise from cover. *The cat sprung forwards on the mouse.* **2** move suddenly by or as if by the action of a spring. *She sprung back as soon as she sat on the couch.* **3** operate or cause to operate by means of a spring mechanism. *The drawer sprung back.* **4** suddenly develop or appear. present something suddenly or unexpectedly to. *The disease suddenly sprung up.* **5** [informal] bring about the escape or release of a prisoner. *The convicts were brought to the court again because they helped spring the accused.* **6** provide with springs. *Workmen springed the couch.* **7** become warped or split. *The new branches sprung together.* **8** [north American] pay for. *He sprung the uniforms for the team. (noun)* **1** the season after winter and before summer, in which vegetation begins to appear. [astronomy] the period from the vernal equinox to the summer solstice. *I love the spring because of the flowers.* 2 an elastic device, typically a helical metal coil, that can be pressed or pulled but returns to its former shape when released. elastic quality. *The spring was very difficult to make straight.* **3**. a wells up from an underground source. *The hot water springs were a popular tourist destination.* **5** an upward curvature of a ship's deck planking from the horizontal. a split in a wooden plank or spar under strain. *The spring of the ship was damaged.* **6** [nautical] a hawser laid out from a ship's bow or stern and secured to a fixed point in order to prevent movement of assist maneuvering. *The spring was too tight.*

Springy – *(adjective)* **1** springing back quickly when squeezed or stretched. *The springy couch was very comfortable to sit on.* **2** light and confident. *He approached the interviewer with a springy steps.*

Sprinkle – *(verb)* **1** scatter or pour small drops or particles over. scatter or pour over an throughout. *I sprinkled salt over my salad.* **2** [north American] rain very lightly. *It sprinkled in the morning. (noun)* **1** a small quantity or amount that is sprinkled. *The sprinkle was just enough for taste.* **2** [north American] a light rain. *The sprinkle increased the humidity.* **3** [north American] tiny sugar strands and balls used for decorating cakes and desserts. *The sprinkle made the cake look beautiful.*

Sprint – *(verb)* run at full speed over a short distance. (noun) an act or spell of sprinting. a short, fast race run over a distance of 400 meters of less. a short, fast race in cycling, horse racing, etc. *He sprinted through the market to catch the rickshaw.*

Sprout – *(verb)* produce shoots. grow plant shoots or hair. start to grow or develop. *My tamarind plant sprouted branches. (noun)* **1** a shoot of a plant. *The sprout was still very fragile.* **2** short for Brussels sprout. *She made sprouts for lunch.*

Spruce – *(verb)* produce shoots. grow start to grow or develop. *The leaves spruced after a month in the plant. (noun)* **1** a shoot of a plant. *The spruce was weak but green.* **2** short for Brussels sprout. *He ate spruce for dinner.*

Spur – *(noun)* **1** a device with a small spike or a spiked wheel, worn on a rider's heel or urging a horse forward. *The rider fell down from the horse and broke the spur.* **2** an incentive. *Money was a good spur for him.* 3 a projection from a mountain or mountain range. botany a slender tubular projection from the base of a flower, e.g. an orchid, typically containing nectar. a short fruit-bearing side shoot. a horny spike on the back of the leg of a cock or male game bird. *The spur was rocky and did not have any trees.* **4** a short branch road or railway line. *The bullock cart took the spur to avoid the traffic.* **5** a small support for ceramic ware in a kiln. *The spur wasn't strong enough to hold the bottle. (verb)* **1** urge forward with spurs. *He spurred the horse to hard.* **2** encourage; give an incentive to. *The manager spurred his team to achieve the targets.* **3** prune in a side shoot so as to form a spur close to the stem. *The gardener spurred the plants.*

Spurious – *(adjective)* false or fake. *The text claimed to be ancient was of spurious origin.*

Spurn – *(verb)* reject with contempt. *She spurned his attention.*

Spurt – *(verb)* gush out suddenly in a forceful way. *The water gushed forwards in a spurt.*

Spy – *(noun)* a person employed to secretly gather information about someone or something. *The spy kept an eye on the suspect.*

Squabble – *(noun)* a trivial noisy quarrel. *The noise of their squabble disturbed the neighbours. (verb)* engage in a squabble. *They squabbled frequently.*

Squad – *(noun)* **1** a small number of soldiers assembled for drill or assigned to a particular task. *The squad worked together as a good team.* **2** a group of sports players from which a team is chosen. *It was difficult to select a few from the squad.* **3** a division of police force dealing with a particular type of crime. *The squad rushed to diffuse the bomb.*

Squadron – *(noun)* **1** an operational unit in an air force consisting of two or more flights of aircraft. *The squadron performed a spectacular stunt.* **2** a principal division of an armoured or cavalry regiment, consisting to two or more troops. *The squadron marched on towards the target.* **3** a group of warships detached on a particular duty or under the command of a flag officer. *The squadron of ship sailed into the enemy territory.*

Squalid – *(adjective)* **1** extremely dirty and unpleasant. *The squalid shop hardly ever got any customers.* **2** showing a contemptible lack of moral standards: a squalid attempt to buy votes. *The voters condemned the squalid attempt to extort money.*

Squall – *(noun)* **1** a sudden violent gust of wind or localized storm, especially one bringing rain, snow, or sleet. *The squall lasted only for about half an hour.* **2** a loud cry. *The squall startled everyone. (verb)* cry noisily and continuously. *The child squalled when her mother didn't buy him a toy.*

Squalor – *(noun)* the state of being squalid. *I am tired of your squalor.*

Squander – *(verb)* waste in a reckless or foolish manner. *He squandered his father's money.*

Square – *(noun)* **1** a plane figure with four equal straight sides and four right angles. *The child drew a square on the paper.* **2** an open, typically four sided, area surrounded by buildings. *Many trees were planted in the square.* **3** an area within a military barracks or camp used for drill. *All soldiers headed to the square for a drill.* **4** cricket a closer cut area at the centre of a ground, any strip of which may be prepared as a wicket. *The square was damp with dew.* **5** [historical] a body of infantry drawn up in rectangular form. *The square moved at a rapid pace.* **6** [US] a block of buildings bounded by four streets. *The square was all grey.* **7** the product of number multiplied by itself. *He can calculate squares of large numbers without using a calculator.* **8** a unit of 100 square ft used as a measure of flooring, roofing, etc. *400 square ft of area needs to be tiled.* **9** an L-shaped or T-shaped instrument used for obtaining or testing right angles. *The child was able to use the square expertly.* **10** [informal] a person considered to be old-fashioned or boringly conventional. *She is such a square.* **11** [astrology] an aspect of 90°. *Please explain me the concept of a square in astrology. (adjective)* **1** having the shape or approximate shape of a square. having or forming a right angle, exactly or approximately. *I am going to the square park for a walk.* **2** denoting a unit of measurement equal to the area of a square whose side is of the unit specified. denoting the length of each side of a square shape or object. *The area of this park is 1500 square feet.* **3** at right angles. cricket & soccer in a direction transversely across the field or pitch. *His position was square to the bowler.* **4** broad and solid in shape. *The square man was very strong.* **5** level or parallel. property arranged. on even terms. *It was a square surface.* **6** fair and honest. *It was a square deal.* **7** [informal] old-fashioned or boringly conventional. *She had some very square views.* **8** simple and straightforward. *I am speaking a square language. (adverb)* **1** directly; straight.

Please work on the assignment square. **2** cricket & soccer in a direction transversely across the field or pitch. *Please stand square to the bowler. (verb)* **1** make square or rectangular. mark out in square. *He squared the paper.* **2** multiply by itself. *He squared the numbers very quickly.* **3** make or be compatible. *You can square yourself to her.* **4** balance or settle a bill or debt. make the score of a match or game even. *They quickly squared the score.* **5** [informal] secure the help or acquiescence or someone, especially by offering an inducement. *He squared an arrangement with the security services.* **6** bring into a position in which they part of a ship at right angles to the keel or other point of reference. *The skipper commanded the ship to be squared to the transit.* **8** [astrology] have a square aspect with another planet or position. *Venus at times has a square aspect with Mars.*

Squash – *(noun)* **1** a gourd with flesh that can be cooked and eaten as a vegetable. *I don't like squash much.* **2** the plant which produces such gourds. *They have squash in their garden.*

Squat – *(verb)* **1** crouch or sit with the knees bent and the heels close to or touching the buttocks or thighs. *The homeless people squatted on the pavement.* **2** unlawfully occupy an uninhabited building or area of land. *They squatted in the abandoned house. (adjective)* short or low, and disproportionately broad or wide. *The teacher told the students not to make fun of their classmate's squat build. (noun)* a squatting position or movement. an exercise in which a person squats down and rises again with a barbell behind their neck. *He does a hundred squats every day.* **2** a building occupied by squatters. an act of squatting in an uninhabited building. *The squat landed them in the jail.* **3** [north American informal] short for diddly-squat. *She only spent a squat amount on the gifts.*

Squawk – *(verb)* **1** make a loud, harsh noise. *The parrot squawked.* **2** say something in a loud, discordant tone. complain about something. *Her mother asked her not to squawk and to speak clearly. (noun)* an act of squawking. *The parrot's squawk was very shrill.*

Squeak – *(noun)* a short, high-pitched sound or cry. a single remark or communication. *I didn't hear a squeak out of them. (verb)* **1** make a squeak. say something in a high-pitched tone. *The child squeaked when she was made to eat cereal.* **2** [informal] inform on someone. *The servant squeaked on the master.* **3** [informal] achieve something by a narrow margin: the bill squeaked through. *She barely managed to squeak a win.*

Squeal – *(noun)* a long, high-pitched cry or noise. *The squeal rang through the hall. (verb)* **1** make a squeal. say something in a high-pitched, excited tone. *The children squealed in excitement.* **2** complain. *Your squealing is getting to me now.* **3** [informal] inform on someone. *The maid squealed on the family.*

Squeeze – *(verb)* **1** firmly press from opposite or all sides, typically with the fingers. extract from something by squeezing. *I squeezed the water out of the sponge.* **2** obtain from someone with difficulty. [informal] put pressure on to supply information, authorization, etc. have a damaging or restricting effect on: the economy is being squeezed by foreign debt repayment. bridge force to discard a guarding or potentially winning card. *The police squeezed the information out of the suspect.* **3** [informal] shoot a round or shot from a gun. take a photograph. *The robbers squeezed in the air.* **4** manage to get into or through a restricted space. move closer to and press tightly against someone or something. manage to find time for someone or something. force someone or something out of a domain or activity. *I squeezed through the crowd to reach the stage. (noun)* **1** an act of amount of liquid extracted by squeezing. *The squeeze from the oranges was very nice.* **4** dated a pressure. [informal] money illegally extorted or exacted from someone. *The squeeze was returned to the rightful owner.* **6** a moulding or cast of an object, or a copy of a design, obtained by pressing a pliable substance round or over it. *The squeeze was used over and over again.*

Squib - *(noun)* **1** a small firework that hisses before exploding. *My nephew didn't find the squib exciting.* **2** a short piece of satirical writing. [north American] a short news item. *The squib was a huge success.* **3** [informal] a small or weak person. *Students were surprised by the strength the squib demonstrated.* **4** [American football] a short kick on a kick-off. *The match started with a squib.* *(verb)* **1** a short distance on a kickoff. *The player squibbed on a kickoff.* **2** [archaic] utter, write, or publish a satirical or sarcastic attack. lampoon. *The writer squibbed and was arrested for it.*

Squid - *(noun)* an elongated, fast swimming cephalopod mollusk with eight arms and two long tentacles. the flesh of this animal as food. an artificial fishing bait resembling a squid. *The squid swam away quickly.* *(verb)* fish using squid as bait. *At times they squid to catch a big fish.*

Squiggle - *(noun)* a short line that curls and loops irregularly. She makes squiggles while talking on the phone. *(verb)* [chiefly north American] wriggle; squirm. squeeze from a tube so as to make squiggles on a surface. *The little girl squiggled on the paper.*

Squint - *(verb)* **1** look at someone or something with party closed eyes. partly close. *He squinted in the sun.* **2** have a squint affecting one eye. *She has squinted since childhood.* *(noun)* **1** a permanent deviation in the direction of the gaze of one eye. *She had a slight squint in one eye.* **2** [informal] a quick or casual look. *The squint suited her.* **3** an oblique opening through a wall in a church permitting a view of the altar. *She saw the ceremony through the squint.* *(adjective)* [chiefly] Scottish not straight or level. *The squint floor needed to be fixed.*

Squire - *(noun)* **1** a country gentleman, especially the chief landowner in an area. US [archaic] a title given to a magistrate, lawyer, or judge in some rural districts. *The squire walked with a lot of poise.* **2** [British] [informal] used as a friendly form of address by one man to another. *"Hey squire! How about meeting at the pub?"* **3** [historical] a young nobleman acting as an attended to a knight before becoming a knight himself. *The squire was a brave man.* *(verb)* accompany or escort a woman. dated have a romantic relationship with a woman. *The gentleman squired the lady through the crowd.*

Squirm - *(verb)* wriggle or twist the body from side to side, especially due to nervousness or discomfort. be embarrassed or ashamed. *The man squirmed in pain.* *(noun)* a wriggling movement. *The squirm proved that he was in a great pain.*

Squirrel - *(noun)* an agile tree-dwelling rodent with a bushy tail, typically feeding on nuts and seeds. used in names of other rodents of the same family e.g. ground squirrel. *The squirrel was running up and down the tree.* *(verb)* **1** hide money or valuables in a safe place. *The rich man squirreled a lot of money at unknown places.* **2** move about inquisitively or busily. *The new reporter squirreled through the party.*

Squirt - *(verb)* **1** be or cause to be ejected in a thin jet from a small opening wet with a jet of liquid. *The water squirted out of the pipe suddenly.* **2** transmit in highly compressed or speeded-up form. *The fire-fighters squirted water at the burning building.* *(noun)* **1** a thin jet of liquid. a device from which liquid may be squirted. *The squirt shocked me.* **2** [informal] a puny or insignificant person. *The squirt stood ground for the class.* **3** a compressed radio signal transmitted at high speed. *The squirt couldn't be heard clearly.*

Stab - *(verb)* **1** thrust a knife or other pointed weapon into. *I stabbed the pumpkin with the knife.* **2** thrust a pointed object at. *I stabbed a skewer at the meat.* **3** cause a sudden sharp sensation. *A sharp pain stabbed through my stomach.* *(noun)* **1** an act of stabbing. a wound made by stabbing. *The stab needed immediate treatment.* **2** a sudden sharp feeling or pain. *The stab of pain was too sharp to bear.* **3** [informal] an attempt to do. *Please take a stab at this.*

Stable - *(adjective)* **1** not likely to give way or overturn; firmly fixed. *The scaffolding was very stable.* **2** not deteriorating in health after an injury or operation. *His condition was stable after the operation.* **3** emotionally well-balanced.

She is a very stable person. **4** not likely to change or fail. *The Government is very stable.* **5** not liable to undergo chemical decomposition or radioactive decay. *Scientists ensure that the radioactive material stored in the lab is stable.*

Stability – *(noun)* the state of being stable. *You can be sure of the program's stability.*

Stack – *(noun)* **1** a pile, especially a neat one. *The clothes were all arranged in a stack.* **2** a rectangular or cylindrical pile of hay, straw, etc. *The stacks lay in the fields for days.* **3** [informal] a large quantity of something. *He ate a stack of rice.* **4** a vertical arrangement of hi-fi or guitar amplification equipment. *The musician crashed through the stack.* **5** a number of aircraft flying in circles at different altitudes around the same point while waiting to land at an airport. *We have a huge stack at the moment.* **6** a pyramidal group of rifles. *No rifle from the stack was ever used.* **7** compact unit of shelving in part of a library normally closed to the public. *Several books that were never borrowed were moved to the stacks.* **8** computing a set of storage locations from which the most recently stored item is the first to be retrieved. *The computer cleared the stack fairly quickly.* **9** a chimney or vertical exhaust pipe. *The stack was full of soot.* **10** [British] a column of rock standing in the sea. *The stack was a resting place for seagulls.* **11** [British] a measure for a pile of wood of 108 cu. ft. *The stack needed to be transported to the construction site.* *(verb)* **1** arrange in a stack. fill, or cover with stacks of things. *He stacked the cupboard with pillows.* **2** cause to fly in stacks. *Many aircrafts were stacked because of the heavy traffic at the airport.* **3** shuffle or arrange dishonestly. *Together the two officers stacked up the funds.* **4** [informal] having large breasts. *She had huge stacks.* **5** computing placed in a queue for subsequent processing. *Several instructions were stacked up as the processor wasn't responding.*

Stadium – *(noun)* **1** an athletic or sports ground with tiers of seats for spectators. *The stadium was being prepared for the games.* **2** a racing track. *The stadium was surrounded by enthusiastic spectators.* **2** an ancient roman or Greek measure of length, about 185 metres. *The field measures more than* **5** *stadiums.*

Staff – *(noun)* a mixture of plaster of Paris, cement, etc. used for temporary building work. *The construction workers had run out of staff.*

Stag – *(noun)* **1** a fully adult male deer. *The stag was a magnificent creature.* **2** an adult male turkey. *The stag followed the female turkeys everywhere.* **3** denoting a social gathering attended by men only. [north American] a man who attends a social gathering unaccompanied by a female partner. *All of the groom's friends enjoyed the stag.* **4** [British] stock exchange a person who applies for shares in a new issue with a view to selling at once for a profit. *The stag made a lot of money.* *(adverb)* [chiefly north American] without a female partner at a social gathering. *He came stag.* *(verb)* **1** [British] stock exchange buy and sell them at once for a profit. *He stagged the stock.* **2** [north American informal] roughly cut off short. *The chairman stagged his speech because of the noise.*

Stage – *(noun)* **1** a point, period, or step in a process or development. a section of a journey or race. *We have reached the second stage in the building project.* **2** each of two or more sections of a rocket or spacecraft that are jettisoned in turn when their propellant is exhausted. *The stages of the rocket were all running out of fuel.* **3** [electronics] a part of a circuit containing a single amplifying transistor or valve. *The electrician couldn't detect current in the stage.* **4** a raised floor or platform on which actors, entertainers, or speakers perform. the acting or theatrical profession. *The stage was decorated very beautifully.* **5** a scene of action of forum of debate. *The stage was set for the discussion.* **6** a floor of a building. *My office is on the third stage.* **7** a raised plate on which a slide or specimen is placed for examination. *The lab assistant placed the specimen on the stage.* **8** [archaic] term for stagecoach. *The stage was full and moved at a leisurely pace.* *(verb)* **1** present a performance of a play or other show. organize and participle in a public event. cause something dramatic or unexpected to happen. *The organizers staged the famous play.* 2 [chiefly medicine] assign to a particular stage in a process. *The doctors staged the disease.*

Stagger – *(verb)* **1** walk or move unsteadily, as if about to fall. [archaic] cause to stagger. *The drunk man staggered across the street.* **2** astonish. *The evidence staggered the jury.* **3** spread over a period of time. *Let us stagger the reforms over 3 years.* **4** arrange so that they are not in line. *The soldiers moved in a stagger.* **5** [archaic] hesitate. *I staggered taking the decision for too long.* *(noun)* **1** arangement of the runners on a track at the start of a race. *The players had to wait on the tracks for some time after the stagger.* **3** an arrangement of the wings of a biplane so that their front edges are not in line. *The plane's wings were arranged in a stagger.*

Stagnant – *(adjective)* motionless and often having an unpleasant smell as a consequence. showing little activity. *The stagnant water needed to be drained.*

Stagnate – *(verb)* become stagnate. *The decisions have stagnated our growth in the company.*

Staid – *(adjective)* respectable and unadventurous. *The staid gentleman didn't have too many friends.*

Stain – *(verb)* **1** mark or discolour with something that is not easily removed. *The turmeric stained my white dress.* **2** damage. *The incident stained the company's reputation.* **3** cololur with a penetrative dye or chemical. *The designer stained the fabric red.* *(noun)* **1** a stubborn discoloured patch or dirty mark. *The stain refused to go away.* 2 a thing that damages a reputation. *They were worried that they will never recover from the stain on their reputation.* **3** a dye or chemical used to colour material. [biology] a dye used to colour organic tissue so as to make the structure visible for microscopic examination. *The stain was quite fast.* **4** [heraldry] any of the minor colours used in blazoning and liveries. *They chose a good stain for the coat of arms.*

Stair – *(noun)* each of a set of fixed steps. a set of such steps leading from one floor of a building to another. *The child climbed down the stairs carefully.*

Staircase – *(noun)* a set of stairs and its surrounding structure. [British] a part of a large building containing a staircase. *The staircase was antique and beautifully ornate.*

Stake – *(noun)* **1** a strong post with a point at one end, driven into the ground to support a tree, form part of a fence, etc. *I used a stake to support my tomato plant.* **2** [historical] a wooden post to which a person was tied before being burned alive as a punishment. *The crime took him to the stake.* **3** a small anvil, typically with a projection for fitting into a socket on a bench. *The stake broke as the carpenters were fitting it.* **4** a long vertical rod used in basket-making. *The stake was too long for the basket.* **5** a territorial division of the Mormon church. *The entire stake attended the ceremony.* *(verb)* **1** support with a stake. *I staked my tomato plant.* 2 mark an area with stakes so as to claim ownership. *The neighbours staked their land.* **3** [informal] keep a place or person under surveillance. *The police staked the main suspect.*

Stale – *(adjective)* **1** no longer fresh or pleasant to eat. *The potatoes were stale.* **2** no longer new and interesting. *The stale news was still playing on the TV.* **3** no longer performing well because of having done something for too long. *The stale news anchor was replaced by a younger one.* **4** invalid because out of date. *The stale chips should be thrown away.* *(verb)* make or become stale. *The curry became stale within two days.*

Stalemate – *(noun)* **1** [chess] a position counting as a draw, in which a player is not in check but can only move into check. *The experienced player soon placed the opponent in a stalemate.* **2** a situation in which further progress by opposing parties seems impossible. *The discussion reached a stalemate pretty soon.* *(verb)* bring to or cause to reach stalemate. *The senior player soon stalemated the junior.*

Stalk – *(noun)* **1** the main stem of a herbaceous plant. the attachment or support of a leaf, flower, or fruit. *The stalk was still strong even though the plant had shed all its leaves.* **2** a similar support for a sessile animal, or for an organ in an animal. *The stalk made the* *movement possible for the animal.* **3** a slender support or stem. *The stalk supported the weight of the vine pretty well.* **4** a lever on the steering column controlling the indicators, lights, etc. *The stake was stuck so she couldn't indicate that she wanted to turn.*

Stall - *(noun)* **1** a stand, booth, or compartment for the sale of goods in a market. *The stall was selling some interesting bags.* 2 an individual compartment for an animal in a stable or cowshed, enclosed on three sides. a stable or cowshed. a cage-like compartment in which a horse is held prior to the start of a race. *The stall was full and needed a bit more room for the animals.* **3** a compartment for one person in a set of toilets, shower cubicles, etc. *I had to use the bathroom but all the stalls were occupied.* **4** [north American] a marked-out parking space. *The vehicle had parked in a stall meant for handicapped people.* **5** a seat in the choir or chancel of a church, enclosed at the back and sides and often canopied, typically reserved for a member of the clergy. *The stall was empty.* **6** [British] the ground-floor seats in a theatre. *I booked two seats in the stalls.* **7** an instance of an engine or vehicle stalling. *The stall ensured that she couldn't make it to the meeting.* *(verb)* **1** stop or cause to stop running. be moving at a speed too low to allow effective operation of the controls. sailing have insufficient wind power to give controlled motion. *The engine stalled in the middle of nowhere.* **2** stop or cause to stop making progress. *The project was stalled because of the lack of finances.* **3** prevaricate. delay or divert by prevarication. *Don't try to stall the discussion.* **4** keep in a stall, especially in order to fatten it. *The farmer stalled the turkey.*

Stallion - *(noun)* an uncastrated adult male horse. *The magnificent stallion trotted around the field.*

Stamina - *(noun)* the ability to sustain prolonged physical or mental effort. *The athlete was asked to work on his stamina.*

Stammer - *(verb)* speak with sudden involuntary pauses and a tendency to repeat the initial letters of words. utter in such a way. *She stammered while addressing the public.* *(noun)* a tendency to stammer. *She went to the speech therapist to consult regarding her stammer.*

Stamp - *(verb)* **1** bring down heavily on the ground or an object. crush, flatten, or remove with a heavy blow from one's foot. crush or pulverize. *The horse stamped the ground.* **2** walk with heavy, forceful steps. *Why are you stamping around?* **3** suppress or put an end to something. *The police stamped out the protest.* **4** impress a pattern or mark on with a stamp. cut out using a die or mould. *They stamped the cattle.* **5** fix a postage stamp to. *The post office employee stamped the envelope.* *(noun)* **1** an instrument for stamping a pattern or mark, especially an engraved or inked block or die. a mark or pattern made by a stamp. *My friend got a good stamp made for his business.* **2** a characteristic or distinctive impression or quality. a particular type of person or thing. *He got the stamp of a spendthrift.* **3** a small adhesive piece of paper recording payment of postage. *I like collecting stamps.* **4** an act or sound of stamping the foot. *The stamp was clearly audible three floors below.* **5** a block for crushing ore in a stamp mill. *The stamp came down upon the ore with force.*

Stampede - *(noun)* **1** a sudden panicked rush of a number of horses, cattle, etc. a sudden rapid movement or reaction of a mass of people due to interest or panic. *Several people were injured in the stampede.* *(verb)* take part of cause to take part in a stampede. *They stampeded without considering the safety.*

Stance - *(noun)* **1** the way in which someone stands, especially when deliberately adopted. *He copied my stance.* **2** a standpoint. *I won't change my stance so easily.* **3** [Scottish] a street site for a market, stall, or taxi rank. *No one was manning the stance.* **4** climbing a ledge or foothold. *The stance was risky as the ladder was quite old.*

Stand - *(verb)* **1** be in or rise to an upright position, supported by one's feet. move in this position to a specified place or be situated in a particular position. remain stationary. remain on a specified course. *They stand in the* *queue every day.* **2** rest without disturbance. *They stood alone without being disturbed.* **3** be in a specified state or condition. remain upright and entire. remain valid or unaltered. be of a specified height. *We stood with her through her court case.* **4** adopt a particular attitude towards an issue. *They stood against corruption.* **5** be likely to do something: investors stood to lose heavily. *The students stood to get good marks because their teacher made them work very hard.* **6** act in a specified capacity: he stood security for the government's borrowing. *She stood a witness to the crime.* *(noun)* **1** an attitude towards a particular issue. a determined effort to hold one's ground or resist something. cricket a partnership. *They took a stand against corruption.* **2** a large raised tiered structure for spectators. a raised platform for a band, orchestra or speaker. a rack, base, or item of furniture for holding or displaying something. a small temporary stall or booth form which promotional goods are sold or displayed. a witness box. *As soon as the ball crossed the boundary, a loud cheer erupted from the stands.* **3** the place where someone usually stands or sits. a place where vehicles wait for passengers. *The bus stand was hardly ever used.* **4** a cessation form motion or progress. *The stand of the ship was disturbed by the waves.* **5** a group of trees or other plants. *The stand was often used as a resting place by the homeless.*

Standard – *(noun)* **1** a level of quality or attainment. a required or agreed level of quality or attainment. [British] historical a grade of proficiency tested by examination. a class or year in a high school. *He met all the requirements demanded by a standard.* **2** something used as a measure, norm, or model in comparative evaluations. principles of honourable, decent behaviour. the prescribed weight of fine metal in gold or silver coins. a system by which the value of a currency is defined in terms of gold or silver. a measure for timber, equivalent to 165 cu.ft tree that grows on an erect stem of full height. a shrub grafted water or gas pipe. *The auditors compared the quality of the material against the standard.* *(adjective)* used or accepted as normal or average. such as is regularly used or produced. viewed as authoritative and so widely read. *His unruly behaviour was thought to be standard amongst the boys of his age.*

Standardize – *(verb)* cause to conform to a standard. adopt as one's standard. determine the properties of by comparison with a standard. *The company standardized its processes.*

Standing – *(noun)* **1** position, status, or reputation. *He has a standing in the community.* **2** duration: a squabble of long standing. *They had a feud of long standing with the family.* **3** a stall for cattle or horses. *The standing was empty because the animals were out grazing.* *(adjective)* **1** performed form rest or an upright position. *His standing act during the play was appreciated by everyone.* **2** long-term or regularly repeated: a standing invitation. *His standing invitation was rejected unceremoniously.* **3** stagnant or still. *The standing water needed to be cleaned.* **4** not yet reaped. *The standing crop was in the risk of damage from unexpected rains.* **5** printing kept set up after use. *They left the printer standing for the next batch.*

Standpoint – *(noun)* **1** an attitude towards a particular issue. *I understand your standpoint.* **2** the position form which a scene or an object is viewed. *This is a good standpoint to see the entire valley.*

Standstill – *(noun)* a situation or condition without movement or activity. *Due to an accident the traffic came to a standstill.*

Stanza – *(noun)* a group of lines forming the basic recurring metrical unit in a poem. a group of four lines in some ancient Greek and Latin meters. *The third stanza of the poem was the most powerful.*

Staple – *(noun)* a small flattened U-shaped piece of wire used to fasten papers together. *We need to buy more staples.* **2** a small U-shaped metal bar with pointed ends for driving into wood to hold electric wires, battens, etc. in place. *The staple was quite strong.* *(verb)* secure with a sample or staples. *Please staple this bunch of papers.*

Star – *(noun)* **1** a fixed luminous point in the night sky which is a large, remote incandescent body like the sun. *Many stars were visible in the pollution-free sky*. **2** a stylized representation to a star, typically with five or more points. a star-shaped symbol indicating a category of excellence. used in names of starfishes and similar echinoderms, e.g. cushion star. *I drew a star in my notebook.* **3** a famous or talented entertainer or sports player. an outstanding person or thing. *He was the star of the team.* **4** [astrology] a planet, constellation, or configuration regarded as influencing one's fortunes or personality. *He was born under good stars.* **5** a white patch on the forehead of horse, or other animal. *The graceful stallion had a star on his forehead.* *(verb)* **1** have as a principal performer. have a principal role in a film, play, etc. *The actress has starred in many feature films.* **2** decorate or cover with star-shaped marks or objects. mark for special notice or recommendation with a star. *The teacher starred the child's notebook.*

Starry – *(adjective)* full of or lit by stars. *The starry sky was treat for the eyes.*

Starboard – *(noun)* the side of a ship or aircraft on the right when one is facing forward. the opposite of port. *The starboard looked clear.* *(verb)* turn to starboard. *The ship starboarded to get the right of the way.*

Starch – *(noun)* **1** an odourless, tasteless carbohydrate which is obtained [chiefly] from cereals and potatoes and is an important constituent of the human diet. *I am off starch for some time.* **2** powder or spray made from this substance, used to stiffen fabric. *My mother got starch to apply to her sari.* **3** stiffness of manner. *He had a certain starch that made everyone uncomfortable.* *(verb)* **1** stiffen with starch. *The dry-cleaner starched the clothes.* **2** [north American] [informal] defeat by a knockout. *The hosts starched the visitors.*

Stardom – *(noun)* the status of being very famous. *He was largely unaffected by stardom.*

Stare – *(verb)* **1** look fixedly at someone or something with the eyes wide open. look fixedly at someone until they feel forced to look away. *If you stare at someone, you may offend them.* **2** be unpleasantly prominent or striking. *People think you are obnoxious because you stare.* *(noun)* an act of staring. *Her stare offended the actress.*

Stark – *(adjective)* **1** severe or bare in appearance. *The stark boat was much older than the other more ornate ones.* **2** unpleasantly or sharply clear. *He was honest but his stark attitude made him unpopular.* **3** complete; sheer: stark terror. *The stark terror written on the boy's face told the story of what he had been through.* **4** rare naked. *The stark man was caught by the police.* **5** [archaic] or poetic/literary rigid or incapable of movement. physically strong. *His stark stand was appreciated by many.*

Starling – *(noun)* a gregarious songbird typically with dark lustrous or iridescent plumage. *The starling sang throughout the day.*

Start – *(abbreviation)* strategic arms reduction talks. *The Start did not lead to any conclusions.*

Starter – *(noun)* **1** [chiefly British] the first course of a meal. *I was full after eating the starters.* **2** an automatic device for starting a machine. a railway signal controlling the starting of trains. *The scooter's starter failed.* **3** a person who signals the start of a race. *The starter whistled and lowered the flag.* **4** a competitor taking part in a race or game at the start. baseball the pitcher who starts the game. *The starter was a fierce player.* **5** a person or thing starting in a specified way: a slow starter. *The man was a slow starter but he performed well in the long run.* **6** a topic or question with which to start a discussion or course of study. *The discussion started with an interesting starter.* **7** a preparation used to initiate souring, fermentation, etc. *The starter was very potent.*

Startle – *(verb)* cause to feel sudden shock or alarm. *You startled me.*

Starve – *(verb)* **1** suffer or die or cause to suffer or die from hunger. force someone out of or into by starving them. deprive of. fee; very hungry. *It is a shame that many poor people still starve to death every year.* **2** [archaic] be freezing cold. *The starving little bird was rescued by the kind boy.*

State – *(noun)* **1** the condition of someone or something. a physical condition as regards internal or molecular from or structure. [informal] an agitated, disorderly, or dirty condition. *He was in a very shocked state.* **2** a nation or territory considered as an organized political community under one government. an organized political community or area forming part of a federal republic. the US. *The country had many states.* **3** the civil government of a country. the legislative body in jersey, Guernsey, and alderney. *The state took some hard decisions.* **4** pomp and ceremony associated with monarchy or government. *The state left everyone in awe.* **5** an impression taken from an etched or engraved plate at a particular stage. a particular printed version of the first edition of a book. *The state had many typos.* *(verb)* **1** express definitely or clearly in speech or writing. [chiefly] law specify the facts of for consideration. *He stated his wishes clearly.* **2** [music] present or introduce in a composition. *She stated the tune in the composition.*

Stately – *(adjective)* dignified, imposing, or grand. *Everyone was in awe of her stately figure.*

Statement – *(noun)* **1** a definite or clear expression of something in speech or writing. a formal account of facts or events, especially one given to the police or in court. *The witness gave his statement to the police.* **2** a document setting out items of debit and credit between a bank or other organization and a customer. *The statement proved that the customer had paid all his debts.* **3** an official assessment of a child's special educational needs. *The school issued a statement for the benefit of the parents.* *(verb)* officially assess as having special educational needs. *Once the school provides statement, I am going to look for alternatives for my child requiring special attention.*

Stateroom – *(noun)* **1** a large room in a palace or public building, for use on formal occasions. *The stateroom was prepared for the meeting.* **2** a captain's or superior officer's room on a ship. a private compartment on a ship. a private compartment on a train. *No one was allowed to enter the stateroom.*

Statesman – *(noun)* a skilled, experienced, and respected political leader or figure. *The statesman addressed the crowd and pacified them.*

Static – *(adjective)* **1** lacking movement, action, or change. *His career had been static for a really long time.* **2** [physics] concerned with bodies at rest or forces in equilibrium. often contrasted with dynamic. *The static force kept the atoms together.* **3** relating to or denoting electric charges acquired by objects that cannot conduct a current. *The sweater gathered static.* *(noun)* **1** static electricity. *The static gave me a slight shock.* **2** crackling or hissing on a telephone, radio, etc. *It was hard to hear the music because of the static.* **3** [informal], angry or critical talk or behaviour. *The static threatened to intensify at any moment.*

Station – *(noun)* **1** a place where passenger trains stop on a railway line, typically with platforms and buildings. *The station was crowded.* **2** a place where a specified activity or service in based: a radar station. a small military base. a subsidiary post office. *They took the pickpocket to the police station.* **3** a broadcasting company of a specified kind. *The radio station had its office in my colony.* **4** the place where someone or something stands or is placed for a particular purpose or duty. one's social rank or position. *He never moves from his station of a senior officer.* **5** a large sheep or cattle farm. *The station was echoing with mooing.* **6** a site at which an interesting or rare plant grows. *The station was of interest to botanists.* *(verb)* assign to a station. *The agile officer was stationed at the most volatile position.*

Stationary – *(adjective)* **1** not moving. *The turtle was stationary for a long time.* **2** not changing in quantity or condition. *The economy was stationary in spite of the depression everywhere else.*

Stationer – *(noun)* a seller of stationery. *The stationer was well stocked.*

Stationery – *(noun)* paper and other materials needed for writing. *I love buying stationery.*

Statistic – *(noun)* a fact or piece of data obtained from a study of a large quantity of numerical data. *Statistics say that the number of boys in the country is much larger than the number of girls.*

Statistical – *(adjective)* of or relating to statistics. *The statistical analysis of the situation revealed some interesting developments.*

Statue – *(noun)* a carved or cast figure of a person or animal, especially one that is life size or larger. *The statue had stood there for centuries.*

Stature – *(noun)* **1** a person's natural height when standing. *He was of a tall stature.* **2** importance or reputation gained by ability or achievement. *No one could question his stature.*

Status – *(noun)* **1** relative social or professional standing. high rank or social standing. the official classification given to a person, country, etc. determining their rights or responsibilities. *He was very much aware of his status while talking to the others.* **2** the position of affairs at a particular time. *The status of the project looks pretty good.*

Status symbol – *(noun)* a possession taken to indicate a person's wealth or high status. *The expensive watch was a status symbol.*

Status quo – *(noun)* the existing state of affairs. *The status quo is very volatile.*

Statute – *(noun)* a written law passed by a legislative body. a rule of an organization or institution. a law or decree made by a sovereign or by god. *The statute helped restore law and order in the city.*

Statutory – *(adjective)* **1** required, permitted, or enacted by statute. *The statutory warning is displayed at the beginning of the movies at times.* **2** having come to be required or expected due to being done regularly: the statutory Christmas phone call to his mother. *She enjoyed her statutory weekly visits to her parents.*

Staunch – *(adjective)* **1** very loyal and committed. *He was a staunch supporter of Gandhian views.* **2** of sturdy construction. watertight. *The staunch container did not break when it fell.*

Stave – *(verb)* look fixedly at something or someone with eyes wide open. *He stared at her in amazement. She sat looking into the sky with mind totally blank.*

Stay – *(noun)* **1** a large rope, wire, or rod used to support a ship's mast. *The stay needed to be tightened.* **2** a guy or rope supporting a flagstaff or other upright pole. *The crew tied the stay.* a supporting wire or cable on an aircraft. *The stay snapped bore the plane took a flight. (verb)* secure or steady by means of a stay. *The crew stayed the boat.*

Stead – *(noun)* the place or role that someone or something should have or fill: appointed in his stead. *The vice-principal was appointed in the principal's stead.*

Steadfast – *(adjective)* resolutely or dutifully firm and unwavering. *He was steadfast in his views.*

Steadfastness – *(noun)* state of being resolutely firm and unwavering. *His steadfastness bordered on stubbornness.*

Steady – *(adjective)* **1** firmly fixed, supported, or balanced. *They had a steady relationship.* **2** not faltering or wavering; controlled. *The army had a steady camp.* **3** sensible and reliable. *He had a steady head on his shoulders.* **4** regular, even, and continuous in development, frequency, or intensity. *The steady rate of growth ensured a bright future. (verb)* make or become steady. exclamatory a warning to keep calm or take care. *The growth steadied over time. (noun)* **1** a person's regular boyfriend or girlfriend. *He is my steady.* **2** a strut for stabilizing a caravan or other vehicle when stationary. *The steady gave way and the caravan rolled on towards the road.*

Steak – *(noun)* **1** high quality beef taken from the hindquarters of the animal, typically cut into thick slices for grilling or frying. a thick slice of other meat or fish. *He liked his steak well done.* **2** poorer quality beef that is cubed or minced and cooked by braising or stewing. *The poor family could only afford steak.*

Steal – *(verb)* **1** take without permission or legal right and without intending to return it. dishonestly pass off as one's own. *The thieves stole the diamond.* **2** give or take surreptitiously or without permission: move somewhere quietly or surreptitiously. *I stole a look at the clock on the wall during the boring lecture.* **3** gain unexpectedly or by exploiting the temporary distraction of an opponent. run to while the pitcher is in the act of delivery. *He stole a win at the last moment. (noun)* **1** a bargain. *This t-shirt was such a steal.* **2** an act of stealing. an idea taken from another work. an act of stealing a base. *The steal was captured on the camera.*

Stealth – *(noun)* **1** cautious and surreptitious action or movement. *He used stealth to win the game.* **2** designed in accordance with technology which makes detection by radar or sonar difficult: a stealth bomber. *The stealth was detected by some alert soldiers.*

Stealthily – *(noun)* in a cautious and surreptitious manner, so as not to be seen or heard. *He approached the base stealthily.*

Steam – *(noun)* **1** the hot vapour into which water is converted when heated, which condenses in the air into a mist of minute water droplets. *Steam was coming out of the boiling water.* **2** the expansive force of this vapour used as a source of power for machines. *The locomotive was powered by steam.* **3** momentum; impetus: the dispute gathered steam. *The war gathered steam as the air force got involved. (verb)* **1** give off or produce steam. become or cause something to become misted over with steam. *I had to stop the car as the windshield steamed over.* **2** cook by heating it in steam from boiling water. *They steamed the vegetables.* **3** clean or otherwise treat with steam. apply steam to so as to open or loosen it. *She steamed the dirty clothes.* **4** travel somewhere under steam power. generate steam in and operate. *The engine steamed towards the destination.* **5** be or become extremely agitated or angry. *The athlete steamed after losing.*

Steamy – *(adjective)* **1** producing, filled with, or clouded with steam. *I love steamy hot soup.* **2** hot and humid. *The steamy weather made me feel tired.* **3** of or involving erotic sexual activity. *The steamy scene was censored.*

Steel – *(noun)* **1** a hard, strong grey or bluish grey alloy of iron with carbon and usually other elements, used extensively as a structural and fabricating material. *The utensils were made of steel.* **2** a rod of roughened steel on which knives are sharpened. *They sharpened their knives against the steel.***3**. strength and determination: nerves of steel. *She displayed a lot of steel during the race. (verb)* mentally prepare to do or face something difficult. *I steeled myself for the encounter.*

Steep – *(verb)* **1** soak or be soaked in water or other liquid. *I steeped the sponge in soap and wiped the slab.* **2** fill or imbue with a particular quality or influence. *The teacher steeped the children with honesty.*

Steeple – *(noun)* a church tower and spire. a spire on the top of a church tower or roof. *Beautiful ringing of the bell issued from the steeple.*

Steer – *(noun)* another term of bullock. *The cart was being pulled by two steers.*

Stem – *(verb)* **1** stop or restrict. *I tried to stem the growth of weeds in my garden.* **2** slide the tail of one ski or both skis outwards in order to turn or slow down. *The skier stemmed just in time.*

Stench – *(noun)* a strong and very unpleasant smell. *The stench was getting stronger by the hour.*

Stencil – *(noun)* a thin sheet of card, plastic, or metal with a pattern or letters cut out of it, used to produce the cut design on the surface below by the application of ink or paint through the holes. *The child used a stencil to label the chart. (verb)* decorate using a stencil. produce with a stencil. *The children stencilled beautiful patterns on the board.*

Stenographer – *(noun)* one who takes notes in short hand and transcribes the same on a typewriter. *The stenographer took notes during the meeting.*

Step – *(noun)* **1** an act or movement of putting one leg in front of the other in walking or running. the distance covered by such a movement. a short and easily walked distance. *She walked in small steps.* **2** one of the sequences of movement of the feet which make up a dance. *The couple performed the steps well.* **3** a flat surface, especially one in a series, on which to place one's foot when moving from one level to another. a doorstep. a rung of a ladder. [British] a stepladder. a foothold cut in a slope of ice. *I missed the step and fell.* **4** a block fixed to a boat's keel in order to take the base of a mast or other fitting. *The step needed to be replaced.* **5** an abrupt change in the value of a quantity, especially voltage. *The step may damage some appliances.* **6** step aerobics. *Steps are a good way to get in shape.* **7** a position or grade in a scale or hierarchy. *She was still on the first step in the organization. (verb)* **1** lift and set down one's foot or one foot after the other in order to walk somewhere or move to a new position. *They stepped towards the lawn.* **2** set up in its step. *He has stepped up in his position.*

Stereo - *(noun)* **1** stereophonic sound. *The stereo was very pleasant on the ears.* **2** a stereophonic CD player, record player, etc. *I take my stereo everywhere I go.* **3** short for stereotype. *I hate any kind of stereos. (adjective)* **1** stereophonic. *The stereo sound brought out the beauty of the song.* **2** stereoscopic. *The stereo movie was a rage amongst the children.*

Stereotype - *(noun)* **1** an image or idea of a particular type of person or thing that has become fixed through being widely held. *One should not judge based on stereotypes.* **2** a relief printing plate cast in a mould made from composed type or an original plate. *Please use the correct stereotype. (verb)* view or represent as a stereotype. *He often stereotypes people.*

Sterile - *(adjective)* **1** not able to produce children or young. not able to produce fruit or seeds. too poor in quality to produce crops. *The sterile seeds were thrown away.* **2** lacking in imagination, creativity, or excitement. *The actor had become sterile over the years.* **3** free from bacteria or other living micro organisms. *The sterile milk was packed in the cartons.*

Sterility - *(noun)* the quality or condition of being sterile. *He was ashamed of his sterility.*

Sterilize - *(verb)* **1** make sterile. *They sterilized the milk before packing it.* **2** deprive of the ability to produce offspring by removing or blocking the sex organs. *The doctor sterilized the man who did not want any more children.*

Sterling - *(noun)* [British] money. *I paid in sterlings for this gift. (adjective)* excellent; of great value. *The toy turned out to be a sterling gift.*

Stern - *(noun)* the rearmost part of a ship or boat. *The crew tied the stern of the boat to the pontoon.*

Stethoscope - *(noun)* a medical instrument for listening to the action of someone's heart or breathing having a small disc shaped resonator that is placed against the chest and two tubes connected to earpieces. *The child started crying as soon as the doctor put on the stethoscope.*

Stew - *(noun)* **1** a pond or large tank for keeping fish for eating. *The stew was full of fish.* **2** an artificial oyster bed. *The stew failed to provide too many oysters.*

Steward - *(noun)* **1** a person who looks after the passengers on a ship or aircraft. *The steward did his job well.* **2** a person responsible for supplies of food to a college, club, etc. *Students often complained to the steward about the quality of the food.* **3** an official appointed to supervise arrangements at a large public event. *The steward made sure that everything was in order at the carnival.* **4** short for shop steward. *The steward represented the workers well.* **5** a person employed to manage another's property, especially a large house or estate. an officer of the [British] royal household, especially an administrator of crown estates. *The steward maintained the property well. (verb)* act as a steward of. *He stewarded the property of the squire.*

Stick - *(noun)* **1** a thin piece of wood that has fallen or been cut off a tree. a stick used for support in walking or as a weapon. *My nephew gathered sticks and used them in his games.* **2** a long, thin implement with a curved head or angled blade, used to hit or direct the ball or puck. the foul play of raising the stick above the shoulder. *The polo player dropped his stick.* **3** goalposts or cricket stumps. *The ball went right into the sticks.* **4** a long, thin object or piece of something: a stick of dynamite. *The terrorists planted sticks of dynamite beneath the bridged.* **5** a conductor's baton. *The conductor waved his stick to let the traffic pass.* **6** a gear or control lever. *The stick was stuck so I had to call the mechanic.* **7**. a mast or spar.. *The stick broke* *and had to be repaired.* **8** a group of bombs or paratroopers dropped from an aircraft. *The stick was aimed at the populous city.*

Sticker – *(noun)* **1** an adhesive label or notice. *I love collecting stickers.* **2** a determined or persistent person. *The sticker never gave up.*

Stickler – *(noun)* a person who insists on a certain quality or type of behaviour. *He was such a stickler for propriety.*

Sticky – *(adjective)* **1** tending or designed to stick; adhesive. glutinous; viscous. *The sticky substance was difficult to wash off with soap.* **2** hot and humid; muggy. *The sticky weather was typical of the season.* **3** damp with sweat. *I felt very sticky after the exercise.* **4** difficult; awkward. *This is a sticky situation.* **5** attracting a long visit or repeat visits from users. *The website has some sticky applications.*

Stiff – *(adjective)* **1** not easily bent; rigid. not moving freely; difficult to turn or operate. unable to move easily and without pain. *Her stiff back made it difficult for her to move.* **2** not relaxed or friendly; constrained. *He was very stiff when they first met.* **3** severe or strong: they face stiff fines. blowing strongly. strong. *The stiff winds made it difficult to sail.* **4** full on. *The children kept up the stiff efforts and kept going.* **5** having a specified unpleasant feeling to an extreme extent: scared stiff. *I was scared stiff when I heard the noise.* *(noun)* **1** a dead body. *They carried the unidentified stiff to the mortuary.* **2** a boring, conventional person. *He was often called a stiff behind his back.* *(verb)* 1 cheat. fail to leave a tip. *The customers stiffed and left.* **2** ignore deliberately; snub. *I feel that he has deliberately stiffed me.* **3** kill. *The criminals stiffed the man.*

Stiffness – *(noun)* the state of not easily bent or changed in shape. *His stiffness is his strength as well as his weakness.*

Stiffen – *(verb)* **1** make or become stiff. *The body stiffened by the hour.* **2** make or become stronger or more steadfast. *The predator's hold stiffened.*

Stifle – *(noun)* a joint in the legs of horses, dogs, and other animals, equivalent to the knee in humans. *The dog hurt his stifle.*

Stigma – *(noun)* eighteenth letter of Greek alphabet. *The children hadn't been taught how to write the symbol of stigma yet.*

Still – *(noun)* an apparatus for distilling alcoholic drinks such as whisky. *The still needed to be sterilized.*

Stilted – *(adjective)* **1** stiff and self conscious or unnatural. *The stilted conversation yielded no results.* **2** standing on stilts. *The stilted clown walked easily across the field.* **3** with pieces of upright masonry between the imposts and the springers. *The stilted house was safe from the Komodo dragons.*

Stimulant – *(noun)* **1** a substance that acts to increase physiological or nervous activity in the body. *The athlete was accused of taking a stimulant just before the race.* **2** something that promotes activity, interest, or enthusiasm. *The workshop was such a stimulant for students.* *(adjective)* acting as a stimulant. *The stimulant exercises warmed the students up for the workshop.*

Stimulate – *(verb)* **1** apply or act as a stimulus to. *Their discussion stimulated the revolution.* **2** animate or excite. *The cartoon stimulated the children.*

Stimulus – *(noun)* **1** a thing that evokes a specific functional reaction in an organ or tissue. *The change in the intensity of light was a stimulus for the pupil.* **2** something that promotes activity, interest, or enthusiasm. *The discussion was a stimulus for the children's creativity.*

Sting – *(noun)* **1** a small sharp pointed organ of an insect, plant, etc. capable of inflicting a painful wound by injecting poison. *The sting of a scorpion is located in its tail.* **2** a wound from such an organ. *Some insects can inflict a sting to defend themselves.* **3** a sharp tingling sensation or hurtful effect. *I felt a sting in my hurt foot.* **4** a carefully planned undercover operation. *Some media houses execute sting operations to gain quick publicity.* *(verb)* wound with a sting. *A bee only stings if it feels threatened.* produce a stinging sensation. hurt; upset. goad someone into. *She made some stinging comments at the end of the altercation.*swindle or exorbitantly overcharge. *The hotel stung me for Rs 3,000 more as charges at the end of my stay.*

Stingy – *(adjective)* mean; ungenerous. *He is so stingy that he doesn't ever dine outside.*

Stink – *(verb)* **1** have a strong unpleasant smell. fill a place with such a smell. *The rotten tomatoes in the refrigerator has started to stink.* **2** be contemptible or scandalous. be highly suggestive of. *The financial records of the company are so excellent that they stink of scandal.* *(noun)* **1** a strong, unpleasant smell. *The stink of the old strawberries is unbearable.* **2** a row or fuss. *She made a great stink when the butler couldn't serve dinner on time.*

Stint – *(noun)* a very small short legged northern sandpiper. *They claimed that they sighted a stint.*

Stipend – *(noun)* a fixed regular sum paid as a salary or as expenses to a clergyman, teacher, or public official. *He says the reason he can't afford a better establishment is because he doesn't get a good stipend in his current job.*

Stipulate – *(verb)* demand or specify as part of a bargain or agreement. *All clauses of the agreement were stipulated in the deed.*

Stir – *(noun)* **1** slight physical movement. *I was straining my eyes and ears for the slightest stir.* **2** a commotion. *The event caused quite a stir.* **3** act of stirring food or drink. *She gave her glass of warlocks a stir.* *(verb)* **1** move a spoon round and round in a liquid in order to mix it thoroughly. *He stirred his tea and ate a few biscuits.* **2** move or cause to move slightly. *A gentle breeze stirred the leaves.*

Stirrup – *(noun)* **1** each of a pair of devices attached at either side of a horse's saddle, in the form of a loop with a flat base to support the rider's foot. *After getting off the horse, the rider lost his balance for a moment, so he grasped the stirrup to gain control.* **2** a pair of metal supports for the ankles used during gynecological examinations and childbirth. *The woman was soon getting tired of her labour pains and was encouraged to place both her feet on the stirrups to support herself better.* **3** another term for stapes. *The stirrup present in our ear is one of the smallest bones in the human body.*

Stitch – *(noun)* **1** a loop of thread or yarn resulting from a single pass or movement of the needle in sewing, knitting, or crocheting. a method of sewing, knitting, or crocheting producing a particular pattern: an embroidery stitch. *The stitch of this dress seems fine.* **2** the smallest item of clothing: swimming around with not a stitch on. *In that horrible incident of theft, the robbers didn't leave a stitch on him.* **3** a sudden sharp pain in the side of the body, caused by strenuous exercise. *I felt a stitch in my abdomen during my regular 30-minute session on the treadmill.* *(verb)* **1** make or mend with stitches; apply a stitch or stitches to. *Can't we apply a quick stitch or two to the torn dress to fix it up for the party in the evening?* **2** manipulate a situation to someone's disadvantage. manipulate a situation or secure a deal to one's own advantage. *He would usually not refrain from stitching a conversation to secure a new deal.*

Stock – *(noun)* **1** a supply of goods or material available for sale or use. *The stock available in the warehouse has been below mark for the past few weeks.* **2** farm animals bred and kept for their meat or milk; livestock. *Stock farming is mostly seen as subsistence farming.* **3** the capital raised by a company through the issue and subscription of shares. a portion of this as held by an individual or group as an investment. securities issued by the government in fixed units with a fixed rate of interest. *The stocks of this company have been on a high for quite some time now, which makes lucrative and risky at the same time.* **4** water in which bones, meat, fish, or vegetable have been slowly simmered. the raw material from which a specified commodity can be manufactured. *Clear stock of chicken is usually good for general health.* **5** a person's ancestry or line of descent. a breed, variety, or population of an animal or plant. *The experiment was successful but only on a particular stock of plants.* *(adjective)* **1** usually kept in stock and thus regularly available for sale. *A basic tablet of paracetamol is usually a stock item in medicine shops.* **2** constantly recurring; common or conventional: the stock characters in every cowboy film. *A rich, mean politician is usually a stock character in most films with a take on* *the political system of our country. (verb)* **1** have or keep a stock of. provide or fill with a stock of something. amass stocks of something. *I like to keep a good stock of snacks at home.* **2** fit with a stock.

Stockbroker – *(noun)* a broker who buys and sells securities on a stock exchange on behalf of clients. *It is worth wondering why during any natural disaster activity of stockbrokers increases manifold.*

Stocking – *(noun)* **1** a woman's garment that fits closely over the foot and leg, typically made of fine knitted nylon yarn, held up by suspenders or an elasticated strip at the upper thigh. a cylindrical bandage or other medical covering for the leg resembling a stocking. *A fine pair of stockings with a skirt is what some woman prefer to wear when stepping out for a formal meeting.* **2** a long sock worn by men. *At one time, football players wore stockings under their uniform in cold weather.* **3** a real or ornamental stocking hung up by children on Christmas eve for father christmas to fill with presents. *When their mother reached home, the children were busy hanging a pair of stocking on the X-mas tree.* **4** a white marking of the lower part of a horse's leg. *The stocking on the hind leg of this horse seems a bit odd.*

Stocky – *(adjective)* especially of a person short and sturdy. *I would describe the accused as being a middle-aged man with a stocky figure.*

Stoke – *(verb)* **1** add coal to. *Stoke the fire well so that it keeps us warm all night in this freezing temperature.* **2** encourage or incite. *His remarks perfectly served to stoke her anger even further.* **3** consume a large quantity of food to give one energy.*From the manner of his eating, the fugitive seemed to be stoking up food.*

Stolid – *(adjective)* calm, dependable, and showing little emotion or animation. *The man seemed to be having a stolid appearance.*

Stomach – *(noun)* **1** an internal organ in which the first part of digestion occurs, being a pear shaped enlargement of the alimentary canal linking the oesophagus to the small intestine. each of four such organs in a ruminant. *It takes about two hours for the stomach to digest a full meal.* **2** the abdominal area of the body; the belly. *The pain seems to be somewhere around my stomach.* **3** an appetite or desire for something. *I don't the stomach for any more desserts now. (verb)* **1** consume without feeling sick. *I somehow managed to stomach the stale food from yesterday.* **2** endure or accept. *The humiliation was too great for him stomach it.*

Stomp – *(verb)* **1** tread heavily and noisily, typically in order to show anger. *After being disobeyed his wife, he stomped about the room in anger.* **2** dance with heavy stamping steps. *The dancing couple stomped on the stage to the beats of the song with much gusto. (noun)* **1** a tune or dance with a fast tempo and a heavy beat. *The stomp immediately gained popularity among young college kids.*

Stone – *(noun)* **1** hard, solid non metallic matter of which rock is made. a small piece of stone found on the ground. a piece of stone shaped for purpose, especially one of commemoration or demarcation. a meteorite made of rock, as opposed to metal. *Protestors were dispersed just when they started throwing stones at the advancing troop of policemen.*

Stonemason – *(noun)* a person who cuts, prepares, and builds with stone. *After losing his job as an architect, the last that I heard about him was that he was working as a stonemason somewhere.*

Stony – *(adjective)* **1** full of stones. *The ground here is generally stony.* **2** of or resembling stone. *Well, the piece of meteorite did feel stony to touch, although we couldn't immediately confirm its exact nature.* **3** cold and unfeeling. *He was left with a stony expression on his face after hearing the news.*

Stool – *(noun)* **1** a seat without a back or arms, typically resting on three or four legs or on a single pedestal. *The envelope was lying on a small stool in a corner of the room.* **2** [chiefly medicine] a piece of faces. *After examining the stool of the patient, the pathologist confirmed he was suffering from jaundice.* **3** a root or stump of a tree or plant from which shoots spring.

The next monsoon saw leaves sprouting from the stool of the tree that remained half-buried in ground. **4** [US] a decoy bird in hunting. *Pigeons are often used as stool birds. (verb)* throw up shoots from the root. cut back to or near ground level to induce new growth. *The stump of that tree will soon stool shoots of leaves.*

Stoop – *(noun)* [north American] a porch with steps in front of a house or other building. *The stoop in front of that house is lined with pots of freshly bloomed purple orchids.*

Stop – *(verb)* **1** come or cause to come to an end. discontinue an action, practice, or habit. *"Stop this evil practice!" cried the tribal leader.* **2** prevent from happening or from doing something. instruct a bank to withhold payment on a cheque. refuse to supply as usual. boxing defeat by a knockout. *We are installing security alarm systems to stop thieves from entering the house.* **3** cease or cause to cease moving or operating call at a designated place to pick up or set down passengers. [British informal] stay somewhere for a short time. *I just stopped by his house to check on his while on my way out of the town.* **4** block or close up a hole or leak. plug the upper end of giving a note an octave lower. *We tried to stop the leak in the boat by plugging a piece of thick cloth in the hole.* **5** obtain the required pitch from by pressing at the appropriate point with the finger. *(noun)* **1** an act of stopping. a place designated for a bus or train to stop. *This morning there was a long queue at the bus stop.* **2** an object or part of a mechanism which prevents movement. bridge a high card that prevent the opponents from establishing a particular suit. nautical a stopper. *This lever acts as a stopper to the device.* **3** phonetics a consonant produced with complete closure of the vocal tract. *The sentence reads a little staccato-like, may be because of the heavy use of stop consonants.* **4** a set of organ pipes of a particular tone and range of pitch. a knob, lever, etc. in an organ or harpsichord which brings into play a set of pipes or string of a particular tone and range of pitch. *The musician pulled out all stops at the event that night, and the crowd thoroughly enjoyed it.* **5** [photography] the effective diameter of lens. a device for reducing this. a unit of change of relative aperture or exposure. *Digital cameras available today do not have a button to control aperture size and can adjust it automatically.*

Stopgap – *(noun)* a temporary solution or substitute. *Shifting into that attic room was just a stopgap arrangement till we found something better.*

Stoppage – *(noun)* **1** an instance of stopping or being stopped. an instance of industrial action. *Agitated at the lack of heed paid by the management to their demands, the workers called for work stoppage.* **2** a blockage. *There is some kind of stoppage in the drainage pipes laid underground.* 3 births deductions form wages by an employer for the payment of tax, national insurance, etc. *The stoppages deducted by the management for taxes took care of half of my salary.*

Stopper – *(noun)* **1** a plug for sealing a hole, especially in the neck of a bottle. *The stopper was broken and the bottle was lying in a pool of the spilled ketchup.* **2** a player whose function is to block attacks on goal from the middle of the field. *Well, the team played great on the defensive with Robin as an excellent stopper.* **3** [baseball] a pitcher who prevents opponents from scoring highly. *One of the main reasons why we couldn't score high was that the opponent team had an excellent stopper on their side.* **4** a rope or clamp for preventing a rope or cable from being run out. *A stopper knot should work fine to stop the load from being dropped. (verb)* **1** seal with a stopper. *Once he realised he had awkwardly clicked open the wine bottle, he quickly stoppered it.*

Stopwatch – *(noun)* a special watch with buttons that starts, stop, and then zero the display, used to time races. *Jim won the race with a record time of 56.65 seconds, strictly by the stopwatch.*

Store – *(noun)* **1** a quantity or supply kept for use as needed. supplies of equipment and food kept for use by members of an army, navy, or other institution. *The store of cereals is fast depleting and we need an urgent refill.* **2** a place where things are kept for future use or sale. [chiefly north American] things are kept for future use or sale. [chiefly north American] a shop. [British] a large shop selling different types of goods. *This grocery store is new in the neighbourhood and keeps almost everything.* **3** [British] a computer memory. *The laptop has a good store of memory.* **4** a sheep, cow, or pig acquired or kept for fattening. *He has a good stock of store pigs. (verb)* **1** keep or accumulate for future use. *We must store some grains for use during our voyage.* **2** retain or enter for future electronic retrieval. *Store the data in the computer with a password.* **3** have a useful supply of. *The shopkeeper had some grains stored away.*

Storey – *(noun)* **1** a part of a building comprising all the rooms that are on the same level. *Three storeys of that building are dedicated to car parking.*

Stork – *(noun)* a very tall long-legged bird with a long heavy bill and typically white and black plumage. *Well, we didn't come across any tigers in the jungle safari, but definitely saw a stork.*

Storm – *(noun)* **1** a violent disturbance of the atmosphere with strong winds and usually rain, thunder, lighting, or snow. *There was a storm last evening.* **2** a sudden violent display of strong feeling. *There was a storm of emotions last night over the family dinner.* 3 a direct assault by troops. *The army stormed the riot scene and dispersed the mob. (verb)* **1** move angrily or forcefully in a specified direction. *He stormed in the room and gave a very sharp reaction before his friends could explain anything to him.* **2**. suddenly attack and capture. *The tiger stormed the prey from behind the bushes and captured it immediately.* **3** shout angrily. *Oh, he looked as if he had been stormed at.* **4** be stormy. *The sea stormed around the boat*

Story – *(noun)* **1** an account of imaginary or real people and events told for entertainment. a storyline. *The manuscript has a good story line.* **2** an account of past events, experience, etc. an item of news. *This is a dry news story and needs some visual support.* **3** [informal] a lie. *I was terribly late for the meeting and had to concoct a story to escape embarrassment.* **4** the commercial prospects or circumstances of a particular company: profitable businesses with solid stories. *"Does the company have a good success story?" asked the investor.*

Stout – *(adjective)* **1** rather fat or heavily built. *He had a stout figure.* **2** sturdy and thick. *It was a stout tree stump that was finally left in the ground.* **3** brave and determined. *He remained stout in the face of danger. (noun)* a king of strong, dark beer brewed with roasted malt or barley. *Given a chance, he would normally settle for stout.*

Stove – past and past participle of stave. *I guess all that we did to stave off the worse all this while was not enough.*

Stow – *(verb)* **1** pack or store tidily in an appropriate place. *Stow the oars away in a dry place when on shore.* **2** conceal oneself on ship, aircraft, etc. so as to travel without paying or surreptitiously. *I stowed myself in a corner of the steamer as I didn't have a single dime on me.*

Strafe – *(verb)* attack with machine-gun fire or bombs from low-flying aircraft. *Strafe the jungle on the territorial border so that we are sure none of the militants have survived.*

Straggle – *(verb)* **1** move along slowly so as to trail behind the person or people in front. *We straggled slowly ahead in the march against inflation.* **2** grow or spread out in an irregular, untidy way. *The tree branches straggled beautifully in different directions. (noun)* an irregular and untidy group. *It was a straggle of disciples for the saint.*

Straight – *(adjective)* **1** extending uniformly in one direction only; without a curve or bend. flat-topped. *The queue went straight ahead at the bus stop.* **2** properly positioned so as to be level, upright, or symphonist. *The frame didn't seem to be hanging straight on the wall.* **3** simple clear and logical. *The interviewers appreciated that she answered straight and to the point.* **4** in continuous succession. *The slides came in straight, one after the other.* **5** undiluted. *I* *prefer a straight drink, without soda.* **6** serious as opposed to comic or musical. *The movie had a straight script that was well executed.* **7** [informal] conventional or respectable. *He lives a straight life.* **8** [informal] heterosexual. *Despite his mannerisms, he is a straight guy.* *(adverb)* **1** in a straight line or in a straight manner. *"Let's get this straight: you are wrong."* **2** [archaic] at once. *The moment she got up in the morning, she went straight into the kitchen.* *(noun)* **1** the straight part of something, especially the concluding stretch of a racecourse. [archaic] a straight from or position. *All horses had reached the straight.* **2** poker a continuous sequence of five cards. *It was a straight for me.* **3** [informal] a conventional person. *The straight was very judgemental about others.* **4** [informal] a heterosexual. *He is straight.*

Straightforward – *(adjective)* **1** easy to do or understand. *It was a straightforward question.* **2** honest and open. *She was straightforward about her live-in relationship with her boyfriend.*

Strain – *(noun)* **1** a distinct breed, stock, or variety of an animal, plant, or other organism. *This strain of bacteria is multi-drug resistant.* **2** a tendency in a person's character. *He has a violent strain in him.*

Strait – *(noun)* **1** a narrow passage of water connecting two seas or other large areas of water. *The Palk Strait lies between India and Sri Lanka.* **2** a situation characterized by a specified degree of trouble or difficulty: in dire straits. *I was in difficult straits with him over our relationship when finally we decided to end it.* *(adjective)* [archaic] **1** narrow or cramped. *It was a strait for me for the first year in this city.* **2.** strict or rigorous. *That was a strait situation for him until Jim came to his rescue.*

Straitened – *(adjective)* characterised by poverty. *After losing his job, his means were straitened.*

Strand – *(noun)* **1** a single thin length of thread, wire, etc, especially as twisted together with others. *There was a loose strand of rope that needed to be tied in.* **2** an element that forms part of a complex whole. *This scan shows just one strand of the DNA helix.*

Strange – *(adjective)* **1** unusual or surprising. *It was a strange incident.* **2** not previously visited, seen, or encountered. [archaic] unaccustomed to or unfamiliar with. *It was a strange place – one he hadn't visited before.*

Stranger – *(noun)* **1** a person whom one does not know. *He is a stranger to me.* **2** a person who does not know, or is not known in, a particular place. *I am a stranger around here.* **3** a person entirely unaccustomed to a feeling, experience, or situation. *He is a stranger to this kind of a situation.* **4** a person who is not a member or official of the house of commons. *In this session of the House of Commons, he will be sitting in the Stranger's Gallery.*

Strangle – *(verb)* **1** squeeze or constrict the neck of, especially so as to cause death. *Based on prima facie evidence, the police said he had been strangled to death.* 2 suppress or hinder an impulse, action, or sound. *I strangled my cry lest the robbers would hear it.*

Strangulation – *(noun)* the action of strangling so as to stop supply of blood. *There were strangulation marks on his neck.*

Strap – *(noun)* **1** a strip of leather, cloth, or other flexible material, used for fastening, securing, carrying, or holding on to. *A pair of leather straps kept the shoe fastened.* **2** a strip of metal, often hinged, used for fastening or securing. *A metal strap was put in place to keep the box from opening.* **3** punishment by beating with a leather strap. *Strapping is a ritual followed in some religions.* *(verb)* **1** fasten or secure with a strap. *Strap on the bag with the leather belt.* **2** [British] bind with adhesive plaster. *The doctor strapped his hand with plaster.* **3** beat with a leather strap. *He strapped himself until blood oozed from his body.*

Strategic – *(adjective)* **1** forming part of a long-term plan or aim to achieve a specific purpose. *This measure is part of our strategic planning.* **2** relating to the gaining of overall or long-term military advantage. done or for use against an enemy's territory or infrastructure. often contrasted. with tactical. *The Siachen Glacier is a strategic location for the Indian Army.*

Strategy - *(noun)* a plan of action designed to achieve a long term aim. *We must have a plausible strategy in place for our firm for the next ten years.*

Straw - *(noun)* **1** adired stalks of grain, used especially as fodder of for thatching, packing, or weaving. *There was a heap of straw kept in the backyard.* **2** a single dried stalk of grain. *He shuddered like a straw in the wind.* **3** a thin hollow tube of paper or plastic for sucking drink form a glass or bottle. *I couldn't sip through the straw; there was probably some blockage.* **4** a pale yellow colour like that of straw. *The lady wore a straw-coloured hat.* **5** anything or at all. *The management didn't care a straw even after the union workers went on strike.*

Strawberry - *(noun)* **1** a sweet soft red fruit with a seed studded surface. *Strawberries are often used in desserts.* **2** the low growing plant which produces this fruit, with white flowers, lobed leaves, and runners. *They planted strawberries in their garden.* **3** a deep pinkish-red colour. *Her skin was strawberry in colour.*

Stray - *(verb)* **1** move away aimlessly form group or from the right course or place. moveably in a specified direction. *The man strayed away from his companions in the jungle.* **2**.be unfaithful to a spouse or partner. *A spouse who strays can ruin a marriage.* *(adjective)* **1** not in the right place; separated from a group. *It was good that the rescue services found the stray zoologist.* **2** having no home or having wandered away from home. *They built a shelter for stray people.* **3** [physics] arising naturally but unwanted and usually detrimental: stray voltages. *The stray voltages are often felt by farm animals.* *(noun)* **1** a stray person or thing, especially a domestic animal. *The stray adopted our family and ended up becoming our family cat.* **2** electrical phenomena interfering with radio reception. *The stray garbled the message on the radio.*

Streak - *(noun)* **1** a long, thin mark of a different substance or colour from its surroundings. *The streak of red on the rock was an evidence of recent violence.* **2** an element of a specified kind in someone's character: a ruthless streak. *She has a certain careless streak in her behaviour.* **3** a spell of specified success or luck. *Her lucky streak lasted the entire tournament.* *(verb)* **1** mark with streaks. *The painter streaked the walls of his room.* **2** move very fast in a specified direction. *The car streaked towards the court.* **3** [informal] urn naked in a public place as to shock or amuse. *Some youngsters streaked during the meeting.*

Streaky - *(adjective)* **1** having streaks. [British] form the belly, thus having alternate strips of fat and lean. *The streaky animal was difficult to spot.* **2** [informal] unpredictable; variable. *The streaky weather hit the island.*

Stream - *(noun)* **1** a small, narrow river. *The stream merged into the river.* **2** a continuous flow of liquid, air, people, or things. *A stream of people exited the metro station.* **3** [British] a group in which schoolchildren of the same age and ability are taught. *He was the brightest in his stream.* *(verb)* **1** run in a continuous flow. move in a continuous flow. *The water streamed out of the rock.* **2** run with tears, swear, or other liquid. *Tears streamed out of her eyes.* **3** float at full extent in the wind. *The kite streamed in the sky.* **4** [British] put in streams. *Small boats were streamed for transportation.*

Streamline - *(verb)* **1** design or provide with a form that presents very little resistance to a flow of air or water. *The engineers streamlined the boat.* **2** make more efficient by employing faster or simpler working methods. *The process needs to be streamlined.* *(noun)* a line along which the flow of a moving fluid is least turbulent. *The streamline was established after several trials.* *(adjective)* free from turbulence. *The streamlined body of the craft made travel very efficient.*

Street - *(noun)* **1** a public road in a city, town, or village, typically with buildings on one or both sides. *I walked down the street to reach the café.* **2** relating to the subculture of fashionable urban youth. *This issue of the magazine focussed on the fashion of the street.*

Strength - *(noun)* **1** the quality or state of being strong. *They tested the wrestler's strength before* *letting him fight the professional.* **2** a good or beneficial quality or attribute. poetic a source of mental or emotional support. *His warmth was his strength.* **3** the number of people comprising a group. a full complement of people: below strength. *The class was present in full strength today.*

Strengthen – *(verb)* make or become stronger. *Unity strengthened their small country.*

Strenuous – *(adjective)* requiring or using great exertion. *Strenuous exercise left him feeling drained.*

Stress – *(noun)* **1** pressure or tension exerted on a material object. physics the magnitude of this measured in units of force per unit area. *The rope gave way to the stress.* **2** a state of mental, emotional, or other strain. *The CEO is under tremendous stress.* **3** particular emphasis given to a syllable or word in speech. *He lay stress on action during his speech.* *(verb)* **1** emphasize. give emphasis to when pronouncing it. *The actress stressed her t's when talking.* **2** subject to stress. *Try not to stress yourself out.*

Stressful – *(noun)* causing mental or emotional stress. *This is a stressful exercise.*

Stretch – *(verb)* **1** be made or be able to be made longer or wider without tearing or breaking. pull tightly form one point to another or across a space. *They stretched the rope to as far as it could go.* **2** straighten or extend one's body or a part of one's body to its full length. *I got up to stretch my legs.* **3** last or cause to last longer than expected. be sufficient for a particular purpose. *They stretched their discussion, much to the dismay of the audience.* **4** extend over an area or period of time. *The debate stretched over two days.* **5** make demands on. *The workers stretched their employer.* *(noun)* **1** an act of stretching. the fact or condition of being stretched. the capacity to stretch or be stretched; elasticity. *The stretch relieved my back pain.* **2** a continuous expanse or period. [informal] a period of time spent in prison. [chiefly] a straight part of a racetrack, typically the home straight. sailing the distance covered on one tack. *He spent two years at a stretch in the prison.* **3** [informal] a motor vehicle or aircraft modified so as to have extended seating or storage capacity. *The stretch made their journeys more comfortable.* **4** a difficult or demanding task. *The children were complaining about the stretch.*

Stretcher – *(noun)* **1** a framework of two poles with a long piece of canvas slung between them, used for carrying sick, injured, or dead people. *The stretchers came in very handy when the ambulance crashed into a tree.* **2** a wooden frame over which a canvas is stretched ready for painting. *The stretcher was too small for the canvas.* **3** a rod or bar joining and supporting chair legs. *The stretcher snapped, causing the chair to break.* **4** a board in a boat against which a rower presses their feet for support. *His legs were too short to reach the stretcher.* **5** a brick or stone laid with its long side along the face of a wall. compare with header. *The stretcher was often used as a step by the children.* **6** [archaic, informal] an exaggeration or lie. *That was such a stretcher.* *(verb)* carry on a stretcher. *The injured were stretchered to the hospital.*

Strew – *(verb)* scatter untidily over a surface or area. cover a surface or area with untidily scattered things. *The little girls strewed flower petals across the road.*

Stricken – [north American] or [archaic] past participle of strike. *People were stricken with grief at the news of the mishap.* *(adjective)* seriously affected by an undesirable condition or unpleasant feeling. showing great distress. *His stricken face told a different story.*

Strict – *(adjective)* **1** demanding that rules concerning behaviour are obeyed. demanding total compliance; rigidly enforced. *The strict principal scolded the students.* **2** following rules or beliefs exactly. *He was a strict vegetarian.* **3** not allowing deviation or relaxation. *I am on a strict diet.*

Stride – *(noun)* **1** walk with long, decisive steps. *She strided across the floor.* 2 cross with one long step. *He strided across the channel.* **3** [poetic] bestride. *The inexperienced horseman strided the horse.* *(noun)* **1** a long, decisive step.

the length of a step or manner of taking steps. *He took a stride towards the trophy.* **2** a step in progress towards an aim. a good or regular rate of progress, especially after a slow start. *He took a confident stride towards his goal.* **3** [British informal] trousers. *This pair of strides was a bargain.* **4** denoting or relating to a rhythmic style of jazz piano playing in which the left hand alternately plays single bass notes on the downbeat and chords and octave higher on the upbeat. *The stride stimulated the listeners to shake a leg.*

Strife – *(noun)* **1** angry or biter disagreement, conflict. *The strife left them stressed.* **2** trouble or difficulty of any kind. *I am learning to deal with strifes.*

Strike – *(verb)* **1** deliver a blow to. accidentally hit against something. come into forcible contact with. hit or kick so as to score a run, point, or goal. ignite by rubbing it briskly against an abrasive surface. bring into being. *We watched him strike the ball across the stadium.* **2** occur suddenly and have harmful effect on attack suddenly. cause a strong emotion in. cause to become suddenly: he was struck dumb. *The lightning struck the tree.* **3** suddenly come into the mind of cause to have a particular impression. find particularly interesting or impressive. [informal] be deeply fond of. *The truth struck me suddenly.* **4** refuse to work as a form of organized protest. [north American] undertake such action against. *They were striking against the reduction in salaries.* **5** cancel or remove by or as if by crossing out with a pen. officially remove someone from membership of a professional group. *They struck his name off the list.* **6** start out on a new or independent course. *They struck out in search of water.* **7** reach by balancing an account. *They strike the accounts tally sheets one by one.* **8** indicate the time by sounding a chime or stroke. *The clock struck two.* **9** make by stamping metal. *They struck the sheet of steel.* **10** discover by drilling or mining. discover or think of, especially unexpectedly. *The miners struck a fortune.* *(noun)* **1** an act of striking by employees. a refusal to do something as an organized protest: a rent strike. *The strike was unsuccessful.* **2** a sudden attack, typically a military one. *The strike took the terrorists by surprise.* **3** an act of striking a ball. an act of knocking down all the pins with one's first ball. baseball a pitch that passes through the strike zone. *The strike won them the game.* **4** [north American] something to one's discredit. *This was a strike against his name.* **5** an act of striking gold, minerals, or oil. *The strike made him a rich man.* **6** the horizontal or compass direction of a stratum, fault, or other geological feature. *The strike led the geologists to the fault.*

Striker – *(noun)* **1** an employee on strike. *The striker was fired by the employer.* **2** the player who is to strike the ball in a game; a player considered in terms of ability to strike the ball. a forward of ability to strike the ball. a forward or attacker. *The team was relying upon the striker to help them win.* **3** [British] a device striking the primer in a gun. *He was saved because the striker failed.*

Striking – *(adjective)* **1** noticeable. *The striking building was an identifying feature of the city's skyline.* **2** dramatically good-looking or beautiful. *Her striking personality could not be ignored.*

String – *(noun)* **1** material consisting of threads of cotton, hemp, etc. twisted together to form a thin length. a piece of such material. *The string broke and the basket fell.* **2** a length of catgut or wire on a musical instrument, producing a note by vibration. the stringed instruments in an orchestra. *Several strings of the guitar needed to be replaced.* **3** a piece of catgut, nylon, etc. interwoven with others to form the head of sports racket. *He struck the racket so hard that the strings broke.* **4** a set of things tied or treaded together on a thin cord. *She wore a string of colourful beads on her wrist.* **5** a sequence of similar items or events. a linear sequence of characters, words, or other data. a group of racehorses trained at one stable. a reserve team or player holding a specified position in an order of preference. a player assigned a specified rank in a team in an individual sport. *The string of* *characters formed a word.* *(verb)* **1** arrange on or as on a string. be arranged in a long line. *Please string the beads.* **2** fit a string or strings to a musical instrument, a racket, or a bow. *The musician strung the guitar.* **3** remove the strings from a bean. *They sat on the floor and strung the beans.* **4** hoax. *They strung a story of a monkey man.* **5** work as a stringer in journalism. *He strung the stories well.* **6** determine the order of play by striking the cue ball from baulk to rebound as far as possible from the top cushion. *The team strung to decide who goes first.*

Stringent – *(adjective)* strict, precise, and exacting. *His stringent action made the students work harder.*

Strip – *(noun)* **1** a long, narrow piece of cloth, paper, etc. steel or other metal in the form of narrow flat bars. *The children decorated the room with colourful strips of paper.* **2** a long, narrow area of land. a main road lined with shops and other facilities. *We often go for a walk on the strip.*

Stripe – *(noun)* **1** a long narrow band or strip of a different colour or texture from the surface on either side of it. *The stripes were visible from a distance.* **2** a chevron sewn on to a uniform to denote military rank. *He was very proud of his stripes.* **3** a type or category. *Everyone in this stripe is a good worker.* **4** a blow with a lash. *The stripe felt raw.* *(verb)* mark with stripes. *The child striped the tiger blue and red.*

Strive – *(verb)* make great efforts. fight vigorously against. *We saw them strive to bring about the change.*

Stroke – *(noun)* **1** an act of hitting: he received three strokes of the cane. an act of hitting the ball with a club, as a unit of scoring. a sound made by a striking clock. *The clock's strokes were quite alarming.* **2** a mark made by drawing a pen, pencil, or paintbrush once across paper or canvas. a line forming part of a written or printed character. a short diagonal line separating characters or figures. *Each stroke by the artist made the portrait come to life.* **3** an act of stroking. *The dog licked my hand in response to my strokes.* **4** one of a series of repeated movements. the whole motion of a piston in either direction. a style of moving the arms and legs in swimming. the mode or action of moving the oar in rowing. the oarsman nearest the stern, setting the timing for the other rowers. *I have learnt the butterfly stroke.* **5** a sudden disabling attack or loss of consciousness caused by an interruption in the flow of blood to the brain. *He suffered a stroke.* *(verb)* **1** move one's hand with gentle pressure over. *I stroked the dog.* **2** manipulate by means of flattery or persuasion. *He tried to stroke his way up the ladder.* **3** act as the stroke of a boat or crew. *He stroked the boat forwards.*

Stroll – *(verb)* **1** walk in a leisurely way. *I strolled through the park.* **2** achieve a sporting victory easily. *She strolled her way through the match.* *(noun)* **1** a short leisurely walk. *I enjoyed my evening stroll.* **2** a victory easily achieved. *She was proud of her stroll.*

Strong – *(adjective)* **1** physically powerful. *He is a strong man.* **2** done with or exerting great force. forceful and extreme. *He gave the boat a strong push.* **3** able to withstand great force or pressure. secure, stable, or firmly established. having steadily high or rising prices. *The rope was strong enough to withstand the pressure.* **4** great in intensity or degree: strong competition for land. not soft or muted. pungent and full flavoured. containing a large proportion of a substance. *We could see a fierce competition amongst the students.* **5** great in power, influence, or ability. *He is a strong partner to have.*

Stronghold – *(noun)* **1** a place that has been fortified against attack. *The palace was a stronghold of the kingdom.* **2** a place of strong support for a cause or political party. *The party was confident of winning in its stronghold.*

Structure – *(noun)* **1** the arrangement of and relations between the parts of something complex. *The structure of the organization was difficult to understand.* **2** a building or other object constructed from several parts. *The structure was strong yet flexible.* **3** the quality of being well organized. *She follows a clear structure.* *(verb)* give structure to. *The new CEO structured the customer service department.*

Structural – *(adjective)* of, relating to, or forming part of a structure. *The building had a structural weakness.*

Struggle – *(verb)* **1** make forceful efforts to get free. *The captives struggled against the ropes.* **2** strive under difficult circumstances to do something. have difficulty in gaining recognition or a living. *They struggled against an oppressive ruler.* **3** contend or compete. *The wrestlers struggled to win.* **4** make one's way with difficulty. *He struggled his way to the top.* *(noun)* **1** an act of struggling. *The struggle for freedom was very rewarding.* **2** a very difficult task. *The task of negotiating with the contractor proved to be a struggle.*

Strum – *(verb)* play by sweeping the thumb or a plectrum up or down the strings. play casually or unskillfully on a stringed instrument. *The guitarist strummed along with the music.* *(noun)* an instance or the sound of strumming. *The strum was not unpleasant.*

Strut – *(noun)* **1** a bar forming part of a framework and designed to resist compression. *The strut was the most reliable part of the structure.* **2** a strutting gait. *His pride reflected in his strut.* *(verb)* **1** walk with a stiff, erect, and conceited gait. *She strutted around in the party.* **2** brace with a strut or struts. *The carpenter strutted the framework to make it stable.*

Stub – *(noun)* **1** the truncated remnant of a pencil, cigarette, or similar shaped object after use. *The stub of the pencil was of no use to the child.* **2** a truncated or unusually short thing: he wagged his little stub of tail. *The dog had but a stub of the tail.* **3** the counterfoil of a cheque, ticket, or other document. *They discarded the stubs after checking the tickets.* **4** denoting a projection or hole that goes only part of the way through a surface. *The stub ended only a few metres into the rock.* *(verb)* **1** accidentally strike against something. *I stubbed my toe.* **2** extinguish by pressing the lighted end against something. *The writer stubbed his half-burnt cigarette.* **3** grub up by the roots. *The planter stubbed the weeds.*

Stubble – *(noun)* **1** the cut stalks of cereal plants left in the ground after harvesting. *The stubble was attacked by parasites.* **2** short, stiff hairs growing on a man's face when he has not shaved for a while. *He thought he looked great with a stubble.*

Stubborn – *(adjective)* **1** determined not to change one's attitude or position. *He was a stubborn man.* **2** difficult to move, remove, or cure. *This is a stubborn disease.*

Stubby – *(adjective)* short and thick. *She wriggled her stubby fingers.* *(noun)* a small squat bottle of beer. *He emptied the stubby in no time.*

Stud – *(noun)* **1** an establishment where horses or other domesticated animals are kept for breeding. *The stud produced some excellent racehorses.* 2 a stallion. *The stud was his favourite.* **3** a sexually active or virile young man. *The stud chatted up many women.* **4** a form of poker in which the first card of a player's hand is dealt face down and the others face up, with betting after each round of the deal. *They played stud throughout the night.*

Student – *(noun)* **1** a person studying at a university or other place of higher education. a school pupil. denoting someone who is studying to enter a particular profession: a student nurse. *He has been a student for 30 years now.* **2** a person who takes a particular interest in a subject. *I will forever be a student of psychology.*

Studio – *(noun)* **1** a room where an artist works or where dancers practice. *His studio was his home.* **2** a room from which television or radio programmes are broadcast, or in which they are recorded. *The anchor invited the speaker to the studio.* **3** a place where films or musical or sound recordings are made. *The studio was very well equipped.* **4** a film production company. *The famous studio produced some great films.* **5** a studio flat. *He kept his studio clean.*

Studious – *(adjective)* **1** spending a lot of time studying or reading. *He is a studious boy but he also enjoys sports a lot.* **2** done deliberately or with great care. *Their studious efforts to create the pamphlet were greatly rewarded.*

Study – *(noun)* **1** the devotion of time and attention to acquiring knowledge, especially from books. *The man devoted a lot of time* *to studies.* **2** a detailed investigation and analysis of a subject or situation. a thing that is or deserves to be investigated. *The study of the evidence revealed several clues.* **3** a room for reading, writing, or academic work. *The writer was mostly to be found in her study.* **4** a piece of work, especially a drawing, done for practice or as an experiment. a musical composition designed to develop a player's technical skill. *The painter's study was a good reflection of his skills.* **5** a good example of: he perched on the bed, a study in misery. *She cried her eyes out, a study in self-pity. (verb)* **1** acquire knowledge on. make a study of. apply oneself to study. learn intensively about something, especially in preparation for a test. try to learn. *I studied literature.* **2** look at closely in order to observe read. *They studied the captured alien.* **3** done with deliberate and careful effort. *The crew studied the changing of the tack.*

Stuff – *(noun)* **1** matte, material, articles, or activities of a specified or indeterminate kind. drink or drugs. one's area of expertise. *The scientists were trying to determine the stuff of which the alien craft was made.* **2** basic characteristic; substance: healey was made of sterner stuff. *She was made of stronger stuff.* **3** woolen fabric, especially as distinct from silk, cotton, and linen. *The stuff was warm and soft.* **4** spin given to a ball. *The stuff was difficult to predict.* **5** nonsense; rubbish. *All of this is just some useless stuff. (verb)* **1** fill tightly with something. force tightly into a receptacle or space. fill out the skin of with material to restore the original shape and appearance. push hastily into a space. have one's nose blocked up with catarrh. eat greedily. *My mother stuffed the pillow with the softest of the cottons.* **2** used to express indifference or rejection. *She stuffed his proposal down.* **3** defeat heavily in sport. *The visitors stuffed the hosts.* **4** have sexual intercourse with. **5** place bogus votes in a ballot box. *The hooligans stuffed the ballot box.*

Stuffing – *(noun)* **1** a mixture used to stuff poultry or meat before cooking. *The stuffing was too rich for my taste.* **2** padding used to stuff cushions, furniture, or soft toys. *Children tore the pillows and took out the stuffing.*

Stuffy – *(adjective)* **1** lacking fresh air or ventilation. *The stuffy room made me feel sick.* **2** conventional and narrow minded. *His stuffy approach suffocated his wife.* **3** blocked up. *She cleared up her stuffy nose.*

Stumble – *(verb)* **1** trip or momentarily lose one's balance. walk unsteadily. *He stumbled towards his home.* **2** make a mistake or repeated mistakes in speaking. *He constantly stumbled upon the words.* **3** find by chance. *The police stumbled upon a clue. (noun)* an act of stumbling. *The stumble left him feeling embarrassed.*

Stump – *(noun)* **1** the part of a tree trunk left projecting from the ground after the rest has fallen or been felled. *Several stumps rose from the ground.* **2** a projecting remnant of something worn away or cut or broken off. *The stump of the rock jutted out of the waterfall.* **3** each of the three upright pieces of wood which form a wicket. close of play. a cylinder with conical ends made of rolled paper or other soft material, used in art for softening or blending pencil or crayon marks. *The ball missed the stumps.***5**. engaged in or involving political campaigning. *Several stumps contributed to his victory. (verb)* **1** baffle. *I was stumped by his reply.* **2** dismiss by dislodging the balls with the ball while the batsman is out of the crease but not running. *The player was stumped by the wicketkeeper.* **3** walk stiffly and noisily. *The soldier stumped through the hall.* **4** pay a sum of money. *They stumped the travel agent.* **5** travel around making political speeches. *He stumped across the country but to no avail.*

Stumpy – *(adjective)* short and thick; squat.*My dachshund looks adorable running around on his stumpy legs.*

Stun – *(verb)* **1** knock unconscious or into a dazed or semi conscious state. *She was stunned after falling from her bed.* **2** astonish or shock so that they are temporarily unable to react. *We were stunned by the large crowd that had come to watch our dance.*

Stunning – *(adjective)* extremely impressive or attractive. *Our hotel room has a stunning view of the lake.*

Stunt – *(noun)* **1** an action displaying spectacular skill and daring. something unusual done to attract attention. *My brother likes to perform stunts on his bike.* **2** *(verb)* perform stunts, especially aerobatics. *The dancers stunted across the stage.*

Stupefy – *(verb)* **1** make unable to think or feel properly. *She was stupefied after the ride on the roller coaster.* **2** astonish and shock. *Everyone was stupefied by the destruction caused by the earthquake.*

Stupendous – *(adjective)* extremely impressive. *The kids gave a stupendous performance on the occasion of diwali.*

Stupid – *(adjective)* **1** lacking intelligence or common sense. used to express exasperation or boredom: stop messing about with your stupid paintings! *It was stupid of him to try and finish the whole cake at once.* **2** dazed and unable to think clearly. *He felt stupid with fatigue.*

Stupidity – *(noun)* behaviour that shows a lack of good sense or judgement. *His stupidity made him lose the race.*

Stupor – *(noun)* a state of near unconsciousness or insensibility. *After the 14 hour-long journey, all of us were in a stupor.*

Sturdy – *(adjective)* strongly and solidly built or made. confident and determined: a sturdy independence. *My father gifted me a sturdy study table on my birthday.* *(noun)* vertigo in sheep caused by a tapeworm larva encysted in the brain. *The farmer was worried that his sheep were suffering from sturdy.*

Stutter – *(verb)* talk with continued involuntary repetition of sounds, especially initial consonants. produce a series of short, sharp sounds. *He often stutters when he is afraid.* *(noun)* a tendency to stutter while speaking. *He stuttered when he was scared.*

Sty – *(noun)* keep in a sty. *She visits the pig in the sty daily.*

Style – *(noun)* **1** a manner of doing something. a way of painting, writing, etc. characteristic of a particular period, person, etc. *The Roman style of architecture fascinates me.* **2** a distinctive appearance, design, or arrangement. *This shop has dresses in different styles.* **3**. elegance and sophistication. *She did her job as a hostess with style.* **4** an official or legal title. *In German-speaking universities, the style for the university president is His/Her Magnificence.* **5** a narrow, typically elongated extension of the ovary, bearing the stigma. *My favourite flower is lily because its styles make it look very pretty.* **6** a small, slender pointed appendage; a stylet. *Some invertebrates may also use style for burrowing.* *(verb)* **1** design, make, or arrange in a particular form. *My sister styled my hair for the party.* **2** designate with a particular name, description, or title. *Hindu priests are styled as pandits or pundits.*

Stylish – *(adjective)* having or displaying a good sense of style. fashionably elegant. *She prepared a stylish bouquet of flowers.*

Stylus – *(noun)* **1** a hard point, typically of diamond or sapphire, following a groove in a gramophone record and transmitting the recorded sound for reproduction. *On my grandmother's birthday, I replaced the stylus of her gramophone.* **2** an ancient writing implement for scratching letters on wax covered tablets. a similar implement for engraving and tracing. a pen like device used to input handwritten text or drawings directly into a computer. *I saw an ancient Egyptian stylus at the museum today.*

Suave – *(adjective)* charming, confident, and elegant. *The Hatter in Alice and the Wonderland was very suave and entertaining.*

Sub – *(noun)* **1** a submarine. *We are going to take the sub ride to see the underwater features of Grand Cayman next month.* **2** a subscription. *My cable was deactivated as I forgot to renew my sub.* **3** a substitute, especially in a sporting team. *The quarterback sub is very talented.* **3** a subeditor. *The new sub was given the charge of the sports section.* **4** an advance or loan against expected income. *I subbed from my friend to get my car repaired.* *(verb)* **1** act as a substitute. *The science teacher subbed for the aerobic teacher on Tuesday.* **2** lend or advance a sum to. *I'll sub you till you receive your pay cheque next week.* **3** subedit. *She got her project subbed before final submission.*

Subconscious – *(adjective)* of or concerning the part of the mind of which one is not fully aware but which influences one's actions and feelings. *She took a subconscious decision to teach in a village.* *(noun)* this part of the mind. *My subconscious did not allow me to cheat in the exam.*

Subcontinent – *(noun)* a large distinguishable part of a continent, such as north America or southern Africa. *He visits the Indian subcontinent every year.*

Subdivide – *(verb)* divide something that has already been divided or that is a separate unit. *The term syllabus was subdivided into three sections.*

Subdue – *(verb)* overcome, quieten, or brig under control. bring under control by force. *It took a long time for the police to subdue the crowd protesting against the price hike.*

Subject – *(noun)* **1** a person or thing that is being discussed or dealt with or that gives rise to something. the part of a proposition about which a statement is made. a person who is the focus of scientific or medical attention or experiment. *Many believe it is cruel to use animals as test subjects for different new treatments.* **2** a branch of knowledge studied or taught in a school, college, or university. *Chemistry is my favourite subject.* **3** a (noun) phrase about which the rest of the clause is predicated. *We were asked to identify the subjects of the sentences in our school today.* **4** a member of a state owing allegiance to its monarch or supreme ruler. *Good rulers always work for the benefit of their subjects.* **5** a theme of a fugue or of a piece in sonata form; a leading phrase or motif. *The theme of her sonata was spring.* *(adverb)* conditionally upon. *The date of the party is subjected to the availability of the venue.* *(verb)* **1** cause or force to undergo. *The poor are often subjected to cruel treatment by the rich.* **2** bring under one's control or jurisdiction, typically by force. *After years of struggle, the state was subjected to army rule.*

Subjective – *(adjective)* **1** based on or influenced by personal feelings, tastes, or opinions. *His review of the book was very subjective.* **2** dependent on the mind for existence. *Ideas and thoughts do not have a physical presence, they are subjective.* **3** relating to or denoting a case of (noun)s and pronouns used for the subject of a sentence. *"He opened the door", "he" is subjective to the verb "open" in this sentence.*

Subjudice – *(adjective)* under judicial consideration and therefore prohibited from public discussion elsewhere. *The media could not provide much about the murder case as it was still sudjudiced.*

Sabjugate – *(verb)* bring under domination or control, especially by conquest. *Alexander the Great subjugated many states in a relatively short time.*

Sublet – *(verb)* lease to a subtenant. *She is subletting the second floor of the house as she doesn't need so much space.* *(noun)* a lease of a property by a tenant to a subtenant. *My sublet of the apartment will expire next month.*

Sublime – *(adjective)* **1** of such excellence, grandeur, or beauty as to inspire great admiration or awe. *The experience of successfully scaling a high mountain is sublime.* **2** extreme or unparalleled: *the sublime confidence of youth. He played the match with sublime confidence.* *(verb)* **1** change directly into vapour when heated, typically forming a solid deposit again on cooling. *Ice can sublime in vaccum.* **2** elevate to a high degree of purity or excellence. *Meditating can help people sublime their thoughts.*

Submarine – *(noun)* **1** a streamlined warship designed to operate completely submerged in the sea for long periods. *I built a model of submarine for my science project.* **2** another term for hoagie. *I had a submarine for lunch today.* *(adjective)* existing, occurring, done, or used under the surface of the sea. *We studied submarine plants in our Biology class last week.*

Submerge – *(verb)* **1** cause to be under water. descend below the surface of water. *The legendary city of Dwarka is believed to have been submerged after Lord Krishna's death.* **2** completely cover or obscure. *The minor faults in his project were submerged by his excellent presentation.*

Submission – *(noun)* **1** the action or fact of submitting. an act of surrendering to a hold by one's opponent. *The labor was forced into submission and made to end the strike.* **2**. a proposal or application submitted for consideration. a proposition or argument presented by counsel to a judge or jury. *They gave a long submission to the authorities demanding a new sports block.* **3** humility; meekness. *He tried to impress the boss with submission and flattery.*

Submissive – *(adjective)* meekly obedient or passive. *The hotel staff is very submissive.*

Submit – *(verb)* **1** accept or yield to a superior force or stronger person. *They submitted to the demands of the workers.* **2** subject to a particular process, treatment, or condition. consent to undergo. agree to refer a matter to a third party for decision or adjudication. *She had to submit to multiple checking before boarding the plane.* **3** present a proposal or application for consideration or judgement. suggest; argue. *She submitted a report on the ways to improve the area's security.*

Subnormal – *(adjective)* not number that can be divided exactly into a specified number. *We learnt the function of subnormal in our computer class today.* *(adjective)* being such a number. *We made a new system including the subnormal numbers today.*

Subordinate – *(adjective)* lower in rank or position. of less or secondary importance. *The subordinate counselors handled the meeting very well.* *(noun)* a person under the authority or control of another. *Her subordinate is very efficient.* *(verb)* treat or regard as subordinate. make subservient or dependent. *The playtime of the class was subordinated to train them in disaster management.*

Subscribe – *(verb)* **1** arrange to receive something, especially a periodical, regularly by paying in advance. contribute or undertake to contribute a sum of money to a project or cause. apply to participate in. apply for an issue of shares. apply for an issue of shares. agree before publication to take a certain number of copies of a book. *I subscribe to two food magazines.* **2** formal sign a will, contract, etc. [archaic] sing oneself as. *He has subscribed to the army for 5 years.* **3** feel agreement with an idea or proposal. *I subscribe to the Gandhian school of thought.*

Subsequent – *(adjective)* coming after something in time. *He won the first round but could not participate in subsequent rounds due to a minor injury.*

Subsequently – *(adverb)* after a particular thing has happened. *Many wanted to cancel the picnic but they subsequently changed their mind.*

Subservient – *(adjective)* **1** prepared to obey others unquestioningly; obsequious. *The new domestic help is very subservient.* **2** less important; subordinate. *As it was getting late, they decided to solve the subservient issues in the next meeting.*

Subside – *(verb)* **1** become less intense, violent, or severe. give way to an overwhelming feeling. *The comic act made even the sulkiest child to subside to laughter.* **2** go down to a lower or the normal level. reduce until gone. *The pain in my hand subsided after taking the medicine.* **3** sink lower into the ground. cave in; sink. [informal] sink into a sitting, kneeling, or lying position. *The island has subsided a little due to rise in water level.*

Subsidiary – *(adjective)* less important than but related or supplementary to. controlled by a holding or parent company. *The subsidiary groups meet every month to get directives for the coming months.* *(noun)* **1** a subsidiary company. *The subsidiary company in Shimla had to be shut down due to lack of funds.*

Subsidy – *(noun)* **1** a sum of money granted from public funds to help an industry or business keep the price of a commodity or service low. a sum of money granted to support an undertaking held to be in the public interest. a grant or contribution of money. *The Indian government provide subsidy on railway service.* **2** [historical] a parliamentary grant to the sovereign for state needs. a tax levied on a particular occasion. *The subsidy provided to the state was discontinued due to misuse of funds.*

Subsidize – *(verb)* support financially. pay part of the cost of producing to reduce its price. *Our school provides us subsidized food in the canteen.*

Subsist – *(verb)* 1 maintain or support oneself, especially at a minimal level. [archaic] provide substances for. *She subsists by giving dance lessons after her classes.* 2 [chiefly] law remain in being, force, or effect. be attributable to. *The scholarship subsisted even after the death of the benefactor.*

Subsistence – *(noun)* 1 the action or fact of subsisting. thc means of doing this denoting or relating to production at a level sufficient only for one's own use or consumption, without any surplus for trade: subsistence agriculture. *Despite the subsistence provided, there was a shortage of medicines at the camp.* 2 [chiefly] law the state of remaining in force or effect.*The subsistence of the program depends on the hard work of the volunteers.*

Substance – *(noun)* 1 a particular kind of matter with uniform properties. an intoxicating or narcotic drug. *The toxic substance from the factory is polluting the river.* 2 the real physical matter of which a person or thing consists. solid basis in reality or fact: the claim has no substance. .dependability or stability. *There was no substance in the complaints of the management.* 3 the quality of being important, valid, or significant. the most important or essential part or meaning. the subject matter of a text or work of art, especially as contrasted with its form or style. wealth and possessions: a woman of substance. *The issue of childcare is of substance for the working parents.* 4 [philosophy] the essential nature underlying phenomena, which is subject to changes and accidents. *The substance of policy is dependent on the needs of the people.*

Substandard – *(adjective)* 1 below the usual or required standard. *The food is usually good at the mess but it was substandard last night.* 2 another term for non standard. *The lights that he installed did not work as he has used substandard parts.*

Substantial – *(adjective)* 1 of considerable importance, size, or worth. strongly built or made. important in material or social terms; wealthy. *We collected a substantial amount in the annual bake sale.* 2 concerning the essentials of something. *There is substantial support for the new law.* 3 real and tangible rather than imaginary. *The court takes decision based on substantial proofs only.*

Substantiate – *(verb)* provide evidence to support or prove the truth of. *She substantiated her report with facts and figure from multiple cases.*

Substitute – *(noun)* 1 a person or thing acting or serving in place of another. *The class was given to a substitute till the teacher got back from her leave.* 2 a sports player nominated as eligible to replace another after a match has begun. *He could not make it to the team but got to play as a substitute for the wicket keeper.* 3 a deputy. *The officer asked the substitute to write the initial report.* *(verb)* 1 use, add, or serve in place of. replace with another. replace with another. *I substituted egg with bananas in the recipe.* 2 replace with a substitute during a match. *He was asked to substitute for the goalkeeper.*

Substitution – *(noun)* replacing something someone with another or person. *The substitution of the LPG with natural gas would be cheap and environment-friendly.*

Subterranean – *(adjective)* 1 existing, occurring, or done under the earth's surface. *Earthquakes and volcanoes are caused by subterranean movements and pressures.* 2 secret. *The idea of working with subterranean security sounds very dangerous and exciting.*

Subtitle – *(noun)* 1 captions displayed at the bottom of a cinema or television screen that translate or transcribe the dialogue or narrative. *We could not really enjoy the French movie that we saw last week as the subtitles were not in sync.* 2 a subordinate title of a published work or article. *The different parts of Pirates of the Caribbean series have the same title but different subtitles to distinguish them.* *(verb)* provide with a subtitle or subtitles. *I subtitled a short film for my friend.*

Subtle – *(adjective)* **1** so delicate or precise as to be difficult to analyse or describe: a subtle distinctin. capable of making fine distinctions. delicately complex and understated: subtle lighting. *There is a subtle taste of saffron in the dish.* **2** making use of clever and indirect methods to achieve something. *He used a subtle approach to get an agreement from the council.* **3** crafty; cunning. *The opposition party used subtle tactics to overthrow the ruling party.*

Subtlety – *(noun)* the quality of being subtle. *She has mastered the subtleties of this crochet design.*

Subtract – *(verb)* take away from another to calculate the difference. remove a part of something. *She subtracted the fancy envelopes to save money for the return gifts.*

Subtraction – *(noun)* the process of taking away one number away from another. *I got all the answers right in the subtraction exercise.*

Suburb – *(noun)* an outlying district of a city, especially a residential one. *I am searching for a flat in the suburbs.*

Suburban – *(adjective)* of or characteristic of a suburb. *The suburban locations often have better residential facilities.*

Subversive – *(adjective)* seeking or intended to subvert an established system or institution. *The writer's article against the government was taken as subversive material.* *(noun)* a subversive person. *The officer was dismissed as he was considered to be subversive.*

Subvert – *(verb)* undermine the power and authority of an established system or institution. *Teenagers often try to subvert their parents' authority.*

Subway – *(noun)* **1** a tunnel under a road for use by pedestrians. *The authorites made a subway to help pedestrians cross the busy road.* **2** an underground railway. *The subway cut the commuting time to half.*

Succeed – *(verb)* **1** achieve an aim or purpose. attain fame, wealth, or social status. *Work hard to succeed in life.* **2** take over an office, title, etc. from someone. become the new rightful holder of an office, title, etc. *The young prince succeeded the king to the throne.* **3** come after and take the place of: her embarrassment was succeeded by fear. *Her embarrassment was succeeded by her fear.*

Success – *(noun)* **1** the accomplishment of an aim or purpose. the attainment of fame, wealth, or social status. a person or thing that achieves success. *The soft drink is a huge success all over the world.* **2** the good or bad outcome of an undertaking. *The success of the conference was evident in the news.*

Successful – *(adjective)* accomplishing an aim or purpose. having achieved fame, wealth, or social status. *She is a successful entrepreneur.*

Succession – *(noun)* **1** a number of people or things following one after the other. *I was so hungry that I ate three bananas in succession.* **2** the action, process, or right of inheriting an office, title, etc. *The boss's son is CEO of the company as boss's succession.* **3** the process by which a plant or animal community successively gives way to another until a stable climax is reached. *The young prince shall become the next king according to the law of succession.*

Successive – *(adjective)* following one another or following others. *The team was happy at winning three successive tournaments.*

Successor – *(noun)* a person or thing that succeeds another. *The captain finally named his successor.*

Succinct – *(adjective)* briefly and clearly expressed. *I will always keep your succinct words in mind.*

Succumb – *(verb)* **1** fail to resist. *The government succumbed to the pressure of the business community.* **2** die from the effect of a disease or injury. *The patient succumbed to the injuries at the hospital.*

Such – *(det.)* predet., & pronoun **1** of the type previously mentioned. *People think they can get away with any crime, but such people should be punished severely.* **2** of the type about to be mentioned. *Please look at such examples, the ones that prove the theory wrong.* **3** to so high a degree; so great. *I respect him such that I cannot find any faults with him.*

Suck – *(verb)* **1** draw into the mouth by contracting the muscles of the lip and mouth to make a partial vacuum. hold in the mouth and draw at it by contracting the lip and cheek muscles. draw in a specified direction by creating a vacuum. make a gurgling sound as a result of drawing air instead of water. *Many children suck their thumbs.* **2** involve in something without their choosing obsequiously. *He tried to suck up to the boss.* **4** be very bad or disagreeable: the weather here sucks. *The meeting sucks.* *(noun)* an act or sound of sucking. *The child was warned about the harms of sucking.*

Suction – *(noun)* the production of a partial vacuum by the removal of air in order to force fluid into a vacant space or procure adhesion. *Suction helped clear the drain.* *(verb)* remove using suction. *The doctors suctioned the water from the patient's lungs.*

Sudden – *(adjective)* occurring or done quickly and unexpectedly. *He felt a sudden pain in his leg.*

Suds – *(plural noun)* **1** froth made from soap and water. *The child played with the suds.* **2** beer. *The suds were warm.* *(verb)* cover or wash in soapy water. form suds. *The child suds himself while taking a bath.*

Sue – *(verb)* **1** institute legal proceedings against, typically for redress. *He stole my patent so I am going to sue him.* **2** appeal formally to a person for something. *The king sued his subjects to restore peace.*

Suede – *(noun)* leather, especially the skin of a young goat, with the flesh side rubbed to make a velvety nap. *The rain muddied my nice new boots made of suede.*

Suffer – *(verb)* **1** experience or be subjected to something bad or unpleasant. be affected by or subject to an illness or ailment. become or appear worse in quality. undergo martyrdom or execution. *The farmers might suffer some losses but no one will starve.* **2** tolerate. allow to do something. *She suffered the naughty child with patience.*

Suffering – *(noun)* the stae of undergoing pain or wardship.*Painkilling drugs were not enough to relieve her suffering.*

Suffice – *(verb)* be enough or adequate. meet the needs of. *They thought that two meals a day would suffice an old man.*

Sufficient – *(adjective & det.)* enough; adequate. *We have sufficient funds for this trip.*

Suffix – *(noun)* **1** a morpheme added at the end of a word to form a derivative. *He used the suffix incorrectly.* **2** another term for subscript. *The font made it difficult to read the suffix.* *(verb)* append, especially as a suffix. *He suffixed "ness" to a lot of words.*

Suffocate – *(verb)* die or cause to die from lack of air or inability to breathe. have or cause to have difficulty in breathing. *Because of faulty respirator the patient suffocated to death.*

Suffocation – *(noun)* feeling of lack of air or inability to breathe. *Because of the suffocation in the crowded carriage, several people felt sick.*

Suffrage – *(noun)* **1** the right to vote in political elections. [archaic] a vote given for a person or in assent to a proposal. *I am going to practise my suffrage this year.* **2** the intercessory petitions pronounced by a priest in the litany. a series of petitions pronounced by the priest with the responses of the congregation. intercessory prayers, especially those for the dead. *The priest pronounced suffrages for those who died in the storm.*

Sugar – *(noun)* a sweet crystalline substance obtained especially from sugar cane and sugar beet, consisting essentially of source and used a sweetener in food and drink. *She added sugar to her tea.* **2** [biochemistry] any of the class of soluble, crystalline, typically sweet-tasting carbohydrates found in living tissues and exemplified by glucose and sucrose. *The fruit was high in sugar.* **3** used as a term of endearment. *Come here, sugar.* **4** a narcotic drug especially heroin or LSD. *They were caught selling brown sugar.* *(verb)* **1** sweeten, sprinkle, or coat with sugar. make more agreeable or palatable. *He sugared the candy.* **2** spread a sugar mixture on a tree trunk in order to catch moths. *They sugared the tree trunk.* **3** the boiling down of maple sap until it thickens into syrup or crystallizes into sugar. *The family sugared the maple sap.* **4** a method of removing unwanted hair by applying a mixture of lemon juice, sugar, and water to the skin and then peeling it off together with the hair. *She chose to sugar her arms even though the process was painful.*

Sugary – *(adjective)* **1** resembling, or containing much, sugar. *He eats too much sugary food.* **2** excessively sentimental. *The soap opera is too sugary for my liking.*

Suggest – *(verb)* **1** put forward for consideration. come into one's mind. *There is strong evidence to suggest that she is telling the truth.* **2** cause one to think that exists or is the case; evoke. state or express indirectly. *He suggested that our policies were not fair.*

Suggestion – *(noun)* **1** an idea or plan put forward for consideration. the action of suggesting. *We like your suggestion.* **2** something that implies or indicates a certain fact or situation. *We were getting strong suggestions that something was wrong in the house.* **3** a slight trace or indication: a suggestion of a smile. *I detected a suggestion of moisture in his eyes.* **4** the influencing of a person to accept a belief or impulse uncritically. *She took the suggestion well.*

Suicide – *(noun)* **1** the action of killing oneself intentionally. a person who does this. relating to or denoting a military operation carried out by people who do not expect to survive it: a suicide bomber. *Several charities work towards preventing suicides.* **2** a course of action which is disastrously damaging to one's own interests. *Why are you bent upon committing professional suicide? (verb)* intentionally kill oneself. *She suicided when she was alone.*

Suicidal – *(adjective)* deeply unhappy or depressed and likely to commit suicide. *The psychologist cured the man's suicidal tendencies.*

Suitable – *(adjective)* right or appropriate for a particular person, purpose, or situation. *This is a suitable dress for the occasion.*

Suitcase – *(noun)* a case with a handle and a hinged lid, used for carrying clothes and other personal possessions. *He dragged his heavy suitcase across the railway station.*

Suite – *(noun)* **1** a set of rooms for one person's or family's use or for a particular purpose. *We booked a suite for the family.* **2** a set of furniture of the same design. *The entire suite fitted the room beautifully.* **3** a set of instrumental compositions to be played in succession. a set of pieces from an opera or musical arranged as one instrumental work. *I bought a CD of the suite.* **4** a group of people in attendance on a monarch or other person of high rank. *The suite never said a word against the king.*

Suitor – *(noun)* a man who pursues a relationship with a woman with a view to marriage. a prospective buyer of a business or corporation. *She had a long queue of suitors to choose from.*

Sulk – *(verb)* be silent, morose, and bad tempered through annoyance or disappointment. *The child sulked when his mom scolded him. (noun)* a period of sulking. *The sulk lasted for two hours.*

Sulky – *(adjective)* morose, bad tempered, and resentful. *She doesn't have too many friends because of her sulky nature. (noun)* a light two wheeled horse drawn vehicle for one person, used [chiefly] in trotting races. *The horse drew the sulky at a fast pace.*

Sullen – *(adjective)* bad tempered and sulky. *She is in a sullen mood again.*

Sulphur – *(noun)* an element in chemistry. *The bottle containing sulphur fell and broke.*

Sultry – *(adjective)* **1** hot and humid. *The sultry weather makes me want to bathe again and again.* **2** displaying or suggesting passion; provocative. *The sultry movie was censured heavily.*

Sum – *(noun)* **1** a particular amount of money. *Please pay me the entire sum at one go.* **2** the total amount resulting from the addition of two or more numbers or amounts. the total amount of something that exists. *The students calculated the sum expertly.* **3** an arithmetical problem, especially at an elementary level. *It took a long time to solve the sum. (verb)* **1** concisely describe the nature or character of someone or something. summarize briefly. *The poem summed up his personality beautifully.* **2** review the evidence at the end of a case, and direct the jury regarding points of law. *The advocate summed up the case beautifully.* **3** find the sum of two or more amounts. *Please sum these numbers.*

Summary – *(noun)* a brief statement of the main points of something. *The summary of our discussion will reach you in a minute.* *(adjective)* **1** dispensing with needless details or formalities. *The summary speech was enough for the everyone.* **2** conducted without the customary legal formalities. made by a judge or magistrate without a jury. *The summary judgement was apt for the crime.*

Summarize – *(verb)* briefly or give main points. *Please summarize your speech.*

Summer – *(noun)* a horizontal bearing beam, especially one supporting joists or rafters. *The summer was old and unstable.*

Summon – *(verb)* **1** authoritatively call on to be present, especially to appear I a law court. *The witness was summoned by the court.* **2** call people to attend. *The priest summoned the people to attend the ceremony.* **3** cause to emerge from within oneself: she managed to summon up a smile. *She summoned up her courage to face the wild tiger.*

Sumptuous – *(adjective)* splendid and expensive looking. *He organized a sumptuous meal for his guests.*

Sun – *(noun)* **1** the star round which the earth orbits. any similar star, with or without planets. *The sun was hidden behind a blanket of fog.* **2** the light or warmth received from the sun. *I am sitting in the sun.* **3** a day or a year. *It will take a sun to complete this task.* *(verb)* sit or lie in the sun. expose to the sun. *The tiger sunned itself on the hill.*

Sunny – *(adjective)* **1** bright with or receiving much sunlight. *The sunny morning was a welcome change from the foggy days.* **2** cheerful. *She was bright and sunny today.*

Sunblind – *(noun)* a window blind used to exclude the sun. *The sunblinds made the room dark.*

Sunburn – *(noun)* inflammation of the skin caused by over exposure to the ultraviolet rays of the sun. *The sunburn was very painful.* *(verb)* suffer from sunburn. *I sunburnt myself.*

Sunlit – *(adjective)* lighted by sunlight. *Violet valleys and the sunstruck ridges.*

Sunrise – *(noun)* the time in the morning when the sun rises. the colours and light visible in the sky at sunrise. *I saw a beautiful sunrise today.*

Sunset – *(noun)* **1** the time in the evening when the sun sets. the colours and light visible in the sky at sunset. *The sunset was spectacular today.* **2** the final declining phase of something. *It was very clear that the business was at its sunset.* **3** denoting a clause or provision under which an agency or programme is to be disbanded or terminated at the end of a fixed period unless it is formally renewed. *The sunset was set at two years from now.*

Sunstroke – *(noun)* heatstroke brought about by excessive exposure to the sun. *Sunstroke can be a dangerous to life.*

Sunday – *(noun)* the day of the week before Monday and following Saturday, observed by Christians as a day of rest and religious worship. *This Sunday, I will spend the time with my family.* *(adverb)* on Sunday. on Sundays; each Sunday. *I will jog each Sunday.*

Sundry – *(adjective)* of various kinds. *They bough sundry stuff from the store.* *(noun)* **1** various items not important enough be mentioned individually. *The sundry items made a heavy load.* **2** Australian term for extra. *I bought some sundry chocolates for the kids.*

Super – *(adjective)* **1** excellent. *You just gave me a super idea.* **2** of extra fine quality. *The super grain will be very popular in the markets.* **3** short for superficial. *He is such a super.* *(adverb)* especially. *He super called her up.* *(noun)* **1** a superintendent. *The super is very particular about discipline.* **2** an extra. *The super loitered around the set.* **3** superphosphate. *The super is often used as a fertilizer.* **4** superfine fabric or manufacture. *The fabric used in making this coat is super.*

Superannuate – *(verb)* **1** retire with a pension. belonging to a superannuation scheme. *My father superannuated 12 years ago.* **2** too old or outdated to be effective or useful. *The air-conditioner superannuated this year.*

Superannuation – *(noun)* regular payment made into a fund by an employee towards a future pension. *The pension from superannuation is a helpful scheme during old age.*

Superb – *(adjective)* **1** excellent. *The superb food was very difficult to resist.* **2** magnificent or splendid. used in names of birds with attractive or colourful plumage, e.g. superb lyrebird. *A superb dancing by peacock was thrilling.*

Supercilious – *(adjective)* having an air of contemptuous superiority. *Her supercilious attitude does not go down too well with her friends.*

Superficial – *(adjective)* **1** existing or occurring at or on the surface. *The burns were just superficial.* **2** apparent rather than actual. *The superficial emotions sickened me.* **3** not thorough or deep; cursory. lacking depth of character or understanding. *Unfortunately, many people misunderstood him to be a superficial person.* **4** denoting a quantity of a material expressed in terms of area covered. *The superficial quantity seems to be about 400 square metres.*

Superfluity – *(noun)* an unnecessary large number of anything. *Superfluity is not recommended in the current economic scenario.*

Superfluous – *(adjective)* unnecessary, especially through being more than enough. *The superfluous kindness appeared fake.*

Superimpose – *(verb)* place or lay over another, typically so that both are evident. *I superimposed the transparent sheet of printed paper over the painted wall.*

Superintend – *(verb)* act as superintendent of. *She superintends the girls' hostel.*

Superintendent – *(noun)* **1** a person who supervises or is in charge of an organization, department, etc. *Everyone ran to their seats as soon as they heard the supervisor arriving.* **2** a police officer ranking above chief inspector. *The superintendent called a meeting with the policemen to take a stalk of the situation.* **3** the chief of a police department. *The superintendent is a man of principles.* **4** the caretaker of a building. *The superintendent failed to get the plumbing fixed.*

Superior – *(adjective)* **1** higher in rank, status, or quality. of high standard or quality. greater in size or power. *He is superior to us in rank.* **2** further above or out; higher in position. situated above the sepals and petals. *The superior part of the flower suffered damage when two butterflies fought for nectar.* **3** written or printed above the line. *The superior text was not legible because of the font.* **4** above yielding to or being influenced by. *She is a superior being when compared to many others in her vicinity.* **5** conceited. *His superior attitude turned many of his friends off.* *(noun)* 1 a person of superior rank. the head of a monastery or other religious institution. *The superior called a meeting.* **2** a superior letter, figure, or symbol. *The superior was very symbolic.*

Superiority – *(noun)* state of being superior. *He often made his superiority clear.*

Superlative – *(adjective)* of the highest quality or degree. *His superlative power of speech was very evident.* *(noun)* a hyperbolical expression of praise. *They used several superlatives to describe their king.*

Supermarket – *(noun)* a large self service shop selling foods and household goods. *I went to the supermarket to buy groceries.*

Supernatural – *(adjective)* **1** attributed to some force beyond scientific understanding or the laws of nature. *People claimed that they felt a supernatural force in the house.* **2** exceptionally or extraordinarily great. *He had some supernatural talents.* *(noun)* upernatural manifestations or events. *I am very curious about the supernatural.*

Supersede – *(verb)* take the place of; supplant. *The director's instructions superseded the ones issued by the HR department.*

Supersonic – *(adjective)* involving or denoting a speed greater than that of sound. *The jet moved at a supersonic speed.*

Superstar – *(noun)* an extremely famous and successful performer or sports player. *He enjoyed being the superstar.*

Superstition – *(noun)* excessively credulous belief in and reverence for the supernatural. a widely held but irrational belief in supernatural influences, especially as bringing good or bad luck. *Our society is plagued by superstitions.*

Superstitious – *(adjective)* having belief in superstitions. *She is a superstitious girl.*

Supervise – *(verb)* observe and direct the execution of or the work of a person. *I supervised the arrangements for the party.*

Supervisor – *(noun)* a person who supervises a person or activity. *I was the supervisor of the party arrangements.*

Supper – *(noun)* **1** a light or [informal] evening meal. *I go for a walk after the supper.* **2** a meal consisting of the specified food with chips: a fish supper. *I had a burger supper in the evening.*

Supplant – *(verb)* supersede and replace. *The boss supplanted the instructions issued by the manager.*

Supple – *(adjective)* flexible or pliant. *She had a supple body.* *(verb)* make more flexible. *He suppled the iron rod.*

Supplement – *(noun)* **1** a thing added to something else to enhance or complete it. *The sugar supplement made the sugar-free dessert edible.* **2** a separate section, especially a colour magazine, added to a newspaper or periodical. *At times I find the supplement more informative than the newspaper.* **3** an additional charge payable for an extra service or facility. *The supplements were higher than the main charge.* **4** the amount by which a given angle is less than 1800. *The supplement could not be calculated accurately.* *(verb)* provide a supplement for. *The doctor supplemented her diet.*

Supplementary – *(adjective)* completing or enhancing something. *She took some supplementary diets to help her recover.*

Supply – *(adverb)* variant spelling of supplely. *She danced supply.*

Support – *(verb)* **1** bear all or part of the weight of. *He supports himself well on the stick.* **2** give assistance, encouragement, or approval to. be actively interested in a sports team. of secondary importance to the leading roles in a play or film. function as a secondary act to at a concert. *The entire film industry supported the newcomer.* **3** provide with a home and the necessities of life. be capable of sustaining. *The charity supported many homeless children.* **4** corroborate. *The evidence supported the defence's plea of innocence.* **5** endure; tolerate. *She supported the incessantly complaining mother-in-law.* *(noun)* 1 a person or thing that supports. the action of supporting or the state of being so supported. *The support was strong and stable.* **2** assistaince, encouragement, or approval. *My family's support was invaluable.*

Supporter – *(noun)* **1** a person who supports a sports team, policy, etc. *The team had many supporters.* **2** a representation of an animal or other figure, typically one of a pair, holding up or standing beside an escutcheon. *The supporters had begun to crack.*

Supportive – *(adjective)* providing encouragement. *Her family were very supportive of her decision to go back to studies.*

Suppose – *(verb)* **1** think or assume that something is true or probable, but without proof. assume or require that something is the case as a precondition. used to introduce a suggestion. *I suppose that you lead a busy life.* **2** be required or expected to do something. *You are supposed to do your work.*

Supposition – *(noun)* an assumption or hypothesis. *The supposition became invalid when the assumption proved to be incorrect.*

Suppress – *(verb)* **1** forcibly put an end to. *The police suppressed the protests.* **2** prevent from being expressed or published. consciously avoid thinking. *The leader suppressed the news to prevent a revolt.* **3** prevent or inhibit. *They successfully suppressed the thieves.*

Supreme – *(adjective)* **1** highest in authority or rank. *The President's word is supreme in some countries.* **2** very great or greatest; most important. involving death. *There are many discussions every day regarding the Supreme being.* *(noun)* a rich cream sauce or a dish served in this. *I don't like the taste of supreme.*

Supremacy – *(noun)* the condition of being superior in authority. *No one could question her supremacy.*

Supreme Being - *(adjective)* highest in authority. *There are several schools of thoughts regarding the Supreme being.*

Surcharge - *(noun)* **1** an additional charge or payment. an amount in an official account not passed by the auditor and having to be refunded by the person responsible. the showing of an omission in an account for which credit should have been given. *There were many surcharges apart from the regular ones.* **2** a mark printed on a postage stamp changing its value. *I misread the surcharge on the stamp.* *(verb)* **1** exact a surcharge from. *The shop surcharged the customers heavily.* **2** mark with a surcharge. *The stamp was surcharged.*

Sure - *(adjective)* **1** completely confident that one is right. *She is very sure of herself.* **2** certain to receive, get, or do something. *It was a sure investment.* **3** undoubtedly true; completely reliable. *It was a sure finding.* *(adverb)* certainly. *He will sure call me*

Surely - *(adverb)* **1** unlikely to stumble or slip. *She treaded the red carpet surely.* **2** confident and competent. *He lived his life surely.*

Surety - *(noun)* **1** a person who takes responsibility for another's undertaking, e.g. the payment of a debt. *He stood as a surety for his friend.* **2** money given as a guarantee that someone will do something. *The organization asked for surety for employment.* **3** the state of being sure. *His surety made his juniors bank on him.*

Surf - *(noun)* the mass or line of foam formed by waves breaking on a seashore or reef. *The surf was tossed high in the air as the waves became steeper.* *(verb)* **1** stand or lie on a surf board and ride on the crest of a wave towards the shore. *She skilfully surfed the steep waves.* **2** ride on the roof or outside of a fast moving vehicle, typically a train, for excitement. *The policeman arrested them when they surfed the train.* **3** occupy oneself by moving from site to site on the internet. *I surf the net for hours every day.*

Surfing - *(noun)* the sport of riding waves towards the shore while standing on a surfboard, the activity of moving from site to site on the internet. *I enjoy surfing.*

Surface - *(noun)* **1** the outside part or uppermost layer of something. the area of this. *The surface of the sphere was smooth.* **2** the upper limit of a body of liquid. *The surface of the water appeared calm.* **3** outward appearance as distinct from less obvious aspects. *On the surface, she appeared calm and collected.* **4** a set of points that has length and breadth but no thickness. *The surface was very wide and long.* *(adjective)* of, relating to, or occurring on the surface. carried by or denoting transportation by sea or overland as contrasted with by air. *The surface temperature was much higher than the temperature at some depth.* *(verb)* **1** rise or come up to the surface. *The sunken ship surfaced after centuries.* **2** become apparent. *Several truths surfaced during the investigation.* **3** provide with a particular surface. *We surfaced the ground for cricket players.* **4** appear after having been asleep. *At last he surfaced.*

Surfeit - *(noun)* **1** an excess. *The surfeit of her emotions disgusted me after a point.* **2** an illness caused or regarded as being caused by excessive eating or drinking. *The surfeit threatened to kill him one day.* *(verb)* **1** cause to be wearied of something through excess. *He surfeited his liver.* **2** overeat. *If you surfeit, your problems will become worse.*

Surge - *(noun)* **1** a sudden powerful forward or upward movement: tidal surges. *The surge uprooted the tree.* **2** a sudden large temporary increase. *The surge in water level made the flood warnings go off.* **3** a powerful rush of an emotion or feeling. *I was overwhelmed by her surge of emotions.* *(verb)* **1** move in a surge. *The mob surged forwards.* **2** increase suddenly and powerfully. *The water level surged resulting in emergency evacuation of the land.* **3** slip back with a jerk. *As soon as the vehicle darted ahead, I surged back.*

Surgeon - *(noun)* **1** a medical practitioner qualified to practice surgery. *He was a respected surgeon.* **2** a doctor in the navy. *They called the surgeon when the naval officer fainted on the deck.*

Surgery - *(noun)* **1** the branch of [medicine] concerned with treatment of bodily injuries or disorders by incision or manipulation, especially with instruments. *He was undergoing surgery for the stones in his kidney.* **2** a place where a medical practitioner treats or advises patients. *The doctor asked them to come to his surgery immediately.* **3** an occasion on which an MP, lawyer, or other professional person gives advice. *Many people waited in the queue during the surgery.*

Surly – *(adjective)* bad tempered and unfriendly. *People stayed away from him because of his surly temper.*

Surmise – *(verb)* suppose without having evidence. *I surmise that they don't care for the cause.* *(noun)* a supposition or guess. *The surmise proved to be correct.*

Surmount – *(verb)* **1** overcome a difficulty or obstacle. *He surmounted his bad finances to become a doctor.* **2** stand or be placed on top of. *He surmounted the benches and gave a mock speech.*

Surname – *(noun)* **1** a hereditary name common to all members of a family, as distinct from a forename. *My surname says a lot about my heritage.* **2** a descriptive or allusive name, title, or epithet added to a person's name. *The artist was better known by his surname.* *(verb)* give a surname to. *They surnamed the poet for the subtle expression in his poetry.*

Surpass – *(verb)* be greater or better than. incomparable or outstanding. *You surpass me in intelligence.*

Surplus – *(noun)* an amount left over when requirements have been met. an excess of income or assets over expenditure or liabilities in a given period. the excess value of a company's assets over the face value of its stock. *The company didn't know what to do with the surplus.* *(adjective)* excess; extra. *The surplus goods were distributed amongst the poor.*

Surprise – *(noun)* **1** a feeling of mild astonishment or shock caused by something unexpected. *I was surprised to see all my friends at my place.* **2** an unexpected or astonishing thing. *The surprise was too much for me.* **3** denoting a complex method of change ringing: surprise major. *(verb)* **1** cause to feel surprise. *My friends surprised me on my birthday.* **2** capture, attack, or discover suddenly and unexpectedly. *The sudden discovery of oil in his fields surprised him.*

Surrender – *(verb)* **1** cease resistance to an opponent and submit to their authority. *The terrorists surrendered before the army.* **2** give up on compulsion or demand. give up before its expiry. *We surrendered the medicines to the store.* **3** abandon oneself entirely to a powerful emotion or influence. *I surrendered to my grief.* **4** cancel and received back a proportion of the premiums paid. *I surrendered my policy.* (noun) the action of surrendering. *His complete surrender to grief was heartbreaking.*

Surreptitious – *(adjective)* cover or clandestine. *Their surreptitious relationship came to light.*

Surrogate – *(noun)* a substitute, especially a person deputizing for another I a specific role or office. a bishop's deputy who grants marriage licences. a judge in charge of probate, inheritance, and guardianship. *She acted as a surrogate to the child's mother.*

Surround – *(verb)* **1** be all round; encircle. *They surrounded their leader eagerly.* **2** be associated with: the killings were surrounded by controversy. *The occurrences in the haunted house were surrounded by myths.* *(noun)* **1** a border or edging. *The tablecloth had a beautiful surround.* **2** surroundings. *His surround was very peaceful.*

Surrounding – *(plural noun)* the conditions or area around a person or thing. *I was happy with my surroundings.*

Surveillance – *(noun)* close observation, especially of a suspected spy or criminal. *She was put under surveillance.*

Survey – *(verb)* **1** look carefully and thoroughly at. *The police surveyed the crime scene thoroughly.* **2** examine and record the area and features of so as to construct a map, plan, or description. *The agency surveyed the locality.* **3** examine and report on the condition, especially for a prospective buyer. *The agent surveyed the apartment complex.* **4** conduct a survey among. *The college authorities surveyed* *the girls. (noun)* **1** a general view, examination, or description. an investigation of the opinions or experience of a group of people, based on a series of questions. *The survey yielded some surprising results.* **2** an act of surveying. *The survey concluded successfully.* **3** a map, plan, or report obtained by surveying. *The survey revealed some interesting truths.*

Surveyor – *(noun)* **1** a person who surveys land, buildings, etc. as a profession. *The surveyor did a good job.* **2** an official inspector, especially for measurement and valuation purposes. *The surveyor visited the building regularly.*

Survival – *(noun)* **1** the state or fact of surviving. *Doctors raised serious doubts on her survival.* **2** an object or practice that has survived from an earlier time. *The survival is still followed with great diligence.*

Survive – *(verb)* continue to live or exist. continue to live or exist in spite of. remain alive after the death of. *Mahatma Gandhi's philosophy will survive for a long time.*

Susceptible – *(adjective)* **1** likely to be influenced or harmed by a particular thing. easily influenced by feelings or emotions. *The hut was susceptible to tornadoes.* **2** capable or admitting of. *She was susceptible of great things.*

Suspect – *(verb)* **1** believe to be probable or possible. believe to be guilty of a crime or offence, without certain proof. *I suspect that what you are telling me is your own story, not your friend's.* **2** doubt the genuineness or truth of. *The police suspected that she was lying. (noun)* a person suspected of a crime or offence. *The suspect was trailed by cops undercover. (adjective)* possibly dangerous or false. *His suspect behaviour made the police put him under scrutiny.*

Suspend – *(verb)* **1** halt temporarily. *I suspended my work to take a break.* **2** debar temporarily from a post, duties, etc. as a punishment. *The DCP was suspended following the violence in the city.* **3** defer or delay. cause to be unenforced as long as no further offence is committed within a specified period. *His sentence was suspended because of unknown reasons.* **4** hang from somewhere. *I suspended the flower basket from the hook.* **5** be dispersed in a suspension. *The swirls suspended in the air for a bit.*

Suspense – *(noun)* **1** a state or feeling of excited or anxious uncertainty about what may happen. *I couldn't stand the suspense any longer.* **2** the temporary cessation or suspension of something. *The authority called off the suspense.*

Suspension – *(noun)* **1** the action of suspending or the condition of being suspended. *The suspension was cancelled at the last moment.* **2** the system of springs and shock absorbers by which a vehicle is supported on its wheels. *The sudden jerks are bad for a vehicle's suspension.* **3** a mixture in which particles are dispersed throughout the bulk of a fluid. *The suspension was beautiful to look at.* **4** a discord made by prolonging a note of a chord into the following chord. *The suspension suited the tune.*

Suspicious – *(adjective)* showing a cautious distrust of something or someone. *The police arrested him for his suspicious activities.*

Sustain – *(verb)* **1** strengthen or support physically or mentally. bear. *The rope sustained the sails well.* **2** keep going over time or continuously. *She sustained her work and received great results.* **3** suffer. *He sustained severe injuries during the fall.* **4** uphold or confirm the justice or validity of. *The high court sustained the ruling of the district court. (noun)* an effect or facility on a keyboard or electronic instrument whereby a note can be sustained after the key is released. *My keyboard had the sustain functionality.*

Sustenance – *(noun)* **1** food and drink regarded as sustaining life. *Everyone needs sustenance to survive.* **2** the sustaining of someone or something in life or existence. *They celebrated the sustenance of unity in their community.*

Swab – *(noun)* **1** an absorbent pad used in surgery and [medicine] for cleaning wounds or applying medication. a specimen of a secretion taken with a swab. *They cleaned the wound with a swab.* **2** a mop or other absorbent device for cleaning or mopping up. *The maid cleaned the floor with a swab.* **3** a contemptible person. US another term for swabbie. *He was such a swab. (verb)* clean or absorb with a swab. *They swabbed the wound.*

Swagger – *(verb)* walk or behave arrogantly or self importantly. *He swaggered through the party, acting snooty and snobbish. (noun)* an arrogant or self important gait or manner. *His swagger irritated quite a few people. (adjective)* **1** denoting a coat cut with a loose flare from the shoulders. *The swagger coat suited his personality.* **2** smart or fashionable. *He is a swagger man.*

Swallow – *(noun)* a migratory swift flying insectivorous songbird with a forked tail. *The swallows were welcome visitors in our city.*

Swamp – *(noun)* a area of waterlogged ground; a bog or marsh. *I squelched my way through the swamp. (verb)* **1** overwhelm or flood with water. *The area was swamped after the Tsunami.* **2** overwhelm with too much of something; inundate. *I was swamped with grief at the news.*

Swampy – *(adjective)* characteristic of a swamp. *The swampy ground was dangerous in foggy conditions.*

Swan – *(noun)* a large water bird, typically all white, with a long flexible neck, short legs, and webbed feet. *Several beautiful swans lived near the lake. (verb)* move or go in a casual, irresponsible, or ostentatious way. *The young man swanned through the streets.*

Swarm – *(noun)* **1** a large or dense group of flying insects. a large number of honeybees that leave a hive with a queen in order to establish a new colony. *A swarm of locusts descended upon the fields.* **2** a large group of people or things. *The swarm poured into the stadium. (verb)* **1** move in or form a swarm. *The football enthusiasts swarmed into the stadium.* **2** move somewhere in large numbers. be crowded or overrun with. *The movie hall was swarmed with students.*

Swat – *(verb)* hit or crush with a sharp blow from a flat object. *I swatted the fly. (noun)* a sharp blow. *Ouch! The swat hurt.*

Swathe – *(verb)* wrap in several layers of fabric. *They swathed the baby to protect it from chill. (noun)* a strip of material in which something is wrapped. *The swathe was clean and smelled of baby powder.*

Sway – *(verb)* **1** move slowly or rhythmically backwards and forwards or from side to side. *The trees swayed in the gentle breeze.* **2** cause to change in opinion, action, etc.; influence. *He swayed from his stand.* **3** rule; govern. *The party had swayed the country for two decades. (noun)* **1** a rhythmical movement from side to side. *The sway of the audience was in sync with the music.* **2** influence; rule. *They swayed the political scene of the country.*

Swear – *(verb)* **1** state or promise solemnly or on oath. admit someone to a position or office by directing them to take a formal oath. compel to observe a certain course of action: I am sworn to secrecy. give an assurance that something is the case. promise to abstain from. have or express great confidence in. [US law] obtain the issue of a warrant for arrest by making a charge on oath. *The spy swore that she would lay down her life before being caught.* **2** use offensive language, especially to express anger. *The young man swore often.*

Swear-word – *(noun)* an offensive or obscene word. *You should not use swear-words.*

Sweat – *(noun)* **1** moisture exude through the pores of the skin, especially as a reaction to heat, physical exertion, or anxiety. *I hate the smell of sweat.* **2** a state of anxiety or distress. hark work; a laborious undertaking. *The success was a result of all his sweat.* **3** a sweatsuit; sweatpants. *I am wearing sweats for jogging. (verb)* **1** exude sweat. get rid of something by exuding sweat. cause to exude sweat by exercise or exertion. exert a great deal of strenuous effort. be or remain in a state of extreme anxiety. worry about. *She sweated the excess calories off.* **2** exude moisture. *The chapattis sweated when kept in an airtight container.* **3** cook slowly in a pan with a small amount of fat. *The chef sweated the meat.*

Sweaty – *(adjective)* exuding, soaked in, or inducing sweat. *She was sweaty after the exercise.*

Sweater – *(noun)* **1** a pullover with long sleeves. *I bought a new pullover from the store.* **2** an employer of sweated labour. *The sweater was fined for the despicable conditions in his factory.*

Sweeper - *(noun)* **1** a person or device that cleans by sweeping. *The sweeper worked hard to keep the school clean.* **2** a player stationed behind the other defenders, free to defend at any point across the field. *The sweeper defended well.*

Sweeping - *(adjective)* **1** extending or performed in a long, continuous curve. *She gestured with sweeping movements of her arms.* **2** wide in range or effect. taking no account of particular cases or exceptions; too general. *The sweeping rains caused flash floods.* *(noun)* dirt or refuse collected by sweeping. *The sweeping was discarded.*

Sweet - *(adjective)* **1** having the pleasant taste characteristic of sugar or honey; not salt, sour, or bitter. *I love sweet porridge.* **2** fresh, pure, and untainted. fragrant. *The sweet fragrance of roses floated in through the open windows.* **3** pleasing in general; delightful. working, moving, or done smoothly or easily. melodious or harmonious. denoting music, especially jazz, played at a steady tempo without improvisation. *She is a sweet girl.* *(noun)* **1** a small shaped piece of confectionery made with sugar. *She loves sweets.* **2** a sweet dish forming a course of a meal; a pudding or dessert. *Let's have something sweet after the meal.* **3** used as a very affectionate form of address. *Hey sweets, what's up?* **4** the pleasures or delights found in something. *He looked at his daughter's antics and sighed "Sweet!"*

Sweeten - *(verb)* **1** make or become sweet or sweeter. *She sweetened the tea.* **2** make more agreeable or acceptable. induce to be well disposed to oneself. *She sweetened her arguments.*

Swell - *(verb)***1** become larger or rounder in size, especially as a result of an accumulation of fluid. *Her injured leg swelled up.* **2** become or make greater in intensity, amount, or volume. *The anger amongst the youth swelled.* *(noun)* **1** a full or gently rounded form. *The swell of the ball rolled towards the people.* **2** a gradual increase in sound, amount, or intensity. a welling up of a feeling. *The swell did not go unnoticed.* **3** a slow, regular movement of the sea in rolling waves that do not break. *The swell was a pleasure to sail on.* **4** a mechanism for producing a crescendo or diminuendo in an organ or harmonium. *The swell worked well in the composition.*

Swelling - *(noun)* an abnormal enlargement of a part of the body as a result of an accumulation of fluid. a natural rounded protuberance. *He cold-pressed the swelling on his injured leg.*

Swelter - *(verb)* be uncomfortably hot. *All of us sweltered in the sun.* *(noun)* an uncomfortably hot atmosphere. *The swelter was getting very difficult to deal with.*

Swerve - *(verb)* abruptly diverge or cause to diverge from a straight course. *The speeding vehicle swerved to the right.* *(noun)* such a change of course. a tendency to swerve imparted to a ball. *The swerve can be very risky at a high speed.*

Swift - *(adjective)* **1** happening quickly or promptly. *I spied a swift movement from the corner of my eye.* **2** moving or capable of moving at high speed. *The swift car overtook the rest in the matter of minutes.* *(adverb)* swiftly: a swift acting poison. *He administered a swift acting drug to reduce her pain.* *(noun)* **1** a fast flying insectivorous bird with long, slender wings, spending most of its life on the wing. *The swift circled my balcony.* **2** a moth, typically yellow brown, with fast darting flight. *The swift was difficult to trace.* **3** a light adjustable reel for holding a skein of silk or wool. *We bought several swifts.*

Swig - *(verb)* drink in large draughts. *He quickly swigged his drink and left.* *(noun)* a large draught of drink. *Even the swig wasn't enough for him.*

Swill - *(verb)* wash or rinse out by pouring large amounts of water over or into it. cause to swirl round a container or cavity. *She swilled the curry out into the sink.* **2** drink greedily or in large quantities. accompany with large quantities of drink. *He swilled the drink down hungrily.* *(noun)* **1** kitchen refuse and waste food mixed with water for feeding to pigs. alcohol of inferior quality. *The pigs enjoyed the swill.* **2** a large mouthful of a drink. *He took a swill and found his parents looking at him.*

Swim – *(verb)* **1** propel oneself through water by bodily movement. cross in this way. float. *I swam the length of the swimming pool.* **2** be immersed in or covered with liquid. *He was swimming in alcohol.* **3** appear to whirl before one's eyes. experience a dizzily confusing sensation. *Her eyes started swimming.* *(noun)* **1** an act or period of swimming. *I enjoy a good swim at the beginning of the day.* **2** a pool in a river which is a particularly good spot for fishing. *The swim was the favourite haunt of the fishermen.*

Swimmer – *(noun)* one who swing in water using limbs. *She is a brilliant swimmer.*

Swindle – *(verb)* use deception to deprive of money or possessions. obtain fraudulently. *The company swindled the customers' funds.* *(noun)* a fraudulent scheme or action. *The scheme sounds like a swindle.*

Swine – *(noun)* **1** a pig. *The swine grew very fat.* **2** a contemptible or disgusting person. *He is such a swine.*

Swing – *(verb)* **1** most or cause to move back and forth or from side to side while or as if suspended. be executed by hanging. *The father swung the child around.* **2** move by grasping a support and leaping. move quickly round to the opposite direction. *He swung himself over the fence.* **3** move or cause to move in a smooth, curving line. attempt to hit or punch, especially with a wide curving movement. throw with such a movement. *He swung his arm blindly.* **4** shift or cause to shift from one opinion, mood, or state of affairs to another. have a decisive influence on. succeed in bringing about. *The news swung his mood from sad to happy.* **5** play music with an easy flowing but vigorous rhythm. *The keyboard player swung the music around easily.* *(noun)* **1** a seat suspended by ropes or chains, on which someone can sit and swing back and forth. *Children enjoyed playing on the swings.* **2** an act of swinging. the manner in which a golf club or a bat is swung. the motion of swinging. sideways deviation of the ball. *The strong swing sent the ball flying out of the ground.* **3** a discernible change in public opinion, especially in an election. *The swing in the public opinion could be felt clearly.* **4** a style of jazz or dance music with an easy flowing but vigorous rhythm. *The swing was beautiful to watch.* **5** a swift tour involving a number of stops. *The bus took the tourists for a swing across the city.*

Swipe – *(verb)* **1** hit or try to hit with a swinging blow. *The cricketer swiped the ball.* **2** steal. *He swiped funds out of their bank account.* **3** pass through an electronic reader. *The merchant swiped my card.* *(noun)* a sweeping blow. an attack or criticism. *The swipe sent the ball out of the court.*

Swirl – *(verb)* move or cause to move in a twisting or spiraling pattern. *The dancers swirled gracefully.* *(noun)* a swirling movement or pattern. *The swirls floating through the air added beauty to the scene of the party.*

Swish – *(verb)* **1** move or cause to move with a hissing or rushing sound. *She swished across the hall.* **2** sink without the ball touching the backboard or rim. *(noun)* **1** a swishing sound or movement. *The swish was caused by the synthetic coat.* **2** a swishing shot. *The swish was caught by the fielder.* *(adjective)* impressively smart and fashionable. *The swish politician charmed his way to the top.*

Switch – *(noun)* **1** a device for making and breaking an electrical connection. a program variable which activates or deactivates a function. *I could hear sparking in the switch.* **2** a change, especially a radical one. *The switch in the mood of the nation was almost instantaneous.* **3** a slender, flexible shoot cut from a tree. *The switch was planted and soon sprouted leaves.* **4** a set of points on a railway track. *The switches were all well maintained.* **5** a trees of hair tied at one end, used in hairdressing to supplement natural hair. *The switch lengthened her hair.* *(verb)* change in position, direction, or focus. exchange. *They switched their stands at the slightest hint of anger.* turn an electrical device off. *We switched off the fan yesterday.* cease to pay attention. *I switched my attention to other things.*

Swivel – *(noun)* a coupling between two parts enabling one to revolve without turning the other. *The canon could swivel to change directions.* *(verb)* turn on or as if on a swivel. *The dancer swivelled for one whole minute.*

Swoon – *(verb)* faint, especially from extreme emotion. *She swooned upon receiving his letter.* *(noun)* an occurrence of swooning. *Her swoon caused her to fall down.*

Sword – *(noun)* **1** a weapon with a long metal blade and a hilt with a handguard, used for thrusting or striking and often worn as part of ceremonial dress. military power, violence. *The warrior drew the sword and entered the fight.* **2** one of the suits in a tarot pack. *The tarot card reader drew a sword.*

Swot – *(verb)* study assiduously or intensively. *He swotted for days.* *(noun)* a person who spends a lot of or too much time studying. *Even though he is a swot, he has his fair share of fun.*

Sycophant – *(noun)* a toady; a servile flatterer. *The sycophant wasn't really liked much.*

Syllable – *(noun)* a unit of pronunciation having one vowel sound, with or without surrounding consonants, and forming all or part of a word. *She pronounced each syllable clearly.* *(verb)* pronounce clearly, syllable by syllable. *He syllabled the poem beautifully.*

Syllabus – *(noun)* **1** the subjects in a course of study or teaching. *The teacher followed the syllabus closely.* **2** a summary of points decided by papal decree regarding heresy. *The syllabus was released by the decree.*

Symbol – *(noun)* **1** a thing that represents or stands for something else, especially a material object representing something abstract. *A white dove is a symbol of peace.* **2** a mark or character used as a conventional representation of something, e.g. a letter standing for a chemical element or a character in musical notation. *She learned how to use symbols to compose music.* *(verb)* symbolize. *Rose symbols love to many people.*

Symbolism – *(noun)* **1** the use of symbols to represent ideas or qualities. symbolic meaning. *She often uses symbolism in her writings.* **2** an artistic and poetic movement or style originating in the late 19th century, using symbolic images and indirect suggestion to express mystical ideas, emotions, and states of mind. *He subscribed to symbolism.*

Symbolize – *(verb)* be a symbol of. represent by means of symbols. *The horse symbolized power.*

Symmetrical – *(adjective)* made up of exactly similar parts facing each other or around an axis; showing symmetry. *Symmetrical designs are out of fashion as of now.*

Symmetry – *(noun)* the quality of being made up of exactly similar parts facing each other or around an axis. correct or pleasing proportion of parts. similarity or exact correspondence. the property of being unchanged by a given operation or process. *He was very particular about the symmetry of things.*

Sympathetic – *(adjective)* **1** feeling, showing, or expressing sympathy. showing approval of an idea or action. *His sympathetic feelings did not appeal to everyone.* **2** likeable. designed in a sensitive or fitting way. *The programme's design is sympathetic to the needs of the elderly.* **3** relating to or denoting the part of the autonomic nervous system supplying the internal organs, blood vessels, and glands, and balancing the action of the parasympathetic nerves. *It is important that the body is able to maintain the balance between the actions of sympathetic and parasympathetic nerves.* **4** of or denoting an effect which arises in response to a similar action elsewhere. *The reaction of the public was sympathetic to the reaction in the rest of the world.*

Sympathy – *(noun)* **1** feelings of pity and sorrow for someone else's misfortune. condolences. *My sympathies are with you.* **2** understanding between people; common feeling. a favourable attitude. relating harmoniously to something else; in keeping. the state or fact of responding In a way corresponding to an action elsewhere. *They dealt with each other with sympathy.*

Symphony – *(noun)* an elaborate musical composition for full orchestra, typically four movements with at least one in sonata form. an orchestral interlude in a large scale vocal work. short for symphony orchestra. *The symphony was beautifully composed.*

Symposium – *(noun)* **1** a conference or meeting to discuss a particular academic or specialist subject. a collection of related papers by a number of contributors. *The symposium turned out to be an interesting event.* **2** a drinking party or convivial discussion, as held in ancient Greece after a banquet. *The men stayed back for the symposium.*

Symptom – *(noun)* a feature which indicates a condition of disease, in particular one apparent to the patient, compare with sign. an indication of an undesirable situation. *She showed all symptoms of a viral infection.*

Synagogue – *(noun)* a building where a Jewish assembly or congregation meets for religious observance and instruction. such an assembly or congregation. *There was a huge crowd outside the synagogue.*

Synchronize – *(verb)* cause to occur or operate at the same time or rate. *Please synchronize your steps with the rest of the troop.*

Synchronous – *(adjective)* **1** existing or occurring at the same time. *I cannot attend both the synchronous events.* **2** of or denoting a satellite which revolves in its orbit I exactly the same time as the primary body rotates on its axis. *Earth has several man-made synchronous satellites.*

Syndicate – *(noun)* a group of individuals or organizations combined to promote some common interest. an agency supplying material simultaneously to a number of news media. a committee of syndics. *The syndicate's cause was to spread peace and tolerance amongst people.* *(verb)* control or manage by a syndicate. publish or broadcast simultaneously in a number of media. *The government syndicated the message from the Prime Minister.*

Syndrome – *(noun)* **1** a group of symptoms which consistently occur together. *She suffers from Down's Syndrome.* **2** a characteristic combination of opinions, emotions, or behaviour. *The company was afflicted by depression syndrome.*

Synonym – *(noun)* a word or phrase that means the same as another word or phrase in the same language, e.g. shut and close. *"Help" is a synonym for "aid".*

Synonymous – *(adjective)* having the same meaning as another word or phrase in the same language. closely associated with something: his name was synonymous with victory. *Her name was synonymous with success.*

Synopsis – *(noun)* a brief summary of something. *The synopsis was too long.*

Synthesis – *(noun)* **1** the combination of components to form a connected whole. often contrasted with analysis. *This school of philosophy was a result of the synthesis of various thoughts.* **2** the production of chemical compounds by reaction from simpler materials. *The synthesis resulted in a compound with the beautiful aroma.* **3** the final stage in the process of dialectical reasoning, in which a new idea resolves the conflict between thesis and antithesis. *The synthesis was beautifully arrived upon.* **4** the process of making compound and derivative words. *Several words used commonly today are a result of synthesis.*

Synthetic – *(adjective)* made by chemical synthesis, especially to imitate a natural product. not genuine; unnatural. *The clothes are made of synthetic fibers.* *(noun)* a synthetic substance, especially a textile fibre. *The synthetic fibres were found to be flexible as well as elastic.*

Syringe – *(noun)* a tube with a nozzle and piston or bulb for sucking in and ejecting liquid in a thin stream, often one fitted with a hollow needle for injecting or withdrawing fluids into or from the body. *The syringe needed to be sterilized.* *(verb)* spray liquid into or over with a syringe. *Doctors syringed the medicine into his veins.*

Syrup – *(noun)* a thick sweet liquid made by dissolving sugar in boiling water, used for preserving fruit. a thick sweet liquid containing [medicine] or used as a drink. a thick, sticky liquid obtained from sugar cane as part of the processing of sugar. *The syrup was too sweet.*

System – *(noun)* **1** a complex whole; a set of things working together as a mechanism or interconnecting network. the human or animal body as a whole. *The entire system failed when a small fault was introduced during the testing.* **2** an organized scheme or method. orderliness; method. *The system was designed to enhance productivity.* **3** the prevailing political or social order, especially when regarded as oppressive and intransigent. *The public revolted against the system.* **4** a major range of strata corresponding to a period in time. *The system could give many hints about the life in the period.* **5** a set of staves joined by a brace. *The system was very strong.*

Tt

T – *(noun)* **1** the twentieth letter of the alphabet. **2** denoting the next after S in a set of items, categories, etc.

Tab – *(noun)* **1** a small flap or strip of material attached to something, for holding, manipulation, identification, etc. a collar marking distinguishing an officer of high rank. [north American] term for ring pull. *The can will open only if you pull the tab.* **2** a restaurant bill. *I asked the waiter if he could put all the drinks on my tab.* **3** short for tableau curtains. *She stepped out of the stage and the tab came down.* **4** a hinged part of a control surface. *The panicking air crew realized that the trim tab was destroyed.* **5** a cigarette. *He asked his friend to pass him a tab.* *(verb)* mark with a tab. *I couldn't quite tab her, but when she spoke, it all came back to me and I recognized her.*

Table – *(noun)* **1** a piece of furniture with a flat top and one or more legs, proving a level surface for eating, writing, or working at. food provided in a restaurant or household. *The newest addition to our house is the fancy dining table.* **2** a set of facts or figures systematically displayed, especially in columns. a league table. multiplication tables. *My son was having a tough time memorizing multiplication tables.* **3** a flat, typically rectangular, vertical surface. a horizontal moulding, especially a cornice. a slab bearing an inscription. *The archaeologists found an ancient table at the digging site.* **4** a flat surface of a gem. a cut gem with two flat faces. *The table was cut beautifully.* **5** each half or quarter of a folding board for backgammon. *We found an old backgammon bird table at the antique shop.*

Tablecloth – *(noun)* a cloth spread over a table, especially during meals. *I bought a bright and flowery tablecloth for our new dining table.*

Tablespoon – *(noun)* a large spoon for serving food. the amount held by such a spoon, in the UK considered to be 15 milliliters when used as a measurement in cookery. *You need to add exactly a tablespoon of milk in the batter.*

Table tennis – *(noun)* an indoor game based on tennis, played with small bats and a small, hollow ball bounced on a table divided by a net. *Being a state level table tennis champion helped her get a seat in the best college.*

Tableau– *(noun)* a group of models or figures representing a scene from history. *The movie was a tableau of a warrior's life.*

Tablet – *(noun)* **1** a flat slab of stone, clay, or wood, used especially for an inscription. another term for table. *They put up a marble tablet in the memory of his father.* **2** a small disc or cylinder of a compressed solid substance, typically a medicine or drug; a pill. *You should take these tablets to get rid of your acne.* **3** a small flat piece of soap. *I bought a tablet of soap from the baby store.* **4** a writing pad. *She left a message on her tablet.* **5** a token giving authority for a train to proceed over a single track line. *Several countries use a form of railway signaling in their single lines called Tyer's Electic Train Tablet.*

Tabloid – *(noun)* a newspaper having pages half the size of those of the average broadsheet, typically popular in style and dominated by sensational stories. *The news of the actress's breakup was fodder for all the tabloids in town.*

Taboo– *(noun)* a social or religious custom placing prohibition or restriction on a particular thing or person. *There was a time in our country when widow remarriage was considered taboo.* *(adjective)* prohibited or restricted by social custom. designated, as sacred and prohibited.

She did a research on taboo customs of the sixth century. (verb) place under such prohibition. *This practice is taboo in our society.*

Tabular– ((adjective)) **1** of data consisting of or presented in columns or tables. *We were asked to arrange all the information in a tabular form.* **2** broad and flat like the top of a table. of a crystal relatively broad and thin, with two well developed parallel faces. *The ship was being battered among the tabular ice bergs.*

Tabulate – (verb) arrange data in tabular form. *Tabulating all the data would be an efficient way of recording it.*

Tacit – (adjective) understood or implied without being stated. *The boss gave a tacit approval to his employee's plan.*

Taciturn – (adjective) reserved or uncommunicative in speech; saying little. *A taciturn man, he replied to my queries in monosyllables.*

Tack – (noun) equipment used in horse riding, including the saddle and bridle. *She straightened the tack and sat upright on the horse.*

Tackle– (noun) **1** the equipment required for a task or sport. *I had to buy better fishing tackle to go for the competition.* **2** a mechanism consisting of ropes, pulley blocks, and hooks for lifting heavy objects. the running rigging and pulley used to work a boat's sails. *I managed to hoist him up with a block and tackle.* **3** in sport an act of talking an opponent. *We got to see rugby tackle never seen before!* **4** a player who lines up next to the end along the line of scrimmage. *The right tackle is a straight A student.* (verb) **1** make determined efforts to deal with a difficult task. initiate discussion with someone about a sensitive issue. *We will have to tackle the situation carefully.* **2** in soccer, hockey, rugby, etc. intercept an opponent in possession of the ball. *Team A tackled B easily.*

Tact – (noun) adroitness and sensitivity in dealing with others or with difficult issues. *You must use your tact while dealing with such issues.*

Tactic– (noun) **1** an action or strategy carefully planned to achieve a specific end. *The teacher knew the student was using some tactic to achieve something.* **2** tactics the art of disposing armed forces in order of battle and of organizing operations, especially during contact with an enemy. often contrasted with strategy. *The government was aware of the guerilla tactics being used in the area.*

Tadpole – (noun) the tailed aquatic larva of an amphibian, breathing through gills and lacking legs until the later stages of its development. *The pond needed urgent cleaning as I could easily spot the tadpoles and the weeds.*

Tag – (noun) **1** a children's game in which one chases the rest, and anyone who is caught then becomes the pursuer. *As soon as we reached the park the children ran and started playing tag.* **2** the action of tagging a runner. *When I touch her, she is tagged.* (verb) **1** touch someone being chased in a game of tag. *She ran super fast to avoid being tagged by me.* **3** put a runner out by touching with the ball or with the hand holding the ball. *He tagged up and scored from third on a long fly to center.*

Tail – (noun) limitation of ownership, especially of an estate or title limited to a person and their heirs. *When she went to demand her rights in the property, his sons told her that the estate was in tail.*

Tailor– (noun) a person whose occupation is making clothes, especially men's outer garments for individual customers. *I searched and searched and finally found a good tailor to stitch his shirts.* (verb) **1** of a tailor make clothes to fit individual customers. *His shirts were tailor made, and hence of superb fitting.* **2** tailor something for/to make or adapt for a particular purpose or person. *He tailored his speech to suit a younger audience.*

Taint – (noun) **1** a trace of a bad or undesirable quality or substance. a contaminating influence or effect. *The government could not shake off the taint of corruption.* **2** an unpleasant smell. *The room was full of the taint of decay.* (verb) **1** contaminate or pollute. affect with a bad or undesirable quality. *Oil has tainted the water.* **2** of food or water become contaminated or polluted. *The meat has been tainted.*

Take -*(verb)* **1** lay hold of with one's hands; reach for and hold. consume as food, drink, medicine, or drugs. occupy a place or position. buy, rent, or subscribe to. ascertain by measurement or observation. capture or gain possession of by force or military means. of illness suddenly strike or afflict. have sexual intercourse with. *We took over the enemy fortress in no time.* **2** remove from a place. subtract. *We took the dishes from the table to the sink.* **3** carry or bring with one; convey or guide. bring into a specified state. use as a route or a means of transport. *Don't forget to take your pencils and pens for the exam.* **4** accept or receive. understand or accept as valid. acquire or assume a position, state, or form. act on an opportunity. experience or be affected by. regard, view, or deal with in a specified way. be attracted or charmed by. submit to, tolerate, or endure. assume. *He didn't take his punishment well.* *(noun)* **1** a scene or sequence of sound or vision photographed or recorded continuously at one time. a particular version of or approach to something: *He was introspecting over his own whimsical take on life.* **2** an amount gained or acquired from one source or in one session. *It added another $11 million to the take.* 3 an amount of copy set up at one time or by one compositor. *She didn't memorize her lines well so we had to do several takes.*

Takings - *(noun)* **1** the action or process of taking. *He knew he would have to analyse the takings of his department thoroughly before giving the presentation.* **2** takings the amount of money earned by a business from the sale of goods or services. *The profit made from the takings this year was not more than 5%.* *(adjective)* captivating in manner; charming. *She had a twinkle in her eyes and a taking smile.*

Talcum-powder - *(noun)* a preparation for the body and face consisting of the mineral talc in powdered form. *The talcum powder she uses was quite visible over her clothes.* *(verb)* powder with this substance. *She dusted the talcum powder off her skin.*

Tale - *(noun)* **1** a fictitious or true narrative or story, especially one that is imaginatively recounted. a lie. *She spun a tale around the whole incident that she could boast to her friends about.* **2** a number or total. *She narrated tales from the Aesop's Fables.*

Talent - *(noun)* **1** natural aptitude or skill. people possessing such aptitude or skill. people regarded as sexually attractive or as prospective sexual partners. *Both her children have a talent for cooking and music right from childhood.* **2** a former weight and unit of currency used by the ancient Romans and Greeks. *Talent is believed to be approximately the mass of water required to fill an amphora.*

Talisman- *(noun)* an object thought to have magic powers and to bring good luck. *The Tantric gave the woman a talisman to be hung around her neck for the next ten days till her desire was fulfilled.*

Talk - *(verb)* speak in order to give information or express ideas or feelings; converse or communicate by speech. have the power of speech. discuss something thoroughly. reply defiantly or insolently. speak patronizingly or condescendingly to. convince someone that they should adopt a particular point of view. persuade or dissuade someone to or from. *We were forbidden from talking inside the seminar hall.* *(noun)* **1** conversation; discussion. rumour, gossip, or speculation. a current subject of widespread gossip or speculation in. formal discussions or negotiations over a period. *There is no issue between two sides that cannot be resolved through talks.* **2** an address or lecture. *Dalai Lama was giving talks at the Habitat Centre this weekend.*

Talkative -*(adjective)* fond of or given to talking. *Her daughter was more talkative than her.*

Tall - *(adjective)* **1** of great or more than average height. measuring a specified distance from top to bottom. *Her daughter was taller than her father.* **2** fanciful and difficult to believe; unlikely: a tall story. *I was used to hearing his tall stories of his heroic exploits.*

Tallow - *(noun)* a hard fatty substance made from rendered animal fat, used in making candles and soap. *The butcher was trying to break the lump of tallow in half.*

Tally - *(noun)* **1** a current score or amount. a record of a score or amount. *Their tally was exact with the list.* **2** a particular number taken as a group pr unit to facilitate counting. a mark registering such a number. *The player improved on his previous year's tally by scoring 38 goals.* **3** also tally stick a piece of wood scored across with notches for the items of an account and then split into halves, each party keeping one. *He kept a tally board to record his score.* **4** a counterpart or duplicate. *Where did you place the tally of your cheque?* **5** an identifying label for a plant or tree. *The tally for the plant says it's a herb.* *(verb)* **1** agree or correspond. *The stories did not really tally.* **2** calculate the total number of. *Did you tally the number of goals they made in today's game?*

Talon - *(noun)* **1** a claw, especially one belonging to a bird of prey. *The bird dug its talons into the skin of the prey.* **2** the shoulder of a bolt against which the key presses to slide it in a lock. *With a swift sound-less movement, the thief undid the talon and the lock opened.* **3** in various card games the cards remaining undealt. *She collected the talons in the end and began the game again.* **4** a printed form attached to a bearer bond that enables the holder to apply for a new sheet of coupons when the existing coupons have been used up. *I filled up the talon since my coupons were over.* **5** an ogee moulding. *The customers were hell bent on having a talon molding in their house.*

Tamarind - *(noun)* **1** sticky brown acidic pulp, from the pod of a tree of the pea family, used as a flavoring in Asian cookery. *Add tamarind extract to the cooked lentil to make the sambhar perfect.* **2** the tropical African tree which yields these pods. *I decided to grow a tamarind tree in my backyard.*

Tame - *(adjective)* **1** of an animal not dangerous or frightened of people; domesticated. of a person willing to cooperate. *The pigeon in my balcony was quite tame.* **2** not exciting, adventurous, or controversial. *The party was too tame for his tastes.* **3** of a plant produced by cultivation. of land cultivated. *He spent his sweat and blood to tame the land.* *(verb)* **1** domesticate an animal. *She tames gorillas for the circus.* **2** make less powerful and easier to control. *The wolf was so tamed it turned into a house dog.*

Tamper - *(verb)* interfere with something without authority or so as to cause damages. *I warned my brother not to tamper with my project.* *(noun)* a machine or tool for tamping down earth or ballast. *She used the tamper to flatten the ground coffee.*

Tan -*(noun)* **1** a yellowish brown colour. *She bought a tan dress for the party.* **2** a golden brown shade of skin developed by pale skinned people after exposure to the sun. *I knew from her tan that she was back from a beach holiday.* **3** also tanbark bark of oak or other trees, bruised and used as a sources of tannin for converting hides into leather. also such bark from which the tannin has been extracted, used for covering paths and in gardening. *The by-products of leather tanning can lead to extensive pollution.* *(verb)* **1** give or acquire a tan after exposure to the sun. *Her pale skin can never tan.* **2** convert animal skin into leather, especially by soaking in a liquid containing tannic acid. *He worked in a tanning factory, much against his own wishes.* **3** beat someone as a punishment. *I'll tan his backside for him.* *(adjective)* having a tan after exposure to the sun. *She was tanned by the sun.*

Tanner - *(noun)* **1** a person employed to tan animal hides. *He sold his leather piece to the tanner.* **2** a lotion or cream designed to promote or simulate the development of a suntan. *Don't forget to carry a tanner with you when you go to the beach.*

Tannery- *(noun)* a place where animal hides are tanned. *He arrived at the tannery early today.*

Tang - *(noun)* **1** a strong taste, flavor, or smell. *She could smell the salty tang of the sea.* **2** the projection on the blade of a knife or other tool by which the blade is held firmly in the handle. *The tang was stuck in the victim's stomach.*

Tangent - *(noun)* 1 a straight line or plane that touches a curve or curved surface at a point, but if extended does not cross it at that point.

The teacher showed how to draw a tangent to three given lines. **2** the trigonometric function that is equal to the ratio of the sides other than the hypotenuse opposite and adjacent to an angle in a right angled triangle. *The teacher explained the relation of sine and cosine to tangent.* **3** a completely different line of thought or action. *The teacher went off on a completely different tangent in his lecture. (adjective)* of a line or plane touching, but not intersecting, a curve or curved surface. *I could not recognize the tangent line since I had missed all the crucial lectures.*

Tangible -*(adjective)* **1** perceptible by touch. *Just because emotions are not tangible does not mean they are insignificant.* **2** clear and definite; real. *We have no tangible evidence to prove the existence of God. (noun)* a thing that is perceptible by touch. *One must not question the tangibility of God.*

Tangle - *(verb)* **1** twist strands together into a confused mass. *The ropes were too tangled to undo.* **2** tangle with become involved in a conflict with. *Don't get into a tangle with the police. (noun)* **1** a confused mass of something twisted together. *Her curly hair was caught in a tangle.* **2** a confused or complicated state; a muddle. a fight, argument, or disagreement. *They carved their way through a tangle of vines.*

Tank - *(noun)* **1** a large receptacle or storage chamber, especially for liquid or gas. the container holding the fuel supply in a motor vehicle. a reservoir. *We ran to switch off the motor when we saw the tank overflowing.* **2** a receptacle with transparent sides in which to keep fish; an aquarium. *I liked the new fish tank he bought though it was too crowded, I felt.* **3** a heavy armoured fighting vehicle carrying guns and moving on a continuous articulated metal track. *A series of tanks were entering the battlefield, ready to fire.* **4** a cell in a police station or jail. *He's been in the tank for twenty five years now. (verb)* **1** drink heavily or become drunk. *One look at him and I knew he was tanked.* **2** fill the tank of a vehicle with fuel. *We were tanked up and ready for the journey!* **3** fail completely or disastrously. in sport deliberately lose or fail to finish a match. *The Stock Market tanked in October 1987*

Tantalize - *(verb)* torment or tease with the sight or promise of something that is unobtainable or with held. *The stripper tantalized her customers at the bar.*

Tantamount - *(adjective)* equivalent in seriousness to; virtually the same as. *His statement was tantamount to an admission of guilt.*

Tantrum - *(noun)* an uncontrolled outburst of anger and frustration, typically in a young child. *The mother lost her temper when the child threw tantrums in the movie hall.*

Tap - *(noun)* **1** a device by which a flow of liquid or gas from a pipe or container can be controlled. *The water wouldn't stop as the washer was broken.* **2** an instrument for cutting a threaded hole in a material. *Since he loves tools, I bought him a tool box, complete with the screw tap, for his birthday!* **3** a device connected to a telephone for listening secretly to conversation. *We knew they had placed a tap on the phone so we had to be careful.* **4** also tapping an electrical connection made to some point between the end terminals of a transformer coil or other component. *The first day as a trainee in the electronics shop, I was taught tapping.* **5** a taproom. *Almost half a dozen drunkards had gathered at the taproom. (verb)* **1** draw liquid through the tap or spout of a cask, barrel etc. *They only have one beer on tap.* **2** draw sap from a tree by cutting into it. *During my short stay at the countryside, I learnt to tap a maple tree for its syrup.* **3** exploit or draw a supply from a resource. obtain money or information from. *She tapped her own experiences for her book.* **4** connected a device to a telephone so that conversation can be listened to secretly. *There are laws allowing the police to tap telephones of even ministers.* **5** cut a thread in something to accept a screw. *Did you tap the nut so I can put the screw in?*

Tape - *(noun)* **1** light, flexible material in a narrow strip, used to hold, fasten, or mark off something. also adhesive tape a strip of paper or plastic coated with adhesive, used to stick things together. *When the vase cracked, I applied tape on it temporarily till I could get a better adhesive.* **2** long, narrow material with magnetic properties, used for recording sound, pictures, or computer data. a cassette or reel containing such material. *I found an old tape that my grandfather used, at the local antique shop.* **3** a strip of material stretched across the finishing line of a race, to be broken by the winner. *The boy ran and with a gap of a millisecond, the African boy had broken the tape.* **4** a tape measure. *The tailor took out the measuring tape to take the customer's measurements.* *(verb)* **1** record sound or pictures on audio or video tape. *Did you tape our son's performance in the school function?* **2** fasten, attach, or mark off with tape. *I taped the base of the feather to the gift box.*

Taper – *(verb)* **1** diminish or reduce in thickness towards one end. *The spire tapers towards the end.* **2** gradually lessen. *The storm had tapered off towards evening.* *(noun)* a slender candle. a wick coated with wax, used for conveying a flame. *She stood at the bottom of the stairs carrying a stick and a taper in her hand.*

Tapestry – *(noun)* a piece of thick textile fabric with pictures or designs formed by weaving coloured weft threads or by embroidering on canvas. *Huge tapestries hung on the wall.*

Tar – *(noun)* a dark, thick flammable liquid distilled from wood or coal, used in road making and for coating and preserving timber. a similar substance formed by burning tobacco or other material. *The newly spread tar on the road was making it impossible for vehicles to pass.* *(verb)* cover with tar. *The road was tarred and we were all asked to take a diversion.*

Tardy – *(adjective)* delaying or delayed beyond the right or expected time; late. slow in action or response; sluggish. *Mother asked me why I have been so tardy with my appointment with the dentist.*

Target – *(noun)* **1** a person, object, or place selected as the aim of an attack. around or rectangular board marked with concentric circles, aimed at in archery or shooting. *He's a good sportsman who has never missed his target in the game.* **2** an objective or result towards which efforts are directed: a sales target. *The sales target was just too hard to achieve this month.* **3** a small round shield or buckler. *The soldier hid behind his target and attacked.* *(verb)* select as an object of attention or attack. aim or direct something. *She has been targeting me ever since she got promoted.*

Tariff – *(noun)* **1** a tax or duty to be paid on a particular class of imports or exports. *India is trying to do away with tariff on items such as electronics.* **2** a table of the fixed charges made by a business, especially in a hotel or restaurant. *Electricity tariffs have escalated.* **3** a scale of sentences and damages for crimes and injuries of different severities. *The sheriff was given a task of analyzing the tariff in his province.* *(verb)* fix the price of something according to a tariff. *The government has fixed a tariff on excess usage of electricity.*

Tarmac – *(noun)* material used for surfacing roads or other outdoor areas, consisting of broken stone mixed with tar. a runway or other area surfaced with such material. *The plane was waiting on the tarmac.* *(verb)* surface with tarmac. *The airport had a new runway where new tarmac had been applied.*

Tarnish – *(verb)* **1** lose or cause to lose luster, especially as a result of exposure to air or moisture. *The old statue of Buddha had tarnished over the years.* **2** make or become less valuable or respected. *The expose by the news channel had tarnished the image of the politician.* *(noun)* dullness of colour, loss or brightness. a film or stain formed on an exposed surface of a mineral or metal. *The tarnished idol fetched a hefty sum at the auction.*

Tarpaulin – *(noun)* **1** heavy duty waterproof cloth, originally of tarred canvas. a sheet or covering of this. *The storm blew away the tarpaulin on the terrace.* **2** a sailor's tarred or oilskin hat. *The sailor's tarpaulin hat ran down with the melting sleet.*

Tarry –*(adjective)* of, like, or covered with tar. *The road was still a bit tarry, so we didn't risk driving on it.*

Tart – *(noun)* an open pastry case containing a sweet or savoury filling. *I am making tarts for tea today.*

Task – *(noun)* a piece of work. *He was given the task of breaking the news to the patient's family.* *(verb)* **1** assign a particular task to. *Did you finish the task I had assigned you yesterday?* **2** make great demands on. *You will be taken to task for this huge blunder you made.*

Taskmaster – *(noun)* a person who imposes an onerous workload on someone. *Your new boss is known for being a hard taskmaster.*

Tassel – *(noun)* a small piece of stone or wood supporting the end of a beam or joist. *On his body, the cord and the tassel hung loosely in the wind.*

Taste – *(noun)* **1** the sensation of flavor perceived in the mouth on contact with a substance. the faculty of perceiving this. *She loved the tangy taste of the curry put on display.* **2** a small portion of food or drink taken as a sample. *I gave her a taste of the curry I just made.* **3** a brief experience of something. *A taste of the sea is enough to draw you back to it again and again.* **4** a person's liking for something. *She has a good taste as far as her dressing style is concerned.* **5** the ability to discern what is of good quality or of a high aesthetic standard. conformity to a specified degree with generally held views on what is appropriate or offensive: a joke in bad taste. *Do not take the joke in bad taste.* *(verb)* **1** perceive or experience the flavor of. have a specified flavor. sample or test the flavor of. eat or drink a small portion of. *Would you like to taste my drink?* **2** have a brief experience of. *She did taste success once in school, but never ever after that.*

Tasteless –*(adjective)* **1** lacking flavor. *This stew is tasteless.* **2** lacking in aesthetic judgment or constituting inappropriate behaviour. *He gave a rather tasteless remark about her performance.*

Tasty – *(adjective)* **1** of food having a pleasant, distinct flavor. *The snacks were tasty at the party.* **2** attractive; appealing. *She was quite tasty with the cutlass.*

Tattered – *(adjective)* old and torn; in poor condition. *I saw a tattered old man begging outside the temple.*

Tattoo – *(verb)* mark with an indelible design by inserting pigment into punctures in the skin. *The couple had tattooed their names on each other's arms.* *(noun)* a design made in such a way. *She had a tattoo in an incomprehensible language on her neck.*

Taunt – *(noun)* a jeering or mocking remark made in order to wound or provoke. *Her taunts fell on deaf ears this time.* *(verb)* provoke or wound with taunts. *She would never cease to taunt me, especially when she saw my reaction.*

Taurus – *(noun)* **1** a constellation the bull, said to represent a bull tamed by Jason a hero of Greek mythology. *The boy was born under the Taurus constellation.* **2** the second sign of the zodiac, which the sun enters about 21 April. *There were two Geminis and a Taurean in our group.*

Taut – *(adjective)* **1** stretched or pulled tight. of muscles or nerves tense. *Her nerves were taut with anxiety.* **2** of writing, music, etc. concise and controlled. *She wrote a taut movie script.* **3** of a ship having a disciplined crew. *The taut crew of the ship came to rescue of the people.*

Tavern – *(noun)* an inn or public house. *I'll meet you in the evening over a drink at the tavern.*

Tawdry – *(adjective)* **1** showy but cheap and of poor quality. *She wore some tawdry costume at the party.* **2** sordid; sleazy. *What tawdry secrets are you going to reveal now?* *(noun)* cheap and gaudy finery. *She wore tawdry jewellery at her friend's wedding.*

Tax – *(noun)* **1** a compulsory contribution to state revenue, levied by the government on personal income and business profits or added to the cost of some goods, services, and transactions. *It was time to file our tax returns.* **2** a strain or heavy demand. *Incurring the additional expenditure of travel would be a tax on our resources.* *(verb)* **1** impose a tax on. pay tax on a vehicle. *The State taxes alcohol heavily.* **2** make heavy demands on. *Your boss is taxing my patience!* **3** charge with a fault or wrongdoing. *I taxed him for dishonesty.* **4** examine and assess the costs of a case. *I tried to tax the costs incurred this year in this department.*

Taxable – *(adjective)* liable to be imposed tax. *The gain from an option is taxable as soon as the shares are acquired.*

Taxing – *(adjective)* physically or mentally demanding. *The whole trip was quite taxing to the nerves.*

Taxation – *(noun)* the levying of tax. money paid as tax. *We had a class on taxation scheduled for this evening.*

Taxi – *(noun)* a motor vehicle licensed to transport passengers in return for payment of a fare. *I took an airport taxi and rushed to catch my flight.* *(verb)* **1** with reference to an aircraft move or cause to move slowly along the ground before takeoff or after landing. *An airplane was taxiing down the runway.* **2** travel in a taxi. *I'll travel in a taxi till the venue.*

Tea – *(noun)* **1** a hot drink made by infusing the dried, crushed leaves of the tea plant in boiling water. the dried leaves used to make tea. a similar drink made from the leaves, fruits, or flowers of other plants. *She makes tea really well.* **2** the evergreen shrub or small tree which produces these leaves, native to south and east Asia. *The hills were full of tea plantations.* **3** a light afternoon meal consisting of sandwiches, cakes, etc. , with tea to drink. a cooked evening meal. *What special are you making for tea today.*

Teach – *(verb)* **1** impart knowledge to or instruct someone in how to do something, especially in a school or as part of a recognized programme. give instruction in a subject or skill. cause to learn by example or experience. *It takes a knack of dealing with children, to be able to teach well.* **2** as a practice or principle. *She teaches racial and religious tolerance in the community.*

Teacher – *(noun)* a person who teaches in a school. *I had the best teacher in the school to give me maths tuitions.*

Teak – *(noun)* **1** hard durable wood used in shipbuilding and for making furniture. *I bought some teak furniture for my guest room.* **2** the large deciduous tree native to India and SE Asia which yields this wood. *She had a huge teak plantation in her estate.*

Team – *(noun)* **1** a group of players forming one side in a competitive game or sport. *The team had to use a unique strategy this time to win.* **2** two or more people working together. two or more horses in harness together to pull a vehicle. *The red team is the best in the business.* *(verb)* **1** come together as a team to achieve a common goal. *We all decided to team up and clean the whole locality of its garbage.* **2** match or coordinate one thing with another. *You must team up the right colours to get the right look.* **3** harness horses together to pull a vehicle. *The horses teamed up quite well.*

Teamwork – *(noun)* the combined effective action of a group. *Nothing succeeds like teamwork.*

Tear – *(noun)* a drop of clear salty liquid secreted from glands in a person's eye when they are crying or when the eye is irritated. *I could make out from her tears that there was something deeply disturbing on her mind.*

Tearful – *(adjective)* **1** crying or inclined to cry. *She stood tearful at the station as the train passed by.* **2** sad. *She was left tearful when her mother left.*

Tease – *(verb)* **1** playfully make fun of or attempt to provoke. tempt sexually. *The young girl bashfully asked the boy to stop teasing her in front of her friends.* **2** gently pull or comb tangled wool, hair, etc. into separate strands. backcomb hair in order to make it appear fuller. comb the surface of woven cloth to raise a nap. *She teased her hair to get a complete look.* **3** find something out by searching through a mass of information. *She teased through the whole lot and found just one man suitable.* *(noun)* **1** an act of teasing. *This question is rather a teaser.* **2** a person who teases. a person who teases someone sexually with no intention of satisfying the desire aroused. *He is a real tease!*

Technical – *(adjective)* **1** of or relating to a particular subject, art, or craft, or its techniques. requiring special knowledge to be understood. *One needs technical knowledge of the product before sitting for an exam.* **2** of, involving, or concerned with applied and industrial science. relating to the operation of machines: a technical fault. *We had to call the specialists to fix the technical fault.* 3 according to a strict application or interpretation of the law or rules. *Technically, you're still not up to the mark.* *(noun)* **1** a small truck with a machine gun mounted on the back. a gunman who rides in such a truck. *We ordered the technical to come to the soldier's rescue.* **2** short for technical foul. *The player was given a card for technical foul.*

Technician – *(noun)* **1** a person employed to look after technical equipment or do practical work in a laboratory. *We need to recruit a new lab technician.* **2** an expert in the practical application of a science. a person skilled in the technique of an art or craft. *He was a technician, well equipped to handle tough situations.*

Technique – *(noun)* a way of carrying out a particular task, especially the execution of an artistic work or a scientific procedure. a procedure that is effective in achieving an aim. *She used a special technique of mixing the icing with the cream and the batter and then frosting the cake.*

Technology – *(noun)* the application of scientific knowledge for practical purposes. machinery and equipment based on such knowledge. the branch of knowledge concerned with applied sciences. *The information technology boom was the greatest leap in industrial development our country could take.*

Teddybear – *(noun)* soft toy bear. *I still have the teddy bear I used to sleep with as a baby.*

Tedious – *(adjective)* too long, slow, or dull. *I had a long tedious day at work today.*

Teem – *(verb)* be full of or swarming with. *The hall was teeming with people of all castes, regions and race.*

Teenager – *(noun)* a person aged between 13 and 19 years. *She has turned 13 and is now a teenager.*

Teens – *(plural (noun))* the years of a person's age from 13 and 19. *Smoking and drugs are most common among teens today.*

Teethe – *(verb)* cut one's milk teeth. *She has been feeling a lot of pain ever since she teethed.*

Teetotaller – *(noun)* a person who never drinks alcohol. *Though he was a drunkard five years back, he is now a teetotaller.*

Telecast – *(noun)* a television broadcast. *They were showing a live telecast of the royal wedding.* *(verb)* transmit by television. *When will the cricket match be telecast?*

Telecommunication – *(noun)* communication over a distance by cable, telegraph, telephone, or broadcasting. the branch of technology concerned with this. *She joined BSNL as a telecommunication engineer.*

Telegram – *(noun)* a message sent by telegraph and delivered in written or printed form, used in the UK only for international messages since 1981. *She rushed to her hometown as soon as she got the telegram about her grandmother's demise.*

Telegraph – *(noun)* **1** a system or device for transmitting messages from a distance along a wire, especially one creating signals by making and breaking an electrical connection. *If only there was a telegraph service on the ship, help would have reached on time and the passengers would have survived the wreck.* **2** a board displaying scores or other information at a sports match or race meeting. *The scores on the telegraph were even so far.* *(verb)* send someone a message by telegraph. send a message by telegraph. *I sent her message through telegraph.*

Telepathy – *(noun)* the supposed communication of thoughts or ideas by means other than the known senses. *I was alarmed at the telepathy, as she called just when I was thinking of her.*

Telephone – *(noun)* **1** a system for transmitting voice over a distance using wire or radio, by converting acoustic vibrations to electrical signals. *Did you get the message on telephone or internet?* **2** an instrument used as part of such a system, typically including a handset with a transmitting microphone and a set of numbered but tons by which a connection can be made to another such instrument. *After a long wait, we finally got our telephone connection fixed.* *(verb)* ring or speak to someone using the telephone. make a telephone call. *I had to urgently make a telephone call, so I rushed to the PCO.*

Telescope – *(noun)* an optical instrument designed to make distant objects appear nearer, containing an arrangement of lenses, or of curved mirrors and lenses, by which rays of light are collected and focused and the resulting image magnified. *He took out his toy telescope and tried to see if he could spy on the girl next door.* *(verb)* **1** with reference to an objects made of concentric tubular parts slide or cause to slide into itself, so that it becomes smaller. crush a vehicle by the force of an impact. *The front of the car was telescoped in the impact.* **2** condense or conflate so as to occupy less space or time. *The novel was telescoped into an abridged version.*

Television – *(noun)* **1** a system for converting visual images with sound into electrical signals, transmitting them by radio or other means, and displayed them electronically on a screen. *We bought a new television transmitter for our audio visual system.* **2** the activity, profession, or medium of broadcasting on television. *She is a television anchor.* **3** also television set a device with a screen for receiving television signals. *The villagers were fascinated by the colours of the film streaming on the television.*

Telex – *(noun)* **1** an international system of telegraphy with printed messages transmitted and received by teleprinters using the public telecommunications network. *The telex system is finally being phased out after nearly 30 years.* **2** a device used for this. *My parents were used to working on the telex for typing out messages and articles.* **3** a message sent by this system. *I received a telex about the company's worrying numbers this evening.* *(verb)* communicate with by telex. send a message by telex. *We telexed this information to our sister company.*

Tell – *(noun)* in the middle east a mound formed by the accumulated remains of ancient settlements. *Abu Hureyra is a tell, exacavated near the Euphrates valley in Syria.*

Temper – *(noun)* **1** a person's state of mind in terms of their being angry or calm. *He is known for his short temper.* **2** a tendency to become angry easily. an angry state of mind. *Stay away from your father when he is in a bad temper.* **3** the degree of hardness and elasticity in steel or other metal. *The waistband had lost its temper.* *(verb)* **1** improve the temper of a metal by reheating and then cooling it. improve the consistency or resiliency of a substance by heating it or adding particular substances to it. *I learnt a new way of tempering glass when I worked at the factory.* **2** often be tempered with serve as a neutralizing or counterbalancing force to. *Temper the curry with mustard and red chillies.* **3** tune a piano or other instrument so as to adjust the note intervals correctly. *Temper the piano, please.*

Temperament – *(noun)* **1** a person's nature with regard to the effect it has on their behaviour. *He was known for his temperament in his social circle.* **2** the adjustment of intervals in tuning a piano or other musical instrument so as to fit scale for use in different keys. an adjustment in which the twelve semitones are equal intervals. *Something was wrong with the temperament of the piano.*

Temperance – *(noun)* abstinence from alcoholic drink. *I was overwhelmed when I saw a reformed alcoholic, rejoicing in the joys of temperance.*

Temperate – *(adj)* **1** relating to or denoting a region or climate characterized by mild temperatures. *We are now in the temperate region.* **2** showing moderation or self restraint. *He now indulges in temperate criticism.*

Temperature – *(noun)* **1** the degree or intensity of heat present in a substance or object. a body temperature above the normal: he was running a temperature. *He has been running a temperature for the last two days.* **2** the degree of excitement or tension present in a situation or discussion. *The temperature was rising and so was the adrenaline!*

Tempest – *(noun)* a violent windy storm. *The ship caught in the tempest never made it to the shore.*

Template – *(noun)* **1** a shaped piece of rigid material used as a pattern for processes such as cutting out, shaping, or drilling. *The boss asked me to follow the template that he had mailed me for the presentation.* **2** something that serves as a model or example. a nucleic acid molecule that acts as a pattern for the sequence of assembly of a protein, nucleic acid, or other large molecule. *I profited a lot from the template he sent.* **3** a timber or plate used to distribute the weight in a wall or under a support. *Stylish body-conscious designs have replaced the baggy template.*

Temple – *(noun)* a building devoted to the worship of a god or gods. a synagogue. *Meenakshi temple is situated in Madurai.*

Tempo – *(noun)* **1** the speed at which a passage of music is played. *The crowd was up on its feet as soon as he increased the tempo.* **2** the pace of an activity or process. *You must increase the tempo of your workout if you want good results.*

Temporal – *(adjective)* **1** of or relating to time. *Specific acts are related to a spatial and temporal context.* **2** relating to worldly affairs; secular. *The clergy should not be occupied with temporal matters.*

Temporary – *(adjective)* lasting for only a limited period. *Everything in life is temporary, the wise sage said.* *(noun)* a person employed on a temporary basis. *He joined on a temporary contract and is on probation now.*

Tempt – *(verb)* **1** entice someone to do something against their better judgment. *Do not tempt me with sweets as I'm trying to lose weight.* **2** attract; charm. *I refused the offer though it was rather tempting.* **3** risk provoking a deity or abstract force. *Don't tempt fate.*

Temptation – *(noun)* the state or quality of being tempted; a desire to do something. a tempting thing. *The first rule for losing weight is to stop fighting your temptations.*

Ten – *(cardinal number)* equivalent to the product of five and two; one more than nine; 10 roman numeral: x or X. *There were ten children in a row.*

Tenth – *(number)* constituting number ten in sequence. *I was talking to the tenth child in the row.*

Tenacious – *(adjective)* not readily relinquishing something; keeping a firm hold. *I had to face a persistent and tenacious interviewer once.*

Tenant – *(noun)* a person occupying rented land or property. a person holding real property by private ownership. *The new tenants in our house are a nice family.* *(verb)* occupy property as a tenant. *We have been living as tenants here for a year now.*

Tend – *(verb)* **1** care for or look after. wait on as an attendant or servant. *We were given the responsibility to tend wounded soldiers.* **2** direct or manage. *The shepherd tends his sheep.*

Tendency – *(noun)* **1** an inclination towards a particular characteristic or type of behavior. *She has a tendency to go off track during her lectures.* **2** a group within a larger political party or movement. *The party leader was silently observing the tendency of the party to move away from their cause.*

Tender – *(verb)* **1** offer or present formally. make a formal written offer to carry out work, supply goods, etc. for a stated fixed price. *She tendered her resignation this evening.* **2** offer as payment. *He tendered for and was awarded the contract.* *(noun)* a tendered offer. *Builders were asked submit tender for road construction.*

Tendon – *(noun)* a flexible but inelastic cord of strong fibrous tissue attaching a muscle to a bone. the hamstring of a quadruped. *He damaged a tendon in his leg in the games.*

Tendril – *(noun)* **1** a slender thread like appendage of a climbing plant, which stretches out and twines round any suitable support. *Her slender hand curled like a tendril around his arms.* **2** a slender ringlet of hair. *Her tendrils flew in the wind.*

Tenement – *(noun)* **1** especially in Scotland or the US a separate residence within a house or block of flats. a house divided into several separate residences. *He gazed at the tenements across the wall, dreaming of having a roof above his head some day.* **2** a piece of land held by an owner. any permanent property, e.g. lands or rents, held from a superior. *He owns a tenement outside the city.*

Tenet – *(noun)* a principle or belief. *Increasing intrusion of scientists has challenged some of the basic tenets of aboriginal life.*

Tennis – *(noun)* a game in which two or four players strike a hollow rubber ball with rackets over a net stretched across a grass or clay court.

Leander Paes is one of our country's best tennis players.

Tenor - *(noun)* **1** a singing voice between baritone and alto or countertenor, the highest of the ordinary adult male range. *His tenor could not be matched.* **2** denoting an instrument of the second or third lowest pitch in its family. *We had to use an instrument with a perfect tenor so it wouldn't stand out in the orchestra.* **3** in full tenor bell the largest and deepest bell of a ring or set. *The bell rang in full tenor and the children ran out of their classes.*

Tense - *(noun)* a set of forms taken by a verb to indicate the time and something the continuance or comspleteness of the action in relation to the time of the utterance. *In English class today, the teacher taught us the application of tenses.*

Tension - *(noun)* **1** the state of being tense. a strained state or condition resulting from forces acting in opposition to each other. *I have noticed that she has been under some sort of tension for the last few days.* **2** mental or emotional strain. a strained political or social state. *The tension between the two states has escalated in the last few months.* **3** the degree of stitch tightness in knitting and machine sewing. *There is nothing very mysterious about setting and adjusting threat tension in your sewing machine.* **4** voltage of specified magnitude: high tension. *The electrician could gauge the high tension that was developing in the transformer.* *(verb)* subject to tension. *She has been under tension for some reason.*

Tent - *(noun)* a portable shelter made of cloth supported by one or more poles and starched tight by cords or loops attached to pegs driven into ground. *As soon as we reached the farm, we took out and fixed our tents.*

Tentacle - *(noun)* **1** a long slender flexible appendage of an animal, used for grasping or moving about, or bearing sense organs. *The jelly fish seemed to be coming nearer with its tentacles almost touching me.* **2** a tendril or sensitive glandular hair on a plant. *The plant had tentacles with thorns on them.* **3** an insidious spread of influence and control. *The party's tentacles reached into every part of people's lives.*

Tentative - *(adjective)* provisional. hesitant. *The college administration has released the tentative timetable for the exams.*

Tenuous - *(adjective)* very weak or slight. very slender or fine. *She was holding on to life by a tenuous thread.*

Tenure - *(noun)* **1** the conditions under which land or buildings are held or occupied. *Lack of security of tenure has led to more unemployment among the youth.* **2** the holding of an office. the period of this. *Her tenure at her workplace was quite short.* *(verb)* give a permanent post to. having or denoting such a post. *The tenure of the highest offices is extended to a definite period.*

Tepid - *(adjective)* **1** lukewarm. *He hates the tepid bath water.* **2** unenthusiastic. *We attended a rather tepid reception party.*

Term - *(noun)* **1** a word or phrase used to describe a thing or to express a concept. a way of expressing oneself. a word or words that may be the subject or predicate of a proposition. *She used some difficult words to comprehend terms in her lecture.* **2** a fixed or limited period for which something lasts or is intended to last. especially in Scotland a fixed day of the year appointed for the making of payments, the start of tenancies, etc. the completion of a normal length of pregnancy. a tenancy of a fixed period. a boundary or limit, especially of time. *She was in the fourth term of her pregnancy.* **3** each of the periods in the year during which instruction is given in a school, college, etc. or during which a law court holds sessions. *Her fifth term exams were round the corner.* **4** stipulated or agreed requirements. conditions with regard to payment. agreed conditions under which a dispute is settled. *Always read the terms and conditions carefully before signing the insurance papers.* **5** each of the quantities in a ratio, series, or mathematical expression. *We were discussing the general term of an algebraic equation of the n-th degree.* **6** a terminus. *I'll be waiting for you at the term.* *(verb)* call by a specified term. *Newton coined and defined the term gravity.*

Terminal -*(adjective)* **1** of, forming, or situated at the end of something. of or forming a transport terminal. *I was waiting for her at the bus terminal.* **2** of a disease predicted to lead to death. having or relating to a terminal disease. *The doctor informed her about the terminal disease she was diagnosed with.* **3** extreme and irreversible. *Her class was terminal boredom!* **4** done or occurring each school, college, etc. term. *Our terminal exams were round the corner.* *(noun)* **1** the end of a railway or other transport route, or a station at this point. a departure and arrival building for passengers at an airport. *My flight would be waiting at Terminal D.* **2** a point of connection for closing an electric circuit. *Four years of electronics engineering and I still cannot recognize the terminal in a circuit.* **3** a device at which a user enters data or commands for a computer and which displays the received output. *She has been working on the terminal to prepare a perfect code for the software.* 4 an installation where oil or gas is stored at the end of a pipeline or at a port. *The oil at the terminal was limited in supply, we knew.* **5** a terminus. *There was a huge traffic jam at the bus terminal.* **6** a patient with a terminal illness. *She was diagnosed with a terminal illness by the doctor today.*

Terminate – *(verb)* **1** bring to an end. end a pregnancy before term by artificial means. of a train or bus service end its journey. *The journey was terminated halfway because of the bomb threat in the area.* **2** have an end at a specified place or of a specified form. *Their relationship terminated amicably.* **3** end the employment of. *He was threatened to be terminated from his job if he didn't work properly.* **4** assassinate. *They were hatching a plan to terminate the minister.* **5** form the physical end or extremity of an area. *My property terminates by the bushes.*

Terminology – *(noun)* the body of terms used in a subject of study, profession, etc. *The terminology the lecturer used in the class was beyond the comprehension of the students.*

Terminus - *(noun)* **1** a railway or bus terminal. an oil or gas terminal. *There was a huge traffic jam at the railway terminus.* **2** an end of extremity. *As Emerson said, the visible creation is the terminus of the invisible world.* **3** a figure of a human bust or animal ending in a square pillar from which it appears to spring, originally a boundary marker in ancient rome. *Do not break the statue of Terminus, the God of boundaries, the soldier warned.*

Termite - *(noun)* a small, pale soft bodied social insect, typically making large nests of earth and feeding on wood. *All our furniture was being eaten up by termites.*

Terracotta - *(noun)* **1** unglazed, typically brownish red earthenware, used chiefly as an ornamental building material and in modeling. *She works in a boutique where they make terracotta items.* **2** a statuette of other object made of terracotta. *I bought her a terracotta Buddha for her birthday.* **3** a strong brownish red colour. *The statue was in beautiful terracotta colour.*

Terrestrial - *(adjective)* **1** of, on, or relating to the earth or dry land. of an animal or plant living on or in the ground. of a planet resembling the earth. *I gave the teacher a list of terrestrial birds, just as she had asked.* **2** denoting television broadcast other than by satellite. *To avoid revealing the plan to terrorists through satellite, the government agencies were working on communicating through terrestrial means.* *(noun)* an inhabitant of the earth. *As Darwin says, there is not a single terrestrial animal that fertilizes itself.*

Terrible - *(adjective)* **1** extremely bad, serious, or unpleasant. *She came from the room with a grim face and revealed the terrible news of the death of her parents.* **2** troubled or guilty. *Every since I lied to Mom about the money, I have been feeling terribly guilty.* **3** causing terror. *The storm was terrible.*

Terrier - *(noun)* **1** a small dog of a breed originally used for turning out foxes and other animals from their earths. *I spotted a fox terrier at the kennel the other day.* **2** a tenacious or eager person. *He was a real terrier when it comes to opportunities!* **3** a member of the territorial army. *He joined as a terrier last year.*

Terrific - *(adjective)* **1** of great size, amount, or intensity. excellent. *Listening to songs in our speakers has a terrific effect.* **2** causing terror. *He was a terrific man of whom children were easily scared of.*

Terrify - *(verb)* cause to feel terror. *Children were terrified of going to the dark house.*

Territory - *(noun)* **1** an area under the jurisdiction of a ruler or state. *The Congress Party ruled most of the territories in India.* **2** especially in the US, Canada, or Australia an organized division of a country not having the full rights of a state. *American troops were stationed in Iraqi terrirtory.* **3** an area defended by an animal against others of the same sex or species. *Dogs are extremely possessive about their territory.* **4** an area defended by a team or player in a game or sport. *The striker was in the wrong territory and he didn't even realize!* **5** an area in which one has certain rights or responsibilities. *Home affairs are not your territory.* **6** an area of knowledge or experience. *Sales is definitely my territory.* **7** land with a specified characteristic: woodland territory. *We were trekking through woodland territory.*

Terror - *(noun)* **1** extreme fear. the use of terror to intimidate people. a cause of terror. the period of the French revolution when the ruling Jacobin faction ruthlessly executed anyone considered a threat to their regime. *Hitler was a terror the world had to live with for a long long time.* **2** a person causing trouble or annoyance. *Dennis was a terror to his teachers and neighbours.*

Terrorism - *(noun)* unauthorised use of violence in pursuit of any political objective. *Terrorism is an evil our world has been facing for a long time now.*

Terrorist - *(noun)* a person who uses violence and intimidation in the pursuit of political aims. *Three terrorists were caught in the recent bomb attacks.*

Terse - *(adjective)* sparing in the use of words; abrupt. *She explained her role to the subordinates in a rather terse manner.*

Tertiary - *(adjective)* **1** third in order or level. relating to or denoting education at a level beyond that provided by schools. *Tertiary education follows secondary education.* **2** relating to or denoting medical treatment provided at a specialist institution. *Symptoms of tertiary syphilis depend on what areas have been affected.* **3** relating to or denoting the first period of the Cenozoic era between the cretaceous and quaternary periods, about 65 to 164 million years ago. *The paleontologists found an area that served as a sanctuary for creatures of the tertiary period which would have otherwise died out like the others.* **4** of an organic compound having its functional group on a carbon atom bonded to three other carbon atoms. derived from ammonia by replacement of three hydrogen atoms by organic groups. *There must have been some model of tertiary transmission. (noun)* a lay associate of certain Christian monastic organizations. *He was a member of the regular tertiaries.*

Test - *(noun)* the shell or integument of some invertebrates and protozoans. *We had to break the test to know what the body composition of the sea urchin was like.*

Testament - *(noun)* **1** a person' will. *She wrote a testament giving all rights to her property to her husband, before she died.* **2** evidence or proof of a fact. event, or quality. *I have testament of the fact that this incident never happened.* **3** in biblical use a covenant or dispensation. *The fourth testament states it is wrong to lie.* **4** a division of the bible. also old testament, new testament. a copy of the new testament. *I received a new copy of the new testament yesterday.*

Testify - *(verb)* **1** give evidence as a witness in a law court. *Bill Clinton was the only President in the USA to have testified for an embarrassing case.* **2** serve as evidence or proof of something.. *Several witnesses testified that they had seen the fight.*

Testimonial - *(noun)* a formal statement testifying to someone's character and qualifications. a public tribute to someone and to their achievements. *She didn't expect him to give testimonials on her skill.*

Tetanus – *(noun)* **1** a bacterial disease causing rigidity and spasms of the voluntary muscles. *We had to get a tetanus vaccination done before the disease spreads.* **2** the prolonged contraction of a muscle caused by rapidly repeated stimuli. *I met a patient suffering from tetanus at the orthopedic clinic.*

Tether – *(noun)* a rope or chain with which an animal is tied to restrict its movement. *The cow was pulling at the string, trying to break the tether to which it was tied.* *(verb)* tie with a tether. *The goat was tethered to the tree.*

Text – *(noun)* **1** a written or printed work regarded in terms of content rather than form. the original words of an author or document. data corresponding to a body of writing. *There were more than a thousand words of text to study and analyse.* **2** the main body of a book or other piece of writing, as distinct from appendices, illustrations, etc. *The text itself was exceeding 300 pages.* **3** a written work chosen as a subject of study. a passage from the bible or other religious work, especially as the subject of a sermon. *The teacher asked her to read a text from the. Reader Book.* **4** fine, large handwriting, used especially for manuscripts. *The author had written in comprehensible text, though the font was a distraction.* *(verb)* send a text message to. *I sent my friend a text message midnight.*

Textile – *(noun)* **1** a type of cloth or woven fabric. *She has been into textile business for quite some time now.* **2** among nudists a person who wears clothes. *Nudists to the left! Textiles to the right!* *(adjective)* of or relating to fabric or weaving. *The crafts fair had a fascinating range of terracotta pottery and textiles.*

Texture – *(noun)* **1** the feel, appearance, or consistency of a surface or a substance. the character of a textile fabric as determined by its threads. *The dress had a rough texture making it itchy when you wear.* **2** the representation of the tactile quality of a surface. *The smooth texture of the soap was indeed alluring.* **3** the quality created by the combination of elements in a work of music or literature. *It was a closely knit symphonic texture.* *(verb)* give a rough or raised texture to. *The art teacher taught us to texture a printing plate by lining and stippling it.*

Than – *(conjunction & preposition)* **1** introducing the second element in a comparison. *She is a better athlete than me.* **2** used to introduce an exception or contrast. *She could run faster than me.*

Thatch – *(noun)* **1** a roof covering of straw, reeds, or similar material. material used for such a covering. *Thatch roofs are a common sight in houses in South India.* **2** the hair on a person's head. *The barber had a tough time clearing his thatch.* **3** dead stalks, moss, etc. on a lawn. *There was too much thatch in the lawn here.* *(verb)* cover with thatch. *The roof of her ancestral house was thatched.*

Thaw – *(verb)* **1** of ice, snow, or a frozen thing become liquid or soft as a result of warming up. the weather becomes warmer and causes snow and ice to melt. cause to thaw. *It was time to thaw the ice.* **2** of a part of the body become friendlier or more cordial. *I left the frozen chicken out until it thawed.* *(noun)* **1** a period of warmer weather that thaws ice and snow. *The thawing of a frozen chicken takes hours.* **2** an increase in friendliness or cordiality. *The thaw between the two countries had led to an unusual smoothness in world affairs.*

The – *(det.)* **1** denoting one or more people or things already mentioned or assumed to be common knowledge; the definite article. used to refer to a person, place, or thing that is unique. with a unit of time the present. used instead of a possessive. used with a surname to refer to a family or married couple. *The river was flowing in the wrong territory, apparently.* **2** used to point forward to a following qualifying or defining clause or phrase. *Ask the man standing outside to clear the gate.* **3** used to make a generalized reference rather than identifying a particular instance. *The medicine is believed to be good for the throat.* **4** enough of. *The singing is awful.* **5** pronounced stressing the used to indicate that someone or something is the best known or most important of that name or type. *The Honourable President will be here soon.* **6** used (adverb)ially with comparatives to indicate how one amount or degree of something varies in relation to another. used to emphasize the amount or degree to which something is affected. *The sooner you come the better.*

Theatre – *(noun)* **1** a building in which plays and other dramatic performances are given. a cinema. *I got a list of movies running at the theatre nearby.* **2** the writing and production of plays. *There is a theatre workshop being organized at the University.* **3** a play or other activity considered in terms of its dramatic quality. *She asked me to quit my theatrical reaction to her remark.* **4** a room for lectures with seats in tiers. *We had our lectures in the theatre near the ground.* **5** an operating theatre. *There were at least five operating theatres in the medical college.* **6** the area in which something happens. denoting weapons intermediate between tactical and strategic. *A new theatre of war has been opened up.*

Theft – *(noun)* the action or crime of stealing. *There has been a theft in my neighbourhood.*

Their – *(possessive)* det. **1** belonging to or associated with the people or things previously mentioned or easily identified. *The principal read out their accomplishments at the end of his speech.* **2** belonging to or associated with a person of unspecified sex. *In several states, they still wash their clothes on the riverbank.* **3** used in titles. *There was a double portrait of Their Majesties.*

Them – *(pronoun)* **1** used as the object of a verb or preposition to refer to two or more people or things previously mentioned or easily identified. used after the verb 'to be' and after 'than' or 'as'. *We saw them at the party.* **2** referring to a person of unspecified sex used in place of either 'him' or 'him or her.' *Let us invite them for dinner.* **3** themselves. *They decided to do it themselves.*

Theme – *(noun)* **1** a subject or topic on which a person speaks, writes, or thinks. the first major constituent of a clause, indicating the subject matter. contrasted with rheme. *The theme of their speech was world peace.* **2** a prominent or frequently recurring melody or group of notes in a composition. frequently recurring in or accompanying the beginning and end of a film, play, etc. *I loved the theme song.* **3** denoting a restaurant or pub in which the décor, food, and drink are intended to suggest a particular country, historical period, etc. *The restaurant we last went to had a jungle theme!* **4** an essay written on a set subject. *We could write on any of the four themes given in the exam.* **5** the stem of a noun or verb. *In the sentence, 'history I do like', history is the theme.*

Then – *(adverb)* **1** at that time. *Back then, there were no cars, only horse carriages.* **2** after that; next. also. *First have rice and then I'll give you the sweet.* 3 therefore. *The case, then, is closed.*

Thence – *(adverb)* **1** from a place or source previously mentioned. *We flew to Norway and thence to Denmark.* **2** as a consequence. *A natural conclusion follows thence.*

Thenceforward – *(adverb)* thenceforth. *With a significant nod of the head, he left the scene, and thenceforward, the world was a happy place to live in.*

Theology – *(noun)* the study of the nature of god and religious belief. religious beliefs and theory when systematically developed. *She wanted to do her post graduate studies in theology.*

Theorem – *(noun)* a general proposition not self evident but proved by a chain of reasoning. a rule in algebra or other branches of mathematics expressed by symbols or formulae. *He proved the theorem he postulated.*

Theoretical – *(adjective)* concerned with or involving theory rather than its practical application. based on or calculated through theory. *After scoring well in the practical exam, it was now time to prepare for the theoretical exam.*

Theory – *(noun)* **1** a supposition or a system of ideas intended to explain something, especially one based on general principles independent of the thing to be explained. an idea accounting for or justifying something. *She postulated a theory* *and was asked to prove it.* **2** a set of principles on which an activity is based: a theory of education. a collection of propositions illustrating the principles of a subject. *The lecture was regarding Einstein's theory of relativity.*

Therapeutic– *(adjective)* of or relating to the healing of disease. having a good effect on the body or mind. *The spa treatment had a therapeutic effect on her.*

There – *(adverb)* **1** in, at, or to that place or position. in that respect; on that issue. *We were asked to sit there.* **2** used in attracting attention to someone or something. *There she goes now.* **3** used to indicate the fact or existence of something. *The answer is out there. (exclamatory)* **1** used to focus attention. *There it is!* **2** used to comfort someone. *There there. Things aren't as bad now.*

Thereabouts – *(adverb)* **1** near that place. *Thereabouts lay the haunted house.* **2** used to indicate that a date or figure is approximate. *We should meet around three or thereabouts.*

Thereby – *(adverb)* by that means; as a result of that. *She knocked the jug, thereby staining the tablecloth.*

Thereupon – *(adverb)* immediately or shortly after that. *Thereupon the whole class gave a standing ovation to their favourite professor.*

Therm – *(noun)* a unit of heat, especially as the former statutory unit of gas supplied in the UK equivalent to 100.000 British thermal units or 1055*10/8 joules. *1 therm of gas produces 100,000 Btu.*

Thermal – *(adjective)* **1** of or relating to heat. another term for geothermal. relating to or denoting particles in thermodynamic equilibrium with their surroundings: thermal neutrons. *The scientists were working on discovering a new source of biothermal energy.* **2** made of a fabric that provides good insulation to keep the body warm. *I bought her a thermal pullover she could wear during the hard winters. (noun)* **1** an upward current of warm air, used by birds, gliders. and balloonists to gain height. *A pyrometer is a non-contacting device that measures and intercepts thermal radiation.* **2** thermal garments, especially underwear. *You'll need almost two levels of thermals in winters in Delhi.*

Thermometer – *(noun)* an instrument for measuring and indicating temperature, typically consisting of a graduated glass tube containing mercury or alcohol which expands when heated. *The thermometer showed that she was running a temperature of 107.*

Thermostat – *(noun)* a device that automatically regulated temperature or activates a device at a set temperature. *Turn down the thermostat, its getting hot!*

Thesaurus – *(noun)* **1** a book that lists words in groups of synonyms and related concepts. *I had to repeatedly refer to the thesaurus to be able to get synonyms for the words.* **2** a dictionary or encyclopedia. *I bought her a dictionary and thesaurus for her birthday.*

These – plural form of this. *These chocolates are mine.*

Thesis – *(noun)* **1** a statement or theory that is put forward as a premise to be maintained or proved. a proposition forming the first stage in the process of dialectical reasoning. compare with antithesis, synthesis. *Now that you've presented the thesis, kindly explain the antithesis and the synthesis.* **2** a long essay or dissertation involving personal research, written as part of a university degree. *The date for submitting our thesis paper was just round the corner.* **3** an unstressed syllable or part of a metrical foot in Greek or Latin verse. often contrasted with arsis. *The Greek philosophy teacher was explaining the significance of the alphabet thesis.*

They – *(pronoun)* **1** used to refer to two or more people or things previously mentioned or easily identified. people on general. people in authority regarded collectively. *They had gathered at the ground for a demonstration.* **2** used to refer to a person of unspecified sex in place of either 'he' or 'he or she'. *If anyone has any objection, they can leave the place.*

Thick – *(adjective)* **1** with opposite sides or surfaces relatively far apart. made of heavy material. *I had to get a thick board that wouldn't* *fall off easily.* **2** made up of a large number of things or people close together. densely filled or covered with. opaque, heavy, or dense: thick fog. *Visibility was low because of thick fog.* **3** relatively firm in consistency; not flowing freely. *You have to bring the batter to a thick consistency.* **4** of low intelligence; stupid. *Stop being so thick headed!* 5 not clear or distinct; hoarse or husky. very marked and difficult to understand. *The thick speech of the drunkard was beyond comprehension. (noun)* the middle or the busiest part of something: in the thick of battle. *We were in the thick of a verbal battle when the boss entered. (adverb)* in or with deep, dense, or heavy mass. *Seashells lay thick on the beach.*

Thickness – *(noun)* **1** the distance through an object, as distinct from width or height. a layer of material. a thicker part of something. *The thickness of her hair was every hair stylists' dream.* **2** the state or quality of being thick. *From the thickness of his speech, we knew he had been drinking a lot. (verb)* plane or cut to a desired thickness. *Each floor had a glass of negligible thickness.*

Thick-skinned – (adjective) not sensitive to criticism. *Your words would have no effect on this thick-skinned man.*

Thicket – *(noun)* a dense group of bushes or trees. *The voice seemed to be coming from the thicket at a distance.*

Thief – *(noun)* a person who steals another person's belongings. *We ran and caught the thief.*

Thigh – *(noun)* the part of the human leg between the hip and the knee. the corresponding part in other animals. *He had cut a deep wound in his thigh that needed urgent treatment.*

Thimble – *(noun)* **1** a metal or plastic cap with a closed end, worn to protect the finger and push the needle in sewing. any short metal tube or ferrule. *She could not stitch unless she had her thimble replaced.* **2** a metal ring, concave on the outside, around which a loop of rope is spliced. *If you're using a thimble, form the look around the thimble.*

Thin – *(adjective)* **1** having opposite surfaces or sides close together. having become less thick as a result of wear. *I gave her a thin book to read.* **2** having little flesh or fat on the body. *She was extremely thin and quite tall.* **3** having few parts or members relative to the area covered or filled; sparse. not dense or heavy. *The thin cold air of the mountains was getting to me.* **4** containing much liquid and not much solid substance. *This milk is too thin for even tea. (adverb)* with little thickness or depth. *Cut the cheese thin for the cannelloni. (verb)* **1** make or become less thick. *You have become thin over the vacation.* **2** remove some plants from to allow the others more room to grow. *The undergrowth has been thinned so we can have more plants.* **3** hit above its centre. *Her thin voice rose above the others'.*

Thin-skinned – *(adjective)* sensitive to criticism. *He is too thin-skinned to survive the competition.*

Thing – *(noun)* **1** an object that one need not, cannot, or does not wish to give a specific name to. personal belongings or clothing. *The sword had a black thing on it.* **2** an inanimate material object, especially as distinct from a living sentient being. a living creature or plant. a person or animal in terms of one's feelings of pity, approval, etc. *You lucky thing!* **3** an action, activity, concept, or thought. unspecified circumstances or matters. *Things are going well now.* **4** what is needed or required. what is socially acceptable or fashionable. *The tote bag is the in thing now.* **5** one's special interest or concern. *The thing that she is into these days is biorecycling.*

Think – *(verb)* **1** have a particular opinion, belief, or idea about someone or something. *She thought good of him.* **2** direct one's mind towards someone or something; use one's mind actively to form connected ideas. take into account or consideration. consider the possibility or advantages of. have a particular mental attitude or approach. have a particular opinion of. *Think rationally before you act.* **3** call something to mind; remember. *I couldn't think of his phone number. (noun)* an act of thinking. *I want to sit down and give it a good think.*

Thinker – *(noun)* a person who thinks deeply and seriously. *Paul Brunton is a famous thinker.*

Thinking – *(adjective)* using thought or rational judgment; intelligent. *I thought he is a thinking man. (noun)* a person's ideas or opinions. thoughts; meditations. *She told me I need to change my thinking and consider a different perspective.*

Third – *(ordinal number)* **1** constituting number three in a sequence; 3rd. *Look at the third boy in the row.* **2** each of three equal parts into which something is or may be divided. *You will need one third of a cup of flour for the batter.* **3** an interval spanning three consecutive notes in a diatonic scale, e.g. C to E or A to C . the note which is higher by this interval than the tonic of a diatonic scale or root of a chord. *Don't sing in the third note.* **4** a place in the third grade in an examination, especially that for a degree. *She is in third grade now.*

Third-rate – *(adjective)* of inferior or very poor quality. *The sun glasses you bought were a third rate commodity.*

Thirst – *(noun)* **1** a feeling of needing or wanting to drink. lack of the liquid needed to sustain life. *We were dying of thirst in the desert.* **2** a strong desire for. *She had a thirst for knowledge which the sage recognized. (verb)* **1** feel a need to drink. *He is thirsting for a drink.* **2** have a strong desire for. *She have a terrible thirst for knowledge.*

Thirsty – *(adjective)* **1** feeling thirst. in need of water; dry or parched. consuming a lot of fuel or water. *I felt sad for the thirsty plants.* **2** causing thirst. *Modeling is thirsty work.*

Thirteen – *(cardinal number)* equivalent to the sum of six and seven; one more than twelve, or seven less than twenty. *There were thirteen children in the room.*

Thirty – *(cardinal number)* the number equivalent to the product of three and ten; ten less forty; 30. *At least thirty people died in the bomb blast.*

Thirtieth – *(number)* constituting number thirty in sequence. *Yesterday was his thirtieth birthday.*

This – *(pronoun & det.)* **1** used to identify a specific person or thing close at hand or being indicated or experienced. referring to the neared of two things close to the speaker. *This is the tree I was talking about.* **2** referring to a specific thing or situation just mentioned. *You said you'll be back before this.* **3** used with periods of time related to the present. *She left early this morning. (adverb)* to the degree or extent indicated. *Drive just this fast and you'll be safe.*

Thistle – *(noun)* **1** a widely distributed herbaceous plant of the daisy family, typically with a prickly stem and leaves and rounded heads of purple flowers. *Thistles were growing in abundance in her garden.* **2** a plant of this type as the Scottish national emblem. *When people look at the Scottish emblem, they cannot help not see the thistle.*

Thistledown – *(noun)* the light fluffy down of thistle seeds, enabling them to be blown about in the wind. *Like a ball of thistledown, it kissed the sea.*

Thorn – *(noun)* **1** a stiff, sharp pointed woody projection on the stem or other part of a plant. *The thorn in the plant pierced into my skin.* **2** a thorny bush, shrub, or tree, especially a hawthorn. *The thorns of cactus plant supposedly possesses cures for several diseases.* **3** an old English and ice landic runic letter, representing the dental fricatives eventually superseded by the digraphth. *The linguistics professor explained the significance of thorn in old English language.*

Thorny – *(adjective)* **1** having many thorns or thorn bushes. *We had to cut and remove the thorny bush that was growing in the garden.* **2** causing distress, difficulty, or trouble. *It was a rather thorny situation.*

Thorough – *(adjective)* **1** complete with regard to every detail. performed with or showing great care and completeness. *She was thoroughly ready for the exam.* **2** absolute; utter used for emphasis. *It was a thorough pleasure having you over.*

Thoroughbred –*(adjective)* **1** of pure breed, especially of a breed of horse originating from English mares and Arab stallions. *One look at the horse and I knew it was a thoroughbred.* **2** of outstanding quality. *What a thoroughbred gentleman he was! (noun)* **1** a thoroughbred animal. *It was a thoroughbred stallion.*

2 an outstanding or first class person or thing. *Naming a thoroughbred horse of the racing track is a demanding and delicate task.*

Thoroughfare – *(noun)* a road or path forming a route between two places. *It was a busy thoroughfare.*

Those – plural form of that. *Those were the people who should have been punished.*

Thought – past and past participiple of think. *You spend too much time in thought.*

Thousand – *(cardinal number)* **1** the number equivalent to the product of a hundred and ten; 1,000. *I received a thousand rupees as prize.* **2** an unspecified large number. *Thousands of people drowned in the ship wreck.*

Thrash – *(verb)* **1** beat repeatedly and violently with or as with a stick or whip. *I will thrash him if he behaves like this again.* **2** move in a violent or uncontrolled way. *He lay thrashing around in pain.* **3** defeat heavily. *The team was thrashed in the hands of the opponents.* **4** discuss something frankly and thoroughly, especially to reach a decision. *He thrashed away at the meeting. (noun)* **1** a violent or noisy movement or beating or thrashing. a fast and exciting motor race or other sporting event. *The car thrashed away at the race.* **2** a party, especially a loud or lavish one. *They thrash around quite often and are not even aware of the surroundings.* **3** a style of fast, loud, harsh sounding rock music, combining elements of punk and heavy metal. *What a thrash they're making!*

Thread – *(noun)* **1**a long, thin strand of cotton, nylon, or other fibres used in sewing or weaving. *The thread on the fabric was standing up.* **2** a long thin line or piece of something. *I noticed a thread of smoke coming from the puja room.***3** a helical ridge on the outside of a screw, bolt, etc. or on the inside of a cylindrical hole, to allow two parts to be screwed together. *The thread of the handle was loosely done and that's why it came off.* **4** a theme or characteristic running throughout a situation or piece of writing. a group of linked messages posted on the internet that share a common subject or theme. a programming structure or process formed by linking a number of separate elements or subroutines. *The thread was so long I lost track of the actual issue being discussed.* **5** clothes. *She wore a hat embroidered with golden threads. (verb)* **1** pass a thread through. pass through something and into the required position for use. put on a thread. *She was threading the beads.* **2** move or weave in and out of obstacles. *She has been threading in and out of issues for so long.* **3** cut a screw thread in or on a hole, screw, or other object. *The handle of the door was not threaded carefully.*

Threat – *(noun)* **1** a statement of an intention to inflict injury, damage, or other hostile action as retribution. a menace of bodily harm, such as may restrain a person's freedom of action. *We received a threat call this evening and immediately informed the police.* **2** a person or thing likely to cause damage or danger. the possibility of trouble or danger. *He is a threat to the company.*

Threaten – *(verb)* **1** make or express a threat to or to do something. *The kidnappers threatened to kill the boy if their ransom was not paid.* **2** put at risk; endanger. seem likely to produce an unwelcome result. *The air was raw and threatened rain.*

Three – *(cardinal number)* equivalent to the sum of one and two; one more than two; 3 *Three men made their way on a horse towards Jerusalem.*

Thresh – *(verb)* **1** separate grain from typically with a flail or by the action of a revolving mechanism. *I found a new technique for threshing.* **2** variant spelling of thrash. *The patient was threshing about on the bed.*

Threshold – *(noun)* **1** a strip of wood or stone forming the bottom of a doorway and crossed in entering a house or room. *She stood at the threshold, waiting for everyone to come out of their shock of seeing her.* **2** a level or point at which something would start or cease to happen or come into effect. a limit below which a stimulus causes no reaction. *She has a low pain threshold.*

Thrice – *(adverb)* **1** three times. *Shake the bottle thrice before consuming the medicine.* **2** extremely; very. *I was thrice blessed.*

Thrift - *(noun)* **1** the quality of being careful and not wasteful with money and other resources. *She was known to be quite smart and thrifty.* **2** another term for saving and loan. *They were praised for their thrift and enterprise.* **3** a plant which forms low growing tufts of slender leaves with rounded pink flower heads, growing chiefly on sea cliffs and mountains. *I found thrifts of all kinds up on the mountain.*

Thrill - *(noun)* **1** a sudden feeling of excitement and pleasure. an experience that produces such a feeling. a wave or nervous tremor of emotion or sensation. *She felt the thrill rising and adrenaline pumping her blood as the rollercoaster started.* **2** a vibratory movement or resonance heard through a stethoscope. a throb or pulsation. *The doctor almost heard the thrill in his heart.* *(verb)* **1** have or cause to have a thrill. *He was thrilled at the thought of space travel.* **2** pass with a nervous tremor. quiver or tremble. *He felt a thrill of fear and adrenaline.*

Thrive - *(verb)* grow or develop well or vigorously. prosper; flourish. *Craves thrive on garbage.*

Throat - *(noun)* **1** the passage which leads from the back of the mouth of a person or animal. the front part of the neck. *She has been having severe throat pain for the last four days.* **2** a voice of a person or a songbird. *We heard a deep throated voice calling from down the corridor.* **3** the forward upper corner of a quadrilateral fore and aft sail. *The throat of the sail was torn.*

Throb - *(verb)* **1** beat or sound with a strong, regular rhythm; pulsate. *I could feel my heart throbbing through my veins.* **2** feel pain in a series of pulsations. *Her hand was throbbing with pain.* *(noun)* a strong, regular beat or sound. *War drums throbbed at the battlefield.*

Throes - *(plural noun)* intense or violent pain and struggle. *He convulsed in his death throes,*

Throne - *(noun)* a ceremonial chair for a sovereign, bishop, or similar figure. the power or rank of a sovereign. *The prince would be the heir to the throne.* *(verb)* place on a throne. *The prince was throned on June 25th.*

Throng - *(noun)* a large, densely packed crowd. *He made his way through the throng of people.* *(verb)* gather in large numbers in. flock or be present in great numbers. *A crowd thronged the station.*

Throttle - *(noun)* **1** a device controlling the flow of fuel or power to an engine. *The devices were at full throttle.* **2** a person's throat, gullet, or windpipe. *It was as if he was being throttled.* *(verb)* **1** attack or kill by choking or strangling. *She badly wanted to throttle him.* **2** control with a throttle. reduce power by use of the throttle. *The machine has two valves that can be throttled.*

Through - *(preposition & adverb)* **1** moving in one side and out of the other side of. so as to make a hole or passage in. expressing the position or location of something beyond. expressing the extent of changing orientation. *The sword went right through his heart.* **2** continuing in time to or towards completion of. from beginning to end of. *The goal came midway through the second half.* **3** so as to inspect all or part of. *We were browsing through some websites.* **4** up to and including a particular point on a sequence. *The festival is on from March 24 through May 7.* **5** by means of. *Viruses enter the body through food or water.* 6 so as to be connected by telephone. *He put a call through the administrative office of the college.* *(adjective)* **1** continuing or valid to the final destination. *We got a through Delhi by a train.* **2** passing continuously from one side and out of the other side. *The village lies on a busy through road.* **3** having successfully passed to the next stage of a competition. *Team A is through to the second round.* **4** having finished an activity, relationship, etc. *You and I are through.*

Throw - *(verb)* **1** propel with force through the air by a rapid movement of the arm and hand. send to the ground in wrestling, judo, etc. unseat. bowl with an illegitimate bent arm action. *She threw the newspaper into the window.* **2** move or put into place quickly, hurriedly, or roughly. *The stewards had thrown a cordon across the fairway.* **3** send suddenly into a particular position or condition. disconcert; confuse. *He threw all* *her emotions into turmoil.* **4** project, direct, or cast in a particular direction. project so that it appears to come from somewhere else, as in ventriloquism. *She can throw her voice.* **5** form on a potter's wheel. turn on a lathe. twist into yarn. *A potter was throwing pots.* **6** have a fit or tantrum. *At the cinema, a child was throwing a tantrum.* *(noun)* **1** an act of throwing. *His throw hit the stumps!* **2** a small rug or light cover for furniture. *She spread the throws neatly.* **3** the extent of vertical displacement in a fault. *The scientists were trying to calculate the throws of the fault.* **4** a machine or device by or on which an object is turned while being shaped. *The throw needed cleaning.* **5** the action or motion of a slide valve or of a crank, eccentric wheel, or cam. the extent of such motion. *How much was the throw of the wheel?*

Thrush – *(noun)* a small or medium sized songbird, typically with a brown back and spotted breast. *The patient called the sad looking doctor a singing thrush.*

Thrust – *(verb)* **1** push suddenly or violently in the specified direction. *She thrust her hand into his box and it got stuck there!* **2** extend so as to project conspicuously. *The boat thrust out into the water.* **3** impose something unwelcome on. *He tried to thrust his way past her.* *(noun)* **1** a sudden or violent lunge or attack. *He pushed the bag up with one powerful thrust.* **2** the principal purpose or theme of a course of action or line of reasoning. *Anti-Americanism became the main thrust of their policy.* **3** the propulsive force of a jet or rocket engine. the lateral pressure exerted by an arch or other support in a building. *The Indian missile had a more powerful thrust than any other in South Asia.* **4** a reverse fault of low angle, with older strata displaced horizontally over newer. *Semi domes assist in containing the thrust within the building.*

Thud – *(noun)* a dull, leaden sound, such as that made by a heavy object falling to the ground. *I heard a thud from somewhere downstairs, around midnight.* *(verb)* move, fall, or strike something with a thud. *The thief fell from the roof with a thud.*

Thug – *(noun)* **1** a violent and uncouth man, especially a criminal. *The thugs were convicted without much delay.* **2** a member of a religious organization of robbers and assassins in India, suppressed by the British in the 1830s. *The thugs had a tough time escaping from the hands of the British police.*

Thumb – *(noun)* the short, thick first digit of the hand, set lower and apart from the other four and opposable to them. *She broke her thumb in the accident.* *(verb)* **1** press, touch, or indicate with one's thumb. *She only had to thumb the button and the door would open.* **2** turn over with or as if with one's thumb. wear or soil by repeated handling. *I can see you've thumbed the glass too much.* **3** request or obtain by signaling with one's thumb. *He thumbed towards the men behind him.*

Thump – *(verb)* **1** hit heavily, especially with the fist or a blunt implement. put down forcefully, noisily, or decisively. beat or pulsate strongly. *My heart was thumping so loud I thought everyone would hear.* **2** play a tune enthusiastically but heavy handedly. *The band was thumping out a tune from their favourite album.* **3** defeat heavily. *England thumped India easily.* *(noun)* a heavy dull blow or noise. *I heard a thumping sound in the sitting room around midnight.*

Thunder – *(noun)* **1** a loud rumbling or crashing noise heard after a lightning flash due to the expansion of rapidly heated air. *There was thunder and lightning all night.* **2** a resounding loud deep noise. *We could hear the thunder of the avalanche on a nearby mountain.* *(verb)* **1** thunder sounds. *Though it started as a drizzle, soon it began to thunder.* **2** move or cause to move heavily and forcefully. *The train thundered through the tunnel.* **3** speak loudly, angrily, and forcefully, especially to protest. *He thundered against the evils of the age.*

Thunderbolt – *(noun)* a flash of lightning with a simultaneous crash of thunder. a supported bolt or shaft believed to be the destructive agent in a lightning flash, especially as an attribute of a god such as Jupiter or Thor. *The news hit her like a thunderbolt.*

Thunderstorm – *(noun)* a storm with thunder and lightning and typically also heavy rain or hall. *The town was struck by a thunderstorm.*

Thunderstruck – *(adjective)* extremely surprised or shocked. *They stood thunderstruck when they heard the news.*

Thursday – *(noun)* the day of the week before Friday and following Wednesday. *I look forward to our Thursday-parties. (adverb)* on Thursday. on Thursdays; each Thursday. *She goes to the temple on Thursdays.*

Thus – *(adverb)* **1** as a result or consequence of this; therefore. *She killed him, thus landing up in jail.* **2** in the manner now being indicated or exemplified; in this way. *While she was thus engaged, someone called the doctor.* **3** to this point; so. *The World Cup is a turning point in Yuvraj Singh's career thus far.*

Thwart – *(verb)* prevent from succeeding in or accomplishing something. *Their plans were thwarted by the teacher who had always had an eye on them. (noun)* a structural crosspiece forming a seat for a rower in a boat. *Perhaps the reason why she fell into the water was because the thwart was loose. preposition & (adverb)* from one side to another side of; across. *A pink cloud spread thwarts the shore.*

Tick – *(noun)* a fabric case stuffed with feathers or other material to form a mattress or pillow. short for ticking. *The sound of the clock ticking was actually comforting.*

Ticket – *(noun)* **1** a piece of paper or card giving the holder a right to admission to a place or event or to travel on public transport. *She ran to get the tickets before the movie starts.* **2** a certificate or warrant, especially an official notice of a traffic offence. *He was used to getting tickets from the traffic police.* **3** a label attached to a rctail product, giving its price, size, etc. *The ticket on the dress says its Rs 799 and size L.* **4** a list of candidates put forward by a party in an election. a set of principles or policies supported by a party in an election. *He stood for the elections on a right wing, no-nonsense ticket.* **5** the desirable thing. *A holiday would be just the ticket.* **6** a person of a specified kind. *You're all a bunch of sick tickets! (verb)* **1** issue with a ticket. *You'll be ticketed if you park on the wrong side.* **2** be destined or heading for a specified state or position. *Passengers in Europe can be electronically ticketed.*

Tickle – *(verb)* **1** lightly touch in a way that causes itching or twitching and often laughter. catch a trout by lightly rubbing it so that it moves backwards into the hand. *She tickled me so badly I was rolling on the floor.* **2** be appealing or amusing to. *She related a few instances that tickled our senses! (noun)* an act of ticking or sensation of being tickled. *Her jokes never ceased to tickle me.*

Tidal – *(adjective)* having to do with rise flow of river or sea water. *The river here is not tidal.*

Tide – *(noun)* **1** the alternate rising and falling of the sea due to the attraction of the moon and sun. *We were asked to stay away from the beach as the tide was higher than usual.* **2** a powerful surge of feeling or trend of events. *A tide of euphoria swept over her. (verb)* **1** help someone through a difficult period, especially with financial assistance. *She helped me immensely to tide over the rough period.* **2** drift with or as if with the tide. move in or out of harbour with the help of the tide. *We moved with the tide.*

Tiding *–plural (noun)* news; information. *If the tiding ever reached her, there would be nothing to save her from dishonor.*

Tidy – *(adjective)* **1** arranged neatly and in order. inclined to keep things or one's appearance neat and in order. not messy; neat and controlled. *She keeps her cupboard quite neat and tidy.* **2** considerable. *Her small work will help bring in a tidy sum. (noun)* **1** an act or spell of tidying. *She's coming to give my house a tidy.* **2** a receptacle for holding small objects. *We should try to keep our surroundings tidy.* **3** a detachable ornamental cover for a chair back. *Why is her tidy so crumpled? (verb)* make tidy. put something away for the sake of tidiness. *The boys finally tidied their room.*

Tie – *(verb)* **1** attach or fasten with string, cord, etc. form into a knot or bow. restrict someone's movement by binding their arms or legs or binding them to something. bring something to a satisfactory conclusion. *The thief tied the hands of the lady with a string.* **2** restrict; limit. restrict someone to a particular situation or place. occupy someone to the exclusion of other activity. invest or reserve capital so that it is not immediately available for use. *She didn't want to be tied down with a bondage so early in her life.* **3** connect; link. be or cause to be in harmony with something. hold together by a crosspiece or tie. unite by a tie. perform as one unbroken note. *Your self-respect is tied to your performance.* *(noun)* **1** a thing that ties. *He tightened the tie of his robe.* **2** a strip of material worn around the neck beneath a collar; tied in a knot at the front. *He wore a blue tie underneath the pullover.* **3** a rod or beam holding parts of a structure together. *He nailed the rafters together with a tie beam.* **4** short for cross tie. *The British often call the cross tie a sleeper.* **5** a curved line above or below two notes of the same pitch indicating that they values. *There was a tie between the two notes that the student could not understand.* **6** a shoe tied with a lace. *He tightened the tie of his shoes.* **7** [British] a sports match between two or more players or teams in which the winners proceed to the next round of the competition: a cup tie. *There was a tie between the teams.*

Tier - *(noun)* **1** one of a series of rows or levels stacked one above the other. *We were travelling on a three-tier AC compartment.* **2** a level or grade within a hierarchy. *He was still in Tier 2 so there was a long way to go.*

Tiff - *(noun)* a quarrel. *The couple were caught in a tiff.*

Tiger - *(noun)* **1** a very large solitary cat with a yellow brown coat striped with black, native to the forests of Asia. *The number of tigers in the country has dwindled.* **2** used in names of tiger moths and striped butterflies, e.g. scarlet tiger, plain tiger. *I caught a tiger moth in my garden between the flower pots.* **3** a dynamic economy of one of the smaller east Asian countries, especially that of Singapore, Taiwan, or south Korea. *He works for a tiger economy.*

Tight - *(adjective)* **1** fixed or fastened firmly; hard to move, undo, or open. close fitting, especially uncomfortably so. very firm. well sealed against something such as water or air. *Her shawl was twisted into a tight knot.* **2** stretched so as to leave no slack. Tense. *Everybody felt a bit unnerved at his tight smile.* **3** strictly imposed. *Security was tight at the ceremony.* **4** concise. *She wrote a tight script.* **5** disciplined and well coordinated. *It was a tightly conducted event.* **6** allowing little room for maneuver. limited; restricted. *They had to work on a tight deadline.* **7** secretive. *Why are you being so tight with me?* **8** miserly. *He was really tight with his money.* *(adverb)* very firmly, closely, or tensely. *The bags were packed tightly.*

Tighten - *(verb)* having to do with fastened firmly. *The noose was tightened around the neck of the culprit.*

Tight-fisted - *(adjective)* not willing to spend or give much money; miserly. *He is extremely tight-fisted with his finances.*

Tight-lipped - *(adjective)* with the lips firmly closed, especially as a sign of suppressed emotion or determined reticence. *Everyone was instructed to be tight-lipped about the incident.*

Tights - *plural (noun)* a close fitting garment made of a knitted yarn, covering the legs, hips, and bottom. *She wore tights under her skirt.*

Tigress - *(noun)* a female tiger. *The tigress roared at the trembling goat.*

Tile - *(noun)* **1** a thin square or rectangular slab of baked clay, concrete, etc., used in overlapping rows for covering roofs. a similar slab of glazed pottery or other material for covering floors or walls. *She was using vitrified tiles for her house.* **2** a thin, flat piece used in scrabble, mahjong, and other games. *We arranged our tiles for the game.* *(verb)* **1** cover with tiles. *The floor of the house was tiled.* **2** arrange on a computer screen so that they do not overlap. *Please tile the icons in your laptop.*

Till - *(noun)* a cash register or drawer for money in a shop, bank, or restaurant. *There were long queues at the till.*

Tiller - *(noun)* a horizontal bar fitted to the head of a boat's rubber post and used for steering. *The tiller was swinging with the ship completely out of control.*

Tilt - *(verb)* **1** move or cause to move into a slopping position. move in a vertical plane. *The windows tilted slightly.* **2** thrust at with a lance or other weapon. engage in a contest with. *He tilted at the prey.* *(noun)* **1** a tilting position or movement. an inclination or bias. *She always had a tilt towards the right wing.* **2** a joust. *She had a tilt at the European Cup.*

Timber - *(noun)* **1** wood prepared for use in building and carpentry. trees grown for such wood. a wooden beam or board used in building and shipbuilding. *They had a timber plantation in their estate.* **2** suitable quality or character. *She is hailed as presidential timber.* *(exclamatory)* used to warn that a tree is about to fall after being cut. *Mark shouted out to Richard, 'Timber! Timber!'*

Time - *(noun)* **1** the indefinite continued progress of existence and events in the past, present, and future, regarded as a whole. *He dreamt of travelling through space and time.* **2** a point of time as measured in hours and minutes past midnight or noon. the favourable or appropriate moment to do something: it was time to go. an indefinite period: he worked for a time as a gardener. a more or less definite portion of time characterized by particular events or circumstances: Victorian times. a period regarded as characteristic of a particular stage of one's life. the length of time taken to run a race or complete an activity. *His time for the mile was 3:49.31* **3** the moment at which the opening hours of a public house end. a moment at which play stops temporarily within a game. *The referee called time.* **4** time as allotted, available, or used. *The party was a complete waste of time.* **5** the normal rate of pay for time spent working. *They are paid time and a half.* *(verb)* **1** arrange a time for. perform at a particular time. *The first performance is timed at 4:45* **2** measure the time taken by. *We were timed and given prizes according to our speed.* **3** cancel an operation automatically because a predefined interval of time has passed. *Connections are timed out when not in use.* **4** multiply a number. *Two times three is six.*

Timeless - *(adjective)* not affected by the passage of time or changes in fashion. *Some of Kishore Kumar's songs are timeless melodies.*

Timely - *(adjective)* done or occurring at a favourable or appropriate time. *Thanks to the doctor's timely arrival, her father was saved.*

Timid - *(adjective)* lacking in courage or confidence. *She was rather timid when she was new to the city.*

Timorous - *(adjective)* lacking in courage or confidence; nervous. *A timorous voice spoke from the last bench.*

Tin - *(noun)* **1** a silvery white metal, the chemical element of atomic number 50. *She bought a tinplate for some lab work.* **2** a lidded airtight container made of tinplate or aluminium. a sealed container for preserving food, made of tinplate or aluminium; a can. an open metal container for baking food. *I bought a biscuit tin from the supermarket.* *(verb)* **1** cover with a thin layer of tin. *The copper pans are tinned inside.* **2** preserve in a tin: tinned fruit. *I was forbidden from having tinned fruits.* **3** tin mining. *He has been working in tin mines for a long time now.*

Tinge - *(verb)* **1** colour slightly. *The pink-tinged cloud was a picture worth being framed.* **2** having a slight influence on. *Though she came after a long time, it was a visit tinged with sadness.* *(noun)* a slight trace. *I felt a tinge of guilt in my heart when I heard my friend bearing the brunt of my activities.*

Tingle - *(noun)* a slight prickling or stinging sensation. *She was tingled all over with joy.* *(verb)* experience or cause to experience a tingle. *A tingle went down my spine at the mere thought of going to that house.*

Tinker - *(noun)* **1** an itinerant mender of pots, kettles, etc. *I met a tinker once in one of my trips.* **2** a gypsy or other person living in an itinerant community. *There are too many tinkers in the outskirts of the village these days.* **3** a mischievous child. *Stop being such a tinker!* **4**

an act of tinkering with something. *Tinker with the planet a little bit and the possibilities of life here will dwindle even more.* *(verb)* attempt in a casual manner to repair or improve. *I found her tinkering with the car engine outside.*

Tinkle – *(verb)* 1 make or cause to make a light, clear ringing sound. *The tinkling of the cycle bells seemed too loud in this quite town.* **2** urinate. *I need to tinkle.* *(noun)* **1** a tinkling sound. a telephone call. *I heard the tinkle of the phone from the other room.* **2** an act of urinating. *We decided to stop for a tinkle on the way.*

Tinsel – *(noun)* **1** a form of decoration consisting of thin strips of shiny metal foil attached to a length of thread. *I decorated her room with tinsels and party lights.* **2** superficial attractiveness or glamour. *The actor's marriage was the hottest issue in tinsel town.*

Tint – *(noun)* **1** a shade or variety of colour. a trace of something. *The sky had a grey tint to it.* **2** the process or dye used in artificial colouring of the hair. *She was checking for grey hair just in case she left any after her last tint.* **3** an area of faint colour printed as a half tone. a set of parallel engraved lines giving uniform shading. *Why don't you give it a blue tint?* *(verb)* colour slightly; tinge. dye hair with a tint. *She got her hair dyed with a blue tint.*

Tiny –*(adjective)* very small. *A tiny little insect was nibbling at my feet.* *(noun)* a very young child. *I recommended books for tinies in every library.*

Tip – *(noun)* the pointed or rounded extremity of something slender or tapering. a small part fitted to the end of an object. *What we saw before us was just the tip of the iceberg.* *(verb)* **1** attach to or cover the tip of. *The mountains were tipped with snow.* **2** colour something at its tip or edge. *Pretty little red roses tipped with white.* 3 paste a page to a neighbouring page with a fine layer of paste down its inner margin. *I had tipped the clipping from the magazine here.*

Tipsy – *(adjective)* slightly drunk. *I asked the others to ignore her as she is tipsy.*

Tiptoe – *(verb)* walk quietly and carefully with one's heels raised and one's weight on the balls of the feet. *We tip-toed through the hall and stealthily entered the kitchen.*

Tirade – *(noun)* a long speech of angry criticism or accusation. *As soon as I entered, I was welcomed with a tirade of complaints.*

Tire – *(verb)* become or cause to become in need of rest or sleep. exhaust the patience or interest of. become impatient or bored with. *I was tired of hearing her complaints everyday.*

Tiresome – *(adjective)* causing one to feel bored or impatient. *Her tantrums were indeed getting quite tiresome.*

Tissue – *(noun)* **1** any of the distinct types of material of which animals or plants are made, consisting of specialized cells and their products. *She had a tear in the tissue near her elbow.* **2** tissue paper. a piece of absorbent paper, used especially as a disposable handkerchief. *I bought a roll of tissue paper from the supermarket.* **3** fabric of a delicate gauzy texture. *She bought a tissue sari from the showroom.* **4** a web like structure or network: a tissue of lies. *What you are telling me is a tissue of lies.*

Tit – *(noun)* a titmouse. *There was a tit mouse in the attic.*

Titbit – *(noun)* **1** a small piece of tasty food. *The little mouse was hunting around for tit bits.* **2** a small and particularly interesting item of gossip or information. *The reporter was hanging around in the party looking out for tit bits.*

Title – *(noun)* **1** the name of a book, musical composition, or other artistic work. a caption or credit in a film or broadcast. *The title of the book had to be mentioned in bold caps.* **2** a name that describes someone's position or job. *She got the title for assistant manager after clearing her exam.* **3** a word used before or instead of someone's name, indicating social or official rank, profession, or academic or marital status. *Her title told me she is married but not whether it was happily so.* **4** a descriptive or distinctive name that is earned or chosen: the title of best restaurant of the year. *The title of best student of the year was awarded to Rahul again.* **5** the position of being the champion of a major sports competition. *He won the world championship* *title.* **6** a right or claim to the ownership of property or to a rank or throne. *She knew she had title to his property.* **7** a fixed sphere of work and source of income as a condition for ordination. a parish church in Rome under a cardinal. *He was under a title when he was in Rome.* *(verb)* give a title to. *The script was titled differently later.*

Title-page – *(noun)* first cover page of a book, film documentary. *The author had unreasonable demands for even the title page.*

To – *(preposition)* **1** expressing direction or position in relation to a particular location, point, or condition. in telling the time before the hour specified. *We were on the way to the station when the accident happened.* **2** identifying the person or thing affected. *She donated Rs 10,000 to the school.* **3** identifying a particular relationship between one person or thing and another. indicating a rate of return on something. *Ten miles to the gallon.* **4** indicating that two things are attached. *She is married to my uncle.* **5** governing a phrase expressing someone's reaction to something. *To her astonishment, he smiled.* **6** used to introduce the second element in a comparison. *The team is nothing to what it was till a few years ago.* **7** placed before a debit entry in accounting. *To account for the Rs 10,000 spent as charity.* *(adverb)* so as to be closed or nearly closed. *He pulled the door to behind him.*

Toad – *(noun)* **1** a tailless amphibian with a short stout body and short legs, typically having dry warty skin that can exude poison. *A rather big toad jumped in front of our vehicle.* **2** a detestable person. *He is such a toad!*

Toadstool – *(noun)* the spore bearing fruiting body of a fungus, typically in the form of a rounded cap on a stalk, especially one that is inedible or poisonous. *Learn to distinguish between a mushroom and a toadstool.*

Toast – *(noun)* accompany a reggae backing track or music with improvised rhythmic speech. *The toast that this DJ does is his USP.*

Tobacco – *(noun)* **1** a preparation of the dried and fermented nicotine rich leaves of an American plant, used for smoking or chewing. *There is too much tobacco in this particular brand of cigars.* **2** the plant of the nightshade family yielding these leaves. *We had tobacco plants in our field.*

Tobacconist – *(noun)* a shopkeeper who sells cigarettes and tobacco. *He worked as a tobacconist for 15 years down the road.*

Today – *(adverb)* on or in the course of this present day. at the present period of time; nowadays. *The effect of the radiation that spread 50 years ago continues even today.* *(noun)* this present day. the present period of time. *What is for lunch today?*

Toddle – *(verb)* move with short unsteady steps while learning to walk. walk or go in a casual or leisurely way. *The baby has started toddling.* *(noun)* an act of toddling. *We are helping him to toddle.*

Toe – *(noun)* **1** any of the five digits at the end of the human foot. any of the digits of the foot of a quadruped or bird. the part of an item of footwear that covers a person's toes. *She had sharp toe nails.* **2** the lower end, tip, or point of something. the tip of the head of a golf club. *The toe of the slopes have eroded and there have been more landslides as well.* *(verb)* **1** push, touch, or kick with one's toes. *Strike the ball with the toe of the club.* **2** walk with the toes pointed in or out. of a pair of wheels converge or diverge slightly at the front. *He toes out when he walks.*

Toffee – *(noun)* a kind of firm or hard sweet which softens when sucked or chewed, made by boiling together sugar and butter. *She was planning to make toffees for Christmas.*

Together – *(adverb)* **1** with or in proximity to another person or people. so as to touch or combine. in combination; collectively. into companionship or close association. married or in a sexual relationship. so as to be united or in agreement. *My parents have been together for 35 years now.* **2** at the same time. *We walked into the room together.* **3** without interruption. *She can sit and listen to him for hours together.* *(adjective)* level headed and well organized. *She's a very together woman!*

Toil – *(verb)* work extremely hard or incessantly. move somewhere slowly and with difficulty. *He has been toiling away at the farm for days now. (noun)* exhausting work. *It is the fruit of his sweat and toil.*

Toilet – *(noun)* **1** a large bowl for urinating or defecating into, typically plumbed into a sewage system. *The public toilet was in desperate need for maintenance.* **2** the process of washing oneself, dressing, and attending to one's appearance. demoting articles used in this process. *She has gone for toilet and will be back shortly.* **3** the cleansing of part of a person's body as a medical procedure. *The doctor was taking the child for toilet after the surgery. (verb)* assist or supervise an infant or invalid in using a toilet. *The baby is being toilet trained now.*

Token – *(noun)* **1** a thing serving to represent a fact, quality, feeling, etc. a badge or favour worn to indicate allegiance to a person or party. a word or object conferring authority on or serving to authenticate the speaker or holder. a device given to a train driver on a single track railway as authority to proceed. *She was given a bonus as a token of appreciation for her hard work.* **2** a voucher that can be exchanged for goods or services. a metal or plastic disc used to operate a machine or in exchange for particular goods or services. *She lost her metro token in the crowd.* **3** an individual occurrence of a linguistic unit on speech or writing. contrasted with type. *The linguistics teacher taught us the application of types and tokens.* **4** a sequence of bits passed between nodes in a fixed order and enabling a node to transmit information. *The token was expiring. (adjective)* **1** done for the sake of appearances or as a symbolic gesture. *Such offenses will only invite a token fine.* **2** chosen by way of tokenism to represent a particular group. *She took offence on being named the token woman on the force.*

Tolerate – *(verb)* **1** allow the existence or occurrence of without interference. *I will not tolerate this disobedience any more.* **2** endure with forbearance. *She has been tolerating his stubbornness for years now.* **3** be capable of continued exposure to without adverse reaction. *Cactus grows in conditions no other plant can tolerate.*

Tolerance – *(noun)* **1** the ability, willingness, or capacity to tolerate something. *Gandhiji is known for his great level of tolerance.* **2** an allowable amount of variation of a specified quantity, especially in the dimensions of a machine or part. *250 parts in his cars were made to tolerances of one thousandth of an inch.*

Tolerant – *(adjective)* **1** showing tolerance. *We must learn to be tolerant of others.* **2** able to endure specified conditions or treatment. *Cactus is completely tolerant of heat.*

Toll – *(noun)* **1** a charge payable to use a bridge or road. a charger for a long distance telephone call. *The toll for this road was increased twice in the last few months.* **2** the number of deaths or casualties arising from an accident, disaster, etc. *The death toll of the fire accident had gone from 25 to 35.* **3** the cost or damage resulting from something. *The environment toll of this policy has been high. (verb)* charge a toll for the use of a bridge or road. *The report advocates motorway tolling.*

Tomato – *(noun)* **1** a glossy red or yellow edible fruit, eaten as a vegetable or in salads. *I like tomato sandwiches better than onion.* **2** the south American plant of the nightshade family which produces this fruit. *We grew tomatoes in our vegetable garden.*

Tomb – *(noun)* **1** a burial place, especially a large underground vault. a monument to a dead person, erected over their burial place. *The Taj Mahal is the greatest tomb of love.* **2** death. *The sea was his tomb.*

Tomboy – *(noun)* a girl who enjoys rough, noisy activities traditionally associated with boys. *She grew up as a tomboy but transformed into a lovely lady later.*

Tombstone – *(noun)* **1** a large, flat inscribed stone standing or laid over a grave. *Her tombstone mentioned her name differently, I noticed.* **2** an advertisement listing the underwriters or firms associated with a new issue of shares, bonds, etc. *Her name appeared in the tombstone advertisement.*

Tomorrow – *(adverb)* **1** on the day after today. *The dress will be delivered tomorrow for sure.* **2** in the near future. *We can never predict for certain what may happen tomorrow. (noun)* **1** the day after today. *Tomorrow will be a special day for her.* **2** the near future. *So what if today was bad, tomorrow will be better.*

Ton – *(noun)* **1** fashionable style or distinction. *You have to have ton for a guaranteed ticket.* **2** fashionable society. *Half the ton was there at the party.*

Tone – *(noun)* **1** a musical or vocal sound with reference to its pitch, quality, and strength. *They were talking in hushed tones.* **2** a modulation of the voice expressing a feeling or mood. *She asked him to put down the knife in a firm tone.* **3** general character. *Trust her to lower the tone of the conversation.* **4** a basic interval in classical western music, equal to two semitones and separating, for example, the first and second notes of an ordinary scale; a major second. *The B flat violin's tone was higher than the designated tone.* **5** the particular quality of brightness, deepness, or hue of a colour. the general effect of colour or of light and shade in a picture. *Could you tone down the sharpness of the picture?* **6** a musical note, warble, or other sound used as a signal on a telephone or answering machine. *I like the polyphonic tones my phone has. (verb)* **1** give greater strength or firmness to the body or a muscle. *The instructor told me I only need to tone down.* **2** make something less extreme or intense. *Can you please tone down your protest?* **3** harmonize with in terms of colour. *The soft pink in your sari tones down the richness of the silk.* **4** give an altered colour in finishing by means of a chemical solution. *Lets sepia tone the print first.*

Toneless – *(adjective)* lacking experssion in a voice or musical sound. *I wonder why he is singing in a toneless voice.*

Tongs -*plural (noun)* **1** a tool with two movable arms that are joined at one end, used for picking up and holding things. *She moved the barbecue away from the fire with the tongs.* **2** short for curling tongs. *She tried to curl her hair often using curling tongs.*

Tongue – *(noun)* **1** the fleshy muscular organs in the mouth, used for tasting, licking, swallowing, and articulating speech. the tongue of an ox or lamb, as food. *The ox has a really long tongue that reaches almost till its eyes.* **2** a person's style or manner of speaking. *He was known for having a caustic tongue.* **3** a particular language. *What is your mother tongue?* **4** a strip of leather or fabric under the laces in a shoe, attached only at the front end. *The tongue of his shoe was torn badly.* **5** the free-swinging metal piece inside a bell which strikes the bell to produce the sound. *The tongue went to and fro as the bell rang loudly.* **6** a long, low promontory of land. *A tongue jutted out of what I thought was the harbor. (verb)* **1** distinctly on a wind instrument by interrupting the air flow with the tongue. *The student had worked out the correct manner of tonguing.* **2** lick or caress with the tongue. *The horse was lovingly tonguing the colt.*

Tonic – *(noun)* **1** a medicinal substance taken to give a feeling of vigour or well being. *You should take this tonic as it will give you energy.* **2** something with an invigorating effect. *I need a tonic at my age.* **3** short for tonic water. *The players were given tonic during lunch break.* **4** the first note in a scale which, in conventional harmony, provides the keynote of a piece of music. *The tonic itself was off tune. (adjective)* **1** relating to or denoting the first degree of a scale. *What a tonic music!* **2** denoting or relating to the syllable within a tone group, that has greatest prominence. *The tonic is extremely important in linguistics.* **3** relating to or restoring muscle tone. of or denoting continuous muscular contraction. *She had a tonic spasm a few days ago.*

Tonight – *(adverb)* on the present or approaching evening or night. *Let's go for a drink tonight. (noun)* the evening or night of the present day. *Tonight is a night to remember.*

Tonnage – *(noun)* **1** weight in tons. *Trucks carry more tonnage than tractors.* **2** the size or carrying capacity of a ship measured in tons. shipping considered in terms of total carrying capacity. *India's total tonnage is nothing in comparison to European Union's.*

Tonne - *(noun)* another term for metric ton. *Six tonnes of iron were being transported.*

Tonsil - *(noun)* either of two small masses of lymphoid tissue in the throat, one on each side of the root of the tongue. *He had to have his tonsils taken out.*

Tonsure- *(noun)* **1** a part of a monk's or priest's head left bare on top by shaving off the hair. *At this rate, he'll soon have a tonsure like a monk.* **2** an act of shaving a monk's or priest's head in this way as a preparation for entering a religious order. *He received the tonsure when he joined the Mission. (verb)* give a tonsure to. *The young boy was tonsured when he joined the monastery.*

Too -*(adverb)* **1** to a higher degree than is desirable, permissible, or possible. very. *I'm sorry, you're too late.* **2** in addition. moreover. *I want the red one, yellow one, and the blue one too.*

Tool - *(noun)* **1** a device or implement, typically hand held, used to carry out a particular function. *I bought him a tool kit for his birthday.* **2** a thing used to help perform a job. *We were all given the tools required for the experiment, in the lab.* **3** a person used by another. *She gave me three people as tools for the project.* **4** a distinct design in the tooling of a book. a small stamp or roller used to make such a design. *Give me the tools for the book.* **5** a man's penis. *She broke his tool with that mighty kick. (verb)* **1** impress a design on with a heated tool. *There were several volumes in the museum bound in leather and tooled in gold.* **2** equip or be equipped with tools for industrial production. *The factory must be tooled for such large scale production.* **3** be or become armed. *They were tooling up for the operation.* **4** drive or ride in a casual or leisurely manner. *I caught him tooling around town in his luxury car.* **5** dress with a chisel. *She had finely tooled the sculpture.*

Toot - *(noun)* **1** a short, sharp sound made by a horn, trumpet, or similar instrument. *I could hear the toot of the school bus from down the street.* **2** a snort of a drug, especially cocaine. cocaine. *He likes a toot occasionally.* **3** a spree. *She is a shopper on a toot! (verb)* **1** make or cause to make a toot. *Someone was tooting non-stop behind my car in the traffic.* **2** snort cocaine. *I tried convincing him about the drawbacks of tooting cocaine.*

Toothache - *(noun)* pain in a tooth or teeth. *She has been having a toothache for the last few days now.*

Top - *(noun)* **1** a conical, spherical, or pear shaped toy that may be set to spin. *The top was her favourite toy throughout her childhood.* **2** used in names of top shells, e.g. strawberry top. *Give me a chocolate top with my cake.*

Topaz - *(noun)* **1** a precious stone, typically colourless, yellow, or pale blue, consisting of a fluorine containing aluminium silicate. *She has been wearing a topaz ring for the last few years now.* 2 a dark yellow colour. *I bought her a topaz top.*

Topic - *(noun)* **1** a subject of a text, speech, conversation, etc. *What exactly is the topic of discussion here?* **2** that part of a sentence about which something is said, typically the first major constituent. *In the exam, the kids were asked to identify the topic of each given sentence.*

Topical -*(adjective)* **1** relating to or dealing with current affairs. *One of my favorite topical affairs programme was We The People.* **2** relating to a particular subject. *It was a rather topical issue.* 3 relating or applied directly to a part of the body. *Stay away from topical steroid creams.*

Topography- *(noun)* **1** the arrangement of the natural and artificial physical features of an area. a detailed description or representation on a map of such features. *I could see the topography change as the train went from the North to the South.* **2** the arrangement of features of an organ or organism. *The doctor was trying to analyse the topography of this organism.*

Topple - *(verb)* overbalance or cause to overbalance and fall. *I laughed at the story of Humpty Dumpty toppling off the wall.*

Topsy-turvy - *(adjective & adverb)* **1** upside down. *Why is the whole house topsy-turvy today?* **2** in a state of confusion. *Her affairs were completely topsy-turvy now.*

Torch – *(noun)* **1** a portable battery powered electric lamp. *I took the torch when I left her house last night as it was really dark outside.* **2** a portable means of illumination such as a piece of wood soaked in tallow and ignited. *I saw a man carrying a lit torch in his hand walking towards the palace.* **3** a valuable quality, principle, or cause, which needs to be protected and maintained: *Britain could carry the torch of freedom.* **4** a blowlamp. *She bought me a torch for my birthday!* *(verb)* set fire to. *The entire village was torched.*

Torment – *(noun)* severe physical or mental suffering. a cause of torment. *She has been the chief cause of my torment.* *(verb)* **1** subject to torment. *I requested my sister to kindly stop tormenting me.* **2** annoy or tease unkindly. *She has been tormenting me for a while now.*

Tornado – *(noun)* a mobile, destructive vortex of violently rotating winds having the appearance of a funnel shaped cloud. *The entire state was devastated by the twin tornadoes that struck yesterday.*

Torpedo – *(noun)* **1** a cigar shaped self propelled underwater missile designed to be fired from a ship, submarine, or an aircraft and to explode on reaching a target. *The torpedo attack was started by the US first.* **2** a railway fog signal. *Switch on the torpedo, quick!* **3** a firework exploding on impact with a hard surface. *The torpedo was lit now.* **4** an electric ray. *They let out a torpedo ray.* *(verb)* **1** attack with a torpedo or torpedoes. *They torpedoed a German submarine last night.* **2** ruin a plan or project. *The fight had torpedoed any scope for peace talks.*

Torrent – *(noun)* **1** a strong and fast moving stream of water of other liquid. *It was pouring in torrents in the neighbouring state.* **2** an overwhelmingly copious outpouring. *She knew a torrent of abuse awaited her at home.*

Torrid – *(adjective)* **1** very hot and dry. *The torrid heat of the desert was getting to me.* **2** full of intense emotions arising from sexual love. *The torrid love affair of the actor and actress was out in the newspapers.* **3** full of difficulty. *He had a torrid time at the elections.*

Torso – *(noun)* **1** the trunk of the human body. *His torso was visible under his tee.* **2** the trunk of a statue without, or considered independently of, the head and limbs. *The statue fell and broke its torso.* **3** an unfinished or mutilated thing, especially a work of art or literature. *The painting was reduced to a torso.*

Tortoise – *(noun)* **1** a slow moving land reptile of warm climates, enclosed in a scaly or leathery domed shell into which it can retract its head and legs. *The zoo kept different kinds of tortoise.* **2** a testudo. *The soldiers held a tortoise above their head.*

Tortuous – *(adjective)* **1** full of twists and turns. *The route is remote and tortuous.* **2** excessively lengthy and complex. *They had a tortuous argument.*

Torture – *(noun)* **1** the action or practice of infliction severe pain as a punishment or a forcible means of persuasion. *The prisoners have been through immense torture.* **2** great suffering or anxiety. *Hitler sent the Jews to a torture chamber.* **3** *(verb)* subject to torture. *I asked him to stop torturing me.*

Toss – *(verb)* **1** throw lightly or casually. throw off its back. throw into the air so as to make a choice, based on which side of the coin faces uppermost when it lands. *She tossed her bag on to the sofa.* **2** move or cause to move from side to side or back and forth. jerk sharply backwards. shake or turn food in a liquid, so as to coat it lightly. *She tossed the salad and got the perfect mix.* **3** drink something rapidly or all at once. produce something rapidly or without thought or effort. *He tossed off a whole bottle of beer!* **4** masturbate. *The doctor explained that tossing is not that bad habit.* *(noun)* an act of tossing. *She gave a defiant toss of her head and walked away.*

Total – *(adjective)* **1** comprising the whole number or amount. *The total figure amounts to $5,000.* **2** complete; absolute. *She was totally indifferent to my worries.* *(noun)* a total number or amount. *He scored a total of 200 runs.* *(verb)* **1** amount on number to. find the total of. *How much do your earnings total to?* **2** destroy or kill. *The car was totaled.*

Totalitarian –*(adjective)* of or relating to a centralized and dictatorial system of government requiring complete subservience to the state. *The country was experiencing a totalitarian regime.* *(noun)* a person advocating such a system. *Most totalitarians seem to be against science.*

Totter – *(verb)* **1** move in an unsteady way. *The old lady came tottering towards the train.* **2** shake or rock as if about to collapse. *The accident site was a sight of tottering, gutted houses.* **3** be insecure or about to collapse. *The economy has been tottering from one crisis to another.* *(noun)* a tottering gait. *Her movement was reduced to a totter.*

Touch – *(verb)* **1** come into or be in contact with. come or bring into mutual contact. bring one's hand or another part of one's body into contact with. strike lightly in a specified direction. *The child was glad his feet touched the ground.* **2** harm or interfere with. take some of for use. consume food or drink. *This food has hardly been touched.* **3** have an effect on. reach a specified level or amount. approach in excellence. *Several companies were touched by the recession.* **4** produce feelings of affection, gratitude, or sympathy in. *I was touched by his words of concern.* **5** have any dealings with. *He took jobs that nobody else would touch.* *(noun)* **1** an act of touching. a musician's manner of playing keys or strings or the manner in which an instrument's keys or strings respond to being played. a light stroke with a pen, pencil, etc. *Her touch was rather hesitant.* **2** the faculty of perception through physical contact, especially with the fingers. *Her touch was enough to calm me down.* **3** a small amount. *Add a touch of vinegar to the milk to make it curdle.* **4** a distinctive detail or feature. *The film's most inventive touch was the special effect.* **5** a distinctive manner or method of dealing with something. an ability to deal with something successfully. *He revealed a surer political touch.* **6** a test of worth or character. *You must put your fate to the touch.*

Touching – *(adjective)* arousing strong emotion; moving. *The scene was indeed touching.* *(preposition)* concerning. *Several discoveries touching the lost traditions of the Andamanese tribes have been made.*

Touchy – *(adjective)* **1** quick to take offence; over sensitive. *He is a touchy guy when it comes to his race.* **2** requiring careful handling. *It's a rather touchy issue.*

Tough – *(adjective)* **1** strong enough to withstand wear and tear. difficult to cut or chew. *The bread you made was too tough.* **2** able to endure hardship, adversity, or pain. *She is known for being really tough with her emotions.* **3** strict and uncompromising. *Of late, the traffic policemen have been really tough with defaulters.* **4** involving considerable difficulty or hardship. *She has been going through a tough period in her life.* **5** rough or violent. *These tough teenagers need tougher punishment.* **6** used to express a lack of sympathy. *If you don't like it, tough.* *(noun)* a rough and violent man. *A gang of toughs have been creating chaos in the complex here.*

Tour – *(noun)* **1** a journey for pleasure in which several different places are visited. *Guided tours may limit your scope for discovering unknown places.* **2** a short trip to or through a place in order to view or inspect something. *If only we could have a tour of the Rashtrapati Bhavan.* **3** a journey made by performers or a sports team, in which they perform or play in several different places. *The team will start their European tour next month.* **4** a spell of duty on military or diplomatic service. *He left on an official tour yesterday.* *(verb)* make a tour of. take on tour. *She is touring the states of Spain, Germany and Denmark.*

Tourism – *(noun)* the commercial organization and operation of holidays and visits to places of interest. *The movie has promoted tourism in the state.*

Tourist – *(noun)* **1** a person who travels for pleasure. *Tourists receive a lot of special attention in this restaurant.* **2** a member of a touring sports team. *India lost to the tourists miserably.* *(verb)* travel as a tourist. *The state government sent a notice to European families touristing in the state.*

Tournament – *(noun)* **1** a series of contests between a number of competitors, competing for an overall prize. *The tournament was organized to improve the relations between the two countries.* **2** a medieval sporting event in which knights jousted with blunted weapons for a prize. *The knights were ready with the weapons for the tournament to begin.* **3** a modern event involving display of military techniques and exercises. *The Royal Tournament was scheduled for the next month.*

Tow – *(noun)* **1** the coarse and broken part of flax or hemp prepared for spinning. *The tow was ready for spinning.* **2** a bundle of untwisted natural or manmade fibres. *The hardware shop had tows of all kinds.*

Towards – *(preposition)* **1** in the direction of. *We drove towards the beach.* **2** getting nearer to a time or goal. *Moves towards peace talks have gained foreground.* **3** in relation to. *She has maintained a hostile attitude towards everyone.* **4** contributing to the cost of. *The state government contributed a huge amount towards the development of transport in the state.*

Towel – *(noun)* a piece of thick absorbent cloth or paper used for drying. *There were clean and fresh towels in the cupboard.* *(verb)* **1** dry with a towel. *Mother asked me to towel myself well after a bath.* **2** thrash or beat. *She toweled the boy mercilessly.*

Tower – *(noun)* **1** a tall, narrow building, either free standing or forming part of a building such as a church or castle. *The bell on the church tower rang non-stop.* **2** a tall structure that houses machinery, operators. etc. *The control tower was beaming the alarm repeatedly.* **3** a tall structure used as a receptacle or for storage. *The CD tower needed an alternative.* *(verb)* **1** rise to or reach a great height. *She towers over the rest of the kids in the class.* **2** soar up to a great, height, especially so as to be able to swoop down on prey. *The eagle towered and then swooped down on the rat.* **3** very important or influential. *She towers in her post over all her peers.* **4** very intense: a towering rage. *I saw a towering rage building up in him.*

Town – *(noun)* **1** a built up area with a name, defined boundaries, and local government, that is larger than a village and generally smaller than a city. the chief city or town of a region. *There were seven towns in the province.* **2** the central part of a neighbourhood, with its business or shopping area. *I thought of going to the town for some grocery shopping.* **3** densely populated areas, especially as contrasted with the country or suburbs. *The town is way more populated than the country.* **4** the permanent residents of a university town. often contrasted with gown. *There's been a growing rift between the town and the gown.* **5** another term for township in sense.*The population in the town has increased in the last few years.*

Town hall – *(noun)* a building used for the administration of local government. *The protestors gathered at the town hall to conduct their demonstration.*

Toxic – *(adjective)* poisonous. of, relating to, or caused by poison. *There have been reports of toxic water in certain areas.* *(noun)* poisonous substances. *The chemicals coming from this factory are toxic for the waterbody nearby.*

Toxin – *(noun)* a poison produced by a microorganism or other organism and acting as an antigen in the body. *The doctor could clearly spot harmful toxins in the patient's bloodstream.*

Toy – *(noun)* **1** an object for a child to play with, typically a model or miniature replica of something. a gadget or machine regarded as providing amusement for an adult. *She had a room overflowing with toys.* **2** denoting a diminutive breed or variety of dog. *I saw a toy poodle at the kennel nearby.* *(verb)* **1** consider casually or indecisively. treat in a superficially amorous way. *Don't toy around with my emotions.* **2** move or handle absent mindedly or nervously. eat or drink in an unenthusiastic or restrained way. *She was toying with the straw.*

Trace – *(noun)* each of the two side straps, chains, or ropes by which a horse is attached to a vehicle that it is pulling. *The traces were wearing off and the horse was revolting too.*

Track - *(verb)* tow a canoe along a waterway from the bank. *He was trying to track the canoe up the rapids.*

Tract - *(noun)* a short treatise in pamphlet form, typically on a religious subject. *I read out the tract we received from the Church.*

Traction - *(noun)* **1** the action of pulling a thing along a surface. the motive power used for pulling, especially on a railway. *There was a primitive vehicle used for animal traction at the museum.* **2** the application of a sustained pull on a limb or muscle, especially in order to maintain the position of a fractured bone or to correct a deformity. *Her arm is in traction.* **3** the grip of a tyre on a road or a wheel on a rail. *Her vehicle hit a huge rock on the road and lost traction.*

Tractor - *(noun)* a powerful motor vehicle with large rear wheels, used chiefly on farms for hauling equipment and trailers. *She worked in a factory that manufactures tractors.*

Trade - *(noun)* **1** the buying and selling of goods and services. a business of a particular kind. *All kinds of trade between the two countries have been stopped.* **2** a job requiring manual skills and special training. the people engaged in a particular area of business. *I learnt the fundamentals of construction trade when I was working with L&T.* **3** the practice of making one's living in business, as opposed to in a profession or from unearned income. *Back then, the king class looked at those in trade with contemptuously.* **4** a trade wind. *The North East Trades were on track this year too.* **5** a transfer; an exchange. *Players can demand a trade after five years.* *(verb)* **1** buy and sell goods and services. buy or sell. be bought and sold at a specified price. *He works as a middleman trading in luxury goods.* **2** exchange, especially as a commercial transaction. exchange a used article in part payment for another. exchange something of value, especially as part of a compromise. transfer to another club or team. *They trade oil for petrol.* **3** take advantage of. *The government is trading on fears of inflation.*

Trademark - *(noun)* **1** a symbol, word, or words legally registered or established by use as representing a company or product. *The invention got the trademark of the company.* **2** a distinctive characteristic or object. *The accident had all the trademark of the gang's planned murder.* *(verb)* provide with a trademark. *They are indulging in hoarding of trademark goods.*

Tradition - *(noun)* **1** the transmission of customs or beliefs from generation to generation, or the fact of being so passed on. a long established custom or belief passed on in this way. *Traditions were made by man and therefore are liable to be changed.* **2** an artistic or literary method or style established by an artist, writer, or movement, and subsequently followed by others. *The metaphysical aspect in Emmanuel Kant's traditions was the topic of the seminar.* 3 doctrine not explicit in the bible but held to derive from the oral teaching of Christ and the apostles. an ordinance of the oral law not in the torah but held to have been given by god to Moses. a saying or act ascribed to the prophet but not recorded in the Koran. *The father taught us the traditions from the Hadith.*

Traditional - *(adjective)* **1** of, relating to, or following tradition. *The traditional festivities of Onam were all set to begin.* **2** in the style of the early 20th century. *He follows the traditional style of jazz.*

Traffic - *(noun)* **1** vehicles moving on a public highway. *The traffic was being diverted to let the VIPs pass.* **2** the movement of ships or aircraft. *It is a peak hour of air traffic.* **3** the commercial transportation of goods or passengers. *There has been increased traffic of goods with aircrafts.* **4** the messages or signals transmitted through a communications system. *Internet is slow at this time because of peak hour data traffic.* **5** the action of trafficking. *The government has caught several people indulging in drug trafficking.* **6** dealings or communication between people. *Traffic has decreased over the years.* *(verb)* deal or trade in something illegal. *There has been illegal trafficking of medicinal drugs in this area.*

Tragedy- *(noun)* **1** an event causing great suffering. destruction, and distress. *The family was struck by a tragedy three years ago.* **2** a serious play with an unhappy ending, especially one concerning the downfall of the protagonist. *Shakespeare's tragedy had a great influence on me.*

Trail – *(noun)* **1** a mark or a series of sign or objects left behind by the passage of someone or something. a track or scent used in following someone or hunting an animal. *The police found a trail of blood at the site of crime.* **2** a long thin part stretching behind or hanging down from something. *We drove down in a trail of tourist cars.* **3** a beaten path through rough country. *The builders were designing country parks with nature trails.* **4** a route planned or followed for a particular purpose. *The zoo is well off the tourist trail.* **5** the rear end of a gun carriage, resting or sliding on the ground when the gun is unlimbered. *The trail lay hanging on the nail waiting for the gun to be limbered. (verb)* **1** draw or be drawn along behind. grow along the ground or so as to hang down. *He trailed a stick through the water.* **2** walk or move slowly or wearily. fade gradually before stopping. be losing to an opponent in a game or contest. *She hated the idea of trailing around the shops.* **3** follow the trail of. *The dog was trailing the smell of the handkerchief.* **4** advertise with a trailer. *The bank's plans have been extensively trailed.* **5** apply through a nozzle or spout to decorate ceramic ware. *She trailed the pot beautifully.*

Trailer – *(noun)* **1** an unpowered vehicle towed by another. the rear section of an articulated truck. a caravan. *He has been living in a trailer for the last few months.* **2** an extract from a film or programme used for advance advertising. *Terrific trailer can surely help mediocre movies.* **3** a trailing plant. *I used to think money plants can be trailing plant. (verb)* **1** advertise with a trailer. *The movie has been extensively trailered.* **2** transport by trailer. *The car can be easily trailered.*

Train– *(verb)* **1** teach a particular skill or type of behaviour through regular practice and instruction. be taught in such a way. *The students were being trained to become good professionals.* **2** make or become physically fit through a course of exercise and diet. *She trains twice a week.* **3** point or aim something at. *The gunman trained his gun behind the window.* **4** cause to grow in a particular direction or into a required shape. *They trained creepers all over their border walls.* **5** go by train. *She trained with me to Delhi.* **6** entice. *She trained him into the deal. (noun)* **1** a series of railway carriages or wagons moved as a unit by a locomotive or by integral motors. *Our train stood on platform 2.* **2** a number of vehicles or pack animals moving in a line. a retinue of attendants accompanying an important person. *A camel train was ready to start.* **3** a series of connected events, thoughts, etc. *The detective related the entire train of events from the beginning of the show till Julie's death.* **4** a long piece of trailing material attached to the back of a formal dress or robe. *She had a wonderful lace train behind her dress.* **5** a series of gears or other connected parts in machinery. *I bought a train of gears from the hardware shop.* **6** a trail of gunpowder for firing an explosive charge. *I warned him against firing as there was a train of gunpowder on the floor.*

Trance – *(noun)* **1** a half conscious state characterized by an absence of response to external stimuli, typically as induced by hypnosis or entered by a medium. *The patient entered into a state of trance as directed by the hypnotist.* **2** a state of abstraction. *The sage was believed to be in a constant state of trance.* **3** a type of electronic dance music characterized by hypnotic rhythms. *I love trance music. (verb)* put into a trance. *The hypnotist put the boy into a state of trance.*

Trainer – *(noun)* **1** a person who trains people or animals. an aircraft or simulator used to train pilots. *He enrolled at the farm as a horse trainer.* **2** a soft suitable for sports or casual wear. *I bought a nice pair of trainers from the shopping website.*

Training – *(noun)* the action of teacing a person or animal a particular skill. *She is undergoing rigorous training for the event.*

Trait – *(noun)* a distinguishing quality or characteristic. a genetically determined characteristic. *She did show instances of self denigration typical to her family trait.*

Tram – *(noun)* **1** a passenger vehicle powered by electricity conveyed by overhead cables, and running on rails laid in a public road. *There have been terror attack threats to the local trams.* **2** a low four wheeled cart or barrow used in coal mines. *Miners were having their lunch on the tram.*

Tramp – *(verb)* **1** walk heavily or noisily. *The little girl was tramping around the whole house.* **2** walk wearily or reluctantly over a long distance. *He was tired of tramping around the whole city.* *(noun)* **1** an itinerant homeless person who lives by begging or doing casual work. *Charlie Chaplin depicted the life of a tramp really well.* **2** the sound of heavy steps. *I could hear tramps downstairs.* **3** a long walk. *She left for a tramp long back.* **4** a cargo vessel running between many different ports rather than sailing a fixed route. *I saw a tramp steamer anchored at the harbor.* **5** a promiscuous woman. *It's a street frequented by tramps.* **6** a metal plate protecting the sole of a boot used for digging. *Save your feet from the tramp.*

Trample – *(verb)* **1** tread on and crush. *The child trampled all over the ants on the doorway.* **2** treat with contempt. *The mother told her daughter not to allow herself to be trampled upon by the world.* *(noun)* an act or sound of trampling. *I could hear the trample of many feet down the walkway.*

Tranquil – *(adjective)* free from disturbance; calm. *The sea was as tranquil as a sleeping baby.*

Tranquility – *(noun)* scene of peacefulness. *We went to the monastery in the hills seeking tranquility and peace of mind.*

Trans – *(prefix)* **1** across; beyond: transcontinental. on or to the other side of: transatlantic. *Their transatlantic journey had just begun.* **2** through: transonic. into another state or place: translate. transcending: transfinite. *One must try to transcend ones lesser energies.* **3** denoting molecules in which two particular atoms or groups lie on opposite sides of a given plane, in particular denoting an isomer in which substituents at opposite ends of a carbon-carbon double bond are also on opposite sides of the bond: 1,2 dichloroethene. *Stilbene has two isomers–trans-stilbene and cis-stilbene.*

Transact – *(verb)* to do business with a person or organisation. *Be careful while transacting on the phone.*

Transaction – *(noun)* **1** an instance of buying or selling. the action of conducting business. *Transactions on the phone are extremely risk prone.* **2** an exchange or interaction between people. *The book encourages a healthy transaction between the reader and the author.* **3** published reports of proceedings at the meetings of a learned society. *The transactions of the Theosophical Society were made public as soon as the investigation began.* **4** an input message to a computer system dealt with as a single unit of work. *You may begin the transaction to work out the software soon.*

Transcend – *(verb)* **1** be or go beyond the range or limits of. *The monk had transcended the limits of phenomenal life.* **2** surpass. *I doubt if I will ever transcend the skills of my mentor.*

Transcendent – *(adjective)* **1** transcending normal or physical human experience. existing apart from and not subject to the limitations of the material universe. often contrasted with immanent. *Philosophy is about the search for a transcendent level of knowledge.* **2** higher than or not included in any of Aristotle's ten categories. *Transcendent almost always means that God is completely outside or beyond the world.* **3** not realizable in experience. *Transcendental philosophy is an important aspect of Kant's theory of knowledge.*

Transcription – *(noun)* **1** a transcript. *They produced a complete transcription of the journal.* **2** the action or process of transcribing. *The funding includes transcriptions of early photocopies of the journal.* **3** a piece of music transcribed for a different instrument, voice, etc. *The teacher wrote a transcription for voice and viola.* **4** a form in which a speech sound or a foreign character is represented. *The usual transcription is given in parenthesis.*

Transfer - *(verb)* **1** move from one place to another. *Your money is being transferred from the headquarters to the home branch.* **2** move or cause to move to another department, occupation, etc. redirect to a new line or extension. *He has been transferred twice in the two years of his service already.* 3 change to another place, route, or means of transport during a journey. *Passengers have to transfer at Mumbai for onward international flights.* **4** make over the possession of to another. *We will transfer full management of the affairs to the locals.* **5** change by extension or metaphor. *The teacher taught us a transferred use of the English.* *(noun)* **1** an act of transferring. *We need an urgent transfer of funds to the state treasury.* **2** a small coloured picture or design on paper, which can be transferred to another surface by being pressed or heated. *The shop sold T-shirts with iron-on transfers.* **3** a ticket allowing a passenger to change from one public transport vehicle to another as part of a single journey. *You must get a ticket to be able to transfer on to that train.*

Transfix - *(verb)* **1** make motionless with horror, wonder, or astonishment. *He was transfixed with the sorrow in her eyes.* **2** piece with a sharp implement or weapon. *The snake was transfixed in the talons of the eagle.*

Transform - *(verb)* subject to or undergo transformation. change the voltage of by electromagnetic induction. *We have learnt that energy can be transformed to light.* *(noun)* the product of a transformation. a rule for making a transformation. *Your transformation needs rules to be implemented.*

Transfusion - *(noun)* act of transferring blood or other fluid into a person or animal. *Blood transfusion was the only option she had for a treatment.*

Transgress -*(verb)* **1** go beyond the limits set by a moral principle, standard, law, etc. *You will be punished if you transgress the rules I have laid out for this house.* **2** spread over an area of land. *Each continent has been transgressed by continental seas.*

Transient - *(adjective)* **1** lasting only for a short time. *Fame is transient, so don't hold on to it.* **2** staying or working in a place for a short time only. *The labour force here is extremely transient.* *(noun)* **1** a transient person. *She is transient in her field of work.* **2** a momentary variation in current, voltage, or frequency. *We were going through a transient voltage spell.*

Transistor - *(noun)* **1** a semiconductor device with three connections, capable of amplification and rectification. *The mechanical professor explained how to fix a transistor connection.* **2** a portable radio using circuits containing transistors. *She carries her transistor everywhere.*

Transit - *(noun)* **1** the carrying of people or things from one place to another. the conveyance of passengers on public transport. *His instrument was damaged in transit.* **2** an act of passing through or across a place. the passage of a planet across the face of the sun, or of a moon across the face of a planet. *The astrologer mentioned something about the transit of mercury over the sun's disc.* *(verb)* pass across or through. *The roads are too small for the new buses to transit through them.*

Transition - *(noun)* **1** the process of changing from one state or condition to another. a period of such change. *The girl has been through a phase of transition and has come out way more mature and sensible than she was.* **2** a momentary modulation. *The transition between the notes was easily visible.*

Transitive - *(adjective)* **1** able to take a direct object e.g. saw in he saw the donkey. the opposite of intransitive. *The English Grammar teacher explained the significance and application of transitive verbs in language.* **2** such that, if it applies between successive members taken in order. *If A is equal to B and B is equal to C, then A is equal to C; this forms a transitive relation in logic and mathematics.*

Translate - *(verb)* **1** express the sense of in another language. be expressed or be capable of being expressed in another language. *She works as a translator at the Embassy.* **2** be converted or convert something into another form or medium. convert to an amino acid sequence during protein synthesis. *The food is translated into a form of amino acid and subsequently into protein.* **3** move from one place or condition to another. move to another see or pastoral charge. *He was translated from Salisbury to Durham.* **4** cause to undergo translation. *It's like she has been translated from familiar surroundings to a foreign court.*

Translucent – *(adjective)* allowing light to pass through partially; semi transparent. *She kept a translucent sheet of cloth over the window.*

Transmission – *(noun)* **1** the action or process of transmitting or the state of being transmitted. *The transmission of the virus is facilitated by the rains.* **2** a programme or signal that is transmitted. *Television transmissions were affected by the meteor shower that happened last night.* **3** the mechanism by which power is transmitted from an engine to the axle in a motor vehicle. *The bike has a three speed automatic transmission.*

Transmit – *(verb)* **1** cause to pass on from one place or person to another. communicate. *The sages of ancient Indian transmitted their knowledge to their students who in turn went on to transmit it down the generations.* **2** broadcast or send out an electrical signal or a radio or television programme. *I asked the reporter when my interview will be transmitted on television.* **3** allow heat, light, etc. to pass through a medium. *It is the three bones in the ear that transmit sound waves to the inner ears.*

Transparent – *(adjective)* **1** allowing light to pass through so that objects behind can be distinctly seen. *There was a transparent sheet on the table.* **2** obvious or evident. *She is very transparent as a person.* 3 open to public scrutiny. *The masses are now seeking a transparent enquiry into the corruption scandal.* **4** transmitting heat or other radiation without distortion. *CFCs and water vapour are virtually transparent to incoming short-wave solar radiation.* **5** functioning without the user being aware of its presence. *They programmed a transparent interface.*

Transparency – *(noun)* **1** the condition of being transparent. *The masses were seeking transparency from the government.* **2** a positive transparent photograph printed on plastic or glass, and viewed using a slide projector. *The photographer was studying the colour transparency of the Niagara Falls.*

Transplant – *(verb)* **1** transfer to another place or situation. replant in another place. *The club was transplanted from its current location to the erstwhile community centre.* **2** take and implant it in another part of the body or in another body. *The kidney was transplanted from the donor's body to the child's.* *(noun)* **1** an operation in which an organ or tissue is transplanted. *The doctor recommended a liver transplant to help the man survive his crisis.* **2** a person or thing that has been transplanted. *It was like the child had been uprooted and transplanted to a completely new surrounding.*

Transport – *(verb)* **1** take or carry from one place to another by means of a vehicle, aircraft, or ship. send to a penal colony. *Arrangements were being made to transport the criminal to the jail in the outskirts of the city.* **2** overwhelm with a strong emotion, especially joy. *She was transported with joy.* *(noun)* **1** a system or means of transporting. the action of transporting or the state of being transported. a large vehicle, ship, or aircraft for carrying troops or stores. a convict who was transported to a penal colony. *New options need to be considered regarding the transport of air freight, apart from lorries alone.* 2 overwhelmingly strong emotions. *Music can often transport people with joy.*

Transpose – *(verb)* **1** cause to exchange places. *You will realize the truth of the situation only if you and the opposing party were transposed.* **2** transfer to a different place or context. write or play in a different key from the original. *The basses are transposed down a octave.* *(noun)* a matrix obtained from a given matrix by interchanging rows and columns. *The new matrix is called Transpose B.*

Transverse – *(adjective)* situated or extending across something. *From the transverse hall, the stairway ascends.*

Trap – *(noun)* basalt or a similar dark, fine grained igneous rock. *There have been sightings of trap in the mines here.*

Trapeze – *(noun)* **1** a horizontal bar hanging by two ropes and free to swing, used by acrobats in a circus. *The trapeze artist is my favorite sight at the circus.* **2** a harness attached by a cable to a dinghy's mast, enabling a sailor to balance the boat by leaning out backwards over the windward side. *The trapeze snapped and the sailor went crashing into the water.*

Trash – *(noun)* **1** waste material; refuse. *The trash was accumulating and the garbage van was late.* **2** worthless writing, art, etc. *There have been too many trash submissions this week, I reported to the editor.* **3** a person or people regarded as being of very low social standing. *The trash class knows little or nothing about sophistication.* **4** the leaves, tops, and crushed stems of sugar cane, used as fuel. *Do not throw away the trash of sugarcanes.* *(verb)* **1** wreck or destroy. *Her dreams were trashed miserably.* **2** criticize severely. *The movie was trashed by the critics.* **3** intoxicated with alcohol or drugs. *You look trashed.* **4** strip of their outer leaves to ripen them faster. *The trash of the plants is nice to watch sometimes.*

Trauma – *(noun)* **1** a deeply distressing experience. *She has been through the trauma of losing her parents.* **2** physical injury. *The trauma of the accident was too much for her body to take.* **3** emotional shock following a stressful event. *She had to relive the whole trauma in the courtroom.*

Travail – *(noun)* painful or laborious effort. labour pains. *The woman in travails was really loud.* *(verb)* undergo such effort. *The travails of life sometimes lead to happy endings.*

Travel –*(verb)* **1** make a journey. journey along or through a region. *I will be travelling across the country next month.* **2** move or go. of a move quickly. *We're planning to conduct a travelling exhibition of his famous works.* **3** withstand a journey without impairment. *Some wines travel poorly.* *(noun)* **1** the action of travelling. journeys, especially abroad. sufficiently compact for use when travelling. *He enjoyed the scenery but hated the travel.* **2** the range, rate, or mode of motion of a part of a machine. *There are two switches that indicate when the valve has reached the end of its travel.*

Traveller – *(noun)* **1** a person who is travelling or who often travels. *I made friends with random travelers during my journey.* **2** a gypsy. *We spotted some travelers in their circus caravans and decided to stop and talk to them.* **3** a person who holds new age values and leads an itinerant and unconventional lifestyle. *I had decided to live a traveler's life for the rest of my life.* **4** an itinerant worker. *He is more a traveler than a diligent worker, I feel.*

Traverse – *(verb)* **1** travel or extend across or through. cross a rock face by means of a series of sideways movements from one practicable line of ascent or descent to another. ski diagonally across losing only a little height. *He traversed the hills and the forests.* **2** move back and forth or sideways. turn to face a different direction. *A pipe was traversed through the tunnel.* **3** deny in pleading. oppose or thwart a plan. *The plaintiff must assert certain facts, which if traversed, he would be put to prove.* *(noun)* **1** an act of traversing. a zigzag course taken by a ship because winds or currents prevent it from sailing directly. *Trekking through the Grand Canyon may involve exposed climbs, traverses and descents.* **2** a part of a structure that extends or is fixed across something. a gallery extending from side to side of a church or other building. *There were three jewels in the traverse of the cross and two in the body.* **3** a mechanism enabling a large gun to be traversed. the sideways movement of a part on a machine. *They used the power traverse to practice firing at multiple targets.* **4** a single line of survey, usually plotted from compass bearings and chained or paced distances between angular points. *The area was surveyed with a traverse.* **5** a pair of right angled bends incorporated in a trench to avoid enfilading fire. *He crept up to the traverse and threw grenade.*

Travesty – *(noun)* an absurd or grotesque misrepresentation. *A travesty of the trial will not* *be dealt with benignly. (verb)* represent in such a way. *By travestying the situations of his family in the play, he has distanced himself from them even more.*

Trawl – *(verb)* **1** fish or catch with a trawl net or seine. *The boat was out in the sea trawling for big fish.* **2** search thoroughly. *They have been trawling through the files to get some evidence for their case. (noun)* **1** an act of trawling. *A simple trawl through their case files will give you enough evidence.* **2** a large wide mouthed fishing net dragged by a boat along the bottom of the sea or a lake. *The trawl followed the boat threateningly.* **3** a long sea fishing line along which are tied buoys supporting baited hooks on short lines. *The fish could see the trawl nearing their territory.*

Tray – *(noun)* a flat, shallow container with a raised rim, typically used for carrying or holding things. *The girl brought a tray of tea to be served to the guests.*

Treacherous – *(adjective)* **1** guilty of or involving betrayal or deception. *The treacherous minister was banished from the kingdom.* **2** having hidden or unpredictable dangers. *The plan was treacherous, so I warned her.*

Treachery – *(noun)* betrayal of trust, faith. *The king accused the minister of indulging in treachery.*

Treacle – *(noun)* molasses, golden syrup. *I bought some treacle syrup from the grocer's and stored it in my larder.*

Tread – *(verb)* **1** walk in a specified way. walk on or along. *Tread carefully on the path as its pebbled and may hurt your tender feet.* **2** press down or crush with the feet. *Tread the grapes to make wine. (noun)* **1** a manner or the sound of walking. *I heard my father treading down the attic.* **2** the top surface of a step or stair. *The tread board was loose so we must climb the stairs carefully.* 3 the thick moulded part of a vehicle tyre that grips the road. the part of a wheel that touches the ground or rail. *The tread was sticking to the tar on the road.* **4** the part of the sole of a shoe that rests on the ground. *The tread of my shoe was flapping noisily.* **5** the upper surface of a railway track, in contact with the wheels. *The engineers were trying to repair the tread on the railway track.*

Treadle – *(noun)* a lever worked by the foot and imparting motion to a machine. *I made a treadle for him to complete his school project. (verb)* operate by a treadle. *He was treadling the machine made for his school project.*

Treason – *(noun)* **1** the crime of betraying one's country, especially by attempting to kill or overthrow the sovereign or government. *The party leader was arrested on charges of treason and corruption.* **2** the crime of murdering a master or husband. *The maid had indulged in treason and was sentenced to death.*

Treasure – *(noun)* **1** a quantity of precious metals, gems, or other valuable objects. a very valuable object. *Legend says that there is a pirate's treasure down in the wreck.* **2** a much loved or highly valued person. *She is a treasure to this company. (verb)* **1** keep carefully a valuable or valued item. *My rag doll is my treasure that I have never parted with for 25 years.* **2** value highly. *I sincerely treasure the moments I got to spend with the team.*

Treasurer – *(noun)* a person appointed to manage finance of a company, society or other body. *He has been working as the party's treasurer for five years now.*

Treasury – *(noun)* **1** the funds or revenue of a state, institution, or society. the government department responsible for the overall management of the economy. *The party leader wondered how he would tell the party that the treasury was almost empty.* **2** a place where treasure is stored. *The king kept the peace and filled the treasury.* **3** a collection of valuable or delightful things. *She has a treasury of the most valuable paintings and sculptures from around the world.*

Treat – *(verb)* **1** behave towards or deal with in a certain way. present or discuss a subject. *You must learn to treat your elders with respect.* **2** give medical care or attention to. *She was treated for a deep wound on her wrist.* **3** apply a process or a substance to. *Please treat this water* *with some cleaning chemical and make it edible.* **4** provide someone with at one's expense. do or have something very pleasurable. *I treated her to a sumptuous feast.* **5** negotiate terms. *There were reports that he was treating with the enemy.* *(noun)* **1** a surprise gift, event, etc. that gives great pleasure. *The friends have been demanding a treat for my promotion.* **2** an act of treating someone to something. *It was my treat, there was no doubt!*

Treatise – *(noun)* a written work dealing formally and systematically with a subject. *She wrote a treatise on Indian political theory.*

Treatment – *(noun)* **1** the process or manner of treating someone or something in a certain way. the presentation or discussion of a subject. *The bill declared equal treatment for men and women in the issue of remarriage.* **2** medical care for an illness or injury. *She needs urgent treatment for her condition.* **3** the use of a substance or process to preserve or give particular properties to something. *Treatment of hazardous waste is very expensive.* **4** used to indicate that something is done enthusiastically or vigorously. *A bit of soft-shoe shuffle got the full treatment.*

Treaty – *(noun)* a formally concluded and ratified agreement between states. *The two countries signed a treaty regarding the distribution of oil.*

Treble – *(noun)* **1** a high pitched voice, especially a boy's singing voice. *The boy had a brilliant treble that got everybody's notice.* **2** denoting a relatively high pitched member of a family of instruments. the smallest and highest pitched bell of a ring or set. *We were asked to reduce the treble to make the melody perfect.* **3** the high frequency output of a radio or audio system, corresponding to the treble in music. *I asked my brother to reduce the treble of the music system.*

Tree – *(noun)* **1** a woody perennial plant typically with a single stem or trunk growing to a considerable height and bearing lateral branches. *We had different kinds of trees in our garden.* **2** a wooden structure or part of a structure. the cross on which Christ was crucified. a gibbet. *Everybody had tears in their eyes by the time the Father reached the part of the Christ and the tree.* **3** a diagram with a structure of branching connecting lines, representing different processes and relationships. *I drew a tree diagram to explain the hierarchy to the team.* *(verb)* **1** force to take refuge in a tree. *This lot should be treed so that the house will be shaded in the summer.* **2** force into a difficult situation. *Dogs like to tree squirrels.*

Trek – *(noun)* a long arduous journey, especially one made on foot. a leg or stage of a journey. *She is planning a trek up the mountains for sometime end of the month.* *(verb)* go on a trek. migrate or journey by ox wagon. draw a vehicle or pull a load. *We've been trekking for five hours now.*

Tremble – *(verb)* shake involuntarily, typically as a result of anxiety, excitement, or frailty. be in a state of extreme apprehension. shake or quiver slightly. *She was trembling with fever.* *(noun)* **1** a trembling feeling, movement, or sound. *I could feel the tremble in his voice.* **2** a physical or emotional condition marked by trembling. *Her Parkinson's disease is what makes her hand tremble.*

Tremendous – *(adjective)* **1** very great in amount, scale, or intensity. inspiring awe or dread. *Scaling that peak was a tremendous achievement by the team.* **2** extremely good or impressive; excellent. *She gave a tremendous performance on stage yesterday.*

Tremor – *(noun)* **1** an involuntary quivering movement. a slight earthquake. *Tremors have been felt in the nearby areas of the epicenter.* **2** a sudden feeling of fear or excitement. *She felt a tremor of joy when she heard the news.* *(verb)* undergo a tremor or tremors. *The old lady could not hide the tremor in her voice.*

Tremulous – *(adjective)* shaking or quivering slightly. timid, nervous. *She gave a tremulous smile.*

Trench – *(noun)* **1** a long, narrow ditch. a ditch of this type dug by troops to provide shelter from enemy fire. *The car was parked at the tip of the trench.* **2** a long, narrow, deep depression in the ocean bed, typically running parallel to a plate boundary and marking a subduction zone. *Scientists have found a wreck in a trench in the Atlantic.* *(verb)* **1** dig a trench or trenches in. turn over the earth of by digging a succession of adjoining ditches. *She trenched the ground for more than 6 feet.* **2** border closely on; encroach upon. *This will surely trench upon the freedom and liberty of citizens.*

Trend – *(noun)* **1** a general direction in which something is developing or changing. *A trend towards part time jobs has begun in the East.* **2** a fashion. *Yellow is the current trend.* *(verb)* bend or turn away in a specified direction. change or develop on a general direction. *Unemployment is still trending down.*

Trepidation – *(noun)* **1** a feeling of fear or agitation about something that may happen. *There was trepidation in the air about the impending blow.* **2** trembling motion. *The trepidation was due to an illness and not anxiety, the doctor informed us.*

Trespass – *(verb)* **1** enter someone's land or property without their permission. make unfair claims on or take advantage of something. *There was a board outside the boundary wall stating that trespassers will be prosecuted.* **2** commit an offence against a person or a set of rules. *Those trespassing against Islamic prescriptions may often have to pay with their lives.* *(noun)* **1** entry to a person's land or property without their permission. *Cross the path but make sure you don't trespass into the land nearby.* **2** a sin; an offence. *The worst trespass against the Islamic law is to throw away the burkha.*

Tresses – *(noun)* long lock of a woman's hair. *Many men have been victims of the charm of her eyes, her long tresses.*

Tri – *comb. form* three; having three: triathlon. containing three atoms or groups of a specified kind: trichloroethane. *Today's experiment was using tri-chloroethylene.*

Trial - *(noun)* **1** a formal examination of evidence in order to decide guilt in a case of criminal or civil proceedings. *The trial for her case is scheduled sometime early next month.* **2** a test of performance, qualities, or suitability. a sports match to test the ability of players eligible for selection to a team. a test of individual ability on a motorcycle. an event in which horses or dogs compete or perform. *The sports trials will begin at 11am.* **3** something that tests a person's endurance or forbearance. *Marriage is about experiencing the trials and tribulations of life together.* *(verb)* **1** test to assess its suitability or performance. *The materials are to be trialed by all the teachers.* **2** compete in trials. *The boys trialed for the college admissions.*

Triangle – *(noun)* **1** a plane figure with three straight sides and three angles. *The teacher taught us equilateral triangles today.* **2** something in the form of a triangle. a drawing instrument in the form of a right angled triangle. a frame of three halberds joined at the top to which a soldier was bound for flogging. *The soldier was hanging from the triangle by the time the forces reached to save him.* **3** a musical instrument consisting of a steel rod bent into a triangle, sounded with a rod. *I love playing the musical triangle.* **4** an emotional relationship involving a couple and a third person with whom one of them is involved. *No one could guess what end this love triangle would come to.* **5** a small brownish moth of oak and beech woods. *There was a weird looking triangle on the tree.*

Tribe – *(noun)* **1** a social division in a traditional society consisting of linked families or communities with a common culture and dialect. each of several political divisions. a distinctive close knit social or political group. large numbers of people. *Relief has been sent to the tribes on the island affected by the tsunami.* **2** a taxonomic category that ranks above genus and below family or subfamily. *Sharks belong to the tribe of fish.*

Tribal – *(adjective)* of or characteristic of a tribe or tribes. characterized by a tendency to form groups or by strong, group loyalty. (noun) members of tribal communities, especially in the Indian subcontinent. *There was tribal jewellery exhibited at the fair.*

Tribulation – *(noun)* a state of great trouble or suffering. a cause of this. *They have been through trials and tribulations all their life.*

Tribunal – *(noun)* **1** a body established to settle certain types of dispute. *The case of the insurance claim was taken to the tribunal.* **2** a court of justice. *The tribunal was to announce the judgment today.* **3** a seat or bench for a judge or judges. *She now works at the tribunal.*

Tributary – *(noun)* **1** a river or stream flowing into a larger river or lake. *The tributary was as big as the river itself.* **2** a person or state that pays tribute to another state or ruler. *Tributaries of the MohenjoDaro were discovered.*

Tribute – *(noun)* **1** an act, statement, or gift that is intended to show gratitude, respect, or admiration. something resulting from and indicating the worth if something else. *His victory was a tribute to his persistence.* **2** payment made periodically by one state or ruler to another, especially as a sign of dependence. *The princely states gave their tributes on a monthly basis.* **3** a proportion of ore or its equivalent, paid to a miner for his work, or to the owner or lessor of a mine. *The owner paid the miner his tribute for the work.*

Trick – *(noun)* **1** a cunning or skilful act or scheme intended to deceive or outwit someone. a mischievous practical joke. a skilful act performed for entertainment. an illusion. intended to mystify or create an illusion: a trick question. liable to fail; defective: a trick knee. *The magician performed a trick of the light.* **2** a peculiar or characteristic habit or mannerism. *She had a trick of playing with words.* **3** a sequence of cards forming a single round of play. *Let's play trick!* **4** a prostitute's client. *The pimp got the wrong trick today.* **5** a sailor's turn at the helm, usually lasting for two or four hours. *How long is your trick?*

Trickery – *(noun)* the practice of deception. *His trickery cannot escape the eyes of the warden.*

Trickle – *(verb)* **1** flow in a small stream. *Water was trickling from the roof.* **2** gradually benefit the poorest as a result of the increasing wealth of the richest. *The relief was beginning to trickle in, much to the benefit of the villagers.* **3** come or go slowly or gradually. *The visitors for the party were trickling in gradually.* *(noun)* **1** a small flow of liquid. *A trickle of blood fell on her arm.* **2** a small group or number of people or things moving slowly. *The trickle of visitors was now an uncontrollable flow!*

Tricky – *(adjective)* **1** requiring care and skill because difficult or awkward. *The question was tricky and needed careful analysis.* **2** deceitful, crafty, or skilful. *She was really tricky for a girl.*

Tricycle – *(noun)* a vehicle similar to a bicycle, but having three wheels, two at the back and one at the front. a three wheels motor vehicle for a disabled driver. *I asked the little girl to first be confident of riding a tricycle before moving on to a grown-up's cycle.* *(verb)* ride on a tricycle. *She has caught on to tricycling big time!*

Trident – *(noun)* a three pronged spear, especially as an attribute of Poseidon or Britannia. *The trident stood proudly on the mast of the pirate ship.*

Trifle – *(noun)* **1** a thing of little value or importance. a small amount. *Don't trouble mother with such trifles when she is working.* **2** a cold dessert of sponge cake and fruit covered with layers of custard, jelly and cream. *I want jelly and fruit trifle for dessert.* *(verb)* **1** treat without seriousness or respect. *Don't trifle matters that are actually more serious than they seem.* **2** talk or act frivolously. *Life is too short to be trifled away.*

Trigger – *(noun)* **1** a device that releases a spring or catch and so sets off a mechanism, especially in order to fire a gun. *The thief's finger was on the trigger, all set to shoot.* **2** an event that causes something to happen. *We were still analyzing what exactly was the trigger to the fire.* *(verb)* **1** cause to function. *Something must have triggered off the fire.* **2** cause to happen or exist. *Stress and working overtime triggered his heart issues.*

Trigonometry – *(noun)* the branch of mathematics concerned with the relations of the sides and angles of triangles and with the relevant functions of any angles. *Trigonometry is one of my favourite topics in mathematics.*

Trillion - *(cardinal number)* large number or amount. *The fraud was of a whopping six trillion dollars.*

Trilogy - *(noun)* a group of three related novels, plays, films, etc. a series of three tragedies performed one after the other. *The Lord of the Rings trilogy is one of Hollywood's best made movies.*

Trim - *(verb)* **1** make neat by cutting away irregular or unwanted parts. cut off irregular or unwanted parts. reduce the size, amount, or number of. *I will pay you to trim the hedges.* **2** decorate especially along its edges. *She added some trims to the decorations.* **3** adjust to take advantage of the wind. adjust the balance of, by rearranging its cargo or using its controls. *The captain began to trim sideways.* **4** adapt one's views to the prevailing political trends for personal advancement. *He is clever enough to trim when required. (noun)* **1** additional decoration, especially along the edges. the upholstery or interior lining of a car. *You need to change the trims in the car this time.* **2** an act of trimming. *He began by trimming the edges of the cake.* **3** the state of being in good order. *He always likes to see the table trimmed to perfection.* **4** the degree to which an aircraft can be maintained at a constant altitude. *The only problem pilot reported was the need to constant readjust the trim of the aircraft.*

Trinity - *(noun)* **1** the three persons of the Christian godhead; father, son, and holy spirit. *We were taught many stories about the Holy Trinity.* **2** a group of three people or things. *These three friends were popularly known as the trinity in school.*

Trio - *(noun)* a set or group of three. a group of three musicians. a composition written for three musicians. the central section of a minuet, scherzo, or march. a set of three aces, kings, queens, jacks, or tens held in one hand. *The trio set out to try their luck in the jungle.*

Trip - *(verb)* **1** catch one's foot on something and stumble or fall. make a mistake. *She tripped and fell flat on her face.* **2** walk, run, or dance with quick light steps. *The kids came tripping and smiling.* **3** activate especially contact with a switch. disconnect automatically as a safety measure. *There has been a power trip so switch off the mains soon.* **4** release and raise from the seabed by means of a cable. turn from a horizontal to a vertical position for lowering. *The engineer suggested we trip the metal sheet.* **5** experience hallucinations induced by taking a psychedelic drug, especially LSD. *He is always on a cocain trip these days. (noun)* **1** a journey or excursion, especially for pleasure. *We are going on a trip to the beach this weekend.* **2** an instance of tripping or falling. a mistake. *I will not tolerate any more tripping from this group.* **3** a hallucinatory experience caused by taking a psychedelic drug. an exciting or stimulating experience. a self indulgent attitude or activity: a power trip. *The drugs entice you by promising a unique trip, but never fall for it.* **4** a device that trips a mechanism, circuit, etc. *The electrician handed me the trip.* **5** a light, lively movement of a person's feet. *She showed me how to trip.*

Triple -*(adjective)* **1** consisting of or involving three parts, things, or people. *Having eggs ensure triple benefits.* **2** having three times the usual size, quality, or strength. *The elephant weighs more than triple that of a dog. (noun)* **1** a thing that is three times as large as usual or is made up of three parts. *Pull out one of the triple boxes and check.* **2** a sporting contest in which each side has three players. *Are you prepared to play triples?* **3** a system of change ringing using seven bells, with three pairs changing places each time. *You can hear the triple every night at twelve.* **4** a hit which enables the batter to reach third base. *He hit a fine triple and won the match for his team. (verb).* make or become three times as much or as many. *Would you like to triple the fun?*

Triplet- *(noun)* **1** one of three children or animals born at the same birth. *We never knew Mary was one of triplets.* **2** a group of three equal notes to be performed in the time of two or four. *He is an expert at playing the triplet.* **3** a set of three rhyming lines of verse. *I have composed a triplet in his honor.* **4** a group of three similar things, e.g. lines in a spectrum. *Count the number of triplets found in this figure.*

Tripod – *(noun)* **1** a three legged stand for supporting a camera or other apparatus. *She set the camera on the tripod and waited.* **2** a stool, table, or cauldron resting on three legs. the bronze altar at Delphi on which a priestess sat to utter oracles. *The tripod is an integral part of any camping trip.*

Trite – *(adjective)* lacking originality or freshness; dull on account of overuse. *I couldn't read through the trite story.*

Triumph – *(noun)* **1** a great victory or achievement. the state of being victorious or successful. joy or satisfaction resulting from a success or victory. a highly successful example: the arrest was a triumph of international co operation. *He has led his side to many a triumphs.* **2** the processional entry of a victorious general into ancient Rome. *There was a triumph march that day. (verb)* **1** achieve a triumph. rejoice or exult at a triumph. *This is the first triumph for his team in a year.* **2** ride into ancient Rome after a victory. *The victorious army walked up a triumph.*

Triumphant – *(adjective)* having won a battle or contest; victorious. jubilant after a victory or achievement. *We heard their triumphant shouts for a mile around.*

Trivia – *plural (noun)* unimportant details or pieces of information. *Do not waste time on such trivia.*

Trolley – *(noun)* **1** a large wheeled metal basket or frame used for transporting heavy or unwieldy items such as luggage or supermarket purchases. a small table on wheels or castors, used especially to convey food and drink. *Take the luggage on this trolley to the train.* **2** a wheel attached to a pole, used for collecting current from an overhead electric wire to drive a tram. *The boys enjoyed watching the trolley brush the wires above and emitting the sparks.* **3** short for trolleybus or trolley car. *The thief jumped into a parked trolley and sped away.*

Trombone – *(noun)* a large brass wind instrument having an extendable slide with which different notes are made. *She couldn't stand her son playing the trombone at night.*

Troop – *(noun)* **1** soldiers or armed forces. *Lead this troop safely.* **2** a cavalry unit commanded by a captain. a unit of artillery and armoured formation. a group of three or move scout patrols. *The troop has been missing since last night.* **3** a group of people or animals of a particular kind. *I think you will be facing troops of people revolting on the streets by tomorrow. (verb)* come or go together or in large numbers. *Let us troop out of the palace with heads held high.*

Trophy – *(noun)* **1** a cup or other decorative object awarded as a prize for a victory or success. a souvenir of an achievement, especially a head of an animal taken when hunting. *She needs an entire room to exhibit all her trophies.* **2** the weapons of a defeated army set up as a memorial of victory. *The trophy was hung in the center of the room for all to see*

Tropic– *(adjective)* **1** relating to, consisting of, or exhibiting tropism. *This plant exhibits tropic behavior against the sun.* **2** variant spelling of trophic. *This leaf is of high tropic value.*

Trot – *(noun)* a Trotskyism or supporter of extreme left wing views. *Do not get into an argument with that trot.*

Trouble – *(noun)* **1** difficulty or problems. malfunction; failure to work property. effort or exertion. a cause of worry or inconvenience. a situation in which one is liable to incur punishment or blame. *I blame you for all out troubles.* **2** public unrest or disorder. *If you take such a decision, there will be trouble for sure. (verb)* cause distress, pain, or inconvenience to. showing or experiencing problems or anxiety. be distressed or anxious about. make the effort required to do something. *Do not trouble me with trivial problems.*

Trough – *(noun)* **1** a long, narrow open container for animals to eat or drink out of. a similar container, e.g. one for growing plants. *Plant the seeds in a trough and place it on the window sill.* **2** a channel used to convey a liquid. a long hollow in the earth's surface. *We need to dig up a trough here.* **3** an elongated region of low barometric pressure. *The cool winds blow into* *the trough.* **4** a hollow between two wave crests in the sea. *The waves rose and fell back to form a rhythmic rise and trough.* **5** a region around the minimum on a curve of variation of a quantity. a point of low activity or achievement. *There seem to be more troughs on the graph as we move from one month to the next.*

Trounce – *(verb)* defeat heavily in a contest. rebuke or punish severely. *He will never forget this trounce.*

Trousers – *plural (noun)* an outer garment covering the body from the waist to the ankles, with a separate part for each leg. *He walked in with completely drenched shirt and trousers.*

Trousseau – *(noun)* the clothes, linen, and other belongings collected by a bride for her marriage. *Have you finalized your wedding trousseau?*

Trout – *(noun)* an edible fish of the salmon family, chiefly inhabiting fresh water. *Let us serve them trout this evening. (verb)* fishing for trout. *This is your night to go fishing for trout.*

Trowel – *(noun)* **1** a small hand held tool with a flat, pointed blade, used to apply and spread mortar or plaster. *The mason used his trowel to flatten the mud.* **2** a small hand held tool with a curved scoop for lifting plants or earth. *Use the trowel to dig out the weeds. (verb)* apply or spread with or as if with a trowel. *Trowel down this rocky path.*

Truant– *(noun)* a pupil who stays away from school without leave or explanation. *He may be a truant so keep an eye on him. (verb)* stay away from school without leave or explanation. *You will be punished for being truant all week. (adjective)* wandering; straying: her truant husband. *She is unaware of having such a truant husband.*

Truce – *(noun)* an agreement between enemies to stop fighting for a certain time. *The king offered a truce in order to avoid a war.*

Truck – *(noun)* **1** barter. the payment of workers in kind or with vouchers rather than money. *Remember you will be payed in truck here.* **2** small wares. odds and ends. *I do not mind being paid a truck as long as I get to work under his guidance.* **3** market garden produce, especially vegetables. *This market is known for its truck produce. (verb)* barter or exchange. *In olden times, one followed the truck method of exchange.*

Trudge – *(verb)* walk slowly and with heavy steps, typically because of exhaustion or harsh conditions. *He trudged up the steep path. (noun)* a difficult or laborious walk. *I cannot trudge any further.*

True – *(adjective)* **1** in accordance with fact or reality. rightly or strictly so called; genuine: true love. real or actual. *This is a true story.* **2** accurate or exact. exactly in tune. north. correctly positioned or aligned; upright or level. *This is the true time for flowering.* **3** loyal or faithful. accurately conforming to a standard or expectation. *I believe you are a true gentleman.* **4** honest: all good men and true. *He is always true to his word. (verb)* bring into the exact shape or position required. *Take up your true positions.*

Truly – *(adverb)* **1** in a truthful way. *This is a truly beautiful scene.* **2** to the fullest degree; genuinely or properly. absolutely or completely. *I am truly repentant today.* **3** in actual fact; really. *This was truly the best birthday ever.* **4** loyally or faithfully. *I am truly indebted to you.*

Trumpet – *(noun)* **1** a brass musical instrument with a flared bell and a bright, penetrating tone. an organ stop with a quality resembling that of a trumpet. *Go out and practice your trumpet someplace else.* **2** something shaped like a trumpet, especially the tubular corona of a daffodil flower. *The wet trumpets gleamed in the sunlight.* **3** the loud cry of an elephant. *We heard the lost cub trumpet to its mother. (verb)* **1** play a trumpet. *I want you to play the trumpet for the band tomorrow.* **2** make its characteristic loud cry. *I nearly jumped when he let out a trumpet.* **3** proclaim widely or loudly. *She always trumpets her disappointments in public.*

Truncate – *(verb)* shorten by cutting off the top or the end. *Truncate the ends and fit the pipe into the slot. (adjective)* ending abruptly as if truncated. *The long scene needs to be truncated to fit into the film.*

Truncheon – *(noun)* **1** a short thick stick carried as a weapon by a police officer. *The robber stared at the police's truncheon.* **2** a staff or baton acting as a symbol of authority, especially that used by the earl marshal. *The naughty subordinates hid their senior's truncheon.*

Trundle – *(verb)* move slowly and unevenly on or as if on wheels. *The drunk trundle out of the bar every night.* *(noun)* an act of trundling. *Stop trundling or you will lose balance and fall on the road.*

Trunk – *(noun)* **1** the main woody stem of a tree as distinct from its branches and roots. the main part of an artery, nerve, or other structure from which smaller branches arise. *This tree has the softest trunk in the world.* **2** a person's or animal's body apart from the limbs and head. *The body bore marks all along its trunk.* **3** the elongated, prehensile nose of an elephant. *The elephant stored water in its trunk and squirted the unsuspecting man.* **4** a large box with a hinged lid for storing or transporting clothes and other articles. *We have kept all the woolens in a trunk in the attic.* **5** the boot of a motor car. *He hid in the trunk of his father's car all night.* **6** of or relating to the main routes of a transport or communication network: a trunk road. *They intend building a trunk road connecting the two cities.*

Trust – *(noun)* **1** firm belief in someone or something. acceptance of the truth of a statement without evidence or investigation. *I trust your decision.* **2** the state of being responsible for someone or something: a man in apposition of trust. *The family always trusted the grandfather.* **3** an arrangement whereby a person is made the nominal owner of property to be held or used for the benefit of one or more others. *I hereby appoint him with the trust to deal with my property.* **4** a body of trustees. an organization or company that has or attempts to gain monopolistic control of a market. *He is on the board of trustees at the hospital.* **5** commercial credit. *I give you this money on trust.* **6** a hope or expectation. *I trust all is well between his parents and him.* *(verb)* **1** believe in the reliability, truth, ability, or strength of. have the confidence to allow someone to have, use, or look after. commit someone or something to the safe keeping of. place reliance on. *She trusts him to help her always.* **2** have confidence; hope: I trust that you have enjoyed this book. *You trust me to like this stuff?* 3 allow credit to. *You can be sure to trust him.*

Trustee – *(noun)* **1** an individual or member of a board given powers of administration of property in trust with a legal obligation to administer it solely for the purposes specified. *He was selected into the board of trustees on account of hard work.* **2** a state made responsible for the government of an area by the united nations. *This state has been officially made a trustee of this land.*

Trusting –*(adjective)* showing trust in or tending to trust others; not suspicious. *His trusting nature will harm him in the long run.*

Trustworthy –*(adjective)* able to be relied on as honest, truthful, or reliable. *He is a trustworthy employee.*

Truth – *(noun)* the quality or state of being true. that which is true as opposed to false. a fact or belief that is accepted as true. *I want to hear the whole truth.*

Truthful – *(adjective)* **1** telling or expressing the truth; honest. *This is an example of a truthful man.* **2** true to life. *We love her for being truthful always.*

Try – *(verb)* **1** make an attempt or effort to do something. test in order to see if it is suitable, effective, or pleasant. attempt to operate, open contact, etc.: I tried the doors, but they were locked. put on an item of clothing to see if it fits or suits one. *Did you try out each and every shirt?* **2** make severe demands on: Mary tried everyone's patience to the limit. *Do not try my patience.* **3** subject to trial. investigate and decide in a formal trial. *He will be tried in court today.* **4** smooth with a plane. *Try this crease quickly.* **5** extract by heating. *Metal is extracted by trying.* *(noun)* **1** an effort to accomplish something; an attempt. an act of testing something new or different. *Try this new battery.* **2** an act of touching the ball down behind the opposing goal line, scoring points and entitling the scoring side to a kick at goal. an attempt to score an extra point after a touchdown. *He scored at the tryouts.*

Tryst – *(noun)* a private, romantic rendezvous between lovers. *There were rumors of their trysts. (verb)* keep or arrange a tryst. *She asked him to arrange a tryst next week.*

Tub – *(noun)* **1** a low, wide, open container with a flat bottom used for holding liquids, growing plants, etc.- a similar small plastic or cardboard container for food. a bath. a container for conveying ore, coal, etc. *Pour the water into the tub*. **2** a short, broad boat that handles awkwardly. *The tub lunged forward into the waters. (verb)* **1** plant or put in a tub. *Put the clothes in the tub.* **2** have a bath. *Go for a tub in the river.*

Tube – *(noun)* **1** a long, hollow cylinder used for conveying or holding liquids gases. a flexible metal or plastic container sealed at one end and having a cap at the other. material forming tubes; tubing. *The doctor passed a tube into the patient's throat.* **2** a hollow cylindrical organ or structure in an animal or plant. a woman's fallopian tubes. *Her main problem lies in her fallopian tubes.* **3** the underground railway system in London. a train running on this system. *From this point you need to take the tube upto two stations.* **4** a sealed container, typically of glass and either evacuated or filled with gas, containing two electrodes between which an electric current can be made to flow. a cathode ray tube, especially in a television set. a thermionic valve. *I am sorry, but the television's tube is not working properly.* **5** television. *Let us check out the tube.* 6 the hollow curve under the crest of a breaking wave. *His favourite sport is water surfing in the tube. (verb)* **1** provide with a tube or tubes. *Please tube this pathway.* **2** convey in a tube. *Be clear and convey in a tube.*

Tuber – *(noun)* **1** a much thickened underground part of a stem or rhizome, e.g. in the potato, serving as a food reserve and bearing buds from which new plants arise. a thickened fleshy root, e.g. of the dahlia. *He has been advised to stay off any tuber.* **2** a rounded swelling or protuberant part. *The rock stood out as a tuber in the barren landscape.*

Tuberous – *(adjective)* **1** resembling, forming, or having a tuber or tubers. *You can identify this root by its tuberous appearance.* **2** characterized by or affected by rounded swellings. *Her knees looked slightly tuberous than normal.*

Tuberculosis – *(noun)* an infectious bacterial disease characterized by the growth of nodules in the tissues, especially the lungs. *Tuberculosis was considered to be incurable till the last century.*

Tuck – *(verb)* **1** push, fold, or turn under or between two surfaces or into a confined space. store something in a secure place. settle someone in bed by pulling the edges of the bedclothes firmly under the mattress. *Her mother tucked her to bed every night and read her a story.* **2** make a flattened, stitched fold in, to improve the fit or for decoration. *She added some tucks in the curtains to make them stand upright.* **3** eat food heartily. *He tucked into the food like a hungry child. (noun)* **1** a flattened, stitched fold in a garment or material. a surgical operation which involves removing a fold of flesh or fat. *The doctor suggested a tuck to make her look thinner.* **2** food eaten by children at school as a snack. *This break is only for having a tuck.* **3** a position with the knees bent and held close to the chest. *The gym instructor began by asking us to tuck and lower our head.*

Tuesday – *(noun)* the day of the week before Wednesday and following Monday. (adverb) on Tuesday. on Tuesdays; each Tuesday. *They hold a market here every Tuesday.*

Tug – *(verb)* **1** pull hard or suddenly. *Please stop tugging at the other end.* **2** tow by means of a tug or tugs. *Try to tug slowly to release the cloth without tearing it. (noun)* **1** a hard or sudden pull. *The boy tugged at his father's shirt.* **2** a small, powerful boat used for towing larger boats and ships, especially in hàrbour. an aircraft towing a glider. *This is just a tug for that ship.* **3** a loop from a horse's saddle which supports a shaft or trace. *He settled the tug carefully before mounting the horse.*

Tugged – *(noun)* pull something hard or suddenly. *The little girl tugged at her pigtails nervously.*

Tuition – *(noun)* teaching or instruction, especially of individuals or small groups. a fee charged for this. *She wants to take tuitions in mathematics.*

Tulip – *(noun)* a bulbous spring flowering plant of the lily family, with boldly coloured cup shaped flowers. *I suggest you gift her a bunch of tulips.*

Tumble – *(verb)* **1** fall suddenly, clumsily, or headlong. perform acrobatic feats, typically handsprings and somersaults. *The clown tumbled down from the staircase.* **2** decrease rapidly in amount or value. *We saw the sales tumble rapidly this last month.* **3** dry in a tumble dryer. *You cannot dry this cloth in a tumble dryer.* **4** rumple; disarrange. *The boy loves to tumble the neatly arranged row of books while his mother is not looking.* **5** have sexual intercourse with. *I think she had a tumble before being murdered.* *(noun)* **1** an instance of tumbling. *Why do you always tumble?* **2** an untidy or confused arrangement or state. *She looked as if her mind was in a tumble.* **3** a handspring or other acrobatic feat. *the acrobat held his tumble firmly.* **4** a friendly sign of recognition or interest. *He showed the least tumble to his own brother at the party.*

Tumbler – *(noun)* **1** a drinking glass with straight sides and no handle or stem. *The giant drinks milk from that huge tumbler.* **2** an acrobat. *Have you seen the antics of the tumbler at the circus?* **3** another term for tumble dryer. *He wishes to gift her a tumbler on their anniversary.* **4** a pivoted piece in a lock that holds the bolt until lifted by a key. a notched pivoted plate in a gunlock. *This lock will not work as its tumbler is damaged.* **5** an electrical switch worked by pushing a small sprung lever. *The electrician suggested we install a tumbler here.* **6** a tumbling barrel. *All the wine was stored in the tumbler.*

Tumor – *(noun)* a swelling of a part of the body, generally without inflammation, caused by an abnormal growth of tissue, whether benign or malignant. *She was shocked to discover a tumor in her stomach.*

Tumult – *(noun)* **1** a loud, confused noise, as caused by a large mass of people. *The shouting was growing really tumult with each passing minute.* **2** confusion or disorder. *The room was a picture of utter tumult.*

Tumultuous – *(adjective)* **1** very loud or uproarious. *She always get her way by being tumultuous with her demands.* **2** excited, confused, or disorderly. *Her mind was so tumultuous that she could not think straight.*

Tuna – *(noun)* a large and active predatory schooling fish of warm seas, extensively fished commercially. *She loves tuna sandwiches.*

Tune – *(noun)* a melody, especially one which characterizes a certain piece of music. *this was a truly haunting tune.* *(verb)* **1** adjust to the correct or uniform pitch. *Please tune your instruments.* **2** adjust to the frequency of the required signal. watch or listen to a television or radio broadcast. *Tune the channels using a set top box.* **3** adjust in order that they run smoothly and efficiently. *It is pure cacophony when they all sing out of tune.* **4** adjust or adapt to a particular purpose or situation. become sensitive to. stop listening or paying attention. *She is always in tune with nature.*

Tuneful – *(adjective)* having a pleasing tune; melodious. *Can you please repeat the tuneful melody?*

Tunic – *(noun)* **1** a loose sleeveless garment reaching to the thigh or knees. a gymslip. *I loved the color of her tunic.* **2** a close fitting short coat worn as part of a uniform. *She forgot to wear her tunic to the hospital.* **3** an integument or membrane enclosing or lining an organ or part. any of the concentric layers of a plant bulb, e.g. an onion. *She peeled through the tunic slowly.*

Tunnel – *(noun)* **1** an artificial underground passage, as built through a hill or under a building or by a burrowing animal. *This is the longest tunnel in the country.* **2** a polytunnel. *The farmer set up lanes of polytunnels to save his crop from the untimely rains.* *(verb)* **1** dig or force a passage underground or through something. *The rat* tunneled through the cupboard. **2** pass through a potential barrier. *You must know there will be tough tunnels to cross on the way.*

Turban – *(noun)* a man's headdress, consisting of a long length of material wound round a cap or the head, worn especially by Muslims and Sikhs. *She thinks she knows the man wearing the blue turban.*

Turbine – *(noun)* a machine for producing continuous power in which a wheel or rotor, typically fitted with vanes, is made to revolve by a fast moving flow of water, steam, gas, air, or other fluid. *The deafening roar of the turbines could be heard for miles.*

Turbulent – *(adjective)* **1** disorderly or confused; not calm or controlled. *The sea turned turbulent within a matter of minutes.* **2** relating to or denoting irregular and disordered flow of fluids. *This liquid is known to be more turbulent than others when poured on a steel surface.*

Turf – *(noun)* **1** grass and the surface layer of earth held together by its roots. a piece of such grass and earth cut from the ground. *The architect has designated a small patch of turf in the front of the house.* **2** horse racing or racecourses generally. *I bet his horse will win on this turf.* **3** an area regarded as someone's territory; a sphere of influence or activity: he did not like poachers on his turf. *The man behaved as if the children trespassed on his turf.* *(verb)* **1** force to leave somewhere: they were turfed off the bus. *The hooligans were turfed out of the cinema.* **2** cover with turf. *The beach was covered with turf.*

Turkey – *(noun)* **1** a large mainly domesticated game bird native to north America, having a bald head and red wattles. *Have you seen the turkey at the zoo?* **2** something that is extremely unsuccessful, especially a play or film. *His entire career seems to have been a turkey.* **3** a stupid or inept person. *Do not behave like a turkey.*

Turmoil – *(noun)* a state of great disturbance, confusion, or uncertainty. *I could sense he was in a great turmoil within.*

Turn – *(verb)* **1** move or cause to move in a circular direction wholly or partly around an axis. move or cause to move into a different position, especially so as to face the opposite direction. change or cause to change direction. change from flood to ebb or vice versa. pass round so as to attack from the side or rear. twist or sprain. bend back so as to make it blunt. *Please turn your face away from the bonfire.* **2** change or cause to change in nature, state, form, or colour; make or become. change colour in the autumn. make or make or become sour. make or become nauseated: the smell would turn the strongest stomach. *The leaves turn orange as autumn approaches.* **3** start doing or becoming involved with. go to for help or information. have recourse to: he turned to drink and drugs for solace. *I always turn to my teacher in times of distress.* **4** shape on a lathe. *Let us turn the wooden piece on the lathe to smoothen the edges.* **5** give a graceful or elegant form to. *makeup turns her into a diva instantly.* *(noun)* **1** an act of turning. a bend or curve in a road, path, river, etc. a place where a road meets or branches off another; a turning. deviation in the direction of the ball when bouncing off the pitch. one round in a coil of rope or other material. *Keep moving on and go past a few turns.* **2** a development or change in circumstances. a time when one period of time ends and another beings. the beginning of the second nine holes of a round of golf. *No one could predict such a turn of events.* **3** an opportunity or obligation to do something that comes successively to each of a number of people. *One good turn deserves another.* **4** a short walk or ride. *Would you care for another turn at the bike?* **5** a shock. a brief feelings or experience of illness: he's had another of his funny turns. *She will have a turn of flu soon.*

Turnip – *(noun)* **1** around root with white or cream flesh which is eaten as a vegetable and also has edible leaves. *The rabbit loves chewing on turnip leaves.* **2** the European plant of the cabbage family which produces this root. *We saw a small turnip garden from her kitchen window.*

Turpentine - *(noun)* **1** an oleoresin secreted by certain pines and other trees and distilled to make rosin and oil of turpentine. *Just apply oil of turpentine and the scar will heal quickly.* **2** a volatile pungent oil distilled from this, used in mixing paints and varnishes and in liniment. *The entire room smelt of turpentine.* *(verb)* apply turpentine to. *The last step is to apply a coat of turpentine.*

Turquoise - *(noun)* **1** a semi precious stone, typically opaque and of a greenish blue colour, consisting of a hydrated phosphate of copper and aluminium. *Her turquoise gown was the talk of the evening.* **2** a greenish blue colour. *The still waters of the lake gleamed a turquoise shade during the day.*

Turret - *(noun)* **1** a small tower at the corner of a building or wall, especially of a castle. *The turret of the medieval era castle was stinking due to neglect.* **2** an armored tower, typically one that revolves, for a gun and gunners in a ship, aircraft, fort, or tank. *The soldiers pointed at the turret.* **3** a rotating holder for tools, especially on a lathe. *The man asked his assistant to take out the turret from his bag.*

Turtle - *(noun)* **1** a marine or freshwater reptile with a bony or leathery shell and flippers or webbed toes. the flesh of a sea turtle, used chiefly for soup. *You can see the migratory turtles on the beach next month.* **2** a directional cursor in a computer graphics system which can be instructed to move around a screen. *I think the turtle is not moving on the screen.*

Tusk - *(noun)* **1** a long, pointed tooth, especially one which protrudes from the closed mouth, as in the elephant, walrus, or wild boar. *The tusk itself weighed nearly 2 kilos.* **2** a long, tapering object or projection. *The strange creature seemed to have a bony tusk below its face.*

Tussle - *(noun)* a vigorous struggle or scuffle. *Freedom always comes after a tussle.* *(verb)* engage in a tussle. *The teacher suspended the students who participated in the tussle.*

Tutor - *(noun)* **1** a private teacher, typically one who teaches a single pupil or a very small group. a university or college teacher responsible for assigned students. an assistant lecturer in a college or university. *He will be your tutor for this semester.* **2** a book of instruction in a particular subject. *This equipment will be accompanied with a tutor explaining its working.* *(verb)* act as a tutor to. work as a tutor. *I want you to tutor these children.*

Tutorial - *(noun)* a period of tuition given by a university or college tutor. an account or explanation of a subject, intended for private study. *(adjective)* of or relating to a tutor or a tutor's tuition. *He attends tutorial classes after work.*

Tweak -*(verb)* **1** twist or pull with a small but sharp movement. *The nail will come off if you tweak it.* **2** improve by making fine adjustments. *Thank you for helping me tweak my work.* *(noun)* **1** an act of tweaking. *He thinks her work needs tweaking.* **2** a fine adjustment. *The musician tweaked the strings of his instrument before the recital.*

Tweed - *(noun)* a rough surface woolen cloth, typically of mixed flecked colours, originally produced in Scotland. clothes made of tweed. *I love wearing my father's tweed coat during winters.*

Tweezers -*plural (noun)* a small instrument like a pair of pincers for plucking out hairs and picking up small objects. *The lab assistant used the tweezers to pick the tiny particles from the bowl.*

Twelve - *(cardinal number)* **1** equivalent to the product of three and four; two more than ten; 12 *There were twelve packets arranged on the bed.* **2** the twelve apostles. *Can you name the twelve apostles?* **3** classified as suitable for people of 12 years and over. *This film has a rating of twelve.*

Twelfth - *(number)* constituting number twelve in a sequence. *Which is the twelfth alphabet in Latin?*

Twenty - *(cardinal number)* the number equivalent to the product of two and ten; ten less than thirty; 20. *I wish to buy twenty books for the class.*

Twentieth - *(number)* constituting number twenty in sequence. *This is his twentieth attempt so far.*

Twice - *(adverb)* **1** two times. *Playing with the kids was twice the fun.* **2** double in degree or quantity. *I had to walk to the store twice today.*

Twiddle - *(verb)* play or fiddle with, typically in a purposeless or nervous way. turn or move in a twirling way. *The boy twiddled his way through the crowded market. (noun)* **1** an act of twiddling. *Stop twiddling and listen carefully.* **2** a rapid or intricate series of musical notes. *This composer is considered to be a master of twiddle.*

Twig - *(noun)* a slender woody shoot growing from a branch or stem of a tree or shrub. a small branch of a blood vessel or nerve. *They saw many dry twigs lying below the tree.*

Twilight - *(noun)* **1** the soft glowing light from the sky when the sun is below the horizon, caused by the reflection of the sun's rays from the atmosphere. *The twilight gave the entire hill an eerie glow.* **2** a period or state of obscurity or gradual decline: the twilight of his career. *We often remember to pray when we touch our twilight years.*

Twin - *(noun)* **1** one of two children or animals born at the same birth. *You two look like twins.* **2** something containing or consisting of two matching or corresponding parts. *Where is the twin blade of the chopper? (adjective)* **1** forming or being one of a twin. *He was always known as being one of the twins.* **2** forming a matching or closely connected pair. *That couple thought as if they were twins.* **3** twinned. *The leaders of the provinces wanted their lands to be twinned. (verb)* **1** link; combine. link with another in a different country, for the purpose of cultural exchange. *Seattle is twinned with Tokyo in Japan.* **2** that is a composite consisting of two parts which are reversed in orientation with respect to each other. *The magnet has twinned poles.* .

Twinge - *(noun)* **1** a sudden, sharp, localized pain. *The boy twinged as the doctor took an injection.* **2** a brief, sharp pang of emotion. *He did not show a twinge of remorse.* (verb) suffer a twinge. *This heartless man will never suffer a twinge of grief.*

Twinkle - *(verb)* **1** shine with a gleam that changes constantly from bright to faint. sparkle, especially with amusement. *I could detect a twinkle in his eyes.* **2** move lightly and rapidly. *The bee twinkled past the flower. (noun)* a twinkling sparkle or gleam. *The firefly looked like it was twinkling in the darkness.*

Twirl - *(verb)* spin quickly and lightly round. *The girl twirled and her skirt formed a neat circle around her.* (noun) an act of twirling. a spiraling or swirling shape, especially a flourish made with a pen. *She always ends her signature with a twirl.*

Twist - *(verb)* **1** form into a bent, curled, or distorted shape. turn or bend round or into a different direction. force or be forced out of the natural position by a twisting action: he twisted his ankle playing tennis. *The woman twisted the towel to drain the water.* **2** rotate or cause to rotate around something that remains stationary; turn. move or cause to move around each other; interlace. take or have a winding course. *Try to twist the wire across the pole.* **3** distort, or misrepresent the meaning of. unpleasantly or unhealthily abnormal. *He will always twist the facts to suit his stand.* **4** dance the twist. *These days the form of dancing the twist is in vogue.* **5** cheat; defraud. *he will twist you of your valuables. (noun)* **1** an act or instance of twisting. *She twisted herself free.* **2** a thing with a spiral shape. a paper packet with twisted ends. a small quantity of tobacco, sugar, etc., wrapped in such a packet. *The toffee was wrapped beautifully with a twist in the end.* **3** force producing twisting; torque. forward motion combined with rotation about an axis. the rifling in the bore of a gun. *The weapon worked on twisting principle.* **4** an unexpected, normally unwelcome, development of events. a new treatment or outlook: she takes conventional subjects and gives them a twist. a swindle. *All her stories carry an unexpected twist in the end.* **5** a fine strong thread consisting of twisted fibres. *Susan selected the thickest rope, made of twisted fibres.*

Twitch - *(verb)* **1** make or cause to make a short, sudden jerking movement. *The boy's arm twitched as the lighted matchstick fell on his palm.* **2** use a twitch to subdue. *Try to slowly* *twitch your jaw. (noun)* **1** a twitching movement. *Be calm and move in a twitching movement.* **2** a pang: he felt a twitch of annoyance. *Her incessant bickering made him twitch in irritation.* **3** a small noose attached to a stick, which may be twisted around the upper lip or ear of a horse to subdue it during veterinary procedures. *He was such an amazing horse that the vet did not even have to use the twitch during his examination.*

Twitter – *(verb)* **1** make a series of light tremulous sounds. *I woke up hearing the twittering of birds on my window sill.* **2** talk rapidly in a nervous or trivial way. *She twittered away in panic. (noun)* **1** a twittering sound. *I can hear the twittering of birds.* **2** trivial talk. *I do not believe in wasting time in such twitters.*

Two – *cardinal number* equivalent to the sum of one and one; one less than three. *There were two eggs in the basket.*

Tycoon – *(noun)* **1** a wealthy, powerful person in business or industry. *He recognized the man to be a business tycoon.* **2** a title applied by foreigners to the shogun of Japan in power between 1857 and 1868. *He was a tycoon in Japan during the late nineteenth century.*

Type – *(noun)* **1** a category of people or things having common characteristics. a person or thing considered as a representative of such a category. a person of a specified character of nature: two sporty types in tracksuits. an abstract category or class of linguistic item or unit. contrasted with token. *The scientists have never seen this type of organism till date.* **2** a person or thing symbolizing or exemplifying the defining characteristics of something. *Milk is a type of liquid.* 3 printed characters or letters. a piece of metal with a raised letter or character on its upper surface, for use in letterpress printing. such pieces collectively. *I want you to rewrite this line using a different type.* **4** a design on either side of a medal or coin. *The type on this coin suggests it does not belong to this country.* **5** a foreshadowing in the old testament of a person or event of the Christian dispensation. *You must read about the type of followers of Christ. (verb)* **1** write using a typewriter or computer. *Please type as I dictate the rules.* **2** determine the type to which belongs. *What type of food do you like to eat?*

Typhoid – *(noun)* an infectious bacterial fever with an eruption of red spots on the chest and abdomen and severe intestinal irritation. *The student missed his examinations as he was suffering from typhoid.*

Typhoon – *(noun)* a tropical storm in the region of the Indian or western Pacific oceans. *We expect the typhoon to hit the coast before tomorrow noon.*

Typical – *(adjective)* **1** having the distinctive qualities of a particular type. characteristic of a particular person or thing. *Feigning innocence is typical of her.* **2** symbolic: the pit is typical of hell. *The screaming is typical of the pain being felt.*

Typify – *(verb)* be typical of. *Snow will typify the winter season in this land.*

Tyranny – *(noun)* **1** cruel and oppressive government or rule. a state under such rule. *Our country ruled under tyranny during the last decade.* **2** cruel and arbitrary exercise of power or control. *We will not allow such tyranny.* **3** rule by a tyrant. *He wishes to unleash his tyranny on his people.*

Tyrranical – *(adjective)* exercising power in a cruel way. *The government formed by Talibans was believed to be tyrannical in nature.*

Tyrant – *(noun)* **1** a cruel and oppressive ruler. *He will always be known as a tyrant in this country.* **2** a person exercising power or control in a cruel and arbitrary way. *Do not behave as a tyrant with your siblings.* **3** a ruler who seized absolute power without legal right. *I will not let that tyrant uproot my family from our home.*

Tyre – *(noun)* **1** a rubber covering, typically inflated or surrounding an inflated inner tube, placed round a wheel to form a soft contact with the road. *The cycle wobbled as the tyre moved on the rocky surface.* **2** a strengthening band of metal fitted around the rim of a wheel, especially of a railway vehicle. *The inspector walked up to take a look at the vehicle's tyres.*

Uu

U – *(noun)* **1** the twenty first letter of the alphabet. **2** denoting the next after T in a set of items, categories, etc.

Udder – *(noun)* the mammary gland of female cattle, sheep, goats, horses, and related ungulates, hanging near the hind legs as a bag like organ with two or more teats. *Udder is an organ shaped like a bag that produces mild and hangs underneath the body of a cow goat etc.*

Ugly –*(adjective)* **1** unpleasant or repulsive in appearance. *Her face is attractive and not ugly.* **2** hostile or threatening; likely to involve unpleasantness. *His behaviour reflects his ugly frame of mind.*

Ulcer – *(noun)* an open sore in an external or internal surface of the body, caused by a break in the skin or mucous membrane which fails to heal. *Harish is suffering from stomach ulcer.*

Ulterior – *(adjective)* **1** other than what is obvious or admitted: *Sachin claims he just wants to help Aman but I suspect he has an ulterior motive.* **2** beyond what is immediate or present. *You cannot control the ulterior motive of a person.*

Ultimate – *(adjective)* **1** being or happening at the end of a process. The ultimate decision about who to employ lies with Bob. **2** being the best or most extreme example of its kind. *Infidelity is considered the ultimate betrayal.* **3** basic or fundamental. *An atom is made up of smaller particles is the ultimate truth.* **4** denoting the maximum possible strength or resistance beyond which an object breaks. *(noun)* **1** the best achievable or imaginable of its kind: *Ramesh is enjoying the ultimate in luxury.* **2** a final or fundamental fact or principle. *The board room was the ultimate in decorative luxury*

Ultimatum – *(noun)* a final demand or statement of terms, the rejection of which will result in retaliation or breakdown in relations. *Shweta has given Sachin an ultimatum – she could either stop seeing him and come back to him.*

Ultra – *(noun)* a person who holds extreme views, especially in politics. *Ultra violet rays can darken our skin when exposed to the sun.* *(adverb)* extremely. *There are a few ultra groups in the animal rights movement.*

Ultrasonic – *(adjective)* of or involving sound waves with a frequency above the upper limit of human hearing. *Under normal conditions our ears can't hear ultrasonic sound.*

Ultrasound – *(noun)* sound or other vibrations having an ultrasonic frequency, particularly as used in medical imaging. *Doctors use ultrasound method to monitor ovaries to see if they're responding to the treatment.*

Umbilical cord – *(noun)* **1** a flexible cord like structure containing blood vessels, attaching a fetus to the placenta during gestation. *He asked the doctor if he could see his wife's umbilical cord.* **2** a flexible cable, pipe, or other line carrying essential services or supplies. *He asks his son to bring the umbilical cord.*

Umbrage – *(noun)* **1** offence or annoyance. *She'll take umbrage if she isn't invited to the wedding.* **2** shade or shadow, especially as cast by trees. *Sita stands on the umbrage of a mango tree.*

Umbrella – *(noun)* **1** a device consisting of a circular fabric canopy on a folding metal frame supported by a central rod, used as protection against rain. *Gauri used to carry her umbrella while walking to school.* **2** a protecting force or influence; a screen of fighter aircraft or anti aircraft artillery. *If you have an umbrella force to support you then it will help you through your life.* **3** a thing that includes or contains many different parts: *United Nations an umbrella organisation composed of many world bodies.* **4** the gelatinous disc of a jellyfish, which contracts and expands to move through the water. *The jellyfish is expanding its umbrella.*

Umpire – *(noun)* **1** in certain sports an official who watches a game or match closely to enforce the rules and arbitrate on matters arising from the play. *Umpires play a significant part in a cricket match.* **2** a person chosen to arbitrate between contending parties. *Both parties agreed to have him act as umpire to arbitrate in their dispute.* *(verb)* act as an umpire; act as umpire in a game or match. *He is umpiring the match between class X and class XII.*

Un – *prefix* **1**added to adjectives, participles, and their derivatives denoting the absence of a quality or state; not*: unacademic*. the reverse of: *unselfish*. **2** added to nouns a lack of*: untruth*.

Unable – *(adjective)* lacking the skill, means, or opportunity to do something. *My father is unable to go to town without a car.*

Unacceptable – *(adjective)* not satisfactory or allowable. *The coach told the players that defeat was unacceptable.*

Unaccompanied –*(adjective)* **1** having no companion or escort. *The baby stayed home unaccompanied.* **2** without instrumental accompaniment. *The singer sings the song unaccompanied by musical instruments.* **3** without something occurring at the same time. *The application form arrived unaccompanied with relevant documents.*

Unanimous – *(adjective)* **1** fully in agreement. *The owner of the house wants a unanimous decision.* **2** of an opinion, decision, or vote held or carried by everyone involved. *The dicision was taken unanimously.*

Unanimity *(noun)* full agreement between a number of people. *People always want for unanimity in opinion.*

Unanimously – *(adverb)* of one mind; without dissent. *The Parliament unanimously approved the bill.*

Unarmed – *(adjective)* not equipped with or carrying weapons. *Unarmed peasants were shot down in the valley.*

Unassuming – *(adjective)* not pretentious or arrogant. *Vinay is unassuming about the value of his work.*

Unattached – *(adjective)* **1** not working for or belonging to a particular organization. *He is unattached to his office.* **2** without a spouse or established lover. *He is unhappy because he is unattached.*

Unattended – *(adjective)* **1** not dealt with. *The bartender dashed out leaving the bar unattended.* **2** not looked after. *Many casualties were lying unattended in our society.*

Unauthorized – *(adjective)* not having official permission or approval. *The employees went on an unauthorized strike.*

Unavoidable – *(adjective)* not able to be avoided or prevented; inevitable. *According to eye witness, the accident was unavoidable.*

Unaware – *(adjective)* having no knowledge of a situation or fact. *Unaware of the danger they entered the room.* *(adverb)* so as to surprise. *Rain caught the family unawares.*

Unbalanced – *(adjective)* **1** upset the mental equilibrium of; derange. *A man who has gone unbalanced is very difficult to manage.* **2** treating aspects of something unequally; partial. *Unbalanced behaviour of parents makes the kids suffer a lot.* *(noun)* a lack of balance or stability. *The method is unbalanced.*

Unbearable – *(adjective)* not able to be endured or tolerated. *Raju suffers an unbearable degree of sentimentality.*

Unbelievable – *(adjective)* **1** unlikely to be true. *The matter is unbelievable to many.* **2** extraordinary. *He drives at unbelievable speed.*

Unborn – *(adjective)* of a baby not yet born. *Please do something good for unborn generations.*

Unbreakable – *(adjective)* not liable to break or able to be broken. *Raju gifted her an unbreakable plastic dinnerware set.*

Unbroken – *(adjective)* **1** not broken; intact. *To retain faith, trust should remain unbroken.* **2** not interrupted. *He loves the unbroken quiet of the afternoon.*

Unburden – *(verb)* relieve of a burden; be relieved of cause of anxiety or distress through confiding in someone. *She unburned the family from giving her economical support.*

Uncalled-for *(adjective)* not required or requested. *Ramesh is not interested in uncalled-for suggestions.*

Uncanny – *(adjective)* strange or mysterious. *She has an uncanny knack of knowing things in advance.*

Uncertain – *(adjective)* **1** not known, reliable, or definite. *He is facing an uncertain recollection of events.* **2** not completely confident or sure. *He is uncertain of his convictions.*

Uncharacteristic – *(adjective)* not typical of a particular person or thing. *The prize goes to a book uncharacteristic of its contents.*

Uncle – *(noun)* **1** the brother of one's father or mother or the husband of one's aunt; an unrelated adult male friend of a child. *Sachin loves his uncle very much.* **2** a pawnbroker. *Ramesh borrowed some money from a uncle for which he had to suffer a lot.*

Uncomfortable – *(adjective)* not physically comfortable. uneasy or awkward. *We spent an uncomfortable day in the hot sun.*

Uncommon – *(adjective)* out of the ordinary; unusual. remarkable great. *Frost and floods are uncommon during these months in many countries.* *(adverb)* remarkably *He has an uncommon sense of humour.*

Uncompromising – *(adjective)* unwilling to make concessions; resolute. harsh or relentless. *The minister of state took an uncompromising stance in the peace talks.*

Unconcerned – *(adjective)* lacking in interest, care or feeling. *He seemed unconcerned during the entire process of negotiation.*

Unconditional – *(adjective)* not subject to any conditions. *Police want unconditional surrender of the criminals.*

Unconscious – *(adjective)* **1** not awake and aware of and responding to one's environment. *He is laying unconscious on the floor.* **2** done or existing without one realizing. *He fell down unconscious.* **3** unaware of. *He is unconscious of his talents.* *(noun)* the part of the mind which is inaccessible to the conscious mind but which affects behaviour and emotions. *Our unconscious mind plays a very important role in our attitude towards everything.*

Uncontrollable – *(adjective)* not controllable. *He is undergoing uncontrollable pain.*

Unconventional – *(adjective)* not based on or conforming to what is generally done or believed. *People look at her unconventional dress and hair style.*

Uncountable – *(adjective)* too many to be counted. *There are uncountable people present in the meeting.*

Uncouth – *(adjective)* **1** lacking good manners, refinement, or grace. *Don't behave like an untutored and uncouth human being.* **2** of a place uncomfortable because of remoteness or poor conditions. *I don't want to speak to the to the people who use uncouth language.*

Uncover – *(verb)* **1** remove a cover or covering from. discover something previously secret or unknown. *Summer uncovers bright clothes in nature.* **2** remove one's hat, especially as a mark of respect. *He uncovered his hat to show respect to his teacher.*

Undecided – *(adjective)* not having made a decision; uncertain. not settled or resolved. *Our position on this bill is still undecided which affects the case significantly.*

Undeniable – *(adjective)* unable to be denied or disputed. *There are undeniable consequences to their actions.*

Under – *(preposition)* **1** extending or directly below. below or behind so as to cover or protect. planted with. *A book is lying under the table.* **2** at a lower level, layer, or grade than. *an undersecretary.* **3** expressing submission or subordination. as provided for by the rules of; in accordance with used to express grouping or classification. *The application has to be submitted under the following guidelines.* **4** lower than a specified amount, rate, or norm. *Children six and under will be admitted free.* **5** undergoing. *(adverb)* **1** extending or directly below something. *The competitors went under the rules.* **2** affected by an anesthetic; unconscious. *This will put the patient under sedation.*

Undercover – *(adjective & adverb)* involving secret work for investigation or espionage: an undercover operation. *Police want an undercover operation to catch the culprits.*

Undercurrent – *(noun)* **1** a current of water below the surface and moving in a different direction from any surface current. *The undercurrent of the river is very strong.* **2** an underlying feeling or influence. *The undercurrent running inside her heart due to the sudden failure will harm her.*

Undercut – *(verb)* **1** offer goods or services at a lower price than a competitor. *The local dealer will actually undercut the foreign dealer by nearly 50% difference.* **2** cut or wear away the part under something, especially a cliff. weaken; undermine. cut away material to leave a carved design in relief. *The carpenter undercut the wood to give a good shape to the furniture.* **3** Strike a ball with backspin so that it rises high in the air. *The young boy undercut the ball strongly.* *(noun)* **1** a spave formed by the removal or absence of material from the lower part of something. a notch cut in a tree trunk to guide its fall when felled. *Ramesh's father gives the undercut properly to the huge tree, so the tree does not fall on their house.* **2** the underside of a sirloin of beef. *Save the undercut of the beef for me safely.*

Underdog – *(noun)* a competitor thought to have little chance of winning a fight or contest. a person who has little status in society. *Our sympathies were always with the underdog.*

Underdone – *(adjective)* of food insufficiently cooked. *The old lady served us underdone bacon and burnt biscuits.*

Underestimate – *(verb)* estimate something to be smaller or less Important than it really is. *Don't underestimate the value of this land, you could get more than what you think.* regard someone as less capable than they really are. *You should not underestimate his capabilites.* *(noun)* an estimate that is too low. *His underestimation of the people atteding the marriage really hampered the reception ceremony.*

Undergo – *(verb)* experience or be subjected to something unpleasant or arduous. *Suddenly his behaviour undergoes a strange change.*

Undergraduate – *(noun)* a student at a university who has not yet taken a first degree. *Only undergraduate students can apply for the post.*

Underground – *(adjective & adverb)* **1** beneath the surface of the ground. *Underground caverns.* **2** in secrecy or hiding, especially as a result of carrying out subversive political activities. *Police want an underground operation to catch the criminals.* **3** seeking to explore alternative forms of lifestyle or artistic expression; radical and experimental. *One portion of today's generation prefers a underground living style than the traditional life style.* *(noun)* **1** an underground railway, especially the one in London. *Delhi metro has many underground tracks.* **2** a group or movement organized secretly to work against an existing regime. *Some people of an unidentified organisation work underground to overthrow the established government.* **3** a group or movement seeking to explore alternative forms of lifestyle or artistic expression. *An underground group of our society is planning to organise a radical marxian gathering.*

Undergrowth – *(noun)* a dense growth of shrubs and other plants, especially under trees. *The ferny undergrowth covers the road to the temple.*

Underhand – *(adjective)* **1** acting or done in a secret or dishonest way. *Anurag achieved success in business by underhand methods.* **2** Underarm; with the palm of the hand upward or outward. *He sent down the delivery underhand.*

Underlie – *(verb)* **1** lie or be situated under. *The electric wires underlie the basement of the studio.* **2** be the cause or basis of. *He is not able to attend school underlying his economic condition.*

Underline – *(verb)* **1** draw a line under a word or phrase to give emphasis or indicate special type. *The teacher advises the students to underline the important sentences.* **2** emphasize. *(noun)* a line drawn under a word or phrase. *Rajesh has the habit of marking important points with underline.*

Underneath – *(preposition & adverb)* **1** situated directly below. *The floor underneath the table.* **2** so as to be concealed by; partly or wholly concealed by a garment. *He was wearing a beautiful shirt underneath the jacket.* *(noun)* the part or side facing towards the ground; the underside. *The underneath part of the car was completely inside water.*

Underpay – *(verb)* pay too little to someone or for something. *The labourers have been underpaid since the inception of the factory.*

Underplay – *(verb)* **1** perform a role or part in a restrained way. *The experienced actor underplayed his role brilliantly.* **2** represent something as being less important than it really is. *Indian parents really underplay the importance of co-curriculum activities.*

Underprivileged – *(adjective)* not enjoying the same rights or standard of living as the majority of the population. *The church brought gifts to the underprivileged children of the neighbourhood.*

Underrate – *(verb)* underestimate the extent, value, or importance of. *She underrated the work that went into the renovation.*

Underscore – *(verb)* Give extra weight to (a communication) *His gesture underscored his words. (noun)* another term for underline.

Undersigned – *(adjective)* appending one's signature to the document in question. *He has to bear the responsibility as the undersigned person. (noun)* the signatory or co signatories to the document in question. *The undersigned pesons were present during the meeting.*

Understand – *(verb)* **1** perceive the intended meaning of words, a language, or a speaker. *I understand what he means*; *She understands French.* perceive the significance, explanation, or cause of; interpret or view in a particular way. *You don't need to explain-I fully understand.* **2** infer from information received. *I understand you're at art school*; supply a missing word, phrase, or idea mentally. assume to be the case; take for granted. *I don't understand his idea.*

Understandable – *(adjective)* **1** able to be understood. *The students weren't getting the simple and understandable lesson.* **2** to be expected; natural, reasonable, or forgivable. Understatement. *His situation is understandable to the people concerned.*

Understudy – *(noun)* an actor who learns another's role in order to be able to act in their absence. *(verb)* study a role or actor as an understudy. *He understudied the role of the most experienced actor of their troupe.*

Undertake – *(verb)* **1** commit oneself to and begin an enterprise or responsibility; take on. *The social worker undertakes the responsibity of opening an English medium school in the village.* **2** formally guarantee, pledge, or promise. *He has undertaken a vow to free the prisoners.*

Undertaking – *(noun)* **1** a formal pledge or promise to do something; a task that is taken on; an enterprise. *The youth organisation is preparing for great undertakings.* **2** a company or business. *People become suspicious of his undertakings.*

Undertaker – *(noun)* a person whose business is preparing dead bodies for burial or cremation and making arrangements for funerals. *The oldest undertaker is suffering from some grave diseases and there is a little time left in him.*

Undertone – *(noun)* **1** a subdued or muted tone of sound or colour. *The doctor spoke in undertones.* **2** an underlying quality or feeling. *It is very difficult to understand undertone feelings of people.*

Underwater – *(adjective & adverb)* situated or occurring beneath the surface of the water. *Many ships get wrecked after colliding with underwater rocks.*

Underwear – *(noun)* clothing worn under other clothes next to the skin. *Always wear good quality underwear.*

Underweight – *(adjective)* **1** below a weight considered normal or desirable. *He is underweight to his age.* **2** having insufficient investment in a particular area. *Uderweight investment will have negative effect on his business. (verb)* apply too little weight to. *He underwighted the matter. (noun)* insufficient weight. *Ramesh's father is suffering from underweight.*

Underworld – *(noun)* **1** the world of criminals or of organized crime. *The underworld is notorious for demanding money from celebrities and kill innocent people for ransom.* **2** the mythical abode of the dead, imagined as being under the earth. *Bollywood movies are believed to be financed by underworld money.*

Underwrite – *(verb)* **1** sign and accept liability under an insurance policy. accept a liability or risk in this way. *The insurance underwrite all* *the damage caused by the devastating fire.* **2** undertake to finance or otherwise support or guarantee. *The owner of the compny underwrites the complete property of the office.* **3** write below something else. *He underwrites the important points below the covering letter.*

Undesirable – *(adjective)* not wanted or desirable because harmful, objectionable, or unpleasant. *It is important to separate the undesirable impurities in steel.* *(noun)* a person considered to be objectionable in some way. *Undesirable persons are not well-accepted in a civilised society.*

Undivided – *(adjective)* **1** not divided, separated, or broken into parts. *All the three brothers keep an undivided interest in the property.* **2** devoted completely to one object *He sought my undivided attention .*

Undo - *(verb)* **1** unfasten, untie, or loosen. *The child requests to undo the shoelace.* **2** cancel or reverse the effects or results of a previous action or measure. *I wish I could undo my actions.* **3** cause the downfall or ruin of. *A single mistake undid the President and he had to resign*

Undoubted - *(adjective)* not questioned or doubted by anyone. *The village sarpanch is the undoubted judge of the entire village.*

Undress - *(verb)* take off one's clothes. take the clothes off someone else. *The mother requested the child not to undress in front of everybody.* *(noun)* the state of being naked or only partially clothed. *He is literally in a state of undress.*

Undue - *(adjective)* unwarranted or inappropriate because excessive or disproportionate. *Please don't show undue excitement in that matter.*

Unearth - *(verb)* **1** find in the ground by digging; *The plice unearthed the town to capture the criminals.* discover by investigation or searching. *The CBI unearthed a plot to kill the Prime Minister.* **2** drive an animal, especially a fox out of a hole or burrow. *The CBI tried its best to unearth the source of black money.*

Unearthly - *(adjective)* **1** unnatural or mysterious, especially in a disturbing way. *He somehow berlieves in unearthly love which is quite strange for others.* **2** unreasonably early or inconvenient. *He reached the village at an unearthly hour.*

Uneasy - *(adjective)* causing or feeling anxiety; troubled or uncomfortable. *The shy girl is feeling uneasy in the crowded marriage reception.*

Uneconomical - *(adjective)* wasteful of money or other resources; not economical. *The main issue is whether a firm would ever operate in the uneconomical region.*

Uneducated – *(adjective)* poorly educated. *Only an uneducated person behaves like this.*

Unemployed - *(adjective)* **1** without a paid job but available to work. *The unemployed workers marched on the capital city.* **2** of a thing not in use. *The old car, so to say, is unemployed now a days.*

Unemployment - *(noun)* the state of being unemployed. the number or proportion of unemployed people. *Unemployment is considered as serious social evil in alomost all countries in the world.*

Unending – *(adjective)* having or seeming to have no end. countless or continual. *I am tired of his unending demands.*

Unequal – *(adjective)* **1** not equal in quantity, size, or value. not fair, evenly balanced, or having equal advantage. *The proposed human resource is unequal to the project.* **2** not having the ability or resources to meet a challenge. *He was unequal to the task assigned.*

Unequivocal - *(adjective)* leaving no doubt; unambiguous. *It is not very difficult to understand the plain and unequivocal language of the presentation.*

Unerring – *(adjective)* always right or accurate. *He is believed to be an unerring shooter.*

Unethical – *(adjective)* not morally correct. *Many social organisations fight to remove unethical business practices.*

Uneven - *(adjective)* **1** not level or smooth. *An uneven colour.* **2** not regular, consistent, or equal. of a contest not equally balanced. *The golfer hit the ball well but his putting was uneven.*

Uneventful – *(adjective)* not marked by interesting or exciting events. *The journey was pleasant but uneventful.*

Unexpected – *(adjective)* not expected or regarded as likely to happen. *He was shocked after hearing the unexpected news.*

Unexpected – *(adjective)* not made clear or accounted for. *It is not possible to accomplish the task with some unexplained process.*

Unfair – *(adjective)* not based on or showing fairness; unjust. contrary to the rules of a game. *It was an unfair trial.*

Unfaithful – *(adjective)* not faithful; disloyal. *She is suffering an account of his unfaithful lover.* engaging in sexual relations with a person other than one's lover or spouse. *Her husband was unfaithful.*

Unfamiliar – *(adjective)* **1** not known or recognized; uncharacteristic. *His name is unfamiliar to most.* **2** unfamiliar with not having knowledge or experience of. *He is unfamiliar with the customs of the society.*

Unfashionable – *(adjective)* not fashionable or popular. *He wears unfashionable clothes.*

Unfasten – *(verb)* open the fastening of; undo. *The airhostess requests the passengers to unfasten their belts.*

Unfavourable – *(adjective)* **1** expressing lack of approval or support. *He will suffer for his unfavourable comments.* **2** adverse; inauspicious. *They are living in unfavourable conditions.*

Unfit – *(adjective)* **1** unsuitable or inadequate for something. *The manager thinks all the project members are unfit for the new challenging project.* **2** not in good physical condition, especially through lack of regular exercise. *He is certified unfit for army service (verb).* make unsuitable; disqualify. *He unfitted the existing working environment with his rude behaviour.*

Unfold – *(verb)* **1** open or spread out from a folded position. *He unfolded the report to have a comprehensible idea.* **2** make or become revealed or disclosed. *A walk through town will unfold many interesting buildings*

Unforeseen – *(adjective)* not anticipated or predicted. *The poor people are preparing to face the unforeseen circumstances.*

Unforgettable – *(adjective)* highly memorable. *Rajesh has recorded all the unforgettable moments of his baby's life on video.*

Unforgiving – *(adjective)* **1** not willing to forgive or excuse faults. *His mother is surly an unforgiving old woman.* **2** of conditions harsh; hostile. *The unforgiving behaviour of the senior members makes it difficult for the newcomers to stay long in that office.*

Unfortunate – *(adjective)* **1** having bad fortune; unlucky. inauspicious. *An unfortunate night for all concerned.* **2** regrettable or inappropriate. *An unfortunate choice of words. (noun)* a person who suffers bad fortune. *He is unfortunate to have lost his right hand in the battle.*

Unfounded – *(adjective)* having no foundation or basis in fact. *He has been facing unfounded suspicion from various people.*

Ungainly – *(adjective)* clumsy; awkward. *What an ungainly creature a giraffe is!*

Ungrateful – *(adjective)* not feeling or showing gratitude. *He left behind all his possession to some ungrateful heirs.*

Unguarded – *(adjective)* **1** without protection or a guard. *The unguarded queen of Mysore was open to attack.* **2** not well-considered; careless. *He made an unguarded remark at the function.*

Unhappy – *(adjective)* not happy; unfortunate. *After the argument all the members lapsed into an unhappy silence.*

Unhealthy – *(adjective)* in poor health. *He seems to be unhealthy.* not conducive to health. *He frequently takes an unhealthy diet of fast foods.*

Unheard – *(adjective)* not heard or listened to. *The teacher will ask questions from the chapters which is unheard to all the students.*

Unicorn – *(noun)* a mythical animal represented as a horse with a single straight horn projecting from its forehead. a representation of this, with a twisted horn, a deer's feet, a goat's beard, and a lion's tail. *He always dreams of riding a unicorn.*

Unidentified – *(adjective)* not recognized or identified. *The prosecutor is talking about an unidentified witness.*

Uniform – *(adjective)* not varying; the same in all cases and at all times. *We are passing through a street of uniform tall white buildings. (noun)* the distinctive clothing worn by members of the same organization or body or by children attending certain school. *It is compulsory in our school to wear uniform while attending school.*

Unify – *(verb)* make or become united or uniform. *We should unify our resources.*

Unilateral – *(adjective)* **1** performed by or affecting only one person, group, etc. *America has decided to take unilateral action against India.* **2** relating to or affecting only one side of an organ, the body, etc. *a unilateral decision.*

Union – *(noun)* **1** the action or fact of uniting or being united. a state of harmony or agreement. *There is strength in union.* marriage; sexual coupling. *God bless this union. The union the uniting of the English and Scottish crowns in 1707, or of the parliaments of Great Britain and Ireland in 1801* **2** a club, society, or association formed by people with a common interest or purpose, especially a trade union. *You have to join the union in order to get a job.* **3** the set that comprises all the elements and no others contained in any of two or more given sets. *Let C be the union of the sets A and B.*

Unique – *(adjective)* being the only one of its kind. *We have seen a unique copy of an ancient manuscript*; unlike anything else. unique to belonging or connected to one particular person, group, or place. remarkable or unusual. *He spoke with a unique accent.*

Unison – *(noun)* simultaneous action or utterance. *The Army is marching in unison. (adjective)* performed in unison. *All the members are singing in unison.*

Unit – *(noun)* **1** an individual thing or person regarded as single and complete; each of the individual components making up a larger whole. a device or pert with a specified function. *The word is a basic linguistic unit.* a self contained or distinct section of a larger military grouping. *After the battle the soldier had trouble rejoining his unit*; a self contained part of an educational course. a single manufactured item. *Units of nucleic acids.* **2** a standard quantity in terms of which other quantities may be expressed. *The dollar is the United States unit of currency of America. (verb)* come or bring together for a common purpose or to form a whole. join in marriage.

Universal – *(adjective)* of, affecting, or done by all people or things in the world or in a particular group. *Universal experience*; applicable to all cases. *The movie opened to universal acclaim;* denoting a proposition in which something is asserted of all of a class. contrasted with particular. *(noun)* **1** a universal proposition. *Some form of religion seems to be a human universal.* **2** a term or concept of general application. a nature or essence signified by a general term. *There is a need to frame universal laws on piracy.*

Universe – *(noun)* all existing matter and space considered as a whole; the cosmos. *They wish to study the evolution of the universe.*

University – *(noun)* a high level educational institution in which students study for degrees and academic research is done. *Delhi University is one of the best universities in the world.*

Unjust – *(adjective)* not just; unfair. *The used unjust methods to earn material gain.*

Unkempt – *(adjective)* untidy or dishevelled. *wild unkempt hair.*

Unkind – *(adjective)* inconsiderate and harsh. *The teacher made a thoughtless and unkind remark of the students.*

Unknown – *(adjective)* not known or familiar. *(noun)* an unknown person or thing. an unknown quantity or variable. *an unknown island; an unknown amount; an unknown poet.*

Unlawful – *(adjective)* not conforming to or permitted by the law or rules. *People are engaged in unlawful banking practices.*

Unleaded – *(adjective)* **1** especially of petrol without added lead. *The use unleaded petrol.* **2** not covered, weighted, or framed with lead. *He baught a unleaded photograph.* **3** not spaced with leads.

Unless – *(conjunction)* except when; if not. *The new rules shall not have effect unless they have been approved.*

Unlike – *(preposition)* different from; not like. in contrast to. uncharacteristic of. *He is very friendly, unlike his father. (adjective)* dissimilar or different form each other. different from. *For twins they are very unlike.*

Unlikely – *(adjective)* not likely; improbable. *He is unlikely to question the legislation.*

Unlimited – *(adjective)* not limited or restricted; infinite. *He wants a internet connection with unlimited downloading.*

Unload – *(verb)* **1** remove a load from. remove goods from a vehicle, ship, etc. *The manager ordered the labourers to unload the truck.* **2** remove ammunition from a gun or film from a camera. *The terrorist unloaded the gun before surrendering.*

Unlock – *(verb)* **1** undo the lock of something using a key. *She quickly unlocked the door.* **2** make something available. *Please unlock the required stuff as soon as possible.*

Unlucky – *(adjective)* having, bringing, or resulting from bad luck. *The unlucky prisoner was put in prison again.*

Unmarried – *(adjective)* not married; single. *He invited only unmarried men and women to the function.*

Unmistakable – *(adjective)* not able to be mistaken for anything else. *His guide's opposition to slavery was unmistakable.*

Unnatural – *(adjective)* **1** contrary to nature; abnormal. *His unnatural interest in death is the only concern of his parents.* **2** affected; not spontaneous. *Unnatural power of concentration.*

Unnecessary – *(adjective)* not necessary; more than is necessary. *Remove the unnecessary stuff from the car.* *(noun)* unnecessary things. *Don't buy unnecessary things in the market.*

Unnerve – *(verb)* deprive of courage or confidence. *The incident shouldn't unnerve him at all.*

Unnoticed – *(adjective)* not noticed. *He has crossed the road unnoticed.*

Unobtrusive – *(adjective)* not conspicuous or attracting attention. *He is living an unobtrusive life of self-denial.*

Unofficial – *(adjective)* not official authorized or confirmed. *He announced an unofficial declaration to the members.*

Unpack – *(verb)* open and remove the contents of a suitcase or container. remove from a packed container. *The child's mother unpacks the birthday presents.*

Unpaid – *(adjective)* **1** of a debt not yet paid. *He notices the unpaid bill.* **2** of work or leave undertaken without payment. of a person not receiving payment for work done. *The firm was run by unpaid employees.*

Unpleasant – *(adjective)* not pleasant; disagreeable. *She can't tolerate his unpleasant personality.*

Unplug – *(verb)* **1** disconnect an electrical device by removing its plug from a socket. *She unplugged the hair drier after using it.* **2** remove an obstacle or blockage from. *Please unplug the heater from the socket.*

Unpopular – *(adjective)* not liked or popular. *The country is ready to wage an unpopular war.*

Unprecedented – *(adjective)* never done or known before. *Our generation is witnessing an unprecedented expansion in population and industry.*

Unpredictable – *(adjective)* not able to be predicted; changeable. *His sudden outburst is completely unpredictable.*

Unprepared – *(adjective)* **1** not ready or able to deal with something. *He is unprepared for today's exam.* **2** of a thing not made ready for use. *The car is unprepared till the race day.*

Unpretentious – *(adjective)* not pretentious; modest. *His quiet unpretentious demeanour attracts all.*

Unprofessional – *(adjective)* below or contrary to the standards expected in a particular profession. *His unprofessional behabviour surprises all.*

Unprovoked – *(adjective)* of an attack, crime, etc. not directly provoked. *The army is not prepared for the unprovoked and dastardly attack.*

Unqualified – *(adjective)* **1** not having the necessary qualifications or requirements. *Raj is unqualified for the post applied for.* **2** without reservation or limitation; total: *She desired an unqualified success.*

Unquestionable – *(adjective)* not able to be disputed or doubted. *He upholds his Unquestionable authority.*

Unravel – *(verb)* **1** undo twisted, knitted, or woven threads; unwind. become undone. *His old grandmother asks him to unravel the thread.* **2** investigate and solve a mystery or puzzle. *The* *kids are very fond of unravel the mystery in the cartoon.* **3** begin to fail or collapse.

Unreal – *(adjective)* **1** imaginary; not seeming real. *She is desirous of unreal success.* **2** unrealistic. *The employees ask the manager not to hope for unreal targets.* **3** incredible; amazing. *His achievements are unreal to most of the people.*

Unreasonable – *(adjective)* **1** not guided by or based on good sense. *The young man's unreasonable attitude distracts all from the goal.* **2** beyond the limits of acceptability. *People find it difficult to meet his unreasonable demands.*

Unreliable – *(adjective)* not able to be relied upon. *People consider our generation unreliable.*

Unremitting – *(adjective)* never relaxing or slackening. *We couldn't go out for picnic because of unremitting rain.*

Unrest – *(noun)* a state of rebellious dissatisfaction and agitation in a group of people: civil unrest. a state of uneasiness or disturbance. *They can't bear the unremitting demands of hunger.*

Unripe – *(adjective)* not ripe. *The vendor is ready to sell unripe fruits to the customers.*

Unrivalled – *(adjective)* surpassing all others. *Her unrivalled mastery of art suppresses all others.*

Unroll – *(verb)* open or cause to open out from a rolled up state. *The activist unrolls the banner before the followers.*

Unruly – *(adjective)* disorderly and disruptive; difficult to control. *The teachers find his attitude unruly.*

Unsafe – *(adjective)* **1** not safe; dangerous. *People think her fortune was increasingly unsafe.* **2** of a verdict or conviction not based on reliable evidence and likely to constitute a miscarriage of justice. *He doesn't want to take the unsafe justice of the landlord.* **3** denoting sexual activity in which precautions are not taken to reduce the risk of spreading sexually transmitted diseases, especially aids. *Unsafe sexual intercourse is responsible for many diseases.*

Unsaid – past and past participle of unsay. *(adjective)* not said or uttered. *Many things left unsaid.*

Unsatisfactory – *(adjective)* **1** Unacceptable; not good enough. *Life is becoming increasingly unsatisfactory.* **2** another term for unsafe. *The joint has been sealed in an unsatisfactory way.*

Unscathed – *(adjective)* without suffering any injury, damage, or harm. *The young man survived unscathed.*

Unscrew – *(verb)* with reference to a screw, lid, etc. unfasten or be unfastened by twisting. *He is asked to unscrew the outlet plate.*

Unscrupulous – *(adjective)* without moral scruples. *Unscrupulous politicians are destroying our country.*

Unsettle – *(verb)* cause to be anxious or uneasy; disturb. *The kids are so comfortably settled, don't disturb them.*

Unshaven – *(adjective)* not having shaved or been shaved. *The young man looked unshaven but energetic.*

Unsightly – *(adjective)* unpleasant to look at; ugly. *Most of the people present get disturbed to see the unsightly adventures of the wannabe man.*

Unskilled – *(adjective)* not having or requiring special skill or training. *He is unskilled in the art of rhetoric.*

Unsound – *(adjective)* **1** not safe or robust; in poor condition. *The new organization is based on an unsound foundation. injured, ill, or diseased. Unsound teeth.* **2** not based on sound evidence or reasoning, unreliable or unacceptable. *They are busy in an unsound argument.* of a person not competent, reliable, or holding acceptable views. *He is considered an unsound person to rely on.*

Unspeakable – *(adjective)* not able to be expressed in words. *He can't express unspeakable happiness in words.* too bad or horrific to express in words. *Never dare to utter the unspeakable name of the witch.*

Unstable – *(adjective)* **1** prone to change or collapse; not stable. *We are witnessing the worst unstable political conditions of the country.* **2** prone to psychiatric problems or sudden changes of mood. *His unstable mind can do harm to the society.*

Unsteady – *(adjective)* **1** liable to fall or shake; not firm. *His hand was unsteady as he poured the wine.* **2** not uniform or regular. *They are climbing carefully up the unsteady ladder.*

Unsuccessful – *(adjective)* not successful. *Ramesh was unsuccessful in his first attempt.*

Unsuitable – *(adjective)* not fitting or appropriate. *The college authority forms new rules unsuitable to students.*

Unsure – *(adjective)* **1** lacking confidence. His father thinks him to be *a very unsure young man.* **2** not fixed or certain. *We are leading towards an unsure future.*

Unsuspecting – *(adjective)* not aware of the presence of danger; feeling no suspicion. *The politicians are deceiving the unsuspecting public.*

Untamed – *(adjective)* not tamed or controlled. of land wild or uncultivated: *The man is fond of the untamed wilderness.*

Untangle – *(verb)* **1** free from tangles. *Untangle the thread.* **2** free from complications or confusion. *She cannot untangle herself from this task.*

Unthinkable – *(adjective)* too unlikely or undesirable to be considered a possibility. *The unthinkable usually remains the unmentionable.*

Unthinking – *(adjective)* without proper consideration. *The unthinking activities of the young prince will bring the doomsday to the kingdom soon.*

Untidy – *(adjective)* not arranged tidily. of a person not inclined to be neat. *He lives in an untidy living room.*

Untie – *(verb)* undo or unfasten something tied. *The people untied the prisoner.*

Until – *(preposition & conjunction)* up to the point in time or the event mentioned. *He sleeps until it gets light.*

Untimely – *(adjective)* happening or done at an unsuitable time; inappropriate. *He makes an untimely remark.* of a death or end happening too soon or sooner than normal. *Alcohol brought him to an untimely end.* *(adverb)* at a time that is unsuitable or premature. *His untimely death brought a lot of difficulties to the family.*

Unto – *(preposition)* **1** archaic term for to. **2** archaic term for until. *The Lord said unto Moses.*

Untold – *(adjective)* **1** too much or too many to be counted; indescribable: *Thieves caused untold damage to the family.* **2** not narrated or recounted. *The untold stories of bravery of the prince should be read.*

Untouchable – *(adjective)* **1** not able to be touched or affected. *He is untouchable for the critics.* **2** unable to be matched or rivaled. *His abilities are untouchable.* **3** of or belonging to the lowest caste Hindu group or the people outside the caste system. *(noun)* a member of the lowest caste Hindu group, with whom contact is traditionally held to defile members of higher castes. *Untouchables suffered a lot in the hands of people.*

Untoward – *(adjective)* unexpected and inappropriate or adverse. *They made a place for themselves under the most untoward conditions.*

Untrue – *(adjective)* **1** false or incorrect. *The statement was simply untrue.* **2** not faithful or loyal. *It is untrue to his highest opportunity and duty.* **3** not upright or level. *It is very difficult to walk on off-level floors and pass on untrue doors and windows.*

Untruth – *(noun)* **1** a lie. His story is bitter untruth. **2** the quality of being false. *Don't tell me any untruth story to save your life.*

Unused – *(adjective)* **1** not used. *He has seen an unused envelop.* **2** not accustomed to. *He is unused to such circumstances.*

Unusual – *(adjective)* **1** not habitually or commonly done or occurring. *Nuclear families are no longer unusual.* **2** remarkable; exceptional. *He is a man of unusual ability.*

Unutterable – *(adjective)* too great or awful to describe. *The small girl can't describe the unutterable incident.*

Unveil – *(verb)* **1** remove a veil or covering from. *Women are not allowed to unveil themselves in public in Islamic societies.* **2** show or announce publicly for the first time. *The minister unveiled the statue of the great person.*

Unwanted – *(adjective)* not wanted. *The family is scared of unwanted guests.*

Unwelcome – *(adjective)* not welcome. *He is unwelcome in the function.*

Unwell – *(adjective)* ill. *He is severely unwell.*

Unwieldy – *(adjective)* hard to move or manage because of its size, shape, or weight. *The person almost dropped the unwieldy parcel.*

Unwilling – *(adjective)* not willing. *She is unwilling the do the homework.*

Unwind – *(verb)* **1** undo or be undone after winding or being wound. *Unwind a ball of yarn.* **2** relax. *She decided to unwound herself in the hot tub.*

Unwitting – *(adjective)* **1** not aware of the full facts: *He is going to encounter an unwitting accomplice.* **2** unintentional. *An unwitting mistake may be overlooked.*

Unwrap – *(verb)* remove the wrapping from. *Let's unwrap the gifts!*

Up – *(adverb)* **1** towards a higher place or position. *The curtain eent up.* to or at a place perceived as higher. *Two of the men hoisted her up.* a walk up to the shops. of the sun visible in the sky. *The sun was already up when they set off.* towards the north. towards or in the capital or a major city. at or to a university. *He is driving up to London to see his friend.* **2** often up and about out of bed. *She made her way up to the bed.* **3** to the place where someone is. **4** at or to a higher level or value. winning by a specified margin. **5** into the desired or a proper condition. so as to be finished or closed. *I dont think anything is going to cheer me up.* *(adjective)* **1** directed or moving towards a higher place or position. *I am going for a walk up to the shops.* **2** of the road being repaired. **3** of a jockey in the saddle. **4** cheerful. *Sales are up by 25 per cent.* **5** of a computer system working properly. **6** at an end. **7** denoting a flavor of quark having a charge of +2/3 *(noun)* a period of good fortune. *You cann't have ups all the time in cricket.* *(verb)* **1** do something abruptly or boldly. *She upped at left hem.* **2** increase a level or amount. *Capacity will be upped by 70 per cent next year.* **3** lift up. *Everyone was cheering up their favourite team.*

Upbeat – *(noun)* in music an unaccented beat preceding an accented beat. *(adjective)* cheerful; optimistic. *His wishes are considered upbeat.*

Upbraid – *(verb)* scold or reproach. *The president upbraided the minister for his irresponsible behaviour.*

Upbringing – *(noun)* the treatment and instruction received from one's parents throughout childhood. *His behaviour reflects his upbringing.*

Update – *(verb)* **1** make more modern. *We updated the bedroom in the old house.* **2** give the latest information to. *Please update me on the new project.* *(noun)* an act of updating or an updated version. *The team leader gives update to the manager.*

Upgrade – *(verb)* raise to a higher standard or rank. *The teacher upgraded the most brilliant student to the next class.* *(noun)* an act of upgrading or an upgraded version. *The upgrade of syllabus makes the students happy.*

Upheaval – *(noun)* **1** a violent or sudden change or disruption. *The industrial revolution was a period of great upheaval in the world.* **2** an upward displacement of part of the earth's crust. **3** a violent disturbance. *The upheavals of the stock market always become the sensational news items.*

Uphill – *(adverb)* towards the top of a slope. *He moves uphill.* *(adjective).* **1** sloping upwards. *This street lay uphill.* **2** difficult: *an uphill struggle.* *(noun)* an upward slope.

Uphold – *(verb)* confirm or support. *He upholds the conditions put forward by the suffering family*; maintain a custom or practice. *The man is trying to uphold the family tradition.*

Upholster – *(verb)* provide furniture with a soft, padded covering. cover the walls or furniture in a room with textiles. *There are many companies that import all types of upholstery frames.*

Upholstery – *(noun)* soft, padded textile used to upholster furniture. *The family is doing the business of importing upholstery for many decades.*

Upkeep – *(noun)* the process of keeping something in good condition. *His upkeep of maintaining the museum is commendable.*

Upland - *(noun)* also uplands an area of high or hilly land.

Uplifting - *(noun)* The rise of something. *The uplifting of the clouds revealed the blue of a summer sky. (verb)* **1** Fill with high spirits; fill with optimism. *Music can uplift your spirits.* **2** Lift up from the earth. *The earth's movement uplifted this part of town.* **3** Lift up or elevate. *We use electric motor pump for uplifting water to the tank.*

Upon - *(preposition)* more formal term for on. *The man balanced upon one leg well.*

Upper - *(adjective)* **1** the topmost one of two. **2** higher in place or position. *The small tree is located in the upper centre of the picture.* **3** superior in rank or accomplishment. *The upper half of the class sits in the front benches. (noun)* **1** The higher of two berths. **2** Piece of leather or synthetic material that forms the part of a shoe or boot above the sole that encases the foot. *Uppers come in many styles.*

Uppermost - *(adjective)* also upmost highest in place, rank, or importance. *Please bring me the uppermost book in the pile. (adverb)* at or to the uppermost position. *The blade turned uppermost.*

Upright - *(adjective)* **1** vertical; erect. of a piano having vertical strings. *She sat bolt upright.* **2** greater in height than breadth. **3** strictly honourable or honest. *He is considered as an upright and respectable man. (adverb)* in or into an upright position. *an upright post. (noun)* a vertical post, structure, or line. *The ball sailed between the uprights.*

Uprising - *(noun)* an act of resistance or rebellion. *The security has been stepped up since the recent uprising in the city.*

Uproar - *(noun)* a loud and impassioned noise or disturbance. a public expression of outrage. *There is a sudden uproar in the city due to a terrorist threat.*

Uproot - *(verb)* **1** pull a plant, tree, etc. out of the ground. *Uproot the vine that has spread all over the garden.* **2** move someone from their home or a familiar location. *The war uprooted many people.* **3** eradicate. *The shadows of political democracy were soon uprooted.*

Upset - *(verb)* **1** make unhappy, disappointed, or worried. *The hostile talks upset the peaceful situation in the room.* **2** knock cover. **3** disrupt. disturb the digestion of a person's stomach. *The spicy foods upset my stomach suddenly.* **4** shorten and thicken the end or edge of a metal bar, wheel rim, or other object. *(noun)* **1** a state of being upset. *He didn't realize the upset he caused me right now.* **2** an unexpected result or situation. *The recent incident is considered the biggest upset since Independence. (adjective)* **1** unhappy, disappointed, or worried. *With everything so upset it is very difficult to go on in life.* **2** of a person's stomach having disturbed digestion. *I have an upset stomach.*

Upshot - *(noun)* the eventual outcome or conclusion. *The recent incidents are the upshot of various happenings occurred two decades ago.*

Upside-down - *(adjective & adverb)* **1** with the upper part where the lower part should be. *The box was lying on the floor upside down.* **2** in or into total disorder. *The things in the room are in upside-down condition,*

Upstairs - *(adverb)* on or to an upper floor. *The younger son lives upstairs. (adjective)* also upstair situated on an upper floor. *(noun)* an upper floor. *No one is allowed to see the upstairs of the building.*

Upstart - *(noun)* a person who has risen suddenly to prominence, especially one who behaves arrogantly. *The man who was so poor one year back is considered an upstart in the city.*

Upstream - *(adjective & adverb)* situated or moving in the direction opposite to that in which a stream or river flows. *He went upstream to look at a sure-enough fish wheel.*

Uptake - *(noun)* the action of taking up or making use of something. *The machine makes paper napkins with a greater uptake of liquids.*

Uptight - *(adjective)* nervously tense or angry. *For some unknown reasons these animals are more laid back than their uptight counterparts.*

Up-to-date - *(adjective)* incorporating or aware of the latest developments and trends. *Read books to keep your knowledge up-to-date.*

Upward – *(adverb)* also upwards towards a higher point or level. *The cards are faced upward.* *(adjective)* moving or leading towards a higher point or level. *The team moves upward.*

Urban – *(adjective)* of or relating to a town or city. *The urban property owners behvaved very rudely with students.*

Urbane – *(noun)* especially of a man suave, courteous, and refined. *The director maintained an urbane tone in his letters.*

Urchin – *(noun)* **1** a mischievous child, especially a raggedly dressed one. *The urchin makes the family members; life very difficult with its mischievous deeds.* **2** a goblin. *Have you even seen a goblin?* **3** a hedgehog. **4** short for sea urchin. *Sea urchin is very rarely seen by people.*

Urge – *(verb)* encourage or entreat earnestly to do something. *Father urged me to finish my studies.* strongly recommend. encourage to move more quickly. *The leader urges the team members to wind up things quickly.* encourage someone to continue. *The teacher urges the students to continue study even if they face difficult situations.* *(noun)* a strong desire or impulse. *I have a very strong urge to drive the bike to Mumbai.*

Urgent – *(adjective)* **1** requiring immediate action or attention. *The old bridge requires urgent need of repair.* **2** earnest and insistent. *There is an urgent need to help the poor students.*

Urine – *(noun)* a pale yellowish fluid stored in the bladder and discharged through the urethra, consisting of excess water and substances removed from the blood by the kidneys. *There was blood in her urine.*

Urn – *(noun)* **1** a tall, rounded vase with a stem and base, especially one for storing a cremated person's ashes. *The son kept his father's ashes in an urn.* **2** a large metal container with a tap, in which tea or coffee is made and kept hot. *Mother put tea in a big urn.*

Us – *(pronoun)* **1** used by a speaker to refer to himself or herself and one or more others as the object of a (verb) or preposition. used after the verb to be and after than or as **2** me. *Give the football to us.*

Usage – *(noun)* **1** the action of using something or the fact of being used. *The Police warned against the usage of narcotic drugs.* **2** habitual or customary practice. *The usage of drug becomes habitual among youth in many countries.*

Use – *(verb)* **1** take, hold, or deploy as a means of accomplishing or achieving something. take an illegal drug. *He used his key to open the front door.* **2** treat in a particular way. exploit unfairly. of a person be worn out. *He used the kid to do all manual jobs.* **3** one would like or benefit from. *Make the best use of coaching classes.* **4** did repeatedly or existed in the past. *(noun)* **1** the action of using or state of being used. the ability or power to exercise or manipulate something. *The poem uses simple words he lost the use of his legs.*

Used – *(adjective)* having already been used. Second hand. *He bought a used car.*

Used to – In the habit. *I am telling you you'll get used to the idea.*

Useful– *(adjective)* **1** able to be used for a practical purpose or in several ways. *The servant is useful to the owner.* **2** very able or competent. *The new employee proves to be very useful to the owner.*

Useless – *(adjective)* **1** serving no purpose. *He is useless in an emergency.* **2** having little ability or skill. *Useless king.*

User – *(noun)* **1** a person who uses or operates something. He is a very careful user. **2** a person who exploits others. *The user exploits his employee.* **3** [Law] the continued use or enjoyment of a right. *The users of RTI should know the law properly.*

Usher – *(noun)* **1** a person who shows people to their seats in a theatre or cinema or at a wedding. *The usher is doing his job properly in the marriage reception.* **2** a person employed to walk before a person of high rank on special occasions. *The usher seems to be nervous while walking before the high ranking officer.* **3** an official in a law court who swears in jurors and witnesses and keeps order. **4** an assistant teacher. *(verb)* show or guide somewhere. *An elderly person ushered us to our seats.*

Usual – *(adjective)* habitually or typically occurring or done. *Mother knows the child's usual bedtime*. *(noun)* the drink someone habitually prefers. the things which is typically done or present. *The usual summer heat in Delhi*

Usurp – *(verb)* **1** take a position of power illegally or by force. *He usurped my rights*. supplant. **2** encroach or infringe upon. *Police try to usurp my rights individuals*.

Usury – *(noun)* the practice of lending money at unreasonably high rates of interest. interest at such rates. *Usuries are very rich persons*.

Utensil – *(noun)* a tool or container, especially for household use. *Use of utensils should be minimum*.

Utilitarian – *(adjective)* **1** useful or practical rather than attractive. *She prefers utilitarian steel tables*. **2** of, relating to, or adhering to utilitarianism. *(noun)* an adherent of utilitarianism. *An utilitarian is always welcomed by wise people*.

Utility – *(noun)* **1** the state of being useful, profitable, or beneficial. in game theory or economics the value of that which is sought to be maximized in any situation involving a choice. *The utility of a computer is known to all people in today's era*. **2** The service (electric power, water or transportation) provided by a public utility. *All the utilities were lost after the earthquake*. **3** a program designed for general support of the processes of a computer. *Computer system provides utility programs to perform the tasks needed by most users a utility program*. *(adjective)* **1**useful, especially through having several functions. *The machine has various utility*. **2** functional rather than attractive. *He buys things based on utility*.

Utilize – *(verb)* make practical and effective use of. *Do you know how do you utilize this tool?*

Utmost – *(adjective)* most extreme; greatest. *He endures to the utmost measure of human endurance*. *(noun)* the greatest or most extreme extent or amount. *She tried her utmost*.

Utopia – *(noun)* an imagined perfect place or state of things. *Some people still think India to be a Utopia*.

Utter – *(adjective)* complete; absolute: utter amazement. *His behaviour shows utter nonsense*.

Utterance – *(noun)* a word, statement, or sound uttered. the action of uttering. an uninterrupted chain of speech or writing. *The sudden utterance of the speech of the political leader disturbs the peaceful environment of the school*.

U-turn – *(noun)* **1** the turning of a vehicle in a U shaped course so as to face the opposite way. *He takes a U-turn as he has mistaken the road to be the right one*. **2** a reversal of policy. *The prosecutor takes a complete U-turn in the court*.

V – *(noun)* **1** the twenty second letter of the alphabet. **2** denoting the next after U in a set of items, categories, etc. *V-shaped sweaters are quite popular during winter.* **3** the roman numeral for five. *He is a student of class V.* **4** denoting an internal combustion engine with a number of cylinders arranged in two rows at an angle to each other. *A V-engine is an internal combustion engine used to convert fuel into energy to run motor car.*

Vacancy – *(noun)* **1** an unoccupied position or job. *There is a vacancy for a DTP operator in our office.* **2** an available room in a hotel, guest house, etc. *There is hardly any vacancy in any of hotels at this time of the year.* **3** empty space. *Aditi stared into job vacancy board, found nothing for her.* **4** lack of intelligence or understanding. *Vacancy, vanity, and inane deception was written all over her face.*

Vacant – *(adjective)* **1** not occupied; empty. of a position not filled. *Nearly half of the office positions are still vacant.* **2** showing no intelligence or interest. *He looked completely dejected and vacant.*

Vacate – *(verb)* **1** leave a place. give up a position or job. *Hotel room must be vacated by noon on the last day of the month.* **2** cancel or annul a judgment, contract, or charge. *The judge vacated a ruling given by the lower court.*

Vaccinate – *(verb)* treat with a vaccine to produce immunity against a disease. *All the children of this school were vaccinated against tuberculosis.*

Vaccinia – *(noun)* cowpox or the virus causing it. *The virus that causes small pox is known as vaccinia.*

Vacillate – *(verb)* waver between different opinions or actions. *He vacillated between teaching and writing.*

Vacuity – *(noun)* lack of thought or intelligence; empty-headedness: *He spoke on the subject of frivolity or vacuity in modern day literature.*

Vacuole – *(noun)* a space or vesicle within the cytoplasm of a cell, enclosed by a membrane and typically containing fluid. *The small cavity developed in nervous tissue as the result of disease is known as vacuole.*

Vacuous – *(adjective)* showing a lack of thought or intelligence. *The vacuous smile he gave out was quite inappropriate at such a serious discussion session.*

Vagabond – *(noun)* **1** a vagrant. *He is a vagabond, here today, there tomorrow.* **2** a rogue. *He is a vagabond, dishonest and no principles at all.* *(adjective)* having no settled home. *He has no job or home and is vagabond in nature and character.* *(verb)* wander about as or like a vagabond. *He went vagabonding about the world.*

Vagary – *(noun)* an unexpected and inexplicable change. *Vagaries of nature are difficult to predict and hard to control.*

Vagina – *(noun)* the muscular tube leading from the vulva to the cervix in women and most female mammals. *Vagina is the passage in the body of a woman or female animal between the outer sex organs and womb.*

Vagrancy - *(noun)* the state of living as a vagrant; homelessness: *Drug abuse may lead to descent into vagrancy.*

Vagrant – *(noun)* a person without a home or job. a wanderer. *A person without a settled home or regular work who wanders from place to place and lives by begging is known as a vagrant.* *(adjective)* of, relating to, or living like a vagrant; wandering. unpredictable or inconstant. *There is no dearth of vagrant beggars or whales who keep wandering from place to place.*

Vague – *(adjective)* of uncertain or indefinite character or meaning. *There are many patients who suffer from vague symptoms.* imprecise in thought or expression. *She has been very vague about her life and activities.*

Vale – *(noun)* valley (used in place names). *The Vale of Glamorgan as a poetic term is popular all over the literary world.*

Valentine – *(noun)* a card sent, often anonymously, on St valentine's day 14 February to a person one loves or is attracted to. a person to whom one sends such a card. *Radha is my valentine, I send her a card but without putting my name on it.*

Valetudinarian – *(noun)* a person who is unduly anxious about their health. *People suffering from poor health are commonly known as valetudinarian.* (*adjective*) showing undue concern about one's health. *Being a valetudinarian, on doctor's advice he promptly joined a health club.*

Valiance – *(noun)* great courage or determination. *He always demonstrates great courage and valiance in all battles.*

Valid – *(adjective)* **1** actually supporting the untended point or claim: *The article carried a valid criticism just below the story.* **2** executed in compliance with the law. *The contract was validated in the court of law.* legally or officially acceptable. *The visa is valid for three months.*

Valley – *(noun)* **1** a low area between hills or mountains, typically with a river or stream flowing through it. *There are many valleys between the mountains in Himachal Pradesh.* **2** an internal angle formed by the intersecting planes of a roof, or by the slope of a roof and a wall. *The architect designed the building to give appearance of a valley between the bedroom and courtyard.*

Valorous – *(adjective)* great courage in the face of danger. *The medal was awarded to the Colonel for his valorous act in the battle area.*

Valuable – *(adjective)* worth a great deal of money. *She bought a valuable antique in London.* extremely useful or important. *I respect my time as highly valuable.* (*noun*) valuable things, especially small items of personal property. *Please keep all your valuable items in the bank's safe vault.*

Value – *(noun)* **1** the regard that something is held to deserve; importance or worth. *Your support would be of great value during election campaigning.* material or monetary worth. *The value of products seldom remains constant.* the worth of something compared to its price: *At Rs.1000/- it is good value for this mobile phone.* **2** principles or standards of behaviour. *The parents were told of the values expected of students in this school.* **3** the numerical amount denoted by an algebraic term; a magnitude, quantity, or number. *Please find the mean value of x in this equation.* **4** in art the relative degree of lightness or darkness of a colour. *The artist has used adjacent colour values to bring better appearance to the scenery.* *(verb)* **1** estimate the value of . *His estate was valued at Rs.5 crore.* **2** consider to be important or beneficial. *He has come to value his opinion.*

Valve – *(noun)* **1** a device for controlling the passage of fluid through a pipe or duct, especially an automatic device allowing movement in one direction only. *This valve will shut off the flow from the boiler when the water is hot enough.* **2** a membranous fold in an organ or vessel which allows blood or other fluid to flow in one direction. *Valve is a delicate structure in the heart or a vein that lets blood flow in one direction only.*

Vampire – *(noun)* **1** in folklore a corpse supposed to leave its grave at night to drink the blood of the living. *In TV serials, we see that vampires have long pointed sharp teeth.* a person who exploits others ruthlessly. *The members who oppose money spent on welfare measures are no less than a blood sucking vampire.* **2** a small bat that feeds on blood by piercing the skin with its incisor teeth, found mainly in tropical America. *Flying winged animals like a mouse that sucks blood of other animals are known as vampires.*

Vanadium – *(noun)* the chemical element of atomic number 23, a hard grey metal used to make alloy steels. *Vanadium is a soft poisonous silver-grey metal that is added to some type of steel to make it stronger.*

Vanguard – *(noun)* **1** the foremost part of an advancing army or naval force. *Vanguards have reported sighting enemy forces near the* *border*. **2** a group of people leading the way in new developments or ideas. a position at the forefront of developments or ideas. *Our company is proud to be in the vanguard of new scientific developments.*

Vanish – *(verb)* **1** disappear suddenly and completely. *The ship vanished into the sea without a trace.* gradually cease to exist. *The environment is under threat since large trees are vanishing due to rising temperature.* **2** become zero. *All hopes of peaceful settlement have now vanished.*

Vanishing Point – *(noun)* the point at which something has been decreasing disappears altogether. *The rates of interest have dwindled to vanishing point.*

Vantage – *(noun)* a place or position affording a good view. *From my vantage point, I could see the whole of Delhi.*

Vaporable – *(adjective)* possible to convert into vapour. *Cold gasoline doesn't vaporize easily.*

Varicosity – *(noun)* something to do regarding vein, especially in the leg. *Following the accident, he has been diagnosed as suffering from varicosity due to poor circulation of blood in the leg.*

Varied – *(adjective)* incorporating a number of different types or elements; showing variation or variety. *His bio data reflects a long and varied career.*

Variety – *(noun)* **1** the quality or state of being different or diverse. *It's the variety that makes my job so enjoyable.* **2** a number of things of the same general class that are distinct in character or quality. *This club offers a variety of leisure activities.* a thing which differs in some way from others of the same general class; a type. a subspecies or cultivar. *This departmental store has fifty varieties of fresh and frozen fishes.* **3** a form of entertainment consisting of a series of different types of act, such as singing, dancing, and comedy. *At this complex you can enjoy a variety of shows every day.*

Variform – *(adjective)* of a group of things differing from one another in form. *India has a variform of languages.* of a single thing or a mass consisting of a variety of forms or things. *Variform education is necessary to succeed in present day competitive world.*

Variola – *(noun)* technical term for smallpox. *In 18th century, smallpox was known as variola.*

Varlet – *(noun)* **1** an unprincipled rogue. *Dishonest people go by the name of varlet.* **2** an attendant or servant. *About a century ago, a man or boy acting as an attendant or servant was usually known as a varlet.*

Varletry – *(noun)* practice of being a varlet. *Practice of varletry was fairly in vogue about a century ago.*

Varnish – *(noun)* **1** a substance consisting of resin dissolved in a liquid, applied to wood to give a hard, clear, shiny surface when dry. *The cupboard was coated with several coats of varnish.* **2** an external or superficial appearance: an outward varnish of civilization. *This latest book on history depicts an outward varnish of Harappan civilization.* *(verb)* apply varnish to. *She painted her finger nails with pink varnish.*

Vary – *(verb)* **1** differ in size, degree, or nature from something else of the same general class. *The properties here vary in size and price.* **2** change from one form or state to another. modify or change something to make it less uniform. *Our skin's moisture content varies with the weather conditions.*

Vascular – *(adjective)* relating to or denoting the system of vessels for carrying blood or in plants sap, water, and nutrients. *Over weight and lack of physical activity have started affecting his vascular system.*

Vasculum – *(noun)* a collecting box for plants, typically a flattened cylindrical metal case with a lengthwise opening. *Vasculum is a metallic container botanists use to collect plants.*

Vase – *(noun)* a decorative container without handles, typically made of glass or china and used as an ornament or for displaying cut flowers. *Porcelain vases containing cut flowers make drawing rooms a showpiece.*

Vaseline – *(noun)* a type of petroleum jelly used as an ointment and lubricant. *The doors glide open as if their rails have been vaselined.*

Vassal – *(noun)* a holder of land by feudal tenure on conditions of homage and allegiance. a person or country in a subordinate position to another. *Macedonia was a vassal state of the Ottoman Empire.*

Vast – *(adjective)* of very great extent or quantity; immense. *Tired of walking we decided to rest at a vast plain full of orchards.* (*noun*) an immense space. *India is a vast country in terms of area and population.*

Vastitude – *(noun)* quality of being vast. *Many neighbouring countries are fearful due to Chinese assertiveness and vastitude.*

Vastly – *(adverb)* the state of being vast. *He vastly exaggerated the inconveniences he faced during training.*

Vaticinate – *(verb)* foretell the future. *The lady spent much of her time vaticinating on learned political panels.*

Vaulter – *(noun)* one who vaults *He is the only vaulter who could jump over twenty feet in the first attempt.*

Vegetable – *(noun)* **1** a plant or part of a plant used as food. *Cauliflower, cabbage, potato, turnip, and bean are vegetables.* **2** a person who is incapable of normal mental or physical activity, especially through brain damage, a person with a dull or inactive life. *Since that accident, the patient has been in a vegetative state unable to respond to any stimulation.*

Vegetal – *(adjective)* **1** of or relating to plants. *A vegetal aroma was coming out strongly when cooking was under way.* **2** denoting the pole or extremity of an embryo containing the less active cytoplasm. *In the early stage of development, the yolk in the ovum or embryo is usually known as vegetal.*

Vegetarian – *(noun)* a person who does not eat meat for moral, religious, or health reasons. *I would like to order a vegetarian lunch today.* (*adjective*) eating or including no meat. *We decided to go to a vegetarian restaurant.*

Vegetate – *(verb)* **1** live or spend a period of time in a dull, inactive, unchallenging way. *If left alone, he would become inactive, sit in front of a TV and vegetate.* **2** of a plant or seed grow or sprout. *The company ordered that seeds be sent in a vegetating condition.*

Vehicle – *(noun)* **1** a thing used for transporting people or goods on land, e.g. a car, truck, or cart. *Mercedes has launched a new series of premium passenger vehicles in India. Heavy vehicles are not allowed to enter the city limit during day time.* **2** a means of expressing, embodying, or fulfilling something. *She uses painting as vehicle to express her ideas.* **3** a substance that facilitated the use of a drug, pigment, or other material mixed with it. *Ink pens are hardly used as a vehicle for writing these days.* **4** a film, programme, song, etc., intended to display the leading performer to the best advantage. *Speeches are a vehicle for politicians to air their views during election time.*

Velarium – *(noun)* a large awning used in ancient Rome to shelter an amphitheatre. *Velariums are still used overhead to protect tennis courts from vagaries of weather.*

Velivolent

Velleity – *(noun)* a wish or inclination not strong enough to lead to action. *The outlandish speech angered me, but I chose to remain a velleity.*

Velocity – *(noun)* the speed of something in a given direction. *There are high-tech machines to increase the velocity of the emitted particles.* in general use speed. *The rocket blasted off with an incredible velocity.*

Velvet – *(noun)* **1** a closely woven fabric of silk, cotton, or nylon with a thick short pile on one side. *The armchair we bought is covered in velvet.* **2** soft downy skin that covers a deer's antler while it is growing. *The moose was still rubbing the velvet from his antlers.*

Venal – *(adjective)* showing or motivated by susceptibility to bribery. *The customs officers at air and seaports are notoriously venal.*

Vend – *(verb)* **1** offer small items for sale, especially from a slot machine. *There was a woman vending cakes and parties at the cinema hall.* **2** sell. *The company manufactures and vends environmentally friendly beauty products.*

Vender – *(noun)* a person offering something for sale, especially in a street. *We buy vegetables from the vendor, he comes here each evening.*

Vendee – *(noun)* a buyer, especially of property. *The real estate developer invited all vendees to lunch and showed them their flats.*

Vendue – *(noun)* a public auction. *Dutch used to call sale by auction as vendue during 18th century.*

Venerability – *(noun)* respect given due to age, character, knowledge. *He is known for great wisdom and, therefore, his venerability is not in doubt.*

Venereal – *(adjective)* **1** of or relating to venereal disease. *There has been a steady increase in venereal infection in South Africa.* **2** of or relating to sexual desire or sexual intercourse. *Every venereal act committed outside of marriage is highly reprehensible.*

Venery – *(noun)* sexual indulgence. *All but a few of them engaged in venery.*

Vengeance – *(noun)* punishment inflicted or retribution exacted for an injury or wrong. *In the ensuing election, voters are ready to wreak vengeance on all politicians.*

Venial – *(adjective)* denoting a sin that is not regarded as depriving the soul of divine grace. *Everything they have disclosed up to now can be seen as venial.*

Venter – *(noun)* relating to abdomen. *The underside of the belly of animal is known as venter.*

Ventiduct – *(noun)* an air passage, especially one for ventilation. *The ventiduct of the air conditioner is not working.*

Ventricle – *(noun)* each of the two larger and lower cavities of the heart. *Each of the two main chambers of the heart, left and right, that pump blood to the body are called a ventricle.*

Ventricular - *(adjective)* something to do with a hollow part or cavity of an organ *An x-ray was done to determine the ventricular positioning of the heart.*

Verdancy – *(noun)* the state of greenery with grass or other rich vegetation *We stayed for a few hours enjoying the alluring verdancy of the hills in Kodaikanal.*

Verderer – *(noun)* a judicial officer of a royal forest. *The verderer arrested the poachers who were trying to kill elephants for their tusk.*

Verdict – *(noun)* **1** a decision on an issue of fact in a civil or criminal case or an inquest. *The jury returned a verdict of not guilty.* **2** an opinion or judgment. *This seems a fair verdict on the state of yellow journalism.*

Verdure – *(noun)* lush green vegetation. *Fresh green colour of lush vegetation is called verdure.*

Verifiable – *(adjective)* anything that can be substantiated, proved correct or otherwise. *His conclusions have been verified by later experiments.*

Verily – *(adverb)* truly; certainly. *Verily, what these people are doing is nothing but madness.*

Veritable – *(adjective)* genuine; actual; properly so called used to qualify a metaphor: a veritable price explosion. *The meal that followed was a veritable feast.*

Vermicelli – *(plural noun)* **1** pasta made in long slender threads. *Fine wheat flower converted into long thin threads is known as vermicelli.* **2** shreds of chocolate used to decorate cakes. *Small pieces of thin chocolate used to decorate cakes are known as vermicelli.*

Vermicide – *(noun)* a substance that is poisonous to worms. *Vermicides are used to kill worms in sewerage lines.*

Vermicular – *(adjective)* like a worm in form or movement; vermiform. *Medical tests confirmed some vermicular movement in his stomach.*

Vermillion – *(noun)* a brilliant red pigment made from mercury sulphide cinnabar. *Married Indian women put vermillion on their head between the partings of hair.* a brilliant red colour. *They coated the outer portion of their house using vermillion coloured paint.*

Vermination – *(noun)* the state of breeding or becoming infected with vermin. *This area, full of filth, need dedicated vermination by municipal authorities.*

Vernacular – *(noun)* **1** the language or dialect spoken by the ordinary people of a country or region. *He writes in the vernacular to reach a larger audience.* the specialized terminology of a group or activity. *When talking to the gardener, I used the gardening vernacular.* **2** vernacular architecture. *In the city suburb, we saw many buildings in which Mughal architecture merged into farmhouse vernacular.* *(adjective)* **1** spoken as or using one's mother tongue rather than a second language. *There is no dearth of vernacular literature with this publisher.* **2** of architecture concerned with domestic and functional rather than monumental buildings. *We came across many vernacular buildings while holidaying in Goa.*

Vernal – *(adjective)* of, in, or appropriate to spring. *The vernal freshness of the land was very alluring.*

Vernier – *(noun)* a small movable graduated scale for obtaining fractional parts of subdivisions on a fixed main scale of a barometer, sextant, or other measuring instrument. *Vernier caliper is used to make small measurements in the laboratory.*

Versant – *(noun)* a region of land sloping in one general direction. *We came down the mountain by using the low gradient eastern versant.*

Versify – *(verb)* turn into or express in verse. *It was never suggested that Wordsworth should simply versify Coleridge's ideas.*

Version – *(noun)* **1** a particular form of something differing in certain respects from an earlier form other forms of the same type of thing. *The revised version of the paper was produced for a later meeting.* **2** an account of a matter from a particular person's point of view. *He narrated his version of what happened yesterday.* **3** a particular edition or translation of a book or other work. *The English version will be published next year.*

Versus – *(preposition)* especially in sporting and legal use against. *England versus Australia cricket test match starts today.* as opposed to; in contrast to. *The company is weighing up the pros and cons of organic versus inorganic produce.*

Vertebra – *(noun)* each of the series of small bones forming the backbone. *The needle was inserted between two of the vertebrae.*

Vertical – *(adjective)* **1** at right angles to a horizontal plane. *The y-axis is at right angle to the x-axis.* having the top directly above the bottom. *Don't move, please keep your back in vertical position.* **2** at the zenith or the highest point. *The resort claims a vertical of 3,100 metres.* **3** involving or passing through all the different levels of a hierarchy or progression. *There is a greater need for more vertical cooperation between manufacturers and service providers.* *(noun)* **1** a vertical line or plane. *The columns incline several degrees away from the vertical.* **2** an upright structure. *We remodelled the opening with simple unadorned verticals.*

Vertiginous – *(adjective)* causing vertigo, especially by being extremely high or steep. *We encountered a vertiginous drop to the valleys below.*

Vertigo – *(noun)* a sensation of whirling and loss of balance, caused by looking down from a great height. *Be warned that looking down from the mountain can bring about vertigo leading to fall.*

Vertu – *(noun)* variant spelling of virtu. *Literary speaking, the good qualities inherent in a person or thing is referred as vertu.*

Verve – *(noun)* vigour, spirit, and style. *Shakira sings with supreme verve and flexibility.*

Very – *(adverb)* in a high degree. *A very large amount of money was deposited yesterday.* without qualification: the very best quality. *He decided to donate his very own car.* *(adjective)* **1** actual; precise: *She might be phoning him at this very moment.* his very words. real; genuine. *The fantastic result was the benevolence of the very God of Heaven.* **2** emphasizing an extreme point in time or space. *I have liked this book from the very beginning.* **3** with no addition; mere. *The very thought of drinking makes him feel sick.*

Vesical – *(adjective)* relating to or affecting the urinary bladder. *The tests confirm that his vesical artery is functioning properly.*

Vesicant – *(adjective)* tending to cause blistering. *Rubbing hands on a stone may be vesicant.* *(noun)* an agent that causes blistering. *Even dilute hydrochloric acid is a vesicant; you must wear hand gloves for protection.*

Vessel – *(noun)* **1** a ship or large boat. *Titanic was the largest sea-going passenger vessel during 1910s.* **2** a hollow container used to hold liquid. *Bronze age drinking vessels have been excavated.* **3** a duct or canal conveying blood or other fluid. *A tube that carries blood through the body of a person is known as a vessel.* any of the tubular structures in the vascular system of a plant, serving to conduct water and nutrients from the root. *Nutrients are passed along the body of a plant through vessels.* **4** chiefly in biblical use a person regarded as embodying a particular quality: *She was inherently the weaker vessel.*

Vestal –*(adjective)* **1** of or relating to the roman goddess Vesta. *Romans even today go to vestal temple to seek blessings of Goddess Vesta.* **2** chaste; pure. *Literary, chaste women are described as vestal.* *(noun)* a vestal virgin. a chaste woman, especially a nun. *Nuns are presumed to be leading a celibate and vestal life.*

Vestiary – *(adjective)* of or relating to dress. *Gender equality demands one to stay away from vestiary.* *(noun)* a room in a monastery in which clothes are kept. *Vestiary is a place similar to a vestibule to keep coats and hats.*

Veteran – *(noun)* **1** a person who has had long experience in a particular field. *Sachin Tendulkar is a veteran Indian cricketer.* **2** an ex-serviceman or servicewoman. *This is a memorial dedicated to the First World War veterans.*

Veterinary – *(adjective)* of or relating to the diseases, injuries, and treatment of farm and domestic animals. *There are not enough veterinary doctors to take care of animals in India.*

Vex – *(verb)* cause to feel annoyed or worried. *Food security is proving to be a vexed issue defying solution at World Trade Organisation meetings.* *(adjective)* angry; annoyed. *Price rise is the most vexing questions for policymakers.*

Vexatious – *(adjective)* **1** causing annoyance or worry. **2** of an action brought without sufficient grounds for winning, purely to cause annoyance to the defendant.

Vexing – *(adjective)* annoying, worrying. *Solution to India-Pakistan border issues are a vexing problem.*

Via – *(preposition)* travelling through a place en route to a destination. *We came to India via Bangladesh.* by way of; *Many people buy a home with a mortgage via a housing society.* through. by means of. *We have a file sent via electronic mail.*

Viaticum – *(noun)* the Eucharist as given to a person near or in danger of death. *Viaticum is an occasion when Christian people eat and drink in memory of last Supper Jesus had with his disciples.*

Vibrancy - *(noun)* youthfulness. *During Christmas time you will find the whole city flirting with vibrancy.*

Vibrant – *(adjective)* **1** full of energy and enthusiasm. *We went around the vibrant cosmopolitan city.* of colour or sounds bold and strong. *The huge ball room was decorated in vibrant blues and greens.* **2** quivering; pulsating. *The lady was vibrant with anger at the maid.*

Vibrissae – *(plural noun)* long stiff hairs growing around the mouth or elsewhere on the face of many mammals; *Vibrissae is one of the characteristics to differentiate animals into kinds.* whiskers. coarse bristle like feathers growing around the gape of certain insectivorous birds that catch insects in flight. *There are many birds that make use of their characteristic of vibrissae to survive.*

Viceregal – *(adjective)* of or relating to a viceroy. *The viceregal carriage moved out drawn with eight horses.*

Vicious – *(adjective)* **1** cruel or violent. *As a result of vicious assault, the person had to be hospitalized with multiple fracture.* of an animal wild and dangerous. *The dog was vicious and likely to bite.* **2** immoral. *Every soul on earth, virtuous or vicious, will perish one day.* **3** of language or a line of reasoning imperfect; defective. *Try to come out of the vicious cycle of bad characters.*

Victor – *(noun)* **1** a person who defeats an enemy or opponent in a battle, game, or competition. *The president congratulated the victors.* **2** a code word representing the letter V, used in radio communication. *The military symbol in radio* *communication for A is alpha, for B is bravo, for C id Charlie, similarly for V it is victory.*

Victorious - *(adjective)* having won a victory; triumphant. of or characterized by victory. *The victorious team was accorded a red carpet welcome on arrival at the airport.*

Victual - *(noun)* food or provisions. *Meat, chicken, fish and other savoury victuals were served at the party. (verb)* **1** provide with food or other stores. *The ship wasn't even properly victualled.* **2** eat. *I invite you to a victual with me next Sunday.*

Vide - *(verb)* see; consult used as an instruction in a text to refer the reader elsewhere. *Vide your comments I have to state the following.*

Videlicet - *(adverb)* more formal term for viz. *Instead of 'videlicet', people are better aware of its short form 'viz'.*

Vie - *(verb)* compete eagerly with others in order to do or achieve something. *Both finalists are vying with each other to win the trophy.*

Vigneron - *(noun)* a person who cultivates grapes for winemaking. *He is the most trusted vigneron for suppling grapes to wine manufacturers.*

Vignette - *(noun)* **1** a brief evocative description, account, or episode. *The function was organized to witness the classic vignette of embassy life.* **2** a small illustration or portrait photograph which fades into its background without a definite border. a small ornamental design in a book or carving, typically based on foliage. *Vignette is a small ornamental design filling a space in a book or carving. (verb)* portray in the style of a vignette. produce a photograph with softened or fading edges. *We asked instructions the studio to make a cropped, oval, vignetted copy of a family group portrait.*

Vigour- *(noun)* physical strength and good health. *His physique reflected a sign of vigour and health.* effort, energy, and enthusiasm. *He set about executing the new task with vigour.*

Village - *(noun)* a group of houses situated in a rural area, larger than a hamlet and smaller than a town. *The coastal areas in Kerala consist essentially of pretty fishing villages.* a self contained district or community within a town or city: *A Olympic village was built for participants to live comfortably.* a small municipality with limited corporate powers. *The village sarpanch ensured that construction of two wells near the dwelling area was completed at the earliest.*

Vim - *(noun)* energy; enthusiasm. *You should go out and play the game with vim, vigour and energy.*

Vindicable - *(adjective)* state of clearing someone of suspicion. *More sober views expressed by respectable citizens were vindicable of proper action taken by police.*

Vindicator - *(noun)* step that removes suspicion. *Immediate action taken by police was indicator of its seriousness to arrest the criminals.*

Vindictive - *(adjective)* having or showing a strong or unreasoning desire for revenge. *The barrage of criticism was both vindictive and personalized.*

Vinegar - *(noun)* **1** a sour tasting liquid containing acetic acid, obtained by fermenting dilute alcoholic liquids, typically wine, cider, or beer, and used as a condiment or for pickling. *Most pickles served at hotels and restaurants are made with the help of vinegar.* **2** sourness or peevishness of behaviour. *His aggrieved and complaining tone held a touch of vinegar.*

Viol - *(noun)* a musical instrument of the renaissance and baroque periods, typically six stringed, held vertically and played with a bow. *Shaped like a violin, early type of musical instrument that produced similar kind of music was known as viol.*

Violate - *(verb)* **1** break or fail to comply with a rule or formal agreement. *Violators of signed agreement would be severely dealt with.* **2** treat with disrespect. *Don't violate the sanctity of mother-child relationship.* **3** rape or sexually assault. *He tried but failed to violate the modesty of a young woman at a lonely place.*

Violet - *(noun)* **1** a small plant typically with purple, blue, or white five petalled flowers. *Violet is a small garden plant that grows in spring with purple or white flowers.* used in names of unrelated plants with similar flowers, e.g. African violet. *She came dressed in violet.*

2 a bluish purple colour seen at the end of the spectrum opposite red. *In a rainbow, violet can be observed at one end and red colour at the other.*

Violin – *(noun)* a stringed musical instrument of treble pitch, having for strings and a body narrowed at the middle and with two shaped sound holes, played with a horsehair bow. *Violin is one of the most popular musical instruments.*

Viper – *(noun)* **1** a venomous snake with large hinged fangs, typically with dark patterns on a lighter background. *Russel viper is one of the most deadly snakes in the world.* **2** a spiteful or treacherous person. *A person who harms interest of others is known as a viper.*

Virgate – *(noun)* a varying measure of land, typically 30 acres. *He purchased in the suburban area a land measuring a virgate for constructing farmhouse.*

Virgo – *(noun)* **1** a large constellation the virgin, said to represent a maiden or goddess associated with the harvest. *Virgo is a large constellation of bright stars, largest of which is Spica.* **2** the sixth sign of the zodiac, which the sun enters about 23 August. *Persons born between the periods 23 August to 22 September are known as belonging to the zodiac Virgo.*

Virility – *(noun)* quality of having strength, energy, sex drive, manliness. *This club lays great importance on a man's virility.*

Virtuosity – *(noun)* great skill in music or another artistic pursui. *The auditorium vibrated with high performance of considerable virtuosity.*

Virtuous – *(adjective)* **1** having or showing high moral standards. *She considered herself virtuous because she neither drank nor smoked.* **2** especially of a woman chaste. *Nuns are believed to be virtuous in character.*

Virulence – *(noun)* extremely severe disease. *The virulence of influenza is causing concern among medical fraternity.*

Virus – *(noun)* **1** a submicroscopic infective particle, typically consisting of nucleic acid coated in protein, which is able to multiply within the cells of a host organism. *The tests have confirmed existence of hepatitis B virus in the sample.* **2** an infection or disease caused by such an agent. *There are many deadly diseases caused by virus.* **3** a piece of code surreptitiously introduced into a system in order to corrupt it or destroy data. *Computers become slow to respond when infected with malicious viruses.*

Visage – *(noun)* a person's face, with reference to the form of the features. *The candidate selected for this position has an elegant, angular visage.* a person's facial expression. *There was lurking sadness behind his visage of cheerfulness.*

Viscera – *(plural noun)* the internal organs in the main cavities of the body, especially those in the abdomen, e. g. the intestines. *The large organs inside the body, such as the heart, lungs and stomach are known as viscera.*

Viscous – *(adjective)* having a thick, sticky consistency between solid and liquid; having a high viscosity. *Diesel is more viscous than petrol or kerosene.*

Viscus – singular form of viscera. *The viscus has been sent for medical examination.*

Visibility – *(noun)* the state of being able to see or be seen. *A reduction in police presence helped improve visibility of people on the streets.* the distance one can see as determined by light and weather conditions. *All trains are running slow because the visibility, because of fog, is down to 15 yards.*

Visible – *(adjective)* able to be seen. *The temple spire is clearly visible from miles away.* of light within the range of wavelengths to which the eye is sensitive. *Silhouette of a man hiding behind the bush was visible even in that dark night.* able to be perceived or noticed easily. *Improvement in cleanliness in the city is clearly visible.* in a position of public prominence. *A highly visible member of the visiting delegation met the President today.*

Vision – *(noun)* **1** the faculty or state of being able to see. *She has a defective vision.* **2** the ability to think about or plan the future with imagination or wisdom. *The firm has completely lost its vision and direction.* a mental image of what the future will or could be like. *He visions India to be a super power by 2050.* **3** an experience of seeing something in a dream or trance, or as a supernatural apparition. *He has visions of becoming the best actor of his time.* a person or sight of unusual beauty. *She was a vision in black velvet.* *(verb)* imagine; envision. *Why don't you display your vision for tomorrow?*

Visit – *(verb)* **1** go to see and spend some time with socially or as a guest. *He went to visit his grandmother.* go to see and spend some time in a place as a tourist or guest. *He went out to visit Qutub Minar in Delhi with his friends.* go to see for any specific purpose, such as to receive or give professional advice. *She went to see a doctor for a thorough check-up of her well-being.* **2** inflict or be inflicted on someone. *The cruel prank visited upon him by his friends caused him extreme pain.* 3 chat. *There was nothing to do but visit with one another.* **4** of god come to in order to bring comfort or salvation. *God shall visit earth to bring solace to all inhabitants.* *(noun)* an act of visiting. *I will pay a visit to him shortly.* a temporary stay at a place. *I don't stay her, I am only visiting.*

Visor – *(noun)* **1** a movable part of a helmet that can be pulled down to cover the face. *He purchased a plastic safety helmet with a transparent visor.* **2** a screen for protecting the eyes from unwanted light, especially one at the top of a vehicle windscreen. *The phone fits comfortably in the driver's visor.* **3** a stiff peak at the front of a cap. *He isn't wearing his visor cap today.*

Vista – *(noun)* **1** a pleasing view, especially one seen through a long, narrow opening. *The telescope allowed us to see the vista of bright stars.* **2** a mental view of an imagined future event or situation. *Vistas of freedom seemed to open ahead of him.*

Visual – *(adjective)* of or relating to seeing or sight. *You should have a visual perception of the landscape before shooting the film.* *(noun)* a picture, piece of film, or display used to illustrate or accompany something. *The music should fit the visuals.*

Vital – *(adjective)* **1** absolutely necessary; essential. *It is vital that the system is regularly checked.* indispensable to the continuance of life: *Her vital organs were showing signs of improvement.* **2** full of energy; lively. *She is a beautiful, vital girl full of enthusism.* **3** fatal. (noun) the body's important internal organs. *The wound appears vital.*

Vitamin – *(noun)* any of a group of organic compounds which are essential for normal growth and nutrition and are required in small quantities in the diet because they cannot be synthesized by the body. *Most people generally don't get all the vitamins they need from a regular diet.*

Viticulture – *(noun)* the cultivation of grapevines. *The study of grape cultivation is known as viticulture.*

Vitreous – *(adjective)* likes glass in appearance or physical properties. *A coarse-grained rock with much grey vitreous quartz was available for sale at a premium..* of a substance derived from or containing glass. *This dinner-set is made of vitreous china.*

Vitriol – *(noun)* **1** sulphuric acid. in names of metallic sulphates, e.g. blue vitriol copper sulphate and green vitriol ferrous sulphate. *It was as if his words were spraying vitriol right in front of her.* **2** extreme bitterness or malice. *He was shocked by his father's sudden gush of fury and vitriol.*

Vituperate – *(verb)* blame or insult in strong or violent language. *For no fault of hers, she was at the centre of vituperative sarcasm.*

Vivacious – *(adjective)* especially of a woman or child attractively lively and animated. *We were amused with the vivaciousness of a little girl jumping all over the park.*

Vivacity – *(noun)* quality, especially in a woman, of being attractively lively. *He was struck by her vivacity, sense of humour and charm.*

Viva-voce – *(adjective)* especially of an examination oral rather than written. *The viva voce examination has been scheduled for today itself.* *adverb)* orally rather than in writing. *(noun)* full form of viva. *We had better discuss this viva voce.*

Vivarium – *(noun)* an enclosure prepared so as to give animals a feeling of semi-natural conditions. *In most zoological parks, at least one vivarium is built to keep animals under observation, when required.*

Viviparous – *(adjective)* of an animal bringing forth live young which have developed inside the body of the parent. *Animals that produce live babies from their body rather than eggs are known as viviparous.*

Vixen – *(noun)* **1** a female fox. *A vixen is a wild animal of the dog family.* **2** a spiteful or quarrelsome woman. *She is a kind of outrageous little shaven-headed vixen who is always ready to get into a tiff with anyone.*

Vogue – *(noun)* often in phr. in/out of vogue the prevailing fashion or style at a particular time. *Child-centred education is quite in vogue these days.*

Voice – *(noun)* **1** the sound produced in a person's larynx and uttered through the mouth, as speech or song. *She raised her voice so that everyone present in the hall could hear her speech.* the ability to speak or sing. vocal condition for singing or speaking: *The soprano is in good voice.* **2** the range of pitch or type of tone with which a person sings. *She had strained and falsified her literary voice to the amusement of all.* **3** an opinion or attitude, or a means or agency by which it is expressed: a dissenting voice. *The opposition parties voiced their concern at the falling standards of education.* *(verb)* **1** express in words. *Please get all teachers to voice their opinions on important subjects.* **2** utter a speech sound with resonance of the vocal cords. *He speaks with a nasal voice.* **3** regulate the tone quality of organ pipes. *Voice quality of this musical instrument is not up to the mark.*

Volition – *(noun)* often in phr. of one's own volition the faculty or power of using one's will. *She went to the carnival on her own volition.*

Voltage – *(noun)* an electromotive force or potential difference expressed in volts. *Electric trains are powered by high voltage traction wires.*

Volubility – *(noun)* the quality of talking fluently, readily, or incessantly; talkativeness. *Her legendary volubility deserted her at the time of making first public speech.*

Volume – *(noun)* **1** a book forming part of a work or series. *We have published a biography of Rabindra nath Tagore in three volumes.* **2** a single book or a bound collection of printed sheets. *Third edition of her volume of short stories has been published.* a consecutive sequence of issues of a periodical. *We have quoted from extensively Chemistry in Britain Volume 28 Number 1.* **3** the amount of space occupied by a substance or object or enclosed within a container. *The sewer pipe could not cope with the volume of rainwater.* **4** the amount or quantity of something, especially when great. *The volumes of data computers handle these days are vast.* **5** fullness or expansive thickness. *This shampoo will give your hair volume and bounce.* **6** quantity or power of sound; degree of loudness. *Please turn down the volume of the music system.*

Voluptuous – *(adjective)* **1** relating to or characterized by luxury or sensual pleasure. *We bought long curtains for our bedroom in voluptuous crimson red.* **2** of a woman curvaceous and sexually attractive. *Everyone present at the floor wanted to dance with that voluptuous lady.*

Volution – *(noun)* a rolling or revolving motion. *A single turn of a spiral or coil is defined as a volution.*

Volvulus – *(noun)* an obstruction caused by twisting of the stomach or intestine. *The doctor advised surgery for caecal volvulus.*

Vomit – *(verb)* eject matter from the stomach through the mouth. *She used to vomit every time she took solid food.* emit in an uncontrolled stream or flow. *The newspaper press vomited fold after fold of paper.* *(noun)* matter vomited from the stomach. *The children's ward smelled of vomit and urine.*

Vowel – *(noun)* a speech sound which is produced by comparatively open configuration of the vocal tract and which is capable of forming a syllable. *He spoke with deep-vowelled German accent.* a letter representing such a sound. *In the English alphabet there are five vowels, namely, A, E, I, O and U.*

Vowelled – *(adjective)* speech which is capable of being formed into a syllable. *A man with heavy vowelled voice came to the restaurant.*

Voyage – *(noun)* a long journey involving travel by sea or in space. *He has decided to go on a voyage to Spain. (verb)* go on a voyage. sail over or along a sea or river. *He spent substantial part of his life voyaging along the Latin American coast.*

Vulcan – *(noun)* God of fire. *In Roman mythology, Vulcan is a name given to the God of fire.*

Vulgarian – *(noun)* an unrefined person, especially one with newly acquired power or wealth. *Due to enormous ancestral wealth coming his way, he has become a sort of jumped-up vulgarian.*

Vulpine – *(adjective)* of, relating to, or reminiscent of a fox or foxes. *She gave a vulpine smile while plotting next course of action.*

Ww

W – *(noun)* **1** the twenty third letter of the alphabet. **2** denoting the next after V in a set of items, categories, etc.

Waddle – *(verb)* walk with short steps and a clumsy swaying motion. *Two geese have waddled across the road.*

Wade – *(verb)* **1** walk through a liquid or viscous substance. *He waded through the knee-deep water.* **2** read laboriously through. *He waded through the book at a rapid pace.* **3** attack, intervene, or become involved in a vigorous or forceful way. *She waded into the crowd and started to beat off the boys.*

Wafer– *(noun)* **1** a very thin light, crisp sweet biscuit. *We purchased a wafer packet with a layer of chocolate.* **2** a small disc of dried paste formerly used for fastening letters or holding papers together. *Postal department has stopped using wafers for sticking envelopes.* **3** a very thin slice of a semiconductor crystal used as the substrate for solid state circuitry. *Millions of electronic circuits are printed on wafer-thin plates.*

Waft – *(verb)* pass easily or gently through the air. *The smell of stale food wafted out from the kitchen.* *(noun)* a gentle movement of air. a scent carried in the air. *A waft of roasting chicken was coming out from the kitchen.*

Wag – *(verb)* move rapidly to and fro. *The dog was wagging its tail.*

Wage – *(noun)* **1** a fixed regular payment for work, typically paid on a daily or weekly basis. *The factory workers were struggling to get better wages.* **2** the result or effect of doing something wrong or unwise. *The wages of crime are time spent in jail.* *(verb)* carry on a war or campaign. *Every country considers it necessary to destroy the enemy's capacity to wage war.*

Waggery – *(noun)* jocular behaviour or remarks. *You can expect such pranks and waggery only from the older boys.*

Waggish – *(adjective)* humorous, playful, or facetious. *Don't try out waggish tales on every occasion.*

Wagonette – *(noun)* a four wheeled horse drawn pleasure vehicle with facing side seats and one or two seats arranged crosswise in front. *Wagonettes are hardly in use today, they have given way to modern sleek cars.*

Wagtail – *(noun)* a slender songbird with a long tail that is frequently wagged up and down. *Wagtails are found wagging up and down over rivers only in Siberia.*

Waif – *(noun)* a homeless and helpless person, especially a neglected or abandoned child. *She is foster-mother to various waifs who have nowhere to go.*

Wail – *(noun)* a prolonged high pitched cry of pain, grief, or anger. *Harish let out a wail as soon as lights went out.* a sound resembling this. *The wail of air siren made them a worried lot.*

Wainscot – *(noun)* **1** an area of wooden panelling on the lower part of the walls of a room. *It has been decided to wainscot the interior to a height of 6 feet.* **2** fine imported oak, as used for such panelling. *These wainscots will be used to panel the walls.*

Waist – *(noun)* **1** the part of the human body below the ribs and above the hips. *He put his arm around her waist.* **2** a narrow part in the middle of something, e.g. a violin, hourglass; etc. the middle part of a ship, between the forecastle and the quarterdeck. *The sand glass had a waist of three inches only.* **3** a blouse or bodice. *She wore a transparent waist that left nothing to imagination.*

Waken – *(verb)* wake from sleep. *She wakened the child and dressed him.*

Walking - *(verb)* move at a regular pace by lifting and setting down each foot in turn, never having both feet off the ground at once. *She walked across the lawn. He turned and walked a few paces.* used to suggest that someone has achieved a state or position easily or undeservedly. *No one has the right to walk straight into a well-paid job for life. (adverb)* guide, accompany, or escort (someone) on foot. *He walked her home to her door.*

Wall - *(noun)* **1** a continuous vertical brick or stone structure that enclose or divides an area of land. *It was difficult to jump over the garden wall.* a side of a building or room. *We entered the drawing room having tapestries on the walls.* **2** a protective or restrictive barrier likened to a wall: *Suddenly there was a wall of silence as soon as the professor entered the class.* **3** a line of defenders forming a barrier against a free kick taken near the penalty area. *The defending side created a wall of defenders to prevent the ball entering the goal post.***4**. the membranous outer layer or lining of an organ or cavity. *The wall of stomach had a few perforations. (verb)* enclose within walls. block or seal a place by building a wall. *Western part of the city has been walled off with concrete to prevent sea water enter the city.*

Walled - *(adjective)* to block or seal something by erecting a barrier. *One doorway has been completely walled up.*

Wall-eyed - *(adjective)* an eye squinting outwards. *Pikeperch is a wall-eyed fish.*

Wall-flower - *(noun)* **1** a southern European plant with fragrant flowers that bloom in early spring. *Wall flower is a garden plant with yellow, orange or red flowers.* **2** a shy or excluded person at a dance or party, especially a girl without a partner. *No one came to partner her as such she was left as a wall flower.*

Wallet - *(noun)* **1** a pocket sized, flat, folding holder for money and plastic cards. *He took out money from his wallet.* **2** a bag for holding provisions when travelling. *She got busy readying her wallet with beauty provisions.*

Wallop - *(verb)* **1** strike or hit very hard. heavily defeat. *He walloped the back of her head with a flexible stick.* **2** strikingly large. *He felt tired of getting walloped with excise duty taxes. (noun)* a heavy blow or punch. potent effect. *I gave the thief a wallop with my left foot.*

Walnut - *(noun)* an edible wrinkled nut enclosed by a hard shell, produced inside a green fruit. *Walnut is a god source of high quality protein.*

Wan - *(adjective)* pale and giving the impression of illness or exhaustion. *He was disappointed when she gave him a wan smile.*

Wander - *(verb)* walk or move in a leisurely, casual, or aimless way. *He wandered aimlessly around the park.* move slowly away from a fixed point or place. move slowly through or over. *The child was found wandering in the streets all alone. (noun)* an act or instance of wandering. *Her thoughts wandered back to her college days.*

Wane - *(verb)* **1** have a progressively smaller part of its visible surface illuminated, so that it appears to decrease in size. *Confidence in dollar has waned considerably around the world markets.* **2** become weaker. *The epidemic of swine flu is on the wane.*

Wangle - *(verb)* obtain by persuading others to comply or by manipulating events. *She succeeded in wangling an invitation to the top flight party. (noun)* an instance of obtaining something in such a way. *The opposition party regarded the coalition as a wangle of opportunist politicians.*

Want - *(verb)* **1** have a desire to possess or do something; wish for. *We want to go to the beach party. I want to speak to her immediately.* **2** be sought by the police. *He is wanted by the police in connection with the theft committed last night.* **3** require to be attended to: *The director wants me to be in the studio.* desirable or essential. *You will want for nothing while you are with me. (noun)* **1** lack or deficiency. poverty. *For want of a better option we went by train.* **2** a desire for something. *These are the expression of our wants and desires.*

Wanted - *(adjective)* being searched for by police. *He is wanted by the police in connection with robberies.*

Wanton – *(adjective)* **1** deliberate and unprovoked. *Properties were destroyed due to sheer wanton vandalism.* **2** sexually immodest or promiscuous. *Her cheeks burned as she recounted how forward he had been, how wanton, how immodest.* **3** growing profusely. *We found wanton growth of bushes around the vacant house.* *(noun)* a sexually immodest or promiscuous woman. *She behaved like a wanton.* *(verb)* **1** play; frolic. *The sea breeze wantoned among the quivering leaves of the chestnut tree.* **2** behave in a sexually immodest or promiscuous way. *These are the women who have wantoned with suitors.*

Warble – *(verb)* sing softly and with a succession of constantly changing notes. *Birds were warbling in the trees.* sing in a trilling or quavering voice. *He warbled in an implausible baritone voice.* *(noun)* a warbling sound or utterance. *Through the wall we could hear a faint warble.*

Warbler – *(noun)* a small, actives songbird, typically living in trees and bushes and having a warbling song. *These are a few warblers that catch insects with the help of their melodious songs.*

Ward – *(noun)* **1** a room in a hospital, typically one allocated to a particular type of patient. *Hospitals designate different wards for different diseases.* **2** an administrative division of a city or borough, typically represented by a councillor or councillors. *Each officer has been given charge of different wards of the city.* **3** a child or young person under the care and control of a guardian appointed by their parents or a court, guardianship. *For the last five years, the boy has been my ward.* **4** prevent someone or something from harming or affecting one, guard, protect. *I saw them keeping ward at one of those huge gates.*

Warden – *(noun)* **1** a person responsible for the supervision of a particular place or procedure. *The warden came down heavily on the boys creating nuisance in the hostel.* **2** the head of certain schools, colleges, or other institutions. *The principal of the college has asked all hostel wardens to attend the emergency meeting.* **3** a prison governor. *The warden was asked to explain how the prisoner managed to escape the jail premises.*

Warder – *(noun)* a prison guard. *Warders have been cautioned to be in a state of high alert in the face of intelligence reports.*

Ware – *(noun)* **1** pottery, typically that of a specified type. *These are the cooking wares recently excavated from this area.* manufactured articles of a specified type. *These wares are of Italian make.* **2** articles offered for sale. *Traders in the street markets displayed their wares.*

Warehouse – *(noun)* **1** a large building where raw materials or manufactured goods may be stored. *Before sending to the distributors, we sent all our products from the factory to our warehouse.* **2** a large wholesale or retail store. *This is a discount warehouse.* *(verb)* store in a warehouse. *The steel ingots were warehoused the following day.* place in a bonded warehouse pending the payment of import duty. *We went to the warehouse to take delivery of imported electronic goods.*

Wares *(noun)* pottery of specified type. *All aluminum wares were on display.*

Warily – *(adverb)* cautiously, carefully. *He walk warily down the street, afraid of being caught.*

Wariness - *(noun)* caution about possible dangers or problems. *I seldom use computer at night because of my mother's wariness.* lack of trust, suspicion. *They had all regarded her presence with wariness.*

Warlock – *(noun)* a man who practices witchcraft. *Stay away from him, he is a warlock.*

Warner – *(noun)* informer of something in advance. *He acted like a warner that police were searching for him.*

Warning – *(noun)* **1** a statement or event that warns or serves as a cautionary example. *The police issued a warning about fake Rs 100 notes.* **2** cautionary advice. *A word of warning says— don't park illegally.*

Warren – *(noun)* a densely populated or labyrinthine building or district. *At the end of this lane is a warren of narrow gas-lit streets.*

Warrior – *(noun)* a brave or experienced soldier or fighter. *Warriors have the last war have been decorated with medals recently.*

Warship – *(noun)* a ship equipped with weapons and designed to take part in warfare at sea. *Indian Navy has more than 100 warships.*

Wary – *(adjective)*. cautious about possible dangers or problems. *I am quite wary of going to that place again.*

Wasp – *(noun)* a social insect with a narrow waisted, typically black and yellow striped body, which carries a sting and builds elaborate nests from wood pulp. *Wasp is a yellow and black flying insect that can sting.*

Wastage – *(noun)* **1** use action or process of wasting. *This is a sheer wastage of natural resources.* an amount wasted. *The government is trying to cut wastage of food grains by 20 per cent.* **2** the reduction in the size of a workforce as a result of voluntary resignation or retirement rather than enforced redundancy. *More than 150 staff was lost through natural wastage.* the number of people leaving a job or further educational establishment before they have completed their training or education. *The influence of academic ability on student wastage turned out to be minimal.*

We – *(pronoun)* **1** used by a speaker to refer to himself or herself and one or more other people considered together or regarded as in the same category. *Nobody knows kids better than we teachers do. May we have a drink now?* people in general. *We should eat as well-balanced a diet as possible.* **2** used in formal contexts for or by a royal person, or by a writer, to refer to himself or herself. *Today we discuss the reasons for this decision.*

Weak – *(adjective)* **1** lacking physical strength and energy. *He was recovering from flu, and was very weak.* **2** liable to break or give way under pressure. *The steel chain may be broken off at a weak joint near the base.* not convincing or forceful. *The argument he advanced is an extremely weak one.* not secure, stable, or firmly established. having a downward tendency. **3** lacking power, influence, or ability. *She could only manage a weak, nervous smile.* **4** lacking intensity. *There was only a weak light from a single street lamp.* heavily diluted. *She only asked for a cup of weak coffee.*

Weal – *(noun)* a red, swollen mark left on flesh by a blow or pressure. a temporarily raised and reddened area of skin, usually accompanied by itching. *He slapped her cheek and a bright red weal sprang up on it.*

Wealth – *(noun)* **1** an abundance of valuable possessions or money. *Many industrialists use their wealth to bribe officials.* the state of being rich. *Many people buy bungalows and cars to display their wealth.* **2** an abundance or profusion of something desirable. *The country's mineral wealth should not be squandered.* a wealth of information. *The tables and maps contain a wealth of information.*

Weasel – *(noun)* **1** a small slender carnivorous mammal related to, but smaller than, the stoat. Irish term for stoat. *Siberian weasels have stormed the city.* **2** a deceitful or treacherous person. *We wanted to trust him but he proved himself to be a double-crossing weasel.* *(verb)* **1** achieve through cunning or deceit. *He suspects me of trying to weasel my way into her affections.* **2** behave or talk evasively. *We wanted her to take a firm stand, but she weaselled.*

Wednesday – *(noun)* the day of the week before Thursday and following Tuesday. *We are going on a picnic next Wednesday.* *(adverb)* on Wednesday. *Parents-teachers meeting is held the first Wednesday of each month.*

Wee – *(adjective)* little. *The lyrics of the song are a wee bit too sweet and sentimental.*

Weeds – *(noun)* **1** a wild plant growing where it is not wanted and in competition with cultivated plants. *The garden was overgrown with weeds.* **2** cannabis. tobacco. *He is addicted to cigarettes but he wants to give up this weed.* **3** a weak or skinny person. *He always believed party games were for weeds and wets.* *(verb)* **1** remove weeds from. *I was weeding a flower bed.* **2** remove unwanted items or members from something. *This research group must raise the level of research and weed out the less productive work.*

Week – *(noun)* **1** a period of seven days. *The training programme lasts twenty six weeks.* the period of seven days generally reckoned from and to midnight on Saturday night. *She has dance classes twice a week.* **2** the five days from Monday to Friday, or the time spent working during this period. *I work during the week, so I can only come to you on Saturdays.*

Ween – *(verb)* think or suppose. *She, I ween, is no sacred personage.*

Weep – *(verb)* **1** shed tears. *He wept over his poor result.* mourn for. *A grieving son wept over the body of his father.* shed tears over. *A young woman is weeping her lost lord.* **2** exude liquid. *He rubbed the sore, making it weep.*

Weir – *(noun)* a low dam built across a river to raise the level of water upstream or regulate its flow. *The government has built a weir on the western side of the river to prevent flood water entering the city.*

Welkin – *(noun)* the sky or heaven. *The crew made the welkin ring with their hurrahs.*

Well – *(adverb)* **1** in a good or satisfactory way. *The whole team played very well.* in a condition of prosperity or comfort. *They lived well and were generous with their money.* luckily; opportunely. *Hail fellow, well met.* **2** in a thorough manner. *Add the coke and lemon juice and mix well.* to a great extent or degree; very much. very; extremely: *He was well out of order.* **3** very probably; in all likelihood. with good reason. '*What are we doing here?' 'You may well ask.' (adjective)* **1** in good health; free or recovered from illness. in a satisfactory state or position. *I am feeling very well.* **2** sensible; advisable. *It would be well to know just what this suggestion entails.*

Wellington – *(noun)* a knee length waterproof rubber or plastic boot. *Wellington boots are hardly used these days.*

Welsh – *(verb)* fail to honour a debt or obligation. *I am not in the habit of welshing on my promises.*

Wen – *(noun)* **1** a boil or other swelling or growth on the skin. *A sebaceous cyst is generally known as a wen.* **2** a very large or overcrowded city. *Tokyo is the largest wen in the world.*

Wench – *(noun)* a girl or young woman. *In the new film about Shaley, she plays the token buxom wench.*

Wend – *(verb)* go slowly or by an indirect route. *He wended his way home through bylanes and not straight.*

Went – past of go. *We went to a party last night.*

Wept – past and past participle of weep. *He literally wept on seeing the poor workmanship.*

Wet – *(adjective)* **1** covered or saturated with liquid. *He followed the leader, slipping on the wet rock in the process.* of the weather rainy. *We had nothing for protection on that wet, windy evening.* involving the use of water or liquid. *He is yet to learn the wet methods of photography.* **2** not yet having dried or hardened. *The waterproof coat can easily be washed off while it is still wet.* **3** lacking forcefulness or strength of character; feeble. *The commander thought the cadets were a bit wet.* **4** allowing the free sale of alcoholic drink. *The programme depends on our willingness to help other alcoholics, both wet and dry. (verb)* past and past participle wet or wetted cover or touch with liquid. *He wetted a finger and flicked through the pages.* urinate in or on. *While dreaming the child wet the bed.* urinate involuntarily. *He was going to wet himself from fear.* infuse by pouring on boiling water. *She said she'd wet the tea immediately because they must be parched. (noun)* liquid that makes something damp. *I could feel the wet of his tears.*

Wetness –*(noun)* liquid that makes something wet. *The child caught cold due to wetness of his body.*

What – *(pronoun)* **1** asking for information specifying something. *What's the time?* asking for repetition of something not heard or confirmation of something not understood. *What did you say?* **2** the thing or things that. *What we need is your commitment.* **3** whatever. She had been robbed of what little money she had. **4** used to emphasize something surprising or remarkable. *Do you know what excuse she gave? (interrogative adverb)* **1** to what extent *What does it matter?* **2** used for emphasis or to invite agreement: poor show. *What a poor show?*

Wheat - *(noun)* a cereal widely grown in temperate countries, the grain of which is ground to make flour for bread, pasta, etc. *Wheat is a staple food in India.*

Wheaten - *(adjective)* made of wheat. *The content of these packets are wheaten products.*

Wheedle - *(verb)* employ endearments or flattery to persuade someone to do something. *He had wheedled us into employing his sister.*

Wheen - *(noun)* a considerable number or amount. *She carried a when of small changes.*

Wheeze - *(verb)* breathe with a whistling or rattling sound in the chest, as a result of obstruction in the air passages. *The sickness often leaves her wheezing.* make an irregular rattling or spluttering sound. *The engine of the motor car coughed, wheezed, and came to a standstill. (noun).* a sound of a person wheezing. *'Don't worry my child,' he wheezed.*

Whelk - *(noun)* a predatory marine mollusc with a heavy pointed spiral shell. *Only a few whelks are edible.*

Whelp - *(noun)* **1** a puppy. a cub. *The lioness was suckling her whelps.* **2** a boy or young man. *It appears too high to call her 'Mam'—isn't that so, whelp?*

When - *(interrogative adverb)* **1** at what time. When are you reaching? how soon. *When can you make it to the station, the train is about to depart?* **2** in what circumstances. *When would such a rule be justifiable? conjunction* 1 at or during the time that. *I loved history when I was at school.* at any time that, whenever. *Can you spare ten minutes when it's convenient?* **2** after which; and just then. *She had drifted off to sleep when the phone rang.* **3** in view of the fact that; considering that. *Why bother to paint it when you can photograph it more or less with the same effect?*

Whence - *(interrogative adverb)* from what place or source. *The Andes Mountains, whence the ore is procured. (adverb)* from which; from where. *Whence does our Parliament derive this power?* to the place from which. *She would be sent back whence she came.* as a consequence of which. *Whence it followed that the strategies were quite obsolete.*

Whenever - *conjunction* at whatever time. *You can seek help whenever you need it.* every time that. *The springs in the chair creak whenever I change my position. (interrogative adverb)* used for emphasis instead of when in questions. *Whenever shall we get to the top of the mountain?*

Where - *(interrogative adverb)* in or to what place or position. *Where are we going?* in what direction or respect. *Where does the argument lead? rel. (adverb)* **1** at, in, or to which. *I first saw her in Delhi, where I lived in the early nineties.* **2** the place or situation in which. *This is where I used to live earlier.* in or to a place or situation in which. *You must sit where I can see you.*

Wherewithal - *(noun)* the money or other resources needed for a particular purpose: *They lacked the wherewithal to pay the dues.*

Wherry - *(noun)* a light rowing boat used chiefly for carrying passengers. *We enjoyed a short sea trip on a wherry.*

Whether - *(conjunction)* expressing a double or choice between alternatives. *She appeared undecided whether to go or stay at home.* expressing an enquiry or investigation. *I'll see whether she's at home.* indicating that a statement applies whichever of the alternatives mentioned is the case. *The only issue arising would be whether or not the publication was defamatory.*

Whew - *(exclamatory)* used to express surprise, relief, or a feeling of being very hot or tired. *Whew—and I thought it was a serious matter!*

Whey - *(noun)* the watery part of milk that remains after the formation of curds. *Whey is very good for health if taken in the morning or afternoon.*

Which - asking for information specifying one or more people or things from a definite set. *Which way is the wind blowing?* used referring to something previously mentioned when introducing a clause giving further information. *It was a crisis for which he was completely unprepared.*

Whiff – *(noun)* **1** a smell that is smelt only briefly or faintly. *I caught a whiff of Lakme perfume.* **2** a trace or hint of something bad or exciting: *There had been a whiff of financial scandal in the past. There was a whiff of danger.* **3** a puff or breath of air or smoke. *Whiffs of smoke emerged from the boiler. (verb)* get a brief or faint smell of. *He whiffed the broth that was simmering on the gas stove.*

Whilst – *(adverb)* while. *The captain was in the pool whilst other players were toying in he field.*

Whimper – *(verb)* make a series of low, feeble sounds expressive of fear, pain, or discontent. *Being alone, the child in a bed nearby began to whimper. (noun)* a whimpering sound. *Her first appearance on the stage ended with a whimper rather than a bang.*

Whimsy – *(noun)* **1** playfully quaint or fanciful behavior or humour. *The movie we watched was an awkward blend of whimsy and moralizing.* a thing that is fanciful or odd. *The stone carvings and whimsies.* **2** a whim. *There was a clean slate on which we were expected to write opinion that suited our whimsy.*

Whinny – *(verb)* make such a sound. *The horse whinnied and tossed his head happily.*

Whisky – *(noun)* **1** a spirit distilled from malted grain, especially barley or rye. *Bottles of whisky were ordered for the party.* **2** a code word representing the letter W, used in radio communication. *Militaries commonly use the word whisky to represent the alphabet w during signalling and communications.*

Whisper – *(verb)* speak very softly using one's breath rather than one's throat. *She was whispering in his ear.* be rumoured. *It was whispered that he would soon join the opposition party. (noun)* a whispered word or phrase, or a whispering tone of voice. *She spoke to him in a whisper.* a soft rustling or murmuring sound. *The thunder became a muted whisper.* a rumour or piece of gossip. *We heard the whispers of their blossoming romance.*

Whither – *(interrogative adverb)* to what place or state. *They asked people whither they would emigrate.* what is the likely future of. *Whither modern architecture.*

Whittle – *(verb)* **1** carve by repeatedly cutting small slices from it. *He was sitting at the door, whittling a piece of wood with a knife.* **2** reduce something by degrees. *The number of shortlisted candidates was whittled down to five.*

Whiz – *(verb)* move quickly through the air with a whistling or whooshing sound. *The missiles whizzed past us.* move or cause to move or go fast. *The weeks whizzed by and the time arrived to go back to hostel. (noun)* **1** a whizzing sound. *We had a quick whizz around the research-and-development facility of this company.* **2** a person who is extremely clever at something. *He is a computer whiz.*

Who – *(pronoun)* **1** what or which person or people. *I wonder who that letter was from.* **2** introducing a clause giving further information about a person or people previously mentioned. the person that *Aron plays the cat who caught the mouse* ; whoever. *Who was I to object?*

Whoa – *(exclamatory)* used as a command to a horse to stop or slow down. *Whoa! That's a huge bargain.*

Whop – *(verb)* hit hard. *Tony whopped him on the nose. (noun)* a heavy blow or its sound. *The loud whop of the helicopter echoed in the still air.*

Whopper – *(noun)* **1** a thing that is extremely large. *The novel is nearly 2000 page whopper.* **2** a gross or blatant lie. *What he is saying is a big whopper, hard to believe.*

Whoso – *(pronoun)* archaic term for whoever. *Whoso comes will be declared a tress passer.*

Wicked – *(adjective)* **1** evil or morally wrong. *There is no dearth of wicked and unscrupulous politicians.* **2** playfully mischievous. *She has a wicked sense of humour.* 3 excellent; wonderful. *Roma makes wicked cakes.*

Wicker – *(noun)* pliable twigs, typically of willow, plaited or woven to make items such as furniture and baskets. *We went to the market looking to buy a set of wicker chairs.*

Wide – *(adjective)* **1** of great or more than average width. *At last we reached a wide road.* from side to side. *This page measures 15 cm long by 12 cm wide.* open to the full extent. *Her eyes were wide with fear.* **2** including a great variety of people or things. *The opinion polls take into consideration a wide range of responses.* spread among a large number or over a large area. *The food security is likely to cover a wide population.* wider share ownership. *It was the government's desire for wider share ownership.* **3** at a considerable or specified distance from a point or mark. *His shot landed wide of the mark.* *(adverb)* to the full extent. *His eyes remained wide open.* *(noun)* a ball that is judged to be to wide of the stumps for the batsman to play. *The bowler sent down a few wide balls in the test match.*

Width – *(noun)* **1** the measurement or extent of something from side to side; the lesser of two or the least of three dimensions of a body. a piece of something at its full extent from side to side. *The cricket pitch was about seven feet in width.* **2** wide range or extent. *The width of experience required for these positions is at least 15 years.*

Wig – *(noun)* a covering for the head made of real or artificial hair. *She wore an auburn coloured wig.*

Wigeon – *(noun)* a dabbling duck with mainly reddish brown and grey plumage, the male having a whistling call. *Penelope and Americana ducks are two prominent species of wigeon.*

Wiggle – *(verb)* move or cause to move with short movements up and down or from side to side. *My teeth were wiggling about due to fear.* *(noun)* a wiggling movement. *The dancer tantalizingly wiggled her hips.*

Wile – *(noun)* a devious or cunning stratagem. *He is a wily politician.* *(verb)* lure; entice. *She could be neither driven nor wiled into flaunting her physical assets.*

Will – *(modal verb)* **1** expressing the future tense. *You will regret it as you become older.* expressing a strong intention or assertion about the future. *I will succeed, come what may.* **2** expressing inevitable events. *Accidents will happen irrespective of traffic rules.* **3** expressing a request. *Will you stay with us here for some more time?* expressing desire, consent, or willingness. *Will you have a drink?* **4** expressing facts about ability or capacity. *This car will hold 10 litres in its tank.* **5** expressing habitual behaviour. *She will go on dancing for hours.*

Willy-nilly – *(adverb)* **1** whether one likes it or not. *The management has been forced to accept labour union's terms willy-nilly.* **2** without direction or planning; haphazardly. *The government expanded food security programmes willy-nilly.*

Windbag – *(noun)* a person who talks a lot but says little of any value. *You can discount 90 percent of anything that windbag says.*

Winder – *(noun)* a device or mechanism for winding something, especially a watch, clock, or camera film. *I am going to get the winder of my mechanical wrist watch repaired.*

Winding – *(noun)* a twisting movement or course. *The windings of the stream pass through the valleys of that mountain.* **2** a thing that winds or is wound round something. a coil of conducting wire in an electric motor, generator, etc. *(adjective)* having a twisting or spiral course. *The winding of the electric motor needs fresh copper wire coiling.*

Window – *(noun)* **1** an opening in a wall or roof, fitted with glass in a frame to admit light or air and allow people to see out. *Thieves smashed a window and took all jewellary and cash.* an opening through which customers are served in a bank, ticket office, etc. *Customers have been advised to queue behind window number three for depositing or withdrawing cash.* a space behind the window of a shop where goods are displayed. *Top quality electronic products are on display at that window.* **2** a transparent panel in an envelope to show an address. *Write the address in such a place that postman can read it through the envelope's window.*

Windpipe – *(noun)* the trachea. *Something has got stuck in his windpipe.*

Wind-up – *(noun)* **1** [British informal] an attempt to tease or irritate someone. *Surely this was a wind-up.* **2** an act of concluding something. *Action has been taken to wind-up the firm.*

Wine – *(noun)* **1** an alcoholic drink made from fermented grape juice. *They decided to celebrate the success by opening a bottle of red wine.* a fermented alcoholic drink made from other fruits or plants. *He ordered a glass of seine wine of*

France. **2** short for wine red. *She wore a wine-coloured suit. verb* entertain someone with drinks and a meal. *We wined and dined at the hotel with our friends.*

Winsome – *(adjective)* attractive or appealing. *She fell for his winsome behaviour.*

Wire – *(noun)* **1** metal drawn out into a thin flexible thread or rod. *We purchased a coil of aluminum wire.* a length or quantity of wire used for fencing, *We have decided to wire our compound to prevent animals from getting near our house.* to carry an electric current, etc. *Stay away from these wires, they carry electric current.* **2** a concealed electronic listening device. *A police informer was wearing a wire to listen to our talks.*3 a telegram or cablegram. *We rushed out on receiving a telegraphic wire. verb* **1** install electric circuits or wires in. *The house was wired with listening devices.* **2** provide, fasten, or reinforce with wire. *The dentist wired his teeth.* **3** send a telegram or cablegram to. *We went to the post office to send an urgent wire.*

Wise – *(noun)* manner, way, or extent. *It would only be wise to discuss the matter with the director.*

Wish – *(verb)* **1** desire something that cannot or probably will not happen. *Every one wished for peaceful election.* **2** want to do something. *We wish to become involved in the management.* ask to do something or that be done. *I wish it to be clearly understood. (noun)* **1** a desire or hope, or an expression of this. an expression of a hope for someone's happiness, success, or welfare. *She wished that he had practiced the routines.* **2** a thing wished for. *We wish her success.*

Wit – *(noun)* **1** the capacity for inventive thought and quick understanding. *She needed all her wits to figure out the way back.* keen intelligence. *I had the wit to realize that the only way out was up.* **2** a natural aptitude for using words and ideas in a quick and inventive way to create humour. *Her caustic wit cuts through the humbug.* 3 a person with this aptitude. *She is such a great wit.*

Witch – *(noun)* **1** a woman thought to have evil magic powers. *Witches are popularly depicted as wearing a black cloak and pointed hat casting spell on unsuspecting people.* **2** an edible north Atlantic flatfish. *Witch is a popular fish consumed by people living near Amazon basin. (verb)* **1** cast an evil spell on. *That old lady is believed to have somehow witched the house.* **2** of a girl or woman enchant a man. *That beauty is a kind of witch able to seduce most male members.*

Withal – *(adverb)* in addition. *She gave him a grateful smile, but rueful withal. preposition* with. *They sat with little to nourish themselves withal but vile water.*

Wither – *(verb)* **1** become dry and shrivelled. *The grass had withered to an unappealing brown.* **2** become shrunken or wrinkled from age of disease. *The old man with a withered arm came to our house.* **3** mortify with a scornful look or manner. *She withered him with a hard glance.*

Within – *(preposition)* **1** inside. *The fire spread fast within the building.* inside the range of. *All illegal buildings within the green belt have been demolished.* inside the bounds set by. *Each member nation extended full cooperation within the terms of the treaty.* **2** not further off than a particular distance. *She lives within the municipal limits of the city.* **3** occurring inside a particular period of time. *(adverb)* **1** Inside, indoors. *We enquired within the college.* **2** internally or inwardly. *Her beauty was coming from within her.*

Without – *(preposition)* **1** not accompanied by or having the use of. *She went to England without him.* **2** in which the action mentioned does not happen. *They sat looking at each other without speaking anything. (adverb)* outside. *He won't be able to go without we know it.*

Witness – *(noun)* **1** a person who sees an event take place. *I was witness to one of the most amazing debut by Arvind Kejriwal in political history.* **2** a person giving sworn testimony to a court of law or the police. *He was a key witness at the trial.* **3** a person who is present at the signing if a document and signs it themselves to confirm this. *The agreement was signed in the presence of two witnesses.* **4** evidence, proof. *The memorial service was witness to the wide circle* *of his interests. verb* **1** be a witness to. *A court official witnessed her signature.* **2** be the place, period, etc. in which a particular event takes place. *The 2010s witnessed an unprecedented increase in the scope of the social media.* **3** give or serve as evidence of. *His writings are witness to our society's inner toughness.*

Witticism – *(noun)* a witty remark. *His witticism was remarkable and harmless.*

Wives – plural form of wife. *He has two wives.*

Wo – *(exclamatory)* variant spelling of whoa.

Woe – *(noun)* great sorrow or distress. *To add to automobile company's woes, customers have been spending less.*

Wold – *(noun)* especially in [British] place names a piece of high, open, uncultivated land or moor. *There are many Wolds in England that have hardly ever been cultivated.*

Wolf – *(noun)* **1** a carnivorous mammal which is the largest member of the dog family, living and hunting in packs. *Tasmanian and Maned wolves are an endangered species.* **2** a rapacious or ferocious person. *Many politically spent forces blame the media as ravening wolves.* a man who habitually seduces women. *He's the archetypal wolf in gentleman's dress. (verb)* devour food greedily. *He wolfed down his breakfast in no time.*

Woman – *(noun)* **1** an adult human female. *The court was composed of seven women and five men.* **2** a female worker or employee. *She is the only woman doctor in this hospital.* a female domestic help. *The woman who works as our domestic help is on leave for five days.* **3** a wife or lover. *He wondered whether Arman had his woman with him.*

Won – past and past participle of win. *India had won five medals at the London Olympic Games in 2012.*

Wonder – *(noun)* **1** a feeling of surprise and admiration, caused by something beautiful, unexpected, or unfamiliar. *She observed the intricacy of the woodwork with the wonder of a child.* **2** a person or thing that causes such a feeling. *New York is a place of wonder and beauty.* having remarkable properties or abilities. *Penicillin was considered to be a wonder drug. (verb)* feel curious. *How many times have I written that, I wonder?* desire to know. used to express a polite question or request. *I wonder whether you have thought more about it?*

Wondrous – *(adjective)* inspiring wonder. *Mumbai is a wondrous city. (adverb)* wonderfully. *She is grown into a wondrous pretty.*

Wood – *(noun)* **1** the hard fibrous material forming the main substance of the trunk or branches of a tree or shrub, used for fuel or timber. *We use only best quality woods in furniture making.* **2** wooden barrels used for storing alcoholic drinks. *These wines are stored in the wood.* **3** a golf club with a wooden or other head that is relatively broad from face to back. *She hit the golf ball with a three-wood.* **4** woods a small forest. *A long thick hedge divided the wood from the field.*

Worry – *(verb)* **1** feel or cause to feel troubled over actual or potential difficulties. *I began to worry whether I had done the right thing.* expressing anxiety. *She was worried about his soldier son in the war.* **2** annoy or disturb. *The music hardly ever stops, but it doesn't worry me.* **3** of a dog or other carnivorous animal tear at or pull about with the teeth. *I found my dog contentedly worrying about a chicken bone.* **4** of a dog chase and attack livestock, especially sheep. *The forest ranger shot a dog that had been worrying sheep.* **5** discover or devise a saluting by persistent thought. *Children should be allowed to pause in their reading to worry out a meaning. (noun)* the state of being worried. a source of anxiety. *He's got financial worries.*

Worst – *(adjective)* of the poorest quality or the lowest standard. *The speech was the worst he had ever made.* most severe or serious. *At least 25,000 people died in Bhopal's worst industrial accident. (adverb)* **1** most severely or seriously. *Manufacturing and mining sectors are the industry's worst affected by falling employment.* **2** least well. *She was voted the worst-dressed celebrity. (noun)* the worst event or circumstance. *When we saw the ambulance* *outside her door, we began to fear the worst.* **3** the worst part or stage of something. *There are enough visible signs that the recession is past its worst. (verb)* get the better of. *This was not the time for a deep discussion—she was tired and she would be worsted.*

Worsted – *(noun)* a fine smooth yarn spun from combed long staple wool, fabric made from such yarn, having a close textured surface with no nap. *He came to the party wearing a worsted three-piece suit.*

Wort – *(noun)* the sweet infusion of ground malt or other grain before fermentation, used to produce beer and distilled malt liquors. *The manufactures add yeast to the wort for production of malted liquor.*

Wot – present of wit. *'Wot a night!' said the old farmer humorously.*

Wound – *(noun)* **1** an injury to living tissue caused by a cut, blow, or other impact. *She slipped and suffered chest wounds.* **2** an injury to a person's feelings or reputation. *The fresh crisis has opened old wounds. (verb)* inflict a wound on. *You really wounded his pride when you turned his request down.*

Wove – past of weave. *He wove a story to escape punishment.*

Woven – past participle of weave. *He came again with woven stories to convince us about his sincerity.*

Wow – *(exclamatory)* expressing astonishment or admiration. 'Wow!' she cried enthusiastically! *(noun)* a sensational success. *Your speech was a real wow. (verb)* impress and excite greatly. *The audiences wowed her thunderous lecture.*

Wraith – *(noun)* **1** a ghost or ghostly image of someone, especially one seen shortly before or after their death. *Constant chest pains had reduced his father to a wraith.* **2** a wisp or faint trace. *A sea breeze was sending a grey wraith of smoke up the slopes.*

Wrangle – *(noun)* a long and complicated dispute or argument. *The compensation was held up due to an insurance wrangle. (verb)* **1** engage in a wrangle. *The bureaucrats continued wrangling over the final draft.* **2** round up or take charge of livestock. *The shepherd wrangled the flock of sheep early.*

Wrap – *(verb)* **1** cover or enclose in paper or soft material. *She wrapped up the marriage gifts attractively.* arrange paper or soft material round something, as a covering or for warmth or protection. *She wrapped herself with a pashmina shawl.* place around so as to encircle. *Please wrap the bandage around the injured finger.* **2** cause a word or unit of text to be carried over to a new line automatically, of a word or unit or text be carried over in such a way. *Words are wrapped automatically to the next line if they are too long.* **3** finish filming or recording. *Please wrap recording of the song. (noun)* **1** a loose outer garment or piece of material. *The girls came and danced in beach wraps.* **2** paper or material used for wrapping. *We went out to purchase plastic food wraps.* **3** the end of a session of filming or recording. *The director ordered to wrap the film shooting.*

Wrath – *(noun)* extreme anger. *The students faced the wrath of the professor for bunking the class.*

Wreak – *(verb)* **1** cause a large amount of damage or harm. *The environmental damage wreaked by years of industrial pollution.* **2** inflict vengeance. *He was determined to wreak his revenge on the girl who had rejected his marriage proposal.*

Wreath – *(noun)* **1** an arrangement of flowers, leaves, or stems fastened in a ring and used for decoration or for laying on a grave. *The visiting president laid a wreath at the Mahatma Gandhi's Samadhi at Rajghat.* **2** a curl or ring of smoke or cloud. *Wreaths of mist were swirling up into the air.*

Wreathe – *(verb)* envelop, surround, or encircle. *She sits wreathed in smoke.* twist or entwine round or over something. *Should I once more wreathe my arms about Anita's waist?* of smoke move with a curling motion. *He watched the smoke wreathe into the cold air.*

Wreck – *(noun)* **1** the destruction of a ship at sea; a shipwreck. *A naval ship brought ashore the survivors of the wreck.* a ship destroyed in such a way. *Another ship was dispatched for salvaging of treasure from wrecks.* brought ashore by the sea from a wreck. *The profits of wreck were deposited with the government.* **2** a building, vehicle, etc. that has been destroyed or badly damaged. a road or rail crash. *The train coaches were reduced to a smouldering wreck.* **3** a person whose physical or mental health or strength has failed: *The scandal left the family an emotional wreck.* *(verb)* **1** cause the destruction of a ship by sinking or breaking up. *He was drowned when his ship was wrecked in the middle of the sea.* the practice of destroying a ship in order to steal the cargo. *The local population reverted to the old practice of wrecking.* **2** destroy or severely damage. spoil completely: *The eye injury wrecked his chances of selection in Air Force.*

Wrest – *(verb)* **1** forcibly pull from a person's grasp. *She tried to wrest her arm from robber's hold.* take power or control after considerable effort or resistance. *They wanted to wrest control of their lives from irresponsible bureaucracy.* **2** distort the meaning or interpretation of. *He seems convinced of my fault, and wrest every reply I have submitted.*

Wrestle – *(verb)* **1** take part in a fight that involves close grappling with one's opponent, either as sport or in earnest. *A shot rang out as the policeman wrestled with the gunman.* force into a particular position in such a way. *The security guards wrestled the ruffians to the ground.* extract or manipulate an object with difficulty and some physical effort. *He wrestled the keys out of the lock after a considerable time.* **2** struggle with a difficulty or problem. *For more than a year he wrestled with a guilty conscience.* *(noun)* **1** a wrestling bout or contest. *Both wrestlers came into the ring.* **2** a hard struggle. *He had a lifelong wrestle with depression.*

Wretch – *(noun)* an unfortunate person. *Can the poor wretch's corpse tell us anything about his death?* a contemptible person. *Ungrateful wretches of the society.*

Wriggle – *(verb)* **1** twist and turn with quick writhing movements. *She kicked and wriggled to free herself from his hold.* move with wriggling movements. *She wriggled to come out of her tight dress.* **2** avoid by devious means. *Don't try to wriggle out of your agreement.* *(noun)* a wriggling movement. *She gave a hurried little wriggle.*

Wright – *(noun)* a maker or builder.. *Carpenters in Scotland are usually called a wright.*

Wring – *(verb)* **1** squeeze and twist to force liquid from. *She wrung the cloth out in the tub.* extract in this way. *She wrung out the excess water from the cloths.* **2** break by twisting forcibly. *The chicken shrieked as the butcher wrung its neck.* squeeze someone's hand tightly. *He fervently wrung Sumita's hand.* **3** after wring something from /out of obtain with difficulty or effort. *Few concessions were wrung from the government.* **4** cause great pain or distress to: *The letter wrung her heart.*

Wrinkle – *(noun)* **1** a slight line or fold, especially in fabric or the skin of the face. *She ironed out the wrinkles from her shirt.* **2** informal a clever innovation, or useful piece of information or advice. *Learning the wrinkles from someone more experienced saves time.* *(verb)* make or become wrinkled. *Her brow wrinkled a bit.*

Wrist – *(noun)* the joint connecting the hand with the forearm. *She fell down and sprained her wrist.* also wrist pin in a machine a stud projecting from a crank as an attachment for a connecting rod. *The parts have elastic wrists and ankles.*

Writ – *(noun)* a form of written command in the name of a court of other legal authority to do or abstain from doing a specified act. *The reinstated employee issued a writ for libel against the* *applicants.* one's power to enforce compliance or submission. *You have business here which is out of my writ and competence.*

Wrong – *(adjective)* **1** not correct or true. mistaken. *That is the wrong answer.* **2** unjust, dishonest, or immoral. *They were completely wrong to take the law into their own hands.* **3** in a bad or abnormal condition; amiss. Something was seriously wrong with the electric motor. *(adverb)* in an unsuitable or undesirable manner or direction. *What is he doing wrong?* with an incorrect result. *She guessed wrong.* *(noun)* an unjust, dishonest or immoral action. *I have done you a great wrong.* *(verb)* **1** act unjustly or dishonestly towards. *He would kill the man who wronged the family.* **2** mistakenly attribute bad motives to. *Perhaps I wrong him.*

Wrote – (past tense of write). *He wrote the article last night.*

Wroth *(adjective)* archaic angry. *The professor is majestically wroth with the students.*

Wrung – past and past participle of wring. *The confession wrung by the police was rejected in the court.*

Wye – *(noun)* name of a river. *Wye is the river which forms part of the border between Wales and England.*

Wynd – *(noun)* narrow street or alley. *Fleet Street is a wynd where leading newspapers have offices.*

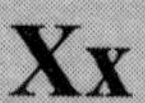

X – *(noun)* **1** the twenty fourth letter of the alphabet. **2** denoting the next after W in a set of items, categories, etc. **3** denoting an unknown or unspecified person or thing. *In mathematics we wre the symbol 'X' to denote an unknown nuber quantity.* **4** the first unknown quantity in an algebraic expression. denoting the principal or horizontal axis in a system of coordinates. *Horizontal axis in co-ordinate geometry is known as X-axis.* **5** a cross shaped written symbol, used: to indicate a position on a map. *The teacher marked my answer with 'X' and gave me zero.*

Xanthine – *(noun)* a crystalline compound formed in the metabolic breakdown of nucleic acids and related to caffeine and other alkaloids. *Xanthine is a chemical compound found in blood and wine.*

Xanthic – *(noun)* Any of a class of unstable organic acids containing sulphur. *Yellow coloured products are also known as xanthic.*

Xanthium – *(noun)* Coarse herbs having small heads of greenish flowers followed by burrs with hooked bristles. *Xanthium is a small flower.*

Xanthoma – *(noun)* an irregular yellow patch or nodule on the skin, caused by deposition of lipids. *People who suffering from Xanthoma should proper care and consult doctor immediately.*

Xanthophyll – *(noun)* a yellow or brown carotenoid plant pigment which causes the autumn colours of leaves. *It is a natural pigment that causes leaves to turn yellow.*

Xanthosis – *(noun)* An abnormal yellow discolouration of the skin. *Xanthosis makes skin colour yellow.*

Xanthous – *(adjective)* of the colour intermediate between green and orange in the colour spectrum; of something resembling the colour of an egg yolk. *Xanthous is a shade of colour that looks like the colour of egg yolk.*

Xebec – *(noun)* a small three misted Mediterranean sailing ship with lateen and square sails.

Xenarthra – *(noun)* Armadillos; American anteaters; sloths. *Xenarthra is a strange looking mammal largely due to its odd shaped vertebrae.*

Xenial – *(adjective)* Pertaining to hospitality or relations with friendly visitors. *His xenial attitude attracts all.*

Xenogamy – *(noun)* fertilization of a flower by pollen from a flower on a genetically different plant, compare with geitonogamy. *Xenogamy is a process of fertilization of flower.*

Xenogenesis – *(noun)* the alternation of two or more different forms in the life cycle of a plant or animal. *Xenogenesis is a name given to there plants that can produce hydrogen cyanide.*

Xenon – *(noun)* the chemical element of atomic number 54, a member of the noble gas series, obtained by distillation of liquid air and used in some specialized electric lamps. *Xenon is a gas used in manufacturing specialised electric camps.*

Xerophilous – *(adjective)* adapted to a dry climate or habitat. *To stay in a desert you need to be Xerophilous.*

Xerophyle – *(noun)* a plant which needs very little water. *Xerophyle grows in desert.*

Xerophytic – *(adjective)* Adapted to a xeric (or dry) environment. *Cacti are xerophytic plants.*

Xerostomia – *(noun)* Abnormal dryness of the mouth resulting from decreased secretion of saliva. *In hot summer days people normally suffer from xerostomia.*

Xerotes – *(noun)* The condition of not containing or being covered by a liquid. *In xerotes condition fishes die in rivers.*

X-ray – *(noun)* **1** an electromagnetic wave of very short wave length. able to pass through many materials opaque to light. denoting an apparent or supposed faculty for seeing beyond an outward form: *X-ray eyes are required to see what is going in the godown of the merchant.*

2 a photography or other image of the internal structure of an object, especially a part of the body, produced by passing X rays through the object. *The fracture in his hand is discovered only after getting the X-ray done.* **3** a code word representing the letter X, used in radio communication. *verb* photograph or examine with X rays. *The doctor x-rayed my chest.*

Xylem – *(noun)* the vascular tissue in plants which conducts water and dissolved nutrients upwards from the root and also helps to from the woody element in the stem. *Xylem tissue is responsible for passing water and nutrients from roots to the whole tree.*

Xylocarp – *(noun)* Life Sciences & Allied Applications/Botany) Botany a fruit, such as a coconut, having a hard woody pericárp. *Xylocarp is a coconut like fruit that some people eat.*

Xylograph – *(noun)* **1** An engraving on wood. **2** An impression from a woodblock. *Xylograph should be avoided as it reduces the life of three.*

Xylographic – *(noun)* Wood engraving, especially of an early period. *Xylographic art was practised widely in older times.*

Xylol – *(noun)* A colourless flammable volatile liquid hydrocarbon used as a solvent. *Xylol is used as solvent in washing powder.*

Y – *(noun)* **1**. the twenty fifth letter of the alphabet. **2**. denoting the next after X in a set of items, categories, etc. **3**. denoting an unknown or unspecified person or thing. **4**. the second unknown quantity in an algebraic expression, usually the dependent variable. denoting the secondary or vertical axis in a system of coordinates. *Vertical axis in co-ordinate geometry is known as 'Y' axis.*

Yacca – *(noun)* West Indian evergreen with medium to long leaves. *Yacca looks very pretty during summer.*

Yahoo – *(noun)* a rude, coarse, or brutish person. *People hate yahoo.*

Yak – *(noun)* a large ox with shaggy hair, humped shoulders, and large horns, used in Tibet as a pack animal and for its milk, meat, and hide. *In Tibet yak is domesticated.*

Yam –*(noun)* **1** the edible starchy tuber of a climbing plant, widely distributed in tropical and subtropical countries. **2** the plant which yields this tuber. **3** a sweet potato. *Have you ever tested yam? People say it is very testy.*

Yank –*(noun)* **1** an American. *He is a yank.* **2** [US] another term for Yankee. *Yankees have yet again move into the world cup final.*

Yap – *(verb)* **1** give a sharp, shrill bark. *The puppies yapped.* **2** talk at length in an irritating manner. *He yapped is an irritating way.* *(noun)* a sharp, shrill bark. *The yap of the puppy is very annoying.*

Yapok – *(noun)* a semiaquatic carnivorous opossum with dark banded grey fur and webbed hind feet, native to tropical America. *Yapok is generally found in tropical America.*

Yardarm – *(noun)* the outer extremity of a ship's yard. *People are resting and enjoying the evening sitting in the yardarm.*

Yare – *(adjective)* moving lightly and easily; easily manageable. *Don't be in hurry, move yare.*

Yarn – *(noun)* **1** spun thread used for knitting, weaving, or sewing. *She uses sharp yarn to sew.* **2** a long or rambling story. especially one that is implausible. a chat. *Her yarn was hesitant.* *(verb)* tell a yarn. chat; talk. *She yarned many impossible incidents she had come across.*

Yarrow – *(noun)* a plant with feathery leaves and heads of small white or pale pink aromatic flowers, used in herbal medicine. *Yarrow is a very useful medicine for many diseases.*

Yataghan – *(noun)* a long Turkish knife with a curved blade having a single edge. *Don't allow children to use the yataghan.*

Yaup – *(verb)* emit long loud cries. *Please don't yaup.*

Yaw – *(verb)* twist or oscillate about a vertical axis. *The yawing motion of the ship.* *(noun)* twisting or oscillation of a moving ship or aircraft about a vertical axis. *Are you sure to see the yaw of the aircraft?*

Yawl – *(noun)* **1** a two masted fore and aft rigged sailing boat with the mizzenmast stepped far aft so that the mizzen boom overhangs the stern. **2** a ship's jolly boat with four or six oars. M*any yawls are lying in the vacant space of the ship.*

Yawn – *(verb)* **1** involuntarily open one's mouth wide and inhale deeply due to tiredness or boredom. *The cute child yawned during the long performance.* **2** be wide open: *a yawning chasm.* *(noun)* **1** an act of yawning. *She could not suppress a yawn* **2** a boring or tedious thing or event. *He finds the marriage ceremony very yawning.*

Yaws – *(plural noun)* a contagious tropical disease caused by a bacterium that enters skin abrasions and causes small crusted lesions which may develop into deep ulcers. *Yaws is considered a very dangerous disease by doctors.*

Yea – *(noun)* an affirmative answer; an affirmative vote or voter. *Yea, I will surely meet you in the function.*

Year – *(noun)* **1** the time taken by the earth to make one revolution around the sun. *Our planet earth takes a year 0072 to complete one* *revolution around the sun.* **2** the period of 365 days starting from the first of January used for reckoning time in ordinary affairs. *A school year;* a period of the same length as this starting at a different point. a similar period used for reckoning time according to other calendars. **3** one's age or time of life. *Ajoy's son is 4 years old.* **4** a very long time. *The 4 days I live alone seems a year to me.* 5. a set of students grouped together as being of roughly similar ages. *He was in my year at the hight school.*

Yearn – *(verb)* **1** have an intense feeling of loss and longing for something. HH*He yearned for a cigarette badly.* **2** be filled with compassion or warn feeling. *He yearned for his mother at the time of crisis.*

Yeast – *(noun)* **1** a microscopic single celled fungus capable of converting sugar into alcohol and carbon dioxide. *Have you ever seen yeast through microscope?* a grayish yellow preparation of this obtained chiefly from fermented beer, used as a fermenting agent, to raise bread dough, and as a food supplement. *Yeast is used as food supplement.* **2** any unicellular fungus that reproduces vegetatively by budding or fission, e.g. candida. *Candila is a yeast produced by fission of fungus.*

Yell –*(noun)* **1** a loud, sharp cry, especially of pain, surprise, or delight. *He uttered a yell of pain.* **2** an organized rhythmic cheer, especially one used to support a sports team. *The speaker was interrupted by loud yells from audience.* **3** an amusing person or thing. *Mr Sharma is a yell in true sense.* *(verb)* shout in a loud or piercing way. *He yelled to her from the window but she couldn't hear him.*

Yellow – *(adjective)* **1** of the colour between green and orange in the spectrum, a primary subtractive colour complementary to blue; coloured like ripe lemons or egg yolks. *My mother wants to know the reason for the yellow tinge on my teeth.* **2** having a yellowish or olive skin. *His skin becomes yellow because of jaundice.* **3** denoting a warning of danger which is thought to be near but not actually imminent. **4** cowardly. showing jealousy or suspicion. *The police officer is too yellow to stand and fight.* 5. unscrupulously sensational. *Yellow news.*(noun) **1** yellow colour or pigment. **2** used in names of yellow butterflies and moths. *clouded yellow.* **3** any of a number of plant diseases in which the leaves turn yellow, typically caused by viruses and transmitted by insects. *(verb)* become a yellow colour, especially with age. *The old man yellowed with age.*

Yen – *(noun)* the basic monetary unit of Japan. *Yen is are of the highly rated currencies in the world.*

Yeoman – *(noun)* **1** a man holding a small landed estate; a freeholder. a person qualified for jury duties, electoral rights, etc. by virtue of possessing free land. *Yeomen are very respectable persons in society.* **2** a servant in a royal or noble household, ranking between a sergeant and a groom or a squire and a page. *Mr Edward is a very courageous yeoman.* **3** a member of the yeomanry force. **4** a petty officer concerned with signaling. a petty officer in the US navy performing clerical duties on board ship. *Yeomen have very significant roles although their job seems petty.*

Yes – *exclamatory* **1** used to give an affirmative response. *Yes! I will do the job for you.* **2** responding to someone addressing one or attracting one's attention. *Yes! I am listening to you.* **3** questioning a remark. **4** expressing delight.(noun) an affirmative answer, decision, or vote. *I am hoping for a yes from my boss.*

Yesterday – *(noun)* **1** the day immediately before today; it was in yesterday's newspapers. **2** the recent past. *Yesterday's solutions are not good enough.* *(adverb)* **1** on the day preceding today. *Yesterday the weather was beautiful.* **2** In the recent past; only a short time ago. *He was not born yesterday.*

Yew – *(noun)* a coniferous tree with poisonous red berry like fruit and dense, springy wood. *Never dare to try the fruit of yew tree.*

Yiddish –*(noun)* a language used by Jews in or from central and eastern Europe, originally a German dialect with words from Hebrew and several modern languages. *The Yiddish language is almost no longer in use now a days.*

Yoke – *(noun)* **1** a wooden crosspiece that is fastened over the necks of two animals and attached to a plough or cart that they pull in unison. *Experienced farmers know well how to use a Yoke properly.* a pair of yoked animals. the amount of land that one pair of oxen could plough in a day. *The small oxen pair can only plough yoke of land each day.* something that represents a bond between two parties: *The yoke of marriage that lasted for almost three years.* **2** a frame fitting over the neck and shoulders of a person, used for carrying pails or baskets. *The shopkeeper uses yoke to carry his vegetable to the market.* something that is regarded as oppressive or burdensome. **3** a part of a garment that fits over the shoulders and to which the main part of the garment is attached. **4** a crosspiece similar to a yoke, such as the crossbar of a rudder. **5** an arch of three spears under which a defeated army was made to march. *verb* put a yoke on; couple or attach with or to a yoke. *The farmer yoked the oxen tightly.*

Yokel – *(noun)* an unsophisticated country person. *The yokel behaved very rudely with the woman.*

Yolk – *(noun)* the yellow internal part of a bird's egg, which is rich in protein and fat and nourishes the developing embryo. *It is very good for health to have yoke every day as breakfast.*

Yon – *(adjective)* distant but within sight; *He asks me what is my yon place. (adverb)* At or in an indicated (usually distant) place. *The coins are scattered here and yon.*

Yonder – *(adverb)* at some distance in the direction indicated; over there. *Ramesh visited the yonder valley last year. (noun)* the far distance. *I want to go to the house yonder.*

You – *(pronoun)* **1** used to refer to the person or people that the speaker is addressing. used to refer to the person being addressed together with other people regarded in the same class. *I love you are they listening?* **2** used to refer to any person in general. *Indians are brilliant in politics. After awhile, you get used to it.*

Younker – *(noun)* a youngster. *He is proud to be a younker.*

Yowl – *(noun)* a loud wailing cry of pain or distress. *The old lady's yowl filled the hallway. (verb)* make such a cry. *The coyotes were yowling in the desert.*

Yucca – *(noun)* a plant of the agave family with sword like leaves and spikes of white bell shaped flowers, native to warm regions of the US and Mexico. *Yucca is native to warm regions like US and Mexico.*

Yuck – *exclamatory* used to express strong distaste or disgust. *Yuck, that's really gross!(noun)* something messy or disgusting. *The environment of the restaurant is yuck to me.*

Yurt –*(noun)* a circular tent of felt or skins used by nomads in Mongolia, Siberia, and Turkey. *Yurt is normally used in Mongolia and Turkey.*

Zz

Z – *(noun)* **1** the twenty sixth letter of the alphabet. **2** denoting the next after Y in a set of iteams, categories, etc. **3** the third unknown quantity in an algebraic expression. denoting the third axis in a three dimensional system of coordinates. *Third unknown quantity in the co-ordinate geometry.*

Zaffre – *(noun)* impure cobalt oxide formerly used to make small and blue enamels. *In today's world zaffre is rarely used.*

Zamia – *(noun)* Any of various cycads of the genus Zamia; among the smallest and most verdant *cycads*

Zarf – *(noun)* an ornamental metal cup-shaped holder for a hot coffee cup. *Rajesh is very fond of having his morning coffee in a zarf.*

Zebu – *(noun)* an ox of a humped breed originally domesticated in India. *Zebu is rarely found in India now a days.*

Zephyr – *(noun)* **1** a soft gentle breeze. *The zephyr was cooled by the river.* **2** a fine cotton gingham; a very light article of clothing. *Cloths made of zephyr are very costly.*

Zeppelin – *(noun)* a large German dirigible airship of the early 20th century. *Zeppelin aircraft were used by German Forces during first world war.*

Zero – *cardinal number* the figure 0; nought; nothing. a temperature of 0 degree c., marking the freezing point of water. a worthless or insignificant person. *The number zero was invented in India. Water freezes at zero degree centigrade.*

Zeus – *(noun)* **1** Type genus of the family Zeidae. **2** (Greek mythology) the supreme god of ancient Greek mythology; son of Rhea and Cronus whom he dethroned; husband and brother of Hera; brother of Poseidon and Hades; father of many gods; counterpart of Roman Jupiter. *The state of Zeus at Olympic is one of the seven wonders of the world.*

Zither – *(noun)* a musical instrument consisting of a flat wooden sound box with numerous strings stretched across it, placed horizontally and played with the fingers and a plectrum. *I have a desire to listen to the music of zither once in my life time.*

Zizania *(noun)* wild rice. *People from different parts of the world are still using zizania.*

Zoetrope – *(noun)* a cylinder with a series of pictures on the inner surface that, when viewed through slits with the cylinder rotating, give an impression of continuous motion. *Collection of zoetrope is found in many renowned museums in the world.*

Zonal *(adjective)* **1** relating to or of the nature of a zone. *Krish will reach the zonal frontier tomorrow.* **2** associated with or divided into zones. *The Railway department has ordered to divide the east wing in zonal division.*

Zonula *(noun)* small beltlike zone. *The zonal is divided into many zonulas.*

Zoo – *(noun)* an establishment which keeps wild animals for study, conservation, or display to the public. *Kamal's parents and children visited the zoo yesterday.*

Zooid – *(noun)* an animal arising from another by budding or division, especially each of the individuals which make up a colonial organism. *Research is going on to find out the advantages and disadvantages of development of zooid.*

Zoolatry – *(noun)* the worship of animals. *The tradition of zoolatry is still in practice in many countries.*

Zoology – *(noun)* the scientific study of the behaviour, structure, physiology, classification, and distribution of animals; the animal life of a particular region or geological period. *Patrick is doing his research in Zoology.*

Zoomorphism – *(noun)* the attribution of animal forms or qualities to a god. *The concept of Zoomorphism reflects the conducts and behaviour of some societies.*

Zoophyte – *(noun)* a plant like animal, especially a coral, sea anemone, sponge, or sea lily. *The life cycle of zoophytes is being telecast in many documentaries in discovery channel.*

Zopilote – *(noun)* American black vulture. *People could see Zopilote in many American Zoos.*

Zoroastrian *(adjective)* of or pertaining to Zoroaster or the religion he founded *(noun)* follower of Zoroaster and Zoroastrianism. *Zoroastrians live in many countries in the world and their population in recognisable in those countries.*

Zoster *(noun)* Eruptions along a nerve path often accompanied by severe neuralgia. *People suffering from zoster have to take proper medication.*

Zulu – *(noun)* **1** a member of a South African people living mainly in Kwaza/natal province. *Zulu people are said to be very adventurous.* **2** the Bantu language of this people. *She speaks Zulu.*

Zwieback *(noun)* slice of sweet raised bread baked again until it is brown and hard and crisp. *American people like to have zwieback in their breakfast.*

Zygomatic *(adjective)* of or relating to the cheek region of the face. *(noun)* the arch of bone beneath the eye that forms the prominence of the cheek. *The zygomatic bone is very delicate, it needs proper care.*

Zymogen – *(noun)* an inactive substance which is converted into an enzyme when activated by another enzyme. *Scientists use various methods to convert zymogen into enzymes.*

Zymoid *(adjective)* resembling an enzyme. *You won't be able to see zymoid with normal eyes.*

Zymotic – *(adjective)* relating to or denoting contagious disease regarded as developing after infection, like the fermenting of yeast. *Sachin is now recovering from cancer, but doctor has advised him to be careful of zymotic diseases.*

Zymurgy – *(noun)* the study or practice of fermentation in brewing, winemaking, or distilling. *Mr Sharma's younger daughter is very much interested in studying zymurgy.*